American Foreign Relations

A History · Since 1895

FOURTH EDITION

THOMAS G. PATERSON

J. GARRY CLIFFORD

KENNETH J. HAGAN

D. C. HEATH AND COMPANY
Lexington, Massachusetts   Toronto

Address editorial correspondence to:

D. C. Heath and Company
125 Spring Street
Lexington, MA 02173

Acquisitions Editor: James Miller
Developmental Editor: Patricia Wakeley
Production Editor: Elizabeth Gale
Designer: Jan Shapiro
Photo Researcher: Nancy Hale
Production Coordinator: Charles Dutton
Permissions Editor: Margaret Roll

Cover: *"The Allied Flags, 1917"* by Childe Hassam. Oil on canvas. 30 1/2 × 49 inches. (Private Collection. Photograph courtesy of Kennedy Galleries, Inc., New York)
Cover research: Sharon Donahue, Photo Editor

Published simultaneously in Canada.

Printed in the United States of America.

International Standard Book Number: 0–669–35156–3

Library of Congress Catalog Number: 94-77212

10   9   8   7   6   5   4   3   2   1

for

Colin Graham Paterson

Carol Davidge

Vera Low Hagan

Preface

Even a casual look at the chapter endnotes and bibliographies of this Fourth Edition of *American Foreign Relations* reveals that we have thoroughly revised the book. It represents the most recent work of both American and foreign scholars in history, political science, and international relations. We include the most influential approaches and interpretations, especially those advanced by younger scholars. This book also reflects the findings of our own archival research as we discover and rediscover the past.

Readers familiar with the last edition will notice that we have changed the title from *American Foreign Policy* to *American Foreign Relations*. We have made this change because the field has evolved in emphasis, interpretation, and research to encompass the myriad interactions of peoples, cultures, economies, national governments, nongovernmental organizations, regional associations, and international institutions. The term *"foreign policy"* seems inadequate to describe these multifaceted intersections because it focuses largely on governmental decisionmaking and on policy itself. *"Diplomacy"* falls short because it refers primarily to negotiations or communications among states or organizations. *"International history"* is so broad a term as to lose meaning, while also underplaying an appropriate emphasis on *American* foreign relations. The phrase *"foreign relations"* comes closest to explaining the totality of interactions—economic, cultural, political, military, environmental, and more—among peoples, organizations, states, and systems.

An historical overview such as this book must draw upon the scholarly work of many colleagues in the United States and abroad. Their expertise informs this book throughout and helps to lend it the authority that instructors and students expect. Our chapter endnotes and Further Reading sections are one way to thank them for their books, articles, and conference papers. We also appreciate their recommendations for revising the text and their suggestions for teaching the courses for which this book is intended. We thank them, too, for challenging us to consider many different approaches and theories, among them world systems, corporatism, dependency, culture, psychology and personality, medical biography, lessons from the past ("thinking in time"), bureaucratic politics, public opinion, executive-legislative competition, gender, national security and power, impact of foreign aid on recipients, the physical environment and ecology, and ideology. As both teachers and writers, we have learned from the lively debates stirred by these different approaches and interpretations. The pages of *American Foreign Relations* demonstrate our participation in these instructive discussions.

We continue to emphasize the theme of expansionism and explain its many manifestations, and we show that on almost every issue in the history of American foreign relations, alternative voices unfailingly sounded among and against official policymakers. Americans have always debated their place in the world, their wars, their overseas commitments, and the status of their principles and power, and they have always debated the people of other nations about the spread of U.S. influence. In this book, we not only engage the ideas of other scholars but also explore the revealing disputes that Americans have frequently had with themselves and with foreigners.

We have reexamined every aspect of this book—every Diplomatic Crossroad section, paragraph, interpretation, quotation, example, illustration, caption, map, chart, endnote, and bibliography. Although retaining the basic structure of previous editions, we have rewritten and reorganized section by section, chapter by chapter. We have updated the story through the Clinton administration, including the tumultuous events following the end of the Cold War and the collapse of the Soviet Union.

The more traditional topics of diplomacy, war, economic relations, and politics are still covered at length, but we have made this edition more comprehensive by extending the discussion of cultural relations, including sports, dress, film, television and popular images, values, and shared memories. Global environmental damage—acid rain, polluted water, industrial waste, pesticides—and the international conferences convened to deal with these phenomena also receive more emphasis in this edition. The ending of the Cold War and the gradual declassification of documents in foreign archives—Russian, East German, Cuban, and Chinese, for example—have permitted new perspectives and more textured discussion of many topics, including U.S. intervention in the Bolshevik Revolution, origins of the Cold War, the Korean War, and the Cuban missile crisis. Because scholars have increasingly explored medical health as a factor in decisionmaking, we have integrated this subject—as in the lives of Woodrow Wilson, Franklin D. Roosevelt, and John F. Kennedy. In this edition, readers will find greater coverage of the nuclear arms race and U.S. relations with Japan, the Philippines, Germany, Puerto Rico, Central America, Cuba, Israel, and the Middle East. We have also expanded our attention to questions of race and gender.

In preparing this edition, we again immersed ourselves in the memoirs, diaries, letters, speeches, recorded tapes, and oral histories of U.S. and international leaders. We often let them speak for themselves in the frankest terms, guarded and unguarded. We have sought to capture their anger and their humor, their cooperation and their competitiveness, their truths and their lies, their moments of doubt and times of confidence, their triumphs and setbacks. *American Foreign Relations,* in short, strives to capture the erratic pulse of international relations through peoples' struggles to plan, decide, and administer policy. We study not only the leaders who made influential decisions but also the world's peoples who welcomed, resisted, or endured decisions that profoundly influenced their lives.

Each chapter opens with a Diplomatic Crossroad section that highlights a significant and dramatic event. This introductory section illustrates the chief characteristics of the period and establishes the themes carried through the chapter. Illustrations, many of them new to this edition, from collections around the world, are closely tied to the narrative in image and caption description. The revised maps, graphs, and Makers of American Foreign Relations tables in each chapter provide essential information. The completely updated bibliographies provide guidance for further reading on the many topics listed and a starting point for term or research papers. The General Bibliography includes reference works, bibliographies, and overviews of U.S. relations with other countries and regions, as well as works on specific subjects such as the Air Force and air power, Congress, cultural relations, drug trade, economic sanctions, food diplomacy and relief, human rights, intelligence, CIA and covert action, nuclear arms, terrorism, isolationism, and the United Nations.

In the late 1970s, the People's Republic of China adopted a new system for rendering Chinese phonetic characters into the Roman alphabet. Called the Pinyin method, it replaced the Wade-Giles technique, which had long been used in English. Use of the Pinyin method has become widespread and we use it in *American Foreign Relations*. Many changes are minor and pose no problem— Shantung has become Shandong and Mao Tse-tung has become Mao Zedong, for example. But when we have a possibly confusing Pinyin spelling, we have placed the Wade-Giles spelling in parentheses—for example, Beijing (Peking) or Jiang Jieshi (Chiang Kai-shek).

Instructors and students who want to continue their study of foreign relations history are invited to join the Society for Historians of American Foreign Relations (SHAFR). This organization publishes a superb journal, *Diplomatic History*, and an informative newsletter; offers book, article, and lecture prizes and dissertation research grants; and holds an annual conference where scholars present their views and research results. Dues are very reasonable. For information, contact the SHAFR Business Office, Department of History, Wright State University, Dayton, Ohio, 45435.

Many colleagues, friends, students, and editors contributed to this edition of *American Foreign Relations* by providing research leads, corrections of errors, reviews of the text, library searches, documents and essays, and editorial assistance. We give our heartiest thanks to Philip J. Avillo, Jr., Ralph DiCarpio, Irwin Gellman, Hope M. Harrison, Ted Hitchcock, Wang Li, Terrence J. Lindell, David McFadden, Charles McGraw, Matt McMahon, Robert McMahon, Shane Maddock, Elizabeth Mahan, Carl Murdock, Brian Murphy, Arnold Offner, Jerry Padula, Carol Petillo, Carol S. Repass, Kent M. Schofield, Kenneth R. Stevens, Mark A. Stoler, Kathryn Weathersby, and Lawrence Wittner. We especially appreciate our reciprocal research agreement with John Rourke. Alexandra Nickerson, as always, has prepared an excellent, comprehensive index. The excellent D. C. Heath staff who guided this edition to publication deserve special mention: James Miller, Sylvia Mallory, Pat Wakeley, Elizabeth Gale, Jan Shapiro, and Nancy Hale.

We also take this opportunity to acknowledge the many people who helped us in previous editions: Richard Baker, Ann Balcolm, Michael A. Barnhart, Kenneth J. Blume, Robert Beisner, R. Christian Berg, Richard Bradford, Kinley J. Brauer, Richard Dean Burns, Charles Conrad Campbell, Chen Jian, John Coogan, Carol Davidge, Mark Del Vecchio, Justus Doenecke, Xavier Franco, Paul Goodwin, James Gormly, Eric Hafter, Alan Henrikson, Gregg Herken, George Herring, Joan

Hoff, Reginald Horsman, Michael Hunt, Edyth Izard, Holly Izard, Richard Izard, Leith Johnson, Burton Kaufman, Melville T. Kennedy, Jr., Thomas Lairson, Lester Langley, Thomas M. Leonard, Li Yan, Martha McCoy, Paul Manning, Herman Mast, Dennis Merrill, Jean-Donald Miller, R. Kent Newmyer, John Offner, David Pletcher, Salvadore Prisco, Stephen G. Rabe, Wayne Repeta, Barney J. Richman III, Michael Roskin, David Sheinin, Anna Lou Smethurst, Elbert B. Smith, Thomas G. Smith, Mark Stoler, William W. Stueck, Jr., Duane Tananbaum, George Turner, Jonathan G. Utley, Ralph E. Weber, Edmund S. Wehrle, Sol Woolman, and Thomas Zoumaras.

We welcome comments and suggestions from students and instructors.

T. G. P.
J. G. C.
K. J. H.

Contents

Chapter 3
War, Peace, and Revolution in the Time of Wilson, 1914–1920

Chapter 4
Descending into Europe's Maelstrom, 1920–1939

Chapter 5
Asia, Latin America, and the Vagaries of Power, 1920–1939   167

Chapter 6
Survival and Spheres: The Allies and the Second World War, 1939–1945   205

Chapter 7
All-Embracing Struggle: The Cold War Begins, 1945–1950   265

Diplomatic Crossroad: The Atomic Bomb at Hiroshima, 1945   266

Chapter 12
The Tests of a New Era: Americans and the World Since 1989   543

Appendix: Makers of American Foreign Relations

General Bibliography

Maps and Graphs

American Foreign Relations

Chapter 1

IMPERIALIST LEAP, 1895–1900

Grover Cleveland (1837–1908). *This caricature of the two-term president, overweight from frequenting saloons as a young man, captured the gruff American attitude toward Britain during the Venezuelan crisis. The historian Dexter Perkins wrote that Cleveland was "so honest, so brave, so independent . . . , but also so rigid and inflexible in his thinking, so unimaginative, so dogmatic." (Courtesy of The New-York Historical Society, New York City)*

✖ *Diplomatic Crossroad*

The Venezuelan Crisis, 1895

Grover Cleveland was pleased. On July 7, 1895, the same day his third daughter was born at the family summer home on Cape Cod, Massachusetts, he wrote an enthusiastic note to Secretary of State Richard Olney. Just a few days before, Olney, who also escaped from the sweltering summer temperatures of Washington to a residence on the Cape, had personally delivered a 12,000-word draft document to the president. The secretary had been on the job only a few weeks, and this draft of a major message to London on the Venezuelan boundary dispute was one of his first efforts. Energetic Olney, a successful corporate lawyer and former attorney general, fretted and fidgeted. He knew that Cleveland wanted the dispute cleared up, and Olney himself liked to keep his desk tidy. The president's note arrived bearing laudatory words: "It's the best thing of the kind I ever read." Cleveland suggested some minor changes, "a little more softened verbiage here and there," and directed Olney to send the document to London, which he did on July 20, 1895. Cleveland later christened it Olney's "twenty-inch gun." It was as much Cleveland's weapon as Olney's.[1]

The gun was aimed at Great Britain, which for decades had haggled with Venezuela over the boundary line separating that country and British Guiana. A Britisher, Robert Schomburgk, had drawn a line in the 1840s, but nobody liked it. Both sides made claims that went deep into the other's territory. In the 1880s, the discovery of gold in the disputed region—the largest nugget ever found, 509 ounces, was unearthed there—heightened competition. At stake, too, was control of the mouth of the Orinoco River, gateway to the potential trade of northern South America. In the 1870s Venezuela had begun to appeal to the United States for help, arguing that the poaching British violated the Monroe Doctrine. Washington repeatedly asked the British to submit the issue to arbitration, but met constant rebuff. In his annual message to Congress in December 1894, Cleveland renewed the call for arbitration. After another British refusal, the impatient president ordered the State Department to prepare a report on the boundary question. The "twenty-inch gun" sounded Olney's memorable answer.

In retrospect it is easy to see why Cleveland and Olney became so agitated about the Venezuelan boundary question. First, the political dimension. In the early 1890s the Venezuelan government hired William L. Scruggs, a former U.S. minister to Caracas, to propagandize its case before the American public. He wrote a widely circulated pamphlet, *British Aggressions in Venezuela, or the Monroe Doctrine on Trial* (1895), which aroused considerable sympathy for the South American nation. Olney himself read it before preparing his blast of July 20. American sentiment soon congealed: The land-grabbing British were picking on a poor hemispheric friend of the United States. A unanimous congressional resolution of February 1895, calling for arbitration, reflected the growing American concern. Cleveland listened attentively to such expressions, because his Democratic party had lost badly in the 1894 congressional elections and his administration was being attacked, particularly by Republicans, as pusillanimous for not annexing Hawaii and for doing nothing when the British briefly landed troops in Nicaragua in April 1895. Cleveland, it seemed, could deflect criticism and recoup Democratic losses by bold action. As one Democrat advised the president: "Turn this Venezuela question up or down, North, South, East or West, and it is a 'winner.'"[2]

The president did not need such political considerations to stimulate his interest. He leaned toward action anyway because of momentous events in the 1890s. This was the golden age of European imperialism, when the powers were carving up territories in Asia, the Near East, and Africa. The British, already holding large stakes in Latin America, seemed intent on enlarging them. Their recent intervention in Nicaragua looked ominous. Everyone remembered the French intervention in Mexico a generation earlier. Americans feared that new incursions could make Latin America another Africa. "Contradictory and palpably unjust," as Olney's predecessor Walter Q. Gresham described it, Britain's claim against Venezuela became a symbol of European intrusion into the Western Hemisphere.[3]

The American depression of the 1890s also helped fix attention on Venezuela. Many, including Cleveland, thought that overproduction had caused the slump and expanding foreign trade could cure it. Might the British close off the Orinoco River and hence the markets of the area? At that time, American economic activity in Venezuela was ripening. For example, the National Association of Manufacturers, organized in 1895 to expand American exports, chose Caracas as the site for its first permanent overseas display of American products. In short, international competition and economic woes suggested that the national interest of the United States was connected to Venezuela's dispute with Britain.

Cleveland's own character and style colored his response. He did not like bullies pushing small fry around. He had already rejected Hawaiian annexation in part because he thought that Americans had bullied the Hawaiians against their will. It appeared to the president, exaggeration though it was, that America's perennial competitor, Britain, was arrogantly manhandling the Venezuelans. What he and the sometimes intemperate Olney needed was an intellectual peg on which to hang the U.S. case. They found it in a refurbished Monroe Doctrine. Olney's "twenty-inch gun" of July 20, 1895, invoked that venerable principle in aggressive, bumptious, and unvarnished language that prejudged the issue against the British.

The brash message noted that the British claim had grown larger and larger, cutting deeper and deeper into Venezuela. Further growth might lead to political control. Olney warned that the European struggle over the partition of Africa might be transferred to Latin America. The "safety," "honor," and "welfare" of the United States were at stake, and the Monroe Doctrine forbade European intervention leading to control in the Western Hemisphere. Using history, Olney cited the successful application of the doctrine in the French-Mexican-American imbroglio of the 1860s. He asserted that "any permanent political union between a European and an American state [was] unnatural and inexpedient."

"The Real British Lion."   A popular American depiction of the British global presence during the crisis over Venezuela. A few years later, President Cleveland himself recalled British behavior as "mean and hoggish." (*New York Evening World*, 1895)

Because its national interest was involved, the United States had to intervene in the dispute. "The states of America, South as well as North, by geographical proximity, by natural sympathy, by similarity of governmental constitutions, are friends and allies, commercially and politically, of the United States. To allow the subjugation of any one of them by a European power is, of course, to completely reverse that situation and signifies the loss of all the advantages incident to their natural relations with us." The forceful overriding theme of Olney's proclamation addressed an international audience: "To-day the United States is practically sovereign on this continent, and its fiat is law upon the subjects to which it confines its interposition." And more: The United States' "infinite resources combined with its isolated position render it master of the situation and practically invulnerable as against any or all other powers."[4] Olney, finally, demanded arbitration, vaguely threatened U.S. intervention, and requested a British answer before the president's annual message to Congress in December.

Ambassador to England Thomas Bayard delivered the document to the giant of European diplomats, Lord Salisbury, then doubling as the British prime minister and foreign secretary. The bearded sixty-five-year-old Salisbury struck an imposing figure—intelligent, aristocratic, cautious, and well-read. He received the missive with some surprise and sent it to the Foreign Office for study. Through the summer months little was done in part because vacations interrupted work.

Salisbury saw no urgency, bothered as he was with crises elsewhere (especially in Africa). Anyway, in the late nineteenth century one expected American Anglophobic bombast. The issue, he thought, would probably fizzle out once American politics calmed down. Furthermore, he disliked arbitrating any question that might weaken the British Empire. Salisbury would never entrust British interests in the Orinoco area to the United States. Obviously he did not grasp how agitated the Cleveland administration was. The British did not complete their reply until November 26, and it arrived in Washington after Cleveland's annual message (actually tame on the Venezuelan controversy). Salisbury's note, which smacked of "the peremptory schoolmaster trying—with faded patience—to correct the ignorance of dullards in Washington," denied the applicability of the Monroe Doctrine and dismissed any U.S. interest in the dispute.[5]

Cleveland, all 250 pounds of him, was duck-hunting in North Carolina when the British response reached Washington. On his return he read it and became "mad clean through."[6] Olney had already been working on a special congressional message. He had not counted on a flat British rejection. Now what? War? Retreat? Neither course would serve the national interest. Olney struggled for alternatives

"If There Must Be War."   Lord Salisbury and President Cleveland slug it out during the Venezuelan crisis as a substitute for full-scale war. According to the historian Richard E. Welch, Jr., Cleveland's "innate talent to identify his personal judgment with righteousness and truth encouraged him to confuse compromise with surrender." (*Life,* 1896)

and finally selected one that left some maneuvering room, kept diplomacy in the hands of the executive branch, and avoided war or backstepping: an American study commission appointed by the president. Cleveland, although tired from his expedition among the ducks, stayed up all night to rewrite Olney's draft. He dispatched his special message to Congress on December 17, and it rang a bell of alarm. England must arbitrate; the United States would create an investigating commission to set the true boundary line; and then American action would follow. Most observers labeled the message an ultimatum, with the possibility of war lurking throughout.

The nation buzzed in anticipation. Congress appropriated funds for the investigating commission. Irish-Americans offered themselves as volunteers to fight the hated British; both Republicans and Democrats lined up behind the president, and Senator Henry Cabot Lodge noted with approval that "Jingoes are plenty enough now."[7] New York City police commissioner Theodore Roosevelt boomed: "Let the fight come if it must; I don't care whether our sea coast cities are bombarded or not; we would take Canada."[8] Many businesspeople rallied behind the administration, with Whitelaw Reid, editor of the *New York Tribune,* hyperbolically declaring that "this is the golden opportunity of our merchants to extend our trade to every quarter of Central and South America."[9] British ambassador Sir Julian Pauncefote reported: "Nothing is heard but the voice of the Jingo bellowing defiance to England."[10]

This high wave of emotionalism subsided rapidly in early 1896. Many bankers and businesspeople became alarmed when the stock market plummeted, in large part because British investors were pulling out. Joseph Pulitzer's *New York World* put out a special Christmas issue with portraits of the Prince of Wales and Lord Salisbury under the headline PEACE AND GOOD WILL, implying that a war was unconscionable with Britain, a country so close in race, language, and culture.[11] Critics like E. L. Godkin, editor of *The Nation,* and respected international law specialist John Bassett Moore pointed out how haughtily Cleveland and Olney had acted. Ambassador Bayard questioned the president's truculent stance: "I fear he has made a gross and great error of judgment and has been too *precipitate,* for I do not see why he should abandon suddenly his attitude of conservatism and go apparently into the camp of aggressiveness."[12] But Cleveland never wanted war. He wanted peace on American terms, even if it required aggressiveness.

U.S. FOREIGN RELATIONS AFTER VENEZUELA

What followed seemed anticlimactic. The British cabinet, on January 11, 1896, instructed Salisbury to seek an "honourable settlement" with the United States.[13] A new dispute with Germany over South Africa necessitated retreat. England needed friends now, not enemies. British troops could not defend Canada, and the Admiralty thought that the Royal Navy was outgunned in the North Atlantic and Caribbean. Formal talks ultimately began and dragged on until November 1896, when Britain and the United States agreed to set up a five-person arbitral board to define the boundary, with each to name two members, who would in turn select the fifth. Finally, in October 1899, the tribunal reached a decision that rejected the extreme claims of each party and generally followed the Schomburgk line. The pivotal Point Barima at the mouth of the Orinoco went to Venezuela, which came out of the dispute pretty well, considering that neither the United States nor Great Britain cared much about what happened to *Venezuela's* national interest.

Indeed, a remarkable characteristic of this controversy was that the United States negotiated directly with Britain without consulting Venezuela. Both parties excluded Venezuela's duly accredited minister in Washington from the talks. Olney never even gave the Venezuelans a copy of his "twenty-inch gun" (they eventually read it in the newspapers), and when they balked over the 1896 Anglo-American agreement he curtly told them what to do. He made one concession: Venezuela could name one of the five members of the arbitration board—so long as that person was not a Venezuelan. Lobbyist William Scruggs complained that the United States sought to "*bull-doze* Venezuela."[14] He had it right, but Washington's vigorous diplomacy targeted others besides that South American nation. The overweening theme of Olney's "twenty-inch gun" merits repeating: "To-day the United States is practically sovereign on this continent, and its fiat is law upon the subjects to which it confines its interposition."

The Venezuelan crisis, most scholars agree, marked a watershed in the history of American foreign relations. Cleveland and Olney helped move the United States toward world-power status. As an example of forceful, even aggressive, American diplomacy, the Venezuelan controversy marked a time in history when the United States determined to demonstrate its weight in international affairs. Besides displaying a self-righteous disregard for the rights and sensibilities of small nations, it revealed a United States more sure of itself, more certain about the components of its "policy," and willing to lecture others. The episode stimulated American nationalism and pride, or what critics at the time called "jingoism." The Monroe Doctrine gained new stature as a warning to European nations to temper, if not abandon, their activities in the Western Hemisphere; the United States, so jingoes boasted, had humbled Great Britain and forced the olympian Salisbury to retreat. The executive branch kept the Venezuelan issue in *its* hands, thereby strengthening the foreign-policy power of the president. Some members of Congress complained that Cleveland was committing the United States to possible war without appropriate consultation with the legislative branch.

Other ramifications became evident. Latin Americans learned once again that the United States intended to establish supremacy in the Western Hemisphere. They realized further that the United States would judge the national interests of other countries and intervene when it saw fit. The United States had always kept an eye on the Caribbean, but the Venezuelan crisis and the outbreak of revolution in Cuba in 1895 intensified North American interest, a significant dimension of which was economic. The Venezuelan issue and the disposition of the Orinoco River also brought more attention to the theory of overproduction as a cause of depression, to be cured by exporting surplus goods. Commercial expansion, always a trend in American history, received another boost.

"Either Caesar or Nothing!"   Uncle Sam protests against imperialism, but refuses to return to his cramped log cabin now that he has taken up "skyscraper" diplomacy, according to this German cartoon. (*Kladderadatsch,* 1899, Courtesy Dartmouth College Library)

The discord with Britain over Venezuela actually fostered Anglo-American rapprochement. Cooperation and mutual interest increasingly characterized relations between Washington and London. British diplomats sought United States friendship as a possible counterweight to growing German power, and one manifestation of the emerging détente was a self-conscious British decision to permit the United States to govern Caribbean affairs. One way, the chief way, the United States could manage events in that area was through naval power. The Venezuelan crisis, joined by crises in Asia and the belief that naval construction would employ those idled by depression, stimulated additional American naval expansion. The Navy Act of 1896, for example, provided for three new battleships and ten new torpedo boats. All told, the Venezuelan boundary dispute advanced the United States farther along the path of expansion.

That path, by the end of the decade, led to new U.S. colonies in the Pacific, Asia, and the Caribbean, a firm hold on independent Cuba, and Europe's recognition of the United States as the overlord of the Caribbean. By 1900, too, the United States had pledged itself to preserve the "Open Door" in China; it had built a navy that had just annihilated the Spanish fleet and ranked sixth in the world; and it had developed an export trade amounting to $1.5 billion. Its industrial might was symbolized by steel and iron production, which almost equaled that of Britain and Germany combined. American acquisition of new colonies after the Spanish-American-Cuban-Filipino War has led some observers to conclude that *only then,* about 1898, did the United States become an imperialist world power. But a continuity of expansionism and imperialism characterized nineteenth-century foreign relations. Seldom do major diplomatic squabbles or wars happen all of a sudden; they flow from cumulative events. Had William H. Seward lived in 1898, for example, he might have triumphantly emphasized the similarities between the 1890s and the 1860s. Had he been a good historian, he would have pointed out also that economic and political changes at home and increased competition with European powers abroad had undermined anti-imperialist arguments and permitted his schemes for empire to be realized. Before the depression decade of the 1890s the United States had often taken halting steps toward a larger empire; in that decade it took the leap.

THE "FOREIGN-POLICY PUBLIC" OF THE 1890S

Assistant Secretary of the Navy Theodore Roosevelt described the anti-imperialists in 1897 as "men of a by-gone age" and "provincials."[15] Indeed, anti-imperialism waned through the late nineteenth century. Increasing numbers of educated, economically comfortable Americans made the case for formal empire (colonies or protectorates) or informal empire (commercial domination). Naval officers, diplomats, politicians, farmers, skilled artisans, businesspeople, and clergy made up what might be called the "foreign-policy public." Better read than most Americans and having access to lecterns to disperse their ideas, this "elite" helped move America to war and empire. Recent scholarly research has shown, contrary to a longstanding assumption, that neither "public opinion," nor the jingoistic "yellow press," nor the "people" in the 1890s compelled the United States to war. Rather, two key elements stand out: a McKinley administration very much in charge of its diplomacy through skillful maneuvering, and a majoritarian view within the articulate "foreign-policy public" in favor of a vigorous outward thrust.

The "hows," rather than the "whys," of decisionmaking can be explained by noting problems with the phrase "public opinion." One often hears that "public opinion" or "the man in the street" influenced a leader to follow a certain course of action. But "public opinion" was not a unified, identifiable group speaking with

Makers of American Foreign Relations, 1895–1900

Presidents	Secretaries of State
Grover Cleveland, 1893–1897	Walter Q. Gresham , 1893–1895
	Richard Olney, 1895–1897
William McKinley, 1897–1901	John Sherman, 1897–1898
	William R. Day, 1898
	John Hay, 1898–1905

one voice. Furthermore, political leaders and other articulate, knowledgeable people often shaped the "public opinion" they wanted to hear by their very handling of events and their control over information. That is, they *led* in the true sense of the word. In trying to determine who the "people" are and what "public opinion" is, social-science studies demonstrate that the people who counted, the people who were listened to, the people who expressed their opinion publicly in order to influence policy—these people in the 1890s numbered no more than 1.5 million to 3 million, or between 10 and 20 percent of the voting public. This percentage—upper- and middle-income groups, educated, active politically—constituted the "foreign-policy public." As Secretary of State Walter Q. Gresham put it in 1893: "After all, public opinion is made and controlled by the thoughtful men of the country."[16] The "public opinion" the president heard in the 1890s was not that of some collection we loosely call the "people," but rather that of a small, articulate segment of the American population alert to foreign-policy issues. Although they counted anti-imperialists in their numbers, the "foreign-policy public" was heavily weighted on the side of imperialism.

The president, as a consummate politician and good tactician, is often the master of policymaking, even thwarting the advice of the "foreign-policy public" itself. President Cleveland, for example, successfully resisted pressure to annex Hawaii and withdrew the treaty from the Senate. He never let Congress or influential public opinion set the terms of his policy toward the Venezuelan crisis. Nor was President William McKinley stampeded into decisions; he tried *his* diplomacy before trying the war that many leaders, especially in Congress, had been advocating for months and years. An imperialist-oriented "foreign-policy public," rather than some immeasurable "public opinion," helped move the United States along a path to war and larger empire, but the administrations determined the speed of the movement. Pressures from jingoes in Congress and a sensationalist press expanded, but the initiative in foreign affairs, unlike the 1860s and 1870s, remained largely in the hands of the executive branch. In most historical periods, the public *reacts* to *immediate* events; the executive *acts, manages,* with *long-term* policy considerations.

THE CUBAN REVOLUTION AND THE UNITED STATES, 1895–1897

Eighteen ninety-five was a year of momentous events. The Venezuelan crisis, Japan's defeat of China in the Sino-Japanese War, and the outbreak of revolution in Cuba—all carried profound meaning for American foreign relations. The sugar-rich island of Cuba, since the close of its unsuccessful war for independence (1868–1878), suffered political repression and poverty. After that war Cuban nationalists prepared for a new assault upon their Spanish overlords. From 1880 to 1895, Cuban national hero José Martí plotted from exile in the United States. In 1892 he organized the Cuban Revolutionary Party, using U.S. territory to recruit men and money for a return to his homeland. Martí's opportunity came when Cuba's economy fell victim in 1894 to a new U.S. tariff, which raised duties on imported sugar and hence reduced Cuban sugar shipments to the United States. On February 24, 1895, with cries of *"Cuba Libre,"* the rebels opened their drive for independence.

The Cuban revolutionaries kept a cautious eye on the United States, for they well knew North America's historical interest in the island and thus feared an ultimate U.S. attempt to control their nation's destiny. José Martí's fifteen-year stay in the United States had turned him into a critic of what he called "the monster."[17] He wrote about an "aggressive" and "avaricious" nation "full of hate" and "widespread spiritual coarseness." And he warned against a U.S. "conquering policy" that "arrogantly" treated Latin American countries as "dependencies."[18] On May 19 Martí was killed in action.

Cuban and Spanish military strategies intended to produce destruction and death. Led by General Máximo Gómez, a veteran of the 1868–1878 war, the *insurrectos* burned cane fields, blew up mills, and disrupted railroads, with the goal of rendering Cuba an economic liability to Spain. "The chains of Cuba have been forged by her own richness," Gómez proclaimed, "and it is precisely this which I propose to do away with soon."[19] Although outnumbered (about 30,000 Cuban troops against 200,000 Spanish) and lacking adequate supplies (often their weapons and ammunition did not match), the insurgents, with the sympathy of the populace, wore the Spanish down through guerrilla tactics. By late 1896 they controlled about two-thirds of the island, with the Spanish concentrated in coastal and urban regions. That year, to break the rebel stronghold in the rural areas, Governor-General Valeriano y Nicolau Weyler instituted the brutal reconcentration program. He divided the island into districts and herded Cubans into fortified camps. A half million Cubans were driven from homes and livelihoods into these centers, where frightful sanitation conditions, poor food, and disease contributed to the death of perhaps 200,000 people. Cubans outside the camps were assumed to be rebels and targets for death. In the countryside Weyler's soldiers destroyed crops, killed livestock, and polluted water sources. This effort to starve the insurgents and deprive them of physical and moral support, combined with the rebels' destructive behavior, made a shambles of Cuba's society and economy.

The Cleveland administration, keeping control of its diplomacy against congressional pressures, faced several alternatives. It could recognize Cuban belligerency. That was ruled out because such an act, Olney noted, would relieve Spain of any responsibility for paying claims filed by Americans for properties destroyed in Cuba. Cleveland and Olney found recognition of Cuban independence even less appetizing, for they believed the Cubans incapable of self-government and feared anarchy and even racial war. That course might also arouse a Spanish declaration of war or force American belligerency because, logically, a Spanish attempt to conquer an "independent" Cuba would constitute a violation of the Monroe Doctrine. War seemed out of the question, as did outright annexation, although apparently Olney toyed with buying the island at one point. The Cleveland administration settled on a dual policy of hostility to the revolution and pressure on Spain to grant some autonomy. Diplomacy and lecturing to a foreign government seemed to work in the Venezuelan crisis; perhaps it would work in the case of Cuba.

Prodded by a Republican Congress (it passed a resolution in April 1896, urging the president to recognize Cuban belligerency), by continued evidence of wholesale destruction, and by Spanish obstinacy in refusing reforms and adhering to force, Olney sent a note to Spain in April 1896. He told Spain it could not win by force, but said the United States preferred continued Spanish control of the island. Because of American sympathy for free institutions, the proximity of Cuba, the loss of U.S. trade and property, and the excesses committed by both combatants, Olney urged on Madrid a political solution that would leave "Spain her rights of sovereignty . . . yet secure to the [Cubans] all such rights and powers of local self-government as they [could] ask."[20] Spain should initiate reforms short of independence. Olney was principally concerned with the interests of Americans, not with those of the Cubans. American property was estimated at $50 million and the decline in sugar production wrought disaster to Cuban-American trade relations. In 1892 Cuba had shipped to the United States goods worth $79 million; by 1898 that figure had slumped to $15 million.

When Spain rejected Olney's advice, the Cleveland administration seemed stymied. It did not desire war, but it meant to protect American interests. Congress kept asking for firm action. And in Havana, hotheaded American consul-general Fitzhugh Lee clamored for American annexation. Cleveland did not feel he could fire Lee, nephew of General Robert E. Lee, because the noisy fellow had some political clout at home, and Cleveland needed political friends at a time when the Democratic party was dumping the incumbent president in favor of William Jennings Bryan. Olney kept Lee at bay by peppering him with endless requests for information. It further nettled Cleveland and Olney that Spain had approached the courts of Europe for diplomatic support, with the argument that the Monroe Doctrine threatened all European powers. Spain's appeal went unheeded, but leaders in Washington still worried about possible European intrusion in Cuba.

British ambassador to Spain H. Drummond Wolff believed "what the United States required for Cuba was 'peace with commerce.'"[21] Cleveland proved this estimate accurate when he sent his annual message to Congress in December 1896. With a slight echo of Olney's "twenty-inch gun" about the United States' "fiat" in the Western Hemisphere, the president reported that neither the Spanish nor the Cuban rebels had established their authority over the island. Americans felt a humanitarian concern, he said, but their trade and investments ("pecuniary interest") were also jeopardized. Furthermore, to maintain its neutrality, the United States had to police the coastline to intercept unlawful expeditions. Spain must grant autonomy or "home rule," but not independence, to "fertile and rich" Cuba to end the bloodshed and devastation. If she did not, he warned, the United States, having thus far acted with "restraint," might abandon its "expectant attitude."[22]

But Cleveland had more bark than bite. Through Olney he successfully buried a Senate resolution urging recognition of Cuban independence and contented himself with some limited Spanish reforms of February 1897. Thereafter he let the Cuban issue fester, bequeathing it to the incoming McKinley administration. His legacy to the new Republican president had grave implications: Cleveland had defined vital U.S. interests in Cuba that U.S. power might have to protect.

McKinley's Road to War, 1897–1898

A veteran Republican politician and deft manager of people, President William McKinley had defeated William Jennings Bryan in the election of 1896 by running as the "Advance Agent of Prosperity" and promising a bright future for America. The teetotaling Ohioan seemed a stable, dignified figure in a time of crisis. He represented deep religious conviction, personal warmth, sincerity, commitment to economic development and the revival of business, party loyalty, and support for expansion abroad. Yet McKinley often gave the appearance of being an infantile follower, a mindless flunky of the political bosses, a spineless leader. One joke went: "Why is McKinley's mind like a bed?" Answer: "Because it has to be made up for him every time he wants to use it." Plucky Theodore Roosevelt allegedly remarked that McKinley had "no more backbone than a chocolate éclair."[23] Such an image was created in large part by bellicose imperialists who believed that McKinley was not moving fast enough and by critics of domestic policy like Bryan who saw McKinley as clay in the hands of big business and party machines. The president certainly was a party regular and friend of large corporations, but he was no lackey. A manager of diplomacy, who wanted expansion and empire without war and a settlement of the Cuban question without U.S. military intervention, McKinley acted as his own man.

McKinley shared America's image of itself as an expanding nation of superior institutions and as a major power in Latin America. He agreed that the United States must have a large navy, overseas commerce, and foreign bases. He believed strongly that America must export its surplus goods. As a tariff specialist, he favored high tariffs on manufactured goods, low tariffs on raw materials, and reciprocity agreements. Although McKinley uttered almost nothing about foreign issues in the campaign of 1896, the Republican party platform overflowed with expansionist rhetoric worthy of William H. Seward himself. Extolling a vigorous diplomacy, it urged American control of Hawaii, a Nicaraguan canal run by the United States, an enlarged navy, purchase of the Virgin Islands, and Cuban independence. Between election and inauguration, however, McKinley quietly joined Cleveland and Olney in successfully heading off a Senate resolution for recognition of Cuba. He wanted a free hand, and he did not believe that Cubans could govern themselves. His appointment of the old and ailing Senator John Sherman as secretary of state suggested further that McKinley would take charge of his own diplomacy. His inaugural address vacuously urged peace, never mentioning the Cuban crisis.

McKinley's first tilt with Congress came in March 1897, after he called a special session for revision of the tariff. Resolutions on Cuba sprang up repeatedly, but the president managed to kill them. He did satisfy imperialists by sending an Hawaiian annexation treaty to the Senate. The president was preparing for his own nonpublic diplomatic assault upon Spain. In June, Madrid received an American reprimand for Weyler's uncivilized warfare and for his disruption of the Cuban economy. "Capitalism and humanitarianism," the scholar Lester Langley has aptly noted, "had joined hands" in the American protest.[24] Spain, however, showed no signs of tempering its military response to the insurrection. American citizens languished in Spanish jails; American property continued to be devastated. Fitzhugh Lee, who remained at his post in Havana, bellowed for American intervention. In July, McKinley instructed the new American minister to Spain, Stewart L. Woodford, to demand that the Spanish stop the fighting. Increasingly convinced that the Cuban *insurrectos* would not compromise, the president sought to persuade Spain to provide autonomy. A new Spanish government assumed power in October and soon moderated policy by offering Cuba a substantial degree of self-government or autonomy. Even more, it removed the hated Weyler and promised to end reconcentration. Never fully implemented, these reforms did not end the fighting, because the Cuban junta demanded full independence.

McKinley's December 6, 1897, annual message to Congress discussed the Cuban insurrection at great length. The crisis caused Americans the "gravest apprehension." McKinley rejected annexation as "criminal aggression." He argued against recognition of belligerency, because the rebels hardly constituted a government worthy of recognition. And he ruled out intervention as premature at a time when the Spanish were traveling the "honorable paths" of reform. He asked for patience to see if Spanish changes would work, but hinted that the United States would continue to consider all policy options, including intervention "with force."[25]

By mid-January evidence had poured into Washington proving that the reforms had not moderated the crisis; in fact, insurgents, conservatives, and the Spanish army all denounced them. Antireform Spaniards rioted in Havana. The United States ordered the warship *Maine* to Havana on January 24, 1898, to protect American citizens and demonstrate concern. On February 9, the State Department received a copy of a private letter written in late 1897 by Spanish minister to the United States Enrique Dupuy de Lôme and sent to a senior Spanish politician touring Cuba. Intercepted in Cuba by a rebel sympathizer, the letter was forwarded to the Cuban junta in New York City. Not only did it reach the State Department; William Randolph Hearst's flamboyant *New York Journal* published it

William McKinley (1843–1901). An Ohioan who studied at Allegheny College, fought in the Civil War, and served several terms as a member of Congress, the twenty-fifth president was a supreme politician and successful imperialist. An assassin killed him in Buffalo, New York. (Library of Congress)

that day with the banner headline: "Worst Insult to the United States in its History." De Lôme labeled McKinley "weak," a "bidder for the admiration of the crowd," and a "would-be politician."[26] McKinley, along with most Americans, was infuriated by de Lôme's remarks. The administration particularly resented another statement that suggested that Spain did not take its reform proposals seriously and would persist in fighting to defeat the rebels. Spain, it appeared, had tricked the United States. De Lôme's hasty recall hardly salved the hurt.

Trying to avoid war, a restless McKinley nevertheless recognized the dangerous trend. On occasion in early 1898 he had to take drugs to sleep. The rush of events did not improve his demeanor. Less than a week after the de Lôme episode,

The U.S.S. *Maine* Before and After. Part of the battleship was raised in 1911, investigated, and sunk at sea with flag flying. The investigators concluded that the explosion that destroyed the vessel was external, but a 1976 navy study by Admiral Hyman G. Rickover blamed the sinking on an internal accident. (Before—*Harper's Weekly*, 1888; after—National Archives)

on February 15, explosions ripped through the *Maine,* anchored conspicuously in Havana harbor. Two hundred and sixty-six of 354 U.S. officers and crew died as the 6,700-ton vessel sank quickly. With no evidence, but considerable emotion, many Americans assumed that Spain had committed the dastardly deed. Few asked why the *Maine* had gone there in the first place—in the troubled waters of a Spanish colony in open rebellion. McKinley ordered an official investigation, but said little publicly. Some decried his caution, but he decided to try diplomacy and threat again. In early March, Woodford protested strongly to the Spanish government about the de Lôme incident and the *Maine.* The "grave" Cuban crisis had to be resolved. On March 6 the president met with Joe Cannon, chairman of the House Committee on Appropriations, and urged him to present a bill providing $50 million for arms. "It seemed as though a hundred Fourths of July had been let loose in the House," a clerk noted, as Congress enthusiastically obliged three days later.[27] Spain, Woodford reported, was stunned by the appropriation.

In mid-March Senator Redfield Proctor of Vermont, a friend of McKinley reportedly opposed to war, graphically told his colleagues about his recent trip to Cuba. He recounted ugly stories about the concentration camps. "Torn from their homes, with foul earth, foul air, foul water, and foul food or none, what wonder that one-half died and that one-quarter of the living are so diseased that they cannot be saved?"[28] Shortly after this moving speech, which convinced many members of Congress and businesspeople that Spain could not bring order to Cuba, the American court of inquiry on the *Maine* concluded that an external mine of unknown origins had destroyed the vessel. The board could not determine who placed it there. A Spanish commission at about the same time attributed the disaster to an internal explosion. We still do not know exactly what set off the forward powder magazine, but in 1898 vocal Americans pinned the crime squarely on Spain. "Remember the *Maine,* to hell with Spain" became the popular chant.

Such events inexorably narrowed options. The president did explore through Minister Woodford the possibility of purchasing Cuba for $300 million—or some other means "by which Spain can part with Cuba without loss of respect and with certainty of American control."[29] But a jingo frenzy had seized the Congress. Following one stormy Senate session, Vice President Garrett Hobart warned McKinley: "They will act without you if you do not act at once." "Say no more," McKinley responded.[30] On March 27 Washington cabled the American demands: an armistice, Cuban-Spanish negotiations to secure a peace, McKinley's arbitration of the conflict if there was no peace by October, termination of the reconcentration policy, and relief aid to the Cubans. Implicit was the demand that Spain grant Cuba its independence under U.S. supervision. As a last-ditch effort to avoid American military intervention, the ultimatum had little chance of success. Spain's national pride and interest precluded surrender. Madrid's answer showed promise: It had already terminated reconcentration, would launch reforms, and would accept an armistice if the rebels did so first. By refusing McKinley's offer of mediation and Cuban independence, the Spanish reply did not satisfy the president or Congress. He began to write a war message in early April. On the ninth, probably in response to the entreaties of other European nations, Spain made a new concession, declaring a unilateral suspension of hostilities "for such length of time" as the

Spanish commander "may think prudent."[31] Too qualified, the declaration still avoided Cuban independence and American mediation. Minister Woodford nonetheless urged that "nothing will now be done to humiliate Spain, as I am satisfied that the present Government is going . . . as fast and as far as it can."[32]

WHY WAR: EXPLOITING OPPORTUNITY

On April 11 McKinley sent a message to Congress asking for the authority to use armed force to end the Cuban war. Since neither the Cubans nor the Spaniards could stem the flow of blood, America would do the job. The United States would do so because of the "cause of humanity" and the "very serious injury to the commerce, trade, and business of our people, and the wanton destruction of property." And, citing the *Maine,* McKinley described the conflict as "a constant menace to our peace." At the very end of the message the president noted that Spain had recently accepted an armistice. He asked Congress to give this new information "your just and careful attention."[33]

As Congress debated an armistice that the Cubans themselves rejected, McKinley beat back a Senate attempt to recognize the rebels. He strongly believed that Cuba needed American tutelage to prepare for self-government. Indeed, as the historian Louis A. Pérez, Jr., has argued, McKinley's decision for war may have been "directed as much against Cuban independence as it was against Spanish sovereignty."[34] Congress did endorse the Teller Amendment, which disclaimed any U.S. intention of annexing the island. Some who voted for the amendment feared that annexation would commit the United States to assume Cuba's large bond debt. On April 19 Congress proclaimed Cuba's independence (but without recognizing the Cuban junta), demanded Spain's evacuation from the island, and directed the president to use force to ensure these results. Spain, on April 21, broke diplomatic relations. On the twenty-second, American ships began to blockade Cuba; two days later Spain declared war. On the twenty-fifth, Congress declared that a state of war had existed from the twenty-first.

Because of the Teller Amendment, the decision for war seemed selfless and humanitarian, and for many Americans it undoubtedly was. But the decision had more complex motives. Different people endorsed war for different reasons. McKinley himself cited humanitarian concern, property, commerce, and the removal of an annoyance. Politics also mattered. Senator Lodge, among others, told the White House that "if the war in Cuba drags on through the summer . . . we [Republicans] shall go down to the greatest defeat ever known."[35] Important businesspeople, initially hesitant, shifted in March and April to demand an end to Cuban disorder. Farmers and businesspeople interested in Asian and Latin American markets thought victory against Spain might open new trade doors by eliminating a colonial power. Many highly moralistic Americans simply felt compelled to end the bloodshed. Republican senator George F. Hoar of Massachusetts, later an anti-imperialist, wrote that "we cannot look idly on while hundreds of thousands of innocent human beings . . . die of hunger close to our doors. If there is ever to be a war it should be to prevent such things as that."[36] Religious leaders, both Protestant and Catholic, marched in the war parade. Lyman Abbott, well-known pastor of Plymouth Church in Brooklyn, thought war the "answer to America to the question of its own conscience: Am I my brother's keeper?"[37] Church missionaries dreamed of new opportunities to convert the "uncivilized." Imperialists hoped war would add new territories to the American empire and encourage the growth of a larger navy. But the "warriors" were not synonymous with the "imperialists." Some people opposed empire and sincerely thought war would halt the long conflict in Cuba, whereas the imperialists seized on war as an opportunity to expand the American empire.

Emotional nationalism also figured in the American thirst for war. The de Lôme and *Maine* incidents stimulated a national anger already infused with notions of American superiority, racial and otherwise. Imperialist senator Albert Beveridge was ebullient: "At last, God's hour has struck. The American people go forth in a warfare holier than liberty—holy as humanity."[38] Journalist Finley Peter Dunne's popular Irish-American characters always seemed to provide the fitting summary: "'We're a gr-reat people,' said Mr. Hennessy, earnestly. 'We ar-re,' said Mr. Dooley. 'We ar-re that. An' th best iv it is, we know we ar-re.'"[39] Excited statements by people like Roosevelt, who looked on war as he looked on horseback riding and cowboying in the Dakotas—it was sport, a game, fun—aroused martial fevers. Newspapers of the "yellow press" variety, like Hearst's *New York Journal* and Pulitzer's *New York World,* sensationalized stories of Spanish atrocities. Others proudly compared the Cuban and American revolutions. The American people, already steeped in a brash nationalism and prepared by earlier aggressive diplomatic triumphs, reacted favorably to this hyperbole.

Both Washington and Madrid had tried diplomacy, but their diplomatic paths never crossed. McKinley wanted "peace" and independence for Cuba under U.S. tutelage. The first Spain could not deliver because the Cuban rebels had become entrenched and bent on independence and Spanish forces remained weak. The second Spain could not grant immediately for fear that ultranationalists might overthrow the Bourbon constitutional monarchy. Spain said it would fight the war more humanely and grant autonomy, but McKinley and Congress wanted more, and they believed they had the right and duty to judge the affairs of Spain and Cuba.

Once McKinley insisted that Spain grant Cuba its independence, war seemed inevitable: Here was one power, the United States, telling another power, Spain, how to manage its national affairs. Critics said America might have been less haughty, letting the Cubans and Spaniards settle their own affairs. McKinley's actions in dispatching the *Maine* and asking Congress for $50 million probably encouraged the Cuban rebels to resist any compromise. He might have given Spain a bit more breathing space. Spain, after all, did fire Weyler, terminate reconcentration, and approve an armistice; most important, Madrid did grant partial autonomy, which ultimately might have led to independence. Some critics said the president should have recognized the Cuban insurgents and covertly aided them, and

"Cuba Reconciling the North and South." Captain Fritz W. Guerin's 1898 photograph trumpeted nationalism in the Spanish-American-Cuban-Filipino War. Golden-haired Cuba, liberated from her chains by her North American heroes, oversees the reconciliation of the Union and Confederacy in a splashy display of patriotism. (Library of Congress)

then American soldiers would not necessarily have had to fight in Cuba, the Philippines, and Puerto Rico. American matériel, not men, in other words, might have liberated Cuba from Spanish rule. "McKinley, of course, did not prefer war," the historian Robert L. Beisner has concluded. "But he did want what only war could provide—an end to violence in Cuba, which outraged his sense of decency, prolonged instability in the economy, smashed investment and trade with Cuba, created the spectacle of an America unable to master affairs close to home, threatened to incite a politically dangerous outburst of jingoism, and diverted policymakers' attention from historic events in China. . . ."[40] The United States, not for the first or last time, chose war to end war.

The Spanish-American-Cuban-Filipino War

Americans flocked to recruiting stations and enlisted in what they trumpeted as a glorious expedition to demonstrate U.S. right and might. They were cocky. Young author Sherwood Anderson joked that fighting Spain would be "like robbing an old gypsy woman in a vacant lot at night after a fair."[41] War almost seemed healthy. U.S. ambassador to England John Hay called it a "splendid little war," and Theodore Roosevelt, who resigned as assistant secretary of the navy to lead the flashy but overrated Rough Riders, remarked that "it wasn't much of a war, but it was the best war we had."[42] Yet the Spanish-American-Cuban-Filipino War, as a veteran recalled, was no "tin-foil" affair.[43] Much of the initial euphoria evaporated in mosquito-infested camps, uncomfortable ships, and inadequate hospitals. It was a short war, ending August 12, but 5,462 Americans died in it—only 379 of them in combat. Most of the rest met death from malaria and yellow fever. The chief surgeon of the U.S. Volunteers witnessed the hundreds of disease-wracked men who came home to be quarantined on the tip of Long Island. "The pale faces, the sunken eyes, the staggering gait and the emaciated forms" marked some as "wrecks for life" and others as "candidates for a premature grave."[44]

That was not how it began. About 200,000 excited men entered army camps in April and May 1898. Tampa, Florida, became the busy base for the Cuban expedition. Camp life was tough. The amateur soldiers had to eat poor food, including poisonous spoiled beef. They wore heavy blue uniforms in a humid climate of rain and warm temperatures; most of the new brown tropical uniforms arrived at Tampa after the troops had left for Cuba. Sanitation earned low marks, diseases visited the camps early, and pungent body odors caused nausea. Black troops, in segregated units led by white officers, found no respite from the stings of racial insult and discrimination. African-American resentment grew in the face of the epithet "nigger" and Jim Crow restrictions that barred them from "white only" public parks, bars, and cafes. A racial battle sparked by drunken whites rocked Tampa in early June; twenty-seven blacks and three whites went to hospitals. Although many blacks hoped to prove in war that they deserved white respect, a black chaplain asked: "Talk about fighting and freeing poor Cuba and of Spain's brutality; of Cuba's murdered thousands, and starving reconcentradoes. Is America any better than Spain?"[45]

Led by officers seasoned in the Civil War and in campaigns against Native Americans, the new imperial fighters embarked from Florida in mid-June. The loading of the ships was chaotic. Men rushed to the transports, fearful that they would be left behind. Roosevelt's Rough Riders muscled out rivals competing for one vessel, but their horses stayed behind for lack of space. Colonel Leonard Wood predicted that if the Americans did not fight the Spanish soon they would tear at one another. Seventeen thousand men, clutching their Krag-Jörgensen rifles, crammed into the flotilla for a week. They ate hardtack and tasteless canned beef, drank bitter coffee, waited anxiously, and got seasick. On the morning of June 22 they disembarked on Cuban soil, finding no Spanish resistance. Cuban insurgents met with the American officers and agreed to help one another against Spanish forces.

Yet the big news had already arrived from the Philippine Islands, Spain's major colony in Asia. Only a few days after the American declaration of war, Commodore George Dewey sailed his Asiatic Squadron from Hong Kong to Manila Bay, where he smashed the Spanish fleet with the loss of one man. Every American ship in Manila Harbor, Senator Orville Platt of Connecticut proclaimed, was "a new *Mayflower* . . . the harbinger and agent of a new civilization."[46] Slipping by the strangely silent Spanish guns at Corregidor, Dewey had entered the bay at night. Early in the morning of May 1 his flagship *Olympia* began to demolish the ten incompetently handled Spanish ships. With his laconic order, "You may fire when ready, Gridley," Dewey quickly became a first-line hero. Some people, ignorant of American interests in the Pacific, the beckoning China market, and the feebleness of Spanish rule over the Philippines, wondered how a war to liberate Cuba saw its first action in Asia. Although probably few Americans knew the location of the Philippines, naval officials had pinpointed them in contingency plans as early as 1896. Often credited alone with ordering Dewey on February 25, 1898, to attack Manila if war broke out, Assistant Secretary of the Navy Theodore Roosevelt actually set in motion preexisting war plans already known and approved by the president. After the war, when the Navy Department balked at revealing its advance preparations, Roosevelt was "naturally delighted at shouldering the responsibility."[47]

By late June, the American troops in Cuba were moving toward Santiago, where ill-equipped and dispirited Spanish soldiers manned antique guns. Joined by experienced Cuban rebels, the North Americans on July 1 battled for San Juan Hill. Having given away their position by sending up an observation balloon, the American troops, spearheaded by the Rough Riders and the black soldiers of the Ninth Cavalry, finally captured the strategic promontory overlooking Santiago despite heavy casualties. Two days later the Spanish fleet, penned in Santiago Harbor for weeks by American warships, made a desperate daylight break for open sea. Some U.S. vessels nearly collided as they hurried to sink the helpless Spanish craft, which went down with 323 dead. Its fleet destroyed, Spain entered its imperial death throes. Santiago soon fell.

American troops also invaded another Spanish colony, Puerto Rico, which expansionists like Roosevelt coveted as a Caribbean base for a "proper navy" and a strategic post that might help protect a Central American canal.[48] In nineteen days General Nelson A. Miles, losing only three soldiers, captured the sugar- and coffee-exporting island. At least at first, the Puerto Rican elite welcomed their new North American masters as an improvement over their Spanish rulers.

Manila collapsed in mid-August, after the Spanish put up token resistance in a deal with Dewey that salvaged Spanish pride and kept insurgent Emilio Aguinaldo from the walled city. Washington soon ordered Aguinaldo and the Filipino rebels, who had fought against the Spanish for independence since 1896 and had surrounded Manila for weeks, to remain outside the capital and to recognize the authority of the United States.

In July, to ensure uninterrupted reinforcement of Dewey, the United States officially absorbed Hawaii, where ships touched en route to Manila. From 1893 to 1897, when Cleveland refused annexation, politics in Hawaii had changed little. The white revolutionaries clung to power. McKinley's election removed the uncertainty. He negotiated a new agreement with the white-led Hawaiian government. But, fearful that the Senate would not give him the two-thirds vote needed for a treaty, the president asked instead for a joint resolution. On July 7, 1898, Congress passed the resolution for annexation by a majority vote (290 to 91 in the House and 42 to 21 in the Senate), thereby formally attaching the strategically and commercially important islands to the United States.

PEACE AND EMPIRE: THE DEBATE IN THE UNITED STATES

Spain sued for peace, and on August 12 the belligerents proclaimed an armistice. To negotiate with the Spanish in Paris, McKinley appointed a "peace commission" loaded with imperialists and headed by Secretary of State William R. Day, friend and follower of the president's wishes. As the talks dragged on into autumn, McKinley, who had made a political tour of the United States to test public opinion and had became convinced that the British would acquiesce in American imperialism, finally instructed the commissioners to demand all of the Philippines and Puerto Rico, as well as to make Cuba independent. Articulate Filipinos pleaded for their country's freedom but met a stern U.S. rebuff. Spanish diplomats accepted this American land grab after the United States offered $20 million as compensation. By early December the treaty was signed, and the American delegates walked out of the elegant French conference room with the Philippines, Puerto Rico, and Guam.

Anti-imperialists howled in protest against the treaty. They had organized the Anti-Imperialist League in Boston in November 1898, but they were never truly united. They counted among their number such unlikely bedfellows as steel magnate Andrew Carnegie, labor leader Samuel Gompers, agrarian spokesman William Jennings Bryan, Massachusetts senator George Hoar, President Charles W. Eliot of Harvard, and Mark Twain—people who had often disagreed on domestic issues. Many of the anti-imperialists took inconsistent positions. Hoar, the most outspoken senator against the treaty, had voted for war and for the resolution to annex Hawaii. An expansionist, Carnegie apparently would accept colonies if they could be taken without force. "I am no little American," he asserted. "The day is coming when we shall own all these West Indian islands. They will gravitate to us of their own accord."[49] He even offered to write a personal check for $20 million to buy the independence of the Philippines. And the anti-imperialists could not overcome the *fait accompli,* possession and occupation of territory, handed them by McKinley. After all, argued the president, could America really let loose of this real estate so nobly taken in battle? The anti-imperialists, rejecting immediacy in favor of principle, denounced the thesis that greatness lay in colonies. They wanted trade too, but not at the cost of subjugating other peoples. Anti-imperialist David Starr Jordan, president of Stanford University, spoke of the "peaceful conquest" of Mexico by trade rather than by annexation.[50] Quoting the Declaration of Independence and Washington's Farewell Address as lessons from the past, these critics recalled America's tradition of self-government and *continental* expansion. Furthermore, the imposition of a government by force on another people was inhumane and immoral. Mark Twain wrote a scathing parody of the *Battle Hymn of the Republic:* "Mine eyes have seen the orgy of the launching of the Sword; / He is searching out the hoardings where the strangers' wealth is stored; / He has loosed his fateful lightning, and with woe and death has scored; / His lust is marching on."[51] Social reformer Jane Addams saw children playing war games in the streets of Chicago. The kids were *not freeing Cubans,* she protested, but rather *slaying Spaniards* in their not-so-innocent play. Some anti-imperialists insisted that the United States had serious domestic problems that demanded attention and resources first; others were racists who predicted that Filipinos and Puerto Ricans would ultimately corrupt Anglo-Saxon blood.

The imperialists, led by Senators Henry Cabot Lodge and Nelson Aldrich, Roosevelt, and McKinley, and backed strongly by articulate business leaders, engaged their opponents in vigorous debate in early 1899. They stressed pragmatic

George F. Hoar (1826–1904). Graduate of Harvard, this Republican became a U.S. senator in 1877. He urged Cuban independence and opposed the annexation of the Philippines. He praised the Filipinos for their written constitution and ability to govern themselves. He compared the lynching of African Americans in the U.S. South to the "lynching" of the Filipino people. (Library of Congress)

considerations, although they communicated common ideas of racial superiority and national destiny to civilize the savage world—to take up "the white man's burden." They could cite the Social Darwinist philosophy that some were more fit than others to survive. The Philippines provided stepping-stones to the rich China market and strategic ports for the expanding navy that protected American commerce and demonstrated American prestige. International competition also dictated that the United States keep the fruits of victory, argued the imperialists; otherwise, a menacing Germany or expansionist Japan might pick up what America discarded. Few believed that the United States should relinquish territory acquired through blood. National honor demanded retention, or so the annexationists argued. Roosevelt, countering the charge that no one had asked the Filipinos if they desired annexation to the United States, cited historical precedent. Jefferson, he delighted in telling Democratic anti-imperialists, took Louisiana without a vote by its inhabitants. Furthermore, said Richard Olney, Washington's Farewell Address had outlived its usefulness; there could be no more American isolation. Duty, destiny, defense, and dollars was the alliterative imperialist litany.

Pro-imperialist Senator Lodge described the treaty fight as the "closest, most bitter, and most exciting struggle I have ever known, or ever expect to see in the Senate."[52] Shortly before the upper house took action, word reached Washington that Filipino insurrectionists and American soldiers had begun to fight. The news apparently stimulated support for the Treaty of Paris. Democrats tended to be anti-imperialists and Republicans imperialists, yet enough of the former endorsed the treaty on February 6, 1899, to pass it, just barely, by the necessary two-thirds vote, 57 to 27. William Jennings Bryan, believing that a rejection of the treaty would mean continued war, that a majority should rule in a democracy, and that the Philippines could be freed after terminating the hostilities with Spain, urged an "aye" vote upon his anti-imperialist friends. The Republicans probably had enough votes in reserve to pass the treaty even if Bryan had opposed it. Eight days later, the tie-breaking vote of the vice president killed a Senate resolution providing for Philippine independence as soon as the Filipinos established a stable government.

IMPERIAL COLLISIONS IN ASIA: THE PHILIPPINE INSURRECTION AND THE OPEN DOOR IN CHINA

Controlling, protecting, and expanding the enlarged U.S. empire became a major chore. The Filipinos proved to be the most obstinate. By the end of the war, Aguinaldo and rebel warriors held control over most of the islands, having routed the Spanish and driven them into Manila. Aguinaldo had arrived from exile in an American warship and believed that American leaders, including Dewey, had promised his country independence if he joined U.S. forces in defeating the

Emilio Aguinaldo (1869–1964). Of mixed Chinese and Tagalog ancestry, this Filipino nationalist was exiled by the Spanish from his country in 1897. He returned with American forces and later clashed with them when he declared independence for the Philippines. Captured in 1901, he then declared allegiance to the United States. During World War II, however, he favored the Japanese, who occupied the islands, and he was briefly imprisoned by American authorities in 1945 when they reestablished U.S. power over Manila. (Library of Congress)

Spanish. After the Spanish-American armistice, he came to resent American behavior. He and his men received U.S. orders to stay out of the city. They were gradually isolated from decisions and insulted by racial slurs, including "nigger" and "goo goo." American soldiers occupying the Manila area considered the Filipinos inferior, the equivalent of Indians and blacks at home. Although one Methodist missionary boasted that the Americans had found Manila "a pesthole, and made it a health resort," critics claimed that imperialism exported the worst in

American life.[53] In the fall and winter of 1898 American officers barred insurgent vessels from Manila Bay and showed no appreciation for the profound Filipino sentiment for independence. The Treaty of Paris angered the Filipinos, as did McKinley's dictate that the authority of the United States was supreme in the Philippines. In open defiance of Washington, Aguinaldo and other prominent Filipinos organized a government at Malolos, wrote a constitution, and proclaimed the Philippine Republic in late January 1899.

Although American anti-imperialist critics were probably correct when they said that the Filipino government was as virtuous as that of Chicago, McKinley believed his new colonials to be ill-fitted for self-government. In February 1899 the Filipinos began fighting better-armed American troops. After bloody struggles, Aguinaldo was captured in March 1901. Before the insurrection collapsed in 1902, more than 5,000 Americans and 200,000 Filipinos died. One hundred and twenty-five thousand American troops quelled the insurrection, which cost the United States at least $160 million. In Batangas province south of Manila, General J. Franklin Bell drove insurrectionists into the hills and killed their livestock. Then malaria-transmitting mosquitoes "were forced to get their meals from people" instead of cattle. The result: an "epidemiological catastrophe" wherein the Batangas population declined by 90,000 (one-quarter of the people) over a six-year period.[54] Anti-imperialist William James, distinguished Harvard University philosopher, poignantly summarized the impact of U.S. intervention on the Philippines: "We are destroying the lives of these islanders by the thousands, their villages and

William Howard Taft (1857–1930) and Animal.   The first U.S. civil governor of the Philippines, Taft weighed more than 300 pounds. He once proudly reported to Washington that he had ridden twenty-five miles to a high mountain spot. Secretary of War Elihu Root replied: "HOW IS HORSE?" (U.S. Army Military History Institute)

"A Fair Field and No Favor." Holding back the militant-minded imperialists of Europe, the United States permits China to inspect American wares. "I'm out for commerce, not conquest," asserts Uncle Sam. The Open Door policy sought to protect U.S. trade in the highly competitive environment. (*Harper's Weekly,* 1899)

their cities. . . . We are destroying down to the root every germ of a healthy national life in these unfortunate people. . . . Civilization is, then, the big, hollow, resounding, corrupting, sophisticating, confusing torrent of mere brutal momentum and irrationality that brings forth fruits like this!"[55]

One of the ugliest wars in American history, this contest saw both sides commit atrocities. After Filipinos massacred an American regiment on Samar and stuffed molasses into disemboweled corpses to attract ants, General Jacob Smith told his officers: "I want no prisoners. I wish you to kill and burn, the more you kill and burn the better you will please me."[56] Americans burned *barrios* to the ground, placing villagers in reconcentration camps like those that had ravaged Cuba. To get information, Americans administered the "water cure" by forcing prisoners to swallow gallons of water and then punching the swollen stomach to empty it quickly. American soldiers were tired, mosquito bitten, and poorly fed, and their patience wore thin. Filipino guerrilla fighters harassed them. Racism and notions of white superiority surfaced. Army captain Frank R. McCoy could not comprehend the Muslim Moros who refused American medical treatment. "You mention Cholera to them," he wrote, "and they throw up their hands [saying,] 'God has given and God has taken away.'"[57] For most soldiers, a new army song had it right: "Civilize 'em with a Krag."[58] The civil governor of the Philippines

American Cigarettes in China. An American soldier in China peddles cigarettes. After the invention of the cigarette machine in 1881, the tobacco tycoon James B. Duke asked to see an atlas. Leafing through the pages, he noticed China's large population of 430 million. "That," he said, "is where we are going to sell cigarettes." Nine years later came the first exports; by 1916 Duke and other American entrepreneurs were selling 12 billion cigarettes in China.(Edward J. Parrish Papers, Duke University Library)

from 1901 to 1904, William Howard Taft, put the question less crudely when he described the American mission as the creation of a Filipino government "which shall teach those people individual liberty, which shall lift them up to a point of civilization . . . , and which shall make them rise to call the name of the United States blessed."[59] Critic Charles Francis Adams, Jr., mocked such thinking: "We are going to make them an independent people by putting them in jail if they mention the word 'independence.'"[60] In fact, Taft administered a sedition act that sought to suppress criticism of the United States. U.S. authorities censored newspapers and jailed recalcitrant dissenters. For years, the Moros would not submit to American rule. In the end, U.S. military policy attempted their extermination. In a June 1913 battle on the island of Jolo, U.S. forces killed 500 Moros. The army's premier "guerrilla warrior," General John J. Pershing, called that bloody encounter "the fiercest [fighting] I have ever seen."[61] Until 1914, moreover, the followers of Artemio Ricarte harassed the U.S. military with their hit-and-run tactics. Ricarte himself, imprisoned from 1904 to 1910 and then deported to Hong Kong and Japan, refused allegiance to the United States and set up a government-in-exile that demanded "immediate and complete independence and the equalization of wealth."[62]

The carrot—what Taft called the policy of "attraction"—joined the stick to pacify the Philippines.[63] Local self-government, social reforms, and American schools, which taught Filipinos of all social classes English and arithmetic, helped win over elites and key minorities. "We'll larn ye our language," said the inimitable Mr. Dooley, "because 'tis easier to larn ye ours thin to larn ourselves ye'ers."[64] As Filipinos developed a colonial mentality, things stateside became preferred. A general amnesty proclaimed by President Theodore Roosevelt on July 4, 1902, also encouraged accommodation. By restricting suffrage at the outset to Filipinos with wealth, education, and previous government service, U.S. administrators successfully wooed Filipino elites, including former revolutionaries, by permitting them to retain their dominant status. American roads, bridges, port improvements, and sanitation projects followed soon after the Filipino submission to alien rule. "Such benefits were no substitute for independence," historian Glenn May has written, "but they served to mollify a sizable segment of a once-hostile populace."[65] In 1916, the Jones Act promised Philippine independence but set no date. Thirty years later the Philippines became an independent nation allied with the United States in world politics.

The proximity of the Philippines to China made the islands especially valuable to U.S. leaders who predicted lucrative markets for American products. In early 1898 American business leaders organized the American Asiatic Association to stimulate public and governmental concern to protect and enlarge U.S. interests in China. Assistant Secretary of the Treasury Frank Vanderlip typically lauded the Philippines as the "pickets of the Pacific, standing guard at the entrances to trade with the millions of China and Korea, French Indo-China, the Malay Peninsula, and the islands of Indonesia."[66] Even though China accounted for only 2 percent of U.S. foreign commerce, American traders had long dreamed of an unbounded China market, and missionaries romanticized a Christian kingdom. These ambitions remained dreams more than reality. Yet dreams became a rationale for action, and during the 1890s the United States, despite limited power, sought to defend its Asian interests, real and imagined. In that decade the European powers and Japan were dividing China, rendered helpless in 1895 after its disastrous defeat in the Sino-Japanese War, into spheres of influence and establishing discriminatory trading privileges in their zones. The McKinley administration in early 1898 watched anxiously as Germany grabbed Jiaozhou (Kiaochow) and Russia demanded and got a lease at Port Arthur on the Liaodong Peninsula. France, already ensconced in Indochina, leased Guangzhou Bay in southern China in April of that year. Japan already had footholds in Formosa and Korea. Britain approached Washington in March 1898 and suggested a joint Anglo-American declaration on behalf of equal commercial opportunity in China. In the midst of the Cuban crisis, the United States gave little attention to the request. Britain, which already had Hong Kong, then forced China to give up part of the Shandong Peninsula. China had become "the Sick Man of Asia."

American economic and religious interests in China seemed threatened. Businesspeople from the American Asiatic Association and missionaries appealed to Washington for help. Drawing on recommendations from William W. Rockhill,

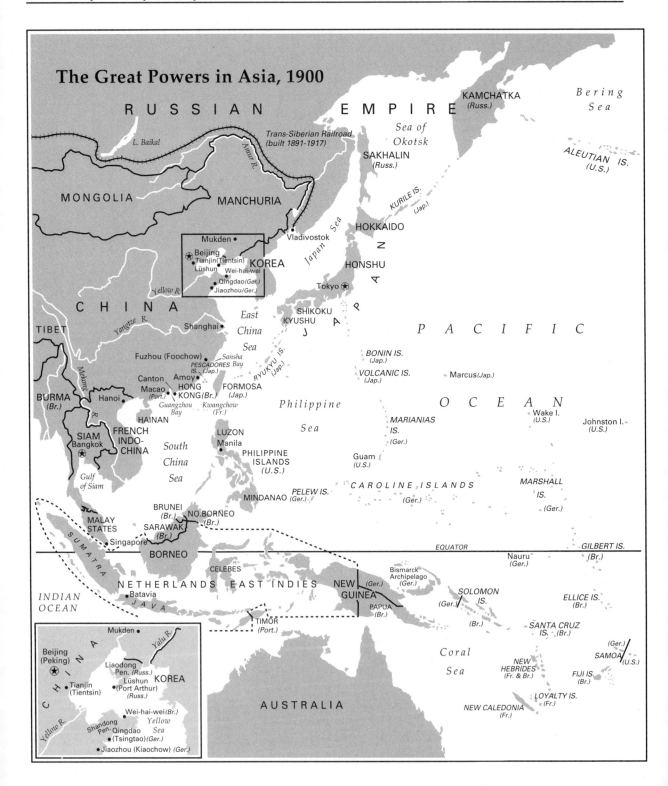

The Great Powers in Asia, 1900

adviser on Asian policy, who in turn drew on advice from his British friend and an officer of the Chinese customs service, Alfred Hippisley, Secretary of State John Hay tried words. Even though President McKinley seemed "to want a slice" of China, Hay sent an Open Door note on September 6, 1899, to Japan, Germany, Russia, Britain, France, and Italy, asking them to respect equal trade opportunity for all nations in their spheres.[67] It was, of course, a traditional American principle, and given minimal military power in Asia, the best the United States could do. Noncommittal replies trickled back, but Hay read into them what he wanted and proclaimed definitive acceptance of the "Open Door" proposal.

Although frail, the Open Door policy carried meaning. Americans knew they were weaker than the other imperialists in Asia, but they also noted that a delicate balance of power existed there that the United States could unbalance. The European powers and Japan might hesitate to exclude American commerce altogether from China, for fear that the United States would tip that balance by joining one of the powers against the others. They also feared that a world war might erupt from competition in Asia. Americans hoped the Open Door policy would serve their goals in an area where the United States had little military power. The United States wanted the commercial advantages without having to employ military force, as it did in Latin America. The policy did not always work, but it fixed itself in the American mind as a guiding principle for Chinese affairs.

The Open Door note notwithstanding, the Manchu dynasty (1644–1912) neared death, unable to cope with the foreign intruders. Resentful nationalistic Chinese, led by a secret society called *Yihequan* ("Righteous and Harmonious Fists," or the "Boxers"), undertook in 1900 to throw out the imperialist aggressors. The Boxers murdered hundreds of Christian missionaries and their Chinese converts, and laid siege to the foreign legations in Beijing (Peking). To head off a complete gouging of China by vengeful Europeans and Japanese, Washington took two steps. It sent 2,500 American troops to Beijing from the Philippines to join 15,500 soldiers from other nations to lift the siege. And Hay, without consulting the Chinese government, issued another Open Door note on July 3, 1900. He defined U.S. policy as the protection of American life and property, the safeguarding of "equal and impartial trade," and the preservation of China's "territorial and administrative entity."[68] In short, keep the trade door open by keeping China intact. Certainly these actions did not save China from continued incursion (it was, for example, assessed more than $300 million to pay for the Boxers' damages). The United States itself even asked for a territorial concession in late 1900 at Sansha Bay, Fujian Province. The Japanese, catching Hay redhanded, politely reminded him of his notes, and he shelved the request. Thereafter Washington buttressed its support for the Open Door by increasing the Asiatic Squadron to forty-eight warships and earmarking army forces in the Philippines for future emergency deployment in China. As the historian Marilyn Blatt Young has concluded: "In the late nineteenth century Americans came to feel that having influence in Asia was a categorical imperative for a world power. America, after the Spanish-American War, was a world power, *ergo* it must take a key part in Far Eastern affairs."[69]

John M. Hay (1838–1905). The author of the Open Door notes graduated from Brown University and served as one of President Abraham Lincoln's secretaries. He became a newspaper editor and diplomat, and in 1897, ambassador to Great Britain. The following year McKinley named him secretary of state, a post he held until his death. The historian Christopher Thorne has described the Open Door policy as a "singular blend of evangelicalism, political calculation, benevolent imperialism, and crude self-interest." (National Portrait Gallery, Smithsonian Institution)

THE ELBOWS OF A WORLD POWER, 1895–1900

Venezuela, Cuba, Hawaii, the Philippines, Open Door notes—together they meant an unprecedented set of commitments and responsibilities for the United States. Symbolic of this thrust to world-power status was the ascendancy of the imperialists' imperialist, Theodore Roosevelt, to the office of the president in 1901. Peering into the twentieth century, Roosevelt warned Americans to avoid "slothful ease and ignoble peace." Never "shrink from the hard contests"; "let us therefore boldly face the life of strife."[70] Indeed, many diplomats looked back upon the triumphs of the 1890s as a testing time when the United States met the international challenge and rightfully asserted its place as a major world power. Europeans watched anxiously. Some, especially Germans, spoke of the "American peril" or "American menace." Italians worried that the United States would grab their poorly defended colonies. With its industrial and naval strength and its string of colonies, the United States, European leaders pointed out, had become a factor in the "balance of power." With whom, they asked in some trepidation, would the nation ally itself?

The odds seemed to favor Great Britain, although the Anglo-American courtship would be prolonged and marriage something for the future. Ever since the eye-opening Venezuelan crisis, the British, in Colonial Secretary Joseph Chamberlain's words, had applauded Washington for "entering the lists and sharing the task which might have proved too heavy for us alone" and pursued what has been called the "great rapprochement."[71] Looking for support against an expansionist Germany, John Bull thought Uncle Sam a fit partner. During the Spanish-American-Cuban-Filipino War the British conspicuously tilted toward the American side and encouraged the subsequent U.S. absorption of Spanish colonies. American leaders, in turn, sympathized with the British suppression of the Boer Republics in South Africa during 1899–1902, comparing that struggle to their own war with the Filipinos. Articulate Americans welcomed Britain's implicit acceptance of their imperialism. Germany seemed to replace Britain as the major power hostile to America. Vague Anglo-Saxonism and cultural ties joined British recognition of the power of the United States to forge more amicable relations. The director of British Naval Intelligence noted in early 1899, moreover, that "the United States means to be the strongest naval power [along their eastern coast] and it will be difficult to prevent it."[72] London decided not to try. Anglophobes continued to twist the lion's tail and Anglo-American commercial competition remained intense, but Anglo-American relations moved from being "cool, grudging, and occasionally hostile" to tolerant and cordial.[73]

Britain still ranked first in naval power, but in the late 1890s the United States was growing, standing sixth by 1900. In 1898 alone, spurred by the war with Spain, the United States added 128 vessels to its navy, at a cost of $18 million. At the 1898 American Historical Association meeting, Professor Edwin A. Grosvenor of Amherst College caught the new times in his address: "Barriers of national seclusion are everywhere tumbling like the great wall of China. Every nation el-

Pears' Soap Advertisement. This unusual mixture of commercial and diplomatic advertising salutes Anglo-American rapprochement. (*Life*, 1898)

bows other nations to-day. . . . What was whispered at evening in the conclave of envoys and ambassadors is shouted the next morning by newsboys thousands of miles distant."[74] Many commentators reported that the United States, although still divided North and South on many issues, had united as never before. Southern racists and northern imperialists now had something in common: the need to keep inferior peoples in their place. Senator Benjamin Tillman of South Carolina claimed that "no Republican leader . . . will now dare to wave the bloody shirt and preach a crusade against the South's treatment of the negro. The North has a bloody shirt of its own. Many thousands of them have been made into shrouds for murdered Filipinos."[75]

The events of the 1895–1900 period further altered the process of decision-making. Both Cleveland and McKinley conducted their own foreign policies, often thwarting or manipulating Congress. They helped establish the authority of the president over foreign policy. In 1907, looking back on the days of 1898, Woodrow Wilson, then president of Princeton University, recorded the historical impact: "The war with Spain again changed the balance of powers. Foreign questions became leading questions again, as they had been in the first days of the government, and in them the President was of necessity leader. Our new place in the affairs of the world has since that year of transformation kept him at the front of our government, where his own thoughts and the attention of men everywhere is centered on him. . . . The nation has risen to the first rank in power and resources. . . . Our President must always, henceforth, be one of the great powers of the world."[76] Wilson exaggerated America's power, for that strength was still largely centered in the Western Hemisphere, but for the United States, as the *Washington Post* editorialized in 1898, "the policy of isolation is dead. . . . A new consciousness seems to have come upon us—the consciousness of strength, and with it a new appetite, a yearning to show our strength. . . . Ambition, interest, land-hunger, pride, the mere joy of fighting, whatever it may be, we are animated by a new sensation. . . . The taste of empire is in the mouth of the people, even as the taste of blood in the jungle."[77] After 1900 the task of managing the expansive empire and the global responsibilities that came with it soon preoccupied U.S. leaders.

Further Reading for the Period 1895–1900

For the 1890s and America's path to empire, see Richard D. Challener, *Admirals, Generals, and American Foreign Policy, 1898–1914* (1973); John A. S. Grenville and George B. Young, *Politics, Strategy, and American Diplomacy* (1967); David Healy, *U.S. Expansionism* (1970); Richard Hofstadter, *Social Darwinism in American Thought* (1955); Walter LaFeber, *The New Empire* (1963); Henry E. Mattox, *The Twilight of Amateur Diplomacy* (1989); Ernest R. May, *Imperial Democracy* (1961); Göran Rystad, *Ambiguous Imperialism* (1981); R. Hal Williams, *Years of Decision* (1978); and William A. Williams, *The Roots of the Modern American Empire* (1969) and *The Tragedy of American Diplomacy* (1962).

The coming and waging of the Spanish-American-Cuban-Filipino War is covered in the works above and in Charles H. Brown, *The Correspondents' War* (1967); Graham A. Cosmas, *An Army for Empire* (1971); Willard B. Gatewood, Jr., *Black Americans and the White Man's Burden, 1898–1903* (1975); John M. Kirk, *José*

Martí (1983); Gerald F. Linderman, *The Mirror of War* (1974); Joyce Milton, *The Yellow Kids* (1989) (journalists); John L. Offner, *An Unwanted War* (1992); Louis A. Pérez, Jr., *Cuba and the United States* (1990) and *Cuba Between Empires, 1878–1902* (1983); Julius Pratt, *Expansionists of 1898* (1938); Hyman G. Rickover, *How the Battleship Maine Was Destroyed* (1976); and David F. Trask, *The War with Spain in 1898* (1981).

Various aspects of imperialism are discussed in "American Empire, 1898–1903," *Pacific Historical Review* (1979) (entire issue); Edward J. Berbusse, *The United States in Puerto Rico, 1898–1900* (1966); Raymond Carr, *Puerto Rico* (1984); Aaron L. Friedberg, *The Weary Titan* (1988) (Britain); Emily Rosenberg, *Spreading the American Dream* (1982); and Tony Smith, *The Pattern of Imperialism* (1982).

For American leaders, see Howard K. Beale, *Theodore Roosevelt and the Rise of America to World Power* (1956); John Braeman, *Albert J. Beveridge* (1971); Charles W. Calhoun, *Gilded Age Cato* (1988) (Gresham); Kenton J. Clymer, *John Hay* (1975); Gerald Eggert, *Richard Olney* (1973); Lewis L. Gould, *The Presidency of William McKinley* (1981); William Harbaugh, *The Life and Times of Theodore Roosevelt* (1975); Margaret Leech, *In the Days of McKinley* (1959); Nathan Miller, *Theodore Roosevelt* (1992); H. Wayne Morgan, *William McKinley and His America* (1963); Edmund Morris, *The Rise of Theodore Roosevelt* (1979); Ronald Spector, *Admiral of the New Empire* (1974) (Dewey); Richard E. Welch, Jr., *The Presidencies of Grover Cleveland* (1988); and William C. Widenor, *Henry Cabot Lodge and the Search for an American Foreign Policy* (1980).

Anti-imperialists and anti-imperialism are treated in William N. Armstrong, *E. L. Godkin and American Foreign Policy* (1957); Robert L. Beisner, *Twelve Against Empire* (1968); Kendrick A. Clements, *William Jennings Bryan* (1983); Paolo E. Coletta, *William Jennings Bryan* (1964–1969); John C. Farrell, *Beloved Lady* (1967) (Addams); Thomas J. Osborne, *"Empire Can Wait": American Opposition to Hawaiian Annexation, 1893–1898* (1981); E. Berkeley Tompkins, *Anti-Imperialism in the United States* (1970); Hans L. Trefousse, *Carl Schurz* (1982); and Joseph F. Wall, *Andrew Carnegie* (1970).

The Open Door policy and Asia are discussed in Thomas A. Breslin, *China, American Catholicism, and the Missionary* (1980); Charles S. Campbell, *Special Business Interests and the Open Door Policy* (1951); Sherman Cochran, *Big Business in China* (1980) (cigarette industry); Michael Hunt, *Frontier Defense and the Open Door* (1973) and *The Making of a Special Relationship* (1983); Akira Iriye, *Across the Pacific* (1967); Robert McClellan, *The Heathen Chinee* (1971); Thomas McCormick, *China Market* (1967); Valentin H. Rabe, *The Home Base of American China Missions, 1880–1920* (1978); and Marilyn Blatt Young, *The Rhetoric of Empire* (1968).

The Philippine rebellion and the American debate receive scrutiny in Teodoro Agoncillo, *Malolos* (1960); A. J. Bacevich, *Diplomat in Khaki* (1989) (General Frank McCoy); Kenton J. Clymer, *Protestant Missionaries in the Philippines, 1898–1916* (1986); John M. Gates, *Schoolbooks and Krags* (1973); Stanley Karnow, *In Our Image* (1989); Brian M. Linn, *The U.S. Army and Counterinsurgency in the Philippine War, 1899–1902* (1989); Glenn A. May, *Battle for Batangas* (1991) and *Social Engineering in the Philippines* (1980); Stuart C. Miller, *"Benevolent Assimilation"* (1982); Daniel B. Schirmer, *Republic or Empire* (1972); Peter Stanley, *A Nation in the Making* (1974); and ed., *Reappraising an Empire* (1984); and Richard E. Welch, *Response to Imperialism* (1979).

For Anglo-American relations, including the Venezuelan crisis, see Stuart Anderson, *Race and Rapprochement* (1981); Charles S. Campbell, *From Revolution to Rapprochement* (1974); R. G. Neale, *Great Britain and United States Expansion, 1800–1900* (1966); Bradford Perkins, *The Great Rapprochement* (1968); and Joseph Smith, *Illusions of Conflict: Anglo-American Diplomacy Toward Latin America, 1865–1896* (1979).

See also the General Bibliography and the following notes. The most comprehensive bibliography is Richard Dean Burns, ed., *Guide to American Foreign Relations Since 1700* (1983).

NOTES TO CHAPTER 1

1. Quoted in Gerald G. Eggert, *Richard Olney* (College Park: Pennsylvania State University Press, 1974), p. 208.
2. Quoted in Ernest R. May, *Imperial Democracy* (New York: Harper & Row, [1961], 1973), p. 33.
3. Quoted in Charles W. Calhoun, *Gilded Age Cato* (Lexington: University Press of Kentucky, 1988), p. 217.
4. *Foreign Relations, 1895,* Part I (Washington D.C.: Government Printing Office, 1896), pp. 545–562.
5. Richard E. Welch, Jr., *The Presidencies of Grover Cleveland* (Lawrence: University Press of Kansas, 1988), p. 184.
6. Quoted in Robert L. Beisner, *From the Old Diplomacy to the New, 1865–1900* (Arlington Heights, Ill.: Harlan Davidson, 1986; 2d ed.) p. 111.
7. Quoted in Howard K. Beale, *Theodore Roosevelt and the Rise of America to World Power* (New York: Collier Books, [1956], 1962), p. 60.
8. Quoted in Nathan Miller, *Theodore Roosevelt* (New York: William Morrow, 1992), p. 235.
9. Quoted in Eggert, *Olney,* p. 223.
10. Quoted in Stuart Anderson, *Race and Rapprochement* (Rutherford, N.J.: Fairleigh Dickinson University Press, 1981), p. 97.
11. Quoted in Joyce Milton, *The Yellow Kids* (New York: Harper & Row, 1989), p. 27.
12. Quoted in Allan Nevins, *Grover Cleveland* (New York: Dodd, Mead, 1932), p. 644.
13. Quoted in Joseph Smith, *Illusions of Conflict* (Pittsburgh: University of Pittsburgh Press, 1979), p. 207.
14. Quoted in George B. Young, "Intervention Under the Monroe Doctrine: The Olney Corollary," *Political Science Quarterly,* LVII (June 1942), 277.
15. Quoted in Richard E. Welch, Jr., *George Frisbie Hoar and the Half-Breed Republicans* (Cambridge, Mass.: Harvard University Press, 1971), p. 209.
16. Walter Q. Gresham to Carl Schurz, October 6, 1893, Walter Q. Gresham Papers, Library of Congress.
17. Quoted in Louis A. Pérez, Jr., *Cuba and the United States* (Athens: University of Georgia Press, 1990), p. 80.
18. Quoted in John M. Kirk, *José Martí* (Gainesville: University Presses of Florida, 1983), pp. 52, 56, 58, 90, 118.
19. Quoted in Philip S. Foner, *The Spanish-Cuban-American War and the Birth of American Imperialism* (New York: Monthly Review Press, 1972; 2 vols.), I, 21.
20. Quoted in John L. Offner, *An Unwanted War* (Chapel Hill: University of North Carolina Press, 1992), p. 26.
21. Quoted in Eggert, *Olney,* p. 265.
22. James D. Richardson, ed., *A Compilation of the Messages and Papers of the Presidents, 1789–1897* (Washington, D.C.: Government Printing Office, 1896–1899; 10 vols.), IX, 716–722.
23. Quoted in Edmund Morris, *The Rise of Theodore Roosevelt* (New York: Coward, McCann, & Geoghegan, 1979), p. 610.
24. Lester D. Langley, *The Cuban Policy of the United States* (New York: John Wiley & Sons, 1968), p. 97.
25. *Congressional Record, XXXI* (December 6, 1897), 3–5.
26. *Foreign Relations, 1898* (Washington D.C.: Government Printing Office, 1901), pp. 1007–1008.
27. Quoted in Offner, *Unwanted War,* p. 129.
28. *Congressional Record, XXXI* (March 17, 1898), 2916–2919.
29. Quoted in Louis A. Pérez, Jr., *Cuba Between Empires, 1878–1902* (Pittsburgh: University of Pittsburgh Press, 1983), p. 172.
30. Quoted *ibid.,* p. 174.
31. *Foreign Relations, 1898,* p. 746.
32. Quoted in Henry E. Mattox, *The Twilight of Amateur Diplomacy* (Kent, Ohio: Kent State University Press, 1989), p. 89.
33. *Congressional Record, XXXI* (April 11, 1898), 3699–3702.
34. Pérez, *Cuba Between Empires,* p. 178.
35. Quoted *ibid.,* p. 174.
36. Quoted in H. Wayne Morgan, *America's Road to Empire* (New York: John Wiley & Sons, 1965), p. 63.
37. Quoted in Winthrop S. Hudson, "Protestant Clergy Debate the Nation's Vocation, 1898–1899" (unpublished ms., 1974).
38. Quoted in John Braeman, *Albert J. Beveridge: American Nationalist* (Chicago: University of Chicago Press, 1971), p. 23.
39. Finley Peter Dunne, *Mr. Dooley in Peace and War* (Boston: Small, Maynard, 1899), p. 9.
40. Beisner, *From the Old Diplomacy to the New,* p. 129.
41. Quoted in Gerald F. Linderman, *The Mirror of War* (Ann Arbor: University of Michigan Press, 1974), p. 125.
42. Quoted in Louis A. Pérez, Jr., "The Meaning of the *Maine,*" *Pacific Historical Review, LVIII* (August 1989), 320.
43. Quoted in Frank Freidel, *The Splendid Little War* (Boston: Little, Brown, 1958), p. 306.
44. Quoted *ibid.,* p. 295.
45. Quoted in Willard B. Gatewood, Jr., *"Smoked Yankees" and the Struggle for Empire* (Urbana: University of Illinois Press, 1971), p. 28.
46. Quoted in Paul C. Nagel, *This Sacred Trust* (New York: Oxford University Press, 1971), p. 252.
47. Quoted in John A. S. Grenville and George B. Young, *Politics, Strategy, and American Diplomacy* (New Haven: Yale University Press, 1966), p. 278.
48. Quoted in Raymond Carr, *Puerto Rico* (New York: Vintage Books, 1984), p. 25.
49. Quoted in David Healy, *U.S. Expansionism* (Madison: University of Wisconsin Press, 1970), p. 55.

50. Quoted in Robert L. Beisner, "1898 and 1968," *Political Science Quarterly, LXXV* (June 1970), 200.

51. Quoted in Hugh Deane, *Good Deeds & Gunboats* (San Francisco: China Books and Periodicals, 1990), p. 65.

52. Quoted in H. Wayne Morgan, *William McKinley and His America* (Syracuse: Syracuse University Press, 1963), p. 422.

53. Quoted in Kenton J. Clymer, *Protestant Missionaries in the Philippines, 1898–1916* (Urbana: University of Illinois Press, 1986), p. 159.

54. Glenn A. May, *Battle for Batangas* (New Haven: Yale University Press, 1991), pp. 267, 291.

55. *Boston Evening Transcript*, March 1, 1899.

56. Quoted in Stanley Karnow, *In Our Image* (New York: Random House, 1989), p. 191.

57. Quoted in A. J. Bacevich, *Diplomat in Khaki* (Lawrence: University Press of Kansas, 1989), p. 29.

58. Quoted in John M. Gates, *Schoolbooks and Krags* (Westport, Conn.: Greenwood Press, 1973), p. vii.

59. Henry F. Graff, ed., *American Imperialism and the Philippine Insurrection* (Boston: Little, Brown, 1969), p. 36.

60. Charles Francis Adams to Moorfield Storey, February 24, 1902, Moorfield Storey Papers, Massachusetts Historical Society, Boston.

61. Quoted in Donald Smythe, *Guerrilla Warrior* (New York: Charles Scribner's Sons, 1973), p. 198.

62. Quoted in Reynaldo C. Ileto, "Orators and the Crowd: Philippine Independence Politics, 1910–1914," in Peter W. Stanley, ed., *Reappraising an Empire* (Cambridge, Mass.: Harvard University Press, 1984), p. 103.

63. Quoted in James C. Thomson, Jr., Peter W. Stanley, and John C. Perry, *Sentimental Imperialists* (New York: Harper & Row, 1981), p. 116.

64. Quoted in Karnow, *In Our Image*, p. 201.

65. May, *Battle for Batangas*, p. 276.

66. Quoted in Thomas J. McCormick, *China Market* (Chicago: Quadrangle Books, 1967), p. 119.

67. Quoted in Louis L. Gould, *The Presidency of William McKinley* (Lawrence: University Press of Kansas, 1981), p. 222.

68. *Foreign Relations, 1901*, Appendix: "Affairs in China" (Washington, D.C.: Government Printing Office, 1902), p. 12.

69. Marilyn Blatt Young, "American Expansion, 1870–1900: The Far East," in Barton J. Bernstein, ed., *Towards a New Past* (New York: Pantheon Books, 1968), p. 196.

70. Quoted in Beale, *Theodore Roosevelt*, p. 84.

71. Quoted in Anderson, *Race and Rapprochement*, p. 127.

72. Quoted in Aaron L. Friedberg, *The Weary Titan* (Princeton: Princeton University Press, 1988), p. 164.

73. Paul M. Kennedy, *The Rise and Fall of the Great Powers* (New York: Random House, 1987), p. 251.

74. American Historical Association, *Annual Report, 1898* (Washington, D.C.: Government Printing Office, 1899), p. 288.

75. Quoted in C. Vann Woodward, *The Strange Career of Jim Crow* (New York: Oxford University Press, 1974; 3d rev. ed.), p. 73.

76. Quoted in Arthur Link's essay in *Wilson's Diplomacy* (Cambridge, Mass.: Schenkman, 1973), p. 6.

77. *Washington Post*, June 2, 1898.

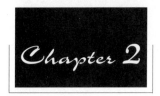

Chapter 2

Managing, Policing, and Extending the Empire, 1900–1914

Theodore Roosevelt the Pirate. *The Colombian minister called the United States a "pirate." When Roosevelt justified to his cabinet the actions he had taken toward Panama in 1903, Secretary of War Elihu Root observed: "You have shown that you have been accused of seduction and you have conclusively proved that you were guilty of rape." Michael C. C. Adams, author of* The Great Adventure: Male Desire and the Coming of World War I *(1990), reads Roosevelt differently, comparing him to Peter Pan, "the boy who would not grow up." (Frank Nankivell, Swann Collection of Caricature and Cartoon)*

✖ *Diplomatic Crossroad*

Severing Panama from Colombia for the Canal, 1903

"Revolution imminent," read the cable from the American consul at Colón, a normally sleepy Colombian seaport on the Atlantic side of the Isthmus of Panama. Acting Secretary of State Francis B. Loomis bridled his curiosity for an hour and five minutes. Then he fired off an inquiry to the U.S. consul at Panama City, on the Pacific slope: "Uprising on Isthmus reported. Keep Department promptly and fully informed." The response came back in four hours: "No uprising yet. Reported will be in the night. Situation is critical." Loomis's anxiety increased sharply five minutes later when he learned that an "important message" intended for the U.S.S. *Nashville* anchored at Colón had miscarried, and troops of the Colombian government had landed in the city.

At the Department of State it was now 8:20 P.M., November 3, 1903. As far as Loomis knew, a revolution had not yet broken out on the isthmus. Nonetheless, he hurriedly drafted instructions for the consuls at Panama and Colón. "Act promptly," he directed in near desperation. Somehow convey to the commanding officer of the *Nashville* this order: "In the interests of peace make every effort to prevent [Colombian] Government troops at Colón from proceeding to Panama [City]." Loomis agonized for another hour. Finally, a new cable arrived: "Uprising occurred to-night . . . no bloodshed. . . . Government will be organized to-night." Loomis no doubt sighed in relief. He had done his part to ensure success in the scheme to acquire a canal controlled by the United States.

If November 3 was a busy day for Francis Loomis, it was far more hectic for José Augustín Arango and his fellow conspirators in Panama. The tiny band of Panamanians and Americans living on the isthmus had actively plotted revolution since August, when the Colombian Congress dashed their hopes for prosperity by defeating the treaty that would have permitted the United States to construct an isthmian canal. By the end of October, they had become convinced that the North American colossus, frustrated in its overtures to Colombia, would lend them moral and physical support. Confident that American naval vessels would be at hand, they selected November fourth as the date of their coup d'état. To their dismay, however, the Colombian steamer *Cartagena* disembarked about 400 troops at Colón early in the morning of November 3. Because the "important message" directing him to prevent the "landing of any armed force . . . either Government or insurgent at Colón" had been delayed in transmission, Commander John Hubbard of the *Nashville* did not interfere with the landing.

Forced to rely on their own wits, the conspirators made good use of the transisthmian railroad. They deviously separated the Colombian commanding general from his troops, lured him aboard a train, and sped him ceremoniously across the isthmus to Panama City. At 6:00 P.M. on the third, the revolutionaries arrested their guest, formed a provisional government, and paraded before a cheering crowd at the Cathedral Plaza. But the revolution would remain perilously unfinished so long as armed Colombian soldiers occupied Colón. Too weak to expel the soldiers by force, the insurgents gave the colonel in charge $8,000 in gold, whereupon he ordered his troops aboard a departing steamer. The American consul at Panama City cabled: "Quiet prevails." At noon the next day, Secretary of State John Hay recognized the sovereign Republic of Panama.

The frantic pace of U.S. isthmian diplomacy continued. The new Panamanian government appointed as its minister plenipotentiary a Frenchman, Philippe Bunau-Varilla, who had long agitated for a Panama canal and who recently had conspired for Panamanian independence from Colombia. With Gallic flourish, Bunau-Varilla congratulated Secretary Hay for rescuing Panama "from the barbarism of unnecessary and wasteful civil wars to consecrate it to the destiny assigned to it by Providence, the service of humanity, and the progress of civilization."[1] John Hay thoroughly understood Bunau-Varilla's rhetoric and eagerly negotiated the treaty both men wanted. On November 18, 1903, less than two weeks after American recognition of Panama, they signed the Hay–Bunau-Varilla Treaty, by which the U.S. government would build, fortify, and operate a canal linking the Atlantic and Pacific oceans.

Hay had at last achieved a goal set by his chief, President Theodore Roosevelt, several years earlier. "I do not see why we should dig the canal if we are not to fortify it," Roosevelt had explained to navalist Alfred Thayer Mahan early in 1900. If an unfortified, neutral canal had existed in Central America during the recent war with Spain, Roosevelt argued, "we could have got the *Oregon* around in time," but the United States would have spent most of the war in "wild panic," fearful that the Spanish fleet would slip through the waterway and rush to the Philippines to attack Commodore Dewey. The obvious lesson: "Better to have no canal at all, than not give us the power to control it in time of war," Roosevelt expostulated.[2] What he really wanted, of course, was a canal run by Americans for the benefit of the United States.

The Clayton-Bulwer Treaty of 1850, stipulating joint Anglo-American control of any isthmian canal, seemed to block the way. In December 1898, flushed with victory over Spain, President William McKinley had directed Secretary Hay to discuss modification of that agreement with the British ambassador, Sir Julian Pauncefote. The Hay-Pauncefote Treaty of February 1900 permitted the United States to build a canal but forbade its fortification, much to the chagrin of Theodore Roosevelt, then governor of New York. He spearheaded an attack that defeated the treaty in the Senate, forcing renegotiation. On November 18, 1901, with Roosevelt now president, Hay and Pauncefote signed a new pact satisfactory to the Rough Rider.

Then began the complex process of determining the route. In November 1901, after an investigation that lasted two years, the Walker Isthmian Canal Commission reported in favor of Nicaragua. The decisive criterion—cost—

seemed exorbitant for Panama because of the obduracy of the New Panama Canal Company, a French-chartered firm that held the Colombian concession for canal rights. The company estimated its assets on the isthmus at $109 million—machinery, property, and excavated soil left by the defunct de Lesseps organization after its failure to cut through Panama in 1888. Purchase of the New Panama Canal Company's rights and holdings would make construction through Panama prohibitively expensive, even though technologically easier. For these reasons, the House of Representatives on January 8, 1902, passed the Hepburn Bill authorizing a canal through Nicaragua.

The New Panama Canal Company's American lawyer, William Nelson Cromwell, described by one irritated member of Congress as "the most dangerous man this country has produced since the days of Aaron Burr—a professional revolutionist," swung into action.[3] A partner in the prestigious New York law firm of Sullivan and Cromwell, he schemed to sell the assets of his French client for the highest possible price. The Walker Commission had estimated the company's worth at $40 million, a figure Cromwell reluctantly accepted after passage of the Hepburn Bill. The attorney began an intense lobbying campaign directed principally at President Roosevelt, Republican senators Mark Hanna and John C. Spooner, and members of the Walker Commission. Bunau-Varilla, formerly chief engineer for de Lesseps, assisted in what has been described as one of the "masterpieces of the lobbyist's art."[4]

On January 18, 1902, the Walker Commission reversed itself and decided for the technologically preferable Panama passage, citing the company's willingness to sell out for the reduced sum of $40 million. Guided by Roosevelt, Spooner, and Cromwell, Congress five months later passed the Spooner Act, approving the Panama route. The State Department soon opened negotiations with Colombia. The annual rent became a stumbling block, which Hay removed only by delivering an ultimatum to the Colombian chargé d'affaires, Tomás Herrán, in January 1903. On January 22 he and Hay signed a treaty granting Colombia an initial payment of $10 million and $250,000 annually. The United States would control the six-mile-wide canal zone for one hundred years, a privilege renewable at the "sole and absolute option" of the North American republic.[5]

The U.S. Senate approved the Hay-Herrán Treaty on March 17, 1903, but the Colombian government deliberated at length. Its treasury drained by a long and costly civil war, Bogotá attempted to extract a $10 million payment from the New Panama Canal Company for permitting the transfer of its assets to the American government. William Nelson Cromwell promptly cried foul, whereupon Secretary Hay bluntly announced that any discussion of a payment by the New Panama Canal Company to Colombia "would be in violation of the Spooner law and not permissible."[6] The Colombians next tried to raise the initial American cash payment from $10 to $15 million. Roosevelt exploded to Hay that "those contemptible little creatures in Bogotá ought to understand how much they are jeopardizing things and imperilling their own future."[7] The president believed that "you could no more make an agreement with the Colombian rulers than you could nail currant jelly to the wall."[8] TR's intransigence and Hay's extraordinary intercession on behalf of a privately owned foreign corporation increased Colombians' resentment against U.S. infringement on their sovereignty over Panama. The Colombian Congress unanimously defeated the treaty on August 12, 1903.

Bogotá's rejection did not catch Roosevelt napping. As early as March 30, Minister Arthur N. Beaupré had cautioned Washington that "without question public opinion is strongly against its ratification," and Roosevelt had begun to ponder undiplomatic alternatives.[9] On June 13 the ubiquitous Cromwell had met with Roosevelt and then planted a story in the *New York World* reporting that, if Colombia rejected the treaty, Panama would secede and grant to the United States "the equivalent of absolute sovereignty over the Canal Zone." The *World* also noted, "President Roosevelt is said to strongly favor this plan."[10] By now the president was peppering his correspondence with contempt for Colombian "jack rabbits," "foolish and homicidal corruptionists," and "cat-rabbits."[11] Even the usually urbane Hay denounced "the government of folly and graft that now rules at Bogotá."[12]

Roosevelt and Hay now considered two options: seizure of Panama by force, or extension of instant recognition and support to any revolutionary regime in Panama. The president inclined sharply toward the latter course after a meeting with Bunau-Varilla on October 10, during which the Frenchman predicted an uprising. When Bunau-Varilla asked what the United States would do, TR replied: "All I can say is that Colombia by her action has forfeited any claim upon the U.S. and I have no use for a government that would do what that government has done."[13] One week later, on October 16, Secretary Hay informed Bunau-Varilla that American naval vessels were heading toward the isthmus. Bunau-Varilla shrewdly calculated the steaming time and cabled the revolutionaries waiting on the isthmus that American warships would arrive by November 2. Early that evening the U.S.S. *Nashville* dropped anchor at Colón as predicted. Although the *Nashville* landed troops to keep order *after* the Panamanian junta had gained control, a Colombian diplomat rightfully complained: "The Americans are against us. What can we do against the American Navy?"[14]

Panama Canal. The U.S.S. *Ohio* passes through the Culebra Cut (now called the Gaillard Cut) of the Panama Canal about a year after the canal opened to traffic—both warships and commercial vessels. (Library of Congress)

In his annual message to Congress after the Panamanian revolution, Roosevelt urged swift ratification of the Hay–Bunau-Varilla Treaty, claiming that Colombia had forced the United States "to take decisive steps to bring to an end a condition of affairs which had become intolerable."[15] When Democratic senators questioned the president's role in the insurrection, Roosevelt disingenuously replied: "No one connected with this Government had any part in preparing, inciting, or encouraging the late revolution."[16] Apparently mollified, on February 23, 1904, the Senate approved the treaty by a vote of 66 to 14. The treaty granted the United States "power and authority" within the zone "in perpetuity" as "if it were the sovereign of the territory."[17] Later, in 1911, TR was widely reported as boasting that "I took the Canal Zone and let Congress debate; and while the debate goes on the Canal does also."[18]

Construction began in mid-1904, and the fifty-mile-long canal opened to traffic on August 15, 1914. During the first year of operation alone, 1,058 merchant vessels slid through the locks, while the Atlantic and Pacific fleets of the U.S. Navy freely exchanged ships. In 1922 the United States paid "conscience money" or "canalimony" of $25 million to Colombia but did not formally apologize for having taken the canal zone. Although Roosevelt's handling of the Panama issue, according to the historian William Harbaugh, constitutes "one of the ineradicable blots on his record," most Americans have applauded his bold meddling in the internal affairs of the sovereign nation of Colombia.[19] Roosevelt himself ranked his accomplishment alongside the Louisiana Purchase and the acquisition of Texas.

THE CONSERVATIVE SHAPERS OF EMPIRE

The taking of Panama symbolized the new activism characteristic of American foreign policy after the Spanish-American-Cuban-Filipino War, and construction of the canal gave the United States virtual hegemony over Latin America. It also plunged Washington into the global contest for empire among the great powers. "The United States will be attacked as soon as you are about to complete the canal," Germany's Kaiser Wilhelm II predicted to an American diplomat in 1907, identifying Japan as the most likely culprit.[20] Britain, which had the power to challenge American preeminence in the hemisphere, chose to acquiesce in the face of a growing political and naval threat from Germany, which was closer to home. In turn, the vigorous German empire, having expanded its markets and investments in Central and South America to more than 2 billion marks by 1900, seemed "desirous of obtaining a foothold in the Western Hemisphere," as the General Board of the U.S. Navy put it.[21] The kaiser boasted to his ambassador in Washington: "We will do whatever is necessary for our navy, even if it displeases the Yankees. Never fear."[22] Revolutionary upheavals in Russia, China, and Mexico produced further shifting in the international balance of power. As European alliances

Makers of American Foreign Relations, 1900–1914

Presidents	Secretaries of State
Theodore Roosevelt, 1901–1909	John Hay, 1898–1905
	Elihu Root, 1905–1909
	Robert Bacon, 1909
William Howard Taft, 1909–1913	Philander C. Knox, 1909–1913
Woodrow Wilson, 1913–1921	William Jennings Bryan, 1913–1915

consolidated and lurched toward a world war, it became the task of President Roosevelt and his successors to defend, develop, and enlarge the new American empire in an era of tumultuous transformation.

In the late nineteenth century, Roosevelt had associated closely with the most vocal pressure group agitating for an American canal, the uniformed "professors of war" at the Naval War College.[23] He corresponded regularly with one of those officers, Alfred Thayer Mahan, the navalist who tirelessly explained the strategic advantages of a canal in the idiom of the 1890s. "Wherever situated, whether at Panama or Nicaragua," Mahan preached, "the fundamental meaning of the canal will be that it advances by thousands of miles the frontiers . . . of the United States."[24] In the course of expanding those frontiers during the "splendid little war" of 1898, the warship *Oregon* dashed at full speed from San Francisco to the tip of South America and through the Strait of Magellan to Cuba in time to help destroy the Spanish fleet off Santiago. The race of more than 14,000 miles fired American imaginations, but it also consumed sixty-eight days and dramatically underscored the need for an interoceanic canal across Central America.

Roosevelt's sense of isthmian strategic necessity reflected a broad worldview he shared with many "progressives" in the reform era of the early twentieth century. A conservative patrician reformer motivated by noblesse oblige, he "feared that unrest caused by social and economic inequities would impair the nation's strength and efficiency."[25] He saw a similar danger to American interests in unrest abroad, and he sought to exert U.S. influence to create order on a global scale. "More and more," Roosevelt told Congress in 1902, "the increasing interdependence and complexity of international political and economic relations render it incumbent on all civilized and orderly powers to insist on the proper policing of the world."[26] A quintessential chauvinist, Roosevelt talked about doing the "rough work of the world" and about the need to "speak softly and carry a big stick."[27] Like his contemporaries, TR had imbibed the Social Darwinist doctrines of "natural selection" and the "survival of the fittest," and he articulated racist notions about Anglo-Saxon superiority and the "white man's burden" to tutor "backward" peoples. For Roosevelt in particular, that superiority was best expressed in war. "All the great masterful races have been fighting races," he lectured to the Naval War College.[28] Not all Progressive Era reformers joined Roosevelt in advocating a vigorous activism abroad. Some, like Wisconsin's Senator Robert M. La Follette, opposed imperialism and contended that the same corporate monopolists they battled at home were dragging the United States into perpetual intervention overseas. Activists in women's organizations bemoaned the "present intoxication with the hashish of conquest" as they urged "women's values" on a male government so as to rein in the "champing steeds" of American militarism and expansion.[29]

Roosevelt vigorously debated his critics and added his unique personal characteristics to American foreign policy. Exuberant and calculating, having the instinct for the jugular, he centralized foreign-policy decisionmaking, frequently bypassed Congress, and believed "the people" so ignorant about foreign affairs that they should not direct an informed president like himself. At the same time, he kept favorite journalists and other "intelligent observers sufficiently enlightened to prevent their going wrong."[30] In the search for a stable world order, Roosevelt could assume the garb of the peacemaker trying to reconcile competing national interests. For example, he won the Nobel Peace Prize in 1906 for his mediating effort at the Portsmouth Conference (see pp. 61–62). The robust president disliked the pomp and ceremony of traditional diplomacy and on one memorable occasion broke up a state luncheon by demonstrating jujitsu holds on the Swiss minister. "The biggest matters," this progenitor of the imperial presidency later wrote, "such as the Portsmouth peace, the acquisition of Panama, and sending the fleet around the world, I managed without consultation with anyone; for when a matter is of capital importance, it is well to have it handled by one man only."[31]

Roosevelt and other shapers of American foreign policy before World War I were members of an American quasi aristocracy and sure-footed devotees of "order." Most had graduated from prestigious eastern colleges and distinguished themselves in high political office or in the professions. They moved comfortably in the affluent, cosmopolitan, upper-class society of the Atlantic seaboard. Roosevelt, a graduate of Harvard College, had been assistant secretary of the navy and governor of New York and was a prolific author. His successor, Ohioan William Howard Taft, a graduate of Yale, had served as a federal circuit court judge, governor of the Philippines (1901–1904), and secretary of war (1904–1908). Woodrow Wilson earned a Ph.D. from Johns Hopkins, wrote books on history, presided over Princeton, and governed New Jersey before entering the White House.

Their secretaries of state, with one exception, belonged to the same elite. John Hay, secretary from 1898 to 1905, was born in Indiana and educated at Brown University. Wealthy and recognized as a poet, novelist, biographer, and editor of the *New York Tribune,* he had served as Lincoln's personal secretary during the Civil War and later as McKinley's ambassador to Great Britain. He thought the "indispensable feature of our foreign policy should be a firm understanding with England," and he was one of the chief architects of the Anglo-American rapprochement of the early twentieth century.[32] His successor, Elihu Root (1905–1909), a cautious conservative who praised Theodore Roosevelt as "the greatest conservative force for the protection of property and capital," was born in upstate New York, graduated from Hamilton College, took a law degree at New

Theodore Roosevelt on Bandanna. This cloth bandanna appeared in 1906 when President Theodore Roosevelt won the Nobel Peace Prize for helping to negotiate an end to the Russo-Japanese War. That this peacemaker was also a warrior is evident from the sketch of the Rough Rider at the top. (The Museum of American Political Life, University of Hartford. Photo by Sally Andersen–Bruce.)

York University, and became one of America's most successful corporation lawyers.[33] As secretary of war from 1899 to 1904, he created mechanisms, such as the Platt Amendment for Cuba, for managing the American empire. Like TR, he believed that the "main object of diplomacy is to keep the country out of trouble" and maintain order abroad.[34] Philander C. Knox (1909–1913) followed Root. A corporation lawyer born in Pennsylvania, he had helped form the giant United States Steel Corporation. He served as attorney general and U.S. senator before entering the State Department. Habitually seeking leisure, Knox liked to play golf at Chevy Chase, spend summers with his trotters at his Valley Forge Farms estate, vacation in Florida in the winter, and delegate departmental work to subordinates. He advocated "dollar diplomacy" as a means of creating order in revolution-prone areas—that is, using private financiers and businesspeople to promote foreign policy, and using diplomacy to promote American commerce and investment abroad. The second man to serve as secretary of state under President Wilson was New Yorker Robert Lansing (1915–1920), a graduate of Amherst College, son-in-law of a former secretary of state, and practitioner of international law. Reserved and conservative, Lansing also would not tolerate disorder in the U.S. sphere of Latin America.

William Jennings Bryan, Wilson's first appointment (1913–1915), did not conform to the conservative elite status of most makers of foreign policy. The "boy orator" of Nebraska could mesmerize crowds by decrying the "cross of gold" on which eastern capitalists were crucifying western and southern farmers, but he could not win a presidential election (he ran in 1896, 1900, and 1908). The "Great Commoner" languished for years as the most prominent has-been of the Democratic party, until Wilson appointed him secretary of state out of deference to his long service to the partisan cause and as a reward for support at the convention of 1912. The president let Bryan appoint "deserving Democrats" to diplomatic posts and indulge his fascination with peace or "cooling off" treaties, but Wilson bypassed him in most important diplomatic decisions, even to the point of composing overseas cables on his own White House typewriter. In 1915, during World War I, Bryan resigned to protest Wilson's pro-British leanings.

These conservative managers of American foreign policy believed that a major component of national power was a prosperous, expanding economy invigorated by a healthy foreign trade. The principle of the "Open Door"—to keep open trade and investment opportunities—became a governing tenet voiced globally, although often tarnished in application. Mahan believed that commerce acted as the "energizer of material civilization," and Roosevelt declared to Congress in his annual message of 1901 that "America has only just begun to assume that commanding position in the international business world which we believe will more and more be hers."[35] In 1900 the United States exported goods valued at $1.5 billion. By 1914, at the start of World War I, that figure stood at $2.5 billion. Exports to Latin America increased markedly from $132 million at the turn of the century to $309 million in 1914. Investments there in sugar, transportation, and banking shot up. By 1913 the United Fruit Company, the banana empire, had some 130,000 acres in cultivation in Central America, a fleet of freighters, and political influence as well. By 1914 the United States dominated nickel mining in Canada and sugar production in Cuba, and total American investments abroad equaled $3.5 billion.

But those statistics were not important solely as contributions to pocketbooks. Americans believed that economic expansion also meant that the best of "Americanism," the core values of industriousness, honesty, morality, and private initiative, were carried abroad. Thus Yale University-in-China and the Young Men's Christian Association (YMCA) joined the Standard Oil Company and Singer Sewing in China as advance agents of civilization. And, as Secretary of War Taft said about the Chinese: "The more civilized they become the more active their industries, the wealthier they become, and the better market they will become for us."[36] President Wilson, who added a conspicuous tinge of missionary paternalism to the quest for order, said simply that he would "teach the South American Republics to elect good men."[37] Some foreign observers did not appreciate American beneficence. The typical "Yankee," one German wrote in 1904, was "a boorish fellow, who condoned corruption in public life and approved of every swindle in economic life; who pursued the dollar and sensation, a barbarian in science and art, a bigoted, sanctimonious hypocrite who chewed tobacco and whose chief amusement was found in lynchings."[38] Whatever Americans' intentions or habits, their compulsion to shape the lives of other peoples while denying any desire to dominate brought mixed results.

THE PROTECTORATE OVER CUBA

In December 1898, President William McKinley promised Cuba "free and independent" status as soon as the American military occupation had achieved "complete tranquility" and a "stable government" on the island.[39] Two months later the Philippine insurrection erupted, sending shock waves through Washington. Secretary of War Elihu Root, charged with formulating Cuban occupation policy, feared that in Cuba the United States stood "on the verge daily of the same sort of thing that happened to us in the Philippines."[40] To accelerate the evolution of Cuban democracy and stability, Root appointed General Leonard Wood the military governor of the island. A Harvard graduate with a degree in medicine, Wood had entered the army for excitement. A spiritual relative and a friend of the adventurous Roosevelt, Wood favored outright annexation of Cuba, but he loyally subordinated his own preferences to the administration's policy of patrician tutelage in the ways of progress and freedom. During his tenure as military governor (1899–1902), he worked to eradicate yellow fever, Americanize education, construct highways, and formulate an electoral law guaranteeing order. He even added "before" and "after" photos of public toilets in his reports. In the historian Emily S. Rosenberg's words, "Mark Twain's Connecticut Yankee could not have done more."[41] The general defined his objectives conservatively: "When money can be borrowed at a reasonable rate of interest and when capital is willing to invest in the Island, a condition of stability will have been reached."[42] Given the war-ravaged Cuban economy, only the North Americans had the resources to generate reconstruction. Those Cuban elites who spoke English and knew American ways could serve as local managers, traders, agents, and advisers. The occupation thus made the teaching of English in the public schools a central goal because, according to one official, "the Cuban people will never understand the people of the United States until they appreciate our institutions."[43] Few Cubans realized that "to be educated by the people who had conquered them was the extension of conquest, only by another name."[44]

Root began construction of a Cuban-American political relationship designed to weather the storms of independence. Working closely with Senator Orville Platt, Root fashioned the so-called Platt Amendment to the Army Appropriation Bill of 1901. By the Platt Amendment's terms, Cuba could not make a treaty with any nation that might impair its independence. Should Cuban independence ever be threatened, or should it fail to protect adequately "life, property, and individual liberty," the United States had the right to intervene. For these purposes, Cuba would cede to the United States "lands necessary for coaling or naval stations."[45] Later putting the issue in global perspective, Root rationalized that "you cannot understand the Platt Amendment unless you know something about the character of Kaiser Wilhelm."[46]

Cubans howled. On Good Friday 1901, the front page of Havana's *La Discusión* carried a cartoon of "The Cuban Calvary" depicting the Cuban people as Christ and Senator Platt as a Roman soldier. Anti-imperialist critics charged that the amendment extinguished Cuban independence. Root claimed that intervention was not "synonymous with intermeddling or interference with the affairs of a Cuban government," but a more straightforward General Wood privately conceded that there was, "of course, little or no independence left Cuba under the Platt Amendment."[47] A reluctant Cuban convention adopted the measure as an amendment to the new constitution on June 12, 1901, and the two governments signed a treaty embodying the provisions of the Platt Amendment on May 22, 1903. In 1903 the U.S. Navy constructed a naval base at Guantánamo Bay;

"If General Wood Is Unpopular with Cuba, We Can Guess the Reason." General Leonard Wood (1860–1927), before he served as military governor of Cuba (1899–1902), was a surgeon who entered the army in 1886 and earned a Congressional Medal of Honor for capturing Indian leader Geronimo. He also commanded the Rough Riders at San Juan Hill during the Spanish-American-Cuban-Filipino War. Later he helped govern the Philippines. (*Minneapolis Tribune* in *Literary Digest,* 1901)

"Gitmo," as the marines christened it, was leased to the United States in perpetuity for a small annual fee. With North American investments pouring into capital-starved Cuba, extending control over the sugar, tobacco (the new Tobacco Trust exported 90 percent of Havana cigars by 1902), mining, and transportation industries, utilities, and cattle ranching, the Reciprocity Treaty of 1902 permitted Cuban products to enter the United States at specially reduced tariff rates, thereby further interlocking the economies of the two countries.

The first president of the Republic of Cuba, Tomás Estrada Palma, has been described as "more plattish than Platt himself."[48] Following his rigged reelection and second inauguration, discontented Cuban nationalists revolted. In a cable of September 8, 1906, the American consul general in Havana reported Estrada Palma's inability to quell the rebellion or "protect life and property."[49] He pleaded for warships. President Roosevelt immediately ordered the cruiser *Denver* to Havana, but his tardy instructions failed to leash the ship's commanding officer, who landed a battalion of sailors at Estrada Palma's request. Roosevelt summarily ordered the men back aboard ship, adding further to the political chaos. "I am so angry with that infernal little Cuban republic," exploded the Rough Rider, "that I would like to wipe its people off the face of the earth." All he wanted from the Cubans, he said, was that "they should behave themselves."[50]

Into this turmoil stepped the portly secretary of war, William Howard Taft, whom Roosevelt ordered to Cuba. Groping for a solution that would "put an end to anarchy without necessitating a reoccupation of the island by our troops," Roosevelt instructed Taft to mediate between the warring factions.[51] "Unless we assure peace," Taft worried that "some $200,000,000 of American property may go up in smoke in less than ten days."[52] Estrada Palma resigned, permitting Taft to establish a new provisional government with himself as governor. Taft soon lectured students in Havana that Cubans needed a "mercantile spirit," a "desire to make money, to found great enterprises."[53] He returned home in mid-October, leaving behind a government headed by an American civilian, administered by U.S. Army officers, and supported by more than 5,000 American soldiers. For twenty-eight months Governor Charles E. Magoon attempted to reinstate Leonard Wood's electoral and humanitarian reforms, while Roosevelt publicly scolded the Cubans that if their "insurrectionary habit" persisted, it was "absolutely out of the question that the Island should continue independent."[54]

Under his successor Taft, and under Taft's successor Woodrow Wilson, American policy toward Cuba consisted of reflexive support for existing governments, by means of force if necessary. Taft and Wilson made no serious effort to reform Cuba in the American image. In what has been called both "a preventive policy" and "Dollar Diplomacy," the United States sought order in Cuban politics and security for American investments and commerce, particularly in sugar.[55] The $50 million invested by Americans in 1896 jumped to $220 million in 1913. By 1920 American-owned mills produced about half of Cuba's sugar. Cuban exports to the United States in 1900 equaled $31 million, by 1914 $131 million, and by 1920 $722 million. American entrepreneurs helped establish missionary schools (such as the Candler school in Havana, named after the founder of Coca-Cola) that, in effect, trained Cubans for employment in North American companies.

When these interests became threatened by revolution, as in May 1912 and February 1917, the marines went ashore. After Havana followed Washington's lead and declared war against Germany in April 1917, some 2,500 American troops went ostensibly to protect the sugar plantations that helped feed the Allied armies. Under the yoke of the Platt Amendment, the U.S. military, and American economic interests, Cuba remained a protectorate of the United States.

POLICING THE CARIBBEAN: VENEZUELA, THE DOMINICAN REPUBLIC, AND THE ROOSEVELT COROLLARY

President Theodore Roosevelt devoted a great deal of thought to Latin America in the winter of 1901–1902. He guided the second Hay-Pauncefote Treaty through the Senate, fretted over the route of his isthmian canal, and helped Elihu Root shape the terms of the occupation of Cuba. He also turned his mind toward the most hallowed of American doctrines, that propounded by James Monroe in 1823. In his first annual message, on December 3, 1901, Roosevelt declared: "It is really a guarantee of the commercial independence of the Americas." The United States, however, as protector of that independence, would "not guarantee any state against punishment if it misconducts itself, provided that punishment does not take the form of the acquisition of territory by any non-American power."[56] If a Western Hemispheric country misbehaved in its relations with a European nation, Roosevelt would "let the European country spank it."[57]

The president was thinking principally of Germany and Venezuela. Under the rule of Cipriano Castro, an unsavory dictator whom Roosevelt once characterized as an "unspeakable villainous monkey," Venezuela perpetually deferred payment on bonds worth more than $12.5 million and held by German investors.[58] Berlin became impatient. Great Britain also became irritated by Venezuela's failure to meet its debts to British subjects. In December 1902, after clearing the way with Washington, Germany and Britain delivered an ultimatum demanding immediate settlement of their claims, seized several Venezuelan vessels, bombarded two forts, and proclaimed a blockade closing Venezuela to commerce. To all of this Theodore Roosevelt initially acquiesced, but American congressional and editorial opinion reacted adversely. The *Literary Digest* of December 20 worried "that England and Germany will overstep the limits prescribed by the Monroe Doctrine" and concluded that many newspapers "think that the allies have already gone too far."[59]

In mid-January 1903, the German navy bombarded two more forts. This time the president delivered a quiet ultimatum to desist. He also sent Admiral George Dewey on naval maneuvers in the Caribbean, which were intended, Dewey later boasted, as "an object lesson to the Kaiser."[60] TR privately mused: "The only power which may be a menace to us in anything like the immediate future is Germany."[61] Shaken by the American reaction, Kaiser Wilhelm II replaced his ill-

Roosevelt Cards. Filling a strong poker hand and completing a winning political platform, Theodore Roosevelt always integrated domestic and foreign policies. (Library of Congress)

informed ambassador with Hermann Speck von Sternburg, an old friend of Roosevelt. The president received him immediately and urged a quick settlement to quell the clamor in Britain and the United States. Thereupon, Britain and Germany in early February lifted the blockade and submitted the dispute to the Permanent Court at The Hague. Prime Minister Arthur Balfour calmed troubled waters by welcoming an "increase of the influence of the United States" in Latin America.[62] Even more, he accepted the Monroe Doctrine as international law. Speck von Sternburg also averred that the kaiser "would no more think of violating that [Monroe] doctrine than he would of colonizing the moon."[63] Not so. In early 1904, The Hague Tribunal awarded preferential treatment to the claims of the two nations that had used force against Venezuela. A prominent State Department official complained that this decision put "a premium on violence" and made likely similar European interventions in the future.[64]

Theodore Roosevelt also worried increasingly about the Dominican Republic, torn continually by revolution since 1899 and seemingly vulnerable to German interests. "I have about the same desire to annex it," Roosevelt said privately, "as a gorged boa constrictor might have to swallow a porcupine wrong-end to."[65] An American firm that formerly handled the country's tariff collections (customs) claimed damages of several million dollars, and European creditors demanded action by their governments. The president had been "hoping and praying . . . that the Santo Dominigans would behave so that I would not have to act in any way." By spring 1904 he thought he might have "to do nothing but what a policeman has to do."[66] He told Root that if they said "'Hands off' to the powers of Europe, then sooner or later we must keep order ourselves."[67]

On December 6, 1904, Roosevelt described to Congress his conception of the United States as hemispheric policeman. "Chronic wrongdoing, or an impotence which results in a general loosening of the ties of civilized society," he proclaimed, "may in America, as elsewhere, ultimately require intervention by some civilized nation, and in the Western Hemisphere the adherence of the United States to the Monroe Doctrine may force the United States, however reluctantly, in flagrant cases of such wrongdoing or impotence, to the exercise of an international police power."[68] With this statement the twenty-sixth president added to the Monroe Doctrine his own corollary, which fundamentally transformed that prohibition on European meddling into a brash promise of U.S. regulation of the Americas.

The Rough Rider soon donned his constable's badge. In December the State Department initiated discussions with the Dominican Republic to provide American collection and distribution of the republic's customs revenues. He assigned an American collector of the Dominican customs, an arrangement finally sanctified in a treaty approved by the U.S. Senate in February 1907. Secretary Root explained that the "inevitable effect of our building the Canal must be to require us to police the surrounding premises," thus gaining "trade and control, and the obligation to keep order."[69] Yet imposing order provoked nationalist resentment from Dominicans who, as one naval officer reported in 1906, "are quieting their children with the threat 'There comes an American. Keep quiet or he will kill you.'"[70]

Taft's secretary of state, Philander C. Knox, applauded Root's customs receivership in the Dominican Republic because it denied to rebels the funds they so eagerly "collected" through the capture of customs houses. Knox credited the receivership with curing "century-old evils."[71] The assassination of the Dominican president the following November 1911 demonstrated that Knox spoke prematurely. And in 1912 revolutionaries operating from contiguous Haiti marauded throughout the Dominican Republic, forcing the closure of several customs houses. To restore order, Taft in September 1912 sent a commission backed by 750 marines. The commissioners redefined the Haitian-Dominican border, forced the corrupt Dominican president to resign by stopping his customs revenues, and avoided direct interference in a new election.

His denunciation of "dollar diplomacy" notwithstanding, Woodrow Wilson had written in 1907 that "concessions obtained by financiers must be safeguarded by ministers of state, even if the sovereignty of unwilling nations be outraged in the process."[72] A reporter interviewing the candidate in 1912 thought him "quite deluded by all that silly jingo talk about Germany making a raid on Latin America."[73] No wonder that President Wilson's search for stability in Latin America retraced familiar steps. When, in September 1913, revolution again threatened the Dominican government, Secretary Bryan warned "that this Government will employ every legitimate means to assist in the restoration of order and the prevention of further insurrections."[74] The Navy Department sent a cruiser, and Wilson urged political and economic reforms. Formal naval occupation followed further revolutionary disorders in spring 1916. As the 400 marines of Admiral William Caperton's landing force entered the city of Santo Domingo at dawn on May 15, they were greeted by empty streets, bolted doors, shuttered windows, and Dominican flags festooned with black crepe—a "*duelo publico* (public mourning)."[75] A new treaty gave the United States full control over Dominican finances. In November, as American involvement in the European war became increasingly probable, President Wilson proclaimed the formal military occupation of the Dominican Republic, ostensibly to curtail the activities of revolutionaries suspected of a pro-German bias. Facing an insurgency by peasants in the eastern region of the Dominican Republic, who waged hit-and-run guerrilla warfare, the U.S. Navy formally governed the country until 1922. The main legacy of the occupation, in the historian Bruce Calder's terse judgment, was "a strong anti-U.S. feeling" among the Dominican people.[76]

THE QUEST FOR STABILITY IN HAITI AND NICARAGUA

The Dominican Republic shares the island of Hispaniola with Haiti, where revolution became an increasingly popular mode of changing governments. American investments in Haiti were limited to ownership of a small railroad and a one-third share in the Haitian National Bank. Nationals of France and Germany controlled the bank, and disorder thus could give either European nation a pretext for intervention. After the outbreak of World War I, the Wilson administration worried about "the ever present danger of German control" of Haiti and Haiti's deepwater harbor of Môle Saint Nicolas.[77] The Navy Department, content with bases in Cuba and Puerto Rico, nonetheless remembered the German cruiser *Panther* sinking a Haitian gunboat in 1902 and the kaiser's inflammatory message, "Bravo, *Panther!*"[78] The State Department sought to buy the Môle "to take it out of the market so that no other nation will . . . secure a foothold there."[79] Instability also invited continued trouble. "Elections . . . do not exist in Haiti," a diplomat reported. "Elections being simply a continuation of the military system under which the country is governed."[80] To impose order on Haiti, Wilson pressed for an American customs receivership on the Dominican model.

The Haitians resisted successfully until July 1915, when the regime of Guillaume Sam fell in an orgy of grisly political murders. Wilson could stomach no more, and he ordered the navy to invade Haiti. While 2,000 marines imposed martial law, Secretary of State Robert Lansing obtained supervision of customs houses and "such financial control over the affairs of the Republic of Haiti as the United States may deem necessary for an efficient administration."[81] He admitted to Wilson that "this method of negotiation, with our marines policing the Haytian Capital, is high handed."[82] The U.S. naval and diplomatic vise meant that Haiti would be ruled until 1934 by what the historian David Healy has called "an American military regime which acted, when it pleased, through the [Haitian] president."[83]

The United States also intervened, virtually at will, in Nicaragua. For Theodore Roosevelt, Nicaragua held importance primarily as a potential canal route, a rivalry decided in Panama's favor in 1903. Subsequently, he manifested interest in Nicaragua only briefly, during 1907, when he and the president of Mexico jointly proposed a peace conference to end the incessant warfare among Central American states. As Secretary Root explained, their conduct was "important to us," because the Panama Canal put them "in the front yard of the United States."[84] When President José Santos Zelaya solicited foreign investors, especially from Germany, for funds to build a second interoceanic canal, because their capital investments were three times greater than U.S. properties in Nicaragua, U.S. diplomats turned against a leader whom some Nicaraguans had compared to Theodore Roosevelt. For Zelaya's crime of seeking a "better economic position for Nicaragua outside the U.S. economic subsystem," as the historian Thomas Schoonover has put it, North Americans labeled him "a tyrannical, self-serving, brutal, greedy disturber of Central American peace, an enemy of U.S. businessmen, and an opponent of all reasonable diplomatic objectives."[85] After Zelaya executed two Americans for joining a revolutionary army in November 1909, the United States broke diplomatic relations, threatened naval intervention, and forced Zelaya into exile. Secretary Knox then negotiated a treaty with the victorious conservatives led by Adolfo Díaz, providing for U.S. control of the customs service and an American loan. The U.S. Senate refused ratification, but Knox and a group of bankers simply acted ad interim without the authorization of a treaty. In September 1912, the administration ordered Major Smedley D. Butler and 354 marines into battle on behalf of the Díaz regime, which the State Department deemed representative "of an educated, property-owning and civilized small minority . . . , [and] the ablest people of the country."[86] After tipping the scales

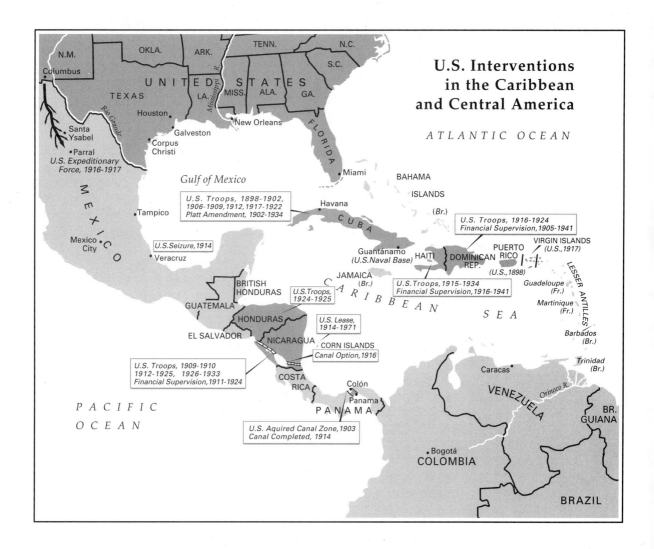

U.S. Interventions in the Caribbean and Central America

ATLANTIC OCEAN

Gulf of Mexico

U.S. Expeditionary Force, 1916-1917

U.S. Troops, 1898-1902, 1906-1909, 1912, 1917-1922 Platt Amendment, 1902-1934

U.S. Seizure, 1914

U.S. Troops, 1916-1924 Financial Supervision, 1905-1941

U.S. Troops, 1915-1934 Financial Supervision, 1916-1941

U.S. Troops, 1924-1925

U.S. Lease, 1914-1971

Corn Islands Canal Option, 1916

U.S. Troops, 1909-1910 1912-1925, 1926-1933 Financial Supervision, 1911-1924

U.S. Aquired Canal Zone, 1903 Canal Completed, 1914

against the newest revolutionary army, the leathernecks returned home, leaving one hundred behind as a legation guard in Managua.

The marines could prevent a coup d'état, but they could not easily put Díaz's house in fiscal order. Bryan in spring 1913 dusted off a shelved draft treaty granting the United States a canal option in Nicaragua in exchange for $3 million. Bryan hoped that this money would "give sufficient encouragement" to American bankers to lend Díaz more.[87] The secretary also added a clause similar to the Platt Amendment before sending the Bryan-Chamorro Treaty to the Senate. The upper house balked at this extension of American commitments and, to gain approval, the Wilson administration had to delete the right of intervention. Ratification in February 1916 did help to shore up Nicaragua's finances. The treaty also effectively excluded European powers from naval bases in the Gulf of Fonseca, and to make that point stick, Wilson ordered U.S. warships to cruise offshore during the 1916 Nicaraguan presidential campaign. Although nominally independent, Nicaragua remained a U.S. protectorate until 1933.

THE MEXICAN REVOLUTION AND THREATENED U.S. INTERESTS

Mexico changed governments with uncharacteristic frequency after the outbreak of revolution in 1910. In 1911 Francisco I. Madero toppled Porfirio Díaz, the aged dictator who had maintained order, personal power, and a healthy environment for North American investments since the late 1870s. U.S. citizens owned more than 40 percent of Mexico's property and Mexico had become the world's third largest oil producer, thanks to Standard Oil Company, Texas Oil Company (Texaco), and Edward L. Doheny's Mexican Petroleum Company. The revolution thus inevitably took on an anti-Yankee tinge. Although angry that the turmoil threatened American lives and property, Taft determined to "sit tight on the lid and it will take a good deal to pry me off."[88] In February 1913, U.S. ambassador Henry Lane Wilson encouraged one of Madero's trusted generals, Victoriano Huerta, to overthrow the revolutionary nationalist. Indeed, Huerta had Madero shot and then set about to consolidate his own power. The Taft administration prepared to recognize Huerta in return for a settlement of claims against Mexico. But one of the state governors, Venustiano Carranza, organized the "Constitutionalist" revolt on February 26. With American residents became caught in the crossfire, the departing Taft administration refused recognition until Huerta punished the "murderers of American citizens" and "put an end to the discriminations against American interests."[89]

Appalled by Madero's murder, President Woodrow Wilson vowed that he would not recognize a "government of butchers."[90] He denounced Huerta as a "diverting brute! . . . seldom sober and always impossible."[91] Seemingly unconcerned about private American properties in Mexico worth some $1.5 billion, Wilson claimed that he was "not the servant of those who wish to enhance the value of their Mexican investments."[92] When Ambassador Henry Lane Wilson, whom the president suspected of complicity in Madero's ouster, continued to advocate recognition of Huerta to protect those American interests, Washington recalled the U.S. envoy in July 1913 and dismissed him from the diplomatic corps. The president thereafter treated with Mexico through special emissaries, only one of whom spoke fluent Spanish.

In August one of these representatives, John Lind, arrived in Mexico City. A rabid anti-Catholic and former governor of Minnesota without diplomatic experience, Lind delivered Wilson's proposal for an armistice between Huerta's federalist troops and all revolutionary groups, "an early and free election," and Huerta's promise not to run for president. In exchange, the United States pledged recognition and aid to "the administration chosen and set up . . . in the way and on the conditions suggested." With sublime arrogance, Woodrow Wilson wondered, "can Mexico give the civilized world a satisfactory reason for rejecting our good offices?"[93] Mexican foreign minister Federico Gamboa did so on August 26, ridiculing Wilson's "counsels and advice (let us call them thus)." Adherence to U.S. dictates would mean that "all the future elections for president would be submitted to the veto of any President of the United States," and no Mexican government would ever perpetrate "such an enormity."[94] After this snub, Woodrow Wilson announced a restrained policy of "watchful waiting," clamped an embargo on arms to Mexico, and advised Americans to leave that country.[95]

Undeterred, Huerta in October dissolved an unruly legislature, arrested its members, and held a special election, which returned an entirely submissive congress ready to extend his presidency indefinitely. Wilson then turned to Carranza in northern Mexico, sending the same proposal Huerta's foreign minister had rejected in August. Equally nationalistic, Carranza contemptuously refused Wilsonian mediation and rejected any solution short of his own triumph. Wilson informed the other powers on November 24 of his policy "to isolate General Huerta entirely; to cut him off from foreign sympathy . . . and so to force him out." If such pressure failed to induce Huerta's retirement, "it will become the duty of the United States to use less peaceful means to put him out."[96]

Most European powers, especially Germany, had recognized Huerta in defiance of Wilson. "Good. Finally unity against the Yankee," Kaiser Wilhelm II had noted in July 1913.[97] The British, however, their capital investments in Mexico ranking second only to those of the United States and their navy relying on Mexican oil as a backup to Middle East sources, did not want to antagonize Wilson when tensions were mounting in Europe. The British Foreign Office therefore notified Huerta that it would not support him against the United States, urged him to resign, and recalled Minister Sir Lionel Carden, whose alleged influence over Huerta had provoked American antipathy—all the while viewing Wilson's policies as "most impractical and unreasonable."[98]

With British compliance assured, Wilson lifted the arms embargo in February 1914 and permitted large quantities of arms to flow to both factions. As Carranza's resupplied forces pushed south, the president sent U.S. naval vessels to the oil-producing town of Tampico on the Gulf of Mexico. On April 9, at Tampico,

William Jennings Bryan (1860–1925), Woodrow Wilson (1856–1924), and Franklin D. Roosevelt (1882–1945), 1913. President Wilson, in white trousers and dark jacket, speaks while Secretary of State Bryan, to the president's right, and Assistant Secretary of the Navy Roosevelt, at the far right of the picture, look on. Wilson spoke proudly of his "missionary diplomacy," for he believed that "every nation needs to be drawn into the tutelage of America." Latin Americans resisted such U.S. paternalism. (FDR Library)

Huerta's troops arrested several American sailors loading gasoline aboard a whaleboat docked provocatively near the Mexican outpost. The Mexican colonel in charge quickly disavowed the arrests, freed the sailors, and apologized orally. The hotheaded U.S. squadron commander, Rear Admiral Henry T. Mayo, demanded a formal twenty-one-gun salute because Mexico had insulted the flag—"a hostile act, not to be excused."[99] Wilson immediately warned the Mexican government "that unless the guilty persons are promptly punished consequences of [the] gravest sort might ensue." Using Huerta's rejection of the Mayo ultimatum as justification, the president undertook to drive the Mexican leader from power. On April 20, Wilson requested congressional approval to use armed force "to obtain from General Huerta and his adherents the fullest recognition of the rights and dignity of the United States."[100] Instead of sending marines to protect American-owned oil fields at Tampico, however, Wilson and Navy Secretary Josephus Daniels ordered U.S. warships to the port city of Veracruz to stop an arms shipment aboard the German-owned steamer *Ypiranga*—weapons intended for Huerta.

On April 21, 1914, eight hundred American sailors and marines landed. Huerta's troops withdrew from the city, but cadets from the naval academy, joined by prisoners liberated from jails and other irregulars, put up a bloody resistance. Nineteen Americans and several hundred Mexicans died. A stunned Wilson told his personal physician that "the thought haunts me that it was I who ordered those young men to their deaths."[101] Although the invasion was designed to undermine Huerta, the historian Ramón E. Ruíz has written, "the capture of Veracruz nearly united Mexicans behind him . . . [because] Mexicans, believing their independence endangered, rushed to enlist in Huerta's army."[102] Rejecting advice from his military advisers, who wanted to march to Mexico City, Wilson accepted mediation when proposed by Argentina, Brazil, and Chile (the ABC powers) on April 25.

A month later, representatives of the United States, Huerta, and the ABC powers met on the Canadian side of Niagara Falls. From the outset, Wilson and Carranza doomed the mediation by their intransigence. The American president refused to discuss the evacuation of Veracruz or Tampico, a major reason for convening the conference. He sought instead "the entire elimination of General Huerta."[103] But Carranza indignantly refused to attend any foreign meeting dealing with Mexico's internal affairs. A newspaper editor sarcastically proposed: "Why should not Abyssinia, Servia, and Senegabia—the A.S.S. powers—tender their good offices? Send out the SOS for the A.S.S."[104] On July 2 the jilted mediators adjourned; two weeks later Huerta fled to Europe, and on August 20 a triumphant Carranza paraded before enthusiastic throngs in Mexico City.

The Constitutionalist triumph did not last. One of Carranza's northern generals, Francisco (Pancho) Villa, soon broke from the ranks, marched south, and in December occupied Mexico City. Wilson saw Villa as a Robin Hood who had spent "a not uneventful life in robbing the rich in order to give to the poor," a potential client who could be "the sword of the revolution" while Wilson offered "capable and disinterested advice."[105] Villa had not criticized the Veracruz operation, and the president reciprocated by facilitating arms exports to him and refusing to recognize Carranza. To avoid danger of a military clash with any Mexican faction, Wilson withdrew all American troops from Veracruz on November 23, 1914. Once again, Wilson watched and waited.

Mexican-American relations remained tense during early 1915. Carranza's forces gradually drove Villa north, but in the process Mexico City became a no-man's-land, with bread riots and starvation threatening its inhabitants, including 2,500 Americans and 23,000 other foreign residents. Wilson contemplated relieving the city by force, perhaps with Pan American cooperation, but deteriorating German-American relations preoccupied him, especially after the *Lusitania* sinking in May. Resigned to failure in Mexico, Wilson seemed to renounce further interference: "Carranza will somehow have to be digested."[106] By then, American oil companies were backing Carranza because he occupied their oil fields. Two months later the United States extended partial, or de facto, recognition to the Constitutionalist government and permitted munitions exports, while embargoing arms to the regime's enemies.

Egged on by German agents who envisaged a Mexican-American war as "a noose . . . to tie the United States to the American continent," Villa denounced *Carranzistas* as "vassals" of the United States.[107] In the predawn hours of March 9, 1916, Villa led a band of *Villistas* across the border into Columbus, New Mexico, initiating a bloody battle that left seventeen Americans and more than a hundred Mexicans dead. Within hours of the attack, Wilson unleashed the U.S. Army against Villa. General John J. "Black Jack" Pershing commanded a Punitive Expedition of some 7,000 men, which penetrated 350 miles into Mexico in a vain search for Pancho Villa. A clash with Carranza's forces in August occurred instead.

Francisco (Pancho) Villa (1878–1923). The intelligent, dedicated revolutionary nationalist bedeviled both Mexico and the United States. His daring raid on an American town was calculated to outrage President Wilson, whom he mocked as "an evangelizing professor of philosophy who is destroying the independence of a friendly people." (W. H. Horne postcard. Southwest Collection, El Paso Public Library)

Carranza kept up drumfire demands for U.S. withdrawal, but Wilson hesitated for fear of appearing weak during a presidential election year. A member of Wilson's cabinet complained that Carranza thought he was "a real god and not a tin god, that he holds thunderbolts in his hands instead of confetti."[108] With the European war looming closer, the president decided to disengage. On January 28, 1917, three days before Germany's resumption of unrestricted submarine warfare, Secretary of War Newton D. Baker announced that Pershing's troops were marching home. All had left Mexico by February 5. In late February, the secret Zimmermann telegram dated January 16, proposing an anti-American alliance between Germany and Mexico (and possibly including Japan), came into the hands of the State Department, courtesy of British intelligence. This dire German ploy accelerated Wilson's movement toward full diplomatic relations with Carranza's government. The United States extended de jure recognition on August 31, 1917, in order to ensure Mexican neutrality during the fight against Germany. After four futile years, Wilson had finally given up trying to tutor the Mexicans. Carranza "may not have fulfilled the social goals of the revolution," as one scholar has written, "but he kept the gringos out of Mexico City."[109]

JAPAN, CHINA, AND DOLLAR DIPLOMACY

Telling Asians how to run their affairs proved even more difficult. Secretary of State John Hay's endorsement of Chinese political and administrative integrity in the Open Door note of July 1900 did not prevent the further emasculation of China. During the Boxer Rebellion Russia stationed 175,000 troops in Manchuria and demanded exclusive rights from China, including a commercial monopoly. President Roosevelt and Hay could do little to stop this infringement of China's sovereignty. The United States, they said, had "always recognized the exceptional position of Russia" in Manchuria and had merely sought the commercial freedom "guaranteed to us by . . . the whole civilized world."[110] Washington retreated because Roosevelt realized that the American people would not fight for nebulous principles of Chinese integrity in Manchuria, an area considered strategically remote and economically inconsequential. He knew it was futile, in historian Akira Iriye's words, "to play the role of an Asian power without military power."[111]

Japan viewed the question quite differently. Russia blocked Japanese economic expansion into Manchuria, posed a potential naval menace, and endangered the Japanese position in Korea. Tokyo covered its flanks with an Anglo-Japanese Alliance in 1902 and prepared for war. On February 8, 1904, the Japanese navy suddenly captured headlines when it destroyed Russia's Asian fleet in a surprise attack at Port Arthur. At first Roosevelt cheered privately, "for Japan is playing our game," but as the enormity of Japanese victories became apparent he hoped for peace "on terms which will not mean the creation of either a yellow peril or a Slav peril."[112] By spring 1905, Japanese soldiers had triumphed at Mukden, where Russia lost 97,000 men. Revolutionary stirrings had hit St. Petersburg, and Admiral Nakagori Togo had sunk the Russian Baltic fleet. Still, the Japanese treasury was drained and the army stretched thin. On May 31, Minister Kogoro Takahira requested Roosevelt "directly and entirely of his own motion and initiative to invite the two belligerents to come together" for direct peace negotiations.[113]

Seizing the opportunity to balance the powers in order to protect America's territorial and commercial interests in the Pacific and Asia, the president invited Japanese and Russian representatives to meet at Portsmouth, New Hampshire, on August 9, 1905. The Japanese delegates demanded Russia's leasehold on the Liaodong Peninsula and the railroad running from Harbin to Port Arthur, evacuation of Russian troops from Manchuria, and Japan's control of Korea. The Russians quickly conceded these points, but rejected additional Japanese requests for an indemnity and cession of the island of Sakhalin. Roosevelt broke the deadlock by proposing division of Sakhalin and agreement "in principle" on an indemnity. Tsar Nicholas II agreed to partition the island but refused any payment. Japan yielded and in late August signed a peace treaty. Roosevelt won the Nobel Peace Prize for his endeavors.

The Roosevelt administration's search for equipoise in East Asia neither began nor ended at Portsmouth. As early as March 1904, TR had conceded to Japan a relationship with Korea "just like we have with Cuba."[114] Secretary of War Taft reaffirmed the concession with Prime Minister Taro Katsura on July 27, 1905. In the Taft-Katsura "agreed memorandum of conversation," the prime minister denied Japanese designs on the Philippines, and Taft, in the words of the historian John Wilz, put an American "seal on the death warrant of an independent Korea."[115] A year later the Japanese reopened southern Manchuria to foreign and American trade, but discouraged foreign capital investments. When Japan formally annexed Korea in 1910, President Taft accepted it as "the final step in a process of control of the ancient empire by her powerful neighbor."[116]

This artful balancing of interests augured well for a continuation of traditional Japanese-American cordiality, until a local dispute in California abruptly undercut Rooseveltian diplomacy. On October 11, 1906, the San Francisco School Board created a special "Oriental Public School" for all Japanese, Chinese, and Korean children. Japan immediately protested, and Theodore Roosevelt denounced the "infernal fools in California" whose exclusion of Japanese from all other public schools constituted "a confession of inferiority in our civilization."[117] He wrote that the "feeling on the Pacific slope . . . is as foolish as if conceived by the mind of a Hottentot."[118] Given existing federal-state jurisdictions, however, he could do little more than rail against the recalcitrant school board, apply political pressure to the California legislature to prevent statewide discriminatory measures, and propose legislation to naturalize Japanese residing permanently in the United States. The president had seriously underestimated the depth of "genuine race feeling" throughout the United States, especially in California.[119] Always the political realist, Roosevelt accepted what he personally disliked and sought accommodation with Japan. By March 1907, he had contrived a "Gentlemen's Agreement" with Tokyo, sharply restricting Japanese immigration on a voluntary basis.

Two months later anti-Japanese riots and yellow journalistic agitation by what Secretary Root called the "leprous vampires" of San Francisco confirmed Roosevelt's apprehensions about further crises with Japan.[120] The president shrewdly pressed for more battleships and fortification of Hawaii and the vulnerable Philippines, now America's "heel of Achilles," so that the United States would "be ready for anything that comes."[121] He also dramatized the importance of a strong navy to Congress and Japan by ordering the battle fleet on a voyage to the Pacific and around the world—a "good will cruise" by the "sixteen messengers of peace."[122] In spring 1908, Congress endorsed a policy of building two battleships per year, and Ambassador Takahira invited the "Great White Fleet" to Tokyo, where it received considerable attention. On the day the ships sailed from Tokyo Bay, Takahira received instructions to reach an agreement with the United States recognizing the Pacific Ocean as an open avenue of trade, pledging the integrity of Japanese and American insular possessions in the Pacific, and promising equal opportunity in China. The ensuing Root-Takahira declaration of November 30,

1908, seemed to restore Japanese-American harmony through mutual understanding of respective national interests.

The new epoch did not materialize. William Howard Taft and Philander C. Knox chose to champion the "Open Door" and encourage Chinese nationalism, thereby threatening Japan. The first explosion of twentieth-century Chinese nationalism had occurred in 1900, when the Boxers challenged both the Manchus and the Western powers exploiting the old dynasty. Even though Washington remitted part of the Boxer indemnity to provide scholarships for Chinese students in the United States, angry Chinese patriots decried the racist law of 1904 whereby Congress permanently barred Chinese immigration. China retaliated in 1905 with a short-lived boycott of American goods and revocation of a railroad franchise held by financier J. P. Morgan. In the turmoil, American missionaries were killed. TR wanted U.S. enterprise to prosper in East Asia, but he thought the Chinese "so helpless to carry out any fixed policy, whether at home or abroad, that it is difficult to have any but the most cautious dealings with them."[123] Placing strategic interests first, Roosevelt chose not to antagonize Japan over the question of China.

Taft thought otherwise. As early as 1905 he had dreamed about Americans capturing "one of the greatest commercial prizes of the world"—the China market.[124] During a trip to East Asia that year, Taft met the impressive, intensely anti-Japanese American consul general in Mukden, Willard Straight. Two years later Straight proposed the creation of a Manchurian bank, to be financed by the American railroad magnate E. H. Harriman, only to have the economic panic of 1907 dash all hopes for subsidizing Chinese administration of Manchuria. When Wall Street revived in 1908, Straight returned to advise New York financiers on Manchuria. He condemned the Root-Takahira agreement as "a terrible diplomatic blunder," because it seemed to recognize Japan's exploitative position in Manchuria.[125] Under Taft, Straight and the State Department quickly inspired several New York banks to form a combination, headed by J. P. Morgan, to serve as the official agency of American railroad investment in China. As acting chief of the department's new Far Eastern Division, Straight instructed Minister William W. Rockhill in Beijing to demand admission of the American bankers into a European banking consortium undertaking construction of the Huguang Railway linking Beijing and Canton. Straight then resigned from the State Department to become the Morgan group's roving representative.

In November 1909, Knox also proposed to Britain the neutralization of Manchurian railroads through a large international loan to China for the purchase of the lines. Britain, however, joined both Japan and Russia to reject the proposal. Knox was "asking us to internationalize what is our own property acquired by us at the cost of much treasure and many lives," one Japanese official complained.[126] Instead of an open door in Manchuria, the scholar A. Whitney Griswold has observed, Knox had "nailed that door closed with himself on the outside."[127] Their Manchurian policy shattered, Knox and Taft continued to seek American entrée to the British, French, and German consortium negotiating the Huguang loan. In fall 1910, an agreement expanded the consortium to include American bankers, and

"Spread-eagleism" in China.   The missionary teacher Grace Roberts teaches a Bible class in 1903 in Manchuria. Americanism and religious work, flag and missionary, became partners. The mission force was feminized—the majority of missionaries were women. (By permission of the Houghton Library, Harvard University)

the loan was floated the following June. Japan and Russia also barged into the deal. But the Chinese Revolution broke out in May 1911 against both the Manchu dynasty and foreign interests and delayed railroad construction until 1913. "'Dollar' diplomacy," Willard Straight ruefully admitted, "made no friends in the Hukuang matter."[128]

Within days of Woodrow Wilson's inauguration, Straight and other banking representatives alerted the new president to the convoluted result of dollar diplomacy in China. Hoping to reap tangible benefits by dissociating from the other powers, Wilson and Secretary Bryan repudiated American participation in the international consortium on March 18, 1913. Failure to cancel the loan, Wilson believed, would have cost the United States "the proud position . . . secured when Secretary Hay stood for the open door in China after the Boxer Uprising." After the American chargé in Beijing reported that nonrecognition "may ignore our own interests and merely promote the aggressive designs of others," Wilson became the first to extend formal diplomatic recognition to the Chinese Republic on May 6.[129] Wilson had renewed America's commitment to the political integrity of China, a goal pragmatically abandoned by Roosevelt, unsuccessfully resuscitated by Taft, and consistently opposed by Japan. Roosevelt warned that "we cannot stop" Japan "unless we are prepared to go to war."[130]

Events at home soon made Wilson's Asian policy resemble Taft's more than Roosevelt's. In April 1913, Democratic and Progressive politicians placed before the California legislature a bill denying residents "ineligible to citizenship" the right to own land. The measure struck directly at the 50,000 Japanese living in California, whose exceptional agricultural productivity had raised fears that they were, in the words of Governor Hiram Johnson, "driving the root of their civilization deep into California soil."[131] Racist passions erupted, with one farmer recoiling from the prospect of racial intermarriage: "What is that baby? It isn't a Japanese. It isn't white. It is a germ of the mightiest problem that ever faced this state; a problem that will make the black problem of the South look white."[132] Basically sharing the Californians' anti-Japanese prejudices, and philosophically sensitive to states' rights, Wilson sent Bryan to Sacramento to beg for a euphemistic statute. But the California legislature passed the offensive bill on May 3, 1913. When Japan protested the "unfair and intentionally racially discriminatory" measure, Wilson and Bryan took refuge in the defense that one state's legislation did not constitute a "national discriminatory policy."[133]

Wilson's antipathy toward Japan reappeared during World War I. In fall 1914 Japan declared war on Germany, seized the German Pacific islands north of the equator, and swept across China's Shandong Peninsula to capture the German leasehold of Jiaozhou. "When there is a fire in a jeweller's shop," a Japanese diplomat theorized, "the neighbours cannot be expected to refrain from helping themselves."[134] Tokyo immediately followed this grab with the Twenty-One Demands of January 18, 1915, by which it insisted on a virtual protectorate over all of China. Despite stout resistance by Beijing, Japan emerged with extensive political and economic rights in Shandong, southern Manchuria, and Mongolia. Preoccupied with Mexico, the British blockade, and the *Lusitania* crisis, the Wilson administration could only refuse in May 1915 to recognize "any agreement . . . impairing the treaty rights of the United States and its citizens in China, the political or territorial integrity of the Republic of China, or . . . the open door policy."[135]

Wilson's nonrecognition policy foundered, however, because of secret treaties in which the European Allies promised to support Japan's conquests at the peace conference. The United States then compromised. In an agreement with Viscount Kikujiro Ishii, signed November 2, 1917, Secretary Lansing admitted that "territorial propinquity creates special relationships between countries, and consequently . . . Japan has special interests in China," while Ishii pledged his nation's dedication to the Open Door and integrity of China.[136] But the Wilson administration also revived the international banking consortium as the only way to check further unilateral Japanese economic penetration of China proper. The wheel had turned full circle for Wilson. Like Taft before him, Wilson had undermined China's fragile sovereignty without conciliating or blocking Japan.

Elihu Root (1845–1937).
Root served as secretary of state (1905–1909). He helped devise methods for managing the American empire. (Library of Congress)

Anglo-American Rapprochement and Empire-Building Before the "Great War"

American policies toward Asia and Latin America often fell short of their proclaimed goals because of the pseudoscientific race thinking of the early twentieth century. So long as Americans viewed Asians as "inscrutable and somnolent," depicted Latin Americans as black children or alluring maidens, imagined Africa as the "dark continent" of "savage beasts and beastly savages," and referred to Filipinos as "our little brown brothers," these biased stereotypes inevitably impeded statecraft and aroused resentment from Bogotá to Beijing, from Managua to Manila.[137] Yet such Darwinist racial attitudes also facilitated much closer relations between the United States and Great Britain. As the historian Michael H. Hunt has written about the ideology of the time, victory "in the international competition among the races . . . might not go to the refined and peaceful peoples but rather to the amoral, the cunning, the fecund, and the power hungry." Thus "Anglo-Americans might then need to cultivate a sense of solidarity and a capacity for cooperation."[138] Theodore Roosevelt certainly thought so when he claimed that "together . . . the two branches of the Anglo-Saxon race . . . can whip the world."[139] So too did the British, as evidenced by their retreat after the Venezuelan crisis of 1895 and their willingness to accept exclusive American control of a canal in Panama. Also prompted by England's search for allies against Germany (evidenced in the Anglo-Japanese Alliance of 1902 and the Entente Cordiale with France in 1904), London's pursuit of what future prime minister Herbert H. Asquith called "the most cordial and constant cooperation" with the United States led to a celebrated "great rapprochement."[140]

The new Anglo-American affinity, however, nearly dissolved in 1903 when "the nationalism of Theodore Roosevelt . . . overwhelmed his Anglo-Saxonism."[141] The Alaska boundary controversy, which involved Canadian claims to large areas of the Alaskan panhandle, produced strained relations. As the power responsible for the Dominion's foreign relations (Canada did not establish a foreign office until 1909), Britain found itself backing Ottawa's dubious contention that much of the panhandle's coastline actually belonged to Canada. Roosevelt and most Americans thought these pretensions absurd; Canada had less right "than the United States did to Cornwall or Kent."[142] The president refused arbitration and sent 800 soldiers to Alaska to awe his opponents. London finally agreed in January 1903 to an American proposal for a mixed boundary commission composed of six "impartial jurists of repute," three from each side.[143] Roosevelt took no chances. He appointed Senator Henry Cabot Lodge and Secretary Root, hardly disinterested judges, to the commission. He informed them that the 1825 treaty "was undoubtedly intended to cut off England, which owned the Hinterland, from access to the sea," and informally warned London he would run the line himself if the commissioners failed to agree.[144] One British commissioner sided with the Americans, and on October 20, 1903, by a vote of 4 to 2, the commission officially

John Bull in Need of Friends. Battered by criticism over its war against the Boers in South Africa and challenged by a rising Germany, Great Britain found a new friend in the United States. According to the historian Thomas Noer: "Forced to decide between support of continued Boer independence or a unified South Africa under direct British control, American leaders gradually became convinced of the advantages of British imperialism. . . . They decided that British control was necessary for the economic development, social changes, and racial policies the United States desired in the area." (*Des Moines Leader* in *Literary Digest*, 1901)

decided for the United States. Canadian prime minister Sir Wilfred Laurier called the settlement "a slap in the face for Canada."[145] The British, in the historian Robert Bothwell's phrase, "made the inevitable choice to please a power ten times the size of Canada and with more than ten times the wealth."[146]

Theodore Roosevelt later claimed that "the Alaskan boundary settled the last serious trouble between the British Empire and ourselves," an observation especially pertinent to Anglo-American policies in the Western Hemisphere.[147] In February 1903, shortly after agreeing to the Alaskan commission, British leaders accepted international adjudication of the Anglo-German claims against Venezuela and publicly praised the Monroe Doctrine. The British ambassador told Roosevelt to "be ready to police the whole American Continent."[148] The Roosevelt Corollary neither surprised nor displeased Great Britain, nor did the denouement in Panama in 1903.

English acquiescence also characterized another Anglo-American settlement of Roosevelt's presidency, the North Atlantic fisheries dispute. Since 1782, American fishermen, especially those from Massachusetts, had insisted on retaining their pre-Revolutionary privileges off Newfoundland. The modus vivendi of 1888, under which they had fished for several years, collapsed in 1905 when Newfoundland placed restrictions on American fishing vessels. Senator Lodge cried for warships to protect his constituents' livelihood. To avoid a heated quarrel with Britain, Roosevelt proposed, and London accepted, arbitration at The Hague Tribunal. In 1910 the tribunal ruled that Britain could oversee fishing off Newfoundland if it established reasonable regulations, that a fisheries commission would hear cases, and that Americans could fish in large bays if they remained three miles from shore. This compromise defused the oldest dispute in American foreign relations and symbolized London's political withdrawal from the Western Hemisphere.

The naval retreat had occurred earlier, when the Admiralty abolished the North Atlantic station based at Halifax. After 1902 the Royal Navy patrolled the Caribbean only with an annual visit by a token squadron of cruisers. Admiral Sir John Fisher, who oversaw this historic retrenchment, wanted to concentrate his heavy ships in the English Channel and North Sea as monitors of the growing German navy, but he acted on the dual premise that the United States was "a kindred state with whom we shall never have a parricidal war."[149]

Even the aggressive hemispheric diplomacy of Taft and Wilson did not undermine Anglo-American rapprochement. Britain criticized dollar diplomacy in Latin America, and Wilson's quixotic efforts to dislodge Huerta from the presidency of Mexico met with little sympathy in England. But Foreign Secretary Sir Edward Grey tersely laid to rest all talk of a challenge: "His Majesty's Government cannot with any prospect of success embark upon an active counterpolicy to that of the United States, or constitute themselves the champions of Mexico or any of these republics against the United States."[150] In reciprocation, Wilson protected British oil interests and made it a "point of honor" to eliminate the one potentially dangerous British grievance inherited from his predecessor.[151] Late in the Taft administration, Congress had enacted a measure exempting American intercoastal shippers from payment of tolls at the Panama Canal. British opinion unanimously condemned this shifting of canal maintenance costs to other users. Wilson soon decided that the law unjustly discriminated against foreign shipping, and in June 1914, Congress revoked the preferential treatment.

In the end, rapprochement between Britain and the United States meant mutual respect for each other's empires. Roosevelt, for example, encouraged London to frustrate native aspirations for independence in India, while the British accepted the American suppression of the Filipinos and U.S. hegemony in Latin America. American leaders usually spoke favorably of independence for colonial peoples, but independence only after long-term education to make them "fit" and "civilized" enough to govern. In 1910 in Egypt, where Roosevelt applauded Britain's "great work for civilization," the ex-president even lectured Muslim nationalists about Christian respect for womanhood.[152] In unstable Liberia, where the United States in 1912 instituted a financial receivership in the African nation similar to that which it had imposed on the Dominican Republic, the British encouraged Washington to use a strong hand in what London called America's "protectorate" and Secretary Knox called America's "ward."[153]

While building an empire, policymakers largely adhered to the tradition of aloofness from continental European political and military affairs, as prescribed in Washington's Farewell Address and Jefferson's First Inaugural. Even Theodore Roosevelt, who worked assiduously behind the scenes, overtly tampered only once with Europe's balance of power. In 1904 France acquiesced in British control of Egypt, in exchange for primacy in semi-independent Morocco. A year later, Germany decided to test the solidity of the new Anglo-French entente by challenging France's extension of power in Morocco. Speaking at Tangier, the kaiser belligerently demanded a German political role in Morocco, which France at once refused. After a brief European war scare, in which Britain stood by her ally, Germany asked Roosevelt to induce France and England to convene a conference to settle Morocco's future. On the grounds that world peace was threatened, Roosevelt accepted the personal invitation only after assuring Paris that he did not act on Berlin's behalf. During the conference, held in early 1906 at Algeciras, Spain, Roosevelt devised a compromise substantively favorable to Paris and persuaded the kaiser to accept it. This political intervention isolated Germany and reinforced the Anglo-French entente, but it generated criticism at home. Roosevelt's successors made sure they did not violate the American policy of nonentanglement with Europe during the more ominous second Moroccan and Balkan crises preceding the "Great War."

Nonentanglement also doomed the sweeping arbitration treaties that Secretary of State Hay negotiated with several world powers. When the Senate attached crippling amendments, Roosevelt withdrew the treaties because they did "not in the smallest degree facilitate settlements by arbitration."[154] After 1905 Secretary Root persuaded Roosevelt to accept watered-down bilateral arbitration treaties, and Secretary Bryan later negotiated a series of supplementary "cooling-off" treaties by which nations pledged to refrain from war during international investigations of serious disputes. None of these arrangements, however, effectively bound any of the signatories, and like the Permanent Court of Arbitration at The Hague, they represented a backwater in international diplomacy. Ambassador Whitelaw Reid compared U.S. participation in The Hague Peace Conference of 1907 to a farmer taking his hog to market: "That hog didn't weigh as much as I expected he would, and I always knew he wouldn't."[155]

The mainstream of American foreign policy between 1900 and 1914 flowed through the Panama Canal, a momentous political, military, and technological achievement. After ratification of the Hay–Bunau-Varilla Treaty, the United States became the unchallenged policeman of the Caribbean region. For Taft, the treaty "permits us to prevent revolutions" so that "we'll have no more."[156] In East Asia, American power paled in comparison. The United States was in no position to challenge Japan or England. As Roosevelt understood, the Open Door "com-

Naval Arms Race.   The international naval competition in the early twentieth century was foreboding. Disarmament talks at The Hague Conferences and arbitration treaties did not curb the arms buildup. Roosevelt's decision to send the "Great White Fleet" around the world in 1907–1908 may have encouraged both Japan and Germany to speed up their naval programs. (*Detroit News* in *Literary Digest,* 1904)

pletely disappears as soon as a powerful nation determines to disregard it."[157] Dollar diplomacy, moreover, antagonized rather than stopped Japan in China. The Philippines needed protection, but congressional distaste for more military spending left the archipelago vulnerable.

One of the legacies of the 1900–1914 period was American insensitivity to the nationalism of other peoples. Filipino resistance to American domination, Cuban anger against the Platt Amendment, Colombian outrage over Panama, and Mexican rejection of Wilsonian intervention bore witness to the depth of nationalistic sentiments. Like the European powers who were carving up Asia, Africa, and the Middle East, the United States was developing its empire and subjugating peoples and compromising their sovereignty in Latin America and the Pacific. As a Panamanian diplomat later explained: "When you hit a rock with an egg, the egg breaks. Or when you hit an egg with a rock, the egg breaks. The United States is the rock. Panama is the egg. In either case, the egg breaks."[158] With the exception of the Virgin Islands, purchased from Denmark for $25 million in 1917 to forestall any wartime German seizure, the empire of the United States grew little from outright territorial gains. It was, instead, an informal empire administered by marines, financial advisers, and reformers who revealed contempt for native peoples' culture, politics, and economies through a paternalistic demeanor. "There is something pathetic and childlike about the people," Roosevelt wrote condescendingly of the Puerto Ricans.[159] Under the Foraker Act (1900), Puerto Rico and its naval base on Culebra became a "new constitutional animal"—an "unincorporated territory" subject to the will of the U.S. Congress and governed by the War Department (until 1934).[160] In a series of decisions called the Insular Cases (1901–1904), the Supreme Court upheld the Foraker Act, providing Washington with a means to govern people it did not wish to organize as a state. In March 1917, Congress granted Puerto Ricans U.S. citizenship. This legislation came just in time for them to be drafted into the U.S. armed forces in the war against

Filipinos at Fourth of July Celebration in Manila, 1900. Not long after the United States took the Philippines from Spain, Filipinos began to encounter American political culture. The puzzled looks on the faces of these children suggest that not all was yet understood or accepted. (Library of Congress)

Germany. To this day, Puerto Rico remains a colony, or "commonwealth," and Puerto Ricans remain divided in their views about statehood, independence, and commonwealth status.

The adventures of American foreign relations under an imperial ideology and the male ethos in the years 1900–1914 attracted many capable, well-educated young men to diplomatic service. "It was TR's call to youth which lured me to Washington," future under secretary of state William Phillips recalled.[161] Career ambassador Joseph C. Grew first gained presidential favor by shooting a tiger in China. Several of these young foreign-service professionals, virtually all graduates of Ivy League colleges, including Phillips, Grew, Willard Straight, former Rough Rider Henry P. Fletcher, and soldier-diplomat Frank R. McCoy, lived in an exclusive bachelors' townhouse at 1718 H Street during their Washington service. Known among themselves as "the Family," these youthful professionals blended camaraderie with careers and "became the elite or legendary 'inner circle' of the State Department" for the next forty years.[162] The New York attorney Henry L. Stimson, himself a protégé of Elihu Root, served as secretary of war under Taft (1911–1913) and continued this tradition of recruiting some of the brightest public servants in a succession of high-level posts through the end of World War II.

Cultural or public foreign relations also flourished during these years. Just as Buffalo Bill Cody's Wild West Show had "hyped" American cultural myths abroad since the 1890s, Wilbur Wright's airplane tour of Europe in 1908 set records, thrilled crowds, and impressed military strategists.[163] The cruise of the "Great White Fleet" was as much pageantry as statecraft—"a feast, a frolic, or a fight," as Admiral Robley D. Evans put it.[164] The Germans guilelessly named a torpedo boat after Alice Roosevelt. Following the example of Alice's father after he left the White House, thousands of wealthy Americans traveled abroad clutching their Baedeker guidebooks, spending American dollars, and sometimes acquiring foreign titles through marriage, as in the case of Jennie Jerome and Lord Randolph Churchill, whose son Winston valued Anglo-American partnership. Boosters took pride in hosting the Olympic Games in St. Louis in 1904, hailed an American victory in the 1908 Round-the-World Automobile race, and cheered the gold medals won by Native American Jim Thorpe at the Stockholm Olympics in 1912. Just as they seemed to take up the great game of empire from Great Britain, so too did Americans become proficient in that most diplomatic of athletic competitions, the royal and ancient Scottish sport of golf. For some Americans, Anglo-American entente did not occur until young Francis Ouimet bested British champions Harry Vardon and Ted Ray in the U.S. Open at Brookline, Massachusetts, in 1913.

Yet beneath the glitter lurked danger. Winston Churchill later wrote of living in two different worlds: "the actual, visual world with its peaceful activities" and "a hypothetical world 'beneath the threshold'"—"a world at one moment utterly fantastic, at the next seeming to leap into reality—a world of monstrous shadows moving in convulsive combination through vistas of fathomless catastrophe."[165] Once the world started spinning around Sarajevo, Bosnia, it became impossible for the growing American empire to escape the maelstrom.

Further Reading for the Period 1900–1914

For presidential and other studies, see Michael C. C. Adams, *The Great Adventure: Male Desire and the Coming of World War I* (1990); A. J. Bacevich, *Diplomat in Khaki* (1989) (General Frank McCoy); William H. Becker, *The Dynamics of Business-Government Relations: Industry and Exports, 1893–1921* (1982); Lester H. Brune, *The Origins of American Security Policy* (1981); Frederick S. Calhoun, *Power and Principle: Armed Intervention in Wilsonian Foreign Policy* (1986) and *Use of Force and Wilsonian Foreign Policy* (1993); Richard D. Challener, *Admirals, Generals, and American Foreign Policy, 1898–1914* (1973); Kendrick A. Clements, *The Presidency of Woodrow Wilson* (1990) and *William Jennings Bryan* (1982); Paolo E. Coletta, *The Presidency of William Howard Taft* (1973); John M. Cooper, Jr.; *The Warrior and the Priest: Woodrow Wilson and Theodore Roosevelt* (1983); Lloyd C. Gardner, *Safe for Democracy: The Anglo-American Response to Revolution, 1913–1923* (1984); Robert C. Hilderbrand, *Power and the People: Executive Management of Public Opinion in Foreign Affairs, 1897–1921* (1981); Michael H. Hunt, *Ideology and U.S. Foreign Policy* (1987); Walter LaFeber, *The American Search for Opportunity, 1865–1913* (1993); Ralph E. Minger, *William Howard Taft and United States Foreign Policy* (1975); John M. Mulder, *Woodrow Wilson: The Years of Preparation* (1978); Thomas J. Noer, *Briton, Boer, and Yankee* (1978) (South Africa); Emily S. Rosenberg, *Spreading the American Dream* (1982); Walter V. and Marie V. Scholes, *The Foreign Policies of the Taft Administration* (1970); E. Berkeley Tompkins, *Anti-Imperialism in the United States* (1970); Richard H. Werking, *The Master Architects* (1977) (foreign service); Rachel West, *The Department of State on the Eve of the First World War* (1978); Rubin F. Westin, *Racism in United States Imperialism* (1972); William C. Widenor, *Henry Cabot Lodge and the Search for an American Foreign Policy* (1980); and Mira Wilkins, *The Emergence of Multinational Enterprise: American Business Abroad from the Colonial Era to 1914* (1970).

Theodore Roosevelt is the subject of Howard K. Beale, *Theodore Roosevelt and the Rise of America to World Power* (1956); John M. Blum, *The Republican Roosevelt* (1954); David H. Burton, *Theodore Roosevelt* (1968); Richard H. Collin, *Theodore Roosevelt, Culture, Diplomacy, and Expansion* (1985); Thomas G. Dyer, *Theodore Roosevelt and the Idea of Race* (1980); Raymond A. Esthus, *Theodore Roosevelt and the International Rivalries* (1970); Lewis L. Gould, *The Presidency of Theodore Roosevelt* (1991); William H. Harbaugh, *The Life and Times of Theodore Roosevelt* (1975); Frederick W. Marks, *Velvet on Iron* (1979); and Natalie A. Naylor et al., eds., *Theodore Roosevelt* (1992).

U.S. relations with Latin America are examined in José A. Cabranes, *Citizenship and the American Empire* (1979) (Puerto Rico); Bruce J. Calder, *The Impact of Intervention* (1984) (Dominican Republic); Raymond A. Carr, *Puerto Rico* (1984); Arturo M. Carrión, *Puerto Rico* (1983); John E. Findling, *Close Neighbors, Distant Friends* (1987) (Central America); Mark T. Gilderhus, *Pan American Visions* (1986) (Wilson); David Healy, *Drive to Hegemony* (1989) and *Gunboat Diplomacy in the Wilson Era* (1976) (Haiti); Warren G. Kneer, *Great Britain and the Caribbean, 1901–1913* (1975); Walter LaFeber, *Inevitable Revolutions* (1993) (Central America); Lester D. Langley, *Struggle for the American Mediterranean* (1976), *The United States and the Caribbean, 1900–1970* (1980), and *The Banana Wars* (1983); Dana Munro, *Intervention and Dollar Diplomacy* (1964); Dexter Perkins, *The Monroe Doctrine, 1867–1907* (1937); Brenda G. Plummer, *Haiti and the United States* (1992) and *Haiti and the Great Powers, 1902–1915* (1988); Hans Schmidt, *The United States Occupation of Haiti, 1915–1934* (1971); and Thomas D. Schoonover, *The United States in Central America, 1860–1911* (1991).

The contest with Colombia over Panama, the U.S. quest for the Panama Canal, and the building of the waterway are explored in Richard H. Collin, *Theodore Roosevelt's Caribbean* (1990); Michael L. Conniff, *Panama and the United States* (1992); Richard L. Lael, *Arrogant Diplomacy* (1987); Walter LaFeber, *The Panama Canal* (1989); David McCullough, *The Path Between the Seas* (1977); and Stephen J. Randall, *Colombia and the United States* (1992).

U.S. hegemony in Cuba is discussed in David Healy, *The United States in Cuba, 1898–1902* (1963); José M. Hernández, *Cuba and the United States* (1993); James H. Hitchman, *Leonard Wood and Cuban Independence, 1898–1902* (1971); Allan R. Millett, *The Politics of Intervention* (1968); and Louis A. Pérez, Jr., *Cuba and the United States* (1990) and *Cuba Under the Platt Amendment, 1902–1934* (1986).

Relations with Mexico are treated in Jonathan C. Brown, *Oil and Revolution in Mexico* (1993); Clarence C. Clendenen, *Blood on the Border* (1969); Jules Davids, *American Political and Economic Penetration of Mexico, 1877–1920* (1976); Mark T. Gilderhus, *Diplomacy and Revolution* (1977); Kenneth J. Grieb, *The United States and Huerta* (1969); John M. Hart, *Revolutionary Mexico* (1988); Larry D. Hill, *Emissaries to a Revolution: Woodrow Wilson's Executive Agents in Mexico* (1973); Friedrich Katz, *The Secret War in Mexico* (1981); Alan Knight, *U.S.–Mexican Relations, 1910–1940* (1987); Robert E. Quirk, *An Affair of Honor* (1962) (Veracruz); Ramón E. Ruíz, *The Great Rebellion: Mexico, 1905–1924* (1980); Karl M. Schmitt, *Mexico and the United States, 1821–1973* (1974); Paul J. Vanderwood and Frank N. Samponaro, *Border Fury* (1988); and Josefina Vázquez and Lorenzo Meyer, *The United States and Mexico* (1985).

For America's interactions with Asia and China, see William R. Braisted, *The United States Navy in the Pacific, 1897–1909* (1958) and *1909–1922* (1971); Jongsuk Chay, *Diplomacy of Asymmetry* (1990) (Korea); Warren I. Cohen, *America's Response to China* (1990); Daniel M. Crane and Thomas A. Breslin, *An Ordinary Relationship: American Opposition to Republican Revolution in China* (1986); Jonathan Goldstein et al., eds., *America Views China* (1991); A. Whitney Griswold, *The Far Eastern Policy of the United States* (1938); Robert A. Hart, *The Great White Fleet* (1965); Michael H. Hunt, *The Making of a Special Relationship* (1983); Akira Iriye, *Across the Pacific* (1967); Jerry Israel, *Progressivism and the Open Door* (1971); Delber L. McKee, *Chinese Exclusion versus the Open Door Policy, 1900–1906* (1976); and Noel H. Pugach, *Paul S. Reinsch* (1979).

Japanese-American relations can be studied in Burton F. Beers, *Vain Endeavor: Robert Lansing's Attempt to End the American-Japanese Rivalry* (1962); Roger Daniels, *The Politics of Prejudice* (1962) (anti-Japanese sentiment); Raymond A. Esthus, *Double Eagle and Rising Sun* (1988) (Portsmouth) and *Theodore Roosevelt and Japan* (1966); Akira Iriye, *Pacific Estrangement* (1972); Charles E. Neu, *An Uncertain Friendship* (1967) and *The Troubled Encounter* (1975); and E. P. Trani, *The Treaty of Portsmouth* (1969).

The work of American missionaries, especially in Asia, is covered in Kenton J. Clymer, *Protestant Missionaries in the Philippines, 1898–1916* (1986); Patricia R. Hill, *The World Their Household* (1985) (women); Jane Hunter, *The Gospel of Gentility* (1984) (women in China); and James Reed, *The Missionary Mind and American East Asia Policy, 1911–1915* (1983).

U.S. relations with Europe and Great Britain, and rivalry with Germany, are discussed in Stuart Anderson, *Race and Rapprochement* (1981); A. E. Campbell, *Great Britain and the United States, 1895–1903* (1960); Charles S. Campbell, *Anglo-American Understanding, 1898–1903* (1957); Holger H. Herwig, *Politics of Frustration: The United States in German Naval Planning, 1889–1941* (1976); Manfred Jonas, *The United States and Germany* (1984); Bradford Perkins, *The Great Rapprochement* (1968); Stephen R. Rock, *Why Peace Breaks Out* (1989); Hans-Jürgen Schröder, ed., *Confrontation and Cooperation* (1993) (Germany); and Frederick F. Travis, *George Kennan and the Russian-American Relationship, 1865–1924* (1990).

The peace movement and the role of The Hague are discussed in Peter Brock, *Pacifism in the United States* (1968); Charles Chatfield, *The American Peace Movement* (1992); Merle E. Curti, *Peace or War* (1936); Calvin Davis, *The United States and the First Hague Conference* (1962) and *The United States and the Second Hague Peace Conference* (1975); Charles DeBenedetti, *The Peace Reform in American History* (1980); Sondra R. Herman, *Eleven Against War* (1969); Charles F. Howlett and Glen Zeitzer, *The American Peace Movement* (1985); C. Roland Marchand, *The American Peace Movement and Social Reform, 1898–1918* (1973); and David S. Patterson, *Toward a Warless World* (1976).

See also the General Bibliography and the following notes. For a comprehensive annotated bibliography, see Richard Dean Burns, *Guide to American Foreign Relations Since 1700* (1983).

Notes to Chapter 2

1. All quotations from U.S. Congress, *Diplomatic History of the Panama Canal*, Senate Doc. 474 (1914), pp. 345–363.
2. Elting E. Morison, ed., *The Letters of Theodore Roosevelt* (Cambridge, Mass.: Harvard University Press, 1951–1954; 8 vols.), II, 1185–1187.
3. Quoted in Gerstle Mack, *The Land Divided* (New York: Alfred A. Knopf, 1944), p. 417.
4. Dwight C. Miner, *The Fight for the Panama Route* (New York: Columbia University Press, 1940), p. 75.
5. *Diplomatic History of the Canal*, p. 261.
6. Quoted in Miner, *Fight*, p. 275.
7. Quoted in Henry F. Pringle, *Theodore Roosevelt* (New York: Harcourt, Brace, 1931), p. 311.
8. Quoted in Howard K. Beale, *Theodore Roosevelt and the Rise of America to World Power* (Baltimore: The Johns Hopkins Press, 1956), p. 33.
9. Quoted in David McCullough, *The Path Between the Seas* (New York: Simon and Schuster, 1977), p. 333.
10. *New York World*, June 14, 1903.
11. Quoted in Pringle, *Roosevelt*, p. 311.
12. Quoted in Tyler Dennett, *John Hay* (New York: Dodd, Mead, 1933), p. 377.
13. Quoted in Thomas Schoonover, "Max Farrand's Memorandum on the U.S. Role in the Panamanian Revolution of 1903," *Diplomatic History, XII* (Fall 1988), 505.
14. Quoted in Stephen J. Randall, *Colombia and the United States* (Athens: University of Georgia Press, 1992), p. 88.
15. Quoted in Lewis L. Gould, *The Presidency of Theodore Roosevelt* (Lawrence: University Press of Kansas, 1991), p. 98.
16. James D. Richardson, ed., *A Compilation of the Messages and Papers of the Presidents, 1789–1897* (Washington, D.C.: Government Printing Office, 1896–1899; 10 vols.), IX, 6919–6923.
17. Quoted in Walter LaFeber, *The Panama Canal* (New York: Oxford University Press, 1989; updated ed.), pp. 225–226.
18. *New York Times*, March 25, 1911.
19. William H. Harbaugh, *The Life and Times of Theodore Roosevelt* (New York: Oxford University Press, 1975; rev. ed.), p. 197.
20. Quoted in Wayne A. Wiegand, *Patrician in the Progressive Era* (New York: Garland, 1988), p. 120.
21. Quoted in Stephen R. Rock, *Why Peace Breaks Out* (Chapel Hill: University of North Carolina Press, 1989), p. 132.
22. Quoted in Holger H. Herwig, *Politics of Frustration* (Boston: Little, Brown, 1976), p. 67.
23. Ronald H. Spector, *Professors of War* (Newport, R.I.: Naval War College Press, 1977).
24. Quoted in Kenneth J. Hagan, "Alfred Thayer Mahan," in Frank Merli and Theodore Wilson, eds., *Makers of American Diplomacy* (New York: Charles Scribner's Sons, 1974), p. 298.
25. John Milton Cooper, Jr., "Progressivism and American Foreign Policy" *Mid-America, LI* (October 1969), 261.
26. Quoted in John Morton Blum, *The Republican Roosevelt* (New York: Atheneum [1954], 1973), p. 127.
27. Quoted in Beale, *Theodore Roosevelt*, p. 77; G. Wallace Chessman, *Theodore Roosevelt and the Politics of Power* (Boston: Little, Brown, 1969), p. 70.
28. Quoted in Beale, *Theodore Roosevelt*, p. 140.
29. Quoted in Judith Papachristou, "American Women and Foreign Policy, 1896–1905," *Diplomatic History, XIV* (Fall 1990), 499, 501, 509.
30. Quoted in Frederick F. Travis, *George Kennan and the Russian-American Relationship, 1865–1924* (Athens: Ohio University Press, 1990), p. 266.
31. Quoted in John Milton Cooper, Jr., *The Warrior and the Priest* (Cambridge, Mass.: Harvard University Press, 1983), p. 75.
32. Quoted in Foster Rhea Dulles, "John Hay," in Norman A. Graebner, ed., *An Uncertain Tradition* (New York: McGraw-Hill, 1961), p. 24.
33. Quoted in Charles W. Toth, "Elihu Root," *ibid.*, p. 41.
34. Quoted in Richard W. Leopold, *Elihu Root and the Conservative Tradition* (Boston: Little, Brown, 1954), p. 50.
35. Quoted in David H. Burton, *Theodore Roosevelt* (Philadelphia: University of Pennsylvania Press, 1968), p. 97; *Congressional Record, XXXV* (December 3, 1901), 82–83.
36. Quoted in Ralph E. Minger, *William Howard Taft and United States Foreign Policy* (Urbana: University of Illinois Press, 1975), p. 179.
37. Quoted in Ray S. Baker, *Woodrow Wilson* (Garden City, N.Y.: Doubleday, Doran, 1927–1939; 8 vols.), IV, 289.
38. Quoted in Rock, *Why Peace*, p. 142.
39. *Foreign Relations, 1898* (Washington, D.C.: Government Printing Office, 1901), pp. lxvi–lxvii.
40. Quoted in Philip C. Jessup, *Elihu Root* (New York: Dodd, Mead, 1938; 2 vols.), I, 286–287.
41. Emily S. Rosenberg, *Spreading the American Dream* (New York: Hill and Wang, 1982), p. 46.
42. Quoted in David F. Healy, *The United States in Cuba, 1898–1902* (Madison: University of Wisconsin Press, 1963), p. 133.
43. U.S. Commissioner Robert P. Porter quoted in Louis A. Pérez, Jr., *Cuba and the United States* (Athens: University of Georgia Press, 1990), p. 127.
44. *Ibid.*, p. 128.
45. *Congressional Record, XXXIV* (February 26, 1901), 3036.
46. Quoted in Richard H. Collin, *Theodore Roosevelt's*

Caribbean (Baton Rouge: Louisiana State University Press, 1990), p. 516.

47. Quoted in H. Hagedorn, *Leonard Wood* (New York: Harper, 1931; 2 vols.), *I*, 362; Healy, *United States in Cuba*, p. 178.

48. Quoted in R. H. Fitzgibbon, *Cuba and the United States, 1900–1935* (New York: Russell & Russell, 1964), p. 112.

49. Quoted in Allan R. Millett, *The Politics of Intervention* (Columbus: Ohio State University Press, 1968), p. 72.

50. Quoted in Burton, *Theodore Roosevelt*, p. 106.

51. Quoted in Millett, *Politics*, p. 78.

52. Quoted in Pérez, *Cuba and the United States*, p. 157.

53. Richardson, *Messages of the Presidents, X*, 7436–7437.

54. Quoted in Minger, *William Howard Taft*, p. 136.

55. Fitzgibbon, *Cuba*, p. 145; Millett, *Politics*, p. 267.

56. Fred L. Israel, ed., *The State of the Union Messages* (New York: Chelsea House, 1967; 3 vols.), *II*, 2038.

57. Morison, *Letters of Roosevelt, III*, 116.

58. *Ibid., IV*, 1156.

59. *Literary Digest, XXV* (December 20, 1902), 823–824.

60. Quoted in John G. Clifford, "Admiral Dewey and the Germans, 1903," *Mid–America, XLIX* (July 1967), 218.

61. Quoted in Manfred Jonas, *The United States and Germany* (Ithaca: Cornell University Press, 1984), pp. 68–69.

62. Quoted in Dexter Perkins, *The Monroe Doctrine, 1867–1907* (Baltimore: The Johns Hopkins Press, 1937), p. 360.

63. Quoted in Jonas, *United States and Germany*, p. 73.

64. Quoted *ibid.*, p. 420.

65. Quoted Lloyd C. Gardner, "A Progressive Foreign Policy, 1900–1921," in William A. Williams, ed., *From Colony to Empire* (New York: John Wiley & Sons, 1972), p. 218.

66. Quoted in Perkins, *Monroe Doctrine*, p. 420.

67. Quoted in Warren G. Kneer, *Great Britain and the Caribbean, 1901–1913* (East Lansing: Michigan State University Press, 1975), p. 103.

68. Israel, *State of the Union Messages, II*, 2134.

69. Quoted in Walter LaFeber, *Inevitable Revolutions* (New York: W. W. Norton, 1993; 2d ed.), p. 37.

70. Quoted in Richard D. Challener, *Admirals, Generals, and American Foreign Policy, 1898–1914* (Princeton: Princeton University Press, 1973), p. 142.

71. *Foreign Relations, 1912* (Washington, D.C.: Government Printing Office, 1919), p. 1091.

72. Quoted in Lloyd C. Gardner, *Safe for Democracy* (New York: Oxford University Press, 1984), p. 41.

73. Oswald Garrison Villard quoted *ibid.*, p. 42.

74. *Foreign Relations, 1913* (Washington, D.C.: Government Printing Office, 1920), p. 426.

75. Bruce J. Calder, *The Impact of Intervention* (Austin: University of Texas Press, 1984), p. 12.

76. *Ibid.*, p. 250.

77. Quoted in Dana G. Munro, *Intervention and Dollar Diplomacy in the Caribbean* (Princeton: Princeton University Press, 1964), p. 336.

78. Quoted in Herwig, *Politics of Frustration*, p. 72.

79. Quoted in Brenda G. Plummer, *Haiti and the Great Powers, 1902–1915* (Baton Rouge: Louisiana State University Press, 1988), p. 188.

80. Quoted in Paul W. Drake, "From Good Men to Good Neighbors: 1912–1932," in Abraham F. Lowenthal, ed., *Exporting Democracy* (Baltimore: The Johns Hopkins University Press, 1991), p. 17.

81. Quoted in David F. Healy, *Gunboat Diplomacy in the Wilson Era* (Madison: University of Wisconsin Press, 1976), p. 109.

82. Quoted *ibid.*, p. 131.

83. *Ibid.*, p. 205.

84. Quoted in Munro, *Intervention*, p. 155.

85. Thomas D. Schoonover, *The United States in Central America, 1860–1911* (Durham: Duke University Press, 1991), p. 130.

86. Quoted in John E. Findling, *Close Neighbors, Distant Friends* (Westport, Conn.: Greenwood Press, 1987), p. 61.

87. Quoted in Baker, *Wilson, IV*, 436.

88. Quoted in Paolo E. Coletta, *The Presidency of William Howard Taft* (Lawrence: University Press of Kansas, 1973), p. 176.

89. *Foreign Relations, 1912*, p. 846.

90. Quoted in Howard F. Cline, *The United States and Mexico* (New York: Atheneum, 1963; rev. ed.), p. 144.

91. Quoted in Arthur S. Link, *Wilson: The New Freedom* (Princeton: Princeton University Press, 1956), p. 360.

92. Quoted in Arthur S. Link, *Wilson: Confusions and Crises, 1915–1916* (Princeton: Princeton University Press, 1964), p. 317.

93. Quoted in Link, *Wilson: New Freedom*, p. 358.

94. Quoted *ibid.*, p. 360.

95. Quoted in Kenneth J. Grieb, *The United States and Huerta* (Lincoln: University of Nebraska Press, 1969), p. 137.

96. Quoted in Link, *Wilson: New Freedom*, pp. 386–387.

97. Quoted in Friedrich Katz, *The Secret War in Mexico* (Chicago: University of Chicago Press, 1981), p. 216.

98. Quoted in Grieb, *United States and Huerta*, p. 135.

99. Quoted in Robert E. Quirk, *An Affair of Honor* (Lexington: University of Kentucky Press, 1962), p. 26.

100. Quoted in Mark T. Gilderhus, *Diplomacy and Revolution* (Tucson: University of Arizona Press, 1977), p. 11.

101. Quoted in Cary T. Grayson, *Woodrow Wilson* (New York: Holt, Rinehart and Winston, 1960), p. 30.

102. Ramón E. Ruíz, *The Great Rebellion: Mexico, 1905–1924* (New York: W. W. Norton, 1980), p. 395.

103. Quoted in Grieb, *United States and Huerta*, p. 160.

104. *Washington Post*, June 3, 1914.

105. Quoted in Gardner, *Safe for Democracy*, p. 58.

106. Quoted in Arthur S. Link, *Wilson: The Struggle for Neutrality, 1914–1915* (Princeton: Princeton University Press, 1960), p. 491.

107. Katz, *Secret War*, p. 560; Villa quoted in Friedrich Katz, "Pancho Villa and the Attack on Columbus, New

Mexico," *American Historical Review, LXXXIII* (February 1978), 111, 114.

108. Franklin Lane quoted in Alan Knight, *U.S.–Mexican Relations, 1910–1940* (San Diego, Cal.: Center for U.S.–Mexican Studies, 1987), p. 113.

109. Lester Langley, *The Banana Wars* (Lexington: University Press of Kentucky, 1983), p. 114.

110. Morison, *Letters of Roosevelt, III,* 497–498.

111. Akira Iriye, *The Cold War in Asia* (Englewood Cliffs, N.J.: Prentice Hall, 1974), p. 35.

112. Morison, *Letters of Roosevelt, IV,* 724, 761.

113. Quoted in Raymond A. Esthus, *Double Eagle and Rising Sun* (Durham: Duke University Press, 1988), p. 39.

114. Quoted in Raymond A. Esthus, *Theodore Roosevelt and Japan* (Seattle: University of Washington Press, 1966), p. 101.

115. John Edward Wilz, "Did the United States Betray Korea in 1905?" *Pacific Historical Review, LIV* (August 1985), 252.

116. Quoted in Jongsuk Chay, *Diplomacy of Asymmetry* (Honolulu: University of Hawaii Press, 1990), p. 170.

117. Quoted in Charles E. Neu, *An Uncertain Friendship* (Cambridge, Mass.: Harvard University Press, 1967), pp. 36, 47.

118. Quoted in Akira Iriye, *Across the Pacific* (New York: Harcourt, Brace & World, 1967), p. 107.

119. Quoted in Esthus, *Roosevelt and Japan,* p. 149.

120. Quoted *ibid.,* p. 173.

121. Morison, *Letters of Roosevelt, V,* 729–730, 761–762.

122. Quoted in Frederick W. Marks, *Velvet on Iron* (Lincoln: University of Nebraska Press, 1979), p. 57.

123. Quoted in Michael H. Hunt, *The Making of a Special Relationship* (New York: Columbia University Press, 1983), p. 207.

124. Quoted *ibid.*

125. Quoted in Herbert Croly, *Willard Straight* (New York: Macmillan, 1925), p. 276.

126. Quoted in Esthus, *Double Eagle,* p. 202.

127. A. Whitney Griswold, *The Far Eastern Policy of the United States* (New Haven: Yale University Press, 1938), p. 157.

128. Quoted in Croly, *Straight,* pp. 392–393.

129. Quoted in Daniel M. Crane and Thomas A. Breslin, *An Ordinary Relationship* (Miami: Florida International University Press, 1986), p. 122.

130. Quoted in William H. Becker, "1899–1920: America Adjusts to World Power," in William H. Becker and Samuel F. Wells, Jr., *Economics and World Power* (New York: Columbia University Press, 1984), p. 198.

131. *New York Times,* May 5, 1913.

132. Quoted in Roger Daniels, *The Politics of Prejudice* (New York: Atheneum, [1962], 1968), p. 59.

133. Quoted in Link, *Wilson: New Freedom,* pp. 300–301.

134. Quoted in Kendrick A. Clements, *The Presidency of Woodrow Wilson* (Lawrence: University Press of Kansas, 1990), p. 108.

135. *Foreign Relations, 1915* (Washington, D.C.: Government Printing Office, 1924), p. 146.

136. *Foreign Relations, 1922* (Washington, D.C.: Government Printing Office, 1938; 2 vols.), *II,* 591.

137. Quoted in Michael H. Hunt, *Ideology and U.S. Foreign Policy* (New Haven: Yale University Press, 1987), pp. 69, 71, 79, 81.

138. *Ibid.,* p. 79.

139. Quoted in Beale, *Theodore Roosevelt,* pp. 81, 152.

140. Quoted in Rock, *Why Peace,* p. 51; Bradford Perkins, *The Great Rapprochement* (New York: Atheneum, 1968).

141. Stuart Anderson, *Race and Rapprochement* (Rutherford, N.J.: Fairleigh Dickinson University Press, 1981), p. 169.

142. Roosevelt quoted in Marks, *Velvet,* p. 168.

143. Quoted in Perkins, *Great Rapprochement,* p. 168.

144. Quoted *ibid.,* p. 169.

145. Quoted in Gould, *Presidency of Theodore Roosevelt,* p. 85.

146. Robert Bothwell, *Canada and the United States* (New York: Twayne, 1992), p. 8.

147. Morison, *Letters of Roosevelt, VII,* 28.

148. Quoted in Perkins, *Monroe Doctrine,* p. 364.

149. Quoted in Arthur Marder, *From the Dreadnought to Scapa Flow* (London: Oxford University Press, 1961–1970; 5 vols.), *I,* 125.

150. Quoted *ibid.,* p. 201.

151. Quoted in Link, *Wilson: New Freedom,* p. 308.

152. Quoted in Burton, *Theodore Roosevelt,* p. 190.

153. Quoted in Emily S. Rosenberg, "The Invisible Protectorate: The United States, Liberia, and the Evolution of Neocolonialism, 1909–40," *Diplomatic History, IX* (Summer 1985), 194, 198.

154. Morison, *Letters of Roosevelt, IV,* 1119.

155. Quoted in Calvin Davis, *The United States and the Second Hague Peace Conference* (Durham: Duke University Press, 1975), p. 296.

156. Quoted in Minger, *William Howard Taft,* p. 106.

157. Quoted in Jerry Israel, *Progressivism and the Open Door* (Pittsburgh: University of Pittsburgh Press, 1971), p. 96.

158. Quoted in Michael L. Conniff, *Panama and the United States* (Athens: University of Georgia Press, 1992), p. 3.

159. Quoted in Arturo Morales Carrión, *Puerto Rico* (New York: W. W. Norton, 1983), p. 163.

160. Raymond Carr, *Puerto Rico* (New York: Vintage Books, 1984), p. 36.

161. William Phillips, *Ventures in Diplomacy* (Boston: Beacon Press, 1952), p. 6.

162. Quoted in A. J. Bacevich, *Diplomat in Khaki* (Lawrence: University Press of Kansas, 1989), p. 48.

163. Rosenberg, *Spreading the American Dream,* p. 35.

164. Quoted in Robert A. Hart, *The Great White Fleet* (Boston: Little, Brown, 1965), p. 45.

165. Winston S. Churchill, *The World Crisis* (New York: Scribner's, 1927; 6 vols.), *I,* 18.

Chapter 3

WAR, PEACE, AND REVOLUTION IN THE TIME OF WILSON, 1914–1920

Mass Grave of Lusitania Victims. *In Queenstown, Ireland, a large burial ground holds more than a hundred victims of the Lusitania disaster of 1915, which rudely brought World War I to American consciousness. (U.S. War Department, National Archives)*

✖ *Diplomatic Crossroad*

THE SINKING OF THE *LUSITANIA,* **1915**

"Perfectly safe; safer than the trolley cars in New York City," claimed a Cunard Line official the morning of May 1, 1915.[1] Indeed, the majestic *Lusitania,* with her watertight compartments and swiftness, seemed invulnerable. The coal-burning steamer had already crossed the Atlantic one hundred times, and in 1907, the year of her maiden voyage, the *Lusitania* had set a speed record for transatlantic crossings. The British government, inspired by a German challenge to Britannia's supremacy of the seas, loaned Cunard the money to build this fast passenger liner, over twice as long as an American football field. The British Admiralty dictated many of the ship's specifications, so that the 30,396-ton vessel could be armed if necessary during war, and stipulated that half the *Lusitania*'s crew belong to the naval reserves. "Lucy's" business was pleasure, not war. Resplendent with tapestries and carpets, the luxurious floating palace dazzled. One impressed American politician found the ship "more beautiful than Solomon's Temple—and big enough to hold all his wives."[2]

A crew of 702 attended the 1,257 travelers for the 101st voyage, leaving from New York's Pier 54 on May 1. Among them were the renowned theatrical producer Charles Frohman and the multimillionaire playboy Alfred Vanderbilt. Deep in the *Lusitania's* storage area rested a cargo of foodstuffs and contraband (4.2 million rounds of ammunition for Remington rifles, 1,250 cases of empty shrapnel shells, and eighteen cases of nonexplosive fuses). The Cunarder thus carried, said a State Department official, both "babies and bullets."[3]

In the morning newspapers of May 1 a rather unusual announcement, placed by the Imperial German Embassy, appeared beside the Cunard Line advertisement. The German "Notice" warned passengers that the waters around the British Isles constituted a war zone wherein British vessels were subject to destruction. One passenger called the warning "tommy-rot" and only a handful canceled their bookings on the *Lusitania.* Few transferred to the *New York,* ready to sail under the American flag that same day. There was little time to shift vessels. Anyway, the unattractive *New York* was slow and for the American "smart set" socially unacceptable. Cunard officials at dockside reassured voyagers, and the State Department did not intercede to warn the 197 American passengers away from the *Lusitania.* Most Americans, in the "business-as-usual" attitude, accepted the statement of the Cunard Line agent: "The truth is that the *Lusitania* is the safest boat on the sea. She is too fast for any submarine. No German war vessel can get her or near her."[4] During this very time, Secretary of State William Jennings Bryan was trying to persuade President Woodrow Wilson that Americans should be prohibited from traveling on belligerent ships. He was making little headway.

The *Lusitania* and *U-20*. The majestic passenger liner (above) was sunk by German submarine *U-20* (below) off the coast of Ireland on May 7, 1915. "Suppose they should sink the *Lusitania* with American passengers on board," King George V had mused to Colonel Edward M. House on that fateful morning. (Peabody Museum of Salem; Bundesarchiv)

Captained by an old sea dog, William T. Turner, the *Lusitania* steamed from New York into the Atlantic at half past noon on May 1. Manned by an ill-trained crew (the best had been called to war duty), "Lucy" enjoyed a smooth crossing in calm water. Perfunctory lifesaving drills were held, but complacency about the submarine danger characterized captain, crew, and passengers alike. Passengers joked about torpedoes, played cards, consumed gallons of liquor, and listened to concerts on deck. During the evening of May 6, as the *Lusitania* neared Ireland, Turner received a warning from the Naval Centre at Queenstown: "Submarines active off south coast of Ireland."[5] Earlier in the day two ships had been sunk in that very vicinity. Captain Turner posted lookouts but took no other precautions, even after receiving follow-up warnings. He had standing orders from the admiralty to take a zigzag path, to steer a midchannel course, and to steam full speed—all to make it difficult for lurking German submarines to zero in on their targets. But Turner ignored these instructions.

May 7 was a beautiful day with unusually good visibility, recorded Lieutenant Walter Schwieger in his log. The young commander was piloting his *U-20* submarine along the southern Irish coast. That morning it had submerged because British ships, capable of ramming the fragile, slender craft, were passing by. Schwieger surfaced at 1:45 P.M. and within a short time spotted a four-funneled ship in the distance. Carrying general orders to sink British vessels, Schwieger quickly submerged and set a track toward the *Lusitania,* eager to take advantage of this chance meeting (his specific orders, had he followed them, would have placed the *U-20* near Liverpool). At 700 meters the *U-20* released a torpedo. The deadly missile dashed through the water tailed by bubbles. A watchman on the starboard bow of the *Lusitania* saw it and cried out. Captain Turner was unaccountably below deck, where he should not have been in those dangerous waters; and for some reason the bridge did not hear the lookout's warning called through a megaphone one minute before the torpedo struck. Had the message been received, the ship *might* have veered sharply and avoided danger. Thirty seconds before disaster a lookout in the crow's nest spied the torpedo and sounded the alarm. Turner rushed to the bridge. He did not see the torpedo, but he heard the explosion as it ripped into the *Lusitania.* Schwieger watched through his periscope as the mighty vessel leaned on its starboard side and its bow dipped. Panic swept the passengers as they stumbled about the listing decks or groped in the darkness below when the cut-off of electric power stranded elevators. Steam whistled from punctured boilers. Less than half the lifeboats were lowered; some capsized or were launched only partially loaded. Within eighteen minutes the "Queen of the Atlantic" sank, killing 1,198—128 of them Americans. A survivor remembered that when the *Lusitania* went down, "it sounded like a terrible moan."[6]

President Wilson had just completed a cabinet meeting in the White House when he received the first sketchy news of the disaster. He was stunned, as was his special assistant, Colonel Edward House, then dining in London with American ambassador Walter Hines Page. "We shall be at war with Germany within a month," uttered the pro-British House, who had actually sailed on the *Lusitania* in February and had witnessed, much to his surprise, the hoisting of an American flag

Captain William T. Turner (1856–1933). He commanded the *Lusitania* to disaster. (U.S. War Department)

as the ship neared the Irish coast.[7] Fearing war, Secretary William Jennings Bryan told the president that "ships carrying contraband should be prohibited from carrying passengers. . . . Germany has a right to prevent contraband going to the Allies and a ship carrying contraband should not rely upon passengers to protect her from attack—it would be like putting women and children in front of an army."[8] Bellicose ex-president Theodore Roosevelt soon seared the air with his declaration that "this represents not merely piracy, but piracy on a vaster scale of murder than old-time pirates ever practiced."[9] American after American voiced horror and demanded that the president express the nation's collective indignation.

**Lieutenant Walter Schwieger
(1885–1917).** His *U–20* sank the
Lusitania. (Bundesarchiv)

But few wanted war. Wilson secluded himself to ponder a response to this ghastly event. Just months before, he had warned Berlin that it would be held strictly accountable for the loss of any American ships or lives because of submarine warfare. Thereafter, Wilson found himself trying to fulfill America's "double wish"—"to maintain a firm front . . . [toward] Germany and yet do nothing that might by any possibility involve us in war."[10]

After three days of reading memoranda from Bryan urging warnings to Americans not to travel on Allied ships carrying contraband, Wilson spoke in Philadelphia on May 10. His words, much misunderstood, suggested he had no backbone: "There is such a thing as a man being too proud to fight. There is such a thing as a nation being so right that it does not need to convince others by force that it is right."[11] Both cheers and boos echoed across the nation, and Wilson regretted his impromptu words. Preoccupied by his intense courtship of his future second wife, the president did "not know just what I said in Philadelphia . . . because my heart was in such a whirl."[12] The next morning he told the cabinet that he would send a note to Berlin insisting that Americans had a right to travel on the high seas and demanding a disavowal by the German government of the inhumane

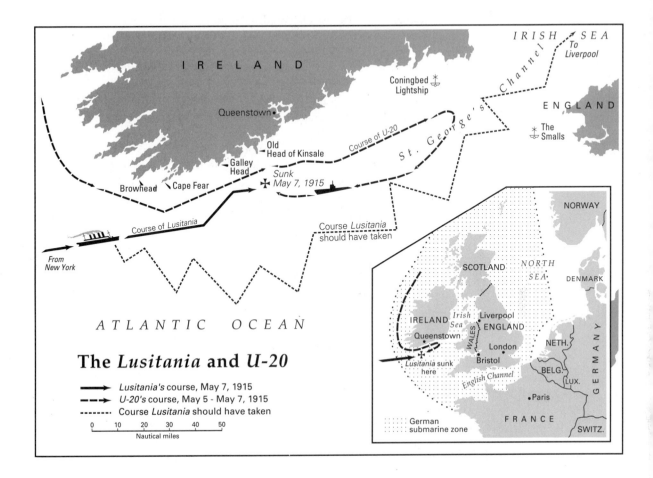

The *Lusitania* and *U-20*

→ *Lusitania's* course, May 7, 1915
--→ *U-20's* course, May 5 - May 7, 1915
······→ Course *Lusitania* should have taken

0 10 20 30 40 50
Nautical miles

acts of its submarine commanders. Bryan sadly approved this first "*Lusitania* note." Long upset about an apparent American double standard in protesting more against German than British violations of American neutral rights, the secretary pleaded with Wilson to send a simultaneous protest to London. But only one note went out on May 13—to Berlin: "The Imperial Government will not expect the United States to omit any word or any act necessary to the performance of its sacred duty of maintaining the rights of the United States and its citizens and of safeguarding their free exercise and enjoyment."[13] In short, end submarine warfare, or else.

The German government took much less pleasure than the German navy did in the destruction of the *Lusitania*. Chancellor Theobold von Bethmann-Hollweg had more than once chastised the navy for inviting war with the United States through submarine attacks on neutral or Allied merchant vessels. On May 28 he sent an evasive reply to Wilson's note. The *Lusitania* case could not be settled, it read, until certain questions were clarified. The German note claimed that the ship was armed, carried munitions, and had orders to ram submarines. Germany asked Washington to investigate. That same day, in a secret meeting with German ambassador Johnann von Bernstorff, Wilson proposed that if Germany would settle the *Lusitania* crisis favorably, he would press the British to suspend their blockade, and then call a conference of neutrals to mediate an end to the war on the following basis: "1. The status quo in Europe; 2. Freedom of the seas. . . . 3. Adjustments concerning colonial possessions."[14]

Wilson convened the cabinet on June 1. When one member recommended a strong note demanding observance of American rights, another suggested as well a note to England to protest British interference with American commerce. Debate became heated. A majority rejected simultaneous notes. Bryan remarked that the cabinet was pro-Ally. Wilson quickly rebuked him for "unfair and unjust" comments.[15] When Germany did not immediately reply to his secret mediation proposal, Wilson sent a second "*Lusitania* note." This note, arguing the case for humanity, vigorously called for an end to warfare by submarine, which could not, given its method of attack, abide by the rules of reason and justice. Wilson rejected Bryan's plea for a warning to passengers and a protest note to England. Sensing that "this will destroy me," Bryan quietly resigned on June 8.[16] Wilson went to the golf links to relax and to free himself from the blinding headaches of the past several days. "He is absolutely *sincere*," the president said of Bryan. "That is what makes him dangerous."[17]

More correspondence on the *Lusitania* followed, but diplomats in Washington and Berlin permitted it to drop from the front pages of newspapers. The crux of the issue was this: The United States insisted that Germany admit it had committed an illegal act; but Germany, unwilling to abandon one of its few effective weapons against British mastery of the ocean, refused to admit wrongdoing and asked for arbitration. "Utterly impertinent," sniffed Kaiser Wilhelm II, who preferred victory to Wilson's mediation.[18] Yet Germany sought a compromise. On February 4 it expressed regret over the American deaths and offered to pay an indemnity (eventually paid in the early 1920s). Semanticists will debate whether this constituted a formal apology, but it surely did not equal an admission of guilt. Wilson nevertheless accepted a German concession.

The horrible deaths from the *Lusitania* nonetheless remained etched on American memories. The torpedoing of the magnificent Cunarder marked a turning point. The Germans suffered a significant propaganda loss, as Britons and Americans alike depicted the "Huns" as depraved. The *Lusitania* disaster became a "naval victory worse than a defeat."[19] The sinking also hardened Wilson's opinion of Germany. After Germany spurned his secret mediation offer, Wilson no longer tried to make diplomatic life easier for the Germans by simultaneously protesting British infractions. No, Germany could not count on equal treatment. The British were violating property rights, but the Germans were violating human rights. He also refused to warn Americans away from belligerent ships. In short, if a U-boat attacked a British ship with Americans aboard, Germany would have to take the consequences. Wilson did not reveal those consequences exactly, but the logical implication was war—just what Bryan feared. His resignation brought pro-Ally Robert Lansing to the secretaryship of state. After the *Lusitania* crisis, Lansing recalled, he held the "conviction that we would ultimately become an ally of Great

Britain."[20] The sinking of the *Lusitania* pointed up, for all to see, the complexities, contradictions, and uncertainties inherent in American neutrality during the European phase of the First World War, 1914–1917.

THE TRAVAILS OF NEUTRALITY

Woodrow Wilson acted virtually as his own secretary of state during those troubled years. "Wilson makes confidant of no one. No one gets his whole mind," an aide wrote. "He is the artistic type which wishes to perfect its own work."[21] British prime minister Lloyd George put it less kindly: Wilson "believed in mankind but . . . distrusted all men."[22] The president defined the overall character of American foreign policy—what historians call "Wilsonianism." Above all else, Wilson stood for an *open* world unencumbered by imperialism, war, or revolution. Barriers to trade and democracy had to be torn down, and secret diplomacy had to give way to public negotiations. The right of self-determination would force the collapse of empires. Constitutional procedures would replace revolution. A free-market, humanized capitalism would ensure democracy. Disarmament programs would restrict the weapons of war. The Open Door of equal trade and investment would harness the economic competition that led to war. Wilson, like so many Americans, believed that the United States was exceptional among nations, that it was the redeemer nation. His reformist, expansionist zeal, often called idealism, blended with realism. The president calculated the nation's economic and strategic needs and devised a foreign policy to protect them. Yet many Americans feared that his world-reforming efforts might invite war, dissipate American resources, and undermine reform at home. Hence Wilson led a divided nation.

Few Americans, Wilson included, desired war, of course. Most watched in shock as the European nations savagely slashed at one another in 1914. Americans of the progressive reform era could no longer argue that decent people had abolished immoral and barbaric war. The progressive faith in human ability to right wrongs, the belief that war was part of the decadent past, the conviction that civilization had advanced too far for such bloodletting—all were ruthlessly challenged. It had seemed before 1914 that the new machine guns, howitzers, submarines, and dreadnoughts were simply too awesome to be unleashed by fair-minded human beings. The outbreak of World War I smashed illusions and tested innocence. Early in the war the president had to "force myself . . . to avoid the kind of numbness that comes from deep apprehension and dwelling upon elements too vast to be yet comprehended."[23] The shock did not become despair, despite the news of poison gas, U-boats, and civilian casualties. The Progressive era was a time of optimism, and Americans, particularly the crusading Wilson, sought to retrieve the happier moments of the past by assuming the role of civilized instructors: America would help Europe come to its senses by teaching it the rules of humane conduct. The carnage justified the mission. In 1915 alone France suffered 1.3 mil-

Woodrow Wilson (1856–1924). Scholar, professor, university president (Princeton), and Democratic governor (New Jersey), Woodrow Wilson was usually cocksure once he made a decision. He protested war and imperialism, but as America's chief diplomat he failed to avoid both. (*Cartoons,* 1912)

Makers of American Foreign Relations, 1914–1920

President	Secretaries of State
Woodrow Wilson, 1913–1921	William Jennings Bryan, 1913–1915
	Robert Lansing, 1915–1920
	Bainbridge Colby, 1920–1921

lion casualties, including 330,000 deaths. Germany suffered 848,000 casualties, and 170,000 deaths. Britain followed with 313,000 casualties, and 73,000 deaths.

Americans had good reason, then, to believe that Europe needed help in cleaning its own house. Furthermore, the outbreak of the war seemed so senseless. By June 1914, the great powers had constructed two blocs, the Triple Alliance (Germany, Austria-Hungary, and Italy) and the Triple Entente (France, Russia, and Great Britain). Some called this division of Europe a balance of power, but an assassin's bullet managed to unbalance it. Between Austria and Serbia lay Bosnia, a tiny province in the Austro-Hungarian empire. Slavic nationalists sought to build a greater Serbia—an independent Slavic state—by annexing Bosnia, which had been absorbed into the Austro-Hungarian empire just a few years before, in 1909. A Slavic terrorist group, the Black Hand, decided to force the issue. On June 28 the heir to the Hapsburg Crown of Austria-Hungary, Archduke Franz Ferdinand, visited Sarajevo, the capital of Bosnia. As his car moved through the streets of the city, a Black Hand assassin gunned him down.

Austria-Hungary sent impossible demands to Serbia. The Serbs rejected them. Austria-Hungary had already received encouragement from Germany, and Serbia had obtained a pledge of support from Russia, which in turn received backing from France. A chain reaction set in. On July 28 Austria-Hungary declared war on Serbia; on August 1 Germany declared "preventive" war on Russia and two days later on France; on August 4 Germany invaded Belgium, and Great Britain declared war on Germany. In a few weeks Japan joined the Allies (Triple Entente) and Turkey the Central Powers, and Italy entered on the Allied side the next year. As the German leader Otto von Bismarck had once prophesied, "some damned foolish thing in the Balkans" would start a world war.[24]

The Atlantic seemed at first an adequate barrier to insulate the United States. In early August, Ambassador Page wrote the president: "Be ready; for you will be called on to compose their huge quarrel. I thank Heaven for many things—first the Atlantic Ocean."[25] Adhering to diplomatic tradition, Wilson on August 4 issued a Proclamation of Neutrality, followed days later by an appeal to Americans to be neutral in thought, speech, and action. Laced with patriotic utterances, the decree sought to cool the passions of immigrant groups who identified with the belligerents. Wilson warned that such ethnically driven alignments would destroy "our peace of mind." America, he implored, must demonstrate to a troubled world that it was "fit beyond others to exhibit the fine poise of undisturbed judgment, the dignity of self-control, the efficiency of dispassionate action."[26] A lofty call for

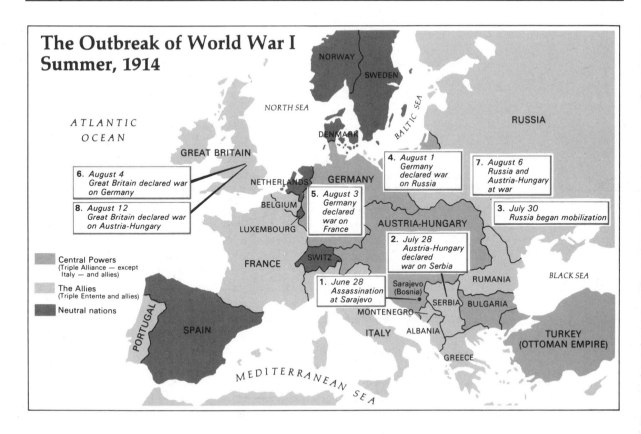

The Outbreak of World War I Summer, 1914

NORWAY

SWEDEN

NORTH SEA

BALTIC SEA

RUSSIA

ATLANTIC OCEAN

DENMARK

GREAT BRITAIN

4. *August 1 Germany declared war on Russia*

7. *August 6 Russia and Austria-Hungary at war*

6. *August 4 Great Britain declared war on Germany*

NETHERLANDS

GERMANY

5. *August 3 Germany declared war on France*

3. *July 30 Russia began mobilization*

8. *August 12 Great Britain declared war on Austria-Hungary*

BELGIUM

LUXEMBOURG

AUSTRIA-HUNGARY

2. *July 28 Austria-Hungary declared war on Serbia*

FRANCE

SWITZ

1. *June 28 Assassination at Sarajevo*

Sarajevo (Bosnia)

SERBIA

RUMANIA

BLACK SEA

MONTENEGRO

BULGARIA

■ Central Powers (Triple Alliance — except Italy — and allies)

□ The Allies (Triple Entente and allies)

■ Neutral nations

PORTUGAL

SPAIN

ITALY

ALBANIA

GREECE

TURKEY (OTTOMAN EMPIRE)

MEDITERRANEAN SEA

restraint, an expression of America as the beacon of common sense in a world gone mad, a plea for unity at home—but difficult to achieve.

Few Americans, including officials of the Wilson administration, proved capable of neutral thoughts and deeds. Loyalties to fatherlands and motherlands did not abate. German Americans identified with the Central Powers. Many Irish Americans, nourishing their traditional Anglophobia at a time when Ireland chafed under British rule and readied for rebellion, wished catastrophe on Britain. But Anglo-American traditions and cultural ties, as well as slogans like "Remember LaFayette," pulled a majority of Americans toward a pro-Allied position. Since the 1890s Anglophobia had weakened in the face of the calming Anglo-American rapprochement. Woodrow Wilson himself harbored pro-British sentiment, believing, he told the British ambassador, that "everything I love is at stake" and that a German victory "will be fatal to our form of Government and American ideals."[27] Then, too, in his days as a scholar, Wilson preferred the British parliamentary system of government to all others, and he had once envisioned himself as a great prime minister. Wilson's advisers, House and Lansing, were ardently pro-British. So was Ambassador Page. Page became so enthusiastic about British-American cooperation that once, after delivering to the British foreign minister an American protest note asserting the rights of neutral traders against British encroachments, he apologized for the U.S. position and helped draft a British reply to his own government.

German war actions, exaggerated by British propaganda, also undermined neutrality. To Americans, the Germans, led by the mustached, arrogant Kaiser Wilhelm II, became symbols of the dreaded militarism and conscription of the Old World, jolters of democracy. Even German chancellor Theobold von Bethmann-Hollweg admitted that "we often got on the world's nerves."[28] Germany, too, seemed an upstart nation, an aggressive latecomer to the scramble for imperialist prizes, and a noisy intruder in the Caribbean where the British had already acknowledged U.S. hegemony. Eager to grasp world power and encouraging Austria-Hungary to war, Berlin certainly had little claim on virtue. The invasion of Belgium alone persuaded thousands of Americans to hate the "Hun." The European powers had guaranteed Belgium neutrality by treaty, but Bethmann-Hollweg dismissed it as a "scrap of paper."[29] On August 4, 1914, hoping to get at France easily, the Germans attacked Belgium and, angered that the Belgians resisted, ruthlessly proceeded to raze villages, unleash firing squads against townspeople, and deport young workers to Germany. One magazine called Belgium "a martyr to civilization, sister to all who love liberty, or law; assailed, polluted, trampled in the mire, heel-marked in her breast, tattered, homeless."[30] American hearts and hands went out in the form of a major relief mission headed by a young, wealthy, and courageous mining engineer, Herbert Hoover. The British did not have to play up these atrocities for them to have an impact, but, in control of transatlantic cables, they launched a hyperbolic propaganda campaign nevertheless, creating fictional stories of babies at the bloody ends of German bayonets and of Belgian women with breasts hacked off.

American economic links with the Allies also undermined Wilsonian appeals for neutrality. England had always been America's best customer and wartime conditions simply intensified the relationship. The Allies needed both war matériel and consumer goods. Americans, inspired by huge profits, a chance to pull out of a recession, and a "business-as-usual" attitude, obliged. In 1914 U.S. exports to England and France equaled $754 million; in 1915 the figure shot up to $1.28 billion; and in 1916 the amount more than doubled to $2.75 billion. Comparable statistics for Germany reveal why Berlin believed the United States was taking sides. In 1914 exports to Germany totaled $345 million; in 1915 they plummeted to $29 million; and in 1916 they fell to but $2 million. In 1914–1917 the prestigious banking house of J. P. Morgan Company of New York City served as an agent for England and France and arranged for the shipment of more than $3 billion worth of goods. In April 1915, Britain ordered shells from the American Locomotive Company costing $63.7 million, and that year Bethlehem Steel contracted for some $150 million in ammunition, to cite two examples. By April 1917, British purchasing missions were spending $83 million a week for American copper, steel, wheat, oil, and munitions.

Britain and France became hard pressed to pay for these huge shipments. First, they sold many of their American securities and liquidated investments. This netted them several billion dollars. Next, in appeals to prominent American bankers and State Department officials, they sought loans. In 1914 Bryan discouraged private American loans to the belligerents, for, as he put it, "money is the worst of all contrabands because it commands everything else."[31] Indeed, loans to belligerents clashed with "the true spirit of neutrality."[32] Yet in early 1915 the Wilson administration did not object to a Morgan credit to France of $50 million. With Bryan's resignation and Lansing's ascent as secretary of state, the practice became common. As Lansing told Wilson, if Americans did not extend loans to the Allies, the United States would invite "restriction of output, industrial depression, idle capital, idle labor, numerous failures, financial demoralization, and general unrest and suffering among the laboring classes."[33] The Wilson administration permitted loans to the Allies amounting to $2.3 billion in the years 1914–1917—a sharp contrast to loans of only $27 million to Germany. Once it joined the war as a belligerent, the American economic powerhouse became even more the dispenser of munitions, food, and money to the Allies. Indeed, as the historian Kathleen Burk has written, "the passing of hegemony from Britain to the United States . . . as the leading financial power can be seen occurring, step by step, in the negotiations between the British Treasury mission and the American government during 1917–18."[34]

Berlin protested that such Allied-American economic ties were "unneutral." Yet for the United States to have curbed trade with Britain, which ruled the seas, would have constituted unneutral behavior in favor of the Germans, for under international law a belligerent could buy, at its own risk, contraband and noncontraband goods from a neutral. Neutral or not, the United States had become the arsenal of the Allied war effort. Berlin determined to interrupt this damaging trade by unleashing *unterseebooten*.

Torpedoes on the High Seas: Submarines and Neutral Rights

To strangle Germany, the British invoked legal doctrines of retaliation and contraband without ever technically declaring a blockade. They mined the North Sea, expanded the contraband list to include foodstuffs and cotton, forced American ships into port for inspection, seized "contraband" from neutral vessels, halted American trade with Germany's neutral neighbors Denmark and Holland, armed British merchant ships, used decoy ships to lure U-boats into traps, flew neutral (often American) flags, and rammed whenever possible any U-boats that complied with international law by surfacing to warn a British merchant vessel of an imminent attack. The British "ruled the waves and waived the rules," as someone put it. Defending traditional U.S. principles of neutral rights, the Wilson administration issued protests, some mild, some tough, against these illegalities. When a defiant London replied, the Foreign Office paid appropriate verbal deference to neutral rights and international law and went right on with its unorthodox behavior. Britain sometimes soothed America's hurt by compensating its businesses for damages and purchasing large quantities of goods at inflated prices. Americans thus came to accept the indignities of British economic warfare. Britain managed brilliantly to sever American economic lines to the Central Powers without producing a rupture in Anglo-American relations.

Germans protested vehemently against this seeming American acquiescence in what Berlin tagged the British "hunger" or "starvation" blockade. To continue the battle against the Allies, Germany had to have imports and had to curb the flourishing Anglo-American trade that fueled the Allied war machine. The German surface fleet, bottled up in ports by British vessels, seemed inadequate for the task, so German leaders hesitantly turned to a relatively new experimental weapon of limited maneuverability, the submarine. At the start they possessed just 21 U-boats, and at peak strength in October 1917 they had but 127. Only a third of this fleet operated at sea at any one time. On February 4, 1915, Berlin announced that it was retaliating against British strangulation by declaring a war zone around Britain. All *enemy* ships in the area would be destroyed. Neutral ships were warned to *stay out* of the zone because of the possibility of mistaken identity, a real possibility given the British practice of hoisting neutral flags. Passengers from neutral countries like the United States were urged, moreover, to *stay off* enemy passenger vessels. Six days later Wilson instructed Germany that it would be held to "strict accountability" for the loss of American life and property.[35]

The British continued to arm their merchant vessels, which thereby became warships and theoretically ineligible to take on arms or munitions in neutral ports. But Washington invoked a fine point of law, making the distinction between offensive and defensive armaments that permitted such "defensively" armed British craft to carry war supplies from American ports. Crying foul, the Germans also argued that old international law, which Wilson invoked, did not fit the submarine. Traditional rules held that enemy merchant vessels about to be captured or sunk had to be adequately warned by the attacking cruiser so that the safety of passengers and crew could be ensured. The submarine could not fulfill this requirement. If it surfaced in its sluggish fashion, the merchant ship's crew might sink it with the blast from a deck gun or even a hand grenade, or ram the vulnerable and slow-moving craft. British vessels like the *Lusitania* had standing Admiralty orders to resist U-boats and to ram them. Before the sinking of the *Lusitania,* the Germans had lost eleven submarines—five by ramming. Imagine the problem for Schwieger of *U-20* when he spotted the *Lusitania.* Had he surfaced to warn her, he would have imperiled his boat and crew. The *Lusitania* would probably have attempted to ram *U-20* or flee and would have sent distress signals to British warships in the vicinity. Even if the *Lusitania* had submitted to the warning, it would have taken at least an hour for the passengers to be placed in lifeboats before the ship could be attacked, and by then British vessels would most likely have closed in on Schwieger. In short, from the German point of view, it was impossible to comply with an international law that did not provide for the submarine. Wilson retorted that differences over international law could be "adjusted after the war," whereas Germany's "sheer acts of piracy on the high seas . . . might easily lead to actual hostilities."[36]

Secretary Bryan tried diplomacy in early 1915, asking Germany to give up use of unannounced submarine attacks in exchange for a British promise to disarm its merchant carriers and permit food to flow to Germany. The Germans seemed interested, but London, which would have to abandon its successful blockade, de-

William Jennings Bryan (1860–1925). The great agrarian reformer went to Congress in 1890 as a Democrat from Nebraska. After several unsuccessful runs for the presidency, Bryan endorsed Wilson and became secretary of state in 1913. He favored the arbitration of international disputes and he perpetuated U.S. interventionist policy in Latin America. Believing that Wilson was tilting toward the British after the *Lusitania* disaster of 1915, Bryan resigned in protest. A colleague called him "too good a Christian to run a naughty world." (National Portrait Gallery, Smithsonian Institution, Washington, D.C.)

murred. Some critics have stated that at this point Wilson should have been tough in pressing the belligerents to alter their naval strategies or face the prospect of American warships convoying America's neutral ships. Or he might have launched a vigorous diplomatic offensive to delay explosive events on the seas. Yet the war was still in infancy, its direction and length uncertain, and American armed convoys in the Atlantic could very well draw America into a war it did not want. A diplomatic offensive, given the intensity of nationalism and war fever in Europe, seemed doomed to an early and inglorious failure. Wilson had to ask if he could risk all this. In March 1915, he did send Colonel House to Europe to sound out possibilities for mediation, but to no avail. Nonetheless, Wilson failed to adjust or shelve ancient international law, which had no provision for the submarine. He accepted British alterations but not German ones, for reasons of both morality and economics.

Between February and early May 1915, marauding submarines sunk ninety ships in the war zone. One American, on the British passenger ship *Falaba,* died in the sinking of that vessel on March 28. Washington did not protest, hoping that a crisis could be avoided and that the belligerents could yet be lured to the conference table. Then came the *Lusitania* in May. Through Wilson's many protest notes, a U.S. posture took shape: uneasy tolerance of British violations of property rights and rejection of German violations of human rights. Despite secret German orders to submarine commanders to avoid a repetition of the *Lusitania* incident, on August 19 the *Arabic,* another British liner, was torpedoed with the loss of two American lives. A worried Ambassador Bernstorff publicly pledged that U-boats would now spare passenger ships.

In early 1916, with the *Lusitania* issue still unresolved, the United States attempted to bring the warring parties to the conference table. Colonel House talked with British officials in London but left with no promises for peace. He journeyed next to Berlin, where German leaders gave no assurances. Both sides would fight on. "Hell will break loose in Europe this spring and summer as never before," House informed Wilson.[37] House then traveled to Paris, where he rashly informed his skeptical French hosts: "If the Allies obtain a small success this spring or summer, the U.S. will intervene to promote a peaceful settlement, but if the Allies have a setback, the United States will intervene militarily and will take part in the war against Germany."[38] House did not tell the president exactly what he had said in Paris.

House returned to London to try to persuade Sir Edward Grey, British foreign secretary, to heed Wilson's call for a peace conference. The American envoy recorded their agreements in the House-Grey Memorandum of February 22, 1916, a document loaded with "ifs." The first paragraph read: "Colonel House told me that President Wilson was ready, on hearing from France and England that the moment was opportune, to propose that a Conference should be summoned to put an end to the war. Should the Allies accept the proposal, and should Germany refuse it, the United States would probably enter the war against Germany." The record of conversation also reported that House had said that the peace conference would secure terms "not unfavourable to the Allies" and that if the conference failed to achieve peace, "the United States would leave the Conference as a bel-

Edward M. House (1858–1938). This Texas "colonel" served as Wilson's trusted emissary abroad. In the House-Grey Memorandum of 1916 he showed signs of the deviousness that led to his break with the president after the Versailles conference. He misled the British by depicting the mediation overture as a pretext for America's entering the war, and he misled Wilson by reporting that the British were genuinely interested in mediation. (National Portrait Gallery, Smithsonian Institution)

ligerent on the side of the Allies, if Germany was unreasonable."[39] President Wilson pronounced the memorandum a diplomatic triumph, but clouded its meaning all the more by inserting a "probably" before the word "leave" in the sentence quoted above. He took the document much more seriously than did the British or French, who shelved it, snubbed American mediation, and vowed victory over Germany.

As House moved among European capitals, Lansing informed the Allied governments that the United States sought a modus vivendi to defuse naval crises: The Allies would disarm merchant vessels and the Germans would agree to follow international law by warning enemy merchant ships. This suggestion revealed that the Wilson administration understood the German argument that armed merchant vessels were in reality offensive craft—that is, warships. The British and Colonel House remonstrated when they received this news. The Germans seemed to endorse the proposal by declaring on February 10 that submarines would henceforth attack only *armed* merchant ships without warning. Suddenly Wilson reversed policy. He abandoned the modus vivendi in order to restore his standing with the British and sustain House's mediation efforts in London. Lansing announced, furthermore, that the United States would not prevent its citizens from traveling on "defensively" armed merchant ships.

WOODROW WILSON AND AMERICA'S DESCENT INTO WORLD WAR

Why let one American passenger and a trigger-happy U-boat captain bring Germany and the United States to war? asked public critics like Bryan. Why not, they inquired, keep Americans off belligerent ships and require them instead to sail on American vessels? From August 1914 to mid-March 1917 only three Americans (on the oil tanker *Gulflight,* May 1, 1915) had lost their lives on an *American* ship torpedoed by a U-boat. In contrast, about 190 Americans, including the *Lusitania's* 128, died on belligerent ships. After the *Falaba* was sunk, Bryan, still secretary of state, recognized that Americans had a right to travel on belligerent vessels, but asked Wilson to ask them to forgo that right. "I cannot see," Bryan wrote the president, "that he [an American on a belligerent ship] is differently situated from those who by remaining in a belligerent country assume risk were of injury." Wilson had, after all, urged Americans to leave war-torn Mexico.[40] Ambassador James W. Gerard in Berlin wrote Wilson that "when Americans have reasonable opportunity to cross the ocean [on American ships] why should we enter a great war because some American wants to cross on a ship where he can have a private bathroom?"[41] Senator William J. Stone, chair of the Foreign Relations Committee, pointed out that the *Lusitania* passengers, duly warned about the risk, were in essence on "British soil." He continued: "Was not their position substantially equivalent to their being in the walls of a fortified city?"[42]

Wilson did not agree: Americans could not give up one right, or all rights would be jeopardized. In January 1916, Congressman Jeff McLemore of Texas, a

Democrat, introduced a resolution to prohibit Americans from traveling on armed belligerent vessels. In February, Senator Thomas P. Gore of Oklahoma, another Democrat, submitted a similar resolution in his chamber. The Gore-McLemore resolution very quickly gained support in both houses. Wilson, a firm believer in presidential supremacy in decisionmaking, bristled at this challenge from Congress. He attacked Gore-McLemore, unleashing Cabinet members with patronage muscle on timid legislators and suggesting that the resolution was a pro-German ploy. He issued a statement marked by lofty, almost embarrassing, phrases. To halt American passage on belligerent ships, Wilson intoned, would be to accept national humiliation and destruction of the "whole fine fabric of international law."[43] In short, he stuck with rigid, archaic concepts, refusing to adjust to the new factor of the submarine or to appreciate the impact on Germany of the obvious British violations of the same law. In early March, the Gore-McLemore resolution lost 68 to 14 in the Senate and 276 to 142 in the House. The Gore-McLemore resolution was one of the more sensible proposals for avoiding German-American conflict. It asked America to give up very little; despite Wilson's exaggerated rhetoric, it did not besmudge national honor. Wilson's message to Berlin rang loud and clear: Do not use your submarines.

In March 1916, another passenger ship, another U-boat, another torpedo, more American injuries: The French ship *Sussex,* moving across the English Channel, took a hit but did not sink. Aboard was a young American scholar, Samuel Flagg Bemis, later to become a renowned historian of foreign relations but then fresh from archival research on Jay's Treaty. Gazing over the calm sea, Bemis glimpsed the swirling wake of a torpedo moments before impact. "The entire bow was blown off and with it the people who were in the dining room," he recalled.[44] Although four Americans sustained injuries, a wet Bemis escaped serious harm. He also saved his little bag of note cards.

The *Sussex* attack violated the "*Arabic* pledge," even though the U-boat commander mistook the ship for a minelayer. Lansing counseled the president to break diplomatic relations with Berlin. Wilson decided instead on an ultimatum. He warned the Germans on April 18 that he would sever relations if they did not halt their submarine warfare against passenger and merchant vessels; to emphasize the point he went to Congress the next day and repeated the warning. Alarmed, German officials fully expected a rupture if they did not rein in the U-boats. With the unsuccessful German offensive at Verdun costing more than half a million lives, Berlin was not willing to invite war with the United States. In early May Germany promised (the "*Sussex* pledge") that submarines would not attack passenger or merchant ships without prior warning. The Germans also reminded Washington that it should try to stop British infractions of international law.

The British, sensing favorable winds, clamped down even harder on trade with the Central Powers. In July, London issued a "blacklist" of firms; more than eighty American companies that had traded with the Central Powers made the list, and even Wilson now fumed that he was "about at the end of my patience with Great Britain and the Allies."[45] He contemplated a prohibition on loans and exports to them, but he did little. Many Americans also condemned the brutal British success in smashing the Irish Easter Rebellion in April 1916.

Shortly after the presidential election of 1916, punctuated with the Democrats' slogan "He Kept Us Out of War," the president launched another diplomatic offensive. In December Wilson boldly asked the belligerents to state their war aims. Neither Berlin nor London, still seeking military victory, welcomed Wilson's mediation, which would deny them the spoils of war. Germany coveted Poland, Lithuania, Belgium, and the Belgian Congo; Britain sought German colonies; France wanted Alsace-Lorraine. Aware of these goals of conquest, Wilson pointedly rejected them on January 22, 1917, when he called for a "peace without victory," because only through a peace founded on the "equality of nations" could a lasting world order be achieved. He proposed that "nations should with one accord adopt the doctrine of President Monroe as the doctrine of the world."[46] Wilson "meant to convey the idea that the United States would not agree to guarantee a peace made on terms so drastic that . . . Germany would be roused into setting them aside," he informed the British. "This did not mean that the Allies' terms, if they won the war, were not to be severe."[47] The grand old man of French letters, Anatole France, nonetheless responded cynically: "Peace without victory is bread without yeast . . . , love without quarrels, a camel without humps, night without moon, roof without smoke, town without brothel."[48]

In early 1917 crises mounted quickly. On January 31 Berlin announced that, starting the next day, German submarines would attack without warning and sink all vessels, enemy and neutral, found near British waters. This declaration of unrestricted submarine warfare expressed Germany's calculated risk that England and France would be defeated before the United States could mobilize and send its soldiers overseas. The cocky German naval minister remarked: "From a military standpoint, America's entrance is as nothing."[49] German naval officers persuaded the kaiser that the U-boats, now numbering about one hundred, could shrink U.S. munitions shipments and hence knock Britain out of the war in six months. Army officers, bogged down in trench warfare, hoped to end their costly immobility through a bold stroke. But an adviser to Chancellor Bethmann-Hollweg fatalistically told his diary that "despite all promises of the navy it remains a leap into the dark."[50]

On February 3 Washington severed diplomatic relations with Berlin. Wilson still did not want war with Germany, even though he had become incensed by Berlin's most recent decision. According to Lansing, moreover, Wilson became "more and more impressed with the idea that 'white civilization' and its domination over the world rested largely on our ability to keep this country intact, as we would have to build up the nations ravaged by the war."[51] Yet Wilson had also committed himself in diplomatic notes and impassioned rhetoric to stand firmly against unrestricted submarine warfare. Allied ships carrying war supplies soon suffered increasing losses, and the few American vessels carrying contraband stayed in port or shifted to trade outside the European war zones. Goods stacked up on wharves. The U.S. economy seemed imperiled.

Added to the threats to economic interests and Wilsonian ideals was an apparent challenge to U.S. security. Washington had already endured espionage and sabotage by German agents, most notably the "thunderous" explosions at the Black Tom munitions factories across from the Statue of Liberty in July 1916.[52] In late

February the British passed to Ambassador Page an intercepted and decoded telegram dated January 16 and sent to Mexico by German foreign minister Arthur Zimmermann. The message proposed a military alliance with the U.S. neighbor. And should war with the United States break out, Germany would help Mexico "reconquer" the territory lost in 1848: Texas, New Mexico, and Arizona. Zimmermann also suggested that Japan be added to the alliance "at the moment war breaks out between Mexico and the United States." Although the skeptical Mexican government never took up the German offer, Wilson saw the telegram as a direct challenge to U.S. security.[53] "This wd [would] precipitate a war between almost any 2 nations," Page confided to his diary.[54]

One day after Wilson learned of Zimmermann's cable, he asked Congress for authority to arm American merchant vessels. On March 1, to create a favorable public opinion for the request, he released to the press the offensive Zimmermann telegram. But antiwar senators Robert La Follette and George Norris led a filibuster—a "little group of willful men," Wilson snarled—that killed the armed ship legislation.[55] Stubbornly ignoring the Senate, Wilson ordered the arming anyway. To no avail: during March 16–18 alone U-boats sunk the American ships *City of Memphis, Illinois,* and *Vigilancia.* Buttressed by the unanimous support of his cabinet, the president decided for war.

After several intense days writing his own speech with some help from Colonel House, Wilson played golf with his new wife before solemnly addressing a special joint session of Congress on the evening of April 2. He asked for a declaration of war against Germany—a war that Berlin had "thrust" on the United States. His words inspired his audience to nationalistic enthusiasm. The "unmanly business" of using submarines, he asserted, constituted "warfare against mankind." Freedom of the seas, commerce, American lives, human rights—the "outlaw" U-boats challenged all. Economic self-interest, morality, and national honor compelled Americans to fight. He characterized the German government as a menacing monster striking at the "very roots of human life." The "Prussian autocracy" stirred up trouble through spies and the Zimmermann telegram. He also hailed the Russian Revolution of March, which made "the great, generous Russian people . . . a fit partner for a league of honor" in a crusade against autocracy. Then came the memorable words: "The world must be made safe for democracy."[56] The address simplified issues and claimed too much for American participation in World War I. But the moment required patriotic fervor, not sophisticated analysis. "It had been a moving oration," the historian Ross Gregory has written, "and when the President had finished, most of his listeners—there remained a few diehard dissenters—were ready to grasp the Hun by the collar, feeling that surely God was on their side, and if He was not, God this one time must be wrong."[57] By votes of 82 to 6 in the Senate on April 4 (La Follette and Norris among the dissenters) and 373 to 50 in the House on April 6 (Majority Leader Claude Kitchin and nine of Wisconsin's eleven representatives among those voting nay), Congress endorsed Wilson's call for a war for peace. "We were children reared in a kindergarten, and now the real thing was coming," a pacifist recalled.[58]

Submarine warfare precipitated the American decision to enter the war. Had there been no submarine to menace American lives, property, and the U.S. defin-

Jeannette Rankin (1880–1973). Native of Montana, Rankin, in 1916, became the first woman to be elected to the House of Representatives. A life-long pacifist, she voted against war in 1917, only to lose her seat the following year. In the inter-war period she lobbied for peace and was again elected to Congress in 1940. Once again she refused to send American soldiers into "the foreign slaughterhouse" and cast the only vote against war in 1941. She later marched against the Vietnam War. (Montana Historical Society)

ition of international law, there would have been no American soldiers sent to France. Critics have argued, however, that from the German perspective, use of the submarine became necessary because of the long list of unfriendly American acts: acquiescence in the British blockade, part of a general pro-British bias; large-scale munitions shipments to, and other commerce with, the Allies; large loans; an interpretation of neutral rights that insisted that American passengers could sail anywhere, even into a war zone, and which thereby rendered the submarine an impotent weapon. Take away those acts, which the Germans considered unneutral, and they might not have launched the U-boats. To dissenters it seemed wrong that American ideals and interests could depend so perilously on armed ships carrying contraband, heading for Britain, and steaming through a war zone. Yet that is how Wilson and his advisers defined the problem.

Evident in Wilson's policies was the traditional American belief that others must conform to U.S. prescriptions, self-professed as they were, and that America's ideals served as a beacon for the world. "We created this Nation," the president once proclaimed, "not to serve ourselves, but to serve mankind."[59] When the Germans defied America's rules, ideals, and property, and threatened its security through a proposed alliance with Mexico, they had to be punished. Here was an opportunity to protect both humane principles and commercial interests. When Wilson spoke passionately of the right of a neutral to freedom of the seas, he demonstrated how intertwined were American moral, economic, and strategic interests. Wilson sought the role of peacemaker and he promised to remake the world in the American image: that is, to create a world order in which barriers to political democracy and the Open Door came down, in which revolution and aggression no longer disturbed world order. This missionary zeal served, at least in Wilson's mind, the national interest (trade and the Open Door) and high principles (respect for human rights, self-determination, and democracy). War came to the United States not simply because German submarines ravaged, but because American leaders, in the expansionist tradition, decided to fight in order to implant in the Old World the best principles and goods America had to offer.

THE DEBATE OVER PREPAREDNESS

Berlin's assumption that American soldiers could not reach France fast enough to reverse an expected German victory proved a gross misjudgment. The Germans underestimated the productive power of the United States. American military muscle and economic power, in fact, decisively tipped the balance against Germany. Given the information available in early 1917, however, the German calculation does not seem so unrealistic. In April the United States was hardly prepared to send a major expedition to the Western Front. At that date the Regular Army counted only 130,000 officers and men, backed by 180,000 National Guardsmen. Although some American officers had been seasoned by military interventions in Cuba, the Philippines, and recently in Mexico, many soldiers had inadequate training. Arsenals had meager supplies of such modern weapons as the machine gun. The "Air Service," then part of the army, did not have a plane of modern design with a machine gun, and some ships in the navy had never fired a gun.

An American "preparedness movement" had been under way for months, encouraged by prominent Americans like the tough-minded Rough Rider and military evangelist General Leonard Wood, who overstated the case when he argued that America's military weakness invited attack, but rang true when he noted that the United States was not recognized as a top-notch military power. After 1914, Wood, Theodore Roosevelt, the National Security League, the Army League, and the Navy League lobbied actively for bigger military appropriations. The belief that "preparedness" offered insurance against war grew more popular. One propaganda film, *The Fall of a Nation,* depicted a helpless United States invaded by spike-helmeted attackers. In mid-1915 one hundred of America's wealthiest men pledged thousands of dollars to help the Navy League plead its case before Congress, and by September of that year twenty-eight governors had joined the National Security League.

Wilson belatedly supported moderate preparedness. After instructing his outspoken senior officers that they "cannot write or talk any more; you can't even say that two and two make four," the president asked Congress in December 1915 for a half-billion-dollar naval expansion program, including ten battleships and one hundred submarines.[60] The president expected the United States to surpass Britain as "incomparably the greatest navy in the world."[61] Land forces would also be enlarged and reorganized.

Perpetuating the antimilitarist tradition of great numbers of Americans, Senator La Follette, Representative Kitchin, and such prominent reformers as Jane Addams, William Jennings Bryan, Lillian Wald, and Oswald Garrison Villard, spurred a movement against these measures. These peace advocates, the Women's Peace Party, and the League to Limit Armaments argued that war would interrupt reform at home, benefit big business, and curtail civil liberties. Several peace leaders also joined the auto manufacturer Henry Ford in December 1915 as he sailed to Europe on his peace ship, *Oscar II,* to establish a Neutral Conference for Continuous Mediation—a quixotic attempt to end the war and get "the boys out of the trenches by Christmas."[62] The American Union Against Militarism agitated against preparedness with its papier-mâché dinosaur, "Jingo," whose collar read "ALL ARMOR PLATE—NO BRAINS."[63] The president, whose support of mediation, disarmament, and a postwar association of nations appealed to antiwar liberals and socialists ("progressive internationalists," in the historian Thomas J. Knock's phrase), hoped that moderate preparedness would not alienate them, for their formidable arguments and numerical strength impressed Congress.[64] Chicago's famed social reformer Jane Addams remembered "moments of uneasiness," but she and others endorsed Wilson in the 1916 presidential campaign, for it seemed "at last that peace was assured and the future safe in the hands of an executive who had received an unequivocal mandate from the people 'to keep us out of war.'"[65]

In January 1916, Wilson set out on a two-month speaking tour, often having to criticize members of his own party for their opposition to a military buildup.

U-boat sinkings aided the president's message. In May 1916, Congress passed the National Defense Act, increasing the Regular Army to some 200,000 men and 11,000 officers, and the National Guard to 440,000 men and 17,000 officers. Provision was made, too, for summer training camps, modeled after one held in Plattsburg, New York, in 1915 for the social and economic elite. In June 1916, Wilson asserted that "mankind is going to know that when America speaks she means what she says."[66] The navy bill passed in August 1916, followed by the shipping bill providing $50 million to enlarge the merchant marine. Theodore Roosevelt thought the measures inadequate, but the anarchist Emma Goldman saw no difference between Roosevelt, "the born bully who uses a club," and Wilson, "the history professor who uses the smooth polished mask."[67]

Once in the war, the Wilson administration mobilized armed forces through the Selective Service Act of May 1917. National military service, proponents believed, would not only prepare the nation for battle but also instill respect for order, democracy, and sacrifice. During the war, the Wilson administration transformed the army "into a potent instrument for citizenship inculcation," the historian Penn Borden has written. "Under the force of reform enthusiasts, the army became sociologist, psychologist, physician, and preacher to the nation."[68] Under the selective service system, 24,340,000 men eventually registered for the draft. Some 3,764,000 men received draft notices, and 2,820,000 were inducted

Senator Robert M. La Follette (1855–1925). This *Life* magazine cartoon depicted the antiwar, progressive reformer as a traitor. La Follette wanted a referendum on the war, certain that the American people would vote "no." Some Americans thought that he should be expelled from the Senate. Others claimed that he took orders from the German kaiser, here shown pinning medals on the Wisconsin senator. La Follette withstood the intolerance of dissent and continued to speak against organized power and for the powerless, who, he said, were the people destined to do the fighting and dying abroad. (State Historical Society of Wisconsin)

(he others failed preinduction tests, never showed up, or claimed conscientious objector—CO—status). Over all, 4,744,000 soldiers, sailors, and marines served in the armed forces during the war. The typical soldier was a white, single, poorly educated (most had not attended high school) draftee between twenty-one and twenty-three years of age. On college campuses, 150,000 students joined the Student Army Training Corps or similar navy units. Although women were excluded from military combat, some of them became navy clerks, telephone operators in the Army Signal Corps, and nurses and physical therapists to the wounded and battle-shock cases.

Officer training camps turned out "ninety-day wonders," thousands of commissioned officers drawn largely from people of elite background. One camper remarked about the spirit of his group: "There are so many Roosevelts that you can't turn around without stumbling over one."[69] Actually, Theodore Roosevelt was not there. The old Rough Rider had asked Wilson for permission to recruit and lead a volunteer unit into battle; no doubt taking some revengeful pleasure in denying the request, Wilson argued that special volunteer divisions would raise havoc with military organization. According to the historian John W. Chambers, Roosevelt's challenge "played the crucial role" in Wilson's decision to raise a wartime army through conscription rather than voluntarism.[70] Roosevelt was to die peacefully in January 1919, after losing his youngest son in the war.

Right after the American declaration of war, Allied military missions begged for soldiers. General John J. "Black Jack" Pershing, veteran fighter against Apaches, Filipinos, and Mexicans, and now head of the American Expeditionary Force to Europe, soon sent a "show the flag" contingent to France to boost Allied morale. Neither Wilson nor Pershing would accept, however, the European recommendation that U.S. troops be inserted in Allied units where needed. American units would cooperate in joint maneuvers with other forces, but the U.S. Army would remain separate and independent. National pride dictated this decision, but so did the realization that Allied commanders had for years wasted the lives of hundreds of thousands in trench warfare. Zigzag trenches fronted by barbed wire and mines stretched across France. Beyond the muddy, stench-ridden trenches lay "no-man's-land," denuded by artillery fire. Soldiers jumped out to charge German lines, also a maze of trenches. Machine guns mowed them down; chlorine gas, first used by Germany in 1915, poisoned them. The United States wanted freedom of choice and no identification with exploitative Allied war aims. Thus did the United States call itself an "associated" rather than an "allied" power in the war.

JOHNNY GET YOUR GUN: THE DOUGHBOYS MAKE THE DIFFERENCE IN EUROPE

On July 4, 1917, General Pershing reviewed the first unit of American troops to arrive in France. A battalion of the 16th Infantry marched proudly through the streets of Paris, as nearly a million Parisians tossed flowers, hugged the "doughboys,"

Red Cross Poster. Women served in many roles in the war. They became workers in weapons factories. They sold Liberty Bonds and publicized government mobilization programs as members of the Women's Committee of the Council of National Defense. They made clothing for refugees and soldiers, and they ran canteens in France to provide American soldiers with food, recreation, and haircuts. Some 10,000 Red Cross nurses cared for the doughboys near at the front. (Library of Congress)

and cheered wildly. The American soldiers were enthusiastic but ill-trained recruits. One company commander recalled that "these men couldn't even slope arms. They were even more dangerous with a loaded rifle."[71] But to the war-weary French, accustomed to viewing haggard men exhausted by the agony of the trenches, these fresh American troops offered inspiration. "Lafayette, we are here!" one U.S. captain proclaimed. A British diplomat commented that American troops had "an ingenious notion that they want to make the rest of the world as democratic as they believe their own country to be."[72]

Preparations continued in the United States. To the tune "Johnny Get Your Gun," draftees and volunteers left their hometowns with fanfare and full stomachs from church dinners. Their six-month training program demanded a seventeen-hour day, including "policing the area" (i.e., picking up cigarette butts), a military custom considered "discipline." The soldiers often drilled without weapons. Some never fired a rifle until stationed in France. The war hero Private Alvin C. York claimed that many of his fellow warriors "missed everything but the sky" during training, but because the army targets were larger than the heads of Tennessee turkeys, they "generally made a tolebly [*sic*] good score."[73]

To the chagrin of American leaders, taverns and brothels quickly surrounded military camps. Alcohol and prostitution, of course, ranked as taboos during the Progressive Era. "Fit to Fight" became the government's slogan, as it moved to close down "red-light districts," designated "sin-free zones" around camps, and banned the sale of liquor to men in uniform. Secretary of the Navy Josephus Daniels preached that "men must live straight if they would shoot straight."[74] The military conquered the venereal-disease problem in the United States. Groups like the YMCA and the Jewish Welfare Board sent song leaders to camps. Movies, athletic programs, and well-stocked stores kept soldiers on the base by making them feel "at home."

These activities could not blunt a major flu epidemic, which first struck camps in spring 1918. The extremely contagious flu virus cut across race, gender, and class lines. At Camp Sherman, Ohio, one of the bases hit hardest, 1,101 people died between September 27 and October 13. Whereas about 51,000 soldiers died in battle during the war, some 62,000 soldiers died from diseases. "Doughboys" infected with the virus carried the flu with them to the European war, where it ignored national boundaries (the Germans called it *Blitzkatarrh*) and turned into a global pandemic that killed more than 21 million people by the spring of 1919.[75]

Approximately 400,000 African-American troops suffered racism and discrimination during this war "to make the world safe for democracy." Camps were segregated and "white only" signs posted. In 1917 in Houston, Texas, whites provoked blacks into a riot that left seventeen whites and two blacks dead. More than a hundred black soldiers were court-martialed; thirteen were executed by hanging. In the army, three out of every four black soldiers served in labor units, where they wielded a shovel, not a gun, or where they cooked or unloaded supplies. They received poor training and became dispirited under the leadership of white officers. Even black officers were assigned second-class quarters during the transatlantic trip. Many black soldiers earned the coveted medal "Croix de Guerre," but Americans preferred to emphasize an uneven performance by two black units in the Meuse-Argonne offensive near the end of the war. To be African American in World War I was to be reminded of a second-class citizenship and the contradiction between America's wartime rhetoric and reality. A statistic revealed the problem: 382 black Americans were lynched in the period 1914–1920.

General Pershing established headquarters outside Paris and tried to acquaint soldiers with the hardships of trench and gas warfare. Although the first official American combat death in Europe actually came only ten days after Congress declared war—that of Edmund Charles Clinton Genet, the great-great-grandson of French Revolutionary diplomat Citizen Genet and member of the famed American volunteer air squadron, the Lafayette Escadrille—not until autumn did large numbers of U.S. troops enter battle. Despite Allied impatience, Pershing hesitated to commit his green soldiers to full-scale battle. As it was, great numbers of troops were shipped over in British vessels and had to borrow French weapons. Disease continued to stalk U.S. forces. American reformers in the camps back home hoped to give the soldiers enough social armor before they reached France so that they would not be tempted by "sin" overseas, but the venereal-disease rate spiraled up. French premier Georges Clemenceau offered to supply the U.S. Army

First Division Troops Encounter German Gas Warfare, 1918.   Near Soissons, France,
U.S. soldiers attacked German lines through air contaminated with poisonous gas. The soldier in the
foreground, wounded by fire, tore off his gas mask. (The Bettmann Archive)

with licensed—health-inspected—prostitutes. When Secretary of War Newton
Baker received the Gallic proposal, he exclaimed: "For God's sake . . . don't
show this to the President or he'll stop the war."[76] The Wilson administration reduced the venereal-disease problem through prevention programs and the threat of
court-martial.

By early 1918 the Allies had become mired in a murderous strategy of throw-
ing ground forces directly at other ground forces. German troops were mauling
Italian forces, and the French army was still suffering from mutinies of the year before. In March, Germany forced Russia out of the war in the draconian Brest-
Litovsk Treaty. President Wilson declared in April that Americans must employ
"Force, Force to the utmost, Force without stint or limit, the righteous and triumphant Force which shall make Right the law of the world, and cast every selfish dominion down in the dust."[77] U.S. soldiers soon trooped into battle.

In March the German armies, swollen by forty divisions from the Russian
front, launched a great offensive. Allied forces retreated, and by late May the
kaiser's soldiers encamped near the Marne River less than fifty miles from Paris.
Saint-Mihiel, Belleau Wood, Cantigny, Château-Thierry—French sites where
U.S. soldiers shed their blood—soon became household words for Americans. In

June at Château-Thierry the doughboys dramatically stopped a German advance. From May through September 1918 more than 1 million American troops went to France—2 million by the November armistice. In mid-July the Allies launched a counteroffensive; nine American divisions fought fiercely near Château-Thierry, helping to lift the German threat from Paris. In the Meuse-Argonne offensive (begun in late September), more than 1 million American soldiers joined French and British units to penetrate the crumbling German lines. The influx of American men and matériel decided the outcome of World War I. "The American infantry in the Argonne [Forest] won the war," German marshal Paul von Hindenburg later commented.[78]

On October 4, as American soldiers fought in the thick Argonne Forest, the German chancellor asked Wilson for an armistice. German troops had mutinied; revolution and riots plagued German cities; Bulgaria had left the war in September. Then Turkey dropped out in late October, and Austria-Hungary surrendered on November 3. Germany had no choice but to seek terms. The kaiser fled to Holland. On November 11, in a railroad car in the Compiègne Forest, German representatives capitulated. In the sports vernacular of the day, the *Rochester Post-Express* concluded that the "trouble with this war game was that it ran into extra innings and Germany had no relief pitcher or pinchhitters."[79]

WILSON IMAGINES A BETTER FUTURE: THE FOURTEEN POINTS AND THE PEACE CONFERENCE

During the combat, President Wilson had begun to explain his plans for the peace. He trumpeted his message of a "peace without victory" most dramatically in his "Fourteen Points" speech before Congress on January 8, 1918. The first five points promised an "open" world after the war, a world distinguished by "open covenants, openly arrived at," freedom of navigation on the seas, equal trade opportunity and the removal of tariffs, reduction of armaments, and an end to colonialism. Points six through thirteen called for self-determination for national minorities in Europe. Point fourteen stood paramount: a "general association of nations" to ensure "political independence and territorial integrity to great and small states alike."[80] His Fourteen Points, joined by later elaborations, signaled a generous, nonpunitive postwar settlement. Pacifists felt like they had been "sent up into the very heaven of internationalism."[81] The Fourteen Points served too as effective American propaganda against revenge-fed Allied aims and Russian Bolshevik appeals for European revolution.

Leaders in France, Britain, and Italy feared that Wilson would deny them the spoils of war. In 1915 the Allies had signed secret treaties carving up German territories, including colonies in Africa and Asia. Nursing deep war wounds and dreaming of imperial expansion at Germany's expense, the Allies did not appreciate the "modern St. George," as the publicist Herbert Croly depicted Wilson, or his attempts to slay the "dragons of reaction" in Europe.[82] In view of the comparative wartime losses, Europeans believed that Wilson "had bought his seat at the peace table at a discount."[83] When, in September and October 1918, Wilson exchanged notes with Germany and Austria-Hungary about an armistice, the Allied powers expressed strong reservations about the Fourteen Points. General Tasker Howard Bliss, the American representative on the Supreme War Council (established in fall 1917 to coordinate the Allied war effort), recognized the Allied thirst for revenge: "I am beginning to despair that the war will accomplish more than the abolition of *German* militarism while leaving *European* militarism as rampant as ever."[84] To counter the Allied assault on the Fourteen Points, Edward House and Wilson hinted that the United States might negotiate a separate peace with the Central Powers. House further warned that the president might go before Congress and publicize the exploitative Allied war aims. Also facing possible economic coercion in the form of reduced American shipments to Europe, London, Paris, and Rome reluctantly agreed, in the armistice of November, to begin peace negotiations on the basis of the Fourteen Points.

Wilson, at the peak of his diplomatic career, relished his opportunity. "Never . . . was the world in such plastic state," one Wilsonian adviser explained.[85] The war had been won by the infusion of American arms, and the United States was about to claim a major role in deciding future international relations. The pictures of dying men dangling from barbed wire fences and the battle-shock victims who staggered home persuaded many Americans of the need to prevent another conflagration. Wilson's call for a just peace commanded the backing of countless foreigners as well. Italians hoisted banners reading *Dio di Pace* ("God of Peace") and *Redentore dell' Humanità* ("Redeemer of Humanity") to welcome Wilson to Europe.

The president weakened his position even before he reached the peace conference. Against much advice he decided to go to Paris to conduct the meetings. Congressional leaders wanted him to stay home to handle domestic problems. Lansing feared that in the day-to-day conference bickering Wilson would lose his exalted image. The president would have only one vote, whereas from Washington he could symbolically marshal the votes of humankind. Wilson retorted that distance contributes to confusion and that his presence would prevent an Allied retreat from the Fourteen Points. The president rejected the apparently sounder advice that he open the conference, engage in preliminary discussions, and then exit, leaving the daily quarreling to American diplomats. No, this would be Wilson's show.

Domestic politics soon set Wilson back. In October 1918, Wilson "hurled a brick into a beehive" by asking Americans to return a Democratic Congress loyal to him.[86] Anything less, he said, would be read abroad as a repudiation of his leadership and ideas. Partisan Republicans, resenting Wilson's attempt to identify himself and the Democratic party with the well-being of the nation, proceeded to capture the November election and majorities in both houses of Congress; now they would sit in ultimate judgment of Wilson's peacemaking. European leaders, some of them fresh from political victories, may have agreed with Theodore Roosevelt that Wilson's stature had been seriously diminished. The president also made the political mistake of not appointing either an important Republican or a senator to the American Peace Commission. Wilson, House, and Lansing sat on it; so did General Bliss and Henry White, a seasoned diplomat and nominal Republican. One editor criticized the members as a handpicked group tied to the president:[87]

Name	Occupation	Representing
Woodrow Wilson	President	Himself
Robert Lansing	Sec. of State	The Executive
Henry White	None	Nobody
Edward M. House	Scout	The Executive
Tasker H. Bliss	Soldier	The Commander in Chief

Wilson also failed to consult with the Senate Foreign Relations Committee before he departed for Paris. Some concessions to his political opposition, and to senatorial prerogatives in foreign affairs, might have smoothed the path later for his peace treaty.

On December 4, with great fanfare, Wilson departed from New York harbor aboard the *George Washington*. He settled into a quiet voyage, surrounded by advisers and nearly 2,000 reports produced by "The Inquiry," a group of scholars who for more than a year had studied international problems likely to arise at the peace conference. Reports proliferated, but the administration had made few plans. In fact, Wilson's friends grew alarmed that the president continued to speak in vague terms and still had not produced a blueprint for the League of Nations. Landing in France December 13, Wilson soon claimed the limelight before appreciative audiences. Enthusiastic Paris crowds cheered him, and thousands in England and Italy greeted him with admiration verging on the religious. Wilson assumed that this

David Lloyd George (1863–1945).
The British prime minister grew annoyed with Wilson's pontificating lectures. (Sketch by Anthony Saris, American Heritage Publishing Company)

Georges Clemenceau (1841–1929). Auguste Rodin's bronze aptly conveys the formidable stature of "The Tiger" from France, eager for revenge against Germany. (The Rodin Museum, Philadelphia)

Wilson in Dover, England, 1919. Of Wilson's reception in Europe, the British historian Antony Lentin has written: "They expected a Prometheus, the Light of the World; and when eventually they understood that he was only a college professor, with an outer carapace of personal vanity and an inner fund of self-delusion, their disenchantment was bitter." (U.S. Signal Corps, National Archives)

generous outpouring meant that *his* peace plan was universally popular and that *he* had a missionary duty to carry it forward. He would soon discover that such "man-in-the-street" opinion and his relentless abstractions did not impress David Lloyd George, prime minister of Britain, French premier Georges Clemenceau, or Italian prime minister Vittorio Orlando, his protagonists at the peace conference.

Germany and Bolshevik Russia were excluded from the conference of January–May 1919, but thirty-two nations sent delegations, which essentially followed the lead of the "Big Four." Most of the sessions worked in secrecy, hardly befitting Wilson's first "point." Clemenceau resented Wilson's "sermonettes" and preferred to work with a more compliant Colonel House. "The old tiger [Clemenceau] wants the grizzly bear [Wilson] back in the Rocky Mountains before he starts tearing up the German Hog," Lloyd George commented on the contest between the two strong-willed leaders.[88] Lloyd George sought to build a strong France and to ensure German purchases of British exports. A fervent Italian nationalist, Orlando concerned himself primarily with issues that would enlarge Italian interests. These leaders distrusted American power and sought bigger empires. Lloyd George, who complained that the United States was bullying Europe, concluded that Wilson "was the most extraordinary compound . . . of the noble visionary, the implacable and unscrupulous partisan, the exalted idealist and the man of rather petty personal rancour."[89]

One of the thorniest issues at the conference was the disposition of colonies and the creation of new countries. Wilson had appealed for self-determination, but the belligerents had already signed secret treaties of conquest. After hard negotiating, the conferees mandated former German and Turkish colonies to the countries that had conquered them, to be loosely supervised under League of Nations auspices. Under the mandate system—a compromise between outright annexation and complete independence—France (with Syria and Lebanon) and Britain (with Iraq, Trans-Jordan, and Palestine) received parts of the Middle East. Japan acquired China's Shandong Province and Germany's Pacific islands. After Wilson's reluctant acceptance of the Shandong arrangement, the president lamented that "the settlement was the best that could be had out of a dirty past."[90] Outraged Chinese students in Beijing protested by launching the May Fourth Movement, an increasingly important anti-imperialist voice. France gained the demilitarization of the German Rhineland and a stake in the coal-rich Saar Basin. Italy annexed South Tyrol and Trieste from the collapsed Austro-Hungarian empire. Some 1,132,000 square miles changed hands. Newly independent countries also emerged from the disintegrating Austro-Hungarian empire: Austria, Czechoslovakia, Hungary, Poland, and Yugoslavia. The Allies further exploited nationalism to recognize a ring of hostile states already established around Bolshevik Russia: Finland, Estonia, Latvia, and Lithuania, all formerly part of the Russian empire (see map). The mandate system smacked of imperialism, in violation of the Fourteen Points, but the new states in Europe did fulfill Wilson's self-determination pledge. To assuage French fears of a revived Germany, Britain and the United States signed a security pact with France guaranteeing its border, but Wilson never submitted it for Senate ratification.

Reparations proved a knotty issue. The peace conference, recalled American adviser Bernard Baruch, dealt "with blood-raw passions still pulsing through people's veins."[91] The United States wanted a limited indemnity for Germany to

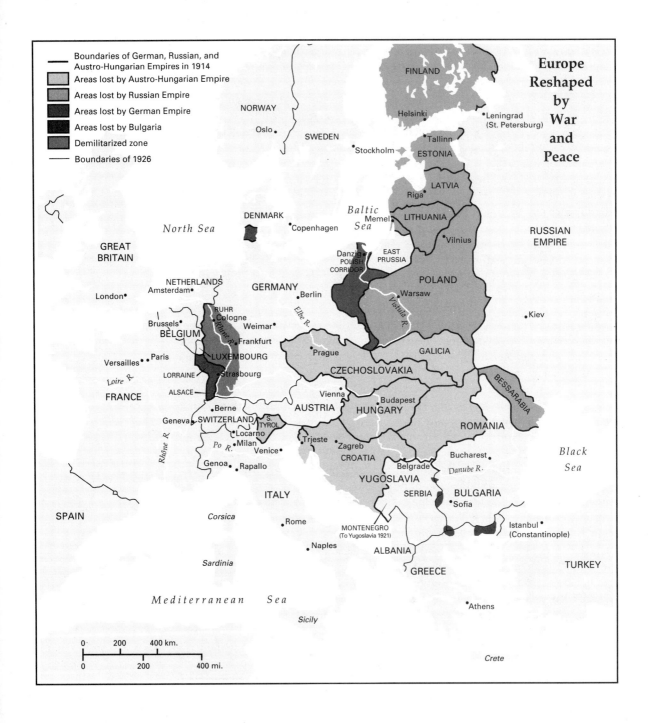

Boundaries of German, Russian, and Austro-Hungarian Empires in 1914
Areas lost by Austro-Hungarian Empire
Areas lost by Russian Empire
Areas lost by German Empire
Areas lost by Bulgaria
Demilitarized zone
Boundaries of 1926

Europe Reshaped by War and Peace

FINLAND
Helsinki
Leningrad (St. Petersburg)
NORWAY
Oslo
SWEDEN
Stockholm
Tallinn
ESTONIA
Baltic Sea
Riga
LATVIA
Memel
LITHUANIA
RUSSIAN EMPIRE
North Sea
DENMARK
Copenhagen
Vilnius
GREAT BRITAIN
Danzig
POLISH CORRIDOR
EAST PRUSSIA
POLAND
NETHERLANDS
GERMANY
Berlin
Warsaw
Vistula R.
London
Amsterdam
Kiev
RUHR
Cologne
Weimar
Elbe R.
Brussels
Rhine R.
BELGIUM
Frankfurt
Prague
GALICIA
Versailles
Paris
LUXEMBOURG
CZECHOSLOVAKIA
Loire R.
LORRAINE
Strasbourg
Vienna
BESSARABIA
FRANCE
ALSACE
Berne
AUSTRIA
Budapest
Geneva
SWITZERLAND
S. TYROL
HUNGARY
ROMANIA
Locarno
Milan
Trieste
Po R.
Venice
Zagreb
Rhône R.
Genoa
Rapallo
CROATIA
Bucharest
Black Sea
Belgrade
Danube R.
YUGOSLAVIA
ITALY
SERBIA
BULGARIA
SPAIN
Sofia
Corsica
Rome
MONTENEGRO (To Yugoslavia 1921)
Istanbul (Constantinople)
Naples
ALBANIA
Sardinia
GREECE
TURKEY
Mediterranean   Sea
Sicily
Athens
Crete

0   200   400 km.
0   200   400 mi.

avoid a harsh peace that might arouse long-term German resentment or debilitate the German economy and politics. "If we humiliate the German people and drive them too far," Wilson remarked before Versailles, "we shall destroy all form of government, and Bolshevism will take its place."[92] To cripple Germany, France pushed for a large bill of reparations. The conferees wrote a "war guilt clause," which held Germany responsible for all of the war's damages. Rationalizing that the League would ameliorate any excesses, Wilson gave in on both reparations and war guilt. "Logic! Logic! I don't give a damn for logic. I'm going to include pensions," he snapped.[93] The Reparations Commission in 1921 presented a hobbled Germany with a huge reparations bill of $33 billion, thereby destablizing international economic relations for more than a decade.

Wilson's primary concern, unlike that of the other participants, was the League of Nations. He directly supervised the drafting of the League's covenant. This charter provided for an influential council of five big powers (permanent) and representatives from smaller nations (by election) and an assembly of all nations for discussion. Wilson argued that the heart of the covenant was Article 10, a provision designed to curb aggression and war: "The Members of the League undertake to respect and preserve as against external aggression the territorial integrity and existing political independence of all Members of the League. In case of any such aggression or in case of any threat or danger of such aggression the Council shall advise upon the means by which this obligation shall be fulfilled."[94] Wilson succeeded in persuading the conferees to merge the League covenant and the peace terms in a package. The League charter, then, constituted the first 26 articles of a 440-article Treaty of Paris. Wilson deemed the League covenant the noblest part of all—"It is practical, and yet it is intended to purify, to rectify, to elevate."[95]

The Germans signed sullenly on June 28 in the elegant Hall of Mirrors at Versailles. By stripping Germany of 13 percent of its territory, 10 percent of its population, and all of its colonies, and by demanding reparations, the treaty humiliated the Germans without crushing them. In the historian Antony Lentin's words, the treaty had emerged from the conference "a witches' brew" with "too little Wilsonianism to appease, too little of Clemenceau to deter; enough of Wilson to provoke contempt, enough of Clemenceau to inspire hatred."[96] Embittered Germans vowed to get even. Indeed, when Wilson died on February 3, 1924, the Weimar Republic in Berlin refrained from issuing an official condolence and the German Embassy in Washington broke custom by not lowering its flag to halfmast.

PRINCIPLE, PERSONALITY, HEALTH, AND PARTISANSHIP: THE LEAGUE FIGHT

Wilson spent almost six months in Europe drawing up his plans for the postwar peace. From February 24 to March 14, he returned to the United States for executive business. On landing in Boston, he castigated critics. "America is the hope of the world," he lectured. Wilson would not let "minds that have no sweep beyond the nearest horizon" reject the American purpose of making people free. "I have fighting blood in me," he asserted.[97] Within days he met with the House Foreign Affairs Committee and Senate Foreign Relations Committee. Republicans peppered him with questions about the degree to which the covenant limited American sovereignty. Senator Frank Brandegee of Connecticut ridiculed Wilson's performance: "I feel as if I had been wandering with Alice in Wonderland and had had tea with the Mad Hatter."[98] In early March, Republican senator Henry Cabot Lodge of Massachusetts engineered a "Round Robin," a statement by thirty-nine senators (enough to deny the treaty a two-thirds vote) that questioned the League covenant and requested that the peace treaty and the covenant be acted on separately. Many of the signers feared that the League would limit U.S. freedom to act independently in international affairs.

A defiant Wilson sailed again for France, cocksure that the "blind and little provincial people" in America would not destroy his beloved League.[99] Still, he was politician enough, and stung enough, to seek changes in Paris. He did not think his senatorial opponents had much sense, but he knew they had votes. So he amended the covenant so that League members could refuse mandates, that the League had no jurisdiction over purely domestic issues, and that the Monroe Doctrine was safeguarded against League action. He would not alter Article 10. When he returned to the United States in July, criticism had not subsided; indeed, it had grown more insistent. Wilson submitted the 264-page Treaty of Paris to the Senate on July 10, with an address that resembled an evangelical sermon: "The stage is set, the destiny disclosed. It has come about by no plan of our conceiving, but by the hand of God, who led us into this way."[100] Asked by the French ambassador if he would accept senatorial "reservations" to the treaty, Wilson snapped: "I shall consent to nothing. The Senate must take its medicine."[101]

Both friends and foes wondered whether Wilson could have avoided the compromises, the land-grabbing, the daunting reparations bill, and the less than open diplomacy at the conference. Most historians agree that Wilson, against strong odds, gained a good percentage of his goals as outlined in the Fourteen Points. Self-determination for nationalities advanced as never before in Europe, and the League ranked as a notable achievement. But Wilson did compromise, especially when faced by formidable opposition like that thrown up by Clemenceau. During the conference, too, both Italy and Japan had threatened to walk out unless they realized some territorial goals. Still, Wilson had so built up a case for his ability to deliver an unselfish peace that when the conquerors' hard bargaining and harsh terms characterized the conference, observers could only conclude that the president had failed badly to live up to his own ideals. Through his millennial rhetoric, Wilson had misled. "How in our consciences are we to square the results with the promises?" asked the journalist Walter Lippmann.[102] Some critics said that he should have left Paris in protest, refusing to sign, or that he should have threatened the European powers with U.S. economic power by curbing postwar loans and trade. Believing ardently that the League, with Article 10, would rectify all, Wilson instead had accepted embarrassing compromises.

Wilson would not compromise at home, however. And he seldom provided systematic, technical analysis to treaty clauses. He simply expected the Senate dutifully to ratify his masterwork. Yet his earlier bypassing of that body and his own partisan speeches and self-righteousness ensured debate with influential critics. Progressive internationalists such as Senator George Norris thought that the League did not go far enough in reducing the possibility of war, that it was an ill-disguised device to continue great-power domination. Conservative senator Henry Cabot Lodge asked a key question: "Are you willing to put your soldiers and your sailors at the disposition of other nations?"[103] Senator James Reed of Missouri feared racial peril from a League initially comprising fifteen white nations and seventeen nations of "black, brown, yellow, and red races," which, he claimed, ranked low in "civilization" and high in "barbarism."[104]

Article 10 seemed to rattle everybody. Two questions stood out: Would League members be obligated to use force? Did the article mean that the status quo would always be upheld? The article did not require members to use force, but it implied they should. Senator William Borah complained that "I may be willing to help my neighbor . . . , but I do not want him placed in a position where he may decide for me when and how I shall act or to what extent I shall make sacrifice."[105] Article 10 also implied that territorial adjustments or rebellions, such as those in Ireland, India, and Egypt, would not be permitted. Senator Robert La Follette called the League an imperialist club, which would likely keep colonies in bondage by invoking Article 10. The article seemed too open-ended. Yet Wilson argued that without such a commitment to halt warmakers the League would become feeble. "In effect," the historian Roland N. Stromberg has noted, "Wilson and the Democrats wanted to accept an obligation that we might thereafter refuse, while Lodge and the Republicans wanted to refuse an obligation we might thereafter accept."[106]

Henry Cabot Lodge towered as Wilson's chief legislative obstacle. Chair of the Senate Foreign Relations Committee, nationalist-imperialist, author, Republican partisan, like Wilson a scholar in politics, Lodge packed his committee with anti-League senators, dragged out hearings for weeks, kept most Republicans together on treaty votes, and nurtured a personal animosity toward Wilson matched only by Wilson's detestation for Lodge. It is frankly unclear whether or not Lodge sought to kill the League in infancy; in any case, he attacked obliquely. He proposed "reservations" to the League covenant. Although in retrospect these reservations, intended to guard American sovereignty, do not appear to have been death blows to the League, at the time they stirred impassioned debate. They addressed the central question of American national interest—the degree to which the United States would limit its freedom of action, the degree to which the United States should engage in collective security. In fact, many of the fourteen reservations stated the obvious—that Congress would retain its constitutional role in foreign policy, for example. Others excluded the Monroe Doctrine from League oversight more explicitly than the covenant's version and denied the League jurisdiction over American domestic legislation such as immigration laws. The reservation that qualified Article 10 emphasized that the United States assumed no obligation to preserve the territorial integrity or political independence of another country unless authorized by Congress.

Henry Cabot Lodge (1850–1924). Wilson's partisan rival complained that the president's speeches in Europe "are all in the clouds and fine sentiments that lead nowhere." As for the League covenant, Lodge ridiculed its scholarship. "It might get by at Princeton," Wilson's alma mater, "but certainly not at Harvard," where the senator had earned a Ph.D. in history. (Library of Congress)

Woodrow Wilson After His Stroke. Recent scholarly assessments of medical evidence reveal that Wilson had a long history of neurological disease. Wilson remained in the White House after his massive stroke in October 1919, while his wife and doctor tried to keep secret the severity of his physical incapacity. Dr. Edwin A. Weinstein, who has studied the relationship among Wilson's health, personality, and decisionmaking, has noted that the president could not maintain his train of thought and was prone to bursts of temper. (Library of Congress)

The Senate divided into four groups. Wilson counted on about forty loyal Democrats called the Non-Reservationists. Another group, the Mild-Reservationists, led by Frank B. Kellogg, numbered about thirteen Republicans. The third faction, managed by Lodge, stood together as the Strong-Reservationists—some twenty Republicans and a few Democrats. The fourth group, consisting of sixteen Irreconcilables, ardently opposed the treaty with or without reservations. Most of them were Republicans, including La Follette, Norris, and Hiram Johnson of California.

While meeting individually with some twenty-three senators over two weeks, Wilson suffered a minor stroke on July 19, 1919. He thereafter rigidly refused to accept any reservations whatsoever. He argued that a treaty ratified with reservations would have to go back to another international conference for acceptance and every nation would then rush in with its pet reservations. This argument seemed hollow after the British announced that they would accept American reservations. In September 1919, noting that Lodge was hoping delay would sour the American people on the treaty, Wilson decided to dig his spade into the grass roots. He set off on a 10,000-mile train trip across the United States. Growing more exhausted with each day, suffering severe headaches and nighttime coughing spells, and showing signs of what the medical historian Bert E. Park has diagnosed as "dementia" from hypertension and cerebrovascular disease, Wilson pounded the podium in forty speeches.[107] He took the offensive, blasting his traducers as "absolute, contemptible quitters."[108] He denounced hyphenated Americans (a response to Irish- and German-American opposition to the treaty) and compared his critics to destructive Bolsheviks. He confused his audiences when he stated that Article 10 meant that the United States had a moral but not legal obligation to use armed force. But he also highlighted often neglected features of the covenant—for example, provisions for the arbitration of disputes and for an international labor conference to abolish child labor and install the eight-hour workday. On September 26, the day after he gave an impassioned speech in Pueblo, Colorado, he awoke to nausea and uncontrollable facial twitching. "I just feel as if I am going to pieces," he said.[109] When his doctor ordered him to cancel the rest of his trip, Wilson cried.

After Wilson returned to Washington, a massive stroke paralyzed his left side. Nearly dying, he lay flat in bed for six weeks and saw virtually no one except his wife and Dr. Cary Grayson. "The government," in the historian Arthur Walworth's terse phrase, "like its president, was paralyzed."[110] For months Mrs. Wilson ran her husband's political affairs, screening messages and banishing House and Lansing, among others, from presidential favor. According to the historian Robert H. Ferrell, Dr. Grayson, in January 1920, "took the courageous step of advising Wilson to resign, right then," but Mrs. Wilson managed to talk her husband out of it.[111] If the president had resigned, the Senate and Vice President James Marshall almost certainly would have reached some compromise agreement on admission to the League with reservations. As it was, Wilson's concentration hampered and his stubbornness accentuated by the stroke, he adamantly refused to change his all-or-nothing position.[112]

In November 1919, the Senate balloted on the complete treaty *with* reservations and rejected it, 39 to 55 (Irreconcilables and Non-Reservationists in the negative). Then it voted on the treaty *without* reservations and also rejected it, 38 to 53 (Irreconcilables and Reservationists in the negative). The president managed to keep loyal Democrats in line, forbidding them to accept any "reserved" treaty. In March 1920, another tally saw many Democrats break ranks to vote in favor of reservations. Still not enough, the treaty failed, 49 to 35, short of the two-thirds majority required for ratification. "It is dead," Wilson lamented to his cabinet. "Every morning I put flowers on its grave."[113] Still a fighter, he avowed that the election of 1920 would be a "solemn referendum" on the treaty. A multitude of other questions actually blurred the League issue in that campaign, and Warren G. Harding, who as a senator had supported reservations, promptly condemned the League after his election as president. In July 1921, Congress officially terminated the war, and in August, by treaty with Germany, the United States claimed as valid for itself the terms of the Treaty of Paris—exclusive of the League articles.

The memorable League fight had ended. The tragic denouement occurred because of political partisanship, personal animosities, senatorial resentment at having been slighted in the peacemaking, and disinterest and confusion in the public, which increasingly diverted its attention to the problem of readjusting to a peacetime economy. Progressive internationalists, many of them harassed by wartime restrictions on civil liberties and disappointed by Wilson's compromises with the imperial powers, no longer backed a president they thought reactionary. "THIS IS NOT PEACE," shouted a headline in *The New Republic*.[114] Then, of course, there was Wilson himself—stubborn, pontificating, combative, and increasingly ill. But for the "marked and almost grotesque accentuation" of personality traits resulting from Wilson's cerebrovascular disease, he might have conceded that the peace had imperfections.[115] He might have provided more careful analysis of a complicated document of 264 pages. He might have remembered when he first learned of the secret treaties. He might, further, have admitted that his opponents held a respectable intellectual position. Instead he chose an often shrill rhetoric and a rigid self-righteousness. Most important, he refused compromise because he saw the difference between himself and his critics as fundamental: whether it was in America's national interest to participate in collective security or seek safety unilaterally. In essence, then, traditional American nationalism and nonalignment, or unilateralism, decided the debate against Wilson.

Although the League came into being without the United States, none of the great powers wished to bestow significant authority on the new organization. Even if the United States had joined, it most likely would have acted outside the League's auspices, especially regarding its own imperialism in Latin America. No international association at that time could have outlawed war, dismantled empires, or scuttled navies. Wilson overshot reality in thinking that he could reform world politics through a new international body: Certainly the League represented a commendable restraint, but hardly a panacea for world peace.

RED SCARE ABROAD: BOLSHEVISM AND INTERVENTION IN RUSSIA

"Paris cannot be understood without Moscow," wrote Wilson's press secretary in France, Ray Stannard Baker.[116] Indeed, throughout the conference "[V. I.] Lenin looms always on the horizon to the East."[117] As he traveled to France aboard the *George Washington,* President Wilson complained about the "poison of Bolshevism."[118] Revolutionary and anticapitalist, the Bolsheviks, or Communists, threw fright into the leaders of Europe and America. At home and abroad the peacemakers battled the radical left. In the United States the Wilson administration trampled on civil liberties during an exaggerated "Red Scare," which sent innocent people to jail or deported them. The fluidity of events abroad, however, and the multiplicity of views among knowledgeable Americans and administration advisers led to a range of policy options—from recognizing and taming the Bolsheviks to overthrowing them. Wilson himself seemed to think that "the only way to kill Bolshevism is . . . to open all the doors to commerce."[119] Only belatedly and hesitantly did the president "cast in his lot" with the other powers in a futile attempt to destroy the new revolutionary regime.[120]

Most Americans applauded the Russian Revolution of March 1917, which toppled Tsar Nicholas II. Wilson himself viewed it as a thrust against autocracy, war, and imperialism. But when the moderate Provisional government under

"Comrade Lenin Sweeps the Globe Clean."   Vladimir Ilyich Lenin (1870–1924) is shown in this Bolshevik art as a revolutionary ridding the world of monarchs and capitalists. But Lenin also craved Western trade and investment to spur his nation's economic reconstruction. As he said in 1919: "We are decidedly for an economic understanding with America—with all countries, but especially with America." (By Mikhail Cheremnykh and Victor Deni in Mikhail Guerman, comp., *Art of the October Revolution,* Leningrad: Aurora Art Publishers, 1979)

ТОВ. ЛЕНИН ОЧИЩАЕТ ЗЕМЛЮ ОТ НЕЧИСТИ.

Alexander Kerensky fell to the radical Bolsheviks in October, Americans responded first with suspicion (the U.S. naval attaché predicted "another Reign of Terror") and then anger in March 1918 when the Bolsheviks signed the Brest-Litovsk Treaty with Germany.[121] The harsh peace forced the Russians to relinquish Ukraine and Finland, among other territories—a total of 1,267,000 square miles, 62,000,000 people, and one-third of Russia's best agricultural land. From the Bolshevik perspective, it was a necessary peace for a ruined nation. From the Allied point of view, the treaty meant a stab in the back, an end to the war's Eastern Front, and a victory for Germany. Some irate American officials began to think that the Bolsheviks were pro-German. Lenin's travel through Germany in early 1917, with the permission of German authorities, fed this mistaken notion.

Lenin actually treated the United States as a special, favored case, and he consistently sought accommodation with Washington. Described by the Red Cross official Raymond Robins as "heavy set, deliberate, always cool . . . , steadfast, patient, utterly courageous, fanatical and confident," Lenin (and other Soviet officials) held a series of cordial conversations from December 1917 to May 1918 with Robins, a de facto U.S. representative.[122] They reached agreements on food relief, purchase of strategic materials, and exemption of American corporations from Bolshevik nationalization decrees. Prior to Brest-Litovsk, Robins urged prompt recognition of the Bolshevik government to keep Russia in the war, but President Wilson paid more heed to Ambassador David Francis's prediction that the Bolshevik regime would soon collapse—a "corpse . . . so putrid that it should be removed in the interest of public health."[123]

Despite a warning from U.S. consul Felix Cole that "we can make more friends . . . by the proper use of sugar, boots, fishnets and machinery," Wilson finally sent troops to northern Russia at Archangel in June 1918.[124] Ordered to avoid military action in the Russian civil war, they inevitably cooperated with British and French forces in attempts to roll back Bolshevik influence. Wilson said publicly that he authorized the expedition only to prevent German seizure of military supplies and a railroad, but he privately hoped to cripple the Red Army. Some 5,000 American troops eventually participated, many comprising the 339th "Polar Bear" Infantry Regiment from Michigan. Two hundred and twenty-two American soldiers died on Russian soil. They suffered through a bitter winter of fifty-below-zero temperatures. Their morale sagged and mutiny threatened. In December 1918, Senator Hiram Johnson of California introduced a resolution to withdraw American troops from Russia. It failed by one vote. U.S. soldiers did not leave Russia until June 1919.

Wilson always said he "hoped to avoid intervention, even the appearance of intervening in Russian affairs," preferring to draw the Bolsheviks peacefully into a new world order.[125] But pressure from the deeply anticommunist French and British and expansionist Japanese and his own anti-Bolshevism inclined him to send another expedition, this time to Siberia, where many envisioned the growth of a non-Bolshevik Russian bastion. In July he approved the expedition, later officially explaining to the American people that he was sending the troops (eventually numbering 10,000) to rescue a group of 70,000 Czechs stranded in Russia. Organized earlier as part of the Tsarist Russian army to fight for a Czech homeland in Austria-Hungary, the Czech legion in 1918 was battling Bolsheviks along the Trans-Siberian Railroad in an effort to reach Vladivostok and possible transportation to the Western Front. Wilson's avowed purpose of evacuating the Czech legion derived also from his "friendly feelings" for Professor Thomas Masaryk and Czechoslovakia's independence, which Wilson soon recognized in October.[126]

Wilson's official explanation evades the larger question of his opposition to Bolshevism. Anti-Bolshevik or not, Wilson's actions became so, for the Czech legion was essentially at war with Lenin's forces. Once Wilson found it impossible to evacuate the Czechs in time to fight in Europe, he reluctantly bowed to Allied pressure and gave support to the anti-Bolshevik White Russian leader Admiral A. V. Kolchak in the hope that he could form a pro-Western constitutional government. Despite money and supplies from the Allies, Kolchak faltered and his armies were routed before they could reach Moscow in June 1919. American troops in Siberia finally withdrew in early 1920 after thirty-six deaths.

At the Paris Peace Conference, the victors tried to isolate what they considered a revolutionary contagion. Yet they vacillated between trying to strangle Bolshevism and doing business with it. Excluding the Soviets from Versailles, of course, ran counter to Wilson's desire for world unity and belied his pledge of self–determination. "Bolshevism is gaining ground everywhere," Colonel House noted in his diary. "We are sitting on an open powder magazine and some day a spark may ignite it."[127] The organization of the Third International in Moscow in early

A. Mitchell Palmer (1872–1936). When U.S. troops were intervening in Bolshevik Russia, Wilson's attorney general, A. Mitchell Palmer, was chasing suspected radicals at home. An architect of the "Red Scare," Palmer believed that the "blaze of revolution" was "eating its way into the homes of the American workmen, its sharp tongues of revolutionary heat . . . licking the altars of the churches, leaping into the belfry of the school bell, crawling into the sacred corners of American homes, burning up the foundations of society." In January 1920, the "Palmer Raids" against meeting halls and homes, without search warrants, put 4,000 people in jail. The attorney general's callous disregard for elementary civil liberties turned even many conservatives against his exaggerations of a communist threat. (Library of Congress)

1919 alarmed postwar leaders, as did communist Bela Kun's successful revolution in Hungary in March 1919, which lasted only until August. At Versailles, the conferees granted territory to Russia's neighbors (Poland, Rumania, and Czechoslovakia) and recognized the nations of Finland, Estonia, Latvia, and Lithuania as a ring of unfriendly states around Russia. During the conference, besides the military interventions, the Allies imposed a strict economic blockade on Russia, sent aid to the White forces, negotiated fruitlessly with the Soviet government about food relief, and extended relief assistance to Austria and Hungary to stem political unrest.

Even though Wilson found the Soviets distasteful for their revolutionary, anticapitalist, anticlerical, authoritarian program, he never settled on a definitive, workable policy to co-opt or smash Bolshevism. The president allowed subordinates and circumstances to determine U.S. policy toward Russia. His growing estrangement at Versailles from Colonel House, who served as a conduit for pro-Soviet liberals, meant that the interventionist Allies and the rabidly anti-Bolshevik Secretary Lansing exerted greater influence.

Wilson's one serious effort to end the civil war in Russia through diplomacy came in January 1919 when he invited the warring groups to meet on Prinkipo (Prince's) Island in the Sea of Marmara off the Turkish coast. The Bolsheviks cautiously accepted the invitation, but the anti-Bolsheviks rejected any meeting. Next, in February, House helped arrange a trip by William C. Bullitt, a member of the American delegation at Versailles, and Lincoln Steffens, radical muckraking journalist, to Russia. Wilson envisioned a fact-finding mission. The ambitious Bullitt, however, negotiated a proposal whereby the Allies would withdraw their troops, suspend military aid to the White forces, and lift the economic blockade. If the Allies accepted these terms, the Soviet government promised to initiate a cease-fire in the civil war and permit its opponents to hold the territories they occupied. Believing the Moscow government firmly established, Bullitt and Steffens returned to Paris convinced that their agreement would satisfy all parties. Lloyd George squelched it; Wilson ignored it. Bullitt, already disgusted by Wilson's compromises with the Allies at Paris, resigned in protest.

The Allied counterrevolution proved costly. "It intensified the civil war and sent thousands of Russians to their deaths," the British official Bruce Lockhart later wrote. "Its direct effect was to provide the Bolsheviks with a cheap victory, . . . and to galvanize them into a strong and ruthless organism."[128] Although the Bolshevik emissary Ludwig Martens laid the foundations for future Soviet-American trade during the height of the Red Scare, Kremlin leaders nurtured long memories. "Never have any of our soldiers been on American soil," Premier Nikita S. Khrushchev lectured Americans as late as 1959, "but your soldiers were on Russian soil."[129] At a time when Soviet leaders waged a life-or-death struggle against internal enemies, they had to resist a foreign invasion. The blatant Allied tactics ultimately backfired, as the Bolsheviks capitalized on the nationalistic feelings aroused by foreign troops on Russian land. Wilson's dream of a cooperative and harmonious world received another blow. William Bullitt resolved to lie on the beaches of the Mediterranean and "watch the world go to hell."[130] "He went. And it did."[131]

SHARING IN THE DISASTER: LEGACIES OF A GLOBAL WAR

More than 116,000 American soldiers died in World War I, and the conflict cost the U.S. government over $30 billion. A third of the figure was paid through taxes; the other two-thirds represented borrowed money, which postwar generations would have to pay back. If one counts the long-term expense of veterans' benefits, the cost to the United States probably equaled three times the immediate direct costs. The price and consequences of World War I can be reckoned in other ways. What President Dwight D. Eisenhower would later call the "military-industrial complex" had its origins in a high degree of government-business cooperation during that war; economic decisionmaking for the nation became centralized as never before; and the increased application of efficient methods in manufacturing contributed to American economic power.[132]

In foreign affairs, the White House, under Wilson's heady leadership, assumed more authority in initiating policy and controlling execution. The State Department read diplomatic messages after Wilson had typed them on his own machine. Wilson bypassed Congress on a number of occasions, failing even to consult that body, for example, about the Fourteen Points, the goals at Versailles, and the intervention in the Russian civil war. He acted, according to his biographer Arthur S. Link, "like a divine-right monarch in the conduct of foreign relations."[133] The Senate finally rebelled by rejecting the League of Nations, but that negative decision did not undercut the trend of growing presidential power in the making of foreign policy.

The era of World War I also witnessed domestic events that impinged on foreign affairs: racial conflict, evidenced by twenty-five race riots in 1919; suppression of civil liberties under the Espionage and Sedition Acts, by which people who dissented from the war were silenced; the stunting of radical commentary (Socialist party leader Eugene Debs went to jail for opposing the war) and hence the imposition of coercive consensus; and the emasculation of the reform impulse. Wars tend to demand conformity at home because leaders insist on patriotism and commitment to the "crusade." Those who question the foreign venture often face ostracism and harassment.

World War I took the lives of some 14,663,400 people—8 million soldiers and 6.6 million civilians (flu pandemic victims not included). Russia led with 3.7 million dead; Germany followed with 2.6 million; then came France with 1.4 million, Austria-Hungary with 950,000, and Britain with 939,000. One out of every two French males between the ages of twenty and thirty-two (in 1914) died during the war. It had been a total war, involving whole societies, not merely their armies. Never before had a war left the belligerents so exhausted, so battered. New destructive weapons made their debut—tanks, airplanes, poison gas, the Big Bertha gun, and submarines. The journalist Hanson Baldwin has noted that World War I "provided a preview of the Pandora's box of evils that the linkage of science

"We Are Making a New World."   The British painter Paul Nash rendered this gloomy commentary on the devastation wrought by World War I. (Imperial War Museum, London)

with industry in the service of war was to mean."[134] Many Americans turned away in disgust, and their desire to avoid another major war and foreign entanglements became strong after the European conflict. Captain Harry S. Truman of Battery D of the 129th Field Artillery Regiment claimed that most soldiers "don't give a whoop (to put it mildly) whether Russia has a Red Government or no government and if the King of the Lollipops wants to slaughter his subjects or his Prime Minister it's all the same to us."[135] Disillusioned intellectuals such as Ernest Hemingway and John Dos Passos mocked the carthaginian peace. E. M. Remarque's *All Quiet on the Western Front* (1929) captured the antiwar mood: "A hospital alone shows what war is."[136]

World War I stacked the cards for the future by bequeathing an unstable international system. Empires broke up—the Turkish, Austro-Hungarian, German, and Russian—creating new and weak nations. The Europe-oriented international order of the turn of the century fragmented and reconfigured to include several new states in central and eastern Europe. Nationalists in Asia, such as Mahatma Gandhi in British-dominated India and Ho Chi Minh in French-controlled Indochina, set goals of national liberation based in part upon Wilson's ideal of self-determination. Sun Yat-sen's Chinese revolution jarred foreign interests, while Japan envisioned hegemony in Asia. In Latin America, prewar European economic ties withered, inviting the United States to expand its interests there, where nationalists resented the greater North American presence. The rise of Bolshevism in Russia and the hostility it aroused around the world made an already fluid international system even more so. Because of fear of a revived Germany, leaders tried to strip it of power, creating bitter resentments among the German people. Because the victors faced reconstruction problems at home, they tagged Germany with a huge reparations bill that would disorient world economics. Nobody seemed happy with the postwar settlement; many would attempt to recapture lost opportunities or to redefine the terms. Wilsonianism enjoyed but a brief prominence; the high-minded lessons Wilson sought to teach went unlearned. World War I had, surely, created as many problems as it had solved.

During World War I the United States became the world's leading economic power. As Wilson confidently put it: "The financial leadership will be ours. The industrial primacy will be ours. The commercial advantage will be ours. And the other countries of the world . . . are looking to us for leadership and direction."[137] During the war years, to meet the need for raw materials, American companies expanded operations in developing nations. Goodyear went into the Dutch East Indies for rubber, Swift and Armour reached into South America, tin interests tapped Bolivia, copper companies penetrated Chile, and oil firms sank new wells in Latin America and gained new concessions in the Middle East. Washington encouraged this economic expansion by building up the merchant marine, which by 1919 had grown 60 percent larger than its prewar size. By 1920, the United States produced about 40 percent of the world's coal and 50 percent of its pig iron.

Because the U.S. government and American citizens loaned heavily to the Allies during the war, the nation shifted from a debtor to a creditor, with Wall Street replacing London as the world's financial center. Whereas before the war Americans owed foreigners some $3 billion, after the conflict foreigners owed Americans and the U.S. government about $13 billion ($10 billion of this figure represented governments' debts). Americans had devised plans to seize the apparent economic opportunities given them by the war—the Edge Act to permit foreign branch banks, and the Webb-Pomerene Act to allow trade associations to continue to combine for export trading without fear of antitrust action, for example—but a key question remained: How could Europeans pay back their debt to the United States? The answer lay somewhere in a complicated tangle of loans, reparations, tariffs, and world trade. "We are on the eve of a commercial war of the severest sort," predicted Wilson in early 1920.[138]

Economic disorder and political instability thus became the twin legacies of global war worked against this result, Wilson, who warned Congress in August 1919: "We must face the fact that . . . in saving Europe, she [United States] will save herself. . . . Europe is our biggest customer. We must keep her going or thousands of our shops and scores of our mines must close. There is no such thing as letting her go to ruin without ourselves sharing in the disaster."[139] More than most Americans, Woodrow Wilson understood global interdependence.

FURTHER READING FOR THE PERIOD 1914–1920

Most books cited in the first paragraph of "Further Reading for the Period 1900–1914" in Chapter 2 also explore events and personalities in the era of World War I. Other general works include John W. Chambers, *The Tyranny of Change* (1992); Ellis W. Hawley, *The Great War and the Search for a Modern Order* (1992); Bernadotte E. Schmitt and Harold C. Vedeler, *The World in the Crucible, 1914–1919* (1984); and David Stevenson, *The First World War and International Politics* (1988).

For Woodrow Wilson and his foreign-policy views, consult Edward H. Buehrig, ed., *Wilson's Foreign Policy in Perspective* (1957); Kendrick A. Clements, *The Presidency of Woodrow Wilson* (1990) and *Woodrow Wilson* (1987); John Milton Cooper, Jr., *The Warrior and the Priest* (1983); Thomas J. Knock, *To End All Wars* (1992); Arthur S. Link, *Wilson* (1960–1965) and *Woodrow Wilson: Revolution, War, and Peace* (1979); and Jan Willem Schulte Nordholt, *Woodrow Wilson* (1991).

Wilson's health problems and their relationship to decisionmaking are examined in Robert H. Ferrell, *Ill-Advised* (1992) and Edwin A. Weinstein, *Woodrow Wilson: A Medical and Psychological Biography* (1981). See also the essays by Dr. Bert E. Park in various volumes of Arthur S. Link et al., eds., *The Papers of Woodrow Wilson,* and Park's *Ailing, Aging, and Addicted* (1993) and *The Impact of Illness on World Leaders* (1986).

Central actors in the period's drama are presented in LeRoy Ashby, *William Jennings Bryan* (1987); Kendrick A. Clements, *William Jennings Bryan* (1982); Paolo Coletta, *William Jennings Bryan* (1956–1969); John Milton Cooper, Jr., *Walter Hines Page* (1977); Ross Gregory, *Walter Hines Page* (1970); Daniel M. Smith, *Robert Lansing and American Neutrality* (1958); Donald Smythe, *Pershing* (1986); Ronald Steel, *Walter Lippmann and the American Century* (1981); David P. Thelen, *Robert M. La Follette and the Insurgent Spirit* (1976); and William C. Widenor, *Henry Cabot Lodge* (1980).

For European questions and the neutrality issue on the road to U.S. entry into World War I, see Thomas A. Bailey and Paul B. Ryan, *The Lusitania Disaster* (1975); Henry Blumenthal, *Illusion and Reality in Franco-American Diplomacy, 1914–1945* (1986); John W. Coogan, *The End of Neutrality* (1981); Patrick Devlin, *Too Proud to Fight* (1975); Robert H. Ferrell, *Woodrow Wilson and World War I* (1985); Ross Gregory, *The Origins of American Intervention in the First World War* (1971); and Ernest R. May, *The World War and American Isolation, 1914–1917* (1959).

The German-American relationship is spotlighted in Reinhard R. Doerries, *Imperial Challenge* (1989); Manfred Jonas, *The United States and Germany* (1984); Hans-Jürgen Schröder, ed., *Confrontation and Cooperation* (1993); and Barbara Tuchman, *The Zimmermann Telegram* (1958).

The Anglo-American relationship is featured in Kathleen Burk, *Britain, America, and the Sinews of War, 1914–1918* (1985); G. R. Conyne, *Woodrow Wilson: British Perspectives, 1912–21* (1992); and Joyce G. Williams, *Colonel House and Sir Edward Grey* (1984).

For the peace movement, see works cited in Chapter 2 and Charles DeBenedetti, ed., *Peace Heroes in Twentieth-Century America* (1986); Allen F. Davis, *American Heroine* (1974) (Jane Addams); and Barbara S. Kraft, *The Peace Ship* (1978).

America's preparedness and warmaking experiences are discussed in John W. Chambers, *To Raise an Army* (1987); J. Garry Clifford, *The Citizen Soldiers* (1972); Edward M. Coffman, *The War to End All Wars* (1968); Henry A. DeWeerd, *President Wilson Fights His War* (1968); Kenneth J. Hagan, *This People's Navy* (1991); Thomas C. Leonard, *Above the Battle* (1978); David F. Trask, *The AEF and Coalition Warmaking, 1917–1918* (1993), *Captains & Cabinets: Anglo-American Naval Relations, 1917–1918* (1980), and *The United States in the Supreme War Council* (1961); and David R. Woodward, *Trial by Friendship: Anglo-American Relations, 1917–1918* (1993).

For the wartime homefront, civil-liberties issues, and propaganda, see George T. Blakey, *Historians on the Homefront: American Propagandists for the Great War* (1970); Allan M. Brandt, *No Magic Bullet* (1985) (venereal disease); Alfred W. Crosby, *America's Forgotten Pandemic: The Influenza of 1918* (1989); Carol S. Gruber, *Mars and Minerva: World War I and the Uses of Higher Learning in America* (1975); David M. Kennedy, *Over*

Here: The First World War and American Society (1980); Seward W. Livermore, *Politics Is Adjourned* (1966); Paul L. Murphy, *World War I and the Origin of Civil Liberties* (1979); Horace C. Peterson and Gilbert C. Fite, *Opponents of War, 1917–1918* (1957); Richard Polenberg, *Fighting Faiths* (1987); Ronald Schaffer, *America in the Great War* (1991); John A. Thompson, *Reformers and War* (1986); Stephen Vaughn, *Hold Fast the Inner Lines* (1980) (Committee on Public Information); and Neil Wynn, *From Progressivism to Prosperity* (1986).

The Versailles peacemaking and debate over the League are discussed in Lloyd E. Ambrosius, *Wilsonian Statecraft* (1991) and *Woodrow Wilson and the American Diplomatic Tradition* (1987); Thomas A. Bailey, *Woodrow Wilson and the Lost Peace* (1944) and *Woodrow Wilson and the Great Betrayal* (1945); Inga Floto, *Colonel House in Paris* (1973); Lawrence E. Gelfand, *The Inquiry* (1963); Warren F. Kuehl, *Seeking World Order* (1969); Antony Lentin, *Lloyd George, Woodrow Wilson, and the Guilt of Germany* (1985); Herbert F. Margulies, *The Mild Reservationists* (1989); Keith Nelson, *Victors Divided: America and the Allies in Germany, 1918–1923* (1973); Stuart I. Rochester, *American Liberal Disillusionment in the Wake of World War I* (1977); Klaus Schwabe, *Woodrow Wilson, Revolutionary Germany, and Peacemaking, 1918–1919* (1985); Alan Sharp, *The Versailles Settlement* (1991); Ralph A. Stone, *The Irreconcilables* (1970); Marc Trachenberg, *Reparations in World Politics* (1986); and Arthur Walworth, *America's Moment, 1918* (1977) and *Wilson and His Peacemakers* (1986).

The U.S. response to Bolshevism, intervention in Russia, and the Red Scare are investigated in Stanley Coben, *A. Mitchell Palmer* (1963); John Lewis Gaddis, *Russia, the Soviet Union, and the United States* (1990); Lloyd Gardner, *Safe for Democracy* (1984); George F. Kennan, *Russia Leaves the War* (1956) and *The Decision to Intervene* (1958); Linda Killen, *The Russian Bureau* (1983); N. Gordon Levin, Jr., *Woodrow Wilson and World Politics* (1968); Arthur S. Link, ed., *Woodrow Wilson and a Revolutionary World, 1913–1921* (1982); Arno Mayer, *Politics and Diplomacy of Peacemaking* (1967); David W. McFadden, *Alternative Paths: Soviets and Americans, 1917–1920* (1993); Robert K. Murray, *Red Scare* (1955); William Pencak, *For God and Country: The American Legion, 1919–1941* (1989); Benjamin D. Rhodes, *The Anglo-American Winter War with Russia, 1918–1919* (1988); Neil V. Salzman, *Reform and Revolution: The Life and Times of Raymond Robins* (1991); John Thompson, *Russia, Bolshevism, and the Versailles Peace* (1966); and Betty Miller Unterberger, *America's Siberian Expedition* (1956) and *The United States, Revolutionary Russia, and the Rise of Czechoslovakia* (1989).

U.S. economic expansion abroad during the war is studied in Burton I. Kaufman, *Efficiency and Expansion* (1974); Emily S. Rosenberg, *World War I and the Growth of United States Predominance in Latin America* (1987); and Jeffrey J. Safford, *Wilsonian Maritime Diplomacy, 1913–1921* (1978).

Also see the General Bibliography, Richard Dean Burns, ed., *Guide to American Foreign Relations Since 1700* (1983), and the following notes.

NOTES TO CHAPTER 3

1. Quoted in Thomas A. Bailey and Paul B. Ryan, *The Lusitania Disaster* (New York: The Free Press, 1975), p. 81.
2. Quoted in Edward Robb Ellis, *Echoes of Distant Thunder* (New York: Coward, McCann & Geoghegan, 1975), p. 195.
3. Quoted in Bailey and Ryan, Lusitania *Disaster,* p. 94.
4. Quoted *ibid.,* p. 82.
5. Quoted *ibid.,* p. 133.
6. Quoted in C. L. Droste and W. H. Tantum, eds., *The Lusitania Case* (Riverside, Conn.: 7 C's Press, 1972), p. 172.
7. Quoted in Burton J. Hendrick, *Life and Letters of Walter Hines Page* (Garden City, N.Y.: Doubleday, Page, 1922–1925; 3 vols.), *II,* 2.
8. William Jennings Bryan and Mary B. Bryan, *Memoirs* (Chicago: John C. Winston, 1925), pp. 398–399.
9. Quoted in William Harbaugh, *The Life and Times of Theodore Roosevelt* (New York: Oxford University Press, 1975), p. 448.
10. John Milton Cooper, Jr., *The Warrior and the Priest* (Cambridge, Mass.: Harvard University Press, 1983), p. 288.
11. R. S. Baker and W. E. Dodd, eds., *Public Papers of Woodrow Wilson* (New York: Harper & Brothers, 1926; 2 vols.), *I,* 321.
12. Quoted in August Heckscher, *Woodrow Wilson* (New York: Charles Scribner's Sons, 1991), p. 365.
13. *Foreign Relations, 1915, Supplement* (Washington, D.C.: Government Printing Office, 1928), p. 396.

14. Quoted in Richard R. Doerries, *Imperial Challenge* (Chapel Hill: University of North Carolina Press, 1989), p. 105.
15. David F. Houston, *Eight Years with Wilson's Cabinet* (Garden City, N.Y.: Doubleday, Page, 1926; 2 vols.), I, 137.
16. Quoted in LeRoy Ashby, *William Jennings Bryan* (Boston: Twayne, 1987), p. 160.
17. Quoted *ibid.*, p. 161.
18. Quoted in Doerries, *Imperial Challenge*, p. 111.
19. Bailey and Ryan, Lusitania *Disaster,* p. 340.
20. Robert Lansing, *War Memoirs* (Indianapolis: Bobbs-Merrill, 1935), p. 128.
21. Ray S. Baker quoted in Arthur S. Link et al., eds., *The Papers of Woodrow Wilson* (Princeton: Princeton University Press, 1989), LXI, 383.
22. Quoted in Rohan Butler, "The Peace Settlement of Versailles, 1918–1933," in C. L. Mowat, ed., *The New Cambridge Modern History,* vol. XII, (Cambridge: Cambridge University Press, 1968), p. 214.
23. Quoted in Jan Willem Schulte Nordholt, *Woodrow Wilson* (Berkeley: University of California Press, 1991), p. 133.
24. Quoted in Barbara Tuchman, *The Guns of August* (New York: Dell, [1962], 1963), p. 91.
25. Quoted in Hendrick, *Life and Letters, I,* 310.
26. Baker and Dodd, *Public Papers, I,* 157–159.
27. Cecil Spring-Rice quoting Wilson in G. R. Conyne, *Woodrow Wilson* (New York: St. Martin's Press, 1992), p. 44.
28. Quoted in Tuchman, *Guns of August,* p. 349.
29. Quoted *ibid.*, p. 153.
30. *Life* quoted in Mark Sullivan, *Our Times* (New York: Charles Scribner's Sons, 1926–1937; 6 vols.), V, 59.
31. Quoted in Ray Stannard Baker, *Woodrow Wilson* (New York: Doubleday, Doran, 1927–1939; 8 vols.), V, 175.
32. Quoted in Kathleen Burk, *Britain, America, and the Sinews of War, 1914–1918* (Boston: Allen & Unwin, 1985), p. 65.
33. Quoted in Paul Birdsall, "Neutrality and Economic Pressures, 1914–1917," *Science and Society, III* (Spring 1939), 221.
34. Burk, *Sinews of War,* p. 5.
35. *Foreign Relations, 1915, Supplement,* p. 99.
36. Frederick Dixon quoting Wilson in Conyne, *Wilson,* p. 51.
37. Quoted in Arthur S. Link, *Woodrow Wilson and the Progressive Era, 1910–1917* (New York: Harper & Row, 1954), p. 203.
38. French report quoted in Joyce G. Williams, *Colonel House and Sir Edward Grey* (Lanham, Md.: University Press of America, 1984), p. 83.
39. Quoted in Arthur S. Link, *Wilson: Confusions and Crises, 1915–1916* (Princeton: Princeton University Press, 1964), pp. 134–135.
40. Bryan and Bryan, *Memoirs,* p. 397.
41. *Foreign Relations, 1915, Supplement,* p. 461.
42. Quoted in Bailey and Ryan, Lusitania *Disaster,* p. 128.
43. Link, *Papers of Wilson, XXXVI* (1981), 213–214.
44. Samuel Flagg Bemis, "A Worcester County Student in Wartime London and Paris (via Harvard): 1915–1916," *New England Galaxy, XI* (Spring 1970), 20.
45. Quoted in Patrick Devlin, *Too Proud to Fight* (New York: Oxford University Press, 1975), p. 517.
46. Link, *Papers of Wilson, XL* (1982), 533–539.
47. Frederick Dixon quoting Wilson in Conyne, *Wilson,* p. 99.
48. Quoted in Arthur S. Link, *Wilson: Campaigns for Progressivism and Peace, 1916–1917* (Princeton: Princeton University Press, 1965), p. 274.
49. Quoted *ibid.*, p. 289.
50. Quoted in Konrad H. Jaransch, *The Enigmatic Chancellor* (New Haven: Yale University Press, 1973), p. 301.
51. Lansing, *War Memoirs,* p. 212.
52. Jules Witcover, *Sabotage at Black Tom* (Chapel Hill, N.C.: Algonquin Books, 1989), p. 12.
53. *Foreign Relations, 1917, Supplement 1* (Washington, D.C.: Government Printing Office, 1931), p. 147.
54. Quoted in John Milton Cooper, Jr., *Walter Hines Page* (Chapel Hill: University of North Carolina Press, 1977), p. 369.
55. Quoted in Thomas W. Ryley, *A Little Group of Willful Men* (Port Washington, N.Y.: Kennikat Press, 1975), p. 2.
56. Link, *Papers of Wilson, XLI* (1983), 519–527.
57. Ross Gregory, *The Origins of American Intervention in the First World War* (New York: W. W. Norton, 1971), p. 128.
58. Max Eastman quoted in Thomas J. Knock, *To End All Wars* (New York: Oxford University Press, 1992), p. 122.
59. Quoted in Robert E. Osgood, *Ideals and Self-Interest in American Foreign Relations* (Chicago: University of Chicago Press, 1953), p. 177.
60. Quoted in Paolo E. Coletta, "The American Navy Leaders' Preparations for War," in R. J. Q. Adams, ed., *The Great War, 1914–18* (College Station: Texas A & M University Press, 1990), p. 170.
61. Quoted in Kenneth J. Hagan, *This People's Navy* (New York: The Free Press, 1991), p. 252.
62. Quoted in Barbara S. Kraft, *The Peace Ship* (New York: Macmillan, 1978), p. 1.
63. Quoted in Knock, *To End All Wars,* p. 63.
64. *Ibid.*, p. 50.
65. Jane Addams, *Peace and Bread in Time of War* (New York: King's Crown Press, 1945), p. 58.
66. Quoted in Ernest R. May, *The World War and American Isolation, 1914–1917* (Chicago: Quadrangle Books, [1959], 1966), p. 337.
67. Quoted in J. Garry Clifford, *The Citizen Soldiers* (Lexington: University Press of Kentucky, 1972), p. 123.
68. Penn Borden, *Civilian Indoctrination of the Military* (Westport, Conn.: Greenwood Press, 1989), p. 143.
69. Quoted in Clifford, *Citizen Soldiers,* p. 234.

70. John W. Chambers, *To Raise an Army* (New York: The Free Press, 1987), p. 138.

71. Quoted in Edward M. Coffman, *The War to End All Wars* (New York: Oxford University Press, 1968), p. 4.

72. Sir William Wiseman quoted in Lloyd E. Ambrosius, *Wilsonian Statecraft* (Wilmington, Del.: Scholarly Resources, 1991), p. 131.

73. Quoted in David D. Lee, *Sergeant York* (Lexington: University Press of Kentucky, 1985), p. 19.

74. Quoted in Allen F. Davis, "Welfare, Reform, and World War I," *American Quarterly, XIX* (Fall 1967), 530.

75. Quoted in Alfred W. Crosby, *America's Forgotten Pandemic* (New York: Cambridge University Press, 1989), p. 26.

76. Quoted in Davis, "Welfare," p. 531.

77. Link, *Papers of Wilson, XLVII,* (1984) 270.

78. Quoted in Donald Smythe, *Pershing* (Bloomington: Indiana University Press, 1986), p. 237.

79. Quoted in *Literary Digest, LIX* (November 30, 1918), 15.

80. Link, *Papers of Wilson, XLV* (1984), 529.

81. Addams, *Peace and Bread,* p. 58.

82. Quoted in Selig Adler, *The Isolationist Impulse* (New York: Collier Books [1957], 1961), pp. 60–61.

83. H. G. Nicholas essay in *Wilson's Diplomacy* (Cambridge, Mass.: Schenkman, 1973), p. 81.

84. Quoted in David F. Trask, *The United States in the Supreme War Council* (Middletown, Conn.: Wesleyan University Press, 1961), p. 155.

85. Ray S. Baker quoted in John A. Thompson, *Reformers and War* (New York: Cambridge University Press, 1988), p. 234.

86. Knock, *To End All Wars,* p. 180.

87. George Harvey quoted in Ralph Stone, *The Irreconcilables* (Lexington.: University Press of Kentucky, 1970), p. 35.

88. Quoted in David W. McFadden, *Alternative Paths* (New York: Oxford University Press, 1993), p. 209.

89. Quoted in Herbert Hoover, *The Ordeal of Woodrow Wilson* (New York: McGraw-Hill, 1958), p. 254.

90. Quoted in Ross Gregory, "To Do Good in the World," in Frank Merli and Theodore Wilson, eds., *Makers of American Diplomacy* (New York: Charles Scribner's Sons, 1974), p. 380.

91. Bernard M. Baruch, *The Making of the Reparation and Economic Sections of The Treaty* (New York: Harper & Brothers, 1920), p. 7.

92. Quoted in Gordon Levin, Jr., *Woodrow Wilson and World Politics* (New York: Oxford University Press, 1968), p. 134.

93. Quoted in Knock, *To End All Wars,* p. 250.

94. U.S. Congress, Senate, *Treaties,* Senate Doc. 348 (Washington, D.C.: Government Printing Office, 1923), pp. 3336–3345.

95. Link, *Papers of Wilson, LV* (1985), 177.

96. Antony Lentin, *Lloyd George, Woodrow Wilson, and the Guilt of Germany* (Baton Rouge: Louisiana State University Press, 1984), p. 132.

97. Link, *Papers of Wilson, LV* (1985), 238–245.

98. Quoted in D. F. Fleming, *The United States and the League of Nations, 1918–1920* (New York: Russell & Russell, 1968), p. 134.

99. Quoted in Robert H. Ferrell, *Woodrow Wilson and World War I,* (New York: Harper and Row, 1985) p. 166.

100. Link, *Papers of Wilson, LXI* (1989), 436.

101. Quoted in Arthur S. Link, *Wilson the Diplomatist* (Chicago: Quadrangle Books [1957], 1963), p. 131.

102. Quoted in Thompson, *Reformers and War,* p. 239.

103. Quoted in William C. Widenor, "The United States and the Versailles Peace Settlement," in John M. Carroll and George C. Herring, Jr., eds., *Modern American Diplomacy* (Wilmington, Del.: Scholarly Resources, 1986), p. 49.

104. Quoted in Lloyd E. Ambrosius, *Woodrow Wilson and the American Diplomatic Tradition* (New York: Cambridge University Press, 1987), p. 139.

105. Quoted in Osgood, *Ideals and Self-Interest,* p. 286.

106. Roland N. Stromberg, *Collective Security and American Foreign Policy* (New York: Praeger, 1963) p. 37.

107. Bert E. Park, "Wilson's Neurological Illness during the Summer of 1919," in Link, *Papers of Wilson, LXII* (1990), 629.

108. Link, *Papers of Wilson, LXIII* (1990), 35.

109. Quoted in Knock, *To End All Wars,* p. 263.

110. Arthur Walworth, *Wilson and His Peacemakers* (New York: W. W. Norton, 1986), p. 533.

111. Ferrell, *Wilson and World War I,* p. 222.

112. Herbert F. Margulies, *The Mild Reservationists and the League of Nations Controversy in the Senate* (Columbia: University of Missouri Press, 1989), p. 261.

113. Quoted in E. David Cronon, ed., *The Cabinet Diaries of Josephus Daniels* (Lincoln: University of Nebraska Press, 1963), p. 520.

114. Quoted in Knock, *To End All Wars,* p. 254.

115. Bert E. Park, "The Aftermath of Wilson's Stroke," in Link, *Papers of Wilson, LXIV* (1986), 525.

116. Quoted in John M. Thompson, *Russia, Bolshevism, and the Versailles Peace* (Princeton: Princeton University Press, 1966), pp. 3–4.

117. Ray S. Baker quoted in McFadden, *Alternative Paths,* p. 240.

118. Quoted in Arno J. Mayer, *Politics and Diplomacy of Peacemaking* (New York: Vintage Books, [1967], 1969), p. 21.

119. Quoted in McFadden, *Alternative Paths,* p. 247.

120. Winston Churchill quoting Wilson in Lloyd C. Gardner, *Safe for Democracy* (New York: Oxford University Press, 1984), p. 239.

121. Newton A. McCully quoted in Charles J. Weeks, Jr., *An American Naval Diplomat in Revolutionary Russia* (Annapolis, Md.: Naval Institute Press, 1993), p. 119.

122. Quoted in McFadden, *Alternative Paths,* p. 104.

123. Quoted *ibid.*, p. 137.

124. Quoted in Benjamin D. Rhodes, *The Anglo-American Winter War with Russia, 1918–1919* (Westport, Conn.: Greenwood Press, 1988), p. 15.

125. Quoted in Betty Miller Unterberger, *The United States, Revolutionary Russia, and the Rise of Czechoslovakia* (Chapel Hill: University of North Carolina Press, 1989), p. 264.

126. Betty Miller Unterberger, "Woodrow Wilson and the Russian Revolution," in Arthur S. Link, ed., *Woodrow Wilson and a Revolutionary World, 1913–1921* (Chapel Hill: University of North Carolina Press, 1982), p. 70.

127. Quoted in Thompson, *Russia, Bolshevism*, p. 389.

128. Quoted in McFadden, *Alternative Paths*, p. 154.

129. Quoted in Rhodes, *Winter War*, p. 123.

130. Quoted in Beatrice Farnsworth, *William C. Bullitt and the Soviet Union* (Bloomington: Indiana University Press, 1967), p. 70.

131. Walter LaFeber, Richard Polenberg, and Nancy Wolloch, *The American Century* (New York: McGraw-Hill, 1992; 4th ed.), p. 126.

132. Dwight D. Eisenhower, *Waging Peace, 1956–1961* (Garden City, N.Y.: Doubleday, 1965), p. 616.

133. Arthur S. Link, *The Higher Realism of Woodrow Wilson* (Nashville: Vanderbilt University Press, 1971), p. 83.

134. Quoted in Gordon A. Craig, "The Revolution in War and Diplomacy," in Jack J. Roth, ed., *World War I* (New York: Alfred A. Knopf, 1967), p. 12.

135. Quoted in Ferrell, *Wilson and World War I*, p. 180.

136. E. M. Remarque, *All Quiet on the Western Front* (London: Putnam, 1929), p. 224.

137. Link, *Papers of Wilson*, LXII (1990), 47.

138. Quoted in John A. DeNovo, "The Movement for an Aggressive American Oil Policy Abroad, 1918–1920," *American Historical Review*, LXI (July 1956), 858.

139. Link, *Papers of Wilson*, LXII (1990), 217.

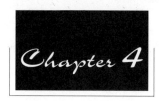
DESCENDING INTO EUROPE'S MAELSTROM, 1920–1939

Trojan Horse?

Trojan Horse? *Many observers thought that President Franklin D. Roosevelt concealed too much in his foreign policymaking—that he not only misled but also lied. Fred O. Seibel of the* Richmond Times Dispatch *(February 4, 1939) portrayed such thinking shortly after a "Boston" bomber with a French pilot aboard crashed in Los Angeles. The British diplomat Lord Halifax saw as much confusion as deviousness in the Roosevelt administration, which he likened to "a disorderly line of beaters out shooting; they do put the rabbits out of the bracken, but they don't come out where you expect." (Courtesy of* Richmond Times Dispatch/*FDR Library)*

✳ *Diplomatic Crossroad*

ROOSEVELT'S ATTEMPT TO EXTEND AMERICA'S FRONTIER TO THE RHINE, 1939

Daubed with red, white, and blue air-corps paint, the new all-metal, twin-engine monoplane performed high-speed acrobatics over Los Angeles's municipal airport on the morning of January 23, 1939. As the sleek craft whipped over the airport and climbed to 3,000 feet at more than 300 miles per hour, only a few observers recognized the aircraft designer Donald Douglas's new light bomber, built to air-corps specifications and destined for fame during World War II as the U.S. Army's A-20 ("Boston") bomber. Test pilot John Cable then apparently cut one motor to attempt a climb on half power. Suddenly the plane went into a spin and hurtled toward the ground. Cable bailed out at 400 feet, but he pulled his parachute ripcord too late. He died on impact. Less than fifty feet from his body the bomber pulverized nine automobiles and injured ten bystanders as it pancaked into the airport parking lot.

Three employees from the adjacent North American Aviation plant extricated a civilian-clad passenger from the wreck just before it burst into flames. An apparent friend of the survivor also rushed to help, speaking excitedly in French. Reporters soon learned that the man with the wrenched back and broken leg was thirty-three-year-old Captain Paul Chemidlin, incognito member of a secret French purchasing mission headed by Jean Monnet to buy American-made warplanes for the French air force. The French were getting ready for World War II, which finally began in September.

Controversy soon engulfed official Washington. General Henry "Hap" Arnold of the U.S. Army Air Corps happened to be testifying before the Senate Military Affairs Committee on budgetary issues. Senator Bennett C. Clark of Missouri, an isolationist, asked how a French officer could be aboard the "secret" bomber that had just crashed. Arnold disingenuously replied that the Frenchman had gone "out there under the direction of the Treasury Department with a view of looking into possible purchase of airplanes by the French Mission."[1] Formal authorization, he added, had come from the War Department, and all secret equipment was removed from the plane before the French saw it. Clark and fellow isolationist Gerald P. Nye of North Dakota then summoned Treasury secretary Henry Morgenthau, Jr., and Secretary of War Harry Woodring for further grilling. Morgenthau acidly pointed out that the army had not yet placed orders for the plane, which remained the sole property of the Douglas Company and could hardly be termed "secret" if flown from a municipal airport where anyone could see it. Woodring, however, admitted that the air corps had originally opposed the French mission but that "everyone [was] . . . in accord before the French went to the West Coast."[2] President Franklin D. Roosevelt muddied matters further by denying to the press that "this Government [had] taken any steps to assist or facilitate France in buying planes in this country." The French wanted to order planes, and "we told them . . . it would be an excellent idea" to help "in building up" U.S. foreign trade, he noted blandly.[3]

A devotee of poker, the president "wasn't ready publicly to show his hand."[4] In seeking to deter a major war through nonmilitary methods, he had talked publicly in recent years about quarantines against aggression, held secret naval talks with the British, and toyed with calling a conference in Washington of six or seven heads of state. His invitation to the king and queen of England to visit America in June 1939 seemed "a safe but effective way of dramatizing Anglo-American amity for the benefit of the dictators and the American public, and as a chance to show off the British monarchy—the epitome in some ways of Anglo-American differences—in the best possible light."[5] Roosevelt had mentioned "methods short of war" to Congress in early January, but he had not explained the details of what would amount to a major shift in American foreign policy in the months prior to World War II.[6]

Ever since the disastrous Munich Conference of September 1938, when England and France had agreed to German territorial demands against Czechoslovakia, FDR had seized on air power as a possible deterrent against another European war and as his "Aladdin's Lamp for instant and inexpensive national security."[7] "Had we . . . 5,000 planes and the immediate capacity to produce 10,000 per year," he had mused, "Hitler would not have dared to take the stand he did."[8] When the French financier-diplomat Jean Monnet visited in October, the president confided that "the Germans can produce 40,000 planes per year, Britain and Canada 25,000 and France 15,000. 20–30,000 more will be needed to achieve decisive superiority over Germany and Italy; and they'll have to be found here, in the United States."[9] He urged England and France to place orders for the latest military models, thereby stimulating the lagging American aviation industry and jumpstarting military rearmament at home. When War Department officials balked at showing top-secret prototypes to foreign buyers, Roosevelt argued that "the only check to a world war, which would be understood by Germany, would be the creation of a great [French] air force and a powerful force in this country."[10] Only after a direct presidential order on January 16, 1939, did General Arnold permit the French to inspect the Douglas bomber.

FDR also wanted to revise America's neutrality laws to permit the sale of arms and munitions to belligerents on a cash-and-carry basis. France and Britain could buy weapons legally in peacetime, but the current law forbade such sales in wartime. The president had secretly promised British prime minister Neville Chamberlain "the industrial resources of the American nation . . . in the event of war with the dictatorships."[11] The crash of the plane with the French officer aboard put his plans in jeopardy. He could explain the secrecy by pointing to the French government's desire to avoid publicity until it had actually placed orders. But Roosevelt needed to avoid at all cost any probe into his own role in initiating the French air mission. The designation of his close friend Morgenthau to oversee all foreign purchases aroused criticism. The bespectacled Treasury secretary served as an "intellectual rough-neck" who "bulled things through" with little regard for bureaucratic sensitivity. In this instance, the chief obstruction proved to be Secretary of War Woodring, a "fourth-rate" former governor of Kansas, whose isolationist views, in Morgenthau's words, stood "in complete opposition to the president's, who not only couldn't see that our frontier was the Rhine, but couldn't see across the Hudson River."[12] A public inquiry could expose the rifts within the administration and abort new foreign-policy initiatives.

Roosevelt invited the Senate Military Affairs Committee to the White House on January 31, 1939. He asked that everything be kept confidential so as not "to frighten the American people." During the meeting, FDR tried to persuade key leaders of Congress that the growing menace from Germany, Italy, and Japan necessitated fundamental changes in U.S. policies. He began by denying that "we can draw a line of defense around this country and live completely and solely to ourselves." He cited Thomas Jefferson's embargo—"the damned thing didn't work" and "the country began to strangle" and "we got into the War of 1812." Roosevelt told the senators that he had "pretty definite information that there was in the making a policy of world domination between Germany, Italy, and Japan." Americans could react to the threat by hoping that "somebody would assassinate Hitler or that Germany will blow up from within." Or they could "try to prevent the domination of the world—prevent it by peaceful means."

Strengthening America's "first line of defense" offered the best approach. In the Pacific, Roosevelt described that defense as "a series of islands, with a hope that through the Army and Navy and the airplanes we can keep the Japanese" from dominating the Pacific and denying "us access to the west coast of South America." In Europe and the Atlantic, the line of defense rested on "the continued independence" of some twenty countries from Finland to Turkey. If England and France fell, however, the others would "drop into the [Axis] basket." Africa would "automatically" capitulate "because Africa is ninety-five percent colonial." The president then outlined ways in which the Germans could dominate South and Central America through subversion and economic penetration. At one point he warned: "The Germans have 1,500 bombing planes that can go from Germany to Colombia inside of forty-eight hours. We have, I think, about eighty that can go down there."

Franklin D. Roosevelt (1882–1945). "Happy Days Are Here Again" was his campaign song. Although crippled by polio in the 1920s, Roosevelt remained energetic and optimistic. A talented politician who won four presidential elections, Roosevelt moved haltingly to shore up Britain and France as they faced an aggressive Hitlerian Germany. (Courtesy of Wide World/FDR Library)

Roosevelt emphatically defended the sale of aircraft to the French, saying that "it is to our interest, quite frankly, to do what we can, absolutely as a matter of peace . . . to help the British and French maintain their independence." The American aviation industry also needed foreign orders to expedite mass production and "turn out nine or ten thousand planes per year" without at the same time delaying the buildup of American air forces. As for giving away secrets, he affirmed that the Norden bomb sight "has not been disclosed to the French and won't." He vowed to "maintain the independence of these other nations by sending them all they can pay for on the barrelhead. . . . Now, that is the foreign policy of the United States."

A bravura performance, to be sure. Yet when asked if he meant to "leave the impression" that the United States had the "duty" to "maintain the independence of these nations . . . by whatever efforts may be necessary," Roosevelt shot back: "No. No! Listen: I probably saw more of the war [World War I] in Europe than any other living person." Describing his three-month tour of the battle zones as assistant secretary of the navy in 1918, he "covered the whole coast of France. . . . I spent days on the Belgian front, on the British front, on the French front, and on the American front. . . . Therefore, you may be quite sure that about the last thing this country should do is ever to send an army to Europe again."[13] Senator Nye, listening intently, went back to his office and immediately wrote a nine-page memorandum. "Get the uniforms ready for the boys," he noted. "I saw troops moving even though the Pres[ident] had declared he had no intent to go to war."[14]

The next day word leaked to the press that FDR had proclaimed that "the frontiers of the United States are on the Rhine."[15] The president angrily hit back at a press conference on February 3, calling the leak "a deliberate lie" that "some boob got off." He accused isolationists of trying to "make political capital" out of words he never spoke. He specifically singled out Senator Nye as "an unscrupulous person."[16] As reverberations echoed in the press, the French ambassador lamented "manifestations of isolation in this country" and Neville Chamberlain noted that "Roosevelt is saying Heaven knows what but anyhow something disagreeable to the dictators."[17]

Did FDR lie? According to a White House transcript of his meeting with the senators, he never said exactly that America's frontier extended to the Rhine, but his argument that the nation's first line of defense depended on the continued independence of England and France carried the same meaning. Several times, Henry Morgenthau later recalled, the president did say privately: "Our frontier is on the Rhine."[18] Yet in all likelihood Roosevelt sincerely believed he spoke the truth. A deft "juggler" who always kept options open, the smiling squire of Hyde Park wanted above all else to deter a European war while at the same time to prepare for possible U.S. participation.[19] He sought, he said, "methods short of war" because "sending a large army abroad was undesirable and politically out of the question."[20] As the historian Michael Sherry has written, "repudiation of armed intervention did not exclude intervention by display of arms. Methods short of war could still embrace the capacity for deterrence that rearmament implied."[21] Roosevelt persisted in selling aircraft to the French and British, even threatening to exile General

Arnold to Guam if he did not "play ball."[22] The 555 combat planes eventually delivered to France did not deter war.

The "cockeyed" affair also caused FDR to abandon any sustained personal effort to educate Congress and public opinion about revising American neutrality laws before the outbreak of war in Europe.[23] Only after the German invasion of Poland in September 1939 did the administration succeed in repealing the arms embargo, and even then the president remained conspicuously in the background. His encounter with the senators over the French air mission remained so traumatic that it made him hesitant to lead boldly: "Recall the colorful and untrue reports of over a year ago about our frontier being on the Rhine; about the sale of war secrets to the Allies; . . . about the death of a French officer caused by the crash of an airplane in California," he told a prominent publisher in June 1940. "The government . . . cannot change its 'editorial' policy overnight. . . . From what extremes do the pendulums swing for us as individuals. Governments, such as ours, cannot swing so far or so quickly."[24] Of course, the French officer had not died, but Roosevelt sometimes exaggerated for effect.

Some six years and two months after FDR made his alleged remarks about America's frontier on the Rhine, U.S. soldiers seized the bridge at Remagen and crossed the Rhine into Germany. Another European war, which American diplomacy and arms sales to France had failed to prevent, had definitively extended the frontiers of the United States.

THE INDEPENDENT INTERNATIONALISTS

The French airplane incident of 1939 illustrates some salient themes of interwar diplomacy. It demonstrates that even on the eve of World War II in Europe, the United States still sought methods short of war to deter potential aggressors in areas vital to the national interest. Because foreign airplane orders also meant "prosperity in this country and we can't elect a Democratic Party unless we get prosperity," as Roosevelt put it, the episode reveals the impact of the Great Depression on foreign trade, domestic politics, and international security.[25] Even in failure, it shows how an activist president can use subterfuge and surrogates to circumvent bureaucratic rivalries and congressional opposition. The incident underlines the lessons learned from America intervention in World War I and the determination to avoid the mistakes allegedly made by Woodrow Wilson. In view of FDR's claim that America's national security had become tied to the independence of France and England, it also proves that important American leaders recognized global interdependence and rejected an ostrichlike, isolationist course during the interwar years.

The United States had emerged from World War I a recognized world power. Under the Treaty of Paris, American military forces even occupied the left bank of the Rhine near Coblenz until early 1923. Postwar American diplomats, closer to a global perspective than ever before, knew that the American frontier had been extended, that even if they wanted to, Americans could not be bystanders in world affairs. True, between World Wars I and II Americans hoped to avoid foreign entanglements and concentrate on domestic matters. But, within the limits of U.S. power, American leaders largely pursued an active foreign policy befitting their nation's high international status. On the whole, they did not put themselves helplessly at the mercy of events, but worked to create a community of peaceful nations characterized by legal and orderly processes, the Open Door, and economic and political stability. Washington emphasized nonmilitary means—treaties, conferences, disarmament, economic and financial arrangements—in its pursuit of world order. President Herbert Hoover pointed to this attempted retreat from military methods when he observed that "we can never herd the world into paths of righteousness with the dogs of war," and Secretary of State Henry L. Stimson remarked that the United States championed a "commercial and non-military stabilization of the world."[26]

America was isolationist between the wars primarily in the sense that it wanted to isolate itself from war, to scale down foreign military interventions, and to preserve the freedom to make independent decisions in international affairs in order to serve the national interest of prosperity and security. The historian Joan Hoff Wilson's apt phrase, "independent internationalism," rather than "isolationism," characterized American practice—active on an international scale, but independent in action.[27] Where the United States lacked viable power, such as in Asia, it moved haltingly. Where it possessed power, as in Latin America, it moved vigorously. As for Europe, according to the historian Melvyn Leffler, "economic imperatives, humanitarian instincts, and ideological impulses compelled American officials to take an active interest."[28] Until 1933 the Republican administrations seriously worked

Charles Evans Hughes (1862–1948) and Warren G. Harding (1865–1923). The secretary of state and president were quite different in background and intellect, but as conservatives both sought a stable, nonrevolutionary world order. (Ohio Historical Society)

to contain but rehabilitate Germany, relieve French strategic anxieties, tame Soviet radicalism while seeking to integrate Russia into the community of nations, advance disarmament proposals, resolve controversies over war debts and reparations, stabilize European currencies, foster American exports, and systematize the flow of private American capital abroad. In attempting to create a world order of peace and prosperity, the U.S. government encouraged private experts in business, finance, labor, and agriculture to cooperate with public officials in what some historians have called a system of "corporatism." By the mid-1930s, with international stability shattered by the Great Depression and Europe torn by conflict, Americans tried to protect themselves from war through neutrality legislation. Not until 1939 did policymakers again risk war to achieve world order.

Weak presidential leadership, congressional-executive competition, and increased professionalism in the Foreign Service characterized U.S. policymaking in the 1920s. Presidents Warren G. Harding and Calvin Coolidge gave minimal attention to foreign affairs, leaving that field to their secretaries of state. Harding's world was his hometown of Marion, Ohio. Wilson's League of Nations fiasco at home persuaded Harding to eschew a conspicuous role in foreign policy. On one occasion, when a European correspondent for the *New York Times* talked with Harding, the president cut him short: "I don't know anything about this European stuff."[29]

Calvin Coolidge managed in his autobiography to avoid mentioning foreign policy, although as a politician he had often waxed noisy on the issue of bolshevism. Member of Congress Lewis Douglas described the taciturn Coolidge as "much like a wooden Indian except more tired looking."[30] Coolidge's relaxed approach to problems, exemplified by the long afternoon naps he took in the White House and by his fawning worship of American business, created a deceptively passive image. Compared with Franklin D. Roosevelt, he certainly was passive—but Coolidge did not withdraw from foreign policymaking as much as Harding did. The simple man from Vermont, preaching the virtues of self-reliance, did grow impatient with Europeans—who, he believed, always looked to the United States to bail them out. "We couldn't help people very much until they showed a disposition to help themselves," he noted in 1926.[31]

Herbert Hoover held much the same philosophy, but he had considerable knowledge about foreign affairs and adopted an active presidential role. He practiced independent internationalism. His distinguished career included experience in international business (mining), food relief (Belgium and Russia), and diplomacy (reparations adviser at Versailles). As secretary of commerce under Harding and Coolidge, he used his office energetically to expand American economic interests abroad. Known as the "Great Engineer," Hoover had a telephone installed at his elbow in the White House, further contributing to his reputation as a specialist in administrative efficiency. A plodding speaker with a shy personality, Hoover entered the presidency as the Great Depression struck, thereby wrecking his political career. True to his Quaker background, he sought nonmilitary, noncoercive solutions to international crises and emphasized cooperative economic relations.

Herbert Hoover (1874–1964). The thirty-first president graduated from Stanford University. Cautious and stubborn, Hoover advocated healthy trade relations, military retrenchment, and foreign loans for "reproductive purposes" as routes to peace. (*The Reporter*, 1953, Copyright 1953 by Fortnightly Publishing Co., Inc.)

Makers of American Foreign Relations, 1920–1939

Presidents	Secretaries of State
Woodrow Wilson, 1913–1921	Bainbridge Colby, 1920–1921
Warren G. Harding, 1921–1923	Charles E. Hughes, 1921–1925
Calvin Coolidge, 1923–1929	Frank B. Kellogg, 1925–1929
Herbert C. Hoover, 1929–1933	Henry L. Stimson, 1929–1933
Franklin D. Roosevelt, 1933–1945	Cordell Hull, 1933–1944

The secretaries of state in the 1920s often compensated for presidential short-comings. Magisterial Charles Evans Hughes, facetiously called by Supreme Court Justice Louis Brandeis the "most enlightened mind of the eighteenth century," was a distinguished jurist (Supreme Court), an experienced politician (governor of New York and unsuccessful candidate for president in 1916), and a confirmed national-ist and expansionist.[32] Under Harding and Coolidge the patient and pragmatic Hughes enjoyed considerable freedom in diplomacy, receiving little presidential in-struction. The observance of international law and the sanctity of treaties served as his primary guides to the attainment of world order. Still, "foreign policies are not built upon abstractions," he said. "They are the result of practical conceptions of national interest arising from some immediate exigency or standing out vividly in historical perspective."[33] Frank B. Kellogg succeeded Hughes. Ingloriously called "Nervous Nellie" because of his shaky appearance (one blind eye and a trembling hand), the former senator and ambassador to Britain moved cautiously, often con-sulting a major critic of interventionism, William Borah, chair of the Senate Foreign Relations Committee. Kellogg left only the much derided Kellogg-Briand peace pact as a legacy. Both he and Hughes had to contend with jurisdictional disputes as Secretary Hoover expanded the international offices and functions of the Depart-ment of Commerce.

President Hoover named as secretary of state the mustachioed Henry L. Stimson, one of America's distinguished public servants. The strong-willed, wealthy lawyer lived on his Long Island estate like an English squire. His social pedigree included Phillips Andover Academy, Yale University, Harvard Law School, and tutelage under the eminent Elihu Root. Tenacious, cold, confident, aloof, reserved, punctual, mannered, stern—Stimson's characteristics befitted an American aristocrat. Before becoming secretary, he had headed the War Depart-ment under Taft. In 1927 he went as a diplomatic troubleshooter to Nicaragua, and during 1927–1929 he served as governor-general of the Philippines. He had been Colonel Stimson in World War I—and let few forget it. Indeed, his athlet-ic and strenuous lifestyle reminded many of Theodore Roosevelt. Hoover did not like Stimson's combative personality and his eagerness to use force in foreign affairs.

That kind of strong personality was just what Franklin D. Roosevelt did not want for his secretary of state. Roosevelt, like Theodore Roosevelt and Woodrow Wilson before him, wanted foreign policymaking in his own hands. FDR came to office with some foreign-affairs experience, having served in the Navy Department under Wilson, and unlike the Republican presidents of the 1920s, he became an activist diplomat. He admired both the big-sticking of his cousin Theodore and the liberal internationlism of Wilson. As a vice-presidential candidate in 1920, Roosevelt had defended the new League and the Versailles treaty, but in the 1932 campaign he abandoned support for the League in order to garner the endorsement of the influential newspaper magnate William Randolph Hearst. Considerable debate has centered on whether Roosevelt was an isolationist. He actually acted as both a Wilsonian and an isolationist. That is, he was a Wilsonian because he believed that collective security through an international organization directed by the large powers would help stabilize world politics. He was an isolationist because he shared, although in differing degrees, the basic components of isolationist thought: (1) abhorrence of war; (2) limited *military* intervention abroad; (3) freedom of action in international relations. In short, he epitomized the era of independent internationalism.

Roosevelt relished personal diplomacy, often taking command of negotiations and appointments and more than once failing to tell the Department of State what he was doing. He centralized decisionmaking in the White House, but, because too often he possessed only a superficial understanding of other national cultures and histories, dangers lurked in his methods. Sometimes he misled diplomats with his easy smile and tendency to be agreeable at the moment; sometimes his agreements lacked precision, depending for their authority on the honor of gentlemen's words; sometimes the formal diplomatic document did not properly capture the "spirit" of a meeting; sometimes U.S. diplomacy moved forward with the dizziness of a confused bureaucracy. As a consummate politician always conscious of hostile opinion, Roosevelt compromised frequently, leaving his ideals a bit tattered. He was not above deception when he believed it would serve his goals. According to the historian Willard Range, FDR was "something of an intellectual jumping-jack . . . hopping helter-skelter in several directions at once," while another scholar has likened him to a college professor who prefers to teach without a syllabus.[34]

Roosevelt's secretary of state was Tennessean Cordell Hull. A powerful senator who focused on the improvement of international trade, the silver-haired, sixty-one-year-old Hull reluctantly accepted the assignment. FDR picked him not for his foreign views (Roosevelt knew little about them), but because the appointment would please old Democratic party members, southern conservatives, and unreconstructed Wilsonians. Roosevelt often undercut him, although Hull and the State Department remained dominant in formulating Asian and Latin American policy. Rexford Tugwell, a presidential aide, noted as early as 1933 that "Hull doesn't know half of what goes on."[35] Indeed, Roosevelt sent Hull to the World Economic Conference in London that June without consulting him on the makeup of the delegation, and then embarrassed him by rejecting a currency stabilization plan and effectively ending the conference. Once dubbed "Miss Cordelia Dull" for his undynamic style, the secretary had contemplated resigning earlier that spring when the president had decided to delay sending to Congress Hull's pet project, the reciprocal trade bill. Hull's deliberate methods wearied the president, who preferred quickness and repartee. The secretary resented the president's practice of dispatching personal envoys like Harry Hopkins overseas, of conspicuously excluding Hull from conferences, and of consulting with friends like Sumner Welles (after 1937 undersecretary of state), Morgenthau, and Ambassador William C. Bullitt, instead of Hull himself. "They all come at me with knives and hatchets," Hull once complained. But he stayed on until 1944, the longest tenure of any secretary of state, forever disliking the pomp of official dinners and receptions, always charming his listeners with his hill-country drawl and lisp, and impressing all with his personal dignity, hard work, and deep commitment to the premise that wars grew out of international economic competition. [36]

The Foreign Service over which Hull presided made important strides toward professionalism in the interwar period. It had certainly needed reform. Frequenting the dark corridors, black leather rocking chairs, and Victorian furnishings of the old State, War, and Navy Building on Pennsylvania Avenue were American diplomats noted for their elite backgrounds (urban, wealthy, eastern, and Ivy League–educated). Some derided them as "cookie pushers" and "striped pants," as purveyors of "pink peppermint and protocol." As the diplomat Joseph Grew lamented, Congress preferred envoys who "talk through their nose and spit on the floor" over "those who talk like an Englishman."[37] Many diplomatic appointees could not speak the language of the country to which they were assigned. Under the spoils system, faithful politicians received diplomatic posts.

The heavy work load imposed on Foreign Service personnel during World War I had exposed the shortcomings. Member of Congress John J. Rogers concluded after the war that, "as adequate as [the Foreign Service] may have been when the old order prevailed . . . , it has ceased to be responsive to present needs."[38] The immigration laws of 1921 and 1924, establishing quotas, demanded a more efficient consular staff; the revolution in China required observers who could intelligently report on that major event; and economic expansion depended on efficient reporting about market conditions abroad. The Rogers Act of 1924 brought some improvements. It merged the previously unequal consular and diplomatic corps into the Foreign Service of the United States and provided for examinations, increased salaries, promotion by merit, and overseas living expense allowances. The legislation also created the Foreign Service School. At about the same time, the State Department began training specialists in Soviet affairs, with George F. Kennan and Charles E. Bohlen (both later ambassadors to Russia) as initiates who mastered the language and culture of Russia. These trainees came to share a set of hard-line attitudes toward the Soviet Union. Although the Great Depression pushed salaries down and forced staff cutbacks, and although cliques, snobbery, politics, and sexist and anti-Semitic attitudes too often still characterized the service, it became more efficient and professional.

Cordell Hull (1871–1955). The long-tenured secretary of state (1933–1944) firmly believed that "we cannot have a peaceful world . . . until we rebuild the international economic structure." Although Roosevelt often ignored him, Hull played a central role in Latin American issues, negotiations with Japan, and trade questions. (National Portrait Gallery, Smithsonian Institution)

Economic and Cultural Expansion in a Rickety World

The Foreign Service helped facilitate conspicuous American economic expansion abroad in the 1920s. After World War I, measured by statistics, the United States had become the most powerful nation in the world, accounting for 70 percent of the world's petroleum and 40 percent of its coal production. Most impressive, the United States produced 46 percent of total world industrial goods (1925–1929 figures). It also ranked first as an exporter, shipping more than 15 percent of total world exports in 1929, and it replaced Great Britain as the largest foreign investor and financier of world trade. Throughout the decade the United States enjoyed a favorable balance of trade, exporting more than it imported. In the period 1914–1929, the value of exports more than doubled, to $5.4 billion, and American private investments abroad grew fivefold—from $3.5 billion in 1914 to $17.2 billion by 1930.

"The growth of U.S. stakes abroad during the 1920s represented not simply an increase in scale," the historian Mira Wilkins has noted. "Rather, U.S. companies were (1) going to *more countries*, (2) building *more plants* in a particular foreign country, (3) manufacturing or mining *more end products* in a particular foreign land, (4) investing in a single alien nation in a *greater degree* of integration, and (5) diversifying on a *worldwide* basis."[39] U.S. Rubber bought its first Malayan plantation; Anaconda moved into Chilean copper mining; General Electric joined international cartels and invested heavily in Germany; oil companies began to penetrate the Middle East; Americans controlled 83 percent of the automobile industry in Canada; General Motors purchased Opel, by 1929 the best-selling automobile in Germany; Henry Ford helped build an automobile plant in Russia; Borden expanded in England; and American firms handled about one-third of oil sales in France.

American culture—including household appliances, foods, language, music, film, and appreciation for machines—also spread worldwide. U.S. government support for the expansion of the communications industry helped International Telephone and Telegraph (ITT), Radio Corporation of America (RCA), Associated Press (AP), and United Press (UP) become international giants by 1930. Hollywood movies so dominated the global market that the "sun . . . never sets on the British Empire and the American motion picture." Indeed, "trade follows the film," and together they so advertised U.S. culture abroad that some foreigners feared that "Americanization" would engulf them.[40] "Culture follows money," the novelist F. Scott Fitzgerald declared. "We will be the Romans in the next generation."[41] In 1929 alone, some 251,000 American tourists visited Europe, where they spent $323 million and displayed American customs and fashions. From mass-production methods to soda fountains and gym shoes, American ways claimed an international clientele. When the Rockefeller Foundation sponsored programs in preventive medicine, hygiene, public health, and nursing in Eastern and Central Europe in the 1920s, this philanthropic institution also introduced America to foreigners. Under Rockefeller auspices, for example, "Kentucky closets" (outdoor toilets) became ubiquitous in Croatian villages.[42]

This economic-cultural activity faced obstacles. Mexican nationalism, confiscation of property in Russia, European resentments, a wrecked German economy, wartime destruction in Europe, growing tariff walls, and the dislocation of international finance caused by World War I debts and reparations—all hindered enterprising Americans. U.S. government decisions offered welcome but limited help. The Webb-Pomerene Act (1918) permitted American companies to combine for purposes of foreign trade without prosecution under the antitrust laws; the Edge Act of 1919 legalized branch banks abroad; and the Merchant Marine Act of 1920 authorized the federal government to sell vessels to private companies and to make loans for the construction of new ships. New tax laws also permitted foreign tax credits for American investors abroad. Secretary Hoover put the Department of Commerce behind trade expansion by providing businesses with research data and advice. To help financiers avoid unproductive foreign lending and the purchase of risky foreign bonds, official Washington tried to oversee loans and bond sales, but the practice never became consistent or thorough. Investors still had considerable freedom to make their own lending choices. For example, the government discouraged the sale in the United States of the bonds of a Czech brewery because it would violate the "spirit" of prohibition laws, but tolerated an unproductive loan for a sports palace in Germany.

The Weight of the United States in the World Economy

Relative Value of Industrial Production, 1925–1929

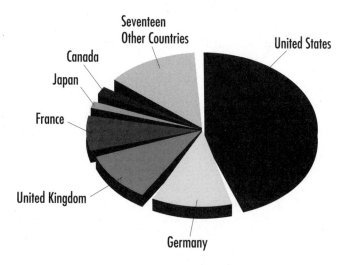

Source: U.S. Department of Commerce, *The United States in the World Economy* (Washington, D.C.: Government Printing Office, 1943), p. 28.

Believing trade essential to domestic prosperity, the United States continued to proclaim the Open Door policy but applied it selectively and imperfectly. U.S. officials usually invoked the policy where the United States faced vigorous competition, as in Asia and the Middle East. In Latin America and the Philippines, however, where American capital and trade dominated, something approximating a "closed door" developed. Europeans complained bitterly that the United States followed a double standard. They also resented American tariff policy, which made it difficult for nations to sell to the United States—as they had to do in order to get the dollars necessary to buy from the United States. The tariff acts of 1922 (Fordney-McCumber) and 1930 (Hawley-Smoot) raised duties to protect domestic producers and invited retaliation against American products. Economists protested the Hawley-Smoot Tariff: "There are few more ironical spectacles than the American Government as it seeks, on the one hand, to promote ex-

The Contracting Spiral of World Trade

January 1929 to March 1933
Total Imports of 75 Countries in Millions of Dollars

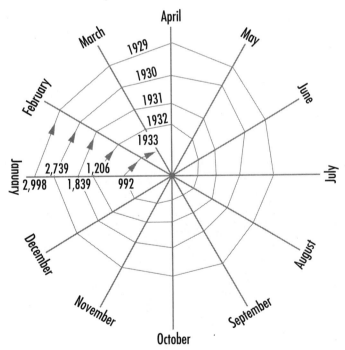

Source: Charles P. Kindleberger, *The World in Depression, 1929–1939* (Berkeley and Los Angeles: University of California Press, 1973), p. 172. Copyright © 1973 by The Regents of the University of California; reprinted by permission of the University of California Press.

ports . . . , while, on the other hand, by increasing tariffs it makes exportation ever more difficult." They predicted "a tariff war" that would disturb world peace.[43] Some twenty-five nations by 1932 had retaliated against American imports. Hoover held that high tariffs and overseas economic expansion could proceed hand in hand, and until the Great Depression struck in 1929 the seeming contradiction appeared to work.

The depression raised havoc with the international economy. Economic nationalism guided most countries as they tried to protect themselves from the cataclysm with higher tariffs, import quotas, and preferential and discriminatory trade agreements. World trade declined 40 percent in value and 25 percent in volume from 1929 to mid-1933. In 1933 the United States exported goods worth $2.1 billion, down from the 1929 figure of $5.4 billion. American capital stayed at home and foreign holders of American loans defaulted. American private investments abroad slumped to $13.5 billion, down from the $17.2 billion figure of 1930. President Hoover simply blamed the economic trouble on the rest of the world. His successor, Franklin D. Roosevelt, confronting 13 million unemployed Americans when he took office in 1933, also succumbed to economic nationalism as he created his New Deal program. He abruptly sabotaged the London Economic Conference, indicating that the United States would henceforth "pursue domestic recovery by means of a policy of unilateralism."[44] But Hull gradually persuaded him that lowered tariffs would spur U.S. foreign trade and spark recovery at home. Hull also preached that healthy world trade would contribute to stable politics and peace at a time when Japan, Germany, and Italy were turning to political extremes and threatening aggression. It would also deter bolshevism from exploiting Europe's economic and social turmoil. "International commerce," Hull avowed, "is not only calculated to aid materially in the restoration of prosperity everywhere, but it is the greatest civilizer and peacemaker in the experience of the human race."[45]

In 1934 Hull piloted through Congress the Reciprocal Trade Agreements Act, which empowered the president to reduce tariffs by as much as 50 percent after making agreements with other nations under the doctrine of the most-favored nation. This principle, which had traditionally guided American trade, did not mean that one nation was more favored than another. Rather, it meant that the United States was entitled to the lowest tariffs imposed by a country (in short, the best favor that country granted any other nation) with which the United States had a reciprocal agreement, and vice versa. The reciprocal trade program did retard the deterioration of world trade, but, as President Roosevelt confessed, "those trade treaties are just too goddamned slow. The world is moving too fast."[46] Hull also created in 1934 the Export-Import Bank, a governmental agency designed to provide loans to expand foreign trade. Washington could give or withhold credits to facilitate foreign-policy goals as well. Yet by May 1937 FDR waxed skeptical: "The more I study the situation the more I am convinced that an economic approach to peace is a weak reed."[47]

The reciprocal trade program and the bank came too late to help solve one of the major troubling legacies of World War I and Versailles—the debts-reparations tangle. Whereas before the war U.S. citizens owed some $3 billion to Europeans, after the war European citizens owed private Americans $3 billion and their governments owed another $10 billion, largely because of wartime loans. America had gone dramatically from a debtor to a creditor nation. But how would Europeans earn dollars to pay such a huge sum? American investments, sale of goods to the United States, U.S. tourist spending, and income from German reparations payments ranked as the most promising sources. But the Germans proved incapable of meeting the indemnity of $33 billion, so in the early 1920s the British began asking for a cancellation of the debts, arguing that they should be considered an American contribution to the Allied victory. Europeans, then, looked on the war loans as essentially political in character, rather than as business transactions. Anyway, they pointed out, they had given lives and had endured destruction and damage of property. The United States, on the other hand, had not suffered military devastation and had enjoyed unprecedented profits from the sale of goods to the Allies. America indignantly rejected this argument, prompting Britons to think "Americans are dirty swine."[48] Coolidge complained that "this money has to be paid by our taxpayers unless it is paid by the taxpayers [of the debtor nations]," and he issued orders to a reparations delegation: "Just remember you are Americans."[49] The humorist Will Rogers captured the American mood in a joke: "There is only one way we could be worse with the Europeans, and that is to have helped them out in two wars instead of one."[50] Congress created the War Debt Commission in 1922 to negotiate full payment. The commission ultimately forgave or canceled about half of the Allied debts. From 1918 to 1931 the United States actually received only $2.6 billion in Allied debts payments.

By stabilizing European finances, restoring trade, and encouraging the private flow of capital to Germany, Republican diplomats, in the historian Michael Hogan's words, sought to "harness Germany's resources to the cause of European recovery without restoring its prewar hegemony or reinvigorating the economic nationalism and autarky" that could lead to world war.[51] The debts-reparations embroglio eventually undercut this strategy. Wild inflation, a crippled economy, inadequate exports, and anti-Versailles hostility prompted the Germans to default on reparations payments in 1922–1923. France and Belgium thereupon aggravated Germany's plight by seizing the rich Ruhr Valley. Britain called again for debt cancellation. In 1924 the State Deparment encouraged the businessman Charles G. Dawes to negotiate the Dawes Plan, whereby American investors like the J. P. Morgan Company loaned millions to Germany and Berlin accepted a systematic reparations payment schedule. But the European economy simply could not bear the heavy debts (Europeans also owed money to other Europeans) and the reparations. Nor could American capital continue to keep Europe afloat. Under the Young Plan of 1929, another salvaging effort reduced German reparations to $9 billion. That year, too, President Hoover informed the British that he would cancel their debt if they transferred Bermuda, British Honduras (Belize), and Trinidad to the United States. London refused. In 1931 Hoover declared a one-year moratorium on debts payments. But thereafter only Finland met its debt obligations, forever winning a place in American hearts. Debtors defaulted, Germany stopped paying reparations, and the world settled into the devastating depression of the 1930s. "It was hardly surprising," the historian Bruce Kent has written, "that this rickety financial structure, the maintenance of which depended on a vigorous expansion of world trade and a buoyant international credit system, should have been shaken to its foundations by the economic contractions" of the depression.[52]

PEACE INITIATIVES BLUNTED

If Europeans and Americans failed to resolve the mammoth problems plaguing the international economy, they also failed to curb a growing arms race, although the Washington Treaties of 1922 held promise (see Chapter 5), and peace sentiment ran high in the United States. In 1923, when the publisher Edward Bok sponsored a contest for the best peace plan, he received more than 22,000 entries. Eleanor Roosevelt, Franklin's wife, helped organize the bipartisan peace prize. The winner of $100,000 was a member of the New York Peace Society who recommended entry into the World Court and partial participation in the League of Nations. Some peace advocates, such as the Carnegie Endowment for International Peace, placed their hopes in such international bodies. Pacifists in the Fellowship of Reconciliation, the War Resisters League, and the Women's Peace Union, on the other hand, renounced individual participation in war. Religious groups pointed to the un-Christian character of war. Salmon Levinson, a Chicago lawyer who organized the American Committee for the Outlawry of War, argued that "war is an institution in the same sense as the church, the school or the home. It will never cease to be an institution until it becomes illegal."[53] Some business leaders, like Thomas J. Watson of International Business Machines (IBM), endorsed the theme of "world peace through world trade."[54] Organizations like the Committee on the Cause and Cure of War, the largest women's peace group in the 1920s, and the Women's International League for Peace and Freedom acted on the belief that "women could and must play a special mediating role in the resolution of conflict between nations."[55] Disarmament and anticolonialism became the missions of many peace-oriented people. Radical pacifists and antiwar advocates agitated for fundamental social and economic change in order to remove social injustice, which they saw as the capitalist wellsprings of imperialism and war. The National Council for the Prevention of War, founded in 1921, served as an organizational umbrella for the divergent peace groups.

Most peace activists or peace-conscious citizens believed that the United States, because of its basically democratic and pacific inclinations, could regenerate habitually war-prone Europe. In the 1920s, such reformist ideas did not seem farfetched: arms seemed controllable (technology had not yet produced global bombers or atomic weapons); domestic economies did not yet rely heavily for their prosperity on defense production; the revulsion against World War I remained intense; and few warmongers had yet seized governments. Still, most Americans devoted more attention to sports, movies, and radio in the decade's consumer culture than to

"Come on in. I'll treat you right. I used to know your daddy." In the 1930s the cartoonist Clarence D. Batchelor recalled the tragedy of World War I in this haunting peace statement. The cartoon won a Pulitzer Prize. (Library of Congress)

questions of peace. The peace advocates floated as "mere chips and foam on the surface of the stream of American life."[56]

One of the peace movement's few achievements was the Kellogg-Briand Pact of 1928. France, prodded by James T. Shotwell, a Columbia University professor and trustee of the Carnegie Endowment for International Peace, asked the United States to sign a bilateral treaty renouncing war between the two nations. The security-conscious French, ever worried about a revived Germany, seemed to want an "American Locarno," in which Washington would support the European guarantee of France's eastern boundary as stipulated in the Locarno Treaty of 1925.[57] Washington cooly received the request. But a publicity compaign for a multilateral treaty launched by Shotwell, Levinson, and Senator William Borah put the State Department on the spot. Secretary Kellogg soon took the lead. In February 1928 he sent a draft treaty to France and other powers. Foreign Minister Aristide Briand fumed; Kellogg and the peace advocates had converted his idea for a Franco-American security treaty into a universal declaration against war. That August in Paris, the signatories, eventually numbering sixty-two, agreed to "condemn recourse to war for the solution of international controversies, and renounce it as an instrument of national policy."[58]

The Kellogg-Briand Pact required no real sacrifices and established no precise responsibilities. On January 15, 1929, the Senate approved it 85 to 1, the lone dissenter being John J. Blaine of Wisconsin, a confirmed Anglophobe. Senator Hiram Johnson of California, who voted "aye," parodied the treaty's lack of enforcement authority by quoting François Villon:[59]

> To Messur Noel, named the neat
>
> By those who love him, I bequeath
>
> A helmless ship, a houseless street
>
> A wordless book, a swordless sheath
>
> An hourless clock, a leafless wreath
>
> A bed sans sheet, a board sans meat,
>
> A bell sans tongue, a saw sans teeth,
>
> To make his nothingness complete.

Hardly lulled into a sense of security by the treaty, the Senate that same day approved funds for fifteen new cruisers. Peace advocates did not naively believe that Kellogg-Briand guaranteed a peaceful world. They saw it as a first step in a long process and championed the pact as a way of alerting the American people to think once again of the costs of war. Thus it held educational value. And the pact gave the Allies the legal grounds after World War II to punish German leaders at the Nuremberg trials for plotting aggressive war.

The League of Nations, itself designed to check wars, opened in Geneva without the United States, and Washington at first ignored League communications.

But by 1925 U.S. diplomats were discreetly participating in League functions. By 1930, unofficial American "observers" had attended more than forty League conferences on such questions as health, prostitution, suppression of obscene materials, codification of international law, and opium. In October 1931 Prentiss B. Gilbert, an American diplomat, formally participated in League Council meetings on the Manchurian crisis, but Washington would only push the League to cite the Kellogg-Briand Pact and condemn Japan for aggression (see Chapter 5). The United States nearly did join the League-sponsored Permanent Court of International Justice (World Court), which sought to arbitrate international disputes when requested to do so. In 1926 the Senate approved U.S. membership but so qualified it that the court could not accept the American proposal. In 1935 a treaty of membership nearly gained the two-thirds vote, aided by FDR's claim that "the sovereignty of the United States [would] in no way be diminished or jeopardized."[60] That eminent jurists such as Charles Evans Hughes did sit as judges in the World Court offered internationalists some solace.

American participation in disarmament conferences in 1922 (Washington), 1927 (Geneva), 1930 (London), 1932–1933 (Geneva), and 1935–1936 (London) also demonstrated America's international but independent diplomatic course. At those conferences, the United States sought arms limitations, especially on navies, in part because it hoped to restrain others at a time when a parsimonious Congress restrained American growth. Except for some naval restrictions negotiated at the Washington and London conferences, little was accomplished. Without building to treaty limits, the United States sought to check the quantitative growth of other navies; France would not endorse disarmament until it received security guarantees; the British had a huge empire to protect and police by sea; Italy and Germany under the dictators Benito Mussolini and Adolf Hitler plotted military buildups; Japan eyed naval expansion in the Pacific. German rearmament under Hitler in the early 1930s and Japanese renunciation of Washington treaty provisions in 1934 presaged a dangerous escalatory course toward war.

COLD AS STEEL: SOVIET-AMERICAN ENCOUNTERS

The Russians signed the Kellogg-Briand Pact and joined the League of Nations in 1934. Yet most European nations and the United States treated Bolshevik Russia as an outsider, a revolutionary disease to be isolated. Only when Europe tottered on the brink of war in 1939 did Germany on the one hand and France and Britain on the other seriously woo Soviet Russia. Most powers, the United States among them, grudgingly established diplomatic and commercial contact with the Soviet Union in the interwar years.

Even though V. I. Lenin had said in 1918 that "with the United States we have friction, encounters, struggle, but there can also be agreement," Republican administrations in the 1920s adhered to the nonrecognition policy set by Woodrow Wilson.[61] The Bolsheviks had confiscated American-owned property valued at $336 million and Russia owed another $192 million to the U.S. government and still another $107 million to American nationals (Tsarist and Provisional government debts). Until Moscow met its obligations, recognition would be denied. Antiradical sentiment in the United States saw the Bolsheviks as godless, uncivilized, anticapitalist, violent, destructive revolutionaries who chained their workers like slaves to an authoritarian system. The *New York Times,* American Legion, and American Federation of Labor, among others, bitterly castigated the Soviet experiment. Secretary Stimson, like other Americans annoyed by the rantings of the American Communist party, declared in 1930 there would be no recognition until Russia "ceased to agitate for the overthrow of American institutions by revolution."[62] Only a few Americans, like Senator Borah and the International Ladies Garment Workers Union, urged tolerance and recognition while they criticized the Soviet system.

If most Americans kept at arm's length from the dreaded Bolsheviks, others, for a variety of reasons, edged closer. In 1921 Russia suffered a devastating famine. After the writer Maxim Gorky appealed for help, Secretary of Commerce Herbert Hoover signed an agreement with Moscow and organized the shipments of valuable food and medicine to needy areas of Russia. Moved by humanitarianism, Hoover also believed that this aid would help implant American influence in Russia and serve as a counterrevolutionary force. From 1921 to 1924 the American Relief Administration collected $50 million from the federal government and private citizens for assistance to approximately 10 million Russians. Colonel William Haskell, who headed the effort in Russia, reported incorrectly that the mission had left communism "dead and abandoned."[63]

American businesses also sought commercial contacts. The State Department separated its distaste for bolshevism from its desire for economic expansion and permitted important commercial relations to develop. International Harvester, General Electric, and DuPont signed trade and technical assistance contracts with the Soviet government, often through its purchasing agency in New York, the Soviet-owned Amtorg Trading Corporation. By 1924 Soviet purchases of American products had jumped seven times over the 1923 figure. In 1925 W. Averell Harriman, two decades later an ambassador to Russia, received monopolistic rights to rich manganese deposits valued at $1 billion, although the project never got under way. In 1928, 24 percent of all foreign investment in Russia was American. Russia's plans for industrialization and collectivization could not have advanced without American machinery, technology, and engineers (1,000 by 1931). Improvements in steel and agriculture in particular depended on American entrepreneurs and technicians, although German trade and investments also figured heavily in Soviet economic growth.

For people who believed that capitalism and communism could never meld, Henry Ford's contract with the Soviet Union in 1929 seemed remarkable. Yet the business hero agreed to supply the technical information needed to build the large Nizhni-Novgorod automobile factory near the Volga River, which would buy Ford parts and produce a car like the Model A and a truck like the Model AA. Ford eventually lost $578,000 on this multimillion-dollar venture, which terminated in 1934. Expecting a "market for Ford products which . . . may someday surpass in volume all the rest of Europe and Asia combined," the auto magnate did sell the Soviets on mass-production techniques (*Fordizatsia*).[64] By 1927, 85 percent of the Soviets' tractors were "Fordsons." An engineer who helped build the Soviet asbestos industry also vowed to "teach them Yankee methods" and make "Americanski Tempo" bywords in Russia.[65]

American-Russian economic ties began to loosen in the early 1930s. The Great Depression had sent capitalism to its knees, and government and business officials resented Soviet announcements in the United States that jobs were available in Russia. Most important, Russia began selling goods in the world market below American prices, whereupon Washington charged Moscow with "dumping." The United States banned imports of Soviet paper pulp because convict labor allegedly produced it. In retaliation and because of inadequate American capital to fund purchases, the Soviets reduced drastically their buying of American goods. In 1932 American exports to Russia declined 90 percent from the 1931 trade. Business executives eager for markets began to argue that official diplomatic recognition might restart stalled commercial relations. The Reconstruction Finance Corporation, a government agency set up to battle the depression, helped by extending Russia a $4 million credit for the purchase of American cotton.

The Roosevelt administration, because it wanted to improve trade and deter further Japanese encroachment on China, and simply because nonrecognition served no useful purpose, recognized the Soviet Union in November 1933. Roosevelt himself conducted the negotiations, even sending Hull away to a Pan American Conference in Montevideo, Uruguay, at the time. Will Rogers quipped that "we would recognize the Devil with a false face if he would contract for some pitchforks."[66] But the exchange of embassies did not smooth relations or halt Japan. American trade with Russia improved little, despite the signing of a trade treaty in 1935, its renewal in 1937, and the establishment of the Export-Import Bank. The loan or credit that Roosevelt and Commissar for Foreign Affairs Maxim Litvinov had discussed at the time of recognition never materialized because the two nations could not agree on compensation for World War I debts. When American communists spoke critically of the United States at Moscow's Seventh International Communist (Comintern) Congress in 1935, Secretary Hull protested, charging a violation of Russia's no-propaganda pledge. To many Americans, the squabbling and dashed hopes meant that the United States could not trust the Russians. President Roosevelt nonetheless continued to seek reconciliation.

Other issues disrupted Soviet-American relations. William Bullitt was named the first ambassador to Moscow; he left America in 1933 as a friend of Russia. Two years later an embittered Bullitt preached the "hard line" and resigned his post. Difficult living conditions in Moscow, spies among his servants, daily indignities at the hands of rude Soviet bureaucrats, and the conspicuous Soviet tyranny—all helped change his mind. The Comintern Congress of 1935 angered him, because

"So You're the Big Bad Bear!"
Roosevelt and Soviet commissar for foreign affairs Maxim Litvinov met in Washington in 1933. The atmosphere was friendly. (*Washington Evening Star*, Library of Congress)

it seemed to violate Russia's promise not to permit propaganda activities to originate from its soil. "Honor" and "fair dealing" were at stake; "friendly" relations with Russia could not be expected. The often hotheaded Bullitt soon "deviled the Russians. I did all I could to make things unpleasant."[67] The American correspondent Louis Fischer, who frequented the embassy rooms in Moscow, remembered that the ambassador urged reporters every day to "fan the flames of anti-Sovietism in America."[68]

The ghastly purges that began in 1935 also moved Bullitt and others toward the hard line. "The last mass trials were a great success. There are going to be fewer but better Russians," quipped an unsmiling Greta Garbo in the movie *Ninotchka* (1939).[69] American observers heard conflicting information and struggled to explain what was happening. Bullitt's successor as ambassador, the wealthy Joseph E. Davies, who thought Stalin "cold as steel" and the trials "a nightmare," speculated that the purge victims (the "outs") had plotted against the "ins."[70] George F. Kennan, a member of the embassy staff, found those days a "liberal education in the horrors of Stalinism."[71] For Kennan, who attended many of the purge trials in person, Russia had become a tortured scene of political murders, secretiveness, conspiratorial thinking, cruelty, and opportunism. Like most diplomats in the suspicious, isolated environment forced on foreigners in Moscow, Bullitt and Kennan became intensely anti-Soviet. So did some liberal and leftist Americans who had previously admired the Soviet experiment. The journalist Eugene Lyons, for example, a United Press correspondent in Russia from 1928 to 1934, became sickened by the callousness of Stalin's regime. When he returned to the United States he wrote a controversial article for *Harper's* magazine (1935) titled "To Tell or Not to Tell," an anguished autobiography that did the former. "The great tragic themes of peasant liquidation, persecution of intellectuals, tightening food shortage were bodied forth in hundreds of individual tragedies," he sadly wrote.[72]

If the purges stunned many Americans, the Nazi-Soviet pact of August 1939 outraged them. Premier Stalin believed he had no choice but to sign this agreement in order to protect his country from a menacing Germany. From the Russian point of view, the Western European powers and the United States had let Hitler expand uninhibited because he harbored conquerer's designs toward Russia. And Stalin had so depleted the officer ranks of his army through the purges that he was in no position to stave off an expected German attack. In the United States, the nonaggression pact, which secretly divided Poland, reinforced charges that Stalin had become Hitler's friend, even that fascism and communism had evolved as similar ideologies. When World War II erupted in September 1939, many Americans blamed Russia.

Lighter moments sometimes mingled with the harshness of Soviet-American relations. Shortly after Bullitt's arrival in Russia, the ambassador threw a party for Red Army generals. Amid the tables covered with plates of caviar, duck, pheasant, and the usual bottles of vodka sat Bullitt and the Soviet commissar of war. With the connivance of Charles Thayer, a prank-prone interpreter bored with his job, the conversation turned to polo. The Russians enthusiastically requested American polo instruction, having learned that the sport improved the cavalry, and in due course the American embassy imported the necessary balls and mallets. The Russians selected their best horsemen and sent them to a field near the Moscow River, where Bullitt tried desperately to explain the game. Once the match started, the refereeing ambassador lost control to the colliding men and horses. Thayer had forgotten to translate Bullitt's words on the relationship between the whistle and the end of the game. Finding no other way to halt the thundering mob of players, Thayer dashed onto the field and sent the ball into the Moscow River. An exuberant Russian rider retrieved it and the melee went on. Thayer then lunged at the ball, tucked it under his arm, and begged the horsemen to stop. Weeks later, after Moscow officials ordered the best ponies shipped to its polo teams, they staged the first formal match before the elite of the Soviet government. As Europe moved toward war, however, the Russian cavalrymen went off on maneuvers, abandoning their "polo for the proletariat."[73]

HITLER'S GERMANY, APPEASEMENT, AND THE OUTBREAK OF WAR

By exploiting the depression-afflicted economy and the vehement attitudes against the Versailles treaty in Germany, the Nazi leader Adolf Hitler came to power in January 1933. Racist toward Jews, emphatically anti-Bolshevik, and fanatical in his quest for personal power, Hitler set out to recapture past glory through the concept of Pan Germanism. In October 1933, Hitler withdrew Germany from the faltering League of Nations and denounced disarmament talks. He told an associate that the European powers would "never act! They'll just protest. And they will always be too late."[74] Indeed, France and Britain settled on a timid policy of "appeasement," hoping to satisfy what they thought were Hitler's limited goals and to avert another European war. By 1935 Hitler was rearming Germany, building an air force and a huge army. Britain, France, Italy, and the League of Nations censured Germany in April 1935. Yet at the same time, Britain agreed that Germany could rebuild its navy to 35 percent of the size of the British navy. This proved a costly concession to German militarism.

Hardly adjusted to the rise of Nazi Germany, the world faced a bold example of military extremism in October 1935 when Italy invaded the African state of Ethiopia. The fascist Benito Mussolini had governed Italy since 1922, and he had long dreamed of creating an Italian empire. Already holding Somaliland and Eritrea as African colonies, Mussolini gradually pressed Ethiopian leader Haile Selassie until military skirmishes broke out. Then Mussolini invaded and annexed Ethiopia. The League imposed an embargo on the shipment of war-related goods (except oil) to Italy. But the French, with their own empire in Africa, and the British, fearful that Italy might impede their imperial lifeline in the Mediterranean, seemed willing to sacrifice Ethiopia, a mere "corridor for camels."[75] They also feared that further

Adolf Hitler (1889–1945). When Hitler took power in 1933, some Americans likened his mustachioed face to that of the actor Charlie Chaplin. In this propagandistic German painting, the anticommunist, anti-Semitic Nazi leader is surrounded by swastikas and saluting followers. Hitler called the United States a "mongrel society" that was "hopelessly weak," but he learned otherwise. (U.S. Army)

hostilities would "play into Germany's hands" and "might mean a general war in Europe."[76]

Apparently encouraged by Anglo-French docility over Ethiopia, Hitler in March 1936 ordered his goose-stepping troops into the Rhineland, the area bordering Belgium and France that the Versailles treaty had declared permanently demilitarized. Gambling that the French would not resist what amounted to German occupation of German territory, Hitler envisioned a potential military avenue through Belgium into France. After World War I, the French had erected the Maginot Line, a series of large gun emplacements and defensive bunkers along the German-French border. By seizing the Rhineland, Germany was now in a position to skirt the supposedly impregnable Maginot. The French, fearful of igniting another war, did not resist the German advance into the Rhineland. Meanwhile, in June, the League of Nations lifted the economic sanctions against Italy. Victories by German athletes at the Berlin Olympiad in summer 1936 proved "as conducive to [Hitler's] self-esteem as a 98% plebiscite—and perhaps more convincing," observed U.S. ambassador William E. Dodd.[77] In October 1936, Germany and Italy arranged a tenuous alignment, the Rome-Berlin Axis; and a month later Germany and Japan, then subjugating China, joined in the Anti-Comintern Pact aimed at Russia.

Spain provided another battleground. "Nationalist" soldiers under General Francisco Franco started the Spanish Civil War in July 1936 by attacking the "Loyalist" Republican government in Madrid. Eager to mold in Spain a Franco government hostile to France, Hitler and Mussolini poured military equipment and troops into the Nationalist effort. The tepid Anglo-French response produced an International Non-Intervention Committee of twenty-seven nations, remarkably including Germany and Italy. Although the signatories pledged to stay out of the Spanish conflict, Hitler and Mussolini continued covert aid, and France and Britain lived with the fiction that they had isolated the Spanish Civil War. Russia and Mexico sent help to the Republicans, and some 3,000 Americans volunteered and fought alongside them in the Lincoln and Washington battalions of the International Brigades. Franco nonetheless prevailed in early 1939.

The mid-1937 election of Neville Chamberlain as British prime minister enshrined the appeasement policy. Chamberlain believed that Germany had good reason to want to throw off the humiliating Versailles treaty (Hitler called it a "dictated treaty")[78] and to claim status as a major power. Tolerant of Hitler's demand for mastery over people of German descent living in Austria, Czechoslovakia, and Poland, Chamberlain also believed, in the historian David Reynolds's words, that "Germany lacked the economic strength and political cohesion seriously to contemplate war and that she could be weaned from aggression by his blend of conciliation and firmness, carrot and stick."[79] Furthermore, an appeased Germany could serve as a useful restraint on Soviet Russia.

In March 1938, German troops crossed into Austria and annexed it to the German Reich. Months of terrorism against Jews and opponents of Nazism in Austria followed. Hitler next demanded the Sudeten region of Czechoslovakia, where 3 million ethnic Germans lived. Hitler assured Chamberlain that this marked Germany's last territorial demand. Britain and France (which had a defense treaty with Prague) granted the Nazi this additional prize. The Czechs had to capitulate.

Benito Mussolini (1883–1945). "Il Duce" excited a revival of Italian imperial grandeur by attacking Ethiopia in 1935. For a time, Roosevelt hoped Mussolini would serve as a moderating influence on Hitler. Will Rogers described Mussolini as a "cross between Roosevelt, Red Grange, Babe Ruth . . . , the elder La Follette, a touch of Borah, Bryan of '96, Samuel Gompers, and Tunney." (National Archives)

The end of Czechoslovakia's independence came at the Munich Conference of September 29–30, 1938, where Italy, Germany, France, and Britain agreed never to make war against one another and to sever the Sudetenland from Czechoslovakia. The conferees never consulted the Czechs themselves, who were not invited to Munich. Nor were the Russians or Americans. Chamberlain proclaimed "peace with honour" and "peace for our time," but as a precaution Britain launched a rearmament program.[80] Hitler soon initiated a brutal program against German Jews and in March 1939 swallowed the rest of Czechoslovakia. The following month Italy absorbed Albania.

Poland came next. Refusing Hitler's demands for the city of Danzig, the Poles soon faced German pressure. But London and Paris, now questioning Hitler's professions about limited goals, announced in March 1939 that they would stand behind an independent Poland. A grim Chamberlain judged it "impossible to deal with Hitler after he had thrown all his own assurances to the wind."[81] Hitler commented privately that "while England may talk big . . . she is sure not to resort to armed intervention in the conflict."[82] Russia then emerged as a central actor in the European tumult. Germany, Britain, and France opened negotiations with Moscow in attempts to gain Russia's allegiance. Germany won. On August 23, Nazi Germany and Soviet Russia signed the nonaggression pact, essentially assuring Berlin that Russia would remain neutral and not align with an Anglo-French coali-

Joachim von Ribbentrop (1893–1946) and Josef Stalin (1879–1953). The German foreign minister and Soviet premier smile their approval of the Nazi-Soviet nonaggression pact signed in August 1939. The news angered but did not surprise American officials, who monitored the secret negotiations through reports from a cooperative German diplomat in Moscow. (World War II Collection of Seized Enemy Records, National Archives)

tion. Poland, the immediate victim, found itself divided between the two powers. As he watched Hitler cavort with the Bolshevik devil, one U.S. senator wrote privately: "If Germany can organize Russia and they make England give up her fleet, look out—we'll have a Nazi, or nasty, world."[83] Yet Western outcries against the Nazi-Soviet pact seemed hypocritical, for Russia had done much the same thing as Britain and France had done at Munich. Hypocrisy or not, Germany stood poised for another conquest. On September 1, German soldiers invaded Poland. Two days later Britain and France buried appeasement and declared war against Germany. On the 17th, Soviet troops struck Poland, engulfing half the nation.

Throughout these years of descent into World War II, Hitler apparently did not consider the United States a nation of consequence. In his warped view, shaped by limited knowledge, the United States could not and would not be a vital factor in international affairs. Although his diplomatic advisers, including German ambassador to the United States Hans Dieckhoff, warned the Fuehrer that American isolationism could not be counted on, Hitler dismissed the United States as a weak, noninterventionist nation. Even in the period 1939–1941, when the United States took measures to aid the Allies, he did not alter his view. The United States, he said, "was incapable of conducting war." It was a "Jewish rubbish heap," incapacitated by economic and racial crisis, crime, and inept political leadership. "The inferiority and decadence of this allegedly new world is evident in its military inefficiency," he claimed. For Hitler a nation was powerful, and thus to be taken seriously, if its racial composition was pure and if it was a land power. Because America seemed to be a "melting pot" of ethnic diversity, "half Judaized, half negrified," and because it was largely a sea power, Hitler underestimated it, although some historians have argued that Hitler's long-range plans included aggressive war against the United States.[84] As the United States after 1938 increasingly tied its fortunes to Britain and France, Hitler's subjective views began to collide with the reality of American power.

AMERICAN ISOLATIONISM AND THE NEUTRALITY ACTS

"This nation will remain a neutral nation," President Roosevelt announced on September 3, 1939, "but I cannot ask that every American remain neutral in thought as well."[85] At the start of the war, the United States was not quite neutral in thought or deed. But this nascent unneutrality came late in the decade. During the early 1930s the United States attempted to shield itself from conflict in Europe and remain neutral. Although most Americans responded hostilely to the rise of Nazism, and strongly disapproved of Hitler's machinations at home and abroad, they tried to isolate themselves from a continent they thought prone to self-destruction. If Britain and France could not handle German aggression in their own backyards, America could not do the job for them.

Americans also drew lessons from World War I. Disillusioned writers and "revisionist" historians argued that Germany alone was not to blame for the outbreak of war in 1914, that an unneutral Wilson had been pro-British and influenced by business leaders and propagandists, and that the costs and results of war—the national interest—did not justify American participation. In 1934 the Book-of-the-Month Club offered a best-selling book titled *Merchants of Death* (by Helmuth Englebrecht and Frank Hanighen). Its message, that profiteering manufacturers of armaments had exploited the American economic and political system to compromise American neutrality, reflected popular opinion. Encouraged by President Roosevelt, Senator Gerald P. Nye held hearings during 1934–1936 to determine if munitions makers and bankers had lobbied Wilson into war. The committee never proved the allegation, but did uncover substantial evidence that these entrepreneurs hardly endorsed peace. As the historian John Wiltz has concluded, the Nye Committee "exhibited documents which shocked Americans into the realization that there was a difference between selling instruments of human destruction and selling sewing machines or automobiles."[86] Nye wailed against "rotten commercialism."[87] Such revelations fed popular sentiment that World War I had been a tragic blunder and that Americans should avoid what Senator Robert M. La Follette, Jr., called "a deadly parallel" by staying out of the next one.[88] Eleanor Roosevelt declared that "anyone who thinks, must think of the next war as they would of suicide."[89]

Peace groups, the scientist Albert Einstein, the celebrated pilot Charles Lindbergh, Herbert Hoover, the anti-Semite Father Charles E. Coughlin, the historian Charles Beard, President Robert Hutchins of the University of Chicago, and Senators William Borah, Hiram Johnson, and George Norris shared some of these ideas. The antiwar movement grew particularly strong on college campuses and among women. Princeton University students organized the Veterans of Future Wars in 1936 and demanded $1,000 each as a bonus *before* going into battle, because few, they predicted, would live through the next war. "Hello Sucker" posters picturing maimed soldiers aroused antiwar consciences. In 1938, member of Congress Louis Ludlow introduced a constitutional amendment calling for a national referendum on decisions for war. Warned Ludlow: "The art of killing people en masse and maiming and wrecking human bodies has been perfected until it is impossible to imagine the next large-scale war being anything less than a vast carnival of death."[90] Roosevelt claimed that the amendment "would cripple any President in his conduct of our foreign relations," and even the isolationist Senator Arthur Vandenberg protested that it "would be as sensible to require a town meeting before permitting the fire department to put out the blaze."[91] A motion to discharge Ludlow's resolution from the Rules Committee failed by only twenty-one votes, 209 to 188.

Many of the so-called isolationists were liberal reformers who believed that American entry into a European war would undercut the New Deal's attempts to recover from the depression. They remembered how the Wilson administration had savaged critics in World War I. They recalled, too, that he had cooperated with big business to win the war. Some reformers had become convinced that business expansionists helped create the conditions that spawned war; hence isolationists sought to curb business adventures abroad that entangled the United States. The statistics were not as readily available to them as they are now to historians. By 1937, for example, twenty of the top one hundred American corporations had negotiated important agreements with Nazi Germany, some of them with the backbone of the German military machine, the I. G. Farben Company. DuPont, Union Carbide, and Standard Oil signed contracts with Germany. Standard Oil helped Germany develop both synthetic rubber and hundred-octane aviation fuel, and, honoring its arrangement with Farben, refused to develop the fuel for the U.S. Army. As the historian Arnold A. Offner has concluded: "American businessmen publicly opposed

Senator Hiram W. Johnson (1866–1945). The fighter from California—a progressive reformer, anti-imperialist, and firm isolationist—served in the U.S. Senate for twenty-eight years. He opposed American membership in the League of Nations and the World Court and called for strict U.S. neutrality as Europe descended into war in the 1930s. The United States, Johnson insisted, "cannot strut as a knight-errant to reform the world." In 1941, however, he voted for U.S. entrance into World War II after the Japanese attack on Pearl Harbor. (Library of Congress)

war as much as anyone else. But it would seem that the one price they would not pay for peace was private profit."[92] A notable exception was the Wall Street law firm of Sullivan and Cromwell, which severed profitable ties with Germany to protest the persecution of Jews.

The abhorrence of war and its potential for harm in the United States, the desire to avoid intervention in the "maelstrom of European controversies," and the nationalist conviction that the United States should protect its freedom of action, all contributed to the passage of neutrality legislation.[93] Roosevelt wanted a neutrality act, but he sought discretionary power to ban sales of arms to aggressors in a war. Suspicious of presidential power in foreign policymaking, Congress instead passed the Neutrality Act of 1935, requiring an American arms embargo against all belligerents after the president had officially declared the existence of war. The president could not, in short, designate and punish the aggressor. Subsequent legislation banned loans to belligerents (Act of 1936) and required belligerents wishing to trade with the United States to carry away American goods in their own ships ("cash and carry"), after payment on delivery (Act of 1937). The latter also forbade American citizens to travel on belligerent vessels. An amendment of 1937 made the United States neutral in the Spanish Civil War.

The Neutrality Acts erred in providing for no discrimination among the belligerents, no punishment of the aggressor. They denied the United States any forceful word in the cascading events in Europe. They amounted to an abdication of power. Yet, at the same time, much of what the isolationists said about the fruits of war rang true. Their criticisms of imperialism and business expansion were honest and telling. They scorned the British Empire and U.S. intervention in Latin America. They compared Italy's subjugation of Ethiopia to Britain's supremacy in India. Many of them warned about increasing the power of the president in foreign affairs beyond congressional reach. Their noble commitment to peace and their rejection of war as a solution to human problems were compelling. "Isolationism was," the historian Manfred Jonas has written, "the considered response to foreign and domestic developments of a large, responsible, and respectable segment of the American people."[94] In condemning all imperialism—American, British, or German—the isolationists often refused to make the choice of the lesser of two or three evils. However praiseworthy their thought, their formulas for the 1930s proved as misguided as Britain's appeasement policy.

ROOSEVELT SHIFTS, CONGRESS BALKS ON THE EVE OF WAR

President Franklin D. Roosevelt, sensitive to the political weight of prevailing American sentiment against U.S. entanglement in Europe's bickering and territorial rearrangements and sharing much of the isolationist loathing of war, responded haltingly to the events of the 1930s. His foreign policy fed appeasement. When Germany began to rearm and when Italy attacked Ethiopia, Roosevelt stated that the United States sought above all to avoid war. America would set a peaceful example for other nations to follow. This idea of the United States as a "showcase" of righteousness drew on American tradition. He and Hull invoked the Neutrality Act in the Italo-Ethiopian conflict, warned Americans not to travel on belligerent ships, and suggested a moral embargo against trade with the warring parties. Actually, American businesses ignored the moral embargo and increased commerce with Italy, especially in oil. In August 1936, the president gave a stirring speech at Chautauqua, New York, recalling World War I: "I have seen war. . . . I have seen blood running from the wounded. I have seen men coughing out their gassed lungs. I have seen the dead in the mud. . . . I have seen the agony of mothers and wives. I hate war."[95]

In January 1937, the Roosevelt administration asked Congress for an arms embargo against Spain, then wracked by civil war. Congress obliged, but the decision sparked considerable debate. It produced "malevolent neutrality" that worked against the "Loyalist" Republican government and in favor of Franco, who received arms from Germany and Italy.[96] Many isolationists protested neutrality—the sacrifice of Spanish democracy—in this case. They agonized: How can one be commited to both peace and liberty? Roosevelt and Hull chose strict neutrality, in essence backing feeble British-French efforts to contain the civil war and aligning themselves with the pro-Franco views of the Catholic hierarchy at home. Yet Roosevelt privately pondered ways to curb the aggressors. In the summer of 1937, the president thought vaguely about calling an international conference, but he took no action. "I haven't got a hat and I haven't got a rabbit in it," he sighed.[97] In July, when Japan plunged into undeclared war against China, Roosevelt favored China by not invoking the Neutrality Act, thereby permitting the Chinese government to buy and import American war goods (see Chapter 5). Then in October he delivered his famous "quarantine" speech, calling for the isolation of international lawbreakers. Hoping that "people realize that war will be a greater danger . . . if we close all the doors and windows than if we go in the street and use our influence to curb the riot," FDR began vague talks with the British ambassador about a joint cruiser blockade against Japan and sent a naval officer to London for secret staff talks.[98] Under Secretary of State Sumner Welles also proposed a world conference on disarmament and international law in Washington, at which Roosevelt might quietly stiffen British diplomacy. Neville Chamberlain, however, blocked the meeting in early 1938; he feared it would interfere with his efforts to negotiate with the aggressors. Convinced that he could "count on nothing from the Americans but words," and that FDR's words on quarantines were the "utterings of a hare-brained statesman," Chamberlain continued to pursue appeasement.[99]

During the Czech crisis of 1938 the United States kept at a safe distance. The president appealed for negotiations to head off war, but he informed Hitler that the United States had "no political involvements in Europe and will assume no obligations in the conduct of the present negotiations."[100] He refrained from criticizing Germany for fear that Czechoslovakia would be encouraged to resist. "Good man," Roosevelt cabled Chamberlain when he heard that the prime minister would go to Munich.[101] Yet the dismemberment of Czechoslovakia, combined with the Japanese terror in China, soon prompted the president to shed his isolationist proclivities. Within months after Munich, he admitted privately that he was ashamed

"Uncomfortable Grandstand." The British cartoonist David Low obviously did not think that a neutral United States could remain safe after the outbreak of war in Europe. President Roosevelt turns a quizzical face to Secretary of State Hull as the bombs fly and burst. (*London Evening Standard*/Solo)

of his earlier response. Worried about the insidious effects of "too much Eton and Oxford," FDR thought the British needed "a good stiff grog, inducing not only the desire to save civilization but the continued belief that they can do it."[102]

In October 1938, Roosevelt asked Congress for $300 million for national defense. He encouraged the State Department and Senator Key Pittman, the hard-drinking, gun-packing, incompetent chair of the Foreign Relations Committee, to lobby for the repeal of the arms embargo law. In November, in protest against Hitler's vicious persecution of the Jews, he recalled Ambassador Hugh Wilson from Berlin and never let him return. Wilson had applauded Munich as opening the way "to a better Europe."[103] Like many other Americans, he hoped that a strong Germany would stand as a bulwark against Soviet Russia. That same month, FDR initiated a program to build more than 10,000 warplanes per year, in order "to have something to back up my words."[104] He also secretly arranged for the French government to place orders for planes. In December the administration rallied behind a declaration of joint defense against aggression in the Western Hemisphere and loaned $25 million to China.

In his annual message to Congress in January 1939, Roosevelt again urged revision of the Neutrality Act so that it would not "actually give aid to an aggressor and deny it to the victim."[105] The crash of the Douglas bomber and FDR's garbled statement about America's frontier on the Rhine stalled this initiative. The president thus delayed until March the introduction of a bill specifically repealing the arms embargo, and throughout the spring he allowed the erratic Pittman to direct legislative strategy. Reluctant to risk battle against sizable political odds, FDR failed to lead at a critical time. In April he asked Hitler and Mussolini to refrain from attacking countries named on a list, but his request met open derision, Il Duce saying that Italy would not respond to "convivial vociferations, or Messiah-like messages."[106] The Senate Foreign Relations Committee, by a 12 to 11 vote, refused in July to report out a bill repealing the arms embargo. "I've fired my last shot," the president groaned.[107] Not until November 1939—after Germany's conquest of Poland—did Congress finally revise the Neutrality Act so that England and France, as belligerents, could purchase American arms on a cash-and-carry basis.

Even in the fall of 1939, however, most Americans joined their president in wanting to avoid participation in World War II. "We cannot expect . . . the United States to evolve quicker than we did," the British ambassador reported.[108] Americans still hoped they could remain outside the melee. By sending Sumner Welles to Berlin, London, Paris, and Rome in the winter of 1939–1940, FDR evidently thought he might somehow mediate the conflict. Hitler's *blitzkrieg* in the west that spring killed any such possibility. The Democratic party platform of 1940, on which Roosevelt ran for a third term, reflected the American desire to avoid war but also to prepare for it: "We will not participate in foreign wars, and we will not send our army, naval or air forces to fight in foreign lands outside of the Americas except in case of attack." Still, it also promised "an invincible air force, a navy strong enough to protect all our seacoasts and our national interests, and a fully equipped and mechanized army."[109] As in the era of World War I, because of their international interests, because U.S. power became intertwined in the war, and because they gradually abandoned neutrality to aid the Allies, Americans once again found themselves risking major war. The interwar quest for world order and peace had failed; the several Neutrality Acts had failed; independent internationalism had failed.

FURTHER READING FOR THE PERIOD 1920–1939

For general studies, see James L. Abrahamson, *America Arms for a New Century* (1981); Selig Adler, *The Isolationist Impulse* (1957) and *The Uncertain Giant* (1965); Warren I. Cohen, *Empire Without Tears* (1987); Robert A. Divine, *The Reluctant Belligerent* (1979); Justus D. Doenecke and John E. Wilz, *From Isolation to War* (1991); Jean-Baptiste Duroselle, *From Wilson to Roosevelt* (1963); L. Ethan Ellis, *Republican Foreign Policy, 1921–1933* (1968); Robert H. Ferrell, *American Diplomacy in the Great Depression* (1957); William E. Leuchtenburg, *Franklin D. Roosevelt and the New Deal* (1963); Sally Marks, *The Illusion of Peace* (1976); Ernest R. May, *Knowing One's Enemies: Intelligence Assessment Before the Two World Wars* (1984); Donald R. McCoy, *Calvin Coolidge* (1967); Robert K. Murray, *The Harding Era* (1969); Arnold Offner, *The Origins of the Second World War* (1975); Robert Schulzinger, *The Making of the Diplomatic Mind* (1975); Michael S. Sherry, *The Rise of American Air Power* (1987); Geoffrey S. Smith, *To Save a Nation* (1992); and Raymond Sontag, *A Broken World, 1919–1939* (1971).

Among studies of Herbert Hoover as secretary of commerce and president are David Burner, *Herbert Hoover* (1978); Martin L. Fausold, *The Presidency of Herbert C. Hoover* (1985); Ellis W. Hawley, ed., *Herbert Hoover, Secretary of Commerce* (1981); and Joan Hoff Wilson, *Herbert Hoover* (1975).

For the secretaries of state: McGeorge Bundy, *On Active Service in Peace and War* (1948) (Stimson); L. Ethan Ellis, *Frank B. Kellogg and American and Foreign Relations* (1961); Robert H. Ferrell, *Frank B. Kellogg* (1963) and *Henry L. Stimson* (1963); Betty Glad, *Charles Evans Hughes and the Illusions of Innocence* (1967); Godfrey Hodgson, *The Colonel* (1990) (Stimson); Elting E. Morison, *Turmoil and Tradition* (1960) (Stimson); Dexter Perkins, *Charles Evans Hughes and American Democratic Statesmanship* (1956); Julius Pratt, *Cordell Hull* (1964); and essays on Hughes, Kellogg, and Stimson in Norman A. Graebner, ed., *An Uncertain Tradition* (1961).

Other diplomats and politicians are studied in Leroy Ashby, *The Spearless Leader* (1972) (Borah); Will Brownell and Richard N. Billings, *So Close to Greatness* (1988) (Bullitt); Wayne S. Cole, *Senator Gerald P. Nye and American Foreign Relations* (1962); Ralph de Bedts, *Ambassador Joseph Kennedy* (1985); Betty Glad, *Key Pittman* (1986); Frank W. Graff, *Strategy of Involvement* (1988) (Welles); Waldo Heinrichs, *American Ambassador* (1966) (Grew); Kenneth P. Jones, *Diplomats in Europe, 1919–1941* (1981); Richard C. Lower, *A Bloc of One* (1993) (Hiram Johnson); Richard Lowitt, *George W. Norris* (1963–1978); Elizabeth K. MacLean, *Joseph E. Davies* (1992); Jesse H. Stiller, *George S. Messersmith* (1987); and other works listed by subject below.

For studies of Franklin D. Roosevelt and his foreign policy, see James M. Burns, *The Lion and the Fox* (1956); Wayne S. Cole, *Roosevelt and the Isolationists* (1983); Robert Dallek, *Franklin D. Roosevelt and American Foreign Policy, 1933–1945* (1979); Kenneth R. Davis, *FDR* (1972–1993); Robert A. Divine, *Roosevelt and World War II* (1969); Frank Freidel, *Franklin D. Roosevelt* (1952–1973) and *Franklin D. Roosevelt* (1990); Frederick W. Marks III, *Wind Over Sand* (1988); Willard Range, *Franklin D. Roosevelt's World Order* (1959); Arthur M. Schlesinger Jr., *The Age of Roosevelt* (1957–1960); and Cornelius A. van Minnen and John F. Sears, eds., *FDR and His Contemporaries* (1992).

Economic foreign relations receive attention in Frederick Adams, *Economic Diplomacy: The Export-Import Bank and American Foreign Policy, 1934–1939* (1976); Derek H. Aldcroft, *From Versailles to Wall Street, 1919–1929* (1977); Joseph Brandes, *Herbert Hoover and Economic Diplomacy* (1962); Herbert Feis, *The Diplomacy of the Dollar* (1950); Lloyd C. Gardner, *Economic Aspects of New Deal Diplomacy* (1964); Michael J. Hogan, *Informal Entente: The Private Structure of Cooperation in Anglo-American Economic Diplomacy* (1977); Burton I. Kaufman, *Efficiency and Expansion: Foreign Trade Organization in the Wilson Administration, 1913–1921* (1974); Charles P. Kindleberger, *The World in Depression, 1929–1939* (1986); Carl Parrini, *Heir to Empire: United States Economic Diplomacy, 1916–1923* (1969); Stephen J. Randall, *United States Foreign Oil Policy, 1919–1948* (1986); William Stivers, *Supremacy and Oil: Iraq, Turkey, and the Anglo-American World Order, 1918–1930* (1982); Mira Wilkins, *The Maturing of Multinational Enterprise: American Business Abroad from 1914 to 1970* (1974); Joan Hoff Wilson, *American Business and Foreign Policy, 1920–1933* (1971); and Gilbert Ziebura, *World Economy and World Politics, 1924–1931* (1990).

The German reparations issue is particularly explored in Bruce Kent, *The Spoils of War* (1989); Stephen A. Schuker, *American "Reparations" to Germany* (1988); and Marc Trachtenberg, *Reparation in World Politics* (1980).

Cultural issues and industries are highlighted in Frank Costigliola, *Awkward Dominion* (1984) (Europe); David H. Culbert, *News for Everyman: Radio and Foreign Affairs in Thirties America* (1976); George Q. Flynn, *Roosevelt and Romanism: Catholics and American Diplomacy, 1937–1945* (1976); Emily S. Rosenberg, *Spreading the American Dream* (1982); Thomas J. Saunders, *Hollywood in Berlin* (1994); Lawrence Spinelli, *Dry Diplomacy* (1989) (Prohibition); Richard W. Steele, *Propaganda in an Open Society* (1985); Arnold H. Taylor, *American Diplomacy and the Narcotics Traffic, 1900–1931* (1969); and Robert C. Williams, *Russian Art and American Money* (1980).

For the peace movement, League of Nations, and disarmament, see Harriet H. Alonso, *The Women's Peace Union and the Outlawry of War* (1989); Thomas Buckley, *The United States and the Washington Conference,*

1921–1922 (1970); Charles Chatfield, *For Peace and Justice* (1971); Merle Curti, *Peace or War* (1936); Charles DeBenedetti, *Origins of the Modern American Peace Movement, 1915–1929* (1978) and *The Peace Reform in American History* (1980); Roger Dingman, *Power in the Pacific: The Origins of Naval Arms Limitation, 1914–1922* (1976); Michael Dunne, *The United States and the World Court* (1988); Robert Ferrell, *Peace in Their Time* (1952); D. F. Fleming, *The United States and World Organization, 1920–1933* (1938); Catherine Foster, *Women for All Seasons* (1989); Harold Josephson, *James T. Shotwell and the Rise of Internationalism in America* (1976); Robert G. Kaufman, *Arms Control During the Pre-Nuclear Era* (1990); Gary B. Ostrower, *Collective Insecurity: The United States and the League of Nations During the Early Thirties* (1979); Stephen Pelz, *Race to Pearl Harbor: The Failure of the Second London Naval Conference and the Onset of World War II* (1974); and Lawrence S. Wittner, *Rebels Against War* (1984).

The internationalist and peace views of Eleanor Roosevelt are explored in Jason Berger, *A New Deal for the World* (1981); Blanche Wiesen Cook, *Eleanor Roosevelt* (1992); Lois Scharf, *Eleanor Roosevelt* (1987); and Joan Hoff Wilson and Marjorie Lightman, eds., *Without Precedent* (1984).

Soviet-American relations and recognition are discussed in Edward Bennett, *Recognition of Russia* (1970) and *Franklin D. Roosevelt and the Search for Security* (1985); Donald G. Bishop, *The Roosevelt-Litvinov Agreements* (1965); Robert Browder, *The Origins of Soviet-American Diplomacy* (1953); Keith D. Eagles, *Ambassador Joseph E. Davies and American-Soviet Relations, 1937–1941* (1985); Beatrice Farnsworth, *William C. Bullitt and the Soviet Union* (1967); Peter Filene, *Americans and the Soviet Experiment, 1917–1933* (1967); John Lewis Gaddis, *Russia, the Soviet Union, and the United States* (1990); Jonathan Haslam, *The Soviet Union and the Struggle for Collective Security in Europe, 1933–1939* (1984); George F. Kennan, *Russia and the West under Lenin and Stalin* (1960); James K. Libbey, *Alexander Gumberg and Soviet-American Relations, 1917–1933* (1977); Thomas R. Maddux, *Years of Estrangement* (1980); Anthony Sutton, *Western Technology and Soviet Economic Development, 1917–1930* (1968); Christine A. White, *British and American Commercial Relations with Soviet Russia, 1918–1924* (1993); and Joan Hoff Wilson, *Ideology and Economics* (1974).

American isolationism, neutrality, interwar European questions, the rise of fascism, and the coming of World War II are treated in many of the works cited above and in James J. and Patience P. Barnes, *Hitler's Mein Kampf in Britain and America* (1980); Edward W. Bennett, *German Rearmament and the West, 1932–1933* (1979); Peter H. Buckingham, *International Normalcy: The Open Door Peace with the Former Central Powers, 1921–29* (1983); Warren I. Cohen, *The American Revisionists* (1967); James V. Compton, *The Swastika and the Eagle* (1967); Jean-Baptiste Duroselle, *France and the United States* (1978); Thomas N. Guinsburg, *The Pursuit of Isolationism* (1981); John Haight, Jr., *American Aid to France, 1938–1940* (1970); Manfred Jonas, *Isolationism in America* (1966); Thomas C. Kennedy, *Charles A. Beard and American Foreign Policy* (1975); Lawrence Lafore, *The End of Glory* (1971); Melvyn Leffler, *The Elusive Quest* (1979) (France); Charles S. Maier, *Recasting Bourgeois Europe* (1975); Brian McKercher, ed., *Anglo-American Relations in the 1920s* (1991); William C. McNeil, *American Money and the Weimer Republic* (1986); Wolfgang Mommsen and Lothar Kettenacker, eds., *The Fascist Challenge and the Policy of Appeasement* (1983); Arnold Offner, *American Appeasement* (1969); R. A. C. Parker, *Chamberlain and Appeasement* (1993); Neal Pease, *Poland, the United States, and the Stabilization of Europe, 1919–1933* (1986); David Reynolds, *The Creation of the Anglo-American Alliance, 1937–41* (1982); William R. Rock, *Chamberlain and Roosevelt* (1988); David F. Schmitz, *The United States and Fascist Italy* (1988); David F. Schmitz and Richard D. Challener, eds., *Appeasement in Europe* (1990); Dan P. Silverman, *Reconstructing Europe after the Great War* (1982); D. C. Watt, *How War Came* (1989); Gerhard Weinberg, *The Foreign Policy of Hitler's Germany* (1970, 1980); and John Wiltz, *In Search of Peace: The Senate Munitions Inquiry* (1963).

For the Spanish Civil War: Mark Falcoff and Frederick B. Pike, *The Spanish Civil War, 1936–1939* (1982); Allen Guttman, *The Wound in the Heart* (1962); Douglas Little, *Malevolent Neutrality* (1985); R. Dan Richardson, *Comintern Army* (1982); and Richard Traina, *American Diplomacy and the Spanish Civil War* (1968).

See also the "Further Reading" sections for Chapters 5 and 6; the General Bibliography; Richard Dean Burns, ed., *Guide to American Foreign Relations Since 1700* (1983); and the following notes.

Notes to Chapter 4

1. Quoted in Kenneth S. Davis, *FDR: Into the Storm* (New York: Random House, 1993), p. 401.
2. Quoted *ibid.*, p. 402.
3. Quoted *ibid.*, p. 401.
4. Henry Morgenthau, Jr., quoted in transcript of conference, March 21, 1946, Box 391, Henry Morgenthau, Jr., Papers, Franklin D. Roosevelt Library, Hyde Park, New York.
5. David Reynolds, *The Creation of the Anglo-American Alliance, 1937–1941* (Chapel Hill: University of North Carolina Press, 1982), p. 43.
6. Quoted in Wayne S. Cole, *Roosevelt and the Isolationists, 1932–45* (Lincoln: University of Nebraska Press, 1983), p. 297.
7. Robert C. Erhart, "The Politics of Military Rearmament, 1935–40: The President, the Congress, and the United States Army" (Ph.D. dissertation, University of Texas, 1975), p. 88.
8. Quoted in Michael S. Sherry, *The Rise of American Air Power* (New Haven: Yale University Press, 1987), pp. 79–80.
9. Quoted in Jean Monnet, *Memoirs* (London: Collins, 1978), p. 119.
10. Quoted in Sherry, *Air Power*, p. 80.
11. Quoted in Cole, *Roosevelt and Isolationists*, p. 301.
12. Quoted in transcript of conference on "The French Airplane Mission," April 25, 1946, Box 391, Morgenthau Papers.
13. Transcript of "Conference with Senate Military Affairs Committee, Executive Offices of the White House, January 31, 1939, 12:45 P.M.," Personal Files, PPF 1-P, Franklin D. Roosevelt Papers, Roosevelt Library.
14. Quoted in J. Garry Clifford, "A Note on the Break Between Senator Nye and President Roosevelt in 1939," *North Dakota History, XLIX* (Summer 1982), 17.
15. *New York Times,* February 1, 1939.
16. Quoted in Clifford, "A Note," 14.
17. Entry of February 7, 1939, diary of J. Pierrepont Moffat, Houghton Library, Harvard University, Cambridge, Mass.; and quoted in Reynolds, *Creation,* p. 37.
18. Transcript, "French Airplane Incident."
19. Warren F. Kimball, *The Juggler* (Princeton: Princeton University Press, 1991), p. 7.
20. Quoted in Sherry, *Air Power,* p. 79.
21. *Ibid.*, p. 82.
22. Henry Arnold quoted in John M. Haight, Jr., *American Aid to France, 1938–1940* (New York: Atheneum, 1970), p. 204.
23. Raymond Clapper to Alfred M. Landon, February 7, 1939, Alfred M. Landon Papers, Kansas State Historical Society, Topeka, Kansas.
24. Franklin D. Roosevelt to Helen Rogers Reid, June 6, 1940, Reid Family Papers, Library of Congress, Washington, D.C.

25. Quoted in John M. Blum, *From the Morgenthau Diaries* (Boston: Houghton Mifflin, 1959–1967; 3 vols.), I, 118.
26. Quoted in Robert F. Smith, "Republican Policy and the Pax Americana, 1921–1932," in William A. Williams, ed., *From Colony to Empire* (New York: John Wiley & Sons, 1972), p. 292; and in Melvyn P. Leffler, "Political Isolationism: Economic Expansionism or Diplomatic Realism?" *Perspectives in American History, VIII* (1974), 419.
27. Joan Hoff Wilson, *American Business and Foreign Policy, 1920–1933* (Boston: Beacon Press, 1973 [c. 1971]), p. *x.*
28. Melvyn P. Leffler, *The Elusive Quest* (Chapel Hill: University of North Carolina Press, 1979), p. 362.
29. Quoted in L. Ethan Ellis, *Republican Foreign Policy, 1921–1933* (New Brunswick, N.J.: Rutgers University Press, 1968), p. 40.
30. Diary, December 9, 1927, Box 87, Lewis Douglas Papers, University of Arizona Library, Tucson, Arizona.
31. Howard H. Quint and Robert H. Ferrell, eds., *The Talkative President* (Amherst: University of Massachusetts Press, 1964), p. 298.
32. Quoted in John Chalmers Vinson, "Charles Evans Hughes," in Norman A. Graebner, ed., *An Uncertain Tradition* (New York: McGraw-Hill, 1961), p. 133.
33. Quoted *ibid.*, p. 132.
34. Willard Range, *Franklin D. Roosevelt's World Order* (Athens: University of Georgia Press, 1959), p. *xii.*
35. Quoted in Frank Freidel, *Franklin D. Roosevelt: Launching the New Deal* (Boston: Little, Brown, 1973), p. 459.
36. Quoted in Jordan A. Schwarz, *Liberal* (New York: The Free Press, 1987), p. 191.
37. Quoted in Waldo H. Heinrichs, Jr., *American Ambassador* (Boston: Little, Brown, 1966), p. 103.
38. Quoted in William Barnes and John H. Morgan, *The Foreign Service of the United States* (Washington D.C.: Department of State, 1961), p. 203.
39. Mira Wilkins, *The Maturing of Multinational Enterprise* (Cambridge, Mass.: Harvard University Press, 1974), p. 138.
40. Edward G. Lowry, "Trade Follows the Film," *Saturday Evening Post, CXCVIII* (November 7, 1925), 12.
41. Quoted in Frank Costigliola, *Awkward Dominion* (Ithaca: Cornell University Press, 1984), p. 175.
42. Quoted in Paul Weindling, "Public Health and Political Stabilization: The Rockefeller Foundation in Central and Eastern Europe Between the Two World Wars," *Minerva, XXXI* (Autumn 1993), 261.
43. *New York Times,* May 5, 1930.
44. Quoted in Robert A. Hathaway, "1933–1945: Economic Diplomacy in a Time of Crisis," in William H. Becker and Samuel F. Wells, Jr., eds., *Economics and World Power* (New York: Columbia University Press, 1984), p. 285.

45. Quoted in Julius W. Pratt, *Cordell Hull* (New York: Cooper Square, 1964; 2 vols.) *I*, 112.

46. Quoted in Blum, *Morgenthau Diaries, I*, 151.

47. Quoted in Richard A. Harrison, "The United States and Great Britain: Presidential Diplomacy and Alternatives to Appeasement in the 1930s," in David F. Schmitz and Richard D. Challener, eds., *Appeasement in Europe* (Westport, Conn.: Greenwood Press, 1990), p. 116.

48. Foreign Office diplomat quoted in Brian McKercher, "Wealth, Power, and the New International Order," *Diplomatic History, XII* (Fall 1988), 421.

49. Quoted in Quint and Ferrell, *Talkative President*, p. 196; and in Frank Costigliola, "The United States and the Reconstruction of Germany in the 1920s," *Business History Review, L* (Winter 1976), 486.

50. Will Rogers, *Letters of a Self-Made Diplomat to His President* (New York: A. & C. Boni, 1926), p. *xii*.

51. Michael J. Hogan, "Revival and Reform," *Diplomatic History, VIII* (Fall 1984), 289.

52. Bruce Kent, *The Spoils of War* (New York: Oxford University Press, 1989), p. 10.

53. Quoted in Harold Josephson, *James T. Shotwell and the Rise of Internationalism in America* (Rutherford, N.J.: Fairleigh Dickinson University Press, 1975), p. 140.

54. Quoted in Charles DeBenedetti, "Peace Was His Profession," in Frank Merli and Theodore A. Wilson, eds., *Makers of American Diplomacy* (New York: Charles Scribner's Sons, 1974), p. 390.

55. Susan Zeiger, "Finding a Cure for War," *Journal of Social History, XXIV* (Fall 1990), 70.

56. Merle Curti, *Peace or War* (New York: W. W. Norton, 1936), p. 262.

57. James Shotwell quoted in Charles DeBenedetti, *Origins of the Modern American Peace Movement, 1915–1929* (Milwood, N.Y.: KTO Press, 1978), p. 187.

58. *The General Pact for the Renunciation of War* (Washington, D.C.: Government Printing Office, 1928).

59. Quoted in Richard C. Lower, *A Bloc of One* (Stanford: Stanford University Press, 1993), p. 197.

60. Quoted in Michael Dunne, *The United States and the World Court, 1920–1935* (New York: St. Martin's Press, 1988), p. 264.

61. Quoted in David McFadden, *Alternative Paths* (New York: Oxford University Press, 1993), p. 26.

62. Quoted in David J. Danelski and Joseph S. Tulchin, eds., *The Autobiographical Notes of Charles Evans Hughes* (Cambridge, Mass.: Harvard University Press, 1973), p. 262.

63. Quoted in Peter G. Filene, *Americans and the Soviet Experiment, 1917–1933* (Cambridge, Mass.: Harvard University Press, 1967), p. 82.

64. Quoted in Christine A. White, *British and American Commercial Relations with Soviet Russia, 1918–1924* (Chapel Hill: University of North Carolina Press, 1992), p. 223.

65. Walter Rukeyser quoted in Costigliola, *Awkward*, p. 159.

66. Will Rogers, *How We Elect Our Presidents* (Boston: Little, Brown, 1952), p. 148.

67. Quoted in Beatrice Farnsworth, *William C. Bullitt and the Soviet Union* (Bloomington: Indiana University Press, 1967), p. 153.

68. Louis Fischer, *Men and Politics* (New York: Duell, 1941), p. 308.

69. Quoted in Melvin Small, "Buffoons and Brave Hearts: Hollywood Portrays the Russians, 1939–1944," *California Historical Quarterly, LII* (Winter 1973), 327.

70. Quoted in Elizabeth Kimball MacLean, *Joseph E. Davies* (Westport, Conn.: Praeger, 1992), pp. 50, 55.

71. George F. Kennan, *Memoirs, 1925–1950* (Boston: Little, Brown, 1967), p. 67.

72. Eugene Lyons, "To Tell or Not to Tell," *Harper's, CLXXI* (June 1935), 102.

73. Charles W. Thayer, *Bears in the Caviar* (Philadelphia: Lippincott, 1951), p. 115.

74. Quoted in Arnold A. Offner, *American Appeasement* (New York: W. W. Norton, 1976 [c. 1969]), p. 50.

75. Quoted in Raymond J. Sontag, *A Broken World, 1919–1939* (New York: Harper & Row, 1971), p. 290.

76. Ambassador Robert Bingham quoted in David F. Schmitz, *The United States and Fascist Italy, 1922–1940* (Chapel Hill: University of North Carolina Press, 1988), pp. 161–162.

77. Quoted in George Eisen, "The Voices of Sanity: American Diplomatic Reports from the 1936 Berlin Olympiad," *Journal of Sports History, XI* (Winter 1984), 75.

78. Quoted in Laurence Lafore, *The End of Glory* (Philadelphia: Lippincott, 1970), p. 158.

79. Reynolds, *Creation*, p. 9.

80. Quoted in A. J. P. Taylor, *The Origins of the Second World War* (New York: Fawcett, 1966 [c. 1961]) p. 181.

81. Quoted in Roy Douglas, "Chamberlain and Appeasement," in Wolfgang J. Mommsen and Lothar Kettenacker, *The Fascist Challenge and the Policy of Appeasement* (London: Allen & Unwin, 1983), p. 87.

82. Quoted in Sontag, *Broken World*, p. 374.

83. Harry S. Truman in Robert H. Ferrell, ed., *Dear Bess* (New York: W. W. Norton, 1983), p. 419.

84. Quoted in James V. Compton, *The Swastika and the Eagle* (Boston: Houghton Mifflin, 1967), pp. 17, 25, 33.

85. Samuel I. Rosenman, ed., *Public Papers . . . of Franklin D. Roosevelt, 1939* (New York: Macmillan, 1938–50; 13 vols.), *VIII*, 463.

86. John E. Wiltz, "The Nye Committee Revisited," *The Historian, XXIII* (February 1961), 232.

87. Quoted in Wayne S. Cole, *Senator Gerald P. Nye and American Foreign Relations* (Minneapolis: University of Minnesota Press, 1962), pp. 126–127.

88. Quoted in Patrick J. Maney, *"Young Bob" La Follette* (Columbia: University of Missouri Press, 1978), p. 226.

89. Quoted in Blanche Wiesen Cook, "Eleanor Roosevelt and Human Rights," in Edward P. Crapol, ed., *Women and American Foreign Policy* (Wilmington, Del.: Scholarly Resources, 1992; 2d ed.), p. 97.

90. Quoted in Thomas G. Paterson, *Meeting the Communist Threat* (New York: Oxford University Press, 1988), p. 216.

91. Quoted in Robert A. Divine, *The Reluctant Belligerent* (New York: John Wiley & Sons, 1979; 2d ed.), p. 52; and in Justus D. Doenecke and John E. Wilz, *From Isolation to War, 1931–1941* (Arlington Heights, Ill.: Harlan Davidson, 1991; 2d ed.), p. 15.

92. Offner, *American Appeasement*, p. 103.

93. Hiram Johnson in *Congressional Record*, LXI (October 18, 1921), 6405.

94. Manfred Jonas, *Isolationism in America, 1935–1941* (Ithaca: Cornell University Press, 1966), p. viii.

95. Rosenman, *Public Papers, 1936, V*, 289.

96. Douglas Little, *Malevolent Neutrality* (Ithaca: Cornell University Press, 1985), p. 265.

97. Quoted in Dorothy Borg, *The United States and the Far Eastern Crisis of 1933–1938* (Cambridge, Mass.: Harvard University Press, 1964), p. 374.

98. Roosevelt to Edward M. House, October 19, 1937, Edward M. House Papers, Sterling Library, Yale University, New Haven, Conn.

99. Quoted in Christopher Thorne, *Allies of a Kind* (New York: Oxford University Press, 1978), p. 38.

100. *Foreign Relations, 1938, I* (Washington, D.C.: Government Printing Office, 1955), 685.

101. *Ibid.*, p. 688.

102. Quoted in Reynolds, *Creation*, p. 43.

103. Quoted in Offner, *American Appeasement*, p. 215.

104. Quoted in Blum, *Morgenthau Diaries, II*, 49.

105. Rosenman, *Public Papers, 1939, VIII*, 4.

106. Quoted in William L. Langer and S. Everett Gleason, *The Challenge to Isolation* (New York: Harper & Brothers, 1952), p. 87.

107. Quoted in Robert Dallek, *Franklin D. Roosevelt and American Foreign Policy, 1932–1945* (New York: Oxford University Press, 1979), p. 192.

108. Lord Lothian to Lord Halifax, September 27, 1939, vol. 24, Halifax Papers, FO/800, Public Record Office, Kew, England.

109. Kirk H. Porter and Donald B. Johnson, eds., *National Party Platforms, 1840–1972* (Urbana: University of Illinois Press, 1973), p. 382.

Chapter 5

ASIA, LATIN AMERICA, AND THE VAGARIES OF POWER, 1920–1939

William E. Borah (1865–1940) and Henry L. Stimson (1867–1950). *The Idaho senator (left) chaired the Foreign Relations Committee, 1925–1933. An isolationist, he opposed U.S. membership in the League of Nations and promoted neutrality; an anti-imperialist, he condemned U.S. interventions in Latin America; a peace advocate, he saluted the Kellogg-Briand Pact. A noted orator, Borah said much on most issues. "Borah this and Borah that, Borah here and there, Borah does and Borah doesn't, until you wish that Borah wasn't," wrote a journalist. In a February 1932 letter to Borah, Secretary of State Stimson explained U.S. defense of the Open Door policy during the Manchurian crisis. (Library of Congress)*

✳ *Diplomatic Crossroad*

The Manchurian Crisis, 1931–1932

It apparently started with thirty-one inches of steel. At 10:20 P.M., a few miles outside the Manchurian capital of Mukden during the night of September 18, 1931, an explosion apparently blasted a short section from the South Manchurian Railway. Japanese soldiers apparently shot and killed some Chinese attempting to escape from the area. Apparently? Yes, because Japanese army officers had a most difficult time explaining the events of that dark night. The Mukden Express had somehow managed to cross over that very section of track *after* the alleged explosion. The train must have jumped the gap, the Japanese lamely answered. American officials who inspected the steel fragments noted that they did not carry the imprint of the Carnegie Steel Works as did the track still in place. Indeed, it appears that independent-minded young officers of the Guandong (Manchurian) army had fabricated the "Mukden Incident" of September 18. They had plotted for months to seize Manchuria and sever it permanently from China. Feverish in their quest for Japanese grandeur and Asian power, they or their followers had already, in 1930, assassinated the Japanese premier. So when the news from Mukden reached Tokyo, one civilian official remarked, "They've done it at last."[1]

For the Japanese—civilian or military—Manchuria ranked as a vital interest. Comprising an area as large as France and Germany with a population of 30 million (including 28 million Chinese), Manchuria served as a defensive buffer against the hated Russians and their communism. More important, the territory teemed with the raw materials (coal, iron, timber, soybeans) so desperately needed by the import-hungry Japanese islands. Manchuria held more than half of Japan's foreign investments. The Japanese-run South Manchurian Railway acted as the nerve center of these large economic holdings. Ever since their victory in the Russo-Japanese War, the Japanese had been driving in their imperial stakes. By treaty they had acquired the right to station troops along the railroad. The United States had recognized Japan's primacy in Manchuria through the Root-Takahira and Lansing-Ishii agreements (see Chapter 2).

Chinese nationalists throughout the 1920s had resisted Japanese intrusions. Nationalist leader Jiang Jieshi (Chiang Kai-shek) encouraged Chinese to move to Manchuria and sought to build a railroad to compete with the South Manchurian. The Chinese boycotted Japanese products, a particularly alarming practice during the Great Depression, when Japan's foreign trade slumped. Chinese and Japanese blood spilled in isolated incidents. Such cumulative provocations amounted to "a case where a thousand pinpricks equalled a slash of the saber."[2] The haughty Japanese response came in the darkness of September 18, 1931.

The Mukden news reached an irritable Secretary of State Henry L. Stimson, worn low by Washington's exceedingly hot, humid temperatures before the age of the air conditioner. The weather accentuated a Stimsonian personality trait—what President Herbert Hoover called his "combat psychology."[3] The forthright secretary shared prevalent American attitudes toward "inferior" races and believed that he understood the "Oriental mind."[4] He also embraced the Open Door policy and the sanctity of law. Japanese aggression in Manchuria violated treaties signed at the Washington Conference (1922), which endorsed the Open Door, and the Kellogg-Briand Pact (1928), which outlawed war. Stimson saw the Manchurian crisis as "an issue between the two great theories of civilization and economic methods."[5]

Stimson hoped at first that the "Mukden Incident" would remain a localized mutiny of the Japanese army. No American wanted the United States to become ensnarled "all by itself" in this Chinese-Japanese-Manchurian imbroglio "full of hidden explosives, dense underbrush, [and] quicksand," noted the chief of the State Department's Division of Far Eastern Affairs, Stanley K. Hornbeck.[6] Caution seemed quite in order. The United States possessed little power in Asia. The British, interested in preserving their own Asian empire and hobbled by economic crisis at home, preferred to appease their former ally Japan. The French foundered in their frequent domestic political confusion. Soviet Russia, still not recognized by the United States, could hardly be called on for help. And the feeble League of Nations, the humorist Will Rogers astutely observed, could "make the little fellows behave" but had "no more power than a Senate investigating committee" to discipline "the big fellows."[7]

"The Open Door." The Japanese thrust into Manchuria in 1931 called into question the peace and disarmament agreements of the previous decade. (*The Outlook*, 1931)

Stimson decided on a meek policy of letting "the Japanese know we are watching them."[8] On September 24, 1931, he urged the Chinese and Japanese to cease hostilities. A few days later the League began to discuss the Manchurian crisis, and the United States permitted an American representative to sit at the League table, but only as an "observer." Stimson and Hoover feared that the international organization would "dump" the "Manchurian baby" in Washington's lap, but the League passed mild peace resolutions and set up the Lytton Commission to investigate.[9] Japanese soldiers kept marching, meeting little resistance from ineptly led Chinese forces, and within months they had seized all of Manchuria.

The secretary of state did not have many options. He could not intervene militarily. He could not call on Britain, France, Russia, or the League. And when he suggested to Hoover, in December 1931, that the United States and others impose economic sanctions on Japan, the president strongly rejected the idea. Stimson knew that the island empire depended on imports of American oil, that it was the third largest buyer of American exports, and that the United States took about 40 percent of Japan's exports. Maybe economic pressure would force Tokyo to disgorge Manchuria. Hoover, however, responded that the United States should not be "sticking pins in tigers."[10] Even more, Hoover wrote privately, Japan's actions "do not imperil the freedom [or] the economic or moral fiber of our people. I do not propose to sacrifice American life for anything short of this."[11]

Thus, nonrecognition. On January 7, 1932, Stimson issued what became known as the Stimson Doctrine. (Hoover, his political fortunes flagging at home, wanted to call it the Hoover Doctrine.) Stimson threw tradition and law against Japan: The United States would not recognize any arrangements in China that might impair American treaty rights, violate the Open Door policy, or subvert the Kellogg-Briand Pact. Defiantly, on January 28, the Japanese marched into Shanghai. A belligerent Stimson persuaded Hoover to reinforce the American military garrison in that city. Reminded of the German attack on Belgium in 1914, the secretary drew an historical lesson and set his jaw against this new aggression.

Stimson had nothing left to try but bluff. He wanted to frighten Japan without its knowing that it had no reason to be afraid. On February 23, 1932, Stimson sent a public letter to Senator William Borah, chair of the Senate Foreign Relations Committee. The secretary privately hoped that the letter would "encourage China, enlighten the American public, exhort the League, stir up the British, and warn Japan."[12] A rather ambitious set of goals, for sure. Employing the Open Door policy as an instrument, Stimson chastised Japan for violating the administrative and territorial integrity of China and the Kellogg-Briand agreement. He repeated his earlier denial of recognition and threatened to fortify Guam and build up the U.S. Navy in the Pacific if Japan did not halt its aggression. This protest made little impact, although Japan soon signed an armistice in Shanghai and the League endorsed nonrecognition. In February, Japan actually reconstituted Manchuria as the puppet state of Manchukuo. In October the Lytton Commission chided the Japanese for misconduct in Manchuria. Perturbed but unchecked, Japan resigned from the League of Nations in early 1933, claiming it was being crucified like Christ on the cross. Stimson's bluff had failed. The secretary, the biographer Elting E. Morison has written, "wound up like a man before a breaking dam with a shovel in his hands." Stimson himself remarked that he brandished "spears of straw and swords of ice."[13]

A QUESTION OF POWER

Stimson's diplomatic efforts raise questions that help explain the choices and limitations facing U.S. leaders in the 1920–1939 period. Was it wise for Stimson to rail against Japanese machinations in Manchuria? Did it do any good? Did it perhaps help the Japanese military gain support from other nationalists who also considered Manchuria vital? Did the nonrecognition policy reveal just how weak the United States was in Asia? Was U.S. policy read as bluff? Did it not also expose China's vulnerability, its abandonment by other nations? Yet, should Stimson have ignored the violations of the treaties? Or would it have been prudent to let the Asians settle their own differences—especially since the United States lacked sufficient naval and military power to intervene in the area? Did the Manchurian crisis threaten America's national interest?

Years after 1931, Stimson admitted that nonrecognition had not worked to restore the balance of power in Asia or restrain Japan. Moral exhortation and lecturing may only have soothed the American conscience and stirred up the aggressor, to nobody's benefit. The diplomat Hugh Wilson reflected on Stimson's tactics: "If the nations of the world feel strongly enough to condemn, they should feel strongly enough to use force. . . . To condemn only merely intensifies the heat." He went on: "Condemnation creates a community of the damned who are forced outside the pale, who have nothing to lose by the violation of all laws of order and international good faith."[14] Still, although American economic interests in Manchuria were small, the principle of the Open Door, both as diplomatic tool and as ideology, was at stake. If Tokyo could violate the Open Door in Manchuria, it could do so elsewhere. Stimson spoke out for the principle that bolstered U.S. economic interests overseas—hence his reference to the struggle in Manchuria as one between different economic methods.

America's timid response to the Manchurian crisis demonstrated that the United States, because it lacked power, could not manage affairs in Asia. U.S. gunboats still chugged on Chinese rivers, American troops garrisoned on Chinese soil, American business interests formed the Shanghai Power Company in 1928 and thus "Americanized" the city, and the Philippines remained a colony, but in the Pacific the Japanese had clear superiority.[15] America could lecture but not enforce. By contrast, the United States held considerable power—economic, naval, military, political—in Latin America. Central America and the Caribbean were to the United States what China, especially Manchuria, was to Japan. The Japanese, in fact, often commented that their actions in China simply resembled U.S. actions in Latin America. In Latin America the United States practiced the "closed door"; in Asia it appealed for the "Open Door." In both areas, the viability of American foreign policy depended on power.

Makers of American Foreign Relations, 1920–1939

Presidents	Secretaries of State
Woodrow Wilson, 1913–1921	Bainbridge Colby, 1920–1921
Warren G. Harding, 1921–1923	Charles E. Hughes, 1921–1925
Calvin Coolidge, 1923–1929	Frank B. Kellogg, 1925–1929
Herbert C. Hoover, 1929–1933	Henry L. Stimson, 1929–1933
Franklin D. Roosevelt, 1933–1945	Cordell Hull, 1933–1944

The Manchurian crisis also revealed the ineffectiveness of the treaties of the 1920s and the reluctance of the European powers to check aggression in the 1930s, when appeasement became the policy of the day. What frightened Stimson and Hoover, in the historian Michael Schaller's words, was "not so much China's fate as the specter of the great powers' seizing new empires to rescue themselves from economic depression."[16] Japan's violation of the Nine Power Treaty eroded what the historian Akira Iriye has called "the Washington Conference system," threatening international stability.[17] Given the timidity of the Europeans and the League of Nations, Americans recognized the limits of their own power and nurtured their independent internationalism. They may have overextended themselves in words, but not in deeds. Still they did not withdraw from international relations. Rather, as already noted in Chapter 4, the United States worked to create with nonmilitary means a world characterized by legal, orderly processes, the Open Door, and economic and political stability. The Hoover-Stimson response to the Manchurian episode typified these goals and methods. Practicing independent internationalism, America hoped to muzzle the dogs of war in order to stimulate domestic prosperity, expand foreign trade, and ensure national security. As in Europe, so in Asia would U.S. efforts come up short.

Facing Japan: The Washington Naval Disarmament Conference and China

The American pursuit of independent internationalism and a nonmilitary foreign policy began conspicuously at the Washington naval conference of November 12, 1921 through February 6, 1922. After World War I a naval arms race loomed among the United States, Britain, and Japan, and all of the parties recoiled from the spiraling financial costs. Japan was pumping as much as one-third of its national budget into naval construction. The United States, possessing the second largest navy in the world, alarmed third-ranked Japan by stationing most of its heaviest fourteen-inch-gun ships in the Pacific Fleet, by developing the base at Pearl Harbor, and by speculating about fortifying the Philippines and Guam. First-ranked Britain already had Singapore, but lacked funds to engage in a naval arms race. The U.S. Congress might not appropriate funds either. Thus all three powers welcomed arms control in order to check one another. With prodding from Senator Borah, the Harding administration invited eight nations (Britain, France, Italy, Japan, China, Belgium, the Netherlands, and Portugal) to Washington to discuss naval arms limitations and competition in Asia.

The Washington conference opened with dramatic words from bewhiskered Secretary of State Charles Evans Hughes. Hughes cut quickly to the problem. Calmly but deliberately he announced that the United States would scrap thirty ships. Then he turned to the British delegation and sank twenty-three of its ships. British admiral Lord David Beatty, noted a reporter, leaned forward like a "bulldog, sleeping on a sunny doorstep, who has been poked in the stomach by the impudent foot of an itinerant soap canvasser." Spellbound now, the delegates heard Hughes scuttle twenty-five Japanese vessels. One commentator wrote that "Hughes sank in thirty-five minutes more ships than all the admirals of the world have sunk in a cycle of centuries."[18]

Despite grumblings of doom from navy officers, the diplomats hammered out a naval limitations pact—the Five Power Treaty. It set a ten-year moratorium on the construction of capital vessels (defined as warships of more than 10,000 tons displacement or carrying guns larger than eight inches in bore diameter) and limited the tonnage for aircraft carriers. The treaty also established a tonnage ratio for capital ships of 5 : 5 : 3 : 1.75 : 1.75 (United States : Britain : Japan : France : Italy; 1 equaling approximately 100,000 tons displacement). The top three naval powers agreed to dismantle sixty-six capital fighting ships, many of them battleships. They also pledged not to build new fortifications in their Pacific possessions, such as the Philippines and Hong Kong, thus reassuring the Japanese, who had sarcastically accepted naval inferiority by translating 5 : 5 : 3 as Rolls Royce : Rolls Royce : Ford. Another treaty—the Four Power—abolished the Anglo-Japanese Alliance and stated simply that the signatories would respect each other's Pacific territories. All delegations also signed the Nine Power Treaty, a polite endorsement of the Open Door for the preservation of China's sovereignty and equal trade opportunity there. In other agreements, Japan consented to evacuate troops from the Shandong Peninsula; the United States obtained cable rights to the Pacific island of Yap; and Japan agreed to end its occupation of parts of Russian Siberia and the northern half of Sakhalin Island. President Harding, who actually had little to do with the conference, bragged that he was "not so much of a duffer as a good many people expected me to be."[19]

The treaties signed in Washington essentially recognized the status quo in Asia. Japan had the upper hand, and the other powers could not challenge it without undertaking massive naval construction and prohibitively expensive fortifications. Hughes knew he could not drive the Japanese out of Manchuria, so he skirted that issue. Geography clearly worked in Japan's favor in Asia, as it did for the United States in Latin America. The United States gave up little in the treaties, except the *potential* of naval superiority. It secured temporary protection of the vulnerable Philippines and abolition of the Anglo-Japanese Alliance, a threatening vestige of the old imperialism against which the Open Door was aimed. Each power accepted some naval disarmament as a way of checking a costly arms race and protecting its Asian interests. But as the Japanese prime minister noted: "While armed conflict has cooled off, economic competition is becoming more and more intense."[20]

Shortcomings emerged. The Five Power Treaty did not limit submarines, destroyers, or cruisers, thus permitting an arms race in those categories, which agreements at the London conference of 1930 only partly curbed. Nor did the Washington naval treaty provide means for verification other than good faith. Russia, which had stakes in Asia, was not invited to the Washington conference, since the major powers were still attempting to isolate the Bolsheviks. The Nine Power Treaty lacked any enforcement provision.

China, torn by factionalism and civil war, lost the most. Represented by the weak Beijing regime, rather than by Sun Yat-sen's Guomindang government in Canton, China could not demand an end to imperial privileges. As the historian Warren Cohen has written: "In answer to China's demand to be allowed to set its own tariff rates, the powers offered a five-percent increase on imports and a promise of subsequent discussion. In answer to the Chinese demand for an end to extraterritoriality, the powers offered only a commission to study the problem. In answer to the Chinese demand for the withdrawal of foreign troops from Chinese soil, nothing was done."[21] The United States did help China negotiate the Japanese out of Shandong, but the imperial powers, including the United States, resisted Chinese nationalist calls for full sovereignty. The Washington Conference took a worthy step toward disarmament, but it still left China at the mercy of foreigners. Hence Japan in 1931 could violate the Nine Power Treaty with impunity.

U.S. policy toward Asia had to contend not only with expansionist Japan but also with anti-imperialist, nationalist Chinese. In 1898 Americans had perceived the Philippines as steppingstones to China; three decades later, in an historical flipflop, a strong China friendly to the United States seemed necessary to protect those defenseless islands. China thus took on strategic importance for Americans in the 1920s and 1930s. Also, many Americans remained mesmerized by the mirage of the China market and the inviolability of the Open Door principle. Stanley K. Hornbeck affirmed that "our people and our Government have, from the beginning of our national life, asserted that in the commercial relationships of sovereign states there should *not* be a 'closed door' *anywhere*."[22] Sentimental considerations partly accounted for the American attachment to China, especially in the 1930s. Pearl Buck's best-selling *The Good Earth* (1931), made into a powerful movie six years later, captured for Americans the romance of the hard-working, persevering Chinese peasants. John Paton Davies, a young Foreign Service Officer in China during the depression decade, recalled America's "righteous infatuation" with China, stemming from years of missionary activity and a misguided and self-congratulatory belief that the United States was China's special friend by virtue of the Open Door notes. In Asia, according to Davies, "Washington preached to everyone, including the Chinese."[23]

Washington directed its preaching at the principal activists in Asia between the world wars: Japan, Russia, and the Chinese Nationalists. Each defined a new "order" that excluded the United States and the other Western imperialists. For the United States, "order" meant peaceful change, the Open Door, protection of American property and citizens, and the treaty rights of trade and judicial extraterritoriality (criminal trials for its nationals in American rather than Chinese courts). To protects its interests, the United States maintained troops on Chinese soil and gunboats on Chinese rivers. Sun Yat-sen, the leader of the Chinese Revolution from its outbreak in 1911 until his death in 1925, bristled when U.S. gunboats from the South China Patrol visited Canton in 1923 to halt a potential Chinese takeover of foreign-dominated customs houses. After declaring that the Chinese Revolution took its inspiration from America, the Christian, English-speaking Sun "might well have expected that an American Lafayette would fight on our side in this good cause. In the twelfth year of our struggle towards liberty there comes not a Lafayette but an American Admiral with more ships of war than any other nation in our waters."[24]

American Gunboat on the Yangtze River, China. The shallow-draft gunboat U.S.S. *Monocacy* served in the Yangtze Patrol, evacuating besieged Americans and protecting missionaries and commerce. After entanglement with Chinese civil disturbances and Japanese military thrusts, the *Monocacy* in 1939 was decommissioned, towed to sea, and sunk. (U.S. Navy)

The United States did little to assist the two potential roadblocks to Japanese expansion—Russia and the Chinese Nationalists. Few American leaders paid heed to the 1921 prophecy of minister to China Jacob G. Schurman that "only the Chinese can solve China's problems and they will do it in a Chinese way."[25] Americans applauded the Chinese nationalistic spirit, preached the Open Door, but then asked that U.S. treaty privileges be perpetuated. Finding minimal sympathy in Washington, the Chinese turned to another possible means of support, Soviet Russia. Seeking to restrain Japan, spank imperialist capitalists, and implant communism, Moscow sent advisers to China. Under the guidance of their agent Michael Borodin, the Soviets helped the Nationalists centralize the structure of the

Guomindang party. Americans understood neither the depth of Chinese nationalism nor Sun Yat-sen's use of Russians for Chinese purposes; Americans compared Sun with the unruly Chinese warlords he was fighting or attributed China's intense antiforeign sentiment to Bolshevik agitation. Although Sun became the major Nationalist leader, he by no means controlled China. Few Americans could foresee who would win in the end.

In 1925, Sun died and the Nationalist outpouring in the May 30th Movement of that year led to attacks on American and other foreign property and citizens. The 10,000 Christian missionaries who lived in China suffered threats and violence. Anti-imperialist opinion at home and Chinese determination prompted Washington to reconsider American treaty privileges. The outbreak of civil war within the Nationalist ranks also dictated a reevaluation. The ambitious Guomindang leader Jiang Jieshi turned fiercely on his communist allies in 1926–1927, booting Borodin back to Moscow and killing Chinese communists by the thousands or chasing them into the hills. The communist leader Mao Zedong fled south to Kiangsi Province, where he set up a rebel government. Jiang told U.S. officials that only American assistance could buttress China in "holding off" Japan and Russia and averting "a great war in the Pacific."[26] Washington responded to Jiang's assertion of power by signing in 1928 a new treaty restoring tariff autonomy to China and providing for most-favored-nation treatment. By 1930 more than 500 American companies were operating in China, with investments amounting to $155 million, yet they represented only 1 percent of total American foreign investments. From 1923 to 1931 the United States sent only 3 percent of its total exports to China. American trade with Japan totaled twice as much.

Despite the continued elusiveness of the China market, Americans waxed hopeful because such American-trained Chinese "cosmopolitans" as H. H. Kung, Hu Shi, and T. V. Soong were gaining influence in the Guomindang.[27] The Rockefeller Foundation was training an English-speaking elite through such institutions as the Peking Union Medical College, where American "modernizers" introduced "scientific medicine" for a country short on physicians.[28] Jiang had joined the crusade against communism. In 1930, furthermore, he announced that he had been converted to Christianity. Even more, he gave up his wife and two concubines to marry Meiling Soong, sister of T. V. Soong and daughter of American-educated Chinese businessman Charles Soong. A Wellesley College honors graduate, she spoke flawless English and soon established ties with prominent Americans in the United States, later called the "China Lobby." Beautiful intelligent, poised, and "Westernized," Madame Jiang captivated Americans. She seemed the right Chinese woman in America's dream of a stable, God-fearing, and Open Door China.

JAPAN'S MARCH FOR A NEW PACIFIC ORDER

Zealous expansionists, the Japanese feared the future. As their population grew, land became short (in 1931, 65 million people lived in an area smaller than Texas) and they became dependent on outside sources for vital raw materials. The Japanese also resented the fact that Western nations had for years intruded into their sphere of influence and come to control products so central to their economy, such as oil. Japan sought self-sufficiency. One Japanese leader argued that "a tree must have its roots," and cited U.S. "roots" in Latin America as an example.[29] Without an empire, many believed, Japan could not survive as a nation. From the Amo Doctrine of 1934, in which Foreign Ministry official Eiji Amo warned "hands off China," to the "Greater East Asia Co-Prosperity Sphere" announced in 1941, the Japanese rationalized their imperial appetite.[30] Compulsive in claiming "equality" with the Occidental powers, they often explained their expansion in the broadest terms: All major powers were doing it. With a high degree of fatalism, the Japanese recognized that an imperialist thrust into Manchuria and China could very well bring them into war with the United States or Russia.

Despite past efforts to defuse their rivalry, Tokyo and Washington took actions in the 1920s and 1930s that accentuated their differences. Indeed, Japan ranked the United States first on its list of potential enemies. A Japanese Navy War College study of 1936 stated that "in case the enemy's [America's] main fleet is berthed at Pearl Harbor the idea should be to open hostilities by surprise attacks from the air."[31] American naval leaders used Japan as the enemy on the war-game board at the Naval War College. Naval competition, despite the Washington conference, continued. That rivalry intensified in 1935–1936 when the London conference broke up without agreement and Japan announced its abrogation of the Washington and London treaties. The American Immigration Act of 1924, blatantly discriminatory in excluding Japanese citizens from entering the United States, rankled the sensitive Japanese. Secretary of State Hughes, less alarmed than West Coast racists about the threat of a domestic "Yellow Peril," lamented that the legislation had "undone the work of the Washington conference and implanted the seeds of an antagonism sure to bear fruit in the future."[32] Angry Japanese contemptuously remarked that, although they could not enter America, they could still go to China. Commercial rivalry also increased. Inexpensive Japanese goods, especially textiles, entered the American market, undercutting some domestic producers. "Buy America" campaigns and public boycotts of Japanese goods followed. Japan began to close the trade and investment door in China, antagonizing the United States. The Japanese considered Western lecturing against expansion a double standard. One diplomat complained that the Western powers taught Japan the game of poker, but after acquiring most of the chips they pronounced the game immoral and took up contract bridge.

Japan and the United States did have two common interests: Their mutual trade continued at high levels and both feared communism and Soviet Russia (Japan joined the Anti-Comintern Pact with Germany in 1936).

When Roosevelt took office in early 1933, his administration continued Stimson's nonrecognition policy. This policy reflected American weakness in Asia. But at least until 1937, the long lull in fighting between China and Japan did not seem to require American action. Roosevelt did move to bring the navy up to the strength permitted by the Washington and London conference treaties. Under New Deal relief programs in 1933, the president allocated funds for thirty-two new vessels, including two aircraft carriers, and by 1937 naval appropriations had doubled. Two years earlier the United States staged large-scale naval maneuvers near

Shanghai, China, 1937. This photograph of a baby amid the ruins of North Station after Japanese bombing galvanized American opinion. Senator George Norris, who gradually abandoned his isolationism because of scenes like this, denounced the Japanese as "disgraceful, ignoble, barbarous, and cruel, even beyond the power of language to describe." (United Press International)

Midway Island in the Pacific to impress the Japanese. American leaders calculated that a large navy would help deter Japanese expansion. The mild American buildup actually reinforced Japan's secret decision in May 1937 to outbuild the Americans and construct warships "above and beyond the quantitative and qualitative limits of the naval treaties"—including the huge 80,000-ton battleships *Yamato* and *Mushashi*.[33] Roosevelt's diplomatic recognition of Soviet Russia in 1933 was intended in part to frighten Japan with the suspicion that Russia and America had linked arms in Asia. Four years later, Captain Claire Chennault, retired from the U.S. Army Air Corps, joined the Chinese air force as chief adviser. By 1940 American volunteer pilots manned his "Flying Tigers" unit. These efforts to strengthen both the United States and China did not risk war for the former. Washington sought to *alert* the Japanese to American disapproval, but not to *threaten* them.

A more complex American policy developed after the eruption of new Sino-Japanese warfare in 1937. During the evening of July 7, Japanese and Chinese units clashed at the Marco Polo Bridge near Beijing. This skirmish grew quickly into the "China Incident" (not a "war" because the Kellogg-Briand Pact outlawed wars). Fighting spread throughout China. Shanghai fell to Japan in November after a costly battle and the cruel bombing of civilians. President Roosevelt refused to invoke American neutrality, thereby permitting valuable trade to continue with the beleaguered Chinese, but this arrangement hardly saved China. To make matters worse, the civil war between Jiang's Guomindang forces and Mao Zedong's communists further sapped China. The communists had declared war on Japan in 1932, charging Jiang with appeasing Tokyo. And until 1937 Jiang fought the communists more than the Japanese. From 1935 to 1937, the communists took the dramatic "Long March" from their southern haven to Yan'an (Yenan) in the north—an expedition of 6,000 miles. In late 1936 dissident Chinese army forces in Manchuria kidnapped Jiang, hoping to end the civil war by creating a coalition government. Josef Stalin and the Chinese communists soon secured his release and persuaded him to institute a tenuous united front against Japan in early 1937. Indeed, a Sino-Soviet nonaggression pact in August led to what the historian John Garver has called a "multifaceted alliance" wherein Moscow increased arms sales and technical assistance to Jiang and Soviet troops actually routed the Japanese in border clashes along the Manchurian and Mongolian frontiers in 1938 and 1939.[34]

Roosevelt addressed a Chicago audience on October 5, 1937, and called vaguely for a "quarantine" on aggressors to check the "epidemic of world lawlessness." Americans, he declared, could not be safe in a "world of disorder."[35] After the speech, FDR admitted that he had no plan ready; indeed, he evoked an attitude more than a "policy." He privately toyed with economic warfare—a naval blockade or embargo—but American isolationists responded to the speech by warning him against any bold action. Senator Gerald P. Nye warned against trying "to police a world that chooses to follow insane leaders" and recalled "our plunge into the European war in 1917."[36] In November Roosevelt sent U.S. representatives to a conference in Brussels, but it disbanded without taking a stand—only the Soviet Union pushed for reprisals against Japan. At the same time, newsreels pricked consciences with images of Chinese "building by hand, rock by rock and one basket of dirt after another, the 'Burma Road' that was going to restore their connection with the outside world."[37] In December the American gunboat *Panay,* escorting on the Yangtze River three small Standard Oil Company tankers flying American flags and well marked with the symbol "S," took destructive fire from zealous Japanese pilots. Two American sailors died. Under pressure from Ambassador Joseph Grew, Tokyo quickly apologized and offered reparations.

As Japan tightened its grip on China in 1938, the Roosevelt administration cautiously initiated new measures. First, through the purchase of Chinese silver, the United States gave China dollars with which to buy American military equipment. Second, Secretary Hull imposed a "moral embargo" on the sale of aircraft to Japan. Third, the United States extended technical assistance to improve the Chinese transportation system. Fourth, a naval bill authorized the construction of two new carriers and the doubling of naval airplanes. Fifth, the United States occupied several Pacific islands (Enderbury, for example) as potential naval bases. Sixth, Roosevelt sent a secret naval emissary to London to discuss contingency plans in the event of war in the Pacific. These actions of 1938 did not deter the Japanese, who by the end of that year controlled virtually all major Chinese seaports and established exploitative development companies. An American trade commissioner in Shanghai charged quite correctly that the "Open Door" was being "banged, barred, and bolted."[38] Japan's "New Order" meant the ouster of Western imperialism and the creation of a self-sufficient Asian bloc united economically and racially.

Japanese Expansion to 1941

Roosevelt and Hull moved cautiously in 1939 because events in Europe clearly carried more weight for the American national interest (see Chapter 4). In mid-1939 the United States abrogated the 1911 Japanese-American Treaty of Commerce and Navigation, hoping the threat of economic leverage would shock the Japanese into tempering their onslaught in China. In 1938 the United States had supplied Japan with 44 percent of its imports, mostly automobiles, machinery, copper, oil, iron, and steel. The abrogation, effective January 1940, by no means ended trade, for Washington remained reluctant to impose a rigid economic embargo. Grew's talks with the Japanese foreign minister in the fall of 1939 failed to secure American trading rights in China but did elicit a Japanese pledge to curtail brutalities against foreigners. In November 1939 another American naval bill authorized two more battleships. By then World War II had begun to bloody Europe, and Japanese-American relations had stalemated. The Roosevelt administration had shown that it would not fight over China. But how would Washington respond if Japan expanded beyond China (see Chapter 6)?

MAKING AND MANAGING GOOD NEIGHBORS IN LATIN AMERICA

In contrast with Asia, U.S. power in the Western Hemisphere remained unmatched and U.S. methods bold. Indeed, shortly after World War I, U.S. armed forces used the Caribbean for maneuvers and planning—as preparation for a possible war with Japan in the Pacific. And when Germany and Japan marched aggressively in the 1930s, the United States brought most of the Latin American states into a virtual alliance to resist foreign intrusions in the U.S. sphere of influence. Japanese leaders observed that their "New Order" in Asia merely copied U.S. hegemony in Latin America. The imperial net in Latin America had been stitched before and during World War I, especially in Central America and the Caribbean, through military occupations, naval demonstrations, the Panama Canal, the management of national finances, the threat of intervention, nonrecognition, and economic ties. The Roosevelt Corollary to the Monroe Doctrine provided the overriding justification (see Chapter 2). In the 1920 presidential campaign, after some Republicans insisted that the United States reject League membership because the British controlled six votes, Democratic vice-presidential candidate Franklin D. Roosevelt crowed that the United States would control twelve votes—eleven from Latin America. The chief of the State Department's Division of Latin America Affairs mentioned in 1925 the "low racial quality" of Latin Americans, but concluded that they were "very easy people to deal with if properly managed."[39] The sight of swaggering American marines in the streets of Havana, Managua, or Port-au-Prince represented only the most conspicuous evidence of North American imperial management.

The use of marines as instruments of policy, however, became unpopular and counterproductive, and nationalist sentiment, especially in Mexico and Argentina, placed limits on U.S. power. Anti-imperialists like Senators George Norris and William Borah, citing the Wilsonian ideal of self-determination, demanded it for Latin Americans. Members of Congress increasingly resented the costs of military interventions, as well as the president's usurpation of their power to declare war when as commander-in-chief he unilaterally dispatched soldiers to the Caribbean. Business leaders came to believe that military expeditions, because they aroused anti-U.S. sentiment and violence, endangered rather than protected their properties. The United States also found its own imperialist behavior in Latin America

Charles A. Lindbergh (1902–1974) Returns from Latin America, 1928. Lindbergh made aviation history on May 20, 1927, when he flew nonstop from New York to Paris in the *Spirit of St. Louis.* To promote U.S. goodwill toward Latin America, the aviator began a tour in December 1927 that first took him to Mexico. There he met Anne Morrow, the daughter of Ambassador Dwight Morrow; later Lindbergh would marry her. After visiting Guatemala, Panama, Venezuela, and other countries, Lindbergh returned from Cuba in February 1928. In the late 1930s Lindbergh became an isolationist, and in his last years he earned yet another reputation as a conservationist. (Lindbergh Picture Collection, Yale University Library)

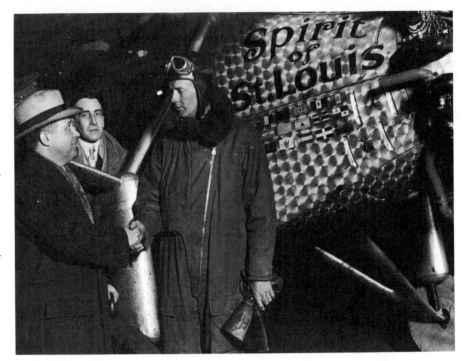

embarrassing when Japan seized Manchuria. Secretary Stimson commented in 1932: "If we landed a single soldier among those South Americans now . . . it would put me absolutely in the wrong in China, where Japan has done all this monstrous work under the guise of protecting her nationals with a landing force."[40] Pragmatic American diplomats recognized that armed interventions undermined their basic goal of stability.

Between the world wars, therefore, the United States sought nonmilitary methods to maintain its hegemony in Latin America. Washington increasingly forswore armed interference and employed economic penetration, political subversion, nonrecognition, support for stable dictators, arbitration treaties, Pan Americanism, Export-Import Bank loans, and the training of national guards. At times U.S. officials pressed for negotiated settlements, as when, in 1929, Secretary Kellogg helped settle the Tacna-Arica dispute between Chile and Peru. These tactics translated into a catchy phrase popularized, but not invented, by Franklin D. Roosevelt—the Good Neighbor policy. The president hailed in early 1933 "the policy of the good neighbor—the neighbor who resolutely respects himself and, because he does so, respects the rights of others—the neighbor who respects his obligations and respects the sanctity of his agreements in and with a world of neighbors."[41] Although Latin Americans welcomed the new spirit, the goal of U.S. hegemony in the hemisphere had not changed, only the means for maintaining it. Now Washington seemed more hesitant to defend exploitative American companies and more willing to entertain shared decisionmaking. Roosevelt defined the "new approach" toward Latin America: "Give them a share. They think they are just as good as we are, and many of them are."[42] As the Axis specter loomed larger in the late 1930s, the Good Neighbor policy came to mean cooperation against the European aggressors.

The history of the famous 1928 memorandum by Undersecretary of State J. Reuben Clark illustrates that the Good Neighbor policy meant new tactics, not new goals. This report repudiated the Roosevelt Corollary by stating that the Monroe Doctrine could not stand as a rationale for U.S. intervention in Latin America, for that doctrine referred specifically to European intrusions, not to the right of the United States to intervene. Yet the report did not denounce the right of intervention, only its sanction by the Monroe Doctrine. In any case, neither the Hoover nor Roosevelt administration paid much attention to the memorandum. For many Latin Americans it simply meant that Washington would find other rationales for intervention. The imperialist elements of coercion, imposition, dependency, and external authority remained.

Economic decisions made by American leaders, private and governmental, held immense importance for the life of Latin American nations, especially in the Caribbean, Mexico, and Central America. In the Dominican Republic, Cuba, and Haiti, for example, officials had to obtain U.S. consent before borrowing foreign capital. The Chilean ambassador to Washington spent much of his time trying to anticipate U.S. decisions on copper purchases and Chilean bonds, both essential to his nation's livelihood. In the 1930s, Chile had never "felt so totally controlled by the unpredictable attitudes of a foreign power."[43] In Cuba, where North American interests accounted for about two-thirds of sugar production, U.S. investments helped lock the country into a risky one-crop economy subject to fluctuating world sugar prices. In Honduras, where the United Fruit Company and Standard Fruit Company accounted for most of the country's revenue, U.S. interests provided essential cannon and machine guns to one political group that conducted a successful coup in 1924. In Venezuela, one-half of the nation's tax revenues came from oil taxes—hence from foreign-owned oil companies. In 1929 American firms produced more than one-half of Venezuela's oil. Their bribery of Venezuelan government officials, including the president, was not uncommon. More than 1,000 American-controlled businesses exercised significant influence in at least three-fourths of the Latin American countries by 1920.

In a process sometimes called "colonialism by contract," professional economists such as Edward Kemmerer of Princeton University served as financial advisers (or "money doctors") to Colombia, Chile, Ecuador, and Peru during the 1920s, usually recommending gold-exchange currency reforms managed by a central bank, new taxes, revised tariffs, and private American loans for public-works projects tied to U.S. firms.[44] Popular at first, such programs aroused nationalist backlashes in the 1930s when declining exports, excessive indebtedness, and contracting capital markets caused massive defaults throughout Latin America.

The Argentine writer Manuel Ugarte bluntly identified a "new Rome" in the mid-1920s. The United States, he explained, annexed wealth rather than territory, thus enjoying the "essentials of domination" without the "dead-weight of areas to

Marine Recruiting Poster.   Americans who joined saw many parts of Latin America, especially the Caribbean. But battle and occupation conditions were hardly as pleasant as depicted in James Montgomery Flagg's drawing. And, asked critics, once you are on the jaguar's back, how do you get off? (Library of Congress)

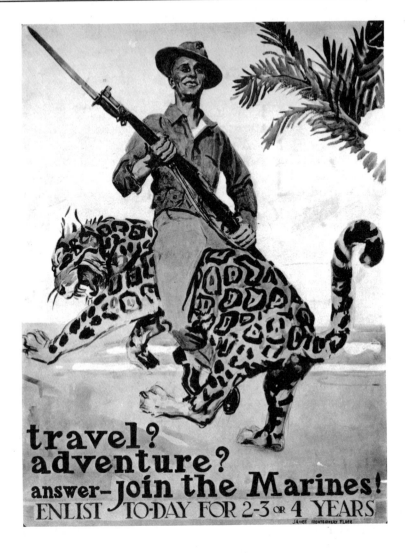

administrate and multitudes to govern." He deplored the consequences of U.S. economic penetration: "Its subtle intrusion into the private affairs of each people has always in consecrated phrase invoked peace, progress, civilization, and culture; but its motives, procedure, and results have frequently been a complete negation of these premises."[45] Latin American leaders, when making economic, political, and diplomatic decisions, always had to consider what North Americans thought and what they owned. Ambassador to Chile William D. Culbertson made no apologies in 1930: "American capital will be the controlling factor in public and private finance in these [South American] countries. . . . American civilization, material and cultural, is bound to impress itself upon, and I believe, benefit these peoples. If anti-American critics wish to describe this as our 'imperialism,' let them make the most of it."[46]

Uncle Sam as Seen by Latin America. This angry cartoon from *Critica* (Buenos Aires) represented one view of the United States in the Western Hemisphere. (*Current History and Forum,* 1927)

Although Latin American intellectuals often regarded North American "intruders as crass émigrés from a materialist culture," a U.S. consul in Brazil appreciated one of the ways the United States cultivated ruling elites.[47] He praised Rotary International, whose "meetings are attended by members of the Federal Cabinet, mayors of cities, and other officials who . . . welcome our support and cooperation."[48] Still, U.S. company managers too often treated foreign peoples with disdain. When a young Nelson Rockefeller visited Venezuela in the early 1930s to look after his oil investments, he noticed that U.S. citizens there seldom learned Spanish. "Why should I?" remarked the wife of an American businessman. "Who would I talk to in Spanish?"[49] Determined to lower cultural barriers when he returned to Venezuela, Rockefeller brought twelve Berlitz instructors with him to inaugurate Spanish classes for his company representatives.

U.S. investments in and trade with Latin America reached a "boom" stage after World War I. Although European, especially British, interests remained important there, U.S. businesses gradually nudged them out of first rank. The direct investments of U.S. citizens (excluding bonds and securities) jumped from $1.26 billion in 1914 to $3.52 billion in 1929, mostly in electric power, railroads, bananas, sugar, oil, and minerals. By 1936, because of the devastating impact of the global depression, the amount dropped to $2.77 billion. These figures represented about one-third of total U.S. investments abroad. One of the nation's largest corporations, Standard Oil of New Jersey, operated in eight countries, and the United Fruit Company held a large stake in the "banana republics" of Central America. International Telephone and Telegraph controlled communications in Cuba, where, between 1919 and 1933, overall U.S. investments increased 536 percent. Worried about diminishing oil reserves in the United States after World War I, Secretary of State Hughes and Secretary of Commerce Hoover decided to "urge our oil companies to acquire oil territory in South America and elsewhere before the European companies preempted all of it." As Hoover further recounted, "a conference of the leading oil producers was called and such action taken that most of the available oil lands in South America were acquired by Americans."[50] Then, too, fourteen Latin American nations floated bonds in the United States in the 1920s, many of them for unproductive public works, such as a marble palace for the Peruvian president. Latin American nationalists complained that large profits went back to the United States. In the period 1925–1929 in Latin America, the average annual income outflow from U.S. investments totaled $100 million more than the U.S. capital inflow.

Confirming the axiom that "trade follows investments," U.S. exports to Latin America tripled in value from 1914 to 1929, reaching the billion-dollar figure, approximately 20 percent of total U.S. exports. Although this impressive trade slumped with the onset of the devastating Great Depression, for many Latin American countries commercial relationships with the United States remained critical. Nicaragua, for example, shipped 96 percent of its exports to the United States by 1941. In 1920 the United States supplied Cuba with 73 percent of its imports; that trade shrank to 59 percent in 1929 because of the depressed state of the Cuban sugar economy. Cuba's exports to the United States also dropped off, although they still comprised 68 percent of all the island's exports. American investments in and trade with Venezuela moved the British out and helped that country to become the world's leading exporter of oil. Trade with Chile in nitrates and copper jumped after U.S. investments there doubled from $200 million in 1920 to $400 million in 1928. Worried by declining world trade during the crippling depression of the 1930s, Secretary of State Cordell Hull sought wider markets in Latin America when he launched the Export-Import Bank (directing some of its loans to inter-American commerce) and the Reciprocal Trade Agreements Program. His efforts helped increase the value of exports to Latin America from $244 million in 1933 to $642 million in 1938.

BUILDING DICTATORS AND GUARDS: THE DOMINICAN REPUBLIC, NICARAGUA, AND HAITI

After Spain left the Dominican Republic in 1865 and until the U.S. military occupation began in 1916, that impoverished Caribbean country knew little peace. Corrupt politics and mismanagement of national revenues produced economic stagnation, political factionalism, and foreign indebtedness. Americans had long shown interest in the Dominican Republic. President Theodore Roosevelt seized control of Dominican finances in 1905, but for years insurrections fractured Dominican order. In May 1916, when a contest between the Dominican congress and president threatened to postpone American demands for expanded U.S. authority, American marines went ashore. Although U.S. forces occupied the major cities and established martial law, the peasants and caudillos in the mountainous eastern regions waged increasingly bloody guerrilla war from 1917 to 1922. The marines retaliated in kind against rebels who "are almost all touched with the tarbrush," as Military Governor Harry Knapp crudely put it.[51] Marine atrocities against Dominican people of color usually went unpunished. Sumner Welles, the American commissioner to the Dominican Republic (1922–1924), later criticized the U.S. officers who ran the occupation—"none of whom had any knowledge or experience of Dominican affairs or problems, and the great majority of whom could not even speak the language of the country."[52]

The military intervention in the Dominican Republic, more so than other U.S. interventions, became a hot political issue at home and abroad. The Republicans went on record in 1920 as favoring withdrawal. *The Nation* (1920) demolished the argument that improved hospitals and schools justified imperialism by noting that the "Germans improved sanitation during their occupation of some of the villages of northern France, but no officer of the Marine Corps ever suggested that these reforms justified the German presence in France."[53] Washington decided to make a virtue out of adversity and to withdraw in 1924. As Hughes ingeniously argued, the departure proved that the United States was "anti-imperialistic."[54] Franklin D. Roosevelt agreed in a 1928 article in *Foreign Affairs:* "We accomplished an excellent piece of constructive work, and the world ought to thank us."[55] With Americans running the country's fiscal affairs until 1941, FDR blithely ignored Welles's observation of "the lasting hostility towards the American people which the occupation created in the hearts of a very great number of the Dominican people."[56]

The U.S. occupation also begot Rafael Leonidas Trujillo. In early 1919 he received a commission as a second lieutenant in the U.S.-created national constabulary. The onetime thief, forger, and pimp earned high marks from American military officers and became chief of staff of the reorganized National Army in 1928. Through the election of 1930, characterized by violence, fraud, and a boycott by political opponents, Trujillo became president. The vote, roughly 224,000 to 1,900, demonstrated his firm grip on the country. Washington worried that his authoritarian methods would spawn new insurrections, but gradually warmed to him when it became clear that his strong-arm tactics would create internal order and thereby eliminate the need for American military intervention. Thanks to beneficent U.S. control of the customs, Trujillo could divert funds to his army for the suppression of internal dissent. Political corruption, military muscle, torture, murder, nepotism, commercial monopolies, and raids on the national treasury enabled Trujillo to quiet opponents and amass a fortune of $800 million.

From 1930 until his assassination in 1961, sometimes as president, sometimes through puppets, Trujillo ruled. U.S. military arms filled Domincan arsenals. American business leaders, who dominated the sugar production of the country,

Rafael Trujillo (1891–1961).
The strongman of the Dominican Republic graduated from an American military training school and went on to rule his nation from 1930 to 1961, when he was assassinated. (*The Reporter*, 1961. Copyright 1961 by The Reporter Magazine Co.)

endorsed him. Most imports came from the United States, and the economic links remained profitable. The National City Bank became the official depository for Dominican revenues. In July 1939, Trujillo traveled to the United States, not as president but as commander of the armed forces. FDR greeted him in good neighborly fashion. By World War II the Dominican Republic stood as a success story for the new Good Neighbor policy. But, asked many critics, good neighbors with whom? Roosevelt reportedly gave an answer in reference to Trujillo: "He may be an S.O.B., but he is our S.O.B."[57]

Nicaragua, like the Dominican Republic, developed in the twentieth century under the weight of U.S. military occupation and the Good Neighbor policy. From 1912 to 1925 the United States ruled Nicaragua and kept in power its favorite group, the Conservative party. Nicaragua by 1925 appeared to be solvent, secure, and stable. The marines departed, but in late 1926 they returned. Even ardent imperialists found it hard to swallow the Coolidge administration's explanation—in an exaggerated report titled "Bolshevik Aims and Policies in Mexico and Latin America"—that communists were fomenting trouble in Nicaragua. It had no evidence of such activity and historians can find none, but such rhetorical rationalization abounded in that era of antibolshevism. In fact, the Nicaraguan Liberals had used Mexico as a sanctuary to organize a countermovement against the Conservatives. "We are not making war on Nicaragua," Coolidge opined, with tones of the Roosevelt Corollary, "any more than a policeman on the street is making war on passersby."[58] Nicaraguans in the Coco River basin saw it differently:

"The Congressional Castigator."
The intervention in Nicaragua sparked debate in the United States. Here Uncle Sam is beleaguered by the terrain, a protesting member of Congress, and the bite of the rebel Sandino. (*The Outlook*, 1928)

"The Machos are coming," they said of the marines. "They will burn our houses."[59]

The Nicaraguan intervention generated heated debate in the United States. The assertion of a communist plot convinced few. Congress again resented a military action taken by the executive, which ignored its power to declare war. Senator Burton K. Wheeler suggested that if U.S. soldiers intended to "stamp out banditry, let's send them to Chicago to stamp it out there. . . . I wouldn't sacrifice . . . one American boy for all the damn Nicaraguans."[60] Bloodshed and destruction in Nicaragua raised further outcries after Secretary of the Navy Curtis D. Wilbur matter-of-factly reported in 1928: "Several houses were destroyed in the village of Quilali in order to prepare a landing field for airplanes so that 19 wounded Marines could be evacuated to a hospital."[61] From 1927 to 1933 the Liberal insurgent César Augusto Sandino, who protested "the corrupting vice of the dollar in Nicaragua," earned an international reputation as he waged guerrilla war against some 5,000 U.S. marines.[62]

Sensitive to the large-scale criticism of the U.S. presence in Nicaragua, the special emissary Henry L. Stimson brought Liberals and Conservatives together in the "Peace of Tipitapa" (1927) and provided for U.S. supervision of the election of 1928. Most important, he and General Frank R. McCoy created an American-trained national guard to perpetuate the domestic order that the marines had im-

César Augusto Sandino (1895–1934). President Hoover called him a "cold-blooded bandit outside the civilized pale," but Nicaraguans have hailed Sandino as a hero. Determined that Nicaragua gain control of its natural resources and shift monies to improvements for the poor, Sandino blasted the Monroe Doctrine as meaning "America for the Yankees." Accused of administering "machete justice" to members of the Guardia Nacional, Sandino explained that "liberty is not conquered with flowers." The revolutionaries who overthrew the Somoza dictatorship in 1979 called themselves "Sandinistas" in his honor. (Library of Congress)

Comic Strips in Nicaragua.   In this 1927 photograph of the tranquil side of intervention, marines read comic strips to Nicaraguan children. (Marine Corps, National Archives)

posed. Shortly after U.S. troops withdrew in 1933, Sandino signed a truce with the Nicaraguan government. But General Anastasio Somoza, who had studied at a business school in Philadelphia and knew colloquial English, and who had "impressed" Henry Stimson "more favorably than any other Liberal," gained command of the American-trained Guardia Nacional.[63] Somoza then captured and executed Sandino, notwithstanding his "word of honor" that no harm would come to the guerrilla hero.[64] In 1936 Somoza seized power and established a family dictatorship that lasted until 1979. Somoza and the United States struck an uneasy alliance. An American collector-general remained to handle customs collections until 1944, and the United States retained canal rights and a naval base. In the late 1930s, when Somoza complained that the United States was undermining the economic development of his country by not building a canal, the Roosevelt administration in 1939 constructed an interoceanic highway (the Rama Road) for several million dollars. Somoza also used the road for moving the guardsmen who suppressed the critics of his self-enriching, brutal regime.

Few benefits accrued to the United States from its years of interference in Nicaragua. Trade never reached important levels, although the United States dominated the Central American nation's economy. From 1914 to 1930 U.S. investments grew from $4.5 million to $13 million, the latter a minuscule part of overall investments in Latin America. Although the stormy occupation of Nicaragua may have indirectly fostered the Good Neighbor policy, for Nicaraguans that policy meant continued foreign financial management and replacement of the U.S. Marine Corps by a home-grown dictator and a constabulary traveling the Rama Road.

Haiti, too, drew Washington's hegemonic attention. A marine officer depicted the Haitians as "real nigger and no mistake—there are some very fine looking, well educated polished men here but they are real nigs beneath the surface."[65] When U.S. soldiers went abroad, of course, they carried American prejudices as well as canteens. For nineteen years, from 1915 to 1934, marines governed the tiny black French-speaking nation of Haiti in the Caribbean. Historians have described the venture as a tragedy that deepened Haiti's distress. The Wilson administration ordered the marines into Haiti on July 28, 1915, after a civil war had erupted there. Interested in the fine harbor at Môle St. Nicholas, the United States feared German intrigue during World War I, sought to protect American financial interests (largely those of National City Bank of New York), and insisted on order in the Caribbean. Franklin D. Roosevelt once boasted, with considerable exaggeration, that as assistant secretary of the navy he had written a "a pretty good little Constitution" for Haiti in 1918.[66]

The occupation touched every aspect of Haitian life. Americans built highways, technical schools, lighthouses, hospitals, and railroads. They improved public health and sanitation. Contemporary critics complained that Haitians could have undertaken most of these projects on their own with some outside assistance and without military subjugation. The improvements never eradicated Haiti's profound human squalor. By the mid-1960s Haiti had the lowest life expectancy (thirty-five years) and the lowest literacy rate (10 percent) in Latin America. Many of the roads had been built in 1916–1918 by forced labor—the *corvée* system under which Admiral William Caperton ordered workers into labor gangs and treated them like prisoners. NAACP official James Weldon Johnson, who toured Haiti, protested: "They were maltreated, beaten and terrorized . . . [like] the convicts in the Negro chain gangs that are used to build roads in many of our southern states."[67] Haitians rebelled against the *corvée;* in 1919 alone the marines killed some 2,000 to quell the insurrection. For many Haitians the marine initials U.S.M.C. meant *Un Salaud Mal Costume* (a sloppy bum).

American racism and Jim Crow reached into Haiti. U.S. personnel introduced to Haitians the words "nigger," "gook," and "coon" and enforced segregation between blacks and whites. Americans bestowed higher status on the mulattoes (the "elites") than on the *authentiques* (blacks), but in contrast to their stance toward other Latin American oligarchies, U.S. officials neither wooed nor entrenched the existing Haitian bourgeoisie. They did not because of intense hostility to mixed bloods based on the belief, in the historian Brenda Plummer's words, "that such persons, as links between the races, endangered the established order in what should be a rigidly color-defined world."[68] Anthropological research in the 1930s by Franz Boaz and others that showed complex linkages among African, European, and indigenous cultures could not displace the prevailing Hollywood stereotype of Haiti as the land of voodoo and zombies.

The United States also meddled in the economic affairs of Haiti, sometimes beneficially. Transportation improvements expanded commercial contacts between cities and rural farmers. Pan American Airways began flights between Miami and Port-au-Prince. Irrigation systems and a telephone network contributed to economic growth. Sugar and cotton exports increased, although the heavy dependence on one crop, coffee, left Haiti susceptible to fluctuations in world prices. The United States became Haiti's largest trading partner. American capital investments grew from $11.5 million in 1914 to $28.5 million in 1930. The National City Bank of New York owned the Banque Nacional. Under U.S. financial supervision, Haiti actually paid its foreign debts (largely French) ahead of schedule. Haiti's economic life depended on decisions in the United States—although the economic rewards for Americans (or Haitians) hardly justified the long occupation.

U.S. military authorities trained a national guard, the *Garde d'Haiti,* to quell revolutions. A majority of the officers of this gendarmerie actually consisted of Americans; no Haitian had reached captain's rank by 1930. The first commandant, Major Smedley D. Butler of the marines, had experience in putting down "natives" in China, Honduras, Nicaragua, Panama, and Mexico. The brash Butler vowed to use "my little chocolate soldiers . . . to make a real and happy nation out of this blood crazy Garden of Eden."[69] The national guard enforced the rules of U.S. occupation; served as judges, tax collectors, and paymasters for teachers; enforced martial law; and wielded the deciding political force.

The United States failed to establish respect for honest government by law and neglected to train efficient civil servants. Washington officials drafted the 1918 constitution and forced it on Haitians; the press was censored and elections were rigged. When President Philippe Sudre Dartiguenave's term ended in 1922, Americans jilted him in favor of Louis Borno, an acquiescent lawyer and perfect stage villain. Borno collaborated with the American high commissioner, General John H. Russell of Georgia, to rule Haiti from 1922 to 1930. Borno "has never taken a step without first consulting me," Russell boasted.[70] The American general wrote Haitian legislation, directed public projects, and when Borno seemed obstinate, ordered the American financial adviser to withhold the president's salary. Despite State Department criticism of Russell's authoritarian rule, one U.S. official believed in 1925 that "these people had never heard of democracy . . . and despotism was the only government they could understand."[71]

Haitians resented their colonial status. The peaking of discontent in 1929 came after a slump in coffee prices and exports and exposure of Borno's political machinations. Protests and strikes spread across the country. President Hoover appointed an investigating commission chaired by W. Cameron Forbes, former governor-general of the Philippines. The commission's report of 1930 combined praise and criticism: "The failure of the Occupation to understand the social problems of Haiti, its brusque attempt to implant democracy by drill and harrow, its determination to set up a middle class . . . all these explain why, in part, the high hopes of our good works in this land have not been realized."[72] The Forbes Commission promoted "Haitianization" to ease Haitians into positions of responsibility. Hoover started the withdrawal; Roosevelt completed it in 1934.

After the marines departed, Haitians celebrated a "Festival of the Second Indepedence." Strong-arm presidents ruled thereafter with the help of Export-

"The Rights of Small Nations: Haiti."   A harshly critical view of the marine occupation of Haiti, 1915–1934. (*Good Morning,* 1921).

Import Bank loans and ties with Washington. During World War II the United States used Haitian bases, and until 1947 American officials supervised Haitian national finances. A revolution in 1946 placed the government in the hands of the *Garde,* and the revolution of 1956–1957 produced the callous dictatorship of Dr. François ("Papa Doc") Duvalier. He ruled until his death in 1971, when his son "Baby Doc" assumed power. Driven out in 1986, he left behind abject poverty and rampant civil strife. A Haitian nationalist summarized the impact of the American occupation: "They have made themselves the allies of the evil past of oppression and tyranny; they have abolished liberty, justice, independence." He concluded bitterly: "How can they teach us when they have so much to learn themselves."[73]

SUBVERTING NATIONALISM IN CUBA AND PUERTO RICO

Cubans bristled under the Platt Amendment and American military interventions (see Chapter 2). Through the 1920s and into the 1930s the United States helped conduct elections, enlarged the national army, managed the national budget, and maintained economic control over the island. North American investment, particularly in sugar, soared to $1.5 billion in 1929. Approximately half a million fun-seeking Americans a year visited the capital city of Havana, where, declared one tourist, "it is hot, it is 'wet,' it is . . . Wide Open."[74]

Gerardo Machado, an admirer of Italy's Benito Mussolini, ruled from 1924 to 1933; he suppressed free speech, jailed or murdered leftists, journalists, labor leaders, and students, and used the army as a political weapon. He received loans from U.S. bankers and gained the approval of North American businesses by prohibiting strikes.

Cuban resentment against Machado intensified in the late 1920s when sugar prices began to drop. Dependent on sugar and exports to the United States, Cuba sank further into economic crisis when the United States instituted the restrictive Smoot-Hawley Tariff of 1931. Unemployment rates shot up, and protests and violence spread. Machado sent his soldiers to club the dissenters and closed the University of Havana. Roosevelt and his advisers decided that an armed U.S. intervention would blatantly violate the newly stated Good Neighbor policy, so the unpopular Machado had to be eased out.

Suave Sumner Welles, the Groton school friend of Roosevelt already experienced in the Dominican Republic, went as ambassador to Havana in 1933. While U.S. warships patrolled Cuban waters, Welles began to subvert the Machado regime. Fearful that fervent nationalists might gain authority once Machado stepped down, the ambassador organized a group of old-style politicians. Welles's pressure, a general strike, and more violence persuaded Machado to flee. But Welles lost control of the revolution; "his" government, led by Carlos Manuel de Céspedes, lasted less than a month. Céspedes counted, said Welles, as a "most sincere friend of the United States," but he was also a lackluster, relatively unknown leader.[75] On September 4, 1933, army men, commanded by Sergeant Fulgencio Batista, staged the "Sergeants' Revolution," deposed Céspedes, and installed Professor Ramón Grau San Martín as president.

An exile under Machado, critic of the Platt Amendment, and friend of the left, Grau, according to the scholar Luis Aguilar, stood as "the hope and the symbol of the forces of nationalism, patriotism, and reform."[76] But the American ambassador would not suffer him, and "no government here can survive for a protracted period without recognition by the U.S.," Welles bragged.[77] Secretary Hull sent a few warships. Grau soon abrogated the Platt Amendment, promulgated economic and social reforms, suspended payment on Chase National Bank loans, and seized some American-owned sugar mills. Welles decried the "confiscatory" decrees of this "social revolution" and conspired with Batista, who, like other military leaders, feared that Grau's economic nationalism would invite U.S. intervention.[78] To Washington, Welles reported that communists were taking over the Grau government, a patently erroneous depiction. Welles left Cuba in December 1933 (he later became assistant secretary of state for Latin American affairs), and in January Batista toppled Grau, who fled to Mexico. A Batista-backed president took over, and the United States quickly granted recognition.

Batista ruled Cuba, sometimes as president, sometimes from the shadows, from 1934 to 1959. At the start of the "Era of Batista," the United States abrogated the

Fulgencio Batista (1901–1973). Born of farm folk in the United Fruit Company town of Banes, Batista joined the Cuban army at age twenty. A smiling, ruthless dictator, he became a staunch U.S. ally, bought real estate in Daytona Beach, Florida, and turned Havana into a playground of casinos and brothels for American tourists. Fidel Castro's 26th of July Movement overthrew the corrupt regime in 1959. Batista died in exile in Portugal. (National Archives)

unpopular Platt Amendment (1934), lowered the sugar tariff, granted a favorable quota to Cuban sugar imports (1934), and issued Export-Import Bank loans ($8 million in 1934). In 1940, Cuba granted American armed forces the use of ports and airfields (besides Guantánamo) in exchange for military aid. One Cuban nationalist, Julio César Fernández, reflected on the lost opportunity of 1933: "American diplomacy has many resources; when the steel of her warships is not convenient, she uses the docile backbone of her native lackeys."[79]

Elsewhere in the Caribbean, Puerto Rico stagnated under American paternalism. Throughout the interwar years, mediocre and often crude American governors who could not speak Spanish castigated Puerto Ricans as "unsteady, unprincipled children" unable to govern themselves.[80] Although the Jones Act of 1917 had granted Puerto Ricans U.S. citizenship, Washington stiff-armed requests for the colony's independence or statehood. Puerto Ricans did not gain the right to elect their own governor until 1947. Absentee American landowners and sugar barons ran the island's economy. Despite improved roads and new schools, Governor Theodore Roosevelt, Jr. (1929–1932) reported "farm after farm where lean underfed women and sickly men repeated again and again the same story—little food and no opportunity to get more."[81] Eighty percent of peasants remained landless and many crowded into urban slums, living six to a room. Puerto Ricans earned an average annual income in 1930 of $130, one-fifth the U.S. figure; by 1933 it had dropped to $85.

Ponce, Puerto Rico, 1938.
The U.S. Farm Security Administration photographer Edwin Rosskam captured class divisions on Puerto Rico, where U.S. imperial neglect helped perpetuate the island's poverty. At the top of the hill sits the villa of the owner of a sugar plantation and refinery. The shacks of workers cling to the hillside. (Library of Congress)

Faculty and alumni of the University of Puerto Rico especially criticized U.S. hegemony. The Harvard-educated lawyer Pedro Albizo Campos headed the Nationalist party, which eventually advocated the violent overthrow of U.S. rule. On Palm Sunday, 1937, police fired on unarmed Nationalist marchers, killing twenty in the "Ponce Massacre." Other Puerto Ricans rallied behind the socialist Luis Muñoz Marín, whose Popular Democratic party ultimately advocated "commonwealth" status (attained in 1952). Muñoz Marín did work with New Dealers in the 1930s to obtain relief and public-works projects amounting to $1 million a month, but when Governor Rexford Tugwell arrived in 1941, he found Puerto Rico "still sunk in hopeless poverty."[82]

COMPROMISING WITH MEXICO: OIL AND NATIONALISM

The ongoing Mexican Revolution, which began in 1910, presented the United States with one of its few major obstacles in Latin America and a test of the non-military emphasis of the Good Neighbor policy. Before the 1920s it had appeared that Mexico would be treated like other U.S. neighbors—invaded, occupied, and owned by Americans, who by 1910 controlled 43 percent of Mexican property and produced more than half of Mexico's oil. Hollywood films perpetuated stereotypes by portraying the Mexican as a bandit or villainous "greaser."[83] Scholars and artists promoted cultural interaction to counter such negative images. Professor Herbert E. Bolton of the University of California, Berkeley, emphasized a shared borderlands history, drawing large numbers of students to his course on "Greater America." In the 1930s at universities in the United States, the Mexican artist José Clemente Orozco painted colorful murals of revolutionary struggle. The Rotary Club and other U.S. associations traveled to Mexico City for conventions. These contacts did not diminish the nationalism of either nation, but they probably did encourage an environment of tolerance and understanding based on mutual experience that undercut war hawks bent on military confrontation. The Mexican Constitution was proclaimed the same day the last American soldier of General John Pershing's army withdrew from Mexico—February 5, 1917. The radical document alarmed capitalist Americans, because its Article 27 held that all "land and waters" and all subsoil raw materials belonged to the Mexican nation. Three hundred million dollars in American investments in oil and mines seemed jeopardized. Mexico also began to tax heavily American oil producers. As the historian Karl M. Schmitt has written, "For the first time in the modern industrial age a weak, underdeveloped, and economically penetrated state insisted on modifying if not abolishing its dependence on a highly industrialized, militarily powerful overlord."[84]

The United States continued to claim economic rights for its nationals in Mexico and refused to recognize the Mexican government. In 1923, however, Mexico and the United States signed the Bucareli Agreements. In exchange for U.S. recognition, Mexico agreed that Americans who held subsoil rights before the 1917 Constitution could continue those concessions and that Americans who had their agricultural lands expropriated would receive Mexican bonds in compensation. At the time Americans owned about 60 percent of Mexico's oil industry. But a new law passed by the Mexican Congress in 1925 stated that oil lands secured before 1917 could only be held for a maximum of fifty years. In part because American oil companies had begun to exploit the rich oil fields of Venezuela, Washington rejected appeals to intervene and resorted to nonmilitary methods instead.

In early 1927, President Coolidge selected Dwight W. Morrow, an old college chum and a partner in the elite Wall Street firm of J. P. Morgan and Company, as the new ambassador to Mexico City. An oil lobbyist advised that Morrow, the "trainer," faced a "vicious animal" in Mexico: "If the trainer showed fear, the animal would attack him, but if he showed courage and force, the animal would submit."[85] Learning a little Spanish, having "Lone Eagle" Charles Lindbergh fly nonstop from Washington, D.C., and even bringing the humorist Will Rogers to the Mexican capital, Morrow ingratiated himself. He then negotiated an agreement that confirmed *pre-1917* ownership of petroleum lands. Thus in 1927–1928 the oil controversy seemed defused through compromise. The United States protected its citizens' oil investments and tacitly conceded that Mexico legally controlled its own raw materials. This arrangement lasted until 1938, when President Lázaro Cárdenas defiantly expropriated the property of all foreign oil companies, then attempting to thwart an oil workers' strike for higher wages. Cárdenas's threat to "burn the oilfields to the ground rather than sacrifice our honour" raised a vital question: What rights did U.S. businesses have in foreign countries?[86]

Josephus Daniels, who became ambassador in 1933 and who as secretary of the navy in 1914 had ordered the marines to Veracruz, dispelled early suspicions and persuaded Mexican leaders that he and Washington had changed. "The oil and other big interests here have no sympathy with the Good Neighbor policy," Daniels informed Hull in 1938. "They go to bed every night wishing that [Porfirio] Díaz were back in power and we carried the Big Stick and had Marines ready to land at their beck and call."[87] Daniels would not tolerate such behavior. Nor would he accept Hull's "get tough" policies, although Daniels disapproved of expropriation. Daniels softened an intemperate State Department blast when he delivered it to the Mexican foreign minister. Refusing to see the Good Neighbor policy "drown in Mexican oil," Daniels opposed Washington's economic coercion through the reduction of U.S. purchases of Mexican silver.[88] "We are strong. Mexico is weak," he wrote to FDR. "It is always noble in the strong to be generous and generous and generous."[89] For their part the American oil companies refused to sell petroleum equipment to Mexico, and they persuaded shipping firms not to carry Mexican oil. Standard Oil of New Jersey financed false propaganda in the United States with the message that Cárdenas plotted to turn Mexico Soviet: The *Atlantic Monthly* magazine ran a pro–Standard Oil article in July 1938 and soon admitted that oil companies had financed the issue.

FDR ruled out U.S. intervention and decided on negotiations to gain compensation for lost properties. Increased purchases of Mexican oil by Germany. Italy, and Japan underscored the urgent need for a diplomatic settlement. Indeed, once war broke out in Europe in September 1939, the "nervous Nelly of American intelligence," FBI director J. Edgar Hoover, reported false rumors about 250 Nazi pilots in Mexico, eight German submarines operating out of Veracruz, and Hitler's promise of British Honduras if Mexico agreed to supply Germany with petroleum during the war.[90] Difficult Mexican-American talks finally produced an agreement in 1941. The United States conceded the principle that Mexico owned its own raw materials, and Mexico promised to pay the oil companies and other Americans for expropriated properties. The Export-Import Bank extended a $30 million loan. Washington's compromise with Mexican nationalism illustrated the Good Neighbor policy's abandonment of military intervention. The change paid strategic dividends as the United States readied itself for World War II.

PAN AMERICANISM AND THE APPROACH OF WAR

In 1889, Secretary of State James G. Blaine spurred formation of the International Bureau of American Republics, renamed in 1910 the Pan American Union. The U.S. secretary of state became its permanent chair. "Pan Americanism" at first focused on the improvement of trade in the Western Hemisphere and symbolized a mythical inter-American unity. The union's elegant quarters, financed by the steel baron Andrew Carnegie, stood, significantly, a short distance from the Department of State building. One Argentine diplomat sneered that "there is no Pan

Americanism in South America; it exists only in Washington."[91] The declarations of neutrality during World War I by seven Latin American governments exposed the hollowness of Pan American solidarity.

In 1923 the Fifth Pan American Conference met in Santiago, Chile. The United States controlled the agenda, and the delegates endorsed a Treaty to Avoid or Prevent Conflicts Between the American States (Gondra Treaty). The Havana Conference of 1928, however, proved quite a different matter. Arriving at Havana shortly after American troops had landed in Nicaragua, the conferees assembled in a rebellious mood. U.S. officials had anticipated trouble and had thus appointed former Secretary of State Hughes to head the American delegation. Even President Coolidge traveled to Cuba to address the conference with soothing banalities. The cooperative Machado dictatorship censored critical newspaper comments about the United States.

At the conference, the delegate from El Salvador moved that "no state has the right to intervene in the internal affairs of another."[92] Mexico and Argentina backed this challenge to the United States. Hughes had the resolution sent to a study committee chaired by himself, whereupon the committee recommended that intervention be considered at the *next* conference. Yet El Salvador's courageous Dr. Gustavo Guerrero reintroduced his nonintervention resolution at the plenary meeting, forcing Hughes to defend the right of intervention—or, as he put it, "interposition of a temporary character."[93] His words did not persuade many, but the power of the United States did, and the issue of intervention was tabled until the next conference.

The Seventh Pan American Conference, in Montevideo, Uruguay (1933), convened with considerable optimism, for it followed Roosevelt's inauguration and met under the aura of the Good Neighbor policy. The expected resolution was introduced ("No state has the right to intervene in the internal or external affairs of another"). Cordell Hull cast an affirmative vote but retained a U.S. right to intervene "by the law of nations as generally recognized and accepted."[94] Further confusion about the meaning of the nonintervention pledge became evident at the 1936 Buenos Aires Conference, where the United States seemingly endorsed an unequivocal statement of nonintervention. The American definition, however, intended to outlaw *military* intervention, whereas many Latin American countries (especially Mexico) interpreted it to mean that the United States could not interfere through economic or political pressure when countries nationalized American-owned property.

Pan Americanism took a decided turn toward hemispheric security in the late 1930s, as Germany, Italy, and Japan attempted to improve their economic and political standing in Latin America. As Germany's trade with Latin America climbed, Cordell Hull thought the danger "not limited to the possibility of a military invasion. It was more acute in its indirect form of propaganda, penetration, organizing political parties, buying some adherents, and blackmailing others."[95] Although Adolf Hitler dreamed of creating "a new Germany" in Brazil and instigated subversive activities there and in Uruguay, Argentina, and Mexico, the United States overreacted to what was at most a long-term Nazi threat.[96] With such fears, Washington decided to form what Assistant Secretary of State Adolf Berle called "a north-south axis" at the Lima Conference of 1938, where Argentina, Uruguay, and Chile fought Hull's proposal to knit the Latin American countries together in a quasi alliance.[97] The anti-German sentiment of most delegates, aroused by the recent Munich crisis, helped Hull beat back attempts to undermine his plan for solidarity. The conferees strongly endorsed the Declaration of Lima, a pledge to resist foreign intervention in the Americas. President Roosevelt warned in April 1939 that German planes "cannot hop directly across our 3,000 miles but they can do it in three hops, middle Europe, Cape Verde, Brazil, Yucatan and Tampico."[98] That autumn the Declaration of Panama established a security belt around the Western Hemisphere to rebuff possible Axis intrusions. At the same time, the United States persuaded Latin American nations to reduce or cease trade with the Axis powers and to ship strategic raw materials to the United States. To advance hemispheric solidarity even more, Roosevelt in 1940 appointed the energetic Nelson Rockefeller to head the new Office of Inter-American Affairs in the State Department.

The post–World War I search for order in international relations had broken down by 1939. In both Asia and Latin America, fervent nationalists challenged the United States. In both areas the viability of American diplomacy derived from the power the United States possessed and exercised. In Asia, after the Manchurian crisis of 1931–1932, the United States sought, without success, to build a counterforce to Japan. Even the Philippines became a virtual hostage that the U.S. military said

FDR Reviews the Fleet.
Aboard the U.S.S. *Houston* with Admiral Claude Bloch, the president, always a "big navy" man, plays commander in chief for a day, July 14, 1938. (Franklin D. Roosevelt Library)

it could not defend. (In the Tydings-McDuffie Act of 1934, the United States promised the Philippines independence in ten years.) By spring 1939 the possibility of simultaneous war with Germany, Italy, and Japan prompted the U.S. Joint Army-Navy Board to modify war plan ORANGE (which emphasized a naval offensive in the Pacific) in favor of RAINBOW plans for hemispheric defense based on the primacy of the Atlantic and Caribbean approaches.

The Great Depression prostrated international relations. World trade and investment collapsed; tariffs went up. The island-bound and trade-conscious Japanese accelerated efforts to build a "co-prosperity" sphere in Asia. In Latin America, many of whose states depended on the exportation of one commodity for economic survival, revolutions and coups erupted, feeding on incipient nationalism. Social unrest and political instability rocked the area from which the United States was withdrawing its marines. The Dominican Republic, Argentina, Brazil, and Chile in 1930, Peru in 1931, Cuba in 1933—these political upheavals in the U.S. sphere of influence threatened U.S. hegemony. Devastated by the depression, Latin Americans gained a new awareness of the extent to which foreigners made their national choices and the degree to which foreign companies drained profits from them. By World War II, Latin Americans held a more favorable image of the United States, because the latter had seemingly abandoned military intervention under the Good Neighbor policy. But they harbored fresh suspicions that invigorated inter-American economic relations would continue U.S. hegemony. Yankeephobia simmered even as Latin Americans joined the United States in the fight against the Axis.

FURTHER READING FOR THE PERIOD 1920–1939

For general studies and biographies covering this period, see some of the works cited in Chapter 4.

For America and Asia, see Irvine H. Anderson, *The Standard-Vacuum Oil Company and United States East Asia Policy* (1974); Richard D. Burns and Edward M. Bennett, eds., *Diplomats in Crisis* (1974); Roger Dingman, *Power in the Pacific* (1976); Herbert Feis, *The Road to Pearl Harbor* (1950); Akira Iriye, *Across the Pacific* (1967), *After Imperialism* (1969), and *The Origins of the Second World War in Asia and the Pacific* (1987); and Gerald Wheeler, *Prelude to Pearl Harbor: The United States Navy and the Far East, 1921–1931* (1963).

For Japan and the United States, consult Michael Barnhart, *Japan Prepares for Total War* (1987); Dorothy Borg and Shumpei Okamoto, eds., *Pearl Harbor as History* (1973); Parks M. Coble, *Facing Japan: Chinese Politics and Japanese Imperialism, 1931–1937* (1991); Justus D. Doenecke, *When the Wicked Rise: American Opinion-Makers and the Manchurian Crisis of 1931–1933* (1984); Saburō Ienaga, *The Pacific War* (1978); Manny T. Koginos, *The Panay Incident* (1967); Frank P. Mintz, *Revisionism and the Origins of Pearl Harbor* (1985); James W. Morley, ed., *Deterrent Diplomacy: Japan, Germany and the U.S.S.R., 1934–1940* (1977); Charles E. Neu, *The Troubled Encounter* (1975); William L. Neumann, *America Encounters Japan* (1963); Sandra C. Taylor, *Advocate of Understanding: Sidney Gulick and the Search for Peace with Japan* (1984); Christopher Thorne, *The Limits of Foreign Policy* (1972); and Jonathan G. Utley, *Going to War with Japan, 1937–1941* (1985).

China and the United States are explored in Russell D. Buhite, *Nelson T. Johnson and American Policy Toward China* (1968); Mary B. Bullock, *An American Transplant: The Rockefeller Foundation and Peking Union Medical College* (1980); Warren I. Cohen, *America's Response to China* (1990) and *The Chinese Connection*

(1978); Bernard Cole, *Gunboats and Marines* (1983); John W. Garver, *Chinese-Soviet Relations, 1937–1945* (1988); David H. Grover, *American Merchant Ships on the Yangtze* (1992); Patricia Neils, *China Images in the Life and Times of Henry Luce* (1990); Youli Sun, *China and the Origins of the Pacific War, 1931–1941* (1993); Barbara Tuchman, *Stilwell and the American Experience in China, 1911–45* (1971); and Stephen J. Valone, *"A Policy Calculated to Benefit China": The United States and the China Arms Embargo, 1919–1929* (1991).

Inter-American relations and the Good Neighbor policy are treated in Cole Blasier, *The Hovering Giant* (1976); John A. Britton, *Carleton Beals* (1987); Alexander DeConde, *Herbert Hoover's Latin American Policy* (1951); Paul J. Dosal, *Doing Business with the Dictators* (1993) (United Fruit, Guatemala); Donald Dozer, *Are We Good Neighbors?* (1959); John Findling, *Close Neighbors, Distant Friends* (1987) (Central America); Alton Frye, *Nazi Germany and the American Hemisphere, 1933–1941* (1967); Irwin F. Gellman, *Good Neighbor Diplomacy* (1979); David Green, *The Containment of Latin America* (1971); Kenneth J. Grieb, *The Latin American Policy of Warren G. Harding* (1976); David G. Haglund, *Latin America and the Transformation of U.S. Strategic Thought, 1936–1940* (1984); Thomas L. Karnes, *Tropical Enterprise: The Standard Fruit and Steamship Company in Latin America* (1978); Michael L. Krenn, *U.S. Policy Toward Economic Nationalism in Latin America, 1917–1929* (1990); Walter LaFeber, *Inevitable Revolutions* (1993); Lester D. Langley, *America and the Americas* (1989); Abraham F. Lowenthal, ed., *Exporting Democracy* (1991); Carlos Marichal, *A Century of Debt Crises in Latin America* (1989); Ivan Musicant, *The Banana Wars* (1990); Richard V. Salisbury, *Anti-Imperialism and International Competition in Central America, 1920–1929* (1989); Hans Schmidt, *Maverick Marine* (1987) (Smedley Butler); James Schwoch, *The American Radio Industry and Its Latin American Activities* (1990); Sarah E. Sharbach, *Stereotypes of Latin America* (1993); Joseph Tulchin, *The Aftermath of War: World War I and U.S. Policy Toward Latin America* (1971); and Bryce Wood, *The Making of the Good Neighbor Policy* (1961).

For relations with Caribbean countries, see G. Pope Atkins and Larman C. Wilson, *The United States and the Trujillo Regime* (1972); Bruce Calder, *The Impact of Intervention* (1984) (Dominican Republic); Raymond Carr, *Puerto Rico* (1984); Arturo Morales Carrión, *Puerto Rico* (1983); Truman P. Clark, *Puerto Rico and the United States, 1917–23* (1975); Ronald Fernandez, *The Disenchanted Island* (1992) (Puerto Rico); Lester D. Langley, *The United States and the Caribbean* (1980); Rayford W. Logan, *Haiti and the Dominican Republic* (1968); Dana Munro, *The United States and the Caribbean Republics, 1921–1933* (1974); Brenda G. Plummer, *Haiti and the United States* (1992); Robert I. Rotberg, *Haiti* (1971); and Hans Schmidt, *The United States Occupation of Haiti* (1971).

For Nicaragua and the U.S. intervention, see Paul C. Clark, Jr., *The United States and Somoza* (1992); Thomas J. Dodd, *Managing Democracy in Central America* (1992); William Kamman, *A Search for Stability* (1968); Neil Macaulay, *The Sandino Affair* (1967); Richard Millett, *Guardians of the Dynasty* (1977); and Knut Walter, *The Regime of Anastasio Somoza* (1993).

For South America: Elizabeth A. Cobbs, *The Rich Neighbor Policy: Rockefeller and Kaiser in Brazil* (1992); Paul W. Drake, *The Money Doctor in the Andes* (1988); Stanley Hilton, *Brazil and the Great Powers* (1975); Michael Grow, *The Good Neighbor Policy and Authoritarianism in Paraguay* (1981); Frank McCann, *The Brazilian-American Alliance* (1973); Michael Montéon, *Chile in the Nitrate Era* (1982); Stephen G. Rabe, *The Road to OPEC* (1982) (Venezuela); and Stephen J. Randall, *The Diplomacy of Modernization* (1977) (Colombia).

Specific studies of U.S.-Mexican relations include Leslie Bethell, ed., *Mexico Since Independence* (1991); E. David Cronon, *Josephus Daniels in Mexico* (1960); Helen Delpar, *The Enormous Vogue of Things Mexican* (1992) (cultural relations); Lorenzo Meyer, *Mexico and the United States in the Oil Controversy, 1917–1942* (1977); W. Dirk Raat, *Mexico and the United States* (1992); Ramón Ruíz, *The Great Rebellion: Mexico, 1905–1924* (1980); and Robert F. Smith, *The United States and Revolutionary Nationalism in Mexico, 1916–1932* (1972).

Cuba's relationship with the United States is studied in Jules R. Benjamin, *The United States and Cuba* (1978); Irwin F. Gellman, *Roosevelt and Batista* (1973); Louis A. Pérez, Jr., *Cuba and the United States* (1990) and *Cuba Under the Platt Amendment* (1968); and Ramón Ruíz, *Cuba* (1968).

See also Richard Dean Burns, ed., *Guide to American Foreign Relations Since 1700* (1983), the General Bibliography, and the following notes.

Notes to Chapter 5

1. Quoted in Elting E. Morison, *Turmoil and Tradition* (New York; Atheneum, 1964), p. 312.
2. Robert H. Ferrell, "The Mukden Incident: September 18–19, 1931," *Journal of Modern History, XXVII* (March 1955), 67.
3. Quoted in Morison, *Turmoil and Tradition*, p. 308.
4. Quoted in Richard N. Current, "Henry L. Stimson," in Norman A. Graebner, ed., *An Uncertain Tradition* (New York: McGraw-Hill, 1961), pp. 171, 169.
5. Quoted in Frank Freidel, *Franklin D. Roosevelt: Launching the New Deal* (Boston: Little, Brown, 1973), p. 120.
6. Quoted in Richard Dean Burns, "Stanley K. Hornbeck," in Richard Dean Burns and Edward M. Bennett, eds., *Diplomats in Crisis* (Santa Barbara, Cal.: ABC-CLIO Press, 1974), p. 103.
7. Quoted in Justus D. Doenecke, *When the Wicked Rise* (Lewisburg, Penn.: Bucknell University Press, 1984), p. 37.
8. Quoted in Christopher Thorne, *The Limits of Foreign Policy* (New York: Capricorn, 1973), p. 158.
9. Quoted in Morison, *Turmoil and Tradition*, p. 310.
10. Quoted *ibid.*, p. 315.
11. Quoted in Doenecke, *When the Wicked*, p. 31.
12. Quoted in Norman A. Graebner, "Hoover, Roosevelt, and the Japanese," in Dorothy Borg and Shumpei Okamoto, eds., *Pearl Harbor as History* (New York: Columbia University Press, 1973), p. 30.
13. Morison, *Turmoil and Tradition*, p. 332.
14. Hugh R. Wilson, *Diplomat Between the Wars* (New York: Longmans, Green, 1941), p. 280.
15. Edgar Snow quoted in James L. Huskey, "The Cosmopolitan Connection," *Diplomatic History, XI* (Summer 1987), 241.
16. Michael Schaller, *The U.S. Crusade in China, 1938–1945* (New York: Columbia University Press, 1979), p. 5.
17. Akira Iriye, *The Origins of the Second World War in Asia and the Pacific* (London: Longman, 1987), p. 16.
18. Quoted in Thomas H. Buckley, *The United States and the Washington Conference, 1921–1922* (Knoxville: University of Tennessee Press, 1970), pp. 72–73.
19. Quoted in Roger Dingman, *Power in the Pacific* (Chicago: University of Chicago Press, 1976), p. 212.
20. Quoted in Akira Iriye, *The Cold War in Asia* (Englewood Cliffs, N.J.: Prentice-Hall, 1974), p. 18.
21. Warren I. Cohen, *America's Response to China* (New York: Columbia University Press, 1990; 3d ed.), p. 89.
22. Stanley K. Hornbeck, *The United States and the Far East* (Boston: World Peace Foundation, 1942), p. 10.
23. John Paton Davies, *Dragon by the Tail* (New York: W. W. Norton, 1972), p. 95.
24. Quoted in Akira Iriye, *Across the Pacific* (New York: Harcourt Brace & World, 1967), p. 148.
25. Quoted in Cohen, *America's Response to China*, p. 88.
26. Quoted in Bernard D. Cole, *Gunboats and Marines* (Newark: University of Delaware Press, 1983), p. 145.
27. Huskey, "Cosmopolitan Connection," p. 228.
28. Mary B. Bullock, *An American Transplant* (Berkeley: University of California Press, 1980), pp. 44, 47.
29. Quoted in Justus D. Doenecke and John E. Wilz, *From Isolation to War, 1931–1941* (Arlington Heights, Ill.: Davidson, 1991; 2d ed.), p. 23.
30. Quoted in Parks M. Coble, *Facing Japan* (Cambridge, Mass.: Harvard University Press, 1991), p. 153.
31. Quoted in Asado Sadao, "The Japanese Navy and the United States," in Borg and Okamoto, *Pearl Harbor*, p. 238.
32. Quoted in William L. Neumann, *America Encounters Japan* (Baltimore: The Johns Hopkins University Press, 1963), p. 176.
33. Robert G. Kaufman, *Arms Control During the Pre-Nuclear Era* (New York: Columbia University Press, 1990), p. 181.
34. John W. Garver, *Chinese-Soviet Relations 1937–1945* (New York: Oxford University Press, 1988), p. 15.
35. Samuel I. Rosenman, ed., *Public Papers and Addresses of Franklin D. Roosevelt* (New York: Macmillan, 1938–1943; 13 vols.), VI, 406–411.
36. Quoted in Wayne S. Cole, "The Role of . . . Congress and Political Parties," in Borg and Okamoto, *Pearl Harbor*, p. 314.
37. Quoted in Patricia Neils, *China Images in the Life and Times of Henry Luce* (Savage, Md.: Rowman & Littlefield, 1990), p. 59.
38. Quoted in Frederick C. Adams, *Economic Diplomacy* (Columbia: University of Missouri Press, 1976), p. 233.
39. Quoted in Robert D. Schulzinger, *The Making of the Diplomatic Mind* (Middletown, Conn.: Wesleyan University Press, 1975), p. 95.
40. Quoted in Arthur P. Whitaker, "From Dollar Diplomacy to the Good Neighbor Policy," *Inter-American Economic Affairs, IV* (Spring 1951), 18.
41. Rosenman, *Public Papers, II*, 14.
42. Quoted in David Green, *The Containment of Latin America* (Chicago: Quadrangle, 1971), p. 38.
43. Frederick B. Pike, *Chile and the United States* (South Bend, Ind.: University of Notre Dame Press, 1963), p. 236.
44. Emily S. Rosenberg and Norman L. Rosenberg, "From Colonialism to Professionalism," *Journal of American History, LXXIV* (June 1987), 79; Paul W. Drake, *The Money Doctor in the Andes* (Durham: Duke University Press, 1989).
45. C. Neale Ronning, ed., *Intervention in Latin America* (New York: Alfred A. Knopf, 1970), pp. 42–49.
46. Quoted in Joan Hoff Wilson, *American Business and Foreign Policy* (Boston: Beacon, 1973 [c. 1971]), p. 160.
47. Lester D. Langley, *America and the Americas* (Athens: University of Georgia Press, 1989), p. 125.
48. Quoted in Emily Rosenberg, *Spreading the American Dream* (New York: Hill and Wang, 1982), p. 112.

49. Quoted in Elizabeth A. Cobbs, *The Rich Neighbor Policy* (New Haven: Yale University Press, 1992), p. 28.
50. Herbert Hoover, *Memoirs: The Cabinet and the Presidency, 1920–1933* (New York: Macmillan, 1952), p. 69.
51. Quoted in Bruce J. Calder, *The Impact of Intervention* (Austin: University of Texas Press, 1984), p. 124.
52. Sumner Welles, *Naboth's Vineyard* (New York: Payson and Clark, 1928; 2 vols.), II, 797–798.
53. Quoted in Joseph R. Juárez, "United States Withdrawal from Santo Domingo," *Hispanic American Historical Review, XLII* (May 1962), 180.
54. Quoted *ibid.*
55. Franklin D. Roosevelt, "Our Foreign Policy," *Foreign Affairs, VI* (July 1928), 583.
56. Quoted in Calder, *Impact of Intervention,* p. 252.
57. Quoted in Robert F. Smith, *The United States and Cuba* (New York: Bookman, 1960), p. 184.
58. Quoted in Albert K. Weinberg, *Manifest Destiny* (Chicago: Quadrangle, 1963 [c. 1935]), p. 441.
59. Quoted in Carleton Beals, "This Is War, Gentlemen!" *The Nation, CXXVI* (April 11, 1928), 406.
60. Quoted in Ivan Musicant, *The Banana Wars* (New York: Macmillan, 1990), p. 328.
61. U.S. Navy, *Operation of Naval Service in Nicaragua* (Senate Doc. 86, 70th Cong., 1st sess., 1928), pp. 5–6.
62. Sergio Ramírez, ed., *Sandino* (Princeton: Princeton University Press, 1990), p. 239.
63. Quoted in John E. Findling, *Close Neighbors, Distant Friends* (Westport, Conn.: Greenwood Press, 1987), p. 94.
64. Quoted in Walter LaFeber, *Inevitable Revolutions* (New York: W. W. Norton, 1993; 2d ed.), p. 70.
65. Colonel Littleton Waller quoted in Robert I. Rotberg, *Haiti* (Boston: Houghton Mifflin, 1971), pp. 137–138.
66. Quoted in Kenneth R. Davis, *FDR: The Reckoning of Destiny, 1882–1928* (New York: G. P. Putnam's Sons, 1972), p. 621.
67. James Weldon Johnson, "The Truth About Haiti," *The Crisis, XX* (September 1920), 223.
68. Brenda G. Plummer, *Haiti and the United States* (Athens: University of Georgia Press, 1992), p. 129.
69. Quoted in Hans Schmidt, *Maverick Marine* (Lexington: University of Kentucky Press, 1987), p. 84.
70. Quoted in Donald B. Cooper, "The Withdrawal of the United States from Haiti, 1928–1934," *Journal of Inter-American Studies, V* (January 1963), 83.
71. Quoted in Paul W. Drake, "From Good Men to Good Neighbors," in Abraham F. Lowenthal, ed., *Exporting Democracy* (Baltimore: The Johns Hopkins University Press, 1991), p. 25.
72. Quoted in Dana G. Munro, *The United States and the Caribbean Republics, 1921–1933* (Princeton: Princeton University Press, 1974), pp. 314–315.
73. Quoted in Emily Greene Balch, ed., *Occupied Haiti* (New York: Winters, 1927), pp. 179–180.
74. Quoted in Louis A. Pérez, Jr., *Cuba and the United States* (Athens: University of Georgia Press, 1990), p. 142.
75. Quoted in Luis E. Aguilar, *Cuba 1933* (New York: W. W. Norton, 1974 [1972]), p. 150.
76. Quoted *ibid.*, p. 167.
77. Quoted in Hugh Thomas, *Cuba* (New York: Harper & Row, 1971), p. 655.
78. Quoted in Louis A. Pérez, Jr., *Cuba Under the Platt Amendment, 1902–1934* (Pittsburgh: University of Pittsburgh Press, 1986), pp. 323–324.
79. Quoted in Aguilar, *Cuba 1933*, pp. 228–229.
80. Arturo Morales Carrión, *Puerto Rico* (New York: W. W. Norton, 1983), p. 206.
81. Quoted in Raymond Carr, *Puerto Rico* (New York: Vintage, 1984), p. 54.
82. Quoted *ibid.*, p. 61.
83. Quoted in Helen Delpar, *The Enormous Vogue of Things Mexican* (Tuscaloosa: University of Alabama Press, 1992), p. 5.
84. Karl M. Schmitt, *Mexico and the United States, 1821–1973* (New York: John Wiley & Sons, 1974), p. 158.
85. Delbert Haff quoted in Michael L. Krenn, *U.S. Policy Toward Economic Nationalism in Latin America, 1917–1929* (Wilmington, Del.: Scholarly Resources, 1990), p. 62.
86. Quoted in Alan Knight, "The Rise and Fall of Cardenismo," in Leslie Bethell, ed., *Mexico Since Independence* (Cambridge, Eng.: Cambridge University Press, 1991), p. 282.
87. Quoted in E. David Cronon, *Josephus Daniels in Mexico* (Madison: University of Wisconsin Press, 1960), p. 185.
88. Quoted in W. Dirk Raat, *Mexico and the United States* (Athens: University of Georgia Press, 1992), p. 145.
89. Quoted in Cronon, *Daniels,* p. 198.
90. David A. Haglund, *Latin America and the Transformation of U.S. Strategic Thought, 1936–1940* (Albuquerque: University of New Mexico Press, 1984), p. 154.
91. Quoted in J. Lloyd Mecham, *A Survey of United States–Latin American Relations* (Boston: Houghton Mifflin, 1965), p. 100.
92. Quoted in Samuel Guy Inman, *Inter-American Conferences,* (Washington, D.C.: University Press, 1965), p. 117.
93. Quoted in Richard V. Salisbury, *Anti-Imperialism and International Competition in Central America, 1920–1929* (Wilmington, Del.: Scholarly Resources, 1989), p. 121.
94. Quoted in Bryce Wood, *The Making of the Good Neighbor Policy* (New York: Columbia University Press, 1961), p. 119.
95. Cordell Hull, *Memoirs* (New York: Macmillan, 1948; 2 vols.), I, 602.
96. Quoted in Holger H. Herwig, *Politics of Frustration* (Boston: Little, Brown, 1976), p. 187.
97. Quoted in Jordan A. Schwarz, *Liberal* (New York: The Free Press, 1987), p. 123.
98. Quoted in John A. Thompson, "The Exaggeration of American Invulnerability," *Diplomatic History, XVI* (Winter 1992), 28.

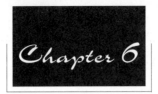

Chapter 6

SURVIVAL AND SPHERES:

THE ALLIES AND THE SECOND WORLD WAR, 1939–1945

***Church Service*, Prince of Wales.**   *On August 10, 1941, President Franklin D. Roosevelt and Prime Minister Winston S. Churchill, with their staffs, attended a stirring service aboard the British vessel during the Atlantic Charter Conference. (Franklin D. Roosevelt Library)*

✳ *Diplomatic Crossroad*

THE ATLANTIC CHARTER CONFERENCE, 1941

It was the longest walk that the tall, graying man had attempted since being stricken by polio twenty years earlier. Holding a cane in his right hand and helped by his son Elliott, President Franklin D. Roosevelt slowly limped the entire length of the battleship H.M.S. *Prince of Wales* to take his place of honor on the quarterdeck. More than 1,500 men, including British prime minister Winston S. Churchill, stood at rigid attention as the president took his tortured steps. "He was making a tremendous effort," observed a Britisher, and "he was determined to walk along that deck even if it killed him."[1] Finally, Roosevelt reached his seat near the bow, side by side with Churchill. British and American chiefs of staff stood behind them, with impressive ranks of sailors and marines on each side. Facing them was the *Prince of Wales*'s forward turret, its fourteen-inch guns protruding "like rigid pythons."[2] Roosevelt and Churchill were attending church services together in the quiet waters of Placentia Bay near the harbor of Argentia, Newfoundland, on Sunday, August 10, 1941.

Sunday services aboard the *Prince of Wales* marked the high point of the four-day summit meeting between the two leaders (August 9–13, 1941), some four months before Pearl Harbor catapulted the United States into World War II as a formal belligerent. The text of the sermon, from Joshua 1:1–9, seemed directed at the president: "There shall not any man be able to stand before thee all the days of thy life; as I was with Moses, so I will be with thee: I will not fail thee, nor forsake thee." And suggesting the need for the United States to aid the British democracy in the war against Hitler was the stirring hymn, "Onward Christian Soldiers," with its call for volunteers "marching as to war." For Roosevelt, who had already supplied destroyers, Lend-Lease, and other aid short of war, the moment evoked a rush of emotion. His handkerchief dabbed at his eyes. "If nothing else had happened," he later told his son, "that would have cemented us. 'Onward Christian Soldiers.' We *are,* and we *will,* go on, with God's help."[3] Churchill found symbolic unity that morning—"the Union Jack and the Stars and Stripes draped side by side on the pulpit; . . . the highest naval, military, and air officers of Britain and the United States grouped together behind the President and me; the close-packed ranks of British and American sailors, completely intermingled, sharing the same books and joining fervently in the prayers and hymns familiar to both."[4] Nobody aboard the *Prince of Wales* could know, of course, that Japanese bombs would destroy the majestic battleship off the coast of Malaya on December 10, 1941.

The four-day meeting in Placentia Bay marked the first of many conferences between Roosevelt and Churchill during World War II; altogether, the two leaders would spend some 120 days in each other's company. Notwithstanding the fears of presidential assistant Harry Hopkins that the meeting foreordained a clash of "prima donnas," the personalities blended well.[5] The tactful British leader's willingness to pay deference to a man he regarded "almost with religious awe" and his own pride in being half-American (his mother) made Churchill an ardent advocate of Anglo-American solidarity.[6] Roosevelt, although he sometimes saw the prime minister as the last of the Victorians, reciprocated Churchill's friendship. Under their leadership the two countries became "mixed up together . . . for mutual and general advantage" to a degree unmatched in modern times.[7] "It is fun to be in the same decade with you," FDR wrote his British partner in early 1942.[8]

Aside from the personal equation, Argentia produced less decisive results. The British asked for men, ships, planes, and tanks. Churchill urged that the American navy extend its convoying of British vessels farther into the German submarine-infested North Atlantic. The British military chiefs, remembering the frightful casualties of World War I, and perhaps hoping to make military intervention more palatable to the Americans, argued that bombing, blockades, and propaganda might so weaken the Germans that they would surrender before a cross-channel operation would have to be launched against France from England. The Americans, particularly Army chief of staff General George C. Marshall, favored a more direct strategy, insisting on large ground armies. Marshall declared further that a U.S. military buildup had to take priority over British requests for weapons and equipment; "the hungry table," as Churchill described the demands on U.S. defense production, simply did not have enough for all who wanted to eat.[9] In the one tangible military commitment at Argentia, FDR promised to order his navy to convoy British merchant ships as far as Iceland. The president delayed any public declaration until September, when a German submarine fired torpedoes at the U.S. destroyer *Greer* off the coast of Iceland. Neglecting to mention that the *Greer* had been shadowing the U-boat for three hours prior to the attack, Roosevelt announced over worldwide radio on September 11 that henceforth American naval vessels would shoot at German submarines. Undeclared naval action (or "war in masquerade")—no further than this would Roosevelt go in the months before Pearl Harbor.[10]

Discussions about Japan exposed British and American differences at Argentia. Foreign Office diplomats argued that Japan, which had recently occupied the southern half of French Indochina, should receive an explicit American warning against further encroachments, and that the United States should commit itself to war if the Japanese attacked British or Dutch territory in Southeast Asia. U.S. officials avoided any definite commitment. Roosevelt did promise to deliver a "mighty swat" to Japan. But when the president returned to Washington, Secretary of State Cordell Hull watered down the proposed statement. Whereas the original draft had stated that further Japanese aggression would cause the United States to take measures that "might result in war," the actual postconference warning to the Japanese ambassador merely read that Washington would take steps necessary "toward insuring the safety and security of the United States."[11] Roosevelt preferred to delay a confrontation in the Pacific until he strengthened his army and navy and cultivated a more favorable public opinion. The president intended to beat Hitler first.

The most famous product of the Churchill-Roosevelt summit conference came in the eight-point statement of war aims—the Atlantic Charter. Reminiscent

Winston S. Churchill (1874–1965) at Placentia Bay, August 1941. Churchill claimed later that after he and Roosevelt signed the Atlantic Charter, "America could not honourably stay out" of the war. One of Roosevelt's speechwriters, the playwright Robert Sherwood, found Churchill "Olympian in his capacity" for alcohol and late-night, earlymorning meetings. "Churchill could talk for an hour or more and hold any audience spellbound." But when the rotund, stubborn Churchill talked about the glories of the British Empire, Americans thought him an Old World colonialist. (Franklin D. Roosevelt Library)

of Woodrow Wilson's Fourteen Points, the Atlantic Charter, in deliberately vague terms, reaffirmed the old Wilsonian principles of collective security, national self-determination, freedom of the seas, and liberal trading practices (see Chapter 3). The signatories also denied themselves any territorial aggrandizement and pledged economic collaboration leading to "social security." Behind the vision of a postwar world in which all people "may live out their lives in freedom from fear and want," however, lay Anglo-American differences. The Americans, particularly Under Secretary of State Sumner Welles, whom Sir Alexander Cadogan said had "swallowed a ramrod in his youth," pressed for a statement explicitly endorsing freer trade.[12] The British wanted to protect their discriminatory system of imperial preferences. The compromise called for "access, on equal terms, to the trade and to the raw materials of the world," leaving the British an escape clause that promised "due respect for their existing obligations." Hull, when he read this vague language later, felt "keenly disappointed."[13] Churchill failed to gain Roosevelt's backing for a new League of Nations. Not wishing to arouse either isolationists or fervent internationalists, Roosevelt accepted only "the establishment of a wider and permanent system of general security."[14] As "both realist and idealist, both fixer and preacher, both a prince and a soldier," the president wanted to be as cautious as he was eloquent about postwar goals.[15]

The Atlantic Charter became a propaganda tool for the war against the Axis. Within a few months the Voice of America's radio broadcasts hailed the Atlantic

Charter's "fight on all the world's battlefields for these essential liberties: liberty of expression, of religion, and the right to live protected from need and from fear."[16] In September 1941, at an Inter-Allied meeting in London, representatives of the nations battling Hitler formally adhered to the "common principles" set forth in the Atlantic Charter.[17] The Soviet Union also gave qualified approval. Twenty-six nations, on January 1, 1942, signed the Declaration of the United Nations, which pledged cooperation in achieving the aims of the Atlantic Charter. Churchill and Roosevelt, however, provided no procedures for enforcement or implementation of the principles. Indeed, on September 9, in the House of Commons, the prime minister insisted that the charter applied only to "nations of Europe now under the Nazi yoke," not to "the regions and peoples which owe allegiance to the British Crown."[18] Roosevelt came to view the principles as a "beautiful idea" rather than as set rules.[19] However much the president believed in the Argentia ideals, he seemed willing to postpone their application or compromise them to accommodate pressing military and diplomatic priorities. "I dream dreams but am, at the same time, an intensely practical person," he once said.[20]

By meeting secretly with Churchill on board a British battleship, Roosevelt demonstrated America's commitment to the defense of Britain by all means short of war. Notwithstanding outcries from American isolationists, and whatever hopes he might have that the theatrics of Argentia would galvanize American opinion for a firmer policy, Roosevelt maintained a "policy of influence without belligerence," as the historian Mark Lowenthal has put it.[21] Not "a single American officer has shown the slightest keenness to be in the war on our side. . . . They are living in a different world from ourselves," one British participant noted.[22] Yet the Atlantic Charter, the Churchill–Roosevelt friendship, the Anglo-American strategic conversations, even the divergent views on international organization and postwar economic policy—all struck chords that would echo through the next four years of war. The fact that the Soviet Union, which Germany had invaded some six weeks earlier, had no representatives at Argentia did not mean that the conferees did not discuss the issue of Soviet cooperation against the Axis. Harry Hopkins, Roosevelt's good friend and Churchill's "Lord Root of the Matter," had visited Moscow two weeks before the Argentia conference, and his assurances that the USSR would withstand the Nazi onslaught buoyed the two leaders. In a joint communication to Stalin from Argentia, Churchill and Roosevelt hailed "the splendid defense that you are making against the Nazi attack" and promised the "very maximum" of supplies.[23] This Anglo-American commitment to cooperation with the Soviet Union against Hitler also carried large implications for the future.

JUGGLING BETWEEN WAR AND PEACE, 1939–1941

The conversations at Placentia Bay exemplified Roosevelt's distinctly personal approach to diplomacy during World War II. A deft juggler who "could keep all his balls in the air without losing his own," as Vice President Henry Wallace quipped,

FDR delighted in face-to-face confrontations, always confident in his ability to charm and understand foreign leaders.[24] The meeting with Churchill whetted his appetite for more. It mattered little to Roosevelt that Secretary of State Cordell Hull learned of the conference when he read about it in the newspapers. The president did not mind that his military and naval advisers often had short notice to prepare for meetings. Roosevelt kept close aides such as Harry Hopkins and Sumner Welles nearby and watched the spotlight focus on himself. His cigarette holder omnipresent, Roosevelt reveled in the power and drama that were his to command. If not the evil Machiavelli of isolationist fantasy, the president, with his formidable style and strong personality, could be unsettling. British foreign secretary Anthony Eden once compared Roosevelt to "a conjurer, skillfully juggling with balls of dynamite, whose nature he failed to understand."[25]

The juggling act had begun some two years before the "Atlantic Charter" Conference, when Germany started World War II by attacking Poland. On September 3, 1939, two days after the German invasion, FDR spoke to the American people in a fireside chat. "This nation will remain a neutral nation," he declared, "but I cannot ask that every American remain neutral in thought as well."[26] Thus, in words pointedly different from Wilson's in 1914, did Roosevelt project for the next twenty-six months U.S. policy toward the war in Europe. The historian Robert A. Divine has compared the evolution of that policy to a game— the president always "moved two steps forward and one back before he took the giant step ahead."[27] Roosevelt proceeded from neutrality to nonbelligerency to undeclared war in the Atlantic and finally, after Pearl Harbor, to full-scale war against the Axis powers. Hoping to avoid war, while at the same time giving as much aid as possible to Hitler's opponents, the president did not always speak candidly to the public about the possible and ultimate contradiction between these two goals.

On September 21, 1939, Roosevelt asked Congress to repeal the arms embargo in the Neutrality Act as the best way to keep the United States from entering the war. He stressed this deceptive argument, knowing that the real purpose of repeal was to permit England and France, with their superior sea power, to purchase arms and munitions on a cash-and-carry basis. He persuaded William Allen White, the Republican sage from Emporia, Kansas, to form a Non-Partisan Committee for Peace through Revision of the Neutrality Act. Although isolationists such as Republican senator Charles Tobey of New Hampshire opposed "our changing the rules after the war has broken out," the president's tactics worked.[28] By a vote of 63 to 30 in the Senate and 243 to 181 in the House, the revised Neutrality Act became law on November 4.

The Pan American Conference at Panama City (September 23–October 3, 1939) also signaled the pro-Allied emphasis of U.S. policy. The conferees proclaimed neutrality, established a committee for economic coordination, and created a neutral zone 300 miles wide along the entire coast of the Western Hemisphere (except Canada), in which belligerent naval operations were prohibited. Roosevelt had told his cabinet as early as April 1939 that the Atlantic fleet would patrol such areas and "if we fire and sink an Italian or German [submarine] . . . we will say it the way the Japs do, 'so sorry.' 'Never happen again.' Tomorrow we sink two."[29]

Makers of American Foreign Relations, 1939–1945

Presidents	Secretaries of State
Franklin D. Roosevelt, 1933–1945	Cordell Hull, 1933–1944
	Edward R. Stettinius, Jr., 1944–1945
Harry S. Truman, 1945–1953	James F. Byrnes, 1945–1947

These "neutrality patrols" actually became the first step toward Anglo-American naval cooperation. By late summer 1940, conversations between staff officers began in London, soon followed by exchanges of personnel and cryptographic intelligence, actual coordination against German naval operations (such as the sighting and sinking of the battleship *Bismarck* in May 1941), and, in autumn 1941, the convoying of merchant ships across the Atlantic. Justified in terms of contingency planning and aid short of war, such naval measures nonetheless led the chief of naval operations, Admiral Harold R. Stark, to conclude in early 1941: "The question as to our entry into the war seems to be *when* and not *whether*."[30]

Germany's *blitzkrieg* humbled Poland in two weeks, and then came, in the winter of 1939–1940, a period of some quiet called the "phony war," or *sitzkrieg*. Most battle news, from November to March, flowed from Northern Europe, where Russia defeated Finland in the "Winter War." Roosevelt sent his sympathies but little else to Finland. The fall of France in June 1940 stung FDR into bold measures. In a speech of June 10, Roosevelt condemned Italy for holding the dagger that "struck . . . the back of its neighbor," and pledged to England "the material resources of this nation."[31] A week later he named the prominent Republicans Henry L. Stimson and Frank Knox, both vocal advocates of aid to Britain, as secretary of war and secretary of the navy, respectively. Then, after careful preparations, and intricate negotiations, the president announced on September 3, 1940, that he was, by executive agreement, transferring to England some fifty old destroyers in exchange for leases to eight British bases stretching from Newfoundland to British Guiana. Two weeks later, he signed into law the Selective Training and Service Act of 1940, the first peacetime military draft in American history.

That Roosevelt could accomplish so much, at a time when isolationist sentiment still prevailed and he sought a controversial third term as president, testifies to his political astuteness. As to both selective service and the destroyers-for-bases agreement, FDR learned that his Republican presidential opponent, Wendell L. Willkie, would not make them campaign issues. In both cases Roosevelt also encouraged influential private citizens (the Century Group for the destroyers deal and the Military Training Camps Association for selective service) to lobby for his objectives. The larger Committee to Defend America by Aiding the Allies, headed by William Allen White, soon rallied behind the president to counter the isolationist America First Committee set up in September 1940. FDR avoided congressional scrutiny of the destroyers deal by presenting it as an executive agreement rather than as a treaty, and he deflected political opposition to conscription by having men of

The German Onslaught 1939–1942

integrity, such as Secretary Stimson and General George C. Marshall, attest to the military's need for a draft. Public sympathy for beleaguered Britain also helped. "Every time Hitler bombed London we got another couple of votes," noted the future selective service director Lewis W. Hershey.[32] Furthermore, Roosevelt continued to promise that his policies would keep America out of war. Although Germany could regard the destroyers deal as a *casus belli,* FDR called it instead "the most important action in the reinforcement of our national defense . . . since the Louisiana Purchase."[33] The president defended his pro-Allied foreign policy in the fall campaign. When Willkie made last-minute charges that Roosevelt secretly sought war, the White House struck back: "Your boys are not going to be sent into any foreign wars." Willkie exploded: "That hypocritical son of a bitch! This is going to beat me!"[34] It did.

As Roosevelt took a postelection cruise in the Caribbean, Churchill spelled out Britain's desperate need for arms and munitions: "The moment approaches when we shall no longer be able to pay cash for shipping and other supplies."[35] Roosevelt soon held one of his breezy, jaunty press conferences, saying that he favored a policy of lending or leasing supplies to Britain. He likened his policy to lending a garden hose to a neighbor whose house was burning. Once the fire is out, "he gives it back to me and thanks me very much for the use of it," or, if damaged, he replaces it with a new product.[36] In a fireside chat on December 29, FDR admitted that sending armaments to Britain risked war, but "our national policy is not directed toward war. Its sole purpose is to keep war away from our country and our people." Then, in a ringing phrase, Roosevelt called on the United States to "become the great arsenal of democracy."[37]

Over the next two months, as FDR later put it, Americans debated the Lend-Lease bill in Congress, "in every newspaper, on every wave length—over every cracker barrel in all the land."[38] Although the vote of 60 to 31 in the Senate and 317 to 71 in the House seemed substantial, the White House did not win without a struggle. Senator Burton K. Wheeler, an isolationist Democrat from Montana, labeled the bill "the New Deal's triple A foreign policy; it will plow under every fourth American boy."[39] Roosevelt called Wheeler's statement "the rottenest thing that has been said in public life in my generation."[40] A bit of benevolent deception occurred in the numbering of the bill in the House. The administration's floor manager, Representative John W. McCormack, worried because his Irish constituents in South Boston would surely protest any "McCormack Bill" designed to aid the British Empire, induced the House parliamentarian to tag the Lend-Lease bill H.R. 1776. When one irate constituent nonetheless berated him, the future speaker of the house thought quickly: "Madam, do you realize that the Vatican is surrounded on all sides by totalitarianism? Madam, this is not a bill to save the English, this is a bill to save Catholicism."[41]

Titled "An Act to Promote the Defense of the United States," the bill became law on March 11, 1941. Under its terms the president could "sell, transfer title to, exchange, lease, lend, or otherwise dispose of" defense articles to "any country whose defense the President deems vital to the defense of the United States."[42] Although the initial appropriation totaled $7 billion, by war's end the United States had expended more than $50 billion on Lend-Lease. The United States even included 900,000 feet of fire hose in the first shipment of goods to England, which eventually received $31.6 billion in Lend-Lease assistance during the war. "If we don't watch our step," one U.S. official grumbled, "we shall find the White House en route to England with the Washington Monument as a steering oar."[43]

With German U-boats operating in wolf packs, sinking more than 500,000 tons of shipping a month, it seemed likely that the United States would use its navy to see that Lend-Lease supplies reached England safely. But FDR hesitated, partly because of public opinion, but also because the Atlantic fleet lacked operational readiness. Instead, he extended naval "patrols" halfway across the Atlantic, announcing in April that American vessels would monitor German warships. "We have got a tadpole that someday may be a frog," Secretary Hull told an aide.[44] U.S. troops also occupied Greenland the same month. Although interventionists urged the president to have the navy convoy British ships, FDR declared a national emergency in late May but took no new action. He told the cabinet that "he expected a clash sooner or later but said the Germans would have to fire the first shots."[45]

When Hitler occupied the Balkans and launched his attack on Soviet Russia in June 1941, the president announced the next month that 4,000 American marines would occupy Iceland for hemispheric defense. Roosevelt also began military Lend-Lease aid to the USSR in November, notwithstanding opinions from State Department and military advisers that the Soviet Union would quickly fall. (By the end of the war Russia had received $11 billion in Lend-Lease.) "Now comes this Russian diversion," FDR wrote four days after the German assault. "If it is more than just that it will mean the liberation of Europe from Nazi domination."[46] As for Churchill, he remarked on his new Russian ally: "If Hitler invaded Hell I would

Lend-Lease to Russia.   A U.S. Lend-Lease official checks American food destined for the Soviet Union's hard-pressed people. The Soviets eventually lost at least 22 million people in the war. (U.S. Information Agency, National Archives)

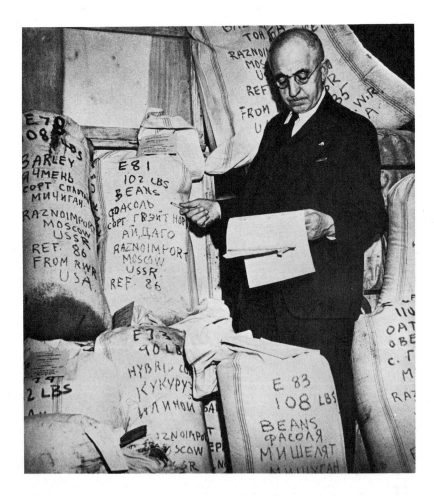

make at least a favorable reference to the Devil in the House of Commons."[47] When bureaucratic tangles and military lethargy inhibited the flow of goods to the USSR, a short-tempered Roosevelt lectured his cabinet that "the only answer I want to hear is that it is under way."[48] Then the president held his dramatic meeting with Churchill at Placentia Bay, and in early September, after German torpedoes just missed the *Greer,* he publicly ordered naval convoys as far as Iceland and issued a "shoot-on-sight" command to the navy.

By autumn 1941, Roosevelt probably sought an "incident" to induce American entry into the war against Hitler. After the Placentia Bay conference, Churchill had told the British War Cabinet that the president "had said that he would wage war, but not declare it, and that he would become more and more provocative. If the Germans did not like it, they could attack American forces."[49] When a U-boat torpedoed the destroyer *Kearny* off Iceland, killing eleven men on October 17, the president seized the moment. "The shooting has started. And history has recorded who fired the first shot," he intoned on October 27. "Hitler's torpedo was directed at every American, whether he lives on our sea coasts or in the innermost part of the country."[50] Roosevelt then flourished a map that purportedly showed how Nazis planned to reorganize Central and South America as vassal states. Through these histrionics the president hoped to persuade Congress to repeal the sections of the 1939 Neutrality Act that prohibited the arming of merchant ships and banned such vessels from war zones. After a U-boat sank the destroyer *Reuben James,* with the loss of more than one hundred men, on October 31, the isolationist America First Committee charged that the White House was "asking Congress to issue an engraved drowning license to American seamen."[51] Following bitter debate, repeal passed in November by narrow margins, 50 to 37 in the Senate and 212 to 194 in the House. For the first time since the outbreak of war in 1939, American merchant vessels could carry arms and munitions to England. Roosevelt must have suspected that Hitler, unless he courted defeat, could not allow American cargo ships to cross the Atlantic unmolested. Naval escorts were provocative enough. Yet even as such moves led to the brink of war with Germany, it is possible, as the historian Manfred Jonas has suggested, that the two countries "might well have teetered on that brink for months or even years."[52]

Roosevelt charted an oblique course toward war because he believed he had no other choice. Although the pollster George Gallup had observed in 1940 that "the best way to influence public opinion" on an issue "is to get Mr. Roosevelt to talk about it and favor it," the president underestimated his power to rally public opinion.[53] "I am doing everything possible," he once explained, "although I am not talking very much about it because a certain element in the press . . . would undoubtedly pervert it, attack it, and confuse the public mind."[54] So worried, FDR chose indirection over candor and relied on events and his own manipulative ability to inch ahead. In the absence of decisive presidential leadership, the internationalist-isolationist debate thus hardened into stalemate by autumn 1941. Some 80 percent of the American people still opposed entering the war, while a higher percentage wanted an Axis defeat. In the Chicago area, for example, "at no time did more than a minority of the proponents of aid view the policy as a spring-

board to full American entry into the war. Until Pearl Harbor, most Americans desired peace. But they wanted even more to see Hitler beaten. They hoped it would
be possible to reconcile these goals."[55] So long as FDR touted aid to the allies as
the best way to avoid war, Americans could think that they had fulfilled both goals.
The narrow vote over repeal of the Neutrality Act in November dramatized the
power of isolationist sentiment and reinforced the president's reluctance to ask for
outright intervention. "The day of the white rabbits has passed," Senator Josiah
Bailey of North Carolina wrote, "and the great magician who could pull them out
of any silk hat . . . cannot find the rabbit."[56]

FDR had said for months that the United States would not enter the war, that
aiding the Allies would prevent the need for American military intervention. Now
he could not easily reverse his position without appearing a hypocrite. He could
only wait for the Germans to fire the first shot. Hitler was slow to oblige, restraining his admirals from all-out war in the shipping lanes while he tried on land to
knock Soviet Russia out. News of the Japanese attack at Pearl Harbor reached
Berlin at a time when German armies had bogged down short of Moscow. In the
mistaken belief that Japanese intervention would keep Americans occupied in the
Pacific, the Fuehrer jubilantly announced war against the United States on
December 11, 1941. Congress soon answered with a resolution affirming a state of
war with Germany.

JAPANESE-AMERICAN RELATIONS AND THE WORLD CONFLICT, 1939–1941

Events in Asia, not Europe, plunged the United States into World War II.
Ambassador Joseph C. Grew expressed surprise at the increased signs of anti-
Japanese sentiment during a trip home in the summer of 1939. The ambassador listened to his old Groton and Harvard friend Franklin Roosevelt talk truculently of
intercepting the Japanese fleet if it moved against the Dutch East Indies. When the
State Department gave formal notice in July that the 1911 commercial treaty with
Japan would terminate in six months, Grew feared that economic sanctions would
follow, and perhaps war as well. "[It] is going to be up to me," he noted, "to let
this American temper discreetly penetrate into Japanese consciousness. Sparks will
fly before long."[57]

Grew, with his Asian preoccupation, had failed to grasp the Europe-first emphasis of Roosevelt's foreign policy. After 1937, when Japan marched deeper into
China, Washington angrily reacted with protests, but limited its intervention. As in
the 1920s and early 1930s, the United States lacked the power to challenge Japanese
predominance in East Asia. Even Roosevelt's much-heralded tactic of refusing to
apply the Neutrality Act to the "incident" in China, thus making it legal to sell arms
and munitions to Jiang Jieshi's government, could not obscure the preponderance
of American trade with Japan. As late as 1940, $78 million in American exports

went to China, whereas $227 million were shipped to Japan. Abrogation of the 1911 commercial treaty permitted economic sanctions against Japan, but oil, the most vital ingredient in Japan's war machine, flowed until stopped in July 1941. In keeping with Roosevelt's policy of all-out aid to England short of war, the navy revised its strategic thinking in November 1940. "Plan Dog" called for a defensive posture in the Pacific, depicted Germany as the country's number one enemy, and made preservation of England its principal goal. Opposed to any appeasement of Japan, Roosevelt still hoped to avoid a confrontation, because "I simply have not got enough Navy to go around—and every little episode in the Pacific means fewer ships in the Atlantic."[58]

Japanese movement into Southeast Asia, in apparent coordination with Hitler's *blitzkrieg* in Europe, placed Washington and Tokyo on a collision course. With the Asian colonies of France and the Netherlands lying unprotected, Japanese expansionists demanded a thrust southward, thus completing the strangulation of China and transforming the whole region into the Greater East Asia Co-Prosperity Sphere. Japan pressed England and France to close down supply routes to the Guomindang through Burma and Indochina. Tokyo also demanded economic concessions from the petroleum-rich Dutch East Indies. Then came the shocking news of late September 1940. Just four days after Vichy French representatives allowed Japanese troops to occupy northern Indochina, Japan, on September 27, signed the Tripartite Pact with Germany and Italy. Each signatory pledged to aid one another if attacked by a nation not currently involved in the war. Because the pact explicitly exempted the Soviet Union, Washington had no doubt about being the target. The aggressors of Europe and Asia had apparently banded together.

A new more militant Japanese government, with Prince Fumimaro Konoe as prime minister and General Hideki Tojo as war minister, took the fateful steps. Foreign Minister Yosuke Matsuoka, who had spent nine years in America as a youth and thought he understood Americans, articulated the advantages of boldness—"one cannot obtain a tiger's cub unless he braves the tiger's den."[59] Matsuoka intended the Tripartite Pact to deter the United States from intervening in either the Atlantic or Pacific, and to facilitate a rapprochement between Japan and the Soviet Union, which remained aligned with Germany in the Nazi-Soviet Pact. Tokyo might then induce Jiang Jieshi to join the Co-Prosperity Sphere, after which Japanese troops would gradually withdraw from China and civilian authorities could reassert control over the army. "Held together by a long chain of 'ifs,'" as the historian Barbara Teters has written, Matsuoka's scenario could also lead to war.[60] The Japanese navy, which would bear the brunt of any war with England and the United States, lobbied against the Tripartite Pact.

Washington flashed warning signals. In July 1940, Roosevelt clamped an embargo on aviation fuel and top-grade scrap iron sought by Japan. In September, at the time of the Tripartite Pact, he extended the embargo to all scrap metals. Even Grew urged firmness. His famous "green light" telegram of September 12, 1940, labeled Japan "one of the predatory powers," lacking "all moral and ethical sense . . . frankly and unashamedly opportunist, seeking at every turn to profit by the weakness of others."[61] Administration "hawks" such as Stimson, Knox, Ickes, Morgenthau, and even Eleanor Roosevelt pressed the president to shut off oil exports as well. Backed by Secretary Hull and the joint chiefs, however, Roosevelt kept the oil flowing to Japan. Recognizing the interconnectness of the "world conflict," the president speculated that Japanese movement southward into the Dutch East Indies and Malay Peninsula would increase Germany's chances of defeating Britain.[62] The president hoped to aid England while avoiding a showdown in the Pacific, which an oil embargo would ensure.

The first six months of 1941 saw vigorous private and official transpacific efforts to avoid war. In February, Admiral Kichisaburo Nomura became ambassador to Washington. Well known for his pro-Western opinions and a personal friend of President Roosevelt, Nomura accepted the appointment only when assured by Konoe and Matsuoka that peace with the United States took precedence over Japan's commitment to the Axis. Otherwise, he said, his task would be "like chasing two rabbits in different directions."[63] A group of private citizens known as the "John Doe Associates" and led by two Catholic missionaries, Father James M. Drought and Bishop James E. Walsh, also tried to effect conciliation. They held interviews with Prince Konoe, Hull, and Roosevelt. The John Doe intermediaries told each government what it wanted to hear. Father Drought enthusiastically forwarded a "Draft Understanding" to Secretary Hull on April 9, which, among other points, called for a Konoe-Roosevelt meeting in Hawaii and U.S. pressure on China to recognize Japanese domination of Manchuria, in exchange for Japanese disavowal of the Tripartite Pact. Hull thought the "Understanding" a Japanese proposal and accepted it as a basis of discussion. But Hull told Nomura that any Japanese-American agreement had to satisfy four basic principles: respect for the territorial integrity and sovereignty of all nations; noninterference in the internal affairs of other nations; respect for the equality of commercial opportunity, or Open Door; and support for peaceful change in the Pacific. Japan, however, thought the "Draft Understanding" an American proposal, and Nomura failed to attach appropriate importance to Hull's four points when he reported to Tokyo. Not until September did Tokyo learn that Hull's four principles were crucial and a major obstacle to any settlement of the China war. The amateur diplomatic activities of the Doe Associates had confused Japanese-American relations, as the question of a Pacific meeting between Konoe and Roosevelt demonstrates. In August the Japanese asked for the meeting they thought the Americans had proposed in April. By August, however, Washington first wanted assurances from Tokyo on outstanding problems and hence rejected a high-level meeting. Japan then grew annoyed, sure that the United States was retreating from its original position.

Japan's determination to hold China and to expand farther doomed these diplomatic efforts. "The Japs are having a real drag-down," Roosevelt observed in early July 1941, "trying to decide which way they are going to jump—attack Russia, attack the South Seas . . . or whether they will sit on the fence and be more friendly with us."[64] When word reached Washington on July 24 that troop transports bearing the Rising Sun were steaming toward Camranh Bay and southern Indochina, FDR signed an executive order freezing all Japanese funds in the United States. Hard-line bureaucrats interpreted the order to mean stopping all trade with Japan—including oil. Thereafter, in the historian Jonathan Utley's words, Washington and Tokyo steered "a collision course that even statesmen of great flexibility would find it difficult to avoid."[65]

The diplomacy of proposals and counterproposals in the remaining months of 1941 proved ineffective. Unless the flow of American oil resumed, Japan determined to seize Dutch and British oil fields. But the United States would not turn on the oil spigot until Tokyo agreed to Hull's four principles, especially the pledge to respect China's sovereignty and territorial integrity. Key American officials also knew from cracking the Japanese diplomatic code (Operation MAGIC) that Japan's forces were massing to strike southward after mid-November. But many in the Roosevelt administration did not think Japan would battle the United States. Hardliners like Henry L. Stimson had advocated embargoes for more than a year, depicting the Japanese as "notorious bluffers" who backed down when confronted firmly.[66] As late as November 27, when MAGIC intercepts revealed a Japanese strike somewhere very soon, State Department Asian expert Stanley K. Hornbeck challenged his colleagues: "Tell me of one case in history when a nation went to war out of desperation."[67] Amid this atmosphere, the urging of army and navy leaders to string out negotiations until the Philippines could be reinforced went unheeded. An eleventh-hour modus vivendi proposed a small trickle of oil to Japan and negotiations between Chongqing and Tokyo, while maintaining American aid to China; Japan would have to abrogate the Tripartite Pact and accept basic principles of international conduct. Exhausted from months of negotiations, Hull advised Roosevelt to shelve the proposal. The secretary of state decided to abandon diplomacy—to "kick the whole thing over."[68]

After months of discussion among civilian and military leaders, the Japanese Imperial Conference of September decided to fight the United States if Washington did not lift the embargo on strategic materials by October 15—a date later extended to November 25 and then to November 30. Tokyo's final decision to attack the United States did not stem from irrationality or suicidal tendencies. Japan required 12,000 tons of oil each day, and desperate moderates and militants alike

The PURPLE Machine. In September 1940, U.S. cryptanalysts of the Signal Intelligence Service cracked Japan's most secret diplomatic cipher—a machine called PURPLE. The American codebreakers thereafter, under Operation MAGIC, not only deciphered thousands of intercepted messages sent by Japanese officials around the world, but also duplicated the machine itself. Important intercepts went to a select group of U.S. officials, including the president. Although these dispatches revealed through 1941 that Japan expected all-out war with the United States, they did not reveal military plans or the planned attack on Pearl Harbor. (National Archives)

read U.S. pressure as provocative and life-strangling. In a choice between fighting the United States or pulling out of China, no Japanese leader recommended the latter. They knew America's power and industrial potential well enough, but, as one Japanese admiral put it, "Japan was like a patient suffering from a serious disease. . . . Should he be let alone without an operation, there was danger of a gradual decline. An operation, which might be extremely dangerous, would still offer some hope of saving his life."[69] The Japanese did not expect America to surrender (an invasion of the United States was out of the question), but they hoped that a stalemated war of endurance might persuade tired Americans to arbitrate. In any case, Japan refused to give up its empire, to "lie prostrate at the feet of the United States."[70]

At dawn on November 25, 1941, a huge task force that included six carriers bearing some 350 airplanes headed across 3,000 miles of the Pacific Ocean. The target: Pearl Harbor, Hawaii. Every ship maintained radio silence to avoid detection and ensure complete surprise. In the early morning of Sunday, December 7, some 220 miles north of Honolulu, the carriers unleashed their planes. They swept down on the unsuspecting American naval base, dropping torpedoes and bombs, strafing buildings. Within a few hours eight U.S. battleships had been sunk or damaged and 2,403 Americans had died. The stunning news shot around the world. Children across the United States heard the story and thought their lives endangered. A girl in Whittier, California, became ill after seeing war newsreels at the movie theater— "the bombed homes, the sick and dying people—children with no homes and no families. I cried."[71] In London, his struggle to get America into the war finally ended, a contented Winston Churchill thought: "So we had won after all!" Indeed, "greater good fortune has rarely happened to the British Empire."[72]

Critics have charged that Roosevelt and his top advisers deliberately sacrificed the Pacific fleet to get into the war with Hitler via the "back door."[73] Most scholars reject the conspiracy theory and explain Pearl Harbor as the consequence of mistakes, missed clues, overconfidence, and plain bad luck. The most authoritative student of the disaster, Gordon Prange, notes intelligence failures in Washington that might have alerted Hawaii, but concludes that American errors weighed less than the enormous care and skill with which the Japanese planned the attack. MAGIC intercepts on November 30, for example, read "that there is extreme danger that war may suddenly break out between the Anglo-Saxon nations and Japan . . . ; this war may come quicker than anyone dreams."[74] Yet the intercepts never revealed military plans and Washington thought Japan would strike Southeast Asia, where troop ships were spotted heading for Malaya; no one thought Tokyo could undertake two major operations at once. As to hints of major Japanese interest in Pearl Harbor, including Grew's warning in February 1941 of a possible sudden attack, the scholar Roberta Wohlstetter has written: "After the event a signal is always crystal clear. . . . But before the event it is obscure and pregnant with conflicting meanings. . . . In short, we failed to anticipate Pearl Harbor not for want of the relevant materials, but because of a plethora of irrelevant ones."[75] Many "ifs" cloud the question. If the radar operator had been able to convince his superiors on Oahu that the blips were really planes, if General Marshall had sent his last-minute warning by navy cable instead of Western Union telegraph, if MAGIC could have read Japan's naval communications as well as its diplomatic cables, if . . .

Pearl Harbor. A Japanese pilot's perspective on Ford Island, Pearl Harbor, Hawaii. The three Pacific U.S. aircraft carriers were not in port and escaped the attack. Of the eight battleships at Pearl Harbor, six were repaired and eventually participated in the war. (Navy Department, National Archives)

For Japan, Pearl Harbor proved a tactical victory but a strategic disaster. Americans rallied to the flag with a national unity not seen in a long time. When President Roosevelt, referring to the "date which will live in infamy," asked for a declaration of war, Congress responded on December 8 with a unanimous vote in the Senate and only one dissent in the House—that of Jeannette Rankin, who had also voted "no" in 1917.[76] For Senator Vandenberg, the Japanese attack on Hawaii "ended isolationism for any realist."[77] Six of the eight battleships damaged at Pearl Harbor were raised from shallow waters and repaired to rejoin the U.S. fleet. At most, then, Pearl Harbor counted as a "military inconvenience" for the United

States, which rebounded with a fury of moral purpose and industrial production that eventually defeated the Axis.[78]

Two days after Pearl Harbor, FDR looked beyond the battlefield to the conference room: "We are going to win the war, and we are going to win the peace that follows."[79]

THE BIG THREE: STRATEGIES AND FISSURES, 1941–1943

The "Atlantic Charter" Conference and the events of 1939–1941 illustrate well the themes of wartime diplomacy. The emphasis on giving material aid to Hitler's opponents through the "arsenal of democracy" foreshadowed the main American contribution to victory in Europe. Washington's commitment to a "Europe First" strategy derived from Anglo-American staff discussions prior to Pearl Harbor, as did the different American and British conceptions of that strategy. Americans favored a "massive thrust at the enemy's heart" and the British preferred "successive stabs around the periphery . . . like jackals worrying a lion before springing at his throat."[80] During the war Americans also revived Wilsonianism but combined it with a pragmatic determination to avoid Wilson's mistakes. This time the United States would join an international organization to maintain peace, even if it meant adding blatant balance-of-power features to the institution and paying court to sensitive Republican senators. There would be no debts-reparations tangle because Lend-Lease would eliminate the dollar sign. This time, too, the enemy would have to surrender unconditionally. The State Department's desire to reduce tariffs abroad and to create an open world became particularly conspicuous during the war, reflecting Secretary Hull's Wilsonian belief that trade discrimination ranked as a prime cause of war. FDR himself frequently irritated European allies by insisting that colonial empires—like the British in India and the French in Indochina—must break up after the war in favor of independence for long-abused people. "We mean to hold our own," Churchill retorted. "I have not become the King's First Minister in order to preside over the liquidation of the British Empire."[81]

If total war inspired visions of total peace, victory over the Axis also required compromises and short-term decisions not always Wilsonian in nature. The marriage of convenience with the Soviet Union marked perhaps the most evident departure from Wilsonian preferences, if only because Soviet security needs and drives in Eastern Europe clashed with the principle of national self-determination. But Franklin Roosevelt had learned as much about statecraft from his cousin Theodore as from Woodrow Wilson. His vision of the "Four Policemen" (the Soviet Union, China, Britain, and the United States) maintaining world peace implied spheres of influence more than true collective security. Roosevelt committed himself to continuing Soviet-American cooperation into the postwar world. Because the Red Army bore the brunt of the fighting until mid-1944, and because the Soviets played down their objective of world revolution after June 22, 1941, it became prudent, even necessary, to postpone difficulties with Moscow until the end of the war. Despite wartime propaganda about similar revolutionary and anti-imperialist pasts, Soviet-American differences remained profound. Fears on both sides that the other would make a separate peace with Germany kept the two nations nervous about one another.

The growing influence of the military suggested that foreign policy sometimes emerged from "a snake pit of influential leaders and faceless bureaucrats working at cross-purposes, striking deals, and not infrequently employing sleight of hand in order to move the nation in the direction each thought most appropriate."[82] That Roosevelt took his joint chiefs, not Secretary Hull, to Argentia and other wartime conferences symbolized the extent to which military decisions determined foreign policy. As a former assistant secretary of the navy, FDR delighted in the duties of commander-in-chief. He liked to devise grand strategy and made the joint chiefs principal advisers during the war. He left postwar planning and congressional liaison to the State Department. Cordell Hull grudgingly acquiesced because he had never been Roosevelt's "complete agent."[83] Hull frequently did not learn of

"Jap . . . You're Next!"   James Montgomery Flagg, already famous for his "I Want You" poster of World War I, offered this version of Uncle Sam in 1942. After Pearl Harbor, posters such as Flagg's helped focus public resentment on Japan, rather than on Hitler. Yet Roosevelt did not want to adopt a "Pacific First" strategy and kept his "Europe First" strategy alive by supporting British proposals to invade North Africa in November 1942. (National Archives)

Roosevelt's decisions until Secretary of War Stimson told him. FDR elevated "fragmentation" to "a first principle" of policymaking.[84] At one point in 1944 the State Department was formulating plans for the occupation of Germany that contradicted decisions made at the Teheran Conference a few months earlier. Roosevelt did not tell Hull what happened at Teheran and Hull apparently never asked.

The ordeal of global war brought new power and confidence to American diplomacy. The Atlantic Charter reflected a commitment to shaping the postwar world in an American image. As Henry Luce's best-selling *American Century* phrased it in 1941, the United States must "exert upon the world the full impact of our influence, for such purposes as we see fit and by such means as we see fit."[85] By rearming, acquiring new bases, raising an army of more than 2 million, welding hemispheric unity, and revving up its industries, the United States built the sinews of global power even before Pearl Harbor. Winston Churchill told Roosevelt in 1944: "You have the greatest navy in the world. You will have, I hope, the greatest air force. You will have the greatest trade. You have all the gold." But Churchill hoped that the Americans "will not give themselves over to vainglorious ambitions, and that justice and fair-play will be the lights that guide them."[86] The United States used its power for both political and military purposes, but, as Roosevelt told Churchill, postwar political settlements and other issues "must be definitely secondary to the primary operations of striking at the heart of Germany."[87]

The diplomacy of the "Grand Alliance" of the United States, Britain, and the Soviet Union centered on two issues: boundaries in Eastern Europe, and the timing of an Anglo-American "second front" in Western Europe. When Anthony Eden went to Moscow just after Pearl Harbor, Premier Stalin said he had no objections to declarations like the Atlantic Charter, which he regarded as "algebra," but he preferred "practical arithmetic"—that is, an agreement guaranteeing Soviet boundaries with Eastern Europe as they stood prior to Hitler's attack in 1941.[88] The British, after an initial refusal, seemed inclined to grant what Stalin wanted. Roosevelt, however, told the Soviet ambassador that "under no conditions would he subscribe to any secret treaty. Nor could he subscribe to any open public treaty with regard to definite frontiers until the war had been won."[89]

FDR did view the second front with greater urgency. The Soviets, fighting some 200 German divisions and dying by the hundreds of thousands, pleaded for a cross-channel attack as quickly as possible, and the American military, despite British reluctance, wished to comply. "We've got to go to Europe and fight," an American staff officer noted as early as January 1942. "If we're to keep Russia in, save the Middle East, India and Burma; we've got to begin slugging with air at West Europe; to be followed by a land attack as soon *as possible*."[90] When the Soviet foreign minister visited Washington that May, Roosevelt "authorized Mr. Molotov to inform Mr. Stalin that [the president] expected the formation of a second front this year."[91] But the Anglo-American invasion of France did not take place until June 6, 1944, and during the interim, as FDR said, "the Russian armies are killing more Axis personnel and destroying more Axis material than all other twenty-five United Nations put together."[92] The delay, to say the least, produced serious fissures in the Grand Alliance.

American military leaders urged a cross-channel attack by spring 1943 at the latest, but the British, with Roosevelt's compliance, decided otherwise. A new plan, Operation TORCH, called for the invasion of French North Africa in November 1942, a decision that led logically to operations against Sicily and Italy in the summer of 1943 and effectively postponed a cross-channel attack (later dubbed Operation OVERLORD) until 1944. When General Dwight D. Eisenhower learned that the second front had been postponed, he muttered that it might be the "blackest day in history" if Russia did not stay in the war.[93] At numerous military conferences in 1942–1943, the Americans always suspected that British fixation on the Mediterranean demonstrated a desire to shore up imperial lifelines, and not, as the British claimed, a coherent strategy to bloody Germany on the periphery before launching a full-scale invasion of France. Sometimes tempers flared, as described by one American general at the Cairo Conference of November 1943, when British chief of staff Alan Brooke exchanged heated words with American admiral Ernest J. King: "Brooke got nasty and King got good and sore. King almost climbed over the table at Brooke. God, he was mad. I wished he had socked him."[94] Apart from Roosevelt's desire to have Americans fighting Germans somewhere in 1942, British strategy predominated in the two years after Pearl Harbor because England had fully mobilized, whereas America had not, and any combined operation had to depend largely on British troops, shipping, and casualties. Once American production and manpower began to predominate in 1943, combined strategy gradually shifted toward Operation OVERLORD. According to the historian Brian Villa, FDR also "enticed" Churchill toward a D-Day pledge of June 1944 by temporarily withholding agreement on a postwar atomic partnership.[95] A symbolic clash between the two competing strategies occurred in early 1944. Churchill insisted on an invasion of Rhodes, off the Turkish coast. "Not one American soldier is going to die on that God damned beach," barked General Marshall.[96] None did.

Roosevelt and Churchill knew how intensely Josef Stalin wanted a full-scale second front in France, not in North Africa or Italy. The Red Army had stopped the Germans short of Moscow in 1941, but in the summer of 1942 German *panzers* drove into the Caucasus oil fields and laid siege to Stalingrad on the Volga River. Churchill told Stalin in August 1942 that a cross-channel attack was planned for spring 1943. Yet a few months later Stalin learned that the attack was postponed until August 1943. Not until June 1943 did the Russians know officially that a cross-channel assault would not happen at all that year. "Need I speak of the dishearteningly negative expression that this fresh postponement of the second front . . . will produce in the Soviet Union?" Stalin wrote Roosevelt.[97] Tensions increased that summer, when the Soviet Union broke off diplomatic relations with the Polish exile government in London after the Poles had asked the International Red Cross to investigate charges that the Russians had murdered more than 10,000 Polish prisoners (many of them senior army officers) in the Katyn Forest in 1941. (Soviet archives opened after the end of the Cold War revealed that Stalin had ordered the Polish executions.) The Russians also protested when the Allies suspended convoys carrying vital Lend-Lease supplies to Murmansk because of shipping needs in the Mediterranean and Pacific. In August 1943 Stalin complained to Roosevelt about the separate peace negotiations that the Americans and British were conducting with Italy. (The Italians formally surrendered in early September, then declared war against Germany, only to have German forces occupy most of the peninsula before Anglo-American troops could land in force.) Britain and the United States, the Soviet leader charged, only "informed" the USSR, and "this situation cannot be tolerated any longer."[98]

Stalin had to be "courted, wooed, constantly chatted up," as Churchill urged the Poles not to protest the Katyn massacre because "nothing you can do will bring them [the dead officers] back."[99] FDR expedited Lend-Lease supplies to Russia without the usual quid-pro-quo arrangements. Probably the most controversial attempt to reassure the Russians came at the Casablanca Conference in January 1943, when Roosevelt announced that "the elimination of German, Japanese, and Italian war power means the unconditional surrender by Germany, Italy, and Japan." He added, "it does . . . mean the destruction of the philosophies in those countries."[100] Coming shortly after the so-called Darlan Deal, wherein the Anglo-Americans made an agreement with the Vichy French collaborator Admiral Jean-François Darlan to gain French cooperation in North Africa, Roosevelt's "unconditional surrender" announcement signaled to a suspicious Stalin that England and the United States would not make a separate peace with one of Hitler's subordinates. Although the doctrine may have encouraged German soldiers to fight harder, as Eisenhower later claimed, its enunciation brought a modicum of Allied unity by concentrating on a total military victory over Hitler, deferring troublesome peace terms until afterward. As long as the United States had to rely on Soviet troops in Europe, however, FDR had little leverage to confront the Soviets over political issues such as the Polish border.

The Russians became less contentious in late August 1943, and called for a Big Three foreign ministers' conference in Moscow. Stalin apparently feared that the Italian surrender might bring the Anglo-Americans quickly into Central Europe at a time when, with postwar boundaries unsettled, the advancing Russian armies were still 600 miles from the 1941 frontiers. The foreign ministers' meeting in Moscow (October 19–30) established an Advisory Council for Italy to coordinate Allied policy and a European Advisory Commission to make recommendations for a final peace settlement. The Russians told Secretary Hull that the 200,000 American battle casualties did not amount to much—"we lose that many each day before lunch. You haven't got your teeth in the war yet."[101] Hull in turn lectured Commissar for Foreign Affairs V. M. Molotov against gobbling up neighbors: "When I was young I knew a bully in Tennessee. He used to get a few things his way by being a bully and bluffing other fellows. But he ended up by not having a friend in the world."[102] Suffering from tuberculosis and "almost mystical in his approach" at Moscow, the seventy-two-year-old Hull got what he wanted: a Declaration of Four Nations on General Security (China included), the first definite commitment to a postwar replacement for the defunct League of Nations.[103]

Moscow seemed a mere appetizer for what the historian Keith Sainsbury has called "the turning point" at Teheran, Iran, November 28–December 1, 1943.[104] Meeting the mustachioed Russian leader for the first time, FDR thought Stalin

Allies in the Soviet Union. These pictures of Roosevelt and Stalin hang over an official Soviet building in 1943 in tribute to the Allied cause. (Courtesy of FDR Library)

"very confident, very sure of himself."[105] The president hoped for a "meeting of the minds."[106] At the first plenary session, as an American general recalled, "Uncle Joe had talked straight from the shoulder," telling Churchill and Roosevelt that he favored a firm commitment to OVERLORD as opposed to any Anglo-American operations in the Balkans.[107] When Churchill backed an Adriatic landing, Stalin asked: "Do the British really believe in OVERLORD or are they only saying so to reassure the Russians?" Churchill lamely replied that "it was the duty of the British Government to hurl every scrap of strength across the channel."[108] At a dinner party two nights later Stalin playfully baited Churchill further by calling for the summary execution of 50,000 German officers. The prime minister protested that the British would "never tolerate mass execution."[109] When Roosevelt joked that only 49,000 should be shot, Churchill walked out in a huff. As General Marshall recalled, Stalin "was turning the hose on Churchill all the time, and Mr. Roosevelt, in a sense, was helping him."[110]

Major Wartime Conferences, 1941–1945

Conference	Date	Participants	Results
Argentia, Newfoundland	August 9–12, 1941	Roosevelt, Churchill	Atlantic Charter
Washington, D.C.	December 22,1941– January 14, 1942	Roosevelt, Churchill	Combined Chiefs of Staff; priority in war effort against Germany; United Nations Declaration
Washington, D.C.	June 19–25, 1942	Roosevelt, Churchill	North African campaign strategy
Moscow, USSR	August 12–15, 1942	Churchill, Stalin, Harriman	Postponement of second front
Casablanca, Morocco	January 14–24, 1943	Roosevelt, Churchill	Unconditional surrender announcement; campaign against Sicily and Italy
Washington, D.C.	May 12–25, 1943	Roosevelt, Churchill	Schedule for cross-channel landing set as May 1,1944
Quebec, Canada	August 14–24, 1943	Roosevelt, Churchill	Confirmation of cross-channel; landing (OVERLORD)
Moscow, USSR	October 19–30, 1943	Hull, Eden, Molotov	Postwar international organization to be formed; Russian promise to enter the war against Japan after Germany's defeat; establishment of European Advisory Commission
UNRRA, Washington, D.C.	November 9, 1943	44 nations	Creation of UNRRA
Cairo, Egypt	November 22–26, 1943	Roosevelt, Churchill, Jiang	Postwar Asia: China to recover lost lands; Korea to be independent; Japan to be stripped of Pacific Islands
Teheran, Iran	November 27– December 1, 1943	Roosevelt, Churchill, Stalin	Agreement on cross-channel landing and international organization; Soviet reaffirmation of intent to enter the war against Japan
Bretton Woods, New Hampshire	July 1–22, 1944	44 nations	Creation of World Bank and International Monetary Fund
Dumbarton Oaks, Washington, D.C.	August 21– October 7, 1944	U.S., Britain, USSR, China	United Nations Organization
Quebec, Canada	September 11–16, 1944	Roosevelt, Churchill	"Morgenthau Plan" for Germany
Moscow, USSR	October 9–18, 1944	Churchill, Stalin	Spheres of influence in Balkans (percentage scheme)
Yalta, USSR	February 4–11, 1945	Roosevelt, Churchill, Stalin	Polish governmental structure, elections, and boundaries; United Nations; German reparations; USSR pledge to declare war against Japan and to recognize Jiang's government; some Japanese territories to USSR
San Francisco, California	April 25– June 26,1945	50 nations	United Nations Organization Charter
Potsdam (Berlin), Germany	July 17– August 2, 1945	Truman, Churchill/ Attlee, Stalin	German reconstruction and reparations; Potsdam Declaration to Japan; Council of Foreign Ministers established

At Teheran, Roosevelt refused to meet with Churchill alone lest the Russians suspect an Anglo-American deal. Yet the president had three conferences *à deux* with Stalin. FDR called for an international organization to be dominated by the "Four Policemen," who would deal immediately with any threat to peace. Stalin commented that Europe might not like domination by the "Four Policemen," and that China was too weak to be of much use as a policeman. The president also told Stalin that the United States would supply only air and naval support in the event of a crisis in postwar Europe; troops would have to come from Britain and Russia. The Soviet leader agreed with Roosevelt that the future United Nations Organization "should be world-wide and not regional" and that France deserved an inconsequential status in the postwar world.[111]

The subjects of Eastern Europe and Germany also came up. Churchill, pushing three matchsticks, had proposed moving Poland's boundaries a considerable distance to the west, incorporating German lands. Polish territory in the east would be transferred to the Soviets to secure their western frontier. Roosevelt told Stalin that he acquiesced in these plans for Poland, but he could not "publicly take part in any such arrangement at the present time." The election of 1944 loomed, and FDR, "as a practical man," did not want to risk losing the votes of millions of Polish-Americans. Roosevelt also mentioned the many Americans of Lithuanian, Latvian, and Estonian origin who wanted self-determination in the Baltic states. Stalin bristled. Those states, he insisted, belonged to the Soviet Union. Roosevelt replied that the American people "neither knew nor understood." Stalin shot back that they "should be informed and some propaganda work should be done."[112] But the president never did explain publicly the differences between the Atlantic Charter and Soviet desires for security in Eastern Europe. On Germany, the conferees debated ways to divide the nation, but they recommended that specific plans for "retribution" against Germany be left to the future.[113]

Although inconclusive on many points, the Teheran discussions pleased the Americans, especially because Stalin had confirmed a previous promise to Hull that, once Hitler was defeated, the USSR would help the United States defeat Japan. In response to this pledge, Roosevelt suggested that the Soviets obtain a Chinese "free port" at Dairen as a reward. Stalin's preference for OVERLORD instead of a Balkans operation also gratified the American joint chiefs and seemed to clinch their position in the interminable debate with the British. General sentiment in favor of a peace dictated by the big powers, an international organization, and a weakened postwar Germany signified important Allied cohesion. Stalin also paid tribute to Lend-Lease and U.S. manufacture of 10,000 aircraft a month: "Without these planes from America the war would have been lost."[114] At a Teheran dinner in celebration of Churchill's sixty-ninth birthday, Roosevelt toasted the Big Three: "We can see in the sky, for the first time, that traditional symbol of hope, the rainbow." Churchill drank to "Stalin the Great." Stalin hailed his "fighting friend Churchill," adding one last jibe, "if it is possible for me to consider Churchill my friend."[115] After Teheran the president optimistically told a national radio audience: "I believe that we are going to get along very well with him [Stalin] and the Russian people— very well indeed."[116] The Grand Alliance had temporarily closed some fissures.

IN SEARCH OF A CHINA POLICY

When Winston Churchill journeyed to Washington in December 1941 to discuss grand strategy, he was astonished that his hosts "rated the Chinese armies as a factor to be mentioned in the same breath as the armies of Russia."[117] America's romanticized infatuation with China, the legacy of the Open Door, the false image of Jiang Jieshi as a democratic leader—all had governed American policy before Pearl Harbor. Some Americans, President Roosevelt included, even envisioned a strong, united China as a postwar client of the United States and bridge to Asian peoples freeing themselves from colonialism. China's military importance soon diminished, however, as Japanese victories in early 1942 sent the British and Americans reeling. The fall of Burma in May closed the last remaining land route to Generalissimo Jiang's capital at Chongqing. The Americans wanted to keep China in the war, yet Roosevelt could not send troops because they were needed elsewhere. He sent General Stilwell instead.

Joseph W. Stilwell was fifty-eight years old when he arrived in Chongqing with the impressive titles of Chief of Staff to Generalissimo Jiang Jieshi and Commanding General of the United States Forces in India, Burma, and China. An aggressive soldier, "diplomacy was not his long suit."[118] As a junior officer he had served two tours of duty in China, had become fluent in Chinese, and had developed great admiration for the Chinese people. But he thought Jiang an untrustworthy scoundrel. In his diary, the always blunt Stilwell called the British "pigfuckers," and Roosevelt "old Rubberlegs."[119] In Chongqing "Vinegar Joe" sought to train and equip Chinese divisions. With these modernized forces, plus British help from India, Stilwell planned to reopen Burma, increase supplies to China, and thus make the mainland the staging point for the final invasion of Japan.

Stilwell's plans for military reform cut at the core of Jiang's power structure. The general sputtered in his diary: "Why doesn't the little dummy [Jiang] realize that his only hope is the 30-division plan, and the creation of a separate, efficient, well-equipped, and well-trained force?"[120] Most of Jiang's armies were actually controlled by twelve commanders, several of them virtually autonomous warlords. Before making a decision, the generalissimo always had to ask: "What orders will my generals accept from me?"[121] Jiang wanted Stilwell's equipment but not his advice. Nor did the Chinese leader want to commit his own forces to battle. Some 500,000 of the Guomindang's best troops had orders to blockade the communists in Yan'an. Jiang wanted to wait out the war and then muster his strength for a final showdown with Mao Zedong. He would not fight in Burma unless the British and Americans gave more support, and the British balked at a Burma campaign. "It is an affectation to pretend that China is a Great Power," said Churchill privately, as he pushed for higher Anglo-American priorities in the Mediterranean.[122] Shortly after the landings in North Africa, Stilwell described his strategic dilemma: "Peanut [Jiang] and I are on a raft, with one sandwich between us, and the rescue ship is heading away from the scene."[123]

President Roosevelt urged a more conciliatory stance toward China. To Chongqing he sent a stream of personal emissaries to buoy Chinese morale and listen to complaints about Stilwell. Jiang received a half-billion dollar loan in 1942, and in January 1943, the State Department negotiated a treaty abolishing the American right of extraterritoriality in China. The following month Roosevelt hosted Madame Jiang at the White House; the immaculately attired Wellesley College alumna also addressed Congress, where she heard cheers that matched those given Churchill. At the Cairo Conference in November 1943, Churchill and Roosevelt met with Jiang and formally pledged the return after the war of Taiwan, Manchuria, and other areas "stolen by Japan."[124] In December Congress repealed the exclusion laws, which had prohibited Chinese immigration. Roosevelt talked confidently of postwar China as one of his "Four Policemen" to keep the peace. Such sentiment derived partly from sincerity, partly from a felt need to compensate China for wartime neglect, and partly from the assumption that the Chinese would be grateful to the United States.

Roosevelt also endorsed a plan of General Claire Lee Chennault. The organizer of the famed "Flying Tiger" volunteers boasted that "the Jap air force could

The Cairo Conference. Jiang Jieshi (1887–1975) and Madame Jiang (1892-   ) with Roosevelt and Churchill in November 1943. Although President Roosevelt publicly heaped praise on the Chinese leader, FDR privately told General Stilwell at the Cairo meeting: "If you can't get along with Chiang [Jiang], and can't replace him, get rid of him once and for all. You know what I mean, put someone in you can manage." (Franklin D. Roosevelt Library)

be destroyed as an effective fighting force within six months by a very modest American air force equipped with modern airplanes."[125] Roosevelt gave Chennault the wares. Disaster nearly struck. When Chennault's bombers began to draw blood in the spring of 1944, Japanese armies launched a massive counterattack and nearly overran all of the American air bases. Jiang then balked at fighting. This time Roosevelt made the extraordinary proposal that Jiang give Stilwell unrestricted command of all forces, Chinese and foreign, in China. The generalissimo stalled for two months; then Roosevelt sent an ultimatum that Stilwell delivered in person. "Mark this day in red on the calendar of life," he wrote in his diary on September 19, 1944. "A hot firecracker. I handed this bundle of paprika to the Peanut and then sank back with a sigh. The harpoon hit the little bugger right in the solar plexus, and went right through him."[126] Jiang never forgave Stilwell for such a personal humiliation, and rather than antagonize Jiang further, FDR soon replaced Stilwell.

In November, General Patrick J. Hurley became ambassador to China. A blunt-talking sixty-one-year-old Oklahoma Republican, Hurley concentrated on forming a coalition between Jiang's government and the communists. Even though the Soviets, like the Americans, sent military supplies to Jiang's forces and not to Mao Zedong's communists, the communist-led troops had waged successful guerrilla war against the Japanese. The Yan'an communists had excellent morale and an effective intelligence network that extended behind Japanese lines. One downed American pilot hiked more than 1,000 miles from eastern Hebei to Yan'an with the aid of "Red" guides. Mao, Zhou Enlai, and other communist leaders welcomed an American "Observer Mission," expected American landings on the China coast, and requested direct military aid. The communist revolutionary leadership, according to Foreign Service Officer John S. Service, "has improved the political, economic and social status of the peasant [and] . . . the Communists are certain to play a large, if not dominant, part in China's future."[127] Because most Americans in China shared the belief that the communists might win over Jiang in a postwar struggle for power, Hurley's initial efforts at coalition building received unified support.

Hurley's first visit to communist Yan'an, in November 1944, provided a grand spectacle. Hurley alighted from his plane "with enough ribbons on his chest to represent every war . . . in which the United States had ever engaged except possibly Shays's Rebellion."[128] Then he completely discombobulated Zhou Enlai by letting out Choctaw war whoops. Later, after the communists rejected Jiang's offer of a virtually worthless seat on the National Military Council in return for merging the Yan'an army under Nationalist control, Hurley accepted Mao's counterproposal for full coalition and communist sharing in Lend-Lease supplies. Jiang continued to insist on a merger of the two armies without real coalition, and Hurley seemed to acquiesce. An angry Mao refused "to submit to being tied hand and foot by the generalissimo. . . . We will yield no further," whereupon Hurley called Mao a "mother——" who "tricked meh!"[129]

At this point Hurley began to diverge markedly from his subordinates, including the young Foreign Service Officers. The ambassador decided on his own that his mission was not to mediate but rather to "sustain" Jiang Jieshi and "to prevent the collapse of the Nationalist government."[130] The communists would undoubtedly have to come to terms. Hurley had formed these views during an earlier visit

The Allies Push Japan Back 1942–1945

NORTH POLE

UNION OF SOVIET SOCIALIST REPUBLICS

ALASKA

UNITED STATES

Attu *ALEUTIAN IS.* 1943

Kiska

OUTER MONGOLIA

MANCHURIA

C H I N A

Beijing

Yan'an

Chongqing

JAPAN

Tokyo

Nagasaki Hiroshima

Midway Is. 1942

HAWAIIAN IS. Oahu

Pearl Harbor 1943

Ledo

Imphal

1944–45

Burma Rd.

Kunming

(TAIWAN) FORMOSA Okinawa

Iwo Jima

Marcus

Mandalay

Lashio

BURMA

Hong Kong

1945

1945

Wake

O C E A N

I N D I A

FR. INDO-CHINA

THAILAND

MARIANAS IS.

Tinian I.

P A C I F I C

Ceylon

Manila

1944

PHILIPPINE ISLANDS

Leyte

Guam

1944

MARSHALL IS.

EQUATOR

MALAYA

Singapore

SUMATRA

BORNEO

1944

C A R O L I N E   I S.

GILBERT IS. 1943

CELEBES

NETHERLANDS EAST INDIES

JAVA

1944–1945

SOLOMON IS. Guadalcanal

1943

NEW GUINEA

TIMOR

I N D I A N

Coral Sea

1942

1942

NEW HEBRIDES

O C E A N

AUSTRALIA

■ Japanese-held areas

⋯⋯ Limit of Japanese conquest

Norman Adams

Mao Zedong (1893–1976) and Patrick J. Hurley (1883–1963). The Chinese communist leader (second from left) seems less than moved by Ambassador Hurley's dramatic gesture of welcome at Chongqing in 1945. Mao thought Hurley a "clown" who favored Jiang; one observer said that Hurley was the only man he ever saw who could strut sitting down; and the dean of American sinologists, John K. Fairbank, has described Hurley as a "flamboyant and simple-minded American." In November 1945, Hurley suddenly resigned and flung wild charges at Foreign Service Officers who had disagreed with him. (National Archives)

to Moscow in August 1944, when Molotov had told him that the Chinese communists "had no relation whatever to Communism" and the Russians would support Jiang Jieshi.[131] The other Americans in China (representatives of the U.S. Army, Office of Strategic Services, and Treasury, as well as Foreign Service Officers) knew that Mao's followers were agrarian-based communists, and they feared that if the United States denied him aid, Mao would obtain assistance from Moscow and thus create a postwar squabble between the United States and the USSR over China. Contrary to Hurley, these "China hands" believed that the rift between the communists and Guomindang ran deep, and that they could obtain Chinese unity only by dealing with Yan'an separately as a way of pressing Jiang. Preliminary talks had already begun in Yan'an, and on January 9, 1945, the head of the American Military Observers Mission cabled that "Mao and Zhou will be immediately available . . . should President Roosevelt express desire to receive them at White House as leaders of a primary Chinese party."[132] The Soviet representative in Yan'an depicted Mao as "clearly offering himself" to the United States to counterbalance Russia.[133] Certain that disloyal subordinates plotted to undermine his position by encouraging the communists, Hurley blocked any meeting between Mao and Roosevelt.

The predictable explosion occurred when Hurley returned to Washington in February 1945 for consultations following the Yalta Conference, where Roosevelt had made concessions to Stalin regarding China without asking the Guomindang for advice. In Hurley's absence, the embassy officers at Chongqing sent a telegram to Washington urging the president to inform Jiang "in definite terms that we are required by military necessity to cooperate with and supply the communists and other suitable groups who can aid in this war against the Japanese."[134] These young "China hands" did not know that Stalin had reaffirmed Soviet entry into the Japanese war at Yalta and, accordingly, that the military rationale for a Guomindang-communist coalition now became less urgent. When Hurley read the telegram, he stormed about Washington telling all who would listen that his subordinates had betrayed him. He called on Roosevelt, then about to take what would be his final journey to Warm Springs, and the president gave him what he wanted—unqualified backing for Jiang's regime. The embassy diplomats, including John S. Service and John Paton Davies, found themselves transferred out of China as a timid State Department bowed to the demands of the rambunctious ambassador.

Roosevelt's wartime policy toward China exposed the disparity between his military strategy and postwar political goals. When it became obvious in 1944 that China would not play a major role in the Japanese war and hardly deserved rank as one of the "Four Policemen," Roosevelt faced a choice. He could accelerate American military activities in China, giving the United States more leverage, and press Jiang to undertake the reforms necessary to maintain him in power. Or the president could scale down his political expectations for China and limit his military operations there. In fact, as the scholar James MacGregor Burns has pointed out, Roosevelt "tried to do both and ran the risk of succeeding in neither. He kept talking to and about China as a great power even while he was giving higher and higher military priorities to other military theaters."[135] When the feud between Hurley and the China hands ignited, moreover, Roosevelt chose to drift with existing policy rather than take a hard look at Chinese politics. As happened often, when the smiling squire of New York could not easily resolve dilemmas, he left them to the future. In this case the future meant intensified civil war, Soviet-American competition for position in a weakened postwar China, the steady deterioration of Jiang's corrupt regime, and the erosion of U.S. influence.

BYSTANDERS TO THE HOLOCAUST: AMERICANS AND THE JEWISH CATASTROPHE

Another problem left to the future was that of the refugees, hundreds of thousands of them Jews from Nazi-occupied territories. Many sought asylum in the United States. Although most Americans denounced Hitler's crusade to preserve the purity of the "Aryan race" through the persecution and extermination of European Jews, translating moral revulsion into effective policy proved difficult. U.S. immigration laws, traditional anti-Semitism, the depression, bureaucratic procedures, wartime fear of spies, and domestic politics shaped the timid American response.

The dark story began in 1933 when Hitler initiated his attacks on "non-Aryans." Throughout the 1930s, the Nazis systematically eliminated Jews from the professions and denied them businesses. In 1935 the Nuremberg Laws stripped Jews of their civil and political rights, in essence making them stateless beings.

Hatemongers plastered signs on buildings: "Whoever buys from a Jew is a traitor."[136] In November 1938 a distraught Jewish boy living in Paris entered the German embassy and killed a German official. He had learned that his parents had been placed in a boxcar for shipment to a concentration camp. Germany erupted in anti-Semitic violence. Nazi thugs beat up Jews on the streets, sacked and burned synagogues, and destroyed Jewish shops. After this *Kristallnacht*, or "Night of the Breaking Glass," the German government fined its Jewish subjects $400 million and sent 50,000 Jews to concentration camps at Dachau and Buchenwald, detention centers later fitted with equipment for extermination. President Roosevelt called the American ambassador home in protest, remarking, "I myself could scarcely believe that such things could occur in a twentieth century civilization."[137]

The brutal events occurred again in Austria, Czechoslovakia, Poland, Hungary, and elsewhere as the Third Reich overran Europe. Americans read about the cruelties in their newspapers. Unprecedented numbers of urgent requests for transit to the United States flooded American embassies and consulates. American immigration law, however, prescribed a quota for each country. The National Origins Act of 1924 openly discriminated against immigrants from eastern and southern Europe, the source, said Member of Congress J. M. Tincher of Kansas, of "Bolshevik Wops, Dagoes, Kikes and Hunkies."[138] The annual quota for Great Britain and Ireland was 83,575, for Germany and Austria 27,370, for Poland 6,000, for Italy 5,500, and for Rumania 300. American consular officers also inhibited immigration to the United States from areas overrun by Nazism by strictly enforcing procedures. Potential immigrants had to present numerous pages of documents attesting to their birth, health, financial status, and crime-free background. Many of these papers had to be obtained from uncooperative Nazi officials. Americans also rigidly denied entry to people "likely to become a public charge." This clause meant that persons could gain a place on the quota list only if they proved that they could support themselves once in the United States. Yet under Nazi law Jews could not take their property or savings from Germany. These restrictions, combined with the evaporation of American jobs during the depression, created a revealing statistic for the period 1933–1938: 174,067 people entered the United States and 221,239 departed, or a net *loss* of 47,172. To have opened America's doors to the persecuted abroad, in short, would not have inundated the United States. The admission of several hundred thousand refugees would not have burdened a nation of 130 million.

Not so, said the restrictionists in the interwar years. The American Federation of Labor and patriotic groups lobbied against any revision in the quotas or relaxation of the visa requirements. Foreigners, they argued, should not compete with American citizens for scarce jobs—a telling argument during the depression. Longstanding anti-Semitism fed such nativist thought. Father Charles E. Coughlin, the fiery Catholic priest from Michigan, equated Judaism and communism in his radio broadcasts, which reached 3.5 million listeners a week. Even the distinguished anti-Nazi diplomat George Messersmith, known as the "Jews' man" in the State Department, opposed the establishment of a University of Exile at the New School for Social Research in New York because he feared that Jews teaching there would undermine the basic Anglo-Saxon Protestant nature of American society.[139] Opinion polls in the 1930s revealed that more than 80 percent of Americans opposed revision of the quotas to admit European refugees. Although the *New Republic* magazine appealed for "common decency," Congress stood firmly behind the quota system.[140] Roosevelt read the political realities. Already blistered by charges that his domestic reform program was a "Jew Deal," a label attached because he appointed Jews like Henry Morgenthau, Jr., and Felix Frankfurter to prominent positions, the president played it safe. Thwarted in his ill-fated "court-packing" attempt in 1937 and his futile effort to purge conservatives from the Democratic party in 1938, Roosevelt would not risk another political setback. "For God's sake," sounded the cry from Congress, "don't send us any more controversial legislation!"[141]

Roosevelt left the refugee problem to the Department of State, which "clung to a policy that was timid, rigidly legal, and without innovation."[142] In 1934 the department lobbied successfully against a Senate resolution condemning Germany's treatment of the Jews, fearful that the resolution would spark German comment about the segregation of black Americans. Secretary Hull also opposed boycotts organized by American Jews against German products because such behavior interrupted normal trade channels. Although he did relax enforcement of the "likely to become a public charge" clause, many Jews, caught in circumstances of fear and chaos, still could not obtain the necessary documents. The result: The German-Austrian quota went unfilled in 1933–1938 and 1940–1945; only in 1939 did it fill. For the entire period 1933–1945, just 35.8 percent of the German-Austrian quota was used. Emanuel Celler, member of Congress from New York, thought the State Department a "heartbeat muffled in protocol."[143]

In 1938 Roosevelt called for an international meeting on refugees, which met in Evian, France, to establish an Intergovernmental Committee on Refugees (IGC). George Rublee, the capable American lawyer who headed the IGC, negotiated with Berlin to permit emigration through a trust fund amounting to 25 percent of Jewish property in Germany. This "undisguised ransom scheme" failed largely because countries outside Germany would not accept large numbers of refugees.[144] Plans for refugee havens in Latin America and central Africa made little progress. Hitler sneered that "the entire democratic world dissolves in tears of pity, but then, in spite of its obvious duty to help, closes its heart to the poor, tortured people."[145] In early 1939 Senator Robert Wagner of New York introduced a bill to allow 20,000 German refugee children to enter above the quota. With revision of the Neutrality Act then pending, the president scratched "File No action FDR," and the bill died in committee.[146] In mid-1939 the ship *St. Louis* steamed toward Cuba from Hamburg carrying 930 Jewish refugees. Havana officials, however, would not permit them to land without proper visas. The ship then headed for Miami, tailed by Coast Guard cutters. American immigration officials would not let the passengers disembark. Despite appeals to Washington from concerned American liberals, the *St. Louis* had to return to Europe. Its passengers ultimately scattered to Britain, the Netherlands, Belgium, and France after refugee societies pressed their governments. "The cruise of the *St. Louis,*" editorialized the *New York Times,* "cries to high heaven of man's inhumanity to man."[147]

The plight of Jewish refugees deepened after the outbreak of war. The State Department actually tightened visa requirements because it feared refugees might include saboteurs and spies. In the State Department, refugee questions fell under the authority of Breckinridge Long, a southern aristocrat, old Wilsonian, former ambassador to Italy, and large financial contributor to the Democratic party. Believing that refugees might become a fifth column in the United States, he and other officials blocked numerous private efforts to save them and later suppressed information about Hitler's plan to exterminate European Jewry. American consuls increasingly rejected applications for visas, and ships headed to American shores half empty. Washington tried futilely to persuade Latin American countries to take refugees. When the State Department asked the British to approach Portugal about opening its African colony of Angola, Lord Halifax snapped: "Let the Americans do it."[148] Resettlement proposals for British Guiana, French Madagascar, Alaska, and Mindanao also fell through; Britain restricted the movement of Jews to Palestine. Other countries thus must share responsibility with the United States. Their failure to provide havens appears even more tragic, according to one scholar who suggests that, prior to 1941, "the Nazis were not operating programmatically toward a premeditated goal" and "were initially quite serious about solving the Jewish question through resettlement" rather than extermination.[149]

In August 1942 reliable evidence reached the State Department that Germany had begun to exterminate the entire Jewish population of Europe. The cruel facts seemed incredible. When Jan Karski, a Polish courier who had winessed mass executions at Belzec and Treblinka, briefed FDR and Hull, they had trouble grasping the full reality of the Holocaust. Even a Zionist like Justice Felix Frankfurter told Karski that "he didn't believe what he was being told."[150] Yet the evidence mounted. After invading Russia in 1941, special German squads rounded up Jews and massacred them; they murdered 33,000 in Kiev in September. The Jewish ghetto in Warsaw became a target of German barbarity; by fall 1942 only 70,000 of its 380,000 residents remained, and they desperately rebelled in the spring of the next year. One million victims died in the most notorious extermination camp at Auschwitz, Poland. Using Zyklon B gas and large crematoria, German officials competed for efficiency ratings in human destruction. Nazi perpetrators shipped Italian and Greek Jews by rail to Auschwitz. Of 10 million Jews in Nazi-occupied Europe in 1940, at least 6 million had died by 1945. The War Department rejected appeals to bomb the rail lines leading to the death camps on the grounds that such diversions would delay victory, the best hope for the Jews. In fact, two massive air raids in 1944 pulverized allegedly more important industrial sites less than five miles from Auschwitz. "How could it be that Government officials knew that a place existed where 2,000 helpless human beings could be killed in less than an hour . . . and not be driven to search for some way to wipe such a scourge from the earth?"[151]

In early 1943 representatives of Britain and the United States met in Bermuda to discuss the refugee problem; in essence they reported that they had done all they could to help. After the conference, Hull informed the president: "The unknown cost of moving an undetermined number of persons from an undisclosed place to an unknown destination, a scheme advocated by certain pressure groups, is, of course, out of the question."[152] Hull never sought to solve the unknowns. Secretary of the Treasury Henry Morgenthau, Jr., did. He asked his general counsel,

Randolph Paul, to study the State Department's handling of the refugee crisis. Paul submitted a *Report to the Secretary on the Acquiescence of This Government in the Murder of the Jews,* a frank critique of Breckinridge Long and the State Department. "It takes months and months to grant the visa and then it usually applies to a corpse," Paul wrote. Morgenthau then told Roosevelt that the rescue of Jews "is a trust too great to remain in the hands of men indifferent, callous and perhaps hostile."[153] In January 1944 the president created the War Refugee Board, outside the auspices of the State Department. Using private and public funds, board operatives established refugee camps in Italy, Morocco, Hungary, Sweden, Palestine, and Switzerland. The board thus saved some 200,000 Jews and 20,000 non-Jews by war's end—too little and too late. In the historian David Wyman's judgment, "Franklin Roosevelt's indifference to so momentous an historical event as the systematic annihilation of European Jewry emerges as the worst failure of his presidency."[154] In large measure, Jewish refugees themselves took command of their survival after the war by leading the "exodus" to Palestine and creating the new nation of Israel in 1948.

Buchenwald Concentration Camp, Germany. Located near Weimer and opened in 1937, this large Nazi concentration camp held Jews and others who served as slave labor for local factories during World War II. Although Buchenwald did not have death-dealing gas chambers, many prisoners nonetheless died there from disease, malnutrition, beatings, medical experiments, and executions. After seeing pictures of the German concentration camps, the writer Susan Sontag wrote: "Nothing I have seen—in photographs or real life—ever cut me as sharply, deeply, instantaneously. . . . I felt irrevocably grieved, wounded, but a part of my feelings started to tighten; something went dead; something is still crying." (Library of Congress)

PLANNING THE POSTWAR PEACE, 1943–1945

The great military battles of 1944, wherein the Anglo-American D-Day invasion of France in June coincided with a massive Russian offensive that reached the Vistula by August, gave postwar planning higher priority. Taking advantage of a "second chance" to overcome isolationism, economic depression, and war, U.S. officials helped launch several international organizations to secure peace and prosperity. Indeed, when FDR saw the Hollywood film *Wilson* (1944) with vivid scenes of his predecessor losing his health and the League, he exclaimed, "By God, that's not going to happen to me."[155] He thus made the Atlantic Charter a more flexible guide than the Fourteen Points. During 1943–1945 the United Nations Relief and Rehabilitation Administration (UNRRA), World Bank, International Monetary Fund, and United Nations Organization took form. Unlike World War I, this time the establishment of postwar institutions would not await the grand deliberations of one conference. Nor would plans to reform Germany.

On November 9, 1943, at the White House, forty-four nations signed the UNRRA Agreement to plan and administer "measures for the relief of victims of war . . . through the provision of food, fuel, clothing, shelter and other basic necessities, medical and other essential services." [156] The humanitarian relief program would, said a State Department official, help create "a more stable world order."[157] Some leaders feared that hungry displaced people might, in desperation, turn to political extremes like communism; food and medicine would help stem postwar political chaos. The Department of State successfully insisted throughout the negotiations that an American head UNRRA. Operating until mid-1947, UNRRA enjoyed a budget of $4 billion, $2.7 billion of which the United States donated. UNRRA dispensed 9 million tons of food; built hundreds of hospitals; prevented epidemics of diphtheria, typhoid, cholera, and venereal disease; revived transportation systems; and cared for at least 1 million displaced persons. China, Italy, Greece, and Austria absorbed about half of UNRRA's assistance. The other half went to Poland, other Eastern European nations, and the Soviet Union. American critics protested that an international organization was spending taxpayers' dollars to shore up communist governments. In fact, UNRRA tried to avoid politics, refusing to apply political tests to the needy. But Americans expected food aid to bring political returns. When it did not, Washington killed UNRRA in 1947 by cutting off funds.

Two other organizations proved more permanent. From July 1 to 22, 1944, the delegates of forty-four nations negotiated at Bretton Woods in the scenic White Mountains of New Hampshire. Working from an Anglo-American proposal, the conferees created the International Bank for Reconstruction and Development (World Bank) and the International Monetary Fund (IMF). The World Bank could extend loans to "assist in the reconstruction and development" of members, to "promote private investment," and to "promote the long-range balanced growth of international trade."[158] The IMF intended to facilitate world trade by stabilizing the international system of payments through currency loans. "The question," Senator Wagner declared in support of the Bretton Woods agreements, "is whether by default we allow the world to repeat the tragic blunders of the 1920s and 1930s."[159]

After much debate, with critics charging "the worst swindle" and "the most efficient propaganda campaign in the history of the nation," Congress passed the Bretton Woods Agreement Act by margins of 345 to 18 and 61 to 16 in July 1945.[160]

From the start, U.S. economic power dominated the two organizations. Located in Washington, D.C., the World Bank has always had an American as president. The United States also possessed one-third of the votes in the bank by subscribing $3.175 billion of the total of $9.100 billion. The United States also held one-third of the votes in the fund. As payer of the "piper," complained the *Manchester Guardian,* the United States would "call the tune."[161] Britain begrudged American control but joined. Although the USSR attended the Bretton Woods Conference, it did not join the bank or fund, because the Soviets practiced state-controlled trade and finance, feared having to divulge economic data, and could not accept the emphasis on "private" enterprise or the U.S. domination. Moscow's absence did not prove disruptive, but it augured poorly for postwar Allied cooperation.

From August to October 1944, representatives of the United States, Britain, the Soviet Union, and China met in the handsome Georgetown mansion at Dumbarton Oaks in Washington, D.C. Cordell Hull had been tooling up for this conference since early in the war. Public opinion polls indicated that Americans strongly endorsed a new world organization, and Congress had passed favorable resolutions. Roosevelt had spoken of the "Four Policemen" as guardians of the peace. At the conference the American delegation helped shape the United Nations Organization (UN) under this concept. With considerable unanimity, the conferees hammered out the UN's preliminary charter, providing for a powerful Security Council dominated by the great powers and a weak General Assembly. The Security Council, empowered to use force to settle crises, had five permanent members. When the United States pushed China as a permanent member, Britain proposed France. Churchill had protested that China was not a world power, but a "faggot vote on the side of the United States."[162] After some grumbling, the Soviet Union accepted both China and France, feeling secure in the veto power that each permanent member of the Security Council possessed.

Two issues dogged the Dumbarton Oaks conferees: voting procedure in the Security Council and membership in the Assembly. The Soviet Union advocated an absolute veto for permanent members, whereas the United States argued that parties to a conflict should not be in a position to veto discussion or action. Not until the Yalta Conference in early 1945 did the Allies agree that the veto could apply only to substantive questions like economic or military sanctions, not to procedural questions. As for membership in the Assembly, Moscow boldly requested seats for all sixteen Soviet republics. That outlandish request derived from Soviet fears of being badly outnumbered in the Assembly by the British Commonwealth "bloc" and the U.S.–Latin America "bloc." As the historian Robert Hilderbrand has written, "the Big Three saw the defense of their own security, the protection of their own interests, and the enjoyment of the fruits of their victory in the world war as more important than the creation of an international organization to maintain world peace."[163] At Yalta the Soviets accepted a compromise of three votes in the Assembly (see p. 248).

United Nations Symbol.
A sign of peace for the new international organization. (United Nations)

During the Dumbarton Oaks Conference, Republican presidential candidate Thomas Dewey criticized the "coercive power" given to the Security Council.[164] Secretary Hull managed to dissuade Dewey from further attacks on the fledgling United Nations Organization. That nonpartisanship, and the inclusion of senators in the Dumbarton Oaks delegation, helped the Roosevelt administration build its case for the UN with the American people. There would be no Wilsonian League of Nations fiasco this time. Still, some critics wondered about the cohesiveness of the new institution. One compared the members to marbles in a dish: "Put your toe on the dish and the marbles will scatter, each to its own corner."[165] On January 10, 1945, the influential Senator Arthur H. Vandenberg of Michigan, an arch prewar isolationist expected to insist on reservations much as Lodge had a generation earlier, delivered a stunning speech urging American participation in collective security as a curb on aggression. He further advised the major Allies to sign a security treaty to keep the Axis nations permanently demilitarized; he hoped thereby to allay Soviet fears of a revived Germany and hence render Soviet expansion unnecessary. Vandenberg could accept American membership in the United Nations, because "this is anything but a wild-eyed internationalist dream of a world State. . . . I am deeply impressed (and surprised) to find Hull so carefully guarding our American veto in his scheme of things."[166]

Roosevelt rewarded Vandenberg for his support by naming him a delegate to the San Francisco Conference of April 25–June 26, 1945, convened to launch the United Nations. The new secretary of state after Hull's retirement in November 1944, Edward R. Stettinius, Jr., managed the conference. "The Conference opens today—with Russian clouds in every sky," Vandenberg noted in his diary. "I don't know whether this is Frisco or Munich."[167] The 282 delegates did not make decisions without prior approval of the representatives of the big powers, who met each evening in Stettinius's penthouse at the Fairmont Hotel. The United States refused to admit Poland, because its government had not reorganized as required by Yalta (see p. 247). But then the American delegation shocked all by requesting participation for Argentina, which had only declared war against Germany in March. Molotov thought it "incomprehensible" that Poland would be refused entry and Argentina admitted.[168] The United States, believing that the Latin American republics would not vote for three Soviet seats in the Assembly unless Argentina were included, would not relent. By the lopsided vote of 32 to 4, with 10 abstentions, Argentina won its seat.

The journalist Walter Lippmann detected an American "steamroller" at San Francisco.[169] So did the Soviet Union, which objected in blunt language. And so did smaller states, which protested their exclusion from key decisions and their impotence in the new United Nations Organization. Fifteen nations abstained, for example, in the vote on the veto formula. The UN Charter, as finally adopted, included the Economic and Social Council and the Trusteeship Council. The latter looked to the eventual independence of colonial areas, but left the British and French empires intact and permitted the United States to absorb former Japanese-dominated islands in the Pacific (Marianas, Carolines, and Marshalls). *Time* magazine aptly termed the United Nations "a charter for a world of power."[170] Indeed, that characterization exemplified not only the veto provision, but also Article 51, which permitted regional alliances such as that the United States and Latin America outlined in the Act of Chapultepec in March. The United States, as War Department official John J. McCloy observed, would "have our cake and eat it too"—freedom of action in the Western Hemisphere and an international organization to curb aggression in Europe.[171] Amid memories of 1919, the Senate debated the UN Charter and approved it on July 28, 1945, by a vote of 89 to 2.

While these plans for the victors unfolded, American officials debated plans for the defeated. The debate over Germany centered on a "constructive" policy (rehabilitation, economic unity, and integration into the European economy) or a "corrective" policy (strict reduction in industry, large reparations, and a decentralized economy).[172] At the center of the controversy stood treasury secretary Henry Morgenthau, Jr. As with the refugee question, Morgenthau stepped outside normal jurisdictional boundaries and proposed a "corrective" plan designed to despoil Germany of industries having potential military value. In early September 1944 he

"Uncle Sam Pulls the Lever at the UN." Many foreign commentators believed that the United States dominated the new United Nations Organization. *(Ta Kung Pao of Shanghai–Hong Kong in United Nations World, 1951)*

Ronald Reagan (1911–   ) and Henry Morgenthau, Jr. (1891–1967). In this 1944 photograph, the actor and future president Reagan (left) helps Secretary of the Treasury Morgenthau promote the sale of war bonds in New York City. (Courtesy of FDR Library)

had informed Roosevelt that the coal- and iron-rich Ruhr area should be stripped of industry. At the Quebec Conference of September 12–16, 1944, the president gained Churchill's reluctant signature to a memorandum: "This programme for eliminating the war-making industries in the Ruhr and in the Saar is looking forward to converting Germany into a country primarily agricultural and pastoral in its character."[173] In an apparent bargain at Quebec, Churchill approved the Morgenthau scheme in exchange for the promise of a postwar American loan.

Back in Washington, however, critics lambasted the "Morgenthau Plan." Secretaries Hull and Stimson opposed a harsh economic peace. "Sound thinking teaches that prosperity in one part of the world helps to create prosperity in other parts of the world," Stimson advised. "It also teaches that poverty in one part of the world induces poverty in other parts."[174] Germany had to be revived to spur postwar prosperity in Western Europe. Using his special access to the president, Morgenthau persuaded Roosevelt in September to approve an interim joint chiefs of staff directive (JSC/1067), the final version of which came in April 1945. JCS/1067 ordered denazification and demilitarization, the dismantling of iron, steel, and chemical industries, a controlled economy, and limited rehabilitation. The new president, Harry S. Truman, however, thought "Morgenthau didn't know sh— from apple butter" and began a gradual retreat from the Morgenthau Plan and JCS/1067, especially after easing Morgenthau out of office in July 1945.[175] By the end of the war, then, American plans for postwar Germany remained unsettled.

COMPROMISES AT THE YALTA CONFERENCE

Near the end of the European war Churchill, Roosevelt, and Stalin met once again, this time at the Livadia Palace near Yalta in the Crimea. The prime minister penned a ditty: "Nor more let us falter! From Malta to Yalta! Let nobody alter!"[176] Meeting from February 4 to 11, 1945, the Big Three, after considerable compromise, made important decisions for the war against the Axis and for the postwar configuration of international affairs, the Yalta "system." After the conclave, Yalta aroused heated controversy akin to the Munich Conference. To some critics, Yalta symbolized a "sell-out" to the Soviets, an example of Roosevelt's coddling of the communist menace. Cocky about his talents in practicing personal diplomacy and worn low by the illness that would take his life two months later, critics have claimed, Roosevelt succumbed to a guileful Stalin and failed to use superior U.S. economic power to force concessions. The president's detractors also pointed an accusing finger at Alger Hiss, a U.S. official at Yalta who later, in the heady days of the early Cold War, went to jail on a perjury charge when he fell victim to right-wing accusations that he served Moscow as a spy. (After the end of the Cold War and the opening of Soviet secret service—KGB—archives, documents suggested that Hiss had *not* spied for the USSR.) The notorious Senator Joseph McCarthy later peddled the nonsense that Hiss "drafted the Yalta agreement."[177] Neither Hiss nor Roosevelt's health decided the outcomes at Yalta.

The Big Three entered the conference with different goals. Britain sought a zone in Germany for France, a curb on Soviet expansion into Poland, and protection of the British Empire. The Soviet Union wanted reparations to rebuild its devastated economy, possessions in Asia, influence over Poland, and a Germany so weakened that it could never again march eastward. The United States wanted a U.S.-managed United Nations for postwar world order, a Soviet declaration of war against Japan, a reduction of communist political power in Poland, and elevation of China to big-power status. Although each participant suspected the others' motives, "a high incidence of consensus was reached at the Conference."[178]

The "consensus" at Yalta reflected not only a willingness to reconcile differences but also the military and diplomatic realities of the moment. Britain and the United States had delayed the opening of the second front until June 6, 1944, and then, from mid-December to mid-January 1945—just before Yalta—Anglo-American troops bogged down in the Battle of the Bulge in Belgium. Churchill had appealed to Stalin to take pressure off the western front by stepping up the Soviet winter offensive in the east. Stalin obliged on January 12. "I am most grateful to you for your thrilling message," a relieved Churchill replied.[179] Throughout 1944 the Red Army had cut deeply into German lines on the eastern front. Indeed, by the time of the Yalta Conference, Russian soldiers were sweeping westward along a wide front through Poland, Czechoslovakia, and Hungary, with Rumania already freed from German clutches. The Red Army, not Roosevelt, gave the Soviet Union influence in Eastern Europe, and "diplomacy can rarely save what is lost by force of arms."[180]

Asian military realities also shaped diplomatic decisions. Japan was fiercely battling American forces in Luzon and the Marianas, and still had 1 million soldiers in China, 2 million in the home islands, and another 1 million in Manchuria and Korea. With some 54 percent of American battle deaths in the Pacific occurring in the last year of the war, both sides fought with increasing savagery. "We shot prisoners in cold blood, wiped out hospitals, strafed lifeboats," one U.S. war correspondent admitted, and "boiled the flesh off enemy skulls to make table ornaments for sweethearts, or carved their bones into letter openers."[181] Japan's suicidal *Kamikaze* resistance on Okinawa still lay in the future. "The military backdrop for the Yalta negotiations," as the historian Forrest Pogue has written, "did not yet afford . . . the luxury of renouncing or forgoing Soviet military cooperation."[182] In short, Roosevelt and Churchill still needed the Soviets to win the war.

The setting itself impressed the conferees with the costs of the war. Gutted buildings, abandoned vehicles, and gnarled railways blotted the snow-blanketed countryside around the resort town on the Black Sea. The villas of bygone dukes and tsars still stood grandly, although retreating Germans had looted Nicholas II's Livadia Palace. The Soviets strained to make their guests comfortable, offering servants and lavish meals. The meetings proceeded amicably, although Stalin once be-

The Yalta Conference.
Looking haggard and slack-jawed in a meeting with Churchill, Roosevelt suffered occasional moments of slurred speech and forgetfulness, as the historians Bert E. Park and Warren Kimball have pointed out. Although he tired easily, FDR's mind still functioned well. Kimball has noted that the frames following this photograph actually show a more energetic president. (Franklin D. Roosevelt Library)

came ruffled when he took Roosevelt's name for him—"Uncle Joe"—as ridicule rather than as a term of endearment, and Molotov wore his customary stone face. Stalin smiled when he heard Churchill's belabored but spirited defense of the British Empire. At the final dinner, Churchill informed Stalin that with general elections scheduled soon "I shall have to speak very harshly about the Communists. . . . You know we have two parties in England." "One party is much better," Stalin dead-panned.[183] Overall, the conferees worked in good humor and frankness because they shared a desire to maintain the Grand Alliance.

For Churchill, Poland counted as "the most urgent reason for the Yalta Conference."[184] Two Polish governments claimed legitimacy. The British and Americans recognized the conservative exiled government in London, led by Stanislas Mikolajczyk. Moscow recognized the Communist-led provisional government in Lublin. Emphatic that any Polish government must lean eastward, Stalin repeatedly reminded everyone that Germany had attacked Russia through the Polish corridor twice in the century. He insisted not only on Allied support for the Lublin government, but also on Polish boundaries that gave Poland part of Germany (Oder-Neisse line in the west) and Russia part of Poland (Curzon line in the east). Churchill and Roosevelt opposed a communist Poland but had no bargaining power because Soviet troops occupied much of the country. Churchill fumed: "Poland [must] be mistress in her own house and captain of her soul."[185] Roosevelt said he had several million Polish voters back home who demanded a more representative Polish government. Stalin, castigating the anti-Sovietism of the conservative London Poles, remained adamant.

Compromises emerged. The Curzon line was temporarily set as the eastern boundary. The Yalta agreement read also that a "more broadly based" government would be created in Poland, that the "Provisional Government which is now functioning in Poland should be therefore reorganized on a broader democratic basis with the inclusion of democratic leaders from Poland itself and from Poles abroad," and that "free and unfettered elections" would be held as soon as possible.[186] Roosevelt wanted the first election in Poland "to be like Caesar's wife. I did not know her but they said she was pure." "They said that about her," Stalin corrected, "but in fact she had her sins."[187] Until such an election, however, the communist Lublin group would comprise the nucleus of the Polish government. "This is so elastic," Admiral William D. Leahy complained, "that the Russians can stretch it all the way from Yalta to Washington without technically breaking it." FDR countered that "it's the best I can do for Poland at this time."[188] Churchill swallowed the bitter pill, in part because Stalin assured him that the Soviet Union would not intrude in British-dominated Greece, then suffering from civil war. Compromises on other issues also made the Polish settlement tolerable.

Britain, although not keen about dividing Germany, accepted "dismemberment" so long as its ally France received a zone of occupation. Noting that Roosevelt had said that American troops would not long remain in Europe, Churchill cited France as a bulwark against Germany. Stalin protested: France had hardly fought during the war; indeed, the Vichy government had collaborated with the Germans. But Stalin finally accepted a French zone. On reparations, which the Soviets vigorously demanded, Britain and America hedged. They agreed on German reparations "in kind," but refused to set a figure until Germany's ability to pay was determined. The Big Three stated only that they would *discuss* in the future the amount of $20 billion, half of which would go to the Soviet Union. Stalin probably assumed that the United States and Britain would henceforth support the $10 billion figure in the new Reparations Commission.

The conferees also reached compromises on Asian issues. The American military and the president sought Soviet participation in the war against Japan. Roosevelt also wanted to break up the British Empire, and prevent a French return to Indochina. The Yalta accords did not treat these imperial questions, and Roosevelt soon retreated from such advanced anticolonial views, but Stalin promised to declare war against Japan two or three months after Hitler's defeat, enough time to permit the transfer of his troops to Asia. Stalin also agreed to sign a pact of friendship and alliance with Jiang Jieshi's regime, not with Mao Zedong's rival communists. In return, the Soviet Union regained what Russia had lost in 1905: the southern part of Sakhalin, Dairen as a free port, Port Arthur as a naval base, and joint operation of the Chinese Eastern and South Manchurian Railroads. The Soviet Union also obtained the Kurile Islands. On these agreements the Big Three never consulted China, a clear loser at Yalta.

The Allies also compromised on the United Nations Organization. Dumbarton Oaks had added France and China as "permanent" members of the Security Council, possessing the veto. Although Churchill thought China would vote with the United States, FDR and Stalin expected France to support British positions. Thus outnumbered in the council, Stalin asked at Yalta for membership of all sixteen Soviet republics in the General Assembly. He also insisted on an absolute veto in the council on all issues, procedural and substantive. Roosevelt agreed to grant the Soviets three seats in the General Assembly and Stalin agreed that the veto could not be cast on procedural questions (such as whether the council should take up an issue to which the permanent member is a party). Before it adjourned, the conference also reaffirmed the Atlantic Charter in the "Declaration of Liberated Europe."

Yalta marked the "dawn of the new day," said Harry Hopkins. "We were absolutely certain that we had won the first great victory of the peace—and, by 'we,' I mean *all* of us, the whole civilized human race."[189] "Poor Neville Chamberlain believed he could trust Hitler," Churchill commented after Yalta. "He was wrong. But I don't think I'm wrong about Stalin."[190] Roosevelt, Churchill, and Stalin had deftly played the great-power game of building spheres of influence. Each went home with some major objectives satisfied. Although they had postponed some tough questions and written some vague language, they had faced military and political realities. None of the leaders, of course, had consulted weak nations on whom the Yalta decisions weighed heavily. France and China did not receive invitations to Yalta, and Poland had no say. Churchill did not apologize for the blatant great-power manipulation: "The eagle should permit the small birds to sing and care not wherefore they sang."[191]

Later, when the Yalta agreements collapsed, critics ignored U.S. gains from the conference—broadening of the Polish government, a UN voting formula, delay of the reparations question, the specific Soviet pledge to enter the Pacific war—and charged that FDR had conceded too much. But he had little to give away. The United States might have used its economic power in the form of reconstruction aid as a diplomatic weapon, but that would have spoiled the spirit of compromise at Yalta, which served American interests. Nor did Stalin play one of his trump cards: the capture of Berlin during the conference. From Yalta Stalin ordered Marshall G. K. Zhukov to halt the Berlin offensive. His generals did not know why, but historians have suggested that Stalin wanted to avoid a dramatic conquest that might have undermined cooperation at Yalta. Churchill recognized the necessity of compromise: "What would have happened if we had quarrelled with Russia while the Germans still had three or four hundred divisions on the fighting front?"[192] Indeed, "had the Grand Alliance fallen apart at Yalta or immediately after because Roosevelt refused to recognize Russia's security needs," the historian Lloyd C. Gardner has written, postwar Europe might have descended into "a series of civil wars or possibly an even darker Orwellian condition of localized wars along an uncertain border."[193] The spheres-of-influence agreement, the Yalta leaders believed, would serve as a transition to peace. In the end, however flawed, the Yalta formula provided an alternative to war.

To Each Its Own: Allied Divergence and Spheres of Influence

Throughout the diplomacy of World War II, the Allies attempted to protect and, if possible, extend their spheres of influence. Churchill's defense of the British Empire, from Argentia through Yalta, reflected this characteristic of wartime diplomacy. "If the Americans want to take Japanese islands which they have conquered," he remarked, "let them do so with our blessing and any form of words that may be agreeable to them. But 'Hands Off the British Empire' is our maxim."[194] With vital interests in the Mediterranean and Persian Gulf, as well as in Asia, Britain resisted postwar United Nations–mandated trusteeships. Some Americans suspected that Churchill's constant postponement of the second front and his strategies for North Africa and Italy aimed at preserving British interests. His advice to American military leaders, near war's end, that they drive quickly to Berlin, and if possible even farther into Eastern Europe, to beat the Soviets there, also raised this suspicion.

The Churchill-Stalin percentage agreement of October 1944 illustrated the movement toward spheres of influence. In early 1944 Churchill concluded that "we are approaching a showdown with the Russians" in the Balkans and he called for a frank settlement. Roosevelt warned against postwar spheres of influence but agreed to a trial division of authority. Instability plagued Rumania, where Soviet troops dominated; Yugoslavia, where independent communist Josip Tito and his Partisans were emerging; Bulgaria, where an indigenous communist movement grew with Soviet influence; and Greece, a British-dominated area in the throes of civil war. At an October conference with Stalin in Moscow, Churchill scribbled some percentages on a piece of paper. In Rumania, Russia would get 90 percent of the power and Britain 10 percent, in Greece Britain would enjoy 90 percent and

Russia 10 percent, in Yugoslavia and Hungary a 50–50 split, and in Bulgaria 75 percent would go to Russia and 25 percent to "others." As Churchill recalled, he "pushed this across to Stalin," who "took his blue pencil and made a large tick upon it."[195] Stalin liked this arrangement that granted the Soviets predominant influence in Eastern Europe. As he later explained: "The United Kingdom had India and the Indian Ocean in her sphere of influence; the United States, China and Japan; the USSR had nothing."[196] Roosevelt did not remonstrate over the bargain, which did not last because local conditions overcame it.

Soviet support for the Lublin government, demands for Polish and Rumanian territory, efforts to exclude the United States and Britain from the joint control commissions in Eastern Europe, and seizure of German-operated property (including Standard Oil equipment in Rumania) alerted American officials to the growing power of the Soviet Union among its neighbors. The Soviet handling of the Warsaw uprising of July 31, 1944, alarmed Western observers. With Soviet armies some twelve miles from Warsaw, the Polish underground gambled and attacked German forces, believing that Soviet troops would dash to their aid. But the Red Army stopped. For two months the Germans pummeled the Polish fighters, who owed their allegiance to the exiled government in London. The Germans killed 166,000 Poles and leveled half the city. Churchill persuaded Stalin in September to drop supplies to the besieged city, but the Soviet leader thought the Warsaw uprising reckless and futile. To requests that American planes be permitted to land at Russian airfields after carrying supplies to Warsaw, Stalin first said *"nyet,"* and then permitted landings in mid-September. Whatever the military realities—Stalin claimed that his soldiers were meeting heavy German resistance—many charged that Stalin abetted the slaughter of the Warsaw Poles. Ambassador to the Soviet Union W. Averell Harriman called the Soviets a "world bully" who "misinterpreted our generous attitude toward them," and British air marshall John Slessor later wrote: "How, after the fall of Warsaw, any responsible statesman could trust any Russian Communist farther than he could kick him, passes the comprehension of ordinary men."[197] The liberation of Poland by Soviet forces in 1944 ultimately fixed a communist regime in Warsaw—one that Roosevelt's compromises at Yalta essentially recognized.

The United States itself was expanding and building spheres of influence during the war. Having drawn most of the Latin American states into a defense community at the Lima Conference (1938) and in the Declaration of Panama (1939), the United States moved to drive German investments and influence from the Western Hemisphere. The Export-Import Bank loaned $130 million to twelve Latin American nations in 1939–1941 to help them oust German businesses, cut trade with the Axis, stabilize their economies, and bring them into alignment with U.S. foreign policy. During the war, the United States increased its stake in Bolivian tin, helped build Brazilian warships, expanded holdings in Venezuelan oil, acquired bases in Panama and Guatemala, and nourished the Dominican dictatorship of Rafael Trujillo. The American military also began to coordinate armaments and military training with Latin American forces. During the war Latin America shipped 50 percent of its exports, largely much needed raw materials, to the United States. At the Rio de Janeiro Conference (January 15–28, 1942), all but Chile and Argentina voted to break diplomatic relations with the Axis nations. In March

Pacific Fleet Carriers.   A major reason for U.S. victories in the Pacific and for a substantial American role in postwar Asia was the air superiority provided by these ships. The light aircraft carrier *Langley* and the heavy carrier *Ticonderoga* lead this Pacific fleet task group. From 1940 to June 1945, the U.S. Navy grew from 1,099 to 50,759 vessels, including 8 new battleships, 92 new aircraft carriers, and 43,255 new landing craft. (Navy Department, National Archives)

1945, in the Act of Chapultepec, the United States and Latin America took another step toward a regional defense alliance. U.S. officials recognized too that Latin Americans would vote with the United States at the new United Nations. In early 1945 Secretary Stettinius unwittingly reminded many that the United States still considered its southern neighbors dependent: "The United States looks upon Mexico as a good neighbor, a strong upholder of democratic traditions in this hemisphere, and *a country we are proud to call our own.*"[198]

U.S. leaders also sought to direct events in postwar Italy and Asia. They essentially excluded the Soviets from the Italian surrender agreement in 1943 and denied them a role in the control commission. Some American officials recognized that Italy, where predominant power rested in their hands, set a precedent for later Soviet predominance in Rumania and Hungary. U.S. officials also insisted on holding the conquered Japanese islands in the Pacific and in unilaterally governing postwar Japan. Roosevelt, an avid philatelist, once showed Churchill a favorite stamp "from one of your colonies." Churchill asked: "Which one?" FDR replied: "One of your last. . . . You won't have them much longer, you know."[199] Thus did Washington envisage closer postwar ties with India, Australia, New Zealand, and Jiang's China.

In the Middle East the United States also expanded. In 1939 the Arabian-American Oil Company (Aramco) began to tap its 440,000-square-mile concession in Saudi Arabia's rich oil fields. By 1944 American corporations controlled 42 percent of the proved oil reserves of the Middle East, a nineteenfold increase since 1936. In 1944, American companies, with Washington's encouragement, applied for an oil concession in Iran, then occupied by British and Soviet troops and used as a corridor for Lend-Lease shipments to the Soviet Union. This request touched off a three-cornered competition for influence in the heretofore British-dominated country. When Roosevelt informed Churchill in 1944 that the United States did not intend to deprive the British of their traditional stakes in the Middle East, the prime minister tartly replied: "Thank you very much for your assurances about no sheeps' eyes at our oil fields in Iran and Iraq. Let me reciprocate by giving you fullest assurance that we have no thought of trying to horn in upon your interests or property in Saudi Arabia."[200]

On a global scale, then, the Big Three jockeyed for power and influence. "Spheres of influence do in fact exist," concluded Roosevelt's State Department in early 1945. "In view of the actual Eastern European sphere and the Western Hemispheric bloc (Act of Chapultepec), we are hardly in a position to frown upon the establishment of measures designed to strengthen the security of nations in other areas of the world."[201] "How many people in the United States do you think will be willing to go to war to free Estonia, Latvia, or Lithuania?" FDR explained to Eleanor Roosevelt after Yalta.[202] But the new Truman administration did frown on the Soviet sphere.

With Germany's surrender on May 8, 1945, the Third Reich collapsed in the rubble of bombed-out Berlin. President Harry S. Truman quickly ended Lend-Lease aid to the Soviet Union (he soon partially restarted it), thereby stirring up a hornet's nest in Moscow, which interpreted the abrupt cutback as diplomatic pressure. With this issue and the Polish question troubling Soviet-American relations, the president sent Harry Hopkins to see Stalin in May, to "use diplomatic language or a baseball bat."[203] The Soviets, said the president, "were like people from across the tracks whose manners were very bad."[204] An irate Stalin warned Hopkins that the Americans had made "a fundamental mistake" in halting Lend-Lease "as pressure on the Russians in order to soften them up."[205] Hopkins denied trying to coerce Moscow, but he expressed growing U.S. dismay about Stalin's apparent obstruction of the Yalta agreement on elections in Poland—a symbol of Soviet-American trust. Stalin frankly explained that he could not permit the anti-Soviet

Harry Hopkins (1890–1946). A progressive reformer, the Iowa-born Hopkins became one of Franklin D. Roosevelt's most trusted New Deal administrators and advisers. During World War II, Roosevelt sent Hopkins on special missions and utilized his counsel at international conferences, including Yalta. When he traveled to Moscow for Truman in May 1945, Hopkins suffered from the cancer that would cause his death within months. (Courtesy of FDR Library)

London Poles (the most likely winners of an election) to govern postwar Poland. The Russians had "not easily forgotten" that Poland twice "served as a corridor for German attacks. . . . It is therefore in Russia's vital interest that Poland should be both strong and friendly."[206] Ambassador Harriman also reported to Truman that Stalin could not "understand why we should want to interfere with Soviet policy in a country like Poland, which he considers so important to Russia's security, unless we have some ulterior motive."[207] Stalin did agree that a few ministries should rest in the hands of non-Lublin Poles. He also promised Hopkins, as at Yalta, that Russia would enter the war against Japan and respect Jiang's government. Pleased momentarily by Stalin's gesture, Truman noted in his diary: "I'm not afraid of Russia. . . . They've always been our friends and I can't see any reason why they shouldn't always be."[208]

THE POTSDAM CONFERENCE AND THE LEGACY OF THE SECOND WORLD WAR

As the war in Asia wound down and the occupation of Germany accelerated, the Big Three gathered in Berlin for the Potsdam Conference (July 16–August 2, 1945). Nearly three-quarters of the capital lay in ruins, and rotting corpses made it "like a city of the dead," remarked General Lucius Clay.[209] One British official toured the battered city with Churchill and grew nauseated: "It was like the first time I saw a surgeon open a belly and the intestines gushed out."[210]

While Churchill "gave me a lot of hooey," Truman's first impression of his Soviet counterpart was favorable: "I can deal with Stalin. He is honest—but smart as hell."[211] That impression soon changed. Truman wrote his family that "you never saw such pigheaded people as are the Russians."[212] Truman grew impatient with the Soviets, Admiral Leahy thought Stalin "a liar and a crook," and Harriman called the Russians "those barbarians."[213] Churchill, who would leave the conference after the defeat of his Conservative party in British elections (Clement Attlee replaced him), took a liking to the new president, whom he described as a "man of exceptional character and ability with . . . simple and direct methods of speech, and a great deal of self-confidence and resolution."[214] Some of that resolution at Potsdam derived from news that "tremendously pepped up" Truman on the second day of the conference: the successful explosion of an atomic device on July 16 in New Mexico.[215]

By the time of Potsdam, American policy toward postwar Germany had moved a good distance from the Morgenthau Plan and JCS/1067 toward a policy of reconstruction. American officials saw Germany as a vital link in the economic recovery of Western Europe. When Germany came up for discussion, Truman resisted dismemberment and large reparations. The final Potsdam accord stated that Germany would be managed by military governors in four zones, treated as "a single economic unit," and permitted a standard of living higher than its low level of 1945.[216] Transportation, coal, agriculture, housing, and utilities industries were to be rehabilitated. As for reparations, desired by the Soviet Union for both revenge and the recovery of its hobbled economy, the United States refused to set a firm figure until Germany's ability to pay was determined. Stalin protested, but he had to settle for an agreement that each occupying power would take reparations from its own zone and that Russia would get some industrial equipment from the Western zones. In return for the latter, the Soviet Union would send food to the other three zones. The diplomat George F. Kennan described the reparations deal as "catch as catch can."[217]

The conferees tangled over Poland. Every time Churchill complained about the absence of free elections in Poland, Stalin mentioned the British domination of Greece. They did agree, however, to set the Oder-Neisse line as Poland's temporary western boundary, thereby granting Poland large chunks of German territory. The Soviet Union agreed to accept Italy as a member of the United Nations. The big powers also established the Council of Foreign Ministers to continue discussion on issues not resolved at Potsdam: peace treaties for the former German satellites; the withdrawal of Allied troops from Iran; postwar control of the Dardanelles; internationalization of inland waterways; and the disposition of Italian colonies. Stalin promised again to enter the war against Japan, but U.S. officials did not push this point as hard as they had at Yalta, in part because they had just learned that they possessed a new atomic weapon that might force Japan's surrender. Britain and the United States issued the "Potsdam Declaration" to Japan, demanding unconditional surrender and threatening it with destruction.

The seemingly minor issue of waterways illustrated the tension at Potsdam and became for Truman a test of Soviet intentions. At the conference he pushed for an international authority to govern the 800-mile-long Danube River, which wound its way through several countries, including the Soviet Union, to the Black Sea. Essentially combining two traditional American principles—free navigation and the Open Door—the proposal antagonized Moscow, which countered with a commission limited to riparian states. For the Soviets, the Danube ranked with America's Panama Canal and Britain's Suez Canal. When Churchill backed Truman on the question, Molotov pressed: "If it was such a good rule why not apply it to the Suez?"[218] Churchill evaded the comparison, and the president drew an exaggerated conclusion: Stalin's attitude on waterways "showed how his mind worked and what he was after. . . . The Russians were planning world conquest."[219]

Potsdam, aptly code-named TERMINAL, left the world much as it had found it—divided and devastated. World War II ended on August 14, 1945, with Japan's surrender after two atomic bombs decimated Hiroshima and Nagasaki (see pp. 266–270). But peace remained elusive because of the war's legacy: the vast social, economic, and political dislocations in Europe and Asia. World War II claimed the lives of 55 million people—22 million of them in a USSR that would never forget this immense tragedy. Poland and Germany lost 6 million each; Yugoslavia suffered at least 1.6 million dead; Britain lost 400,000. The toll mounted in Asia, too: 10 million Chinese, 4 million Indonesians, 2.5 million Japanese, 1 million Vietnamese, 120,000 Filipinos, and more. A total of 405,395 Americans died fighting in the war. A generation of young European people in their twenties and thirties virtually disappeared. Millions of displaced persons became separated from their homelands. Transportation systems and communications networks did not function. Factories shut down. Cities entered the postwar era as rubble heaps, including the German city of Dresden, which Allied planes had punished in February 1945 in a merciless attack of questionable necessity. The firebombing of Tokyo killed 100,000. The war's devastation upended societies, economies, and politics everywhere. An unprecedented reconstruction task faced awed world leaders.

With the imperial powers in disarray, their Asian colonies, long yearning for the moment and encouraged by Japan during the waning days of the war, became rebellious. Unable to apply the necessary resources and manpower to curb the nationalist revolutions, the European empires began to crumble. The Dutch battled their Indonesian subjects; France fought the Vietnamese in Indochina; Britain reluctantly began its exit from Burma, India, and Ceylon (Sri Lanka).

The rise of the Soviet Union as a major international player counts as another legacy of World War II. The "greatest crime of Hitler," said Ambassador Harriman, was that his defeat opened parts of Europe to Soviet influence.[220] Russia resented any intimation that it should not have an influential voice in postwar questions. Reeling from heavy wartime losses, the Soviets asked for much and grabbed what they could before the war ended. "You know we have never been accepted in European councils on a basis of equality," Maxim Litvinov complained. "We were always outsiders."[221] Never again.

Bombed-out French Town, 1944. Europe lay in ruins at the end of the war, and American help became essential to the reconstruction effort. (U.S. Office of War Information, National Archives)

The USSR rose, Britain declined, China floundered, and the United States galloped. The American economy, untouched by enemy bombers or marauding armies, moved in high gear at war's end. The U.S. gross national product jumped from $90.5 billion in 1939 to $211.9 billion in 1945. Observers spoke of an American "production miracle."[222] By the end of the war, in the historian Thomas McCormick's words, the United States had become "the global workshop and banker, umpire and policeman, preacher and teacher."[223] One Briton penned a jealously derogatory poem:[224]

> In Washington Lord Halifax
> Once whispered to Lord Keynes:
> "It's true *they* have the money bags
> But *we* have all the brains."

A British Foreign Office diplomat complained that "we shall have to suffer from American arrogance."[225] Alone in a position to provide the capital and goods for recovery abroad, Washington felt flushed with power. Imbibing lessons from the 1930s about the need to avoid Munichs, Americans looked forward to shaping a world of peace and prosperity. With greatly increased power, the United States seemed capable of creating the stable world order that had eluded it between the two world wars. State Department official Dean Acheson observed that the "great difference in our second attempt to establish a peaceful world is the wide recognition that peace is possible only if countries work together and prosper together. That is why the economic aspects are no less important than the political aspects of the peace."[226] Through the war years the United States had constructed institutions—UNRRA, World Bank, International Monetary Fund, United Nations—to ensure that peace.

The war also wrought changes in the decisionmaking process in the United States. The United States underwent a "bureaucratic revolution."[227] Agencies in the government handling national security matters ballooned in size. The defense establishment became more active in making diplomatic choices. In comparison, the State Department, so frequently bypassed by President Roosevelt, slipped in power. The war spawned a large espionage establishment, beginning with the Office of Strategic Services (OSS) in 1942 and culminating in the Central Intelligence Agency (CIA) five years later. The president centralized decisionmaking in the White House, while Congress gave up its foreign-affairs prerogatives in the constitutional system and applauded bipartisanship. War wrought "a complacent faith in the superior intelligence and disinterestedness of the executive branch," the historian Arthur M. Schlesinger, Jr., has noted.[228] Another consequence of the war was an enlarged "military-industrial complex," a partnership between business executives eager for lucrative defense contracts and military brass eager for increased budgets. The recruitment of universities bequeathed a long-term legacy. Professors of the sciences had developed the atomic bomb at the Universities of Chicago and California, Berkeley. Princeton received grants for ballistics research. "The universities transformed themselves into vast weapons development laboratories," the editor of *Scientific American* observed.[229] Postwar federal subsidies flowed to colleges not only for arms development but also for research on Russian studies and intelligence gathering.

"The world was fluid and about to be remade" in 1945, the journalist Theodore White remembered.[230] After the setbacks of depression and war, the historian Allan Nevins wrote, "the old self-confident America is coming into its stride again."[231]

FURTHER READING FOR THE PERIOD 1939–1945

For general accounts, see Robert Dallek, *Franklin D. Roosevelt and American Foreign Policy, 1933–1945* (1979); Robert A. Divine, *Roosevelt and World War II* (1969); Jean-Baptiste Duroselle, *France and the United States* (1978); Herbert Feis, *Churchill, Roosevelt, Stalin* (1957); Julian G. Hurstsfield, *America and the French Nation, 1939–1945* (1986); Lloyd C. Gardner, *Spheres of Influence* (1993); Manfred Jonas, *The United States and*

Germany (1984); Gabriel Kolko, *The Politics of War* (1968); Ralph B. Levering, *American Opinion and the Russian Alliance* (1976); William H. McNeill, *America, Britain, & Russia* (1953); James E. Miller, *The United States and Italy, 1940–1950* (1986); Michael Sherry, *The Rise of American Air Power* (1987); Gaddis Smith, *American Diplomacy During the Second World War* (1985); John L. Snell, *Illusion and Necessity* (1963); Richard W. Steele, *Propaganda in an Open Society* (1985); and works cited in Chapters 4 and 5.

Among biographical studies that stress foreign relations are Rudy Abrahamson, *Spanning the Century* (1992) (Harriman); Michael Beschloss, *Kennedy and Roosevelt* (1980); John M Blum, ed., *From the Morgenthau Diaries* (1959–1972) and *The Price of Vision* (1973) (Henry Wallace); James M. Burns, *Roosevelt: The Soldier of Freedom* (1970); Kenneth R. Davis, *FDR* (1972–1993); Martin Gilbert, *Winston S. Churchill* (1983); Waldo H. Heinrichs, *American Ambassador* (1966) (Grew); Warren F. Kimball, *The Juggler* (1991) (FDR); Joseph P. Lash, *Roosevelt and Churchill, 1939–1941* (1976); George McJimsey, *Harry Hopkins* (1987); Elting E. Morison, *Turmoil and Tradition* (1960) (Stimson); Forrest C. Pogue, *George C. Marshall* (1963–1987); Mark A. Stoler, *George Marshall* (1989); and works cited in Chapters 4 and 5.

FDR's health is the subject of Kenneth R. Crispell and Carlos F. Gomez, *Hidden Illness in the White House* (1988); Robert H. Ferrell, *Ill-Advised* (1992); and Bert E. Park, *The Impact of Illness on World Leaders* (1986).

For the United States and Europe, 1939–1941, and debates at home, see Patrick Abbazia, *Mr. Roosevelt's Navy* (1975); Robert Boyce and Esmonde M. Robertson, eds., *Paths to War* (1989); Mark Chadwin, *The Hawks of World War II* (1968); J. Garry Clifford and Samuel R. Spencer, Jr., *The First Peacetime Draft* (1986); Wayne S. Cole, *America First* (1953) and *Roosevelt and the Isolationists* (1983); James V. Compton, *The Swastika and the Eagle* (1967); Robert A. Divine, *The Reluctant Belligerent* (1979); Saul Friedlander, *Prelude to Downfall: Hilter and the United States, 1939–1941* (1967); Martin Gilbert, *Winston S. Churchill* (1983–1986); Silvo Hietanen, ed., *The Road to War* (1993); Travis B. Jacobs, *America and the Winter War, 1939–1940* (1981); Warren F. Kimball, *The Most Unsordid Act* (1969) (Lend-Lease); William L. Langer and S. Everett Gleason, *The Challenge to Isolation, 1937–1940* (1952); James R. Leutze, *Bargaining for Supremacy: Anglo-American Naval Collaboration, 1937–1941* (1977); Mark A. Lowenthal, *Leadership and Indecision: American War Planning and Policy Process, 1937–1942* (1988); Arnold A. Offner, *The Origins of the Second World War* (1975); David L. Porter, *The Seventy-Sixth Congress and World War II, 1939–1940* (1979); Anthony Read and David Fisher, *The Deadly Embrace* (1989) (Nazi-Soviet Pact); David Reynolds, *The Creation of the Anglo-American Alliance, 1937–1941* (1982); James C. Schneider, *Should America Go to War?* (1989); Grigory Sevost'ianov, ed., *Soviet-American Relations, 1933–1942* (1989); D. C. Watt, *How War Came* (1989); and Theodore A. Wilson, *The First Summit* (1991).

For the advent of war with Japan, see the books by Borg and Okamoto, Burns and Bennett, Feis, and Neu cited in Chapter 5; Michael A. Barnhart, *Japan Prepares for Total War* (1987); Robert J. C. Butow, *Tojo and the Coming of the War* (1961) and *The John Doe Associates* (1974); Hilary Conroy and Harry Wray, eds., *Pearl Harbor Reexamined* (1990); Ladislas Farago, *The Broken Seal* (1967) (MAGIC); Akira Iriye, *The Origins of the Second World War in Asia and the Pacific* (1987); Robert W. Love, Jr., ed., *Pearl Harbor Revisited* (1994); Peter Lowe, *Great Britain and the Origins of the Pacific War* (1977); Martin V. Melosi, *The Shadow of Pearl Harbor* (1977); Samuel Eliot Morison, *The Rising Sun in the Pacific* (1973); James Morley, ed., *The Fateful Choice: Japan's Advance into Southeast Asia, 1939–1941* (1980); Gordon W. Prange, *At Dawn We Slept* (1981) and *Pearl Harbor* (1986); Bruce M. Russett, *No Clear and Present Danger* (1972); Paul W. Schroeder, *The Axis Alliance and Japanese-American Relations, 1941* (1958); Charles C. Tansill, *Back Door to War* (1952); Jonathan Utley, *Going to War with Japan* (1984); and Roberta Wohlstetter, *Pearl Harbor* (1962).

Wartime issues, Allied relations, and plans for the postwar world are explored in Michael C. C. Adams, *The Best War Ever* (1993); Stephen Ambrose, *The Supreme Commander* (1970); Robert Beitzell, *The Uneasy Alliance* (1972); Edward M. Bennett, *Franklin D. Roosevelt and the Search for Victory* (1990); Douglas Brinkley and David Facey-Crowther, eds., *The Atlantic Charter* (1994); A. Russell Buchanan, *The United States and World War II* (1964); Thomas M. Campbell, *Masquerade Peace: America's UN Policy, 1944–1945* (1973); R. D. Cuff and J. L. Granatstein, *Canadian-American Relations in Wartime* (1975); Robert A. Divine, *Second Chance* (1967); Alan P. Dobson, *U.S. Wartime Aid to Britain* (1986); Robin Edmonds, *The Big Three* (1991);

Kent R. Greenfield, *American Strategy in World War II* (1963); George C. Herring, Jr., *Aid to Russia, 1941–1946* (1973); Gary R. Hess, *The United States at War, 1941–1945* (1986); Robert C. Hilderbrand, *Dumbarton Oaks* (1990); Gregory Hooks, *Forging the Military-Industrial Complex* (1990); Barry M. Katz, *Foreign Intelligence* (1989); Helen Keyssar and Vladimir Posner, eds., *Remembering War* (1990) (USSR); Warren F. Kimball, ed., *America Unbound* (1992); Clayton R. Koppes and Gregory D. Black, *Hollywood Goes to War* (1987); Eric Larrabee, *Commander in Chief* (1987); Michael Leigh, *Mobilizing Consent* (1976); David MacIsaacs, *Strategic Bombing in World War Two* (1976); Vojtech Mastny, *Russia's Road to the Cold War* (1979); Steven M. Miner, *Between Churchill and Stalin* (1988); Samuel Eliot Morison, *Strategy and Compromise* (1958); William O'Neill, *A Democracy at War* (1993); David Reynolds et al., eds., *Allies at War* (1994); Keith Sainsbury, *Churchill and Roosevelt at War* (1994); Ronald Schaffer, *Wings of Judgment: American Bombing in World War II* (1985); Michael S. Sherry, *Preparing for the Next War* (1977); Holly C. Shulman, *The Voice of America* (1991); Richard W. Steele, *The First Offensive, 1942* (1973); Mark A. Stoler, *The Politics of the Second Front* (1977); Dwight W. Tuttle, *Harry L. Hopkins and Anglo-American-Soviet Relations, 1941–1945* (1983); Piotr S. Wandycz, *The United States and Poland* (1980); Russell F. Weigley, *Eisenhower's Lieutenants* (1981); Gerhard L. Weinberg, *A World at Arms* (1994); Randall B. Woods, *A Changing of the Guard* (1990) (U.S.-Britain); and Llewellyn Woodward, *British Foreign Policy in the Second World War* (1970–1971).

Big Three summit meetings are treated in Russel O. Buhite, *Decisions at Yalta* (1986); Diane Shaver Clemens, *Yalta* (1970); Keith Eubank, *Summit at Teheran* (1985); Herbert Feis, *Between War and Peace* (1960) (Potsdam); Keith Sainsbury, *The Turning Point* (1985) (Cairo and Teheran); and John L. Snell, ed., *The Meaning of Yalta* (1956).

For the Pacific theater, China, and decolonization, see Wesley M. Bagby, *The Eagle-Dragon Alliance* (1992); David D. Barrett, *Dixie Mission* (1970); Russell D. Buhite, *Patrick J. Hurley and American Foreign Policy* (1973); Warren I. Cohen, *America's Response to China* (1990); John W. Dower, *War Without Mercy* (1986); Herbert Feis, *The China Tangle* (1953); John W. Garver, *Chinese-Soviet Relations, 1937–1945* (1988); Suburō Ienaga, *The Pacific War* (1978); Akira Iriye, *Power and Culture: The Japanese-American War, 1941–1945* (1981); E. J. Kahn, Jr., *The China Hands* (1975); William R. Louis, *Imperialism at Bay* (1978) (decolonization); Michael Schaller, *The U.S. Crusade in China, 1938–1945* (1978); John J. Sbrega, *Anglo-American Relations and Colonialism in East Asia* (1983); Leon V. Sigal, *Fighting to the Finish: The Politics of War Termination in the United States and Japan, 1945* (1988); Ronald H. Spector, *Eagle Against the Sun* (1984); Christopher Thorne, *Allies of a Kind* (1977) and *The Issue of War* (1985); Tang Tsou, *America's Failure in China, 1941–1950* (1963); Barbara Tuchman, *Stilwell and the American Experience in China, 1911–1945* (1971); and Odd Arne Westad, *Cold War and Revolution* (1993) (China).

For U.S. wartime relations with Latin America, see works cited in Chapter 5; Michael J. Francis, *The Limits of Hegemony* (1977) (Argentina and Chile); Michael Grow, *The Good Neighbor Policy and Authoritarianism in Paraguay* (1981); Frank D. McCann, Jr., *The Brazilian-American Alliance, 1937–1945* (1973); Stanley Hilton, *Hitler's Secret War in South America, 1939–1945* (1981); and Randall B. Woods, *The Roosevelt Foreign Policy Establishment and the "Good Neighbor"* (1980) (Argentina).

For U.S. interest in the Middle East and oil, consult Irvine H. Anderson, *Aramco, the United States, and Saudi Arabia* (1981); Philip J. Baram, *The Department of State in the Middle East, 1919–1945* (1978); Aaron D. Miller, *Search for Security* (1980) (Saudi Arabia); and Michael B. Stoff, *Oil, War, and American Security* (1980).

The Holocaust and refugee problem are recounted in Robert H. Abzug, *Inside the Vicious Heart* (1985); Richard Breitman and Alan M. Kraut, *American Refugee Policy and European Jewry* (1987); Christopher Browning, *The Path to Genocide* (1992); Leonard Dinnerstein, *America and the Survivors of the Holocaust* (1982); Henry L. Feingold, *Politics of Rescue* (1970); Martin Gilbert, *Auschwitz and the Allies* (1981); Walter Laqueur, *The Terrible Secret* (1980); Deborah E. Lipstadt, *Beyond Belief* (1993); Arthur D. Morse, *While Six Million Died* (1968); William E. Nawyn, *American Protestantism's Response to Germany's Jews and Refugees, 1933–1941* (1982); Arnold Offner, *American Appeasement* (1964); Monty N. Penkower, *The Jews Were Expendable* (1983); and David Wyman, *Paper Walls* (1968) and *The Abandonment of the Jews* (1984).

See also the General Bibliography; Richard D. Burns, *Guide to American Foreign Relations Since 1700* (1983); and the following notes.

Notes to Chapter 6

1. Quoted in Theodore A. Wilson, *The First Summit* (Lawrence: University Press of Kansas, 1991; rev. ed.), p. 98.
2. H. V. Morton quoted *ibid.,* p. 78.
3. Elliott Roosevelt, *As He Saw It* (New York: Duell, Sloan, and Pearce, 1946), p. 33.
4. Winston S. Churchill, *The Grand Alliance* (Boston: Houghton Mifflin, 1950), p. 431.
5. Quoted in Robert E. Sherwood, *Roosevelt and Hopkins* (New York: Harper & Brothers, 1948), p. 236.
6. Harold Nicolson, *Diaries and Letters* (New York: Atheneum, 1966–1968; 3 vols.), II, 385.
7. Churchill quoted in David Reynolds, "Churchill, Roosevelt, and the Wartime Anglo-American Alliance, 1939–1945," in Wm. Roger Louis and Hedley Bull, eds., *The "Special Relationship"* (New York: Oxford University Press, 1986), p. 40.
8. Quoted in Warren F. Kimball, "Churchill and Roosevelt," *Prologue, VI* (Fall 1974), 179.
9. Quoted in Forrest C. Pogue, *George C. Marshall* (New York: Viking, 1963–1973; 3 vols.), II, 46.
10. David Reynolds, *The Creation of the Anglo-American Alliance, 1937–1941* (Chapel Hill: University of North Carolina Press, 1981), p. 195.
11. Quoted in Raymond Esthus, "President Roosevelt's Commitment to Britain to Intervene in a Pacific War," *Mississippi Valley Historical Review, L* (June 1963), 31.
12. David Dilks, ed., *The Diaries of Sir Alexander Cadogan, 1938–1945* (New York: G. P. Putnam's Sons, 1971), p. 399.
13. Cordell Hull, *Memoirs* (New York: Macmillan, 1948; 2 vols.), II, 975–976.
14. *Foreign Relations, 1941* (Washington, D.C.: Government Printing Office, 1958), I, 368–369.
15. James MacGregor Burns, *Roosevelt: The Soldier of Freedom* (New York: Harcourt Brace Jovanovich, 1970), p. 550.
16. Quoted in Holly C. Shulman, *The Voice of America* (Madison: University of Wisconsin Press, 1990), p. 72.
17. *Foreign Relations, 1941, I*, 378.
18. Quoted in William H. McNeill, *America, Britain, & Russia* (London: Oxford University Press, 1953), p. 41.
19. Quoted In Lloyd C. Gardner, *Spheres of Influence* (Chicago: Ivan R. Dee, 1993), p. 241.
20. Quoted in Burns, *Soldier of Freedom,* p. 609.
21. Mark A. Lowenthal, *Leadership and Indecision* (New York: Garland, 1988), p. 633.
22. Ian Jacob quoted in Martin Gilbert, *Winston S. Churchill* (Boston: Houghton Mifflin, 1983), p. 1161.
23. Quoted in Wilson, *First Summit,* p. 182.
24. Quoted in J. Garry Clifford, "Juggling Balls of Dynamite," *Diplomatic History, XVII* (Fall 1993), 636.
25. Anthony Eden, *The Reckoning* (Boston: Houghton Mifflin, 1965), p. 433.
26. Samuel I. Rosenman, ed., *Public Papers . . . of Franklin D. Roosevelt, 1939* (New York: Macmillan, 1938–1950; 13 vols.), *VIII,* 463.
27. Robert A. Divine, *Roosevelt and World War II* (Baltimore: The Johns Hopkins University Press, 1969), p. 37.
28. Charles Tobey to James Richardson, September 28, 1939, Charles Tobey Papers, Baker Library, Dartmouth College, Hanover, New Hampshire.
29. Quoted in John M. Blum, *From the Morgenthau Diaries: Years of Urgency* (Boston: Houghton Mifflin, 1965), p. 91.
30. Quoted in Patrick Abbazia, *Mr. Roosevelt's Navy* (Annapolis: Naval Institute Press, 1975), p. 142.
31. Rosenman, *Public Papers, 1940, IX,* 263.
32. Quoted in John G. Clifford, "Grenville Clark and the Origins of Selective Service," *Review of Politics, XXXV* (January 1973), 31–32.
33. Rosenman, *Public Papers, 1940, IX,* 391.
34. Quoted in Robert A. Divine, *Foreign Policy and U.S. Presidential Elections, 1940–1948* (New York: New Viewpoints, 1974), pp. 82-83.
35. Warren F. Kimball, ed., *Churchill & Roosevelt* (Princeton: Princeton University Press, 1984; 3 vols.), I, 108.
36. Rosenman, *Public Papers, 1940, IX,* 607.
37. *Ibid.,* pp. 640–643.
38. Quoted in George C. Herring, Jr., *Aid to Russia, 1941–1946* (New York: Columbia University Press 1973), p. 4.
39. Quoted in Warren F. Kimball, *The Most Unsordid Act* (Baltimore: The Johns Hopkins University Press, 1969), p. 154.
40. Rosenman, *Public Papers, 1940, IX,* 711–712.
41. Quoted in Kimball, *Most Unsordid Act,* p. 153.
42. *Congressional Record, LXXVII* (March 8, 1941), 2097.
43. Emory S. Land to Roosevelt, April 4, 1941, OF 48, Franklin D. Roosevelt Papers, Franklin D. Roosevelt Library, Hyde Park, New York.
44. Breckinridge Long Diary, May 12, 1941, Breckinridge Long Papers, Library of Congress, Washington, D.C.
45. Claude Wickard Diary, May 2, 1941, Claude Wickard Papers, Roosevelt Library.
46. Quoted in Calvin L. Christman, "Franklin D. Roosevelt and the Craft of Strategic Assessment," in Williamson Murray and Allen R. Millett, eds., *Calculations* (New York: The Free Press, 1992), p. 256.
47. Churchill, *Grand Alliance,* p. 370.
48. Quoted in Blum, *Morgenthau Diaries,* p. 264.
49. August 19, 1941, CAB 65/19, War Cabinet Records 84, Public Record Office, London, England.
50. Rosenman, *Public Papers, 1941, X,* 438, 439.
51. Quoted in Wayne S. Cole, *America First* (Madison: University of Wisconsin Press, 1953), p. 163.
52. Manfred Jonas, *The United States and Germany* (Ithaca: Cornell University Press, 1984), p. 258.

53. George Gallup, "Influencing and Evaluating Public Opinion," lecture, April 1940, G-1, No. 7, Army War College Records, U.S. Military Institute, Carlisle, Pennsylvania.

54. Roosevelt to Lewis Douglas, June 7, 1940, PPF 1914, Roosevelt Papers.

55. James C. Schneider, *Should America Go to War?* (Chapel Hill: University of North Carolina Press, 1989), p. 219.

56. Josiah Bailey to I. M. Meekins, September 6, 1941, Josiah Bailey Papers, Perkins Library, Duke University, Durham, North Carolina.

57. Quoted in Edward M. Bennett, "Joseph C. Grew," in Richard Dean Burns and Edward M. Bennett, eds., *Diplomats in Crisis* (Santa Barbara, Cal.: ABC-CLIO, 1974), p. 78.

58. Harold L. Ickes, *The Secret Diary of Harold L. Ickes* (New York: Simon and Schuster, 1953; 3 vols.), III, 567.

59. Quoted in Charles E. Neu, *The Troubled Encounter* (New York: John Wiley & Sons, 1975), p. 168.

60. Barbara Teters, "Yosuke Matsuoka," in Burns and Bennett, *Diplomats*, p. 288.

61. *Foreign Relations, 1940* (Washington, D.C.: Government Printing Office, 1955), *IV*, 602.

62. Quoted in Christopher Thorne, *The Issue of War* (New York: Oxford University Press, 1985), p. 22.

63. Quoted in Hilary Conroy, "Nomura Kichisaburo," in Burns and Bennett, *Diplomats*, pp. 300–301.

64. Quoted in Herbert Feis, *The Road to Pearl Harbor* (New York: Atheneum, 1967), p. 206.

65. Jonathan Utley, *Going to War with Japan, 1937–1941* (Knoxville: University of Tennessee Press, 1984), p. 156.

66. Ickes, *Secret Diary, III*, 346.

67. Quoted in James C. Thomson, Jr., "The Role of the Department of State," in Dorothy Borg and Shumpei Okamoto, eds., *Pearl Harbor as History* (New York: Columbia University Press, 1973), p. 101.

68. Quoted in Jonathan G. Utley, "Cordell Hull and the Diplomacy of Inflexibility," in Hilary Conroy and Harry Wray, eds., *Pearl Harbor Reexamined* (Honolulu: University of Hawaii Press, 1990), p. 82.

69. Quoted in Scott D. Sagan, "The Origins of the Pacific War," *Journal of Interdisciplinary History, XVIII* (Spring 1988), 895.

70. Japanese Liaison Conference quoted *ibid.*, p. 912.

71. Quoted in William M. Tuttle, Jr., *"Daddy's Gone to War"* (New York: Oxford University Press, 1993), p. 11.

72. Quoted in Thorne, *Issue of War*, p. 10.

73. Charles Tansill, *Back Door to War* (Chicago: Regnery, 1952).

74. Quoted in Carl Boyd, *Hitler's Japanese Confidant* (Lawrence: University Press of Kansas, 1993), p. 36.

75. Roberta Wohlstetter, *Pearl Harbor* (Stanford: Stanford University Press, 1962), p. 387.

76. Rosenman, *Public Papers, 1941, X*, 514.

77. Arthur H. Vandenberg, Jr., ed., *The Private Papers of Senator Vandenberg* (Boston: Houghton Mifflin, 1952), p. 1.

78. John Mueller, "Pearl Harbor: Military Inconvenience, Political Disaster," *International Security, XVI* (Winter 1991/92), 172–203.

79. Rosenman, *Public Papers, 1941, X*, 530.

80. Samuel E. Morison, *Strategy and Compromise* (Boston: Little, Brown, 1958), p. 25.

81. Quoted in Warren F. Kimball, *The Juggler* (Princeton: Princeton University Press, 1991), p. 136.

82. Utley, *Going to War*, p. *xiii*.

83. Memorandum of Conversation with Cordell Hull, September 29, 1944, "Black Notebooks," Box 1, Arthur Krock Papers, Princeton University Library, Princeton, New Jersey.

84. Townsend Hoopes and Douglas Brinkley, *Driven Patriot: The Life and Times of James Forrestal* (New York: Alfred A. Knopf, 1992), p. 228.

85. Quoted in Geoffrey Perrett, *Days of Sadness, Years of Triumph* (Baltimore: Penguin, 1973), p. 197.

86. Quoted in Kimball, "Churchill and Roosevelt," p. 181.

87. Winston S. Churchill, *Triumph and Tragedy* (Boston: Houghton Mifflin, 1953), p. 338.

88. Eden, *Reckoning*, pp. 336–337.

89. Quoted in Steven M. Miner, *Between Churchill and Stalin* (Chapel Hill: University of North Carolina Press, 1988), p. 217.

90. Alfred D. Chandler et al., eds., *The Papers of Dwight David Eisenhower* (Baltimore: The Johns Hopkins University Press, 1970; 5 vols.), I, 66.

91. Quoted in Sherwood, *Roosevelt and Hopkins*, p. 563.

92. Quoted in Herbert Feis, *Churchill, Roosevelt, Stalin* (Princeton: Princeton University Press, 1957), p. 42.

93. Quoted in Harry C. Butcher, *My Three Years with Eisenhower* (New York: Simon and Schuster, 1946), p. 29.

94. Quoted in Arthur Bryant, *Triumph in the West, 1943–1946* (London: Collins, 1959), p. 78.

95. Brian L. Villa, "The Atomic Bomb and the Normandy Invasion," *Perspectives in American History, XI* (1978), p. 497.

96. Quoted in Mark A. Stoler, *George Marshall* (Boston: Twayne, 1989), p. 106.

97. *Correspondence between the Chairman . . . U.S.S.R. and the Presidents of the U.S.A. and the Prime Ministers of Great Britain* (Moscow: Foreign Languages Publishing House, 1957; 2 vols.), *II*, 70–71.

98. Quoted in Robert Beitzell, *The Uneasy Alliance* (New York: Alfred A. Knopf, 1972), p. 159.

99. D. C. Watt, *Succeeding John Bull* (Cambridge, Eng.: Cambridge University Press, 1984), p. 101; Winston S. Churchill, *The Hinge of Fate* (Boston: Houghton Mifflin, 1950), p. 759.

100. Quoted in Raymond G. O'Connor, *Diplomacy for Victory* (New York: W. W. Norton, 1971), p. 52.

101. Memorandum of Conversation with Cordell Hull,

November 30, 1943, "Black Notebooks," Box 1, Krock Papers.

102. Hull, *Memoirs, II*, 1297.

103. Robert Murphy, *Diplomat Among Warriors* (Garden City, N.Y.: Doubleday, 1964), p. 208.

104. Keith Sainsbury, *The Turning Point* (New York: Oxford University Press, 1985), p. 307.

105. Quoted in Keith Eubank, *Summit at Teheran* (New York: Morrow, 1985), p. 248.

106. Quoted in Divine, *Roosevelt and World War II*, p. 62.

107. Henry H. Arnold, *Global Mission* (New York: Harper & Brothers, 1949), p. 465.

108. Quoted in Mark A. Stoler, *The Politics of the Second Front* (Westport, Conn.: Greenwood Press, 1977), p. 149.

109. Churchill, *Hinge of Fate*, p. 374.

110. Quoted in Pogue, *Marshall, III*, 313.

111. Quoted in Beitzell, *Uneasy Alliance*, p. 348.

112. *Foreign Relations, Cairo and Teheran*, (Washington, D.C.: Government Printing Office, 1961) pp. 594–595.

113. Churchill quoted in Sainsbury, *Turning Point*, p. 300.

114. Quoted in Burns, *Roosevelt: Soldier*, p. 411.

115. *Foreign Relations, Cairo and Teheran*, pp. 583, 585; (New York: Norton, Charles Bohlen, *Witness to History, 1973*) p. 149.

116. Rosenman, *Public Papers, 1943, XII*, 558.

117. Churchill, *Hinge of Fate*, p. 133.

118. Warren I. Cohen, *America's Response to China* (New York: Columbia University Press, 1990; 3d ed.), p. 127.

119. Quoted in Jonathan Spence, *To Change China* (Boston: Little, Brown, 1969), p. 236; Christopher Thorne, "Indochina and Anglo-American Relations, 1942–1945," *Pacific Historical Review, XLIV* (February 1976), 76.

120. Theodore H. White, ed., *The Stilwell Papers* (New York: William Sloane Associates, 1948), p. 157.

121. Quoted in Robert P. Newman, *Owen Lattimore and the "Loss" of China* (Berkeley: University of California Press, 1992), p. 70.

122. Quoted in Sainsbury, *Turning Point*, p. 156.

123. Quoted in Herbert Feis, *The China Tangle* (Princeton: Princeton University Press, 1953), p. 51.

124. Quoted in Akira Iriye, "Japan Against the ABCD Powers," in Akira Iriye and Warren Cohen, eds., *American, Chinese, and Japanese Perspectives on Wartime Asia, 1931–1949* (Wilmington, Del.: Scholarly Resources, 1989), p. 233.

125. Quoted in Martha Byrd, *Chennault* (Tuscaloosa: University of Alabama Press, 1987), p. 174.

126. White, *Stilwell Papers*, p. 333.

127. *Foreign Relations, 1944* (Washington, D.C.: Government Printing Office, 1967), VI, 631–632.

128. David D. Barrett, *Dixie Mission* (Berkeley: University of California, 1970), p. 56.

129. Quoted in Odd Arne Westad, *Cold War and Revolution* (New York: Columbia University Press, 1993), p. 64; John Paton Davies, *Dragon by the Tail* (New York: W. W. Norton, 1972), p. 381.

130. Quoted in Feis, *China Tangle*, p. 213.

131. Quoted in Russell D. Buhite, *Patrick J. Hurley and American Foreign Policy* (Ithaca: Cornell University Press, 1973), p. 152.

132. Quoted in Barbara W. Tuchman, "If Mao Had Come to Washington," *Foreign Affairs, L* (October 1972), 44.

133. Pyotr Vladimirov quoted in Wesley M. Bagby, *The Eagle-Dragon Alliance* (Newark: University of Delaware Press, 1992), p. 122.

134. Quoted in Feis, *China Tangle*, p. 269.

135. Burns, *Roosevelt: Soldier*, p. 545.

136. Quoted in Moshe Gottlieb, "The Berlin Riots and Their Repercussions in America," *American Jewish Historical Quarterly, LIX* (March 1970), 306.

137. Quoted in Cyrus Adler and Aaron M. Margalith, *With Firmness in the Right* (New York: American Jewish Committee, 1946), p. 381.

138. Quoted in Saul S. Friedman, *No Haven for the Oppressed* (Detroit: Wayne State University Press, 1973), p. 21.

139. Quoted in Jesse H. Stiller, *George S. Messersmith* (Chapel Hill: University of North Carolina Press, 1987), p. 123.

140. Quoted in Robert A. Divine, *American Immigration Policy, 1924–1952* (New Haven: Yale University Press, 1957), p. 98.

141. Quoted in James M. Burns, *Roosevelt: The Lion and the Fox* (New York: Harcourt, Brace and World, 1956), p. 339.

142. Arnold A. Offner, *American Appeasement* (New York: W. W. Norton, 1976 [c. 1969]), p. 92.

143. Quoted in Henry L. Feingold, *Politics of Rescue* (New Brunswick, N.J.: Rutgers University Press, 1970), p. 19.

144. *The Nation* quoted in David Wyman, *Paper Walls* (Amherst: University of Massachusetts Press, 1968), p. 54.

145. Quoted in Friedman, *No Haven*, p. 83.

146. Quoted in Wyman, *Paper Walls*, p. 97.

147. Quoted in Irwin F. Gellman, "The *St. Louis* Tragedy," *American Jewish Historical Quarterly, LXI* (December 1971), 156.

148. Quoted in A. J. Sherman, *Island Refuge* (Berkeley: University of California Press, 1973), p. 207.

149. Christopher Browning, *The Path to Genocide* (Cambridge, Eng.: Cambridge University Press, 1992), pp. 87, 89.

150. Quoted in Henry L. Feingold, "'Courage First and Intelligence Second: The American Secular Jewish Elite, Roosevelt, and the Failure to Rescue," in Michael Marrus, ed., *The Nazi Holocaust: Bystanders to the Holocaust* (Westport, Conn.: Meckler, 1989; 9 vols.) II, 781.

151. David S. Wyman letter, *New York Times*, March 6, 1979.

152. Quoted in Arthur D. Morse, *While Six Million Died* (New York: Random House, 1968), p. 63.

153. Quoted *ibid.*, pp. 93, 95.

154. David Wyman, *The Abandonment of the Jews* (New York: Pantheon, 1986), p. xi.

155. Henry Bruenn quoted in Keith W. Olson, "Franklin D. Roosevelt, the Ghost of Woodrow Wilson, and World War II," in Silvo Hietanen, ed., *The Road to War* (Tampere, Finland: University of Tampere, 1993), p. 62.

156. Quoted in George Woodbridge et al., *The History of the United Nations Relief and Rehabilitation Administration* (New York: Columbia University Press, 1950; 3 vols.), I, 4.

157. Francis B. Sayre in *Department of State Bulletin, IX* (October 23, 1943), 275.

158. *Treaties and Other International Acts* (Washington, D.C.: Government Printing Office, 1946), series 1501–1502.

159. Quoted in Thomas G. Paterson, *Soviet-American Confrontation* (Baltimore: The Johns Hopkins University Press, 1973), p. 147.

160. Congresswoman Jesse Sumner and Senator Robert Taft quoted in Randall B. Woods, *A Changing of the Guard* (Chapel Hill: University of North Carolina Press, 1990), pp. 236–37.

161. Quoted in Richard N. Gardner, *Sterling-Dollar Diplomacy* (New York: McGraw-Hill, 1969; rev. ed.), p. 267.

162. Quoted in Diane Shaver Clemens, *Yalta* (New York: Oxford University Press, 1970), p. 48.

163. Robert C. Hilderbrand, *Dumbarton Oaks* (Chapel Hill: University of North Carolina Press, 1990), p. 246.

164. Quoted *ibid.*, p. 133.

165. Quoted in Robert A. Divine, *Second Chance* (New York: Atheneum, 1967), p. 229.

166. Quoted in Gabriel Kolko, *The Politics of War* (New York: Random House, 1968), pp. 270–271.

167. Vandenberg, *Private Papers*, p. 176.

168. Quoted in Divine, *Second Chance*, p. 290.

169. Quoted *ibid.*, p. 291.

170. Quoted *ibid.*, p. 297.

171. Quoted in Kolko, *Politics of War*, p. 470.

172. Arnold Wolfers, *United States Policy Toward Germany* (New Haven: Yale Institute of International Studies, 1947), p. 3.

173. *Foreign Relations, Conference at Quebec, 1944* (Washington, D.C.: Government Printing Office, 1972), p. 467.

174. Henry L. Stimson to the president, September 15, 1944, Box 100, James Forrestal Papers, Princeton University Library.

175. Notebooks, Interview with Harry S. Truman, November 12, 1949, Box 85, Jonathan Daniels Papers, University of North Carolina Library, Chapel Hill.

176. Churchill, *Triumph and Tragedy*, p. 338.

177. Quoted in George C. Herring, "Yalta as Cold War Metaphor," in F. Kevin Simon, ed., *The David A. Sayre History Symposium* (Lexington, Ky.: Sayre School, 1991), p. 21.

178. Clemens, *Yalta*, p. 287.

179. *Correspondence Between the Chairman, I*, 295.

180. Theodore Draper, *A Present of Things Past* (New York: Hill and Wang, 1990), p. 251.

181. Edgar Jones quoted in John W. Dower, *War Without Mercy* (New York: Pantheon, 1986), p. 64.

182. Forrest C. Pogue, "The Struggle for a New Order," in John L. Snell, ed., *The Meaning of Yalta* (Baton Rouge: Louisiana State University Press, 1956), pp. 33–34.

183. Quoted in Martin Gilbert, *Winston S. Churchill: Road to Victory, 1941–1945* (Boston: Houghton Mifflin, 1986), p. 1208.

184. Churchill, *Triumph and Tragedy*, p. 366.

185. Quoted in Vojtech Mastny, *Russia's Road to the Cold War* (New York: Columbia University Press, 1979), p. 245

186. *Foreign Relations, Yalta* (Washington, D.C.: Government Printing Office, 1955), p. 973.

187. Quoted in Gardner, *Spheres*, p. 236.

188. William D. Leahy, *I Was There* (New York: Whittlesey House, 1950), pp. 315–316.

189. Quoted in Sherwood, *Roosevelt and Hopkins*, p. 870.

190. Quoted in Kimball, *Juggler*, p. 173.

191. Quoted in Charles E. Bohlen, *Witness to History, 1929–1969* (New York: W. W. Norton, 1973), p. 181.

192. Churchill, *Triumph and Tragedy*, p. 402.

193. Gardner, *Spheres*, p. xiii.

194. Quoted in Kolko, *Politics of War*, p. 465.

195. Churchill, *Triumph and Tragedy*, pp. 227–228.

196. Quoted in Robin Edmonds, *The Big Three* (New York: W. W. Norton, 1991), p. 419.

197. Harriman quoted in Rudy Abrahamson, *Spanning the Century* (New York: Morrow, 1992), p. 383; Slessor in John Wheeler-Bennett and Anthony Nicholls, *The Semblance of Peace* (New York: W. W. Norton, 1974 [c. 1972]), p. 191.

198. Quoted in Richard L. Walker, *E. R. Stettinius, Jr.* (New York: Cooper Square Publishers, 1965), p. 333. Emphasis added.

199. Quoted in Peter Davis interview with Laura Delano, probably 1959, Roosevelt television series scripts, Roosevelt Library.

200. *Foreign Relations, 1944* (Washington, D.C.: Government Printing Office, 1965), III, 103.

201. Quoted in Kolko, *Politics of War*, p. 482.

202. Quoted in Edward M. Bennett, *Franklin D. Roosevelt and the Search for Victory* (Wilmington, Del.: Scholarly Resources, 1990), pp. 173–174.

203. Harry S. Truman, *Memoirs* (Garden City, N.Y.: Doubleday, 1955–1956; 2 vols.), I, 258.

204. Quoted in John M. Blum, *The Price of Vision* (Boston: Houghton Mifflin, 1973), p. 451.

205. *Foreign Relations, Berlin* (Washington, D.C.: Government Printing Office, 1960; 2 vols.), I, 33.

206. *Ibid.*, I, 39.

207. *Ibid.*, I, 61.

208. Quoted in James L. Gormly, *From Potsdam to the Cold War* (Wilmington, Del.: Scholarly Resources, 1990), p. 21.

209. Lucius D. Clay, *Decision in Germany* (Garden City, N.Y.: Doubleday, 1950), p. 21.

210. Lord Moran quoted in Thomas G. Paterson, *On Every Front* (New York: W. W. Norton, 1992; rev. ed.), p. 5.

211. Quoted in Eduard Mark, "'Today Has Been a Historical One'," *Diplomatic History, IV* (Summer 1980), 320, 322.

212. Truman, *Memoirs, I,* 402.

213. Journal, August 1, 1945, Box 19, and Memorandum of Conversation with Harriman, July 17, 1945, Box 18, Joseph Davies Papers, Library of Congress.

214. "Note of the Prime Minister's Conversation with President Truman at Luncheon, July 18, 1945," Premier 3, 430/8, Prime Minister's Office Records, Public Record Office.

215. Quoted in Robert L. Messer, "World War II and the Coming of the Cold War," in John M. Carroll and George C. Herring, eds., *Modern American Diplomacy* (Wilmington, Del.: Scholarly Resources, 1986), p. 121.

216. *The Tehran, Yalta & Potsdam Conferences: Documents* (Moscow: Progress Publishers, 1969), p. 323.

217. George F. Kennan, *Memoirs, 1925–1950* (Boston: Little, Brown, 1967), p. 260.

218. *Foreign Relations, Berlin, II,* 365.

219. Truman, *Memoirs, I,* 412.

220. Quoted in Walter Millis, ed., *The Forrestal Diaries* (New York: Viking, 1951), p. 79.

221. "Notes on Conversation in Moscow with Maxim Litvinov," by Edgar Snow, December 6, 1944, Box 68, President's Secretary's File, Roosevelt Papers.

222. Peter F. Drucker, *The Concept of the Corporation* (New York: New American Library, 1964; 2d ed.), p. xi.

223. Thomas J. McCormick, *American's Half-Century* (Baltimore: The Johns Hopkins University Press, 1989), p. 33.

224. Quoted in Gardner, *Sterling-Dollar Diplomacy,* p. xvii.

225. H. D. Clarke in Minutes on the Political Situation in the United States, August 20, 1945, AN2505/4145, Foreign Office Correspondence, Public Record Office.

226. *Department of State Bulletin, XXII* (April 22, 1945), 738.

227. Richard J. Barnet, *Roots of War* (Baltimore: Penguin, 1973 [c. 1972]), p. 23.

228. Arthur M. Schlesinger, Jr., *The Imperial Presidency* (New York: Popular Library, 1974), p. 128.

229. Quoted in Barnet, *Roots of War,* p. 42.

230. Theodore H. White, *In Search of History* (New York: Warner, 1979), p. 224.

231. Allan Nevins, "How We Felt About the War," in Jack Goodman, ed., *While You Were Gone* (New York: Simon and Schuster, 1946), p. 23.

Chapter 7

All-Embracing Struggle:
The Cold War Begins, 1945–1950

Atomic Blast. *The second atomic bomb fell on Nagasaki August 9, 1945, killing at least 60,000. When the renowned scientist Albert Einstein heard that Japan had been blasted with an atomic bomb, he said; "Ach! The world is not ready for it." (U.S. Air Force)*

✖ *Diplomatic Crossroad*

The Atomic Bomb at Hiroshima, 1945

The crew of the B-29 group scrawled rude and poignant anti-Japanese graffiti on the "Little Boy." A major, thinking about his son in the states and a quick end to the war, scratched "No white cross for Stevie" on the 10,000-pound orange and black bomb.[1] The 509th Bombardment Group had been training on the Mariana Island of Tinian since May. At last, it seemed that the United States' secret atomic development program ("the Manhattan Project") neared fruition. In the evening of August 5, 1945, Colonel Paul "Old Bull" Tibbets informed his crew members for the first time that their rare cargo was "atomic." He did not explain the scientific process in which two pieces of uranium (U-235), placed at opposite ends of a cylinder, smashed into one another to create tremendous energy. They knew what the equivalent of 20,000 tons of TNT meant, however. At midnight they settled down to a preflight meal, played poker, and waited.

At 1:37 A.M. on August 6 three weather planes took off in the darkness for the urban targets of Hiroshima, Kokura, and Niigata. At 2:45, after photo snapping and well wishing, Tibbets's heavily laden B-29, the *Enola Gay,* named after his mother, lifted ponderously off the Tinian runway. The six-hour flight was uneventful, marked by the dodging of cumulus clouds and the nerve-wracking final assembly of the bomb's inner components. Followed by two observation planes stocked with cameras and scientists, the *Enola Gay* spotted the Japanese coast at 7:30 A.M. The weather plane assigned to Hiroshima, the primary target, reported that "everything was peachy keen."[2] Tibbets headed for that city.

"This is history," he intoned over the intercom, "so watch your language."[3] But in those anxious moments someone actually forgot to switch on the tape recorder. At 31,600 feet and 328 miles per hour the *Enola Gay* began its run on Hiroshima. Crew members fastened on welder's goggles. Bombardier Thomas Ferebee prepared to cross the hairs in his bombsight. At 8:15 A.M. he shouted "bombs away." The *Enola Gay* swerved quickly to escape. The hefty "Little Boy" fell for fifty seconds and then exploded about 2,000 feet above ground, a near perfect hit at hypocenter. A brilliant flash of light temporarily blinded the fliers. The ship trembled, hit by a wave of sound like a baseball bat hitting an ash can. Crew members looked back. "My God," sighed copilot Captain Robert Lewis, as he watched the huge, purplish cloud of smoke, dust, and debris rise 40,000 feet into the atmosphere. "Even though we had expected something terrific," he remembered, "what we saw made us feel that we were Buck Rogers twenty-fifth century warriors."[4]

Enola Gay. On August 6, 1945, just before takeoff, Colonel Paul Tibbets waved from the cockpit of his aircraft *Enola Gay.* Tibbets hailed from Miami and had served in the European theater. For commanding the atomic mission, Tibbets received the Distinguished Service Cross. (U.S. Air Force)

"Little Boy." The nuclear weapon detonated over Hiroshima was 120 inches long and 28 inches in diameter, and weighed about 10,000 pounds. (Los Alamos Scientific Laboratory, courtesy of the Harry S. Truman Library)

Hiroshima ranked as Japan's eighth largest city, with 250,000 people. Manhattan Project director Lieutenant General Leslie Groves, with the president's approval, had put it first on the target list because it housed regional military head-quarters, but it was largely a residential and commercial city. On the cloudless, warm morning of August 6, 1945, Hiroshima's inhabitants heard the bombing alert siren. An "all clear" sounded when only a weather plane passed over. Everything seemed routine, for Hiroshima had largely escaped American bombs during the war. Forty-five minutes later, at 8:15 A.M., people labored near their jobs or moved in the streets. Few heard the *Enola Gay* overhead. Suddenly a streak of light raced through the sky. A blast of lacerating heat traveling near the speed of light rocked the city. The temperature soared to suffocating levels. Trees were stripped of their leaves. Buildings blew apart like firecrackers. Debris shot through the air like bullets. Permanent shadows etched themselves into concrete. The sky grew dark, lighted only by the choking fires that erupted everywhere. Winds swirled violently and raindrops intermittently struck the cluttered ground. "Nobody there looked like human beings," a survivor recalled. "They just sat catching fire."[5]

As the giant mushroom cloud churned above, dazed survivors stumbled about like scarecrows, their arms raised to avoid the painful rubbing of burned flesh. The victims remembered skin peeling off like ribbons, gaping wounds, vomiting and diarrhea, intense thirst. A badly wounded Dr. Michihiko Machiya noted that "no one talked, and the ominous silence was relieved only by a subdued rustle among so many people, restless, in pain, anxious, and afraid, waiting for something else to happen."[6] The nightmare registered in statistics: about 130,000 dead, as many wounded, and 81 percent of the city's buildings destroyed. Some twenty-three American prisoners of war also perished there.

American aircraft continued their destructive conventional bombing of other Japanese cities. On August 9, a second atomic bomb smashed Nagasaki, killing at least 60,000. The next day a sobered President Harry S. Truman decided not to unleash a third atomic bomb. He now had qualms about killing "all those kids."[7] The Japanese surrendered four days later. "We cried with relief and joy," a twenty-one-year-old lieutenant recalled. "We were going to grow up to adulthood after all."[8] Presidential aide Admiral William D. Leahy regretted, however, that "in being the first to use it, we had adopted the ethical standard common to the barbarians of the

Victims at Hiroshima.   Flash-burned victims shortly after the destruction of Hiroshima. Estimates are that in the five years after Hiroshima and Nagasaki another 130,000 people died. Although the atomic bombings took a large toll, General Curtis LeMay noted the effects of the earlier firebombing of Tokyo: "We scorched and boiled and baked to death more people in Tokyo on that night of 9–10 March [1945] than went up in vapor at Hiroshima and Nagasaki combined." (Photographs courtesy of Dr. A. A. Liebow, Army Institute of Pathology)

Dark Ages. I was not taught to make war in that fashion; and wars cannot be won by destroying women and children."[9]

As Leahy's comment attests, the decision to use the atomic bomb against an urban center met criticism within the small circle of government officials and scientists privy to the Manhattan Project. Although Truman claimed that his atomic bomb decision became necessary to end the war and thus save American lives, some advisers and scientists disagreed. They presented what they considered viable alternatives to dropping the bomb on a civilian population: (1) follow up Japanese peace feelers; (2) blockade and bomb Japan conventionally; (3) have Russia declare war on Japan; (4) warn Tokyo about the bomb and threaten its use; (5) demonstrate the bomb on an unpopulated island or area with international observers, including Japanese; (6) conduct a military landing on the outlying Japanese island of Kyushu. Many scientists believed that use of the bomb would constitute a moral blot on the American record, that it would jeopardize chances of postwar international control of the awesome weapon, and that it was unnecessary because Japan tottered on the verge of surrender.

Those who chose to drop the atomic bomb on populated targets stressed that they wanted to end the war as quickly as possible to save American lives. "Think of the kids who won't be killed!" Truman wrote from the Potsdam Conference.[10] That simple reason helps to explain the decision, but decisions seldom derive from single factors and this one is no exception. Three primary and intertwined motives induced policymakers to inflict atomic horror on the citizens of Japan. Together, the three suggest the central point: Truman found no compelling reasons against dropping atom bombs on Hiroshima and Nagasaki and important advantages in doing so.

The first motive—emotion—dated from December 7, 1941, when the Japanese bombed Pearl Harbor without warning. Vengeful Americans never forgot or forgave that disaster. The Japanese, as Truman said time and time again, could not be trusted. Revenge became the order of the day; they had to be repaid. The traditional racist American image of the Japanese as treacherous agents of a "Yellow Peril" strengthened this popular wartime attitude. Comics and movies crudely disparaged this people of color as "yellowbellies" and "yellow monkeys." One weapons manufacturer acclaimed its machine gun for "blasting red holes in little yellow men."[11] The *kamikaze* air attacks in 1945 persuaded many that the Japanese, suicidal and bloodthirsty, deserved the worst of punishments. Americans hated the Japanese—the "slant-eyes"—more than the Germans, and 13 percent in a Gallup poll of December 1944 recommended the extermination of all Japanese. Others advised sterilization. "We are drowning and burning the bestial apes all over the Pacific," Admiral William Halsey boasted on a newsreel, "and it is just as much pleasure to burn them as to drown them."[12] This feverish emotion carried influence. Truman himself said on August 11, 1945: "When you have to deal with a beast you have to treat him as a beast."[13]

The second motive—military momentum—merged with the first and dated from the establishment of the Manhattan Project in August 1942. This program began after European scientists, through a letter from Albert Einstein to President Franklin D. Roosevelt, warned that Germany might develop a nuclear device for

Hiroshima.   The ruins of Japan's eighth largest city bespoke the birth of the atomic age. (U.S. Air Force)

military purposes. From the start, officials in charge of the $2 billion project as-
sumed that once they developed a bomb they would use it to end the war. Truman
inherited this assumption from the Roosevelt administration. Put another way,
Truman really did not make a decision to drop the bomb. Rather, as General Leslie
Groves remarked, the president made a decision to honor the assumption, to sustain the momentum, to practice "noninterference—basically a decision not to upset the existing plans."[14] By 1945, furthermore, the large-scale bombing of civilians, as in Dresden and Tokyo, had become accepted conduct. By August 1945,
however, compelling momentum had taken on an irrational quality, for the
Germans had surrendered and Japan faced certain defeat.

The third factor that helped persuade Truman to unleash the atomic bomb was the diplomatic advantage that might accrue to the United States. The diplomatic bonus materialized when American leaders, while at the Potsdam Conference, learned about the successful test explosion at Alamogordo, New Mexico, on July 16, 1945. "Japs will fold up before Russia comes in," Truman wrote on learning the details. "I am sure they will when Manhattan appears over their homeland."[15] Throughout the war, Churchill and Roosevelt tried to keep the secret of the bomb from Soviet Russia, in part to use it for diplomatic leverage in the postwar period. Some scientists and advisers protested that excluding the Soviet Union, an ally, from any knowledge, would jeopardize or kill opportunities for successful postwar negotiations. At Potsdam, Truman did casually and cryptically inform Stalin that the United States had "a new weapon of unusual destructive force."[16] Stalin muttered that he hoped America would use it against the Japanese. Already aware of the

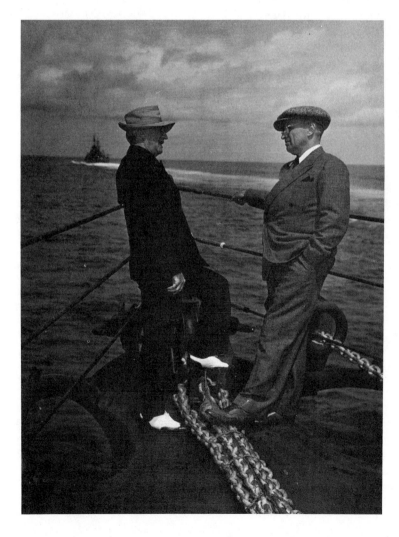

James F. Byrnes (1879–1972) and Harry S. Truman (1884–1972). Both the secretary of state and the president, here on their way back from the Potsdam Conference, welcomed the atomic bomb as a diplomatic bargaining weapon in the postwar period. The South Carolinian Byrnes, as secretary of state for 1945–1947, attended so many international conferences that, reportedly, "the State Department fiddles while Byrnes roams." At Potsdam, Truman wrote to his wife, Bess: Stalin "seems to like it when I hit him with a hammer." (U.S. Navy, courtesy of the Harry S. Truman Library)

Manhattan Project through Soviet espionage, Stalin soon ordered his scientists to speed up their own nuclear program. Truman jotted in his diary: "It is certainly a good thing for the world that Hitler's crowd or Stalin's did not discover this atomic bomb."[17]

Churchill learned about the test in New Mexico directly from the American delegation at Potsdam. "Now I know what happened to Truman yesterday," the prime minister noted. "When he got to the meeting after having read this report [from New Mexico] he was a changed man. He told the Russians just where they got on and off and generally bossed the whole meeting."[18] Two diplomatic advantages suggested themselves. First, the bomb might gain important concessions by strengthening the United States' negotiating position vis-à-vis the Soviets. An intimidated Russia might offer concessions on Eastern Europe if the bomb revealed its destructive power on a Japanese city. Second, the bomb might end the war in the Pacific before the Soviets could declare war against Japan; such a circumstance would deny the USSR any part in the postwar control of Japan and perhaps forestall Soviet military entry into Manchuria. Until the explosion at Alamogordo the United States had sought Soviet military action against Japan; the bomb's triumph in the sands of New Mexico ended that desire.

All three factors—emotion, military momentum, and diplomatic advantage—explain the tragedies at Hiroshima and Nagasaki. The diplomatic aspect emerged as a late bonus; the bomb would have been dropped whether such a consideration existed or not. To have decided against dropping the atomic bomb, Truman would have had to deny the passion and momentum that had built up by midsummer 1945. He could avenge Pearl Harbor, end the war quickly, save American lives, and shore up the U.S. diplomatic position—the advantages far outweighed the disadvantages in the American mind. Still, the costs were not inconsequential. Some of the alternatives, or a combination of them, might have terminated the war without the heavy death toll and the grotesque suffering of the survivors. The failure to discuss atomic development and control with the Soviets during the war bequeathed to the postwar generation both division and fear. "Seldom, if ever," CBS radio commentator Edward R. Murrow stated, "has a war ended leaving the victors with such . . . a realization that the future is obscure and survival is not assured."[19]

THE BIG TWO AND THE INTERNATIONAL SYSTEM: SOURCES OF THE LONG WAR

Because World War II left the international system in utter disarray, the transition to peace proved rough and contentious. Broken societies and economies needed repair, and competing models for a new future produced wrenching political turmoil. Some 35 million people died in Europe during the war, and hungry, homeless survivors, many of them "displaced persons," struggled to live in the rubble. The contrast with prosperous Americans, untouched by enemy bombers or soldiers, became stark. The war so weakened the French, British, and Dutch, moreover, that they could no longer manage their rebellious colonies, particularly in Asia. The once mighty imperialists had to retreat from empire. Britain, for example, granted independence to India in 1947 and Burma in 1948, and the Dutch left Indonesia a year later. Throughout the postwar period, the decolonization process accelerated in what became known as the Third World. Failure by the colonial regimes to relinquish power to the people clamoring for freedom "would be like failing to install a safety valve and then waiting for the boiler to blow up."[20]

As Washington moved to fill the power vacuums left by the defeated Axis and the victorious but retrenching colonial powers, it encountered an obstreperous competitor in Josef Stalin's Soviet Union. Soon a bipolar international structure emerged from the Soviet-American rivalry—the Cold War. The Soviets' pushy behavior, suspiciousness, and blunt language rankled Americans. Truman complained that they negotiated "with a boorishness worthy of stable boys."[21] At the end of the war, the Soviet Union had troops in several Eastern European countries and part of Germany. It lacked an effective navy or air force and had no atomic bomb, but it possessed strong regional power by virtue of its military exploits. Motivated by traditional Russian nationalism and communist ideology, craving security against a revived Germany and facing a huge task of reconstruction, the Kremlin determined to make the most of the limited power it held. Often rude and abusive, yet cautious and realistic, Josef Stalin determined never again to see his country invaded through Eastern Europe. Still, compared with the United States, as chargé d'affaires George F. Kennan reported from Moscow, the Soviet Union stood as the "weaker force."[22]

The United States emerged from World War II a full-fledged global power for the first time in its history. An asymmetry—not a balance—of power existed. Washington possessed what political scientists call "compellent" power and flexed its multidimensional muscle to build even more power. Because of domestic public pressure, Washington may have demobilized its troops faster than Truman wished, but the Soviet Union also demobilized millions of soldiers. Overall the United States emerged as the premier postwar military power. With troops in Asia and Europe, the world's largest navy and air force, a monopoly of the atomic bomb, and a high-gear economy, the United States demanded first rank in world affairs. As one scholar has put it, the United States held the "prime weapon of *de*struction—the atomic bomb—and the prime weapon of *recon*struction—such wealth as no nation hitherto had possessed."[23] President Truman heralded America as the "giant of the economic world," and British ambassador Lord Halifax reported that "by contrast with the exhausted and devastated countries of western Europe, the United States sees itself, as a result of the war, endowed with colossal productive and fighting capacity."[24]

American ideology and economic needs influenced U.S. leaders to project the nation's power. American ideology integrated political and economic tenets in a "peace and prosperity" philosophy. This thinking held that world peace and order depended on the existence of prosperity and political democracy. Poverty and economic depression bred totalitarianism, revolution, communism, the disruption of world trade through economic competition, and war. Prosperity became the handmaiden of stability, political freedom, unrestricted trade, and peaceful international

Josef Stalin (1879–1953).   General secretary of the Soviet Communist party since 1922, he ran an authoritarian state and conducted a foreign policy of suspiciousness. His daughter recalled that "he saw enemies everywhere." (*The Reporter*, 1952. Copyright 1952 by Fortnightly Publishing Co., Inc.)

relations. This thinking did not begin in the postwar era; Americans had long believed that they were prosperous because they were democratic and democratic because they were prosperous.

American leaders determined that *this time,* unlike after World War I, the United States would seize the opportunity to fulfill its ideological premises. As the historian Gaddis Smith has described diplomat Dean Acheson's historical understanding, "only the United States had the power to grab hold of history and make it conform."[25] The lessons of the 1920s and 1930s tugged at the leaders of the 1940s to generate a desire to throw off the mistakes of the past. Americans believed themselves a successful people, with admirable institutions and ideals worthy of universal adoption. The postwar period seemed an opportune time to install America's concept of "peace and prosperity" as the world's way—a time to express traditional American expansionism.

Postwar expansionism also fed off another fundamental factor: the vital needs of the American economy. Truman and other leaders frankly stated the facts: the United States *had* to export American goods and *had* to import strategic raw materials. By 1947 U.S. exports accounted for one-third of total world exports and were valued at $14 billion a year. Pivotal industries, such as automobiles, trucks, machine tools, steel, and farm machinery relied heavily on foreign trade for their well-being. Farmers exported about half of their wheat. Many Americans, remembering the

Makers of American Foreign Relations, 1945–1950

President	Secretaries of State
Harry S. Truman, 1945–1953	Edward R. Stettinius, Jr., 1944–1945
	James F. Byrnes, 1945–1947
	George C. Marshall, 1947–1949
	Dean G. Acheson, 1949–1953

Great Depression, predicted economic catastrophe unless U.S. foreign trade continued and expanded. Although less than 10 percent of the GNP, exports exceeded in volume such elements of the GNP as consumers' expenditures on durable goods, total expenditures by state and local governments, and private construction. Furthermore, imports of manganese, tungsten, and chromite, to name a few, had become essential to America's industrial system. Foreign trade, however, was threatened by the sickness of America's best customer, Europe, which lacked the resources to purchase American products, and also by nationalists in former colo-

"What Next?"   Jack Lambert's 1946 cartoon of Harry S. Truman captured the feeling of many Americans that the president, new at his job, was overwhelmed by postwar problems. FDR had kept Truman in the dark on foreign affairs. (Jack Lambert, *Chicago Sun Times*)

nial areas, who controlled raw materials sources for both Europe and America. To protect its interests and to fulfill its ideology the United States undertook foreign aid programs that eventually became global in scale.

President Truman, who loved the game of poker, felt the flush of American power, shared the ideology, and knew well the economic needs of the country. A Democratic party regular from the Pendergast machine in Kansas City, Truman had long experienced rough-and-tumble politics. Whereas Roosevelt had been charming and often evasive, Missouri-bred Truman waxed blunt and straightforward. "The buck stops here" read a sign on his desk. He prided himself on simple, direct language and quick decisions. The British ambassador considered Truman "an honest and intelligent mediocrity"—"a bungling if well-meaning amateur."[26] "Give 'em hell Harry," the crowds shouted. Truman had the "steady energy of a commission salesman, the aplomb and brashness of a riverboat gambler," and the "sass" of a bantam rooster, wrote one biographer.[27] With intense eyes peering through thick lenses, Truman relished the verbal brawl. His hurried simplification of issues, his superficial application of lessons from the past, and his quick-tempered style spawned jokes that often fit the truth. Why did the president arrive late for a press conference? "He got up this morning a little stiff in the joints and had trouble putting his foot in his mouth." Somebody rewrote a proverb: "To err is Truman." Although intelligent and energetic, Truman was a provincial nationalist of narrow vision who believed he could win the Cold War through the projection of U.S. power, and he expected the world to go America's way. When it did not, he sometimes lost his temper and spoke carelessly. He once admitted that he "was not a deep thinker."[28] His assistant Clark Clifford observed the president's preference for "rapid, intuitive decision-making rather than careful, analytical staff work."[29] Truman saw the world in black and white terms, seldom grasping the grays—the nuances and subleties.

In April 1945, Soviet foreign minister V. M. Molotov visited the White House. President Truman gave him a vigorous tongue-lashing, charging that Moscow had not honored the Yalta accords. Molotov stormed out of the office, stung by language more suitable for a ward politician in Missouri who had not delivered enough votes to the machine. After the encounter, the first meeting between the new president and a high-ranking Soviet official, Truman gloated to a friend: "I gave it to him straight 'one-two to the jaw.' I let him have it straight."[30] Truman's assertive style drew strength from actual American power. He could "get tough," as the saying went at the time, because the United States had impressive power. Truman told Ambassador to Russia W. Averell Harriman that he did not fear the Soviets, because they "needed us more than we needed them." He did not expect to win 100 percent of the American case, but "we should be able to get 85 percent."[31] Indeed, although U.S. resources did not always reach as far as American goals because the unstable international system, political leftists, and nationalists put up obstacles, Washington possessed unusual power.

The confrontation between the United States and the Soviet Union derived from the different postwar needs, ideology, style, and power of the two rivals and drew on an historical legacy of frosty relations. Each saw the other, in mirror image, as the world's bully. Each charged the other with assuming Hitler's aggressive mantle. Americans compared Nazism and communism, Hitler and Stalin, and coined the phrase "Red Fascism." Each exaggerated the intentions of the other. As the historian Melvyn Leffler has pointed out, Moscow and Washington became trapped in a "security dilemma": Every step taken by one side to ensure its security appeared to the other to be provocative. Still, "in view of the overwhelming power of the United States and in view of the relative restraint exhibited by the Kremlin *outside its immediate periphery,* U.S. officials might have displayed more tolerance for risk."[32]

Because the international system lay in shambles, the task of configuring a new one generated inevitable conflict. Uncertain in the tumultuous transition from war to peace, world leaders feared falling dominoes and "chain reactions" that might overwhelm them.[33] The advent of the air and nuclear ages, moreover, made all nations vulnerable to surprise attack. "We are for all time de-isolated," wrote one observer.[34] And the Soviet and American quests for spheres of influence kindled a global contest for advantage—an "all embracing struggle" with an expensive arms race, military alliances, trade restrictions, and repeated interventions and client-state wars.[35] The Cold War era lasted more than forty years, claimed the lives of millions of victims, and nearly bankrupted the main protagonists because they eventually suffered decline from "imperial overstretch."[36] In the end, nobody won.

CHALLENGING THE SOVIET SPHERE IN EASTERN EUROPE

By the end of the war Eastern Europe had become a Soviet sphere of influence, largely closed off to American penetration. Although some observers considered Eastern Europe an impenetrable and solid Soviet bloc, the region looked more like a patchwork quilt. The Soviet presence in Eastern Europe before 1947–1948 was neither uniform nor consistent. Moscow had no imperial blueprint for its neighbors. Poland, with its communist Lublin government in control, fell firmly within the Soviet grasp. Rumania, an anti-Soviet German satellite during the war, suffered under a Soviet-imposed government. The Soviet Union gained territory at the expense of Poland, Finland, and Rumania after postwar boundary settlements. Bulgaria had a large indigenous communist movement, which gained control through elections without much help from Moscow.

Hungary and other nations developed differently. The conservative Hungarian Smallholders' party of Ferenc Nagy won national elections in November 1945 by routing the communists, who gained only 17 percent of the vote. The Nagy government remained in office until a communist coup in spring 1947. In Finland, to demonstrate further the political complexity in Eastern Europe, noncommunist leaders recognized their precarious position with respect to neighboring Russia and adopted a neutral position vis-à-vis the Soviet-American confrontation. Finland thus retained its independence and in 1948 even ousted from its cabinet the lone communist member. Yugoslavia, although a communist state, established its independence from Moscow under the leadership of Josip Broz Tito. The growing

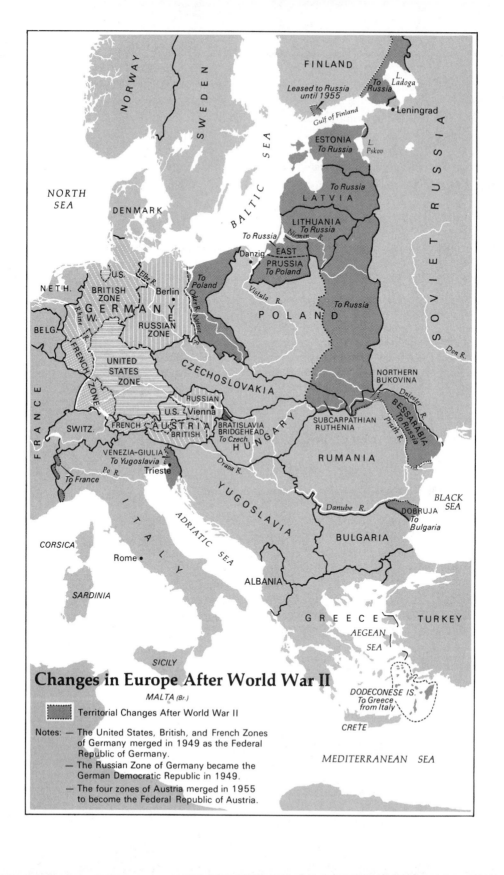

NORWAY

SWEDEN

FINLAND

Leased to Russia until 1955

To Russia

L. Ladoga

• Leningrad

Gulf of Finland

NORTH SEA

DENMARK

BALTIC SEA

ESTONIA
To Russia

L. Pskov

SOVIET RUSSIA

LATVIA
To Russia

LITHUANIA
To Russia

Niemen R.

NETH.

U.S.

Elbe R.

Danzig

To Russia

EAST PRUSSIA
To Poland

BRITISH ZONE

Berlin

To Poland

G E R M A N Y

W.

E.

Rhine R.

BELG.

RUSSIAN ZONE

Oder R.

Neisse R.

Vistula R.

P O L A N D

To Russia

FRENCH ZONE

UNITED STATES ZONE

C Z E C H O S L O V A K I A

Don R.

FRANCE

SWITZ.

RUSSIAN

U.S. Vienna

A U S T R I A

FRENCH

BRITISH

BRATISLAVIA BRIDGEHEAD
To Czech.

NORTHERN BUKOVINA

Dniester R.

BESSARABIA
To Russia

Pruth R.

SUBCARPATHIAN RUTHENIA

VENEZIA–GIULIA
To Yugoslavia

Po R.

Trieste

To France

H U N G A R Y

Drava R.

R U M A N I A

I T A L Y

ADRIATIC SEA

Y U G O S L A V I A

Danube R.

BLACK SEA

DOBRUJA
To Bulgaria

CORSICA

Rome •

B U L G A R I A

SARDINIA

ALBANIA

G R E E C E

TURKEY

AEGEAN SEA

Changes in Europe After World War II

SICILY

MALTA (Br.)

Territorial Changes After World War II

DODECONESE IS.
To Greece from Italy

CRETE

Notes: — The United States, British, and French Zones of Germany merged in 1949 as the Federal Republic of Germany.
    — The Russian Zone of Germany became the German Democratic Republic in 1949.
    — The four zones of Austria merged in 1955 to become the Federal Republic of Austria.

MEDITERRANEAN SEA

schism became public in 1948 when Belgrade and Moscow bitterly split. In Czechoslovakia, an independent socialist country with a democratic political process and ties with the West, officials recognized the advisability of a middle course in the developing Cold War. A coalition government under noncommunist president Eduard Beneš and Foreign Minister Jan Masaryk assumed office after free elections in May 1946. Communists held membership in the government, with 9 of 26 top-level positions and 114 of 300 National Assembly seats, but the Soviet Union for a time refrained from meddling directly in Czech affairs. Not until February 1948, after the Cold War had intensified, did the communists seize control of Czechoslovakia during a domestic crisis.

The Soviet presence in Eastern Europe before 1948, then, became conspicuous and often repressive, but not absolute. Communists sometimes gained control of repressive ministries of interior (police). Stalin seemed hesitant and uncertain, having a different policy for each Eastern European country. The Soviet leader said he wanted "friendly governments," not satellites. In early 1945, in stating his case regarding Poland, Stalin emphasized security: "Throughout history Poland has been the corridor for attack. . . . Poland was weak. Russia wants a strong, independent, and democratic Poland. . . . It is not only a question of honor for Russia, but one of life and death."[37] Still bitter over the *cordon sanitaire* the Western powers constructed around Russia after World War I and staggering from the loss of 22 million dead during the recent war, Soviet leaders demanded security through influence among their neighbors. "Give them twelve to fifteen years and they'll be on their feet again," Stalin said of the Germans.[38] They also believed that the 1944 Moscow percentage bargain, armistice agreements, and Yalta accords acknowledged their primary position in Eastern Europe. Thus the Soviets began building their own *cordon sanitaire*.

U.S. goals for the area clashed with those of the Soviet Union. Washington sought "free elections" and the "Open Door" for trade, both traditional principles calculated in part to reduce Soviet influence. The Soviets signed bilateral trade treaties with many Eastern European states, which established favors anathema to America's multilateral approach to trade. Although Americans had minimal commercial ties with Eastern Europe, U.S. diplomats preached the Open Door as a way of driving a wedge into the area. The application of the principle of "free elections" also proved difficult in Eastern Europe. First, except for Czechoslovakia, the region lacked democratic traditions. Second, free elections in most of those nations would have produced strongly anti-Soviet governments threatening Soviet security (such as the London Poles). The question of elections in Hungary demonstrates the complexity of the question. During late 1946 it was the *noncommunist* Nagy who delayed elections, because he knew that the communists would lose badly, alarming Moscow and perhaps triggering Soviet intervention. Both the United States and the Soviet Union wanted in Eastern Europe not democratic, but friendly governments. After all, critics asked, if "free elections" remained the ultimate and universal goal of U.S. diplomacy, why not apply it to the U.S. sphere of influence in Latin America, where Washington recognized and sustained military dictators?

The Soviets hence charged the United States with a double standard. When American leaders consciously excluded the USSR from participation in the post-

"Red Fascism." This popular notion among Americans suggested that German Nazism and Soviet communism were really one and the same and that the 1940s would suffer totalitarian aggression like that of the 1930s. Such thinking aroused fears of another "Munich" or "appeasement" and thereby hindered negotiations. (*The Reporter,* 1950. Copyright 1950 by Fortnightly Publishing Co., Inc.)

war reconstruction of Italy and Japan, the Soviets cited the Italian example as a precedent for their machinations in Eastern Europe. Secretary of War Henry L. Stimson remarked: "Some Americans are anxious to hang on to exaggerated views of the Monroe Doctrine and at the same time butt into every question that comes up in Central Europe."[39] The Soviets also feared U.S. economic power. Molotov contended that an Open Door in Eastern Europe would mean ultimate American economic domination of war-weakened nations. In short, the Soviet Union looked on American goals in Eastern Europe as guises for U.S. expansion in an area vital to Soviet security.

At the Yalta and Potsdam conferences, at the Foreign Ministers's conferences in London (September–October 1945) and Moscow (December 1945), at the Paris Peace Conference (April–October 1946), and in numerous diplomatic notes, the United States sought influence in Eastern Europe to counter the Soviets. It tried nonrecognition of the pro-Soviet governments, but abandoned that tactic after slight Soviet concessions, such as adding a handful of noncommunists to the Polish government. Some American leaders thought the continued U.S. monopoly of the atomic bomb would act as a compellent. Stimson recorded in his diary that Byrnes "looks to having the presence of the bomb in his pocket" at the London Conference.[40] A telling incident occurred at that conference. Molotov, as if he had been reading Stimson's diary, asked Byrnes if he had "an atomic bomb in his side pocket." "You don't know Southerners," Byrnes replied. "We carry our artillery in our pocket. If you don't cut out all this stalling and let us get down to work, I am going to pull an atomic bomb out of my hip pocket and let you have it."[41] The humorless Molotov apparently laughed. Still, the implied threat of the bomb did not budge the Soviets from Eastern Europe, and the United States never practiced a conscious "atomic diplomacy" of direct threat.

Stimson opposed the use of the bomb as a diplomatic weapon in September 1945. He had earlier thought of compelling Soviet concessions, but reversed himself when he told Truman that the United States should share the secret of the bomb to spur postwar cooperation. "For if we fail to approach them now and merely continue to negotiate with them, having this weapon rather ostentatiously on our hip, their suspicions and their distrust of our purposes and motives will increase." Stimson, then seventy-eight, and a former cabinet officer under William Howard Taft, Herbert Hoover, and Franklin Roosevelt, offered the president some sage advice: "The chief lesson I have learned in a long life is the only way you can make a man trustworthy is to trust him; and the surest way you can make a man untrustworthy is to distrust him and show your distrust."[42] Stimson gained the support of Secretary of Commerce Henry Wallace, but Secretary of the Navy James V. Forrestal rejected any effort to "buy [Russian] understanding and sympathy. We tried that once with Hitler."[43] Truman sided with Forrestal.

The United States also used foreign aid as a diplomatic weapon in Eastern Europe. Byrnes stated the policy in 1946: "We must help our friends in every way and refrain from assisting those who either through helplessness or for other reasons are opposing the principles for which we stand."[44] In short, no loans or aid for Eastern Europe. This policy backfired, for it left those countries dependent on Soviet aid and drove them deeper into the Soviet orbit. In Czechoslovakia, for ex-

"I Can't Give You All Up For One Angel of Peace." The burly Russian savors the attention of the Eastern Europeans in this critical Turkish cartoon. (*ULUS*, Ankara, in *United Nations World*, 1947)

ample, the United States abruptly severed an Export-Import Bank loan to press Beneš to remove the communists from his government. Noncommunist foreign trade minister Hubert Ripka complained bitterly in late 1947, "These idiots started the usual blackmail: 'Okay, you can have 200,000 or 300,000 or even 500,000 tons of wheat, but on one condition only—that you throw the Communists out of the Czechoslovak Government.' " The result: "And now these idiots in Washington have driven us straight into the Stalinist camp."[45]

The United States, through such pressure tactics on the Soviet sphere of influence, helped intensify the Cold War. That is, Moscow leaders read American policies, including encouragement to dissident anti-Soviet political groups, as threats to their security and so tightened their grip. George F. Kennan has suggested, for example, that the Czech coup of 1948 represented the Soviet response to the Marshall Plan, a major American aid program that the Soviets considered a challenge to their tenuous position in Eastern Europe (see pages 292–295). Overall, Washington exaggerated the extent of Soviet control in Eastern Europe and pressed the peoples of that region to align with the West. Yet the Eastern Europeans, so close to Soviet power, could not and would not affront the Soviet Union. Washington treated only Finland and Yugoslavia as exceptions, forwarding some aid to them. American policymakers showed little understanding of the difference between an independent country (like Czechoslovakia) influenced by the Soviet Union and a subjugated country (like Poland). To Americans all Soviet "satellites" deserved stiff-arming.

Yet, as contemporary critics asked, would the Eastern Europeans have retained some of their independence had Washington cooled its rhetoric, meddled less, recognized what it ultimately could not change, and maintained economic and political ties through foreign aid? Perhaps. In any case, the manipulative, often brutal Soviet behavior did not happen in a vacuum. American pressure aroused Soviet fears and hence countermeasures damaging to the Eastern Europeans.

STIFFENING UP: EARLY COLD WAR CRISES

The question of Eastern Europe broke up the London Conference of Foreign Ministers (September–October 1945). Byrnes demanded representative governments in Bulgaria and Rumania before he would sign any peace treaties with the former German satellites. Molotov countered with questions about British-dominated Greece and American-dominated Japan. The conferees left London unable to agree even on a public communiqué. The Grand Alliance was breaking up. At the Moscow Conference in December 1945, the secretary of state tempered his tough stand somewhat, and Stalin permitted a token broadening of the Rumanian and Bulgarian regimes. The Soviets also accepted Byrnes's ideas for a general peace conference to be held in Paris and a United Nations Atomic Energy Commission to prepare plans for international control.

Yet Truman grew impatient. In early 1946 he snapped that he intended to "stop babying the Russians," and he instructed Byrnes to "stiffen up," to make no compromises with the Soviets.[46] The new "get tough" policy developed through the early months of 1946. Republican senator Arthur Vandenberg of Michigan helped shape it with his denunciations of "appeasement." The news of a Canadian spy ring that had sent atomic secrets to Moscow broke in February, about the same time that Stalin gave a cocky preelection speech that persuaded some Americans that the Soviets had become intractable. From Moscow, on February 22, chargé d'affaires George F. Kennan wrote an alarmist and influential cable that declared that "we have here a political force committed fanatically to the belief that with [the] US there can be no permanent modus vivendi." The "long telegram" circulated widely in Washington, and people who believed that the United States could never negotiate with the Soviet Union devoured it with relish. Kennan explained what made the Soviets tick: an implacable communist ideology and a "neurotic view of world affairs" stemming from an "instinctive Russian sense of insecurity."[47] Kennan later apologized that the cable read like a primer published by "the Daughters of the American Revolution, designed to arouse the citizenry to the dangers of the Communist conspiracy."[48]

On March 5, Winston Churchill, no longer prime minister, spoke in Fulton, Missouri. President Truman sat prominently on the platform and heard the eloquent orator declare that the United States "stands at this time at the pinnacle of world power." Churchill then lashed out at the Soviets: "From Stettin in the Baltic to Trieste in the Adriatic, an iron curtain has descended across the Continent."[49]

Winston S. Churchill (1874–1965) in Fulton. Churchill (far left) received applause from President Harry S. Truman (far right) during the former British prime minister's visit to Westminster College in Fulton, Missouri. There Churchill delivered his provocative oration against the "iron curtain." He had been defeated for reelection in 1945, but he returned as prime minister in 1951, retiring in 1955. (Truman Library and Westminster College)

Most Americans applauded his stiff anti-Soviet tone, but they warmed much less to his call for an Anglo-American alliance outside the fledgling United Nations Organization. "Winnie, Winnie, go away, G.I. Joe is home to stay," students chanted at Harvard University.[50] Churchill's forceful speech pleased Truman. Secretary Henry A. Wallace, a dissenter from the "get tough" approach, feared that the Anglo-Americans were trying to "strut around the world and tell people where to get off."[51] An angry Stalin asserted that nations would not exchange the "lordship of Hitler for the lordship of Churchill."[52]

The Iranian crisis disturbed Soviet-American relations at the same time. The crisis began quietly in 1944 when British and American oil companies applied for Iranian concessions. It became a classic example of competition for spheres of influence. Unwilling to be excluded from a bordering country, the Soviet Union soon applied for an oil concession too. The British, who had long dominated Iran, no longer had the power to sustain their position. London discovered that the wartime and postwar American quest for petroleum in the Middle East served as a counterweight against the Soviets. By 1944 American corporations controlled 42 percent of the "proved" oil reserves of the Middle East, a nineteenfold increase in American holdings there since 1936.

A 1942 treaty with Iran allowed the British and Soviets to occupy the country and required them to leave six months after the end of the war. American soldiers and supply units also went to Iran, primarily to facilitate Lend-Lease shipments to the Soviet Union. In mid-1945 the Soviets backed an indigenous rebellion in northern Iran (Azerbaijan) against the central government in Teheran. In January 1946, working with American officials, Iran took the question of Soviet meddling to the new United Nations Organization. The indignant Soviets pointed out that British troops remained. Iran and Russia entered direct negotiations, but they did not reach an accord by March 2 when all foreign troops, by treaty, had to depart. U.S. soldiers had withdrawn in January, but left military advisers behind; British troops departed in early March. The Soviets thus stood alone in defiance of the treaty and, in Truman's exaggerated view, the Soviets threatened a "giant pincers movement" toward the Mediterranean and the Near East.[53] In April, however, Moscow and Teheran concluded an agreement and Soviet forces left. In exchange for this withdrawal, Iran agreed to establish a joint Iranian-Soviet oil company, subject to approval by its parliament. After this agreement, the Iranian prime minister took a strong stand against the Soviet Union and the rebels in Azerbaijan, often following the advice of American ambassador George V. Allen. In late 1946, Iranian armed forces, advised by Major General Robert W. Grow of the U.S. Army, squelched the insurrection in northern Iran. The Soviets took no steps to defend their Azerbaijani friends. Not until October 1947 did the legislature consider the joint oil company; it rejected the agreement by a vote of 102 to 2.

The Soviets exploded in anger. They had departed Iran while Britain and the United States had driven in stakes. Arthur C. Millspaugh, former U.S. financial adviser to the Iranian government, pinpointed the security issue: "Iran's geographic relation to the Soviet Union is roughly comparable to the relation of Mexico or Canada to the United States."[54] The Soviets wanted what the British and Americans already had—oil and influence—and feared the foreign penetration of a neighboring state. Years later, Truman embellished the Iranian story by claiming that he had sent the Soviets an ultimatum to get out of Iran or face American troops, but the State Department has denied the existence of such a message. Yet this myth suggests the simple lesson Americans drew from the conflict: "Get tough" and the Soviets will give way. Secretary Wallace saw it differently and told a Madison Square Garden audience in September 1946: "'Getting tough' never brought anything real and lasting—whether for schoolyard bullies or businessmen or world powers. The tougher we get, the tougher the Russians will get."[55] Truman fired him from the cabinet. "The Reds, phonies and 'parlor pinks' seem to be banded together and are becoming a national danger. I am afraid they are a sabotage front for Uncle Joe Stalin," the president steamed.[56]

Other issues heightened friction in 1946 and illustrated Truman's "get tough" policy. During the war, Moscow asked Washington for a major postwar reconstruction loan. Although some U.S. diplomats thought such economic assistance would help improve Soviet-American relations, others anticipated leverage to pry concessions from the Soviets. Seeing U.S. aid as one of America's "cards" in the Cold War game, Truman decided to brandish assistance for the USSR's massive reconstruction task as a weapon rather than as a tool.[57] But as Ambassador Harriman

W. Averell Harriman (1891–1986). Graduate of Yale, heir to the Harriman railroad empire, investment banker of Brown Brothers, and diplomat, Harriman was one of America's great public servants in the twentieth century. He served as ambassador to Russia (1943–1946), ambassador to Great Britain (1946), secretary of commerce (1946–1948), and U.S. representative in Europe for the Marshall Plan. Later he advised Presidents John F. Kennedy and Lyndon B. Johnson. Maxim Litvinov once asked: "How can a man with a hundred million dollars look so sad?" (*The Reporter,* 1950. Copyright 1950 by Fortnightly Publishing Co., Inc.)

admitted, the U.S. rejection of the Soviet loan request in early 1946 actually "may have contributed to their avaricious policies" in Eastern Europe.[58] In contrast, Washington granted Britain a $3.75 billion loan in mid-1946 in return for British promises to open trade in their Sterling Bloc.

The Baruch Plan, presented to the United Nations Atomic Energy Commission in July 1946, also divided the United States and the Soviet Union. The plan emerged from months of intra-administration talks, but its final touches belonged to Bernard Baruch, the uncompromising American negotiator. He outlined the proposal for control of atomic weapons: (1) the creation of an international authority; (2) the international control of fissionable raw materials by this authority; (3) inspections to prevent violations; (4) no Security Council vetoes of control or inspections; (5) global distribution of atomic plants for peaceful purposes; (6) cessation of the manufacture of atomic bombs; (7) destruction of existing bombs; (8) these procedures to occur in stages, with abandonment of the U.S. atomic bomb monopoly coming last.

Not until the last stage, after the Soviets had given up atomic bomb development and fissionable materials within their country, and submitted to inspections, would the United States relinquish its monopoly. The United States would also control a majority of the members of an international authority, and most of the plants would be in areas friendly to the United States. "In other words," Wallace wrote the president, "we are telling the Russians that if they are 'good boys' we may eventually turn over our knowledge of atomic energy to them."[59] About the same time, the Soviet ambassador in Washington, Nikolai Novikov, warned his superiors that the United States was "striving for world supremacy."[60] Moscow not surprisingly rejected the Baruch Plan, and the stalemate persisted until 1949, when the Soviets successfully exploded their first atomic device.

The issue of Germany—zones, reparations, central administration, demilitarization, and the dismantling of war-oriented factories—deepened the schism between the former Allies. France, Britain, the USSR, and the United States each had a zone in defeated Germany and in Berlin, and each did what it liked. The vengeful French proved the most obstructionist, refusing to permit any centralized German agencies and pushing for permanent dismemberment. The Soviets tried with mixed success to grab reparations, thereby weakening the entire German economy. The British tried to bestow socialism on their district, but generally wanted a strong Germany to which they could sell goods and from which they could receive coal. The United States sought, according to the Potsdam accords, to treat Germany as one economic unit to speed reconstruction. Never again, vowed Truman, would America "pay reparations, feed the world, and get nothing for it but a nose thumbing."[61] With the Morgenthau Plan near death by 1946, new plans evolved to reconstruct steel- and coal-rich Germany as the vital center of a revived European economy. Washington also implemented Project Paperclip to bring German scientists and technicians to the United States to assist in the "development of new types of weapons."[62]

Berlin Airlift.   In May 1949, at the close of the crisis over the Berlin blockade, American military personnel celebrate victory for "Operation Vittles." During the blockade, Soviet-sponsored Radio Berlin aired propaganda against the West: "What has American imperialism to offer us in the way of culture? Is it the boogie-woogie culture and the sensational and immoral films which appeal to the lowest instincts? . . . Is it the shameless exploitation of the poverty of our young women which makes them into soldiers' prostitutes and infects our girls with American syphilis at the price of a bar of chocolate and a few Camels?" (U.S. Air Force)

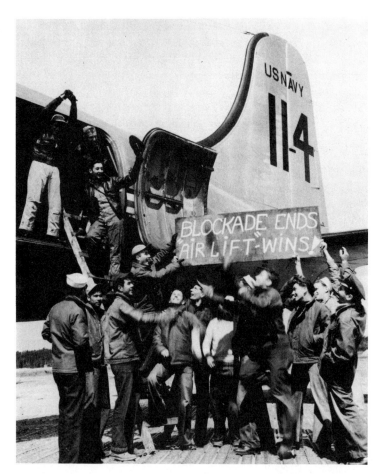

The dismantling of industrial plants slowed down, and in May 1946, American military governor Lucius Clay halted all reparations shipments from the American zone. No more reparations, he told the Soviets, until they contributed to German economic unity. As former president Herbert Hoover concluded after a fact-finding mission: "We can keep Germany in these economic chains but it will also keep Europe in rags."[63] In December 1946, the British and Americans combined their zones into "Bizonia." The Federal Republic of Germany (West Germany), a consolidation of "Bizonia" with the French zone, formed in May 1949. The Soviets, however, economically exhausted their zone and retaliated in October 1949 with the establishment of their client, the German Democratic Republic (East Germany).

The Soviets initiated the Berlin blockade (June 1948–May 1949) to impede the unilateral Western issuance of a new German currency, which they read as another sign of a unified nation tied to the West. They sealed off land access to Berlin, perhaps hoping to prompt negotiations. One U.S. general urged that an armored column proceed down the East German access road and another advised bombing Soviet troops. Truman chose a less provocative airlift. U.S. planes soon swept into the western part of the city with food, fuel, and other supplies. He also ordered B-29 bombers to England, concealing the fact that they went without any of the fifty atomic bombs then in the U.S. arsenal. Although Truman thought it "no time to be juggling an atom bomb," his public comment that he would use "the bomb" if necessary chilled people everywhere.[64] For their part, the Soviets never shot down an American cargo plane. Moscow lifted the blockade, but only after suffering worldwide reproach and the creation of the West Germany it had so wanted to prevent. Americans drew another Cold War lesson: to win, never flinch in the face of communist aggression.

THE TRUMAN DOCTRINE, ISRAEL, AND CONTAINMENT

On March 12, 1947, President Harry S. Truman spoke dramatically to a special joint session of Congress. Greece and Turkey, he said, faced grave threats. Unless the United States offered help, "we may endanger the peace of the world—and we shall surely endanger the welfare of this Nation." History seemed to be repeating itself. The Greek-Turkish crisis raised the specter of Hitler and World War II all over again. Truman invoked the peace and prosperity idiom when he declared that the "seeds of totalitarian regimes are nurtured by misery and want." His most famous words became known as the Truman Doctrine, the commanding guide to U.S. foreign policy in the Cold War: "I believe that it must be the policy of the United States to support free peoples who are resisting attempted subjugation by armed minorities or by outside pressures."[65] Truman asked for $400 million to ensure this policy's success. The president's address was short on analysis of the civil war in Greece and the Soviet-Turkish controversy over the strategic Dardanelles, but long on clichés, alarmist language, and panacea. He played on the words *free* and *democratic,* leaving the mistaken impression that they fit the Greek and Turkish governments. Presidential aide Clark Clifford called it "the opening gun in a campaign to bring the people up to [the] realization that the war isn't over by any means."[66]

A lingering squabble over the Dardanelles and a British request for help in Greece served as immediate catalysts for the Truman Doctrine. When the Germans withdrew from hobbled Greece in 1944, much of the countryside had come under the control of communist and other leftist Greek nationalist resistance fighters, the ELAS (National Popular Liberation Army) and their political arm, the EAM (National Liberation Front). Intent on reestablishing their imperial rule in Greece, the British soon installed a government in Athens. Violence erupted in December 1944. British troops, transported to Greece on U.S. ships, joined by rightist sympathizers, and spurred by Churchill's pledge of "no peace without victory," engaged the leftists in vicious warfare.[67] The rebels, thinking themselves within reach of political power through elections, signed a peace treaty in February 1945.

From then until March 1946, when the civil war flared again, the corrupt British-sponsored Athens regime set about to eliminate its political foes. The United States sent warships to Greek ports and offered aid through the Export-Import Bank. In September, Secretary Forrestal announced that the United States would maintain a permanent fleet in the Mediterranean. Although wary about a Greek government that one American official described as "completely reactionary, . . . incredibly weak, stupid, and venal," Washington still considered a friendly regime better than a leftist or communist one.[68] Greece limped along, staggered by war-wrought devastation and civil turmoil. Britain, suffering its imperial death throes, could no longer pay the Greek bill. On February 21, 1947, the British informed Washington that they were pulling out. Truman's special message to Congress answered the British appeal with uncommon alacrity.

Many members of Congress resented Truman's having handed them a fait accompli on March 12, 1947. Critics argued that Truman bypassed the United Nations by giving direct aid to Greece and Turkey and backed a ruthless Greek regime. Others worried about the cost of the program, preferred economic over military aid, and feared that the Soviets would read the Truman Doctrine as threatening a world crusade. The Truman administration enlisted the support of Senator Vandenberg in a prime example of bipartisan foreign policy. The Michigan Republican, who often warned against another Munich, predicted a "Communist chain reaction from the Dardanelles to the China Sea and westward to the rim of the Atlantic."[69] Most leaders accepted what would later be called the "domino theory." On April 22 the Senate passed the bill for aid to Greece and Turkey, 67 to 23; the House followed on May 15 with a positive voice vote.

Critics had challenged the administration's contention that Soviet aggression threatened Greece and Turkey, but received lame answers. It became clear why. The EAM, although communist-led, had minimal ties with the Soviet Union. Churchill more than once said that Stalin had kept the bargain he made at their 1944 Moscow conference to stay out of the Greek imbroglio. In fact, Stalin disliked the nationalist Greek communists because they admired the independent-minded Yugoslav leader Tito, who gave them aid. Yet Truman believed that all communists took their orders from Moscow.

The Dardanelles question also had more complexity than Truman acknowledged. The United States urged international control over the straits. The Soviets saw the issue quite differently, for they had witnessed Turkish behavior during World War II that permitted German warships to pass through the straits into the Black Sea. Stalin insisted at Yalta that Russia could no longer "accept a situation in which Turkey had a hand on Russia's throat."[70] For its part, Turkey refused joint control with the Soviets. The Soviets lambasted the Turks, threatening to take action. Turkey, stated one State Department report, "constitutes the stopper in the neck of the bottle through which Soviet political and military influence could most effectively flow into the eastern Mediterranean and Middle East."[71] Stalin once asked: "What would Great Britain do if Spain or Egypt were given this [Turkish] right to close the Suez Canal, or what would the United States Government say if some South American Republic had the right to close the Panama Canal?"[72] The Truman administration exaggerated the issue: The Soviets wanted to subjugate Turkey. U.S. aid to Turkey under the Truman Doctrine pulled that Mediterranean nation and Soviet neighbor into the U.S. orbit.

The Dardanelles issue became a perennial Cold War subject, whereas the Greek civil war ended when the rebels capitulated in October 1949. American aid and advisers had flowed to Greece after 1947, with U.S. officials taking charge of the Greek government. More than 350 American officers accompanied the Greek army in its campaign against the EAM. Greece became dependent on American assistance, and it too entered the U.S. sphere of influence. Truman claimed another Cold War victory, but the Greek insurgents lost not only because of American intervention, but because the Soviet Union refused to help them and Tito sealed off the Yugoslav border to deny Greek leftists a sanctuary. Soothing and distorting simplicity had overcome complexity in U.S. thinking. As one student of America's response to revolutions has concluded: "The fifth-column analogy from World War II dominated official thinking. The possibility that men had taken to the hills for reasons of their own and not as agents of a foreign power was never seriously considered."[73]

U.S. interest in the Mediterranean region also entangled the United States in the Palestine question, "an open sore, the infection from which tends to spread rather than to become localized."[74] Zionists had long sought a Jewish homeland, and at the end of World War II they pressed London and Washington to open British-mandated Palestine to Holocaust survivors. As Britain stalled, blocking immigration and turning back ships like the *Exodus* loaded with Jewish refugees, extremist Zionists vowed to take up arms. At first, U.S. Mideast policy sought to satisfy the Arabs, who opposed increased Jewish immigration and a new Jewish state, because Washington valued Mideast oil and Arab anticommunism. At the same time, many Americans, including President Truman, welcomed the humanitarian opportunity to assist displaced persons whose lives had been so terrorized by Nazism. The astute politician in Truman also spoke: "I have to answer to hundreds of thousands who are anxious for the success of Zionism," he told U.S. diplomats posted in the Middle East. "I do not have hundreds of thousands of Arabs among my constituents."[75]

George F. Kennan (b. 1904). Graduate of Princeton, Pulitzer Prize–winning historian, career diplomat, and recognized expert on Soviet affairs, Kennan was Mr. "X" in 1947 when he articulated the containment doctrine. This brilliant man served Ambassador Harriman in Moscow and then headed the State Department's Policy Planning Staff (1947–1949). Later he became ambassador to Russia (1952) and Yugoslavia (1961–1963). In the 1970s and 1980s he emerged as a leading critic of the nuclear arms race, imploring leaders to "cease this madness." (The Institute for Advanced Study, Princeton, New Jersey)

The beleaguered British decided to abandon the Palestine question to the United Nations, whose special commission recommended partition into Jewish and Arab states, with 56 percent of the mandate area assigned to the Zionists. America's UN ambassador embarrassingly exhorted Arabs and Jews to "settle this problem in a true Christian spirit."[76] Truman groped for a policy while he exploded against Zionists who castigated him for not demanding an independent Jewish nation: "Jesus Christ couldn't please them when he was here on earth, so how could anyone expect that I would have any luck?"[77] Although such statements smacked of anti-Semitism, the president hoped to win the large Jewish vote in the forthcoming presidential election, and he resented unyielding State Department officials who kept predicting that acceptance of partition would alienate Arabs and lose the United States allies in the Cold War. In fall 1947 Truman chose partition. The Syrian delegate to the United Nations joined other Mideast leaders in denouncing the "flagrant" American "partisanship toward the Zionists."[78] Fighting between Arabs and Jews escalated, and millions of private dollars from Jewish Americans flowed to compatriots in Palestine to buy weapons. (By war's end in early 1949, some 780,000 of 1,300,000 Arab residents had been displaced; many of these Palestinians became refugees in Lebanon and Jordan. Having jettisoned the partition plan, Jews came to occupy 77 percent of Palestine.)

Truman tilted further toward the Zionists after his old business partner Eddie Jacobson arranged a visit from Chaim Weizmann in March 1948. This Zionist leader (and soon to be the first president of Israel) had once thought Truman "will never jeopardize his oil concessions for the sake of the Jews, although he may need them when the time of election arrives."[79] For reasons of politics and Cold War strategy, Truman formally extended diplomatic recognition to a new Jewish state on May 14, 1948, just nine minutes after Zionists declared the existence of Israel. Two presidential aides and Zionist sympathizers, David Niles and Max Lowenthal, had persuaded Truman that Israel would "line up on the side of the United States a far abler force" than the Arabs, thereby bolstering the American position vis-à-vis the Soviet Union in the Middle East.[80] And Clark Clifford, another pro-Zionist as-

Chaim Weizmann (1874–1952) in Israel, 1948. A Russian-born Zionist and first president of Israel, Weizmann visits women soldiers of the new Jewish nation. (UPI/Bettmann)

sistant, advised that "shilly-shallying appeasement" of the Arabs would cause "contempt" for the United States around the world, thus serving Soviet ambitions.[81] Despite Secretary of State George Marshall's blunt comment that he "would vote against the president" in the election if Truman recognized Israel for political expediency, subsequent Israeli military victories over the armies of five Arab states prompted even the State Department to reassess Israel's importance as a strategic Cold War asset and potential ally in the containment of the Soviet Union.[82] Moscow itself recognized Israel, reducing the risk that U.S. recognition would drive angry Arabs into the Soviet camp.

Containment became the byword of the time, and George F. Kennan, director of the State Department's Policy Planning Staff, wrote the definitive statement. The July 1947 issue of the prestigious journal *Foreign Affairs* carried an article titled "The Sources of Soviet Conduct," written by a mysterious Mr. "X," soon revealed as Kennan. The United States must adopt a "policy of firm containment," he wrote, "designed to confront the Russians with unalterable counterforce, at every point where they show signs of encroaching upon the interests of a peaceful and stable world." Such pressure might force the "mellowing" of Soviet power. Kennan sketched a picture of an aggressive, uncompromising Soviet Union driven by ideology. Mechanistic Soviet power, he wrote, "moves inexorably along a prescribed path, like a persistent toy automobile wound up and headed in a given direction, stopping only when it meets some unanswerable force."[83] Kennan seemed vague on whether to use economic or military means to implement containment—a key question thereafter.

One of the most vocal critics of containment, the journalist Walter Lippmann, predicted trouble. In a series of articles published as *The Cold War* (1947), Lippmann called containment a "strategic monstrosity" because it did not distinguish vital from peripheral areas. Containment would test American resources and patience without limit. What if Congress should decide not to fund some presidential ventures in "counter-force"? Lippmann also prophetically observed that the "policy can be implemented only by recruiting, subsidizing and supporting a heterogeneous array of satellites, clients, dependents and puppets." Instead of a global crusade, he proposed the removal of all foreign troops from Europe to ease tension. He denied the popular notion that Soviet forces stood poised to attack Western Europe, a point on which he and Kennan agreed. Finally, Lippmann sadly concluded that Truman and Mr. "X" in their major statements had abandoned their essential responsibility—diplomacy. "For a diplomat to think that rival and unfriendly powers cannot be brought to a settlement is to forget what diplomacy is about."[84]

THE MARSHALL PLAN, NATO, AND THE DIVISION OF EUROPE

In 1947–1948, under the banner of containment, U.S. goals for Western Europe crystallized: economic reconstruction and hunger relief, linkage of Germany's western zones with a Western European economic system, reinvigorated trade with the United States, prevention of leftist political gains, ouster of communists from governments (especially in Italy and France), settlement of colonial disputes (as in Indochina and Indonesia) that were draining funds, blockage of neutralist tendencies, and building military allies. By 1947 the United States had already spent $9 billion in the region. Despite assistance through the United Nations Relief and Rehabilitation Administration, the World Bank, and the International Monetary Fund, plus the loan to Britain and expenditures for the military occupation of Germany, Washington had failed to secure peace and prosperity. Europe remained prostrate, and Americans predicted that communists would exploit the economic chaos. Europe's multibillion-dollar deficit, furthermore, posed a real danger to the American economy—Europeans could not buy American products unless they received dollars from the United States.

On June 5, 1947, at Harvard University, Secretary of State George C. Marshall called for a comprehensive, coordinated program to put Europe back on its feet. A halting, quiet orator, Marshall delivered a monumental message in only 1,500 words. A distraught Europe had to have help to face "economic, social and political deterioration of a very grave character."[85] He vaguely called on the European nations to initiate a collective plan. Recognizing that "if we want to act singlehandedly, we lose everything," British foreign secretary Ernest Bevin and French foreign minister Georges Bidault conferred and soon accepted Marshall's proposal, ultimately shaping it according to American specifications.[86] They reluctantly invited Soviet foreign minister V. M. Molotov to join them for a meeting in Paris.

The seemingly open Marshall invitation and the Bevin–Bidault request stimulated intense discussion among Kremlin leaders. They sniffed a capitalist trap. Yet Molotov, according to two Russian scholars using newly opened archives, "initially planned to join the European recovery program. Only after he sensed Stalin's mood did he make a U-turn."[87] The scowling commissar thus convened with the French and British in Paris in late June and early July. Bevin and Bidault maneuvered to forestall Soviet participation. Opposed to any program dominated by the United States, Molotov suggested loosely structured arrangements designed to protect national sovereignties. Bevin and Bidault, knowing that Washington insisted on an integrated effort, rejected national shopping lists. Molotov abruptly left town, and he recalled in his unrepentant memoirs that "if *they* think we made a mistake in rejecting the Marshall Plan, that means we acted correctly."[88]

The United States had never wanted or expected Soviet participation in the European Recovery Program (ERP), as the Marshall Plan became known. "At best," the historian Michael J. Hogan has written, "American officials saw Marshall's plan as a way to break Soviet influence in Eastern Europe; at worst, they were counting on Soviet opposition to galvanize support for the plan in Congress."[89] Moscow rejected the Marshall Plan because Eastern Europe was expected to ship raw materials to industrial Western Europe, ensuring dependency on the West; because a large influx of dollars into the Soviet sphere of influence would directly challenge Soviet interests; and because the plan intended to revive West Germany. In any case Congress would probably have shunned funding a recovery program that included the Soviet Union and its neighbors. The Soviets ultimately organized a feeble Molotov Plan for Eastern Europe to counter the Organization of European Economic Cooperation set up to administer the Marshall Plan.

V. M. Molotov (1890–1986). Popularly known as "stone ass," the Soviet foreign minister (1939–1949; 1952–1956), a tough-minded negotiator, cleared most decisions with Stalin. When he became angry, a bump appeared on his forehead, alerting adversaries of trouble. American diplomats uniformly disliked him. (*The Reporter*, 1956. Copyright 1956 by The Reporter Magazine Co.)

After months of discussion about how much to spend and after a huge administration advertising campaign, Congress in March 1948 passed the Economic Cooperation Act. The coup in Czechoslovakia, scheduled elections in Italy (would they go communist?), and the growing crisis over Germany, together with a March 17 Truman war scare speech to a joint session of Congress, garnered the Marshall Plan a vote of 69 to 17 in the Senate and 329 to 74 in the House. Congress approved $4 billion for the program's first year. Before ending in December 1951, the Economic Cooperation Administration had sent 12.4 billion Marshall Plan dollars into the needy European economy. The Marshall Plan proved a mixed success. In Europe it caused inflation, failed to solve a serious balance-of-payments problem, and took only tentative steps toward economic integration. But it sparked impressive Western European industrial production and investment and started the region toward self-sustaining economic growth. The ERP, remarked Bevin, acted "like a lifeline to sinking men."[90]

From the American perspective, the Marshall Plan served both self-interested and humanitarian purposes. It stimulated the U.S. economy by requiring recipients to spend some aid in the United States on American goods; in this way, the valuable flow of American exports to traditional European markets continued. It helped put people back to work in the factories and mines of the devastated continent, it

Essen, Germany. In the rubble of this German city rested a new citizen, who because of American reconstruction aid apparently enjoyed a full stomach. According to the historian Thomas A. Schwartz, "the United States pursued a 'dual containment' policy in Europe, designed to keep both the Soviet Union and Germany from dominating the Continent. . . . The two policies, which were inextricably linked, were always in a delicate balance; the United States could not contain the Soviet Union in Europe without German strength, and it could not maintain its hold over the German Federal Republic without the Soviet threat." (Harry S. Truman Library)

"aided and accelerated . . . the anti-Communist shift of the European trade union movement," and it won friends and votes for those nonradical political parties that backed the generous U.S. project.[91]

The Marshall Plan had shortcomings, too. Europe became dependent on American aid, less able to make its own choices. The French complained about "Coca-colonization."[92] The publisher of *Le Monde* remarked to Walter Lippmann, no doubt with exaggeration for effect, that "France under the Marshall Plan and the Truman Doctrine was becoming a sort of Philippines."[93] Some American money funded European resistance to colonial wars. The program bypassed the United Nations and the Economic Commission for Europe, where it might have operated with less divisiveness. The Marshall Plan created a deeper rift between the two rivals. It encouraged restrictions on East-West trade, and helped revive West Germany, thereby arousing Moscow's fears of its nemesis. A European Recovery Program was sorely needed, but how the United States presented and shaped it in part explains why it became divisive. The Marshall Plan, in the end, gave way to military aid. In 1951 the Economic Cooperation Administration merged into the

Mutual Security Administration, and by 1952 80 percent of American aid to Western Europe had become military in nature.

From the beginning of the Cold War, American foreign policy had included a military dimension. Much of Greek-Turkish aid, for example, consisted of military hardware. In July 1947, Congress passed the National Security Act, which streamlined the military establishment. The act created the Department of Defense, the National Security Council (NSC) to advise the president, and the Central Intelligence Agency (CIA) to gather and collate information through spying and other unspecified functions, which later came to mean covert activities against foreign governments or citizens. In Europe in March 1948, Britain, France, and the three Benelux nations, with U.S. encouragement, signed the Brussels Treaty for collective defense. In June the Senate passed (64 to 4) Vandenberg's resolution applauding that effort and suggesting American participation.

Dollar and Atomic Diplomacy. In this Soviet view of U.S. foreign policy, Truman wields the atomic bomb and the money bag. Note Winston S. Churchill on the right. (*Krokodil,* USSR)

Truman summarized American foreign policy in his Inaugural Address of January 20, 1949. Articulating simple juxtapositions of "communism" and "democracy," the president listed four central points. First, he endorsed the United Nations. Second, he applauded the European Recovery Program. Third, he announced that the United States was planning a North Atlantic defense pact. And fourth, "we must embark on a bold new program" of technical assistance for "underdeveloped areas," a reference to the Point Four Program, to be launched in 1950.[94] The new secretary of state, Dean Acheson, concluded negotiations on the defense pact. "He was present only on the sixth, the last day of creation," a Canadian diplomat later wrote of Acheson, "but that was a particularly busy day."[95] On April 4, 1949, the North Atlantic Treaty was signed in Washington by the five Brussels Treaty countries of Britain, France, Belgium, the Netherlands, and Luxembourg, as well as by Denmark, Iceland, Italy, Norway, Portugal, Canada, and the United States. (Greece and Turkey joined in 1952 and West Germany in 1954.) Article 5 provided "that an armed attack against one or more . . . shall be considered an attack against them all."[96]

Acheson anticipated heated debate at home. After all, the United States had not participated in a European alliance since the days of George Washington, and by 1949 an entangling alliance for some Americans seemed worse than original sin. Article 5, said critics, meant that the United States was creating a Pearl Harbor in every NATO country, drawing America into a war even if it did not want to go. "Mr. Republican," Senator Robert Taft of Ohio, recoiled from NATO, considering it a threat to Russia that would eventually force the United States to send military aid to Europe and a stimulant to an arms race. Taft noted that the president could commit American troops almost at will without constitutional restraint. Some dissenters questioned the precise nature of the Soviet threat: Was it military, political, or ideological? After all, no Soviet military attack seemed imminent. Other critics from both the left and right thought that the United States was overextending itself—in short, weakening rather than strengthening its position.

The critics made little impact. James Reston of the *New York Times* reported that "there seems to be ignorance about specific parts of the treaty, indifference or a certain fatalistic approach to the future, combined with an acceptance of the idea

Dean Acheson (1893–1971). A graduate of Yale and Harvard and a wealthy lawyer, Acheson described himself as "always a conservative." Polished and arrogant, he served as secretary of state for 1949–1953. "There's no way to argue with a river," Acheson once said about the Soviets. "You can channel it; you can dam it up. But you can't argue with it." (Portrait by Gardner Cox, National Portrait Gallery, Smithsonian Institution, Gift of Covington and Burling)

of 'doing something' about the Russians."[97] Vandenberg endorsed NATO as a healthy reversal of the Neutrality Acts, which, he said, had encouraged Hitler. When asked in Senate hearings whether the United States planned to send substantial numbers of American troops to Europe to stand in the way of a potential Soviet attack, Secretary Acheson replied "no." Without U.S. troops, one British official remarked, the alliance looked "like the Venus de Milo, plenty of SHAPE, but no arms."[98] But, even though Soviet divisions far outnumbered those of Western Europe, the United States possessed atomic weapons and planned to destroy USSR cities if Soviet forces ever started a war by moving westward. Soviet knowledge of these war plans provided deterrence enough. George F. Kennan, increasingly disaffected from the American militarization and nuclearization of the Cold War, argued that, because few U.S. leaders anticipated a Soviet military thrust, NATO served no military need.

Although NATO did stand as a "trip wire" warning to the Soviets, the United States welcomed NATO as much for political as for military purposes. A popular saying explained that NATO kept the Soviets out, the Americans in, and the Germans down. That is, NATO gave the United States influence in Europe—an extension of the Monroe Doctrine, one senator claimed. Through NATO Washington could blunt neutralist tendencies or revival of an "appeasement psychology."[99] The alliance also permitted the United States to rearm West Germany while reassuring Europeans that Germany would be controlled by a multinational organization. With the Marshall Plan launched, moreover, U.S. officials believed that Western Europe needed a "general stiffening of morale" through the creation of NATO, to stimulate capital investment and encourage an energetic reconstruction effort.[100] "Europe under American water cans handled by British gardeners blossoms into a happy Garden of Eden," as one diplomat phrased it.[101]

On July 21, 1949, the Senate ratified the NATO Treaty by a handsome 82 to 13 margin. Truman, who had had an enduring respect for the military ever since his own Battery "D" days in World War I, signed the treaty two days later. That day he also sent the Mutual Defense Assistance Bill to Congress asking for a one-year appropriation of $1.5 billion for European military aid. Containment had taken a distinct turn to military means, and the stakes became bigger. In January 1950, shortly after the Soviets exploded an atomic device, Truman ordered speedier development of a thermonuclear or hydrogen "superbomb." George F. Kennan and the scientist J. Robert Oppenheimer opposed the decision, warning that the United States risked accelerating the arms race. By mid-1950 the U.S. arsenal already included some 300 atomic bombs and more than 260 aircraft that could drop them on Soviet targets. The Soviets responded to NATO with the Warsaw Pact in 1955, the same year that they detonated their first hydrogen bomb.

In late January 1950, Truman ordered the State and Defense Departments to prepare a comprehensive review of U.S. military and foreign policy. Eventually tagged National Security Council Paper Number 68 (NSC-68), the April report predicted prolonged global tension, Soviet military expansion, and relentless communist aggression (some read Mao's recent triumph in China as an example of an international conspiracy). According to one student of national security policy, "conventional rearmament and strategic superiority were now deemed indispensable for the risk-taking necessary to co-opt the industrial core of Eurasia, integrate it with the Third World periphery, and maintain America's preponderant position in the international system."[102] Washington had to persuade the public to support larger defense budgets and higher taxes. Paul Nitze, who soon shared "Acheson's wave length" and replaced Kennan as head of the Policy Planning Staff, wrote most of NSC-68, and he glossed over complexities and ambiguities.[103] The document treated communism as a monolith, ignoring differences within the communist community. It spoke of the "free world," overlooking the many nations allied with the United States that had undemocratic governments. It postulated that communism orchestrated the world's troubles, neglecting the indigenous character of nationalist movements that challenged the imperial powers. It made sweeping assumptions about Soviet motives and capabilities without evidence. The report, in short, exaggerated the "threat." Lippmann's counsel against indiscriminate globalism went unheeded; the United States prepared to become the world's policeman. But how to convince Americans to support the report's prescriptions? "We were sweating over it, and then—with regard to NSC-68—thank God Korea came along," recalled an Acheson aide.[104] In September 1950, a few months after the outbreak of the Korean War, Truman ordered NSC-68's implementation.

Just as the United States moved to a harder line in the Cold War, the Soviet Union seemed to shift to a softer one by calling for "peaceful coexistence."[105] In the wake of the Marshall Plan, triumph over the Berlin blockade, and launching of NATO, whereby the United States consolidated its sphere of influence, the Soviets not only reaffirmed their authority over Eastern Europe but also appealed for a Soviet-American dialogue to reduce tensions. Although Winston Churchill and UN leaders urged a summit conference, Washington flatly rejected the Soviet initiative. Acheson ridiculed the Soviet "Trojan dove," vowing to contest the Soviets by building U.S. "situations of strength" throughout the world.[106] As Walter Lippmann had predicted, diplomacy became a victim of the Cold War.

Asian Allies: Restoring Japan and Backing Jiang's China

Asia entered a major process of reconstitution at the end of World War II. In Indochina, Burma, and Indonesia the old imperial system crumbled. Japan suffered defeat and occupation. Korea, formerly dominated by Japan, was divided along the thirty-eighth parallel by the Soviet Union and the United States. Civil war loomed in China. The colonial powers, recognizing their diminished position, looked to the United States to help them salvage what they could. The Pacific Ocean, they agreed quite reluctantly, would become an American sphere of influence.

If the Soviets ran some of the Eastern European countries, the Supreme Commander for the Allied Powers, General Douglas MacArthur, ran Japan. Unlike Germany, Japan had no zones. Despite the establishment of a Far Eastern Advisory

Commission with Soviet membership, the United States rejected Soviet requests for shared power and MacArthur treated Stalin's representative like "a mere piece of furniture."[107] The United States also assumed control over Micronesia (the Marianas, Marshalls, and Carolines), Okinawa, Iwo Jima, and more than a hundred other Pacific outposts. As if to demonstrate the point, on July 7, 1946, the United States tested an atomic bomb on the Marshall Island of Bikini. To avoid the charge of imperial land grabbing, Washington had the United Nations place Micronesia under an American trusteeship. In 1949 MacArthur declared that "now the Pacific had become an Anglo-Saxon lake," and State Department official Dean Rusk wanted "to control every wave in the Pacific."[108]

Although occupation officials planned at first to reform Japan, they reversed course as the Cold War progressed and it appeared that communist Mao Zedong would win in China. Americans now needed a "stable Japan, integrated into the Pacific, friendly to the U.S., and, in case of need, a ready and dependable ally."[109] During 1947–1950, labor unions were restricted, the reparations program curtailed, production controls in war-related industries relaxed, the antitrust program suspended, communists barred from government and university positions, and former Japanese leaders reinstated. But Japan buried its militarism as a more pacifist culture evolved.

The restoration of Japan carried international ramifications. The Chinese communists feared a "devilish scheme" to rebuild Japan as a base for aggression against China.[110] Japanese recovery, U.S. officials argued in early 1950, also required the development of markets for Japanese products in Southeast Asia, Indonesia, the Philippines, Southern Korea, and India, and hence, application of the containment doctrine to undercut communists. The Soviet Union suspiciously eyed the expansion of U.S. power in Asia and protested America's peace treaty negotiations with Japan. In September 1951, the United States and fifty other nations signed a peace treaty that restored Japanese sovereignty, gave the United States a base on Okinawa, and permitted the retention of foreign troops in Japan. The Soviet Union refused to sign. A separate Japanese-American security pact also permitted American troops and planes on Japanese soil. From Pearl Harbor, a merciless war, and the atomic blasts to a peaceful occupation and Japanese-American cooperation—how does one explain the dramatic shift? Continued demonic images and punishment no longer served the interests of either party. Americans sought a Cold War ally, and the Japanese sought a helping hand, an end to militarism, and peace. More, "the same stereotypes that fed superpatriotism and outright race hate were adaptable to cooperation." For example, because Americans viewed the Japanese as lesser men and women, as children, then they could become "good pupils" under U.S. tutelage. And the Japanese philosophy of "proper place" meant that the Japanese could become "good losers" who lose the war but win the peace.[111]

Americans wanted a peaceful China within their sphere of influence too. For decades they had preached the Open Door, dreamed of vast Chinese markets and Christian havens, and considered China a special friend, if not client, of the United States. "With God's help," Senator Kenneth Wherry of Nebraska avowed, Americans would "lift Shanghai up and up, ever up, until it looks just like Kansas City."[112] The Chinese communists in particular had other ideas, challenging the

American-backed regime of Jiang Jieshi. During 1945–1949, the United States became a counterrevolutionary force in a revolutionary country.

American postwar goals, at least as understood in Washington, sought a united noncommunist country under Jiang, trade with the United States, China as a keeper of the balance of power in Asia, and an American ally. At the end of the war, American troops took positions in northern China, including Beijing and Tianjin. They transported Jiang's soldiers to Manchuria in a race to beat the communists there. Hundreds of American military officers advised the Nationalist armed forces.

Changes in Asia After World War II

Countries gaining independence after World War II with dates of independence

*Some of the islands once governed by the United States became independent in 1978 as Tuvalu and in 1979 as Kiribati.

The Soviets, honoring their pledge at Yalta, signed a treaty of friendship with Jiang's regime in August 1945. Moscow appeared to abandon the Chinese communists of Mao Zedong and Zhou Enlai. The Soviets preferred a divided, weak China that would pose no threat along the 4,150 miles of the Sino-Soviet border. Mao seemed too independent-minded, too "Titoist" for the Soviet taste. Stalin called the Chinese "margarine" communists.[113] U.S. Foreign Service Officers such as John Paton Davies and John S. Service reported from China that relations between Moscow and Mao remained fractious and that the communists would probably defeat Jiang without much help from Moscow, despite the presence of Soviet troops in Manchuria.

American ambassador Patrick J. Hurley saw an opportunity (see pages 232–235). If Moscow was jilting the Chinese communists, Hurley reasoned, then Jiang might be able to defeat Mao. The swashbuckling ambassador managed to bring Mao and Jiang together for talks in fall 1945, but Jiang refused to make concessions, confident that the United States was backing him. The talks failed. In November, Hurley, with his typical blast-furnace approach, resigned and charged that "a considerable section of our State Department is endeavoring to support communism in . . . China," in favor of "Mouse Dung" and "Joe N. Lie" (as he called Mao and Zhou).[114] Hurley's vituperative attack on the professional diplomats fed the conspiracy-minded who needed scapegoats for the American frustration over China. The "China experts" had not preferred Mao; they had simply reported that Jiang was corrupt, reactionary, and unlikely to gain the allegiance of the Chinese people, and that the communists would thus gain support. The experts paid for their accuracy; in the early 1950s many of them were ousted from the State Department under pressure from red-baiting Senator Joseph McCarthy. If only the Foreign Service Officers had supported Jiang, bellowed Hurley and McCarthy, then he would have won. History knows few more simplistic distortions of reality.

After the Hurley debacle, in December 1945, Truman sent the "Marshall Mission" to China. Headed by the highly respected General George C. Marshall, it sought to unite the factions under a noncommunist government. The communists, not wanting a bloody civil war and seeing coalition government as a nonviolent route to power, accepted Marshall's cease-fire in January 1946. About the same time, the Soviets pulled out of Manchuria, after having seized equipment as war booty, leaving the area to superior communist forces. By the end of April 1946, 90 percent of Manchuria rested in communist hands. Jiang's decision to storm into Manchuria to challenge Mao doomed the cease-fire. Marshall and the 1,000 U.S. military and naval personnel who advised Jiang's forces could not restrain the overconfident generalissimo, whereupon Chinese communists claimed to "have found out that the real intention of the United States is to dominate China alone."[115] A chagrined Marshall returned to the United States in January 1947 to become secretary of state.

Still hopeful of preventing a communist victory, Truman dispatched a new delegation. The "Wedemeyer Mission" went to China in July 1947. General Albert C. Wedemeyer criticized the disarray of the nationalists, but concluded that China, like Greece, needed an aid program to end the communist menace. He also suggested that a UN commission govern Manchuria. Secretary Marshall vetoed both proposals as impractical. And a UN role in China might prompt the Soviets to suggest one for Greece, where the United States preferred to act alone. But Marshall did release undelivered Lend-Lease goods to Jiang. In autumn 1947 Marshall offered the nationalists arms and ammunition and authorized the Army Advisory Group to train Chinese combat troops on Formosa. In part to answer critics who asked why Greece should be saved from communism but not China, the White House asked Congress in early 1948 for $570 million in China aid. Under the China Aid Act of April, China obtained $400 million—enough to anger Mao further, but far too little to save Jiang. Many members of Congress saw it as a futile gesture to a dying regime, a Truman tactic to deflect criticism.

Despite $3 billion in aid to Jiang since V-J Day, military advisers, and diplomatic missions, Washington failed to stop Mao's ascent. Jiang let inflation run rampant, neglected tax and land reforms, launched risky military expeditions, tolerated corruption, and rejected negotiations. Dispirited soldiers defected from his army. American military equipment fell into communist hands; ironically, in this roundabout way, Mao's troops got more aid from America than from the Soviet Union. "We picked a bad horse," the president lamented.[116] For many Americans, however, "the atheists defeated the Christians in 1949."[117]

THE PEOPLE'S REPUBLIC OF CHINA AND U.S. NONRECOGNITION

In June 1949, Mao Zedong stated that he was leaning to the side of socialism (the Soviet Union) against that "one great imperialist power" (the United States).[118] For many Americans, Mao's strident address simply confirmed Moscow's creation of another puppet state. Despite little evidence of Soviet direction or supply of the Chinese communists and contrary facts that suggested an actual Sino-Soviet schism, Americans preferred the words of Secretary of State Dean Acheson, in the famous *China White Paper* of August 1949, that "the Communist regime serves not [Chinese] interests but those of Soviet Russia."[119] This bald assumption has not enhanced Acheson's reputation. As the historian Akira Iriye has written: "Since the documents in the *White Paper* did not warrant the assertion that the Soviet Union had systematically sought to extend its power and influence in China, Acheson must have come to such a sweeping conclusion through the medium of Cold-War visions."[120] The documents in fact showed little the United States could have done because Jiang himself would do so little. In January 1949 he sent China's gold supplies to the island of Formosa (Taiwan); in December, his Nationalist government followed. Mao's People's Republic, established on October 1, assumed power.

The Truman administration had a difficult time explaining the "fall" of China. Critics such as the publisher Henry R. Luce of *Time* magazine, Republican members of Congress, and missionaries charged that Truman had "lost" China as if it had once "belonged" to the United States. Senator Styles Bridges and Representative

"The Open Door."   The communists, led by Mao Zedong, defeated the crumbling forces of Jiang Jieshi in 1949, opening a door that the United States had tried to keep closed. The American imperialists, Mao claimed, would "make trouble, fail, make trouble again, fail again . . . till their doom." (*The Reporter,* 1950. Copyright 1950 by Fortnightly Publishing Co., Inc.)

Walter Judd headed an informal, noisy, and influential "China Lobby," which for years had advocated a major U.S. intervention in the Chinese civil war. They asked: If American foreign policy sought the containment of communism without geographical limit, as stated in the Truman Doctrine and the "X" article, why did not the United States intervene in China? Truman administration officials answered that China was too large, that a land war in Asia was unthinkable, that Jiang was unmanageable, and that the monetary costs were prohibitive. The administration had tried to apply containment to China. "China lost itself," Acheson once remarked.[121]

The United States did not fail in China because of insufficient aid or lack of concern; rather, more fundamental, top American leaders never understood the dynamic force of a peasant society ripe for change and the real appeal the land-reforming communists had among the Chinese people. Americans never marshaled the courage to admit their mistake in clinging to those whom Truman privately viewed as "grafters and crooks."[122]

After Mao's victory over Jiang, the United States refused to recognize the People's Republic of China. Behind the nonrecognition policy lay mounting Sino-American animosities. In June 1949 communist leaders asked American ambassador J. Leighton Stuart to meet with them. The Truman administration vetoed contact. Not only did Truman fear howling protest from the "China Lobby," but he also resented Chinese communist behavior. In bombastic speeches, they rudely reminded Americans of their imperialist past, including military participation in the Boxer Rebellion, support for Japan's seizure of Shandong in 1919, and naval gunboat patrols on Chinese rivers in the 1920s and 1930s. They confiscated American property and harassed Americans. They kept the U.S. consul general at Mukden under house arrest for two years before expelling him as a spy in October 1949.

From December 1949 through February 1950, in Moscow, Mao negotiated a treaty of friendship and alliance. Fearful of a revived Japan and of the expanded U.S. presence in Asia, Mao needed an ally. Stalin hesitated, wary of a Chinese Tito and a strong China. Despite acrimonious talks because of Soviet desires to retain their spoils won at Yalta, the United States looked on the treaty as evidence of a cohesive Communist monolith. The treaty provided for the withdrawal of Soviet troops from Port Arthur, the transfer of Soviet interests in railroads to China, Soviet commercial rights in Xinjiang (Sinkiang) and Soviet control of Outer Mongolia. Analysts should have noticed the inconsequential foreign aid Moscow promised and the clash of traditional Russian-Chinese national interests. Yet Americans largely ignored the schism, stressed Sino-Soviet ideological affinity, and denounced the treaty as the Soviet conquest of China. The "Chi Commies," as official U.S. telegrams tagged the new Chinese leaders, would not receive U.S. diplomatic recognition. Born in failure, misinterpretation, and exaggeration, the nonrecognition policy set the United States firmly against the largest (650 million people) and potentially most influential nation in Asia. Hoping eventually to drive a wedge between the two communist powers, Assistant Secretary of State Dean Rusk in early 1951 taunted the Chinese: "The Peiping regime may be a colonial Russian government—a Slavic Manchukuo on a larger scale. It is not the Government of China. It does not pass the first test. It is not Chinese."[123]

THE COLD WAR MENTALITY TAKES ROOT

"We thought we could do anything," noted a U.S. writer who recalled the end of World War II. "We were heirs to a smiling and victorious confidence."[124] Indeed, Americans in 1945 exuded a sense of power; the British, the Soviets, and many other foreign observers mentioned it, sometimes with apprehension. Although Western Europeans welcomed American assistance, they regretted their frequent powerlessness against U.S. influence and the "ham-fisted" way Americans pressed the U.S. agenda.[125] America's confidence contributed to a zealous pursuit of goals in the postwar period, as did American ideology, economic needs, and strategic doctrine. Shorn of their ignoble "isolationism," determined to throw off the failures of the depression decade, and committed to a world of peace and prosperity on their terms, Americans grew outraged when the Soviet Union challenged the American mission and opportunity. In their frustration to explain how the grand ideals of the Allies had deteriorated to the bickering of the Cold War, Americans—leaders and common folk alike—often adopted superficial assumptions and an uncompromising diplomatic style.

"After World War II," Senator J. William Fulbright remembered, "we were sold on the idea that Stalin was out to dominate the world. I didn't have the knowledge or the foresight to make a judgment at the time. . . . Henry Wallace sensed it, he had a feeling about it, but he was ridiculed for being a visionary, an appeaser, unrealistic."[126] As Fulbright suggested, a popular idea captivated many Americans in the early Cold War: The Soviet Union had launched a crusade to communize the world. Appearances fed such a notion. Austere, intransigent, and ruthless, Stalin became in American eyes an obstructionist. Soviet diplomatic machinations and strong-arm rule in Eastern Europe alarmed Washington, and simple-minded communist ideology and propaganda offended. The Soviet diplomatic style struck Americans as rude, with threats as common as compromises.

In the turmoil of the immediate postwar years, Americans exaggerated the Soviet/communist threat, imagining an omnipresent force. Americans made the communist adversary into something it was not, claiming for it a strength it did not possess, blaming it for trouble it did not start, identifying a monolith it did not resemble, and attributing to it accomplishments it did not achieve. To be sure, the tough-talking Soviets eventually turned Eastern Europe into client states and probed in Berlin, but right after World War II the Soviets acted cautiously because they suffered extreme economic weakness and lacked a long-range air force, air defenses, atomic bomb, and surface fleet. Moscow actually snubbed independent communists like Tito and Mao, could not control communists in Western Europe, and hesitated to challenge the United States and its allies except in areas where Soviet security seemed vulnerable—that is, in areas contiguous to the Soviet Union.

In the heat of the Cold War, Americans nonetheless came to believe that Moscow ignited, fueled, and exploited unrest around the world, including revolutions. Most upheaval actually sprang from indigenous sources—colonial, tribal, ethnic, religious, cultural, economic. Downplaying the internal causes for political and social disorder and the diversity among nations, Americans posited a mechanistic "domino theory." Intent on erecting a global wall against communism, the United States supported imperialist allies such as France, which attempted to restore its colonial power in Vietnam against a popular nationalist movement (see pages 377–380). Believing that the Soviet Union masterminded revolutions directed specifically against the interests of the United States, Washington sniffed international conspiracy and refused to recognize the People's Republic of China, hardly a Soviet puppet. Dependent on imports of uranium and other strategic minerals from South Africa to sustain a Cold War nuclear strategy and economy, the Truman administration backed white, anticommunist regimes that suppressed black nationalism, acting, in the historian Thomas Borstelmann's phrase, "as a reluctant uncle—or godparent—at the baptism of apartheid."[127] In the "zero-sum" thinking of the Cold War era (holding that any loss for the United States was a gain for the Soviet Union), Washington exercised its extraordinary power to win and hold friends, however unsavory.

The American Cold War mentality explained international relations in simple "good guys–bad guys" terms. The malevolent Soviets acted; the heroic Americans reacted. The Soviets aggressed; Americans defended. The expansive term "national security" took on an almost sacred aura, justifying huge military budgets that starved the infrastructure, the suspension of diplomacy in favor of confrontation, interventions far distant from the United States, a secrecy that shrouded foreign-policy decisions and undermined constitutional procedures, and actions Americans condemned others for—manipulating foreign governments, assassinating political foes abroad, and disseminating false information ("disinformation"). Because the Soviets acted similarly, they share responsibility for the extremes and costs of the long Cold War.

To meet the communist threat and to protect and extend traditional overseas interests through "preponderant power," American diplomats in the early Cold War pursued a self-conscious, expansionist, often unilateral foreign policy.[128] In a world ravaged by war, American business and government officials cooperated to expand U.S. foreign trade. By 1947 the United States accounted for one-third of the world's exports. Americans exploited opportunities for Middle Eastern oil and tapped the raw materials of the Third World, importing manganese ore from Brazil and India, for example. The United States continued to preach the Open Door policy to help spur this trade and facilitate the investment of $12 billion abroad by 1950, but other nations complained that they could not compete; therefore the Open Door really invited American domination. Stalin thought the "Open Door policy as dangerous to a nation as foreign military invasion."[129] The foreign aid program of the postwar years aimed in part to keep trade and investments flowing; foreigners could not purchase American products unless they had dollars. One of the chief legacies of the Truman period, then, was the establishment of foreign aid as a major tool of American diplomacy—a way of curbing revolution, thwarting communism, and stimulating the American economy.

The containment doctrine became the commanding principle of American Cold War foreign policy. When Americans had doubts, the containment doctrine told them what to do. There were enough successes, enough "lessons," that it became fixed as a cure-all. "Like medieval theologians," Fulbright noted, "we had a philosophy that explained everything to us in advance, and everything that did not fit could be readily identified as a fraud or a lie or an illusion. . . . The perniciousness of the anti-Communist ideology of the Truman Doctrine arises not from any patent falsehood but from its distortion and simplification of reality, from its universalization and its elevation to the status of a revealed truth."[130] Americans henceforth applied the historical lessons of the 1940s, failing to define precisely the "threat," placing few geographical limits on containment, and increasingly adopting military methods. Whereas Washington explained its mission as containment, Moscow read encirclement. Newly opening Russian archives should help scholars answer the basic question: Did U.S. policies "curb Soviet expansion, or did they rather contribute to the siege mentality, in other words helping to prolong the totalitarian regime and the cold war?"[131]

Another legacy of the early Cold War reshaped the American political process. The Truman administration, sometimes using scare tactics, influenced the thinking of the "foreign-policy public." Most foreign-policy debates centered on how much to spend, not whether to spend. Congress sometimes proved obstinate, but on the whole Truman got what he wanted. The contest with the communists seemed too important to leave to the people, because, as the historian Thomas A. Bailey reasoned, "the masses are notoriously short-sighted and generally cannot see danger until it is at their throats." Concluded Bailey, in an unabashed endorsement of executive infallibility in 1948: "Deception of the people may in fact become increasingly necessary, unless we are willing to give our leaders in Washington a free hand. . . .[T]he yielding of some of our democratic control of foreign affairs is the price that we may have to pay for greater physical security."[132]

"Uncle Sam's World Wide Umbrella." As the donor of large amounts of foreign aid, as the chief partner in military alliances, and as the professor of the containment doctrine, the United States undertook new global responsibilities after World War II. (*The Reporter*, 1950. Copyright 1950 by Fortnightly Publishing Co., Inc.)

Bipartisanship also helped the president control the making of foreign policy. Americans had to speak with unity. As bipartisan leader Vandenberg proudly concluded, "our Government did not splinter. It did not default. It was strong in the presence of its adversaries."[133] But bipartisanship meant too often that legislation received superficial analysis, that debate became pro forma, and that Congress permitted the president considerable freedom in foreign policy, abdicating its own responsibilities. Acheson bluntly remarked: "Bipartisan foreign policy is the ideal for the executive because you cannot run this damned country any other way except by fixing the whole organization so it doesn't work the way it is supposed to work. Now the way to do that is to say politics stops at the seaboard—and anyone who denies that postulate is a son-of-a-bitch and a crook and not a true patriot. Now if people will swallow that, then you're off to the races."[134]

People swallowed it. Debate—testing assumptions and holding government leaders accountable—became shallow. Tolerance of dissenting views and the fearless inquiry so essential to democracy deteriorated during the early Cold War. Unprincipled demagogues exploited public anxiety about personal and national security, charging that communist conspiracies wormed through official Washington. Timid members of Congress, afraid of recrimination if they did not join the anticommunist crusade, fell into line. Officials tried to isolate critics by suggesting that they threatened the nation itself, that they might even be communists. During the 1948 campaign, Truman practiced the "red-baiting" so common to Cold War politics when he deliberately attempted to link Progressive party candidate Henry A. Wallace, dissenter from the "get-tough" policy, to the communists. Three years before demagogic Senator Joseph McCarthy charged government officials with treason, the Truman administration itself instituted a federal employee loyalty program to identify and ferret out suspected subversives. With no precise definition of disloyalty, zealous witch-hunters confused criticism with subversion. In this milieu of suspicion, an ever-increasing public cynicism infected politics. Credibility gaps opened wide to reveal that the American people believed that their leaders were lying to them. Later exposure of government abuse of power—in scandals such as Watergate and Iran-Contra—deepened the cynicism.

Public apprehension about the future fed into Cold War extremism and exaggeration. Because people recognized that the Cold War "might not end in *one* Rome but with *two* Carthages," that nuclear war invited apocalypse, leaving no winners, Americans and other people worldwide lived with a unique nervousness.[135] Government officials, magazine editors, strategic analysts, scientists, and fiction writers alike, again and again, issued doomsday forecasts, sketching pictures of a radioactive global wasteland if nuclear weapons were not controlled. In a bestselling book, *No Place to Hide* (1948), David Bradley, a physician who witnessed the Bikini atomic test, chillingly depicted "the shadow of the colossus which looms behind tomorrow."[136] In late 1949, after the Soviet atomic success, the *Bulletin of the Atomic Scientists* moved the hands of its "doomsday clock" to three minutes before midnight. In 1953, a few months after the United States exploded the first thermonuclear or hydrogen bomb, the hands moved to two minutes before midnight. America, the poet Robert Frost wrote, had "invented a new Holocaust."[137]

FURTHER READING FOR THE PERIOD 1945–1950

Some works cited in Chapter 6 cover particular leaders and the transition from war to peace.

For general studies of the Cold War, relevant to this chapter and others that follow, see Stephen Ambrose, *Rise to Globalism* (1993); Richard Barnet, *Roots of War* (1972); H. W. Brands, *The Devil We Knew* (1993); Gordon A. Craig and Francis L. Lowenheim, eds., *The Diplomats, 1939–1979* (1994); John P. Diggins, *The Proud Decades* (1988); Philip J. Funigiello, *American-Soviet Trade in the Cold War* (1988); John Lewis Gaddis, *The Long Peace* (1987) and *Russia, the Soviet Union, and the United States* (1990); Alexander L. George et al., eds., *U.S.-Soviet Security Cooperation* (1988); Alexander L. George and Richard Smoke, *Deterrence in American Foreign Policy* (1974); Roger E. Kanet and Edward A. Kolodziej, eds., *The Cold War as Cooperation* (1991); Charles W. Kegley, ed., *The Long Postwar Peace* (1991); Paul Kennedy, *The Rise and Fall of the Great Powers* (1987); Gabriel and Joyce Kolko, *The Limits of Power* (1972); Walter LaFeber, *America, Russia, and the Cold War* (1993); Ralph Levering, *The Cold War* (1988); Geir Lundestad, *The American "Empire"* (1990); Michael Mandelbaum, *The Fate of Nations* (1988); Ernest R. May, *"Lessons" of the Past* (1973); Thomas J. McCormick, *America's Half Century* (1989); Thomas G. Paterson, *Meeting the Communist Threat* (1988) and *On Every Front: The Making and Unmaking of the Cold War* (1992); Marshall D. Shulman, *Stalin's Foreign Policy Reappraised* (1963); Adam Ulam, *The Rivals* (1971) and *Expansion and Coexistence* (1974); and Thomas W. Wolfe, *Soviet Power and Europe: 1945–1970* (1970).

U.S. leaders in the early Cold War period are studied in Rudy Abramson, *Spanning the Century* (1992) (Harriman); H. W. Brands, *Inside the Cold War* (1991) (Henderson); Douglas Brinkley, ed., *Dean Acheson and the Making of U.S. Foreign Policy* (1993); David Callahan, *Dangerous Capabilities* (1990) (Nitze); Robert H. Ferrell, *George C. Marshall* (1966) and *Harry S. Truman* (1994); James G. Hershberg, *James B. Conant and the Birth of the Nuclear Age* (1993); Townsend Hoopes and Douglas Brinkley, *Driven Patriot* (1992) (Forrestal); Walter Isaacson and Evan Thomas, *The Wise Men* (1986); David McCullough, *Truman* (1992); David McLellan, *Dean Acheson* (1976); William E. Pemberton, *Harry S. Truman* (1989); Forrest C. Pogue, *George C. Marshall* (1963–1987); Alan R. Raucher, *Paul G. Hoffman* (1986); T. Michael Ruddy, *The Cautious Diplomat* (1986) (Bohlen); Jordan A. Schwarz, *The Speculator* (1981) (Baruch); Gaddis Smith, *Dean Acheson* (1972); Ronald Steel, *Walter Lippmann and the American Century* (1980); Mark A. Stoler, *George C. Marshall* (1989); and J. Samuel Walker, *Henry A. Wallace and American Foreign Policy* (1976).

Many books, all with the main title *Stalin,* include and critique the Soviet leader's foreign policy: Robert Conquest (1991); Isaac Deutscher (1967); Walter Laqueur (1990); Robert H. McNeal (1988); and Dmitri Volkogonov (1991).

The ideas and career of George F. Kennan are explored in Barton Gellman, *Contending with Kennan* (1984); Walter Hixson, *George F. Kennan* (1990); David Mayers, *George Kennan and the Dilemmas of U.S. Foreign Policy* (1988); Wilson D. Miscamble, *George F. Kennan and the Making of American Foreign Policy* (1992); and Anders Stephanson, *George Kennan and the Art of Foreign Policy* (1989).

For the origins of the Cold War, including the contest over Eastern Europe, see Barton J. Bernstein, ed., *Politics and Policies of the Truman Administration* (1970); Michael M. Boll, *Cold War in the Balkans* (1984); Kendrick A. Clements, ed., *James F. Byrnes and the Origins of the Cold War* (1982); Audrey K. Cronin, *Great Power Politics and the Struggle over Austria, 1945–1955* (1986); Arthur B. Darling, *The Central Intelligence Agency* (1990); Robert J. Donovan, *Conflict and Crisis: The Presidency of Harry S. Truman, 1945–1948* (1977); John L. Gaddis, *The United States and the Origins of the Cold War* (1972); Lloyd Gardner, *Architects of Illusion* (1970); James L. Gormly, *The Collapse of the Grand Alliance* (1987); Fraser J. Harbutt, *The Iron Curtain* (1986); John L. Harper, *America and the Reconstruction of Italy* (1986); George Herring, *Aid to Russia, 1941–1946* (1973); Lynn B. Hinds and Theodore O. Windt, Jr., *The Cold War as Rhetoric* (1991); Frank Kofsky, *Harry S. Truman and the War Scare of 1948* (1993); Gabriel Kolko, *The Politics of War* (1968); Deborah W. Larson, *Origins of Containment* (1985); Melvyn P. Leffler, *A Preponderance of Power* (1992); Richard C. Lukas, *Bitter Legacy* (1982) (Poland); Geir Lundestad, *The American Non-Policy Towards Eastern Europe, 1943–1947* (1975); Stanley M. Max, *The United States, Great Britain, and the Sovietization of Hungary, 1945–1948* (1985); Donald R. McCoy,

The Presidency of Harry S. Truman (1984); Robert Messer, *The End of an Alliance* (1982); James E. Miller, *The United States and Italy, 1940–1950* (1986); Frank A. Ninkovich, *The Diplomacy of Ideas* (1981); Thomas G. Paterson, ed., *Cold War Critics* (1971); Thomas G. Paterson and Robert J. McMahon, eds., *The Origins of the Cold War* (1991); David Reynolds, ed., *The Origins of the Cold War in Europe* (1994); William Taubman, *Stalin's American Policy* (1982); Walter Ullmann, *The United States in Prague, 1945–1948* (1978); Piotr S. Wandycz, *The United States and Poland* (1980); Patricia D. Ward, *The Threat of Peace* (1979); Donald R. Whitnah and Edgar L. Erickson, *The American Occupation of Austria* (1985); and Daniel Yergin, *Shattered Peace* (1977).

For the early years of the United Nations Organization, see James Barros, *Trygvie Lie and the Cold War* (1989); Thomas Campbell, *Masquerade Peace* (1973); Robert A. Divine, *Second Chance* (1967); Robert C. Hilderbrand, *Dumbarton Oaks* (1990); Evan Luard and Derek Herter, *The United Nations* (1993); and George Mazuzan, *Warren R. Austin at the U.N., 1946–1953* (1977).

The atomic bomb and nuclear questions are discussed in Gar Alperovitz, *Atomic Diplomacy* (1985); Barton J. Bernstein, ed., *The Atomic Bomb* (1975); Paul Boyer, *By the Bomb's Early Light* (1986); McGeorge Bundy, *Danger and Survival* (1990); Robert J. C. Butow, *Japan's Decision to Surrender* (1954); Committee for the Compilation of Materials on Damage Caused by the Atomic Bombs in Hiroshima and Nagasaki, *Hiroshima and Nagasaki* (1981); Herbert Feis, *The Atomic Bomb and the End of World War II* (1966); Jonathan E. Helmreich, *Gathering Rare Ores: The Diplomacy of Uranium Acquisition* (1986); Gregg Herken, *The Winning Weapon* (1981); Richard Hewlett and Oscar Anderson, *The New World* (1962); David Holloway, *The Soviet Union and the Arms Race* (1984); John Newhouse, *War and Peace in the Nuclear Age* (1989); Martin Sherwin, *A World Destroyed* (1975); Samuel R. Williamson and Steven L. Rearden, *The Origins of U.S. Nuclear Strategy* (1993); Allan M. Winkler, *Life Under a Cloud* (1993); Lawrence S. Wittner, *One World or None* (1993) (disarmament movement); and Peter Wyden, *Day One* (1984). The H-bomb decision is treated in Herbert F. York, *The Advisors* (1975).

Anglo-American relations are discussed in Terry H. Anderson, *The United States, Great Britain, and the Cold War, 1944–1947* (1981); Elisabeth Barker, *The British Between the Superpowers, 1945–1950* (1983); Richard A. Best, Jr., *"Co-operation with Like-Minded Peoples"* (1986); Alan Bullock, *Ernest Bevin* (1984); Robin Edmonds, *Setting the Mould* (1987); Robert M. Hathaway, *Ambiguous Partnership* (1981); John Kent, *British Imperial Strategy and the Origins of the Cold War* (1993); Ritchie Overdale, *The English Speaking Alliance* (1985); and Kenneth W. Thompson, *Winston Churchill's World View* (1983).

The United States in the world economy and economic expansion are treated in Irvine H. Anderson, *Aramco, the United States, and Saudi Arabia* (1981); Fred L. Block, *The Origins of International Economic Disorder* (1977); Alfred E. Eckes, Jr., *A Search for Solvency* (1975) (Bretton Woods) and *The United States and the Global Struggle for Minerals* (1979); Aaron D. Miller, *Search for Security* (1980) (Saudi Arabia's oil); David S. Painter, *Oil and the American Century* (1986); Stephen J. Randall, *United States Foreign Oil Policy, 1919–1984* (1985); and Michael B. Stoff, *Oil, War, and American Security* (1980).

For Western European issues, economic reconstruction, and the Marshall Plan, see Josef Becker and Franz Knipping, *Power in Europe?* (1986); Anthony Carew, *Labour under the Marshall Plan* (1987); Frank Costigliola, *France and the United States* (1992); David W. Ellwood, *Rebuilding Europe* (1992); Richard Gardner, *Sterling-Dollar Diplomacy* (1969); John L. Harper, *America and the Reconstruction of Italy* (1986); Michael J. Hogan, *The Marshall Plan* (1987); Richard Mayne, *Recovery of Europe* (1973); James E. Miller, *The United States and Italy, 1940–1950* (1986); Alan S. Milward, *The Reconstruction of Western Europe, 1945–51* (1984); Thomas G. Paterson, *Soviet-American Confrontation* (1973); Sallie Pisani, *The CIA and the Marshall Plan* (1991); Robert A. Pollard, *Economic Security and the Origins of the Cold War* (1985); Federico Romero, *The United States and the European Trade Union Movement* (1992); Irwin M. Wall, *The United States and the Making of Postwar France* (1991); and Imanuel Wexler, *The Marshall Plan Revisited* (1983).

For Germany, see Stephen Ambrose, *Eisenhower and Berlin, 1945* (1967); John H. Backer, *Winds of History* (1984); Tom Bower, *The Paperclip Conspiracy* (1988); Anne Deighton, *The Impossible Peace* (1990); John Gimbel, *The American Occupation of Germany* (1968), *The Origins of the Marshall Plan* (1976), and *Science,*

Technology, and Reparations (1990); Bruce Kuklick, *American Policy and the Division of Germany* (1972); Clarence G. Lasby, *Project Paperclip* (1971); Edward N. Peterson, *The American Occupation of Germany* (1978); Thomas A. Schwartz, *America's Germany* (1991); Avi Shlaim, *The United States and the Berlin Blockade, 1948–1949* (1983); Christopher Simpson, *Blowback* (1988) (recruitment of Nazis); and Jean Smith, *The Defense of Berlin* (1963).

For the Truman Doctrine and containment, consult G. M. Alexander, *The Prelude to the Truman Doctrine* (1984); David J. Alvarez, *Bureaucracy and Cold War Ideology* (1980) (Turkey); Richard Barnet, *Intervention and Revolution* (1972); Robert Frazier, *Anglo-American Relations with Greece* (1991); Richard Freeland, *The Truman Doctrine and the Origins of McCarthyism* (1971); John L. Gaddis, *Strategies of Containment* (1981); Charles Gati, ed., *Caging the Bear* (1977); John O. Iatrides, *Revolt in Athens* (1972) and ed., *Greece in the 1940s* (1981); Howard Jones, *"A New Kind of War"* (1989); Bruce R. Kuniholm, *The Origins of the Cold War in the Near East* (1980); and Lawrence S. Wittner, *America Intervention in Greece, 1943–1949* (1982).

NATO and military questions are studied in John Baylis, *The Diplomacy of Pragmatism* (1993) (Britain); Timothy P. Ireland, *Creating the Entangling Alliance* (1981); Lawrence S. Kaplan, *NATO and the United States* (1988) and *The United States and NATO: The Formative Years* (1984); Robert Osgood, *NATO: The Entangling Alliance* (1962); Steven L. Rearden, *History of the Office of the Secretary of Defense* (1984); Olav Riste, ed., *Western Security* (1985); Edward J. Sheehy, *The U.S. Navy, the Mediterranean, and the Cold War* (1992); Michael S. Sherry, *The Rise of American Air Power* (1987); Nicholas Sherwen, ed., *NATO's Anxious Birth* (1985); E. Timothy Smith, *The United States, Italy, and NATO* (1991); and Joseph Smith, ed., *The Origins of NATO* (1990). See also Samuel F. Wells, Jr., "Sounding the Tocsin: NSC-68 and the Soviet Threat," *International Security* (1979).

U.S. relations with Asia, including decolonization, are discussed in Robert Blum, *Drawing the Line* (1982); Russell Buhite, *Soviet-American Relations in Asia, 1945–1954* (1982); Edward Friedman and Mark Selden, eds., *America's Asia* (1971); Marc S. Gallicchio, *The Cold War Begins in Asia* (1988); Gary Hess, *America Encounters India, 1941–1947* (1971) and *The United States' Emergence as a Southeast Asian Power 1940–1950* (1987); Akira Iriye, *The Cold War in Asia* (1974); Akira Iriye and Warren Cohen, eds., *American, Chinese, and Japanese Perspectives on Wartime Asia, 1931–1949* (1990); James I. Matray, *The Reluctant Crusade* (1985) (Korea); Robert J. McMahon, *Colonialism and Cold War* (1981) (Indonesia) and *The Cold War on the Periphery* (1994) (India and Pakistan); Yōnosuke Nagai and Akira Iriye, eds., *The Origins of the Cold War in Asia* (1977); Anita I. Singh, *The Limits of British Influence* (1994) (South Asia); and William W. Stueck, Jr., *The Road to Confrontation* (1981).

For Japan and the American occupation, see William S. Borden, *The Pacific Alliance* (1984); Roger Buckley, *Occupation Diplomacy* (1982); John W. Dower, *War Without Mercy* (1986); Herbert Feis, *Contest Over Japan* (1967); D. Clayton James, *The Years of MacArthur* (1985); Richard B. Finn, *Winners in Peace: MacArthur, Yoshida, and Postwar Japan* (1992); Philip R. Piccigallo, *The Japanese on Trial* (1979); Michael Schaller, *The American Occupation of Japan* (1985) and *Douglas MacArthur* (1989); and Gary H. Tsuchimochi, *Education Reform in Postwar Japan* (1993).

For the Chinese civil war and the recognition question, see Dorothy Borg and Waldo Heinrichs, eds., *Uncertain Years* (1980); Russell Buhite, *Patrick J. Hurley and American Foreign Policy* (1973); Gordon Chang, *Friends and Enemies* (1990); Warren Cohen, *America's Response to China* (1990); Herbert Feis, *The China Tangle* (1953); Harry Harding and Yuan Ming, eds., *Sino-American Relations, 1945–55* (1989); E. J. Kahn, Jr., *The China Hands* (1975); Ronald C. Keith, *The Diplomacy of Zhou Enlai* (1989); Ross Koen, *The China Lobby in American Politics* (1974); Paul G. Lauren, ed., *The China Hands' Legacy* (1987); Gary May, *China Scapegoat: The Diplomatic Ordeal of John Carter Vincent* (1979); Robert P. Newman, *Owen Lattimore and the "Loss" of China* (1992); James Reardon-Anderson, *Yenan and the Great Powers* (1979); William Stueck, *The Wedemeyer Mission* (1984); Nancy B. Tucker, *Patterns in the Dust* (1983); Odd Arne Westad, *Cold War and Revolution* (1993); Shaw Yu-Ming, *John Leighton Stuart and Twentieth-Century Chinese-American Relations* (1992); and Shu Guang Zhang, *Deterrence and Strategic Culture* (1992).

For the Middle East, Iran, and the new state of Israel, see books on oil cited above and Michael J. Cohen, *Palestine and the Great Powers, 1945–1948* (1983) and *Truman and Israel* (1990); Leonard Dinnerstein,

America and the Survivors of the Holocaust (1982); Bruce J. Evensen, *Truman, Palestine, and the Press* (1992); Louise L. Fawcett, *Iran and the Cold War* (1992) (1946 crisis); Zvi Ganin, *Truman, American Jewry, and Israel, 1945–1948* (1979); James F. Goode, *The United States and Iran, 1946–51* (1989); George Lenczowski, *American Presidents and the Middle East* (1989); Wm. Roger Louis, *The British Empire in the Middle East, 1945–1951* (1984); Wm. Roger Louis and Robert W. Stookey, eds., *The End of the Palestine Mandate* (1986); Mark H. Lytle, *The Origins of Iranian-American Alliance, 1941–1953* (1987); John Quigley, *Palestine and Israel* (1990); Barry Rubin, *The Great Powers in the Middle East, 1941–1947* (1980); David Schoenbaum, *The United States and the State of Israel* (1993); John Snetsinger, *Truman, the Jewish Vote, and the Creation of Israel* (1974); and Robert W. Stookey, *America and the Arab States* (1975). See also works on the Middle East cited in following chapters.

Relations with other Third World nations are explored in Scott L. Bills, *Empire and Cold War* (1990); Thomas Borstelmann, *Apartheid's Reluctant Uncle* (1993) (South Africa); Walter LaFeber, *Inevitable Revolutions* (1993); and Thomas M. Leonard, *The United States and Central America, 1944–1949* (1984). Works on Indochina and Vietnam are cited in Chapter 9.

For domestic politics, anticommunism, interest groups, and public opinion in the early Cold War period, see Robert Divine, *Foreign Policy and U.S. Presidential Elections, 1940–1960* (1974); Justus Doenecke, *Not to the Swift: The Old Isolationists in the Cold War Era* (1979); Richard M. Fried, *Nightmare in Red* (1990); Robert Griffith and Athan Theoharis, eds., *The Specter* (1974); Earl Latham, *The Communist Controversy in Washington* (1966); Ronald Radosh, *American Labor and U.S. Foreign Policy* (1969); Colin Shindler, *Hollywood Goes to War* (1979); Peter L. Steinberg, *The Great "Red" Menace* (1984); Athan Theoharis, *Seeds of Repression* (1971), *The Yalta Myths* (1970), and ed., *Beyond the Hiss Case: The FBI, Congress, and the Cold War* (1982); and Lawrence Wittner, *Rebels Against War: The American Peace Movement, 1941–1960* (1984). For works on McCarthyism, see Chapter 8.

See also the General Bibliography, the following notes, and Richard Dean Burns, ed., *Guide to American Foreign Relations Since 1700* (1983).

Notes to Chapter 7

1. Quoted in Hanson W. Baldwin, "Hiroshima Decision," in *Hiroshima Plus 20* (New York: Delacorte, 1965), p. 41.
2. Harold M. Agnew quoted in *Time*, CXXVI (July 29, 1985), 46.
3. Quoted in John Toland, *The Rising Sun* (New York: Random House, 1970), p. 780.
4. Quoted in William L. Laurence, *Dawn Over Zero* (New York: Alfred A. Knopf, 1946), pp. 219, 221.
5. Yamaoka Michiko, "Eight Hundred Meters from the Hypocenter," in Haruko Taya Cook and Theodore F. Cook, eds., *Japan at War* (New York: The New Press, 1992), p. 385.
6. Michihiko Hachiya, *Hiroshima Diary* (Chapel Hill: University of North Carolina Press, 1955; trans. by Warner Wells), p. 6.
7. Quoted in John M. Blum, ed., *The Price of Vision: Diary of Henry A. Wallace* (Boston: Houghton Mifflin, 1973), p. 474.
8. Paul Fussell, "Hiroshima," in Michael B. Stoff, ed., *The Manhattan Project* (New York: McGraw-Hill, 1991), p.276.
9. William D. Leahy, *I Was There* (New York: Whittlesey, 1950), p. 441.
10. Quoted in Robert Messer, "American Perspectives on the Origins of the Cold War in Asia, 1945–1949," in Akira Iriye and Warren Cohen, eds., *American, Chinese, and Japanese Perspectives on Wartime Asia, 1931–1949* (Wilmington, Del.: Scholarly Resources, 1990), p. 251.
11. Quoted in John W. Dower, *War Without Mercy* (New York: Pantheon, 1986), p. 162.
12. Quoted in Richard Barnet, *Roots of War* (Baltimore: Penguin, 1973), p. 46.
13. Quoted in Barton J. Bernstein, "Roosevelt, Truman and the Atomic Bomb, 1941–1945," *Political Science Quarterly*, XC (Spring 1975), 61.
14. Quoted in Michael S. Sherry, *The Rise of American Air Power* (New Haven: Yale University Press, 1987), p. 341.
15. Quoted in Marc S. Gallicchio, *The Cold War Begins in Asia* (New York: Columbia University Press, 1988), p. 44.
16. Harry S. Truman, *Memoirs* (Garden City N.Y.: Doubleday 1955–56; 2 vols.), I, 416.
17. Quoted in McGeorge Bundy, *Danger and Survival* (New York: Random House, 1988), p. 133.
18. Quoted in Martin J. Sherwin, *A World Destroyed* (New York: Alfred A. Knopf, 1975), p. 224.
19. Quoted in Lawrence S. Wittner, *One World or None* (Stanford: Stanford University Press, 1993), p. 58.

20. Sumner Welles quoted in Lloyd C. Gardner, *Approaching Vietnam* (New York: W. W. Norton, 1988), p. 25.

21. Harry S. Truman to Eleanor Roosevelt, December 12, 1948, Box 4560, Eleanor Roosevelt Papers, Franklin D. Roosevelt Library, Hyde Park, New York.

22. *Foreign Relations, 1946,* (Washington, D.C.: Government Printing Office, 1969), VI, 707.

23. Jeanette P. Nichols, "Dollar Strength as a Liability in United States Diplomacy," *Proceedings of the American Philosophical Society, III* (February 17, 1967), 47.

24. Quoted in Thomas G. Paterson, *Soviet-American Confrontation* (Baltimore: The Johns Hopkins University Press, 1973), p. ix; Halifax to Bevin, August 9, 1945, AN2560/22/45, Foreign Office Correspondence, Public Record Office, London, England.

25. Gaddis Smith, *Dean Acheson* (New York: Cooper Square Publishers, 1972), p. 416.

26. Lord Inverchapel quoted in Peter Boyle, "America's Hesitant Road to NATO, 1945–1949," in Joseph Smith, ed., *The Origins of NATO* (Exeter, Eng.: University of Exeter Press, 1990), p. 76.

27. Bert Cochran, *Harry Truman and the Crisis Presidency* (New York: Funk and Wagnalls, 1973), p. 232.

28. Quoted in Thomas G. Paterson, *On Every Front* (New York: W. W. Norton, 1992; rev. ed.), p. 127.

29. Clark Clifford, *Counsel to the President* (New York: Random House, 1991), p. 77.

30. Quoted in John Lewis Gaddis, *The United States and the Origins of the Cold War* (New York: Columbia University Press, 1972), p. 205.

31. Quoted in John Lewis Gaddis, "Harry S. Truman and the Origins of Containment," in Frank Merli and Theodore Wilson, eds., *Makers of American Diplomacy* (New York: Charles Scribner's Sons, 1974), p. 500.

32. Quoted in Melvyn P. Leffler, *A Preponderance of Power* (Stanford: Stanford University Press, 1992), p. 99.

33. Michael Mandelbaum, *The Fate of Nations* (Cambridge, Eng.: Cambridge University Press, 1988), p. 137.

34. Lester Markel, "Opinion—A Neglected Instrument," in Lester Markel et al., *Public Opinion and Foreign Policy* (New York: Harper, 1949), p. 4.

35. *Public Papers, Truman, 1952–53* (Washington, D.C.: Government Printing Office, 1966), p. 1199.

36. Paul Kennedy, *The Rise and Fall of the Great Powers* (New York: Random House, 1987), p. 515.

37. *Foreign Relations, Yalta* (Washington, D.C.: Government Printing Office, 1955), p. 669.

38. Quoted in Vladislav Zubok and Constantine Pleshakov, "The Soviet Union," in David Reynolds, ed., *The Origins of the Cold War in Europe* (New Haven: Yale University Press, 1994), p. 62.

39. Quoted in Lloyd C. Gardner, *Economic Aspects of New Deal Diplomacy* (Madison: University of Wisconsin Press, 1964), p. 308.

40. Quoted in Barton J. Bernstein, "American Foreign Policy and the Origins of the Cold War," in Barton J. Bernstein, ed., *Politics and Policies of the Truman Administration* (Chicago: Quadrangle, 1970), p. 36.

41. Quoted in Gregg Herken, *The Winning Weapon* (New York: Alfred A. Knopf, 1980), p. 48.

42. Henry L. Stimson and McGeorge Bundy, *On Active Service in Peace and War* (New York: Harper & Brothers, 1948), p. 644.

43. Walter Millis, ed., *The Forrestal Diaries* (New York: Viking, 1951), p. 96.

44. *Foreign Relations 1946, VII,* (Washington, D.C.: Government Printing Office, 1969) 223.

45. Quoted in Alexander Werth, *Russia: The Post-War Years* (New York: Taplinger, 1971), pp. 328–329.

46. Quoted in James L. Gormly, *The Collapse of the Grand Alliance, 1945–1948* (Baton Rouge: Louisiana State University Press, 1987), p. 147.

47. Quoted in Thomas G. Paterson, *Meeting the Communist Threat* (New York: Oxford University Press, 1988), pp. 114–115.

48. George F. Kennan, *Memoirs, 1925–1950* (Boston: Little, Brown, 1967), p. 294.

49. Quoted in Fraser J. Harbutt, *The Iron Curtain* (New York: Oxord Univerity Press, 1986), p. 186.

50. Quoted in Boyle, "America's Hesitant Road," p. 74.

51. Quoted in Gaddis, *United States and Origins,* p. 315.

52. *New York Times,* March 14, 1946 (*Pravda* interview).

53. Quoted in Louise L. Fawcett, *Iran and the Cold War* (Cambridge, Eng.: Cambridge University Press, 1992), p. 125.

54. Arthur C. Millspaugh, "Memorandum on Recent American Diplomacy in Iran," September 8, 1948, Box 20, John W. Snyder Papers, Harry S. Truman Library, Independence, Missouri.

55. *Vital Speeches, XII* (October 1, 1946), 738–741.

56. Quoted in William Hillman, *Mr. President* (New York: Farrar, Straus and Young, 1952), p. 128.

57. Paraphrase by Colonel Bernard Bernstein in U.S. Congress, Senate, Judiciary Committee, *Morgenthau Diary (Germany),* (Washington, D.C.: Government Printing Office, 1967; 2 vols.), II, 1555.

58. W. Averell Harriman, "Certain Factors Underlying Our Relations with the Soviet Union," November 14, 1945, W. Averell Harriman Papers, Library of Congress, Washington, D.C.

59. Henry A. Wallace, "The Path to Peace with Russia," *The New Republic, CXV* (September 30, 1946), 401–406.

60. "The Novikov Telegram, Washington, September 27, 1946," *Diplomatic History, XV* (Fall 1991), 527.

61. Quoted in Arnold A. Offner, "Harry S. Truman as Parochial Nationalist," in Thomas G. Paterson and Robert J. McMahon, eds., *The Origins of the Cold War* (Lexington, Mass.: D. C. Heath, 1991; 3d ed.), p. 56.

62. Quoted in John Gimbel, "Project Paperclip," *Diplomatic History, XIV* (Summer 1990), 351.

63. Quoted in Thomas A. Schwartz, *America's Germany* (Cambridge, Mass.: Harvard University Press, 1991), p. 31.

64. Quoted in John Newhouse, *War and Peace in the Nuclear Age* (New York: Alfred A. Knopf, 1989), p. 67.

65. *Public Papers, Truman, 1947* (Washington, D.C.: Government Printing Office, 1963), pp. 176–180.

66. Quoted in David W. Ellwood, *Rebuilding Europe* (London: Longman, 1992), p. 69.

67. Quoted in John O. Iatrides, *Revolt in Athens* (Princeton: Princeton University Press, 1972), p. 208.

68. Paul Porter quoted in Howard Jones, *"A New Kind of War"* (New York: Oxford University Press, 1989), p. 30.

69. *Congressional Record, XCIII* (April 22, 1947), 3772–3773.

70. *Foreign Relations, Yalta*, p. 903.

71. *Ibid., 1946, VII*, 895.

72. "Record of Meeting at the Kremlin, Moscow, 9th October, 1944, at 10 p.m.," Premier 3, 434/4, Prime Minister's Office Records, Public Record Office.

73. Richard Barnet, *Intervention and Revolution* (New York: New American Library, 1968), p. 121.

74. Loy Henderson quoted in H. W. Brands, *Inside the Cold War* (New York: Oxford University Press, 1991), p. 177.

75. Quoted in George Lenczowski, *American Presidents and the Middle East* (Durham, N.C.: Duke University Press, 1990), p. 30.

76. Warren Austin quoted in Mark A. Stoler, *George C. Marshall* (Boston: Twayne, 1989), p. 172.

77. Quoted in Michael J. Cohen, *Truman and Israel* (Berkeley: University of California Press, 1990), p. 136.

78. Quoted in Walid Khalidi, "The Arab Perspective," in Wm. Roger Louis and Robert W. Stookey, eds., *The End of The Palestine Mandate* (Austin: University of Texas Press, 1986), p. 120.

79. Quoted in Cohen, *Truman and Israel*, p. 122.

80. Quoted *ibid.*, p. 193.

81. Quoted in Bruce J. Evensen, *Truman, Palestine, and the Press* (New York: Greenwood Press, 1992), p. 180.

82. Quoted in David Schoenbaum, *The United States and the State of Israel* (New York: Oxford University Press, 1993), p. 34.

83. "X," "The Sources of Soviet Conduct," *Foreign Affairs, XXV* (July 1947), 566–582.

84. Walter Lippmann, *The Cold War* (New York: Harper & Brothers, 1947), pp. 18, 21, 60.

85. *Department of State Bulletin, XVI* (July 15, 1947), 1159–1160.

86. Bidault quoted in René Girault, "The French Decision-Makers and Their Perception of French Power in 1948," in Josef Becker and Franz Knipping, eds., *Power in Europe?* (Berlin: Walter de Gruyer, 1986), p. 61.

87. Zubok and Pleshakov, "Soviet Union," p. 67.

88. Quoted in Woodford McClellan, "Molotov Remembers," *Cold War International History Project Bulletin*, Issue 1 (Spring 1992), 18.

89. Quoted in Michael J. Hogan, *The Marshall Plan* (New York: Cambridge University Press, 1987), p. 52.

90. Quoted in Richard D. McKinzie and Theodore A. Wilson "The Marshall Plan in Historical Perspective" (unpublished paper, American Historical Association, 1972), p. 8.

91. Frederico Romero, *The United States and the European Trade Union Movement, 1944–1951* (Chapel Hill: University of North Carolina Press, 1992), p. 216.

92. Quoted in Irwin M. Wall, *The United States and the Making of Postwar France, 1945–1954* (Cambridge, Eng.: Cambridge University Press, 1991), p. 122.

93. Diary, November 23, 1948, Walter Lippmann Papers, Yale University Library, New Haven, Connecticut.

94. *Public Papers, Truman, 1949* (Washington, D.C.: Government Printing Office, 1964), p. 114.

95. Escott Reid quoted in Alex Danchev, "Taking the Pledge," *Diplomatic History, XV* (Spring 1991), 203.

96. *Department of State Bulletin, XX* (March 20, 1949), 340.

97. *New York Times*, May 19, 1949.

98. Fitzroy Maclean quoted in David Reynolds, "Introduction," in Reynolds, *Origins in Europe*, p. 16.

99. Quoted in Paterson, *On Every Front*, p. 87.

100. John Hickerson in *Foreign Relations, 1948* (Washington, D.C.: Government Printing Office, 1974), *III*, 183.

101. Pierson Dixon quoted in Anne Deighton, *The Impossible Peace* (New York: Oxford University Press, 1990), p. 190.

102. Leffler, *Preponderance of Power*, p. 314.

103. William Bundy quoted in David Callahan, *Dangerous Capabilities* (New York: HarperCollins, 1990), p. 95.

104. Edward W. Barrett in "Princeton Seminar," October 10–11, 1953, Box 65, Dean Acheson Papers, Truman Library.

105. Quoted in Marshall D. Shulman, *Stalin's Foreign Policy Reappraised* (New York: Atheneum, [1963], 1966), p. 51.

106. Dean Acheson, *Present at the Creation* (New York: W. W. Norton, 1969), p. 379; *Department of State Bulletin, XXII* (March 20, 1950), 1037.

107. Stalin quoted in D. Clayton James, *The Years of MacArthur: Triumph and Disaster, 1945–1964* (Boston: Houghton Mifflin, 1985), pp. 26–27.

108. Quoted in John W. Dower, "Occupied Japan and the American Lake, 1945–1950," in Edward Friedman and Mark Selden, eds., *America's Asia* (New York: Vintage, 1971), p. 170; Dean Rusk, *As I Saw It* (New York: W. W. Norton, 1990), p. 123.

109. John Paton Davies quoted in Michael Schaller, "Securing the Great Crescent," *Journal of American History, LXXIX* (September 1982), 395.

110. Quoted in Nancy B. Tucker, "American Policy Toward Sino-Japanese Trade in the Postwar Years," *Diplomatic History, VIII* (Summer 1984), 192.

111. Dower, *War Without Mercy*, pp. 302, 305.

112. Quoted in Michael Schaller, *The United States and China in the Twentieth Century* (New York: Oxford University Press, 1990; 2d ed.), p. 119.

113. Quoted in Herbert Feis, *The China Tangle* (New York: Atheneum, 1965), p. 140.

114. Quoted in John Maxwell Hamilton, *Edgar Snow* (Bloomington: Indiana University Press, 1988), p. 171; Robert A. Hart, *The Eccentric Tradition* (New York: Charles Scribner's Sons, 1976), p. 156.

115. Zhou Enlai quoted in Shuguang Zhang, "'Preparedness Eliminates Mishaps,'" *Journal of American–East Asian Relations, I* (Spring 1992), 46.

116. Quoted in Thomas G. Paterson, "If Europe, Why Not China?" *Prologue, XIII* (Spring 1981), 37.

117. Robert P. Newman, *Owen Lattimore and the "Loss" of China* (Berkeley: University of California Press, 1992), p. 200.

118. Quoted in William Stueck, *The Road to Confrontation* (Chapel Hill: University of North Carolina Press, 1981), p. 124.

119. *United States Relations with China* (Washington, D.C.: Department of State, 1949), p. *xvii.*

120. Akira Iriye, *The Cold War in Asia* (Englewood Cliffs, N.J.: Prentice-Hall, 1974), p. 170.

121. Transcript, "A Conversation with Dean Acheson," by Eric Sevareid, September 28, 1969, CBS Television, p. 2.

122. Quoted in Gordon H. Chang, *Friends and Enemies* (Stanford: Stanford University Press, 1990), p. 13.

123. *Department of State Bulletin, XXIV* (May 28, 1951), 847.

124. L. E. Sissman, "Missing the Forties," *Atlantic Monthly, CCXXXII* (October 1973), 35.

125. M. E. Dening quoted in Wm. Roger Louis, *Imperialism at Bay* (New York: Oxford University Press, 1978), p. 550.

126. Quoted in Daniel Yergin, "Fulbright's Last Frustration," *New York Times Magazine,* November 24, 1974, p. 87.

127. Thomas Borstelmann, *Apartheid's Reluctant Uncle* (New York: Oxford University Press, 1993), p. 197.

128. Policy Planning Staff quoted in Melvyn P. Leffler, "Negotiating from Strength," in Douglas Brinkley, ed., *Dean Acheson and the Making of U.S. Foreign Policy* (New York: St. Martin's Press, 1993), p. 177.

129. Quoted in W. Averell Harriman and Elie Abel, *Special Envoy to Churchill and Stalin* (New York: Random House, 1975), p. 528.

130. J. William Fulbright, "Reflections: In Thrall to Fear," *The New Yorker, XLVII* (January 8, 1972), 43.

131. Zubok and Pleshakov, "Soviet Union," p. 56.

132. Thomas A. Bailey, *The Man in the Street* (New York: Macmillan, 1948), p. 13.

133. Arthur H. Vandenberg, Jr., ed., *The Private Papers of Senator Vandenberg* (Boston: Houghton Mifflin, 1952), pp. 550–551.

134. Quoted in Theodore A. Wilson and Richard D. McKinzie, "White House versus Congress" (unpublished paper, Organization of American Historians, 1973), p. 2.

135. Harold D. Lasswell, *Power and Personality* (New York: W. W. Norton, 1948), p. 180.

136. Quoted in Paul Boyer, *By the Bomb's Early Light* (New York: Pantheon, 1985), p. 92.

137. Quoted in Allan M. Winkler, *Life Under a Cloud* (New York: Oxford University Press, 1993), p. 50.

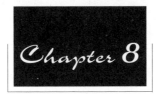
GLOBAL WATCH:
THE KOREAN WAR
AND EISENHOWER FOREIGN RELATIONS, 1950–1961

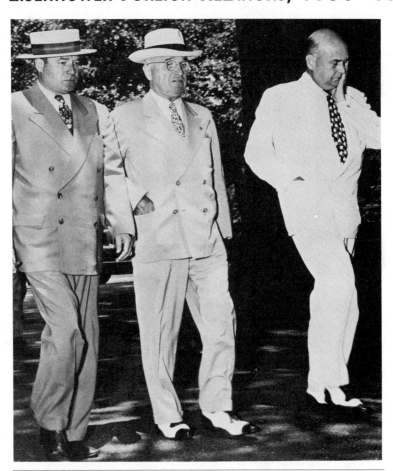

Blair House Meeting. *Attorney General J. Howard McGrath, President Harry S. Truman, and Secretary of Defense Louis Johnson break for lunch on June 27, 1950, after discussing the Korean crisis. Truman believed that "punishment always followed transgression," and he intended to punish the "pagan wolves" of North Korea. (Harry S. Truman Library)*

✖ *Diplomatic Crossroad*

THE DECISION TO INTERVENE IN THE KOREAN WAR, 1950

American ambassador to South Korea John J. Muccio was awakened by a telephone call at 8:00 A.M. "Brace yourself for a shock," his chief deputy said, "the Communists are hitting all along the front!"[1] Muccio dressed hurriedly and rushed out to check the alarming reports. United Press correspondent Jack James, also in Seoul, alertly did the same and earned himself a rare scoop. At 9:50 A.M. he cabled the UP in the United States that North Korean troops had crossed the thirty-eighth parallel. Approximately the same time Muccio cabled Washington about "an all-out offensive."[2]

At 4:00 A.M. that rainy Sunday morning of June 25, 1950, some 75,000 troops of the Democratic People's Republic of Korea (North Korea) bolted across the thirty-eighth parallel, the boundary drawn after World War II by the United States and the Soviet Union, cutting Korea into North and South. North Korean units attacked along a 150-mile front with heavy artillery and a spearhead of well-armored tanks that followed the valley roads into the South. The Soviet-made tanks rumbled forward, seemingly invulnerable to South Korean resistance. South Korean forces quickly collapsed in a rout. General Douglas MacArthur remembered that the North Korean army "struck like a cobra."[3]

James's cable beat Muccio's to the United States, more than 7,000 miles away, by a few minutes. It was a hot, humid Saturday evening (June 24) in Washington, D.C., thirteen hours behind Seoul time. The UP called the Department of State to verify James's report. Dumbfounded officers had no information. They phoned Assistant Secretary of State Dean Rusk, then dining with journalist Joseph Alsop in the Georgetown section of Washington. Rusk left the Alsop party about the same time that Muccio's cable reached the State Department. About 10:00 P.M., after Muccio's message had been decoded, the bad news began to spread by telephone and messenger across official Washington. Secretary of State Dean Acheson, resting at his Maryland farm just outside the capital, had begun reading himself to sleep when his official phone rang. When General MacArthur received word at his Tokyo post, he told visiting envoy John Foster Dulles: "This is probably only a reconnaissance in force. . . . I can handle it with one hand tied behind my back."[4] Dulles expected worse, and he cabled Washington to resist the North Korean attack: "To sit by while Korea is overrun . . . would start a disastrous chain of events leading most probably to world war."[5]

Acheson and State Department officials agreed that they should notify the United Nations Organization and convene an emergency session of the Security Council. The United States dominated that body, Korean issues had been handled there before, and the principle of collective security in the face of aggression seemed at issue. At 11:20 P.M. Acheson rang up President Harry S. Truman, at home in Independence, Missouri, with his family. "Mr. President, I have very serious news."[6] Acheson told Truman that the president could do little at that point, so he should remain in Missouri, get a good night's sleep, and come to Washington the next day, Sunday, June 25. State Department personnel worked through the night drafting a Security Council resolution that charged North Korea with a "breach of the peace."[7] Meetings in the Pentagon and the State Department debated courses of action. Orders went out to evacuate Americans from Seoul. World War III, thought some officials, had started.

President Truman boarded his plane early Sunday afternoon for the trip to the capital. According to one biographer, the president possessed "an appetite, too much of one, really, for unhesitating decision."[8] Truman stood low in the public opinion polls at the time, in large part because Senator Joseph McCarthy of Wisconsin was charging him with softness toward communism. Former State Department official Alger Hiss, to right-wing critics the epitome of the "sell-out" spy, had been convicted of perjury in January, and China had "fallen" just a few months before. Bold action now would disarm the president's critics. As Truman sat alone in his airplane, he pondered history. He frequently drew facile lessons from the past. Korea was the American Rhineland, he thought. The 1930s all over again: "Communism was acting in Korea just as Hitler, Mussolini, and the Japanese had acted ten, fifteen, and twenty years earlier."[9] No appeasement this time! Meanwhile, the Security Council passed the U.S. resolution of condemnation of North Korea. Except for Yugoslavia's abstention, all members present voted "yes." The Soviet delegation, which could have cast a veto to kill the measure, remained surprisingly absent, still boycotting the United Nations over its refusal to seat the new communist government in China.

A stern, short-tempered Truman, familiar bow tie snugly in place, deplaned in Washington and headed for a dinner meeting of top officials at Blair House, that elegant federal-style building on Pennsylvania Avenue, then being used as a residence during the renovation of the White House. Nobody present doubted that the Soviet Union had engineered the attack, using its North Korean allies to probe for a soft spot in the American containment shield. The relationship between the Soviet Union and North Korea, an assistant secretary of state remarked, was "the same as that between Walt Disney and Donald Duck."[10] Here was a test of American will and power. Worse still, they speculated, the thrust into South Korea might be only one component of a worldwide communist assault. Would Tito's Yugoslavia be next? Then Iran? Formosa? French Indochina? The Philippines? Japan? "If we let Korea down," Truman predicted, "the Soviet [*sic*] will keep right on going and swallow up one piece of Asia after another. . . . [Then] the Near East would collapse and no telling what would happen in Europe."[11] The State Department cabled its overseas posts to be vigilant. Truman ordered General MacArthur in Japan to send arms and equipment to the South Koreans and to use U.S. war planes to attack the North Korean spearhead. Further, he sent the Seventh Fleet into the waters between the Chinese mainland and Formosa to forestall conflict between the two Chinas.

Dean Acheson (1893–1971). He, like the president, assumed that Moscow had initiated the Korean War and urged resolute American reaction. The new crisis, coming after his National Press Club speech of January 12, 1950, and other foreign-policy woes such as Mao's recent victory in China, emboldened some of his critics to ask once again for his resignation. (*The Reporter,* 1952. Copyright 1952 by Fortnightly Publishing Co., Inc.)

Although Truman received widespread bipartisan support for his decisions, some conservative Republicans seized the moment to indulge in McCarthyite recriminations. Senator William E. Jenner of Indiana, one of the anticommunist tramplers of civil liberties in the postwar period, waxed splenetic: "The Russian bear is sprawled across the Eurasian continent, biding its time, digesting its prey, and digging itself in for a long and cruel international winter. The Korean debacle also reminds us that the same sell-out-to-Stalin statesmen, who turned Russia loose, are still in the saddle, riding herd on the American people."[12]

By Monday evening, North Korean forces neared Seoul. At 9:00 P.M. another Blair House conference convened. Truman learned about a downed North Korean plane, which he hoped "was not the last."[13] Diplomats and military leaders believed that the reputation of the United States stood at risk. If America did not back its word—its principle of containment—its image would tarnish and its power erode. As Acheson said later: "To back away from this challenge, in view of our capacity for meeting it, would be highly destructive of the power and prestige of the United States. By prestige I mean the shadow cast by power, which is of great deterrent importance."[14] Korea, then, became a supreme test, a symbol, a link in a Cold War chain of events. To falter would forfeit world leadership, Truman officials claimed. They decided on firm action: They ordered U.S. aircraft and warships into full-scale action below the thirty-eighth parallel; they declared Formosa (Taiwan) off limits to the mainland Chinese; and they dispatched military aid to Indochina and the Philippines.

Truman did not ask Congress for a declaration of war. Senator Tom Connally of Texas, chair of the Foreign Relations Committee, advised: "You might run into a long debate in Congress which would tie your hands completely. You have the right to do it as Commander-in-Chief and under the UN Charter."[15] Truman simply informed key legislators about his decisions. Critics would soon label it "Mr. Truman's War." On Tuesday, June 27, Americans applauded Truman's response. "Never . . . have I felt such a sense of relief and unity pass through the city," wrote one veteran reporter.[16] The United Nations passed another U.S.-sponsored resolution urging members to aid South Korea. The United Nations in essence approved actions the United States had already taken. Seoul nonetheless fell. The American embassy staff burned secret documents in a farewell bonfire.

The news of the continued North Korean push into the South sparked talk on June 28 and 29 of sending U.S. troops. Presidential supporters cited historical precedent to counter criticism that Truman had bypassed the congressional right to declare wars: Jefferson had ordered action against the Barbary pirates and McKinley had sent troops into China during the Boxer Rebellion without prior congressional sanction. On the twenty-ninth, Truman ordered U.S. pilots to attack above the thirty-eighth parallel. On Friday, June 30, after visiting the war front, MacArthur asked Truman to send American soldiers to Korea. The president soon gave the order. Amid reports that the North Korean surge was pushing the South Koreans into a small area at the bottom of the peninsula, the Pusan perimeter, Truman left Washington for a weekend yacht cruise on the Chesapeake. He had made his tough decisions, and characteristically did not brood over them. The nation mobilized for an undeclared but initially popular war against communism. Truman tagged it a "police action."

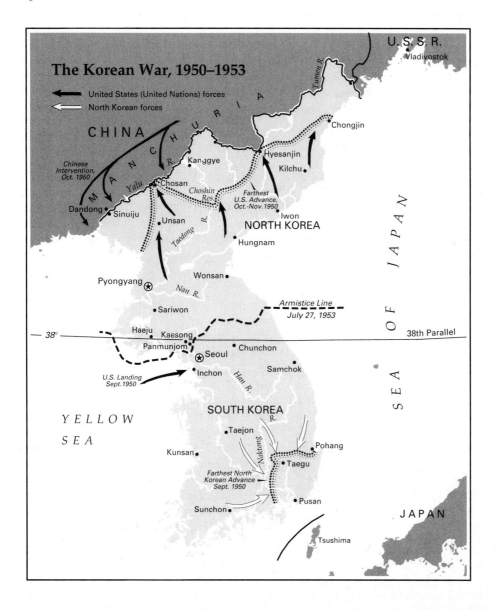

The Korean War, 1950–1953

← United States (United Nations) forces
← North Korean forces

THE KOREAN WAR SPURS THE COLD WAR

"If the best minds in the world had set out to find us the worst possible location to fight a war, the unanimous choice would have to have been Korea," Secretary Acheson later remarked.[17] At first the war went badly for the United States, South Korea, and the small number of troops offered by allies, all nominally under United Nations auspices. America's initial combat units took heavy losses, buying time for General MacArthur to equip and transport a substantial force for offensive operations in Korea. The president and his advisers began discussing the question whether American troops should cross the thirty-eighth parallel and attempt to unite the two Koreas—in short, to "liberate" the North from the communist camp. In August the president decided in favor of this drastic change in U.S. war aims.

Meanwhile, MacArthur persuaded a reluctant Joint Chiefs of Staff to approve an amphibious assault at Inchon, hundreds of miles behind North Korean lines. The area's high tides, narrow approach channels, mud flats, and well-fortified enemy positions did not deter the general. "For a five-dollar ante, I have an opportunity to win fifty thousand dollars," he told the chiefs.[18] On September 15, 1950, American marines landed at Inchon, pushed the North Koreans back, and quickly cut to Seoul. North Korean troops evacuated Seoul and retreated north. "We want you to feel unhampered tactically and strategically to proceed north of the 38th Parallel," Secretary of Defense George C. Marshall cabled MacArthur.[19] Farther south, the American Eighth Army broke out of the Pusan bridgehead.

The Chinese warily watched these events. When Truman sent the Seventh Fleet to neutralize Formosa on June 27, Beijing called the decision "armed aggression against Chinese territory," revealing the "true imperialist face" of the United States.[20] Shortly after the Inchon landing, Mao Zedong decided to send "volunteers" to fight in Korea. Worried about Chinese security, Mao and Zhou Enlai also warned the United States to keep its troops away from the Yalu River boundary. American officials thought the Chinese were bluffing. "We are no longer fearful of their [Chinese] intervention," MacArthur assured the president. "They have no Air Force . . . [and] if the Chinese tried to get down to Pyongyang there would be the greatest slaughter."[21]

On October 8, United Nations forces (90 percent American) moved across the thirty-eighth parallel and marched deep into North Korea. Even after Stalin reneged on a promise of Soviet air support, 250,000 Chinese troops quietly crossed the Yalu on October 19 to prevent "the American aggressors" from running "even more wild to the detriment of all of East Asia."[22] On October 26, Chinese forces hit back. After fierce fighting, however, they retreated—either Beijing's signal to the United States to stop pushing northward unless it wanted full-scale war or an "attempt to deceive the enemy" about its intentions.[23] In any case, U.S. officials abandoned caution. On November 8, for the first time, B-29 bombers struck bridges across the Yalu—bridges that linked North Korea and China. Then, on November 24, MacArthur sent his troops northward on a major offensive. Victory appeared near. Two days later, what one U.S. general called "a glut of Chinamen"

Central Korea, 1951. In war-scarred terrain, soldiers of the 25th Infantry Division take cover from mortar shells in April 1951. (Library of Congress)

swept down on MacArthur's unsuspecting armies.[24] Within weeks Chinese engulfed the North. MacArthur asked Washington, without success, to approve air strikes against China. The United Nations soon branded China an "aggressor," and Truman hinted publicly that using nuclear weapons was under "active consideration."[25] "You can use the atomic bomb," Mao reportedly boasted. "I will respond with my hand grenade. I will catch the weak point on your part and defeat you."[26] British prime minister Clement Attlee hastened to Washington to protest that the United States should seek negotiations, not a dangerously expanded war. To Truman's assertion that China had become a Soviet satellite and the "only way to meet communism is to eliminate it," Attlee wondered "when it is that you scratch a communist and find a nationalist."[27] In fact, Truman and his advisers rejected a wider war because they deemed the nuclear arsenal too small and feared Soviet retaliation in Europe.

By March 1951 MacArthur had managed to shove communist forces back across the thirty-eighth parallel. The fighting stabilized at roughly the prewar boundary. Truman contemplated negotiations at this point, but MacArthur grew restless, hell-bent on reversing earlier defeats and slashing China on behalf of the crusade against international communism. Truman would not let him attack China proper or use nationalist Chinese forces in Korea, so the general with the Napoleonic ego began to make public statements suggesting that his commander in chief practiced appeasement. To Representative Joseph Martin, he wrote, in a letter made public in April: "There is no substitute for victory."[28] Asia, not Europe, argued the general, provided the key to defeating communist aggression. On April 11 Truman, backed strongly by the Joint Chiefs of Staff, fired the seventy-one-year-old MacArthur for insubordination.

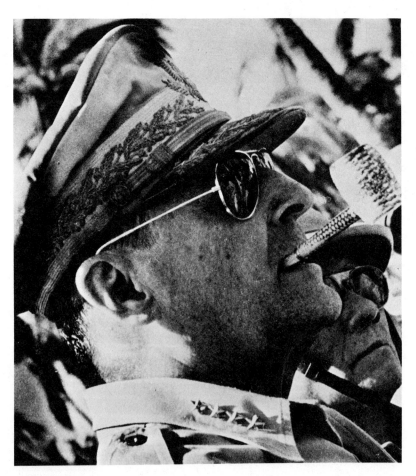

Douglas MacArthur (1880–1964).
The West Point graduate commanded U.S. forces in Asia during World War II, directed the postwar occupation of Japan, and headed the "United Nations" effort in Korea until relieved of duty by the president in April 1951. MacArthur later said he could have ended the Korean War in ten days: "I would have dropped between 30 and 50 atomic bombs" on China. (Library of Congress)

The vain general, who had so badly miscalculated Chinese reactions, returned home to ticker-tape parades. In a televised address that left many in tears, he told Congress on April 19 that the war had to be expanded. He closed with now famous words: "Old soldiers never die; they just fade away."[29] Congressional hearings featuring the old hero who wanted to be elected president revealed that many Americans shared MacArthur's frustrations over military restraint. Americans were used to winning wars; Truman was now talking about something alien—a "limited war," localized and without atomic weapons. Senator McCarthy spewed his venom, too. The president, he declared on the Senate floor, "is a rather sinister monster of many heads and many tentacles, a monster conceived in the Kremlin, and then given birth to by Acheson . . . , and then nurtured into Frankenstein proportions by the Hiss crowd, who still run the State Department."[30] The debate, as the historian Bruce Cumings writes, focused on different strategies for rolling back communism. "There was MacArthur's, which resembled a locomotive with no brakes. And there was Acheson's, a controlled rollback limited to Korea."[31]

Truman and Acheson replied to the charges of appeasement, and talk of impeachment, by pointing to the risk of world war. Acheson compared MacArthur and other opponents to the farmer who "goes out every morning and pulls up all his crops to see how they have been doing during the night."[32] The chairman of the Joint Chiefs of Staff, General Omar Bradley, pointed out that an enlargement of the war would by no means guarantee victory, that it might bring the Soviets in, and that the United States would lose angry allies. He rejected a showdown with Soviet communism in Korea, for it would be "the wrong war, at the wrong place, at the wrong time, and with the wrong enemy."[33] As the historian Marc Trachtenberg points out, Bradley implied that the *right war* should be against the Soviet Union, "and the *right place* to fight it was not at the periphery, but at the heart of Soviet power," and the *right time* only after the requisite buildup of American power under NSC-68.[34]

Peace talks began at Panmunjom in July 1951. They made little headway and the fighting continued. In June 1952, American aircraft blasted the large hydroelectric plants along the Yalu. During the 1952 presidential campaign, Republican candidate Dwight D. Eisenhower pledged, if elected, to go to Korea to find a way to end the conflict. Elected in good part because of American frustration with limited war, Ike did go to Korea but found no easy solution. The most serious difference between Chinese and American negotiators centered on the disposition of prisoners of war (POWs). Thousands of Chinese and North Korean soldiers, encouraged by a "re-education" program in the South, refused repatriation. A few hundred captives in the North, having undergone communist "brainwashing," elected to remain above the thirty-eighth parallel. The usual international practice called for the return of all prisoners, but Truman and Eisenhower wanted to liberate from communist rule those POWs who resisted repatriation.

By 1953 the military buildup under NSC-68 had erased doubts about U.S. capabilities that had precluded escalation earlier in the war. Announcing that the United States considered "the atomic bomb as simply another weapon in our arsenal," Eisenhower tried to intimidate the Chinese.[35] Secretary of State John Foster Dulles also hinted at the use of nuclear weapons when he advocated "a stronger rather than a lesser military exertion [which] . . . might well extend the area of conflict."[36] And Washington "unleashed" Jiang Jieshi to attack the mainland; nationalist bombing raids soon followed. The March death of Stalin, combined with these actions, probably helped bring the peace talks to a conclusion. A more flexible Moscow urged Beijing to settle the prisoner question. When South Korean president Syngman Rhee tried to sabotage the talks by releasing thousands of North Korean POWs, the Chinese launched a final offensive against South Korean positions.

On July 27, 1953, the adversaries signed an armistice. They agreed to turn over the POW issue to a committee of neutral nations (ultimately the POWs stayed where they chose—including twenty-one Americans in North Korea). The conferees drew a new boundary line close to the thirty-eighth parallel, which gained South Korea 1,500 square miles of territory. The agreement also provided for a demilitarized zone between the two Koreas.

Although called the "Korean Conflict" in the armistice document, the war ranks as one of the costliest in twentieth-century history. Close to 5 million Asians died: 2 million North Korean civilians and 500,000 North Korean soldiers; 1 million South Korean civilians and nearly 100,000 South Korean soldiers; and 1 million Chinese soldiers (estimates reach as high as 3 million, but to this day the Chinese government has not released official numbers).

The United States lost 54,246 dead and 105,000 wounded, and spent some $20 billion. The United States supplied more than 80 percent of the naval power and more than 90 percent of the air support, as well as half the combat troops, in this "United Nations" effort. The war had no victors—no dancing, cheering crowds in Times Square. The U.S. military drew a lesson of caution. "Never, never again should we be mousetrapped into fighting another defensive ground war," declared General Mark Clark. "Never should we commit numerically inferior American troops . . . against numerically superior forces of the enemy's second team unless we are prepared to win."[37]

The Korean War has left many questions, some of which the recent partial opening of Chinese and Russian archives are helping to answer. Did Moscow start the Korean War? Truman officials claimed that the Soviet Union induced its North Korean client to attack. Perhaps Moscow sensed an opportunity, because Secretary Acheson had indicated in a speech before the National Press Club on January 12, 1950, that South Korea lay outside the American defense perimeter. Acheson's speech "produced a certain influence" on the young North Korean leader Kim Il Sung, who visited Moscow in April and promised a surprise attack that would win the war in three days without American intervention.[38] But Stalin was skeptical. The Soviet leader asked Mao for his opinion, and the Chinese leader reportedly approved Kim's plan. Stalin, it seems, then reluctantly backed Kim's scheme, probably gambling that North Korea could score a quick victory.

The "gamble thesis" raises some difficult questions. Why did the Soviet delegate absent himself from the United Nations at such a crucial time, especially if the Soviets had approved the attack? More important, why did Stalin give such inadequate aid to the North Koreans and Chinese during the war? Why did Moscow launch a European movement for peaceful coexistence and then torpedo that effort by provoking war in Asia? As the historian Bruce Cumings writes, "we are thus left to reconcile the ubiquitous American assumption that Stalin started the war with the unambiguous evidence that he distanced Soviet interests, prestige, and armed might from the conflict, allowing the United States ultimately to pulverize North Korea."[39]

Soviet relations with China may have determined Stalin's decisions on Korea. If he refused to support Kim Il Sung's goal of unifying Korea, Stalin might invite the charge that he hindered revolution in Asia, thereby boosting Mao's China as a potential rival. As the historian Kathryn Weathersby suggests, Stalin may further have calculated that even if the United States did not defend South Korea, Washington would never permit the additional loss of Taiwan. The Americans would then move to protect Jiang Jieshi's government on the island, thus preventing any rapprochement between the United States and the People's Republic of China and forcing Mao to "continue to turn to the Soviet Union for economic and military aid."[40] Whatever Stalin's precise motives, he hesitated, because a war in Korea risked Soviet economic and strategic interests in Northeast Asia. The initiative, and probably the timing, for the war came from Pyongyang, not from Moscow; from Kim, not Stalin.

This interpretation seems plausible because since 1945 a two-part civil war had wracked Korea: the conflict in the South and the conflict between South and North. In the South, "people's committees" resisted the rightist state backed by the United States. Peasant uprisings, leftist-initiated labor strife, and guerrilla warfare claimed tens of thousands of lives. The North encouraged the rebellions in the South, and skirmishes between northern and southern soldiers intensified in 1949 along the dividing parallel. Both Kim Il Sung's North Korean communist government and Syngman Rhee's Republic of Korea in the South craved national unification. Both tapped foreign sources for material aid. Rhee, who had lived in the United States for almost four decades and who held a Ph.D. from Princeton University, used his American political connections well. In February 1950, Congress authorized $60 million in economic aid for South Korea; in March it voted almost $11 million in military assistance; and on June 5 it added another $100 million in military aid. Although U.S. occupation troops had departed in mid-1949, a U.S. Military Advisory Group remained to train Rhee's forces. In May elections, Rhee lost control of the South Korean National Assembly. All the while, Rhee "seemed like a tethered hound, constantly pulling at the [U.S.] leash."[41]

With a 150,000-soldier army well supplied with Soviet arms, including 150 T-34 tanks, Kim's authoritarian regime probably decided to strike before Rhee could utilize U.S. aid and stabilize his precarious political position. The preponderance of evidence indicates a premeditated North Korean strategy of taking Seoul by a tank-led *blitzkrieg*. Other circumstantial evidence, however, suggests that South Korean units may have provoked the northern assault by attacking, on the morning of June 25, the town of Haeju, several miles inside North Korea. In any case, scholars interpret the major war that exploded in June 1950 as an extension of the ongoing civil war waged by North and South Korea, not as a conflagration ignited by the two Cold War superpowers.

If we do not know for certain how the war began, or why, we *can* measure its consequences. At home in the United States, it meant the repudiation of the Democrats in 1952 and the election of a Republican administration, both made possible by popular exasperation with the stalemate in Korea. The Korean War wounded bipartisanship and fueled McCarthyism. It helped set off a "great debate" in the early 1950s over whether Europe or Asia ranked higher in the campaign against communism and whether the United States had overcommitted itself around the globe. Truman's handling of the American response to the Korean War also confirmed presidential supremacy in foreign policy; he neither consulted Congress nor asked for a declaration of war. Acheson did not wish to invite hearings which might produce that "one more question in cross-examination which destroys you, as a lawyer. We had complete acceptance of the President's policy by everybody on both sides of both houses of Congress." He did not wish to answer "ponderous questions" that might have "muddled up" Truman's policy.[42] As the historian Arthur Schlesinger, Jr., has concluded, Truman "dramatically and dangerously enlarged the power of future Presidents to take the nation into major war."[43] Truman, a former senator, thought most members of Congress "do not have the guts of a gnat."[44]

The Korean War poisoned Sino-American relations while it strengthened Japanese-American relations. The United States continued to intervene in the Chinese civil war by aiding Jiang on Formosa. Washington more than ever adamantly refused to recognize Mao's government, now that it had shed American blood. At the same time, the war enabled the Chinese communists to consolidate their revolution at home and gain international prestige from battling the United States to a draw. The Korean War also bolstered Japan. Some $3 billion in U.S. procurement orders during the war revived Japanese industry ("divine aid," said the president of the Bank of Japan) and solidified Tokyo's status as an ally. The historian Roger Dingman has noted that the continued presence of foreigners "helped shape the ability of mid-century Japanese to open the markets of the world to the products of their economy and culture."[45]

The Korean War also intensified the Cold War, further dividing the world into two competing camps and drawing Third World nations into its destructive wake as the domino theory took on new vigor. "We are fighting in Korea," Truman proclaimed in fall 1952, "so we won't have to fight in Wichita, or in Chicago, or in New Orleans, or on San Francisco Bay."[46] South Korea became a staunch ally, receiving, in 1953–1972, $5.5 billion in foreign aid from the United States. Viewing nationalist movements as threats to U.S. interests and as potential Soviet allies, and determined to back allies in the aggravated Cold War, Washington increased aid to the French in their battle against Vietnamese nationalists (see Chapter 9).

The Truman administration utilized the Korean War to fulfill other goals. As Acheson noted, the dispatch of troops to Korea "removed the recommendations of NSC-68 from the realm of theory and made them immediate budget issues."[47] The Defense Department budget for fiscal year 1953 reached $52.6 billion, up from $17.7 billion in 1950. American military expansion impressed observers: a much enlarged army; development of tactical nuclear weapons; four more army divisions for Europe, making a total of six there; the 1952 maiden flight of a new jet bomber, the B-52; the explosion of a thermonuclear device in November 1952. The United States also expanded its military ties abroad. It acquired bases in Saudi Arabia and Morocco, began successful talks with fascist Spain for an air base, and initiated plans for the rearmament of West Germany. In 1951 the United States, Australia, and

New Zealand formed the ANZUS Pact. The United States formed a military alliance with Pakistan in 1954. Strategies for psychological warfare and propaganda culminated in the creation of the United States Information Agency in 1953. CIA covert operations to overthrow unfriendly foreign leaders also increased (see pp. 328–329). The Korean War's most lasting legacy was its acceleration of the militarization of the cold war.

Ambivalent Cold Warrior: Dwight D. Eisenhower

The stalemated Korean War and the "loss" of China provided Republicans with considerable political ammunition in the 1952 presidential campaign. Bipartisanship eroded, because the political stakes—removing the Democratic party from its twenty-year hold on the White House—were high. Although Republican candidate General Dwight D. Eisenhower conducted a smiling, moderate campaign, his party's right wing attacked vehemently. The Truman administration, which had launched containment, gotten "tough" with the Soviets, and established an internal security system, had somehow grown soft on communism. Vice presidential candidate Richard M. Nixon, already famous for his anticommunist zeal as a senator, ridiculed Democratic candidate Adlai E. Stevenson as a graduate of "Acheson's Cowardly College of Communist Containment."[48] The Republican party platform, written by John Foster Dulles, hurled invective at the Truman administration for ineptly squandering American power.

The containment doctrine became a target of abuse. Republicans called it defensive and immoral. Dulles proposed "liberation" as a replacement.[49] By that he meant lifting the communist yoke from Eastern Europe. He never explained precisely how to do this; he often merely advocated a propaganda program to arouse Eastern Europeans against their Soviet masters. Democrats retorted that meddling in Eastern Europe would do those people little good because the Soviets would crush them—an assumption the Democrats themselves had rejected during the first years of the Cold War.

"Liberation" did not decide the election of 1952, but the rhyme "I like Ike" may have. Eisenhower came across as a sincere, modest, wholesome, and honest person, whose simple rhetoric and homespun illustrations made him attractive to millions. Because the Cold War seemed more than ever a military matter, this professional soldier seemed better qualified for the job than Adlai Stevenson. Although no less a Cold Warrior than Eisenhower, the Democratic governor of Illinois became tainted by his association with the unpopular Truman administration. Eisenhower's "I shall go to Korea" statement of October 24 certainly helped ensure his election with 55 percent of the popular vote.[50]

The first Republican president since Hoover, Eisenhower appeared, but was not, simple-minded. He lacked a surefootedness for grammar. His utterances often displayed mangled syntax and Eisenhowerese colloquialisms that produced dizziness in his listeners. This idiosyncratic style masked a skillful politician whose "hidden hand" leadership dominated the policy process.[51] But the president's meandering

Richard M. Nixon (1913–1994). Before being elected vice president in 1952, Nixon graduated from Whittier College, took a law degree from Duke University, served in Congress (1946–1951), and represented California as senator (1951–1953). An anticommunist alarmist who often used excessive language to score debating points, Nixon was, said Adlai Stevenson, "the kind of politician who would cut down a redwood tree, and then mount the stump and make a speech for conservation." (*The Reporter,* 1960. Copyright 1960 by The Reporter Magazine Co.)

Makers of American Foreign Relations, 1950–1961

Presidents	Secretaries of State
Harry S. Truman, 1945–1953	Dean G. Acheson, 1949–1953
Dwight D. Eisenhower, 1953–1961	John Foster Dulles, 1953–1959
	Christian A. Herter, 1959–1961

remarks, platitudes, and apparent moments of confusion permitted Democrats to claim that the president was a shallow, aging hero, out of touch with details, and vulnerable to the wiles of demagogic right-wingers in his party.

Born in Texas and raised in Abilene, Kansas, Eisenhower graduated from West Point and led an obscure military life until appointed the supreme allied commander in Europe during World War II. After the war he served as army chief of staff, president of Columbia University, and NATO commander. He liked fishing and golf and most of his companions in sport belonged to the business elite. Eisenhower admired business leaders and their financial success and appointed many to high office in agencies shaping foreign policy. Representatives of business, finance, and law held 76 percent of such posts under Eisenhower, whereas the figure for Truman had been 43 percent. Conservative advocates of "private enterprise" in a world increasingly turning toward revolution and socialism, these "national security managers" sought to impose order on international relations.[52]

Fearing class conflict and believing in a "mutually cooperative, voluntarist society," Eisenhower and his advisers saw capitalist development as a deterrent to communism.[53] Healthy world trade, they argued, helped stimulate cooperative capitalism. Eisenhower appointed a Commission on Foreign Economic Policy in 1953, and it urged a more liberal trade policy through tariff reduction. The president soon extended the reciprocal trade agreements program, expanded the lending authority of the Export-Import Bank, and relaxed controls on trade with Eastern European nations. Total American exports expanded from $15 billion in 1952 to $30 billion in 1960. At first Eisenhower favored trade over aid. But by the mid-1950s he had shifted to a mix of trade and aid to help developing nations. He also emphasized military aid. This emphasis carried benefits for a president determined to balance the budget. Military aid constituted sound economics, said the president, because it cost less to maintain a Greek soldier than an American one. During the 1950s, the United States spent more than $3 billion a year in foreign military assistance under the Mutual Security program. Eisenhower also added a new program in 1954, later called "Food for Peace," wherein the United States disposed of its agricultural surplus overseas. In ten years this program accounted for $12.2 billion in farm exports. And in 1959, after years of ignoring ardent Latin American requests, the United States established the Inter-American Development Bank to spur hemispheric economic projects.

The Eisenhower administration elevated the CIA as a major instrument of foreign policy. Under its director Allen W. Dulles, brother of Secretary of State John

Foster Dulles, the CIA hired bright Ivy League–educated lawyers and academicians to gather data on foreign governments and groups and to prepare "estimates"—predictions about their policies, motives, and capabilities. But the agency also provided the president with the "quiet option," including "termination with extreme prejudice" or "health alteration"—that is, assassination.[54] Working under the assumption that the Cold War had "no rules" and that "longstanding American concepts of 'fair play' must be reconsidered," the CIA became empowered "to subvert, sabotage, and destroy our enemies."[55] Among those included on the CIA's assassination hit list were the Congo's Patrice Lumumba and Cuba's Fidel Castro. When it was not trying to kill foreign leaders, the agency covertly bribed foreign politicians, hired mercenaries, conducted sabotage, coopted labor unions, planted stories in newspapers, and staged coups. The CIA helped overthrow governments in Iran (1953) and Guatemala (1954) but failed to overthrow the Indonesian government in 1958.

At home, the CIA put American journalists and professors on its payroll, recruited business executives as "fronts," financed the National Student Association, funded research projects at universities, and used philanthropic foundations to pass money to organizations for anticommunist activities. By the mid-1960s, the CIA had clandestinely subsidized publication of some 1,000 books. In the name of Cold War research and without the knowledge of the victims, the agency used Americans as guinea pigs to study the effects of "mind control" drugs.[56] Under a program called MKULTRA, for example, researchers subjected unwitting, nonvolunteer Americans to the mind-altering drug LSD. Other governmental projects sought to measure the effects of radioactivity by injecting unsuspecting Americans at schools and hospitals with radioactive materials. Researchers usually targeted the powerless, especially people suffering mental impairment or terminal illnesses. Eisenhower once remarked privately that as president he "knew so many things that I am almost afraid to speak to my wife."[57] Indeed, revelations and scandals have revealed that the CIA, with very lax congressional oversight but broad presidential authority, ran amok in the Eisenhower-Dulles years.

Unlike Truman and Acheson, Eisenhower at least seemed willing to negotiate with the Soviets. Stalin's death in March 1953 removed one of the original Cold War architects, and in April Eisenhower seized the opportunity to deliver a stirring address titled "The Chance for Peace." The president berated the Soviets for disrupting the postwar world, but he also invited more friendly relations and revealed his discomfort with militarism. "Every gun that is made, every warship launched, every rocket fired signifies, in the final sense, a theft from those who hunger and are not fed. . . . The cost of one modern heavy bomber is this: a modern brick school in more than 30 cities."[58]

Fearing nuclear war, Eisenhower often recommended arms-control measures, and he regretted that technology kept pushing nuclear weapons to more dangerous levels. Eisenhower's "Atoms for Peace" speech in December 1953 called for contributions of fissionable materials to an International Atomic Energy Agency that would then develop nonmilitary uses for atomic energy. Hardly slowing the arms race, the proposal did lead to the United States's signing agreements with thirty-nine nations to develop nuclear energy for peaceful purposes. In 1954 the president

Dwight D. Eisenhower (1890–1969). Well experienced in world affairs before becoming president, Eisenhower nurtured a "deeply rooted anti-Communism" and "an obsession with falling dominoes," writes his biographer Stephen E. Ambrose. Patient and deliberate, Eisenhower managed problems more than he solved them. About his style, Ike once said that he had no respect for the "desk-pounder" or the "loud and slick talker." (Dwight D. Eisenhower Library)

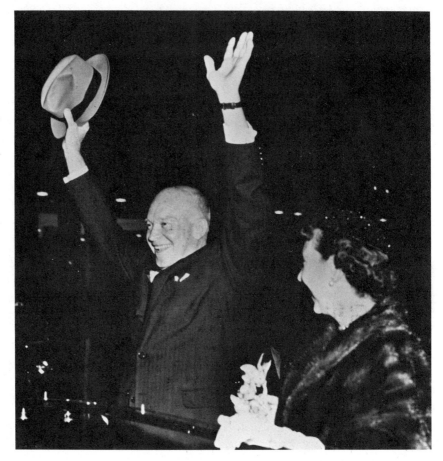

rejected advice that the United States use nuclear weapons or send troops to Indochina to forestall a Vietnamese victory over the French. In his "Farewell Address" of early 1961, Eisenhower warned against a "military-industrial complex"—the powerful lobby of "an immense military establishment and a large arms industry"—which threatened peace and "democratic processes."[59]

Ike's peace initiatives fizzled and his antimilitarist sentiments seldom translated into effective policies. He unilaterally halted the testing of nuclear weapons in 1958, yet two years later the U.S. atomic stockpile had tripled from 6,000 to 18,000 weapons. He sent troops to Lebanon, and by 1959 one million Americans served overseas in forty-two countries. By 1960 the Defense Department controlled 35 million acres of land at home and abroad. Defense budgets averaged more than $40 billion a year, although Eisenhower kept limits on them because he feared "'busting' ourselves" by overspending.[60] Defense expenditures ate up one-half of the 1960 U.S. budget.

JOHN FOSTER DULLES, MCCARTHYISM, AND THE NEW LOOK

Although Secretary of State John Foster Dulles (1953–1959) seemed, from his stern public image, a less flexible Cold Warrior than Eisenhower, he and the president "held strikingly parallel views," and "the documents confirm that it was the president who made the decisions."[61] Dulles's grandfather, John W. Foster, had served as secretary of state in 1892–1893 and the grandson had more than once trooped behind him in foreign capitals. Tutelage from his Presbyterian minister father, education at Princeton and George Washington Law School, service as a negotiator on reparations at the Paris Peace Conference at Versailles, membership in the prestigious Wall Street firm of Sullivan and Cromwell, and worldwide activity on behalf of the Federal Council of Churches gave Dulles a varied, cosmopolitan experience before World War II. After the war he helped promote bipartisanship. In 1952 he assailed the very policies of the Truman administration he had helped to shape, but he later admitted that his desire to elect Eisenhower had fueled this political gambit.

Forceful, ambitious, sharp, self-righteous, Dulles combined moral idealism with hard-nosed realism. He pursued ideals through the exercise of power. He once told a journalist that the United States "is almost the only country strong enough and powerful enough to be moral."[62] A dull, flat speaker with a lecturing tone, he preferred "personal diplomacy"—face-to-face negotiations with foreign diplomats. He disliked compromise. "We must be constantly vigilant lest we fall into a trap," he warned.[63] Winston Churchill once remarked that Dulles was the only bull he knew who carried his own china shop with him. Although Dulles publicly portrayed the Cold War as a biblical contest between atheistic communism and Western Christianity, Dulles thought with more sophistication. Still, foreigners thought his incantations too hectoring, and his public, if not his private, stances too rigid.

Eisenhower-Dulles defense policy took the name "New Look." It emphasized nuclear weaponry and air power in order to ensure "massive retaliation."[64] Under this concept, Washington apparently would drop atomic bombs on a communist aggressor if it stepped across the line. The idea derived from the administration's desire to enhance deterrence and to lower military costs by relying more on nuclear weapons than on conventional forces. The administration did not neglect conventional forces, alliances, covert actions, psychological warfare, or foreign aid as means to deter adversaries, but its pledge of massive retaliation did reflect a "more bang for the buck" mentality (or as one wag commented in Soviet terms, "more rubble for the ruble"). Later in the decade, Eisenhower and Dulles moved toward the idea of a "firebreak"—a delay between the beginning of a crisis and the launching of strategic nuclear weapons.[65]

With its huge nuclear arsenal and strong armed forces, the United States practiced "brinkmanship": not backing down in a crisis, even if it meant going to the brink of war. "Victory goes to him who can keep his nerve to the last fifteen minutes," Dulles wrote.[66] Keep enemies guessing, Dulles advised. But what if they guessed wrong? asked critics.

John Foster Dulles (1888–1959). Although the president sincerely admired his secretary of state, Eisenhower did question Dulles's "practice of becoming a sort of international prosecuting attorney." More biting, Soviet foreign minister V. M. Molotov described Dulles and his brother Allen, who was CIA director, as "the sort who would pick your pockets and cut off your head in one stroke." (*The Reporter*, 1956. Copyright 1956 by the Reporter Magazine Co.)

Joseph McCarthy (1909–1957). The notorious Republican senator from Wisconsin used the "big lie" to advance his political career. He castigated former secretaries Marshall and Acheson. Graduate of Marquette University, judge, and marine, the demagogic senator was once known as the "Pepsi-Cola Kid" for protecting the interests of that company. The Senate "condemned" him in December 1954. (*The Reporter*, 1951. Copyright 1951 by Fortnightly Publishing Co., Inc.)

As for the Third World, Eisenhower in 1954 uttered the "falling domino principle": "You have a row of dominoes set up, you knock over the first one, and what will happen to the last one is the certainty that it will go over very quickly."[67] Thus if one country in Asia fell to the communists, others supposedly would fall in rapid succession. The 1957 "Eisenhower Doctrine" read that the United States would intervene in the Middle East if any government threatened by a communist takeover requested aid. Sold as dynamic departures from the Truman administration, such slogans offered only tactical changes in a continuing containment strategy.

Eisenhower once said that "sometimes Foster is just too worried about being accused of sounding like Truman and Acheson."[68] Dulles had witnessed the harassment of Acheson by Republican right-wingers in endless congressional hearings. Dulles avoided a similar fate by showing his anticommunist colors early and by permitting McCarthyites to investigate the State Department, which Senator Joseph McCarthy claimed harbored communists or their sympathizers. Dulles appointed an ex-FBI man and McCarthy henchman, Scott McLeod, the chief security officer. McLeod's distaste for Democrats and "New Dealers" soon manifested itself in witch-hunting tactics that confused criticism with treason. He soon hired 350 zealous investigators to ferret out drunkards, homosexuals, incompetents, and "incompatibles."[69] In early 1953, Dulles ordered books authored by "Communists, fellow travellers, et cetera" to be removed from the libraries of American overseas information centers.[70] Who was an "et cetera"? Bureaucrats gave the broadest interpretation and tossed out the books of such people as Bert Andrews (Washington bureau chief of the *New York Herald Tribune*), Joseph Davies (former ambassador to the Soviet Union), Walter White (deceased former head of the NAACP), and the historian Foster Rhea Dulles, the secretary of state's own cousin.

"I Hear There's Something Wrong With Your Morale." Secretary Dulles launched a damaging purge of Foreign Service Officers. President Eisenhower, refusing to get into "a pissing contest with that skunk" McCarthy, whom he privately viewed as "a pimple on [the] path of progress," did nothing to halt the political onslaught against the State Department. (*Herblock's Here and Now,* Simon & Schuster, 1955)

One of the more prominent and tragic cases centered on Foreign Service Officer John Carter Vincent, an independent-minded "China hand" who during World War II reported that Jiang Jieshi would probably lose. McCarthyites took this professional analysis to mean that Vincent plotted to defeat Jiang. A State Department Loyalty Board cleared Vincent, but the Civil Service Loyalty Review Board, by a vote of 3 to 2, doubted his loyalty to the United States. Dulles at first rejected that decision, but he forced Vincent out by questioning his standards as an officer. Dulles once asked Vincent if he had read Stalin's *Problems of Leninism*. Vincent said he had not and Dulles replied that Vincent would not have advocated the China policy he did if he had read it. One student of China affairs has commented that "since Stalin failed in China no less than Truman, one may wonder whether Stalin read his own book."[71] Another China specialist, John Paton Davies, also lost his job even though nine security reviews had cleared him. By 1961, the purged Bureau of Far Eastern Affairs had become "dominated by Cold Warriors and staffed largely by the cowed."[72] "The wrong done," the journalist Theodore A. White has written, "was to poke out the eyes and ears of the State Department on Asian affairs, to blind American foreign policy."[73]

THE GLACIER GRINDS ON: KHRUSHCHEV, EISENHOWER, AND THE COLD WAR

Like a huge glacier, the Cold War continued to move across the international landscape. After Stalin's death, Eisenhower asked "what is the Soviet Union ready to do?"[74] The early signs for improved Soviet-American relations seemed auspicious. Moscow helped end the deadlock over Korea, opened diplomatic relations with Yugoslavia and Greece, abandoned territorial claims against Turkey, toned down its anti-American rhetoric, and launched a "peace offensive." Although the Soviet crushing of an East Berlin riot in June reminded Americans of the past, the freeing of Stalinist victims from forced labor camps conversely suggested that Stalin's heirs would not mimic their long-time autocrat.

Soviet leaders scrambled for position in the succession crisis. Nikita S. Khrushchev, son of a farmer, and for years the Communist party boss of the Ukraine, eventually climbed to the top of the Kremlin hierarchy. By September 1953, Khrushchev had become first secretary of the Central Committee of the party; five years later he became premier. Portly and amiable, Khrushchev impressed people as an impulsive, competitive person of coarse speech. Eisenhower found him "shrewd, tough, and coldly deliberate even when he was pretending to be consumed by anger."[75] Khrushchev thought Eisenhower "a good man, but he wasn't very tough."[76]

Eisenhower and Khrushchev continued their nations' military buildups, driving up defense budgets. Although Soviet ground forces outnumbered their American counterparts by a 2 to 1 margin, the United States possessed a far wider margin in strategic bombers, and they stood ready to vaporize hundreds of Soviet targets with nuclear bombs. In an attempt to bolster Western defenses through

Nikita S. Khrushchev (1894–1971). The short, stocky Soviet leader denounced Stalin in a "de-Stalinization" speech in 1956. He became premier in 1958 and fell from power in 1964. "How can this fat, vulgar man with his pig eyes and ceaseless flow of talk, really be the head—the aspirant Tsar—of all those millions of people?" British prime minister Harold MacMillan once crudely asked. (*The Reporter,* 1956. Copyright 1956 by The Reporter Magazine Co.)

greater integration, including West German units, Dulles sponsored the European Defense Community (EDC). When the French balked, he warned them that the United States would undertake an "agonizing reappraisal"of U.S. security commitments.[77] Paris called his bluff and rejected EDC. The secretary did gain West German membership in NATO in May 1955. That year became notable for ringing communist nations with military alliances: SEATO went into effect, the American defense treaty with nationalist China became active, the Baghdad Pact formed, and West Germany joined NATO. In response,the Soviets formed their own military organization, the Warsaw Pact of Eastern European states.

On one issue, Austria, the two great powers also competed, but then cooperated in a rare example of productive Cold War diplomacy. Each side had hoped to pull occupied Austria into its own orbit, but the Austrians preferred neutrality and neither Vienna nor Moscow nor Washington desired a partitioned state. After years of negotiations in which the Austrians actively participated, the Soviet Union and the United States agreed by treaty in May 1955 to end their ten-year occupation and to create an independent, neutral Austria. The agreement emerged not only because the Austrians adeptly pressed for it but because both the Soviets and the Americans found elements of "victory" in it. First, each side effectively denied Austria to the other's sphere. Second, Moscow demonstrated a commitment to peaceful coexistence. Finally, Washington welcomed a possible model for Eastern European nations eager to roll back Soviet power. As Secretary Dulles remarked, he expected the Red Army's withdrawal from Austria to become "contagious" among nationalists and "carry a whole lot of new problems into the satellite area."[78]

Also in May 1955, the Soviet Union and the United States, under United Nations–sponsored negotiations, seemed close to an agreement to prohibit the use and manufacture of nuclear weapons, reduce conventional forces, and create an inspection system to monitor compliance—all terms that the United States had insisted on for years and that post-Stalinist Kremlin leaders now seriously advanced in order to halt the drain on the Soviet economy from swelling military expenses.

"The whole thing looks too good to be true," remarked the French representative on the UN Disarmament Subcommittee.[79] So it was. Within several months, the United States backed away from the disarmament proposal. Why? Steeped in the Cold War mentality, U.S. officials, especially the military high brass of the Joint Chiefs of Staff, still did not trust the Soviets and expected them to cheat. But more important, John Foster Dulles and Dwight D. Eisenhower sought to win the Cold War, not negotiate its end. As a former policymaker has written, "what Dulles feared about proposals for disarmament in 1955 was simply that they might lead to agreement."[80]

Throughout 1954–1955, from several corners of the globe, came calls for a summit meeting of the great powers. Winston Churchill made an eloquent plea and Democrats in Congress urged negotiations. Dulles responded with a long list of reasons why Americans should not meet with the Soviets: a summit conference would permit them to use propaganda on a grand scale; it would let them appear equal to Americans; a summit might encourage neutralism, for other countries would fear less and align less; better to wait until West Germany had rearmed; and the Soviets would not bargain seriously because totalitarianism depended upon an outside enemy. Eisenhower, however, decided to test Soviet intentions through discussions. Overruled, Dulles nonetheless advised the president to avoid social settings with Soviet officials and to maintain "an austere countenance on occasions where photographing together is inevitable."[81]

The Soviet Union, the United States, Britain, and France met in Geneva July 18–23, 1955. Just before leaving for that beautiful city where diplomats historically seek international peace, Eisenhower and Dulles assured members of Congress that "Geneva was not going to be another Yalta."[82] The reference was timely, for early in 1955 Dulles had engineered the publication of the secret *Yalta Papers* in an abortive attempt to embarrass the Democrats. Geneva did not repeat Yalta, because the Big Four struck no concrete agreements. Everybody tried to score points for prestige. Even evangelist Billy Graham journeyed to the city of John Calvin and preached to a throng of 35,000. Eisenhower ignored Dulles's advice and behaved in his usual amiable manner. The Soviet delegates worried about appearances; Khrushchev, for example, became embarrassed because the Soviets flew into Geneva in a two-engine plane, whereas Eisenhower and Dulles disembarked from a more imposing four-motor aircraft. A peasant of little schooling, Khrushchev knew that he was being tested by graduates of West Point, Eton, Oxford, and the Sorbonne. "Would we be able to represent our country competently?" Khrushchev thought before Geneva.[83]

American officials believed before Geneva that they would have the upper hand in bargaining. As Ike told a press conference, the United States approached negotiations "from a greater position of strength than we ever had before."[84] Dulles said before Geneva that the Soviet Union wobbled on the verge of economic collapse. That drew a heated rebuttal from Khrushchev. At the conference itself, East and West split over the issues of German reunification, European security, and arms control, but the conferees "disagreed so nicely."[85] Each side wanted to unite Germany but to set the terms. Americans sought a unified Germany in NATO. Both sides favored arms control, but parted over methods. Eisenhower dramatically presented his "Open Skies" proposal, which called for the Soviet Union and the United States to exchange maps and submit their military installations to aerial inspection to ensure compliance with control agreements.[86] On this American propaganda ploy designed to counter pre-Geneva Soviet appeals for disarmament, Eisenhower later remarked: "We knew the Soviets wouldn't accept it. We were sure of that, but we took a look and thought it was a good move."[87] "A bald espionage plot," sniffed Khrushchev.[88] Indeed, secrecy comprised one of the Soviets' deterrents, keeping Americans guessing on whether the inferior Soviets were catching up in airborne striking power. That secrecy ended in 1956 when the United States began secret reconnaisance flights of high-altitude U-2 planes over the Soviet Union.

When Eisenhower returned home, he applauded a "new spirit of conciliation and cooperation" and assured Americans that he had not penned any secret agreements.[89] After the largely ceremonial conference, Moscow recognized West Germany and Khrushchev endorsed "détente." Yet, he went on: "If anybody thinks that for this reason we shall forget about Marx, Engels, and Lenin, he is mistaken. This will happen when shrimps learn to whistle."[90] The Geneva summit did initiate cultural exchanges, most notably Vice President Nixon's 1959 trip to the Soviet Union, where at a display of American products in a Moscow exhibition, he engaged Khrushchev in the "kitchen debate" on capitalism, communism, and the "commodity gap."[91] And the journalist I. F. Stone wrote in 1955 about the visits of communists to the Kiwanis Club of Des Moines, Iowa, and about the excursions of American farmers to the fields of Kharkov: "Nothing is more deadly for the war spirit than the discovery that the enemy, too, is human."[92]

The thaw of 1955 marked a brief interlude in the Soviet-American confrontation in Europe. Neither Moscow nor Washington had the power to force significant changes in European alignments, and neither side wanted to risk war to alter the status quo. Disillusionment followed Geneva because differences remained great. Moscow still wanted Germany removed from NATO and NATO expunged from Europe. The United States still wanted the Soviets excluded from Eastern Europe and the indefinite perpetuation of U.S. nuclear superiority. Former ambassador W. Averell Harriman, a partisan Democrat, charged that the "free world was psychologically disarmed" by the "spirit of Geneva," which served only as a Soviet "smokescreen" for further aggression.[93] Harriman's extreme conclusion missed the degree to which Dulles was perpetuating the Cold War diplomacy that Harriman himself had helped launch in the 1940s.

After Geneva, Eisenhower contemplated not seeking reelection in 1956. That possibility almost became reality when he collapsed in September 1955 from a coronary thrombosis after playing twenty-seven holes of golf. But within months he recovered and won a substantial victory over Democratic candidate Adlai Stevenson, who had charged that the Eisenhower administration was losing the Cold War to the Soviets.

In February 1956, Khrushchev, once the loyal follower of Stalin and supporter of the bloody purges of the 1930s, delivered a momentous speech to the Twentieth Party Congress. He denounced Stalin for domestic crimes, initiated a "de-Stalinization" program, endorsed peaceful coexistence, and suggested that the

Preparation for the "Kitchen Debate." Khrushchev and Vice President Richard M. Nixon sip Pepsi-Cola at the American National Exhibition in Moscow in July 1959, just before their "kitchen debate" over what the Soviet leader called American "gadgets" that "are not needed in life." (PepsiCo, Inc.)

Kremlin would now recognize different brands of communism. In the communist nations of Eastern Europe, Khrushchev's apparent acceptance of Titoism emboldened nationalists and victims of Stalinism to challenge Stalinist leaders. The abolition of the Cominform in April seemed to demonstrate Moscow's new tolerance for diversity. Young people and intellectuals especially insisted on self-determination. In Poland, for example, a labor dispute in mid-1956 ballooned into national resistance to Soviet tutelage. After using force to put down riots, Moscow compromised with Polish nationalism by reluctantly accepting as the Polish Communist party chairman Wladyslaw Gomulka, heretofore denied influence because Stalin thought him too "Titoist." The United States, which had been giving aid to Tito himself for years, soon offered Poland economic assistance. Washington encouraged any crack in the communist edifice. "Our hearts go out" to the Poles, the president declared.[94]

Revolt erupted next in Hungary. Young revolutionaries marched and fought in the streets of Budapest. A new government, backed by local revolutionary councils throughout the country, took a drastic step when it announced that Hungary was pulling out of the Warsaw Pact and becoming neutral in the Cold War. Khrushchev looked on neutrals in Eastern Europe much as Dulles looked on them elsewhere—with utter disdain. The Soviet Union began to move troops into Hungary and on November 4 crushed the resistance with brute force. The courageous hand-to-tank combat of underarmed students and workers in the streets of

"I'll Be Glad to Restore Peace to the Middle East, Too." The ugly Soviet suppression of the Hungarian rebellion of 1956 prompted this telling cartoon by Herblock. (*Herblock's Special for Today,* Simon & Schuster, 1958)

Budapest stirred global sympathy. Approximately 4,000 Hungarians died. The West would have scored some propaganda points against the Soviets had not British, French, and Israeli troops invaded Egypt shortly before the Soviets smashed the Hungarian Revolution (see p. 357). The West now had to share the moral revulsion against aggression.

The Polish and Hungarian rebellions seemed to satisfy Dulles's dream of "liberation." In 1953, Congress had passed the first annual Captive Peoples' Resolution as a spur to self-determination in Eastern Europe. The Eisenhower administration had been encouraging discontent in Eastern Europe through the Voice of America and the CIA-financed Radio Free Europe, which beamed anti-Soviet propaganda broadcasts into the Soviet sphere. A covert CIA program called RED SOX/RED CAP trained East European emigrés for paramilitary missions. Dulles also hinted that nations that split from the Soviet orbit would receive U.S. foreign aid.

Although Hungarian dissidents appealed for some kind of U.S. intervention and expected it, Washington found itself boxed. The United States simply lacked the means to direct or influence events in the Soviet sphere, short of full-scale war. "To annihilate Hungary," Eisenhower commented, "is in no way to help her."[95] Budapest was "as inaccessible to us as Tibet."[96] Hungary exposed "liberation" as a sham slogan that was aimed largely at winning votes in elections from Americans of East European background. The Eisenhower administration lowered immigration

Propaganda Balloons for Eastern Europe. Although the United States did not send troops or military supplies to Hungary during the 1956 uprising, in the 1950s the Free Europe Committee floated message-filled balloons across the "iron curtain" from West Germany to stir up unrest with Soviet rule. (Franklin D. Roosevelt Library)

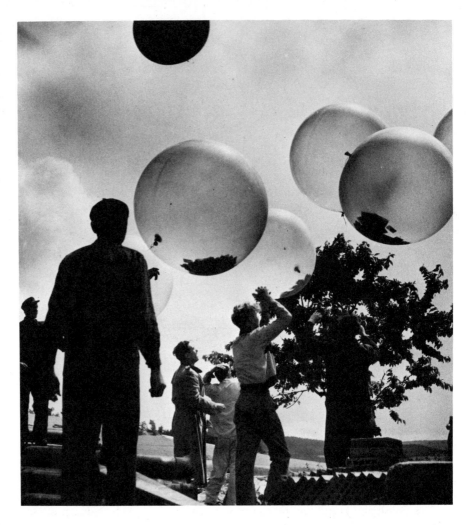

barriers to permit more than 20,000 Hungarian refugees to enter the United States and introduced a resolution condemning Soviet force in the General Assembly of the United Nations. Washington could do nothing more. Still, Dulles acclaimed "an irreversible trend" toward decentralization in the Soviet empire.[97]

MISSILES, BERLIN, AND THE U-2 MESS

In 1956–1957, the United States seemed on the defensive and the Soviets on the offensive. Washington's adjustment to this appearance took a familiar military course. The United States hastened to patch up its crumbling European alliance, rocked by American disapproval of British-French military actions in the Middle

East. Washington reinvigorated NATO and deployed intermediate range ballistic missiles in Britain and tactical nuclear weapons in Western Europe. Still, the French became bogged down in a colonial war in Algeria and had to transfer many of their NATO contingents to Africa. Many Western Europeans remained suspicious of the American push for German rearmament, worried about a resurgence of McCarthyism, and resented U.S. strictures on trade with communist countries. People in NATO nations also expressed doubt about America's credibility as an ally. That is, might not Americans fail to defend Western Europe against a Soviet attack lest U.S. countermeasures in Europe invite a Soviet nuclear onslaught against the United States itself? An economic recession in the United States in 1957 further sapped Western vitality. Unsettling, too, was the news of November 2, 1956, that John Foster Dulles had to undergo cancer surgery. The secretary of state lay incapacitated for weeks, and President Eisenhower had to steer the United States through Eastern European and Mideast crises without his trusted adviser. The United States and its allies were by no means weak or defenseless, but their unity and confidence waned.

On October 4, 1957, Cold War competition took a new turn. That day the Soviets launched into outer space the world's first man-made satellite, *Sputnik*. Two months earlier the Soviets had fired the first intercontinental ballistic missile (ICBM). These achievements in rocketry shocked Americans, for the Soviets had surpassed them in missile development. In June and again in September the United States had failed to launch an Atlas ICBM. Some Americans chastised Eisenhower for apparently letting American power and prestige slip. "The idea of *them* [Democrats] charging *me* with not being interested in *defense!*" President Eisenhower snapped. "Damn it, I've spent my whole life being concerned with defense of our country."[98] Even though the Soviets had test-fired only six ICBMs and the United States still had a significant lead in strategic weapons, prominent Americans had worried about a "bomber gap"; next, after *Sputnik*, they spoke of a "missile gap." Khrushchev fed worries by bragging about turning out rockets "like sausages."[99] A presidential commission study, the "Gaither Report," fed popular fears that the Soviets were outstripping the United States both militarily and economically. This "Gaither Report" of November 1957 urged a large expensive military buildup to improve U.S. "deterrent power."[100]

Eisenhower recoiled from the prospects of expanding the budget deficit, but he did agree to develop more ICBMs and disperse Strategic Air Command bombers. He nonetheless knew that *Sputnik* had not undermined U.S. security, because since 1956 American U-2 spy planes, flying at high altitude with sensitive instruments, had been gathering information on Soviet military capabilities. The president tried to explain without releasing the intelligence data. Yet when critics such as the nuclear strategist Albert Wohlstetter wrote about "our deep pre-Sputnik sleep" and charged that the strategic balance "is in fact precarious," Eisenhower could not reassure the American public.[101]

In January 1958, rocket scientists, many of them former Germans like Werner von Braun brought to the United States at the end of World War II, successfully launched an American satellite named Explorer I. In July, the National Aeronautics and Space Administration (NASA) was created; its high-priced operations culminated in 1969 in the landing of Americans on the moon. America's educational system received a jolt from *Sputnik,* too. Why did not "Johnny" keep up with "Ivan"? Many answered that Soviet schools offered superior instruction in mathematics and science. The National Defense Education Act (NDEA), passed in September 1958, provided for federal aid to finance new educational programs in the sciences, mathematics, and foreign languages. Soviet-American competition made education a Cold War issue. One university president observed that the nation's colleges and universities had become "bastions of our defense, as essential as . . . supersonic bombers."[102]

The continued militarization of the Cold War and the new emphasis on missile development alarmed George F. Kennan, an earlier architect of the containment doctrine. In November and December 1957 Kennan delivered the "Reith Lectures" in London, calling for the "disengagement" of foreign troops from Eastern Europe and Germany, restrictions on nuclear weapons in that area, and a unified, nonaligned Germany. Earlier in the year, Polish foreign minister Adam Rapacki had advocated a "denuclearized zone" in Central and Eastern Europe.[103] The "Rapacki Plan" seemed a sensible way to reduce the atomic arms race, but the Eisenhower administration, despite its own appeals for disarmament, did not pursue the proposal. Kennan tried to keep the idea alive through his eloquent lectures, widely broadcast over BBC radio. Also, in order to reduce Moscow's security fears, he sought to remove Germany from the Cold War and thereby permit a withdrawal of Soviet troops from Eastern Europe. Finally, Kennan urged the administration to "put our military fixations aside," to exercise diplomacy rather than to strengthen NATO.[104]

Kennan's suggestions elicited instant hostility and sparked a debate over strategy. Former secretary of state Dean Acheson spared Eisenhower and Dulles the task of debating "disengagement." "Next to the Lincoln Memorial in moonlight," the

"Braggers." In this Japanese cartoon, Khrushchev and Eisenhower brag about their missiles. "Everyone knows," General Nathan Twining told Eisenhower in 1958, "we already have a stockpile large enough to completely obliterate the Soviet Union." (Nasu, courtesy of the State Historial Society of Missouri)

columnist James Reston wrote, "the sight of Mr. Dean G. Acheson blowing his top is without doubt the most impressive view in the capital."[105] Acheson warned against a new American isolationism. Should Kennan's plan become reality, he scolded, the Soviet Union might reintroduce troops into Eastern Europe, threaten Western Europe, and actually sign an anti-American military pact with the new united Germany. A rearmed West Germany must remain in the American camp. German-born Henry A. Kissinger, a Harvard political scientist, also argued the need for a German defense line against a potentially aggressive Soviet Union. In his *Nuclear Weapons and Foreign Policy* (1957), Kissinger also criticized Dulles's concept of "massive retaliation" and appealed instead for a mobile, tactical missile system tied to flexible fighting units so that conventional wars would not ignite nuclear annihilation. The United States, Kennan answered, would never know Moscow's intentions unless it negotiated. He spoke of new "realities" in Europe that made the 1950s different from the 1940s. Walter Lippmann, who had criticized Kennan's containment in 1947, stood with him in 1957. People like Acheson and Kissinger, Lippmann complained, resembled "old soldiers trying to relive the battles in which they won their fame and glory. . . . Their preoccupation with their own past history is preventing them from dealing with the new phase of the Cold War."[106]

The "disengagement" debate had hardly subsided before a crisis over Berlin demonstrated the importance of Kennan's suggestions for defusing European issues. West Berlin, 110 miles inside communist East Germany, stuck like a bone in the

Soviet throat, as Khrushchev put it. Some 3 million East German defectors, many of them skilled workers, had used West Berlin as an escape route since 1949. For Americans and their allies, including the West German government of Konrad Adenauer, the city operated as an espionage and propaganda center for activities. West Berlin's prosperity, induced by billions of dollars in U.S. aid, glittered next to drab East Berlin. Washington heated Soviet tempers by crowing about West Berlin's economic success and applauding the East German exodus. The United States also insisted that the two Germanies unite under free elections and refused to recognize the East German government. Finally, the continued rearmament of West Germany, including American planes capable of dropping nuclear bombs, alarmed Moscow, which had endorsed the Rapacki Plan.

In November 1958 the Soviet Union boldly issued an ultimatum to solve the German "problem" through negotiations. Within six months, warned Khrushchev, unless East-West talks on Germany had begun, Moscow would sign a peace treaty with East Germany, thereby ending the occupation agreements still in effect from World War II and turning East Berlin over to the East German regime. He recommended that Berlin become a "free city" without foreign troops. Washington knew that to deal with East Germany would confirm the Soviet claim of two Germanies. Such an acceptance would in turn call into question the post–World War II occupation rights and hence the U.S. presence within West Berlin itself. Fearful that "if we let the Germans down they might shift their own position and even go neutralistic," Eisenhower balked at negotiating "disengagement" with the Soviets.[107] Dulles braced for an episode in brinkmanship. Dean Acheson and Army Chief of Staff Maxwell Taylor urged the president to test Soviet intentions by sending U.S. military units through the corridors to West Berlin. Eisenhower rejected such inflammatory advice and stalled. Eisenhower said privately that "in this gamble, we are not going to be betting white chips, building up the pot gradually and fearfully. Khrushchev should know that when we decide to act, our whole stack will be in the pot."[108] Khrushchev wanted to talk, not fight. "Do not hurry. The wind does not blow in your face. . . . The conditions are not ripe as yet for a new scheme of things," he told the militant East German leaders.[109] He backed away from his ultimatum and agreed to a foreign ministers conference for May 1959, which proved inconclusive, a trip in September 1959 to the United States to speak directly with Eisenhower, and ultimately a Paris summit meeting in May 1960.

Khrushchev's tour of the United States in September 1959 provided a real spectacle. Eisenhower personally welcomed him, hoping to "soften up the Soviet leader even a little bit. Except for the Austrian peace treaty, we haven't made a chip in the granite in seven years."[110] Dulles had died of cancer in April, so Eisenhower stood more in the forefront of diplomacy now. Khrushchev and his party took a national tour. The premier, seeming altogether human, inspected an IBM plant, fell in love with the city of San Francisco, cuddled babies just like an American politician, and visited a Hollywood movie set where he took offense at the bare legs exposed in a cancan dance—a sign to him of the decadence of Western capitalism. He heard Frank Sinatra sing "Live and Let Live." Khrushchev plugged "peaceful coexistence" and said that no one should take his "we will bury capitalism" statement in a literal or military sense. "I say it again—I've almost worn my tongue thin re-

Titan II Missile. Ten stories high and packing in one nuclear warhead the explosive power of 9 million tons of TNT (equivalent to 700 Hiroshima bombs), this intercontinental ballistic missile (ICBM) stands ready for launching from its underground silo. The decision to develop the Titan I came in 1955; the Titan booster was successfully tested four years later; and in 1962 the bigger and longer Titan II was launched. In 1963, this missile became part of the Strategic Air Command, deployed at bases in Arizona, Kansas, and Arkansas. (U.S. Air Force)

peating it—you may live under capitalism and we will live under socialism and build communism. The one whose system proves better will win."[111] Khrushchev reminded Americans that they had sent troops into the Russian civil war during the World War I period, and they reminded him that they had also sent relief aid in the early 1920s. "The plain people of America like me," he exulted. "It's just those bastards around Eisenhower that don't."[112] After ten days on the road, the Soviet premier went to Camp David, that quiet, secluded presidential retreat near the Catoctin Mountains in Maryland. For two days the two leaders exchanged war stories and discussed Berlin. Eisenhower would not agree to a new summit meeting until Khrushchev abandoned his Berlin ultimatum. The premier agreed to do so. Although the president and premier moved no closer to a German settlement, observers identified a "Spirit of Camp David"—a willingness on both sides to talk their way to détente.

In 1959–1960 Eisenhower himself made a number of foreign trips in a deliberate effort to ease tensions. Just before Khrushchev's visit to the United States, the president had flown to London, Paris, and Bonn for talks with European leaders. In December he traveled 22,000 miles to eleven nations in Europe, Asia, and North Africa. Television viewers "saw him call on Pope John XXIII, receive a Persian rug from the Shah of Iran, tour the Taj Mahal with India's [Jawaharlal] Nehru, and

U-2. The United States began work on this high-altitude reconnaissance aircraft in 1954. The following year a prototype flew for the first time. In 1956, the Lockheed-built forty-nine-foot-long spy plane began overflights of the Soviet Union to gather intelligence on Soviet missile development. With a range of 2,200 miles and a cruising speed of 460 miles per hour, the U-2 also conducted surveillance during the Suez crisis. On May 1, 1960, a U-2 piloted by Francis Gary Powers crashed near Sverdlovsk, an industrial area 1,200 miles inside the Soviet Union. Washington's clumsy handling of the incident and refusal to apologize, and President Eisenhower's announcement that flights over Soviet territory would continue, so angered Premier Nikita Khrushchev that he cancelled the Paris summit meeting scheduled for mid-May. (National Air and Space Museum, Smithsonian Institution, Photo No. 85-7309)

steam from Athens to Tunis aboard the cruiser *Des Moines,* the flagship of the U.S. Sixth Fleet."[113] Ike relished this "goodwill" tour. In February 1960, he toured Latin America for two weeks and encountered a mixed reception. And then he departed for the Paris summit meeting in May. There the "goodwill" ended.

Two weeks before that summit meeting, on May 1, 1960, an American airplane carrying high-powered cameras and other reconnaissance instruments was shot down over Sverdlovsk in the Ural Mountains of northern Russia, 1,200 miles inside the Soviet Union. On a CIA mission, the U-2 intelligence plane was flying from a base in Pakistan to one in Norway. Although such flights had gone on for four years and the Soviets had learned about them, this was the first time that Soviet firepower had reached the high–altitude craft. Pilot Francis Gary Powers's U-2 evidently had engine trouble and dropped several thousand feet before being shot down. He parachuted and was captured immediately, unable or unwilling to kill himself by taking his CIA-issued poison. CIA officials in the United States knew only that a plane was missing. NASA, used as "cover," announced routinely on May 3 that a "research airplane" studying weather patterns over Turkey had apparently crashed. Two days later Khrushchev cryptically announced that an American airplane had been shot down after it had violated Soviet air space. Thereafter, the Eisenhower administration bungled badly. The State Department fabricated a statement that a weather plane piloted by a civilian had probably strayed over Soviet territory by mistake. On May 6 Premier Khrushchev demolished that story by displaying photographs of the uninjured pilot and his spy equipment. The Soviets also had the crashed U-2. No longer able to keep the truth hidden, Eisenhower took responsibility for the U-2 reconnaissance flights as necessary to prevent another Pearl Harbor.

The fiasco came on the eve of the Paris summit meeting, where the status of Berlin and the question of controls on nuclear-weapons testing stood high on the agenda. Apparently preferring to wait until a new president took office, perhaps seizing an opportunity to show domestic hard-liners and Chinese critics of peaceful coexistence that he could be tough, and certainly angry about U.S. violations of Soviet air space, Khrushchev wrecked the conference. He denounced American aggression, demanded an apology for the U-2 flights, and stalked out. Thinking that a real opportunity to wind down the Cold War had been lost, Eisenhower bemoaned "the stupid U-2 mess" and looked forward to retirement on his Gettysburg farm.[114]

To the Brink with China, to the Market with Japan

The Chinese communists did not mourn this deterioration in Soviet-American relations. From the mid-1950s onward, Beijing castigated any sign of Soviet-American rapprochement. China repeatedly criticized Khrushchev for "yielding to evil" and "coddling wrong."[115]

As the Sino-Soviet schism widened, it became less tenable for U.S. officials to speak of a communist monolith, although many still did. But even John Foster Dulles admitted the split, and, seizing the opportunity, he worked to drive a wedge between Moscow and Beijing by "exerting maximum strain" on the Chinese communists to force them to ask the Soviets for help, "thereby placing additional stress on Russian-Chinese relations."[116] Many reasons other than U.S. pressure explain the Sino-Soviet split, including Moscow's refusal to help China develop nuclear capability. It remains unproven that the hard-line U.S. posture produced better results than a softer policy of trade and engagement might have achieved. In any case, under Eisenhower-Dulles policies, the Sino-American chasm gaped ever wider.

In early 1953, to press the People's Republic of China to accept an armistice in the Korean War, President Eisenhower "unleashed" Jiang Jieshi by announcing that the Seventh Fleet would no longer block his attempts to attack the mainland.[117] Jiang actually lacked the resources for a major fight, but the decision alarmed Beijing, especially after nationalist bombing raids began to hit coastal regions. Throughout the 1950s Jiang pledged a return to China. He received an annual average of more than $250 million in American economic and military assistance. The Seventh Fleet remained in the Taiwan Strait, for U.S. policy valued Jiang's Formosa as a military partner in Asia. In December 1954, Taiwan and the United States signed a mutual defense treaty. The following month, Congress, by an overwhelming vote of 83 to 3 in the Senate and 410 to 3 in the House, gave the president authority in the Formosa Resolution to employ American troops if necessary to defend Taiwan and adjoining islands.

In fall 1954 the United States created SEATO, an alliance with France, Britain, Australia, New Zealand, Thailand, Pakistan, and the Philippines. The new pact essentially targeted "Red China" and Beijing's support of nationalist revolution in Indochina. Washington also resisted cultural or economic contacts with China. American officials forbade American journalists to accept China's 1956 invitation to visit the mainland. The State Department even banned the shipment of a panda bear to the United States, because the animal had been born in China. At the 1954 Geneva Conference on Indochina (see next chapter), Chinese and American diplomats barely mixed. At one point Foreign Minister Zhou Enlai approached Secretary Dulles intending to shake hands, but Dulles, afraid that photographers would record this contaminating event, brusquely shunned Zhou's outstretched hand by turning his back. The United States also imposed a trade embargo on China.

In a crisis that "illustrates the danger of mutual isolation," China and the United States lurched toward the brink in 1954–1955.[118] Jinmen (Quemoy) and Mazu (Matsu) lay just a few miles off the southeastern China coast in the Taiwan Strait, two of some thirty small offshore islands that the nationalists had managed to hold when they fled to Taiwan in 1949. Jiang had fortified the two islands with thousands of troops and used the outposts to raid the mainland. As the United States negotiated the defense treaty with Jiang in summer 1954, Beijing unfurled a "Liberate Taiwan" global propaganda campaign to counter the clear implication of the treaty: that the United States recognized an independent Taiwan. On September 3, 1954, the local Chinese commander ordered his shore batteries to bombard Jinmen. The decision did not seem out of the ordinary to him, because communist and nationalist forces had been exchanging fire for more than a year, and his immediate goal was to intercept a nationalist supply ship—to answer a provocation. The Chinese did not intend to invade Jinmen, and they certainly did not anticipate the U.S. response.

Mao Zedong (1893–1976). Chief of the Communist party in "Red China," father of the successful Communist Revolution, and radical philosopher-poet, Mao vigorously criticized United States "imperialism." Yet he helped launch Sino-American détente before his death. (*The Reporter*, 1956. Copyright 1956 by The Reporter Magazine Co.)

American officials had never considered the offshore islands militarily valuable to Taiwan (more than 100 miles away), and they had cautioned Jiang against escalating coastal warfare. "Quemoy is not our ship," Eisenhower said at first. People would ask, "What do we care what happens to those yellow people out there?"[119] After September 3, however, the president changed his view, interpreting the shelling as a stab at American credibility, as a Cold War probe. Jinmen and Mazu, Vice President Nixon asserted, had become "stakes" in the "poker game of world politics."[120] U.S. officials also learned that two American servicemen, members of the Military Assistance Advisory Group, had died in the bombardment.

Wanting to avoid a long-term commitment, seeking flexibility, and hoping to deter further Chinese military action, Eisenhower decided to keep Mao puzzled about U.S. intentions. The United States signed the defense treaty with Taiwan, and Congress gave the president a blank check in the Formosa Resolution. Mao also practiced brinkmanship: In mid-January 1955, he activated a standing plan and sent the People's Liberation Army to overrun a nationalist garrison in the offshore island group called the Dachens. Heeding U.S. advice, Jiang pulled his troops out; then Washington took up Mao's challenge. Eisenhower brandished nuclear weapons, stating publicly that he would use them "just exactly as you would use a bullet or anything else."[121] The Joint Chiefs of Staff readied plans to drop several Hiroshima-size bombs on coastal cities with expected casualties in the millions.

Dismissing the atomic threat, but lacking guaranteed support from the Soviet Union and reacting to alarms voiced by Asian nations attending the Bandung Conference (see p. 355), China offered in April to discuss tensions with the United States. The crisis quickly quieted. Beginning in Geneva, and after 1958 in Warsaw, Chinese and American officials talked at the ambassadorial level about Taiwan, trade, and other topics. These limited discussions constituted the only sensible, civil element in Sino-American relations.

After the deployment of U.S. tactical nuclear weapons on Taiwan, and after Jiang had augmented his forces to more than 100,000 on the offshore islands, Mao answered in August 1958 by once again shelling Jinmen and Mazu. During the new crisis, Eisenhower resisted military advice for "an immediate counter-attack with atomic weapons" and instead ordered U.S. airlifts and Seventh Fleet escorts for nationalist supply ships.[122] Recalling Munich, the president disavowed appeasement. America's European allies protested against a wastage of U.S. resources over Jinmen and Mazu. Beijing vowed "to deal resolute blows and take necessary military action" against Jiang's "clique."[123] Mao told Soviet foreign minister Andrei Gromyko that "it's getting so hot, and we want Eisenhower to take a shower."[124] Gromyko urged a peaceful settlement instead.

Eisenhower and Dulles stepped back from the brink, as did the People's Republic. After Dulles and Jiang signed an agreement in October that the Formosan leader would not use force against the mainland, Jiang withdrew some troops from Jinmen and Mazu and the United States suspended escorts of nationalist vessels. Beijing relaxed its bombardment of the islands. "Who would have thought when we fired a few shots," Mao asked, "that it would stir up such an earth-shattering storm?"[125] After the Taiwan Strait crises, Beijing became more determined than ever to acquire its own nuclear deterrent, setting off alarm bells in both Moscow and Washington.

As it went to the brink with the People's Republic, the United States continued to rebuild Japan, cultivating it as a dependent, anticommunist partner, all the while worrying China, the Soviet Union, the Koreas, and other past victims of Japanese aggression. Two September 8, 1951, agreements guided Japanese-American relations for the decade. The first, a peace treaty signed by the United States and forty-seven other nations, provided for the ending of American occupation on April 28, 1952. The second, the Mutual Security Treaty signed by Washington and Tokyo, provided for U.S. defense of Japan and the stationing of American arms and forces on Japanese soil. Japan agreed to create a small military, eventually called Self-Defense Forces, which could not be used outside the nation. The military pact provoked considerable friction. Many Japanese resented the U.S. bases and the U.S. pressure to rearm, and throughout the 1950s, with popu-

Neighborhood Street and Coca-Cola in Tokyo, Japan. Although Japan developed a booming export economy in the 1950s, it also imported famous U.S. products. In this way, the American and Japanese cultures intersected, sometimes with ease, sometimes not. (Library of Congress)

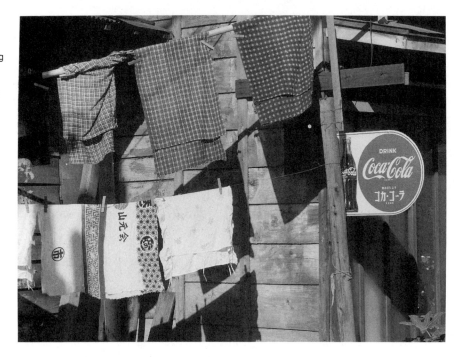

lar opinion favoring "rice before guns," mass street demonstrations strained relations.[126] Meanwhile, American leaders who insisted that Japan pay for more of its own defense sharply criticized the Tokyo government for obstructing rearmament.

The plight of the *Fukuryu Maru* (*Lucky Dragon*), a Japanese fishing boat, heightened the debate. On March 1, 1954, the United States tested its new hydrogen bomb in the Bikini Atoll (Marshall Islands). The *Lucky Dragon* was fishing for tuna near the area. After the huge fireball erupted, shifting winds sprinkled radioactive fallout on the crew. The contaminated ash caused severe nausea, fever, and blisters. One crew member died, igniting international protest against nuclear testing in the atmosphere. When the American ambassador in Tokyo dismissed Japanese complaints as emotionalism and Washington waited many months before compensating the victims, Japanese citizens protested American insensitivity.

After negotiators signed a renewed Japanese-American defense pact in January 1960, hundreds of thousands marched and rioted against the retention of U.S. bases. Although the Japanese government pushed the new treaty through the Diet (the parliament), the prime minister was forced to resign and President Eisenhower had to cancel his goodwill trip to Japan.

Even though huge U.S. military purchases in Japan during the Korean War—for Toyota trucks, for example—spurred economic recovery, Secretary Dulles still complained in 1954 that Japan "has been listless and drifting and apparently expecting merely to be taken care of by [the] U.S."[127] Eager to lower the costs of subsidizing Japanese reconstruction and to blunt possible communist exploitation of economic instability, U.S. officials encouraged Japan to develop a prosperous export-oriented economy. Tokyo launched an economic hyper-expansion—the "Japanese miracle." By the mid-1950s, Japan began to enjoy double-digit economic growth by using large sums of U.S. foreign aid, buying and copying American technology (Motorola helped the electronics industry get started), inviting an industrious and loyal workforce to cooperate closely with management for efficiency and quality control, practicing trade protectionism, and spending money on research and development rather than on military weaponry. With conspicuous national self-confidence, Japan became not only America's military ally but also eventually its economic competitor.

THE THIRD WORLD RISES: REVOLUTIONARY NATIONALISM AND NONALIGNMENT

In the years 1946–1960, thirty-seven new nations emerged from colonial status in Asia, Africa, and the Middle East. In 1958, twenty-eight prolonged guerrilla insurgencies raged. Eighteen countries became independent in 1960 alone. Revolutions and the collapse of empires thus claimed a central place in international affairs. These great changes occurred in the "Third World"—a term for those nations that belonged neither to the capitalist "West" nor to the communist "East." At first called "backward" and then "developing" countries, Third World nations generally consisted of nonwhite, agricultural peoples in the southern half of the globe. Once the Cold War lines stabilized in Europe, the Soviet-American confrontation shifted to the Third World. The stakes remained high. These countries abounded in raw materials and had for decades served the needs of the industrial nations. In 1959 more than one-third of American direct private investments abroad were in the Third World. These nations also bought manufactured goods and provided sites for air and naval bases and intelligence facilities.

The volatile conditions in these "emerging" nations did not permit easy management by outsiders. Many of their leaders were anticolonial revolutionaries who established leftist, undemocratic regimes. Long exploited, these poor countries eagerly sought economic improvement without foreign ownership. Nationalism flourished. Many new nations declared themselves uncommitted, nonaligned, or neutral in the Cold War. In longer-established Third World nations, particularly in Latin America, in an effort to beat back rebel challenges, the United States continued to support governments controlled by military, political, or economic elites.

The Eisenhower administration and its successors fared poorly. American leaders did not deal with the new nationalism as a force in itself, but as part of the Cold War struggle. They disparaged "nationalism" and "neutralism," claiming that the phenomena only helped the communist cause. They assumed that Moscow inspired much of the trouble in the Third World. "Yet to blame the danger of these [explosions] on the presence of Communists," one scholar has written, "is like blaming the inherent danger in a huge mass of exposed combustible materials on the

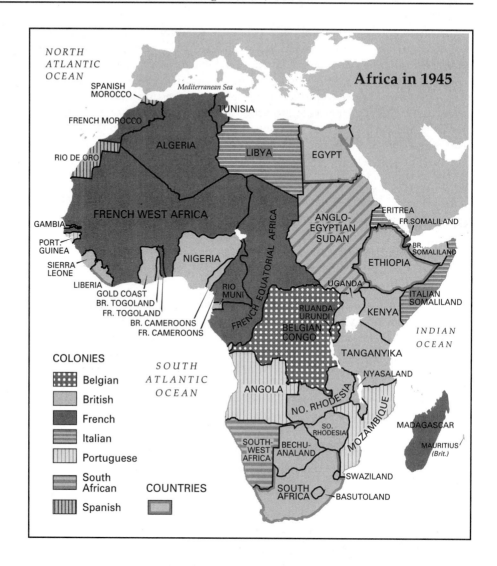

possible presence of arsonists."[128] The Eisenhower–Dulles team tried to apply the venerable containment doctrine to these regions in a futile effort to curb the new challenge.

The nation's great wealth proved a handicap. Known as the "People of Plenty," to borrow the title of a 1954 book by the historian David M. Potter, Americans found that foreigners both envied and resented America's unmatched abundance; some wanted to acquire American material culture—from blue jeans to sports cars—and grew indignant over the difficulty of doing so. The image of the "Ugly American" exacerbated foreign resentment. In 1958 William J. Lederer and Eugene Burdick wrote a novel with that title to underscore the tarnished U.S. reputation in the Third World. They noted, among other problems, that Americans abroad flaunted their wealth and that U.S. diplomats often isolated themselves from the poor countryside by living lavishly in a "Golden Ghetto."[129] The authors ap-

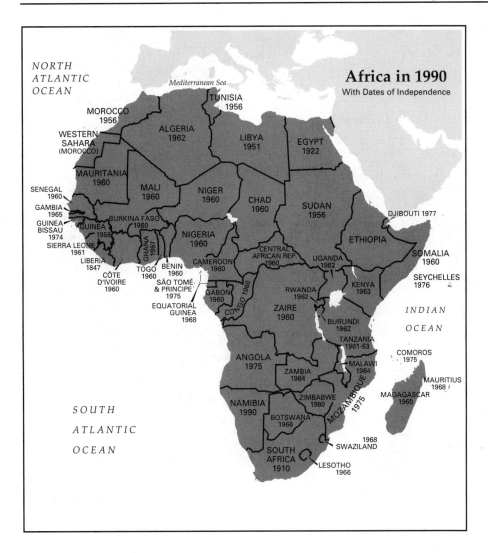

pealed for Foreign Service Officers who spoke the language of the host country. Unless American officials moved more among "the people," they argued, the United States would lose the struggle against communism.

American racism, symbolized by Jim Crow practices, also handicapped the United States. In December 1952, when the attorney general asked the Supreme Court to strike down segregation in public schools, his brief read that "it is in the context of the present world struggle between freedom and tyranny that the problem of racial discrimination must be viewed." American segregation, in short, "furnished grist for the Communist propaganda mills."[130] It did. In 1955 an airport restaurant in Texas refused service to the Indian ambassador because of his dark skin. In 1957, on Route 40 leading into Washington, the finance minister of Ghana was denied food at a Howard Johnson's. President Eisenhower tried to assuage the insult by inviting him to breakfast at the White House. In the same year, when

Anti-Imperialist Protest. During his tour of Asia in 1953, Vice President Nixon encountered this nationalist sign of disapproval. (Department of State, National Archives)

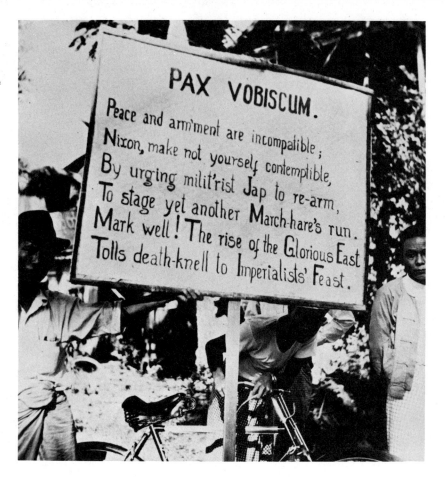

PAX VOBISCUM.

Peace and arm'ment are incompatible;
Nixon, make not yourself contemptible,
By urging milit'rist Jap to re-arm,
To stage yet another March-hare's run.
Mark well! The rise of the Glorious East
Tolls death-knell to Imperialists' Feast.

Eisenhower sent federal troops to Little Rock, Arkansas, to escort black children to school in the midst of ugly white protest, the president criticized that state for a "tremendous disservice . . . to the nation in the eyes of the world."[131] With Soviet propaganda in the Third World mocking the blatant contradiction between America's professed principles and actual practice, the Voice of America struggled to create a more favorable image.

Americans professed a revolutionary tradition ("the Spirit of '76") and often said they identified with the revolutionary aspirations of others. But that tradition and American foreign policy diverged in the post–World War II period. Americans had become propertied representatives of the status quo. Revolution now threatened America's national interest because it destabilized a world order that guaranteed Americans both a prominent position in international relations and an affluent society. Mr. Dooley had remarked at the start of the century: "A riv'lution can't be bound be th' rules iv th' game because it's again' the rules iv th' game."[132] Americans at mid-century clung to the "rules."

The American Revolution hardly resembled the wrenching social revolutions of the twentieth century. "The men who pushed the American Revolution were not nationalists compelled to spend years in the jails of the colonial power," the historian Carl N. Degler has written, "but political leaders seeking only to continue their free governments as they knew them all their lives."[133] Many Americans had been soured by the bloody excesses of the French Revolution. In the 1830s, Alexis de Tocqueville observed that "in no other country in the world is love of property more active and more anxious than in the United States; nowhere does the majority display less inclination for those principles which threaten to alter, in whatever manner, the laws of property."[134] As early-twentieth-century revolutions, like those in Mexico, China, and Russia, rocked international equilibrium, the United States increasingly found itself a target rather than a model of revolution. One government report put the problem frankly in 1945: "The United States leans toward propertied classes who place a premium on order and trade."[135] So it was during the Eisenhower years. In late 1960, when forty-three Afro-Asian states, led by India, sponsored a United Nations resolution championing liberation from colonialism, the United States abstained from voting, not wishing to offend Cold War friends like Portugal.

The Soviets, with their own brand of revolutionary past, had their troubles in the Third World, too. On the ideological level, both Marxism and the professed anticolonialism of the Soviet Union enjoyed wide appeal. In the mid-1950s Khrushchev toured India, Burma, and Afghanistan; and the Soviet Union, however inexpertly, launched a foreign aid offensive. It agreed, for example, to build a $91 million steel plant in India and the Aswan Dam in Egypt. Between 1954 and 1959 Indonesia received the equivalent of a quarter-billion dollars in Soviet aid. At the Bandung Conference of April 1955, where twenty-nine "nonaligned" states representing about one-quarter of the world's population met to applaud "neutralism" and the Soviet call for "peaceful coexistence," it became evident that the "free world" held less popularity than the "Communist world" in the Third World.

Yet the Soviet Union bumped up against nationalism, too, and gained few allies. Egypt's Gamal Abdul Nasser and India's Jawaharlal Nehru would not become Soviet clients. As Nehru once said, India refused to become the "plaything" or "pawn" of other nations.[136] Khrushchev, during a 1955 trip in India, vehemently denounced the West, and the neutralist Indians resented this blatant effort to bring the Cold War into their country. Then, too, Arab nationalism, not Soviet communism, dominated the Middle East. And in Latin America, between 1945 and 1955, sixteen nations outlawed the Communist party. The Soviets, like the Americans, could not tolerate or exploit independent nationalism. Nor did they have the economic resources to make good on many of their foreign aid promises. Finally, they could not explain away the giant contradiction between their rhetoric on self-determination and their suppression of Eastern European countries.

American officials remained fearful, however, that communism would exploit nationalistic sentiment and poverty in the Third World. Foreign aid became a primary U.S. tool for combating the perceived threat. So did the Central Intelligence Agency, noted for its manipulation of Third World events. Whereas during the 1949–1952 period some three-quarters of total U.S. economic assistance went to

Europe, in the years 1953–1957 three-quarters flowed to developing countries. By 1961 more than 90 percent of U.S. aid went to the Third World. But to Washington's distress, many of the recipients refused to choose sides in the Cold War. Third World nonalignment drew fire from Americans seeking political returns from foreign aid. To Dulles, neutralism seemed but a deceitful stage on the road to communism. So he declared it an "immoral and shortsighted conception."[137] With such negative statements the United States separated itself from the Third World, becoming the New Rome—a counterrevolutionary in a revolutionary world.

Stormy Weather: Nationalism in the Middle East and Latin America

Crises in the Middle East and Latin America illustrated troubled U.S. relations with the Third World. The Middle East became a particularly tumultuous region (see map, pages 442–443). In 1952 Gamal Abdul Nasser led young Egyptian army officers against King Farouk, their vulgar, pro-Western ruler, who fled to Europe with his harem and his wealth. Nasser initiated land reform and pledged to eliminate British control of the Suez Canal. A 1954 agreement, reluctantly signed by London, provided for a phased withdrawal. To maintain Western influence in the Middle East, thwart Soviet expansion, and fill what U.S. officials thought was a defense "vacuum," Washington in 1955 promoted the Baghdad Pact, a military alliance of Britain, Turkey, Iran, Iraq, and Pakistan.[138] Iran had been won over in 1953 when the United States, through the intervention of the CIA and a cut-off of foreign aid, helped overthrow the nationalist regime of Mohammed Mossadegh, who had attempted to nationalize foreign oil interests. American companies produced about 50 percent of the Middle East's petroleum. Of Europe's crude oil imports in 1955, 89 percent came from that region.

Israel drew closer to the United States through foreign aid totaling $374 million from 1952 to 1961. Yet bitter Arab-Israeli conflict thwarted U.S. hopes for order in the Middle East. After the Israelis raided the Gaza Strip in 1955 and exposed Egypt's military weakness, Cairo signed an arms agreement with Czechoslovakia. Heretofore Western nations had monopolized arms sales in the Middle East. Meanwhile, Palestinian refugees languished in squalid camps, growing more militant each year. As Israel rejected Washington's advice to compensate the homeless Palestinians, U.S. officials became annoyed. "Drop the attitude of a conqueror and the conviction that force . . . is the only policy that your neighbors will understand," Assistant Secretary of State Henry Byroade lectured the Israelis. He also implored Arabs to accept Israel's existence "as an accomplished fact."[139]

Despite his dislike for Nasser's pan-Arabism and neutralism, Dulles used foreign aid to entice him toward the West. In December 1955 the secretary offered to fund Nasser's dream of the Aswan Dam on the Nile, a potential source of electrical power and irrigation. During the next year the World Bank worked out the details of a $1.3 billion project utilizing British, American, and World Bank monies. About the same time, Egypt joined an anti-Israeli military alliance with Saudi Arabia, Syria, and Yemen. Jewish Americans chastised Washington, while southern members of Congress asked why the United States should support a project that would permit Egypt to produce competitive cotton. Eisenhower and Dulles worried that the Czech arms deal signified Egyptian alignment with the Soviets. Cairo had also recognized the People's Republic of China. Dulles asked: "Do nations which play both sides get better treatment than nations which are stalwart and work with us?"[140] Nassar always replied that nationalism provided the best defense against communism, and that Zionism and Western imperialism, not communism, ranked as Egypt's greatest enemies.

To no avail. On July 19, 1956, Dulles informed the Egyptian ambassador that the United States would not fund the Aswan Dam. The State Department publicly insulted the Egyptians by explaining that their credit was no good—this despite the World Bank's decision that the dam represented a sound investment. "May you choke to death on your fury," Nasser jeered.[141] As an American warning to Egypt and others neutrals to align with the United States, this hardknuckled economic diplomacy failed miserably. Nasser quickly seized the Suez Canal, intent on using its $25 million annual profit to help build the Aswan Dam.

Without consulting Washington, and defiant of U.S. advice to avoid violence, the British and French huddled with Israel and planned a military operation. In late October and early November 1956, British, French, and Israeli forces invaded Egypt and nearly captured the canal. "Nothing justifies double-crossing us," an irate Eisenhower told his aides. "We're going to apply sanctions, we're going to the United Nations, we're going to do everything we can to stop this thing."[142] To make matters worse, Dulles had just entered the hospital for treatment of his cancer. Eisenhower publicly upbraided the British and French for taking military action that might draw the Soviets into the Middle East and that took the spotlight off the simultaneous Soviet invasion of Hungary (see pp. 338–340). The Soviets, preoccupied with Eastern Europe, actually did little during the Suez crisis except wail against the invaders.

U.S. officials introduced a UN resolution demanding withdrawal and refused to meet Britain's need for oil shipments to make up for losses due to the closing of the Suez Canal and the destruction of oil pipelines. Washington also refused to aid Britain financially when its currency (the pound) faltered and Bank of England reserves dwindled because of a dollar drain. British officials grumbled that Eisenhower officials treated them like "naughty boys" who had not minded their "nanny."[143] Still, they bowed to U.S. pressure. By late December, French and British troops had pulled out. Only after Washington threatened sanctions (economic aid had already been suspended) did Israel disengage its forces from the Sinai in March 1957. A UN peacekeeping unit then took positions and returned the canal, now clogged with sunken ships, to Egypt.

After the Suez crisis, although the United States retained its oil interests, Washington failed to persuade much of the Muslim world to accept the United States as anything more than another Western usurper. After all, the United States

Gamal Abdul Nasser (1918–1970). The bold Egyptian leader once told John Foster Dulles that the Russians "have never occupied our territory . . . but the British have been here for seventy years." Nasser went on: "How can I go to my people and tell them I am disregarding a killer with a pistol sixty miles from me at the Suez Canal to worry about somebody who is holding a knife a thousand miles away?" (*The Reporter,* 1956. Copyright 1956 by The Reporter Magazine Co.)

still stood at odds with the most popular Arab leader, Nasser, whom Eisenhower labeled an "evil influence" but whom Arabs hailed as a hero for his daring confrontation with Western imperialism.[144] "The power of Nasser's personality was enhanced," one scholar has written, and "the policy of appealing over the heads of governments to their peoples seemed to have succeeded," because radical Nasserist movements sprang up everywhere.[145] By withdrawing the High Dam offer and handing Moscow the opportunity to build the imposing structure, as the Soviets eventually did, Eisenhower saw no choice but to assume the role of Middle East policeman—because "the Bear is still the central enemy."[146] Anti-imperialist and anti-Israeli Arabs bristled against the U.S. presumption that they needed a protective sheriff. Relations with Britain and France had fractured, but Eisenhower's ire soon subsided in favor of strengthening the NATO alliance. Suez nonetheless accelerated Britain's decline, confirming Winston Churchill's 1954 comment on his nation's status: "I feel like an aeroplane at the end of its flight, in the dusk, with the petrol running out."[147] As for Israel, Eisenhower coveted it as an anticommunist ally, and in August 1958 Washington made its first arms sale to the Jewish state.

Claiming that communists schemed to exploit the Mideast "vacuum" and that "it is 'curtains' for Israel" if the United States did not take action in the Middle East to halt Soviet-backed Arab radicals, the president and a healthier Dulles revitalized containment in the Eisenhower Doctrine.[148] In a speech before Congress on January 5, 1957, Eisenhower requested authority to use U.S. armed forces in the Middle East to help nations there resist "overt armed aggression from any nation controlled by International Communism" and authority to send military and economic assistance to the region.[149] On January 30, both houses approved the request in a resolution, but not before Senator J. William Fulbright protested that the administration "asks for a blank grant of power . . . , to be used in a blank way, for a blank length of time, under blank conditions with respect to blank nations in a blank area. . . . Who will fill in all these blanks?"[150] Although Iran and Lebanon endorsed the doctrine, Syria, Egypt, and Jordan soundly rejected it, and Iraq and Saudi Arabia seemed lukewarm.

Tests came soon. In April 1957, when pro-Nasser Jordanians threatened to overthrow King Hussein, Eisenhower ordered the Sixth Fleet to patrol off the coast of Lebanon and suggested that he would send U.S. marines too. Although the king had appealed for implementation of the Eisenhower Doctrine, this first application of the doctrine actually targeted Nasserite Arabs, not communists. In any case, the revolt failed. The second test came in Syria, where pro-Nasser radical military officers gained power and negotiated aid from the Soviet Union. Syrian officials exposed a CIA plot to oust them, and Dulles declared Syria a virtual Soviet satellite. In fact, the anticommunist Syrians looked mostly to Cairo, not Moscow. In February 1958, Syria and Egypt merged as the United Arab Republic; Nasser quickly banished the Communist party from Syria.

Lebanon and Iraq claimed attention next. In May 1958, a civil war erupted between Christians and pro-Nasser Muslims in multireligious Lebanon. A few months later, when Nasserites overthrew the regime in Iraq, Washington, fearing the spread of Arab radicalism, took firm action to save the Christian-led, pro-American government in Lebanon. On July 15, 14,000 U.S. marines rushed the beaches of

Lebanon. They departed in October after U.S. diplomats negotiated an end to the civil war. Although the Eisenhower Doctrine receded from use after Lebanon, the fundamental U.S. posture toward the Middle East changed little. In the end, Eisenhower had "exaggerated the Soviet threat, misunderstood Arab nationalism, and stimulated Arab anti-Americanism."[151]

Nationalism also tightened its grip on the United States' most immediate sphere of influence, Latin America. Through the Rio Pact (a defensive military alliance formed in 1947), the Organization of American States (launched the following year but formally established in 1951 to help settle inter-American disputes), investments of $8.2 billion by 1959, economic assistance totaling $835 million for the period 1952–1961, and support for military dictators like Fulgencio Batista in Cuba, the United States perpetuated its hegemony over neighbors to the south. But many Latin Americans grew restless, and their nationalism became strident. Latin American poverty remained stark; illiteracy rates stood high; health care proved inadequate; a population explosion threatened scarce resources; productivity showed minuscule growth; profits from raw materials such as sugar and oil flowed through American companies to the United States. As the Cold War shifted to the Third World, Washington worried more about Latin American discontents. "To arrest the drift in the area toward radical and nationalistic regimes," Dulles said, the United States would intervene, the Good Neighbor policy notwithstanding.[152]

Guatemala became a test case in which U.S. anticommunism, economic stakes, and hegemonic presumption prompted intervention. Jacobo Arbenz won election as president by a wide margin, and after his inauguration in spring 1951, he set land reform as the central goal of his administration. Only 2 percent of the population owned 70 percent of the land. Under the agrarian reform law of mid-1952, the government eventually expropriated about one-quarter of the nation's arable land and distributed it to some 500,000 peasants. Food production increased. Soon after expropriation, however, Arbenz clashed with the United Fruit Company (UFCO), the U.S.-owned banana exporter and Guatemala's largest landowner. UFCO had to give up more than 400,000 acres of uncultivated land. When Arbenz offered compensation in government bonds, using the value of the land the company itself, for tax purposes, set at $1.2 million, UFCO claimed the expropriated properties represented $19 million. The State Department sided strongly with UFCO, which hired lobbyists and propagandists to spread a story in the United States: Communism had secured a beachhead in Central America.

The Soviet Union, prudently honoring the law of "geographical fatalism" in the face of superior U.S. regional power, actually showed little interest in Latin America in the 1950s.[153] Moscow looked skeptically at Arbenz and other anti-Yankee leftists who seemed more reformist than radical or communist. The Guatemalan Communist party received no money from the Soviets. Still, indigenous communists backed Arbenz. He welcomed their help in the struggle against entrenched interests, and he appointed some of them to administer land reform projects. Arbenz insisted that he would become neither a communist nor an anticommunist, but he defended the communists as servants of Guatemalan nationalism who respected the electoral process. Given their Cold War mentality, however, U.S. diplomats suspected the worst. As Ambassador John Peurifoy remarked,

Arbenz "talked like a Communist, he thought like a Communist, he acted like a Communist, and if he is not one . . . , he will do until one comes along."[154]

The desire to save UFCO properties also motivated U.S. actions, but what worried Washington most was "the strong appeal" among Central American neighbors of Guatemala's "broad social program of aiding workers and peasants."[155] Simply put, Arbenz challenged U.S. hegemony in the region. "They would have overthrown us even if we had grown no bananas," Arbenz's friend José Manual Fortuny recalled.[156] Washington opposed radical reform and grew alarmed that it might become contagious in the primary sphere of influence of the United States.

Eisenhower approved a CIA plan to overthrow the Arbenz government. Using a base in Florida and $5–7 million, the CIA began to hire Guatemalan exiles. Training camps in Nicaragua and Honduras prepared them for an invasion. Colonel

Rioters Stone Nixon in Venezuela.   His car surrounded by hostile Venezuelans, Vice President Nixon experienced a grueling outbreak of anti-Americanism in May 1958. He was forced to leave Caracas ahead of schedule, his experience highlighting problems in Latin America for the United States. (United Press International)

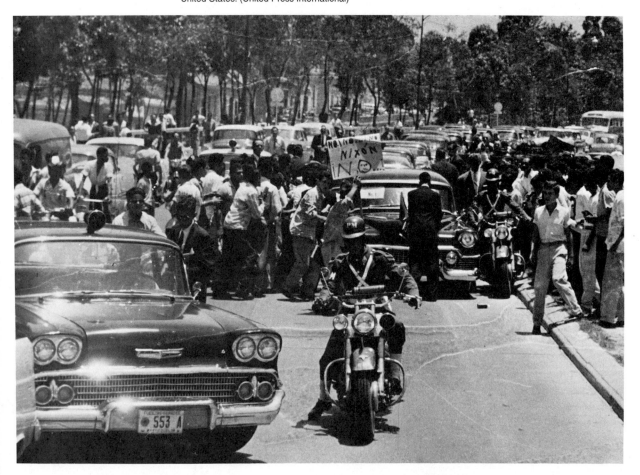

Carlos Castillo Armas, a graduate of the army staff school at Fort Leavenworth, Kansas, won favor as the president-to-be. In early 1954 the United States prodded the Organization of American States to declare, by a 17 to 1 vote, that the domination of any American state by the international communist movement would constitute a threat to the hemisphere. Washington also cut off technical assistance funds to Guatemala. After learning that the United States plotted his overthrow, Arbenz turned to Czechoslovakia. A Czech arms shipment triggered the last stage of the CIA operation called PBSUCCESS.

On June 18, after the CIA bribed Guatemalans, planted fictitious news stories about Arbenz's submission to the Soviets, and dropped supplies at United Fruit facilities, Castillo Armas's small force attacked from Honduras. U.S.-supplied rebel planes bombed Guatemala City. Abandoned by his military and fearful that Washington would order U.S. marines to Guatemala if Castillo Armas's invasion failed, an anguished Arbenz fled to Mexico, where he died in 1971.

Castillo Armas soon returned UFCO lands, jailed his detractors, and set Guatemala on a course of government-sponsored terror that by 1990 had left 100,000 Guatemalans dead. In 1957 he fell to assassination, but the new regime remained a staunch U.S. ally. Although encouraged by their successful covert operation in Guatemala to stage coups elsewhere, U.S. officials had to endure loud protest from Latin Americans who saw a repeat of past U.S. hubris.

Vice President Richard Nixon felt the protest firsthand in April–May 1958 when he traveled south on a goodwill tour. In Montevideo, Uruguay, anti-Yankee pickets mingled with the cheering crowds when Nixon motored through the city. Determined to counter what he considered communist agitation, Nixon stopped at the University of the Republic and engaged students in an emotional debate on U.S. foreign policy. Nixon claimed a rhetorical "victory" and went on to Peru, where anti-Yankee sentiment welled up at San Marcos University. Nixon went there anyway, vowing to contest a "bunch of Communist thugs."[157] Stoned and spat on, he then headed for Caracas.

In Venezuela all hell broke loose. Earlier in 1958 the ruthless dictatorship of Marcos Pérez Jiménez ("P.J.") had been overthrown by a military junta. "P.J." had been a special friend of the United States during his seven-year rule. In 1954 the United States had decorated him with the Legion of Merit. The following year Dulles declared that Venezuela "has adopted the kind of policies which we think that other countries of South America should adopt. Namely, they have adopted policies which provide in Venezuela a climate which is attractive to foreign capital to come in."[158] When Jiménez fled Caracas and the Eisenhower administration gave him asylum, Venezuelan bitterness toward the United States deepened.

Into this volatile environment stepped Nixon, emboldened by his earlier tangles with protesting students. Crowds blocked Nixon's motorcade en route to a wreath-laying ceremony at the tomb of Simón Bolívar; demonstrators stoned his car, shattering windows. They smashed fenders, rocked the automobile, and threatened the vice president's life. A Secret Service agent drew his pistol: "Let's get some of these sons-of-bitches."[159] Before shooting broke out, however, Nixon's car somehow sped away. In Operation Poor Richard, Eisenhower dispatched two airborne infantry companies to the Caribbean, but Nixon left Venezuela without further trouble. His toughness under stress gained him public admiration in the United States. "A national defeat," noted one journalist, "has been parlayed into a personal political triumph."[160]

After Nixon's trip, Washington began to send more economic and military aid below the border. In 1959 the United States subscribed $500 million to the new Inter-American Development Bank. To combat communist propaganda and dissuade opinion makers in Latin America from criticizing the United States, Nixon recommended that Washington distance itself somewhat from unpopular rulers: "a formal handshake for dictators; an *embraso* [*abrazo*] for leaders in freedom."[161] That advice proved inadequate. In 1959, students and other nationalists in Panama rioted against U.S. control of the Canal Zone and tried to plant Panamanian flags there. Zone police and U.S. infantry beat them back, wounding more than 120. Eisenhower eventually permitted the Panamanian flag to fly over the zone for the first time since the early twentieth century. In Cuba, too, the United States met challenge. Nationalistic insurgents led by Fidel Castro overthrew Fulgencio Batista and launched a revolution to expel U.S. economic and military interests from the island (see Chapter 9). "You fellows better batten down the hatches," Assistant Secretary Thomas Mann told Latin American specialists in the State Department. "There's going to be some real stormy weather."[162]

EISENHOWER IN A MULTIPOLAR WORLD

When the Eisenhower administration gave way to the Democratic administration of John F. Kennedy in January 1961, it was holding the line—against Arab nationalism, against Latin American revolution, against Third World neutralism, against communism, against the Soviet Union, against China. Despite the catchy phrases of the Eisenhower-Dulles years, no dramatic new departures occurred in foreign policy. "Liberation" and "rollback" had always been the ultimate goal of "containment." The "Eisenhower Doctrine" extended the "Truman Doctrine." Dulles's strictures against neutralism sounded very much like Truman's declaration that all nations must choose between two ways of life. The "domino theory" in Asia differed little from the Truman administration's alarmist predictions that if Greece fell, the Middle East would fall and then Europe collapse. Eisenhower and Dulles reinforced the Truman-Acheson hostility to "Red China." Both administrations intervened, with different methods, in the Middle East. Both expanded the covert spoiling operations of the Central Intelligence Agency. Both sped the growth of the nation's nuclear arsenal. Both nourished overseas economic interests as essential to U.S. and world stability. Both sought to draw West Germany into Western Europe. Indeed, the continuity in American foreign relations from Truman through Eisenhower is conspicuous. America's Cold War institutions, its high defense budgets, its large foreign-affairs bureaucracy, its assumptions from the past—all ground on.

But the world had changed. In 1945 the United States sat atop the hierarchical structure of international relations. Few restraints obstructed its exercise of power. Americans confidently placed restraints on others. A bipolar world developed. But as the Soviet Union and the United States built their economies and military forces toward a stalemate, particularly in Europe, the bonds of stability loosened elsewhere. Throughout the 1950s new nations claimed independence and threw off the shackles of colonialsim. These new nations of the Third World refused to join sides in the Cold War. Troubles for the two major powers also erupted in their own spheres of influence. Independent-minded client states and allies challenged great-power hegemony. Latin America became less responsive to U.S. tutelage, and political turmoil and anti-Yankeeism ran rampant. The 1959 victory of nationalists in the Cuban Revolution symbolized the new challenge (see next chapter). Anti-American Japanese rioters forced Eisenhower to cancel a trip to Japan in 1960, and Europeans like Charles de Gaulle of France sought restrictions on U.S. influence. The Soviets faced the Hungarian Revolution, growing discontent in Eastern Europe, and the Sino-Soviet split. Both great powers grew alarmed by the proliferation of nuclear weapons: Britain developed an atomic bomb in 1952, France in 1960, and China in 1964.

The bipolar world gradually became multipolar. Neither the Soviet Union nor America, tied to rigid policies and military programs, adjusted well to the new more fluid international system. Although both professed an understanding of Third World needs and aspirations, both sought to place curbs on nationalism. After all, notwithstanding their propaganda, they wanted friends or allies, not fulfillment of the principle of self-determination. The two antagonists, in their drive to accumulate friends through foreign aid and subversion, saw Third World nations manipulate the Cold War competition to gain economic assistance and military hardware from both sides. The U.S. antipathy toward revolutionary nationalism, socialism, the nationalization of land and industry, and neutralism created a formidable barrier between the United States and the Third World. Nor did alliances like SEATO and Baghdad, CIA activities in Iran and Guatemala, training of counterrevolutionaries in South Vietnam (see next chapter), and sending of troops to Lebanon reveal an American grasp of the new challenge.

If, as critics said, the Eisenhower administration showed little imagination in dealing with the Third World, it also lacked innovation in its relations with the Soviet Union or China. The arms race continued, evolving into a space race and missile race. Washington seemed only minimally interested in considering ideas for reducing tension in Central Europe and Germany, quickly rejecting the Rapacki Plan and "disengagement" proposals. The Soviet Union seemed serious about cooling the arms race, but Moscow too so distrusted the intentions of the other side that negotiations produced little. Nonrecognition of China simply isolated the United States from one of the world's important nations. Standing firmly with Jiang on Formosa revealed obstinacy, not wisdom, when many other Western nations recognized Beijing and traded with the People's Republic.

Domestic constraints did not prevent Eisenhower from pursuing a more innovative foreign policy. McCarthyism inhibited, but it had waned by 1954. The president also deflected another challenge, a proposed amendment to the Constitution.

Khrushchev at the United Nations, 1960. The Soviet premier's temper flared into outbursts that rudely interrupted speakers. At one point, a devilish smirk on his face, he took off his shoe and banged it on the table. In October 1964, his Soviet colleagues forced Khrushchev into retirement. (United Nations)

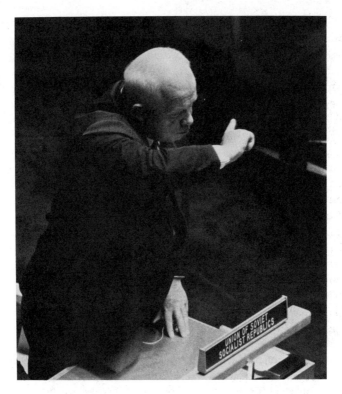

The Bricker Amendment, first offered in 1951 by Republican senator John Bricker of Ohio, sought primarily to limit the effects in the United States of UN–sponsored agreements on human rights. But it also included restrictions on executive agreements to ensure that presidents did not skirt the treaty-making power of the Senate. Hoping to force the president to consult more with Congress on foreign-policy issues and to forestall another Yalta, the amendment's backers insisted that executive agreements be voted on like treaties. Seeing an assault on presidential authority, Eisenhower, with help from liberal Democrats and moderate Republicans, beat back the amendment in a close Senate vote in February 1954. Eisenhower thereafter consulted regularly with legislators on major foreign policies, with the conspicuous exception of covert operations. Congress usually granted his requests. The Formosa Resolution of 1955, for example, passed 83 to 3 in the upper chamber and 410 to 3 in the lower body. The Eisenhower Doctrine of 1958 earned a 72 to 19 vote from the Senate and a 350 to 60 count in the House. The Cold War consensus shaped in the 1940s continued strong. The Eisenhower administration failed to devise new policies for new realities, then, not because of Joe McCarthy and the China Lobby but because of its own uncompromising assumptions.

In the election of 1960, the Democrats charged that the Cold War should be won. They differed from Eisenhower in the methods with which to continue the old fight and to reverse the declining position of the United States in the Third World. The Democratic party and its presidential candidate, Senator John F.

Kennedy, embraced the anticommunist absolutes of the era as heartily as John Foster Dulles ever had. Eisenhower's political critics charged that he and his secretary of state had caused the United States to fall behind in the missile race and that they had squandered American power.

Historical assessments of the Eisenhower administration used to stress its conservatism, passive style, limited achievements, and hesitancy to adjust to new circumstances. They bemoaned the president's apparent failure to keep abreast of events and his timidity in coming down hard on Joe McCarthy. Eisenhower's loyalty program damaged the Foreign Service. His expansion of the CIA and covert operations proved dangerous and short-sighted. Subsequent revelations of CIA assassination plots tarnished Ike's reputation. Whatever his doubts about the insanity of the nuclear-arms race, he advanced it and left a legacy of nuclear fear. The 1950s generation would long remember going through the duck-and-cover drills of civil defense and watching Hollywood films of nuclear holocaust like *On the Beach* (1959). Eisenhower distrusted Jiang Jieshi's nationalists and seemed to prefer a "two Chinas" policy, but a hard-line posture toward the People's Republic of China tempted nuclear war on more than one occasion.[163] In recent years, scholars have been researching the now declassified documents of the 1950s. Many now emphasize Eisenhower's influential style, command of the policymaking process, political savvy, taming of hawks like Dulles and Nixon, sensibly moderate approach to most problems, commitment to nuclear-arms control, and curbing of the military. He was, in short, not an aging bystander in the 1950s. Such "Eisenhower revisionism" has stimulated a healthy reconsideration of the period. But we should not praise him too much for not going over the brink, for Eisenhower remained a zealous anticommunist of little flexibility whose diplomatic record is at best mixed.

A Saddened "Ike." The end of his administration included cancellation of a trip to Japan, the U-2 crisis, and the breakup of the Paris Conference. Just before leaving office, the general warned Americans against a military-industrial complex. At the time, 1,400 retired military officers above the rank of major, including 261 generals and admirals, were employed by the top 100 corporations that received defense contracts. (*The Reporter,* 1960. Copyright 1960 by The Reporter Magazine Co.)

FURTHER READING FOR THE PERIOD 1950–1961

Some works cited in Chapter 7 also cover this period.

The Korean War, both its civil and international character, is explored in Frank Baldwin, ed., *Without Parallel* (1975); Ronald Caridi, *The Korean War and American Politics* (1969); Bruce Cumings, *The Origins of the Korean War* (1981 and 1990) and ed., *Child of Conflict* (1983); Robert J. Donovan, *Tumultuous Years* (1982); Rosemary Foot, *A Substitute for Victory* (1990) and *The Wrong War* (1985); Sergei N. Goncharov, John W. Lewis, and Xue La-tai, *Uncertain Partners: Stalin, Mao, and the Korean War* (1994); John Halliday and Bruce Cumings, *Korea* (1988); D. Clayton James, *Refighting the Last War* (1992) and *The Years of MacArthur* (1985); Burton I. Kaufman, *The Korean War* (1986); Callum A. MacDonald, *Korea* (1987); John Merrill, *Korea* (1989); Glenn D. Paige, *The Korean Decision* (1975); Michael Schaller, *Douglas MacArthur* (1989); John W. Spanier, *The Truman-MacArthur Controversy* (1959); John Toland, *In Mortal Combat* (1991); and Allen Whiting, *China Crosses the Yalu* (1960). Roy E. Appleman has written several military histories of the Korean War.

For studies of foreign relations in the 1950s and President Dwight D. Eisenhower, see Craig Allen, *Eisenhower and the Mass Media* (1993); Stephen E. Ambrose, *Eisenhower* (1983–1984) and *Nixon* (1987); Michael R. Beschloss, *MAYDAY* (1986) (U-2); H. W. Brands, Jr., *Cold Warriors* (1988); Jeff Broadwater, *Eisenhower and the Anti-Communist Crusade* (1992); Blanche W. Cook, *The Declassified Eisenhower* (1981); Robert A. Divine, *Eisenhower and the Cold War* (1981); Fred I. Greenstein, *The Hidden-Hand Presidency* (1982); Burton I. Kaufman, *Trade and Aid* (1982); Michael T. Klare, *American Arms Supermarket* (1985); Elaine Tyler May, *Homeward Bound* (1988); Richard A. Melanson and David A. Mayers, eds., *Reevaluating Eisenhower*

(1986); G. Bernard Noble, *Christian A. Herter* (1970); Chester J. Pach, Jr., and Elmo Richardson, *The Presidency of Dwight D. Eisenhower* (1991); Herbert S. Parmet, *Eisenhower and the American Crusades* (1972); James Patterson, *Mr. Republican* (1972) (Taft); Duane Tananbaum, *The Bricker Amendment Controversy* (1988); and W. W. Rostow, *Eisenhower, Kennedy, and Foreign Aid* (1985).

John Foster Dulles is the centerpiece in Louis Gerson, *John Foster Dulles* (1968); Richard Goold-Adams, *The Time of Power* (1962); Michael Guhin, *John Foster Dulles* (1972); Townsend Hoopes, *The Devil and John Foster Dulles* (1973); Richard H. Immerman, ed., *John Foster Dulles and the Diplomacy of the Cold War* (1990); Frederick W. Marks, *Power and Peace* (1993); and Ronald W. Pruessen, *John Foster Dulles* (1982).

For relations with the Soviet Union and European questions, consult George W. Breslauer, *Khrushchev and Brezhnev as Leaders* (1982); Frank Costigliola, *France and the United States* (1992); Audrey K. Cronin, *Great Power Politics and the Struggle over Austria* (1986); Ennio Di Nolfo, ed., *Power in Europe? II* (1992); Michael P. Gehlen, *The Politics of Coexistence* (1967); Alexander L. George et al., eds., *U.S.-Soviet Security Cooperation* (1988); Alfred Grosser, *The Western Alliance* (1975); Wolfram F. Hanrieder, *Germany, America, Europe* (1989); Wm. Roger Louis and Hedley Bull, eds., *The Special Relationship* (1986) (Britain); Jack M. Schick, *The Berlin Crisis* (1971); Michel Tatu, *Power in the Kremlin* (1969); and William Zimmerman, *Soviet Perspectives on International Relations, 1956–1967* (1969).

The nuclear arms race, missile development, and antinuclear views are treated in Edmund Beard, *Developing the ICBM* (1976); Howard Ball, *Justice Downwind* (1986); McGeorge Bundy, *Danger and Survival* (1988); Barbara B. Clowse, *Brainpower for the Cold War: The Sputnik Crisis and the National Defense Education Act of 1958* (1981); Robert A. Divine, *Blowing on the Wind* (1978) and *The Sputnik Challenge* (1993); Gregg F. Herken, *Counsels of War* (1985); Richard G. Hewlett and Jack M. Holl, *Atoms for Peace, 1953–1961* (1989); Jerome H. Kahan, *Security in the Nuclear Age* (1975); Fred Kaplan, *The Wizards of Armageddon* (1983); Milton S. Katz, *Ban the Bomb* (1986); Michael Mandelbaum, *The Nuclear Question* (1979); Walter A. McDougall, *The Heavens and the Earth* (1985); George H. Quester, *Nuclear Diplomacy* (1970); Chalmers M. Roberts, *The Nuclear Years* (1970); Marc Trachtenberg, *History and Strategy* (1991); and Ernest J. Yanarella, *The Missile Defense Controversy* (1977).

Asian questions, including China, the offshore islands crises, and Japan, are studied in Stanley D. Bachrack, *The Committee of One Million* (1976) (China Lobby); William D. Borden, *The Pacific Alliance* (1984) (Japan); Roger Buckley, *U.S.-Japan Alliance Diplomacy, 1945–1990* (1992); Gordon H. Chang, *Friends and Enemies: The United States, China, and the Soviet Union, 1948–1972* (1990); Warren I. Cohen, *America's Response to China* (1990); Warren I. Cohen and Akira Iriye, eds., *The Great Powers in East Asia, 1953–1960* (1990); Harry Harding and Yuan Ming, eds., *Sino-American Relations, 1945–1955* (1989); Akira Iriye and Warren I. Cohen, eds., *The United States and Japan* (1989); David A. Mayers, *Cracking the Monolith: U.S. Policy Against the Sino-Soviet Alliance* (1986); Kenneth T. Young, *Negotiating with the Chinese Communists* (1968); and Shu Guang Zhang, *Deterrence and Strategic Culture* (1992) (China). Studies of Indochina/Vietnam appear in Chapter 9.

Third World questions and countries are covered in Richard J. Barnet, *Intervention and Revolution* (1972); H. W. Brands, *The Specter of Neutralism* (1989); Melvin Gurtov, *The United States Against the Third World* (1974); Gabriel Kolko, *Confronting the Third World* (1988); Robert J. McMahon, *The Cold War on the Periphery* (1994) (India and Pakistan); Thomas J. Noer, *Cold War and Black Liberation* (1985) (Africa); and L. S. Stavrianos, *Global Rift* (1981). See also works cited in Chapters 7, 9–12.

For U.S. relations with the Middle East, especially with Egypt and Israel, see Isaac Alteras, *Eisenhower and Israel* (1993); George W. Ball and Douglas B. Ball, *The Passionate Attachment* (1992) (Israel); William J. Burns, *Economic Aid and American Policy Toward Egypt, 1955–1981* (1985); Steven Z. Freiberger, *Dawn Over Suez: The Rise of American Power in the Middle East, 1953–1957* (1992); Peter L. Hahn, *The United States, Great Britain and Egypt, 1945–1956* (1991); George Lenczowski, *The Middle East in World Affairs* (1980); S. Neil MacFarlane, *Superpower Rivalry and Third World Radicalism* (1985); Gail E. Meyer, *Egypt and the United States* (1980); William R. Polk, *The Arab World Today* (1991); Cheryl Rubenberg, *Israel and the American National Interest* (1986); Barry Rubin, *The Arab States and the Palestine Conflict* (1981); Nadav Safran, *From War to War: The Arab-Israeli Confrontation, 1948–1967* (1969); David Schoenbaum, *The United States and the State of Israel*

(1993); Steven L. Spiegel, *The Other Arab-Israeli Conflict* (1985); and Robert W. Stookey, *America and the Arab States* (1975).

The Suez crisis is included in many of the works above, but especially see Chester L. Cooper, *The Lion's Last Roar* (1978); Diane B. Kunz, *The Economic Diplomacy of the Suez Crisis* (1991); Donald Neff, *Warriors at Suez* (1981); Wm. Roger Louis and Roger Owen, eds., *Suez 1956* (1989); and Selwyn Troen, ed., *The Sinai-Suez Crisis, 1956* (1990).

Latin American–U.S. relations and the intervention in Guatemala are treated in Samuel L. Baily, *The United States and the Development of South America, 1945–1975* (1976); Cole Blasier, *The Hovering Giant* (1976); Elizabeth A. Cobbs, *The Rich Neighbor Policy* (1992); Piero Gleijeses, *Shattered Hope* (1991) (Guatemala); Richard Immerman, *The CIA in Guatemala* (1982); Stephen Kinzer and Stephen Schlesinger, *Bitter Fruit* (1982) (Guatemala); Walter LaFeber, *Inevitable Revolutions* (1993) (Central America) and *The Panama Canal* (1989); Abraham F. Lowenthal, ed., *Exporting Democracy* (1991); Nicola Miller, *Soviet Relations with Latin America, 1959–1987* (1989); Thomas G. Paterson, *Contesting Castro* (1994); Stephen G. Rabe, *Eisenhower and Latin America* (1988); Ramón Ruíz, *Cuba* (1968); Gaddis Smith, *The Last Years of the Monroe Doctrine* (1994); and Bryce Wood, *The Dismantling of the Good Neighbor Policy* (1985).

For the Central Intelligence Agency and its covert activities, see Stephen E. Ambrose, *Ike's Spies* (1981); Sigmund Diamond, *Compromised Campus: The Collaboration of Universities with the Intelligence Community, 1945–1955* (1992); Loch K. Johnson, *America's Secret Power* (1989); Ludwell L. Montagne, *General Walter Bedell Smith as Director of Central Intelligence* (1992); John Ranelagh, *The Agency* (1986); and Robin W. Winks, *Cloak & Gown* (1987).

For the impact of McCarthyism, consult some works cited in Chapter 7 and Michael R. Belknap, *Cold War Political Justice* (1977); Robert Griffith, *The Politics of Fear* (1987); William W. Keller, *The Liberals and J. Edgar Hoover* (1989); Stanley I. Kutler, *The American Inquisition* (1982); Mary S. McAuliffe, *Crisis on the Left* (1978); Thomas C. Reeves, *The Life and Times of Joe McCarthy* (1982); Ellen W. Schrecker, *No Ivory Tower: McCarthyism and the Universities* (1986); Athan Theoharis and John S. Cox, *The Boss* (1988) (J. Edgar Hoover); and Stephen J. Whitfield, *The Culture of the Cold War* (1991).

Richard Dean Burns, ed., *Guide to American Foreign Relations Since 1700* (1983), is an extensive, annotated bibliography. See also the General Bibliography and the following notes.

NOTES TO CHAPTER 8

1. Quoted in Glenn D. Paige, *The Korean Decision* (New York: The Free Press, 1968), p. 82.
2. Glenn D. Paige, ed., *1950: Truman's Decision* (New York: Chelsea House Publishers, 1970), p. 49.
3. Quoted in David Rees, *Korea* (London: Macmillan, 1964), p. 36.
4. Quoted in John Toland, *In Mortal Combat* (New York: William Morrow, 1991), p. 34.
5. Quoted in Ronald W. Pruessen, *John Foster Dulles* (New York: The Free Press, 1982), p. 454.
6. Harry S. Truman, *Memoirs* (Garden City, N.Y.: Doubleday, 1955–1956; 2 vols.), II, 332.
7. Paige, *1950*, p. 63.
8. Robert J. Donovan, *Tumultuous Years* (New York: W. W. Norton, 1982), p. 202.
9. Truman, *Memoirs*, II, 333.
10. Quoted in *New York Times*, June 26, 1950.
11. Quoted in Melvyn P. Leffler, *A Preponderance of Power* (Stanford: Stanford University Press, 1992), p. 366.
12. *Congressional Record*, XCVI (June 26, 1950), 9188.
13. *Foreign Relations, 1950, VII* (Washington, D.C.: Government Printing Office, 1976), 179.
14. Dean Acheson, *Present at the Creation* (New York: W. W. Norton, 1969), p. 405.
15. Quoted in Toland, *In Mortal Combat*, p. 41.
16. Joseph C. Harsch quoted in Bruce Cumings, *The Origins of the Korean War* (Princeton: Princeton University Press, 1981, 1990; 2 vols.), II, 628.
17. Quoted in Walter Isaacson and Evan Thomas, *The Wise Men* (New York: Simon and Schuster, 1986), p. 507.
18. Quoted in Joseph C. Goulden, *Korea* (New York: Times Books, 1982), p. 194.
19. Quoted in D. Clayton James, *Refighting the Last War* (New York: The Free Press, 1993), p. 16.
20. Mao Zedong quoted in Hao Yufan and Zhai Zhihai, "China's Decision to Enter the Korean War," *China Quarterly*, No. 121 (May 1990), 101.
21. *Foreign Relations, 1950, VII*, 953–954.
22. Mao quoted in Michael H. Hunt, "Beijing and the Korean

Crisis, June 1950–June 1951," *Political Science Quarterly, CVII* (Autumn 1992), 464.

23. General Peng Dehuai quoted in Hao and Zhai, "China's Decision," 114.

24. Edward Almond quoted in Cumings, *Origins, II,* 742.

25. Quoted in Callum A. MacDonald, *Korea* (New York: The Free Press, 1987), p. 71.

26. Quoted in Philip West, "Confronting the West," *Journal of American–East Asian Relations, II* (Spring 1993), 6–7.

27. *Foreign Relations, 1950, VII,* 1368.

28. Quoted in Michael Schaller, *Douglas MacArthur* (New York: Oxford University Press, 1989), p. 335.

29. *Congressional Record, XCVII* (April 19, 1951), 4125.

30. *Ibid.,* April 24, 1951, p. 4261.

31. Cumings, *Origins, II,* 713.

32. *Department of State Bulletin, XXIII* (November 27, 1950), 839.

33. Quoted in Burton I. Kaufman, *The Korean War* (New York: Alfred A. Knopf, 1986), p. 173.

34. Marc Trachtenberg, "A 'Wasting Asset': American Strategy and the Shifting Nuclear Balance," *International Security, XIII* (Winter 1988/89), 27.

35. Quoted in Rosemary Foot, *A Substitute for Victory* (Ithaca: Cornell University Press, 1990), p. 162.

36. Quoted in Roger Dingman, "Atomic Diplomacy During the Korean War," *International Security, XIII* (Winter 1988/89), 86.

37. Quoted in MacDonald, *Korea,* p. 225.

38. General Chung Sang-chin of North Korea quoted in Kathryn Weathersby, "Soviet Aims in Korea and the Origins of the Korean War, 1945–1950," Working Paper No. 8, *Cold War International History Project* (Washington, D.C., November 1993), p. 26.

39. Cumings, *Origins, II,* 643.

40. Weathersby, "Soviet Aims," p. 31.

41. John Halliday and Bruce Cumings, *Korea* (New York: Pantheon, 1988), p. 34.

42. "Princeton Seminar," February 13–14, 1954, Box 66, Dean Acheson Papers, Harry S. Truman Library, Independence, Missouri.

43. Arthur M. Schlesinger, Jr., *The Imperial Presidency* (New York: Popular Library, 1973), p. 138.

44. Entry of September 15, 1950, in Robert H. Ferrell, ed., *Truman in the White House: The Diary of Eben A. Ayers* (Columbia: University of Missouri Press, 1991), p. 374.

45. Roger Dingman, "The Dagger and the Gift: The Impact of the Korean War on Japan," *Journal of American–East Asian Relations, II* (Spring 1993), 43, 55.

46. *Public Papers, Truman, 1952–1953* (Washington, D.C.: Government Printing Office, 1966), p. 708.

47. Acheson, *Present at the Creation,* p. 420.

48. Quoted in Stephen E. Ambrose, *Nixon* (New York: Simon and Schuster, 1987), p. 297.

49. Quoted in John Lewis Gaddis, *Russia, the Soviet Union, and the United States* (New York: McGraw Hill, 1990; 2d ed.), p. 216.

50. Quoted in Stephen E. Ambrose, *Eisenhower, 1890–1952* (New York: Simon and Schuster, 1983), p. 569.

51. Fred I. Greenstein, *The Hidden-Hand Presidency: Eisenhower as Leader* (New York: Basic Books, 1982).

52. Richard J. Barnet, *Intervention and Revolution* (New York: New American Library, 1972; rev. ed.), p. 36.

53. Quoted in Robert Griffith, "Dwight D. Eisenhower and the Corporate Commonwealth," *American Historial Review, LXXXVII* (February 1982), 91.

54. Quoted in Loch K. Johnson, *America's Secret Power* (New York: Oxford University Press, 1989), pp. 17, 27.

55. Hoover Commission quoted *ibid.,* p. 10.

56. John Ranelagh, *The Agency* (New York: Simon and Schuster, 1986), p. 202.

57. Quoted in Stephen E. Ambrose, *Eisenhower, the President* (New York: Simon and Schuster, 1984), p. 226.

58. *Public Papers, Eisenhower, 1953* (Washington, D.C.: Government Printing Office, 1960), pp. 182–183.

59. *Public Papers, Eisenhower, 1960–61* (Washington, D.C.: Government Printing Office, 1961), pp. 1035–1040.

60. "Discussion at the 309th Meeting of the National Security Council, Friday, January 11, 1957," Box 7, NSC Summaries, NSC Series, Ann Whitman File, Dwight D. Eisenhower Papers, Dwight D. Eisenhower Library, Abilene, Kansas.

61. Richard H. Immerman, "Conclusion," in Richard H. Immerman, ed., *John Foster Dulles and the Diplomacy of the Cold War* (Princeton: Princeton University Press, 1990), p. 266.

62. Quoted in Herbert S. Parmet, "Power and Reality," in Frank Merli and Theodore Wilson, eds., *Makers of American Diplomacy* (New York: Charles Scribner's Sons, 1974), p. 593.

63. Quoted in John Lewis Gaddis, *Strategies of Containment* (New York: Oxford University Press, 1982), p. 141.

64. Quoted in Alexander L. George and Richard Smoke, *Deterrence in American Foreign Policy* (New York: Columbia University Press, 1974), p. 27.

65. Wolfram F. Hanrieder, *Germany, America, Europe* (New Haven: Yale University Press, 1989), p. 70.

66. Quoted in Gordon H. Chang, *Friends and Enemies* (Stanford: Stanford University Press, 1990), p. 116.

67. *Public Papers, Eisenhower, 1954* (Washington, D.C.: Government Printing Office, 1960), p. 383.

68. Quoted in Emmett John Hughes, *The Ordeal of Power* (New York: Dell, 1964 [c. 1962]), p. 98.

69. Quoted in Isaacson and Thomas, *Wise Men,* p. 565.

70. Quoted in Earl Latham, *The Communist Controversy in Washington* (New York: Atheneum, 1969), p. 338.

71. Ross Terrill, "When America 'Lost' China," *Atlantic Monthly, CCXXIV* (November 1969), 79.

72. James C. Thomson, Jr., "On the Making of U.S. China Policy, 1961–9," *China Quarterly,* No. 50 (April–June, 1972), p. 222.
73. Theodore H. White, *In Search of History* (New York: Warner, 1978), p. 395.
74. *Public Papers, Eisenhower, 1953,* p. 187.
75. Quoted in Steven I. Levine, "Soviet Asian Policy in the 1950s," in Warren I. Cohen and Akira Iriye, eds., *The Great Powers in East Asia, 1953–1960* (New York: Columbia University Press, 1990), p. 298.
76. Nikita S. Khrushchev, *Khrushchev Remembers* (New York: Bantam Books, 1971; trans. by Strobe Talbott), p. 434.
77. Quoted in Gaddis, *Strategies,* p. 153.
78. Quoted in Kurt Steiner, "Negotiations for an Austrian State Treaty," in Alexander L. George et al., eds., *U.S.-Soviet Security Cooperation* (New York: Oxford University Press, 1988), p. 75.
79. Quoted in Matthew Evangelista, "Cooperation Theory and Disarmament Negotiations in the 1950s," *World Politics, XLII* (July 1990), 503.
80. McGeorge Bundy, *Danger and Survival* (New York: Random House, 1988), p. 301.
81. Quoted in Townsend Hoopes, *The Devil and John Foster Dulles* (Boston: Atlantic, Little, Brown, 1973), p. 295.
82. Sherman Adams, *Firsthand Report* (New York: Popular Library, 1962 [1961]), p. 177.
83. Khrushchev, *Khrushchev Remembers,* pp. 430, 438.
84. *Public Papers, Eisenhower, 1955* (Washington, D.C.: Government Printing Office, 1959), p. 507.
85. James Reston in *New York Times,* July 24, 1955.
86. Quoted in Richard G. Hewlett and Jack M. Holl, *Atoms for Peace and War* (Berkeley: University of California Press, 1989), p. 299.
87. Quoted in Herbert S. Parmet, *Eisenhower and the American Crusades* (New York: Macmillan, 1972), p. 406.
88. Quoted in Michael R. Beschloss, *MAYDAY* (New York: Harper & Row, 1986), p. 103.
89. *Public Papers, Eisenhower, 1955,* P. 730.
90. Quoted in Denis Healey, " 'When Shrimps Learn to Whistle,' " *"International Affairs, XXXII* (January 1956), 2.
91. Elaine Tyler May, *Homeward Bound* (New York: Basic Books, 1988), p. 164.
92. I. F. Stone, *The Haunted Fifties* (New York: Random House, 1963), p. 104.
93. Averell Harriman, "The Soviet Challenge and the American Policy," *Atlantic Monthly, CXCVII* (April 1956), 45.
94. Dwight D. Eisenhower, *The White House Years: Waging Peace, 1956–1961* (Garden City, N.Y.: Doubleday, 1965), p. 60.
95. Quoted in H. W. Brands, Jr., *Cold Warriors* (New York: Columbia University Press, 1988), p. 133.
96. Quoted in Chester J. Pach, Jr., and Elmo Richardson, *The Presidency of Dwight D. Eisenhower* (Lawrence: University Press of Kansas, 1991), p. 132.
97. Quoted in John Lewis Gaddis, "The Unexpected John Foster Dulles," in Immerman, *Dulles,* p. 72.
98. Quoted in Hughes, *Ordeal,* p. 216.
99. Quoted in Gregg Herken, *Counsels of War* (New York: Oxford University Press, 1987), p. 130.
100. Quoted in Michael Mandelbaum, *The Nuclear Question* (New York: Cambridge University Press, 1979), p. 66.
101. Quoted in Bundy, *Danger,* pp. 346–347.
102. Quoted in Richard Barnet, *Roots of War* (Baltimore: Penguin Books, 1973), p. 43.
103. Noble Frankland, ed., *Documents on International Affairs, 1957* (London: Oxford University Press, 1960), p. 157.
104. George F. Kennan, *Russia, the Atom, and the West* (New York: Harper & Brothers, 1958), p. 92.
105. *New York Times Book Review,* March 2, 1958.
106. Quoted in Thomas G. Paterson, ed., *Containment and the Cold War* (Reading, Mass.: Addison-Wesley, 1973), p. 116.
107. Quoted in William Burr, "New Sources on the Berlin Crisis, 1958–1962," *Cold War International History Bulletin,* Issue 2, (Fall 1992), 22.
108. Quoted in Hoopes, *Devil,* p. 470.
109. Quoted in Hope M. Harrison, "Ulbricht and the Concrete 'Rose,'" Working Paper No. 5, *Cold War International History Project* (Washington, D.C., May 1993), p. 21.
110. Eisenhower, *Waging Peace,* p. 432.
111. *Khrushchev in America* (New York: Crosscurrents, 1960), p. 120.
112. Quoted in Beschloss, *MAYDAY,* p. 201.
113. Craig Allen, *Eisenhower and the Mass Media* (Chapel Hill: University of North Carolina Press, 1993), p. 169.
114. Quoted in Ambrose, *Eisenhower, President,* p. 580.
115. Quoted in Edward Crankshaw, *The New Cold War* (Baltimore: Penguin, 1965 [c. 1963]), p. 81.
116. Quoted in John Lewis Gaddis, *The United States and the End of the Cold War* (New York: Oxford University Press, 1992), p. 75.
117. Quoted in Shu Guang Zhang, *Deterrence and Strategic Culture* (Ithaca: Cornell University Press, 1992), p. 200.
118. Gordon H. Chang and He Di, "The Absence of War in the U.S.-China Confrontation over Quemoy and Matsu in 1954–1955," *American Historical Review, XCVIII* (December 1993), 1523.
119. Quoted in Waldo Heinrichs, "Eisenhower and the Sino-American Confrontation," in Cohen and Iriye, *Great Powers,* p. 99.
120. Richard M. Nixon, *Six Crises* (Garden City, N.Y.: Doubleday, 1962), p. 273.
121. Quoted in Zhang, *Deterrence,* p. 214.
122. Nathan Twining quoted in Chang, *Friends,* p. 189.
123. Quoted in Melvin Gurtov, "The Taiwan Strait Crisis Revisited," *Modern China, II* (January 1976), 79.

124. Quoted in Zhang, *Deterrence,* p. 255.

125. Quoted in John Gittings, "New Light on Mao," *China Quarterly,* No. 60 (December 1974), p. 755.

126. Quoted in Roger Buckley, *U.S.-Japan Alliance Diplomacy, 1945–1990* (Cambridge, Eng.: Cambridge University Press, 1992), p. 57.

127. Quoted in Stuart Auerbach, "How the U.S. Built Japan Inc.," *Washington Post National Weekly Edition,* July 26–August 1, 1993.

128. Robert L. Heilbroner, "Making a Rational Foreign Policy Now," *Harper's, CCXXXVII* (September 1968), 65.

129. William J. Lederer and Eugene Burdick, *The Ugly American* (New York: Fawcett, 1958), p. 234.

130. C. Vann Woodward, *The Strange Career of Jim Crow* (New York: Oxford University Press, 1974; 3d ed.), p. 132.

131. *Public Papers, Eisenhower, 1957* (Washington, D.C.: Government Printing Office, 1958), p. 694.

132. Finley Peter Dunne, *Dissertations of Mr. Dooley* (New York: Harper & Brothers, 1906), p. 130.

133. Carl N. Degler, "The American Past," *American Scholar, XXXII* (Spring 1963), 194.

134. Quoted in Michael H. Hunt, *Ideology and U.S. Foreign Policy* (New Haven: Yale University Press, 1987), p. 124.

135. SWNCC, "Political and Military Problems in the Far East," November 29, 1945, James F. Byrnes Papers, Clemson University Library, Clemson, South Carolina.

136. Quoted in Robert J. McMahon, *The Cold War on the Periphery* (New York: Columbia University Press, 1994), p. 38.

137. *Department of State Bulletin, XXXIV* (June 18, 1956), 1000.

138. Quoted in Thomas G. Paterson, *Meeting the Communist Threat* (New York: Oxford University Press, 1988), p. 161.

139. Quoted in William R. Polk, *The Arab World Today* (Cambridge, Mass.: Harvard University Press, 1991), p. 388.

140. Quoted in Hoopes, *Devil,* p. 337.

141. Quoted in Gail E. Meyer, *Egypt and the United States* (Rutherford, N.J.: Fairleigh Dickinson University Press, 1980), p. 146.

142. Quoted in Peter L. Hahn, *The United States, Great Britain, and Egypt, 1945–1956* (Chapel Hill: University of North Carolina Press, 1991), p. 230.

143. Lord Harcourt quoted in Diane B. Kunz, *The Economic Diplomacy of the Suez Crisis* (Chapel Hill: University of North Carolina Press, 1991), p. 140.

144. Cablegram, December 12, 1956, Box 20, DDE Diary Series, Whitman File, Eisenhower Papers.

145. Albert Houranie, "Conclusion," in Wm. Roger Louis and Roger Owen, eds., *Suez 1956* (New York: Oxford University Press, 1989), p. 408.

146. Quoted in David Schoenbaum, *The United States and the State of Israel* (New York: Oxford University Press, 1993), p. 117.

147. Quoted in Anthony Adamthwaite, "Overstretched and Overstrung," in Ennio Di Nolfo, ed., *Power in Europe? II* (Berlin: Walter de Gruyter, 1992), p. 41.

148. John Foster Dulles quoted in Douglas Little, "The Making of a Special Relationship: The United States and Israel, 1957–68," *International Journal of Middle East Studies, XXV* (1993), 564.

149. Quoted in Ambrose, *Eisenhower, President,* p. 382.

150. Quoted in Cecil Crabb, *The Doctrine of American Foreign Policy* (Baton Rouge: Louisiana State University Press, 1982), p. 170.

151. Stephen G. Rabe, "Eisenhower Revisionism," *Diplomatic History, XVII* (Winter 1993), 109.

152. Quoted in Thomas G. Paterson, *Contesting Castro* (New York: Oxford University Press, 1994), p. 10.

153. Quoted in Nicola Miller, *Soviet Relations with Latin America, 1959–1987* (Cambridge, Eng.: Cambridge University Press, 1989), pp. 5–6, 10.

154. Quoted in Richard H. Immerman, *The CIA in Guatemala* (Austin: University of Texas Press, 1982), p. 181.

155. U.S. official Burrows quoted in Piero Gleijeses, *Shattered Hope* (Princeton: Princeton University Press, 1991), p. 365.

156. Quoted *ibid.,* p. 4.

157. Nixon, *Six Crises,* pp. 198–199.

158. U.S. Senate, Committee on Finance, *Trade Agreements Extension* (Hearings), 84th Cong., 1st Sess. (1955), Part 4, p. 2049.

159. Quoted in Nixon, *Six Crises,* p. 219.

160. James Reston quoted in J. Fred Rippy, "The Hazards of Dale Carnegie Diplomacy," *Inter-American Economic Affairs, XII* (Summer 1958), 35.

161. Quoted in Stephen G. Rabe, *Eisenhower and Latin America* (Chapel Hill: University of North Carolina Press, 1988), p. 104.

162. Quoted in Robert A. Stevenson Oral History, Foreign Affairs Oral History Program, Lauinger Library, Georgetown University, Washington, D.C., p. 29.

163. Nancy B. Tucker, "John Foster Dulles and the Taiwan Roots of the 'Two Chinas' Policy," in Immerman, *Dulles,* p. 238.

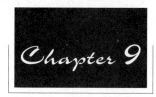

Chapter 9

PASSING THE TORCH:
THE VIETNAM YEARS, 1961–1969

The U.S. Embassy in Saigon. *American soldiers inspect the outer wall of the embassy compound, blasted open by Vietcong commandos in one of the first attacks of the Tet offensive in early 1968. (Richard Swanson, Life Magazine, © Time, Inc.)*

�֎ *Diplomatic Crossroad*

THE TET OFFENSIVE IN VIETNAM, 1968

"They're coming in! They're coming in! VC in the compound," the young MP shouted into his radio.[1] Seconds later Vietcong (VC) commandos gunned him down. Moments before, about 3:00 A.M. that January 30, 1968, the compound of the American embassy in Saigon, South Vietnam, was quiet, the only noise coming from the whirring air conditioners and the fireworks exploding in celebration of the Lunar New Year, or Tet. Only a few Americans guarded the grounds. Completed in 1967 at a cost of $2.6 million, the six-story embassy building was protected by shatterproof Plexiglas windows, a concrete sun shield covering the entire structure, and a thick, eight-foot-high outer wall. Topped by a helicopter pad, the fortified building, remarked one Vietnamese observer, had become "the symbol of America's power to stay, to destroy, to change a whole way of life, to propose and dispose at will."[2]

At 2:45 A.M., a Renault taxi cab and Peugeot truck moved without lights into the darkness from a repair shop near the embassy. About fifteen Vietcong leaped from their vehicles and fired at two embassy MPs (military police). The stunned Americans fired back and hastily bolted the heavy steel gate to the compound. Soon a hugh explosion blew a three-foot hole in the wall. The VC scrambled through, firing automatic rifles. The two MPs managed to radio for help before they died. The invaders then unleashed their antitank guns and rockets, transported into Saigon weeks before under shipments of tomatoes and firewood. The thick teakwood embassy doors took a direct hit, sending the U.S. seal crashing to the ground. Inside, a skeleton crew of Central Intelligence Agency and Foreign Service officials felt as if they were "in a telephone booth in the *Titanic* while the ship was going down."[3] A few blocks away, aides roused Ambassador Ellsworth Bunker and whisked him away to a secret hiding place. Just weeks earlier, Bunker had hosted a New Year's Eve party at the embassy, inviting guests to come "see the light at the end of the tunnel."[4]

The news of the attack spread quickly across Saigon. Flash bulletins reached the United States. Few American leaders could believe that the enemy had breached "Bunker's bunker." After all, on January 17, in his State of the Union message, President Lyndon B. Johnson himself had called most of South Vietnam secure, and the embassy seemed the most secure of any site.

In Saigon's dim morning light, American soldiers counterattacked, using a jeep to knock down the steel gate. Paratroopers landed by helicopter on the roof. By 9:15 A.M., with the compound secure, General William C. Westmoreland arrived to survey the littered yard. He counted nineteen dead Vietnamese (four were friendly embassy employees), five dead Americans, and two Vietcong prisoners. He

"What the Hell's Ho Chi Minh Doing Answering Our Saigon Embassy Phone . . . ?" Paul Conrad's cartoon expressed well the startled American response to the attack on the U.S. Embassy in South Vietnam, in January 1968. President Lyndon Johnson had earlier reported that most of South Vietnam had been secured against the Vietcong and North Vietnamese. (© 1968, *Los Angeles Times.* Reprinted with permission Los Angeles Times Syndicate)

then declared an American victory. One reporter described the compound as a "butcher shop in Eden."[5]

The bold sally against the embassy comprised but one part of the massive, well-coordinated Tet offensive conceived in communist North Vietnam by General Vo Nguyen Giap, famous for his defeat of the French at Dienbienphu in 1954. The forays struck thirty-six of the forty-four provincial capitals, some one hundred other villages, the gigantic Tan Son Nhut airbase, and numerous sites in Saigon (see map, page 413). The communist forces attacked when about half of the South Vietnamese Army (ARVN) had gone on leave for the Tet holiday. The VC, or National Liberation Front (NLF), and North Vietnamese hoped to seize the cities, foment a general sympathetic uprising, force ARVN and U.S. forces to move to the cities—leaving a vacuum in the countryside—and disrupt the governmental bureaucracy. In the end, Washington would have to negotiate American withdrawal. The NLF Order of the Day prophesized "the greatest battle ever fought throughout the history of our country. It will bring forth worldwide changes, but will also require many sacrifices."[6] U.S. officials soon grasped this "climactic" moment in the "struggle in Southeast Asia."[7] When Secretary of Defense Robert McNamara suggested sending troops with limited training to "rear areas," a general replied, "Mr. Secretary, there are no rear areas in Vietnam anymore."[8]

Yet the ARVN and U.S. armies struck back "with the fury of a blinded giant," according to the Pulitzer Prize-winning journalist Frances FitzGerald. "Forced to fight in the cities, they bombed, shelled, and strafed the most populous districts as if they saw no distinction between them and the jungle."[9] Americans at home watched the counterattacks on color television and many recoiled from the carnage. To fight enemy troops in Hue, South Vietnam's old imperial capital and third largest city, American and ARVN forces used everything from nausea gas to rockets. "Nothing I had seen during the Second World War in the Pacific [and] during the Korean War" matched the "destruction and despair" in Hue, recalled a journalist.[10] After three weeks of vicious warfare, the communists fled; 100,000 people had become refugees, thousands lay dead, and American bombings had reduced a once-beautiful city to rubble. The Vietcong executed hundreds, perhaps thousands, of civilians, most of them connected with the South Vietnamese government or Americans. The Vietcong commander at Hue later wrote: "There is never an easy 'political' victory . . . without first having to shed blood and scatter bones on the battlefield."[11]

In the northwest corner of South Vietnam, U.S. soldiers bravely resisted a siege of their two-square-mile hillside at Khe Sanh, which, according to Westmoreland, "served to lure North Vietnamese to their deaths."[12] Hundreds of Americans died during the first months of 1968, as enemy rockets zeroed in on the strategic but vulnerable base. American B-52s countered by dropping tons of bombs on the surrounding area. By the end of March, remembered a colonel, "the jungle had become literally a desert—vast stretches of scarred, bare earth with hardly a tree standing, a landscape of splinters and bomb craters."[13] The communists never launched a major assault. Still, to many Americans, the sight of pinned-down GIs at Khe Sanh represented a new defensive posture for the United States in Vietnam.

The provincial capital of Ben Tre symbolized the costs of the Tet offensive. To ferret out the VC, American and ARVN forces leveled Ben Tre, killing a thousand civilians. In unforgettable words, a U.S. officer declared that "it became necessary to destroy the town to save it."[14] That statement joined one newsreel to sear American memory. The NBC Huntley-Brinkley news program of February 1 showed a brief film clip of the national police chief of South Vietnam pointing a pistol at the head of a suspected VC. As reporter John Chancellor narrated "rough justice on a Saigon street," General Nguyen Ngoc pulled the trigger and blasted the young man. The fifty-two seconds of footage, said an NBC producer, broadcast the "rawest, roughest film anyone had ever seen."[15]

The Johnson administration, having claimed before Tet that South Vietnam had gained the upper hand in the war and having said that U.S. officials had expected a communist offensive, suffered an ever-growing "credibility gap" with the American people. January proved a bad month for Lyndon B. Johnson. On the twenty-third the North Koreans captured the American spy ship *Pueblo* and its entire crew off the Korean coast. The international balance of payments for the United States, Johnson learned, was running at an adverse annual rate of $7 billion. A B-52 with four H-bombs aboard crashed in Greenland. And Senator Eugene McCarthy, a "dove" on Vietnam, continued to challenge Johnson's renomination to the presidency.

Vietnamese Widow and Her Husband's Coffin. Pham Thi Cuc weeps at the coffin of her husband, killed during the battle for Hue in 1968. (Turner Collection, Hoover Institution Archives)

Rough Justice on a Saigon Street. The South Vietnamese national police chief executes a suspected Vietcong guerrilla in the street during the Tet offensive, 1968. Associated Press photographer Eddie Adams caught this terrible incident, as did an NBC television crew. (Wide World Photos)

Critics and doubters probed the administration's assertion that Tet counted as a triumph. Senator Robert F. Kennedy, soon to declare himself a candidate for the Democratic presidential nomination, said "it is as if James Madison [had claimed] victory in 1812 because the British only burned Washington instead of annexing it to the British Empire."[16] Senator Stuart Symington quizzed Secretary of State Dean Rusk: "It is clear what we are losing, but what do we win if we win?"[17] After Secretary McNamara recited enemy casualties, a reporter asked: "Isn't there something Orwellian about it, that the more we kill, the stronger they get?"[18] A testy Rusk asked the press: "Whose side are you on?"[19] When the popular television newscaster Walter Cronkite of CBS judged the war a stalemate, LBJ confided: "If I've lost Cronkite, I've lost middle America."[20]

Some 45,000 Vietcong, 2,000 ARVN, and 1,000 American soldiers died. Vietnamese civilians suffered a heavy toll, too. More than 14,000 died and 24,000 were wounded. One-eighth of the South Vietnamese people became homeless refugees in their own land. A Vietnamese villager concluded: "The important thing about Tet . . . is that the Communists made the Government very weak."[21] Although the NLF had not generated a national rebellion, had failed to hold the cities, and had suffered huge casualties, they had freed thousands of prisoners, disrupted the South Vietnamese governmental structure, crippled the American pacification program in the countryside, gained more influence in rural areas, heaped monstrous refugee and reconstruction problems on the Saigon regime, and proved that they could mount massive assaults.

Johnson decried the "chorus of defeatism" in the United States.[22] He authorized 10,500 more troops for Vietnam, gave hawkish speeches against quitting under fire, and flamboyantly toured American military bases. In late February Johnson

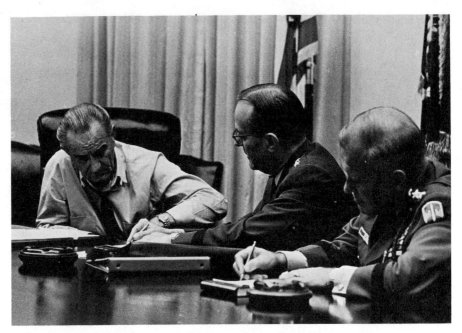

Lyndon B. Johnson (1908–1973). A tired president confers with Generals Creighton Abrams and Earl Wheeler at the National Security Council meeting of March 27, 1968. A few days later, Johnson removed himself as a candidate in the presidential race. The historian George C. Herring writes that Lyndon Johnson now appears less a warmonger and more "a tragic figure, trapped in a dilemma not entirely of his own making and stubbornly persisting despite the enormous pain he was inflicting on the nation and himself." (Courtesy of The Lyndon B. Johnson Library)

ordered the new secretary of defense, Clark Clifford, a former Truman adviser, to undertake a major review of Vietnam policy. General Westmoreland had recommended that an additional 206,000 American troops join the more than 500,000 already there. The generals, one student of Tet has written, "hoped that Clifford would be a *tabula rasa* on which they could write their plan."[23] They planned a major new ARVN-American offensive. Within the Pentagon, formerly timid dissenters pleaded for deescalation of the violence. Americans could not save Vietnam by destroying it, advisers such as Under Secretary of the Air Force Townsend Hoopes and Deputy Secretary of Defense Paul Nitze counseled. Furthermore, Vietnam was draining America's resources from its more serious confrontation with the key enemy, the Soviet Union. In early March, too, Rusk suggested curtailing the bombing of North Vietnam to induce peace talks. In the New Hampshire Democratic primary on March 12, McCarthy made a surprisingly strong showing by polling 42 percent of the vote to Johnson's 49 percent. Johnson also talked with the quintessential Cold Warrior. Dean Acheson responded bluntly: "With all due respect, the Joint Chiefs of Staff don't know what they're talking about."[24]

Clifford came to the same conclusion when he fired a series of questions at the military brass. He grew appalled that the generals could not say how long the fighting would continue or how many more troops might be needed. "Nothing had prepared me for the weakness of the military's case," he recalled.[25] Clifford's review committee, the Ad Hoc Task Force on Vietnam, recommended in early

March increasing the bombing of North Vietnam and sending 20,000 additional American troops. But Clifford expressed private doubts to the president. Later in the month, another advisory body, the "Wise Men," comprised largely of Truman-era diplomats and generals, told the president that victory had become impossible. "The establishment bastards have bailed out," roared Johnson.[26] They also expressed alarm that the Vietnam war had initiated a gold and dollar crisis that threatened the economic well-being of the United States. Nervous foreigners—especially Europeans—rushed to exchange their dollars for gold. On March 14 alone, foreigners redeemed $372 million for gold. A post-Tet military buildup would cost billions more, further bloat the deficit-burdened budget, and panic foreign owners of dollars even more. Clifford heard from his associates in the business community, who found America "in a hopeless bog."[27] The "sheer accumulation" of negative views from advisers, opinion polls, the news media, and Congress, one scholar has written, turned Johnson toward deescalation—but "he did so in secret."[28] In a dream he also saw himself as Woodrow Wilson paralyzed from the neck down.

On March 31 Johnson spoke on prime-time television. "We are prepared to move immediately toward peace through negotiations," he announced. Although the United States was sending another 13,500 soldiers to South Vietnam and more military aid to ARVN, he reported that U.S. airplanes would halt their bombing of a major portion of North Vietnam. "Even this limited bombing of the North could come to an early end—if our restraint is matched in Hanoi [the North Vietnamese capital]."[29] The president appealed for peace talks. He also asked Congress to raise taxes. Then, to the amazement of viewers and even some of his advisers, Johnson declared that he would not seek reelection. On April 3 the North Vietnamese agreed to go to the conference table. Discussions began on May 14. The fighting and talking—and dying—would go on for several years more. Many GIs no longer thought the war worth fighting, as they said in their familiar slogan: "It don't mean nothin'."[30]

VIETNAMESE WARS: THE HISTORY BEFORE 1961

Why Vietnam? Why did this Southeast Asian land of peasant farmers become the site of America's longest war? The American-Vietnamese intersection began long before Tet and comprised but one part of a centuries-long story of Vietnamese resistance to foreigners—Chinese, French, Japanese, and American. In 1867 France colonized Vietnam and soon began to exploit the country's raw materials, as well as those of Laos and Cambodia, which became protectorates in 1883 and part of French Indochina in the 1890s. Rice, rubber, tin, and tungsten from the area flowed to European markets. France constructed a haughty and repressive imperial government and monopolized land holdings, while some 80 percent of the Vietnamese people existed as poor, rural peasants. From 1867 onward the embittered Vietnamese battled their French overlords.

Vietnam's most famous nationalist leader was Ho Chi Minh, born in 1890 to a low-level government employee. Later described as a "small man, with a face the

Ho Chi Minh (1890–1969). The Vietnamese nationalist and communist led his nation's battle against foreigners for decades. In 1945 Ho told an American agent of the Office of Strategic Services (OSS): "Your statesmen make eloquent speeches about helping those with self-determination. We are self-determined. Why not help us? Am I different from . . . even your George Washington? I, too, want to set my people free." (*The Reporter,* 1950. Copyright 1950 by Fortnightly Publishing Co., Inc.)

color of tea, a beard the color of rice, a piercing look beneath a forehead crowned by a somewhat absurd lock of hair," Ho traveled to Europe and at the time of World War I lobbied for independence.[31] In Paris, Ho sent a memorandum to the Big Four leaders at Versailles, but his upstart anticolonial ideas, despite their deliberate reference to Woodrow Wilson's principle of self-determination, did not move the conferees. Because the Communist party seemed the only political force vigorously denouncing colonialism, Ho and other nationalists joined it. Throughout the twenties and thirties he lived and agitated in China and Russia. In 1930–1931 the French brutally suppressed a Vietnamese peasant rebellion, killing 10,000 and deporting another 50,000. "If the French had . . . employed all available means for eliminating rural poverty," the scholar Joseph Buttinger has written, "the Communist movement in Vietnam would never have gained its extraordinary strength."[32]

During 1940–1941 the Japanese took over Vietnam but left collaborating French officials in charge. Vietnamese nationalists, including Ho's communists, went underground, used China as a base, and in 1941 organized the Vietminh, a coalition of nationalist groups led by the Communist party. In the final days of World War II, Vietminh guerrillas tangled with Japanese troops, liberated some northern provinces, and cooperated with the U.S. Office of Strategic Services (OSS). Agents grew fond of Ho, designated him OSS Agent 19, gave him weapons, and hoped that he would work with Americans after the war. Ho sent formal messages to Washington, asked for recognition, and often mentioned the American Declaration of Independence and the Atlantic Charter. In late August 1945, Ho's Vietminh organized the Democratic Republic of Vietnam (DRV) in Hanoi. On September 2, he proclaimed Vietnam's independence, borrowing phrases from America's document of July 4, 1776. Still, jilted in the past, Ho remained privately suspicious of Americans as "only interested in replacing the French. . . . They want to reorganize our country to control it. They are capitalists to the core."[33]

During World War II, U.S. officials speculated about Vietnam's future. President Franklin D. Roosevelt remarked on a number of occasions that France should relinquish Indochina, because the French had exploited and brutalized the region's people. He toyed with the idea of a trusteeship. The Department of State valued the Southeast Asian countries as "potentially important markets for American exports. They lie athwart the southwestern approaches to the Pacific Ocean and have important bearing on our security and the security of the Philippines."[34] Some American officials also worried that denying France the restoration of its empire would alienate a potential European ally needed to stabilize the postwar world. French power could help to counter Soviet power. Ambassador W. Averell Harriman predicted that the Soviet Union would become a "world bully" and "reach into China and the Pacific."[35] Prime Minister Winston Churchill, moreover, informed Roosevelt in no uncertain terms that Britain opposed the breakup of empires. Just before he died, Roosevelt retreated. Judging it "better to keep quiet now," he did not discuss Indochina with an agitated Churchill at Yalta.[36] Roosevelt's anticolonial instincts never became policy.

So the French, with British military help and American tolerance, returned to Vietnam. Ignored by the United States, receiving no support from Moscow, and now facing French forces, the embittered Vietminh accepted a compromise with

France in March 1946: DRV status as a "free state" in the French Union and French military occupation of northern Vietnam. It soon became clear that Paris intended to reestablish its imperial grip. Vietminh and French soldiers clashed in December. One French bombardment of Haiphong killed several thousand civilians. The Vietminh responded with guerrilla terror. For the next eight years Vietnam endured bloody combat, with the French holding the cities and the Vietminh the countryside.

Indochina, Truman administration adviser Clark Clifford recalled, seemed at first a "French problem."[37] To win Paris's favor for its postwar policies in Europe, Washington acquiesced in the return of French colonialism to Vietnam. Although in the early postwar months Ho Chi Minh had requested economic assistance and support for independence, he never received replies from Washington. As the Cold War intensified in 1946–1947, Ho's Moscow "training" became a topic of American discussion. By late 1946 the Department of State had designated him an "agent of international communism," although some State Department officers dissented and pointed out that Vietnamese leaders were nationalists, not servants of Moscow, and that Ho stood as an Asian Tito. Ho himself chafed at accusations that he had become a mere tool of international communism. He had earlier described himself to an OSS officer as a "progressive-socialist-nationalist"—that is, the leader of both a colonial rebellion against France and a social revolution for Vietnam.[38]

In 1948 the French installed Emperor Bao Dai, who had served the Japanese in World War II, as their Vietnamese leader. U.S. officials knew that Bao Dai had become a French puppet, but they accepted him as an alternative to "Commie domination of Indochina."[39] In February 1950, in what now appears as a momentous decision based on mistaken Cold War notions that the Soviet Union instigated nationalist rebellions and that Mao's China might engulf the region, Washington recognized the Bao Dai government. In May, moreover, the Truman administration extended aid to the French for their war in Vietnam.

The Korean War stirred even more American interest in the outcome of the Vietnamese rebellion. In 1950 Washington sent $150 million and a contingent of military advisers to Vietnam. For 1945–1954 the United States gave $2 billion of the $5 billion that Paris spent to keep Vietnam within the French empire. In 1954 U.S. aid covered 78 percent of the cost of the war, and some 300 Americans went to Vietnam as part of the Military Assistance Advisory Group—all to no avail.

In spring 1954, at Dienbienphu, a fortress where the besieged French had chosen to stand or fall, Vietminh forces moved toward a major, symbolic victory. To save the fortress the French sought American intervention. Eisenhower received conflicting advice from the U.S. military. The chairman of the Joint Chiefs of Staff, Admiral Arthur Radford, urged massive night attacks on Vietminh positions by 300 U.S. carrier aircraft, possibly including tactical nuclear weapons. Army chief of staff Matthew Ridgeway, however, judged intervention "altogether disproportionate to the liability it would incur."[40] A Defense Department analyst agreed, fearing a wider commitment: "One cannot go over Niagara Falls in a barrel only slightly."[41]

The president cited the "falling domino" theory to explain American interests in Southeast Asia and then sounded out Congress, France, and Britain about internationalizing the war through "United Action." But members of Congress warned against an air strike that might lead next to ground troops and another Korea. The British also balked. "Without allies," a stymied Eisenhower remarked, "the leader is just an adventurer like Genghis Khan."[42] Without U.S. intervention, French forces at Dienbienphu surrendered on May 7. Determined to hold Vietnam in the Western camp, Ike had to find another way to intervene.

A few days earlier, on April 26, 1954, representatives from France, the Soviet Union, Britain, China, the United States, Bao Dai's Vietnam, the DRV, Laos, and Cambodia met in Geneva to discuss Asian issues. The Eisenhower administration, fearing a French retreat, reluctantly agreed to discuss Vietnam at the conference. In fact, a new French government, headed by Pierre Mendès-France, came to power on June 12 and pledged a political settlement to end the war. President Eisenhower expected to "gag" on any Geneva agreement, but he vowed to "salvage something" by organizing Southeast Asian states into a military pact and defending the southern half of Vietnam.[43] At the time, Ho's Vietminh controlled two-thirds of Vietnam.

On July 20 the DRV and France signed the Geneva agreements. Ho's government did so only after pressure from the Soviet and Chinese representatives. The terms: temporary partition of Vietnam at the seventeenth parallel; French withdrawal to below that latitude; neither North nor South Vietnam to sign military alliances or permit foreign bases on Vietnamese soil; national elections to be held in 1956; unification of the country after elections; and elections also in neighboring strife-torn Laos and Cambodia, the other territories in French Indochina. Refusing to endorse the accords, the United States did state that it would not disturb the agreements—it would "refrain from the threat or the use of force."[44] The National Security Council found the Geneva settlement a "disaster" that represented a "major forward stride of Communism which may lead to the loss of Southeast Asia."[45] Quite an exaggeration, but the United States believed that Communist China, which had sent some aid to the Vietminh, would use Vietnam as a base for expansion. As the French reporter Bernard Fall observed, the "struggle now began to rebuild a truncated land into a viable non-Communist Vietnamese state."[46]

Not about to "mourn the past," as Dulles remarked, the United States moved deliberately.[47] It created the Southeast Asia Treaty Organization in September 1954 to protect Cambodia and Laos from supposed communist aggression and South Vietnam from the Vietminh. SEATO violated the spirit of the Geneva accords by specifying protection over the southern half of Vietnam—now treated as a separate state. After SEATO, the seventeenth parallel seemed less a provisional and more a permanent line.

In the South, the United States backed the new government of Prime Minister Ngo Dinh Diem, a noncommunist Vietnamese nationalist and Catholic who had spent a few years in the United States cultivating prominent friends such as Cardinal Francis Spellman, Supreme Court Justice William O. Douglas, and Senators Hubert H. Humphrey and John F. Kennedy. An enlarged contingent of American advisers, in violation of Geneva, began to train a South Vietnamese army, and millions of dollars in U.S. military and economic aid flowed to Diem's regime. Diem and U.S. officials cooperated to displace Bao Dai and the remnants of French influence. In mid-1955 the North proposed preliminary talks to plan the national election scheduled by Geneva for 1956. Diem refused, and the Eisenhower administration, certain that Ho would win an election, endorsed cancellation of the electoral provisions of the Geneva Accords, thereby thwarting unification. In October 1955 Diem held his own referendum in the South. That blatant fraud gave him 98.2 percent of the vote. In Saigon, his backers so stuffed the ballot boxes that 605,000 votes emerged from 450,000 registered voters.

The two Vietnams went their separate ways, with Ho's North receiving aid from both the Soviet Union and China, but cautiously avoiding dependence on either by deftly shifting intimacy from one to the other. Ho launched land reform, ending a landlord system that had largely excluded peasants. Diem's Republic of Vietnam received U.S. aid of about $300 million a year (80 percent of it for the military). Working under CIA contract, Michigan State University police experts began to train a "Civil Guard" to capture suspected Vietminh. Fresh from putting down the radical Hukbalahap movement in the Philippines, Air Force colonel Edward Lansdale, on loan to the CIA, inaugurated a propaganda campaign. It consisted of alarmist disinformation about an impending communist-engineered bloodbath intended to scare Catholics in the North into moving to the South. Some 900,000 people, most of them Catholics, made the trek. Lansdale also organized sabotage operations in the North. Most important, he helped Diem overcome powerful competitors through bribes and threats, thereby reassuring skeptical U.S. officials that Diem had the backbone to lead in crisis. In 1956 Diem jailed 20,000 to 30,000 suspected communists in "reeducation" camps. Tortures became

Eisenhower, Ngo Dinh Diem (1901–1963), and Dulles. The South Vietnamese nationalist Diem, from a mandarin and Catholic family, spent time in exile in the United States before returning to his country as premier (1954–1963). His police-state rule did not seem to upset President Eisenhower or Secretary Dulles in May 1957 when they met with Diem in Washington. (Dwight D. Eisenhower Library)

routine. In 1957 and 1958 angry southern rebels retaliated by killing village teachers, police, officers, and government officials.

Capitalizing on widespread rural support and general anti-Diem dissent, the Vietminh organized the National Liberation Front (NLF) in December 1960 as an umbrella organization. Hanoi, which had been sending aid to allies in the South only since 1959, encouraged this communist-dominated group. Diem labeled the front the "Vietcong," meaning Vietnamese communists, to discredit it. In the rural areas they controlled, NLF cadres won favor from peasants by distributing land and reducing rents. In contrast, Diem resisted land reform and placed family members in profitable positions, grafting corruption onto an already unpopular regime. Ambassador Elbridge Durbrow criticized Diem for not initiating reforms, but American military advisers defended the premier, and Eisenhower hailed him as a "tough miracle man" and the "savior" of South Vietnam.[48]

U.S. officials charged that North Vietnamese aggression initiated this new war in the South, but most scholars have concluded that the NLF sprang from the peculiar, repressive environment of Diem's South. Vietnam's history had thus evolved from a colonial rebellion to expel the French from Vietnam into several interacting wars and revolutions: post-Geneva social revolution in the North; civil war within Diem's South; civil war between North and South; and, finally, an anti-imperialist war to force the Americans out. Imbued with the Cold War mentality that crammed events into an East-West frame, however, Americans failed to understand the singularly *Vietnamese* character of the Vietnamese wars. Senator John F. Kennedy in 1956 called Diem's Vietnam the "cornerstone of the free world in Southeast Asia, the keystone of the arch, the finger in the dike."[49] In 1961 Kennedy became president.

JOHN F. KENNEDY AND HIS "ACTION INTELLECTUALS"

Vietnam actually figured little in the 1960 presidential contest between the Republican vice president, Richard M. Nixon, and Democratic candidate John F. Kennedy, both Cold Warriors who differed more on style than on policy. Kennedy, who beat Nixon by a narrow margin, aroused support through the slogan: "I think it's time America started moving again."[50] Both Nixon and Kennedy belonged to the "containment generation" that matured politically in the 1940s and imbibed the popular lessons of World War II and the Cold War. Both Nixon and Kennedy had won seats in Congress in 1946 and endorsed the "Truman Doctrine" the following year. In 1960, Kennedy charged that the Eisenhower-Nixon administration had neglected the Third World, thus consigning it to communism without a fight. With the U-2 affair, the abrupt demise of the Paris summit meeting, an adverse balance of payments, cancellation of a presidential visit to Japan, and crises in Cuba, the Congo, and Indochina as the immediate backdrop, Kennedy and many Americans believed that the United States was losing the Cold War. "I think there is a danger that history will make a judgement," Kennedy stated during the

1960 campaign, "that these were the days when the tide began to run out"—"when the communist tide began to pour in."[51] His words smacked of John Foster Dulles himself when he described the Cold War as a "struggle for supremacy between two conflicting ideologies: Freedom under God versus ruthless, godless tyranny."[52] Kennedy pledged to move the Cold War from stalemate and potential communist victory to American triumph.

Kennedy did not mind being called Truman with a Harvard accent. Born in 1917 to wealthy, Catholic, politically active parents, John Fitzgerald Kennedy graduated from Harvard College and served with honor in World War II. At the time his father served as ambassador to Great Britain, his senior thesis appeared as a book titled *Why England Slept* (1940), with the theme that England should have resisted Nazi aggression with force, rather than embraced weakness. For Kennedy's generation, the Munich agreement became the "Munich syndrome" or appeasement lesson. As he said in 1962: "The 1930s taught us a clear lesson: aggressive conduct, if allowed to go unchecked and unchallenged, ultimately leads to war."[53] He also remembered the 1940s. As the grand theorist Walt W. Rostow reported, the "first charge of the Kennedy Administration in 1961—somewhat like the challenge faced by the Truman Administration in 1947—the was to turn back the Communist offensive."[54] History both tugged at the Kennedy advisers and pushed them.

So did the distinctive style and personality of the young president. "All at once you had something exciting," recalled a student campaigner in comparing Eisenhower and Kennedy. "You had a young guy who had kids, and who liked to play football on his front lawn. . . . Everything they did showed that America was alive and active. . . . To run a country it takes more than just mechanics. It takes a psychology."[55] Call it psychology, charisma, charm, image, or mystique, Kennedy had it. Photogenic and quick-witted, he became a television star. Observers marveled at his alleged speed-reading abilities. Decrying softness in the American people, he launched a physical fitness program. Handsome, articulate, ingratiating, dynamic, energetic, competitive, athletic, cultured, bright, self-confident, cool, analytical, mathematical, zealous—these were the traits universally ascribed to the president. People often listened not to what he said but to how he said it, and he usually said it with verve. Dean Rusk remembered him as an "incandescent man. He was on fire, and he set people around him on fire."[56] For the historian-politician and presidential assistant Arthur M. Schlesinger, Jr., JFK had "enormous confidence in his own luck," and "everyone around him thought he had the Midas touch and could not lose."[57]

Style and personality influence diplomacy. Many of his friends have commented that a desire for power drove John F. Kennedy, because power ensured victory. His father, Joseph P. Kennedy, "pressed his children hard to compete, never to be satisfied with anything but first place. The point was not just to try; the point was to win."[58] Although Kennedy suffered from near-fatal Addison's disease and received regular injections of potent drugs, all of which he concealed through public disclaimers, JFK nonetheless projected the image of a healthy, vigorous man who played to win. His appearances with Hollywood actresses such as Marilyn Monroe and his frequent extramarital sexual liaisons with many women reflected his macho self-image. John F. Kennedy also saw foreign affairs as an arena for proving his

John F. Kennedy (1917–1963). Before becoming president, JFK represented Massachusetts in the House (1947–1953) and the Senate (1953–1961). His ghostwritten book *Profiles in Courage* (1957) won a Pulitzer Prize. One of the president's underpublicized achievements was the Trade Expansion Act of 1962 and the subsequent "Kennedy Round" of trade negotiations, which reduced tariffs. (*The Reporter*, 1962. Copyright 1962 by The Reporter Magazine Co.)

Arthur M. Schlesinger, Jr. (b. 1917) and Kennedy. The distinguished historian-politician became a special assistant to the president in 1961 and helped plan policies for Latin America. His partisan defense of JFK, *A Thousand Days* (1965), won a Pulitzer Prize. Dean Acheson did not share Schlesinger's high opinion of the young president, calling Kennedy an "Indian snake charmer . . . who lives only in his dream. Someday one of the snakes will wake up, and no one will be able even to run." (John F. Kennedy Library)

coughness. "Who gives a shit about the minimum wage?" he once asked.[59] Stung in the 1960 campaign by anti-Catholic bias, by misplaced right-wing charges that he was soft on communism, and by his narrow victory over Nixon, Kennedy soon gave Americans box scores on the missile race, the arms race, and the space race. Cocky, thinking themselves the "right" people, Kennedy and his advisers were, a skeptical Under Secretary of State Chester Bowles complained, "sort of looking for a chance to prove their muscle."[60] Schlesinger captured the mood: "Euphoria reigned; we thought for a moment that the world was plastic and the future unlimited."[61] Kennedy's alarmist inaugural address demonstrated the new spirit. Its swollen Cold War language announced that "the torch has been passed to a new generation." He paid homage to historical memories when he noted that his generation had been "tempered by war" and "disciplined by a hard and bitter peace." Then came those moving, but in hindsight dangerously expansive, words: "Let every nation know that we shall pay any price, bear any burden, meet any hardship, support any friend, oppose any foe to assure the survival and the success of liberty."[62]

The Kennedy people considered themselves "can-do" types, who with rationality and careful calculation could revive an ailing nation and world and manage crises. Theodore H. White tagged them "the Action Intellectuals."[63] "Management" became one of the catchwords of the time. They had an inordinate faith in data. When a White House assistant attempted to persuade Secretary of Defense Robert McNamara, the "whiz kid" from Ford Motor, that the Vietnam venture would fail, McNamara shot back: "Where is your data? Give me something I can put in the computer. Don't give me your poetry."[64] Danger lurked in a heavy reliance on quantified information. "Ah, *les statistiques,*" said a Vietnamese general to a U.S. official. "If you want them to go up, they will go up. If you want them to go down, they will go down."[65] A diplomat once told McNamara: "Bob, you're trying to put a Ford motor into a Vietnamese ox-cart. You will break it down."[66] Nonetheless, with its faith in formulas, the self-confident Kennedy team introduced fresh slogans: "The Grand Design" for Europe; the "New Africa" policy; "Flexible Response" for the military; the "Alliance for Progress" for Latin America; and the "New Frontier" at home.

Kennedy's secretary of state, Dean Rusk, worked uncomfortably with the crusading "action intellectuals," but he remained a loyal member of the team. A Rhodes Scholar, Rusk had served as a military intelligence officer in Asia during World War II, as an assistant secretary of state under Truman, and as president of the Rockefeller Foundation in the 1950s. Truman warhorses Robert Lovett and Dean Acheson enthusiastically recommended Rusk to Kennedy, who liked Rusk's quiet, modest, and unflappable manner. The president wanted to design his own foreign policy and did not relish a secretary of state who was too independent-minded. The relatively unknown Rusk fit the bill. "The gentle, gracious Rusk," the presidential assistant Theodore C. Sorenson later noted, "deferred almost too

Robert Strange McNamara (b. 1916). The mathematically minded secretary of defense graduated from the University of California, Berkeley. A former Ford Motor executive, McNamara applied efficiency methods to his department and served as war minister for Vietnam. In 1968 he became president of the World Bank. In the 1980s he became a major critic of the nuclear-arms race that he had accelerated in the 1960s. (*The Reporter*, 1967. Copyright 1967 by The Reporter Magazine Co.)

Makers of American Foreign Relations, 1961–1969

Presidents	Secretary of State
John F. Kennedy, 1961–1963 Lyndon B. Johnson, 1963–1969	Dean Rusk, 1961–1969

amiably to White House initiatives and interference."[67] A native of Georgia and the son of a Presbyterian minister, Rusk formed his worldview in the 1930s and 1940s. In his eight years as secretary, Rusk agonized over Vietnam, opposing Americanization of the war but refusing to withdraw until a noncommunist government stood secure. So he ended up backing military escalation. Lyndon Johnson appreciated his loyalty: "He has the compassion of a preacher and the courage of a Georgia cracker. When you're going in with the Marines, he's the kind you want at your side."[68]

Next to Attorney General Robert F. Kennedy, the president's brother who served as troubleshooter and confidant, McGeorge Bundy became Kennedy's chief foreign-relations counselor. The brilliant forty-one-year-old former Harvard dean had helped Henry L. Stimson write his memoirs and had worked for the Marshall Plan. As national security affairs adviser, Bundy centralized decisionmaking in the White House and controlled the flow of information to the president. One Kennedyite, in a reference to a famed FDR adviser, called Bundy "Harry Hopkins with hand grenades."[69] "Almost antiseptically clear in his views," Bundy intimidated others and found it "hard to reverse field."[70] A self-professed member of the

Dean Rusk (b. 1909). A graduate of Davidson College and a Rhodes Scholar at Oxford, Rusk served Kennedy and Johnson as a loyal secretary of state. "Personally, I made two mistakes," he recalled. "I underestimated the tenacity of the North Vietnamese and overestimated the patience of the American people." (Lyndon B. Johnson Library)

well-born elite dedicated to public service, Bundy lived the motto of his prepara-
tory school, Groton: "To Serve Is to Rule." Bundy worked loyally to make
Presidents Kennedy and Johnson look decisive, foreign policy look coherent, and
crises look managed.

ARMS BUILDUP, BERLIN CRISIS, AND NATION BUILDING

The Kennedy administration emphasized military expansion. Kennedy had charged
that the Eisenhower administration was losing the Cold War by tolerating a "missile gap" favorable to the Soviets. Part politics, part exaggeration by the military establishment, part frustrating symbol of the post-Sputnik shock, and part guesswork,
the charge derived from conflicting intelligence estimates. Democrats, led by
Senator Stuart Symington, declared that the Soviets would have a 3 to 1 edge in intercontinental ballistic missiles (ICBMs) by 1962. Eisenhower, who had warned in
1959 against the "feverish building of vast armaments to meet glibly predicted moments of so-called 'maximum peril,'" knew the charge was nonsense.[71] U-2 intelligence flights revealed a modest Soviet missile program. The United States had immense superiority. Kennedy and McNamara learned this, too, but, worried by
Soviet boasting and Third World insurgencies, they began a mighty expansion of
the military.

The administration called its defense strategy "flexible response," providing a
method for every conceivable kind of war.[72] The Special Forces or Green Berets
would conduct counterinsurgency against wars of national liberation; conventional
forces would handle limited wars; more and better missiles would deter war or serve
as primary weapons in nuclear war; at home, fallout shelters would protect
Americans under a civil defense plan; and, when required, the United States would
participate in collective security arrangements through the United Nations. In 1961
Kennedy increased the defense budget by 15 percent. Eisenhower's farewell address
notwithstanding, Kennedy enlarged the armed services and missile arsenal. By 1963
the United States had 275 major bases in 31 nations, 65 countries hosted U.S.
forces, and the American military trained soldiers in 72 countries. Also, one and a
quarter million military-related American personnel were stationed overseas. In
1961 the United States had 63 ICBMs; by 1963, 424. During 1961–1963, NATO's
nuclear firing power increased 60 percent. Kennedy also created the U.S. Arms
Control and Disarmament Agency, but his military buildup took priority.

The more missiles Americans acquired, the more vulnerable they became, because the Soviets tried to catch up by also building more. With Berlin continuing
to rattle nerves, the Kennedy administration decided to reassure Americans about
U.S. supremacy and warn Moscow. Kennedy calculated that Nikita Khrushchev
might go to the brink expecting to win because the Kremlin premier assumed that

U.S.S. *Sam Rayburn*.   Launched in 1962, this Polaris submarine with sixteen missile tubes and a missile range of 2,875 miles became part of a large Kennedy-inspired military buildup. The first Polaris submarine was commissioned in 1959. (U.S. Navy, Naval Photographic Center)

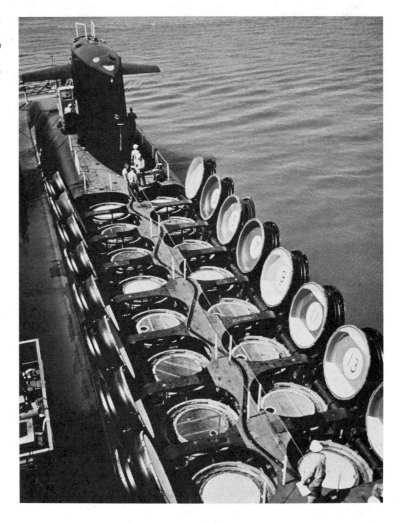

Americans still thought that the "missile gap" was in Moscow's favor. On October 21, therefore, Secretary McNamara's deputy, Roswell Gilpatric, itemized U.S. strategic forces and announced that the United States had such a powerful nuclear retaliatory force that any enemy which triggered it would invite self-destruction. The United States, moreover, could withstand a Soviet nuclear strike and still have enough missiles remaining to annihilate the Soviet Union. By all accounts, the message disturbed Soviet leaders, who sped up their ICBM program.

Kennedy met with Khrushchev at Vienna in June 1961, to discuss a test ban treaty, Berlin, and Laos. Aides warned that Khrushchev's style ranged from "cherubic to choleric."[73] Kennedy went to Vienna to show the Soviets that they "must not crowd him too much."[74] With 30,000 refugees each month escaping from East

"The Purpose of the Meeting Is to Take Measurements." Nikita S. Khrushchev and John F. Kennedy met at the summit in Vienna in June 1961. Kennedy told his brother Robert that talking with Khrushchev was "like dealing with Dad. All give and no take." (Parrish, Chicago Tribune–New York News Syndicate, Inc.)

Germany to West Berlin, Khrushchev speculated that "soon there will be nobody left in the GDR [East Germany] except for [Communist boss Walter] Ulbricht and his mistress."[75] Khrushchev told Kennedy that Berlin must become a "free city," thereby ending Western occupation. If the United States did not negotiate, Moscow would sign a separate treaty with East Germany, thus terminating the Soviet commitment to postwar occupation rights in Berlin. "Berlin is the testicles of the West," Khrushchev privately quipped. "Every time I want to make the West scream, I squeeze on Berlin."[76] Kennedy exploded: "That son of a bitch won't pay any attention to words. He has to see you move."[77] Although Khrushchev may have left Vienna thinking that he had outdueled the young president, records of their meetings reveal that a tenacious Kennedy gave as good as he got in disagreements on almost every issue. Still, because news accounts depicted Kennedy as "shaken and angry," the public perception developed that the Soviet leader had pushed Kennedy around.[78]

After Vienna, with the president remarking that Khrushchev had behaved like a "barbarian," the administration decided to force the Berlin question.[79] On July 25, calling Berlin "the great testing place of Western courage and will," he asked Congress for a $3.2 billion addition to the regular defense budget and authority to call up military reservists. He also requested $207 million to begin a civil defense, fallout shelter program—"in the event of an attack."[80] In a meeting with East German comrades, Khrushchev denounced Kennedy's "blustering" and snorted that "if he starts a war then he would probably become the last president of the United States of America."[81]

On August 13 the East Germans, backed by Moscow, suddenly put up a barbed wire barricade, followed by an ugly concrete block barrier, between the two Berlins. Worried that his East German ally Walter Ulbricht intended to capture West Berlin, provoking more confrontation than Moscow could tolerate, Khrushchev welcomed the wall solution to contain the uncompromising Ulbricht

The Berlin Wall.   East German soldiers replace barbed wire with concrete slabs at the Berlin Wall. Willy Brandt, later Germany's chancellor, grew disillusioned with the United States because it "merely frowned" when the wall went up. "What was called my Ostpolitik was formed against this background. . . . Traditional formulas of Western policies had been shown to be ineffective and unrealistic." (United Press International)

and defuse the crisis. The wall did shut off the exodus of refugees. Judging that "a wall is a hell of a lot better than a war," Kennedy acquiesced.[82] But he speculated that "we shall probably come very close to the edge" of nuclear war.[83] Unbeknownst to the president, his special representative in Berlin, General Lucius Clay, took it upon himself to arm U.S. tanks with bulldozer attachments to knock down the wall. Soviet intelligence learned of these preparations. Ten American M-48 tanks suddenly found themselves facing ten Russian tanks on opposite sides of Checkpoint Charlie on October 27, nearly precipitating "a nuclear-age equivalent of the Wild West Showdown at the OK Corral."[84] With the NSC staff simulating war games in which European fatalities reached tens of millions, Kennedy used a secret channel to negotiate with Khrushchev. After sixteen tense hours, both Soviet and U.S. tanks withdrew, and the crisis passed. West Germans scowled at Kennedy's unwillingess to knock the wall down. To assuage bruised feelings, Washington filled the airwaves with rhetorical commitments to the reunification of Germany. Kennedy himself had visited West Berlin in June 1963 to underscore the American will to stay.

As Kennedy dealt with the Cold War, he also attended to the Third World, the region he thought most vulnerable to revolution and communism and at the same time most susceptible to American influence. "Nation building" became his watch-

"Could You Point Out the Ground You've Taken? We're Here to Secure and Develop It Economically." A "nation-building" team cooperates with a counterinsurgency team in this parody of the "modernization" efforts of Americans overseas. (Editorial cartoon by Pat Oliphant, © 1976, *Los Angeles Times.* Reprinted with permission of Universal Press Syndicate)

word. The Kennedy team acknowledged the force of nationalism in the Third World; rather than flatly oppose it, the "action intellectuals" sought to use or channel it. Through modernization, or what the Kennedy team called peaceful revolution or middle-class revolution, Third World nations would grow from economic infancy to economic and political maturity. Evolutionary economic development hopefully would ensure noncommunist political stability. "Modern societies must be built," one of the chief theoreticians of the concept, Walt W. Rostow, declared, "and we are prepared to help build them."[85] Kennedy, for example, counted populous India as a particularly good candidate because it followed a noncommunist model of economic development, bordered the People's Republic of China, and led the nonaligned movement. India might be won for the West through U.S. economic and military aid. Although dollar assistance to India angered Pakistan, with which the United States had a military alliance, Washington nonetheless tilted toward New Delhi, especially during the Sino-Indian border war of fall 1962. In the early 1960s, India became the world's largest recipient of U.S. economic aid, for, if "we lose" the neutrals, "the balance of power could swing against us."[86]

Khrushchev's pledge of January 1961 to support wars of national liberation—such as that in Vietnam—seemed to raise the stakes in the Third World. A U.S. intelligence report of August 1961 claimed that other Asian countries saw Vietnam as a "gauge of U.S. willingness to help an anti-Communist Asian government stand against a Communist 'national liberation' campaign."[87] Counterinsurgency became the U.S. means to meet this test. Counterinsurgency took several forms, all reflecting the "can-do" philosophy: the training of native police forces and bureaucrats, flood control, transportation and communications, and community action projects. The American Special Forces units, or Green Berets, received special attention. Kennedy personally elevated their status in the military and supervised their choice of equipment. Washington assumed it could apply America's finest technology in Vietnam to succeed where the French had failed.

Besides enlarging counterinsurgency forces and extending foreign aid, the Kennedy administration created the Peace Corps. Established by executive order in 1961, this volunteer group of mostly young Americans numbered 5,000 by early 1963 and 10,000 a year later. They went into developing nations as teachers, agricultural advisers, and technicians. The Peace Corps, although certainly a selfinterested arm of U.S. foreign policy, blunted some of the sharper edges of poverty and hardship. Hundreds of dedicated individuals worked to improve living conditions. Peace Corps monuments—irrigation systems, water pumps, larger crops—arose throughout Latin America and Africa, but the corps's humanitarian efforts fell far short of resolving the Third World's profound squalor. Some nations, suspecting CIA infiltration of the Peace Corps, refused to cooperate. In some cases, as in Ethiopia, Peace Corps Volunteers went abroad with too little understanding of foreign languages and cultures. But, said one volunteer, "I still think it's a good basic way to approach problems—at the grass roots level—unlike policymakers who never understand things at the grass roots."[88]

The Kennedy administration also embarked on the Alliance for Progress in Latin America to head off Cuban-style revolution and communist subversion. Launched at the Punta del Este meeting of the Organization of American States in August 1961, the alliance envisioned spending $20 billion in funds from the United States and international organizations. In return, the Latin Americans promised land and tax reforms, housing projects, and health improvements. Initiated with great fanfare, the alliance soon sputtered. American businesses did not invest as expected; the State Department dragged its feet; Latin American nationalists disliked U.S. control; elites resisted reforms and pocketed American money; the gap between rich and poor widened; middle-class Latin Americans, whom Washington counted on, proved selfish. In the end, adult literacy and infant mortality rates improved, but Latin American economies registered unimpressive growth rates, class divisions remained stark, unemployment climbed, and agricultural production per person declined. The *Alianza para el Progreso* became another tool to maintain U.S. hegemony

Peace Corps Pamphlet.   Launched in 1961, the Peace Corps by 1963 had 5,000 volunteers. Most were college graduates with liberal arts degrees; although some middle-aged and elderly Americans joined the Corps, most volunteers were between the ages of twenty-two and twenty-eight. Teaching was the most common occupation, but many worked in community development programs: fish farms in Togo, roads in Colombia, poultry cooperatives in India, and bridges in Sierra Leone. (The Peace Corps)

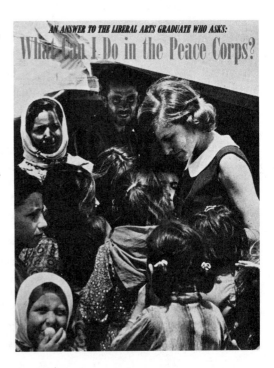

in the hemisphere and to wage the Cold War. By the mid-1960s, under the leadership of the staunchly conservative diplomat Thomas Mann, the alliance had turned its resources to military purposes, such as internal security forces. Washington abandoned its requirement that political democracy accompany economic change. Cuba's Fidel Castro acknowledged the alliance as "a politically wise concept put forth to hold back the tide of revolution." But it did not work, he keenly pointed out, "because those in charge of seeing that the agrarian reform was implemented in Latin America were the very owners of the lands."[89]

The difficulties of nation building appeared dramatically in the Congo (now called Zaire), which obtained hurried independence from Belgium in mid-1960. Civil war quickly erupted. Backed by American and European cobalt and copper interests, Moise Tshombe tried to detach Katanga Province from the new central government headed by Patrice Lumumba. The United States, fearing Soviet influence in "another Laos" or "another Cuba," helped a UN mission quell the Katanga insurrection.[90] Secretary Rusk worried about the consequences of the U.S. intervention for African views of the United States: "One or two more Congos—and we've had it."[91] Although Lumumba died in 1961, by early 1963 the central Congolese government had defeated Tshombe. About a year later, however, a major leftist revolt supported by the Soviet Union, China, and Ghana broke out. With UN forces gone, the CIA soon bolstered former enemy Tshombe as the new leader

Where Are We? The Alliance for Progress suffered sluggishness, and it eventually abandoned its initial objective of reforming military dictatorships in Latin America. The diplomat Willard L. Beaulac concluded: "We told people whom we did not know how to solve problems that we did not understand. We aroused expectations that could not be met." (Edmund Valtman, *The Hartford Times*)

of the central government, and with direct American aid, including military advisers, he recruited white mercenaries. The rebels responded by terrorizing white foreigners. In November 1964 a small force of Belgian paratroopers dropped from U.S. aircraft into the Congo to rescue Belgian and American citizens. Although a serious communist threat never emerged in the Congo, the Kennedy administration, reading Cold War lessons, had thrust America into the shaky politics of Africa. American ambassador to Guinea William Attwood noted that leading African nationalists felt humiliated by the American and foreign intervention in the Congo, because "the white man with a gun, the old plunderer who had enslaved his ancestors, was back again, doing what he pleased, when he pleased, where he pleased. And there wasn't a damn thing Africa could do about it, except yell rape."[92] Attwood identified the chief source of resistance to American nation building—nationalism itself.

A COMPLETE BREAK: FIDEL CASTRO AND THE CUBAN REVOLUTION

Africa counted as a sideshow compared to Latin America, formerly a secure U.S. sphere of influence. Cuba claimed center stage. On July 26, 1953, a young lawyer and Cuban nationalist, Fidel Castro, attempted to overthrow the American-backed regime of Fulgencio Batista. Imprisoned and later released, Castro fled to Mexico. In late 1956, under the banner of the 26th of July movement, he returned to Cuba. Almost captured, he escaped into the mountains, where for three years he augmented his guerrilla forces, gained popular support, and fought Batista's American-supplied army. In January 1959, despite CIA plots to deny him power, the bearded rebel marched into Havana and initiated social and economic programs designed to reduce extensive U.S. interests that had developed since 1898 and had come to dominate Cuba's sugar, mining, and utilities industries.

Determined to reduce the North American cultural influence that they believed had undermined Cuba's national identity, the Castroites crippled the gangster-run gambling casinos and ousted from government the *batistianos* who had profited from close contact with U.S. investors. Calling the new Cuban leaders "children" who needed a fatherly hand, U.S. officials nonetheless saw that Castro intended "a complete break" with the past and an end to U.S. hegemony in the Caribbean.[93] Declaring the Platt Amendment mentality dead, Castro remarked that "we no longer live in times when one had to worry when the American Ambassador visited the [Cuban] Prime Minister."[94] Indeed, "what happened in Guatemala will not happen here."[95] When Castro visited Washington in April 1959, Eisenhower refused to meet with him and headed south to play golf instead.

Fearing that a successful Cuban revolution would cause the United States to "get kicked around in the hemisphere," but finding no evidence that Castro was a communist, Washington soon applied a series of tests: Cuba must respect North

American–owned property, continue alignment with the United States on international questions, and adhere to a democratic politics that permitted pro-U.S. "moderates" to sustain ties.[96] Cuba failed to satisfy these U.S. requirements. Land reform struck at U.S. interests, the execution of Batista supporters reduced U.S. influence, and the moderates faltered in their competition with Castroite radicals. Castro postponed elections, and he defiantly evicted the U.S. military missions that had supported Batista. In vehement anti-Yankee orations, Castro also called for revolutions throughout Latin America. Washington warned against his "Nasser-like ambition" and his apparent turn toward neutrality in the Cold War.[97] In late 1959 the CIA began to work with Castro's rivals to "check" or "replace" the revolutionary regime.[98] When President Eisenhower made a goodwill tour to Latin America in February 1960, he spotted a sign in Rio de Janeiro: "We like Ike. We like Fidel too."[99] In March 1960, Eisenhower ordered the CIA to train Cuban exiles for an invasion of their homeland—this shortly after Cuba signed a trade treaty with the Soviet Union.

In mid-1960, as the revolutionary government nationalized foreign properties, the United States suspended imports of Cuban sugar and then forbade U.S. exports to the island in an effort to bring down the Castro government. These strong measures only pushed Cuba toward a new economic lifeline—the Soviet Union. As Ambassador Philip Bonsal explained, "Russia came to Castro's rescue only after the United States had taken steps to overthrow him."[100] Now embracing the thesis that Castro had moved from neutralism to communism, Washington broke diplomatic relations with Cuba in early January 1961.

Cuba had hardly become a Soviet puppet or a threat to U.S. security by 1961. "The Castro regime is a thorn in the flesh," Senator J. William Fulbright argued, "but it is not a dagger in the heart."[101] Still, ignoring the U.S. contribution to Castro's anti-Americanism, President Kennedy defined Cuba as a test of will, a new Cold War battleground, and he decided to remove the Cuban irritation. The CIA assured him that it could deliver another Guatemala, just like 1954—or even better. The CIA predicted that the Cuban people would rise up against Castro and a CIA-hired assassin's bullet would kill him. The CIA pinpointed Bahía de Cochinos (Bay of Pigs) as the invasion site and organized a Cuban Revolutionary Council to take office. Uneasy with the plan, Kennedy nonetheless approved it, although he prohibited direct U.S. military participation. The CIA did not protest this prohibition because "we felt that when the chips were down," Allen Dulles later wrote, "any action required for success would have been authorized [by the president] rather than permit the enterprise to fail."[102] Kennedy had made Cuba an issue in the 1960 campaign and eagerly sought to oust Castro, and CIA assurances seemed incontrovertible. The administration also worried that the trained exiles would embarrass him politically if he scotched the expedition—the "disposal" problem.[103] The Kennedy administration never tried to talk with the Castro government, and it never consulted Congress on launching this war against Cuba.

In mid-April 1961, 1,453 CIA-trained commandos departed from Nicaragua for Cuba (see map, page 492). They met early resistance from Castro's militia, no sympathetic insurrection occurred, and within two days the invasion had become a fiasco. One hundred and fourteen commandos died, and more than 1,100 were captured. Some one hundred and fifty Cuban defenders were killed. Four American pilots also died in the operation. Like his brother John, Attorney General Robert Kennedy found defeat difficult to accept: "We just could not sit and take it"; Moscow might think Americans "paper tigers." Walt Rostow, sensitive to Kennedy machismo, reassured him that "we would have ample opportunity to prove we were not paper tigers in Berlin, Southeast Asia, and elsewhere."[104] After the disaster, President Kennedy, who had vetoed a desperate CIA request for U.S. air attacks during the last hours of the failing invasion, blamed the CIA and Joint Chiefs of Staff for faulty intelligence and sloppy execution. He had no qualms about overthrowing a sovereign government, only the methods for doing it.

Little sobered by the Bay of Pigs setback, Kennedy vowed a "relentless struggle in every corner of the globe" with communism.[105] During the next year, the United States imposed a tighter economic blockade on Cuba, evicted the island nation from the Organization of American States, refused to recognize Castro, directed U.S. Information Agency propaganda at the Havana regime, and continued assassination plots on Castro's life. Under Operation Mongoose, CIA agents cooperated with anti-Castro exiles to stage hit-and-run sabotage raids against oil facilities and other island targets. This multitrack campaign did not knock Castro from his perch. What next? "If I had been in Moscow or Havana at that time," Secretary of Defense McNamara later remarked, "I would have believed the Americans were preparing for an invasion."[106]

"Now It's Official." Jeff Yohn's anti-Castro, anti-Soviet cartoon appeared in the *San Bernadino Sun-Telegram* (California) newspaper in 1961. In July 1960, when the Soviet Union agreed to purchase Cuban sugar after the Eisenhower administration ended sugar imports from the island, Soviet premier Nikita Khrushchev declared the Monroe Doctrine dead and pledged military aid to Cuba—"if it became necessary." During the April 1961 Bay of Pigs crisis, Khrushchev told President Kennedy that the Soviets would give "to the Cuban government all the necessary assistance to repel aggression." In 1962 such aid included nuclear-tipped SS-4 missiles, setting off yet another crisis. (Library of Congress)

SPINNING OUT OF CONTROL: THE CUBAN MISSILE CRISIS

Critical to understanding the missile crisis of fall 1962 is the relationship and timing between U.S. activities and Soviet/Cuban decisions to place on the island forty-two nuclear-tipped SS-4 missiles that could strike areas of the United States where 92 million people lived. In May 1962 Soviets and Cubans first discussed the idea of such missiles; in July, during a trip by Raúl Castro to Moscow, representatives probably initialed a draft agreement; in late August/early September, during a trip by the Cuban leader Che Guevara to Moscow, an accord probably became final. These decisions emerged at the same time that the United States was pressing Cuba on all fronts.

Not only did Castro learn about the assassination plots and witness the sabotage attacks, he also heard reports that the United States was creating an anti-Castro Cuban unit in the U.S. military. At about the same time, American military planning and activities, some public, some secret, demonstrated a determination to cripple the Castro government. The director of Operation Mongoose, Brigadier General Edward Lansdale, planned to ignite a revolt against Castro in October 1962, and he endorsed the use of U.S. forces to ensure its success. Because the plan required close cooperation with Cuban exiles, it is likely that Castro's spies picked up from the leaky Cuban community in Miami suggestions that the U.S. military was contemplating military action against Cuba. American military maneuvers heightened Cuban fears. One well-publicized U.S. exercise, staged during April, included 40,000 troops and an amphibious landing on a small island near Puerto Rico. Some noisy American politicians, throughout 1962, called for the real thing: an invasion of Cuba.

By late spring/summer 1962, when Havana and Moscow were contemplating defensive measures that included medium-range missiles, Cuba felt besieged from several quarters. The Soviet Union had become its trading partner; and the Soviets, after the Bay of Pigs, had begun military shipments that ultimately included small arms, howitzers, armored personnel carriers, patrol boats, tanks, MIG jet fighters, and SAMs. Yet all this weaponry did not seem to deter the United States. And, given the failure of Kennedy's multitrack program to unseat Castro, "were we right or wrong to fear direct invasion" next, asked the Cuban leader.[107]

Had there been no exile expedition at the Bay of Pigs, no destructive covert activities, no assassination plots, no military maneuvers and plans, and no economic and diplomatic steps to harass, isolate, and destroy the Castro government in Havana, there would not have been a Cuban missile crisis. The origins of the October 1962 crisis derived largely from the concerted U.S. campaign to quash the Cuban Revolution and from the Soviet-Cuban effort to save it by deterring the United States through missile deployment. Scholars have attributed other motives to the Soviets, such as their wanting to force negotiations on Berlin, to compel a trade for U.S. missiles stationed in Turkey and pointed at the Soviet Union, or to undermine Chinese criticism that Moscow had become too tolerant of the West. Perhaps because Pentagon officials had publicly announced a decisive American nuclear superiority (the U.S. had more than 170 ICBMs and the Soviets perhaps a dozen), Moscow also may have hoped to leap forward in the nuclear-arms race. But to stress only the global, Cold War dimension slights the local or regional sources of the conflict and misses the central point: Premier Nikita Khrushchev would never have had the opportunity to install dangerous missiles in the Caribbean if the United States had not been attempting to overthrow the Cuban government. To say this is to explain, not condone, the Cuban-Soviet decisions on missile deployment that raised the level of nuclear terror, invited confrontation with the United States, and left so much to chance.

On October 14, a U-2 reconnaissance plane photographed medium-range (1,100-mile) missile sites under construction in Cuba. After gathering more data, American officials informed the president on October 16 that the Soviet Union had indeed placed missiles in Cuba. Kennedy created an Executive Committee of the National Security Council (Ex Com), consisting of his "action intellectuals" and experienced diplomats from the Truman years. Besides McNamara, brother Robert, McGeorge Bundy, and Theodore Sorenson, there were Dean Acheson, Paul Nitze, and Robert Lovett, among others.

Kennedy's immediate preference became clear: "We're certainly going . . . to take out these . . . missiles."[108] Ex Com considered four options: "talk them out," "squeeze them out," "shoot them out," and "buy them out."[109] Officials initially gave only slight attention to negotiations and concentrated on military action. Dean Acheson, among others, favored an air strike. Robert Kennedy listened and passed a note to his brother: "I now know how Tojo felt when he was planning Pearl Harbor."[110] Robert said that he did not want his brother to become a Tojo. Anyway, air force officials reported they could not guarantee 100 percent success; some missiles might remain in place for firing against the United States. The Joint Chiefs of Staff recommended a full-scale military invasion. Although alluring, such a scheme could mean a prolonged war with Cuba, heavy American casualties, and a Soviet retaliatory attack on Berlin. Ex Com ruled out a private overture to Castro. Ambassador to the United Nations Adlai Stevenson's proposal that the United States publicly offer to trade the missiles in Turkey for those in Cuba met open derision. Ex Com members, tired and irritable, finally settled on a naval blockade or quarantine of future arms shipments to Cuba. The quarantine, pushed ardently by McNamara, constituted a compromise between armed warfare and doing nothing and left open options for further escalation.

Kennedy went on national television on October 22 and set off a war of nerves with Moscow. He announced a blockade and insisted that Khrushchev "halt and eliminate this clandestine, reckless and provocative threat to world peace."[111] More than 180 American ships patrolled the Caribbean, and marines reinforced the American naval base on Cuba, Guantánamo. A B-52 bomber force loaded with nuclear bombs took to the skies. On October 24, Soviet vessels sailed toward the blockade. The president awaited a collision. But the ships stopped, even as assembly of the missiles already in Cuba continued. Secretary General of the United Nations U Thant urged talks; Khrushchev called for a summit meeting. Kennedy demanded removal of the missiles first. On October 26 a Soviet agent contacted correspondent John Scali of the American Broadcasting Company and offered to

Soviet Missile Site at San Cristóbal, Cuba. This revealing U-2 photograph was taken in October 1962, when Soviet technicians were busily trying to assemble the various components of medium-range missiles. (U.S. Air Force)

disengage the missiles if the United States promised publicly not to invade Cuba in the future. Then came a long letter from Khrushchev stating much the same offer but still insisting that the missiles were defensive, not offensive.

The next day, October 27, the crisis accelerated. A Soviet commander shot down a U-2 plane over Cuba. The Americans prepared to retaliate, not knowing that Soviet commanders had tactical nuclear weapons to use against an invasion. Later in the day, a U.S. spy aircraft strayed into Soviet air space, nearly setting off a dogfight with Soviet MIGs. By this time U.S. officials were analyzing another Khrushchev letter. The premier raised the stakes with a tougher tone: He would withdraw the missiles from Cuba if the United States removed its missiles from Turkey. "We can't very well invade Cuba," JFK mused, "when we could have gotten them [missiles] out by making a deal on . . . Turkey."[112] Robert Kennedy proposed to ignore the last letter and answer the first, whereupon the president endorsed Khrushchev's first proposal: removal of the missiles in Cuba in exchange for a public U.S. pledge not to invade Cuba. Robert Kennedy assured the Soviets in private that the Jupiter missiles would be withdrawn from Turkey, but he warned that if Moscow divulged this secret deal, Washington would disavow it. On the 28th Khrushchev agreed to these terms. If Khrushchev had balked, Rusk had secretly arranged for the United Nations to propose removing missiles from both Turkey and Cuba; "Kennedy would not let the Jupiters in Turkey become an obstacle," Rusk has insisted.[113] But Khrushchev withdrew his missiles. The military forces at his command could not prevent or repel a U.S. invasion, he worried that Castro would provoke some incident, and the imminence of doomsday frightened the Kremlin gambler. Khrushchev nonetheless gained what Ambassador Llewellyn Thompson thought was the "important thing" for the Soviet leader: being able to say, "I saved Cuba. I stopped an invasion."[114]

Although popular opinion applauded Kennedy's venture with brinkmanship, critics questioned the president's willingness to risk nuclear war and his resort to public confrontation rather than quiet diplomacy. Walter Lippmann on October 25 wrote a widely read column asking why, when the president met privately in the White House with Soviet foreign minister Andrei Gromyko on October 18, Kennedy did not show the diplomat the U-2 photographs and seek a diplomatic solution then and there.

"We were in luck," John Kenneth Galbraith later commented, "but success in a lottery is no argument for lotteries."[115] As McGeorge Bundy remembered, the crisis became "so near to spinning out of control."[116] Close calls (the U-2 incidents), flawed intelligence (Soviet troops in Cuba numbered 42,000, not the estimated 10,000), an inability to control local events (an Operation Mongoose sabotage team prowled in Cuba during the crisis but could not be recalled), and fatigue if not nervous breakdown (some participants have said that both Rusk and Stevenson suffered incapacitating stress)—all reveal something quite short of the artful crisis management often attributed to the president. Even the aftermath of the crisis proved messy. Washington demanded that the IL-28 bombers that the Soviets had given to Cuba must be removed along with the missiles. Embittering negotiations followed, and not until November 13 did Khrushchev agree to pull the IL-28s out. The three protagonists, moreover, never signed a formal agreement, leaving enough ambiguity to cause later crises in Cuban-Soviet-American relations (see pp. 449, 503). A quarter century after the 1962 crisis, McNamara offered a somber reassessment: "You *can't* manage" crises because of all the "misinformation, miscalculation, misjudgment, and human fallibility."[117]

The Cuban missile crisis both slowed and accelerated the Cold War. Having found communication difficult during the event, both sides installed a "hot line" or teletype link between the White House and Kremlin. Both sides seemed frightened enough by nuclear danger to move toward a more accommodating relationship, producing the Limited Test Ban Treaty of July 1963, which prohibited atmospheric and underwater nuclear testing. In a high-minded speech at American University

Adlai Stevenson (1900–1965). Governor of Illinois and twice an unsuccessful Democratic presidential candidate, Stevenson became ambassador to the United Nations under Kennedy. Stevenson worried about the Kennedys' muscular diplomacy, once complaining to a friend that "they've got the damndest bunch of boy commandos running around . . . you ever saw." During the Cuban missile crisis, the ambassador urged negotiations rather than confrontation. He believed "that the existence of nuclear missile bases anywhere is NEGOTIABLE before we start anything." (National Portrait Gallery, Smithsonian Institution)

the month before, Kennedy revealed uneasiness with large weapons spending, appealed for arms control, and asked Americans to reexamine Cold War attitudes.

Later Kennedy speeches, however, sounded hawkish once again. Indeed, the missile crisis carried long-term detrimental effects. The Soviet Union, revealed as a nuclear inferior, pledged to catch up in the arms race. That part of the Cold War contest ratcheted up with new and more dangerous weapons systems. As for Cuba, despite a Castro initiative for rapprochement, U.S. officials schemed anew to "tighten the noose."[118] The CIA quickly launched new dirty tricks and revitalized its assassination option by making contact with a traitorous Cuban official, Rolando Cubela Secades. Codenamed AM/LASH, he plotted with the CIA to kill Fidel Castro. On the very day that President Kennedy fell to assassination, AM/LASH rendezvoused with CIA agents in Paris, where he received a ballpoint pen rigged with a poisonous hypodermic needle intended to produce Castro's instant death. Like all other assassination plots against Castro, this one failed. The new Johnson administration put Cuban–American contacts at the United Nations "on ice."[119] From that time onward, U.S.-Cuba relations remained frozen.

After their success in the Caribbean crisis, U.S. officials may have become emboldened to use military threat elsewhere, to face down communists in other parts of the globe. "That Cuba was the precedent for Vietnam there can be no doubt," one student of the missile crisis has concluded.[120]

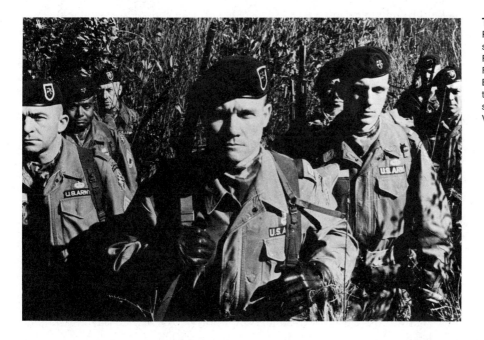

The Green Berets.
President Kennedy helped select equipment for Special Forces units like this one at Fort Bragg. The Green Berets were trained in counterguerrilla methods and sent into the jungles of Vietnam. (U.S. Army)

Laos, Vietnam, and the Kennedy Legacy

Continued unrest in Laos and Vietnam placed those Asian trouble spots high on President John F. Kennedy's foreign-policy list. Rostow saw an opportunity to use "our unexploited counterguerrilla assets"—helicopters and Special Forces units. "We are not saving them for the Junior Prom," he told Kennedy.[121] The land-locked agricultural nation of Laos, wracked by civil war, became a testing ground. Granted independence at Geneva in 1954, Laos chose neutralism in the Cold War when the nationalist leader Souvanna Phouma organized a coalition government of neutralists and the procommunist Pathet Lao in 1957. The Eisenhower administration opposed the neutralist government and initiated a major military aid program to build up the rightist Laotian army. The money also disrupted the Laotian economy through inflation and graft. In 1958 CIA-backed rightists displaced Souvanna Phouma and shaped a pro-American government without Pathet Lao participation. Washington soon dispatched military advisers to the new but shaky regime.

Souvanna Phouma returned to power after a coup in August 1960, but the United States undermined him by again equipping rightist forces. Seeking a counterweight, Souvanna took assistance from Moscow and North Vietnam. But in December he fled his country. "How can they [the Americans] think I am a Communist?" he sighed. "I am looking for a way to keep Laos non-Communist."[122] For Eisenhower, "the fall of Laos to Communism" would initiate "a chain of events [that] would open the way to Communist seizure of all Southeast Asia."[123] The neutralists and the Pathet Lao, it appeared to Eisenhower, had joined a global communist conspiracy.

The incoming Kennedy administration did not perceive the Laotian problem much differently. In a rephrasing of the "domino theory," adviser Arthur M. Schlesinger, Jr., later explained: "If Laos was not precisely a dagger pointed at the heart of Kansas, it was very plainly a gateway to Southeast Asia."[124] As conspicuous Soviet aid flowed to the Pathet Lao, Kennedy ordered the Seventh Fleet into the South China Sea, alerted American forces in Okinawa, and moved 500 marines with helicopters into Thailand. Then the Bay of Pigs disaster struck. Fearing to appear weak with one arm tied down in Cuba, Kennedy swung the other in Laos. The president instructed the several hundred American military advisers in Laos, heretofore under cover in covert operations, to discard their civilian clothes and dress in more ostentatious military uniforms as a symbol of U.S. resolve. The Soviets wanted no fight in Laos. In April 1961 they endorsed Kennedy's appeal for a cease-fire. But the independent-minded Pathet Lao battled on alone. Kennedy asked the Joint Chiefs of Staff if an American military expedition could succeed. The military experts demurred, but "if we are given the right to use nuclear weapons," remarked the Joint Chiefs of Staff chairman, General Lyman L. Lemnitzer, "we can guarantee victory."[125]

The solution came in Geneva, where a conference on Laos began in May 1961. Although it took deft diplomatic pressure from W. Averell Harriman, continued bloodshed in Laos, and hard bargaining lasting until June 1962, the major powers did sign a Laotian agreement. Laos would become neutral; it could not enter military alliances or permit foreign military bases on its soil. Souvanna Phouma headed the new government. Bernard Fall, veteran observer of Southeast Asia, measured the U.S. maneuvering in Laos by comparing the neutralist government of the 1950s with that of 1962: "Instead of two communists in Cabinet positions, there would be four now; instead of having to deal with 1,500 poorly armed Pathet Lao fighters, there were close to 10,000 now well-armed with new Soviet weapons."[126] Still, peace did not come to that ravaged land. In late 1962, in clear violation of the agreement it had just signed, Washington secretly shipped arms to Souvanna's government, which increasingly turned to the right. Small numbers of North Vietnamese soldiers in the north served as the pretext, and Washington resumed its policy of building a sturdy pro-American outpost in Indochina. Unbeknownst to the American people, the United States began secret bombing raids against Pathet Lao forces in 1964, after a right-wing coup had diminished Souvanna's authority. By then Laos's problem derived from its proximity to Vietnam.

"This is the worst one we've got, isn't it," Kennedy asked Rostow. "You know, Eisenhower never mentioned it. He talked at length about Laos, but never uttered the word Vietnam."[127] Eisenhower may actually have advised "*against* unilateral action," but Kennedy took steps that did make Vietnam America's "worst one" over the next decade.[128] As two scholars have explained, "with Laos neutralized, Cuba hostile, and East Berlin sealed off, Vietnam became a testing ground by his own definition."[129] Kennedy ignored Charles de Gaulle's warning that "we failed and you will fail."[130] Kennedy advisers considered the conservative, corrupt Ngo Dinh Diem a liability, but as Vice President Lyndon B. Johnson put it privately—after having publicly annointed Diem the Winston Churchill of Asia—"Sh, man, he's the only boy we got out there."[131]

Kennedy hesitated to tie U.S. fate to the "repressive" Diem.[132] The president said he did not want to launch a white man's war in Asia; Asians had to fight their own battles. But because he accepted the domino theory, interpreted communists as part of an international conspiracy, thought that China fomented Vietnamese turmoil, and believed that nation building promised success, he expanded the U.S. presence. In January 1961, Kennedy authorized $28.4 million to enlarge the South Vietnamese army and another $12.7 million to improve the civil guard. In May he ordered 400 Special Forces soldiers and another 100 military "advisers" to South Vietnam. Meanwhile the Vietcong captured more territory and accelerated the violence through assassinations of village chiefs. In October a U.S. intelligence report indicated that 80–90 percent of the 17,000 Vietcong in South Vietnam came from the South, not from North Vietnam, and that most of their supplies originated in the South. Although this estimate exploded the theory of advisers such as Walt W. Rostow that the Vietnamese crisis started because of aggression by North Vietnam, the report apparently did not influence Kennedy.

Still troubled by conflicting viewpoints, the president in October dispatched two hawks, General Maxwell Taylor and Walt W. Rostow, to South Vietnam to study the war firsthand. Diem asked for more American military aid. Taylor soon urged Kennedy to send U.S. combat troops. Rusk questioned such advice, arguing

Market Place

School

Dispensary

Guard Post

Gate

Arms Storage

Radio Station

Earthen Mound with Bamboo Spears

Bamboo & Barbed Fence

Moat

Bamboo Barrier

House

Watchtower

GENERALIZED STRATEGIC HAMLET

Scale: 6 Inches — 1 Mile

Strategic Hamlet, South Vietnam.
Introduced by the Diem regime in 1962, inspired by British counterinsurgency expert Sir Robert Thompson (based on his experience in Malaya and the Philippines), and funded by the United States, the strategic hamlet program sought to separate the Vietcong from their supporters among the people. Peasants had to move from ancestral lands and live in quarters surrounded by barbed wire and bamboo spears. Many of the 6,000 hamlets were poorly managed and defended, alienating the very people the Saigon government tried to win over. (Courtesy of M. W. Dow, from M. W. Dow, *Nation Building in Southeast Asia.* Boulder, Colorado: Pruett Press, 1966; rev. ed.)

that Diem must first reform his conservative government. McNamara supported Taylor. Conscious that his decision violated the Geneva Accords but unwilling to say so publicly, Kennedy authorized in November an increase in U.S. forces or "advisers" in South Vietnam. By the end of 1961 they numbered 3,205. During the next year the figure jumped to 9,000, and at the time of Kennedy's death in November 1963 these forces had reached 16,700. American troops, helicopter units, minesweepers, and air reconnaissance aircraft went into action. In 1962, 109 Americans died and in 1963, 489. The strategic hamlet program fortified villages and isolated them from Vietcong influence. This population control through barbed wire, however, proved disruptive and unpopular with villagers and permitted the Vietcong to appear as Robin Hoods. Then, too, many of the American weapons actually ended up in Vietcong hands. In February 1963, Rusk announced that the "momentum of the Communist drive has been stopped."[133] "Go ahead and fight in the jungles of Vietnam," Khrushchev told Dean Rusk. "The French fought there for seven years and still had to quit in the end. Perhaps the Americans will be able to stick it out for a little longer, but eventually they will have to quit too."[134]

In May 1963 the difficulties of nation building became exposed when South Vietnamese troops opened fire on protesting and unarmed Buddhists in Hue, massacring nine. The incident erupted after a Catholic provincial chief had enforced an old decree prohibiting the flying of Buddhist flags. A Catholic oligarchy, which included Diem's brother Ngo Dinh Thuc as the bishop of Hue, governed the pre-

A Suicide in Protest, Saigon. Quang Duc, a Buddhist monk aged seventy-three, set his gasoline-drenched yellow robes afire in June 1963 at a main intersection in Saigon to protest Diem's restrictions on Buddhists. (Wide World Photos)

dominantly Buddhist population. The Buddhist demonstrations also expressed longstanding nationalist sentiment, an appeal for peace talks with the NLF, and resentment against U.S. interference in Vietnamese politics. On June 10 a Buddhist monk sat in a Saigon street, poured fuel over his body, and immolated himself. The appalling sight led Diem's sister-in-law Madame Nhu to chortle about Buddhist "barbecues."[135] During the late summer and fall the protest spread; so did Diem's military tactics, including an attack on Hue's pagoda. Also, authorities arrested thousands of students. Kennedy publicly chastised Diem and reduced aid. Senior South Vietnamese generals, now aware that Diem no longer had American favor, asked U.S. officials how they would respond to a coup d'état. The new ambassador, Henry Cabot Lodge, unsuccessful Republican vice presidential candidate in 1960, wanted to dump Diem, but officials in Washington hesitated. McNamara sent a new study mission. Marine general Victor H. Krulak and State Department officer Joseph Mendenhall took a hurried tour; Krulak reported that the war was going well despite the Buddhist squabble, whereas Mendenhall argued that the Vietnamese disliked Diem more than the Vietcong. A puzzled Kennedy asked: "You two did visit the same country, didn't you?"[136]

Washington continued cool relations with Diem, who proved more and more resistant to U.S. advice. In early October 1963 the Vietnamese generals prepared to overthrow the recalcitrant premier. Lodge did not discourage them, a signal the generals fully appreciated. On November 1 the generals took Diem prisoner and murdered him. A few weeks later, on November 22, Kennedy himself was assassinated in Dallas. Some Kennedy advisers have suggested that after the presidential election of 1964 he would have withdrawn from Vietnam. But none of Kennedy's decisions pointed in that direction, and the removal of Diem only accentuated the political instability that undercut U.S. efforts to defeat the NLF and thus necessitated continued intervention. "I had hundreds of talks with John F. Kennedy," Dean Rusk recalled, "and never once did he say anything of this sort" about withdrawal.[137] Given his Cold War mentality, his unwillingess to change U.S. nonrecognition policy toward China, his personal aversion to defeat, his political alertness to charges of being soft on communism, and the persistently poor prospects of victory in Vietnam, Kennedy probably would have pushed on in Vietnam, much as did his successor, Lyndon B. Johnson.

No More Munichs, No More Cubas: Lyndon B. Johnson's World

The presidential transition from John F. Kennedy to Lyndon B. Johnson (LBJ) went smoothly. Johnson kept on many of Kennedy's advisers. McNamara stayed until early 1968; Rusk remained until the end; when McGeorge Bundy stepped down in 1966, Walt Rostow replaced him and became one of LBJ's most ardent supporters. If Johnson lacked Kennedy's zeal for nation building, he had his own brand of international reform, derived from a sensitivity to the travails of poverty. Influenced by his New Deal reform years, he declared: "I want to leave the footprints of America there [Vietnam]. I want them to say, 'This is what the Americans left—schools and hospitals and dams. . . .' We can turn the Mekong [River area] into a Tennessee Valley."[138] "Old Ho can't turn me down," he asserted.[139] Johnson shared the Cold War assumptions of most Americans, declaring: "I am not going to be the President who saw Southeast Asia go the way China went."[140]

An experienced political operator, Johnson came from the poor, dusty hill territory of Texas between Fort Worth and San Antonio. "It is unrelenting country," his wife, Lady Bird, commented, "and Lyndon is unrelenting, too."[141] He gulped his meals and talked incessantly. "When you got the Johnson treatment," remembered Benjamin Bradlee of the *Washington Post,* "you really felt as if a St. Bernard had licked your face for an hour, had pawed you all over."[142] Dean Acheson once called him "a real centaur—part man, part horse's ass."[143] He reminded Clark Clifford of "a powerful old-fashioned locomotive roaring unstoppably down the track."[144] Often raging against "gutless" bureaucrats who leaked "defeatist" information to "simpleton" reporters, he once complained that "you can't have intercourse with your wife without it being spread around by traitors."[145] A "credibility gap" dogged the administration, not so much because Johnson told barefaced lies, but because he embellished the actual record with exaggerations and trite analogies in a drawl that sometimes made him appear stupid. He was not. His mind was quick and retentive, although very much a captive of the past. The chair of the Senate Foreign Relations Committee, J. William Fulbright of Arkansas, thought Americans under Johnson suffered an "arrogance of power" that left the United States by the end of the 1960s a "crippled giant."[146]

Johnson left relations with the Soviet Union and China much as he had found them—calmer after the Cuban missile crisis, but still strained and based on intense military competition. He met Soviet premier Aleksei Kosygin in Glassboro, New Jersey, in 1967, but the heralded "spirit of Glassboro" did not last. That year the Johnson administration asked Congress for an antiballistic missile system (ABM) to maintain the posture of massive retaliation or deterrence. The Soviets already had a limited ABM system. The heated debate over further enlargement of the arms race via the ABM still raged when Johnson left office (see Chapter 10). The United States, the Soviet Union, and more than fifty other nations signed a nuclear non-proliferation treaty in 1968 (ratified in 1969), a pledge not to spread nuclear weapons to other nations. But France and China, both members of the nuclear club, refused to sign. Nonsigner India joined the elite club in 1974, demonstrating again the diffusion of power in the international system.

In Latin America, smoldering nationalism, frequent military coups, and Castro's defiant survival defined Johnson's policies. Johnson put Assistant Secretary of State Thomas C. Mann in charge of the Alliance for Progress and it soon withered away from neglect. Mann declared that the United States preferred to support anticommunist governments through economic assistance rather than to oppose military regimes. In 1964 Washington officials "did not try to hide their elation" over a military takeover in Brazil, and when Panamanians rioted against U.S. control of the Canal Zone, Johnson lectured the president of Panama that the United States would not tolerate insults to the American flag.[147] In 1965, fearing another Cuba, Johnson sent more than 20,000 American soldiers into the Dominican Republic. The trouble had started when, in late 1962, after the assassination of the dictator Rafael Trujillo the year before, radical reformer Juan Bosch won election

General William C. Westmoreland (b. 1914) and President Lyndon B. Johnson (1908–1973). Graduate of the U.S. Military Academy, Westmoreland commanded American troops in Vietnam during 1964–1968. He kept asking for more soldiers and the president usually obliged. Here they meet at Cam Ranh Bay, South Vietnam, in December 1967. After Tet, Johnson named him army chief of staff. (Lyndon B. Johnson Library)

as president of the economically depressed Caribbean country. Ten months later a military coup ousted him. But in April 1965, pro-Bosch rebels launched a new civil war against the military regime. Johnson and his advisers, with trigger-finger quickness and fragmentary evidence, assumed that "the choice is: Castro in the Dominican Republic or U.S. intervention."[148] They ordered a U.S. invasion. "This was a democratic revolution smashed by the leading democracy of the world," Bosch lamented.[149] The Dominican generals took over once again.

The president announced that the United States would henceforth prevent a communist government from taking office in the hemisphere. A frank statement of hegemony, it attempted to maintain the U.S. sphere in Latin America. (In 1968, after the Soviets had ruthlessly invaded rebellious Czechoslovakia, the Kremlin's explanations sounded much like those of Johnson in 1965.) Senator Fulbright, who opposed the Dominican venture, protested: "We have made ourselves the prisoners of the Latin American oligarchs who are engaged in a vain attempt to preserve the status quo—reactionaries who habitually use the term communist very loosely . . . in a calculated effort to scare the United States into supporting their selfish and discredited aims."[150]

THE AMERICANIZATION OF THE VIETNAM WAR

During Johnson's five years in office, Vietnam consumed his energies, his ambitions, his reputation. After Diem's death, the time seemed propitious for a political settlement. The National Liberation Front, Secretary General U Thant of the United Nations, the French government, and many Americans who recoiled from an unwinnable Asian land war called for a coalition government in Saigon and the neutralization of Vietnam. Johnson would have none of it. In December 1963, he insisted on "victory" to prevent "a communist takeover."[151] For Johnson and his advisers, Vietnam occupied only one front in the Cold War; to falter in Southeast Asia, they believed, would send a false signal that the United States would retreat elsewhere, too.

By early 1964, however, the war fared poorly for America's South Vietnamese ally. The Saigon government suffered factionalism, unable to unite feuding Buddhists and Catholics or contain bickering among ambitious military officers. The Army of the Republic of Vietnam (ARVN) proved ineffective in the field, and desertions ran high. The strategic hamlet program collapsed, and governmental administration in rural areas weakened. In January 1964, General Nguyen Khanh seized power in a coup that U.S. officials in Vietnam had helped plot. But neither political stability nor military success followed Khanh's power grab. Secretary McNamara reported in March that the Vietcong controlled some 40 percent of the South Vietnamese countryside, and in those areas governed by the Saigon regime, people had become apathetic or indifferent.

This deterioration in Vietnam gave Johnson's political foes an issue in the 1964 presidential campaign. Republican candidate Barry Goldwater urged military action against Ho Chi Minh's North. But, more, so did some of Johnson's advisers, especially Walt Rostow and Maxwell Taylor. The president publicly chided Goldwater as a dangerous warmonger. But in private his administration was already implementing plans and developing new contingencies to increase both the American presence in South Vietnam and U.S. pressure against North Vietnam. In early 1964, Washington dispatched additional military advisers (reaching 23,000 by the end of the year). Air strikes hit Laos, through which supplies flowed south. In February a covert operation, tagged OPLAN 34-A, began to air-drop commando's into the North to conduct sabotage. To encourage the Khanh government and to give Johnson flexibility to reverse the negative trend in Vietnam, McGeorge Bundy and other aides urged the president in June to ask Congress for a resolution endorsing a vigorous anticommunist effort.

Events in the Gulf of Tonkin soon dramatically escalated the U.S. role in Southeast Asia. On August 2, 1964, North Vietnamese torpedo patrol boats opened fire on the American destroyer *Maddox* some ten miles offshore. American aircraft from the U.S.S. *Ticonderoga* entered the fray. U.S. forces drove off the attackers, sinking one boat and damaging others, with no American casualties. The *Maddox* was on an espionage mission, called a "DeSoto patrol," collecting intelligence on radar and coastal defenses. The North Vietnamese probably concluded that the destroyer was assisting an OPLAN 34-A operation that had struck two nearby is-

Vietcong Tunnels. After the war, when a Vietnamese communist was told that his side had never beaten U.S. troops in a major battle, he replied: "That is correct. It is also irrelevant." That is, guerrillas win so long as they do not lose. Well-hidden tunnels helped the Vietcong defy superior U.S. military power. The most famous tunnels, in the Cu Chi region near Saigon, served as a staging area for the Tet offensive. (U.S. Army)

lands the night before. After the incident, almost as if to bait North Vietnam, the *Maddox* and *C. Turner Joy* steered within four miles of the islands. "The other side got a sting out of this," Rusk remarked. "If they do it again, they'll get another sting."[152]

On August 4, in the dark of the evening and in heavy seas, the captain of the *Maddox* read his sonar instruments to mean that North Vietnamese gunboats had attacked his ships. The *Maddox* and *C. Turner Joy* fired away wildly and American warplanes flew in to help. Hours later the captain wondered if his ship had been attacked at all. Indeed, no evidence has ever confirmed a North Vietnamese attack. The ship's sonar may have picked up the sound of waves, a thunderstorm, or the destroyer's own propellers. James B. Stockdale flew a Crusader jet from the *Ticonderoga* that night. Asked whether he had seen North Vietnamese attack craft, he answered: "Not a one. No boats, no wakes, no richochets off boats, no boat impacts, no torpedo wakes—nothing but black sea and American firepower."[153]

Despite the CIA's report that the North Vietnamese were simply defending their territory against commando raids, Johnson exploited the moment to punish North Vietnam and to seek a congressional resolution. On August 4, the president announced air strikes against the North. Saying nothing about destroyer operations against the North, he charged the enemy with deliberate aggression in international waters. Johnson self-consciously misled the American people and the Congress. The "Tonkin Gulf Resolution" passed on August 7 without much debate and by huge margins, 416 to 0 in the House and 88 to 2 in the Senate. Many voted "aye" unenthusiastically. "We are there but don't want to be. We want to get out but can't," Senator Richard Russell of Georgia commented.[154] Only Senators Ernest Gruening of Alaska and Wayne Morse of Oregon dissented. The resolution authorized the president to "take all necessary measures to repel armed attack against the forces of the United States and to prevent further aggression."[155] The resolution, said Johnson, was "like grandma's nightshirt—it covered everything."[156] In 1970, regretting this open-ended concession to the president, the Senate repealed it.

On February 7, 1965, the Vietcong attacked an American airfield at Pleiku and killed eight Americans. Johnson immediately ordered retaliatory strikes against the North. By March the United States had undertaken a sustained bombing program—Operation Rolling Thunder. By July 80,000 U.S. troops were operating in the South. The Joint Chiefs of Staff asked for 100,000 more. On July 21 the president convened his high-level advisers. Only Under Secretary of State George W. Ball spoke against escalation. He argued that the United States could not win a protracted war in an Asian jungle. "Take our losses, let their government fall apart, negotiate, discuss, knowing full well there will be a probable take-over by the Communists," he advised. Sending more troops would be "like giving cobalt treatment to a terminal cancer case." In the long run, then, the war "will disclose our weakness, not our strength." Johnson jumped in: "But, George, wouldn't all these countries say that Uncle Sam was a paper tiger," with America losing its credibility? "No sir," Ball answered. "The worse blow would be that the mightiest power on earth is unable to defeat a handful of guerrillas."[157]

With other advisers, including former president Eisenhower, urging support for the Joint Chiefs of Staff recommendation, Johnson further Americanized the

Going for Medical Aid, 1968. During a July 1968 operation called Lancaster II, marines of the Second Battalion, Third Marine Division, help a wounded buddy reach medical aid near the Demilitarized Zone (DMZ) in South Vietnam. (U.S. Marine Corps photo)

war by sending ground forces in gradual increments. Ball warned: "Once on the tiger's back we cannot be sure of picking the place to dismount."[158] By the end of the year nearly 200,000 American troops were fighting in Vietnam; a year later the number reached 385,000. Not wanting to jeopardize Great Society reforms, Johnson built up forces without mobilizing the reserves or raising taxes. As Rusk later said, "In a nuclear world it is just too dangerous for an entire people to get too angry and we deliberately tried to do in cold blood what perhaps can only be done in hot blood."[159] In 1966 American bombers hit oil depots in the North, and by midyear 70 percent of the North's storage capacity had been destroyed. Hanoi nonetheless increased its flow of arms and men to the South, the heavy bombing apparently having had little impact on the enemy's ability to resist. During 1965–1968 the United States tried, in General Curtis LeMay's infamous phrase, "to bomb them back into the stone age" by dropping 400 tons of ordnance per day. But the United States lost 918 aircraft valued at $6 billion.[160] By war's end more than 7 million tons of U.S. bombs had battered Vietnam, the equivalent of 400 Hiroshima atomic blasts. General William Westmoreland kept asking for more troops, even though Secretary McNamara reported in October 1966 that "pacification has, if anything, gone backward."[161] The president nonetheless kept sending troops—reaching a peak of 543,400 in early 1969. Saigon's Tan Son Nhut airport became the second busiest in the world (after Chicago's O'Hare).

At a "Wise Men" meeting in November 1967, George Ball made "his usual plea for extrication to the usual deaf ears." Then he lost his temper: "You're like a flock of buzzards sitting on a fence, sending the young men off to be killed."[162] President Johnson took comfort in simplistic historical analogies: "Just like FDR and Hitler, just like Wilson and the Kaiser," Americans had to stop "aggression."[163]

In this period of escalation, 1965–1968, the bloodshed and dislocation staggered the Vietnamese people. In "search and destroy" missions under a strategy of "attrition," American and South Vietnamese forces bombed and destroyed villages that harbored suspected Vietcong, the "Charlie." Hundreds of thousands of civilians died, many from fiery napalm attacks in areas called "free fire zones." "After you've done it for a while you forget that there are people down there," an American pilot explained.[164] Psychiatrists later attributed certain post-traumatic stress disorders in Vietnam War veterans to the unparalleled killing of women, children, and elderly people." To deny the enemy food and to expose hideouts, moreover, American defoliation teams sprayed millions of pounds of chemicals such as Agent Orange on crops and forests, denuding the landscape and inadvertently exposing GIs to the dioxin-tainted herbicide. After the war, some 39,000 veterans with cancer and nerve diseases filed claims with the U.S. government. Beginning in 1967 the CIA supervised the Phoenix program, in which South Vietnamese operatives infiltrated rural areas and "neutralized" thousands of suspected Vietcong.

Military Operation Near the Provincial Capital of Phuoc Vinh, 1967. Helicopters not only lifted soldiers to battle sites in Vietnam's rough terrain, but in "dust-off" or medevac missions they also carried the wounded to military hospitals. Here GIs of the U.S. Army's 1st Infantry Division scramble for cover after leaping from a chopper during an offensive operation fifty miles north of Saigon. (U.S. Army photo)

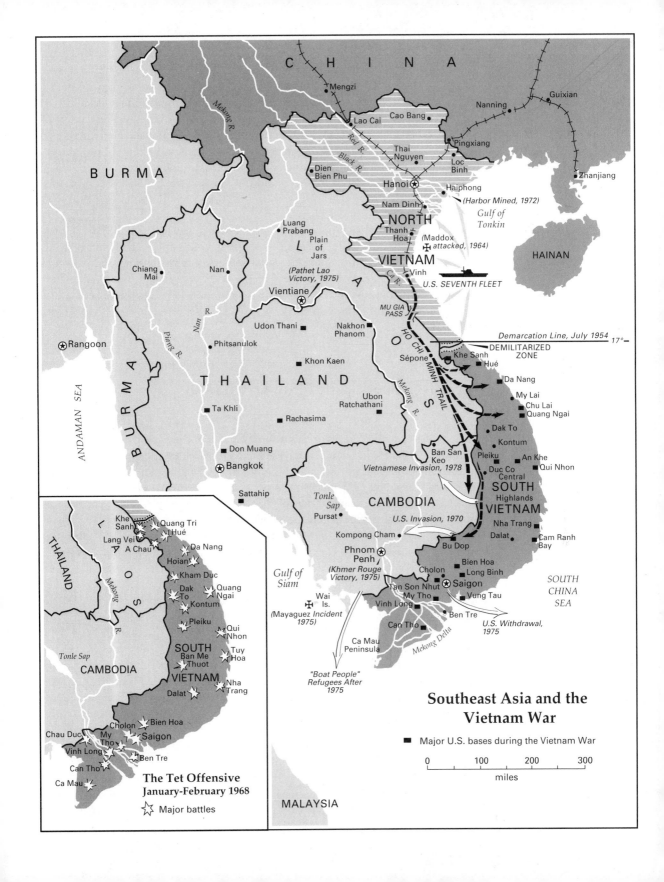

CHINA

Mengzi

Guixian

Cao Bang

Nanning

Lao Cai

Pingxiang

Thai
Nguyen

Loc
Binh

Mekong R.

Zhanjiang

BURMA

Red R.

Black R.

Dien
Bien Phu

Hanoi

Haiphong

(Harbor Mined, 1972)

Nam Dinh

Luang
Prabang

Plain
of
Jars

NORTH

*Gulf of
Tonkin*

Thanh
Hoa

L

Chiang
Mai

Nan

*(Maddox
attacked, 1964)*

VIETNAM

HAINAN

A

Ca R.

Vinh

Vientiane

*(Pathet Lao
Victory, 1975)*

U.S. SEVENTH FLEET

O

Nan R.

Rangoon

Udon Thani

MU GIA
PASS

Nakhon
Phanom

Phitsanulok

S

Demarcation Line, July 1954 17°—

HO CHI MINH TRAIL

Sépone

Khe Sanh

DEMILITARIZED
ZONE

Hué

Da Nang

B
U
R
M
A

THAILAND

Ping R.

Khon Kaen

My Lai

Chu Lai

Quang Ngai

Ta Khli

Ubon
Ratchathani

Mekong R.

Dak To

Kontum

Pleiku

Rachasima

An Khe

Don Muang

Ban San
Keo

Duc Co

Qui Nhon

ANDAMAN SEA

Bangkok

Vietnamese Invasion, 1978

Central

SOUTH

Highlands

VIETNAM

Sattahip

*Tonle
Sap*

CAMBODIA

Nha Trang

Dalat

Pursat

U.S. Invasion, 1970

Bu Dop

Cam Ranh
Bay

Kompong Cham

Bien Hoa

Long Binh

Cholon

Phnom
Penh

*(Khmer Rouge
Victory, 1975)*

Tan Son Nhut

Saigon

*SOUTH
CHINA
SEA*

*Gulf of
Siam*

Wai
Is.

*(Mayaguez Incident
1975)*

My Tho

Vinh Long

Vung Tau

Ben Tre

*U.S. Withdrawal,
1975*

Can Tho

*"Boat People"
Refugees After
1975*

Ca Mau
Peninsula

Mekong Delta

Southeast Asia and the
Vietnam War

■ Major U.S. bases during the Vietnam War

MALAYSIA

0   100   200   300

miles

The Tet Offensive
January–February 1968

☆ Major battles

Khe
Sanh

Quang Tri

Hué

Lang Vei

A Chau

Da Nang

THAILAND

Hoian

Kham Duc

Dak
To

Quang
Ngai

Kontum

LAOS

Mekong R.

Pleiku

Qui
Nhon

Tuy
Hoa

Tonle Sap

SOUTH

Ban Me
Thuot

VIETNAM

CAMBODIA

Nha
Trang

Dalat

Chau Duc

Cholon

Bien Hoa

My
Tho

Saigon

Vinh Long

Ben Tre

Can Tho

Ca Mau

"We never feared a division of troops," a Vietcong leader later admitted, "but the infiltration of a couple of guys into our ranks created tremendous difficulties for us."[165] To many Americans, the Phoenix program and massacres like that at My Lai on March 16, 1968, where a U.S. Army platoon commanded by Lieutenant William Calley shot to death scores of helpless women and children, or "gooks," represented a depravity unbecoming to a civilized nation. Because of official cover-ups, the story of the My Lai massacre did not become public until twenty months later.

Many incidents of the deliberate shooting, raping, and torturing of civilians and prisoners have been documented, but most American soldiers were not committing atrocities. They were trying instead to save their young lives—the average age of the Vietnam GI was only nineteen—from snipers, booby traps, ambushes, mortar attacks, and firefights. Etched in their memories, too, was the inhospitable environment, "as if the sun and land were in league with the Vietcong," recalled the marine officer Philip Caputo in *A Rumor of War* (1977), "wearing us down, driving us mad, killing us."[166]

THE DOVES DISSENT, THE PEACE EFFORTS FAIL

"Can the tortoise of progress in Vietnam stay ahead of the hare of dissent at home?" one official asked.[167] It could not. Students and faculties at universities began to hold "teach-ins" in 1965, first at the University of Michigan in March. Hundreds refused military draft calls and went to jail or fled to Canada. Others strove to obtain deferments. The protest songs of Bob Dylan, Pete Seeger, and Joan Baez inspired rallies. Many denounced the expenditure of billions of dollars in Vietnam when social maladies at home begged for attention. Johnson tried a "guns-and-butter" approach, but the government spent more and more on guns for Vietnam and his reformist Great Society programs suffered. The National Student Association, secretly funded by the CIA, found itself upstaged by the radical Students for a Democratic Society (SDS). Sit-ins greeted representatives of major corporations such as Dow Chemical, a maker of napalm, when they attempted to recruit on campus. In early 1967, 300,000 demonstrators marched in New York City and in November, 100,000 surrounded the Pentagon. Often vitriolic and impolite, they shouted down prowar speakers: "Hey, hey, LBJ, how many kids did you kill today?" "Don't pay any attention to what those little shits on the campuses do," Johnson commented. "The great beast is the reactionary elements in this country. Those are the people we have to fear."[168] With LBJ's encouragement, the CIA and FBI spread rumors that antiwar activists had come under the control of communists. Prominent intellectuals, like the linguist Noam Chomsky, the political scientist Hans Morgenthau, Jr., and a disaffected Arthur M. Schlesinger, Jr., called for withdrawal from Vietnam. Business executives, lawyers, and members of the clergy, too, joined antiwar groups. Benjamin Spock, the best-selling author of books on baby care, and Dr. Martin Luther King, Jr., the civil rights leader, added their voices to the antiwar movement. Widely watched television commentators such as CBS's Walter Cronkite increasingly editorialized the evening news with an antiwar slant. Radical pacifists, liberal reformers, conservative constitutionalists, strategic realists, religious moralists, hippies, trade unionists, and many others melded into a national, largely unstructured antiwar movement. Often stereotyped as the haven for long-haired, bearded college-age youth, the movement actually encompassed a wide spectrum of people. The strongest opposition to the war came from older, black, female, and lower-class Americans. Younger, white, male, and middle-class citizens tended to support escalation of the war and follow the president's lead—at least until 1968. In February of that year, after Tet, a majority of polled Americans for the first time said that the United States had made a "mistake" in sending troops to Vietnam.

The critics offered multifaceted arguments: The war cost too much and weakened needed reform at home; America's youth was dying—30,000 by 1968; inflation and a worsening balance of payments damaged the economy; the ghastly bloodshed and U.S. conduct of the war were immoral; the United States neglected diplomacy in favor of militarism; the war damaged relations with allies and foes alike; Washington and Saigon could not win the war; the president was undermining the constitutional system of checks and balances; U.S. behavior in Vietnam debased the American principles of fair play and right to self-determination; and dissension was ripping domestic America apart. America had stepped into a traditional struggle that it could not control. Above all else, the critics argued, the United States had succumbed to a debilitating globalism of anticommunism, overcommitment, and overextension. In short, some critics complained about how the war was being conducted, whereas others, more searching, criticized globalism and the containment doctrine itself.

The growing public disaffection with the war encouraged dissent in Congress. Senator J. William Fulbright and some of his colleagues had had lingering doubts about the Tonkin Gulf Resolution. In February 1966 his Senate Foreign Relations Committee conducted publicly televised hearings. LBJ ridiculed him as Senator Halfbright, the "stud duck of the opposition."[169] But dissenting senators kept asking the administration to explain exactly what in Vietnam the United States was trying to contain. The Soviet Union? China? North Vietnam? The Vietcong? Wars of national liberation? Communism? Revolution? Secretary Rusk settled on China as the main culprit, especially after Chinese leader Lin Piao declared in 1965 that China would encourage wars of national liberation in the Third World. "It is on this spot," as Rostow once asserted, "that we have to break the liberation war— Chinese type. If we don't break it here we shall have to face it again in Thailand, Venezuela, elsewhere."[170] Although China supplied most arms to North Vietnam until the mid-1960s, the Soviet Union took over that role in an attempt to match American armaments and curry favor in Hanoi. Many administration officials overlooked the fundamental fact that the conflict in South Vietnam grew from indigenous roots—that it was a civil war. The surprise testimony at the Fulbright hearings came from the poised, persuasive George F. Kennan. He insisted that the containment doctrine, designed for a stable European nation-state context in the

Harvard Strike, 1969. The clenched fist and V-shaped fingers became symbols of the antiwar movement. (Homer Babbidge Library, University of Connecticut)

Vietnam War "Doves."   Left to right, Senators J. William Fulbright, Mike Mansfield, Frank Church, and Wayne Morse—all members of the Foreign Relations Committee and critics of U.S. intervention in Vietnam. In this 1966 meeting, Church presented a portrait of William E. Borah, who chaired the committee in the years 1925–1933 and, like the four senators here, earned a reputation for anti-imperialism. (Frank Church Collection, Boise State University Library)

1940s, did not fit Asia. Facile analogies with the 1940s did not solve the new realities of the 1960s. He urged a gradual withdrawal from Vietnam. So did Senator Eugene McCarthy, who declared in late 1967 that he would challenge President Johnson for the 1968 Democratic nomination. "A lot of little people in a lot of little places were doing a lot of little things" to support McCarthy, observed one reporter.[171] In March 1968, Senator Robert F. Kennedy, the slain president's brother, also entered the Democratic race as an antiwar candidate.

The Johnson administration lashed back, citing polls showing that most Americans, before 1968, favored escalation, not withdrawal. Rostow tried to reassure Johnson with statistical charts showing the enemy's large losses, yet the most heavily industrialized, the most militarily powerful, the richest nation on earth could not subdue small, rural Vietnam. Doubters grew within administration ranks. In 1967 Johnson's advisers generally favored the "stick it out" option, but by Tet the president heard words such as "disengagement," "deescalation," "withdrawal," and "sinkhole."[172] McNamara's increasing disenchantment and 1967 resignation angered the president. White House national security adviser McGeorge Bundy, Under Secretary of State George Ball, and close political adviser Bill Moyers had already departed. With victory an increasingly elusive goal by 1967–1968, Johnson seemed determined at least not to lose.

Critics said that the administration should pursue opportunities for negotiations. Throughout the 1965–1968 escalation period, international groups, including the United Nations and the Vatican, reached for peace. In 1965, through Italy, North Vietnam offered a peace plan resembling the 1954 Geneva agreements. Believing that "you can't fertilize a field by farting thru the fence," LBJ sent prominent emissaries to foreign capitals to promote peace.[173] In January 1966, Johnson halted the bombing of North Vietnam. But during this bombing pause, he also increased U.S. troop strength in Vietnam, raising doubts about the seriousness of the U.S. peace offensive. The obstacles to negotiations stood high in any case. Washington would not talk until North Vietnam ceased its "aggression" and would not recognize the National Liberation Front as a political force in the South. Hanoi, increasingly speaking for the Vietcong, would not negotiate until U.S. bombing stopped and Saigon granted the NLF political rights. Assistant Secretary of Defense John McNaughton, another "hawk" rapidly becoming a "dove," concluded that the United States wanted "capitulation by a Communist force that is far from beaten."[174] A promising diplomatic contact (codenamed MARIGOLD) through a Polish representative, in December 1966, aborted when American bombers stepped up air strikes around Hanoi, which then scuttled the Polish peace initiative. Another bombing pause came in February 1967, in part induced by McNamara's argument that the bombing did not seriously impede the flow of arms and soldiers into the South, much of it on bicycles over narrow, jungle paths (the "Ho Chi Minh Trail" see map on p. 413). Johnson in his "San Antonio formula" insisted on an end to infiltration before discontinuing bombing or beginning to negotiate. After each pause, the bombing intensified.

And then the Tet offensive of early 1968 wrought its havoc; military escalation and Johnson's political career derailed; the bombing scaled down; and the peace talks finally began in Paris. In November, Richard M. Nixon defeated Vice President Hubert Humphrey for the presidency. Back in Texas, Lady Bird Johnson remarked that "the coach has turned back into a pumpkin and the mice have all run away."[175] In 1961 John F. Kennedy had asked Americans to "pay any price" and "bear any burden." By 1969, many refused. The new Nixon administration faced the task of halting the decline of U.S. power and maintaining American interests abroad while at the same time mollifying the evident discontent with globalism. As Americans asked, "How could Vietnam happen?" and heard the critics variously say kneejerk anticommunism, the domino theory, inflexible containment, the arrogance of power, presidential hubris, economic expansion and the military-industrial complex, bureaucratic politics, an inadvertent and ignorant walk into a quagmire, racist views of Asians, welfare imperialism, right-wing political pressure, insensitivity to morality, violation of noble principles, and a failure to understand an alien culture—the incoming administration was asking, "How can the United States get out?"

Antiwar Buttons. Opponents of the Vietnam War demonstrated their protest in a panoply of buttons urging withdrawal and peace. (Division of Political History, Smithsonian Institution)

FURTHER READING FOR THE PERIOD 1961–1969

Several works cited in Chapters 7 and 8 on the Cold War and the Third World also survey this period, and not all are repeated here.

For John F. Kennedy and his foreign relations, see James D. Barber, *The Presidential Character* (1992); Irving Bernstein, *Promises Kept* (1991); Michael Beschloss, *The Crisis Years* (1991); Thomas Brown, *JFK* (1988); Kenneth R. Crispell and Carlos F. Gomez, *Hidden Illness in the White House* (1989); Robert H. Ferrell, *Ill-Advised* (1992); James N. Giglio, *The Presidency of John F. Kennedy* (1991); Doris Kearns Goodwin, *The Fitzgeralds and the Kennedys* (1987); David Halberstam, *The Best and the Brightest* (1972); Montague Kern et al., *The Kennedy Crises* (1983); William E. Leuchtenburg, *In the Shadow of FDR* (1989); Timothy P. Maga, *John F. Kennedy and New Frontier Diplomacy* (1994); Bert Park, *Ill-Fated History* (1993); Herbert S. Parmet, *JFK* (1983); Thomas G. Paterson, ed., *Kennedy's Quest for Victory* (1989); Richard Reeves, *President Kennedy* (1993); Thomas C. Reeves, *A Question of Character* (1991); Gerald T. Rice, *The Bold Experiment* (1985) (Peace Corps); J. Richard Snyder, ed., *John F. Kennedy* (1988); and Garry Wills, *The Kennedy Imprisonment* (1982). For Kennedy and specific countries and crises, see below.

For Lyndon B. Johnson and his administration (Vietnam is covered separately below), see Vaughn D. Bornet, *The Presidency of Lyndon B. Johnson* (1983); Paul K. Conkin, *Big Daddy from the Pedernales* (1986); Robert A. Divine, ed., *The Johnson Years* (1987–1994) and *Exploring the Johnson Years* (1981); Peter Geyelin, *Lyndon B. Johnson and the World* (1966); Paul Y. Hammond, *LBJ and the Presidential Management of Foreign Relations* (1993); Doris Kearns, *Lyndon Johnson and the American Dream* (1976); Diane Kunz, ed., *The Diplomacy of the Crucial Decade* (1994); and Emmette Redford and Richard McCulley, *White House Operations* (1986).

Other prominent Americans are studied in Leroy Ashby and Rod Gramer, *Fighting the Odds* (1994) (Frank Church); William C. Berman, *William Fulbright and the Vietnam War* (1988); Douglas Brinkley, *Dean Acheson* (1992); Jeff Broadwater, *Adlai Stevenson* (1994); Eugene Brown, *J. William Fulbright* (1984); Warren I. Cohen, *Dean Rusk* (1980); David L. DiLeo, *George Ball, Vietnam, and the Rethinking of Containment* (1991); Gilbert C. Fite, *Richard B. Russell, Jr.* (1991); Dorothy Fosdick, ed., *Staying the Course* (1987) (Henry Jackson); Walter Isaacson and Evan Thomas, *The Wise Men* (1986); John B. Martin, *Adlai Stevenson and the World* (1977); Thomas McCormick and Walter LaFeber, eds., *Behind the Throne* (1993) (Bundy and Mann); Barry Riccio, *Walter Lippmann* (1989); Howard B. Schaffer, *Chester Bowles* (1993); Thomas J. Schoenbaum, *Waging Peace and War* (1988) (Rusk); Deborah Shapley, *Promise and Power* (1993) (McNamara); Carol Solberg, *Hubert Humphrey* (1984); and Ronald Steel, *Walter Lippmann and the American Century* (1980).

Economic issues and trade policy are scrutinized in David P. Calleo, *The Imperious Economy* (1982); John W. Evans, *The Kennedy Round* (1971); and Thomas Zeiler, *American Trade and Power in the 1960s* (1992).

Europe, the Berlin crisis, and the nuclear-arms race are the subjects of Desmond Ball, *Politics and Force Levels* (1980); McGeorge Bundy, *Danger and Survival* (1988); Curtis Cate, *The Ides of August* (1978) (Berlin); Honoré Catudal, *Kennedy and the Berlin Wall Crisis* (1980); Frank Costigliola, *France and the United States* (1992); Bernard Firestone, *The Quest for Nuclear Stability* (1982); Alfred Grosser, *The Western Alliance* (1980); Michael Harrison, *The Reluctant Ally* (1981) (France); Michael Mandelbaum, *The Nuclear Question* (1979); David Nunnerly, *President Kennedy and Britain* (1972); Jack Schick, *The Berlin Crisis* (1971); Glenn T. Seaborg and Benjamin S. Loeb, *Kennedy, Khrushchev, and the Test Ban* (1981) and *Stemming the Tide* (1987) (arms control); Robert Slusser, *The Berlin Crisis of 1961* (1973); Peter Wyden, *The Wall* (1989); and Ernest J. Yanarella, *The Missile Defense Controversy* (1977).

Aspects of relations with the Third World in the 1960s include Melvin Gurtov, *The United States and the Third World* (1974); Gabriel Kolko, *Confronting the Third World* (1988); Timothy P. Maga, *John F. Kennedy and the New Pacific Community* (1990); Robert J. McMahon, *Cold War on the Periphery* (1994) (India and Pakistan); Robert A. Packenham, *Liberal America and the Third World* (1973); and David L. Schalk, *War and the Ivory Tower* (1991) (Algeria).

For the Cuban Revolution, Fidel Castro, Bay of Pigs, and missile crisis, see Graham Allison, *Essence of Decision* (1971); Jules Benjamin, *The United States and the Origins of the Cuban Revolution* (1990); James G.

Blight, *The Shattered Crystal Ball* (1990); James G. Blight and David A. Welch, *On the Brink* (1989); James G. Blight et al., *Cuba on the Brink* (1993); Dino A. Brugioni, *Eyeball to Eyeball* (1991); Herbert Dinerstein, *The Making of a Missile Crisis* (1976); Jorge Domínguez, *Cuba* (1978) and *To Make a World Safe for Revolution* (1989); Raymond L. Garthoff, *Reflections on the Cuban Missile Crisis* (1989); Alexander L. George, ed., *Avoiding War* (1991); Trumbull Higgins, *The Perfect Failure* (1987) (Bay of Pigs); Morris Morley, *Imperial State and Revolution* (1987); James A. Nathan, ed., *The Cuban Missile Crisis Revisited* (1992); Thomas G. Paterson, *Contesting Castro* (1994); Louis A. Pérez, Jr., *Cuba and the United States* (1990); Tad Szulc, *Fidel* (1986); Lucien S. Vandenbroucke, *Perilous Options* (1993) (Bay of Pigs); Richard E. Welch, Jr., *Response to Revolution* (1985); and Peter Wyden, *Bay of Pigs* (1979).

U.S.–Latin America relations in the 1960s, including the Alliance for Progress, are explored in Samuel Baily, *The United States and . . . South America* (1976); Jan K. Black, *United States Penetration of Brazil* (1977); Cole Blasier, *The Hovering Giant* (1976); Theodore Draper, *The Dominican Revolt* (1968); Piero Gleijeses, *The Dominican Crisis* (1978); Walter LaFeber, *Inevitable Revolutions* (1993); Lester D. Langley, *America and the Americas* (1989) and *The United States and the Caribbean in the Twentieth Century* (1982); Ruth Leacock, *Requiem for Revolution* (1990) (Brazil); Jerome Levinson and Juan de Onís, *The Alliance That Lost Its Way* (1970); Abraham F. Lowenthal, *Exporting Democracy* (1991); John D. Martz, ed., *United States Policy in Latin America* (1988); Phyllis Parker, *Brazil and the Quiet Intervention* (1979); L. Ronald Scheman, ed., *The Alliance for Progress* (1988); and W. Michael Weis, *Cold Warriors & Coups D'Etat* (1993) (Brazil).

Studies of U.S. relations with Africa include Julius A. Amin, *The Peace Corps in Cameroon* (1992); David N. Gibbs, *The Political Economy of Third World Intervention* (1991) (Congo); Madeline G. Kalb, *The Congo Cables* (1982); Richard D. Mahoney, *JFK* (1983); Thomas J. Noer, *Cold War and Black Liberation* (1985); Joseph E. Thompson, *American Policy and African Famine* (1990) (Nigeria); and Stephen Weissman, *American Foreign Policy in the Congo* (1974).

Narratives and analyses of the United States and Vietnam, especially the experience of the 1960s, include David L. Anderson, ed., *Shadow on the White House* (1993); Loren Baritz, *Backfire* (1985); David M. Barrett, *Uncertain Warriors* (1993); Larry Berman, *Lyndon Johnson's War* (1989) and *Planning a Tragedy* (1982); Larry Cable, *Unholy Grail* (1991); Phillip B. Davidson, *Vietnam at War* (1988); Frances FitzGerald, *Fire in the Lake* (1972); Leslie Gelb and Richard Betts, *The Irony of Vietnam* (1979); William C. Gibbons, *The U.S. Government and the Vietnam War* (1986–1988); Allan E. Goodman, *The Lost Peace* (1978); Fred Greenstein et al., eds., *How Presidents Test Reality* (1989); Ellen J. Hammer, *A Death in November* (1987) (Diem); Patrick L. Hatcher, *The Suicide of an Elite: American Internationalists and Vietnam* (1990); Patrick J. Hearden, ed., *Vietnam* (1990); George C. Herring, *America's Longest War* (1986) and *LBJ and Vietnam* (1994); Gary R. Hess, *Vietnam and the United States* (1990); Susan Jeffords, *The Remasculinization of America: Gender and the Vietnam War* (1989); George McT. Kahin, *Intervention* (1986); Stanley Karnow, *Vietnam* (1991); Gabriel Kolko, *Anatomy of a War* (1985); David W. Levy, *The Debate Over Vietnam* (1991); Bill McCloud, *What Should We Tell Our Children About Vietnam?* (1989); Douglas Pike, *Vietnam and the Soviet Union* (1987); William J. Rust, *Kennedy in Vietnam* (1985); William Y. Schandler, *The Unmaking of a President* (1977) (Johnson); Neil Sheehan, *A Bright Shining Lie* (1988); Anthony Short, *The Origins of the Vietnam War* (1989); Ronald H. Spector, *After Tet* (1993); William S. Turley, *The Second Indochina War* (1986); Brian VanDeMark, *Into the Quagmire* (1991) (Johnson); Jayne S. Werner and Luu Doan Huynh, eds., *The Vietnam War* (1992); Marilyn Young, *The Vietnam Wars* (1991); and James J. Wirtz, *The Tet Offensive* (1992).

Laos and Cambodia are discussed in many of the studies above and in Timothy N. Castle, *At War in the Shadow of Vietnam* (1993) (Laos); David P. Chandler, *The Tragedy of Cambodian History* (1991); Michael Haas, *Cambodia, Pol Pot, and the United States* (1991); William Shawcross, *Sideshow* (1979) (Cambodia); and Charles Stevenson, *The End of Nowhere* (1972) (Laos).

The colonial history of Vietnam, its wars against foreigners, and the development of its politics are examined in Joseph Buttinger, *Vietnam* (1970); William Duiker, *The Communist Road to Power in Vietnam* (1981); Bernard Fall, *The Two Viet-Nams* (1967); James P. Harrison, *The Endless War* (1982); Ronald E. Irving, *The First Indochina War* (1975); David Marr, *Vietnamese Anti-Colonialism, 1885–1925* (1971) and *Vietnamese*

Tradition on Trial, 1920–1945 (1981); John T. McAlister, Jr., *Vietnam* (1971); and Douglas Pike, *History of Vietnamese Communism* (1978) and *Viet Cong* (1972).

Specific studies of the Truman and Eisenhower administrations and Vietnam are David L. Anderson, *Trapped by Success* (1991) (Eisenhower); Melanie Billings-Yun, *Decision Against War* (1988) (Dienbienphu); Lloyd C. Gardner, *Approaching Vietnam* (1988); Ellen J. Hammer, *The Struggle for Vietnam, 1945–1955* (1966); Lawrence S. Kaplan et al., eds., *Dien Bien Phu and the Crisis of Franco-American Relations* (1990); and Andrew J. Rotter, *The Path to Vietnam* (1987).

For province- and village-level studies that probe American interactions with a peasant society, see William Andrews, *The Village War* (1973); Eric M. Bergerud, *The Dynamics of Defeat* (1991); Jeffrey Race, *War Comes to Long An* (1972); and James W. Trullinger, Jr., *Village at War* (1980).

Military decisions and operations and the soldier's experience in Vietnam are studied in Christian G. Appy, *Working-Class War* (1993); Jeffrey J. Clarke, *United States Army in Vietnam* (1988); Mark Clodfelter, *The Limits of Power* (1989) (bombing); Robert L. Gallucci, *Neither Peace Nor Honor* (1975); Douglas Kinnard, *The Certain Trumpet* (1991) (Taylor) and *The War Managers* (1977); Andrew F. Krepinevich, Jr., *The Army and Vietnam* (1986); Otto J. Lehrack, *No Shining Armor* (1992) (marines); Guenter Lewy, *America in Vietnam* (1978); Donald J. Mrozek, *Air Power & the Ground War in Vietnam* (1989); Edgar O'Ballance, *The Wars in Vietnam* (1975); Douglas Pike, *PAVN: People's Army of Vietnam* (1986); John Prados and Ray Stubbe, *Valley of Decision* (1991) (Khe Sanh); Ronald H. Spector, *United States in Vietnam* (1983); Shelby Stanton, *The Rise and Fall of an American Army* (1985); Harry G. Summers, *On Strategy* (1981); and James C. Thompson, *Rolling Thunder* (1980).

American public opinion, media, and politics and the antiwar movement are discussed in many of the works above and specifically in Peter Braestrup, *Big Story* (1977); Charles DeBenedetti and Charles Chatfield, *An American Ordeal* (1990) (antiwar movement); Terry Dietz, *Republicans and Vietnam* (1986); G. David Garrow, *Bearing the Cross* (1986) (Martin Luther King, Jr.); Daniel C. Hallin, *The "Uncensored War"* (1986); Kenneth J. Heineman, *Campus Wars* (1993); Allen J. Matusow, *Unraveling of America* (1984); Melvin Small, *Johnson, Nixon, and the Doves* (1988); Melvin Small and William D. Hoover, eds., *Give Peace a Chance* (1992); Amy Swerdlow, *Women Strike for Peace* (1993); Kathleen J. Turner, *Lyndon Johnson's Dual War* (1985); Tom Wells, *The War Within* (1994); Lawrence S. Wittner, *Rebels Against War* (1984); and Nancy Zaroulis and Gerald Sullivan, *Who Spoke Up?* (1984).

See also the General Bibliography, Richard D. Burns, *Guide to American Foreign Relations Since 1700* (1983), and the following notes.

Notes to Chapter 9

1. Quoted in J. L. Dees, "The Viet Cong Attack that Failed," *Department of State News Letter,* No. 85 (May 1968), p. 22.
2. Tran-van Dinh, "Six Hours That Changed the Vietnam Situation," *Christian Century, LXXXV* (March 6, 1968), 289.
3. Don Oberdorfer, *Tet!* (Garden City, New York: Doubleday, 1971), p. 25.
4. Quoted in Marilyn B. Young, *The Vietnam Wars* (New York: HarperCollins, 1991), p. 216.
5. Quoted in Oberdorfer, *Tet!,* p. 33.
6. Quoted in Robert Shaplen, *Time Out of Hand* (New York: Harper Colophon, 1970; rev. ed.), p. 408.
7. *Department of State Bulletin, LVIII* (March 4, 1968), 304.
8. Harold Johnson quoted in David M. Barrett, *Uncertain Warriors* (Lawrence: University Press of Kansas, 1993), p. 115.
9. Frances FitzGerald, *Fire in the Lake* (New York: Vintage, 1972), p. 524.

10. Shaplen, *Time Out of Hand*, p. 416.
11. Tran Van Tra, "Tet," in Jayne S. Werner and Luu Doan Huynh, eds., *The Vietnam War* (Armonk, N.Y.: M. E. Sharpe, 1992), p. 58.
12. William C. Westmoreland, *A Soldier Reports* (Garden City, N.Y.: Doubleday, 1976), p. 348.
13. Quoted in Townsend Hoopes, *The Limits of Intervention* (New York: David McKay, 1969), p. 213.
14. Quoted in George McT. Kahin and John W. Lewis, *The United States in Vietnam* (New York: Dell, 1969; rev. ed.), p. 373.
15. Quoted in George A. Bailey and Lawrence W. Lichty, "Rough Justice on a Saigon Street," *Journalism Quarterly, XLIX* (Summer 1972), 222.
16. Quoted in *Newsweek, LXXI* (February 19, 1968), 24.
17. U.S. Senate, Foreign Relations Committee, *Foreign Assistance Act of 1968—Part 1—Vietnam* (Washington, D.C.: Government Printing Office, 1968), p. 100.

18. *Department of State Bulletin, LVIII* (February 26, 1968), 261.
19. Dean Rusk, *As I Saw It* (New York: Penguin, 1991), p. 477.
20. Quoted in Philip B. Davidson, *Vietnam at War* (Novato, Cal.: Presidio Press, 1988), p. 486.
21. Quoted in James W. Trullinger, Jr., *Village at War* (New York: Longman, 1980), p. 129.
22. Lyndon B. Johnson, *The Vantage Point* (New York: Holt, Rinehart and Winston, 1971), p. 384.
23. John B. Henry II, "February, 1968," *Foreign Policy,* No. 4 (Fall 1971), p. 19.
24. Quoted in Marvin Kalb and Elie Abel, *Roots of Involvement* (New York: W. W. Norton, 1971), p. 211.
25. Clark Clifford, *Counsel to the President* (New York: Random House, 1991), p. 494.
26. Quoted in Gabriel Kolko, *Anatomy of a War* (New York: Pantheon, 1985), p. 317.
27. Barrett, *Uncertain Warriors*, p. 111.
28. Quoted in Ronald Spector, *After Tet* (New York: The Free Press, 1993), pp. 21–22.
29. *Public Papers, Johnson, 1968* (Washington, D.C.: Government Printing Office, 1970), p. 470.
30. Quoted in Christian G. Appy, *Working-Class War* (Chapel Hill: University of North Carolina Press, 1993), p. 208.
31. Jean Lacouture, *Ho Chi Minh* (New York: Vintage [1967], 1968), p. 3.
32. Joseph Buttinger, *Vietnam* (New York: Praeger, 1967; 2 vols.), I, 174–175.
33. Quoted in Lloyd C. Gardner, *Approaching Vietnam* (New York: W. W. Norton, 1988), p. 65.
34. Quoted in Christopher Thorne, "Indochina and Anglo-American Relations, 1942–1945," *Pacific Historical Review, XLIV* (February 1976), 93.
35. Quoted in Walter LaFeber, "Roosevelt, Churchill, and Indochina: 1942–45," *American Historical Review, LXXX* (December 1975), 1289.
36. Quoted in Gary R. Hess, "Franklin Roosevelt and Indochina," *Journal of American History LIX* (September 1972), 364.
37. Clark M. Clifford, "A Viet Nam Reappraisal," *Foreign Affairs XLVII* (July 1969), 603.
38. Quoted in Archimedes L. A. Patti, *Why Vietnam?* (Berkeley: University of California Press, 1980), p. 203.
39. Dean Acheson in *Foreign Relations, 1950* (Washington, D.C.: Government Printing Office, 1976), VI, 692.
40. Quoted in Melanie Billings-Yun, *Decision Against War* (New York: Columbia University Press, 1988), p. 91.
41. Quoted in George C. Herring, *America's Longest War* (New York: Alfred A. Knopf, 1986; 2d ed.), p. 32.
42. Quoted in George C. Herring and Richard H. Immerman, "Eisenhower, Dulles, and Dien Bien Phu," in Lawrence S. Kaplan et al., eds., *Dien Bien Phu and the Crisis of Franco-American Relations, 1954–1955* (Wilmington, Del.: Scholarly Resources, 1990), p. 95.
43. Quoted in Herring, *America's Longest War*, p. 39.
44. Quoted in Young, *Vietnam Wars*, p. 42.
45. Quoted in *New York Times, The Pentagon Papers* (New York: Bantam, 1971), p. 14.
46. Bernard Fall, *The Two Viet-Nams* (New York: Praeger, 1967; 2d ed.), p. 233.
47. Quoted in Kahin and Lewis, *U.S. in Vietnam*, p. 61.
48. Quoted in David L. Anderson, "Dwight D. Eisenhower and Wholehearted Support of Ngo Dinh Diem," in David L. Anderson, ed., *Shadow on the White House* (Lawrence: University Press of Kansas, 1993), p. 54.
49. Quoted in George W. Ball, *The Past Has Another Pattern* (New York: W. W. Norton, 1982), p. 364.
50. Quoted in Theodore C. Sorensen, *Kennedy* (New York: Harper & Row, 1965), p. 199.
51. *New York Times*, August 25, 1960.
52. Quoted in Richard J. Walton, *Cold War and Counterrevolution* (Baltimore: Penguin, [1972], 1973), p. 9.
53. *Public Papers, Kennedy, 1962* (Washington, D.C.: Government Printing Office, 1963), p. 807.
54. Walt W. Rostow, "The Third Round," *Foreign Affairs, XLII* (October 1963), 5–6.
55. Don Ferguson in Peter Joseph, *Good Times* (New York: Morrow, 1974), p. 4.
56. Quoted in Thomas G. Paterson, "Introduction," in Thomas G. Paterson, ed., *Kennedy's Quest for Victory* (New York: Oxford University Press, 1989), p. 14.
57. Arthur M. Schlesinger, Jr., *A Thousand Days* (Boston: Houghton Mifflin, 1965), p. 259.
58. James Barber, *The Presidential Character* (Englewood Cliffs, N.J.: Prentice-Hall, 1992; 4th ed.), p. 345.
59. Quoted in Michael R. Beschloss, *The Crisis Years* (New York: HarperCollins, 1991), p. 48.
60. Oral History Interview by Chester Bowles, pp. 49, 90, John F. Kennedy Library, Boston, Massachusetts.
61. Schlesinger, *Thousand Days*, p. 217.
62. *Public Papers, Kennedy, 1961* (Washington, D.C.: Government Printing Office, 1962), pp. 1–3.
63. Theodore H. White, "The Action Intellectuals," *Life, LXII* (June 1967), 43.
64. Quoted in David Halberstam, "The Programming of Robert McNamara," *Harper's, CCXLII* (February 1971), 62.
65. Quoted in Roger Hilsman, *To Move a Nation* (Garden City, N.Y.: Doubleday, 1967), p. 523.
66. Frederick Nolting, *From Trust to Tragedy* (New York: Praeger, 1988), p. 62.
67. Sorensen, *Kennedy*, p. 270.
68. "Memorandum of Conversation with President Johnson," by Max Frankel, July 8, 1965, "Black Notebooks," Box 1, Arthur Krock Papers, Princeton University Library, Princeton, New Jersey.
69. Quoted in Lloyd Gardner, "Harry Hopkins with Hand Grenades?" in Thomas J. McCormick and Walter LaFeber, eds., *Behind the Throne* (Madison: University of Wisconsin Press, 1993), p. 204.
70. Harry McPherson, *A Political Education* (Boston: Houghton Mifflin, 1988), p. 257.

71. *Public Papers, Eisenhower, 1959* (Washington, D.C.: Government Printing Office, 1960), p. 8.

72. Quoted in Michael Mandelbaum, *The Nuclear Question* (New York: Cambridge University Press, 1979), p. 90.

73. "Biographic Briefing Book," June 1961, Box 126, President's Office File, John F. Kennedy Papers, Kennedy Library.

74. Schlesinger, *Thousand Days*, p. 348.

75. Quoted in Vladislav M. Zubok, "Khrushchev and the Berlin Crisis," Working Paper No. 6, *Cold War International History Project* (Washington, D.C., May 1993), p. 20.

76. Quoted in Rusk, *As I Saw It*, p. 227.

77. Quoted in Schlesinger, *Thousand Days*, p. 391.

78. James Reston quoted in James N. Giglio, *The Presidency of John F. Kennedy* (Lawrence: University Press of Kansas, 1991), p. 78.

79. Quoted in Thomas J. Schoenbaum, *Waging Peace and War* (New York: Simon and Schuster, 1988), p. 336.

80. *Public Papers, Kennedy, 1961*, pp. 534, 536.

81. "Khrushchev's Secret Speech on the Berlin Crisis," *Cold War International History Project Bulletin*, Issue 2 (Fall 1993), 59.

82. Quoted in Beschloss, *Crisis Years*, p. 278.

83. Quoted in Frank Costigliola, "The Pursuit of Atlantic Community," in Paterson, *Kennedy's Quest*, p. 40.

84. Raymond L. Garthoff, "Berlin 1961," *Foreign Policy*, No. 84 (Fall 1991), 142.

85. Marcus G. Raskin and Bernard B. Fall, eds., *The Viet-Nam Reader* (New York: Vintage, 1967; rev. ed.), p. 113.

86. John F. Kennedy quoted in Robert J. McMahon, *The Cold War on the Periphery* (New York: Columbia University Press, 1994), p. 273.

87. Quoted in Gary R. Hess, "Commitment in the Age of Counterinsurgency," in Anderson, *Shadow*, p. 71.

88. Carol Miller Reynolds quoted in Gary May, "Passing the Torch and Lighting Fires," in Paterson, *Kennedy's Quest*, p. 315.

89. Quoted in Frank Mankiewicz and Kirby Jones, *With Fidel* (New York: Ballantine, 1975), p. 175.

90. Quoted in Thomas Noer, "New Frontiers and Old Priorities in Africa," in Paterson, *Kennedy's Quest*, p.262.

91. Dean Rusk to G. Mennen Williams, January 8, 1962, Box 29, Records of G. Mennen Williams, Department of State Records, National Archives, Washington, D.C.

92. William Attwood, *The Reds and the Blacks* (New York: Harper & Row, 1967), p. 219.

93. Allen Dulles in *Foreign Relations, 1958–1960* (Washington, D.C.: Government Printing Office, 1991), *VI*, 398; Daniel M. Braddock quoted in Thomas G. Paterson, *Contesting Castro* (New York: Oxford University Press, 1994), p. 242.

94. Quoted in Jules Benjamin, *The United States and the Origins of the Cuban Revolution* (Princeton: Princeton University Press, 1990), p. 182.

95. Quoted in Paterson, *Contesting*, p. 242.

96. Roy R. Rubottom, Jr., in *Foreign Relations, 1958–1960,VI*, 656.

97. Quoted in Paterson, *Contesting*, p. 257.

98. *Foreign Relations, 1958–1960, VI*, 656–657.

99. Dwight D. Eisenhower, *The White House Years: Waging Peace, 1956–1961* (Garden City, N.Y.: Doubleday, 1965), p. 527.

100. Philip W. Bonsal, *Cuba, Castro, and the United States* (Pittsburgh: University of Pittsburgh Press), p. 192.

101. Quoted in Schlesinger, *Thousand Days*, p. 251.

102. Quoted in Lucien S. Vandenbroucke, "The 'Confessions' of Allen Dulles," *Diplomatic History, VIII* (Fall 1984), 369.

103. Allen Dulles quoted in Lucien S. Vandenbroucke, *Perilous Options* (New York: Oxford University Press, 1993), p. 22.

104. Walt W. Rostow, *The Diffusion of Power* (New York: Macmillan, 1972), pp. 210–211.

105. *Public Papers, Kennedy, 1961*, pp. 304–306.

106. Quoted in *New York Times*, February 5, 1989.

107. Quoted in Mankiewicz and Jones, *With Fidel*, p. 130.

108. Transcript, "Off-the-Record Meeting on Cuba," 11:50 A.M.–12:57 P.M., October 16, 1962, Presidential Recordings, Kennedy Library.

109. Maxwell Taylor quoted in J. Anthony Lukacs, "Class Reunion," *New York Times Magazine*, August 30, 1987, p. 58; Abram Chayes quoted in James A. Nathan, "The Heyday of the New Strategy," in James A. Nathan, ed., *The Cuban Missile Crisis Revisited* (New York: St. Martin's Press, 1992), p. 24.

110. Robert F. Kennedy, *Thirteen Days* (New York: W. W. Norton, 1969), p. 31.

111. *Public Papers, Kennedy, 1962*, p. 808.

112. Transcript, "Cuban Missile Crisis Meetings," October 27, 1962, Presidential Recordings, Kennedy Library.

113. Quoted in Barton J. Bernstein, "Reconsidering the Missile Crisis," in Nathan, *Cuban Missile Crisis*, p. 100.

114. Quoted in Thomas G. Paterson, "Commentary," *Diplomatic History, XIV* (Spring 1990), 256.

115. John Kenneth Galbraith, "The Plain Lessons of a Bad Decade," *Foreign Policy*, No. 1 (Winter 1970–1971), 32.

116. Quoted in McGeorge Bundy, *Danger and Survival* (New York: Random House, 1988), p. 426.

117. Quoted in James Blight and David Welch, *On the Brink* (New York: Hill and Wang, 1989), p. 100; Marc Trachtenberg, "Commentary," *Diplomatic History, XIV* (Spring 1990), 242.

118. "Review of the Cuban Situation and Policy," February 28, 1963, Box 115, President's Office File, Kennedy Library.

119. "Meeting with the President," December 19, 1963, Box 19, Aides Files—Bundy, National Security File, Lyndon B. Johnson Papers, Lyndon B. Johnson Library, Austin, Texas.

120. Quoted in Richard Ned Lebow, "The Traditional and Revisionist Interpretations Reevaluated," in Nathan, *Cuban Missile Crisis,* p. 180.

121. Walt W. Rostow, Memorandum, March 29, 1961, Box 193, National Security File, *Kennedy Papers.*

122. Quoted in Schlesinger, *Thousand Days,* p. 330.

123. Eisenhower, *Waging Peace,* p. 607.

124. Schlesinger, *Thousand Days,* p. 324.

125. Quoted *ibid.,* p. 338.

126. Bernard Fall, *Anatomy of a Crisis* (Garden City, N.Y.: Doubleday, 1969), p. 229.

127. Quoted in Rostow, *Diffusion of Power,* p. 265.

128. Robert McNamara memorandum quoted in Fred I. Greenstein and Richard H. Immerman, "What Did Eisenhower Tell Kennedy about Indochina?" *Journal of American History,* LXXIX (September 1992), 575.

129. Lawrence J. Bassett and Stephen E. Pelz, "The Failed Search for Victory," in Paterson, *Kennedy's Quest,* p. 222.

130. Quoted in Frank Costigliola, *France and the United States* (Boston: Twayne, 1992), p. 140.

131. Quoted in David Halberstam, *The Best and the Brightest* (Greenwich, Conn.: Fawcett, 1973), p. 167.

132. Rusk, *As I Saw It,* p. 436.

133. U.S. Senate, *Foreign Assistance Act of 1968,* p. 218.

134. Quoted in Beschloss, *Crisis Years,* p. 649.

135. Quoted *ibid.,* p. 651.

136. Quoted in Herring, *America's Longest War,* p. 100.

137. Quoted in William J. Rust, *Kennedy in Vietnam* (New York: Scribner's, 1985), p. x.

138. Quoted in Jim F. Heath, *Decade of Disillusionment* (Bloomington: Indiana University Press, 1975), p. 186.

139. Quoted in Brian VanDeMark, *Into the Quagmire* (New York: Oxford University Press, 1991), p. 123.

140. Quoted in Barber, *Presidential Character,* p. 25.

141. Quoted in Robert W. Sellen, "Old Assumptions versus New Realities," *International Journal,* XXVIII (Spring 1973), 206.

142. Quoted in *Boston Globe,* September 15, 1980.

143. Quoted in Douglas Little, "Crackpot Realists and Other Heroes," *Diplomatic History, XIII* (Winter 1989), 103.

144. Clifford, *Counsel,* p. 385.

145. Quoted in Stanley Karnow, *Vietnam* (New York: Viking, 1991 rev. ed.,), p. 526.

146. J. William Fulbright, *The Arrogance of Power* (New York: Vintage, 1966); *The Crippled Giant* (New York; Vintage, 1972).

147. W. Michael Weis, *Cold Warriors & Coups D'Etat* (Albuquerque: Uni-versity of New Mexico Press, 1993), p. 163.

148. Jack Valenti quoted in Walter LaFeber, "Latin American Policy," in Robert A. Divine, ed., *The Johnson Years* (Lawrence: University Press of Kansas, 1987–1994; 3 vols.), I, 76.

149. Quoted in *Newsweek, LXV* (May 17, 1965), 52.

150. Fulbright, *Arrogance of Power,* pp. 91–92.

151. Quoted in Kahin and Lewis, *U.S. and Vietnam,* p. 152.

152. Quoted in Herring, *America's Longest War,* p. 120.

153. Quoted in George McT. Kahin, *Intervention* (New York: Alfred A. Knopf, 1986), p. 223.

154. Quoted in Gilbert C. Fite, *Richard B. Russell, Jr.* (Chapel Hill: University of North Carolina Press, 1991), p. 441.

155. *Congressional Record, CX* (August 7, 1964), 18471.

156. Quoted in Karnow, *Vietnam,* p. 374.

157. Quoted in Jack Valenti, *A Very Human President* (New York: W. W. Norton, 1975), pp. 329, 334, 335.

158. Quoted in Young, *Vietnam Wars,* p. 127.

159. Quoted in George C. Herring, "The Reluctant Warrior," in Anderson, *Shadow,* p. 93.

160. Quoted in James P. Harrison, "History's Heaviest Bombing," in Werner and Huynh, *Vietnam War,* p. 135.

161. Quoted in Eric M. Bergerud, *The Dynamics of Defeat* (Boulder, Colo.: Westview Press, 1991), p. 163.

162. Quoted in David L. DiLeo, *George Ball, Vietnam, and the Rethinking of Containment* (Chapel Hill: University of North Carolina Press, 1991), p. 170.

163. Quoted in Doris Kearns, *Lyndon Johnson and the American Dream* (New York: Harper & Row, 1976), p. 329.

164. Quoted in Jonathan Mirsky, "The Root of Resistance," *The Nation, CCVII* (August 5, 1968), 90.

165. Quoted in Karnow, *Vietnam,* p. 617.

166. Philip Caputo, *A Rumor of War* (New York: Ballantine, 1977), p. 100.

167. Nicholas Katzenbach quoted in Larry Berman, *Lyndon Johnson's War* (New York: Oxford University Press, 1989), pp. 106–107.

168. Quoted in Clifford, *Counsel,* p. 417.

169. Quoted in Charles DeBenedetti, "Lyndon Johnson and the Antiwar Opposition," in Divine, *Johnson Years, II,* 34.

170. Quoted in Stephen Ambrose, *Rise to Globalism* (Baltimore: Penguin, 1993; 7th ed.), pp. 201–202.

171. Richard T. Stout quoted in Charles DeBenedetti and Charles Chatfield, *An American Ordeal* (Syracuse: Syracuse University Press, 1990), p. 213.

172. Barrett, *Uncertain Warriors,* p. 158.

173. Quoted in Clifford, *Counsel,* p. 436.

174. Quoted in Donald F. Lach and Edmund S. Wehrle, *International Politics in East Asia* (New York: Praeger, 1975), p. 338.

175. Quoted in Johnson, *Vantage Point,* p. 568.

DÉTENTE AND DISEQUILIBRIUM, 1969–1977

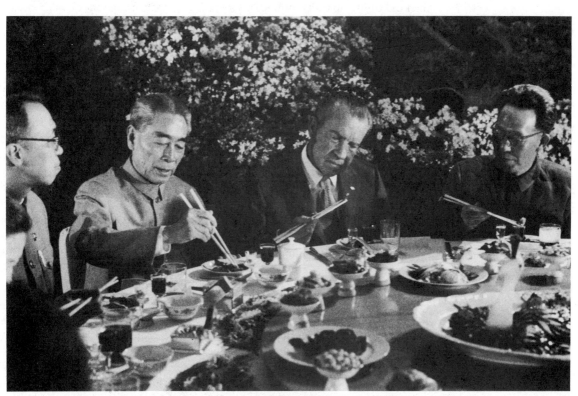

Zhou Enlai (1898–1976) and Richard M. Nixon (1913–1994), 1972. *One of the fine meals the president enjoyed during his dramatic visit to China in February. Nixon also visited the Great Wall, where he uttered a memorable banality: "I think that you would have to conclude that this is a great wall. . . . As we look at this wall, we do not want walls of any kind between peoples." Zhou is second from left. (Nixon Presidential Library)*

✳ *Diplomatic Crossroad*

Richard M. Nixon's Trip to China, 1972

The president's chief security officer aboard the aircraft radioed an American agent at the Beijing airport below: "What about the crowd?" The answer came back: "There is no crowd." The disbelieving officer asked: "Did you say, 'No crowd'?"[1] Indeed, when President Richard M. Nixon's blue and silver jet, the *Spirit of '76*, touched down on the Chinese runway that wintry morning of February 21, 1972, the reception was decidedly restrained and spartan. Apparently the Chinese wanted observers to think that the United States desired this dramatic meeting more eagerly than did the People's Republic of China (PRC). Cheering schoolchildren usually greeted visiting dignitaries, but only "a vast silence" welcomed Nixon.[2] The president awkwardly kept his arms at his sides, difficult for one who habitually waved his hands when departing an aircraft.

At the foot of the stairs stood trim seventy-three-year-old Premier Zhou Enlai, a veteran communist who had served Chairman Mao Zedong as key administrator since the success of the Chinese Revolution in 1949. Nixon and Zhou formally shook hands—the very gesture that Secretary John Foster Dulles had spurned at Geneva in 1954. The premier noticed Nixon adviser Henry A. Kissinger and purred, "Ah, old friend."[3] The television cameras whirred, sending back to the United States, via satellite, picture postcards of the historic encounter. The American visitors could not miss a large banner: "Make trouble, fail; make trouble again, fail again; make trouble until doom: that is the logic of the imperialists and reactionaries."[4] Zhou and Nixon sped toward Beijing, passing a gray landscape of communes, their caretakers indoors to escape the freezing temperatures. Portraits of Mao and political signs hung everywhere. The Chinese had painted over one poster that read: "We Must Defeat the U.S. Aggressors and All Their Running Dogs Wherever They May Be."[5]

Nixon's "journey for peace" contrasted sharply with the previous quarter century in which formal diplomatic relations had not existed between the two countries.[6] For years they had harangued each other as aggressors and had gone to war against one another in Korea. The United States maintained close ties with the PRC's archenemy Jiang Jieshi in Taiwan, while China aided America's foe in Vietnam. Nixon and Zhou had not forgotten this history of hostility, but each now recognized that cooperation best served his own country's interests.

In 1969, newly inaugurated President Nixon had asked his assistant for national security affairs, Henry A. Kissinger, to review relations with China. When border fighting between the Soviet Union and China broke out that year, Nixon told his cabinet: "The worst thing that could happen to us would be for the Soviet Union to gobble up Red China."[7] He soon sent private and public signals to Beijing by scaling back U.S. Seventh Fleet operations in the Taiwan Straits and relaxing trade restrictions with China. China picked up the signals. Early in 1970 PRC diplomats once again began meeting with U.S. officials in Warsaw—talks that China had suspended two years earlier as a protest against American warfare in Vietnam. In December, Mao told the visiting American journalist Edgar Snow that he would welcome Nixon to China, "either as a tourist or as President."[8] Nixon responded by lifting restrictions against Americans wanting to travel to the People's Republic. In April 1971 an American table tennis team competing in Japan accepted an invitation to visit China. Quips about "Ping-Pong diplomacy" and "the Ping heard round the world" did not detract from the symbolic significance of the trip.[9]

Using Pakistan as an intermediary, Kissinger made plans to go to China himself. In Islamabad, the Pakistani capital, Kissinger feigned illness and dropped from public view. On July 9, 1971, he secretly boarded a plane for Beijing. He soon reported that "the process we have now started will send enormous shock waves around the world."[10] A few days later, on July 15, President Nixon made the startling announcement that he would go to China to "seek the normalization of relations."[11]

Renewed Sino-American relations seemed to promise a number of advantages. Because of the gaping Sino-Soviet split, American recognition of the People's Republic would keep Moscow wondering what Washington intended. The United States conceivably could pit the antagonistic communist nations against one another. As one journalist put it, "The president is in the position of the lovely maiden courted by two ardent swains [China and the Soviet Union], each of whom is aware of the other but each of whom is uncertain of what happens when the young lady is alone with his rival."[12] With the American economy sagging, moreover, the legendary China market once again loomed large in American imaginations. Nuclear-arms race questions also shaped U.S. motives. China had rejected the 1968 Treaty on the Nonproliferation of Nuclear Weapons, and Washington sought Beijing's adherence. Then, too, U.S. recognition of China might encourage Beijing to reduce its aid to North Vietnam and to urge on Hanoi a political settlement of the Vietnam War.

The China trip also promised Nixon political profits at home. An antiwar Democrat, Senator George McGovern, had launched a conspicuous campaign against the Nixon administration's continued intervention in Vietnam, and in March, New Hampshire would hold the first presidential primary of 1972. "Look," Kissinger frankly remarked, "it wasn't just a matter of this summit—[Nixon's] political ass was on the line."[13] Liberal-left Americans had been calling for relations with China for years, and Democrats soon applauded the Nixon journey. At the same time, the right wing of the Republican party could hardly charge that Nixon, a proven anticommunist, had turned soft on communism. Finally, dominating all was the importance of the China journey to the general Nixon-Kissinger policy of "détente"—the relaxation of international tensions with communist nations to protect American interests. As Kissinger said: "We needed China to enhance the flexibility of our diplomacy."[14]

Marco Polo. Political cartoonist Ray Osrin portrayed two reasons for the Nixon journey to China, 1972. Kissinger's secret 1971 trip to China was code-named "Polo." (Ray Osrin in *The Cleveland Plain Dealer*)

The Chinese had their own reasons for inviting Nixon. From their vantage point the United States no longer ranked as their number-one threat, for Sino-Soviet relations had seriously deteriorated. The military skirmishes in 1969 on the shared 4,150-mile border caused many Chinese, recalling the Soviet invasion of Czechoslovakia in 1968, to fear a Soviet attack on China. The Soviet Union constructed an air base in Mongolia; the Chinese dug bomb shelters and tunnel networks. Resuming Sino-American ties, then, might deter the Soviets. In classic Chinese practice, Beijing hoped to play one barbarian against the other to "aggravate the contradictions between the United States and the Soviet Union."[15] China also feared a revived Japan, and a Sino-American rapprochement might unsettle Japan, keeping Tokyo off-guard and cautious. Or it might, as actually happened, lead to the opening of Sino-Japanese relations, thereby also strengthening China against the Soviet Union. Finally, China wanted American trade and a reduction of the U.S. commitment to Taiwan.

On the flight to China, Nixon, Kissinger, and their aides studied black notebooks about Chinese politics, culture, and diplomacy. Included were CIA analyses of Mao and Zhou and "talking points" that Nixon committed to memory. Joining the presidential party of thirty-seven—which included Secretary of State William Rogers, upstaged as always by Kissinger—was a press corps of eighty-seven, heavy with television news personalities. Americans carried specially printed souvenir matchbooks and wore flags in their lapels. Following his maxim that "one TV picture is worth 10,000 words," the president carefully staged his pageant for the prime-time screens back home.[16]

Only after arriving at his guesthouse did Nixon learn that he would have the "privilege" of meeting Chairman Mao.[17] Soon seated in overstuffed chairs, Nixon, Kissinger, Mao, and Zhou talked warmly for about an hour. Tang Wensheng, a Brooklyn-born Radcliffe graduate who had become a Chinese citizen, served as interpreter. Seventy-eight-year-old Mao, although ill, remained an imposing figure, esteemed by the Chinese as the leader of the Long March and father of the People's Republic. "He has the quality of being at the center wherever he stood," remarked Kissinger. "It moved with him wherever he moved."[18] Mao smiled and bantered. "Your book, *Six Crises,* is not a bad book," Mao commented. After Nixon heard the translation of that lukewarm review of his prepresidential memoirs, he looked at Zhou and said: "He reads too much."[19] Always gracious, the crew-cut, bushy-browed Zhou seemed tireless. Born into a well-to-do mandarin family, he spoke English, Russian, French, and Japanese as well as his native Chinese. A skillful negotiator with a sharp memory, Zhou never sought the limelight. American diplomats contrasted his quiet, patient style with the blunt, haggling manner of Soviet diplomats.

That evening, in the Great Hall of the People, Zhou hosted a massive banquet for 800 guests. Sipping glasses of *mao tai,* a 150-proof rice liquor "roughly equivalent to lawn mower fuel," Nixon and Zhou, Americans and Chinese, generously toasted one another.[20] A Chinese military band somewhat stiltedly played "Home on the Range." Then, tearing a page from Chinese communist history, Nixon called for a "long march together." And he even quoted Mao himself: "Seize the day, seize the hour. This is the hour."[21]

On February 22, Nixon and Zhou conferred while journalists filed reports on the Chinese lifestyle—clean streets, gauze masks to prevent infectious diseases, acupuncture techniques for surgery, anti-imperialist banners, expertise in table tennis, regimented schools, puritanical social habits, improved nutrition and health since 1949, Mao's photographs plastered on walls, bicycles, the monotony of blue dress, a pioneering and diligent character. Chinese authorities gave students lists of

"A Brick, A Bamboo, A Brick, A Bamboo . . ."
A French cartoonist's view of the delicate process of building Sino-American relations in the late 1960s and early 1970s. (Pierre, *Aux Ecoutes*)

questions reporters might ask "so that everyone could practice giving appropriate answers."[22] The fervent anticommunist William Buckley did not appreciate the ribbing from a Nixon aide who found the journalist in a souvenir shop: "Doing a little trading with the enemy, Bill?"[23] Although Nixon's meeting with Mao reminded Buckley of a Nuremberg prosecutor embracing "Goering and Goebbels and Doenitz and Hess, begging them to join . . . in the making of a better world," most American attitudes changed.[24] After years of thinking the Chinese a bestial enemy, Americans now found them loving and suffering like the rest of humanity. Whereas in the 1960s Americans used words like "ignorant, warlike, treacherous, and sly" to describe the "Red Chinese," after the 1972 trip they described them as "hard-working, intelligent, progressive, artistic, and practical."[25] As for Chinese images of Americans, the *Peking Daily* of February 22, in what analysts saw as a unique issue, carried pictures of Nixon's meeting with Mao. No longer the demonic traducer, any friend of Mao's became a friend of China's.

After late-night social events, an exhausted Kissinger sat down with the vice-foreign minister to fashion language for a joint communiqué. Issued on February 27, after much bickering, the document followed Zhou's formula of "seeking common ground while reserving differences."[26] For their part, the Americans stated their opposition to "outside pressure or intervention" in Asia—meaning Vietnam. They reaffirmed their friendly relations with South Korea and Japan. The Chinese, on the other hand, declared that they would continue to support "the struggles of all oppressed people" against large nations that attempt to "bully" the small. All foreign troops should withdraw from Asia, especially Vietnam. On the issue of Taiwan, which the United States still recognized as the official government of China, the Chinese part of the communiqué admonished the United States to remove its military forces from the island. There was only one China. The Americans equivocated, calling for a "peaceful settlement of the Taiwan question by the Chinese themselves." Both parties agreed, however, that "neither should seek hegemony in the Asia-Pacific region and each is opposed to efforts by any other country or group of countries to establish such hegemony"—a thinly veiled slap at the Soviet Union. Finally, both sides appealed for increased cultural and commercial contacts.[27]

Diplomacy done, on the seventh day of his trip, February 28, the president bade farewell at Shanghai and proclaimed that "this was the week that changed the world."[28] Typically, Nixon had rushed to judgment.

Nixon, Kissinger, and Their Critics

Nixon and Kissinger, quite different individuals who shared basic assumptions about American foreign relations, orchestrated this surprising turnabout in Sino-American relations. Richard Milhous Nixon, the grocer's son from Whittier, California, relished the "big play" in politics and saw himself walking "on the edge of a precipice because over the years you have become fascinated by how close to the edge you can walk without losing your balance."[29] He apparently wanted the

Pinocchio and Jiminy Cricket. The lies President Richard Nixon told during the Watergate crisis forced him from office. Using characters from the popular story of Pinocchio, the cartoonist Robert Grossman depicts the president as the untruthful youngster and Henry A. Kissinger as his faithful adviser. (© Robert Grossman)

Soviets and North Vietnamese to think him irrational and unpredictable. This self-professed "madman theory" would supposedly deter adversaries or cause them to settle on American terms.[30] A secretive, suspicious man, Nixon privately said about Kissinger, "I don't trust Henry, but I can use him."[31] Although his old adversary Dean Acheson found him "a curiously appealing person," Nixon did not trust many people.[32] He complained that the CIA was too liberal, staffed by Ivy Leaguers; he had little confidence in the State Department; he thought the news media schemed to "get" him; he scorned intellectuals and protesters. His administration guarded itself against these "enemies" through secrecy and through a variety of executive crimes and corrupt political practices later known collectively as Watergate. In part because he did not trust his aides, and in part because he wanted a record to write his memoirs and guard against misinformation, Nixon secretly taped conversations in the White House. When made public by court order, the tapes inspired an impeachment process that Nixon himself, caught in barefaced lies, terminated by resigning from the presidency on August 8, 1974, thereby elevating Vice President Gerald Ford to the White House. The Watergate scandal included the wiretapping of foreign-policy advisers and journalists. The uncovering of this illegal behavior weakened the executive branch in its ongoing struggle with Congress over policymaking and stripped the sacred garb from the phrase "national security," which Nixon had invoked for months to block public exposure of the incriminating tapes.

After Nixon's ignoble departure, Henry A. Kissinger stayed on. Presidential assistant for national security affairs (1969–1976) and secretary of state (1973–1977), Kissinger thought Nixon an "egomaniac" apparently "obsessed by the fear that he was not receiving adequate credit" for foreign-policy triumphs such as the change in China policy.[33] An ambitious political scientist of German-Jewish ancestry, with an Old World accent, Kissinger had escaped from Nazism in 1938. He spent much of his academic life advising government officials and politicians, presidential aspirant Nelson A. Rockefeller included. In his widely read book *Nuclear Weapons and Foreign Policy* (1957), Kissinger criticized "massive retaliation" for limiting U.S.

Makers of American Foreign Relations, 1969–1977

Presidents	Secretaries of State
Richard M. Nixon, 1969–1974	William P. Rogers, 1969–1973
Gerald Ford, 1974–1977	Henry A. Kissinger, 1973–1977

choices and rejected George F. Kennan's "disengagement" proposals. He also wrote an earlier book on European relations after the 1815 Congress of Vienna, extolling the conservative balance-of-power techniques Austria's Prince Metternich had used to curb revolution.

Reflective, witty, seldom rattled, energetic, persistent, and vain, "Henry the Navigator" became one of the most traveled diplomats in American history. He reveled in personal diplomacy, in the give-and-take, the head-to-head contest, the battle of words, the manipulation of power and people. His "devilish nimbleness" and evident rapport with people of different cultures brought him negotiating successes.[34] As the nation's unrivaled diplomatic leader in the 1969–1977 period, Kissinger managed an impressive number of roles: theorist, policymaker, negotiator, presidential adviser, bureaucratic infighter, and public spokesperson. He and Nixon agreed early that they would make policy in the White House, often sidestepping the State Department and other parts of the foreign-affairs bureaucracy. Kissinger used private, secret "back channels" to communicate with foreign governments, thereby creating a serious problem of morale in the Foreign Service. William P. Rogers served as a loyal secretary of state until 1973, but Nixon granted him little authority. Also resenting its exclusion from policymaking, Congress reasserted its prerogatives by passing, over Nixon's veto, the War Powers Resolution (1973): The president could commit American troops abroad for no more than sixty days, and after that period he had to obtain congressional approval. Congress also vexed Kissinger by cutting foreign aid to Turkey, Cambodia, South Vietnam, and Angola. Without Watergate and without congressional interference, Kissinger lamented, he could have accomplished so much more. He nonetheless shared with North Vietnamese negotiator Le Duc Tho the Nobel Peace Prize in 1973.

Despite the intragovernmental tussles and complaints against his "one-man authoritarianism," Kissinger remained a popular figure.[35] He charmed journalists and leaked secret information to them to generate favorable newspaper stories. He amused detractors and well-wishers alike. To an admirer who said, "Dr. Kissinger, I want to thank you for saving the world," the secretary replied, "You're welcome."[36] Kissinger also cultivated a "swinger" image until his 1974 marriage. He visited nightclubs arm-in-arm with attractive women, including movie star Jill St. John. "I've always acted alone," he told an interviewer. "Americans admire the cowboy leading the caravan alone astride his horse. . . . This romantic, surprising character suits me." [37] Soviet ambassador Anatoly Dobrynin found Kissinger "intelligent and erudite" but "prone . . . to brag of his influence."[38] Foreign Minister

"Some Chicken, Some Egg."
Henry A. Kissinger (b.1923) received his doctorate in 1954 from Harvard, where he taught until Nixon appointed him national security affairs adviser in 1969. An architect of détente, Kissinger also undertook extensive travel to trouble spots such as the Middle East and Africa to conduct personal negotiations. Critics on the left compared him to "Dr. Strangelove," the slightly deranged fictional character in the movie by that name who perpetrated a nuclear holocaust. Critics on the right thought Kissinger too conciliatory to the communists. (*The Economist,* London, 1975)

Andrei Gromyko dubbed him "*kisa*" (pussycat) but thought him "slippery as a snake."[39]

Kissinger's critics rarely underestimated him. They questioned the secrecy that surrounded foreign relations. When academicians, business executives, and lawyers, many of whom frequented the Council on Foreign Relations or wrote for its prestigious journal *Foreign Affairs,* became disenchanted, Kissinger exploded: "What the hell is an Establishment for, if it's not to support the President?"[40] Critics argued that Kissinger followed the ruthless maxim that the ends justify the means: He wiretapped aides and journalists because unauthorized leaks were breaking his seal of secrecy; he defended the president in the lowest days of Watergate; He relied recklessly on huge arms sales; he sponsored CIA plots abroad that held America up to ridicule for advocating democracy but undermining it; and he approved the deadly bombing of the peoples of Southeast Asia. When critics questioned him for first aiding and then abandoning the Kurds of Iraq, contributing to the deaths of thousands of them, Kissinger coldly replied that "one must not confuse the intelligence business with missionary work."[41] U.S. Ambassador Hermann F. Eilts admired Kissinger as a "conceptualizer," but conceded that "Henry is a master of half the story, of half the truth."[42]

Kissinger and Nixon prided themselves on being pragmatists rather than ideologues. "[Woodrow] Wilson had the greatest vision of America's world role," the president once remarked. "But he wasn't practical enough."[43] Kissinger sought to purge "sentimentality" from American foreign relations.[44] The term that most generally described the thrust of the Nixon-Kissinger diplomacy was "détente": limited cooperation with the Soviet Union and the People's Republic of China within a general environment of rivalry. Détente became a means, a process, a climate in which to reduce international tensions and sustain U.S. leadership in world politics. Détente was supposed to produce a geopolitical balance of power, or "equilibrium," by containing the Soviet Union and China and curbing radical revolution.[45] To Nixon and Kissinger, the world divided into roughly five power centers: Russia, America, China, Japan, and the Common Market nations of Western Europe. Under détente, each great center had the responsibility to keep order among smaller states and clients in its region and to refrain from intervening in another's sphere. Because the "five great economic superpowers will determine the economic future," Nixon explained, "and, because economic power will be the key to other kinds of power, [they will determine] the future of the world."[46]

The Nixon-Kissinger team, like those before it, saw Soviet-American competition as the primary element in world affairs. But the Nixon administration recognized 1970s realities and sought to exploit them to U.S. advantage. It understood that by 1970 the Soviet Union had achieved nuclear parity or equality with the United States, that the Soviets suffered severe internal economic problems and needed outside help, that the Sino-Soviet split had widened, and that world power (capital and weaponry) had become diffused as nations had recovered from World War II and colonies had broken away from empires. These conditions placed limits on American activity, but they also provided opportunities to shape new relationships. Nixon and Kissinger moved the United States from containment through confrontation to containment through negotiation.

Détente, SALT, and the Nuclear-Arms Race

The Nixon administration emphasized the triangular relationship formed by Soviet Union, China, and the United States—that is, it attempted to play the two communist states off against one another, to keep one worrying about what the United States was doing with the other; thus the two could contain one another. For the Soviets there would be both incentives (such as capital and trade) to encourage restraint, and penalties (such as large arms sales to Soviet adversaries or closer ties to China) to punish unacceptable behavior. Washington officials believed, moreover, that they could moderate the Soviets. "The bear would be treated like one of [the psychologist] B. F. Skinner's pigeons," one scholar wrote. "There would be incentives for good behavior, rewards if such behavior occurred, and punishments if not."[47]

The new approach to the major communist countries made sense to European allies who abhorred the U.S. "obsession with Southeast Asia."[48] Moscow and Beijing might help the United States extricate itself from war in Vietnam. The Cold War was also costing too much; détente supposedly offered a cheaper way of pursuing the containment doctrine by reducing the necessity for interventions, spiraling military expenditures, and new nuclear weapons systems. The Nixon administration reduced the armed forces from 3.5 million in 1968 to 2.3 million in 1973, ended the draft, and in 1972 negotiated a strategic arms limitation treaty (see page 439). At a time when U.S. foreign trade needed a boost to eliminate a billion-dollar deficit in the balance of payments, détente conjured up images of expanded markets. Massive grain shipments flowed to the Soviet Union—in 1972, 25 percent of the American wheat crop—and corporations such as Pepsi-Cola and Chase Manhattan Bank started operations in the USSR. American exports to Russia reached $2.3 billion in 1976. Businesses also revived the great China market dream.

Nixon-Kissinger grand strategy rested on some questionable assumptions. It overestimated the usefulness of China as a check on Moscow. It assumed wrongly that the Soviets could manage their "friends" in North Vietnam or India or the Middle East and that great-power cooperation could calm Third World problems. Still viewing small states as proxies of the great powers, the Nixon administration paid too little attention to the local sources of disputes and the fierce independence of nationalist and neutralist governments. Kissinger spent much of his time trying to keep détente glued together against the backdrop of violent conflicts in Asia, Africa, and the Middle East, and economic challenges from the Organization of Petroleum Exporting Countries (OPEC). Even America's friends caused difficulty: Iran insisted on huge arms shipments but raised oil prices, threatening the U.S. economy; Saudi Arabia demanded sophisticated weaponry but refused to help resolve the Arab-Israeli conflict.

Détente also ran afoul of domestic dissenters. In 1974 conservatives and liberals in Congress joined in what a disapproving Kissinger called "a rare convergence, like an eclipse of the sun" to deny most-favored-nation trade status to the Soviet Union until it permitted Jewish emigration.[49] Americans of Eastern European descent berated détente as sellout—an abandonment of their homelands to Soviet domination. Liberals criticized Kissinger's arrogant presumption of superpower domination and his tolerance of authoritarian regimes that trampled on human rights. Not only did morality seem absent; the Nixon and Ford administrations also seemed to contradict themselves. For example, they appealed for arms control while they broke records for arms sales abroad ($10 billion in 1976 alone). Hard-line anticommunists labeled Kissinger an appeaser who conceded the communists too much and who squandered U.S. supremacy in the international system. By 1976 the secretary of state had concluded that "the principal danger we face is our own domestic divisions."[50]

The Nixon administration nonetheless claimed diplomatic triumphs. The opening to China ranked highest. Although Nixon exaggerated the effects of Sino-American rapprochement, the turnaround helped thwart reconciliation between the two communist giants. It tied down several Soviet military divisions in Asia—away from NATO. It spawned new ties between Japan and China that contributed to Asian stability. And it nurtured a promising trading partnership. In 1973 large companies such as Boeing, Radio Corporation of America, and Monsanto Chemical signed contracts with the Chinese. Sino-American trade began to climb, reaching $700 million in 1973. Also, cultural exchanges and travel between the once-distant nations reduced mutual ignorance. In 1973 Washington and Beijing

Beijing Ball Park. This American magazine advertisement, titled "Yankees come here," appeared after Nixon's trip. It read: "The way things are going in China, hot dogs will be sold right along with egg rolls." Mao, of course, never donned a baseball uniform nor blasted a home run over the Great Wall, but Sino-American détente inspired exaggerations like this. (Lucy Gould, *Parade*. Courtesy of Frankfurt Communications, Inc., New York)

exchanged "Liaison Offices" or miniembassies. Formal diplomatic relations would wait until 1979, after Watergate, Nixon's resignation, the 1976 presidential election, the deaths of Mao and Zhou, and new political alignments within China.

The improvement in Sino-American relations did have some tragic side effects. In 1971 the Bengalis of East Pakistan rebelled against the military dictatorship of West Pakistan and declared the independent nation of Bangladesh. The Pakistani government attempted to crush the revolution and carried out a slaughter that U.S. officials at the scene called genocide. India, which had just signed a treaty of friendship with the Soviet Union, intervened in the civil war on behalf of the rebels. The White House, against considerable State Department objection, ordered a "tilt" in favor of Pakistan.[51] As an ally, Pakistan had granted the United States bases for U-2 flights over the Soviet Union and intelligence-gathering posts to monitor Soviet nuclear testing. American weapons soon flowed to Pakistan, foreign aid to India stopped, and a naval task force steamed into the Bay of Bengal without specific orders. "We can't allow a friend of ours and China's [Pakistan] to get screwed in a conflict with a friend of Russia's [India]," Kissinger fumed.[52] Indeed, the White House took a global rather than regional view of the crisis and saw India acting as Moscow's surrogate. But India never attacked an expectant West Pakistan, and the Soviet Union never encouraged it to attack. The Indian navy received orders: "If you encounter U.S. Navy ships, invite their captains aboard for a drink."[53] Pakistan, India, China, and the Soviet Union—*before* Kissinger's "stress on the need for a confrontation with the Soviet Union," his "histrionic signals," and his "acrobatics"—all had indicated support for an agreement that matched the outcome: an end to hostilities and independence for Bangladesh.[54]

Although Washington and Moscow swapped blunt words over the hot line during the Indo-Pakistani conflict, détente remained U.S. policy. The president and his national security affairs adviser traveled to the Soviet capital in May 1972 for a productive summit meeting. "My reputation is one of being a very hard-line, cold-war-oriented, anti-communist," Nixon told President Leonid Brezhnev, but he now believed that capitalism and communism could "live together and work together."[55] They struck agreements on cooperation in space exploration (culminating in a joint space venture in 1975) and trade (large grain sales soon followed). The leaders also discussed Vietnam and concluded that small nations should not disrupt détente. Only a few weeks earlier, when Nixon had escalated the bombing of North Vietnam, he feared that an angry Moscow might cancel the summit. The Soviets did not; to them détente came first.

The summit conferees concentrated on the Strategic Arms Limitation Talks (SALT) agreements. When the Nixon administration entered office, it inherited a legacy of doctrines and missiles that defined U.S. nuclear strategy. (See glossary, p.438.) In the 1960s, the doctrine of "massive retaliation" evolved into the concept of "mutual assured destruction," or MAD. MAD's viability depended on each side's "second-strike capability": the capacity to absorb a first strike and still destroy the attacker with a retaliatory or second strike. By 1969 American strategists sought a superiority of forces through the triad: land-based intercontinental ballistic missiles (ICBMs), long-range B-52 bombers, and submarine-launched ballistic missiles (SLBMs), all armed with nuclear weapons. To help guarantee superiority, the United States had also begun to flight-test the "multiple independently targetable reentry vehicle" (MIRV). Finally, President Nixon inherited initial planning for an "antiballistic missile" (ABM) system to defend cities and ICBMs vulnerable to Soviet attack. Because ABMs theoretically (their efficiency was questionable) protected offensive weapons from attack, critics feared that the ABM would stimulate the Soviets to build more missiles to overwhelm the ABM protection, thus further accelerating the nuclear-arms race.

By 1968 the United States had deployed 1,054 ICBMs to the Soviets' 858; the United States also led in SLBMs, 656 to 121, and in long-range bombers 545 to 155. The United States ranked first in total nuclear warheads, about 4,200 to 1,100, and in the accuracy of its weapons systems. Yet American officials knew that the Soviets were constructing new missiles, submarines, and bombers at a faster pace. In a few years these new weapons would give the Soviets nuclear parity with the United States. The two great nuclear powers had become "fencers on a tightrope: each facing the other, weapon in hand, balancing precariously; neither willing to

The Nuclear-Arms Race: A Glossary

Antiballistic missile (ABM):   A defensive missile designed to destroy an incoming enemy ballistic missile before its warhead reaches its target.

Ballistic missile: A rocket-propelled missile that leaves the atmosphere and returns to earth in a free fall.

Cruise missile: A guided missile that flies to its target within the earth's atmosphere, close to the surface. The cruise missile can carry a nuclear warhead and can be launched from the air, land, or sea.

Delivery vehicle: A missile or strategic bomber that delivers a warhead to its target.

Deployment: Installing weapons, making them ready for action.

First strike: An initial nuclear attack by one country intended to destroy an adversary's strategic nuclear forces.

Intercontinental ballistic missile (ICBM):   A land-based missile capable of traveling more than 3,000 nautical miles to deliver one or more warheads.

Intermediate-range nuclear forces (INF):   Sometimes called theater nuclear forces, these weapons have a range of about 3,000 miles.

Missile experimental (MX):   An American ICBM capable of carrying as many as ten MIRVs.

Multiple independently targetable reentry vehicle (MIRV):   A vehicle loaded with a warhead and mounted, along with similar vehicles, on one ballistic missile. Once separated from the missile, each MIRV can be directed against a different target.

Mutual assured destruction (MAD):   The ability of both the United States and the Soviet Union to inflict damage so severe that neither is willing to initiate a nuclear attack.

Neutron bomb: An "enhanced radiation weapon," this nuclear bomb is designed primarily to kill people and to inflict less damage on buildings than other bombs.

Nuclear freeze: The immediate halt to the development, production, transfer, and deploy ment of nuclear weapons.

Second strike: A retaliatory nuclear attack launched after being hit by an opponent's first strike.

Strategic Defense Initiative (SDI):   Popularly known as "Star Wars," SDI was President Ronald Reagan's 1983 proposal to build a space-based, defensive system that could establish a protective shield over the United States and its allies with the capability to shoot down incoming ballistic missiles.

Strategic weapon or arms: A long-range weapon capable of hitting an adversary's territory. ICBMs, SLBMs, and strategic bombers are so classified.

Submarine-launched ballistic missile (SLBM):   A ballistic missile carried in and launched from a submarine.

Surface-to-air missile (SAM):   A missile launched from the earth's surface for the purpose of knocking down an adversary's airplanes.

Tactical nuclear weapons: Short-to medium-range, low-yield nuclear weapons for battlefield use.

Triad: The three-part structure of American strategic forces (ICBMs, SLBMs, and strategic bombers).

Warhead: That part of a missile which contains the nuclear explosive intended to inflict damage.

drop his weapon and give way to the other; each fearing to thrust decisively because such a thrust would topple them both, attacker and victim, to mutual disaster."[56]

President Nixon soon abandoned the untenable doctrine of superiority and accepted "sufficiency," or parity of forces with the Soviet Union.[57] Still, he decided to phase in the ABM system. Nixon also ordered the installations of MIRVs. Thus the United States could enter the SALT talks, he said, from a position of strength.

The first SALT talks began in Helsinki in November 1969, and alternated between that city and Vienna until 1972. SALT-I culminated on May 26, 1972 at the Moscow summit with the signing of two agreements. The first, a treaty, limited the deployment of ABMs for each nation to two sites only. In essence the accord sustained the MAD doctrine, because it left urban centers in both countries vulnerable. The other accord, an interim agreement on strategic offensive arms, froze the existing number of ICBMs already deployed or in construction. At the time, the Soviet Union led 1607 to 1054. The interim agreements also froze SLBMs at 740 for the USSR and 656 for the United States, although the two nations could raise these numbers to 950 and 710 respectively if they dismantled one ICBM for every SLBM added. SALT-I did not limit the hydra-headed MIRVs, thus leaving the United States superior in deliverable warheads, 5,700 to 2,500. Nixon and Kissinger underestimated the speed with which the Soviets would deploy their own MIRVs on heavier missiles, and by not seeking a ban on MIRVs, rendered American ICBMs theoretically vulnerable to a first strike. Kissinger later wished that he "had thought through the implications of a MIRVed world more thoughtfully."[58] Nor did the agreement restrict long-range bombers, in which the United States ranked first with some 450, compared to about 200 for the Soviets. Finally, SALT-I did not prohibit the development of new weapons. The United States, for example, moved ahead on the Trident submarine (to replace the Polaris-Poseidon fleet), the B-1 bomber (to replace the B-52), and the cruise missile (a highly accurate, low-flying guided missile). Indeed, as Kissinger remarked: "The way to use this freeze is for us to catch up."[59]

Still, SALT-I marked an unprecedented step in advancing frank strategic arms talks and in placing limits on specified nuclear weapons. In August 1972, the Senate passed the ABM treaty by an 88 to 2 vote; a joint congressional resolution later endorsed the interim agreement. Détente's reputation soared. Conservative critics charged, however, that even though the American arsenal contained many more nuclear warheads than did the Soviets', the United States still lagged behind the Soviet Union in delivery vehicles (ICBMs, SLBMs, and strategic bombers). "What in the name of God is strategic superiority?" Kissinger challenged his critics. "What do you do with it?"[60]

Negotiations on SALT-II opened in late 1972, but progress came slowly. At Vladivostok, in November 1974, Presidents Ford and Brezhnev initialed a set of principles to guide the talks. They agreed, first, to place a ceiling of 2,400 on the total number of delivery vehicles permitted each side. They agreed, second, that each side could equip no more than 1,320 missiles with MIRVs. Critics who thought the United States was dodging real arms control complained that the numerical ceilings actually projected higher levels than either side had reached. "Using the Vladivostok agreement to slow the arms race," one analyst has written, "is analogous to attempting to dam a wide stream by dropping one large rock in its middle."[61]

After 1974 the SALT-II talks bogged down over which types of weapons should be included in the 2,400 ceiling. The United States insisted that the new Soviet bomber, the Backfire, be included, and the Soviets demanded inclusion of the U.S. cruise missile. Each side thought the other sought superiority. Neither Moscow nor Washington yielded before 1977, the year the SALT-I agreements expired. By then the United States wielded 8,500 warheads, compared with 5,700 in 1972; comparable Soviet figures equaled 4,000 and 2,500. Total strategic delivery vehicles by January 1978 numbered 2,059 for the United States and 2,440 for the Soviet Union. Détente had not checked the nuclear-arms race.

In Europe, however, détente worked to ease tensions. Willy Brandt, the West German chancellor, pursued a policy of *Ostpolitik* to remove the two Germanies from great-power competition. A West German–Soviet treaty of August 1970 identified détente as the goal of both countries and recognized the existence of two Germanies. A few months later Brandt signed an agreement with Poland that con-

The Last Washington Painting.   Alan Sonneman's painting reflected the alarm that some Americans felt over the ever-expanding nuclear-arms race. The Department of Defense reported that, in a massive nuclear exchange, as many as 165 million Americans and 100 million Soviet citizens would be killed. (Courtesy of Alan Sonneman, © 1979–1980)

firmed the latter's postwar absorption of German territory to the Oder-Neisse line. Then, in June 1972, the four powers occupying Berlin signed an agreement wherein Russia guaranteed Western access to the city and relaxed restrictions on travel between the two Berlins. Finally, in December 1972, the two Germanies themselves initialed a treaty that provided for the exchange of diplomatic representatives and membership in the United Nations for both (effected in 1973). European East-West trade boomed, with the West German economy the chief beneficiary. "European countries look upon us as suckers," said Republican senator Charles Percy, because of "restrictions by the U.S. government on our doing business with Eastern European countries."[62]

At the Conference on Security and Cooperation in Helsinki, Finland, in summer 1975, thirty-five nations, including Canada, the United States, and all of Europe (save Albania), assembled in what some observers called the peace conference that officially ended World War II. That is, the delegates accepted the permanence of existing European boundaries, including adjustments made in Germany and Eastern Europe three decades earlier. The conferees pledged themselves to détente and endorsed human rights for all Europeans. Although many Americans greeted the last accord with skepticism, dozens of "Helsinki groups" sprang up to press communist governments to honor the pledges about human rights. Such groups included Charter 77, headed by Václav Havel in Czechoslovakia, and Solidarity, led by Lech Walesa in Poland. Instead of the "consolidation of the postwar order that Moscow had so long desired," a Kissinger aide later noted, "the political status quo in Eastern Europe began to unravel."[63] In the short run, however, the Kremlin arrested Soviet intellectuals who demanded freedom of speech. When the dissident writer Aleksandr Solzhenitsyn, whose *Gulag Archipelago* (1974) described and condemned Soviet oppression, asked to visit the White House, President Ford turned down the expatriate because he did not want to jeopardize progress toward SALT-II.

ARAB-ISRAELI WAR AND THE MIDEAST ARMS RACE

The Nixon Doctrine, announced in July 1969, declared that henceforth the United States would supply military and economic assistance but not soldiers to help nations defend themselves. "We must avoid that kind of policy that will make countries in Asia so dependent upon us that we are dragged into conflicts such as the one that we have in Vietnam."[64] Washington sought to build up regional surrogate powers, such as Iran and Israel, thus apparently retiring its badge as the world's policeman. Not quite. Third World countries held a place in the Nixon-Kissinger scheme for equilibrium because of their vulnerability to destabilizing radicalism and hence to pernicious Soviet influence. Kissinger cited Moscow's endorsement of national liberation movements to argue, therefore, that the internal politics of developing nations intertwined with the "international struggle."[65] When troubles arose

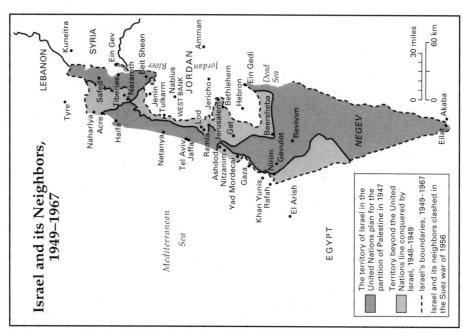

Israel and its Neighbors, 1949–1967

Legend:
- The territory of Israel in the United Nations plan for the partition of Palestine in 1947
- Territory beyond the United Nations line conquered by Israel, 1948–1949
- --- Israel's boundaries, 1949–1967
- Israel and its neighbors clashed in the Suez war of 1956

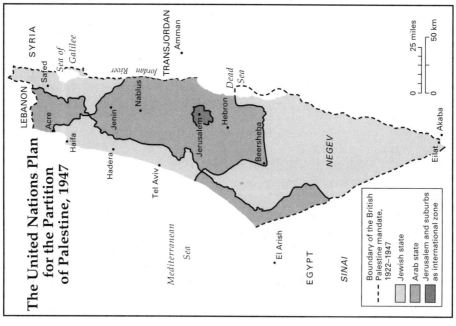

The United Nations Plan for the Partition of Palestine, 1947

Legend:
- --- Boundary of the British Palestine mandate, 1922–1947
- Jewish state
- Arab state
- Jerusalem and suburbs as international zone

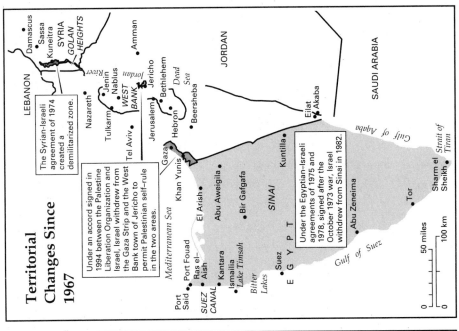

Territorial Changes Since 1967

The Syrian-Israeli agreement of 1974 created a demilitarized zone.

Under an accord signed in 1994 between the Palestine Liberation Organization and Israel, Israel withdrew from the Gaza Strip and the West Bank town of Jericho to permit Palestinian self-rule in the two areas.

Under the Egyptian-Israeli agreements of 1975 and 1978, signed after the October 1973 war, Israel withdrew from Sinai in 1982.

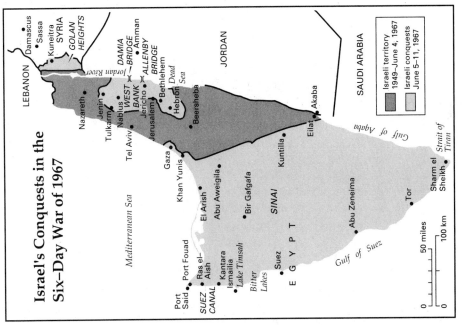

Israel's Conquests in the Six–Day War of 1967

Israeli territory 1949–June 4, 1967

Israeli conquests June 5–11, 1967

in the Third World, Nixon, Ford, and Kissinger reflexively interpreted them as moves in the game of great-power politics.

Problems in the Middle East sorely tested détente. Basic American goals since World War II had been consistent for the region: ensure oil supplies; contain the Soviet Union; protect Israel; challenge neutralism; and blunt the appeal of Arab nationalism. After the 1956 Suez crisis (see Chapter 8), the Soviet Union and the United States armed Egypt and Israel respectively. In June 1967, after years of growing friction and months of threats and counterthreats, Israel attacked Egypt and Syria. In the Six-Day War, the Israelis, using American-supplied weapons, scored a devastating victory by capturing the West Bank, including the ancient city of Jerusalem, from Jordan, the Golan Heights from Syria, and the entire Sinai Peninsula, including the eastern bank of the Suez Canal, from Egypt (see maps on pp. 442–443). Half of the Arab states broke diplomatic relations with Washington. Soviet vessels obtained access to Arab ports. With pressure from the pro-Israeli lobby, the United States sold fifty F-4 Phantom jets to Israel in December 1968.

The Middle East, said Nixon, had become a "powder keg."[66] His administration worried that the persistent Arab-Israeli conflict would open a Soviet avenue into the Middle East. In the spirit of détente, Washington and Moscow began talks on the Middle East that proved futile. Egypt insisted on Israeli withdrawal from occupied territory; Israel, nonetheless, steadfastly refused to "be sacrificed by any power or interpower policy and will reject any attempt to impose a forced solution on her."[67] As American Phantom jets began to arrive in Israel, as Washington wrestled with a new Israeli request for many more aircraft and tanks, and as the Israelis conducted bombing raids deep into Egypt in January 1970, the Soviets began their own military escalation. In spring 1970 the Soviets shipped surface-to-air missiles (SAMs) to Egypt to defend against the Phantoms. Thousands of Soviet troops, advisers, and pilots answered Egypt's call for assistance. Washington gave Israel more F-4s and electronic equipment to improve Israeli accuracy. U.S. military credits for Israel totaled $1.2 billion, 1971–1973.

Meanwhile, Palestinian Arabs, many of them refugees ousted from their homes in 1948 when Israel won nationhood, grew more frustrated. The Palestine Liberation Organizaion (PLO), formed in 1964 by several guerrilla groups, came under the aggressive leadership of Yasir Arafat four years later. Many Arab leaders backed the organization in its demand for the elimination of the Jewish state and for the creation of a Palestinian homeland. In 1970 a radical wing of the PLO hijacked airliners and temporarily seized passengers, including Americans, as hostages. That same year, PLO troops with Syrian help battled King Hussein's armies in Jordan. Palestinian terrorists murdered Israeli athletes at the 1972 Olympic Games in Munich. The Israelis retaliated, assassinating PLO figures abroad.

Soviet relations with the PLO and Egypt grew frosty in the early 1970s, as Moscow tried to restrain both of them out of fear that Washington would scuttle détente if Mideast tensions continued. For its part, the Nixon administration, from 1970 to 1973, followed a "standstill diplomacy."[68] Israel possessed military superiority, Moscow displayed restraint, and a new, seemingly more moderate Egyptian government under the leadership of Anwar el-Sadat came to power after Nasser's death in September 1970. Under pressure from radical Egyptians to win back the

Sinai, Sadat plotted a new war against Israel. He withstood a Soviet-supported coup d'état attempt, and in summer 1972 he abruptly expelled several thousand Soviet technicians and military advisers. The United States continued to arm Israel; in early 1973 Washington promised more airplane deliveries. On October 6, 1973 (Yom Kippur, the holiest day on the Jewish calendar), Egyptian forces struck across the canal into Sinai, while Syrian troops attacked Israel's northern border. The attack took Israel and the United States by surprise. At first the Israelis suffered heavy losses and the Arabs regained land lost in 1967. Tel Aviv pressed Washington for stepped-up military aid. Nixon promised more Phantoms. "We will not let Israel go down the tubes," he vowed.[69] Moscow hurried military equipment to Syria.

In the midst of the crisis, the shadow of Watergate lengthened over the Nixon administration. On October 10, Vice President Spiro Agnew resigned after evidence surfaced that he had accepted payoffs as governor of Maryland years before. Ten days later Nixon fired the special Watergate prosecutor for getting too close to damaging evidence. The concatenation of domestic and foreign crises frayed nerves. The White House staff feared that Moscow might think the U.S. government weak or incapacitated.

On October 13, Nixon ordered a massive airlift of military matériel to Israel, an operation that some in the Pentagon looked on "in much the way the three bears regarded Goldilocks."[70] Soviet premier Aleksei Kosygin flew to Cairo to persuade Sadat to accept a cease-fire. Suspicious, Kissinger expedited delivery of more American equipment to Israel than the USSR could match. Kissinger himself flew to Moscow on October 20, learning en route that the Saudis had embargoed oil to the United States. By October 21 most Arab members of the Organization of Petroleum Exporting Countries had joined the embargo. Kissinger and the Soviets finally arranged a cease-fire on October 22. But the Israelis ignored the truce and surrounded the Egyptian Third Army. When Moscow angrily threatened inter-

Golda Meir (1898–1978), Nixon, and Kissinger. In early 1973, the prime minister of Israel met with the president, who promised more U.S. airplanes. (Department of State *Newsletter*)

vention, Kissinger, noting that "two can play chicken," ostentatiously ordered all U.S. forces on nuclear alert, a calculated ploy to gain "the attention of Soviet decision-makers because it was several times more alarming than their own action."[71] The Soviets did not intervene, and Kissinger pressed the Israelis to honor the truce. A new cease-fire held.

The Arab-Israeli contest threatened the American economy as well as the economies of U.S. allies. Arab states such as Saudi Arabia, which for three decades had supplied Western nations with inexpensive petroleum, now used their black riches as a weapon: They embargoed petroleum shipments to the United States and quadrupled the price of crude oil for Western Europe and Japan. "We are masters of our own commodity," the Saudi oil minister announced.[72] The United States, importing between 10 and 15 percent of its oil from the Middle East, suffered an energy crisis. Gasoline prices at the pumps spun upward and anxious drivers lined up, sometimes for hours, hoping to fuel their automobiles. The embargo ended in March 1974, but prices remained high and America's vulnerability had been exposed.

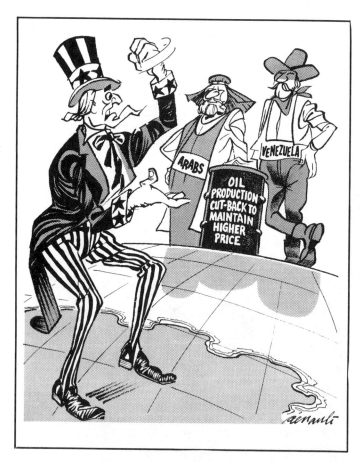

"You're Like a Bunch of . . . of . . . of . . . CAPITALISTS!!"   The oil embargo by the OPEC nations in 1974 produced anger among Americans who found that gasoline stations ran out of fuel or that what they could buy had drastically risen in price. Venezuela and the Arab nations replied that they were only doing what the developed nations had done to them for decades. (Dennis Renault, *Sacramento Bee*)

Kissinger launched "shuttle diplomacy" to prevent another Mideast blowup. With impressive stamina and patience, he bargained in Cairo and Tel Aviv and other capitals intermittently for two years. "I hear [Saudi Arabia's king] is anti-Jewish. I'm Jewish. Tell me, how do I deal with him," Kissinger asked the U.S. diplomat Hermann F. Eilts. "Just let Feisal talk, talk, talk," the Arabist replied.[73] Eilts soon became ambassador to Egypt, where he developed trust with Sadat, who in turn trusted Kissinger. "Dr. Henry, you are my favorite magician," said Sadat.[74] At one point, in March 1974, Kissinger thought he had failed because of Israeli intransigence. "It's tragic to see people dooming themselves to a course of unbelievable peril," he told top Israeli officials.[75] Yet, finally, on September 1, 1975, Egypt and Israel initialed an historic agreement that provided for an eventual Israeli pullback from part of the Sinai, created a United Nations–patrolled buffer zone, and placed U.S. technicians in "early warning" stations to detect military activities. Washington also promised substantial foreign aid to both Egypt and Israel.

Thorny problems remained. The Palestinian Arabs still lived in refugee camps and demanded a homeland, while Israelis entrenched themselves in occupied territories, building industries, farms, and houses. Jordan still demanded the return of the West Bank, and Syrian-Israeli hostility persisted with the Golan Heights in Israel's hands. A bloody civil war broke out in Lebanon, which prompted Syria to send in troops in 1976. Washington continued to ship weapons to both the Arabs and Israelis after the October war, and Sadat warned that military conflict could erupt again. Egypt's economy remained unstable, fanning political unrest. In March 1976, Sadat, who needed American technology and mediation, denounced the Soviet Union, saying that "99 percent of the cards in the game are in America's hands whether the Soviet Union likes it or not."[76] Once Cairo turned emphatically toward the United States, American policy in the Middle East looked more like old-fashioned containment than détente. Critics surmised that Kissinger's failure to include the Soviets (and the Palestinians) in Middle Eastern diplomacy blocked a full Arab-Israeli settlement. Moscow reacted ominously by backing Libya's President Moammar Gadhafi, a radical anti-American, pan-Arabist who came to power in 1969 and denounced all peace efforts.

As a counterweight to the Soviets and radical Arabs in the Middle East, the Nixon and Ford administrations fashioned a closer alliance with the Shah of Iran. Nixon and Kissinger visited Teheran in 1972 and promised the Shah all the non-nuclear weapons he wanted and U.S. technicians to help Iranians operate the sophisticated hardware. "I am the army," said the Shah, as his military gorged itself on huge amounts of modern American arms, paid for by galloping oil revenues ("petro-dollars").[77] American corporate executives rushed to Iran to display their submarines, fighter aircraft, assault helicopters, and missiles. In 1977 his nation ranked as the largest foreign buyer of American-made arms, spending $5.7 billion that year alone. For 1973–1978 the bill totaled $19 billion. His armed forces became the most powerful in the region. But doubters in the shahdom thought such excessive military spending foolhardy when the Iranian per capita income stood at only $350 and such funds could help alleviate the nation's economic woes. Also, the Shah's CIA-trained secret service jailed or killed critics with a ruthlessness that drew protest from many Americans. To improve his image in the United States, the Shah hired a New York advertising agency and lavishly bestowed gifts on prominent Americans. Official Washington regarded Iran as a pillar of stability in the turbulent Middle East and the Shah as "an unconditional ally," but critics argued that the huge infusion of weapons further fueled a dangerous regional arms race.[78]

COVERT ACTION AGAINST RADICALS IN LATIN AMERICA AND AFRICA

Compared with the Middle East, Latin America seemed quiet and manageable. Thousands of Latin American military officers still trained in the United States, some at the Inter-American Defense College in Washington, D.C., where they learned urban counterinsurgency and jungle warfare techniques. U.S. trade with the Western Hemisphere remained large. In the early 1970s about one-third of Latin American exports went to the United States and about two-fifths of the region's imports came from the United States. In 1976, Latin American countries supplied 34 percent of the United States' petroleum imports, 68 percent of its coffee, 57 percent of its sugar, 47 percent of its copper, and 98 percent of its bauxite. In that year U.S. direct investments in its southern neighbors totaled some $17 billion. Despite these strong ties, Latin American governments increasingly flung challenges at Washington. Soon after taking office, Nixon sent Governor Nelson Rockefeller on a fact-finding mission to Latin America. Demonstrations erupted and parts of his trip had to be canceled. The governor reported to the president in August 1969 that the United States caused deep resentment through its "paternalistic attitude" and attempts to "direct the internal affairs of other nations to an unseemly degree."[79]

Mexico refused to honor the economic blockade of Cuba, strongly criticized the 1965 Dominican intervention, and, in its 1972 Charter of Economic Rights and Duties of Nations, boldly proclaimed the economic independence of small states and their right to expropriate foreign enterprises. The charter further urged that developed nations share their wealth with poorer countries. In 1974 the United Nations approved the charter by a 120 to 6 vote, with the United States voting "no." The United States also engaged Peru and Ecuador in a "tuna war," after those nations declared a 200-mile territorial limit and began seizing American fishing vessels in coastal waters. After 1968, a new, radical (noncommunist) military government in Peru deliberately set out to break the country's economic dependence on the United States by nationalizing an Exxon oil subsidiary and other American-owned properties. Lima also defiantly purchased Soviet MIGs. Venezuela also searched for ways to reduce its economic reliance on the United States. A founding member of OPEC in 1960, Caracas joined the Arabs in drastically raising petroleum prices in the 1970s, and in 1976 it too nationalized American-owned oil companies.

Although Kissinger once dismissed Chile as "a dagger pointed at the heart of Antarctica," that South American nation attracted his rapt attention as a threat to U.S. hegemony in September 1970.[80] That month Chileans elected as their president Salvador Allende, an unabashed Marxist, a physician by profession, and a founder of Chile's Socialist party. The CIA had sent hundreds of thousands of dollars in bribe and propaganda money to Chile to thwart his electoral victory. The CIA also cooperated with the International Telephone and Telegraph Company's covert effort to back a right-wing candidate. "I don't see why we have to let a country go Marxist just because its people are irresponsible," Kissinger said at the time.[81] Having failed to prevent Allende's election, Nixon ordered the CIA to stimulate a military coup before the Chilean Congress confirmed Allende's triumph. When that tactic also failed, the CIA initiated an elaborate project to undermine the Allende government. Following presidential advice to "make the economy scream" in Chile in order to unsettle Allende's policies, which included the nationalization of American-owned copper corporations (Kennecott and Anaconda), the CIA worked with U.S. companies to block credit and the shipment of spare parts.[82] Washington cut off economic aid and denied Export-Import Bank loans to Chile. Military assistance continued as the CIA conspired with Chilean army officers and also spent $6 million to subsidize newspapers and political parties opposed to Allende. Allende criticized U.S. pressure—"an always oblique attack, covert, sinuous, but nonetheless harmful for Chile."[83]

In 1973 a military junta overthrew Allende. In the chaos, military officers murdered him, or he committed suicide. Most scholarly accounts and a Senate intelligence committee report conclude that U.S. complicity stopped short of direct participation in the coup. "U.S. authorities did not create the factors" that overthrew the government, Allende's foreign minister has written, "but rather increased and intensified the impact of those factors."[84] Most Americans remember Allende's ouster from watching the 1982 film *Missing*, starring Jack Lemmon and Sissy Spacek, a taut thriller in which Chilean authorities kill an American journalist fin-

Frank Church (1924–1984). Graduate of Stanford University and Democratic senator from Idaho (1957–1981), Church became a major figure on the Foreign Relations Committee, serving as its chair, 1979–1981. A critic of the Vietnam War and a great orator, Church also headed a special Senate committee that revealed U.S. complicity in the overthrow of Chile's elected president Salvador Allende. (Frank Church Collection, Boise State University Library)

gered by the U.S. Embassy because he detected U.S. machinations. Although Ambassador Nathaniel Davis subsequently refuted the main thesis of the film, it still reinforced the culpability many Americans felt about meddling in the internal politics of a sovereign state and about the many Chileans who lost their lives under the junta's iron-fisted tyranny. The new government returned companies to private hands, suspended freedom of speech and press, jailed dissenters, and gained notoriety for torturing and killing political opponents.

The Nixon and Ford administrations also sought to keep Cuba isolated. Under Fidel Castro, Cuba had become a communist state and close Soviet ally. "There'll be no change toward that bastard while I'm President," snapped Nixon.[85] In fall of 1970, after the election of Allende, a friend of Castro's, Nixon concluded from sketchy U-2 evidence that the Soviets were building a nuclear submarine base at Cienfuegos, Cuba, in violation of their understanding after the 1962 missile crisis to refrain from placing offensive weapons on the island (see Chapter 9). The president and Kissinger decided "to face the Soviets down."[86] Moscow assured Washington that the Soviets were not building a naval facility. The crisis quickly passed, but the Nixon administration claimed a victory that "reaffirmed," "clarified," and "amplified" the 1962 understanding by prohibiting Soviet nuclear submarine facilities in Cuba.[87] In mid-1971, swine fever swept Cuba, causing health authorities to slaughter half a million pigs to prevent further spread of the disease. Although Cubans suspected sabotage of a major food source, not until 1977 did U.S. investigative journalists reveal that the CIA and an exile group had introduced the deadly virus into Cuba—another CIA dirty trick. Still seeking some accommodation with North America in the early 1970s, Castro deemphasized the export of revolution and aid to insurgencies, and in 1973 he signed an antihijacking treaty with the United States to discourage terrorism on the airways. Two years later the Organization of American States lifted its economic blockade of Cuba. During 1974–1975, U.S. officals met secretly with Cuban diplomats to explore possibilities for détente. But these positive steps ended when Cuban troops in Africa helped Angolan radicals come to power.

Until the mid-1970s, Africa stood low on the Nixon-Ford-Kissinger list of diplomatic priorities. Administration policy sought to expand U.S. material interests, strengthen ties with white minority regimes in Portuguese Angola, Rhodesia, and South Africa, and yet encourage progress toward racial harmony. The National Security Council explained in a memorandum (NSSM 39) that "the whites are here to stay and the only way that constructive change can come about is through them."[88] Washington calculated that the black majorities feared white military superiority and would therefore refrain from major violent confrontation. In February 1970, Nixon told Kissinger, then preparing a presidential message to Congress on foreign policy, to "make sure there's something in it for the jigs, Henry."[89] This crude, condescending remark about black Africans reflected the attitude underlying U.S. policy. Washington relaxed the arms embargo to white South Africa; Congress in 1971 passed the Byrd Amendment permitting the United States to buy chromium from Rhodesia despite a United Nations–declared economic boycott of Ian Smith's white minority government. Although the chair of the Congressional Black Caucus resigned from the U.S. delegation to the United Nations because of the "stifling hypocrisy" of Nixon's policy toward Africa, CIA director Richard

Helms claimed "they [black Africans] need us."[90] Americans pointed to the more than $2 billion invested in black Africa and to U.S. purchases of cobalt, oil, manganese, and platinum.

Events in Angola eventually shattered American complacency and forced a shift in policy. Since the early 1960s, black rebel groups had battled the Portuguese in Angola. Playing a double game in that decade, the CIA channeled funds to a faction of freedom fighters while Washington officially backed Portugal and sold it military equipment to quell the nationalist rebellion. The Soviets began to support one of the guerrilla groups, the Popular Movement for the Liberation of Angola (MPLA). As Portugal floundered in 1974–1975, the independence movement gained momentum. Kissinger decided that the outcome in Angola held global implications, that America had to thwart Soviet expansionism by confronting the MPLA. In 1975 the CIA spent $32 million on covert operations for propaganda, arms, communications gear, the hiring of white mercenaries, and payments to anti-MPLA political figures. The State Department official in charge of African affairs, Nathaniel Davis, vigorously argued that a commitment of American prestige and resources would not succeed because the United States simply could not control the revolution or local events in Africa. It would merely stimulate increased Soviet activity. Davis urged that the United States appeal to African leaders in Tanzania and Zambia to negotiate a diplomatic solution. For "a test of strength with the Soviets," he advised Kissinger, "we should find a more advantageous place."[91] When President Ford nevertheless decided on covert intervention, Davis resigned.

Gerald R. Ford (b. 1913). In October 1973, after Spiro Agnew pleaded no contest to charges of income-tax evasion and acceptance of bribes, and resigned, Ford assumed the office of vice president. A longtime conservative member of Congress from Michigan, Ford aroused controversy when, as president, he pardoned Richard M. Nixon. Ford tried to maintain a U. S. presence in Vietnam and Angola, but Congress rejected funding. (The White House)

In November 1975, Portugal granted independence to Angola. The insurgent factions then fought one another in a civil war, with the American clients doing poorly despite support from the United States and China. South Africa and Zaire also dispatched troops to support an American-backed group. The Soviets and Cubans substantially increased their aid to the MPLA in late 1975, flying advisers and troops into Angola. In fall 1975, Davis's resignation and leaks about the secret intervention stirred Congress. Another Vietnam? Actually, the select representatives and senators had been briefed earlier in the year and had acquiesced in the covert operations. But doubts multiplied after the escalation of warfare, major foreign intervention, and the steady gains of the MPLA. The administration prepared to spend another $25 million for arms. "That's when Congress pulled the plug," President Ford later wrote.[92] In December the Senate voted to stop military expenditures for action in Angola; the House followed suit in January 1976. Kissinger upbraided Congress for missing a strategic opportunity to confront the Soviets.

Opponents replied that the United States should never have viewed an African civil war through a Cold War, ideological prism. The MPLA, after all, did not molest American oil companies, and it never ranked as a Soviet puppet. Given the MPLA's success, the United States hurt itself by choosing the losing side. Discussions with the MPLA—preventive diplomacy—might have reduced the violence. "You may be right in African terms, but I'm thinking globally," Kissinger retorted.[93] That kind of thinking, replied one African specialist, "betrays an obsessional self-defeating preoccupation with superpower global antics reminiscent of the grimmest days of the cold war."[94] When in early 1976 the MPLA won the civil war, the Ford administration denounced the Soviets and stopped using the word *détente*.

The Angolan experience prompted reconsideration of U.S. policy toward Africa. So did the outbreak of racial violence in South Africa, where the white government in 1976 crushed a black rebellion in the township of Soweto. America's desire for bountiful Nigerian oil also recommended a change of course. The United States, reasoned Kissinger, faced isolation from the continent, with black radicals, Soviets, and Cubans denying Americans economic links and naval facilities. The United States must do something to "avoid a race war," to contain foreign intervention, and to "prevent the radicalization of Africa," Kissinger belatedly concluded.[95] Arms shipments went to Kenya and Zaire. Economic ties were strengthened through investments by companies such as Bethlehem Steel and Kaiser Aluminum, in pursuit of titanium and bauxite, respectively. The secretary of state began to disengage the United States from white regimes in Rhodesia and South Africa, urging the latter to abandon its segregationist policy of *apartheid*. Such changes could not disguise the fact that Africa had become an expanded arena for the Cold War adversaries.

ECONOMIC COMPETITION, ENVIRONMENTAL DISTRESS, AND THE NORTH-SOUTH DEBATE

"History has shown that international political stability requires international economic stability," Kissinger said in 1975.[96] He had cause for worry, because the 1970s marked a disturbing watershed in the history of the world economy. The international economic order created in the wake of World War II foundered. The Bretton Woods monetary mechanism (see pages 240–241) faltered; the dollar skidded; famines starved millions of people at a time when grain stocks fell to record postwar lows; dwindling natural resources spawned political tensions; and the former colonies of the Third World challenged the industrial nations to share decision-making power. Crisis after crisis jolted the international system. The worldwide recession of the early 1970s became the worst since the 1930s. Inflation raised the cost of industrial goods for developing countries. Dramatically climbing OPEC oil prices hit poor and rich nations alike, while the price of some other commodities, like copper, slumped, causing economic downturns in nations dependent upon the export of one product. Economists coined the term "Fourth World"—poor, less developed countries (LDCs) that lacked profitmaking raw materials, relied heavily on imports of food, and built up large debts owed to governments and private banks. Nations began raising protectionist barriers, further impeding world trade.

The Soviet Union and the People's Republic of China engaged in world trade as never before, in quest of agricultural products and high technology, and enlarged East-West trade became a headline issue. So did the questions of how to avoid a fierce race among nations to exploit the mineral riches on the ocean's floor and how

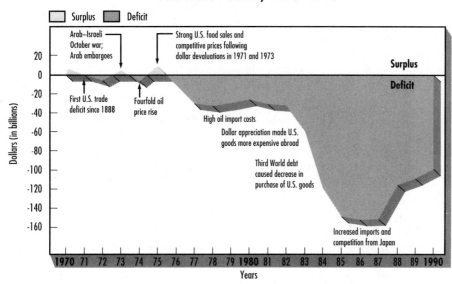

U.S. Trade Balance, 1970–1990

☐ Surplus ☐ Deficit

Arab–Israeli October war; Arab embargoes

Strong U.S. food sales and competitive prices following dollar devaluations in 1971 and 1973

Surplus

Deficit

First U.S. trade deficit since 1888

Fourfold oil price rise

High oil import costs

Dollar appreciation made U.S. goods more expensive abroad

Third World debt caused decrease in purchase of U.S. goods

Increased imports and competition from Japan

Dollars (in billions)

20 0 -20 -40 -60 -80 -100 -120 -140 -160

1970 71 72 73 74 75 76 77 78 79 1980 81 82 83 84 85 86 87 88 89 1990

Years

Source: U.S. Department of State

"America's prosperity," Kissinger noted, "could not continue in a chaotic world economy."[97] The United States produced about one-third of all the world's goods and services. It remained the world's largest trading nation. In 1970 U.S. exports stood at $27.5 billion; by 1977 they had climbed to $121.2 billion. Large firms such as Coca-Cola, Gillette, and IBM earned over half of their profits abroad. Many American jobs depended on a healthy foreign trade. In 1976, for example, one out of every nine manufacturing workers produced goods for export. Exports accounted for one out of every four dollars of agricultural sales in 1977.

American industry also relied on imports of raw materials: 75 percent of the tin, 91 percent of the chrome, 99 percent of the manganese, and 64 percent of the zinc consumed by Americans in 1975 came from foreign sources. In 1977 the nation imported more than 40 percent of the petroleum it used. These import needs had become conspicuous in 1971 when, for the first time since the depression decade of the 1930s, the United States suffered a trade deficit, importing more than it exported (see chart). Six years later, the trade imbalance reached $26.5 billion, due in large part to imported energy sources.

American direct investments abroad—about half of the world's total of foreign direct investments—equaled $75.5 billion in 1970 and $149.8 billion in 1977, thus further defining the United States as a pivot of the international economy. The greatest part of these investments remained in developed countries (73 percent in 1975). These investments faced political unrest, terrorist acts, and nationalization.

Overall in the world economy, the United States seemed to be losing its competitive edge, and foreigners had less confidence in the once-vaunted American ability to sustain a global economic order. In the 1970s, ninety-eight nations had higher rates of economic growth than the United States. Japan and West Germany, strategic allies but commerical rivals, challenged America in the international marketplace. In fact, Japanese automobiles, televisions, and electronic equipment seized a large share of markets within the United States. Once dominant, American producers of computers, high technology, and aerospace machinery now struggled to retain high rank. Then, too, Americans became alarmed when it appeared that wealthy Arabs were buying up American banks, companies, and real estate.

The descent of the once mighty dollar further demonstrated the declining U.S. position. A "dollar glut" developed abroad, induced by U.S. foreign-aid programs, military expenditures ($90 billion in 1970 alone), private investments, inflation, and purchases of higher-priced oil. Foreigners held $78 billion in 1969; by 1977 the figure had jumped to $373 billion. Foreign holders of dollars wanted to exchange them for gold, thus putting pressure on America's diminishing gold stock. "We're broke, anyone can topple us," bemoaned one Nixon adviser about the diminishing gold supply.[98] The dollar declined in value against such currencies as the German mark and Swiss franc. The United States faced a serious balance-of-payments crisis.

In its first two years, the Nixon administration paid scant attention to economic foreign relations. Then, when the president finally acted, he turned to unilateral policies that shocked foreign capitals and upset the Bretton Woods system of cooperation. In August 1971, after the dollar had fallen to its lowest point against the mark since World War II, he announced that the United States was devaluing the dollar (by increasing the dollar price of an ounce of gold) and suspending it's convertibility into gold. The president also cut foreign aid by 10 percent, and imposed a 10 percent surtax on all imports, seeking thereby to reduce the influx of Japanese and European goods and to put diplomatic pressure on other nations to revalue their currencies to make them less competitive with the dollar. The new Treasury secretary, John Connally, asserted that "all foreigners are out to screw us and it's our job to screw them first."[99] Kissinger later called this "declaration of economic war on the other industrial democracies" an example of "brutal unilateralism."[100]

In December, representatives of ten leading trading nations gathered at the Smithsonian Institution in Washington to try to stabilize the international monetary system. After stormy sessions, America's economic competitors agreed to revalue their currencies to bring them more into line with the dollar. The United States then lifted its import surcharge and once more made the dollar exchangeable for gold. But the Smithsonian agreement did not work for long; in early 1973 the United States again devalued the dollar. The United States also withdrew the dollar from a fixed rate system and let it "float," its value determined no longer by agreement but by supply and demand in the monetary marketplace. Efforts by the International Monetary Fund to restore an orderly system fell short.

America's international money problems intersected with foreign trade problems. Not only were American goods priced too high to compete with Japanese or

European products, but also the European Economic Community (Common Market) engaged in preferential trade arrangements and export subsidies that hurt American sales abroad. Japan remained highly protectionist at home, yet its products penetrated worldwide markets. In reaction, protectionists in Congress, wanting to limit imports of textiles, steel, and shoes, introduced a bill in 1970 to impose import quotas and thus reverse America's liberal trade policy. This bill never came to a vote, but it denoted the attraction of protectionism, as did the 1971 10 percent surcharge on imports. Nixon himself sent a strong signal to Tokyo that year when he threatened quotas on textile imports. The Japanese agreed voluntarily to limit their textile exports to the United States, averting a trade war.

From 1967, when the Trade Expansion Act of 1962 expired, to 1975, when a new trade act became law, the president had no authority to conclude trade agreements. Nonetheless, multilateral trade negotiations, under the auspices of the long-working General Agreement on Tariffs and Trade (1947), began in Tokyo in 1974. Five years later the "Tokyo Round" of negotiations finally produced accords, largely liberal in character. Overall, tariffs were reduced about 30 percent. The signatories, including the United States, also wrote codes to regulate other practices such as subsidies and dumping. Yet they failed to liberalize trade in agriculture. Many protectionist practices continued, prompting the chief American negotiator in 1980 to remark that "the free flow of world trade remains largely an ideal."[101]

Economic relations with Third World nations also grew troubled. Kissinger warned: "The division of the planet between rich and poor could become as grim as the darkest days of the Cold War."[102] In 1972, although the developing world

The Rich and Poor Countries: A Comparison, 1960 and 1972 (percentages)

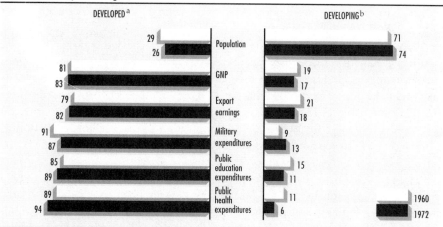

Source: Roger D. Hansen and the staff of the Overseas Development Council, *The U.S. and World Development: Agenda for Action, 1976* (New York: Praeger Publishers, Inc., 1976), p. A-9. Based on Ruth Leger Sivard, *World Military and Social Expenditures, 1974*, published under the auspices of the Institute for World Order (New York), pp. 6 and 17; export figures from *International Trade, 1973-74* (Geneva: General Agreement on Tariffs and Trade, 1974), Publication Sales No. GATT/1974-4, Table E.

[a] Includes North America, USSR, most European countries, Oceania, Israel, Japan, and South Africa.
[b] Includes Latin America, a few southern European countries, Asia (except Israel and Japan), and Africa (except South Africa).

had 74 percent of the world's population, it represented only 17 percent of the world's combined gross national product (GNP). In 1976, GNP per capita stood at $6,414 in the industrialized world, but only at $538 in the developing nations (excluding the oil-rich countries). From the perspective of the developing nations (the "South"), it seemed imperative that wealthier industrial nations (the "North") reduce their profits by charging less for manufactured goods and technology, offer foreign assistance and loans at low rates, reduce tariff barriers, pay more for imported raw materials through commodity price agreements, and refrain from interference when Third World nations nationalized or restricted foreign-owned corporations. Developing countries also insisted on a greater voice in international institutions such as the World Bank. Behind these economic demands lay political purpose: Economic improvement would supposedly decrease dependency on foreigners, enhance political autonomy and neutralism, and redress the balance of international power. "The object is to complete the liberation of the Third World countries from external domination" by changing the "structure of power," explained Tanzania's Julius K. Nyerere.[103]

The Group of 77, a coalition of developing nations organized in 1964, articulated the Third World's economic demands. Numbering more than one hundred countries by the 1970s, this consortium used the United Nations as a forum. They dominated the General Assembly, and in 1974 that body endorsed a New International Economic Order encompassing their goals. The United States, Japan, and Western European nations agreed to talk, and struck some compromises, but by the early 1980s a stalemate existed. U.S. officials did not take kindly to charges of American self-interest when many Third World nations themselves indulged in corruption, imposed tyrannies on their people, and wasted their precious national resources on weaponry. India, fearing Chinese and Pakistani nuclear capabilities, allotted billions to produce a nuclear bomb in 1974 instead of devoting those funds to fertilizers and agricultural research to overcome severe food shortages. The ruthless regime of Idi Amin ordered the murder of thousands in Uganda. Third World leaders, critics argued, should put their own house in order before demanding that rich nations share their wealth.

Global leaders also made little headway toward alleviating food shortages. Insufficient fertilizer, inadequate farm acreage, environmental pollution, droughts, and shrinking fish supplies due to overharvesting condemned one-quarter of humankind to hunger. The drought that swept Africa in the early 1970s caused at least 10,000 deaths a day. A high birth rate and falling death rate put severe pressure on available food supplies. In 1975 the world population passed 4 billion. Nutritionists estimated that between a half billion and one billion people ate less than the number of calories required to sustain ordinary physical activity.

At the 1974 World Food Conference in Rome, the United States voted to help finance an International Fund for Agricultural Development to expand food production in developing countries. But the United States continued to market surplus food for profit, most notably in large grain sales to the dollar-paying Soviet Union. And food aid, always political, became more so; in 1973–1974 more than half of American food assistance went to clients South Vietnam, Cambodia, and South

Korea. At the same time, because of the OPEC oil embargo and rising petroleum costs, the United States reduced its exports of petroleum-derived fertilizers, thus contributing to a deficiency of fertilizer in the developing world. The shortage meant 15 million fewer tons of grain produced worldwide in 1974. As the CIA noted, "in bad years . . . Washington would acquire virtual life-and-death power over the fate of the multitudes of the needy."[104] The 1970s ranked as bad years.

U.S. foreign-aid strategy in the early 1970s aimed to assist especially the most impoverished people through projects to improve nutrition, family planning, health, and education, and the production of food. But developing nations complained that the United States was cutting back when the need was greatest.

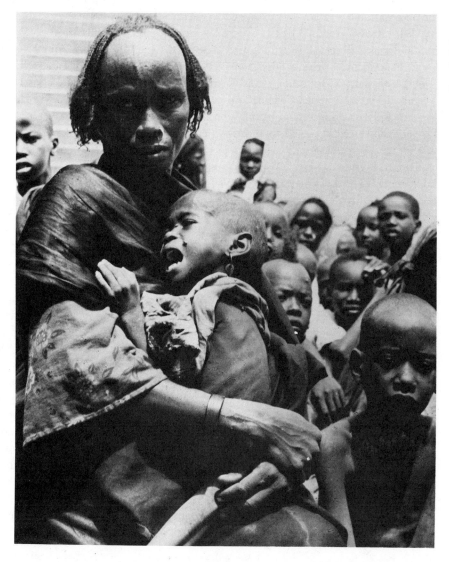

Famine in Chad, Africa. Drought-stricken Chad was only one of many poor nations that suffered in the world hunger crisis of the 1970s. Millions died. (CARE, New York)

Although total foreign aid (economic and military) had increased from $6.6 billion in 1970 to $7.8 billion in 1977, the proportion of the U.S. GNP devoted to development assistance actually decreased. Because of fast-paced inflation, moreover, the aid dollars bought less. In 1977 Americans spent about four times as much on tobacco products as their government expended on development aid. Kissinger attempted to meet some of the South's demands; he nonetheless reflected a growing American impatience with the "confrontational" manner in which the developing nations pressed their case and their assumption that growth was "a quick fix requiring only that the world's wealth be properly redistributed through tests of strength instead of a process of self-help over generations."[105] American popular support for foreign aid began to erode.

North-South relations also became contentious over environmental changes that carried the potential of destabilizing governments and redistributing power in the international system. "The threats to security," the Worldwatch Institute's Lester R. Brown wrote, "may now arise less from the relationship of nation to nation and more from the relationship of man to nature."[106] In the United States, books like Rachel Carson's *Silent Spring* (1962), Paul Erlich's *The Population Bomb* (1968), and Barry Commoner's *The Closing Circle* (1971) raised public consciousness about environmental degradation and the growing imbalance between food supplies and burgeoning populations, and they spurred a grassroots movement. In 1969 Greenpeace organized to protest nuclear-weapons tests, and the following year Americans celebrated the first Earth Day. Although hostile to environmental regulation, President Nixon bowed to congressional pressure and helped create the Environmental Protection Agency (EPA). Oil spills from oceangoing tankers, unsafe disposal of hazardous wastes, and the contamination of precious water sources revealed environmental questions as borderless, transnational issues requiring international attention. As environmental groups around the world pressed for action, countervoices challenged the doomsday forecasts and "eco-hysterics" of "econuts."[107]

Swedish scientists and diplomats alarmed by increasing air pollution and the resultant acid rain championed an international conference. In June 1972 the United Nations sponsored the Conference on the Human Environment. The Soviet Union and most of its Eastern European clients boycotted the meeting in Stockholm, but 113 nations, 19 intergovernmental organizations (IGOs), and 400 nongovernmental organizations (NGOs) attended. North-South differences surfaced. Third World nations feared that measures to protect the environment would slow their economic development. Might not they be told to remain "green areas so that the constructed areas could continue to develop without being disturbed?" asked the Brazilian foreign minister.[108] Might not poor countries have to suspend use of pesticides, which they depended on for agricultural production? The South demanded compensation for the losses they expected to suffer under stricter environmental controls. The South also asked for the North's commitment to additional foreign-assistance funds earmarked for environmental projects. Developed nations in turn worried that Third World industrialization would overwhelm the biosphere.

Although long disparaging of both the Third World and the United Nations, President Nixon endorsed the global conference, pledged U.S. monies to the new environmental fund, supported a global monitoring system, and joined the popular call for a ten-year moratorium on commercial whaling. But the administration balked at calls for more financial assistance to Third World countries and resented delegates' complaints that the United States had battered the natural environment in Indochina. Less developed nations voted for principles that insisted on a link between development and environmental progress, but the United States held the purse strings, and conference resolutions did not bind any states that opposed them. Still, the global conference effectively stimulated national environmental policies, set up Earthwatch to survey environmental conditions, and spotlighted the problem of transboundary pollution.

Water covers 70 percent of the earth's surface. Disputes over navigation and fishing rights had divided nations for generations, but in the 1960s a new question became urgent: Who owned the rights to the gas, petroleum, and minerals such as manganese and nickel that rested in the deep seabed? Offshore oil drilling was well advanced, but the exploitation of the ocean's mineral riches was just beginning. American companies like Kennecott Copper and United States Steel began to invest large sums in new technology to explore the ocean floor. From the perspective of developing nations, the seabed resources belonged to all nations as a "common heritage of mankind."[109] The United States endorsed this general principle in 1970, but at the United Nations–sponsored Law of the Sea Conference, which opened in 1973 and continued into the early 1980s, American officials rejected the South's call for a powerful international seabed agency with exclusive rights over the mining of ocean resources. Because the new authority would operate on a one-nation, one-vote basis, the United States and other industrial nations would become the minority and lose their competitive advantage. Washington insisted on the right of private commercial exploitation, with no limits on profits or access to sites. But in 1976–1977 the United States compromised, now recommending a dual system: private development and an international authority, the latter to be assigned exclusive exploitation of certain mining sites. Until such an agreement, Kissinger insisted, the United States would explore and mine on its own.

The South and North also debated restrictions on multinational corporations, the South seeking tighter controls and a larger proportion of the giant companies' profits earned from operations in developing nations. Ten of the top twelve multinationals in the mid-1970s were American, including General Motors, Exxon, and Ford Motor. As economic powers, they ranked higher than most of the world's nations. They sometimes intervened in the politics of other nations or bribed foreign leaders to gain contracts. Investigations revealed that Lockheed Aircraft and Exxon, among others, spent millions to bribe overseas politicians—a practice Congress tried to halt through the 1977 Foreign Corrupt Practices Act. The multinationals' economic decisions—where to locate a plant, for example—held real importance for developing nations that welcomed multinational investments but resented outside control. The South also protested that the multinationals employed too few "locals" in high positions and exploited natural resources without adequate compensation. The multinationals, some charged, had become global mini-empires, beyond the reach of national laws. Business executives and U.S. officials replied that multinational enterprises brought benefits to developing nations in higher wages, tax revenues, and technology transfers. Whether beneficial or detrimental, multinational corporations by the early 1970s had become major actors in the international system. Washington balked at restraining them because they brought profits home, but the South vowed to restrict them—one of the many economic issues that challenged the Nixon-Kissinger quest for "equilibrium."

VIETNAMIZATION, CAMBODIA, AND A WIDER WAR

"What we are doing now with China is so great, so historic, the word 'Vietnam' will be only a footnote when it is written in history," Kissinger declared in 1971.[110] With superpower relations paramount in Nixon-Kissinger foreign relations, Vietnam became, in the words of a senior White House official, simply a "cruel side show."[111] Cruel, but no side show. America's longest war continued to claim central attention until 1975. The Nixon administration constantly worried that the persistent war could damage the president at home and spoil détente. At the same time, the administration hoped that through détente, the United States might enlist Moscow and Beijing to press North Vietnam into concessions at the on-again, off-again Paris peace talks. "I'm not going to end up like LBJ," Nixon early assured his advisers. "I'm going to stop that war. Fast."[112] But under what terms would the United States withdraw and still achieve a "peace with honor?" to quote Nixon's refrain. During the 1968 presidential campaign Nixon stated that he had a plan for ending the war. He avoided details and recalled that President Eisenhower had brought the Korean War to a close shortly after taking office. Nixon also mentioned that Ike had threatened the use of nuclear weapons. But, like Ike in 1952, Nixon had no plans in 1968.

At the outset, Nixon weighed his options. He could simply pull out of the war, "lock, stock and barrel," as Senate majority leader Mike Mansfield advised.[113] Nixon vetoed that suggestion. He would not sacrifice an ally. Nixon vowed to end the war but not lose it. He allowed to aides that his purpose was not to defeat North Vietnam but "to avoid [the] defeat of America."[114] Nixon's strategy had several components. First, Washington capitalized on détente, trying to persuade China and the Soviet Union, suppliers of the Vietnamese communists, to force Hanoi to compromise. Second, the United States itself, through military escalation, signaled Ho Chi Minh that Nixon intended to punish the enemy harshly where Johnson had not. North Vietnam had to have a breaking point. Third, Nixon exploited his "madman" image to keep Hanoi wondering if he might order an atomic attack on the North Vietnamese capital. Fourth, the president sought to strengthen South Vietnam through huge infusions of foreign aid and the training of a larger South Vietnamese army (ARVN). This "Vietnamization" dovetailed with the emphasis of the Nixon Doctrine on self-help. It meant, Ambassador Bunker said, "changing the color of the bodies."[115] And last, to pacify the American people while he negotiated an acceptable peace, Nixon gradually withdrew U.S. troops from Vietnam and issued tough-tongued speeches to counteract the doves. In the cynical belief that most antiwar protesters simply feared "getting their asses shot off," he cut back draft calls, announced a draft lottery in May 1969, removed the controversial General Lewis B. Hershey Selective Service head, and promised to end the draft soon.[116]

The multifaceted scheme did not work. Ho Chi Minh and the Vietcong leaders did not bow to foreign wishes, no matter whether from Washington, Moscow, or Beijing, and the Soviet Union and China continued to supply their ally. Having outlasted the Japanese and the French, Ho's legions had no intention of surrendering to the Americans, seemingly in retreat after Tet. As for Nixon's attempts to quiet dissent at home, every new escalation swelled the ranks of the critics and finally prompted Congress to limit the president's ability to enlarge the war. By summer 1971, according to one survey, only 31 percent of the American people approved Nixon's Vietnam policies. Nor did Vietnamization convert South Vietnam into a powerful military state. Although U.S. ships, planes, helicopters, rifles, and millions of dollars poured in, the detrimental effects outweighed the positive. South Vietnam became dependent on U.S. aid to keep its gorged army in the field, thus undermining the ultimate objective of helping South Vietnam stand on its own feet. America's aid sustained the notoriously corrupt regime of General Nguyen Van Thieu, a government bloated with self-serving officials and a top-heavy bureaucracy—"a network of cliques held together by American subsidies," unpopular and ultimately incapable of conducting a winning effort.[117] Finally, Vietnamization diminished *American* military effectiveness. "Why get killed now?" a U.S. marine recalled. "If the shit hit the fan . . . you didn't have that 'let's go out and find them' attitude anymore."[118]

In early 1969 the Paris peace negotiations stalled over the basic issues of troop withdrawals (Nixon wanted North Vietnam's forces to pull out of the South) and the survival of the Thieu government. The communists continued to advance on the ground in Vietnam. The National Security Council prepared a new war plan, codenamed DUCK HOOK, calling for massive bombing of Haiphong and Hanoi, destruction of the dike system, mining of harbors and rivers, possible invasion of North Vietnam, and optional use of tactical nuclear weapons. Nixon decided instead to bomb communist sanctuaries in Cambodia—but secretly so that neither Congress nor the American people knew about it. Codenamed MENU, the secret bombing of Cambodia began in March 1969 with punishing B-52 sorties. But leaks soon brought the story into the newspapers. A self-proclaimed "paranoiac . . . with regard to secrecy," Nixon ordered the FBI to wiretap several journalists and thirteen government officials in a futile attempt to catch the leakers.[119]

As Vietnamization proceeded, Nixon grew impatient with the enemy for insisting on complete victory. Kissinger, in August 1969, began a series of secret meetings with North Vietnamese representatives that lasted into 1973. In the first encounter in Paris, Kissinger warned North Vietnam to change its rigid stance or face grave consequences. Meanwhile, American soldiers were coming home, so that by the end of 1971 the troop level had dropped to 139,000. Protest against the war continued nonetheless. On October 15, 1969, a quarter of a million people peacefully marched in Washington, calling for a moratorium on the war. "Don't get rattled—don't waver—don't react," Nixon told himself.[120] The president asked the "great silent majority of my fellow Americans" to help him "win the peace," and he urged Vice President Spiro Agnew to attack the news media.[121]

Events in Cambodia actually prompted the Nixon administration to expand the war. In March 1970, a pro-American general, Lon Nol, overthrew the neutralist government of Prince Norodom Sihanouk. Nixon saw new opportunities: Aid Lon Nol against the Khmer Rouge (Cambodian communists) and the North Vietnamese, who used Cambodian territory for supplies and as a staging area to attack South Vietnam; step up the attack on the North Vietnamese in Cambodia, already targets of American bombing raids; send unmistakable signals to Hanoi that it had better relent; and show his critics "who's tough."[122] Despite considerable opposition from the State and Defense departments, the president ordered U.S. troops to invade Cambodia in late April. "You have to electrify people with bold decisions," Nixon asserted.[123]

A cascade of protest rolled across America. Antiwar demonstrations rocked college campuses. As Nixon belittled the protesters, inexperienced National Guard troops shot and killed four students at Kent State University in Ohio. Two students at all-black Jackson State College in Mississippi died when state police without

"We Demand: Strike!"
The U.S. thrust into Cambodia in 1970 prompted a new wave of protests, including a demand from the radical Boston paper *Old Mole* that students go on strike. Many universities temporarily suspended classes to discuss the costly war. In some cases, radical campus groups trashed buildings and police and troops occupied college grounds. (*Old Mole,* 1970, University of Connecticut Library)

warning sprayed a women's dormitory with automatic-weapons fire. Within the administration, three Kissinger aides, including Anthony Lake, resigned in protest against the thrust into Cambodia. More than one hundred Foreign Service Officers also resigned. In June the Senate terminated the Tonkin Gulf Resolution of 1964 and passed the Cooper-Church Amendment cutting off funds for military operations in Cambodia. Although the House failed to pass this measure, Nixon reacted by lengthening his enemies list. A "siege mentality" gripped the White House.[124]

Nixon declared the Cambodian operation a complete success. Communist arms, equipment, and food had been captured and hundreds of enemy troops killed. Although Americans did not find or destroy the headquarters that Nixon cited as a major objective, the invasion probably slowed the communist momentum and bought time for Vietnamization. But the bold venture also widened the war, caused the sanctuaries to spread out, and further bloodied Cambodia. North Vietnam substantially increased its aid to the Khmer Rouge insurgents, who gained new recruits radicalized by the American invasion. Lon Nol became another besieged Asian leader dependent on U.S. assistance. South Vietnamese units, which entered Cambodia with American troops, stayed there to sustain Lon Nol's army after the Americans withdrew on June 30, thus stretching South Vietnam's resources to another front.

North Vietnam and the Vietcong answered the sally into Cambodia by boycotting the Paris peace negotiations. The war dragged on. Nixon refused to alter course. In November 1970 he launched an unsuccessful raid on the Sontay prisoner-of-war camp in North Vietnam, despite his fear that antiwar protesters "will probably knock down the gates and I'll have a thousand incoherent hippies urinating on the Oval Office rug."[125] He ordered "protective reaction strikes" against North Vietnam after American reconnaissance planes were shot down. In early 1971, Nixon approved a South Vietnamese invasion of Laos, where North Vietnamese forces met the invaders head-on in some of the fiercest fighting of the war. After heavy losses on both sides, ARVN forces beat a hasty retreat.

At home the wider war wrought more turmoil. After a court-martial in March 1971 found First Lieutenant William Calley guilty of murdering unresisting children, women, and old men at My Lai in 1968 (see page 414), Nixon had Calley placed under house arrest only before he received the sentence of life imprisonment. (Calley won parole in November 1974). The uproar over Nixon's display of moral obtuseness in the Calley case had hardly subsided when, in June 1971, the *New York Times* began to print the *Pentagon Papers,* a long, secret Defense Department history of U.S. intervention in Vietnam, complete with classified documents. Leaked by a former Pentagon official, Daniel Ellsberg, the papers fortified critics in their argument that American presidents consistently had tried to win a military victory and had frequently withheld facts from the American public. More and more Americans believed their highest officials had lied and that the United States should never have become involved in Southeast Asia in the first place. "This will totally destroy American credibility forever," groaned Kissinger.[126] After the Supreme Court refused to halt publication of the *Pentagon Papers,* Nixon set up a "plumbers" group to stop leaks and to find ways to discredit Ellsberg. Watergate soon followed.

The year 1972 brought the presidential trip to China and SALT-I—and even greater escalation of the war in Vietnam. In Paris, Kissinger continued to meet intermittently in secret with North Vietnamese representatives, always rejecting the communist demand that the United States abandon Thieu. The North Vietnamese claimed that Thieu would rig any postwar election, as he had rigged the one that elected him president in 1972. When the talks again faltered, North Vietnam sent its own message to Washington in March of that year by way of a surprise onslaught that struck deep into South Vietnam and threw the Saigon government into disarray. Soon American B-52 bombers pummeled fuel depots around Hanoi and Haiphong, where four Soviet merchant ships were sunk by accident. Kissinger warned the Soviets that détente was threatened unless the communist offensive ceased. "Why are you turning against *us* when it is Hanoi that has challenged you?" asked Ambassador Anatoly Dobrynin.[127] In May the president announced the mining of Haiphong harbor, a naval blockade of the North, and more massive bombing raids code-named LINEBACKER-I. "The bastards have never been bombed like they're going to be bombed this time," he growled.[128] During the seven months of LINEBACKER-I, American aircraft flew 41,653 sorties and dropped some 155,000 tons of bombs on North Vietnamese storage facilities, air bases, power plants, bridges, tunnels, and by mistake, hospitals. "They used planes worth millions to attack a bamboo pontoon bridge!" General Vo Nguyen Giap recalled.[129] Supplies to the South slowed but did not stop.

THE PEACE AGREEMENT, WITHDRAWAL, AND DEFEAT

In early October 1972, Kissinger and the North Vietnamese negotiator Le Duc Tho finally reached an agreement that provided for U.S. withdrawal sixty days after a cease-fire, the return of American prisoners of war, and a political arrangement in the South that ultimately included elections. In short, both sides made concessions—North Vietnam gave up its demand that Thieu resign, and the United States dropped its insistence that North Vietnamese troops pull out of the South. When Kissinger traveled to Saigon, however, Thieu balked. "I wanted to punch Kissinger in the mouth," the South Vietnamese president recalled.[130] Resentful at not having been consulted and opposed to continuation of North Vietnamese troops in the South, Thieu refused to sign. When Kissinger bemoaned "the greatest failure of my diplomatic career," Thieu asked: "Are you rushing to get the Nobel Prize?"[131] Fearing that Thieu might propagandize a sellout to the communists just a few days before the presidential election in the United States, Nixon sent Kissinger back to the negotiating table. The communists, suspecting trickery, published the agreement that they had crafted with Kissinger. And they made new demands. Still, on October 31, Kissinger told the press "peace is at hand."[132] Not so.

Back in Paris, on November 20, Kissinger and Le Duc Tho resumed their meetings. In early December, after heated exchanges, they reached terms very much like those Thieu and Nixon had torpedoed in October. But a final agreement faltered over the status of the Demilitarized Zone (DMZ). Kissinger suspected the communists of stalling, perhaps counting on an unconditional military victory. So he broke off the talks. "Tawdry, filthy shits," Kissinger said of his adversaries.[133]

The carrot for Saigon (more arms), the stick for Hanoi. Nixon ordered the bombing of North Vietnam above the 20th parallel. "I don't want any more of this crap about the fact that we couldn't hit this target or that one," he told the Joint Chiefs.[134] From December 18 to 20, LINEBACKER-II planes pounded North Vietnam hour-upon-hour in saturation bombing that one Kissinger aide called "calculated barbarism."[135] Everything from factories to water supplies took hits in the so-called "Christmas bombing." Fifty-foot bomb craters gaped in Hanoi and Haiphong. North Vietnam's largest hospital was destroyed in error—"by bombs escaping the normal bomb train."[136] At least 2,000 civilians perished. Swedish prime minister Olof Palme (a graduate of Kenyon College) cited such atrocities as "Guernica, Oradour, Katyn, Lidice, Sharpville, Treblinka. Now there is another name to add to the list—Hanoi, Christmas 1972."[137] Kissinger angrily pointed out that Sweden had remained neutral in World War II.

On December 22 Washington informed Hanoi that the bombing would stop if the North Vietnamese would reopen negotiations. The talks resumed, and on January 27, 1973, Kissinger and Tho signed an agreement. The United States promised to withdraw its remaining troops within sixty days; both sides would exchange prisoners; an international commission would oversee the cease-fire; and a coalition would conduct elections in the South. New language settled the DMZ issue. Although the Vietcong accepted the terms, Thieu as before stood aloof.

American officials dealt bluntly with him this time: Accept or suffer a cut-off of American aid. Thieu bitterly capitulated. "Ah, these great powers who divide the world among themselves!" he remarked. "They have an open market everywhere and what does it matter if this market costs the life of a small country?"[138] American critics noted that in the four years of the Nixon-Kissinger war, more than 20,000 Americans and half a million Vietnamese had died when "we could have gotten essentially the same deal anytime after the 1968 bombing halt," as one diplomat put it.[139]

Nixon believed that the bombings had forced the enemy to the bargaining table. A Kissinger aide stated more accurately: "We bombed the North Vietnamese into accepting our concessions."[140] The United States itself took heavy losses in the twelve days of bombing. The Pentagon lost twenty-six planes over North Vietnam, fifteen of them expensive B-52s, the backbone of the strategic bomber force. Could the United States afford to lose more? The final agreement, moreover, resembled the one reached in October, before the bombing. The North Vietnamese did not agree to anything important that they had not already accepted, and the U.S. position did not improve. But the bombing, in combination with Nixon's pledge to Thieu that the United States would come to his aid if the communists violated the agreement, apparently persuaded the South Vietnamese leader to sign. "Brutality is nothing . . . if this son-of-a-bitch doesn't go along," Nixon fulminated.[141] Finally, the popular outcry in the United States against the president grew deafening, and Nixon could not ignore it. Congress was about to reconvene, and many legislators wanted to eliminate funds for the bombing. Perhaps through North Vietnam's willingness to resume negotiations, "Nixon got himself off the hook," as the historian George C. Herring has written.[142]

The cease-fire broke down quickly as each side moved to strengthen itself militarily. The United States maintained military and CIA "advisers" in Vietnam and

Uncle Sam.   The cartoonist Bill Mauldin depicted a bedraggled and bruised Uncle Sam after the hasty withdrawal from Vietnam that spelled defeat in America's longest war. (Copyright 1975, *Chicago Sun-Times.* Reproduced by courtesy of Bill Mauldin)

transferred millions of dollars worth of equipment and bases to the Saigon regime. One peace term called for the United States to provide Hanoi with substantial reconstruction funds. But when the cease-fire collapsed, that agreement died. American warships still cruised off Southeast Asian coasts, and the bombing of Cambodia continued. Congress acted again, this time against a president weakened by Watergate revelations, voting in June 1973 to require the president to cease military actions in all parts of Indochina. Nixon vetoed the measure, but he accepted a compromise deadline of August 15. In November came the War Powers Resolution. In 1974 Congress rejected Kissinger's appeal for $1.5 billion in military aid for Thieu's faltering government, voting $700 million instead.

Cut loose from the American umbilical cord and pressed by North Vietnamese and Vietcong advances, Thieu and his coterie seemed paralyzed by early 1975. Then the communists launched an offensive whose swift success surprised even themselves. The Army of the Republic of Vietnam disintegrated as a fighting force. Many ARVN troops deserted, were captured, or were killed. Refugees clogged highways; the turmoil in the countryside and cities left some civilians near starvation. ARVN forces abandoned vast amounts of American-made military hardware to the enemy.

On April 30, 1975, both the war for Vietnamese independence and the civil war in the South abruptly ended. That day the victorious Vietcong and North Vietnamese streamed into Saigon and renamed it Ho Chi Minh City in honor of the nationalist leader who had died in 1969. For days, frantic Vietnamese had surged toward the Tan Son Nhut airbase near Saigon, where American planes loaded evacuees. But there were not enough airplanes, people blocked the runways, and enemy rockets smashed into frightened crowds. Thousands of people engulfed the U.S. Embassy, whose roof served as a landing pad for helicopters from offshore ships. American troops and officials fought back the scrambling, crying Vietnamese. Thieu, the generals, other high-ranking officials, and those who had the money to bribe their passage, had managed to escape earlier, but they abandoned thousands of panic-stricken Vietnamese compromised by their years of cooperation with the United States. Some were sent to communist "reeducation camps." Others escaped as "boat people" and sailed away in unseaworthy craft with inadequate water and food. Human tragedy also struck Cambodia and Laos, where, in 1975, the communist insurgents also triumphed. In Cambodia the Khmer Rouge imposed a genocidal regime that killed millions.

The Americans exited from their longest war without victory. More than 58,000 Americans died in Vietnam. At least 1.5 million Vietnamese died. Hundreds of thousands of people had been maimed, and millions had become refugees. Civilian deaths in Cambodia and Laos, before and after 1975, also numbered in the millions. The United States had spent at least $170 billion in Southeast Asia. Perhaps another $200 billion would be paid to American veterans of the war in the future. The prolonged Vietnam War alienated U.S. allies, undercut détente, and spoiled relations with the Third World. At home the war fueled inflation and political instability. Nixon's Watergate abuses stemmed in large part from the strains the war placed on the White House and from frustrations over leaks. The war wrecked two presidencies—Johnson's and Nixon's—and weakened the institution of the presidency. Believing that their highest officials had too often lied and deceived, Americans' trust in their government plummeted. In the end, President Nixon savored one positive result. In the words of his biographer Stephen Ambrose, Nixon achieved "the withdrawal of American troops from Vietnam without a right-wing revolt in the United States."[143]

THE MANY LESSONS AND QUESTIONS OF VIETNAM

Not accustomed to defeat, some Americans wondered along with a U.S. official who asked "how so many with so much could achieve so little for so long against so few."[144] Americans only reluctantly searched for lessons after the Vietnam debacle, and most discussion took place among the intellectual and governmental elite. Most citizens seemed more relieved that it had ended than inquisitive about consequences. They switched it off like a TV set. The 1976 presidential campaign passed with barely a word uttered about Vietnam. "Coming back to America," recalled a Vietnam veteran, "I was shocked . . . that no one even talked about it."[145]

Hawkish leaders feared that defeat in Vietnam had weakened U.S. credibility, inviting the nation's adversaries to exploit Washington's setback. They bemoaned a "Vietnam syndrome" that allegedly prevented America from sustaining its role as world leader. Nixon's secretary of defense, James Schlesinger, regretted that the military had operated with too many restraints during the war. Next time, he advised, the United States should bomb earlier the enemy's cities, the heart of its military power. Generals Maxwell Taylor and William Westmoreland lamented that they could have gained victory if only the American people had not suffered a failure of will during the Tet offensive. Just let the military do its job next time, unencumbered by fickle public opinion, inquisitive journalists, and public congressional watchdogs. Other hawks considered Vietnam the wrong terrain on which to battle communism: Next time the United States should choose a more strategically advantageous site and use aerial and naval power rather than troops. Or the United States should change its strategy to emphasize limited or theater nuclear warfare. America should also find more reliable allies, more dependable instruments of containment. General Taylor later admitted that "we didn't know our ally." But he added, "we knew even less about the enemy. And, the last, most inexcusable of our mistakes, was not knowing our own people."[146]

McGeorge Bundy joined others in insisting that the Vietnam War was unique and therefore should not govern responses to future crises. The lesson, then, was to draw no lessons. Arthur M. Schlesinger, Jr., argued that the United States had stepped inadvertently deeper and deeper into a quagmire without really knowing what it was getting into. The war, then, evolved as an accident, a mistake.

Some political scientists, such as Graham Allison in *Essence of Decision* (1971), emphasized a bureaucratic politics model to interpret events. They suggested that it is difficult to hold individuals accountable for decisions and "outcomes," because of the way the impersonal, oversized bureaucracy resists change, follows standard op-

Vietnam Refrain.
Presidents Eisenhower through Ford kept predicting victory in Vietnam but kept losing the war. In 1975, Ford made a last-ditch effort to gain a small victory in the tragic *Mayaguez* affair. (Mike Peters, *Dayton Daily News,* 1975)

erating procedures, and becomes rutted in traditional channels.[147] The bureaucracy in Washington takes on a momentum of its own that no one seems able to control. This bureaucracy, these theorists argued during and after the Vietnam debacle, had to be reformed to encourage more intragovernment dissent and debate, eschew fixed doctrines and kneejerk anticommunism, and "think in time"—that is, become alert to the historical record in order to avoid making the same mistakes again and again.[148] Critics of this school of thought, however, blamed Vietnam on strong presidents like Johnson, who actually controlled the bureaucracy through appointments, an overpowering personality, and a pervasive ideology. This viewpoint implied that a future change in presidents would bring about diplomatic reformation. Some commentators noted that the Vietnam War's causes and consequences exposed the "imperial presidency" and executive abuses in the constitutional system. They concluded that Congress, with larger committee staffs for investigative research, should rein in headstrong presidents.

Other opinions differed radically. Vietnam was neither unique, inadvertent, accidental, presidential, nor bureaucratic, but rather a prime example of American global expansionism and arrogance, encouraged by a zealous belief that the United States, through superior power and ideals, could and should manage events almost everywhere. Richard J. Barnet of the Institute for Policy Studies in Washington, D.C., in his *Roots of War* (1972), wrote that the nation had to examine "those drives . . . that impel us toward destruction," among them a capitalist economy and business creed that required intervention abroad.[149]

The *Mayaguez* incident of May 1975 seemed to suggest as much. At a time when the United States was retreating from Southeast Asia, Cambodian patrol boats seized the American merchant ship *Mayaguez*. The United States, claimed President Ford, had to demonstrate "resolve" to refute charges that it had become a helpless giant after Vietnam.[150] U.S. Marines assaulted Koh Tang Island off the Cambodian coast, and U.S. warships and planes attacked Cambodian boats and bases, nearly killing the *Mayaguez* crew in the process. Cambodians released the *Mayaguez* and its crew, but forty-one Americans died in the "tactical fiasco." Indeed, notes one scholar, "eighteen Americans were lost . . . landing at the wrong place to rescue prisoners whom the Cambodians were about to set free."[151] Although most Americans applauded and Senator Barry Goldwater crowed "we've still got balls," public boasts about clobbering a much weaker nation suggested that Americans had learned all too little from the traumatic experience in Vietnam.[152]

The Vietnam War, said other critics, revealed the shortcomings of the containment doctrine, which had failed to make distinctions between peripheral and vital areas and which applied military force to political problems. The analyst Edmund Stillman wrote: "Freedom *is* divisible. Some places are worthy of defense. Some are not. Some are capable of being defended. Some are not."[153] Ronald Steel, an eloquent critic of *Pax Americana,* likewise commented that "you win some and lose some, but . . . you should never confuse knights and bishops with pawns."[154] The United States fought a limited war but Hanoi and the Vietcong fought an unlimited war to win independence. The communists prevailed despite battle losses in proportion to population that stood "probably twice as high as those suffered by the fanatical, often suicidal Japanese in World War II."[155]

The historian Henry Steele Commager, sickened by the use of napalm and atrocities, wondered why "we find it so hard to accept this elementary lesson of history, that some wars are so deeply immoral that they must be lost, that the war in Vietnam was one of these wars, and that those who resist it are the truest patriots."[156] To some, then, defeat became a victory for humane values. In contrast to those who blamed the antiwar activists for encouraging the enemy and weakening congressional resolve, historians of the peace movement offer a more modest judgment. Antiwar opponents, according to Charles DeBenedetti, "produced an awareness of an alternative America that stripped away through dissent and resistance the rational, moral, and political legitimacy of Washington's war in Indochina."[157] He adds: "The dissidents did not stop the war. But they made it stoppable."[158]

Some commentators urged "neo-isolationism" as an appropriate posture after Vietnam. "Compared to people who thought they could run the universe," remarked Walter Lippmann, "I *am* a neo-isolationist and proud of it."[159] Never again should the United States practice unrestrained global interventionism. Neo-isolationism might check presidential ambitions for foreign ventures and undeclared wars. Yet neo-isolationism seemed short-lived. The political scientist Robert Tucker, for example, wrote a book in 1972 titled *A New Isolationism,* defending the new thinking. But after the OPEC oil embargo and heightened Middle Eastern tensions, he advocated a rejuvenated containment, including the creation of permanent U.S. military bases in the Middle East, and military intervention if necessary, to provide "countervailing power" against either Soviet or Arab threats to the oil fields that sustained the Western allies and Japan.[160]

By the late 1970s public discussion of the Vietnam experience and its consequences increased. Such films as *Coming Home* (1978), *The Deer Hunter* (1978), and

Vietnam Memorials. These statues, part of the memorial site in Washington, D.C., honor the men and women who served in the Vietnam War. On the left is the Vietnam Veterans Memorial by Frederick Hart, and on the right is the Vietnam Women's Memorial by Glenna Goodacre. Both stand near the long wall on which the names of Americans who died in Vietnam are etched. (National Park Service)

Apocalypse Now (1979) heightened public attention. Memoirs such as C.D.B. Bryan's *Friendly Fire* (1976), Ron Kovic's *Born on the Fourth of July* (1976), Philip Caputo's *A Rumor of War* (1977), and Michael Herr's *Dispatches* (1977); oral histories such as Al Santoli's *Everything We Had* (1981) and Mark Baker's *Nam* (1981); and novels such as James Webb's *Fields of Fire* (1978) depicted the soldier's Vietnam.

The dedication of the Vietnam Veterans Memorial in Washington in November 1982 gave the 2.8 million survivors of service in the war "a wailing wall. We came to find the names of those we lost in the war, as if by tracing the letters cut into the granite we could find what was left of ourselves."[161] As many as 800,000 veterans suffered from post-traumatic stress disorder. An ex-marine remembered crawling "around on the floor with my .357 Magnum in my house looking for North Vietnamese soldiers with my wife and kids terrorized."[162] For thirteen years a former army nurse woke up each night to wash her hands. "I felt like Lady Macbeth. I couldn't get the blood of Vietnam off my hands," she recalled.[163] By the early 1990s, thousands of veterans of the Vietnam War had committed suicide.

Debate on the war came to center largely on the major issue of whether the United States could have won. Many conservatives articulated a "stab-in-the-back" theory, namely, that the United States could have won had protesters not impeded the war effort and had civilian officials not restrained the military.[164] In the 1980 presidential campaign, for example, the Republican candidate Ronald Reagan claimed that "ours was, in truth, a noble cause."[165] Then, as president, Reagan declared that American troops "were denied permission to win."[166] "It takes the full strength of a tiger to kill a rabbit," argued General William C. Westmoreland.[167]

Doubters have raised imposing questions about such thinking. Because the bombing of North Vietnam did not significantly impede the flow of matériel and men to the South, perhaps only a U.S. invasion of the North would have sufficed to defeat the enemy. This strategy would have entailed heavy American casualties and a long occupation of a hostile population that had demonstrated its tenacity against foreigners through decades of warfare. Would Americans accept the killing of tens of thousands of people by bombing the irrigation dikes of the North? Would Americans volunteer for a cause with such an uncertain end? Would they tolerate huge draft calls? An invasion of the North, moreover, would have risked war with both the Soviet Union and China. Détente might have restrained the Soviets from rescuing the North, but China had promised publicly that it would intervene as it had in Korea in 1950 if the United States moved north. Could the United States have won in a conflagration of the great powers? Those who contend that the United States lacked the "will" to win have misunderstood the real limits on American power. "What distinguishes me from [Lyndon] Johnson," Nixon once wrote, "is that I have the *will* in spades."[168] Yet Nixon wisely rejected tactical nuclear weapons or an invasion of the North, because he recoiled from the domestic and international consequences.

To have won, suggested some, the United States would also have had to destroy what it was trying to save. That is, using more military power would have produced more deaths and more refugees. What would remain after "victory"? Perhaps at best an internally divided, economically feeble nation needing huge infusions of American aid, but still vulnerable to collapse. Even with the military unleashed— and dropping on Indochina three times the tonnage of bombs used in all theaters during World War II hardly suggests restraint—it would still have faced intractable problems: an inhospitable terrain and climate; jungle, leeches, malaria, and enemy booby traps; an elusive adversary deeply committed to its cause, battle-tested, and able to live off the land (*its* land); and a South Vietnamese people who often sheltered communist soldiers. Doubters of the "win" thesis also note that the United States received very little help from its allies. In fact most European partners urged Washington to stop wasting its resources on a fruitless venture. Of America's forty allies by treaty, only Australia, New Zealand, South Korea, and Thailand sent combat troops. As for exercising the option of nuclear weapons "no matter how remote the threat of nuclear war," one scholar notes, "American political leaders must respect that threat when fighting an enemy with superpower backing."[169]

The United States could not have won, others have argued, because it lacked a political base on which to build. Coups and attempted coups too often rocked the unpopular Saigon governments. The South Vietnamese desertion rate ran high. "I served as an adviser to three separate ARVN battalions," recalled one veteran marine officer, "every one of which, every time we were in combat, split."[170] ARVN forces suffered the same problems that afflicted their government: poor morale, corruption, and nepotism. The "war of attrition" alienated many South Vietnamese, as did the unsettling strategic-hamlet program, disruptive "search and destroy" missions, leveling of villages, requiring of identity cards, bombings of innocents, and spraying of Agent Orange. Cultural differences also separated Americans from Vietnamese. Bars and prostitution flourished in a rural Buddhist society made rapidly urban by fleeing refugees. High-tech computers hummed and giant war machines rumbled in a land of water buffalo, rice paddies, and traditional peasant folk.

Problems in the U.S. military itself reduced the chances for victory. Because officers wanted to reassure superiors that they were turning back the enemy, some suppressed intelligence information and submitted false reports on the numbers killed. One colonel recalled an exaggerated "scorecard": When two different reports of four Vietcong and two Vietcong killed reached headquarters, personnel there joined the figures to read forty-two killed."[171] "If he's dead and Vietnamese, he's VC [Vietcong]" became the prevailing assumption in the field.[172] Decision-makers in Washington did not fully know how badly the war was going. The military also suffered from corruption and mismanagement—even a black market for equipment developed. By early 1971 some 40,000 GIs had become heroin addicts. "For ten dollars," one helicopter pilot reported, "you could get a vial of pure heroin the size of a cigarette butt, and you could get liquid opium, speed, acid, anything you wanted."[173] Racial tension between "bloods" (blacks) and "honkies" (whites) and "fragging"—the murder of officers by enlisted soldiers by means of a hand grenade or other weapon—further reduced combat effectiveness. Educational deferments under the draft system meant that "high school dropouts were three times more likely to experience heavy combat than were college graduates."[174] The rotation system for officers—one year in Vietnam to "punch your ticket"—undermined military cohesion and the benefits of experience. Thus, the United States would have had to replace its military leaders and reform its army—an impossible undertaking in wartime—and even then victory would have been elusive.

The United States also faced tenacious adversaries who suffered remarkable losses but kept coming. Defending their nation against outsiders, as their ancestors had done for generations, the Vietnamese enemy seemed indomitable. "Everything we knew commanded us to fight," a Vietcong veteran remembered. "Our ancestors called us to war. Our myths and legends called us to war. Our parents' teachings called us to war."[175] General Bruce Palmer, Jr., remembered that "their will to resist was inextinguishable."[176]

Whatever the answer to the Vietnam tragedy, succeeding administrations would have to operate in a domestic political setting of uncertainty about the post-Vietnam direction of American foreign relations. Conservative defenders of the war stood ready to criticize any policy that smacked of retrenchment or "another Munich." Liberals and radicals stood alert to dispute any policy that seemed to offer "another Vietnam." And in this highly-charged environment, the unfulfilled Nixon-Kissinger grand design disintegrated further.

Further Reading for the Period 1969–1977

Some of the works on the Cold War, the Third World, and other topics cited in earlier chapters are also relevant for this period.

For foreign relations during the Nixon and Ford presidencies, and for Richard M. Nixon the person, see Stephen E. Ambrose, *Nixon: Ruin and Recovery* (1991) and *Nixon: The Triumph of a Politician* (1989); Seyom Brown, *The Faces of Power* (1983); Terry L. Deibel, *Presidents, Public Opinion, and Power* (1987); Thomas M. Franck and Edward Weisband, *Foreign Policy by Congress* (1979); Michael Genovese, *The Nixon Presidency* (1990); John R. Greene, *The Limits of Power* (1992); Seymour Hersh, *The Price of Power* (1983); Stanley Hoffmann, *Primacy or World Order* (1978); Ole Holsti and James R. Roseneau, *American Leadership in World Affairs: Vietnam and the Breakdown of Consensus* (1984); Robert C. Johansen, *The National Interest and the Human Interest* (1980); Loch K. Johnson, *A Season of Inquiry: The Senate Intelligence Investigation* (1985); Anthony Lake, *The "Tar Baby" Option: American Policy Toward Southern Rhodesia* (1976); Roger Morris, *Richard Milhous Nixon* (1989); Jonathan Schell, *The Time of Illusion* (1976); Franz Schurmann, *The Foreign Politics of Richard Nixon* (1987); Lewis Sorley, *Arms Transfers Under Nixon* (1983); John Spanier and Joseph Nogee, eds., *Congress, the Presidency and American Foreign Policy* (1981); Laurence Stern, *The Wrong Horse* (1977) (Cyprus, Greece, and Turkey); C. L. Sulzberger, *The World and Richard Nixon* (1987); Tad Szulc, *The Illusion of Peace* (1978); and Garry Wills, *Nixon Agonistes* (1970).

Henry A. Kissinger and his ideas are the subject of Dan Caldwell, ed., *Henry Kissinger* (1983); Gregory D. Cleva, *Henry Kissinger and the American Approach to Foreign Policy* (1989); Stephen Gaubard, *Kissinger* (1973); Walter Isaacson, *Kissinger* (1992); Bernard and Marvin Kalb, *Kissinger* (1974); Roger Morris, *Uncertain Greatness* (1977); Robert D. Schulzinger, *Henry Kissinger* (1989); Harvey Starr, *Henry Kissinger* (1984); and John Stoessinger, *Henry Kissinger* (1976).

For Soviet-American relations, détente, and SALT, see Richard J. Barnet, *The Giants* (1977); Coral Bell, *The Diplomacy of Détente* (1970); Robert F. Byrnes, *Soviet-American Academic Exchanges, 1958–1975* (1976); Robin Edmonds, *Soviet Foreign Policy* (1983); Michael B. Froman, *The Development of the Idea of Détente* (1992); Raymond L. Garthoff, *Détente and Confrontation* (1985); Alexander L. George et al., eds., *Managing U.S.-Soviet Rivalry* (1982); Marshall I. Goldman, *Détente and Dollars* (1975); Jonathan Haslam, *The Soviet Union and the Politics of Nuclear Weapons in Europe, 1969–87* (1990); David Holloway, *The Soviet Union and the Arms Race* (1983); Thomas B. Larson, *Soviet-American Rivalry* (1978); Robert S. Litwak, *Détente and the Nixon Doctrine* (1984); Michael Mandelbaum, *The Nuclear Question* (1979); John Newhouse, *Cold Dawn* (1973); Morton Schwartz, *Soviet Perceptions of the United States* (1978); Gordon B. Smith, ed., *The Politics of East-West Trade* (1984); Paula Stern, *Water's Edge* (1979) (Jackson Amendment); Richard W. Stevenson, *The Rise and Fall of Détente* (1985); and Adam B. Ulam, *Dangerous Relations* (1983).

Policy toward China is studied in Warren I. Cohen, *America's Response to China* (1990); Gene T. Hsiao, ed., *Sino-American Détente and Its Policy Implications* (1974); Arnold Xiangze Jiang, *The United States and China* (1988); Ronald C. Keith, *The Diplomacy of Zhou Enlai* (1989); Michael Schaller, *The United States and China* (1990); David Shambaugh, *Beautiful Imperialist* (1991); Robert G. Sutter, *The China Quandary* (1983); and Ross Terrill, *Mao* (1993).

The end and lessons of the Vietnam War are discussed in Anthony S. Campagna, *The Economic Consequences of the Vietnam War* (1991); Walter H. Capps, *The Unfinished War* (1982); John H. Ely, *War and Responsibility* (1993); Leslie H. Gelb and Richard K. Betts, *The Irony of Vietnam* (1979); Allan E. Goodman, *The Lost Peace* (1978); John Hellmann, *American Myth and the Legacy of Vietnam* (1986); Anthony Lake, ed., *The Vietnam Legacy* (1976); Timothy J. Lomperis, *The War Everyone Lost—and Won* (1984); Myra MacPherson, *Long Time Passing* (1984); Richard A. Melanson, *Writing History and Making Policy* (1983) and *Reconstructing Consensus* (1990); Gareth Porter, *A Peace Denied* (1975); Earl C. Ravenal, *Never Again* (1978); William Shawcross, *Sideshow* (1979) (Cambodia); and W. Scott Thompson and Donaldson D. Frizzill, eds., *The Lessons of Vietnam* (1977). See also works listed in Chapter 9.

International economic questions, including the North-South debate, are covered in Richard J. Barnet, *The Lean Years* (1980); Richard J. Barnet and Ronald Müller, *Global Reach* (1974); David P. Calleo, *The Imperious Economy* (1982); Albert L. Danielson, *The Evolution of OPEC* (1982); I. M. Destler, *Making Foreign Economic Policy* (1980); I. M. Destler, Haruhiro Fukui, and Hideo Sato, *The Textile Wrangle* (1979); Jeffrey A.

Hart, *The New International Economic Order* (1983); Charles A. Jones, *The North-South Dialogue* (1983); Stephen Krasner, *Defending the National Interest* (1978); David Morawetz, *Twenty-five Years of Economic Development, 1950–1975* (1977); Robert K. Olson, *U.S. Foreign Policy and the New International Economic Order* (1981); Robert A. Pastor, *Congress and the Politics of U.S. Foreign Economic Policy, 1929–1976* (1980); Joan E. Spero, *The Politics of International Economic Relations* (1985); and Brian Tew, *The Evolution of the International Monetary System, 1945–81* (1982).

Environmental issues, population, food, and their intersection with the international economy and world politics are examined in Robert Boardman, *International Organization and the Conservation of Nature* (1981); Lynton K. Caldwell, *International Environmental Policy* (1984); Alfred E. Eckes, Jr., *The United States and the Global Struggle for Minerals* (1977); Ann L. Hollick, *U.S. Foreign Policy and the Law of the Sea* (1981); Raymond F. Hopkins and Donald J. Puchala, *Global Food Interdependence* (1980); John McCormick, *Reclaiming Paradise: The Global Environmental Movement* (1989); William Murdoch, *The Poverty of Nations* (1980); William and Paul Paddock, *Time of Famines* (1976); Clyde Sanger, *Ordering the Oceans* (1987); Ross B. Talbott, *The Four World Food Agencies in Rome* (1990); Mitchel B. Wallerstein, *Food for War–Food for Peace* (1980).

For the Middle East, oil, and the Arab-Israeli conflict, see George W. Ball and Douglas B. Ball, *The Passionate Attachment* (1992) (Israel); James A. Bill, *The Eagle and the Lion* (1988) (Iran); George W. Breslauer, *Soviet Strategy in the Middle East* (1990); Trevor N. Dupuy, *Elusive Victory* (1978); Robert D. Kaplan, *The Arabists* (1993); George Lenczowski, *The Middle East in World Affairs* (1980); Donald Neff, *Warriors Against Israel* (1988); William R. Polk, *The Arab World Today* (1991); William B. Quandt, *Decade of Decisions* (1977); Bernard Reich, *Quest for Peace* (1977); Cheryl A. Rubenberg, *Israel and the American National Interest* (1986); Barry Rubin, *Paved with Good Intentions* (1977) (Iran); David Schoenbaum, *The United States and the State of Israel* (1993); Mohammed K. Shadid, *The United States and the Palestinians* (1981); Edward R. F. Sheehan, *The Arabs, Israelis, and Kissinger* (1976); Benjamin Shwadran, *Middle East Oil* (1977); Steven L. Spiegel, *The Other Arab-Israeli Conflict* (1985); Robert W. Stookey, *America and the Arab States* (1975); and Daniel Yergin, *The Prize* (1991) (oil).

Latin America–U.S. relations, including Chile, are treated in Robert J. Alexander, *The Tragedy of Chile* (1978); Richard R. Fagen, ed., *Capitalism and the State in U.S.–Latin American Relations* (1979); T. H. Moran, *Multinational Corporations and the Politics of Dependence: Copper in Chile* (1974); Morris H. Morley, *Washington, Somoza, and the Sandinistas* (1994); James Petras and Morris Morley, *The United States and Chile* (1975); Stephen G. Rabe, *The Road to OPEC* (1982) (Venezuela); Paul E. Sigmund, *The United States and Democracy in Chile* (1993); and Arthur P. Whitaker, *The United States and the Southern Cone* (1976).

See also the General Bibliography, Richard D. Burns, *Guide to American Foreign Relations Since 1700* (1983), and the following notes.

NOTES TO CHAPTER 10

1. Quoted in Bernard Kalb and Marvin Kalb, *Kissinger* (Boston: Little, Brown, 1974), p. 266.
2. Hugh Sidey in *Life*, LXXII (March 3, 1972), 12.
3. Quoted in Kalb and Kalb, *Kissinger*, p. 267.
4. Joseph Kraft, *The Chinese Difference* (New York: Saturday Review Press, 1973), p. 19.
5. *Newsweek*, LXXIX (February 28, 1972), 13.
6. *Department of State Bulletin*, LXVI (March 6, 1972), 290.
7. Quoted in John Lewis Gaddis, *Strategies of Containment* (New York: Oxford University Press, 1982), p. 296.
8. Quoted in John Maxwell Hamilton, *Edgar Snow* (Bloomington: Indiana University Press, 1988), p. 269.
9. Quoted in Robert D. Schulzinger, *Henry Kissinger* (New York: Columbia University Press, 1989), p. 85.
10. Henry Kissinger, *White House Years* (Boston: Little, Brown, 1979), p. 754.
11. *Public Papers, Nixon, 1971* (Washington, D.C.: Government Printing Office, 1972), p. 819.
12. Harry Schwartz in *New York Times*, February 21, 1972.
13. Quoted in William L. Safire, *Before the Fall* (Garden City, N.Y.: Doubleday, 1975), p. 452.
14. Kissinger, *White House Years*, p. 1049.
15. Quoted in Raymond L. Garthoff, *Détente and Confrontation* (Washington, D.C.: Brookings, 1985), p. 240.
16. Quoted in Seymour M. Hersh, *The Price of Power* (New York: Summit, 1983), p. 500.
17. U. Alexis Johnson, *The Right Hand of Power* (Englewood Cliffs, N.J.: Prentice-Hall, 1984), p. 555.

18. Quoted in Henry Brandon, *The Retreat of American Power* (New York: Dell, 1972), p. 190.
19. Richard Nixon, *RN* (New York: Grosset & Dunlap, 1978), p. 564.
20. Walter Isaacson, *Kissinger* (New York: Simon and Schuster, 1992), p. 402.
21. *Department of State Bulletin, LXVI* (March 20, 1972), 421.
22. Chen Jo-shi quoted in Steven W. Mosher, *China Misperceived* (New York: Basic Books, 1990), p. 15.
23. Quoted in Safire, *Before*, p. 12.
24. Quoted in Mosher, *China Misperceived*, p. 13.
25. George Gallup in *Hartford Courant*, March 12, 1972.
26. Quoted in Ronald C. Keith, *The Diplomacy of Zhou Enlai* (New York: St. Martin's Press, 1989), p. 199.
27. *Department of State Bulletin, LXVI* (March 20, 1972), 435–438.
28. Nixon, *RN*, p. 580.
29. Quoted in Safire, *Before*, p. 102; Stephen E. Ambrose, *Nixon: Ruin and Recovery, 1973–1990* (New York: Simon and Schuster, 1991), p. 587.
30. H. R. Haldeman, *The Ends of Power* (New York: Times Books, 1978), p. 98.
31. Quoted in Roger Morris, *Uncertain Greatness* (New York: Harper & Row, 1977), p. 3.
32. Dean Acheson to J. H. P. Gould, March 12, 1970, Box 13, Dean Acheson Papers, Yale University Library, New Haven, Connecticut.
33. Quoted in Richard Valeriani, *Travels with Henry* (New York: Berkley, 1980), p. 123; Kissinger, *White House Years*, p. 1094.
34. Stanley Hoffmann, *Primacy or World Order* (New York: McGraw-Hill, 1978), p. 33.
35. A senator quoted in *New York Times*, February 22, 1975.
36. Quoted in Kalb and Kalb, *Kissinger*, p. 13.
37. "An Interview with Oriana Fallaci: Kissinger," *New Republic, CLXVII* (December 16, 1972), 21–22.
38. Quoted in *New York Times*, February 8, 1993.
39. Quoted in *Time, CXXV* (February 11, 1985), 65.
40. Quoted in J. Garry Clifford, "Change and Continuity," in James Patterson, ed., *Paths to the Present* (Minneapolis: Burgess, 1975), p. 137.
41. Quoted in Thomas G. Paterson, "Oversight or Afterview?" in Michael Barnhart, ed., *Congress and United States Foreign Policy* (Albany: State University of New York Press, 1987), p. 155.
42. Quoted in Robert D. Kaplan, *The Arabists* (New York: The Free Press, 1993), p. 145.
43. Quoted in Garry Wills, *Nixon Agonistes* (Boston: Houghton Mifflin, 1970), p. 20.
44. Kissinger, *White House Years*, p. 191.
45. *Ibid.*, p. 55.
46. *Public Papers, Nixon, 1971*, p. 806.
47. Stanley Hoffmann, *Primacy*, p. 46.
48. Memorandum of White House meeting, December 7, 1970, Box 68, Acheson Papers.
49. Quoted in John Newhouse, *War and Peace in the Nuclear Age* (New York: Alfred A. Knopf, 1989), p. 241.
50. Elaine P. Adam and Richard P. Stebbins, eds., *American Foreign Relations, 1976* (New York: New York University Press, 1978), p. 13.
51. Quoted in Robert J. McMahon, *The Cold War on the Periphery* (New York: Columbia University Press, 1994), p. 346.
52. Quoted in Nixon, *RN*, p. 527.
53. Quoted in Isaacson, *Kissinger*, p. 377.
54. Garthoff, *Détente and Confrontation*, p. 277.
55. Nixon, *RN*, p. 527.
56. Michael Mandelbaum, *The Nuclear Question* (Cambridge, Eng.: Cambridge University Press, 1979), p. 218.
57. *Public Papers, Nixon, 1969*, p. 19.
58. Quoted in Gregg Herken, *Counsels of War* (New York: Oxford University Press, 1987), p. 255.
59. Kissinger, *White House Years*, p. 1245n.
60. Quoted in Donald R. Baucom, *The Origins of SDI, 1944–1983* (Lawrence: University Press of Kansas, 1992), p. 75.
61. Robert C. Johansen, *The National Interest and the Human Interest* (Princeton: Princeton University Press, 1980), p. 55.
62. Quoted in Thomas J. McCormick, *America's Half-Century* (Baltimore: The Johns Hopkins University Press, 1989), p. 173.
63. William Hyland quoted in Isaacson, *Kissinger*, p. 663.
64. *Public Papers, Nixon, 1969*, p. 548.
65. Kissinger, *White House Years*, p. 117.
66. Quoted in David Schoenbaum, *The United States and the State of Israel* (New York: Oxford University Press, 1993), p. 171.
67. Quoted in William B. Quandt, *Decade of Decisions* (Berkeley: University of California Press, 1977), p. 91.
68. *Ibid.*, p. 127.
69. Nixon, *RN*, p. 924.
70. Schoenbaum, *U.S. and Israel*, p. 205.
71. Quoted *ibid.*, p. 208; Kissinger paraphrased in Barry M. Blechman and Douglas M. Hart, "The Political Utility of Nuclear Weapons," *International Security, VII* (Summer 1982), 145.
72. Ahmed Zakhi Yamani quoted in Daniel Yergin, *The Prize* (New York: Simon and Schuster, 1991), p. 606.
73. Quoted in Kaplan, *Arabists*, p. 144.
74. Quoted in Edward R. F. Sheehan, "How Kissinger Did It," *Foreign Policy*, No. 22 (Spring 1976), p. 48.
75. Quoted in Edward R. F. Sheehan, *The Arabs, Israelis, and Kissinger* (New York: Reader's Digest Press, 1976), p. 162.
76. Quoted in *New York Times*, March 15, 1976.
77. Quoted in James A. Bill, *The Eagle and the Lion* (New Haven: Yale University Press, 1988), p. 196.
78. Kissinger quoted *ibid.*, p. 203.
79. Quoted in Samuel Baily, *The United States and the Development of South America* (New York: New Viewpoints, 1976), p. 118.

80. Quoted in Paul E. Sigmund, *The United States and Democracy in Chile* (Baltimore: The Johns Hopkins University Press, 1993), p. 9.
81. Kissinger, *White House Years*, p. 673.
82. Quoted in U.S. Senate, Select Committee to Study. . . Intelligence Activities, *Covert Action in Chile, 1963–1973* (Washington, D.C.: Government Printing Office, 1975), p. 33.
83. Quoted in William F. Sater, *Chile and the United States* (Athens: University of Georgia Press, 1990), p. 184.
84. Clodomiro Almeyeda quoted *ibid.*, p. 187.
85. Quoted in Morris, *Uncertain Greatness*, p. 106.
86. Kissinger, *White House Years* , p. 645.
87. Quoted in Garthoff, *Détente and Confrontation*, p. 80.
88. Quoted in Stephen Weissman, "CIA Covert Action in Zaire and Angola," *Political Science Quarterly*, XCIV (Summer 1979), 281.
89. Quoted in Morris, *Uncertain Greatness*, p. 131.
90. Quoted in Steven Metz, "Congress, the Antiapartheid Movement, and Nixon," *Diplomatic History, XII* (Spring 1988), 177; Morris, *Uncertain Greatness*, p. 117.
91. Nathaniel Davis, "The Angola Decision of 1975," *Foreign Affairs, LVII* (Fall 1978), 114.
92. Gerald R. Ford, *A Time to Heal* (New York: Harper & Row, 1979), p. 345.
93. Quoted in *New York Times*, March 14, 1976.
94. John A. Marcum, "Lessons of Angola," *Foreign Affairs, LIV* (April 1976), 418.
95. *Department of State Bulletin, LXXV* (July 12, 1976), 46.
96. *Ibid., LXXII* (June 2, 1975), 713.
97. *Ibid.*
98. John Connally quoted in Michael A. Genovese, *The Nixon Presidency* (Westport, Conn.: Greenwood Press, 1990), p. 69.
99. Quoted in Hersh, *Price of Power*, p. 462.
100. Kissinger, *White House Years*, pp. 955, 962.
101. Reuben Askew quoted in Charles W. Kegley, Jr., and Eugene R. Wittkopf, *World Politics* (New York: St. Martin's Press, 1981), p. 181.
102. *Department of State Bulletin, LXXIII* (September 22, 1975), 425.
103. Quoted in Thomas G. Paterson, *On Every Front* (New York: W. W. Norton, 1992; 2d ed.), p. 217.
104. Quoted in Johansen, *National Interest*, p. 13.
105. Quoted in Adam, *American Foreign Relations, 1976*, p. 478.
106. Lester R. Brown, *Human Needs and the Security of Nations* (New York: Foreign Policy Association, 1977), p. 6.
107. Petr Beckmann quoted in John McCormick, *Reclaiming Paradise* (Bloomington: Indiana University Press, 1989), p. 85.
108. Mario Gibson Barbaroza quoted in Charles McGraw, "Removed from Planet Earth" (Unpub. paper, University of Connecticut, 1994), p. 7.
109. United Nations, General Assembly, *Official Records*, 22nd Session, August 18, 1967, Document A/6695, p. 1.
110. Quoted in Michael Roskin, "An American Metternich," in Frank J. Merli and Theodore A. Wilson, eds., *Makers of American Diplomacy* (New York: Scribner's, 1974), p. 698.
111. Quoted in Tad Szulc, "How Kissinger Did It," *Foreign Policy*, No. 15 (Summer 1974), p. 35.
112. Quoted in Haldeman, *Ends of Power*, p. 81.
113. Quoted in Stanley Millet, ed., *South Vietnam* (New York: Facts on File, 1973–1974; 7 vols.), IV, 64.
114. H. R. Haldeman notes quoted in Genovese, *Nixon Presidency*, p. 134.
115. Quoted in James A. Nathan, "Commitments in Search of a Roost," *Virginia Quarterly Review, L* (Summer 1974), 337.
116. Quoted in Melvin Small, "Containing Domestic Enemies," in David L. Anderson, ed., *Shadow on the White House* (Lawrence: University Press of Kansas, 1993), p. 137.
117. Frances FitzGerald, *Fire in the Lake* (New York: Vintage, 1972), p. 544.
118. Ken George quoted in Otto J. Lehrack, *No Shining Armor* (Lawrence: University Press of Kansas, 1992), pp. 337–338.
119. Quoted in *Time, CXXIII* (April 16, 1984), 24.
120. Nixon, *RN*, p. 403.
121. *Public Papers, Nixon, 1969*, p. 909.
122. Quoted in Morris, *Uncertain Greatness*, p. 175.
123. Quoted in William Shawcross, *Sideshow* (New York: Pocket Books, 1979), p. 152.
124. Charles Colson quoted in George C. Herring, *America's Longest War* (New York: Alfred A. Knopf, 1986), p. 239.
125. Quoted in Lucien S. Vandenbroucke, *Perilous Options* (New York: Oxford University Press, 1993), p. 63.
126. Quoted in Isaacson, *Kissinger*, p. 329.
127. Quoted in Nixon, *RN*, p. 605.
128. Quoted in Herring, *America's Longest War*, p. 247.
129. Quoted in Peter Macdonald, *Giap* (New York: W. W. Norton, 1993), p. 316.
130. Quoted in Nguyen Tien Hung and Jerrold L. Schecter, *The Palace File* (New York: Harper & Row, 1986), p. 88.
131. Quoted *ibid.*, p. 105.
132. Kissinger, *White House Years*, p. 1399.
133. Quoted in Nixon, *RN*, p. 733.
134. Quoted in Jeffrey P. Kimball, " 'Peace with Honor,' " in Anderson, *Shadow*, p. 173.
135. Morris, *Uncertain Greatness*, p. 190.
136. Guenter Lewy, *America in Vietnam* (New York: Oxford University Press, 1978), p. 414.
137. Quoted in Fredrik Logevall, "The Swedish-American Conflict over Vietnam," *Diplomatic History, XVII* (Summer 1993), 441.
138. Quoted in Oriana Fallaci, *Interview with History* (Boston: Houghton Mifflin, 1976), p. 56.
139. Richard Holbrooke quoted in Isaacson, *Kissinger*, p. 483.
140. John Negroponte quoted in Marilyn B. Young, *The Vietnam Wars* (New York: HarperCollins, 1991), p. 279.

141. Quoted in Ambrose, *Nixon*, p. 51.

142. Herring, *America's Longest War*, p. 255.

143. Ambrose, *Nixon*, p. 57.

144. Robert Komer quoted in W. Scott Thompson and Donaldson D. Frizzell, eds., *The Lessons of Vietnam* (New York: Crane, Russak, 1977), p. 211.

145. Quoted in Mark Baker, *Nam* (New York: Morrow, 1981), p. 314.

146. Quoted in Thomas G. Paterson, "Historical Memory and Illusive Victories," *Diplomatic History*, XII (Winter 1988), 14.

147. Quoted in J. Garry Clifford, "Bureaucratic Politics," in Michael J. Hogan and Thomas G. Paterson, eds., *Explaining the History of American Foreign Relations* (New York: Cambridge University Press, 1991), p. 141.

148. Richard E. Neustadt and Ernest R. May, *Thinking in Time* (New York: The Free Press, 1986).

149. Richard J. Barnet, *Roots of War* (Baltimore: Penguin, 1972), p. 9.

150. Ford, *Time to Heal*, p. 275.

151. Vandenbroucke, *Perilous Options*, p. 113.

152. Quoted in Young, *Vietnam Wars*, p. 301.

153. Edmund Stillman, in "America Now: A Failure of Nerve?" *Commentary*, LX (July 1975), 83.

154. Ronald Steel in *ibid.*, p. 79.

155. John E. Mueller, "The Search for the 'Breaking Point' in Vietnam," *International Studies Quarterly*, XXIV (December 1980), 498.

156. Henry Steele Commager, "The Defeat of America," *New York Review of Books*, October 5, 1972, p. 13.

157. Charles DeBenedetti, *The Peace Reform in American History* (Bloomington: Indiana University Press, 1980), p. 174.

158. Charles DeBenedetti, "On the Significance of Peace Activism," *Peace and Change*, IX (Summer 1983), 14.

159. Quoted in Ronald Steel, *Walter Lippmann and the American Century* (Boston: Little, Brown, 1980), p. 586.

160. Robert W. Tucker, *The Purposes of American Power* (New York: Praeger, 1981), pp. 113, 178.

161. Bruce Weigl quoted in Young, *Vietnam Wars*, p. 328.

162. Jim Yost quoted in Lehrback, *No Shining Armor*, p. 356.

163. Joan Furey quoted in Laura Palmer, "How to Bandage a War," *New York Times Magazine*, November 7, 1993, p. 40.

164. Jeffrey P. Kimball, "The Stab-in-the-Back Legend and the Vietnam War," *Armed Forces and Society*, XIV (Spring 1988), 433–458.

165. Quoted in *New York Times*, August 19, 1980.

166. Quoted in George C. Herring, "The 'Vietnam Syndrome,'" *Virginia Quarterly Review*, LVII (Fall 1981), 595.

167. Quoted in Thomas G. Paterson, *Meeting the Communist Threat* (New York: Oxford University Press, 1988), p. 259.

168. Quoted in Gaddis, *Strategies*, p. 300.

169. Mark Clodfelter, *The Limits of Air Power* (New York: The Free Press, 1989), p. 210.

170. Robert Müller quoted in "After Vietnam," *Washington Post*, May 25, 1980, p. B4.

171. John B. Keeley quoted *ibid.*, July 6, 1981.

172. Quoted in Philip Caputo, *A Rumor of War* (New York: Ballantine, 1977), p. 69.

173. Quoted in Stanley Karnow, *Vietnam* (New York: Viking, 1991; rev. ed.), p. 646.

174. Christian G. Appy, *Working Class War* (Chapel Hill: University of North Carolina Press, 1993), p. 26.

175. Le Ly Hayslip, *When Heaven and Earth Changed Places* (Garden City, N.Y.: Doubleday, 1989), p. xiv.

176. Bruce Palmer, Jr., *The 25-Year War* (Lexington: University Press of Kentucky, 1984), p. 176.

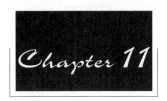

Chapter 11

To Begin the World Over Again:
Carter, Reagan, and Revivalism, 1977–1989

American Hostage in Iran. *On November 8, 1979, this blindfolded, hand-tied American captive was paraded on the grounds of the U.S. Embassy in Teheran. A jeering crowd taunted the frightened American early in the Iranian hostage crisis. (AP/Wide World Photos)*

✳ *Diplomatic Crossroad*

THE IRANIAN HOSTAGE CRISIS, 1979–1981

"Death to the Shah! Death to Carter! Death to America!" chanted the radical Islamic student demonstrators outside the U.S. Embassy in Teheran, Iran.[1] Suddenly, they stormed the embassy that their religious leader Ayatollah Ruhollah Khomeini had branded a "nest of spies."[2] After snipping the gate chains with boltcutters and scaling the eight-foot wall, hundreds of shouting students spread over the twenty-seven-acre compound. On that cold, rainy morning of November 4, 1979, recalled a American trapped inside, the attackers were "lowing for death."[3] In the chancery, American officials, including CIA officers operating undercover as Foreign Service personnel, hurried to shred classified documents. Marine guards fired tear gas, but the armed militants broke into rooms and seized frightened Americans, including Ann Swift, a political officer who maintained contact with the Operations Room of the Department of State in Washington until she put down the telephone and surrendered. "We're paying you back for Vietnam," snarled one attacker.[4]

All told, sixty-six Americans were captured—some of them on the streets after they fled from the breached compound, others in nearby apartments. Three were visiting the Iranian Foreign Ministry at the time; they remained there throughout the crisis. A few American officials escaped, and Canadian diplomats later spirited them out of Iran. To the jubilant students, the kidnapped Americans would go free only after Shah Mohammad Reza Pahlavi returned to Iran for trial.

What had set off this angry outpouring of anti-Americanism? Why were Iranian revolutionaries "blind drunk with their hatred" for the United States?[5] The admission of the exiled Shah to a New York hospital two weeks earlier had provided the immediate catalyst for seizing the embassy. But Iranian hostility had been smoldering since the 1950s. The Shah had risen to power in 1941, replacing his father, who had claimed the Peacock Throne by force in the 1920s. The young Shah increasingly relied on American advice and assistance—a dependence demonstrated most emphatically in 1953 after he left Iran, when nationalists, led by Prime Minister Mohammad Mossadegh, gained control of the government and nationalized the Anglo-Iranian Oil Company. In Operation AJAX, the CIA plotted with royalist Iranians and British officials, restored the Shah to the throne, and drove Mossadegh from the country. The Shah soon became a staunch anticommunist ally of the United States and a pillar of American influence in the Middle East. In 1957, with CIA assistance, he organized SAVAK, a secret police organization that suppressed dissent and terrorized the population. "We will teach the CIA not to do these things in our country," said a militant student to one hostage.[6]

In the 1970s popular discontent with the Shah swelled. Muslim clergy resented Western influences, including Hollywood movies and rights for women. Intellectuals and students protested the suppression of civil liberties. Social democrats who had fled with Mossadegh in the 1950s demanded a constitutional government. For different reasons, merchants, young workers, and feudal landholders felt aggrieved by the Shah's "white revolution," or modernization of the Iranian economy. Inflation, unemployment, inadequate housing for the millions who moved from village to city, and preferential jobs for skilled foreigners also created unrest. Ethnic separatists in Kurdistan fought for autonomy. SAVAK, symbol of the Shah's police state, committed untold brutalities that ultimately helped to unite disparate groups against the monarch and his sponsor, the United States.

Some Iranians also objected to massive purchases of arms from the United States. In the period 1973–1978, the Shah spent $19 billion of the nation's oil wealth on American weapons. He bought helicopters, fighter aircraft, destroyers, and missiles, because, he argued, Iran had to fend off numerous enemies—the Soviet Union, Iraq, radical Arabs, domestic radicals—and had to police the Persian Gulf. Iran possessed the mightiest military in the Middle East, but many Iranians thought that the Shah squandered the nation's resources. The arms deals also made the Shah appear to be a stooge of the United States.

President Jimmy Carter, visiting Teheran in late 1977, toasted the Shah for making Iran "an island of stability" and for earning "the respect and admiration and love which your people give to you."[7] American diplomats in attendance were "dumbfounded" by Carter's remarks, for the president had identified the pursuit of human rights (hardly the Shah's strongest point) as a major U.S. foreign-policy goal.[8] The president, of course, was paying polite deference to an ally and hinting to the Shah that the United States would back him against his internal critics. After Vietnam, American leaders looked to regional powers like Iran to assist the United States in preserving its global interests. But pell-mell events in Iran had created a condition in which "the regional tail [was] wagging the super-power dog."[9] Because of American intelligence reporting deficiencies, Carter did not know that the Shah was dying of cancer—a condition perhaps making him fatalistic and lethargic.

In 1978, demonstrations, riots, and strikes shook Iran. The Shah declared martial law, and the United States equipped his forces with tear-gas cannisters and other riot-control equipment. "Hang firm and . . . count on our backing," Carter told him.[10] U.S. officials pondered options. The National Security Affairs Adviser Zbigniew Brzezinski spoke for a vigorous military course: The Iranian army should smash the opposition and stage a coup. Secretary of State Cyrus Vance rebutted that the "iron fist" belied the central thrust of Carter's foreign policy and would not work because the largely conscript Iranian army would disintegrate.[11] From Teheran, U.S. ambassador William Sullivan sided with Vance. Brzezinski telephoned the ambassador and asked whether he could arrange a military coup. "I regret that the reply I made is unprintable," Sullivan later wrote.[12] He exploded because officials in Washington had rejected his advice to open direct communication with Khomeini, the evident leader of the revolution, then in exile in Paris. All

American leaders agreed, however, that the United States would welcome the Shah should he leave his country.

After appointing a civilian government acceptable to his generals, the Shah flew to Egypt on January 16, 1979. Making it clear that Islamic clerics intended to govern Iran, the Ayatollah rejected the new regime and soon installed his own. When he fueled rampant anti-Americanism in angry speeches to cheering Iranians, American citizens began to depart the convulsed nation. On February 14 a revolutionary group seized the U.S. Embassy, but the Iranian government forced the intruders to abandon the compound.

After leaving Teheran, the Shah moved from Egypt to Morocco to the Bahamas to Mexico. Few nations wanted to give sanctuary to a repudiated despot. As Americans learned that "our problem in Iran is us," Carter rescinded the offer of welcome to the Shah.[13] Former secretary of state Henry A. Kissinger and David Rockefeller, whose Chase Manhattan Bank had substantial financial ties to Iran, petitioned the White House to remain loyal to a longtime ally, to cease treating the Shah like "a flying Dutchman" in search of a safe place to land.[14] In October the president learned that the Shah would die of a malignant lymphoma unless a New York hospital admitted him. Embassy officials in Teheran warned that such a move could ignite protest against Americans in Iran. Carter nonetheless invited the Shah to the United States. "We threw a burning branch into a bucket full of kerosene," recalled Moorhead C. Kennedy, Jr., one of the American hostages.[15] "It is as if Franco's Spain had offered to treat Hitler for cancer immediately after the Second World War," explained Iran's new foreign minister.[16] The Shah arrived in New York on October 22; on November 4 militant students seized the embassy.

As stunned Americans watched "America Held Hostage" instead of Johnny Carson each night, it became clear that the hostage-takers wanted more than the Shah.[17] First, the hostage-grabbing was Iran's way of preventing the Shah from launching a counterrevolution from the United States; many Iranians painfully remembered 1953. Second, the hostage-taking helped Iran break diplomatic relations with the United States, which Khomeini called a "global Shah" never to be trusted.[18] Finally, the hostage drama permitted the eighty-one-year-old Khomeini—whose dark, piercing eyes glared from posters hung throughout the country—to use anti-Americanism as a vehicle to overwhelm civilian moderates who competed with him and his clerics for control of the revolution.

Spending sleepless nights, President Carter felt "the same kind of impotence that a powerful person feels when his child is kidnapped."[19] Carter adopted a policy of "restrained anger."[20] "If I wasn't President," he told an aide while pro-Khomeini pickets marched outside the White House, "I'd probably take a swing at any Khomeini demonstrator I could get my hands on."[21] Within the administration, Vance and Brzezinski differed bitterly. The latter advocated retaliatory action to preserve U.S. honor, even at the cost of lives. Vance countered that the crisis called "not for rhetoric, but for quiet, careful and firm diplomacy."[22]

Carter first ordered a review of the visas of 50,000 Iranian students in the United States; those not enrolled in a college or university would be deported. But this plan proved ineffective because the government could not easily locate the

Iranians, and cases stalled in the courts. On November 14 the president froze Iranian assets in the United States valued at about $8 billion. American officials secretly asked Palestine Liberation Organization leader Yasir Arafat to help. He did, persuading the revolutionary government to release thirteen hostages (most of those released were women and African Americans). Washington also enlisted the help of other foreign governments, international organizations, and private emissaries. These efforts came to naught.

As the diplomats struggled to negotiate with an Iranian government that often seemed incapable of functioning, the hostages languished in captivity. Although never mutilated or sexually abused, the hostages suffered through an ordeal lasting 444 days. At first blindfolded with their hands and feet tied, they thought that they would be either released quickly or killed. Some had to parade before jeering mobs. For a long time they could not speak or read newspapers. The hostages slept in soiled clothes, lost weight, and became sick. They received books and games later, but they constantly fought boredom, melancholy, and fear. The worst terror they endured was a mock execution, preceded by abusive interrogation. Some captives came to pity their captors, concluding that they had become naive followers of power-crazed Islamic clerics. Asked later if he would ever return to Iran, however, one freed hostage shot back: "Yeah, in a B-52."[23]

At home Americans debated who had "lost" Iran. Many people could not tolerate the White House's patience in the face of daily insult. Kissinger upbraided the administration for "self-abasement" and urged a "reassertion of American will."[24] The veteran diplomat George Ball retorted that it was "fatuous" for Kissinger to claim that he would never have let the Shah fall in the first place. "What would Mr. Kissinger have done [against the internal revolt]? Sent the Sixth Fleet steaming up the Gulf?"[25]

On April 7, 1980, after Teheran jettisoned another secret diplomatic opportunity, the United States broke relations with Iran. Four days later, Carter ordered the Joint Chiefs of Staff to launch a complicated rescue mission. "Stunned and angry that such a momentous decision had been made in my absence," Vance asked for reconsideration when he returned from a trip.[26] Carter called a meeting of the National Security Council to hear Vance's objections. First, the secretary said, the United States had just pressed its allies to impose economic sanctions on Iran; a military maneuver, without prior warning, would make them feel deceived. Second, the Iranian parliament, about to meet, might provide a solution to the crisis. Third, the hostages faced no immediate physical danger. Even if the raid succeeded, numerous hostages would die as the military blasted its way in. Fourth, the Iranians might retaliate by seizing U.S. journalists and other Americans in Teheran, creating another hostage crisis. Fifth, the whole Middle East might become inflamed. And last, such a military venture might push the Iranians into the arms of the Soviets. No one at the meeting agreed with Vance. "I will stick with the decisions I made," stated a grim-faced Carter.[27] The time had now come to "lance the boil" of American frustration, Brzezinski concluded.[28] "America needs a win. We need one real, real bad," remarked "Chargin' Charlie" Beckwith, the rescue mission's ground commander.[29] Later he admitted that "the probability of success was about 50 percent."[30]

Jimmy Carter's World. The Iranian crisis joined domestic economic turmoil to trouble President Carter. A White House aide remembered that "before conferring with a foreign leader, Carter would often sit by his globe . . . trying to imagine the political, economic, and military pressures experienced by the leader." (Cartoon by Tony Auth. Reprinted with permission from *Foreign Policy* magazine, no. 31, Summer, 1978. Copyright 1978 by the Carnegie Endowment for International Peace)

On April 24, eight large helicopters lifted off the deck of the supercarrier *Nimitz* in the Arabian Sea. At the same time, six C-130 Hercules transports took to the skies from a base in Egypt. All the aircraft headed for a rendezvous in the Iranian desert; from there rescue teams of Green Berets and Rangers planned to infiltrate Teheran and assault the U.S. Embassy to free the hostages. But the helicopters had to fly through unexpected dust clouds, and two of them malfunctioned before reaching Iran; another lost a hydraulic line at the rendezvous point, "Desert One." "It was a zoo," an army officer recalled.[31] The president accepted Colonel Beckwith's recommendation to abort the mission. In the hasty and dusty exit, a helicopter and a C-130 collided, killing eight crew members. When he heard about the tragedy, the saddened president asked his staff for a copy of the speech that John F. Kennedy had made after the disastrous 1961 Bay of Pigs invasion; then he told the nation the news. Vance, who had informed the president that he would resign whether or not the rescue attempt succeeded, quietly left the administration. Critics pounded Carter for undertaking a project sure to cause the deaths of many hostages. "Thank God for the sandstorm," remarked one hostage later.[32] While some speculated that Carter may have ordered the risky operation to bolster his sagging political fortunes, others asked if "the Three Stooges now directed foreign policy."[33]

After the rescue attempt, Americans seemed resigned to a prolonged crisis. Many citizens displayed yellow ribbons to symbolize their prayers, while others pasted stickers on their car bumpers: NUKE THE AYATOLLAH and "Ayatollah Assa Hola." After Vance resigned, an aide told Carter: "Zbig needs to drop from public view for the next few months at least."[34]

Four major events finally facilitated a resolution. First, the Shah died in Egypt in July 1980. Second, Khomeini's Islamic clerics won control of the parliament and thus no longer needed the hostages for their political purposes. Third, in September, Iraq and Iran went to war, and Iran found that it had few friends or funds. Iran's oil exports, a major source of government revenue, had slowed because of equipment breakdowns and war-related destruction of petroleum facilities and pipelines. And fourth, Ronald Reagan, who promised a tougher posture, was elected president. The Carter administration official Gary Sick later charged that Reagan's campaign director, William J. Casey, may have secretly negotiated with Iranian officials to prevent any release of the hostages before the election, thus avoiding an "October Surprise."[35] Reagan dismissed the charge as "complete fiction."[36]

As these events unfolded, American and Iranian diplomats met with Algerian mediators. On the day before Reagan took office, an agreement was struck: release of the hostages in exchange for the unfreezing of Iranian assets in the United States. On January 20, 1981—shortly after Reagan's inauguration—the hostages gained their freedom. After 444 days of imprisonment, they returned home to a relieved nation that celebrated briefly and then tried to forget.

"*No one* spoke to any of the Persian-speaking political officers among the hostages to find out what happened" until months later, because U.S. officials "just didn't care," one hostage recalled.[37] Americans tried to forget quickly, but some second-guessing occurred. Should Carter have played up the hostage issue so much, thereby signaling to the Iranians that they had in fact stung and would continue to sting Americans? But with the Iranians jeering Washington day after day, with

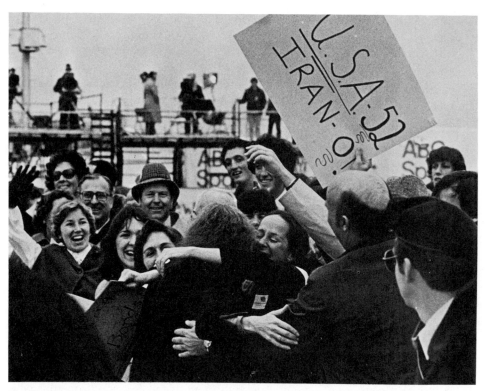

The Hostages Return.   After 444 days in captivity, the fifty-two Americans held prisoner in Iran came home to celebrations. At the start, sixty-six had been seized. Fourteen had been released from bondage earlier. This placard awarded victory to the United States. (U.S. Department of State. Photograph by Rover Kaiser)

Kissinger harping on America's weakness, with television cameras daily chronicling the crisis, with this gross violation of diplomatic immunity, with Carter's vaunted compassion for other human beings—could the president have removed the issue from the spotlight? And had the glare of publicity perhaps helped deter the Iranians from executing the hostages?

What did it all mean? The United States had lost an ally with a large army, huge quantities of oil, intelligence posts that yielded critical data on Soviet missile tests, and billions of dollars to spend on American-made weapons. The long crisis had wounded American pride and diminished its prestige, raising questions in the post-Vietnam era about the ability of the United States to lead. The hostage ordeal helped bring down the Carter presidency. President Reagan drew a simple lesson from the crisis: America had to build up its military to deter enemies. Other Americans urged separation from right-wing regimes and clients so that the United States could avoid becoming the target of revolutionary ire. Perhaps the hostage travail reinforced a lesson of Vietnam: Large infusions of American aid and weaponry, such as had flowed to the Shah, cannot guarantee the survival of an unpopular regime. As the Iranian revolution descended into tyranny, executions of Khomeini foes, and disputes with other Muslims in the Middle East, some Americans prided themselves on once having supported the Shah. Others found comfort in the fact that Washington's loss did not automatically become Moscow's gain: The Iranians remained ardently anti-Soviet.

The outpouring of emotional patriotism that greeted the returning hostages suggested another conclusion: The nation hungered for heroes who could rekindle American pride—a pride matched by assertiveness. "If television coverage of Vietnam had converted the American people into temporary pacifists," wrote one analyst, "the video images from Iran turned them into a pack of snarling wolves."[38] An Oklahoma man who judged Carter too timid looked to the imperial past for inspiration: "I agree with Teddy Roosevelt. Walk softly and carry a big stick," the Oklahoman said. "And club the hell out of them if you need to."[39]

ZBIGS AND ZAGS: CARTER'S DIVIDED ADMINISTRATION

Teddy Roosevelt's "big stick" was exactly what Jimmy Carter had found wrong with American foreign policy when he came to office in 1977—too much bluster, too much military, and too much insensitivity toward Third World peoples. During the 1976 campaign, Carter joined critics of the Nixon-Ford-Kissinger years in demanding "no more Vietnams" and "no more Chiles." He promised to reduce military budgets, bring some of America's overseas forces home, trim arms sales abroad, and slow nuclear proliferation. He berated the Republicans for tarnishing America's moral integrity by supporting dictatorial regimes. Yet at times Carter sounded more like an inveterate Cold Warrior than a reformist peacemaker. He claimed that the Republicans had permitted a decline of U.S. power. He mocked détente: "We've been outtraded in almost every instance."[40] He criticized the White House for accepting Soviet domination of Eastern Europe and authorizing huge grain sales to the Soviet Union. President Gerald Ford thought that Carter was playing politics—attracting the hawks by bemoaning the descent of American power and wooing the doves by advocating cuts in defense spending. "He wavers, he wanders, he wiggles, and he waffles," Ford complained.[41]

After the downbeat years of Watergate, Vietnam, CIA abuses, corporate bribes of foreign leaders, and soaring OPEC oil prices, the election of the wealthy peanut farmer with a toothy smile inspired hope. After graduating from the Naval Academy and serving on a nuclear submarine, Carter had entered politics as a Georgia state senator in the 1960s and, in 1970, had become governor. After a four-year gubernatorial term, this relatively obscure Democrat had set out to win the presidency. He astounded the professionals by doing so. Carter cherished hard work, family responsibility, and religion. A devout Baptist, he became a "born again" Christian, awakened to a religious revival by his evangelical sister Ruth, a faith-healer. Energetic, ambitious, and self-confident, Carter seemed to some people sanctimonious and arrogant. A quick learner, he paid meticulous attention to details. A Pentagon official noted that some decisionmakers were "forest men"—

Makers of American Foreign Relations, 1977–1989

Presidents	Secretaries of State
Jimmy Carter, 1977–1981	Cyrus R. Vance, 1977–1980
	Edmund Muskie, 1980–1981
Ronald Reagan, 1981–1989	Alexander M. Haig, Jr., 1981–1982
	George P. Shultz, 1982–1989

seeing the big picture—and others "treemen." Carter? "My God, he was a leaf man!"[42]

An "outsider" to Washington politics, Carter brought little experience in foreign affairs to the White House. He did hold membership in the Trilateral Commission, organized by the Columbia University political scientist Zbigniew Brzezinski and the banker David Rockefeller to bring together business, political, and academic notables for discussions of global problems bedeviling the industrial nations of Western Europe, North America, and Japan. And Carter had followed the fractious debate over Vietnam and its lessons, and he knew that a new national foreign-policy consensus had not yet taken form. "Deeply troubled by the lies our people had been told," he sensed a need for national redemption.[43]

Carter selected Cyrus Vance as his secretary of state. A wealthy, West Virginia–born, Yale-educated lawyer widely respected as a selfless public servant, Vance had held top posts in the Department of Defense in the 1960s. He doubted the efficacy of military intervention. He had learned from Vietnam, he said, that the United States could not "prop up a series of regimes that lacked popular support," and that "there can be no going back to a time when we thought there could be American solutions to every problem."[44] He did not believe that the Soviets fomented most local conflicts, and he advised quiet diplomacy to find avenues toward Soviet-American cooperation. When Vance resigned in April 1980, he did so not

Cyrus R. Vance (b. 1917). Yale graduate and former deputy secretary of defense, "Cy" Vance brought extensive diplomatic experience to his post as secretary of state. Vance won plaudits for negotiating the Panama Canal treaties and SALT-II. His resignation in 1980 was the first such act made in protest by a secretary of state since that of William Jennings Bryan in 1915. (National Archives)

only to protest the hostage rescue mission, but also to register his disenchantment with Carter for embracing military means and for his accepting the "visceral anti-Sovietism" of Zbigniew Brzezinski, the national security affairs adviser.[45]

Outspoken and tenacious, arrogant and aggressive, Brzezinski blamed most of the world's troubles on the Soviets. He sought military superiority and worked to play China off against the Soviet Union. To counter Vance's argument that a military coup in Iran would not save the Shah but would produce bloodshed, Brzezinski coldly lectured President Carter that "world politics was not a kindergarten."[46] State Department officers often bristled over Brzezinski's strong-arm bureaucratic methods and his attempts to become a public spokesperson for policy. He also sidestepped the professional diplomats by initiating back-channel contacts with foreign leaders. "While Mr. Vance played by the Marquis of Queensberry rules," remarked one American diplomat, "Mr. Brzezinski was more of a street fighter."[47]

The president believed that Vance and Brzezinski would balance one another in both style and substance, and that he could manage any conflict: "Zbig would be the thinker, Cy would be the doer, and Jimmy Carter would be the decider."[48] But acrimonious infighting soon made the administration's foreign policy appear inconsistent and contradictory, marked by zigs and zags between caution and hyperbole.

Despite personal and bureaucratic tussles, the Carter administration pursued basically traditional goals. "U.S. foreign policy is like an aircraft carrier," remarked Brzezinski. "You simply don't send it into a 180-degree turn; at most you move a few degrees to port or starboard."[49] At the start Carter officials rejected the extreme

Carter (b. 1924) and Zbigniew Brzezinski (b. 1928). This Warsaw-born son of a Polish diplomat emigrated to the United States in 1953. A long-time professor of political science at Columbia University, Brzezinski became noted for his Cold War views before serving as Carter's adviser. According to one White House staffer, Brzezinski relished his role as "the first Pole in 300 years in a position to really stick it to the Russians." Brzezinski told an interviewer: "I'm pretty good at winning. I win a great deal. I seldom lose, very seldom." (Carter Presidential Materials Project, Atlanta)

options of "Fortress America" (isolationism) and "Atlas America" (global police-man) in favor of "Participant America."[50] That meant emphasizing worldwide diplomatic activism or preventive diplomacy: advancing the peace process in the Middle East; reducing nuclear arms; normalizing relations with China; mediating conflict in the Third World; stimulating improvements in human rights; and creat-ing economic stability through talks on the law of the sea, energy, and clean air and water. The president wanted to concentrate on long-range issues and to avoid a re-active foreign policy enmeshed in short-term, day-to-day crises. With traditional American reformist zeal, Carter set out to apply "morality, reason, and power" to American diplomacy.[51]

Carter especially sought to restore American power and influence in the Third World. He preferred to emphasize North-South rather than East-West issues and to make concessions to nationalism, even to leftist regimes. The president declared that the "intellectual and moral poverty" of military intervention had been demon-strated in Vietnam.[52] Third World problems, he argued, sprang not from commu-nist plots but from deep-seated, indigenous economic, social, racial, and political problems. The appointment of Andrew Young as ambassador to the United Nations symbolized Carter's sympathetic approach. An African American once ac-tive in the civil rights movement, Young gradually improved the U.S. dialogue with suspicious Third World diplomats. But in 1979 Carter had to fire Young af-ter the ambassador made unauthorized contact with representatives of the Palestine Liberation Organization, a group that the United States refused to recognize. It later became known that the U.S. ambassador to Lebanon also held thirty-five secret yet officially sanctioned meetings with PLO representatives during the same period.

The "soul" of American foreign policy, Carter insisted, should be the defense and expansion of human rights for foreign peoples.[53] The president intended this as his personal contribution to world affairs. By internationalizing the Bill of Rights, America could recover its prestige and pride and add moral force to the nation's ar-senal. Drawing on Woodrow Wilson's ideas, the 1948 United Nations Universal Declaration of Human Rights, and his own religious commitment, Carter vowed to win for all peoples the freedom to work, vote, worship, travel, speak, assemble, and receive a fair trial. Slavery, genocide, torture, forced labor, arbitrary arrest, rigged elections, and suspensions of civil liberties all became anathema. Dictators must respect human rights or face cutbacks in American foreign aid.

Although Carter emphasized that Americans should put their "inordinate fear of communism" behind them, he actually reinvigorated the containment doctrine by initiating new weapons systems and streamlining conventional forces, by en-couraging nationalism in Eastern Europe, and by cultivating Third World govern-ments.[54] Improved Sino-American ties (the "China card"), continued strategic arms limitations talks, and public denunciations of Soviet violations of human rights also might check the Soviets. By 1979 Carter, having moved closer to Brzezinski's views, sounded the familiar Cold War tones of "a more muscular foreign policy."[55] The following year he proclaimed the Carter Doctrine, or containment in the Middle East. Confrontation more than cooperation came to mark Soviet-American relations under Carter.

Andrew Young (b. 1932). A graduate of Howard University and the Hartford Theological Seminary, the Reverend Young had been Dr. Martin Luther King's right-hand man in the civil rights movement of the 1950s–1960s and a member of Congress from Georgia be-fore Carter named him am-bassador to the United Nations. Young was forced to resign in 1979 when he ad-mitted meeting with represen-tatives of the Palestine Liberation Organization, whose participation in negoti-ations he deemed essential to Middle East peace. (United Nations. Photograph by Y. Nagata)

THE PANAMA CANAL AND NATIONALISM IN HIGH VOLTAGE: LATIN AMERICA

Although the Iranian hostage crisis and the bipolar rivalry with the Soviet Union came to dominate the president's foreign policy, at the outset Carter launched an active diplomacy toward Latin America, the Middle East, and Africa. In Latin America, still beset by poverty, rapid population growth, and natural disasters, Carter championed human rights and democratization and worked to accommodate the United States to nationalism. More than ever before, the Latin American governments claimed an independent role in world politics and shunned U.S. advice. Latin Americans petitioned Washington for lower tariffs, higher commodity prices, less diplomatic backing of North American corporations locked in disputes with their governments, and the transfer of technology on convenient terms. The Carter administration saw high stakes: $59 billion in trade (1979); investments of $24.4 billion (1979); vital imports of petroleum, copper, and tin; and Latin America's thirty votes in the United Nations. Foreign aid ($726 million in 1977–1978) continued as one means of exerting influence, but Carter also sought to reduce hostility by initiating negotiations.

Panama became the first testing ground. Panamanians had long resented the 1903 treaty granting the United States the Canal Zone, a ten-mile-wide, 500-square-mile slice of territory that cut their nation in half (see pages 38–43). "What nation of the world can withstand the humiliation of a foreign flag piercing its own heart?" asked Panamanian General Omar Torrijos.[56] After bloody anti-American riots in 1964, President Lyndon B. Johnson had started talks, but they barely crawled forward.

Carter brought the negotiations to fruition. Two treaties were signed in 1977 and ratified the following year. One treaty, abrogating the 1903 document, provided for the integration of the Canal Zone into Panama. The United States also agreed to increase Panama's percentage of the canal's revenues to boost the small nation's ailing economy. The other treaty stated that the United States had the right to defend the "neutrality" of the canal forever. In a national vote, Panamanians approved the treaties by a 2 to 1 margin, but nationalistic sentiment against a continued U.S. role in Panamanian affairs ran high. Torrijos identified "lots of electric currents" in his country that had to be controlled. The American negotiator Ellsworth Bunker thanked him for "keeping the voltage down."[57]

Conservative critics in the United States soon denounced the treaties as diabolical instruments of appeasement, isolationism, retreat, and surrender. After Vietnam, Americans had to draw the line somewhere: "Panama is the place and now is the time."[58] Many Americans thought that the United States owned the canal. Ronald Reagan, running hard for the Republican presidential nomination, mangled the historical record: "We bought it, we paid for it, it's ours, and we're going to keep it."[59] Other detractors argued that giving up a key waterway would weaken American defense and leave Panama vulnerable to Soviet or Cuban subversion. The American Legion and other veterans' groups lined up against the treaties, and the Conservative Caucus flooded senatorial offices with antitreaty mail. Many people were "still riding up the hill with Teddy Roosevelt," observed Senator Gale McGee of Wyoming, a supporter of the treaties.[60]

The Carter administration countered with "a full-court press."[61] The Committee of Americans for the Canal Treaties enlisted the veteran diplomat W. Averell Harriman, the former CIA director William Colby, the labor leader George Meany, and army general Maxwell Taylor, among others. Gerald Ford and Henry Kissinger also worked for approval. Executives of the National Association of Manufacturers and multinational corporations holding large investments in Latin America endorsed the agreements. Treaty advocates stressed the goodwill that the United States would gain after terminating the imperialistic document of 1903. If the United States insisted on staying in Panama, it might invite a protracted guerrilla war; a few well-placed sticks of dynamite could render the canal useless. Some argued that the canal's strategic value had declined because modern aircraft carriers had too much beam to pass through the waterway. Others pointed out that the canal's economic worth had also dwindled because less than 10 percent of U.S. foreign trade went through it, and the new, large cargo ships and supertankers could not squeeze through the locks.

As the debate peaked in early 1978, the administration used arguments that alarmed Panamanians. A "memorandum of understanding," signed by Torrijos and Carter and later added to the neutrality treaty by the Senate, provided for U.S. intervention after the year 2000 to thwart "any aggression or threat directed against the Canal or against the peaceful transit of vessels through the Canal."[62] When asked what the United States would do after 2000 if the Panamanians closed the canal for repairs, Brzezinski answered: "We will move in and close down the Panamanian government for repairs."[63]

On March 16, 1978, the Senate approved the neutrality treaty 68 to 32; the other treaty passed on April 18 by a similar count—in both cases with only one vote more than the two-thirds tally mandated by the Constitution. Carter later acknowledged that "some fine members of Congress had to pay with their political careers for their votes."[64] But the treaties did not gain approval without amendments. A "condition," which an annoyed Torrijos accepted only after Carter's personal plea, stated that if canal operations ever stopped, the United States had the right to intervene, "including the use of military force in the Republic of Panama."[65]

The Carter administration also contended with nationalist stirrings in Nicaragua. Since 1936 the Somoza family had ruled that Central American state (see pages 190–191). Dictatorial, brutal, and corrupt, the Somoza dynasty nevertheless had gained grudging U.S. support as a stable, reliable anticommunist ally and had received military aid, which it often used to suppress critics. Nicaragua had served as a staging area for CIA operations against Guatemala (1954) and Cuba (1961), and Nicaraguan troops had joined U.S. marines during the occupation of the Dominican Republic (1965). All the while, Nicaraguans suffered high rates of poverty, malnutrition, and illiteracy, and the Somozas amassed great wealth, coming to own much of the country's land and industry. After a devastating 1972

The United States and Latin America Since 1945

CANADA

UNITED STATES

Washington, D.C.

Inter-American Development
Bank Began Operations, 1961
Inter-American Defense
College Founded, 1962

ATLANTIC OCEAN

MEXICO

Miami

Castro, 1959
Bay of Pigs, 1961
Missile Crisis,
1962

U.S. Efforts to
Restore
Democracy, 1990s

U.S. Military
Intervention, 1965

DOMINICAN
REPUBLIC

Issues with U.S.
over Drugs, Debt,
and Migrants
NAFTA, 1994

Mexico City

Chapultepec
Conference,
1945

Havana

CUBA

GUANTÁNAMO
(U.S.)

HAITI

VIRGIN IS (U.S.)

PUERTO RICO (U.S.)

CIA–sponsored Intervention, 1954

GUATEMALA

BELIZE

JAMAICA

HONDURAS

U.S. Intervention
in Civil War, 1970s –1990s

EL SALVADOR

NICARAGUA

Anti-Nixon Riots, 1958
Founding Member
of OPEC, 1960

U.S. Invasion,
1983

GRENADA

Somoza Ousted, 1979
Contra War, 1982 –1990
Sandinistas Defeated in Election, 1990

COSTA
RICA

PANAMA

Caracas

TRINIDAD and TOBAGO

VENEZUELA

GUYANA

SURINAME

CANAL
ZONE

Bogotá

FR. GUIANA

Anti-U.S. Riots, 1959, 1964
Panama Canal Treaties, 1978
U.S. Invasion, 1989 –1990

COLOMBIA

U.S.-backed Military
Coup, 1964
U.S.-supplied Fuel for
Nuclear Reactor, 1978
Rain Forest Crisis, 1990s

O.A.S. Charter, 1948
Drug War, 1989 –

Quito

ECUADOR

Tuna War with U.S., 1971

PERU

BRAZIL

PACIFIC OCEAN

Lima

Radical Military Junta to Power, 1968
Major Cocaine Source for U.S. Market, 1980s –1990s

BOLIVIA

La Paz

Brasilia

Che Guevara killed, 1967
Major Cocaine Source for
U.S. Market, 1980s –1990s

PARAGUAY

Rio de Janeiro

Asunción

Rio Pact Concluded,
1947

CHILE

URUGUAY

Alliance for Progress
Launched, 1961

U.S. Helped Oust
Allende, 1973

Santiago

Buenos Aires

Montevideo

ARGENTINA

Rule of Juan Perón,
1943 –1955, 1973 –1974

Pan-American Highway

U.S. Military sites

Soviet Missile sites, 1962

U.S. Direct Investments in Latin America:
1950 = $4.4 bil. 1970 = $11.1 bil.
1960 = $7.5 bil. 1980 = $38.7 bil.
          1990 = $71.6 bil.

U.S. Foreign Aid (Grants and Credits):
1946 –1990 = $31.47 bil.

Argentine-British
War, 1982

FALKLAND IS.
(MALVINAS)

earthquake, the Somoza family callously drained off international relief aid. A long-smoldering popular rebellion exploded in 1978, led by the leftist Sandinista National Liberation Front (FSLN). Founded in 1962, the FSLN took its name from the insurgent César Augusto Sandino, who had fought American occupation in the 1920s and 1930s (see pages 189–190). As the insurgency gained momentum, business executives, Catholic clergy, and intellectuals joined the crusade to unseat the Somozas and reduce U.S. influence. General Anastasio Somoza Debayle, a graduate of West Point (1946), answered with torture, executions, and bombings of civilians.

Wanting neither Somoza nor the revolutionary Sandinistas, Carter tried to shape a new government that would ensure Somoza's departure and restrict the radical Sandinistas. Somoza balked and the effort failed. After the FSLN opened its final offensive in mid-1979, Washington encouraged the national guard—Somoza's hated personal army—to preserve order. When this tactic also faltered, diplomats pressed the new, broadly based provisional government to share power with more nonradicals or else forfeit reconstruction assistance. "The only way to characterize this is blackmail," decried the Reverend Miguel D'Escoto, the foreign minister–designate.[66] On July 17, 1979, Somoza and his entourage fled the battle-scarred country; he was later assassinated in Paraguay. Carter had abandoned a client government supported by seven previous U.S. administrations.

The new Nicaraguan government promised a mixed economy and pluralistic politics. But only after Mexico, Venezuela, and others offered loans did Carter ask Congress to appropriate $75 million in economic assistance for Nicaragua. Congress waited until July 1980 to allocate funds; conservatives had delayed the bill with emotional charges that the Nicaraguan government was becoming communist because it welcomed Cuban advisers and indulged in caustic anti-Yankee propaganda. Many Nicaraguans naturally resented the United States' longtime ties with Somoza, the initial tampering with their revolution, and then the long delay in extending foreign aid. Tension between Managua and Washington soon ran high, especially when Carter suspended economic aid in early 1981 on the grounds that the Sandinistas aided rebels who were challenging the U.S.-backed government of El Salvador (see pages 521–523).

Mexico's announcement in 1981 that it was "tightening the links of friendship that bind us with the revolutions of Cuba and Nicaragua" suggested diplomatic troubles even closer to home.[67] Mexico and the United States shared a 2,000-mile border. Goods and people moved across it with ease. In the 1970s hundreds of thousands of Mexicans entered the United States without immigration papers. These illegal immigrants or undocumented aliens—popularly called wetbacks—numbered some 2 to 4 million by 1980. In 1978 alone, American border patrols captured 1 million Mexicans trying to cross the international boundary, but perhaps as many as 500,000 migrants slipped across unnoticed that year, most of them young males escaping the depressed economy of Mexico to work. Great numbers returned to Mexico each year. "It is not a crime to look for work," remarked President José López Portillo, especially when American employers offered jobs.[68] U.S. critics contended that these illegal laborers displaced American workers, drove down wages, and burdened taxpayers by ending up on the welfare roles. The migrants flouted U.S. law. Yet on this point confusion abounded: It was illegal for undocumented migrants to take jobs but legal for employers to hire them. Carter tackled the *indocumentado* controversy early. In August 1977, he asked for new legislation, but not until 1986 did Congress pass the Immigration Reform and Control Act, which provided amnesty and legal residence for illegal migrants already in the United States, fines for employers who hired undocumented workers, and stricter border controls.

Commercial questions also troubled Mexican-American relations. By 1980 Mexico ranked as the United States' third most important trading partner, after Canada and Japan. The United States bought about three-quarters of Mexico's exports, valued at $12.5 billion, and provided about 70 percent of Mexico's imports, valued at $15.1 billion. U.S. citizens held 69 percent of total foreign investments in Mexico, or more than $5 billion. Mexican nationalists railed against their economic dependency. Mexico appeared to gain leverage in the late 1970s, when geologists discovered vast deposits of oil and natural gas. Energy-hungry North Americans hailed the find, anticipating that Mexico, not a member of OPEC, would sell at bargain prices. Mexico did sell most of its petroleum to the United States, but at a price *higher* than that charged by Saudi Arabia. Mexicans asked why they should bail the United States out of its energy crisis at the expense of their own economy.

U.S. companies signed agreements with Mexico to purchase large amounts of natural gas, and in 1977, the Mexicans began construction of an expensive pipeline to transport the gas northward. But Washington refused to accept the Mexican price, and the deal fell through. They struck a new agreement in September 1979. "We received much less gas at a much higher price at a much later date," observed a U.S. diplomat, and the "adverse political fallout was being felt long after the event."[69] Still, in 1980, oil and natural gas accounted for 50 percent of U.S. imports from Mexico.

The "political fallout" from the Cuban Revolution continued to rain down as well. The Carter administration initially sought to reduce tensions with Fidel Castro's government. In March 1977, U.S. and Cuban negotiators began to discuss the normalization of relations. In September of that year, Cuba and the United States each established "interests sections" in the other's country (essentially embassies without full diplomatic recognition). Carter also lifted the ban on travel to Cuba. Castro in 1978 made gestures toward improved relations by releasing 3,600 political prisoners. Several irritants diminished these positive steps. The Soviet Union was pouring about $3 million a day into Cuba to sustain the island's fragile economy, much weakened by the longstanding U.S. trade embargo and Castro's mismanagement. Washington argued that Cuba had become a Soviet puppet and charged that Cuban troops in Angola and Ethiopia served as Soviet surrogates. Castro retorted that he was pursuing Cuba's commitment to revolutions in the Third World. The Cubans had entered Angola as early as the 1960s, independently of the Soviets. Secret, high-level U.S.-Cuba talks in 1978–1980 failed to normalize relations or relax the trade embargo. And the question of a Soviet brigade in Cuba poisoned chances for rapprochement with Havana (see page 503).

An unusual crisis in spring 1980 further soured Cuban-American relations. Castro announced that Cubans wishing to leave the country could use Peruvian visas if they could get them. Thousands jammed into the Peruvian embassy grounds in Havana. Carter thereupon announced that the United States would accept Cubans who wanted to join their families already in the United States. Castro soon declared that any Cuban who wanted to emigrate could do so by boat from the port of Mariel. All makes and shapes of watercraft began to shuttle between Cuba and Florida in a "freedom flotilla"; about 100,000 Cubans entered U.S. processing centers. Castro emptied his jails of "undesirables" and cynically put them on boats to the United States. "Fidel has flushed his toilet on us," the mayor of Miami bitterly charged.[70] Many of the new arrivals languished in detention centers in the United States; others rioted. Americans felt tricked, especially as evidence mounted that many *Marielitos* had criminal records.

Elsewhere in Latin America, right-wing governments resisted Carter's efforts to improve human rights, although Haiti, Argentina, and the Dominican Republic did release hundreds of political prisoners. In 1977 Carter suspended military aid to Guatemala when its regime sanctioned the murder and torture of political opponents; two years later he froze U.S. aid to Bolivia after that nation's military seized power. Democratic leaders in Latin America praised Carter's efforts to put distance between the United States and the dictatorships. Henry Forde, prime minister of Barbados, remarked that Carter had done much "to correct the image of the United States as an unfeeling giant."[71]

CARTER'S ACTIVISM IN THE MIDDLE EAST AND AFRICA

The Middle East emerged as the most tense and dramatically changing area of the world in the Carter years. The Iranian revolution and hostage crisis, civil war in Lebanon, Arab-Israeli conflict, Iran-Iraq War, Soviet thrust into Afghanistan (see page 504), and Western reliance on Persian Gulf oil put the region in the headlines. The United States had significant economic, military, and diplomatic interests in the Middle East. Saudi Arabia served as America's largest supplier of imported oil. In 1980 Israel and Egypt together received about one-third of all U.S. foreign aid. During the period 1971–1981, the United States sold $47.7 billion worth of armaments to Middle Eastern countries. American weapons became the instruments of war in the region: Israel used U.S. warplanes to attack Palestinian communities in Lebanon and revolutionary Iran used American arms to battle Iraq. Syrians and Iraqis, on the other hand, brandished Soviet armaments.

Building on Kissinger's earlier efforts, the Carter administration concentrated on bringing Egypt and Israel to the peace table. Israeli leaders encouraged the president, because "if you take one wheel off a car, it won't drive. If Egypt is out of the conflict, there will be no more war."[72] President Anwar el-Sadat of Egypt personally advanced the peace process. In November 1977 he astonished the world by journeying to Jerusalem to offer peace and security to Israel in exchange for an Israeli withdrawal from lands occupied since 1967. When the Sadat initiative faltered, Carter interceded, inviting Sadat and Israeli prime minister Menachem Begin

Signatures on the Egyptian-Israeli Peace Treaty of March 26, 1979. The historic document, hammered out under the patient guidance of the American president, was signed by Egypt's president Anwar el-Sadat, Israeli prime minister Menachem Begin, and President Jimmy Carter. (U.S. Department of State)

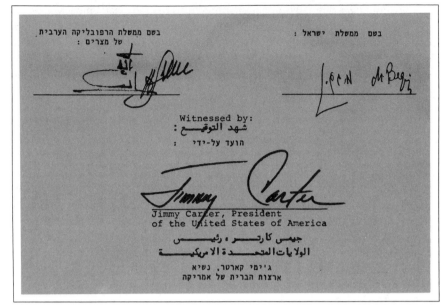

to Camp David. Carter brought an annotated Bible, "which I predicted . . . would be needed in my discussions with Prime Minister Begin."[73] From September 5 to 17, 1978, the three leaders and their aides engaged in often heated discussion. Carter pressed Begin to withdraw to Israel's 1967 borders in the hope that the restored territories might become a homeland for Palestinians. Israel could not have both peace and captured territories, Carter reasoned. Like his predecessors, Carter favored an agreement based on the 1967 United Nations Resolution 242, by which Arabs would recognize Israel's right to live in peace and security in exchange for Israeli withdrawal from territories seized in the war. Playing "the role of draftsman, strategist, therapist, friend, adversary, and mediator," Carter wooed and cajoled.[74] But, alert to the Jewish vote in the United States and confronted with Begin's stubbornness, Carter retreated from a comprehensive peace and persuaded Sadat to accept compromises. Sadat wanted an agreement more than Begin did. Carter promised both sides huge amounts of foreign aid if they would settle some of their differences.

Egypt and Israel signed two Camp David Accords. The first agreement stated goals: negotiations leading to self-government for the West Bank and Gaza and future involvement of Jordanian and Palestinian representatives in the peace process. The second agreement, a "framework" for peace, provided for Israeli withdrawal from the Sinai in exchange for Egyptian diplomatic recognition. Once resumed, the Egyptian-Israeli negotiations stumbled again. Carter pressed for compromise. In March 1979, he flew to the Middle East to meet separately with Begin and Sadat. Once more Carter flattered and implored.

The presidential presence worked again. Signed on March 26, 1979, the Egyptian-Israeli Peace Treaty provided for the phased withdrawal of Israel from the

Sinai, to be completed in 1982; the stationing of United Nations forces along the Egyptian-Israeli boundary to monitor the agreement; full economic and diplomatic relations between Cairo and Tel Aviv (they exchanged ambassadors in early 1980); and the opening of negotiations on Palestinian rights in the occupied West Bank and Gaza (see map, page 443). After thirty years of war, peace formally came to part of the Middle East. Carter candidly called the treaty "the first step of peace. . . . There now remains the rest of the Arab world."[75] Other Arabs, especially the PLO, denounced the treaty for not recognizing the right of Palestinians to a homeland. Even Jordan's King Hussein, long considered an Arab moderate, blasted the peace as a "dead horse" because it ignored the homeland question.[76] By the end of Carter's administration, the troops of Israel and the PLO, the latter with Syrian help, were shooting at one another in Lebanon (see page 528).

Although sub-Saharan African issues did not carry the urgency of Middle Eastern problems, the Carter administration strove to identify the United States with black African nationalism and to end the "last vestiges of colonialism" in Zimbabwe/Rhodesia and Namibia.[77] Ambassador Andrew Young became the president's chief adviser, with "African solutions for African problems" as his motto.[78] He believed that American support for a strong and stable black Africa, through foreign aid and trade, would reduce Soviet influence on the continent. African nationalism, not American intervention, would contain the Soviet Union and protect U.S. interests.

Much seemed at stake in Africa. First, the continent had political clout—a third of the membership in the United Nations. Second, Africa possessed a bulging storehouse of raw materials. For example, Zaire ranked as the United States' largest supplier of cobalt; Nigeria provided the second largest source of imported oil; Gabon supplied manganese; Namibia had the world's largest uranium mine; and South Africa shipped manganese, platinum, chromium, and antimony to the United States. Third, Africa held great trade and investment potential, because the fifty nations hungered for development capital and modern technology. By 1979 Americans had invested some $4 billion in black Africa and about $2 billion in South Africa. Total annual trade with Africa passed the $30 billion figure. Fourth, Africa's strategic location aroused interest. Its ports and airfields lay along major sea lanes through the Persian Gulf, Indian Ocean, and Atlantic Ocean. Fifth, the region's political instability made it an arena for great power competition. Sixth, because American blacks had descended from Africans, they kept national leaders alert to African issues and politically accountable for their decisions.

The Carter administration worked especially hard to cultivate Nigerian friendship. Africa's most populous nation, Nigeria, ranked seventh in world oil production and carried weight in African politics. Nigeria became independent in 1960 and in 1967 suffered a civil war in which victory over Biafran separatists cost more than half a million lives. World opinion, including that of the United States, grew hostile toward the military regime that had perpetrated this tragedy. But in the 1970s, when America endured its energy crisis and Nigeria expanded its oil production, relations improved. Both Carter and Young visited Nigeria, acknowledging the nation's importance to Africa's future.

South Africa stood near the forefront of African-American relations. Its riches, traditional ties to the United States, occupation of Namibia, blatant racism, and white minority government ensured its continuing prominence on the U.S. diplomatic agenda. Carter chided white South African rulers for apartheid—an official system of segregating nonwhites and whites that included removals of blacks to designated homelands, discriminatory wages based on race, and the denial of voting rights, absence of civil liberties, and arbitrary arrest for blacks. During a visit to South Africa, Vice President Walter Mondale angered whites by calling for a one-person, one-vote policy (85 percent of South Africa was nonwhite), not only because he thought it right, but because "perpetuating an unjust system is the surest incentive to increase Soviet influence and even racial war."[79] Carter rejected economic sanctions as a means to foster change in the Republic of South Africa, because trade stood at $4 billion in 1979, and the largest concentration of American investment in the continent rested in South Africa. In the mid-1970s, twenty-nine of America's top fifty corporations operated there, with General Motors, Mobil, Exxon, Ford, General Electric, and Firestone heading the list. Although American critics argued for disinvestment to press South Africa to halt apartheid, the most some American companies would do was to accept the Sullivan Principles. Devised by the black Philadelphia minister Leon H. Sullivan, also a member of the General Motors board of directors, the guidelines amounted to a voluntary pledge to follow nondiscriminatory employment practices in South Africa. By 1979 only 116 of the 300 American firms active there had endorsed the Sullivan Principles, and very few

Breaking the Rules in South Africa. The policy of apartheid sought to separate blacks (the majority of South Africa's population) from whites (the minority). But black South Africans protested the oppressive rules in a host of ways—including this man's daring violation of the law by sitting on a bench reserved for "Europeans" or whites. (UPI/Bettmann)

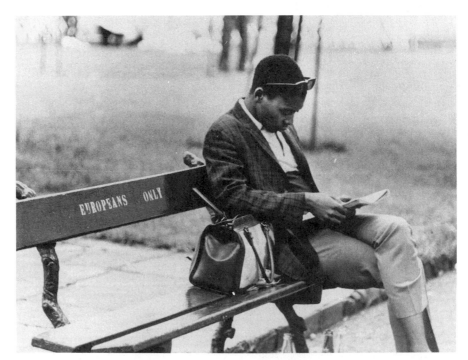

blacks held managerial positions in American-owned companies operating in South Africa.

Many black African leaders favored a U.S. economic boycott and protested the sale of American aircraft to the regime. They criticized Carter's approval of Export-Import Bank loans (subsequently stopped by Congress). One Nigerian official condemned America's "outright collaboration with South Africa" and pressed Washington to honor its rhetoric of human rights.[80] The Carter administration defended its policies: The United States needed strategic minerals from South Africa; disinvestment would hurt native blacks by causing unemployment; if American investors pulled out, competitors would simply move in, denying the United States both profits and leverage on the regime; and economic warfare would have limited impact, given South Africa's unusual self-sufficiency. Carter officials believed that steady pressure, short of economic sanctions, would move South Africa to reform. But the white regime's minor changes, argued critics, amounted to little more than the "desegregation of the deck chairs on the *Titanic*."[81]

Nor did change occur in Namibia, a former German colony governed by South Africa since World War I. In 1966 the United Nations revoked South Africa's mandate over Namibia and demanded independence, but Pretoria defiantly continued to rule the mineral-rich territory. The radical South West African People's Organization (SWAPO) battled South African armies from sanctuaries in Angola and Zambia and vowed a war of national liberation that U.S. leaders feared might enmesh the great powers in further conflict in Africa (see page 532).

In contrast, in Zimbabwe/Rhodesia, the bitter civil war between whites and insurgent blacks finally ended. Ian Smith's white government, formed in 1965, had made token gestures to black majority rule, but Carter insisted on real change. The president persuaded Congress in early 1977 to repeal the Byrd Amendment (1971), which had permitted the United States to trade with Zimbabwe/Rhodesia in chromium, despite the UN-declared economic boycott of Smith's regime. Carter in 1979 refused to accept the results of white-manipulated elections. Finally, British-led negotiations culminated in an all-races, nationwide election held in April 1980, which produced a new government led by the former black rebel Robert Mugabe. The outcome served as a rare example of a civil war resolved by diplomacy.

By the end of Carter's term, U.S. influence in Africa stood higher than ever, and trade with black Africa was improving. The United States gained access to military facilities in Somalia after that nation had expelled the Soviets in 1977. At the UN General Assembly, many African countries joined the United States in a 104 to 18 vote to condemn the Soviet invasion of Afghanistan. Soviet and Cuban influence in Africa confined itself mainly to Ethiopia and Angola, and even the latter reached out for better relations with Western nations. Nigeria's President Obasanjo reflected widespread opinion when he warned Moscow and Havana that Africa would not welcome a "new imperial power."[82] Zambian president Kenneth Kaunda hailed President Carter for bringing "a breath of fresh air to our troubled world."[83]

U.S. Dependence on Imports of Raw Materials, 1980

RAW MATERIALS	PERCENT OF DOMESTIC CONSUMPTION DERIVED FROM IMPORTS	MAJOR FOREIGN SOURCES AND USES
Columbium	100%	Brazil, Canada, Thailand — Boiler steel, refinery equipment, jet engines, gas turbines
Mica (sheet)	100%	India, Brazil, Madagascar — Electrical and electronic equipment
Strontium	100%	Mexico — Color television picture tubes, pyrotechnics
Graphite	100%	Mexico, South Korea, Madagascar, U.S.S.R. — Steel, refractories, lubricants
Industrial diamonds	100%	Ireland, South Africa, Belg.-Lux., U.K. — Abrasives, drills, phonograph needles, glass cutters
Manganese	97%	South Africa, Gabon, Brazil, France — Steel, dry cell batteries, chemicals, paints
Tantalum	97%	Thailand, Canada, Malaysia, Brazil — Electronic components, machinery
Bauxite & alumina	94%	Jamaica, Guinea, Australia, Suriname — Pots and pans, window frames, house siding, abrasives
Cobalt	93%	Zaire, Belg.-Lux., Zambia, Finland — Gas turbine engines, magnetic materials, mining tools
Chromium	91%	South Africa, U.S.S.R., Philippines, Turkey — Metals, chemicals, refractories, jet engines
Platinum — Group metals	87%	South Africa, U.S.S.R., U.K. — Jewelry, chemicals, fuel cells, electrodes, dental fillings
Fluorspar	84%	Mexico, South Africa, Spain — Chemicals, water fluoridation
Tin	84%	Malaysia, Bolivia, Thailand, Indonesia — Cans, containers, ceramics, pigments
Asbestos	76%	Canada, South Africa — Asbestos-cement pipe, flooring, insulation, gaskets
Nickel	73%	Canada, Norway, New Caledonia, Dom. Rep. — Steel, electroplating, nuclear reactors
Potassium	62%	Canada, Israel — Fertilizers, chemicals, soap
Cadmium	62%	Canada, Australia, Mexico, Belg.-Lux. — Hardware, batteries, pigments, plastics
Zinc	58%	Canada, Spain, Mexico, West Germany — Galvanizing iron and steel, die castings, bleaches, paints
Tungsten	54%	Canada, Bolivia, Thailand, South Korea — Incandescent lamps, jet engines, high pressure equipment
Antimony	53%	South Africa, Mexico, Bolivia, China — Ammunition, flame retardants, batteries, glass
Mercury	49%	Spain, Algeria, Italy, Canada, Yugoslavia — Catalyst for plastics and resins, gauges, thermostats
Titanium (ilmenite)	47%	Australia, Canada, South Africa — Jet engines, missile parts, pigments, bottle helmets
Selenium	40%	Canada, Japan, Yugoslavia — Electronic components, photocopiers, glass, chemicals
Barium	38%	Peru, Ireland, Mexico, Morocco — Well-drilling, television picture tubes, optical glass
Gypsum	38%	Canada, Mexico, Jamaica — Plasters, cements
Petroleum	31%	Saudi Arabia, Nigeria, Libya, Mexico — Fuels, asphalt, plastics, synthetic rubber
Gold	28%	Canada, U.S.S.R., Switzerland — Jewelry, electronics, dental fillings, investment bars
Iron ore	22%	Canada, Venezuela, Brazil, Liberia — Steel, ships, machine tools, razor blades, nuts and bolts
Vanadium	15%	South Africa, Chile — Construction equipment, pipelines, welding rods
Copper	14%	Canada, Chile, Zambia, Peru — Electrical wire, bearings, coins, steel cases

Source: 1976–1979 data from U.S. Department of the Interior, U.S. Department of Energy, and the U.S. Department of the Navy.

The Red Thread: SALT-II, Afghanistan, and the Carter Record

Carter's efforts to improve relations with the Third World ultimately became over-shadowed by the old question of containing the Soviet Union. From the outset, conflicting interpretations of Soviet behavior beset the Carter administration. Some officials believed that North-South relations ranked as more important than the East-West rivalry. Global problems did not always stem from Soviet intrigue, and the Soviet Union suffered domestic troubles, an unimaginative and aged leadership, and nationalist stirrings in Eastern Europe. "Are the Soviets five feet tall or ten feet tall?" asked Marshall Shulman, an aide to Vance.[84] Shulman and others in the State Department saw the Soviets as adversaries with whom the United States could ne-gotiate, but Brzezinski and his NSC staff countered that Soviet expansionism in the Middle East and Africa had to be faced down, not negotiated away. Brzezinski wanted the Soviets to sense an American "challenge to their legitimacy and thus to their very existence."[85]

Buffeted by these competing views, Carter vacillated, settling on a mix of "competition and cooperation."[86] He once asked Vance and Brzezinski to submit separate memoranda for a major 1978 speech on Soviet-American relations. Predictably, two contrasting statements reached the Oval Office. In essence stapling the different papers together, the president gave an address marked by a glaring con-tradiction between toughness and conciliation, between the "mailed fist and the dove's coo."[87] Still, as Vance learned, the president increasingly leaned toward Brzezinski's counsel of confrontation.

Barely a month in office, the administration exhorted Moscow to permit Dr. Andrei Sakharov, a leading dissident, to speak freely against the Soviet government. The Kremlin testily warned Americans to stop meddling in Soviet domestic affairs. To Moscow, Carter's call for human rights counted as yet another example of Washington's abandonment of détente. The Soviets still smarted from the 1974–1975 controversy over the Jackson-Vanik Amendment to the 1974 Trade Act (requiring the Soviets to relax restrictions on Jewish emigration before the United States would grant most-favored-nation tariff treatment), from the anti-Soviet tone of the 1976 presidential campaign, and from American overtures to Soviet archenemy China. They defied Carter's sermons by harassing Jews who ap-plied to emigrate from the Soviet Union to Israel and dissident intellectuals who criticized the communist regime. From the American perspective, too, the Soviets seemed bent on a military buildup: Cuban troops and Soviet advisers stayed in Angola; the Soviet navy and Warsaw Pact forces modernized; and greater numbers of missiles pointed at NATO countries. U.S. arms improvements and activism abroad, Moscow retorted, explained the Soviet steps. In any case, détente never meant to them that they must abandon their support for leftist Third World nations. In this environment laced with suspicion and hostility, Secretary Vance journeyed to Moscow in March 1977 to reenergize the SALT (Strategic Arms Limitation

Talks) process with a sudden, publicized proposal for deep cuts in ICBMs—precisely the category in which the Soviets were strongest. "Too sudden, too public, too narrow and even too discourteous," said George F. Kennan of the Vance proposal after the Soviets quickly rejected it.[88] The Soviets did not believe Carter was "serious."[89]

Carter next tried toughness. In March 1978 he denounced the Kremlin for conducting a proxy war in Ethiopia by using Cubans to battle Somalia, a newfound American friend that had futilely invaded Ethiopia to seize disputed land. The president's blunt speech, boasted Brzezinski, meant "we weren't soft."[90] British prime minister James Callaghan downplayed any Soviet threat, ridiculing "Columbuses who have lately discovered Africa."[91] In May, Brzezinski traveled to China with the intention of signaling the Soviets that they should worry about Sino-American "parallel interests."[92] After the NSC adviser challenged his hosts to a footrace at the Great Wall, saying the "last one to the top fights the Russians in Ethiopia," the Chinese called him "the polar bear tamer."[93] Hints of American arms sales to the People's Republic prompted one Soviet official to complain that the United States was "smuggling" weapons aimed against the USSR through the "back door" in Asia.[94]

As Soviet-American trade increased, Moscow understandably expressed puzzlement over "constant zigzags and inconsistency" in U.S. behavior.[95] Still, the two superpowers, like "apes on a treadmill," moved toward a new strategic arms limitation agreement.[96] SALT-II talks, which had begun in November 1972, produced some guidelines in the form of the 1974 Vladivostok accord but then fizzled. The giants had continued to deploy new missiles and enlarge their arsenals of warheads (see pages 439–440). In the SALT-II talks of 1977–1979, the Soviets tried but failed to block American development of the new MX (missile experimental), an improved ICBM designed to carry ten MIRVs; the Trident-II submarine-launched ballistic missile, capable of carrying fourteen warheads; and the cruise missile (see Glossary page 438). The Americans sought but failed to restrict the new Soviet supersonic "Backfire" bomber. Its range of 5,500 miles threatened Western Europe and China, and in a desperate one-way mission it could also strike the United States. Prolonged negotiations nonetheless culminated in the SALT-II treaty, signed at the Vienna summit in June 1979.

One of the most complex treaties ever negotiated, SALT-II for the first time established numerical equality between the United States and the Soviet Union in total strategic nuclear delivery vehicles, each limited to 2,400 (reduced to 2,250 in 1982). The treaty capped MIRVed launchers at 1,200 and limited the number of warheads per delivery vehicle. Whereas the treaty required the Soviets to dismantle more than 250 existing delivery vehicles, the Americans could expand from their current 2,060 to the ceiling of 2,250. The treaty also provided that each nation could conduct technical verification of the other's compliance without interference.

SALT-II soon fell victim to the deteriorating Soviet-American relationship and fears that détente had cost the United States its world supremacy. The influential Paul Nitze, conservative adviser to six presidents on national security, said that he opposed the agreement in order to stem the "weakness and inconsistency" of American foreign policy: "The United States is being pushed around in the world . . . ; it is time for the United States to stand up and not be a patsy."[97] The treaty ran into trouble in the Senate, where hawkish opponents argued that progress on nuclear-arms control should be linked to Soviet behavior on other issues, such as human rights and Africa. Just before Carter went to Vienna, Democratic senator Henry Jackson of Washington, who took a "stick-it-to-the-Russians" approach to diplomacy, charged the president with "appeasement in its purest form."[98] Jackson and other hawks also claimed that the Soviets, by the mid-1980s, could destroy America's land-based missiles in a first strike. SALT-II therefore endangered American security. Conservatives also asserted that accurate verification could not be guaranteed. Dovish critics, however, found SALT-II limitations too meager, permitting continued nuclear-weapons growth. But at least the treaty codified the arms race.

Admitting that SALT-II was but a small step toward deep-cut agreements, the Carter administration concentrated on rebutting conservative critics. Without SALT-II, the State Department explained, the Soviets would enlarge their nuclear forces at a brisker pace. Compelled to keep up, the United States would fuel an expensive, spiraling arms race. SALT-II, moreover, curbed the Soviets but placed minimal restraints on U.S. nuclear weapons development. As for the alleged vulnerability of American ICBMs, Carter officials explained that the Soviets would have to deposit two warheads squarely on every ICBM silo to ensure destruction— an unlikely scenario. First, in a "single cosmic roll of the dice," the timing would have to be near-perfect so that one incoming warhead would not explode and destroy other warheads before they reached their targets ("fratricide").[99] Second, wind speed, changes in atmospheric density, and irregularities in gravitational field could alter a missile's course. Third, the Soviets would have to assume that the president would stand by—even with twenty to thirty minutes' warning—and let American ICBMs be destroyed in their silos. Fourth, even if a Soviet first strike somehow destroyed the land-based ICBMs, it could damage only 30 percent of U.S. nuclear forces; the rest of the triad—SLBMs and strategic bombers—would remain to annihilate tens of millions of Soviet people. "They [Soviets] are not supermen; they are not fools either," remarked the State Department officer Leslie H. Gelb.[100]

The president tried to mollify his critics. To ensure the survivability of the ICBMs, Carter decided to deploy MX missiles in an expensive network of tracks and underground shelters. In a giant shell game, 200 missiles would constantly shuttle through the 9,000-mile system, a tactic that would prevent the Soviets from targeting them. Dovish critics thought the highly accurate MX would stimulate a feverish arms race by providing the United States with a "counterforce" capability—that is, the ability to knock out Soviet ICBMs in a first strike.

If Carter clouded the meaning of SALT-II by injecting the MX issue, he further jeopardized ratification by mishandling a "pseudo-crisis" in fall 1979.[101] He accused the Soviets of sneaking a combat brigade of 2,600 troops into Cuba to threaten other Caribbean islands. When the surprised yet conciliatory Soviets replied that the unit had been stationed there for many years, Carter retreated from the storm he had stirred up. Asked later why the episode had ever occurred, Under Secretary of State David D. Newsom fingered politics: "The White House is naturally conscious of the Presidential image."[102] The episode further poisoned the atmosphere for SALT-II by suggesting that the Soviets were once again up to no good and that Carter was inept. "Jimmy Carter's Cuban fiasco," wrote one columnist, "ranks right up there with the Dewey campaign of 1948 for snatching defeat from the jaws of victory."[103] Senator Frank Church of Idaho, chair of the Foreign Relations Committee, temporarily postponed hearings on SALT-II and exploited the brigade issue in order to improve his own chances in a tough reelection campaign.

With senatorial ratification of the treaty in doubt in early December, and with the hostage crisis raising fears that the Soviets might meddle in Iran, Carter tried to win votes from hawks through other decisions. He announced an expensive five-year military expansion program and NATO approval of an American plan to deploy 572 Pershing-II ballistic missiles and ground-launched cruise missiles in Western Europe to counter the Soviet medium-range SS-20 missiles aimed at America's allies.

The Soviet invasion of Afghanistan in late December 1979 killed the SALT-II treaty and elevated to orthodoxy Brzezinski's hard-line views about a malevolent Soviet Union. Thousands of Red Army troops marched into neighboring Afghanistan to sustain a Soviet client challenged by Islamic rebels. According to the scholar Raymond Garthoff, the security-conscious Soviets intervened because they wanted to maintain Afghanistan as a "buffer" against the spread of Islamic fundamentalism in central Asia.[104] Carter used the "hot-line" to vent his rage at Soviet premier Leonid Brezhnev, because the invasion marked a "quantum jump in the nature of Soviet behavior."[105] Carter claimed that the Soviet invasion posed the most serious threat to peace since World War II. Washington worried, too, because about one-third of America's oil imports came from the Persian Gulf region; Japan and allies in Western Europe imported three-quarters and two-thirds, respectively. Did the invasion of Afghanistan signal a Soviet master plan to deny America and its allies vital fuel? Would the Soviets take advantage of the chaos in Iran and move against that nation too? With an eye on domestic opinion, the Carter administration acted as if it feared the worst. "Putting 'a Red thread' through the complexities of the Gulf area seemed to us to be a desirable and justified simplification" to arouse the American people, Brzezinski later admitted.[106]

In early 1980 Carter announced punishments for the Soviet Union. He withdrew the SALT-II treaty from the Senate. He stopped high technology sales and grain shipments to the USSR. He pulled the United States out of the Summer Olympic Games scheduled for Moscow and urged other nations to boycott the event. And he curtailed Soviet commercial fishing privileges in American waters. Carter also outlined military measures: arms assistance for Pakistan, a state bordering the Soviet Union; creation of U.S. naval facilities in Oman, Kenya, Somalia, and Egypt; formation of a rapid deployment force for use in the Middle East; positioning of two aircraft carrier groups in the region; and a much increased defense budget. Further, the president asked an obliging Congress to require young men to register for the draft so as to mobilize forces quickly in the event of war. And last, the CIA secretly aided the Afghan rebels. Carter, wrote a former Nixon assistant, had turned to "the hawks for quick fixes."[107]

MX Launch Test. The "missile experimental" carried ten warheads and was first deployed in 1986. Following the recommendation of the Scowcroft Commission, a study group he appointed to advise him on a basing system, President Reagan decided to place MX missiles in fixed ICBM silos. (U.S. Air Force)

In his State of the Union address of January 24, 1980, the president proclaimed the Carter Doctrine: "An attempt by any outside force to gain control of the Persian Gulf region will be regarded as an assault on the vital interests of the United States of America, and such an assault will be repelled by use of any means necessary, including military force."[108] As a statement of containment, it sounded familiar themes. But serious problems impeded implementation. When Washington offered $400 million to Pakistan, its prime minister said "peanuts" and demanded more.[109] The Saudis refused to let the U.S. military use their facilities. West Germany and Japan declined to interrupt their lucrative trade with the Soviet Union. West German chancellor Helmut Schmidt thought Carter unpredictable: "We do not need nervousness, war cries, or excited or provocative speeches."[110] Brazil and Argentina increased their commerce with the Soviets, further diminishing the impact of trade restrictions. Many nations rejected the Olympics boycott; Lord Killanin, head of the international Olympics committee, bewailed the use of athletes "as pawns in political problems that politicians cannot solve themselves."[111]

The Carter Doctrine also sparked debate at home. Unlike the Truman and Eisenhower Doctrines, it did not go to Congress for approval. George F. Kennan scolded Carter for unnecessarily creating a war atmosphere. Kennan and others denied that the Soviet attack on Afghanistan marked a prelude to further aggression. A "thundering" Carter, moreover, carried a "small stick," Kennan lamented.[112] Carter had played all of his cards at the outset and the Soviets remained in Afghanistan. Other critics thought that Carter had capitulated fully to Cold Warriors like Brzezinski in another diplomatic lurch, going too far too fast, and that he had exaggerated the issue to boost his low political standing. A State Department official later revealed that the Carter Doctrine "grew out of last-minute pressures for a presidential speech" rather than from a cool calculation of policy.[113]

As Soviet-American relations deteriorated, Sino-American relations continued to improve. After formal recognition of the People's Republic of China in early 1979, Washington and Beijing began to use each other to contain the Soviet Union. While Washington played its "China card" in the anti-Soviet game, Beijing played its "America card." A U.S.-China trade agreement took effect in early 1980, and the Export-Import Bank extended credit to China. American companies began work on a major Chinese hydroelectric project and explored for oil in the China Sea. Chinese markets beckoned American farmers; in 1977–1980 China ranked fourth in the world as a buyer of U.S. agricultural exports, taking about half of the nation's cotton exports in 1979 alone. Mineral-short America eyed China's large deposits of tin, chrome, and tungsten. In 1980 American exports to China totaled $4 billion, up from $807 million in 1974. China replaced the Soviet Union as the United States' largest communist trading partner; in 1980 American exports to the Soviet Union stood at a comparatively low $1.5 billion.

Taiwan's status, however, remained contentious. The United States severed formal diplomatic relations with the Republic of China on Taiwan, unilaterally terminated the 1954 mutual defense treaty, and withdrew all U.S. forces and military installations from the island. But private Americans maintained strong economic links, and the U.S. government continued low-level official ties through an "Institute." Washington also kept up the flow of military aid. The People's

Republic insisted on ultimately repossessing Taiwan, but threats of force subsided. On the question of Taiwan, then, China and the United States still agreed to disagree.

During the Carter presidency, many Americans sensed that the nation's power had slipped, that its role as the world's sheriff, banker, business manager, and teacher had eroded. Some complained that a meek Carter administration had done too little to reverse the negative trend. A Nashville woman lamented, "Growing up, we learned in history that America was the best at everything. We had the respect of the whole world. But where can you go today and be respected for being American?"[114] High OPEC prices, huge deficits in the balance of payments, haunting memories of Vietnam, revolution in Nicaragua, return of the Canal Zone to Panama, Castro's defiance, Soviet nuclear equivalence and the jilted SALT-II, the Iranian hostage crisis, and Afghanistan—all seemed to project an image of American weakness. Carter had failed to persuade Americans that a decline in U.S. power was inevitable in an interdependent, multipolar world of some 150 nations. He talked bluntly of the 1970s and 1980s as decades of limits and scarcity. Accustomed to rhetoric from other presidents about boundless growth and influence, Americans rejected both the new message and the messenger. The American people, concluded one historian, suffered "a serious case of empire shock for the first time in their cultural history."[115]

Carter left a mixed record. Too often, administration policy appeared erratic because of the constant feuding between the State Department and Brzezinski's National Security Council. Carter also seldom gave a rousing speech or pounded the bully pulpit—too "de-pomped," wrote the noted specialist on presidential power Richard E. Neustadt.[116] Carter lacked FDR's charm, Eisenhower's popularity, JFK's television presence, LBJ's ability to handle Congress, and Nixon's talent for exploiting the spectacular. Carter also violated some of his stated goals. Despite his pledge to reduce the American military presence abroad, more military personnel served overseas in 1980 (489,000) than in 1976 (460,000). Carter promised to withdraw U.S. forces from South Korea but then reversed himself. Strongly advocating nuclear nonproliferation, he nonetheless agreed in 1980 to ship 38 metric tons of enriched uranium fuel to India, even though New Delhi had rejected international inspection to guard against nonpeaceful uses and had snubbed the nonproliferation treaty. He promised to reduce defense spending but actually increased the Pentagon's budget, recommending for fiscal year 1982 a 14.5 percent rise over 1981. Although the president vowed to trim arms sales abroad, they climbed from $12.8 billion in 1977 to $17.1 billion in 1980.

Coke in China.   In 1981 the Coca-Cola Company opened a plant in China, where the famous soft drink is known as "tasty happiness." The humorist Art Buchwald commented: "I don't mind 800 million Chinese drinking a bottle a day, but I don't want them to bring back the empties." (Courtesy The Coca-Cola Company, 1979)

Carter's human-rights policy also appeared inconsistent. While condemning Soviet mistreatment of dissidents, he muted criticism of abuses by U.S. friends such as Egypt, the Philippines, China, and Saudi Arabia. Amnesty International, the London-based independent organization founded in 1961 to monitor the worldwide status of human rights, cited the governments of Argentina, Brazil, Guatemala, Indonesia, Iran, Morocco, the Philippines, South Korea, Taiwan, and Thailand for condoning or practicing torture, political terrorism, or arbitrary arrest. In 1976–1980 the United States delivered $2.3 billion in military aid to those ten nations and sold them weapons worth $13.7 billion. "The United States stands at the supply end of a pipeline of repressive technology" and "will remain a party to any violations of human rights committed in those countries," concluded two students of the subject.[117] The United States also trained thousands of foreign officers and police at U.S. military schools. Conservative critics, in contrast, complained that Carter was behaving like an evangelical preacher in a world of sinners, that he invited revolutions such as the one in Iran by weakening leaders whom America needed as strategic partners. Although the United States opposed multilateral loans to Bolivia, the Central African Republic, Chile, and Guatemala, and Carter's human-rights efforts led to the freeing of hundreds of political prisoners abroad, the president's detractors faulted his effort as either too little or too meddlesome.

The president's defenders attributed his uneven record to domestic politics. Carter may have played politics with the Cuban brigade issue, the rescue attempt in Iran, and the Afghan crisis, they admitted, but vigorous right-wing pressure made him do so. They blamed noisy Cold Warriors in the Committee on the Present Danger. Founded in 1976 and modeled after a similar anti-Soviet organization of the early 1950s, this pressure group included such hawks as former under secretary of state Eugene V. Rostow, former secretary of state Dean Rusk, the Harvard historian Oscar Handlin, and the veteran policymaker Paul Nitze, who had composed NSC-68 in 1950. The organization advocated scrapping SALT-II and enlarging the military. Carter's bow to the conservatives violated the dictum that "smart politics produce bad policies."[118]

Did Congress thwart Carter? Foreign policy became highly partisan in the Carter years, and Congress proved susceptible to special-interest lobbyists for Israel and Greece, among others. Foreign leaders, moreover, hired American public relations firms to improve their image with politicians. In fact, South Korean intelligence agents made payments to some members of Congress in an influence-peddling scandal dubbed "Koreagate." Congress did intrude into policymaking: It stopped certain military shipments, placed stipulations on foreign aid, warned against certain covert operations, and tinkered with the Panama Canal treaties. Still, Carter, not Congress, made and executed most policies.

Carter officials believed that the administration had pursued noble goals and achieved diplomatic successes. They brought the rhetoric, if not always the substance, of morality to American foreign policy in an effort to prove that U.S. power lay not simply in military capabilities but also in the nation's values. The administration candidly explained the limits of American influence in a world of diffused power and made people conscious of the need to deal with long-range issues, not just immediate crises. Pointing to the Egyptian-Israeli peace, Panama Canal treaties, normalization of relations with China, progress on the law of the sea, North-South dialogue, end to civil war in Zimbabwe, nuclear modernization of NATO, creation of a rapid deployment force, and an improved American status in Africa, Professor Brzezinski proudly filled out the administration's report card as A−/B+.

The 1980 Republican presidential candidate, Ronald Reagan, disputed that high grade. The former Hollywood actor and California governor slammed Carter for leading America into decline. In a display of raw anticommunism, Reagan declared that an expansionist Soviet Union "underlies all the unrest that is going on. If they weren't engaged in this game of dominoes, there wouldn't be any hot spots in the world."[119] Analysts wondered whether Reagan really believed such over-simplifications of world politics; they came to think that he did and that he had reenergized exaggeration of the communist threat. Confounded by domestic economic troubles, the unresolved Iranian hostage crisis, and Carter's unsteady leadership, and rallying to Reagan's promise to "make America great again," the electorate turned Carter out by giving him only 41 percent of the popular vote.[120] The Republicans also gained control of the Senate; liberal, dovish Senators Birch Bayh of Indiana, Frank Church of Idaho, John Culver of Iowa, and George McGovern of South Dakota joined Carter in defeat.

RONALD REAGAN'S MISSION TO REVIVE HEGEMONY

Ronald Reagan had no experience in national government or foreign affairs before he became president. He preferred movies and television to reading books, riding horses to roundtable discussions. Time and time again, he revealed an ignorance of fundamental information. After returning from his first trip to South America, he announced: "Well, I learned a lot. You'd be surprised. They're all individual countries."[121] He once called Liberian president Samuel K. Doe "Chairman Moe."[122] He also became noted for reckless and exaggerated statements, factual inaccuracies, and right-wing sloganeering. "His is a kind of 1952 world," remarked a Reagan aide. "He sees the world in black and white terms."[123] Reagan acted more on his instincts than on patient reasoning. His staff, fearing ill-thought utterances, carefully managed his public performances. Surrounded by pollsters and communications specialists who tapped his natural talent, Reagan proved an effective communicator. His "aw shucks" style deflected criticism and camouflaged his shallow grasp of many issues. Representative Patricia Schroeder of Colorado remarked that Reagan had perfected "the Teflon-coated presidency"—no mess would stick to him.[124] "Being a good actor pays off," he told students at China's Fudan University.[125]

Reagan became a very popular president, winning a landslide reelection in 1984 against former vice president Walter Mondale. Americans liked Reagan, even when he suffered setbacks. They applauded his poised, amiable, down-to-earth, speak-from-the-heart manner, his self-deprecating humor (especially about his age), and his dogged consistency in voicing his convictions. The optimistic septuagenarian made Americans feel good, and they liked his steady focus on long-range goals. "When you are up to your ass in alligators," he reminded his advisers, "you sometimes forget that we are here to drain the swamp."[126]

Several beliefs rooted in the American past guided the Reagan administration. First, Reagan and his conservative allies believed in a devil theory: A malevolent Soviet Union instigated international insecurity—the bully on the block who ignited civil wars, promoted terrorism, and built an "evil empire."[127] In an avalanche of strident rhetoric, Reagan buried détente. Soviet leaders, the president avowed, stood poised "to commit any crime, to lie, to cheat" to achieve a communist world.[128] Such rhetoric poisoned the diplomatic environment. A British diplomat described the approach as "facing [the] Russians down in a silent war of nerves, broken only by bursts of megaphone diplomacy [and] crude, one-dimensional moralism."[129] Reagan's dark view of the Soviets overlooked the many successful Soviet-American agreements of the recent past. He also left the United States open to charges of a double standard, because Washington itself sponsored "disinformation" programs and engaged in covert skullduggery. Analysts pointed out as well that civil wars in Central America derived not from Soviet meddling but from deep-seated, local sources of economic instability, poverty, and class oppression; Arab-Israeli rivalry and the Palestinian problem, not Soviet behavior, fanned Mideast tensions; ethnic and racial differences, the legacy of colonialism, and economic woes underlay African troubles. Reagan officials, nonetheless, thought in terms of an earlier age of bipolarism, global containment, and confrontation—with one exception: They lifted the grain embargo so that American farmers could sell billions of dollars of wheat and corn to the Soviet Union.

Second, Reagan officials believed that a major U.S. military buildup would thwart the Soviet threat and intimidate Moscow into negotiating on terms favorable to the United States. "Defense is not a budget item," Reagan told the Pentagon. "Spend what you need."[130] They did—and more. Although running up huge federal deficits, he launched the largest peacetime arms buildup in American history, spending $2 trillion. Reagan pushed plans for the B-1 bomber (Carter had refused to fund this plane); ordered the stockpiling of the neutron bomb (Carter had vetoed this weapon); and resumed the production of poison gas for chemical warfare. The administration, moreover, expanded the navy, beefed up special forces units for counterinsurgency warfare, and continued the Trident-II submarine, MX, cruise missile, Stealth bomber, and mobile Midgetman missile programs. Conspicuous military maneuvers in various parts of the globe showed off the enlarged forces. "We're not going to spend all this money on the military and then keep it parked in the garage," observed one defense expert.[131] In 1985 the Pentagon was spending $28 million an hour, twenty-four hours a day, seven days a week. More than 500,000 military personnel served abroad, mostly in West Germany, Japan, and South Korea. Seeing "Uncle Sam as an enterprising, self-reliant fix-it man with more trust in his own common sense than in what the know-it-alls might say," Reagan also embraced a nuclear abolitionist's faith that American technology could devise an invulnerable space shield that would protect civilian populations from nuclear annihilation.[132] The former actor likened the arms race to "two Westerners standing in a saloon aiming their guns at each other's heads—permanently. There had to be a better way."[133]

Third, Reagan believed it important to change America's mood to gain public support for a more militarized, interventionist foreign policy. He therefore implored the American people to abandon their post-Vietnam "self-doubt" in favor of a "national reawakening."[134] Whereas the 1970s revealed "self-criticism bordering on masochism," observed former defense secretary James Schlesinger, the 1980s witnessed a mood of "self-congratulation to the point of narcissism."[135] Using his exceptional communicating skills to whip up emotional patriotism, Reagan reassured Americans that "we've closed the door on a long, dark period of failure."[136]

Ronald Reagan (b. 1911). Born in Illinois, a graduate of Eureka College, a longtime professional actor, and governor of California 1967–1975, Reagan displayed a sunny disposition that helped return optimism, even chauvinism, to the national mood. "By the time he got to the White House," remarked one journalist, "Reagan had spent more than fifty years using every communications medium save Morse code and smoke signals." (Peter Souza Photo, The White House)

The fourth driving force became known as the Reagan Doctrine. As the president declared in 1985, the United States would openly support anticommunist "freedom fighters" who battled the Soviets or Soviet-backed governments.[137] The CIA, with congressional approval, accordingly funneled aid to Islamic rebels in Afghanistan and to the *contras* assaulting Nicaragua, as well as to other anticommunist insurgents and terrorists in Angola, Cambodia, and Ethiopia. Reagan made overt what had been covert: the attempted overthrow of governments deemed inimical to U.S. interests. The Reagan Doctrine emphasized a commitment to low-intensity conflict: military action through allies, proxies, and paramilitary assets so that fewer American soldiers would fight and die in foreign lands as elite forces organized others to do the dirty work of shadow wars.

Fifth, Reagan and his advisers believed that nations must embrace private capitalism and "privatize" managed economies. American leaders frequently lectured Third World nations on the "magic of the marketplace."[138] The United States even cast the only "no" vote against a UN resolution to restrict the sale of baby formula in developing nations. Medical authorities had complained that companies marketed their infant products so aggressively that many mothers were forgoing healthy breastfeeding in favor of the artificial liquid, which they then mixed with polluted water. Diseases spread and children needlessly died, yet Reagan officials would tolerate no interference with private business. The Reagan administration also refused to sign the long-awaited Law of the Sea Treaty, protesting that the agreement did not adequately protect American deep-sea mining companies. Overall, Reagan's Washington tried to silence the North-South dialogue.

Sixth, drawing lessons from the failure of the Carter administration to support friendly dictators in Iran and Nicaragua, the Reaganites accepted Ambassador to the United Nations Jeane Kirkpatrick's distinction between "authoritarian" and "totalitarian" regimes.[139] Authoritarian regimes in such countries as the Philippines, Chile, South Korea, and South Africa sustained capitalist economies and would supposedly respond to U.S. suggestions for reform. Communist totalitarian regimes imposed managed economies and resisted change. Given such thinking, Reagan officials further downgraded the need for more human-rights tests for friendly authoritarian governments.

Finally, another central belief of the Reagan team was that the United States must serve as a model for other nations and that it had a mission to reform a reprobate world. "The United States is the economic miracle," bragged the president. "The world's hopes rest with America's future."[140] Indeed, "There is sin and evil in the world, and we are enjoined by Scripture and the Lord Jesus to oppose it with all our might."[141] This reformist zealotry found expression through such institutions as the National Endowment for Democracy, created in 1983 as a propaganda agency using federal and private funds to promote free enterprise and democratic politics. The endowment gave millions of dollars to foreign political parties, labor unions, and publishers, many with an antileft bias. Reagan manifested his evangelical mood when he quoted Tom Paine of the American Revolution: "We have it in our power to begin the world over again."[142]

Reagan named General Alexander M. Haig, Jr., as his first secretary of state. A steely-eyed military professional who became famous for his mixed metaphors and

July 4, 1986. Here, with Nancy Reagan, the president stands before a ship's gun on Independence Day. Nancy Reagan often advised her husband, especially on personnel changes. She thought Chief of Staff Donald Regan had an "oversized ego" and helped get him fired. She was "ever protective of me," the president said. (Terry Arthur Photo, The White House)

"Give War a Chance." During his confirmation hearings in January 1981, Secretary of State–designate Alexander M. Haig, Jr., said: "There are more important things than peace—there are things which we Americans must be willing to fight for." Some people thought him too eager to apply military solutions to political problems and too inclined toward confrontation with the Soviet Union and leftist Third World nations. As for El Salvador, where Haig and Reagan thrust the United States into a civil war, the secretary declared: "We are going to succeed and not flounder as we did in Vietnam." (Bob Englehart, *Hartford Courant*)

his ambition, Haig feuded with just about everybody. "Sometimes our right hand doesn't know what our far-right hand is doing," Reagan once joked.[143] The volatile secretary abruptly resigned in June 1982. Haig found the White House "as mysterious as a ghost ship; you heard the creak of the rigging and the groan of the timbers and even glimpsed the crew on deck. But which one of the crew was at the helm?"[144] George P. Shultz followed Haig. A founding member of the Committee on the Present Danger, Shultz was a self-confident and loyal Princeton graduate (he had a tiger tattoo on his buttocks), University of Chicago economist, and business executive who had served in Nixon's cabinet. Shultz often clashed with Secretary of Defense Caspar W. ("Cap") Weinberger, especially after Weinberger announced in 1984 that the United States should use military force only under certain conditions: with long-term public and congressional support; for "clearly defined political and military objectives"; and with "the clear intention of winning."[145] Shultz chastised Weinberger as a big spender who refused to use newly augmented U.S. forces. Despite having "the charisma of a drowsy clam," Shultz battled other high-level administration officials such as Weinberger, Kirkpatrick (no "ventriloquist's dummy"), and CIA director William J. Casey (whom Shultz saw "as independent as a hog on ice" and "as confident [as he was] wrong"). [146] As one scholar has put it, "in a monastery of friars," Shultz "was the lawyer brought in to negotiate with the heathen."[147] Unlike Haig, Shultz accepted his role as the president's servant and team player.

Richard V. Allen, a business consultant noted for his anticommunist zeal, became Reagan's first assistant for national security affairs. After Allen departed in 1982 under suspicion of scandal, the office of national security adviser suffered instability, further undistinguished leadership, and more scandal. Under William Clark, Reagan's political crony from California, NSC staffwork became so cumbersome that Shultz thought it "worse than a university."[148] Then came Robert C. McFarlane, a former marine who never argued against misguided policies because "if I'd done that, Bill Casey, Jeane Kirkpatrick, and Cap Weinberger would have said I was some kind of commie."[149] John M. Poindexter, an active-duty admiral with a Ph.D. in nuclear physics, succeeded McFarlane, but he had to resign in late 1986 when the Iran-Contra affair erupted.

Despite strong opposition from Weinberger and Shultz, President Reagan ordered the National Security Council to carry out a dubious covert project to trade arms to Iran in return for the release of U.S. hostages held in Lebanon. Because he also empowered the NSC to secretly aid the Nicaraguan *contras* (see page 525), the two operations eventually commingled. To ensure secrecy and deniability, McFarlane and Poindexter ran both schemes in total disregard of Congress and almost completely outside the purview of the Defense and State departments. Relying on CIA connections, the action officer in charge of both operations, marine lieutenant colonel Oliver North, flaunted his contempt for Congress, professional diplomats, and traditional bureaucrats. "Colonel North was given a very broad charter," Poindexter later testified, "and I did not micromanage him."[150] When North discovered a way to divert profits from the Iranian arms sales to the *contras,* Poindexter approved but said he did not tell Reagan, because he wanted the president "to have some deniability so that he would be protected."[151] Shultz later portrayed Reagan as an innocent dupe misled by his inner circle. Yet the record shows that at all top-level meetings on Iran-Contra, President Reagan spoke more than any of his advisers, forcefully steered discussions, and made the basic decisions,

Reagan in Doubt.
When the crisis over the arms sale to Iran and aid to the *contras* erupted in 1986–1987, President Reagan revealed that he could not remember the timing or details of some of his decisions. This cartoon plays on words often heard during the Watergate crisis of the 1970s. (Bill Schorr © 1987, The Los Angeles Times Syndicate)

" WHAT DO I KNOW ... AND WHEN WILL I KNOW IT ? "

whether or not he approved every operational detail. The extent to which the president participated in the later cover-up remains cloudy.

Reagan's appointment of Frank C. Carlucci, a seasoned diplomat and administrator, and then General Colin Powell, as his next NSC advisers did not quiet a national crisis that badly besmirched the Reagan presidency. In 1989 North was found guilty of three felonies (obstructing a congressional inquiry, destroying documents, and receiving illegal gratuities), and in early 1990 Poindexter was convicted of five felony charges, including lying to Congress. A federal appeals court later overturned both convictions because Congress had granted immunity to the two men for testimony given to congressional committees. President George Bush later pardoned CIA officers guilty of a cover-up, and when Secretary of Defense Caspar Weinberger was indicted, Bush also pardoned him before a trial could take place.

REAGAN, THE SOVIETS, AND THE NUCLEAR-ARMS RACE

Reagan assumed that the Soviet Union outspent the United States on armaments and outdistanced it in nuclear weapons. He had campaigned on an anti–SALT-II platform and displayed undisguised distaste for nuclear-arms control talks. The United States had to close the the "window of vulnerability"—the theoretical vulnerability of American land-based ICBMs to a Soviet first strike—by deploying the MX and enlarging the American nuclear arsenal.[152] The Soviets outranked the United States in ICBMs and SLBMs but lagged behind in strategic bombers and nuclear warheads. And at least two-thirds of Soviet nuclear arms consisted of vulnerable ICBMs resting in fixed silos. The president failed to count on the American side the defense spending of NATO allies. As for the "window of vulnerability," it soon disappeared from parlance. In 1983 the president's own Commission on Strategic Forces (the Scowcroft Commission) reported that the window did not exist and that America's triad of air-, sea-, and land-based nuclear weapons provided sufficient deterrence.

Casual statements by Reagan officials about winning a nuclear war stimulated a transatlantic debate. The evangelist Billy Graham, World Council of Churches, and Union of Concerned Scientists urged restraint in the nuclear-arms race. The American Medical Association declared that "there is no adequate medical response to a nuclear holocaust," and one doctor called nuclear war the "final epidemic."[153] If Boston were hit, a half-million people would die; hundreds of thousands would suffer ghastly burns, deep lacerations, radiation poisoning, and multiple fractures; and hospitals, including the famed Massachusetts General, would be reduced to rubble. George F. Kennan added his voice to the antinuclear movement. "Cease this madness," he implored.[154] Complaining that Reagan's views on the USSR represented "an intellectual primitivism," Kennan recommended an immediate 50 percent cut in nuclear arsenals on both sides, the denuclearization of much of Europe, a complete ban on nuclear testing, and a freeze on new weapons.[155] In early 1982, 17 senators (one-sixth of the Senate) and 128 House members (30

George Shultz (b. 1920).
A graduate of Princeton University and the Massachusetts Institute of Technology (Ph.D., 1949), Shultz went on to become a professor of industrial relations at the University of Chicago. President Nixon tapped him to be secretary of labor, director of the Office of Management and Budget, and secretary of the Treasury. In 1974 he became an executive with the Bechtel Group, Inc. Eight years later he joined the Reagan cabinet as secretary of state. (Department of State)

percent of that body) endorsed the freeze, as did many states, cities, and towns across America. The House of Representatives in 1983 also passed a freeze resolution. Proponents argued that America's infrared satellites and other intelligence techniques could verify a freeze on the testing and deployment of ballistic missiles. But Reagan disparaged the freeze as a "very dangerous fraud" that would ensure Soviet nuclear supremacy.[156]

In May 1983 the Roman Catholic Bishops of the United States issued a pastoral letter that further annoyed the White House. "We are the first generation since Genesis with the power to virtually destroy God's creation," read the 150-page document. The bishops condemned nuclear arms as "immoral" because they killed indiscriminately. They asked for an end to the nuclear-weapons race, "which robs the poor and the vulnerable" and "places before humankind indefensible choices of constant terror or surrender."[157] In November an ABC television dramatization titled "The Day After" sent shudders through the American people with its vivid depiction of the human costs of a nuclear war. Scientists postulated that even people who survived a nuclear exchange would face a devastating "nuclear winter": clouds of debris, dust, and smoke from mass fires would block the sun's rays, cooling the earth's temperatures (perhaps to zero in summer months) and killing plant and animal life.

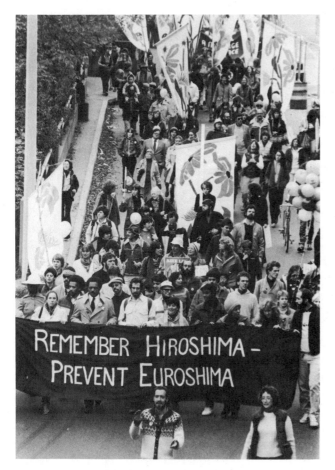

Antinuclear March. In October 1983, the civil rights leader Jesse Jackson (front, on left) led a Cambridge, Massachusetts, march against nuclear weapons, especially the Pershing-II missiles scheduled for deployment in Europe. This protest was part of an international weekend campaign, which included Jackson's speech at a rally on Boston Common. (AP/Wide World Photos)

Europeans also vigorously spoke to the issue. In the fall of 1981, for example, huge crowds in Bonn, London, Rome, and Amsterdam called for a ban on the installation of Pershing and cruise missiles. "The most important mass-based challenge to NATO in its entire history" demanded that both Washington and Moscow sit down to talk and that the NATO countries forswear the new weapons.[158] American leaders thought the Europeans too jittery, but statements by U.S. officials evoked alarm. Reagan mentioned the possibility of a limited nuclear war in Europe, thus sparing the two great powers. On other occasions he revealed his "stunning ignorance about the capabilities of the weapons over which he had authority."[159] He once stated that cruise missiles were defensive weapons—in fact, they were designed to penetrate Soviet defenses and to strike targets deep in the USSR. He even said that SLBMs could be recalled after firing.

To satisfy Western European leaders who welcomed U.S. missiles but wanted less domestic protest, and to quiet the American antinuclear movement, Reagan reluctantly agreed to begin talks in Geneva on intermediate-range nuclear forces

(INF) in Europe. For these negotiations, which opened in November 1981, the United States proposed to stop planned deployment of the new Pershings and cruise missiles in NATO nations if the Soviet Union would dismantle its growing arsenal of SS-20, SS-4, and SS-5 missiles pointed at Western Europe. The Soviets initially rejected this "zero option," because it excluded British and French nuclear forces and U.S. weapons on submarines and aircraft. Also, argued Moscow, the new NATO missiles could reach the USSR, but the SS-20s could not hit America. When Reagan shelved an agreement proposed by the INF negotiator Paul Nitze that fell short of the "zero option," the president said: "You just tell the Soviets you're working for one tough son-of-a-bitch."[160] The Soviets soon deployed more triple-warhead SS-20s and the United States began to put Pershing-IIs into NATO countries, first Great Britain and then West Germany. Mass rallies in Western Europe protested the deployment. In November 1983, to express their displeasure over the emplacement of the new missiles, the Soviets suspended the INF talks. Meetings did not resume until early 1985, only to falter again. Pentagon hardliners did not mind. Without an agreement, the U.S. arms buildup continued.

Negotiations on strategic nuclear weapons did not fare much better. Reagan replaced SALT with START—Strategic Arms Reduction Talks. ("How about 'Faster Arms Reduction Talks'?" one White House aide suggested.)[161] Negotiations began in Geneva in 1982, but the U.S. proposal for deep cuts got nowhere. The reason became obvious: The American plan sought drastic reductions in those very weapons that constituted the bulk of Soviet deterrent power. Reagan apparently failed to grasp this point, for in late 1983 he told incredulous legislators that he had just realized that 70 percent of the Soviet Union's missiles were land-based.

Chances for a START agreement also became complicated because of President Reagan's fascination with the Strategic Defense Initiative (SDI), which he announced in March 1983. Joint Chiefs of Staff chairman General John Vessey once asked: "Wouldn't it be better to protect the American people rather than avenge them?" Reagan perked up and said: "Don't lose those words."[162] Soon dubbed "Star Wars," SDI envisioned an antiballistic missile defense system in space—a laser or particle beam shield over the United States that could intercept Soviet ballistic missiles and destroy them in space. Skeptical scientists reported that the SDI simply would not work. Jerome B. Wiesner, former scientific adviser to the White House, pointed out that "there are 10,000 or more nuclear weapons on each side. A defense system that would knock out 90 or 95 percent would be a miracle—and the remaining 5 or 10 percent would be enough to totally destroy civilization."[163] Others argued that defensive space stations could be converted to offensive uses for a first strike and that if SDI ever did work, it would undermine deterrence itself by eliminating the danger of Soviet attack, thus freeing the United States to use nuclear weapons without fear of retaliation (effective defense theoretically undermines deterrence). Although some saw SDI as a multibillion-dollar "turkey" (by 1993 $30 billion had been spent with minimal results), it had a certain appeal.[164] "I'd rather shoot missiles than shoot people," said SDI's scientific godfather Dr. Edward Teller.[165] As SDI research advanced, with some test results actually faked to keep congressional funds flowing, START stalled.

Pershing-II Missile.
First deployed in 1983 in NATO countries in Western Europe, this highly accurate missile targeted the Soviet Union. It was intended to counter Soviet SS-20 missiles targeted on Western Europe. (U.S. Army)

"Star Wars" in 1984. President Reagan made a passionate case for the Strategic Defense Initiative to prevent a "madman" with missiles from blackmailing "all of us." Some scientists assured him that they could create his "dream"—an effective ballistic missile defense system. In this artist's sketch, a space-based electromagnetic railgun destroys a nuclear-armed reentry vehicle presumably launched from the Soviet Union. Ten years after this sketch, although still heavily funded, SDI technological development seemed stalled. (Courtesy of U.S. Army/Department of Defense, Still Media Records Center)

Other events muddled the negotiating environment. As the Reagan administration closed out its first year, the Solidarity labor movement in Poland, having earned concessions from the communist government through strikes and protests, called for a national referendum on the future of that government and for a reexamination of Poland's military alliance with the Soviet Union. For months Moscow had warned the Poles against weakening the communist regime. In December the Polish military cracked down, imposing martial law and arresting Solidarity leaders. Washington reacted quickly. It suspended economic arrangements with Poland and blamed Moscow for unleashing the "forces of tyranny" against its neighbor.[166] Reagan cut back Soviet-American trade and banned Soviet airline flights to the United States but elected to do no more. NATO countries reacted cautiously, in part because they possessed little leverage in Polish affairs and in part because they did not want to interrupt their own lucrative trade with the Soviets and Soviet clients.

On September 1, 1983, Korean Air Lines Flight 007, en route from Anchorage, Alaska, to Seoul, South Korea, strayed some 300 miles off course and for a time cruised in Soviet airspace near the site of a strategic nuclear base. Soviet planes scrambled. When the Korean pilot did not acknowledge warning signals and shots, a Soviet jet blasted the Boeing 747 with one missile, killing all 269 passengers aboard. Reagan branded the shootdown a "crime against humanity," "an act of barbarism."[167] The Soviets may have confused KAL 007 with an American RC-135 spy plane that was flying in the same area before the Korean airliner. After the tragedy, the Soviets charged that KAL 007 was on a spy mission for the United States. Moscow authorities later revealed that the shootdown had occurred in international airspace, that Soviet authorities had found the wreckage and "black box" from KAL 007, and that they had crudely covered up the pilot's error. Washington officials chose to explain the event as premeditated treachery. "White hot, thoroughly white hot," a Soviet Politburo member described relations at the end of 1983.[168]

Another obstacle to an arms-control agreement was the instability and incapacity of Soviet leadership—until the arrival of Mikhail S. Gorbachev in 1985. Leonid Brezhnev died in 1982; his first successor, Yuri Andropov, died in 1984; and his second successor, Konstantin Chernenko, died the following year after a prolonged illness. One Soviet leader later depicted Chernenko and others as "absolute mediocritics" who had spent most of their lives "among dull and half-educated bureaucrats."[169] But the so-called new thinking actually began under Andropov. Gorbachev became the new general secretary of the Communist party, at age fifty-four one of the Soviet Union's youngest leaders and certainly its most charming. Determined to reform the sluggish Soviet economy through restructur-

Mikhail Gorbachev (b. 1932) and Reagan.   In May 1988, at the Moscow summit meeting, the two leaders continued their warm personal relationship that ended the Cold War. (Photo by Bill Fitz-Patrick, The White House, Courtesy Ronald Reagan Library)

ing (*perestroika*) and to open the suffocating authoritarian political system through liberalization (*glasnost*), Gorbachev initiated stunning changes in his own nation and across the globe (see Chapter 12).

The new secretary general altered the Soviet position on nuclear weapons. He unilaterally stopped further deployment of intermediate-range missiles. He halted nuclear-weapons tests and proposed mutual on-site inspection to verify the suspension of tests. In November 1985 Gorbachev and Reagan met in Geneva to try to break the impasse over nuclear weapons reductions. Although they could not agree on SDI or an extension of SALT-II, they established warm personal relations during two days of talks. "I bet the hard-liners in both our countries are bleeding," whispered Reagan as he shook Gorbachev's hand.[170] Then in early 1986 Gorbachev called for an end to all nuclear weapons by the year 2000. Another summit meeting in Reykjavík, Iceland, in October 1986, seemed close to producing a substantial treaty. The conferees made tremendous progress by agreeing to reduce warheads, missiles, and bombers on each side and to remove all American and Soviet intermediate missiles from Europe. Reagan found the results "breathtaking." But when Gorbachev said that "this all depends, of course, on your giving up SDI,"

Destruction of a Cruise Missile Under the INF Treaty. Under the terms of the Intermediate-Range Nuclear Forces Treaty, signed in late 1987 and effective in mid-1988, both the United States and the Soviet Union (and its successor states) eliminated theater nuclear forces in Europe, including Soviet SS-20 missiles and U.S. Pershing-II and cruise missiles. To destroy this cruise missile, a demolition crew cut it in half. (Courtesy of U.S. Arms Control and Disarmament Agency)

Reagan "blew my top."[171] The meeting quickly ended. Yet the atmosphere had clearly changed for the better. "Gorbachev decided that Reagan had meant what he said at Geneva. He did want to rid the world of nuclear weapons," the U.S. ambassador to Moscow recalled.[172] Gorbachev hailed Reykjavík as "a major event. . . . Nobody [could] now act in the same way as he had acted before."[173]

The Washington summit meeting in December 1987 finally saw the signing of the Intermediate-Range Nuclear Forces (INF) Treaty. This agreement provided for the elimination of all U.S. and Soviet INF missiles anywhere and verification of their destruction through on-site inspections. What had changed? First, Gorbachev had taken the initiative by accepting the "zero option" and by constantly asking American leaders to respond. Second, the warmth between Reagan and Gorbachev facilitated negotiations. "When I told him [Gorbachev] we should put our cards on the table, he took out his Visa and Mastercard," Reagan later joked.[174] Shultz similarly found Soviet foreign minister Eduard Shevardnadze (who "could smile, engage, converse") a welcome change from the dour Andrei Gromyko.[175] Third, many of the hard-liners in the Reagan administration—Weinberger, Assistant Secretary of Defense Richard Perle, and Director of the Arms Control and Disarmament Agency Kenneth Adelman—had resigned. Fourth, the antinuclear movement had produced strong antinuclear public opinion in Europe. Last and most obvious, the two superpowers saw the treaty as beneficial to their quite different national interests. Both faced economic troubles spawned by the long Cold War. "Our economy," one Soviet official told his colleagues, "has been literally eviscerated by military spending."[176] "How long," Reagan wondered, "can the Russians keep on being so belligerent and spending so much on the arms race when they can't feed their own people?"[177] Some Americans asked the question of themselves. In May the Senate approved the treaty by a 93 to 5 vote. On June 1, 1988, the INF Treaty went into force and missiles began to be destroyed.

Gorbachev also advanced other issues. In April 1988 he signed a UN-mediated accord providing for the withdrawal of all Soviet forces from Afghanistan by early 1989. They departed on schedule, acknowledging in their retreat a conspicuous defeat for the Soviet military, caused in part by the "Stinger" antiaircraft weapons that the United States had shipped to the Afghan *mujahedeen* ("holy warriors"). In December 1988 the Soviet leader announced a unilateral Soviet cut of 500,000 ground troops. Moscow also reduced its support for the Sandinistas in Nicaragua and negotiated for the removal of Cuban troops from Angola. "I'm doing this because there's a revolution taking place in my country," Gorbachev told Vice President George Bush.[178]

"Low Intensity Conflict" in the "Backyard"

The Reagan administration read events in the Third World as related chapters in an East-West, Cold War book written by the two superpowers, not as independent short stories composed by distinct, indigenous sources. In the Third World, argued

Reagan officials, U.S. influence had to be restored to halt Soviet expansionists. But more than anticommunism drove U.S. policy. Hegemony was at stake. Reagan quoted the Truman Doctrine, resuscitated the domino theory, and stressed military means over negotiations. Central America, long in the United States' grip but restless under the burden of profound economic, political, and social divisions, figured prominently in Reagan's counterrevolutionary crusade.

The "Moscow-Havana axis," claimed the State Department, had used Cuba to propagandize revolution, train insurgents, and promote the proliferation of "Cuba-model states" that would "provide platforms for subversion, compromise vital sea lanes, and pose a direct military threat at or near our borders. This would undercut us globally and create economic dislocation and a resultant influx of illegal immigrants."[179] At times President Reagan imagined radicals crossing the border from Mexico into Texas, but increasingly he made a strategic case: As a major trade route, the Caribbean provided "our lifeline to the outside world," and "Soviet military theorists want to destroy our capacity to resupply Western Europe in case of an emergency. They want to tie down our attention and forces on our own southern border and so limit our capacity to act in more distant places such as Europe, the Persian Gulf, the Indian Ocean, the Sea of Japan."[180] Fearing "another Cuba," Reagan officials determined to defeat leftist insurgents in El Salvador, to topple the Sandinista government in Nicaragua, and to draw Guatemala and Honduras into a tighter U.S. military network. Through billions of dollars in aid (including the Caribbean Basin Initiative announced in 1982), CIA operations, weapons and advisers, splashy military maneuvers, and support for the anti-Sandinista army known as the *contras,* Washington plunged more deeply into Central American affairs (see map, page 492).

Critics, many of them in Congress, charged that Reagan exaggerated the Soviet-Cuban threat, underplayed the local causes of disorder, bypassed opportunities for negotiations, and shored up the right wing and military, thus spurring further political polarization. Such policies threatened regional war and helped invite what Washington wanted most to prevent: Soviet influence in the area. Senator Christopher Dodd, a Democrat from Connecticut and former Peace Corps volunteer in Latin America, decried the "ignorance" of the Reagan diplomats who "seem to know as little about Central America in 1983 as we knew about Indochina in 1963." Downplaying a Soviet threat and emphasizing instead the United States' own responsibility for instability in the region, not to mention Central America's economic underdevelopment, inadequate medical care, illiteracy, and class structure, Dodd declared that "if Central America were not racked with poverty, there would be no revolution."[181]

In El Salvador, the Reagan administration nevertheless found "a textbook case of indirect armed aggression by Communist powers."[182] A hastily prepared "White Paper" identified Cuba and the Soviet Union as masterminds of a civil war. El Salvador seemed a place where the United States could "win one for a change," as one senator put it.[183] A presidential assistant explained that "El Salvador itself doesn't matter—we have to establish credibility."[184] Reagan said it simply: "We are the last domino."[185]

El Salvador was a poor country plagued with a high infant mortality rate, illiteracy, and violence. The army and a small landed elite had long ruled the nation. Two percent of the people owned half the land. In October 1979, however, reform-minded colonels seized power and organized a new government under José Napoleón Duarte, a Christian Democratic party leader. The elite responded by organizing "death squads" to assassinate reformers and radicals alike. (Some assassins belonged to the government security forces, which Duarte could not control.) Leftists formed the Farabundo Martí Front for National Liberation (FMLN), and moderate reformers organized the Democratic Revolutionary Front (FDR). As hundreds of FDR members were murdered each month, others fled to the hills to join the FMLN. In 1980 alone, at least 13,000 Salvadorans died at the hands of "death squads"; by 1985, 40,000 civilians had been slaughtered. In 1980 national guard troops raped and killed four American churchwomen, but the Salvadoran government refused to prosecute the officers who ordered the murders. Ambassador Jeane Kirkpatrick seemed to excuse the slayings by saying "the nuns were not just nuns" but "political activists" for the FMLN.[186]

"Communism." Critics of Reagan's interventionism in Central America believed that the president misread the sources of instability in the region. (Dennis Renault, *Sacramento Bee*)

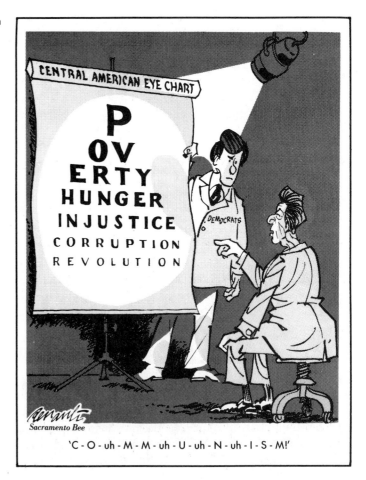

Determined to find a non-Marxist solution to the Salvadoran civil war through land reform, the Carter administration had extended economic aid to the Duarte government. But it had also dispatched military advisers and military aid. The Reagan administration dramatically increased the military assistance program ($128.3 million in 1985 alone) and expanded economic aid ($310.7 million in 1985). Reagan explained that "we have training squads in more than thirty countries, so this isn't an unusual thing that we are doing."[187]

While reluctantly funding Reagan's Salvadoran programs, Congress insisted that the administration certify human-rights progress in the country. Every six months officials dutifully issued optimistic but disingenuous statements. "Everybody *knew,* Congress *knew,* what they [Salvadoran military forces] were doing," a U.S. Embassy official recalled. "So they beat their breasts and tore their hair . . . and made us jump through this hoop called certification. . . . What's improvement, any way? You kill eight hundred and it goes down to two hundred, that's improvement. The whole thing was an exercise in the absurd."[188] The UN Truth Commission reported in 1993 that 85 percent of the 75,000 people killed in the Salvadoran civil war died at the hands of government forces and gun-for-hire death squads. U.S. military advisers trained some of the units responsible for murdering civilians, while U.S. officials often failed to investigate crimes or covered up atrocities. Ambassador William Walker cited "management control problems."[189] Although they said that they sought reforms to curb death-squad killings, U.S. diplomats did not exert "high-level pressure for change on Salvadoran military leaders."[190] Americans recalled Vietnam. "The White House did not appreciate how rapidly El Salvador would take off in the minds of the press as a Vietnam," a presidential aide observed.[191] "They thought it was like rolling a drunk," former ambassador to El Salvador Robert E. White remarked.[192] White lost his job for advocating negotiations rather than a military solution.

Hoping to establish a stable political system that could win the war against the insurgents, the Reagan administration helped El Salvador conduct elections. The election of 1982, boycotted by the FMLN, installed a right-wing government without Duarte. But in the 1984 election, U.S. officials helped ensure Duarte's victory by using the CIA to distribute funds. To the apparent surprise of U.S. officials, Duarte opened talks with rebel leaders who had long urged negotiations on sharing power. As these talks faltered, the Reagan administration improved the Salvadoran military's ability to stage air assaults and bombing raids. This strategy actually undermined Duarte's struggle to strengthen moderates. And the growing civilian death count from the air war actually may have facilitated the FMLN's recruitment of followers. Although Reagan spent $4.5 billion in El Salvador during the 1980s, victory in the bloody civil war still eluded him when he left office. An editorial cartoon depicted the president waist deep in quicksand, doggedly plunging ahead with a rifle upraised, telling a nervous Uncle Sam: "Quit grousing! . . . It's not Vietnam." Uncle Sam replies: "It doesn't look like Munich, either."[193]

The Reagan administration blamed much of the Salvadoran trouble on Cuba and Nicaragua, which sent small supplies of arms to the insurgents. Secretary Haig announced that the Soviets had a "hit list" of Central American states, with Nicaragua first, El Salvador second.[194] Reaganites became convinced that

Nicaragua had already fallen into Soviet hands, for not only had the Sandinistas invited thousands of Cuban medical specialists and teachers into their poor country, but they were using Cuban advisers and Soviet weapons to build a strong military, limiting free speech as they moved to a one-party government, and defiantly snubbing U.S. demands that they sever ties with Cuba and conduct free elections. Nicaraguans bent on fulfilling their revolution faced a Reagan administration determined to stamp out revolutionary contagion. "Nicaragua has been an appendage of the United States. . . . Our function was to grow sugar, cocoa, and coffee for the United States; we served the dessert at the imperialist dinner table," remarked Minister of Agrarian Reform Jaime Wheelock. "We have to be against the United States in order to reaffirm ourselves as a nation."[195]

As the United States had treated Cuba in the 1950s and 1960s, so it treated Nicaragua in the 1980s: putting pressure on a small, proud, doggedly radical government to the point where it seemed to face a choice between capitulation or seeking outside help for defense. The Nicaraguans remembered the Bay of Pigs, the invasion of the Dominican Republic, and Allende's Chile. Reagan first cut off all foreign aid. In November 1981, he ordered the CIA to train and arm the anti-Sandinista *contras* in a prime example of the low-intensity-conflict strategy. If the United States did not stop radicals "in our own backyard, it was far less likely that

The Vietnam Syndrome Cured by the Reagan Doctrine. President Reagan's interventionism in the Third World supposedly ended the Vietnam syndrome, but many critics, including a majority of the American people, feared another Vietnam. (Dan Wasserman for *The Boston Globe* © 1985, Los Angeles Times Syndicate. Reprinted with permission)

we could do so in the years ahead in more distant locations," a top U.S. official later explained.[196] "Let's make the bastards sweat," CIA director William Casey told his covert operators.[197] The *contras* by 1986 had grown into a mercenary army of 15,000–20,000 dependent upon the United States. The *contras* operated out of bases in Honduras and Costa Rica. They raided Nicaragua, sabotaging bridges, oil facilities, and crops, and brutalizing civilians.

Although in 1982 Congress had prohibited the use of funds to overthrow the Nicaraguan government, Reagan officials winked at the restriction. In early 1984 Congress discovered that the CIA had worked with *contra* commandos to mine three Nicaraguan ports. "I am pissed off," roared Senator Barry Goldwater at the CIA's Casey. "It is an act of war. . . . I don't see how we're going to explain it."[198] When Nicaragua went to the World Court to charge the United States with a breach of international law, Washington refused to recognize the court's jurisdiction. (In June 1986, the court decided that the United States had violated international law by funding the *contras* and ordered Washington to pay an indemnity to Nicaragua; Reagan ignored the ruling.) In mid-1984, Congress banned aid to the *contras*. Meanwhile, Nicaraguan-American talks in Mexico produced no agreement, largely because the Nicaraguans refused U.S. demands for political change.

The congressional prohibition did not stop aid to the *contras*. In an operation described by one senator as "part James Bond and part Jimmy Durante," CIA, Pentagon, and NSC officials worked with private, right-wing Americans to channel millions of dollars of supplies to anti-Sandinista forces.[199] Retired general John K. Singlaub, head of the World Anti-Communist League, retired air force major general Richard V. Secord, other conservatives, and Cuban Americans in Miami cooperated with Lieutenant Colonel Oliver L. North of Reagan's NSC. In 1985–1986, North shifted to the *contras* profits from arms sales to Iran by using Israeli intermediaries and a Swiss bank account. North also coordinated a network of planes and ships and funded the building of a large airstrip in Costa Rica—all without informing Congress. As an independent federal prosecutor later concluded, President Reagan "created the conditions which made possible the crimes committed by others" and "knowingly participated" in the illegal aid effort.[200] Reagan told his advisers that if the "story gets out, we'll all be hanging by our thumbs in front of the White House."[201] U.S. support for the *contras* forced the Sandinistas to look increasingly to the Soviets for help. "Reagan has become an obsession for us," Nicaragua's minister of interior remarked, "and we've become an obsession for him."[202]

In early 1985 Reagan admitted publicly what he had long denied: Washington sought to oust the Sandinista government—he wanted it to say "uncle."[203] In May he imposed an economic embargo. The United States also blocked loans to Nicaragua from the World Bank and the Inter-American Development Bank. Congress grew more obliging; it appropriated $27 million for "humanitarian" aid to the *contras*. Still, the *contra* war did not go well. The insurgents constantly feuded among themselves; they generated little popular support in Nicaragua; and they could not seize and hold towns. But they destroyed, and they forced the Sandinistas to shift funds from social programs to defense and to tighten controls on civil liberties, thus slowing the revolution and arousing internal dissent. In 1986 Congress voted $100 million in military aid for the *contras*. An opponent of *contra* aid, Republican Mark O. Hatfield of Oregon, remembered Vietnam: "Here we are again, old men creating a monster for young men to destroy. What a waste of life."[204]

Washington showed no interest in a negotiated settlement. The administration snubbed the Contadora group (Mexico, Venezuela, Panama, and Colombia), which in 1983 had persuaded the five Central American states to limit foreign advisers, reduce arms, and promote democracy. Meanwhile, the *contras* proved a poor fighting force whose leaders squandered funds. Washington knew by 1987 that the counterrevolutionaries could not win. Still, Reagan officials stiff-armed the 1987 peace plan offered by Costa Rican president Oscar Arias Sánchez for a cease-fire and national reconciliation. In February 1988 *contra* attackers murdered eight people, including three children, at a farm cooperative in central Nicaragua. Total deaths in the CIA-directed war now numbered at least 20,000, and the Niacaraguan economy lay in shambles. Congress banned further military aid to the *contras* ("humanitarian" aid continued). The Sandinistas endorsed the Arias plan, but talks broke down, and the Sandinistas soon cracked down on their opponents. Hobbled by the Iran-Contra scandal, Reagan resisted appeals from hard-liners to send more aid to the *contras*. "Those sonsofbitches won't be happy until we have 25,000 troops in Managua, and I'm not going to do it," the president snapped.[205] When Reagan left office, the Sandinistas still governed their much ravaged country.

To Reaganites, Cuba instigated the trouble in both El Salvador and Nicaragua. Haig advocated a naval blockade of Cuba, if not more. "Give me the word," he crowed, "and I'll make that island a fucking parking lot."[206] Reagan rejected such extremes but banned tourist and business visits to Cuba, denied Cuban officials visas for travel in the United States, restricted importation of Cuban newspapers and magazines, and relentlessly propagandized Cuban perfidy. "All I hear from you . . . is Cuba, Cuba, Cuba!" complained Soviet ambassador Anatoly Dobrynin.[207] The United States insisted that Cuba evict the Soviets and halt support for Third World revolutions, and the Cubans demanded an end to the U.S. economic embargo. As for Central America, Cuba endorsed the Contadora process and urged the Salvadoran rebels and Nicaraguans to negotiate in order to obviate U.S. intervention. Castro welcomed an agreement to ban foreign advisers and foreign weapons from Central America. The United States, seeking victory through just such means, replied that the Cubans could not be trusted. In December 1984 Havana and Washington did manage to sign an immigration agreement: The United States would return to Cuba about 2,700 "excludables" (people with criminal records) who had come by boat in the 1980 Mariel exodus, and Cuba would let Cubans reunite with families in the United States.[208] But when the United States, in mid-1985, started up Radio Martí to beam American news and propaganda into Cuba, Castro angrily abrogated the accord. Isolated Cuba remained dependent on Soviet aid and defiantly independent of the United States.

When U.S. troops invaded the tiny Caribbean island of Grenada on October 25, 1983, Washington intended to send an unvarnished message to both Cuba and

Grenada. After U.S. troops invaded this small Caribbean island of 113,000 people in 1983 to oust a leftist government, many Grenadians expected an influx of U.S. foreign aid to energize a depressed economy. After the invasion, American assistance helped bring an airfield project to conclusion to improve Grenada's tourist industry. (By David Alan Harvey © 1984 National Geographic Society)

Nicaragua: Beware. More than 6,000 Americans went ashore to oust a Marxist regime with close ties to Cuba. During the invasion, more than 100 people died, including about 25 Cubans helping to build an airstrip. Reagan claimed that the airfield would serve the Cuban and Soviet militaries, but British engineers explained that its purpose was to boost Grenada's tourist trade. The administration also justified the invasion as the rescue of 1,000 Americans, many of them medical students, from factional strife among Marxists. But critics argued that the Americans faced no immediate danger. By mid-December, having deported surviving Cubans from the island and closed the Soviet embassy, U.S. forces evacuated Grenada. The mission had cost $75.5 million. World opinion disapproved this modern example of gunboat diplomacy; when the UN Security Council deplored the invasion, the United States vetoed the resolution. OAS members protested that the OAS charter had been violated. North Americans, in contrast, rejoiced that the United States had "won one for a change," especially only days after a bomb had killed 241 American soldiers in Lebanon (see page 528).

ENDANGERED INTERESTS IN THE MIDDLE EAST, AFRICA, AND ASIA

The Reagan administration failed to sustain Carter's initiatives in the Middle East. A "Hollywood poolside Zionist" who had resigned from a country club in 1948 to protest Jewish exclusion, Reagan sought to gain some sort of homeland for the Palestinians and to guarantee Israel's security through a new Arab-Israeli accord.[209] But the peace process stalled. Lebanon descended into savage civil war and suffered a punishing Israeli invasion and Syrian occupation; the Iran-Iraq War disrupted oil shipments; Libya and the United States skirmished; Israel and the United States bickered bitterly; and terrorists victimized the innocent, including many Americans. Concluding that Middle Easterners seemed bent on self-destruction, Secretary of State Shultz grumbled, "Somehow or other we have to get over the notion that every time things don't go just to everybody's satisfaction in the Middle East, it's the U.S.'s fault or it's up the U.S. to do something about it."[210] Indeed, the United States had few answers to Middle Eastern questions, especially when moderate Arab states like Saudi Arabia and Jordan refused to help relieve tensions with Israel yet kept placing large orders for arms. (For example, Reagan in 1981 approved the sale of high-tech military equipment valued at $8.5 billion to the Saudis.) Reaganites assumed that the Soviet Union coveted the region. But Israel considered the PLO and Arab nationalism the greater threats; and the Arabs designated Israel, not the Soviet Union, as enemy number one.

In late 1981, in open defiance of Reagan's position, Israel suddenly announced its annexation of the Golan Heights. Secretary Weinberger complained, "How long do we have to go on bribing Israel," getting little cooperation in return?[211] When Reagan suspended an Israeli-American military agreement, Prime Minister Menachem Begin exploded, "Are we a banana republic?" To American protests against Israeli bombing raids of PLO camps in Lebanon, Begin barked that he had read about American bombing in Vietnam—"You don't have a right, from a moral perspective, to preach to us."[212] Then came the Egyptian radicals' assassination of President Sadat and Israel's invasion of Lebanon.

Lebanon had long suffered factionalism, especially between Muslims and Christians. For decades, displaced Palestinians had moved into the country, and in 1970–1971 PLO fighters driven from Jordon joined them. When civil war erupted in the mid-1970s, Lebanon invited Syria to restore order; Syrian troops arrived and stayed. From bases in Lebanon the PLO harassed and murdered Israelis. Israel invaded Lebanon in June 1982 in the hope of "cleansing" the nation of Palestinians.[213] Israeli forces drove all the way to Beirut, helping to destroy much of the capital city. Reagan finally telephoned Begin. "Menachem, this is a holocaust," he said. "Mr. President," Began replied, "I think I know what a holocaust is."[214] Nonetheless the Israeli bombing of Beirut stopped.

U.S. officials arranged the withdrawal of both the PLO and Israel from Beirut and the introduction of a peace-keeping force that included American marines. Soon Americans became targets because they were perceived as backing the Christians, thus taking sides in the civil war. One member of Congress thought the marines "too few to fight and too many to die."[215] In April 1983 bombs hit the U.S. Embassy in Beirut, killing 63 people; mortar and sniper fire took the lives of marines over the next several months. Then, in October, a terrorist drove a truck loaded with explosives into a building full of sleeping American troops, killing 241 of them. President Reagan still insisted that keeping the marines in Lebanon had been "central to our credibility on a global scale."[216] A shaken Secretary Shultz, however, told aides: "If I ever say send in the Marines again, somebody shoot me."[217] In February 1984, with the military mission a proven failure and public criticism rising, Reagan withdrew the marine contingent.

After 533 days and scores of deaths, the marines could not quell Lebanon's multifaceted war. Critics chastised the administration for compliantly following Israel's lead into disaster and for not penalizing Israel for its use of American weapons in violation of contractual restrictions. The veteran diplomat George W. Ball regretted that the United States had intervened in a "neighborhood quarrel that was none of our business" and that detracted America's energies from trying to resolve the Palestinian issue.[218] The Reagan administration soon patched up relations with Israel, which in 1985 received the largest U.S. foreign-aid package of any nation— $3 billion, or more than $700 per person.

Israeli-American relations soured again after the Palestinian uprising (in Arabic, the *intifada*) began in December 1987 in the West Bank and Gaza. The Israelis had been ruling the 1.5 million inhabitants since 1967. Like other Palestinians in the Middle East (some 5 million), the PLO-backed participants in the *intifada* wanted a homeland. As youthful demonstrators were shot down by Israeli troops, and as shopkeepers organized anti-Israeli boycotts, Shultz tried to intercede. In 1988 he urged convocation of an international conference to work out the details of a "land for peace" solution. Both Israel and the PLO adamantly rejected the idea. Jordan decided to relinquish the West Bank to the PLO, which then declared an independent Palestinian state and endorsed UN Resolution 242 (see page 496). PLO leader Yasir Arafat launched a peace initiative of his own, but when he asked to

The Muddle East. To many Americans, including the cartoonist Toles, the turbulent Middle East seemed a strange, even irrational region. (TOLES © 1986 The Buffalo News. Reprinted with permission of UNIVERSAL PRESS)

speak before the General Assembly, Shultz denied him a visa. In an open rebuff to the United States, UN members voted to convene in Geneva to hear Arafat. In Switzerland, Arafat spoke, in obfuscating language, about "rejecting" and "condemning" terrorism and respecting Israel's "right to exist, to peace and security."[219] Shultz firmly signaled that he wanted a more precise commitment, and when Arafat soon offered it, the United States announced that U.S. diplomats would open official talks in Tunisia with the PLO for the first time ever. The first meeting was held December 16, 1988. The Israeli government denounced this step toward negotiations.

Terrorism spread beyond the Middle East (the Baader-Meinhof gang operated in West Germany, and death squads killed in El Salvador). In 1985 alone, more than 800 terrorist incidents in the world claimed some 900 lives, 23 of them Americans. But Mideast terrorists drew the greatest attention. Passengers on American commercial jets became hijack and murder victims, American-owned buildings were bombed, and U.S. citizens were taken hostage. In one case in 1985, U.S. warplanes forced to the ground an Egyptian airliner known to be carrying four Palestinians who had earlier seized the Italian cruise ship *Achille Lauro* and murdered a wheelchair-bound American. "You can run but you can't hide," asserted Reagan.[220]

The Reagan administration especially blamed Libyan radical Islamic ruler Moammar Gadhafi for much of the terrorism in the Middle East, and it tried to remove him from power. Diplomatic relations between Libya and the United States were severed in early 1981, the following year Washington imposed an embargo on oil imports from Libya, and in early 1986 Reagan banned all trade. After a series of terrorist attacks at busy European airports, Reagan officials fingered Libyan responsibility and sent U.S. warships into the Gulf of Sidra, waters claimed by Libya. "We have to put Qaddafi [Gadhafi] in a box and close the lid."[221] When the Libyans sent out patrol boats, American planes attacked them as well as shore batteries and radar sites. A few months later, in April 1986, the bombing of a West Berlin discotheque killed one American soldier and wounded others. Reagan declared Gadhafi the "mad dog of the Middle East."[222] Within days U.S. planes again bombed Libya, coming close to killing Gadhafi himself. The raid did slay his adopted infant daughter and wound two of his sons. Later investigation indicated that Libya had not been directly involved in the West Berlin bombing that triggered the U.S. attack.

The Iran-Iraq War also engaged the U.S. military. Deaths ran in the hundreds of thousands as each side savagely attacked the other. Iraq had initiated the war in 1980 to gain Iranian oil lands, control the Shatt al Arab waterway, and topple the Khomeini regime, which had incited Shiite Muslims in Iraq to rebel at every opportunity. Iraq began to sink oil tankers in the Persian Gulf. As Iran retaliated in the "tanker war," the United States vowed to keep the Gulf open to international commerce. In May 1987 two sea-skimming missiles fired by an Iraqi aircraft hit the U.S. frigate *Stark;* 37 crewmen were killed. Iraq apologized. Reagan soon beefed up the U.S. naval presence in the Gulf and "reflagged" Kuwaiti oil tankers as American vessels; minesweepers combed the Gulf for deadly underwater mines. In October, after Iranian missiles struck a reflagged Kuwaiti tanker, American aircraft attacked two Iranian oil platforms. The next year, in July, the U.S.S. *Vincennes,* thinking that it was under attack despite sophisticated equipment that should have told its captain otherwise, shot down a civilian Iranian airliner, killing all 290 aboard. Unlike Moscow's callous defense of its downing of the Korean airliner, Washington admitted error while covering up the fact that the *Vincennes,* violating international law, was inside Iranian territorial waters at the time of the shootdown. At last, in August 1988, Iran and Iraq agreed to end their costly war.

In Africa, too, Reagan had to deal with knotty, long-term issues. Death-dealing famine, as in the Sudan in the mid-1980s; civil wars in Angola and Ethiopia, where Soviet and Cuban troops assisted ruling regimes and covert CIA aid helped insurgents; the unresolved status of South Africa–dominated Namibia; and especially the dehumanizing policy of apartheid in South Africa demanded attention. Reagan again espied Soviet adventurism. Toward white-ruled South Africa he launched "constructive engagement."[223] Because the United States could not coerce South Africa to abandon its oppression of the black majority, Assistant Secretary of State Chester Crocker argued, Americans should disapprove apartheid but refrain from overt pressure (such as economic sanctions), and instead encourage gradual reform. This policy amounted to a "kid-glove, all carrot-and-no-stick approach," complained some analysts.[224]

Hunger in Africa.   These refugees in a camp in Ethiopia in 1984 await food or death. During the 1980s, several African countries experienced severe drought and famine. Concerned people around the world raised money and sent food and supplies, but millions of Africans still starved to death. (Sebastiano Salgado, Jr./Magnum)

Reagan shifted from "constructive engagement" for several reasons. The South African government would not entertain serious reform, and black South Africans marched, protested, and died for their freedom, demanding that people around the world take sides. World opinion had become highly critical of American policy, which appeared to tolerate racism. As violence spread across South Africa and moderates seemed to flirt with radical measures, Reagan also worried that the opportunistic Soviets might exploit the turmoil. Protest in the United States, led by the Free South Africa Movement, a broad-based coalition, forced the issue onto the American political agenda. Members of Congress joined with church, labor, and intellectual leaders to picket the South African embassy in Washington, D.C., and even submitted to arrest to publicize the issue. South African bishop Desmond M. Tutu, the 1984 Nobel Peace Prize recipient, toured the United States appealing for economic pressure against his government. Cities (Boston, Philadelphia, and others) and states (Connecticut, Maryland, and Nebraska among them) passed divestiture laws requiring the sale of stock they owned in American companies operating in South Africa. Anti-apartheid groups also pressed American corporations to begin divestment—the sale of their businesses in South Africa. Some companies pulled out; by the end of 1985, American investments had dropped to $1.3 billion from $2 billion in 1981.

To quiet American protest and head off congressional action, Reagan, in September 1985, added a few sanctions to the earlier (1962) embargo on arms sales to South Africa. This time he restricted nuclear and computer sales and prohibited American bank loans to the South African government. But in October 1986, with

Race War in South Africa.   Doug Marlette's biting 1986 cartoon depicted President Reagan using his famed humor at a time when his "constructive engagement" policy toward South Africa was failing and South Africa was bleeding. (Reprinted by permission: Tribune Media Services)

"WHAT'S BLACK AND WHITE AND RED ALL OVER?...THAT'S EASY, SENATOR DOLE— A NEWSPAPER!...NO?...A SUNBURNED ZEBRA!...NO?...AN EMBARRASSED NUN!...NO?..."

an unusual bipartisan consensus and over Reagan's veto, Congress passed a stiffer bill for economic sanctions, including a ban on new American investments in and oil exports to South Africa and on imports of certain South African products. Good news came out of South Africa in December 1988, when Angola, Cuba, and South Africa signed a U.S.-mediated agreement for a Cuban troop withdrawal from Angola and black majority rule in Namibia.

In Asia, Ferdinand Marcos's Philippines became a troublesome ally. Elected president in 1965, Marcos had created a dictatorship marked by corruption, martial law, and personal enrichment. By the early 1980s his country groaned under a huge foreign debt of more than $20 billion, high unemployment, and economic stagnation. He jailed critics, whom security forces tortured and murdered. Business, Roman Catholic Church, civil libertarian, and professional leaders demanded reform. Two insurgencies fed on Filipino discontent: the New People's Army led by communists and the Moro National Liberation Front of Muslims in the south. The accelerating discontent with Marcos came suddenly to a head in August 1983, after assassins gunned down the anti-Marcos leader Benigno S. Aquino on his return from exile in the United States. The evidence pointed to a successful military conspiracy.

American investments of $2 billion, trade sales of similar value, and outstanding debts owed to American banks seemed in jeopardy. So, too, did two major American bases: Subic Bay Naval Station and Clark Air Base. "There is no hope for my naval base with that guy as president of that country," remarked Admiral William Crowe. "Choose between Marcos and that base."[225] The Reagan administration distanced itself from Marcos and pressed for reforms. When Marcos stole an election from Benigno Aquino's widow, Corazon Aquino, turmoil tore across the Philippines. Besieged by his own people and abandoned by the United States, Marcos, on February 25, 1986, went into exile in Hawaii. U.S. aid soon flowed to the Aquino government.

An altogether different kind of issue stood at the center of Japanese-American relations: a huge trade deficit. Although Japan remained a solid strategic partner, providing bases for the U.S. military and foreign aid to such American allies as South Korea, Turkey, and Pakistan, it also grew dramatically as an economic competitor. Imported Japanese products flooded American stores and won customers who appreciated their price, quality, and durability. In 1985 the total U.S. trade deficit (more imports than exports) mounted to an all-time high of $148.5 billion— $50 billion of it with Japan. The overall deficit derived in large part from the strong dollar abroad (making American goods expensive in other countries and imports less expensive in the United States) and the indebtedness of Third World nations, which forced them to buy fewer American products. But many Americans complained that Japan's tariff barriers, cartels, and government subsidies made it difficult for American goods such as plywood, paper, and cosmetics to penetrate Japanese markets. Protectionists demanded retaliatory, higher tariffs on Japanese goods so that ailing American industry could better meet import competition and American workers could hold their jobs. In 1985 Japan voluntarily set quotas on automobile and carbon-steel shipments to the United States and promised trade liberalization at home, but Washington wanted something more than this piece-by-piece approach. In 1987 Reagan imposed restrictions on some Japanese imports. The 1988 Omnibus Trade and Competitiveness Act authorized U.S. retaliation against nations that refused to negotiate reductions in trade barriers. Economic conflict with Japan persisted (see pages 590–592).

TRIUMPHS AND TIME BOMBS: THE REAGAN LEGACY

In the election of 1988 domestic issues predominated. Reagan's foreign-policy record received only minimal attention from the Democratic candidate, Michael Dukakis, and the Republican nominee, Vice President George Bush. Dukakis questioned the value of Reagan's heavy military spending, doubted the wisdom of U.S. intervention in Central America, and berated officials for doing business with Panama's dictator Manuel Noriega (see page 573). Dukakis also warned that unless the United States put its economic house in order, it would slip from its status as a world power. Bush sidestepped the huge federal budget and trade deficits, his involvement in the Iran-Contra scandal, and the ailing infrastructure and instead cheered American prosperity and hammered Dukakis on domestic issues like abortion and crime. Bush overwhelmed the Democrat at the polls, handing the Republicans their fifth victory in the last six presidential races. But the Democrats made gains in the House and Senate.

The Reagan record included foreign-policy successes, especially in the twilight of his presidency: Namibia, the INF Treaty, the departure of dictators in Haiti (Jean-Claude Duvalier) and the Philippines (Ferdinand Marcos), termination of the Iran-Iraq War, talks with the PLO, and Cuban withdrawal from Angola. At the end Reagan seemed less ideological, more adaptable. Improved U.S. relations with the Soviet Union suggested that the Cold War was winding down (see Chapter 12). The Soviets pulled out of Afghanistan and loosened their grip on Eastern Europe.

Some analysts argued that the huge Reagan military spending forced the economically hobbled Soviets to make concessions. Others noted that much of the money was misspent and wasted (especially on SDI), and that the remarkable changes initiated by Gorbachev sprung not from U.S. pressure but from a new generation of Soviet leaders and courageous Eastern European dissidents. The large U.S. defense buildup may actually have delayed the end of the Cold War by undermining Soviet moderates in their struggle against Kremlin hawks. Reagan very well may have undercut American power and prestige in the long run by spending the United States into tremendous debt and neglecting to repair the American economy or to improve American education to make the United States competitive in the international marketplace. The conservative columnist George F. Will wrote that Reagan "has been a great reassurer, a steadying captain who calmed the passengers and, to some extent, the sea." But, Will added, Reagan's "cheerfulness" was "a narcotic, numbing the nation's senses about hazards just over the horizon."[226]

President Reagan bequeathed to Bush several failures and unresolved international issues. Reagan (and Bush as vice president) had paid little attention to global environmental questions. Soil erosion reduced food production at a time when the world's population was growing rapidly. Toxic wastes, acid rain, shortages of clean water, the overcutting of forests, and the overgrazing of fields hurried environmental decline, which in turn burdened governments. Tons of valuable topsoil were being swept down rivers to the sea. "Encroaching deserts now pose a greater threat to national security, and indeed national survival, than do invading armies," warned one development specialist.[227] A warming of the earth's climate owing to the "greenhouse effect" of carbon dioxide and other gases building up in the atmosphere, scientists reported, might raise ocean levels, flooding farmlands and dislocating millions of people. Political analysts predicted that unless corrected, these environmental and economic problems would spawn political unrest. Some positive signs appeared: population-control programs in many Third World nations; public-health programs providing an effective vaccine against malaria; oral rehydration therapy to reduce child deaths from diarrhea; massive immunization programs against measles and polio; India's attainment of self-sufficiency in food production; and the conservation of dwindling supplies of minerals. But the Reagan administration barely noticed.

Environmental questions also figured in Canadian-American relations. Canadians grew alarmed that polluted American air in the form of acid rain was destroying their forests and contaminating their water. Tension between Ottawa and Washington reached an awkward high. Former Canadian prime minister Pierre Trudeau once mused, "Living next to you is in some ways like sleeping with an elephant. No matter how friendly and even-tempered is the beast, if I may call it that, one is affected by every twitch and grunt."[228] Although Reagan showed scant interest in acid rain, he did launch negotiations leading to the United States–Canada Free Trade Agreement of 1988. This accord created the world's largest free trade area. The two nations exchanged more goods and services each year, worth about $166 billion in 1989, than any other two countries. With the tariff walls eliminated and an influx of American products expected, many Canadians quipped that Canada was destined to become the fifty-first state. "It all started [when] I woke up singing the American anthem," read an editorial cartoon under a sketch of a Canadian worker explaining his identity crisis to a psychiatrist. "I began to repeat the Pledge of Allegiance and then I started having this incredible urge to purchase a handgun."[229]

Any accounting of the Reagan legacy would have to include the president's failure to energize the peace process in the Middle East. The Iran-Contra scandal and intervention in Lebanon must rank as major foreign-policy blunders. In Central America, Reagan registered a large death count, continued civil wars, economic disarray, and a bankrupt attachment to the *contras*. On South Africa, Congress had to push Reagan to express serious disapproval of apartheid. On economic questions, the trade and budget deficits grew to dangerous proportions in the Reagan years (the national debt tripled to $2.8 trillion), and the United States became a debtor nation. Trade conflict with Japan intensified as the United States found it more and more difficult to compete with the trans-Pacific power. The Third World "debt bomb" also jeopardized a stable economic future.

In the 1980s, after Vietnam and the Iranian hostage crisis, Americans worked to reassert their international supremacy. Great powers have seldom relinquished their domains and commanding positions without reluctance and without a good deal of violence: witness Spanish, Dutch, Portuguese, French, and British imperial death throes. Americans, too, clung to declining power in the 1980s. They stoutly hurled challenges at their detractors; they built up massive military and nuclear forces; they financed insurgencies; they defended their global interests; they continued to assume that they had answers to others' problems; they reaffirmed their self-appointed mission to purify an imperfect world; they restated their belief in American exceptionalism. In his upbeat farewell address, Ronald Reagan declared that "America is respected again in the world, and looked to for leadership."[230] Other voices suggested that he "may have left time bombs ticking away for the future."[231]

FURTHER READING FOR THE PERIOD 1977–1989

For overviews of the period and various topics, see William C. Berman, *America's Right Turn* (1994); Tom J. Farer, *The Lost Consensus* (1987); Raymond L. Garthoff, *The Great Transition* (1994) and *Détente and Confrontation* (1985); Robert C. Gray and Stanley J. Michalak, Jr., eds., *American Foreign Policy Since Détente* (1984); Ole R. Holsti and James N. Rosenau, *American Leadership in World Affairs* (1984); Robert C. Johansen, *The National Interest and the Human Interest* (1980); Paul Kennedy, *The Rise and Fall of the Great Powers* (1987); and Sanford Ungar, *Estrangement* (1985). See also books listed in Chapters 7, 10, and 12.

For Jimmy Carter and his foreign relations (specific policies and regions listed in later paragraphs), see John Drumbell, *The Carter Presidency* (1993); Betty Glad, *Jimmy Carter* (1980); Erwin C. Hargrove, *Jimmy Carter as President* (1988); Charles O. Jones, *The Trusteeship Presidency* (1988); Burton I. Kaufman, *The Presidency of James Earl Carter, Jr.* (1993); David S. McLellan, *Cyrus Vance* (1985); A. Glenn Mower, *The United States, the United Nations, and Human Rights* (1979) and *Human Rights and American Foreign Policy* (1987); Nancy P. Newell and Richard S. Newell, *The Struggle for Afghanistan* (1981); Kenneth A. Oye et al., eds., *Eagle Entangled* (1979); Jerel A. Rosati, *The Carter Administration's Quest for Global Community* (1987); Herbert O. Rosenbaum and Alexej Ugrinsky, eds., *Jimmy Carter* (1993); Gaddis Smith, *Morality, Reason, & Power* (1986); and Sandy Vogelgesang, *American Dream, Global Nightmare* (1980) (human rights).

Ronald Reagan's worldview, record as president, advisers, and legacy are studied in Coral Bell, *The Reagan Paradox* (1989); Larry Berman, ed., *Looking Back on the Reagan Presidency* (1990); Sidney Blumenthal and Thomas B. Edsall, eds., *The Reagan Legacy* (1988); Paul Boyer, ed., *Reagan as President* (1990); Lou Cannon, *President Reagan* (1991); Robert Dallek, *Ronald Reagan* (1984); Theodore Draper, *A Very Thin Line* (1991) (Iran-Contra); Ronnie Duggar, *On Reagan* (1983); Allan Gerson, *The Kirkpatrick Mission* (1991) (UN); Fred I. Greenstein, ed., *The Reagan Presidency* (1983); J. David Hoeveler, Jr., *Watch on the Right* (1991); Haynes Johnson, *Sleepwalking through History* (1991); David E. Kyvig, ed., *Reagan and the World* (1990); Alexandre Laurien, *The Voice of America* (1988); Thomas E. Mann, *A Question of Balance* (1990) (Congress); Jeff McMahan, *Reagan and the World* (1986); Morris Morley, *Crisis and Confrontation* (1988); Roger Morris, *Haig* (1982); Kenneth A. Oye et al., eds., *Eagle Defiant* (1983) and *Eagle Resurgent?* (1987); Michael Rogin, *Ronald Reagan* (1987); Michael Schaller, *Reckoning with Reagan* (1992); and Garry Wills, *Reagan's America* (1987). Specific topics and regions are listed below.

International economic and environmental issues can be explored in C. Fred Bergsten and William R. Cline, *The United States–Japan Economic Problem* (1987); Margaret P. Doxey, *Economic Sanctions and International Enforcement* (1980); Robert Gilpin, *The Political Economy of International Relations* (1987); Edward Goldsmith and Nicolas Hildyard, eds., *The Earth Report* (1988); Gary C. Hufbauer et al., *Economic Sanctions Reconsidered* (1985); Anne G. Keatley, ed., *Technological Frontiers and Foreign Relations* (1985); John H. Makin, *The Global Debt Crisis* (1984); John McCormick, *Reclaiming Paradise* (1989); Jürgen Schmandt et al., eds., *Acid Rain and Friendly Neighbors* (1988); Gilbert R. Winham, *International Trade and the Tokyo Round Negotiations* (1986); and Donald Worster, ed., *The Ends of the Earth* (1988).

For relations with the Soviet Union (except for the nuclear-arms race listed below), see Garthoff above; Seweryn Bialer, *The Soviet Paradox* (1986); Seweryn Bialer and Michael Mandelbaum, eds., *Gorbachev's Russia and American Foreign Policy* (1988); Alexander Dallin, *Black Box: KAL 007 and the Superpowers* (1985); Seymour M. Hersh, *"The Target Is Destroyed"* (1986); Jerry Hough, *Russia and the West* (1988); Robert G. Kaiser, *How Gorbachev Happened* (1991); Michael MccGwire, *Perestroika and Soviet National Security* (1991); Michael Mandelbaum and Strobe Talbott, *Reagan and Gorbachev* (1987); Jerry Sanders, *Peddlers of Crisis* (1983); and Strobe Talbott, *The Russians and Reagan* (1984).

For the nuclear-arms race, SALT-II, SDI, and the antinuclear movement, see Ruth Adams and Susan Cullen, eds., *The Final Epidemic* (1981); William Arkin and Richard Fieldhouse, *Nuclear Battlefields* (1985); Donald C. Baucom, *The Origins of SDI, 1944–1983* (1992); Dan Caldwell, *The Dynamics of Domestic Politics and Arms Control* (1991) (SALT-II); David Callahan, *Dangerous Capabilities* (1990) (Nitze); Sidney D. Drell et al., *The Reagan Strategic Defense Initiative* (1985); Lynn Eden and Steven E. Miller, eds., *Nuclear Arguments* (1989); Matthew Evangelista, *Innovation and the Arms Race* (1988); Harvard Nuclear Study Group, *Living with Nuclear Weapons* (1983); Jonathan Haslam, *The Soviet Union and the Politics of Nuclear Weapons in Europe, 1969–87* (1990); Robert Jervis, *The Meaning of the Nuclear Revolution* (1989); William W. Kaufmann, *A Reasonable Defense* (1986); Michael T. Klare, *American Arms Supermarket* (1984); Edward T. Linenthal, *Symbolic Defense* (1989) (SDI); David S. Meyer, *A Winter of Discontent* (1990) (freeze); John Mueller, *Retreat from Doomsday* (1989); National Academy of Sciences, *Nuclear Arms Control* (1985); John Newhouse, *War and Peace in the Nuclear Age* (1989); Janne E. Nolan, *Guardians of the Arsenal* (1989); Andrew J. Pierre, *The Global Politics of Arms Sales* (1982); Jerome Price, *The Antinuclear Movement* (1989); Thomas R. Rochon, *Mobilizing for Peace* (1988); Scott D. Sagan, *Moving Targets* (1989); Jonathan Schell, *The Fate of the Earth* (1982); David N. Schwartz, *NATO's Nuclear Dilemmas* (1983); Leon V. Sigal, *Nuclear Forces in Europe* (1984); Steven K. Smith and Douglas A. Wertman, *U.S.–Western European Relations During the Reagan Years* (1992); Strobe Talbott, *Endgame* (1979) (SALT-II), *Deadly Gambits* (1984), and *The Master of the Game* (1988) (Nitze); Douglas C. Waller, *Congress and the Nuclear Freeze* (1987); Daniel Wirls, *Buildup* (1992); and Thomas W. Wolfe, *The SALT Experience* (1979).

The CIA and U.S. attraction to covert operations, counterinsurgency, and counterrevolution are explored in Daniel P. Bolger, *Americans at War, 1975–1986* (1988); Loch Johnson, *America's Secret Power* (1989); Michael T. Klare and Cynthia Arnson, *Supplying Repression* (1981); Michael T. Klare and Peter Kornbluh, eds., *Low-Intensity Warfare* (1988); David C. Martin and John Wolcott, *Best Laid Plans* (1988); Michael McClintock, *Instruments of Statecraft* (1992); Joseph E. Persico, *Casey* (1990); John Prados, *Presidents' Secret*

Wars (1986); John Ranelagh, *The Agency* (1986); D. Michael Shafer, *Deadly Paradigms* (1988); and Gregory F. Treverton, *Covert Action* (1987).

For U.S. relations with the Third World, see Richard E. Feinberg, *The Intemperate Zone* (1983); John L. Girling, *America and the Third World* (1980); Melvin Gurtov and Ray Maghroori, *Roots of Failure* (1984); Gabriel Kolko, *Confronting the Third World* (1988); Stephen D. Krasner, *Structural Conflict* (1985); Barry Rubin, *Modern Dictators* (1987); Peter J. Schraeder, *Intervention in the 1980s* (1989); and Marshall D. Shulman, ed., *East-West Tensions in the Third World* (1986).

Middle East topics, Arab-Israeli conflict, and the peace process are examined in Fouad Ajami, *The Arab Predicament* (1981); George W. Ball, *Error and Betrayal in Lebanon* (1984); Mahmoud G. ElWarfally, *Imagery and Ideology in U.S. Policy Toward Libya* (1988); George Lenczowski, *American Presidents and the Middle East* (1989) and *The Middle East in World Affairs* (1980); Zachary Lochman and Joel Beinin, eds., *Intifada* (1989); A. F. K. Organski, *The $36 Billion Bargain* (1990) (aid to Israel); Don Peretz, *Intifada* (1990); William R. Polk, *The Arab World Today* (1991); William B. Quandt, *Camp David* (1986), *Peace Process* (1993), and *The United States and Egypt* (1990); Cheryl Rubenberg, *Israel and the American National Interest* (1986); David Schoenbaum, *The United States and the State of Israel* (1993); Steven L. Spiegel, *The Other Arab-Israeli Conflict* (1985); and Daniel Yergin, *The Prize* (1991) (oil).

For U.S.-Iranian relations and the hostage crisis, see James A. Bill, *The Eagle and the Lion* (1988); Richard Cottam, *Iran and the United States* (1988); Mark J. Gasiorowski, *U.S. Foreign Policy and the Shah* (1991); Nikki R. Keddie, *Iran, the United States, and the Soviet Union* (1990); R. K. Ramazani, *Revolutionary Iran* (1987); Barry Rubin, *Paved with Good Intentions* (1980); Paul Ryan, *The Iranian Rescue Mission* (1985); Amin Saikal, *The Rise and Fall of the Shah* (1980); William Shawcross, *The Shah's Last Ride* (1988); Gary Sick, *All Fall Down* (1985) and *October Surprise* (1991) (hostages and Reagan election); and Marvin Zonis, *Majestic Failure* (1991).

For events in Asia, including the Philippines, see David Bain, *Sitting in Darkness* (1984) (Philippines); C. Fred Bergsten and William R. Cline, *The United States–Japan Economic Problem* (1987); Raymond Bonner, *Waltzing with a Dictator* (1987) (Marcos); H. W. Brands, *Bound to Empire* (1992) (Philippines); John Bresnan, ed., *Crisis in the Philippines* (1986); Roger Buckley, *U.S.-Japan Alliance Diplomacy* (1992); Sandra Burton, *Impossible Dream* (1989); Warren I. Cohen, *America's Response to China* (1990); Lynn D. Feintech, *China's Four Modernizations and the United States* (1982); Yufan Hao and Guocang Huan, eds., *The Chinese View of the World* (1989); Harry Harding, *A Fragile Relationship* (1992) (China); Akira Iriye and Warren I. Cohen, eds., *The United States and Japan* (1989); Stanley Karnow, *In Our Image* (1989); Richard J. Kessler, *Rebellion and Repression in the Philippines* (1989); S. P. Linder, *The Pacific Century* (1986); Michael Schaller, *The United States and China in the Twentieth Century* (1989); Stephen R. Shalom, *The United States and the Philippines* (1981); Richard H. Solomon, ed., *The China Factor* (1981); and Robert G. Sutter, *The China Quandary* (1983).

For the Panama Canal treaties and Latin America, see Paul Drake and Iván Jaksić eds., *The Struggle for Democracy in Chile, 1982–1990* (1991); Richard R. Fagen, ed., *Capitalism and the State in U.S.–Latin American Relations* (1979); William L. Furlong and Margaret E. Scranton, *The Dynamics of Foreign Policymaking: The President, the Congress, and the Panama Canal Treaties* (1984); J. Michael Hogan, *The Panama Canal in American Politics* (1986); Walter LaFeber, *The Panama Canal* (1989); Gordon K. Lewis, *Grenada* (1987); Abraham F. Lowenthal, ed., *Exporting Democracy* (1991) and *Partners in Conflict* (1987); Christopher Mitchell, ed., *Western Hemisphere Immigration and United States Foreign Policy* (1992); Louis A. Pérez, Jr., *Cuba and the United States* (1990); and Lars Schoultz, *Human Rights and United States Policy Toward Latin America* (1981) and *National Security and United States Policy toward Latin America* (1987).

Mexican-American relations are the subject of Wayne Cornelius, *Building the Cactus Curtain* (1980); Paul R. Erlich et al., *The Golden Door* (1981); George W. Grayson, *The Politics of Mexican Oil* (1980) and *Oil and Mexican Foreign Policy* (1988); Robert H. McBride, ed., *Mexico and the United States* (1981); Robert A. Pastor and Jorge G. Castañeda, *Limits of Friendship* (1988); Susan K. Purcell, ed., *Mexico–United States Relations* (1981); W. Dirk Raat, *Mexico and the United States* (1992); Peter H. Smith, *Mexico* (1980); and Stanley Weintraub, *Marriage of Convenience* (1989).

For Central America, especially Nicaragua and El Salvador, see Thomas P. Anderson, *Politics in Central America* (1988); Cynthia J. Arnson, *Crossroads* (1994); Bruce M. Bagley, ed., *Contadora and the Diplomacy of*

Peace in Central America (1987); Leslie Bethell, ed., *Central America Since Independence* (1991); Morris J. Blachman et al., eds., *Confronting Revolution* (1986); Kenneth M. Coleman and George C. Herring, eds., *Understanding the Central American Crisis* (1991); Richard E. Feinberg, ed., *Central America* (1982); Roy Gutman, *Banana Diplomacy* (1987) (Nicaragua); Martha Honey, *Hostile Acts* (1994) (Costa Rica); Stephen Kinzer, *Blood of Brothers* (1991) (Nicaragua); Peter Kornbluh, *Nicaragua* (1988); Clifford Krauss, *Inside Central America* (1991); Walter LaFeber, *Inevitable Revolutions* (1993); Anthony Lake, *Somoza Falling* (1989); Tommie Sue Montgomery, *Revolution in El Salvador* (1990); Morris H. Morley, *Washington, Somoza, and the Sandinistas* (1994); Robert Pastor, *Condemned to Repetition* (1987) (Nicaragua); Holly Sklar, *Washington's War on Nicaragua* (1988); Gaddis Smith, *The Last Years of the Monroe Doctrine, 1945–1993* (1994); and Thomas W. Walker, *Revolution and Counterrevolution in Nicaragua* (1990) and, ed., *Reagan vs. the Sandinistas* (1987).

South Africa and African questions are treated in Pauline H. Baker, *The United States and South Africa* (1989); James Barber and John Barratt, *South Africa's Foreign Policy* (1990); Gerald J. Bender et al., eds., *African Crisis Areas and U.S. Foreign Policy* (1985); Christopher Coker, *The United States and South Africa* (1986); Alexander deWaal, *Famine That Kills: Darfur, Sudan, 1984–1985* (1989); Peter Duignan and Lewis H. Gann, *The United States and Africa* (1987); Arthur Gaushon, *Crisis in Africa* (1981); Richard W. Hull, *American Enterprise in South Africa* (1990); Janice Love, *The U.S. Anti-Apartheid Movement* (1985); Martin Meredith, *In the Name of Apartheid* (1988); William Minter, *King Solomon's Mines Revisited* (1986); Robert I. Rotberg, *Suffer the Future* (1980); and Jennifer S. Whitaker, *Conflict in Southern Africa* (1978) and *How Can Africa Survive?* (1987).

See also the General Bibliography and the following notes.

Notes to Chapter 11

1. Quoted in Robert D. McFadden et al., *No Hiding Place* (New York: Times Books, 1981), p. 3.
2. Quoted in William B. Quandt, "The Middle East Crisis," *Foreign Affairs: America and the World, 1979*, LVIII (1980), 544.
3. Quoted in McFadden, *No Hiding Place*, p. 4.
4. Quoted in Doyle McManus, *Free at Last!* (New York: New American, 1981), p. 16.
5. William D. Hartley quoted in *U.S. News & World Report*, LXXXVIII (January 28, 1980), 32.
6. Quoted in Tim Wells, *444 Days* (San Diego: Harcourt Brace Jovanovich, 1985), p. 70.
7. *Public Papers, Carter, 1977* (Washington, D.C.: Government Printing Office, 1977–1978; 2 vols.), II, 2221.
8. Pierre Salinger, *America Held Hostage* (Garden City, N.Y.: Doubleday, 1981), p. 5.
9. Gary Sick, *All Fall Down* (New York: Random House, 1985), p. 21.
10. Jimmy Carter, *Keeping Faith* (New York: Bantam, 1982), p. 439.
11. Cyrus Vance, *Hard Choices* (New York: Simon and Schuster, 1983), p. 331.
12. William H. Sullivan, "Dateline Iran: The Road Not Taken," *Foreign Policy*, No. 40 (Fall 1980), p. 186.
13. Former U.S. official quoted in David Schoenbaum, "The United States & Iran's Revolution," *Foreign Policy*, No. 34 (Spring 1979), p. 20.
14. Quoted in *New York Times*, November 18, 1979.
15. Quoted in McFadden, *No Hiding Place*, p. 9.
16. Sadegh Ghotbzadeh quoted in Eric Rouleau, "Khomeini's Iran," *Foreign Affairs*, LIX (Fall 1980), 10.
17. Quoted in Daniel Yergin, *The Prize* (New York: Simon and Schuster, 1991), p. 701.
18. Quoted in Harold H. Saunders, "Diplomacy and Pressure," in Warren Christopher et al., *American Hostages in Iran* (New Haven: Yale University Press, 1982), p. 102.
19. Quoted in McFadden, *No Hiding Place*, p. 214.
20. Benjamin Civiletti, "Oral Argument . . . World Court," December 10, 1979, Department of State Current Policy No. 118.
21. Quoted in Hamilton Jordan, *Crisis* (New York: G. P. Putnam's Sons, 1982), p. 40.
22. Quoted in Burton I. Kaufman, *The Presidency of James Earl Carter, Jr.* (Lawrence: University Press of Kansas, 1993), p. 160.
23. Quoted in Wells, *444 Days*, p. 439.
24. Quoted in McFadden, *No Hiding Place*, p. 198.
25. Quoted in Barry Rubin, *Paved with Good Intentions* (New York: Oxford University Press, 1980), p. 257.
26. Vance, *Hard Choices*, p. 409.
27. Zbigniew Brzezinski, *Power and Principle* (New York: Farrar, Straus & Giroux, 1985; rev. ed.), p. 494.
28. Zbigniew Brzezinski, "The Failed Mission," *New York Times Magazine*, April 18, 1982, p. 64.
29. Quoted in Phillip Keisling, "Desert One," *Washington Monthly*, XV (December 1983), 56.
30. Quoted in Lucien S. Vandenbroucke, *Perilous Options* (New York: Oxford University Press, 1993), p. 140.

31. Logan Fitch quoted in David C. Martin and John Walcott, *Best Laid Plans* (New York: Simon and Schuster, 1988), p. 35.
32. Quoted in Paul B. Ryan, *The Iranian Rescue Mission* (Annapolis, Md.: Naval Institute Press, 1985), p. 127.
33. Michael Schaller, *Reckoning with Reagan* (New York: Oxford University Press, 1992), p. 21.
34. Jody Powell quoted in Kaufman, *Carter,* p. 176.
35. Gary Sick, "The Election Story of the Decade," *New York Times,* April 15, 1991.
36. Quoted in Schaller, *Reckoning,* p. 33.
37. John Limbert quoted in James A. Bill, *The Eagle and the Lion* (New Haven: Yale University Press, 1988), p. 303.
38. Sanford J. Ungar, "The Roots of Estrangement," in Ungar, ed., *Estrangement* (New York: Oxford University Press, 1985), p. 7.
39. Quoted in Steven V. Roberts, "The Year of the Hostage," *New York Times Magazine,* November 2, 1980, p. 63.
40. Quoted in Jules Witcover, *Marathon* (New York: Viking, 1977), p. 596.
41. Quoted in Betty Glad, *Jimmy Carter* (New York: W. W. Norton, 1980), p. 391.
42. Quoted in Hedley Donovan, *Roosevelt to Reagan* (New York: Harper & Row, 1985), p. 235.
43. Carter, *Keeping Faith,* p. 143.
44. Quoted in *Washington Post,* January 12, 1977; *New York Times,* May 2, 1979.
45. Vance, *Hard Choices,* p. 394.
46. Brzezinski, *Power and Principle,* p. 380.
47. Leslie H. Gelb in *New York Times,* April 29, 1980.
48. Jordan, *Crisis,* p. 47.
49. Quoted in *Newsweek,* LXXXVIII (December 27, 1976), 19.
50. Marina v. N. Whitman, "Leadership without Hegemony," *Foreign Policy,* No. 20 (Fall 1975), p. 138.
51. Gaddis Smith, *Morality, Reason, & Power* (New York: Hill and Wang, 1986).
52. *Public Papers, Carter, 1977, I,* 956.
53. *Ibid., 1978* (Washington, D.C.: Government Printing Office, 1979; 2 vols.), *II,* 2164.
54. Quoted in John Lewis Gaddis, *Strategies of Containment* (New York: Oxford University Press, 1982), p. 345.
55. Smith, *Morality, Reason, & Power,* p. 9.
56. Quoted in Richard Hudson, "Storm Over the Canal," *New York Times Magazine,* May 16, 1976, p. 24.
57. Quoted in William J. Jorden, *Panama Odyssey* (Austin: University of Texas Press, 1984), p. 436.
58. Quoted in William L. Furlong and Margaret E. Scranton, *The Dynamics of Foreign Policymaking* (Boulder, Colo.: Westview Press, 1984), p. 55.
59. Quoted in Lou Cannon, *President Reagan* (New York: Simon and Schuster, 1991), p. 342.
60. Quoted in Walter LaFeber, *The Panama Canal* (New York: W. W. Norton, 1979; rev. ed.), p. 213.
61. Carter, *Keeping Faith,* p. 164.
62. *Department of State Bulletin, LXXVIII* (May 1978), 52.
63. Brzezinski, *Power and Principle,* p. 136.
64. Quoted in Charles O. Jones, *The Trusteeship Presidency* (Baton Rouge: Louisiana State University Press, 1988), p. 160.
65. *Department of State Bulletin, LXXVIII* (May 1978), 53.
66. Quoted in Richard R. Fagen, "Dateline Nicaragua," *Foreign Policy,* No. 36 (Fall 1979), p. 188.
67. López Portillo quoted in W. Dirk Raat, *Mexico and the United States* (Athens: University of Georgia Press, 1992), p. 161.
68. Quoted in Michael S. Teitelbaum, "Right versus Right," *Foreign Affairs, LIX* (Fall 1980), 46.
69. Robert H. McBride, "The United States and Mexico," in McBride, ed., *Mexico and the United States* (Englewood Cliffs, N.J.: Prentice-Hall, 1981), p. 16.
70. Quoted in Saul Landau, "The Bay of Pigs," *Los Angeles Times,* April 19, 1981.
71. Quoted in *Hartford Courant,* November 20, 1980.
72. Moshe Dayan quoted in William B. Quandt, *Peace Process* (Washington, D.C.: Brookings, 1993), p. 268.
73. Quoted in David Schoenbaum, *The United States and the State of Israel* (New York: Oxford University Press, 1993), p. 260.
74. William B. Quandt, *Camp David* (Washington, D.C.: Brookings, 1986), p. 258.
75. *Department of State Bulletin, LXXIX* (May 1979), 1.
76. Quoted in *Hartford Courant,* December 22, 1980.
77. Andrew Young in Elaine P. Adam and Richard P. Stebbins, eds., *American Foreign Relations, 1977* (New York: New York University Press, 1979), p. 301.
78. Quoted in Walter LaFeber, *America, Russia, and the Cold War, 1945–1992* (New York: McGraw-Hill, 1993; 7th ed.), p. 292.
79. In Adam and Stebbins, *American Foreign Relations, 1977,* p. 309.
80. General Obasanjo quoted in Donald Rothchild, "U.S. Policy Styles in Africa," in Kenneth A. Oye et al., eds., *Eagle Entangled* (New York: Longman, 1979), p. 327.
81. Clyde Ferguson and William R. Cotter, "South Africa," *Foreign Affairs, LVI* (January 1978), 262.
82. Quoted in Foreign Policy Association, *Great Decisions, '79* (New York: Foreign Policy Association, 1979), p. 60.
83. Quoted in Kaufman, *Carter,* p. 91.
84. Quoted in *New York Times,* December 7, 1978.
85. Zbigniew Brzezinski, "From Cold War to Cold Peace," in G. K. Urban, ed., *Détente* (New York: Universe, 1976), pp. 264–265.
86. Quoted in Garthoff, *Détente and Confrontation,* p. 567.
87. Hodding Carter III, "Life Inside the Carter State Department," *Playboy, XXVIII* (February 1981), 215.
88. Quoted in John Newhouse, *War and Peace in the Nuclear Age* (New York: Knopf, 1989), p. 302.
89. Georgi Arbatov quoted in Garthoff, *Détente and Confrontation,* p. 566.

90. Quoted in Lawrence Caldwell and Alexander Dallin, "U.S. Policy Toward the Soviet Union," in Oye, *Eagle Entangled*, p. 220.

91. Quoted in Gerry A. Andrianopoulos, *Kissinger and Brzezinski* (New York: St. Martin's Press, 1991), p. 268.

92. Quoted in *New York Times*, May 29, 1978.

93. Quoted in Thomas J. McCormick, *America's Half-Century* (Baltimore: The Johns Hopkins University Press, 1989), p. 206.

94. Georgi Arbatov quoted in Joseph Kraft, "Letter from Moscow," *The New Yorker, LIV* (October 16, 1978), 122–124.

95. Quoted in George McGovern, "How to Avert a New 'Cold War,'" *Atlantic Monthly, CCXLV* (June 1980), 52.

96. Paul C. Warnke, "Apes on a Treadmill," *Foreign Policy*, No. 18 (Spring 1975), p. 12.

97. Quoted in David Callahan, *Dangerous Capabilities* (New York: HarperCollins, 1990), p. 409.

98. Leslie H. Gelb, "A Draw Is a Win," *New York Times Book Review*, November 4, 1979; quoted in Strobe Talbott, *Endgame* (New York: Harper & Row, 1980), p. 5.

99. Harold Brown quoted in Christopher A. Kojm, *The ABC's of Defense* (New York: Foreign Policy Association, 1981), p. 29.

100. Leslie H. Gelb, "The Facts of SALT II," April 1979, Department of State Current Policy No. 65.

101. Senator Robert Byrd quoted in *New York Times*, October 4, 1979.

102. Quoted in Robert Shaplen, "Eye of the Storm—III," *The New Yorker, LVI* (June 16, 1980), 76.

103. Tom Wicker quoted in David D. Newson, *The Soviet Brigade in Cuba* (Bloomington: Indiana University Press, 1987), p. 53.

104. Garthoff, *Détente and Confrontation*, p. 928.

105. Quoted in John G. Stoessinger, *Why Nations Go to War* (New York: St. Martin's Press, 1982; 3d ed.), p. 193.

106. George Urban, "A Long Conversation with Dr. Zbigniew Brzezinski," *Encounter, LVI* (May 1981), 18.

107. William Safire, "Bay of Tonkin Time," *New York Times*, January 10, 1980.

108. *Department of State Bulletin, LXXX* (February 1980), Special B.

109. Quoted in Smith, *Morality, Reason, & Power*, p. 232.

110. Quoted in *New York Times*, January 22, 1980.

111. Quoted in Glad, *Carter*, pp. 461–462.

112. *New York Times*, February 1, 1980.

113. David D. Newsom, "America Engulfed," *Foreign Policy*, No. 43 (Summer 1981), p. 17.

114. Quoted in Roberts, "Year of the Hostage," p. 60.

115. William A. Williams letter in *The Nation, CCXXXII* (February 14, 1981), 162.

116. Richard E. Neustadt, *Presidential Power and the Modern Presidents* (New York: The Free Press, 1990), p. 261.

117. Michael T. Klare and Cynthia Arnson, *Supplying Repression* (Washington, D.C.: Institute for Policy Studies, 1981), p. 7.

118. Cyrus Vance quoted in *New York Times*, June 6, 1980.

119. Quoted in Hedrick Smith, "Reagan," *New York Times Magazine*, November 16, 1980, p. 172.

120. Quoted in Cecil V. Crabb, Jr., "The Reagan Victory," in Ellis Sandoz and Cecil V. Crabb, Jr., eds., *A Tide of Discontent* (Washington, D.C.: Congressional Quarterly Press, 1981), p. 158.

121. Quoted in Robert G. Kaiser, "Your Host of Hosts," *New York Review of Books*, June 28, 1984, p. 38.

122. Quoted in Cannon, *President Reagan*, p. 131.

123. John P. Sears quoted in Smith, "Reagan," p. 174.

124. Quoted in *Washington Post National Weekly Edition*, April 30, 1984.

125. Quoted in Kaiser, "Your Host," p. 39.

126. Quoted in *Time, CXX* (December 13, 1982), 12.

127. Quoted in Strobe Talbott, *The Russians and Reagan* (New York: Vintage, 1984), p. 32.

128. *Public Papers, Reagan, 1981* (Washington, D.C.: Government Printing Office, 1982), p. 57.

129. Lord Carrington quoted in S. R. Ashton, *In Search of Détente* (New York: St. Martin's Press, 1989), p. 197.

130. Quoted in Schaller, *Reckoning*, p. 47.

131. Quoted in *New York Times*, March 13, 1983.

132. Strobe Talbott, *The Master of the Game* (New York: Vintage, 1989), p. 195.

133. Ronald Reagan, *An American Life* (New York: Simon and Schuster, 1990), p. 547.

134. *Public Papers, Reagan, 1981*, p. 464; *ibid., 1983* (Washington D.C.: Government Printing Office, 1984–1985, 2 vols.), I, 265.

135. James Schlesinger, "Eagle and Bear," *Foreign Affairs, LXIII* (Summer 1985), 961.

136. *Public Papers, Reagan, 1983, II*, 1189.

137. *Weekly Compilation of Presidential Documents, XXI* (February 11, 1985), 146.

138. *Department of State Bulletin, LXXXIV* (May 1984), 4.

139. Quoted in Walter LaFeber, *Inevitable Revolutions* (New York: W. W. Norton, 1993; 2d ed.), p. 276.

140. *Weekly Compilation of Presidential Documents, XXII* (February 10, 1986), 136, 140.

141. *Public Papers, Reagan, 1983, I*, 362.

142. *Department of State Bulletin, LXXXIV* (November 1984), 7.

143. Quoted in Cannon, *President Reagan*, p. 160.

144. Alexander M. Haig, Jr., *Caveat* (New York: Macmillan, 1984), p. 85.

145. Quoted in Michael McClintock, *Instruments of Statecraft* (New York: Pantheon, 1992), p. 378.

146. George Will quoted in *New York Times*, September 7, 1983; Jeane Kirkpatrick quoted in Judith Ewell, "Barely in the Inner Circle," in Edward Crapol, ed., *Women and American Foreign Policy* (Wilmington, Del.: Scholarly Resources, 1992; 2d ed.), p. 158; George P. Shultz, *Turmoil and Triumph* (New York: Charles Scribner's Sons, 1993), p. 84.

147. Ronald Steel, "Shultz's Revenge," *New York Review of Books*, September 23, 1993, p. 38.

148. Shultz, *Turmoil and Triumph*, p. 275.

149. Quoted in Robert A. Pastor, "The Centrality of Central America," in Larry Berman, ed., *Looking Back on the Reagan Presidency* (Baltimore: The Johns Hopkins University Press, 1990), p. 40.

150. Quoted in Theodore S. Draper, *A Very Thin Line* (New York: Simon and Schuster, 1991), p. 565.

151. Quoted *ibid.*, p. 560.

152. Quoted in Robert E. Osgood, "The Revitalization of Containment," *Foreign Affairs: America and the World, 1981, LX* (1982), 475.

153. Quoted in *New York Times*, December 10, 1981.

154. George F. Kennan, "Cease this Madness," *Atlantic Monthly, CCXLVII* (January 1981), 25–28.

155. George F. Kennan, "On Nuclear War," *New York Review of Books*, January 21, 1982, pp. 10, 12.

156. Quoted in *New York Times*, March 11, 1983.

157. Quoted *ibid.*, May 4, 1983.

158. Steven K. Smith and Douglas A. Wertman, *US–West European Relations During the Reagan Years* (New York: St. Martin's Press, 1992), p. 58.

159. Talbott, *Master of the Game*, p. 5.

160. Quoted in Strobe Talbott, *Deadly Gambits* (New York: Vintage, 1984), p. 144.

161. James Baker quoted *ibid.*, p. 223.

162. Quoted in Donald R. Baucom, *The Origins of SDI, 1944–1983* (Lawrence: University Press of Kansas, 1992), pp. 192–193.

163. Quoted in *New York Times*, March 27, 1983.

164. Paul C. Warnke quoted *ibid.*, April 22, 1986.

165. Quoted in William J. Crowe, Jr., *The Line of Fire* (New York: Simon and Schuster, 1993), p. 301.

166. Reagan quoted in *Washington Post*, December 24, 1981.

167. Ronald Reagan, "Korean Airline Massacre," September 5, 1983, Department of State Current Policy No. 507.

168. Quoted in Arnold Horelick, "U.S.-Soviet Relations," *Foreign Affairs: America and the World, 1984, LXIII* (1985), 517.

169. Georgi Arbatov, *The System* (New York: Times Books, 1992), p. 244.

170. Quoted in Robert G. Kaiser, *How Gorbachev Happened* (New York: Simon and Schuster, 1991), p. 119.

171. Reagan, *American Life*, pp. 675, 677.

172. Arthur Hartman quoted in Newhouse, *War and Peace*, p. 387.

173. Quoted in Michael MccGwire, *Perestroika and Soviet National Security* (Washington, D.C.: Brookings, 1991), p. 202.

174. Quoted in LaFeber, *America, Russia*, p. 325.

175. Shultz, *Turmoil and Triumph*, p. 702.

176. Arbatov, *System*, p. 350.

177. Quoted in Edwin Meese III, *With Reagan* (Washington, D.C.: Regnery Gateway, 1992), p. 167.

178. Quoted in Michael R. Beschloss and Strobe Talbott, *At the Highest Levels* (Boston: Little, Brown, 1993), p. 11.

179. Quoted in Harold Molineu, *U.S. Policy Toward Latin America* (Boulder, Colo.: Westview Press, 1986), p. 176; NSC paper of April 1982 quoted in *New York Times*, April 7, 1983.

180. *Public Papers, Reagan, 1983, I*, 373, 601.

181. Quoted in *New York Times*, April 28, 1983.

182. *Department of State Bulletin, LXXXI* (March 1981), 7.

183. Quoted in *New York Times*, April 26, 1981.

184. Quoted in William M. LeoGrande, "A Splendid Little War," *International Security, VI* (Summer 1981), 27.

185. Quoted *ibid.*, p. 45.

186. Quoted in LaFeber, *Inevitable Revolutions*, p. 277.

187. *Department of State Bulletin, LXXXI* (April 1981), 12.

188. Howard Lane quoted in Mark Danner, "The Truth of El Mozote," *The New Yorker, LXIX* (December 6, 1993), 118.

189. Quoted in *Washington Post National Weekly Edition*, March 29–April 4, 1993.

190. Thomas Carothers, "The Reagan Years," in Abraham F. Lowenthal, ed., *Exporting Democracy* (Baltimore: The Johns Hopkins University Press, 1991), p. 93.

191. Quoted in Sidney Blumenthal, "Marketing the President," *New York Times Magazine*, September 13, 1981, p. 112.

192. Quoted in Marvin E. Gettleman et al., eds., *El Salvador* (New York: Grove, 1981), p. 355.

193. Quoted in George C. Herring, "Vietnam, Central America, and the Uses of History," in Kenneth L. Coleman and George C. Herring, eds., *Understanding the Central American Crisis* (Wilmington, Del.: Scholarly Resources, 1991), p. 184.

194. Quoted in *New York Times*, March 19, 1981.

195. Quoted in Stephen Kinzer, "Nicaragua," *New York Times Magazine*, August 28, 1983, p. 24.

196. Quoted in Peter Kornbluh, "The U.S. Role in the Counterrevolution," in Thomas W. Walker, ed., *Revolution & Counterrevolution in Nicaragua* (Boulder, Colo.: Westview, 1991), p. 325.

197. Quoted in Bob Woodward, *Veil* (New York: Simon and Schuster, 1987), p. 281.

198. Quoted in Thomas G. Paterson, "Oversight or Afterview?" in Michael Barnhart, ed., *Congress and United States Foreign Policy* (Albany: State University of New York Press, 1987), p. 154.

199. Paul Trible quoted in Ann Wroe, *Lives, Lies, and the Iran-Contra Affair* (London: I. B. Tauris, 1991), p. 50.

200. Lawrence Walsh quoted in Theodore Draper, "Walsh's Last Stand," *New York Review of Books*, March 3, 1994, p. 27.

201. Quoted in Joel Brinkley, "The Cover-Up That Worked," *New York Times*, January 23, 1994.

202. Tomas Borge quoted in Pastor, "Centrality," p. 37.

203. Quoted in *New York Times,* February 23, 1985.

204. Quoted *ibid.*, August 13, 1986.

205. Ken Duberstein quoting Reagan in Cannon, *President Reagan*, p. 337.
206. Michael Deaver quoting Haig in Schaller, *Reckoning*, p. 123.
207. Quoted in Haig, *Caveat*, p. 107.
208. Wayne S. Smith, *The Closest of Enemies* (New York: W. W. Norton, 1987), p. 276.
209. Quoted in Schoenbaum, *U.S. and Israel*, p. 273.
210. Quoted in *Washington Post National Weekly Edition*, April 9, 1984.
211. Quoted in Haig, *Caveat*, p. 328.
212. Quoted in *New York Times*, December 21, 1981.
213. General Ariel Sharon quoted in Quandt, *Peace Process*, p. 346.
214. Quoted in Schoenbaum, *U.S. and Israel*, p. 285.
215. Sam M. Gibbons quoted in *Washington Post National Weekly Edition*, November 7, 1983.
216. Quoted in *New York Times*, October 25, 1983.
217. Quoted in Martin and Walcott, *Best Laid Plans*, p. 148.
218. George W. Ball, *Error and Betrayal in Lebanon* (Washington, D.C.: Foundation for Middle East Peace, 1984), p. 23.
219. Quoted in Quandt, *Peace Process*, p. 374.
220. Quoted in *New York Times,* October 15, 1985.
221. Quoted *ibid.* November 4, 1985.
222. Quoted *ibid.,* April 20, 1986.
223. Chester A. Crocker, "South Africa: Strategy for Change," *Foreign Affairs, LIX* (Winter 1980/1981), 346.
224. Donald Rothchild and John Ravenhill, "From Carter to Reagan," in Kenneth Oye et al., eds., *Eagle Defiant* (Boston: Little, Brown, 1983), p. 349.
225. Quoted in H. W. Brands, *Bound to Empire* (New York: Oxford University Press, 1992), p. 329.
226. George F. Will, "How Reagan Changed America," *Newsweek, CXIII* (January 9, 1989), 13, 17.
227. Lester R. Brown quoted in *World Development Forum, IV* (August 31, 1986), 1.
228. Quoted in Ivo D. Duchacek, *Nations and Men* (Hinsdale, Ill.: Dryden Press, 1975; 3d ed.), p. 146.
229. Quoted in *Washington Post National Weekly Edition*, December 5–11, 1988.
230. Quoted in Foreign Policy Association, *Great Decisions 1990* (New York: Foreign Policy Association, 1990), p. 16.
231. Terry Deibel, "Reagan's Mixed Legacy," *Foreign Policy*, No. 75 (Summer 1989), p. 49.

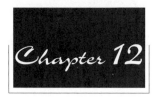

THE TESTS OF A NEW ERA:
AMERICANS AND THE WORLD SINCE 1989

Dancing on the Berlin Wall. *Berliners cavort atop the Berlin Wall in front of the Brandenburg Gate. The opening of the Wall on November 9, 1989, led to the reunification of East and West Germany. The breaching of the Wall, explained a U.S. presidential aide, occurred because Mikhail Gorbachev "put his foot on it and shoved it." (AP/Wide World Photos)*

✖ *Diplomatic Crossroad*

THE BERLIN WALL COMES DOWN, 1989

The partying began at midnight. Earlier on that afternoon of November 9, 1989, East Berlin Communist party boss Gunter Schabowski had announced almost offhandedly that starting at midnight, citizens of the German Democratic Republic (GDR) could leave the country at any spot along the GDR's borders, including the crossing points along the infamous twenty-eight-mile-long Berlin Wall, where since 1961 guards had shot dead 191 people who had tried to scale the barricade. The news sped through both parts of the divided city, to the 1.3 million inhabitants of East Berlin and the 2 million in the West. At Checkpoint Charlie in the American sector of West Berlin, a huge crowd gathered well before midnight, carrying bottles of beer and *Sekt* (sparkling wine) to celebrate. As the hour approached, the crowds grew raucous, taunting the East Berlin border guards with the cry *"Tor Auf!"* ("Open the gate!").

At the stroke of midnight, thousands of East Berliners proceeded to file through, some triumphantly waving their heretofore obligatory blue ID cards. Soon all West Berlin exploded with trumpet blasts, fireworks, and dancing. Strangers embraced amid a cacophony of honking horns and joyous shouts. Atop the ten-foot wall in front of the Brandenburg Gate, Berliners linked arms, pranced, and sang the popular folk song, "Such a Beautiful Day Should Last Forever."[1] The Berlin novelist Christoph Hein jotted in his diary: "One of the most insurmountable borders in Europe has become a German dance floor."[2]

The jubilant celebration that followed was, as one West German radio station put it, "Christmas, New Year's and Easter rolled into one."[3] New signs covered the graffiti along the Wall: "Stalin Is Dead, Europe Lives" and "Only Today Is the War Really Over."[4] During the ensuing three-day weekend, more than 2 million Easterners crossed into West Berlin to walk along the Kurfurstendamm boulevard, that mecca of capitalist success with its fancy stores, elegant hotels, and chic coffeehouses, where the migrants eagerly spent the hundred Deutschemarks given to them by West German authorities as "welcome money." The main east-west subway line reopened after being sealed off for twenty-eight years.

Everywhere people grabbed their new freedom. Thousands of East Germans in their two-cylinder Trabant cars wheezed onto the autobahns to pay their first visits to friends and relatives inside West Germany. Traffic jams delayed cars at border crossings for more than five hours, but no one seemed to mind. In the northern city of Lubeck, the city council ran out of welcome money and had to appeal to banks and retailers for more. Hundreds of thousands of East Germans had entered the country over the weekend, but only 3,742 had applied for immigrant status. "This is the true reunification, the reunification of people," observed a shopkeeper in Helmstedt. "But it is also good that they are returning to their homes."[5]

The British scholar Timothy Garton Ash also participated in "the greatest street party in the history of the world." As he strolled through the Potsdamer Platz on Sunday morning, November 12, he could see workers dismantling the famous platform where distinguished visitors, including John F. Kennedy and Ronald Reagan, had hurled defiant speeches across the Berlin Wall. Soon the platform had disappeared "like an unneeded stage prop. . . . Clear the stage for another show." To Garton Ash, the Easterners looked "the same as they make their way home—except for the tell-tale shopping bag. But everyone is inwardly changed, changed utterly." The weekend, he thought, had a certain "magic, Pentecostal quality . . . when you feel that somewhere an angel has opened his wings."[6] Watching the scenes on television, President George Bush told his aides: "If the Soviets are going to let the Communists fall in East Germany, they've got to be really serious—more serious than I realized."[7] The journalist Michael Meyer watched a giant crane pull down a section of the concrete Wall. "The panel jerks back and forth like a broken tooth, then gives way," he recorded. "Floodlights illuminate graffiti on the slab's broken surface. The word [is] *Freiheit:* 'Freedom.'"[8]

The foundations of the Wall had begun to crumble the previous May, when Hungary had opened its border with Austria. In August tens of thousands of East Germans went on holiday to Hungary, then traveled across the Austro-Hungarian border and eventually to West Germany, where they could obtain automatic rights of citizenship. East Germany soon banned travel to Hungary, but this restriction only temporarily stemmed the flood, as more East Germans voted with their feet. Some sought asylum in the West German embassy in Prague, Czechoslovakia. By

Exodus of East Germans. On October 4, 1989, some 10,000 refugees from East Germany milled outside the West German embassy in Prague, Czechoslovakia, waiting for special buses to take them to West Germany, where they could obtain automatic citizenship. "Ich bin ein out of here," quipped the comedian Johnny Carson, as the tide of refugees swelled. Five weeks later, the Berlin Wall opened. (AP/Wide World Photos)

late October the number of refugees from the GDR had swelled to 200,000, a mass exodus on the scale that had prompted the East German government to erect the Berlin Wall in 1961. That same month, popular demonstrations in Leipzig and East Berlin led to the resignation of Erich Honecker's government. His successor, Egon Krenz, tried to stop the hemorrhaging by opening the Wall on November 9 and promising free elections for 1990, a signal that East Germany would soon join Hungary and Poland in abandoning orthodox Communism for some combination of democratic socialism and market capitalism. The day after the Wall came down, moreover, a bloodless coup in Sofia, Bulgaria, ousted Todor Zhivkov, the hard-line Communist party boss for the past thirty-five years. By the end of November, mass demonstrations were peacefully terminating communist rule in Czechoslovakia, and during Christmas week a bloody popular uprising toppled the tyrannical regime of Nicolae Ceausescu in Rumania.

The breaching of the Wall also raised the prospect of German reunification. West German chancellor Helmut Kohl interrupted an official visit to Poland to fly to West Berlin to join the festivities. "The wheel of history is turning faster now," he proclaimed. "We are and remain one nation. Long live a free German father-land!"[9] The precise blueprints and timetables for reunification remained vague, but the effects on international relations promised to be revolutionary. "It was one of those rare times," according to *Time,* "when the tectonic plates of history shift beneath men's feet, and nothing after is quite the same."[10]

MIKHAIL GORBACHEV AND THE REVOLUTIONS OF 1989

The seismic events of the *annus mirabilis* (year of miracles) 1989 would not have occurred without major impetus from Soviet president Mikhail S. Gorbachev. Since his accession to leadership in the Kremlin in March 1985, Gorbachev's bold effort at reforming the USSR through political liberalization (*glasnost*) and economic restructuring (*perestroika*) had acquired a momentum of its own. To revive the sick Soviet economy, plagued by declining productivity and a demoralized work force, the Soviet leader warned at the outset that "everyone must change, from the worker to the minister to the secretary of the central committee."[11] Freeing up emigration, permitting religious freedom, eliminating censorship, guaranteeing opposition parties and free elections, and overhauling the economy required changes in external policies. What started out as a fairly limited foreign-policy agenda—ending the war in Afghanistan, improving relations with China, and negotiating arms-control agreements with the United States—quickly mushroomed. "For five years," the historian Michael Howard has written, "the world watched astounded as, like an expert skier, Gorbachev used the very steepness of the slopes down which he hurled himself to maintain his balance . . . fearful that at any moment he would come crashing to the ground."[12]

Meeting at Camp David, 1990. Secretary of State James Baker (b. 1930), Barbara Bush (b. 1925), President George Bush (b. 1924), Raisa M. Gorbachev (b. 1936), and President Mikhail S. Gorbachev (b. 1932) left to right, at an informal meeting on June 2, 1990, at the Maryland presidential retreat. Raisa Gorbachev impressed people during the Gorbachevs' tour of the United States. The first wife of a Soviet leader to appear prominently in public with her husband, she held a graduate degree in the philosophy of science and could lecture on Marxism or missiles. (Courtesy of the Bush Presidential Materials Project)

Gorbachev identified the huge drain on Soviet resources caused by the superpower competition as one area of potential savings. Eliminating the cost of occupying Eastern Europe was another. Gorbachev decided on military cuts *despite* the Reagan military buildup. "These were unnecessary and wasteful expenditures that we were not going to match," he later insisted.[13] Improving East-West trade and achieving serious arms reductions meant that Gorbachev could not simultaneously reform Soviet society and carry on the Cold War as usual. Thus, on December 7, 1988, Gorbachev astounded the world by announcing that over the next two years his country would unilaterally cut its military forces by 500,000 men and 10,000 tanks, approximately 10 percent of the total Soviet manpower and 25 percent of the Red Army's tanks in Eastern Europe. In visits to Western Europe in spring and summer 1989, the charismatic Soviet leader elaborated on his proposals for a "common European home" that would eliminate "the probability of an armed clash and the very possibility of the use of force."[14] Even before the bloody massacre in June 1989 of Chinese students in Tiananmen Square (see pages 587–588), Gorbachev quietly passed the word to East European officials that Soviet troops would not intervene to put down uprisings—the Brezhnev Doctrine was dead. That interventionist doctrine would be replaced, quipped one Soviet commentator, by the Frank Sinatra doctrine—"They'll do it their way."[15]

The veteran communist oligarchs of Eastern Europe heard the message and lost their nerve. "Imagine an ultra-conservative cardinal being told that the Pope had been converted to Judaism," wrote one political scientist.[16] In early 1989 the Solidarity trade union movement in Poland, led by Lech Walesa, regained its legal status and cooperated with the communist regime in framing a new representative constitution. In June Solidarity won control of the new parliament, and two months later, Tadeusz Mazowiecki, editor of Solidarity's weekly paper, became the first noncommunist prime minister in Poland since the 1940s. In May 1990 Poland held its first free election in sixty-eight years. In Hungary the pace of reform quickened under the moderate leadership of Karoly Grosz, spurred especially by ceremonies in Budapest in June 1989, when the remains of ex-Premier Imre Nagy, executed by the Soviets for his role in the 1956 revolution, were exhumed from an unmarked grave and reburied with honor. By October the Hungarian Communist party had reconstituted itself as the Hungarian Socialist party; the parliament adopted a new constitution guaranteeing multiparty elections; and the Hungarian People's Republic formally ceased to exist. During the winter, Budapest and Moscow reached an agreement to withdraw all Soviet troops.

Perhaps the most memorable events occurred in Prague. On November 17, 1989, only a week after the Berlin Wall opened, some 500 university students marched toward Wenceslas Square in the center of the city, waving Czech national flags and calling for the rights of free speech and assembly. Riot police and special antiterrorist squads suddenly assaulted the marchers with tear gas, wooden truncheons, and attack dogs. Those in the front line tried to hand flowers to the police. Placing lighted candles on the ground and raising their arms, the students cried out: "We have bare hands!"[17] The savage beatings continued with methodical fury. More than a hundred students suffered wounds.

The "massacre" in Wenceslas Square—no one actually died—triggered more demonstrations. Every afternoon for eight consecutive days, crowds crammed into the square chanting *"Svoboda! Svoboda!"* ("Freedom! Freedom!") and calling on the communist leadership to resign. On the first afternoon 50,000 came; the next day, more than 300,000. "With as much civility as passion, as much wit as rage," the Prague demonstrators took care to make a revolution without litter or broken windows. When it was announced during one rally that a little boy named Honza had become separated from his mother, a quarter million people joined in the chant, "Honza, be brave!"[18] Smaller crowds mounted similar protests in other cities. On November 24, in the same piazza where Soviet tanks had crushed Alexander Dubĉek's democratic reforms in 1968, more than half a million people, the largest assemblage in Czechoslovakia's history, waved banners reading "Down with Communism," as that same Dubĉek spoke to his people for the first time in twenty-one years. Within hours General Secretary Milos Jakes and the entire Politburo had resigned.

The acknowledged hero of "Prague Autumn" was Václav Havel, a reddish-haired, fifty-three-year-old playwright whose parable about a greengrocer became the text for what he called the "velvet revolution." In the parable, the authorities order a grocer to hang a sign in his shop window saying, "Workers of the World, Unite." No one pays much attention. The grocer cares little for the slogan, but he displays the sign so that his son can get into the university. He conforms. The system, Havel seemed to say, was held together by a whole series of ideologically articulated lies. The system would collapse the moment greengrocers mustered the courage to remove the slogans. "A single seemingly powerless person who dares to cry out the truth," according to Havel, "has surprisingly greater power, though

Transformations: Russia, the Former Soviet Republics, Eastern Europe, and Germany

MONGOLIA

CHINA

TAJIKISTAN

INDIA

KYRGYZSTAN

Alma Ata

Bishkek

PAKISTAN

Dushanbe

ARABIAN SEA

Tashkent

KAZAKHSTAN

UZBEKISTAN

AFGHANISTAN

TURKMENISTAN

Ashkhabad

ARAL SEA

IRAN

PERSIAN GULF

CASPIAN SEA

Baku

AZERBAIJAN

RUSSIA

GEORGIA

Tbilisi

Yerevan

ARMENIA

IRAQ

SAUDI ARABIA

Moscow

Gorbachev in Power, 1985–1991
U.S.S.R. Dissolved, 1991

SYRIA

JORDAN

St. Petersburg

Declared
Independence,
1990

FINLAND

Renounced
Soviet Law,
1990

UKRAINE

TURKEY

LEBANON

ISRAEL

SWEDEN

Kiev

Chisinau

Odessa

Ceausescu Falls,
1989

BLACK SEA

EGYPT

Minsk

MOLDOVA

Tallinn

ESTONIA

BELARUS

MEDITERRANEAN SEA

Declared
Independence, 1990

Riga

LATVIA

RUMANIA

Bucharest

BULGARIA

NORWAY

BALTIC SEA

Vilnius

LITHUANIA

RUSSIA

Solidarity to Power,
1989

Warsaw

POLAND

Yugoslavia
Breaks Up,
1991

Belgrade

SERBIA

Sofia

Skopje

MACEDONIA

GREECE

German
Reunification,
1990 DENMARK

NORTH
SEA

Berlin

GERMANY

CZECH.
REP.

Prague

Bratislava

SLOVAKIA

AUS.

Budapest

HUNGARY

Zagreb

CROATIA

Ljubljana

SLOVENIA

Sarajevo

BOSNIA AND
HERZEGOVINA

ADRIATIC
SEA

Tirane

ALBANIA

LIBYA

MALTA

NETH.

BEL.

FR.

SWITZ.

ITALY

Václav Havel (b. 1936) of Czechoslovakia.
When this former Prague brewery worker, playwright, and political prisoner was sworn in as president of Czechoslovakia by communist officials, who had jailed him twice, one observer said "it was as though Kafka's Joseph K. had been retried and acquitted." Havel eloquently proclaimed that "all of us are responsible, each to a different degree, for keeping the totalitarian machine running. None of us is merely a victim, because all of us helped to create it together." Havel is pictured here outside the White House in February 1990. When Czechoslovakia splintered, Havel became president of the Czech Republic. (Courtesy of the Bush Presidential Materials Project, photo by Carol T. Powers)

formally disenfranchised, than do thousands of anonymous voters."[19] The "powerless" coalition of intellectuals, workers, discussion groups, artists, and students that composed the Civic Forum, Czechoslovakia's opposition, soon propelled Havel to the presidency of his country on December 29. The new Czech president, on visiting Washington in February 1990, told Congress: "You can help us most of all if you help the Soviet Union on its irreversible but immensely complicated road to democracy."[20]

On the day of Havel's inauguration in Prague, a large sign tallied up the score: "Poland—10 Years / Hungary—10 Months / East Germany—10 Weeks / Czechoslovakia—10 Days / Rumania—10 Hours."[21] The last referred to the gore-soaked ouster of the seventy-one-year-old Rumanian dictator Nicolae Ceausescu. The corrupt Stalinist strongman, who had once boasted that reform would come to Rumania only "when pears grow on poplar trees," stood on a balcony haranguing a sullen crowd in Bucharest's Victory Square on the morning of December 21.[22] He was attempting to blame recent killings by police in the western city of Timisoara on provocation by Hungarian nationalists. The crowd grew restive. Shouts of "Freedom!" and "Democracy!" interrupted the speech. Irritated and surprised, Ceausescu gestured for quiet. When the chanting grew louder, he angrily stalked from the balcony. That afternoon, large crowds surged into the streets, and that same evening, the Securitate, Ceausescu's secret police, fired into the crowds and massacred hundreds. The Rumanian army, however, soon joined the fighting against the security forces. As students jubilantly pushed Christmas trees into tank cannon barrels and fraternized with soldiers, Ceausescu and his wife Elena were captured and executed by firing squad on Christmas Day. The new Rumanian

National Salvation Front took control of the government. In mid-1990 this re-named Communist party won the Rumanian presidency through an election that some citizens thought rigged. When public protest arose, the new government vi-olently crushed it and held on to power. Events proved less volatile in Bulgaria, which held its first free election in June 1990, and in Albania, where the Communist party retained power but began to relax its tight grip, by granting, for example, its citizens the right to travel abroad.

Whether or not Gorbachev expected Eastern Europe "to crumble like a dry Saltine cracker in just a few months," he encouraged the process.[23] He urged General Wojciech Jaruzelski to try to co-opt Solidarity; he also warned Jakes and Honecker against resisting the forces of history. "Life itself punishes delay," Gorbachev told cheering crowds in Berlin on October 7, the fortieth anniversary of the founding of the GDR.[24] Gorbachev advised Krenz to open the Wall—it would "let off steam" and "avoid an explosion."[25] Even before Ceausescu's ouster, the Soviet news agency Tass denounced the Rumanian president as "one of the

Lenin Statue Removed in Rumania.   In March 1990 two cranes lifted the twenty-five-foot high, seven-ton bronze statue of Vladimir I. Lenin in front of the State Public House in Bucharest, Rumania. Just as the re-moval of the hammer and sickle from public buildings symbolized the demise of communist rule in Eastern Europe, so too did the symbolic tearing down of statues and structures associated with Soviet domination serve to assert the independence of nations heretofore sub-servient to Moscow. As the spiritual leader of Soviet communism, Lenin represented the God that failed in 1989–1990. (AP/Wide World Photos)

most odious dictators of the twentieth century."[26] Most important, throughout these dramatic months Soviet troops stayed in their barracks. "Like the little boy who pointed out the emperor's nakedness," the political scientist Michael MccGwire later wrote, Gorbachev "saw the established approach to international relations as not only absurd, but highly dangerous and inherently unnecessary."[27]

Just as *glasnost* and *perestroika* accelerated the liberation of Eastern Europe, so too did the toppling of communist regimes have repercussions inside the Soviet Union. During late August, in one of the most astonishing events of 1989, more than a million citizens of Estonia, Latvia, and Lithuania linked arms to form a human chain some four hundred miles long in protest against the fiftieth anniversary of the Nazi-Soviet Pact that had led to Stalin's annexation of the Baltic states. In December the Lithuanian Communist Party Congress broke with the party leadership in Moscow. In March 1990 the Lithuanian Parliament declared formal independence from the Soviet Union, and Estonia's governing body renounced Soviet law. In May Latvia declared independence, and in July the Ukraine proclaimed itself sovereign. Gorbachev tried to slow down, if not reverse, the surging separatist tide, but he promised not to use force.

Elsewhere in the multinational Soviet Union, long-smoldering ethnic rivalries ignited. Violent clashes between Muslim Azerbaijanis and Christian Armenians finally prompted Gorbachev in January 1990 to send 40,000 troops to Baku, Azerbaijan. Rioting in Tajikistan and Uzbekistan led to Moscow's imposition of martial law in those Central Asian republics. In addition, nationalist stirrings in Moldavia and Georgia conjured up the specters of separatism, anarchy, and disintegration—with the USSR losing all but its central Russian component.

McDonald's in Moscow. A worldwide symbol of capitalist bounty came to Moscow in early 1990 when McDonald's opened a fast-food restaurant in Pushkin Square. McDonald's Canadian subsidiary had spent fourteen years negotiating a contract with Soviet authorities. (McDonald's Corporation)

Gorbachev also faced daunting economic problems. Moscow's superpower military status masked the economy of a Third World nation: "Upper Volta with rockets," according to one wag.[28] Notwithstanding the hoopla surrounding the opening of a Moscow McDonald's restaurant, the Soviet economy was floundering in early 1990. *Perestroika* had caused the stick of a command economy to shrink, but the carrots of a market economy only slowly took root. Although rubles were plentiful, according to one visitor, "there has been so little to buy for so long, so little on the store shelves, so little coming out of the state farms and factories, that even the poorest intellectuals . . . have rubles in the tea tin. There is rarely tea in the tea tin."[29]

Facing hard-line communists who accused him of abandoning the Leninist faith and losing Eastern Europe, Gorbachev lobbied vigorously for his program. On March 6, 1990, the Supreme Soviet approved new legislation permitting Soviet citizens to open businesses and to employ other people to work for them. Thus was laid the foundation for a mixed economy, based on state, collective, and private enterprise. "Russians are believers," wrote the journalist Jane Kramer, "and they have decided to believe in the miracle-working market. They wait for the market the way the Pacific Islanders used to wait for the strong white god who was going to arrive with the next boat and bring them grace and cargo."[30]

Over the next two years, Gorbachev went from confident master of events to bewildered victim of forces he had unleashed. He won the Nobel Peace Prize, but he

Nobel Peace Prize Winners, 1981–1993

1981	Office of the United Nations High Commissioner for Refugees.
1982	Alva Myrdal of Sweden and Alfonso García Robles of Mexico, disarmament advocates.
1983	Lech Walesa of Poland, leader of the Solidarity trade union movement.
1984	Bishop Desmond M. Tutu of South Africa, a leader of the antiapartheid movement.
1985	International Physicians for the Prevention of Nuclear War, an organization jointly headed by a Soviet and an American doctor.
1986	Elie Wiesel, American writer on the Holocaust and a Nazi death camp survivor.
1987	President Oscar Arias Sánchez of Costa Rica, author of a peace plan for Central America.
1988	United Nations peacekeeping forces.
1989	Dalai Lama, exiled leader of Tibet.
1990	Mikhail S. Gorbachev, Soviet leader who launched *glasnost* and *perestroika*.
1991	Daw Aung San Suu Kyi, Burmese woman who organized political opposition to the repressive military government in her country.
1992	Rigorberta Menchú, Guatemalan woman who struggled for the rights of indigenous peoples.
1993	Frederick W. de Klerk, president of South Africa, and Nelson Mandela, head of the African National Congress, who cooperated to end apartheid and initiate majority rule in South Africa.

hesitated, gradually turning against Soviet reformers, democrats, and nationalists. He tried for a time to conciliate old-guard communists. When Eduard Shevardnadze resigned in December 1990, the disaffected foreign minister warned against "the onset of dictatorship."[31] The following month Gorbachev looked callous when he allowed hard-liners to massacre civilians in Riga and Vilnius. But he still rejected a return to terror. In August 1991, just prior to the scheduled signing of a new union treaty that would turn the USSR into a genuine confederation, prominent hard-liners, including Defense Minister Dimitri Yazov and Prime Minister Valentin Pavlov, attempted a coup. For three tense days, while Gorbachev remained under house arrest in the Crimea, the president of the new Russian republic, Boris Yeltsin, rallied huge crowds in Moscow against the disorganized conspirators. The coup collapsed, the plotters either committed suicide or surrendered, and Gorbachev returned to Moscow.

By the end of 1991 the Soviet Union had disintegrated into sixteen squabbling independent nations. Following the abortive coup attempt, the Communist party disbanded, the weakened central government recognized the independence of the three Baltic states, and most of the republics signed a new union treaty that left the Soviet government virtually impotent. Russia declared its independence and with many of the republics formed the Commonwealth of Independent States in December. The USSR had ceased to exist. Yeltsin's Russian government soon took over the Kremlin, the KGB, and the Soviet Foreign Ministry. A president without a country or even an office, Gorbachev told reporters: "I did all I could; maybe other people who come will be better."[32] On Christmas Day 1991, at 7:32 P.M. (Moscow time), the red hammer-and-sickle flag atop the Kremlin fluttered downward for the last time, soon replaced by the red, white, and blue Russian flag.

Gorbachev visited the United States in May 1992, arriving as the guest of the publisher Malcolm Forbes aboard his corporate jet, *Capitalist Tool*. President Bush feted the former Soviet leader at the White House. "A class act, that guy. A lot to admire there—a lot to miss," said Bush in a valedictory judgment.[33]

CAUTION, PRUDENCE, AND PRIORITIES: THE BUSH AND CLINTON ADMINISTRATIONS

As the world turned upside down in 1989, the U.S. government seemed to be a passive spectator. Studied nonchalance appeared to be the official reaction to the opening of the Berlin Wall. An outward show of calm prevailed. No special "Berlin task force" monitored events. The State Department professed to worry more about the latest rebel offensive in El Salvador. President Bush remained subdued and noncommittal. In the scholar Richard Barnet's words, the president left "the impression that he didn't know quite what to do but was determined to do it prudently."[34]

Makers of American Foreign Relations Since 1989

Presidents	Secretaries of State
George Bush, 1989–1993	James A. Baker III, 1989–1992
	Lawrence Eagleburger, 1992–1993
Bill Clinton, 1993–	Warren M. Christopher, 1993–

Appearances were partly deceiving. Although the process of reassessment took several months, by the time the Berlin Wall came down the Bush administration had made up its collective mind that Gorbachev was "for real," that his reforms in the Soviet Union and Eastern Europe served America's national interest, and that Washington would cooperate with Moscow in smoothing the transition to a post–Cold War world.[35] The conspicuously quiescent response to events in Berlin was deliberate—one of several signals to the Soviet Union that the United States did not seek to exploit the upheavals in Eastern Europe. Cautiousness suited both the unstable international setting and Bush's self-defined "cautious and prudent" style.[36] Most analysts agreed that George Bush and his foreign-policy team were cautious about almost everything. "People say I'm indecisive." Bush joked at a Gridiron Club dinner. "Well, I don't know about that."[37] Reactive, ad hoc, adaptable rather than ideologically zealous, conservative, eager to satisfy the right wing in the Republican party while still appealing to moderates, fearful of doing the wrong thing, Bush at times seemed to deserve the scornful question posed by Senator Edward M. Kennedy of Massachusetts during the 1988 presidental campaign—"Where was George?"[38]

A manager who liked to deal with facts and not visions, a doer rather than an intellectual, Bush did not seem to think long-term. "He's not interested in a lot of airy stuff," remarked Secretary of the Treasury Nicholas F. Brady.[39] He also lacked that ability to inspire people as Franklin D. Roosevelt and Winston S. Churchill had done during earlier periods of great historical change. A former Yale University baseball captain who still played golf and tennis, Bush once quoted the famed Yankee catcher Yogi Berra: "I'll make plenty of mistakes, but I don't want to make the wrong mistakes."[40] Bush's style seemed passive and his speeches flat. Although many applauded the absence of Reaganite hyperbole and misstatement, others thought that Bush should shape fast-moving events. The *New York Times* editorialized, "Why Not Prudence Plus Leadership?"[41] Brent Scowcroft, Bush's assistant for national security affairs, put it succinctly: "We prefer what is, as opposed to the alternative. . . . This is not an administration that is hell-bent on change."[42]

Bush's conservatism had deep roots. "George Bush was born on third base and thinks he hit a triple," quipped a fellow Texan.[43] Born in Massachusetts in 1924 to a wealthy, old Yankee family, Bush became a decorated navy pilot in World War II, attended Yale (B.A., 1948), and then moved to Texas, where he amassed greater wealth in the booming oil industry of the 1950s. Elected in 1966 to the first of two terms in Congress, Bush in 1970 went down to defeat in a bid for a Senate seat. President Nixon then appointed him ambassador to the United Nations. Two years later, Bush became chair of the Republican National Committee and part of the "damage control" team during Nixon's Watergate troubles; in 1974–1975 Bush represented the United States in China; and during 1976–1977 he served as CIA director. He unsuccessfully battled Ronald Reagan for the Republican presidential nomination in 1980 but enthusiastically accepted the second spot on the ticket. Always a loyalist as vice president, Bush supported Reagan's policies and traveled widely to broaden an international experience that few men have brought to the White House.

Bush liked to be his own secretary of state—practicing a "Rolodex diplomacy" by often using the telephone to call around the world. He nonetheless had a compatible secretary of state in James A. Baker III, a close friend from Texas who had skillfully managed his political campaigns. Like Bush, born (1930) to the elite, Baker had become a Texas corporate lawyer after graduation from Princeton University, where he majored in history and classics. A methodical problem solver, competitor, and workaholic, Baker had won high marks as Reagan's White House chief of staff and secretary of the treasury. "This is a man I can accomplish things with," Soviet foreign minister Eduard Shevardnadze reported after his first meeting with Baker.[44] Reactive and conservative like Bush, Baker preferred to deal with the task at hand rather than with the opportunity ahead. The journalist Elizabeth Drew has observed that the secretary "cultivates international figures and he cuts deals." With the president, Baker shared a "view of politics—domestic or international—as having very much to do with the art of massage."[45] Brent Scowcroft, national security affairs adviser, worked well with Baker and with Baker's successor, Lawrence Eagleburger, thus avoiding the feuding that had marred previous administrations. The sixty-three-year-old Scowcroft, a former army general from Utah, held a doctorate in international relations from Columbia University. He defined his role as facilitator, broker, and coordinator, not as architect of policy.

The election of former five-term Arkansas governor Bill Clinton in 1992 seemed to bring a different generational perspective to the White House. A graduate of Georgetown University and Yale Law School, Rhodes scholar, intern to Senator J. William Fulbright, Vietnam War protester and draft avoider, self-confessed "policy wonk," and at age forty-six the second youngest elected president, Clinton pledged during the campaign to maintain America's global leadership—to "build a world of security, freedom, democracy, free markets, and growth."[46] Yet he came to Washington hoping to defer major foreign-policy initiatives until he had conquered such pressing issues as taxes, deficits, economic growth, health care, welfare reform, and other domestic priorities. One journalist called him "an internationalist with a small-town touch . . . the detail man, the policy pointillist, who nonetheless loves to paint visionary landscapes."[47] The scholar Richard Neustadt observed that Clinton had "a vision of the Presidency that is charmingly naive—the place that can get things done."[48] Another student of the presidency compared Clinton's extemporaneous, "perfectly grammatical 100-odd-word sentences" with Bush's "fractured prose," and noted Clinton's "energy, enthusiasm, intelligence, and devotion to policy." But Fred I. Greenstein also discovered an "absence of self-discipline; hubristic confidence in his own views and abilities; and difficulty in narrowing his goals, ordering his efforts, and devising stratgies."[49]

Clinton appointed sixty-seven-year-old Warren M. Christopher as secretary of state. An alumnus of the University of Southern California and Stanford Law School, this "lawyer's lawyer," who had served as deputy secretary of state during the Carter years, had negotiated the release of American hostages from Iran in 1980–1981.[50] Disciplined and dignified, dour and aloof, Christopher "practiced diplomacy as though it were a contract that needed a bit more work before it was ready for signature."[51] Picked by Clinton as "a sure thing who would make no mistakes," Christopher received criticism for "lawyering everything to such an extreme that there is no visible enthusiasm when he talks about it."[52]

Christoper maintained collegial relations with Clinton's national security affairs adviser, Anthony Lake. Educated at Harvard and Cambridge, with a Ph.D. in international relations from Princeton, Lake had entered the foreign service in 1962 but resigned from Henry Kissinger's National Security Council staff in protest against the U.S. invasion of Cambodia in 1970. He later served in the Carter State Department and during the Reagan-Bush years taught political science at Mount Holyoke College. Described by associates as "a stalwart Puritan," "immensely kind," "the opposite of a self-promotor," Lake exhibited little of the egotism and manipulative qualities often found in White House advisers.[53] Miscast in the role of a George F. Kennan (see page 291) supposed to define a new grand strategy for the post–Cold War era, Lake seemed to balk because he believed that the NSC adviser "should be strictly an inside operator" rather than a public advocate.[54] In fall 1993, however, he espoused the "enlargement" of free markets and democracies to replace "containment." His speech mentioned the word *market* forty-one times.[55] "Banality on stilts," sniffed the historian Gaddis Smith.[56]

Under Christopher and Lake, administration policy seemed hesitant, troubled by false starts and retreats, lacking in clear advice and direction from a president preoccupied with domestic issues. Inherited troubles in Somalia, Bosnia, and Haiti soon revealed confusions and inconsistencies. In Somalia, Clinton transformed a successful relief operation into a nation-building project and wound up with a military fiasco (see page 584). In Bosnia, Clinton talked tough against Serbian aggression but stepped back in the face of European and congressional dissent (see page 586). In Haiti, Clinton tried to return deposed president Jean-Bertrand Aristide to office, but backed down when the Haitian military organized resistance. Then Clinton tightened economic sanctions that hurt the Haitian people more than the military dictatorship. In each instance Clinton committed U.S. military prestige without clearly articulating the national interest or explaining the risks involved. In each crisis he failed to educate an increasingly isolationist American public that seemed to be saying: "Don't get engaged. Stay back. We've got too many problems back at home."[57]

President Bill Clinton and the Global Puzzle. Although he held a bachelor's degree in international affairs from Georgetown University and had studied at Oxford University as a Rhodes Scholar, William Jefferson Clinton hoped to devote his energies more to serious domestic problems than to foreign policy. Violent disputes around the world nonetheless demanded his attention, requiring the administration to face a hard, traditional question: When should U.S. forces be deployed? (© Kevin Kallaugher/Cartoonists & Writers Syndicate)

Although a pundit described Clinton's policy lurches as "Mr. Toad's Wild Ride," the administration seemed most consistent in its handling of foreign economic relations.[58] Clinton explained repeatedly that the health of the U.S. economy depended on the openness of the world economy; he recognized, as he put it, that Asia "has become the new economic main street."[59] Clinton skillfully lobbied the North American Free Trade Agreement (NAFTA) through Congress, bluntly demanded that Japan open its markets to more U.S. exports, and vowed to "expand and strengthen the world's community of market-based democracies."[60] In April 1994, the Clinton administration's trade representative, Mickey Kantor, signed the "Uruguay Round" GATT accords liberalizing world trade. Negotiated for seven years, this General Agreement on Tariffs and Trade also created a new world trade organization to replace the GATT regime.

The New Europe: Soviet Disintegration, German Reunification

Given the conservative makeup of the Bush foreign-policy team, it was not surprising that the administration failed to reach an immediate consensus on how to handle Gorbachev's initiatives. Hard-line "squeezers" who sought to harass the Kremlin into choosing between collapse and the abandonment of communism still competed with "dealers" who thought the time ripe to negotiate with the Soviets on a whole spectrum of issues.[61] The Bush administration undertook a national security review that eventually endorsed the banal goal of "status quo plus."[62] "Early on," one senior official later recalled, "we were thinking in terms of counter-punching—if he [Gorbachev] did this, what do we do? As things unfolded in Eastern Europe, we moved from counter-punching to 'what can we offer?'"[63]

The turning point seems to have been Secretary Baker's visit to Moscow in early May 1989. The dapper American followed protocol as he walked casually toward the midpoint of the long rectangular meeting room, only to have the buoyant Gorbachev stride well past the center line as he thrust out his hand to the secretary of state. "If Mr. Baker was in no hurry," noted one reporter, "Mr. Gorbachev certainly seemed to be."[64] During Baker's visit Gorbachev offered specific reductions for the Conventional Forces in Europe negotiations (CFE) under way in Vienna; the numbers were so close to NATO's proposals that Washington officials became persuaded that Gorbachev seriously sought further arms agreements. In late May, Bush announced that it was time to "move beyond containment" and to focus on "integrating the Soviet Union into the community of nations."[65] A cordial meeting in September between Baker and Foreign Minister Shevardnadze in picturesque Jackson Hole, Wyoming, broke the impasse over Strategic Arms Reduction Talks (START) when the Soviets dropped their demand that the United States abandon its SDI research. Baker soon affirmed that the United States wanted *perestroika* to "succeed at home and abroad because we believe that it will bring about a less aggressive Soviet Union."[66] At the end of the year, Bush promised that the United States would remove discriminatory trade barriers as soon as Moscow passed formal legislation permitting free emigration. "The United States has declared that it has stopped economic warfare against the Soviet Union," cheered Georgi Arbatov, the dean of Soviet Americanologists.[67] Soon entering Eastern Europe were American Peace Corps volunteers, who went first to Poland and Hungary in mid-1990 to teach English to teachers. At the Washington summit of June 1990, the new détente strengthened. Bush and Gorbachev signed agreements to improve trade, to reduce chemical weapons, to expand university undergraduate exchanges, and to negotiate deeper cuts in strategic arms. To congressional complaints about his use of economic coercion against Lithuania, Gorbachev retorted that if Americans loved freedom so much, they should not have invaded Panama (see pages 573–576). At least *he* was not using *troops* to change an enemy government.

As the Soviet Union and its empire gradually disintegrated over the next two years, Bush continued to solicit a special relationship with Gorbachev. During Germany's rapid reunification Bush and Baker helped to ensure Soviet acquiescence by emphasizing that only Germany's membership in NATO could keep the new Germany from ever moving hostilely eastward. When Iraq invaded Kuwait in early August 1990, Washington and Moscow jointly called for an "international cutoff of all arms supplies" to Iraq.[68] As the United States contemplated military action against Iraq, Shevardnadze told Baker: "If you go down this path—and I'm going to suggest . . . that we go down it with you—the critical factor here is that you must succeed. It must be decisive."[69] Bush kept in telephone touch with Gorbachev throughout the Gulf crisis (see pages 576–580). When a Baltic-American delegation accused the White House of appeasement in January 1991 for not condemning a Soviet crackdown against Latvia and Lithuania, an angry Bush shot back: *"Don't—use—that—word!"*[70] The president's prudence paid off when the Soviet Foreign Ministry reaffirmed the "principle that all problems will be solved peacefully," saying that violence in Riga and Vilnius had not been "presidential policy."[71]

The Bush-Gorbachev relationship also paid off in the START-I accord signed in Moscow in July 1991. Bypassing hard-liners in their respective military bureaucracies, the two presidents ironed out the final compromises in personal correspondence. They inked the forty-seven-page treaty and accompanying protocols using pens made of metal salvaged from missiles banned under the earlier INF Treaty. "Thank God, as we say in Russian, that we stopped this," said Gorbachev.[72] The treaty limited each nuclear superpower to 1,600 delivery vehicles and 6,000 strategic nuclear devices. Only 4,900 such devices could be carried by intercontinental ballistic missiles (ICBMs) or sea-launched missiles (SLBMs) deployed on submarines. The remaining 1,100 devices permitted under the treaty included warheads and bombs carried by cruise missiles and strategic bombers. In effect, the United States and the Soviets pledged to reduce their nuclear arsenals by half.

The subsequent dissolution of the Soviet Union left the status of START-I in limbo, as Belarus, Kazakhstan, Russia, and Ukraine inherited Soviet nuclear weaponry. In May 1992 Belarus, Kazakhstan, and Ukraine agreed in a treaty with the United States to destroy all of their nuclear weapons by 1999; they also pledged to sign the nuclear nonproliferation treaty. Russia's parliament ratified this agreement in November, but made ratification contingent on positive action by the other three republics. Because they were bargaining for political and economic concessions from both Russia and the United States, the three republics did not comply immediately.

If START-I marked the high point of Bush-Gorbachev cooperation in July 1991, détente's nadir soon came during in the abortive coup of August 18–21. CIA analysts had downplayed the likelihood of a hard-line coup, even though Eduard Shevardnadze had repeatedly warned Secretary Baker of such a possibility. Joint Chiefs of Staff chairman Admiral William Crowe also had a hint when his Soviet counterpart, Marshal Sergei Akhromeyev, told him that "I don't support any man unconditionally."[73] The coup conspirators proved inept. Russian president Boris Yeltsin and his top aides holed up in the Russian Parliament (or "White House") and called for a general strike. When Bush failed to condemn the coup, critics compared his reticence to his restrained response to the Tiananmen Square massacre the previous summer (see page 588). Bush tried several times to telephone Gorbachev, but not until the third day did he call Boris Yeltsin, who boomed: "I am *extremely* glad to hear from you!"[74] By this time Yeltsin had rallied mass demonstrations, and crowds outside the Russian White House climbed on tanks to fraternize with soldiers, most of whom turned against the coup. By the fourth day the revolt had fizzled. Bush and his advisers understood immediately that legitimate authority had shifted to Yeltsin and the Russian republic.

During the 1992 presidential campaign Bill Clinton criticized Bush for his fixation on Gorbachev and his belated support for Yeltsin. He also took Bush to task for his so-called "Chicken Kiev" speech in August 1991 to the Ukrainian parliament and for being "a reluctant bridegroom" in extending diplomatic recognition to the Baltic republics.[75] Bush in fact preferred Gorbachev to Yeltsin, whom he thought too volatile, and the U.S. president feared the centrifugal forces surging through the Soviet Union. Bush saw a strong central government as essential for keeping control over the Soviet nuclear arsenal and fending off renegade military units. In the end, Bush's caution did not prevent Washington from working harmoniously with a Yeltsin-led Russia, as evidenced by a $24-billion Western-aid package to Russia and further negotiations on nuclear arms reductions. When Yeltsin visited Washington in June 1992 and addressed Congress, he proclaimed: "I think this is the greatest day of my life."[76] Just before Bush left office in January 1993, he and Yeltsin signed a START-II agreement in Moscow that provided for the cutting of nuclear warheads and bombs to 3,500 (U.S.) and 2,997 (Russia) and for eliminating all multiple warhead (MIRV) intercontinental missiles by the year 2003.

Although Secretary Christopher promised "a new strategy to direct America's resources at something other than superpower confrontation," the Clinton administration still pursued what one scholar has called a "Russia first" policy.[77] The administration's principal expert (or "Tsar") on Russian affairs, Strobe Talbott, had been a Russian literature major at Yale, a roommate and fellow Rhodes scholar with Clinton at Oxford, and a reporter and editor at *Time* magazine.[78] As journalist and private citizen, he had visited the Soviet Union more than forty times, and his cultivation of high-level sources in both Washington and Moscow helped him write impressive inside accounts of bureaucratic warfare and diplomatic wrangling on arms control during the 1970s and 1980s. Talbott advised Clinton to back Yeltsin's free-market reforms with financial assistance even though they resulted in short-term hardship for the Russian people, including high unemployment and the removal of social-security safety nets. Clinton wrote Yeltsin detailed letters twice a month and gave Yeltsin unconditional support when he dissolved the Russian parliament in October 1993 and then turned army guns on recalcitrant legislators holed up in the building. But the favorable showing of the ultranationalist Vladimir Zhirinovsky, whose party won 23 percent of the vote for a new parliament, reinforced Clinton's decision not to offer more than a loose partnership status in NATO to former Warsaw Pact members. "Do our people really want to be dragged into some ethnic fight because of a security guarantee?" asked Secretary of Defense Les Aspin.[79] Russia nonetheless accepted partnership status.

Clinton's critics charged that he feared too much being hit by the charge "Who lost Russia?" and that by putting all his chips on Boris Yeltsin, Clinton had repeated Bush's mistake with Gorbachev. Like others who feared a revival of Russian imperialism, Zbigniew Brzezinski thought a close Russian–American relationship "premature."[80] Other critics contended that U.S. policy should concentrate on larger security issues, especially the safety and security of the vast stockpile of nuclear weapons scattered in more than 200 different locations. "Russia today . . . cannot confidently assert effective control over 99.9 percent of anything," one analyst worried.[81] The Clinton administration nonetheless claimed that Russia's struggle to establish a new democracy was succeeding in the face of continued economic woes, an increase in crime, bureaucratic corruption, and embittered intellectuals. Optimists found hope in the military's support for Yeltsin against the old parliament and the loss of political influence by entrenched managers of the economy. Taking on legitimacy, the new regime seemed capable of resisting right-wing demagogues. "A fledgling Russian republic may succeed where the Weimar Republic [of Germany in the 1920s] failed," one expert speculated.[82]

The German question temporarily strained the new détente. In late fall 1989, without consulting his NATO allies, German chancellor Helmut Kohl put forward a plan for confederation between East and West Germany. Kohl intended to "stake out reunification as a matter for Germans to decide."[83] Gorbachev warned Bonn against "blowing on the flames" of German nationalism and insisted that "no harm" should come to the German Democratic Republic. Both Washington and Moscow stressed the "importance of stability" during the process of German unification.[84] Once again, however, the pell-mell rush of events upset expectations and orderly procedures. After the border opened in November, the best and the brightest of

East Germany's citizens continued to migrate to the West at a rate of 2,000 to 3,000 a day. Local government, public services, the economy, and civic morale in the GDR steadily eroded. In early 1990, West German politicians and parties began to funnel campaign money to new political groups in order to build alliances in the East for an anticipated post-election unification.

Using a formula called "two-plus-four," the negotiators for the two Germanies met to determine their economic, political, and legal unification. Representatives of the United States, Great Britain, France, and the Soviet Union also sat down with the Germans and discussed the status of German military forces and security guarantees for Germany's neighbors. In theory, according to the political scientist Michael Mandelbaum, this formula for reunification, approved in February 1990 by all six nations, was meant "to reassure Germany and the Soviet Union about each other and . . . to reassure the countries between them about both."[85]

German reunification now became, in the words of former CIA director Richard Helms, "a kind of runaway freight train that nobody—East or West—seems able to contain."[86] The Kohl-supported center-conservative coalition won a landslide victory in the March GDR elections. Kohl initiated currency union and economic merger in July 1990. Then, in September, the four powers agreed to end their postwar occupation. In October the two Germanies formally reunited.

A new juggernaut seemed to loom in the center of Europe—nearly 80 million people between the Rhine and the Oder, with a potential combined military force of 1.8 million, and a strong export-driven economy. Notwithstanding the multibillion-dollar investment needed to rehabilitate the East German economy,

A United Germany in NATO. Mikhail Gorbachev, remembering with many other Soviet citizens the German onslaught of World War II, at first resisted the U.S. push for a united Germany in the North Atlantic Treaty Organization (NATO). But Gorbachev recognized that he could not stop the realignment of European power. Struggling to overcome domestic woes, Gorbachev at least received promises of foreign aid from Western nations. (By permission of Mike Luckovich and Creators Syndicate)

many economists believed that another *Wirtschaftwunder* (economic miracle) could be achieved within a few years. Volkswagen, Siemens, and other West German firms invested in the East. As new markets opened up in Eastern Europe, the Germans stood ready to provide the very products most needed—machinery, chemicals, high-tech manufactures, and top-quality consumer goods. "We want to lead," boasted a top Kohl aide. "Perhaps in time the United States will take care of places like Central America, and we will handle Eastern Europe."[87]

Washington backed Kohl's quest for rapid reunification because of the chancellor's continued commitment to NATO and European integration. "German unification is going to happen," explained one American official. "The more you resist it, the more likely you are to create the kind of Germany you don't want—resentful, angry."[88] Bush advisers believed that in the long run the Soviets would prefer a Germany anchored within NATO to an unrestrained, neutral Germany facing eastward—like "a cannon not being fixed to the deck of a ship."[89] Still, as one Soviet Foreign Ministry official explained, "having our enemies of the '40s, the Germans, join our enemies of the '50s, '60s, and '70s in an alliance whose whole reason for being is anti-Soviet—that makes us feel as though we lost World War II."[90] In July 1990 Gorbachev dropped objections to a reunited Germany in NATO in exchange for a promise of Western economic aid and a smaller German army. An old saying had it that NATO's true purpose had always been to "keep the Russians out, the Americans in, and the Germans down." With the Russians leaving and the Germans reviving, some U.S. officials quietly claimed that a continued American presence was still needed precisely to keep the Germans down or at least to retain some leverage over what a new German state could do in a new Europe. Bush had "provided a skillful accompaniment" to European events, the political scientist Stanley Hoffmann has noted, "but the main musicians were not in Washington; they were in Bonn and in Moscow."[91]

The course of events after unification did not clearly indicate the future posture of the new Germany. Kohl assuaged fears of German military power by limiting future troop strength and pledging never to build nuclear, chemical, or biological weapons. A poll in 1992 indicated that 42 percent of all Germans thought they could do without a military, with 11 percent undecided. Germany became the dominant voice in the European Community (EC), pressed for aid to Eastern Europe and the former Soviet republics, pledged billions of dollars (but not troops) to the Gulf War, and extended quick diplomatic recognition to Croatia and Slovenia as they broke from Yugoslavia in 1992. Germany also sent a token warship and three reconnaissance planes to the Adriatic to participate in UN sanctions against the former Yugoslavia in July 1992. Germany's new constitution also explicitly welcomed refugees, thus implying "some sort of national atonement for past aggressions," as one scholar put it.[92] In 1992 alone, nearly a million people sought refuge in Germany, including refugees from Yugoslavia.

Doubts and problems persisted. What one scholar called "the benign takeover of the bankrupt G.D.R. by Bonn Inc." cost more than anyone had expected.[93] When the Kohl government chose to pay the annual reunification bill of $20 billion by borrowing capital rather than by raising taxes, inflation shot up. The Bundesbank raised interest rates to the point where Britain and Italy had to devalue the pound and lira; by September 1992 the European Monetary Union was unraveling. German reunification, some thought, had torpedoed European integration. By 1993 Germany suffered a recession in which unemployment rose to 7.5 percent in the West and 14.5 percent in the East. The opening of the GDR Stasi (secret police) files revealed widespread corruption, even implicating some prominent individuals who had publicly opposed the Ulbricht and Honecker regimes. Divisions remained. "East Germans are given to self-pity, West Germans to arrogance and exasperation," observed the historian Fritz Stern.[94] A new, extreme, right-wing party scored impressive victories in local elections. During 1992, authorities recorded some 18,000 incidents ranging from the public display of Nazi swastikas to desecration of Jewish graves to firebombs and killings. Although German citizens by the hundreds of thousands organized silent marches to protest right-wing violence against immigrants, historical memories remained strong. British prime minister Margaret Thatcher's unguarded opinions on Germany leaked to the press, including her assessment of "the German character: in alphabetical order, aggressiveness, angst, assertiveness, bullying, egotism."[95] Both President Bush and President Clinton vowed to maintain America's special relationship with a Germany preoccupied, at least temporarily, with healing the past.

The conversion of the Economic Community into the European Union through ratification of the Maastricht Treaty in fall 1993 advanced continental integration but hardly decreased wariness about Germany. A Belgian diplomat described squabbling Western Europe as "an economic giant, a political dwarf, and a

"Now That You're a Capitalist." The Poles and other Eastern Europeans may have abandoned communism, but, the cartoonist Jeff Danziger reminds us, they may have exchanged one set of problems for a new set all too familiar to capitalist countries. The rough transition to a postcommunist world grafted harsh reality onto the initial euphoria many felt when the failed communist regimes collapsed. (Jeff Danziger/*Christian Science Monitor.* © 1989 Los Angeles Times Syndicate)

military worm."[96] European reluctance to intervene in the Bosnian crisis underscored the region's disunity. In the Eastern European nations, Poland, Hungary, and Czechoslovakia (divided into Czech and Slovak republics in 1993) progressed most quickly in organizing market economies and democratic governments and looked to membership in the European Union. Bulgaria, Rumania, Albania, Slovenia, Croatia, Estonia, Latvia, Lithuania, and other former Soviet republics faced tremendous obstacles, not the least of which were smoldering ethnic and national rivalries long frozen by the Cold War. The specter of chauvinistic Russian nationalism still hovered over the region, too. The U.S. offer of NATO "Partnership for Peace" status (without a formal military guarantee) to former Warsaw Pact members seemed little more than a gesture. Whatever its future, Europe represented a microcosm of "the centrifugal and centripetal forces that pull international systems in opposite directions."[97]

Adapt or Die: South Africa and the End of Apartheid

If the year 1989 marked communism's collapse in Eastern Europe, another system driven by ideology—apartheid—began its descent in South Africa. As with the dynamics of change in Europe, the main impetus for reversing decades of social, political, and economic discrimination came from within—in this case, from within a nation of 35 million blacks, people of mixed race, and Asians ruled by 6.7 million whites (1992 figures). And as with Eastern Europe, the United States played a modest role in nurturing the process.

One of the last diplomatic achievements of the Reagan administration, the mediation of the Namibia-Angola agreement in New York in December 1988 prepared the way. Not only did these accords establish independence for Namibia (effective March 1990), but they also called for the staged withdrawal of Cuban and South African troops from Angola. UN-supervised elections held in Namibia in November 1989 delivered a decisive victory to the black nationalist South West African People's Organization (SWAPO). Pacification in Namibia and Angola meant that South Africia's antiapartheid organizations found it increasingly difficult to obtain outside assistance and weapons to mount guerrilla campaigns inside South Africia. Harsh measures by Pretoria's security police during four years of the state of emergency since 1986 also neutralized most armed revolutionary activity by black nationalists. Thus when South Africa's white leaders, P. W. Botha and his successor, F. W. de Klerk, began to make serious proposals for negotiating an end to apartheid, beleaguered black activists responded positively.

The Bush administration helped to persuade Pretoria to negotiate by maintaining sanctions against South Africa as mandated by the Comprehensive Anti-

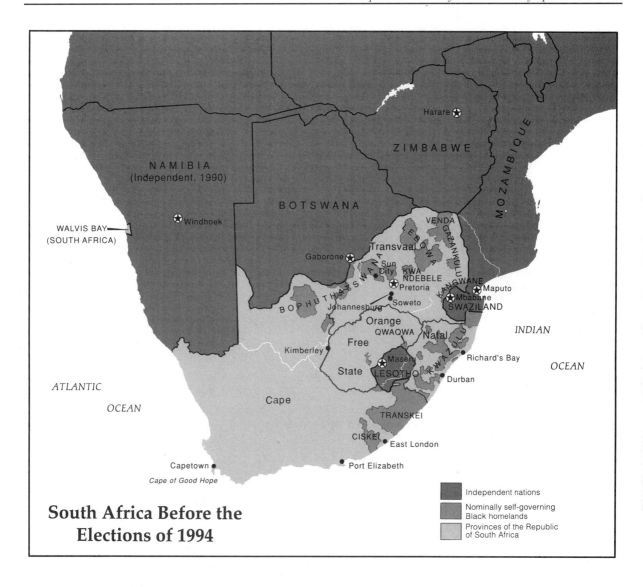

South Africa Before the Elections of 1994

Independent nations

Nominally self-governing Black homelands

Provinces of the Republic of South Africa

Apartheid Act of 1986. From 1986 to 1989, sanctions cost South Africa $32 to $40 billion, including $11 billion in capital outflows and $4 billion in lost export earnings. To what extent economic pressure induced negotiations is difficult to determine. As early as 1979, well before sanctions had become a reality, President Botha had told his Afrikaner *volk* that they must "adapt or die."[98] When de Klerk became president in September 1989, reforms quickly followed. He lifted prohibitions against dissent, stopped executions, freed selected political prisoners, legalized banned organizations like the African National Congress (ANC), and desegregated beaches and a few housing areas. He also offered to talk with black leaders to devise a new constitution in which blacks would share governing power. Conservative white Afrikaners vowed to reverse the stunning changes.

De Klerk also released the political prisoner Nelson Mandela on February 11, 1990. When the gray-haired, seventy-one-year-old Mandela, the symbol of resistance to apartheid, walked through a police cordon outside a prison near Cape Town, he raised his right arm in the black nationalist salute—the first time he could freely do so in nearly twenty-eight years. *"Amandla! Amandla! i-Africa mayibuye!"* ("Power! Power! Africa, it is ours!") Mandela defiantly chanted in his first public speech later that evening.[99] Another antiapartheid activist in prison with Mandela recalled that the black leader preferred peaceful change: "He taught us to confront the regime where it was weakest—at the bargaining table—rather than where it was strongest, on the battlefield."[100]

It soon became apparent that de Klerk's commitment to reform stopped short of black demands for majority rule. He hoped to maintain Afrikaner dominance regardless of institutional changes. During Mandela's triumphant tour of the United States in mid-1990, therefore, the ANC chief asked Americans to continue their economic sanctions until South African whites relented. At a packed Yankee Stadium in New York City, Mandela won over even die-hard Boston Red Sox fans when he donned a Yankee baseball cap and proclaimed: "You now know who I am. I am a Yankee."[101]

Serious talks for a democratic South Africa did not begin until December 1991. They stalled the following year as bloody skirmishes and massacres erupted from rivalry between the ANC and the Zulu-based Inkatha Freedom Party, headed by Chief Mangosuthu Buthelezi and—scandals revealed—backed by government and police officials. Despite continued violence—among black groups (especially Zulus versus Xhosas), between blacks and the government, and by white extremists such as the Afrikaner Resistance Movement—twenty-six parties resumed constitutional talks in early 1993. Four straight years of zero economic growth helped to spur compromises.

Agreement on a constitutional democracy finally came in September 1993, and South Africa's first all-race elections were held in April 1994. The ANC handily won the elections and Mandela became South Africa's first black president. The new parliament began to draw up a new constitution. The ten black "homelands" set up by the white government in the 1970s were reincorporated into South Africa. The U.S. Congress repealed most sanctions, and U.S. companies began to invest once again in South Africa. Mandela and de Klerk received the Nobel Peace Prize later that year.

Nelson Mandela (b. 1918). A founder of the African National Congress (ANC), this attorney and member of the Xhosa tribe was still a young man when the white South African government jailed him in November 1962. Following his release from prison in February 1990, Mandela gave the black-power salute. (Reuters/Bettmann)

Mandela faced daunting tasks. Buthelezi's Inkatha Party remained a challenger, and extremist groups such as the Afrikaner Volksfront still sought an independent white homeland. Radical blacks in the Pan African Congress, chanting "one settler, one bullet," wanted immediate redistribution of land.[102] Political and criminal violence continued, the economy grew slowly after prolonged recession, and unemployment hit 40 percent. South Africa's future seemed precarious. Arguing for increased U.S. foreign assistance to the new democracy, the director of Clinton's Agency for International Development called it a "once-in-a-generation opportunity" to make South Africa "the engine that drives Africa."[103]

MARKET FORCES IN LATIN AMERICA

The Bush administration did not break with the past in its policies toward Latin America. The president himself held traditional proprietary North American ideas about the region, and he had helped devise and administer Reagan's interventionism. The Western Hemisphere seemed to be advancing from military regimes to popularly elected governments (as in Argentina, Chile, and Brazil), yet at the time of Bush's inauguration many of the 1980s interventionist U.S. policies had failed: Narcotics continued to flow into the profitable U.S. marketplace despite expensive antidrug operations; the Latin American debt, rampant inflation, and sluggish growth rates imperiled economies; the civil war in El Salvador ground on; a graying but seemingly unalterable Fidel Castro still bedeviled Washington; an escalating crisis with Panama threatened further instability in the Caribbean; and the *contras* faltered in their violent effort to seize control of Nicaragua and end the Sandinista revolution through force. Latin America's economic linkage with the United States nonetheless remained strong: In 1990 40 percent of the region's exports flowed to the United States.

When Bush took office, the war against Nicaragua—a test case of the Reagan Doctrine—had not succeeded (see pages 523–526). The Sandinista National Liberation Front remained in power. Bush continued economic sanctions and aided the *contras*. A meeting of Central American presidents in February 1989 devised a plan for free elections in Nicaragua and the disbanding of the *contras*. The Sandinistas endorsed this "Tesoro Beach Accord" and granted civil liberties to opposition groups. Bush and Congress then reached a bipartisan compromise on aid for the *contras;* the ban on military assistance held, but humanitarian assistance would continue until the Nicaraguan elections of February 1990. Meanwhile, the *contras* did not desist from their sabotage and killing. In eight years of civil war 30,000 lives had been lost.

In the 1990 election the United States openly supported the National Opposition Union (UNO) and its presidential candidate Violeta Barrios de Chamorro, publisher of the anti-Sandinista newpaper *La Prensa,* which the Nicaraguan government had closed down in 1986 because officials claimed that it was receiving CIA subsidies. Chamorro ran against Sandinista President Daniel Ortega Saavedra, who dismissed the UNO as Washington's "rented opposition," tainted by the millions of dollars that the Bush administration poured into the UNO campaign.[104] In an election monitored extensively by foreign observers, including former president Jimmy Carter, the UNO soundly defeated the Sandinista Front, which had expected to win. Although U.S. leaders claimed that the *contra* war and economic sanctions had paid off by creating so much destabilization in Nicaragua that the electorate voted the Sandinistas out, others applauded the leadership of Costa Rica's President Oscar Arias Sánchez and the Sandinistas themselves for initiating and implementing peace plans that permitted free elections to go forward. Despite millions of dollars in U.S. reconstruction aid, the devastated Nicaraguan economy faltered. Per capita income, which stood at $1,396 in 1981, had shrunk to $425 in 1992. Only Haiti ranked lower in the hemisphere.

Another Central American state, El Salvador, still suffered instability and deadly civil war despite substantial U.S. assistance (see pages 521–523). The Salvadoran government could not subdue the Farabundo Martí National Liberation Front (FMLN). The murder of six Jesuit priests by government forces aroused critical American opinion, already sickened by years of death-squad activities linked to the military and by FMLN human-rights abuses (including the killing of several mayors). Like other nations in Central America, El Salvador had seen per capita income fall and infant mortality rates and malnutrition increase. The unemployment rate in 1990 reached 50 percent. That year, talks between the rebels and the government began, with the two sides finally signing a United Nations–sponsored agreement on January 1, 1992. But neither peace nor democracy came to the battered people of El Salvador, because full implementation of the accord proved elusive.

Debt joined violence in burdening Latin America. By 1990 Latin American nations owed more than $400 billion (total Third World debt stood at more than $1.3 trillion). Brazil, Mexico, and Argentina owed the most, and much of it to U.S. banks. One economist spread the blame for the huge debt run up in the 1970s: "Stupid bankers made stupid loans to stupid countries."[105] Others pointed to global trends: the worldwide economic recession of the early 1980s, rising interest rates, higher oil prices, and falling export earnings. The debt crisis hurt the United States. As debtors struggled to meet debt-service payments, they trimmed their imports; U.S. exports then slumped by billions of dollars, and North American jobs were lost. Latin migrants trying to escape grinding poverty pressed against U.S. immigration gates. The narcotics trade expanded as poor farmers and laborers turned to lucrative drug crops for income. Because health services and educational outlays had

Violeta Barrios de Chamorro (b. 1929) and Daniel Ortega Saavedra (b. 1945). In April 1990, Ortega placed the sash on Chamorro after she defeated him for the presidency. Inspired by the Cuban Revolution, Ortega had fought the Somoza dictatorship; he spent the years 1967 to 1974 in prison, where he was tortured. From 1985 to 1990 he served as Nicaragua's president. In the 1980s Violeta Chamorro turned *La Prensa* into an anti-Sandinista newspaper and then led the UNO to victory. (AP/Wide World Photos)

to be reduced and economic-development projects scuttled throughout Latin America, political unrest spread.

The Brady Plan, initiated by Secretary of the Treasury Nicholas F. Brady in March 1989, provided for some debt forgiveness and lower interest rates, but the U.S. government increasingly urged banks "to paddle their own leaky canoes."[106] Several agreements between commercial banks and Latin American governments, and backed by the International Monetary Fund, cut debt burdens by about one-third. In return, Latin American debtors accepted market-opening requirements—controlling inflation, attracting foreign investment, and reducing trade restrictions. As Latin American governments in the early 1990s instituted reforms to improve "investor confidence" and advanced regional economic integration based on a "free trade" philosophy, "swelling flows of foreign direct investment" helped ease the debt crisis and raised hopes that the hemisphere's groaning poverty and environmental deprivation could find relief.[107] Still, as former Argentine president Raúl Alfonsín, head of his nation's Social Democratic Movement, remarked, "'market forces' are not enough to provide welfare."[108]

Many Americans also believed that the flourishing drug trade endangered international stability and hence U.S. security. President Bush declared drugs "the gravest domestic threat facing our nation today."[109] By 1990 the U.S. drug market probably topped $100 billion; American prisons filled to capacity with people convicted of drug-related crimes. "This is more serious than the Vietnam War," claimed the governor of Maryland.[110] As the Cold War receded, the "Drug War" accelerated, and Washington began using the military to fight the new enemy. "The Medellín [Colombian drug] cartel was marching across Central America," wrote two *Miami Herald* journalists, "infecting governments far more readily than communism ever had."[111]

In the 1980s, U.S. policy had aimed at stopping *supply* through interdiction and eradication programs. In 1986, for example, American troops and army Blackhawk helicopters had helped the Bolivian military swoop down on jungle cocaine laboratories. Bush continued to urge Latin American governments to quash the drug growers and traffickers, and U.S. counternarcotics aid flowed to the Andean nations of Peru, Bolivia, and Colombia. But President Bush increasingly stressed the importance of halting *demand* inside the United States itself. This apparent change stemmed in part from pressure from Latin Americans who feared new U.S. interventionism; they had grown bitter over the drug issue, because they contended that North Americans unfairly blamed them for the problem. "Most Mexicans believe that the responsibility for the drug traffic . . . falls squarely on the existence of a multibillion-dollar market in the United States," wrote the Mexican scholar Jorge G. Castañeda. "Without the demand generated by that market, supply would wither away."[112]

Mexico had become a major source of marijuana (a hemp plant, *Cannabis sativa*) and heroin (a white powder processed from opium poppies) and a major highway for South American cocaine shipments destined for the United States. From Bolivia, Peru, and Colombia came coca, which was processed into cocaine and crack. (Tons of opium/heroin also entered the United States from the "Golden

THE AMERICAN ADDICTION

The American Addiction.
This political cartoon from a Honduran newspaper reflected the Latin American perspective that the drug crisis in the United States stemmed not from the production of cocaine in Latin America but from the consumption of dangerous drugs in North America. Could the cartoonist also be suggesting that the drug trade was destroying Latin America? (McDonald/Diario El Heraldo, San Pedro Sula, Honduras)

Major Foreign Drug Producers for the U.S. Market, 1989
(in metric tons)

Opium	Burma	2,625
	Afghanistan	585
	Laos	375
	Iran	300
	Pakistan	130
	Mexico	85
	Thailand	50
Cocaine	Peru	124,408
	Bolivia	65,998
	Colombia	33,487
	Ecuador	270
Marijuana	Mexico	47,590
	Colombia	2,800
	Jamaica	190
	Belize	66

Source: U.S. Department of State

Triangle" of Burma, Thailand, and Laos and the "Golden Crescent" of Iran, Afghanistan, and Pakistan.) Any nation that came into contact with the drug trade became exposed to corruption, drug addiction, violence, and death. Illegal drug money bribed politicians in some Latin American states, where governments lost legitimacy as their efforts to control traffickers repeatedly proved ineffective. In Colombia the sharpshooters of the militarized drug cartels assassinated judges, journalists, police officers, and government officials. "Narcoterrorism" destabilized Peru: Leftist guerrillas called the *Sendero Luminoso* (Shining Path) used the drug trade to help finance their rebellion.[113] Drug profits, not reinvested in long-term development, distorted regional economies; the "laundering" of "narcodollars" befouled banking systems. Colombia took courageous steps to defeat the drug lords of the Medellín and Cali cartels, and some cartel members were extradicted to the United States for prosecution. But the drug crisis did not relent—"a shared tragedy for both halves of the hemisphere."[114]

In contrast, the North American Free Trade Agreement forecast a brighter future, at least according to its enthusiastic supporters. Initiated by the Bush administration, signed by Canada, Mexico, and the United States in 1992, approved by Congress in 1993, and operative in 1994, NAFTA created the world's largest free-trade bloc, comprising 370 million people with a combined gross domestic product of $6.5 trillion. Because critics warned that U.S. companies would move south of the border to exploit low-wage workers in *maquiladoras* (assembly factories) and lax environmental controls, President Clinton negotiated side agreements with Mexico to protect workers' rights and environmental standards. In the face of opposition from organized labor, the president mobilized an effective lobbying effort that included former presidents and secretaries of state. Under the agreement, tariffs on goods sold in the triangular relationship would be phased out. NAFTA also promised to expand an already burgeoning "Mexamerica," the 2,000-mile border society where two cultures blended "like reluctant lovers in the night, embracing for fear that letting go could only be worse."[115]

THE INVASION OF PANAMA

The drug issue became central to Panamanian–United States relations. After the United States signed the 1978 canal treaties with Panama's military government (see pages 490–491), the Carter administration tried to nudge the country toward civilian rule. But the military solidified its hold. In 1983 General Manuel Antonio Noriega took power and molded the Panamanian Defense Forces (PDF) into an instrument of personal authority. Noriega had served as the intelligence chief of the PDF, and as such he had come to know Panama's thriving world of drug trafficking. As Panamanian banks laundered drug money, Noriega became a millionaire by cutting deals with Colombia's cocaine barons. By the late 1980s his dictatorial rule and drug-running had stirred anger in North Americans eager to blame the swaggering Panamanian for U.S. drug problems.

Little did the American people know that official Washington and General Noriega had long been allies. As a young officer in the 1960s, Noriega received regular payments from the Central Intelligence Agency. During the 1980s he helped the United States aid and train the *contras*. Grateful for this cooperation, Washington turned a blind eye to reports of his links with drug traffickers. American officials also knew that Noriega funneled intelligence information to their nemesis, Cuba's Fidel Castro. "We knew he was a double agent," remarked a Reagan official. "The CIA calculated that we were getting more than we were giving away."[116] In fact, Noriega acted as at least a quadruple agent or worse, because he traded with all comers—Sandinistas, *contras,* Cubans, Libyans, the CIA, drug lords, and more. At times he won Washington's favor by cooperating with the U.S. Drug Enforcement Agency to capture narcotics traffickers and to intercept cocaine cargos.

In mid-1987 a former Noriega aide exposed in detail the general's corrupt practices. Anti-Noriega protests rocked Panama, and a widening spectrum of Panamanian opinion called for his resignation. But the strongman would not budge. "One reason for Noriega's steadfastness," a student of Panama has written, "was his confidence that certain sectors of the U.S. government would support him."[117] Sensing the popular Panamanian resentment against the general, however, American officials urged Noriega to step down. To make their point, they halted foreign aid to Panama. The Reagan administration took stronger action in February 1988, after two Florida grand juries indicted the dictator for shipping Colombian drugs to the United States, for taking payoffs to launder drug money in Panamanian banks, and for allowing Colombia's drug cartel to build cocaine-processing plants on Panamanian soil. Soon Washington not only urged civilians and PDF members to remove Noriega but also froze Panamanian assets in the United States. State Department officials offered Noriega safe haven in another country (such as Spain). Yet Noriega would agree to nothing until the indictments were dropped. Washington broke off the talks in May 1988. In apparent violation of the canal treaties, the United States also held back canal toll revenues due Panama. In the belief that such economic coercion would work, Reagan officials boasted that Noriega would quickly flee his distressed nation. He did not.

During the 1988 presidential election campaign George Bush faced tough questions about why he and Reagan had taken so long to distance the United States from Noriega and had done so little to interrupt the Panamanian's drug business. Bush lamely contended that the U.S. government had lacked hard evidence. Once president, Bush came to suffer what he called "an enormous frustration" because of his inability to topple Noriega.[118] A "wet-noodle approach to Panama," complained one Washington journalist; "Bush is a wimp" became a familiar phrase.[119] Political pressure for bold action mounted.

In late fall 1989, Noriega's rhetoric heated up in angry anti-*yanqui* public rallies. "He was getting backed into a corner," recalled an administration official. "We knew he was going to have to respond to us."[120] Violent and harassing incidents involving U.S. military personnel in Panama soon grabbed front-page headlines. "Enough is enough," snapped Bush. "This guy [Noriega] is not going to lay off. It will only get worse."[121]

In the early hours of December 20, 1989, Operation Just Cause commenced. The largest military activity since the Vietnam War, the invasion of Panama by 22,500 troops proved a bloody success. A billion dollars' worth of property in Panama City suffered damage and more than 300 Panamanian civilians died in the assault. The Pentagon reported that only 23 American soldiers perished. American

General Colin Powell's Briefing on the Invasion of Panama. Born in New York City in 1937, Powell earned a B.S. degree from the City University of New York before he began a successful military career. In 1987–1989 the army general served as assistant to the president for national security affairs, and in 1989 he was named chairman, Joint Chiefs of Staff. Here he gives a briefing, on December 20, 1989, shortly after U.S. paratroopers attacked Panama. (R. D. Ward, Department of Defense)

The Commander in Chief Directs the Invasion of Panama. President Bush liked to use the telephone. Here, on December 20, 1989, he communicates with U.S. officials in Panama after he ordered the invasion. Critics bemoaned another example of "gunboat diplomacy," but Bush's popularity at home rose. Pummeled by massive U.S. firepower, Panama staggered into deep economic crisis. Hundreds of Panamanian lives were lost. As many as 60 percent of American casualties were caused by "friendly fire"—Americans killed or wounded by mistake by other Americans. (Carol T. Powers, The White House)

forces neutralized the PDF and captured many of its members. But the resistance had been greater than anticipated. Reflecting North American prejudice about the character of Latin Americans, one U.S. official remarked that "we thought if there was a lot of noise outside of the front door, they would go out the back."[122] American officials also had not prepared for the anarchy that soon swept Panama City. With the PDF destroyed and no police force to take its place, looters pillaged at will. Thousands of civilian refugees and wounded overwhelmed hospitals; the American military had not brought adequate supplies of food and medicine to meet needs. What worried American officials the most, however, was their inability to capture General Noriega. They eventually located him at the Vatican Embassy in Panama City, where church officials persuaded him to surrender to American authorities. On January 4, 1990, Manuel Antonio Noriega, tagged #41586, became a federal prisoner in Miami awaiting trial on drug charges. Foiled in his efforts to reveal CIA secrets and embarrass President Bush, Noriega was convicted of cocaine smuggling in April 1992 and went to prison.

Bush's popularity shot up after the military invasion of Panama. Democrats and Republicans alike cheered even though Bush had not consulted Congress about his decision for war against Panama. "It's always nice," said a senior Bush official, "when you can intervene on behalf of democrats, but that's not always possible."[123] Critics, however, lambasted the administration for violating the UN Charter and the OAS Charter, which contain nonintervention provisions. The Organization of American States censured the United States for its use of force, and only a U.S. veto prevented passage of a UN Security Council resolution condemning the invasion. Former senator George McGovern reminded the celebrants of intervention that the United States had nurtured Noriega for years and that the appropriate solution lay in the Panamanian people's hands, not in Washington's; it was "ironic that when Mikhail Gorbachev is winning worldwide acclaim for standing clear of other countries' political struggles—even on the borders of the Soviet Union—our government continues its efforts to control Central America."[124] As for the other Latin

American governments, most applauded the Noriega ouster, but they did not think a U.S. military attack the best way to oust him. President Alan García Pérez of Peru branded the invasion a "criminal act."[125]

Although the United States withdrew its invasion force in February, stability eluded Panama. The new government looked like Washington's puppet. When U.S. troops had seized the television station in Panama City, on screen flashed the seal not of the sovereign government of Panama but of the U.S. Department of Defense. Another difficulty for postinvasion Panama was its economic disarray. Already weakened by two years of U.S. economic sanctions, capital flight, and foreign debt, Panama suffered major destruction from the attack. Finally, nationalist resentment against the United States resurfaced. "There is a love-hate relationship between Panamanians and North Americans that arose from the very outset of our independence [in 1903]," explained the publisher of the Panamanian newspaper *La Prensa*. Like the "love-hate relationship that develops between a teen-age son and his overbearing father, there is a rebellious attitude to make your own way."[126] Little, it seemed, had changed in almost a century.

Mideast Tests: Persian Gulf War and Arab-Israeli Peace Process

The invasion of Kuwait by 140,000 Iraqi troops and 1,800 tanks on August 2, 1990, led to an even more significant exercise of U.S. power. Instead of paying back billions of dollars in loans received from Kuwait during the eight-year war between Iran and Iraq, Iraq's dictator, Saddam Hussein, resurrected old territorial claims and tried to annex Kuwait in the name of all "zealous Arabs who believe in one Arab nation."[127] Washington feared that Saddam might next invade Saudi Arabia and thus control 40 percent of the world's oil. Bush also saw the Iraq-Kuwait crisis as the first post–Cold War "test of our mettle" at a time when "declinists" questioned the U.S. capacity to lead.[128] "This will not stand," he vowed only two days after the invasion.[129] He organized an international coalition of thirty countries to liberate Kuwait, and he lobbied UN Security Council members. By November the UN had imposed economic sanctions and demanded Iraqi withdrawal. Bush initially had sent some 200,000 American troops as part of a multinational peacekeeping force to defend Saudi Arabia (Operation Desert Shield). In early November he increased the size of the expeditionary force to more than 500,000; contingents from other allied countries brought the troop level to 700,000. Security Council Resolution 678 commanded Iraq to evacuate Kuwait by January 15, 1991, or else face military attack.

What Saddam Hussein had hoped to contain as an isolated regional quarrel provoked instead unprecedented international unity among the United States and most NATO members; Iraq's former military patron, the Soviet Union; and several Arab states, including Egypt and Syria. The Iraqi dictator no doubt found Washington's outraged reaction especially puzzling in view of recent efforts by the Reagan and Bush administrations to befriend Iraq. Off-the-books arms transfers to Iraq were kept secret from Congress from 1982 to 1987, in violation of the law. Washington had supplied intelligence data to Baghdad during the Iran-Iraq War, and Bush had blocked congressional attempts to deny agricultural credits to Iraq because of human-rights abuses. The Bush administration had also winked at secret and illegal bank loans that Iraq had used to purchase some $5 billion in Western technology for its burgeoning nuclear and chemical weapons programs. Assistant Secretary of State John Kelly told Congress in early 1990 that Saddam Hussein acted as "a force of moderation" in the Middle East.[130] Only a week before the invasion, Ambassador April Glaspie informed Saddam Hussein that Washington had no "opinion on inter-Arab disputes such as your border dispute with Kuwait."[131]

"Maybe I'll turn out to be a Teddy Roosevelt," mused Bush in the first weeks of the crisis.[132] Pursuing what one scholar has called a "policy of minimum candor," Bush and his advisers, without informing Congress or the American people, apparently decided early in August to use military force to expel Saddam Hussein from Kuwait.[133] "It must be done as massively and decisively as possible," the Vietnam-conscious JCS chairman General Colin Powell advised. "Choose your target, decide on your objective, and try to crush it."[134] Yet the president described the initial deployments as defensive, even after General H. Norman Schwarzkopf had begun to plan offensive operations. Bush did not announce the offensive

World Orders, Old and New.   In 1991, as the United States fought the Persian Gulf War, the cartoonist Jim Borgman linked past (Theodore Roosevelt) and present (George Bush) to suggest that the United States still saw itself as—and acted like—an international policeman. Not much had changed, it seemed to many Americans, since the early twentieth-century days of the Roosevelt Corollary and the Big Stick. (Jim Borgman, Cincinnati Enquirer © 1991. Reprinted with special permission of King Features Syndicate)

buildup until after the November mid-term elections. All the while he expanded U.S. goals from defending Saudi Arabia, to liberating Kuwait, to crippling Iraq's war economy, even to stopping Saddam Hussein from acquiring nuclear weapons. UN sanctions cut off 90 percent of Iraq's imports and 97 percent of its exports. Iraq still refused to consider withdrawal from Kuwait unless the United States forced Israel to relinquish its occupied territories. Baker vetoed any direct linkage, as well as any Arab solution whereby Iraq would retain parts of Kuwait. Iraq's aggression, which the president likened to Adolf Hitler's, should gain no reward. "If we get into an armed situation, [Saddam Hussein] is going to get his ass kicked," Bush boasted in the masculine overtones so common to the language of foreign policy.[135] For the president, it became "the right war, at the right place, at the right time, and against the right enemy."[136]

Although Bush claimed that he had the constitutional authority to order U.S. troops into combat under a UN resolution, he reluctantly requested congressional authorization. There followed a searching four-day debate. Senator Joseph Biden of Delaware declared that "none [of Iraq's] actions justify the deaths of our sons and daughters."[137] Senator George Mitchell of Maine cited the risks: "an unknown number of casualties and deaths, billions of dollars spent, a greatly disrupted oil supply and oil price increases, a war possibly widened to Israel, Turkey or other allies, the possible long-term American occupation of Iraq, increased instability in the Persian Gulf region, long-lasting Arab enmity against the United States, a possible return to isolationism at home."[138] Senator Robert Dole of Kansas rebutted these critics, saying that "Saddam . . . may think he's going to be rescued, maybe by Congress."[139] On January 12, 1991, after Congress defeated a Democratic resolution to sustain the policy of sanctions, a majority in both houses then narrowly approved Bush's request to use force under UN auspices. Nearly every Republican voted for war; two-thirds of House Democrats and forty-five of fifty-six Democratic senators cast negative votes. Those few Democratic senators voting for war (among them Tennessee's Albert Gore and Joseph Lieberman of Connecticut) provided the necessary margin.

Operation Desert Storm began with a spectacular aerial bombardment of Iraq and Kuwait on January 16. For five weeks satellite television coverage via Cable News Network (CNN) enabled Americans to watch as Tomahawk cruise missiles sped to Iraqi targets and U.S. Patriot missiles intercepted Iraqi Scud missiles. Bush and Baker masterfully kept the coalition intact, persuading Israel not to retaliate after Iraqi Scud attacks and keeping Gorbachev aboard as allied bombs devastated Russia's erstwhile client. Finally, on February 23, General ("Stormin' Norman") Schwarzkopf sent hundreds of thousands of allied ground forces into Kuwait and eastern Iraq. Notwithstanding Saddam Hussein's warning that Americans would sustain thousands of casualties in the "mother of all battles," Iraq's largely conscript army put up little resistance.[140] Iraqi troops scrambled to leave Kuwait, blowing up as many as 800 oil wells as they retreated. Allied aircraft flew hundreds of sorties along what became known as the "Highway of Death" from Kuwait City to Basra. After only one hundred hours of fighting on the ground, Iraq accepted a UN-imposed cease-fire. An exultant Bush proclaimed: "By God, we've kicked the Vietnam syndrome once and for all."[141]

Estimates vary and remain disputed, but Iraq's casualties numbered some 25,000 dead; U.S. forces suffered only 148 deaths and 458 wounded (out of a coalition total of 240 and 776). A public-health crisis soon beset the Iraqi people, who had seen their infrastructure disabled by pounding air attacks; cholera and typhoid spread through the population. A UN inspection team reported that Iraq had been "relegated to a preindustrial age, but with all the disabilities of postindustrial dependency on an intensive use of energy and technology."[142]

Bush chose not to send U.S. forces to Baghdad to capture Saddam Hussein, despite his earlier designation of the Iraqi leader as Public Enemy Number One. Attempts during the fighting to target Saddam had failed, and Bush undoubtedly hoped that the Iraqi military or disgruntled associates in the Ba'ath party would oust Saddam in a coup. Yet when Kurds in northern Iraq and Shi'ites in the south rebelled, Bush did little to help. "If you want to go in and stop the killing of Shi'ites, that's a mission I understand," said General Powell. "But to what purpose? If the Shi'ites continue to rise up, do we then support them for the overthrow of Baghdad and the partition of the country?" Powell opposed "trying to sort out two thousand years of Mesopotamian history."[143] Bush, ever wary of a Mideast quagmire, backed away, saying: "We are not going to permit this to drag on in terms of [a] significant U.S. presence à la Korea."[144] Saddam used his remaining tanks and helicopters to crush both rebellions, sending streams of Kurdish refugees fleeing toward the Turkish border. Public pressure persuaded Bush to send thousands of U.S. troops to northern Iraq, where the United Nations designated a security zone and set up tent cities. Saddam Hussein's remarkable survival left a sour taste—"like an exasperating endgame in chess, when the winning player never seems to trap the other's king even though the final result is inevitable."[145] America may have won the war, said some, but it lost the peace and sullied its moral standing by failing to come to the rescue of people it had urged to challenge Saddam.

Under Security Council Resolution 687, Iraq had to accept the inviolability of the boundary with Kuwait; tolerate the presence of UN peacekeepers on its borders; and fully disclose all chemical, biological, and nuclear weapons, including missiles, and cooperate in their destruction. Bush had boasted during the air war that "our pinpoint attacks have put Saddam out of the nuclear bomb-building business for a long time to come."[146] Not so. What allied bombs had missed, UN inspectors did not. Saddam Hussein's scientists and engineers had built more than twenty nuclear facilities. Air attacks had only inconvenienced Iraqi efforts to build a bomb. Inspectors also found and destroyed more than 100 Scud missiles, 70 tons of nerve gas, and 400 tons of mustard gas. By fall 1992, the head of the UN inspection team rated Iraq's capacity for mass destruction at zero.

Other results from the Gulf War included the restoration of Kuwait's independence, a drop in oil prices sent up during the war crisis, and at least a temporary revitalization of the United Nations. Improved Western relations with Iran and Syria eventually brought an end to hostage-taking in Beirut. In the fall of 1991 firefighters extinguished the last of the blazing oil wells ignited by the retreating Iraqis, but only after the suffocating smoke had spread across an area twice the size of Alaska and caused long-term environmental damage. Millions of barrels of oil befouled the Persian Gulf, killing tens of thousands of seabirds. The financial costs of

Burning Oil Fields in Kuwait.   Months after Operation Desert Storm freed Kuwait from Iraqi rule, oil fields blazed, creating an environmental disaster. Some oil facilities were hit in the fighting. Retreating Iraqi forces also torched Kuwait's oil industry. Soot and unburned crude oil billowed into the air and then polluted soils, vegetation, and Persian Gulf waters. (U.S. Navy/Department of Defense, Still Media Records Center)

the war to the Arab countries amounted to $620 billion, with Iraq and Kuwait each paying about a third. The Japanese, Germans, and Arabs contributed $54 billion (or 90 percent) to cover the costs of the allied campaign.

The Persian Gulf War refueled the debate over American decline that the best-selling *The Rise and Fall of the Great Powers* (1987) had helped to set off. The historian Paul Kennedy had argued in this meaty book that the United States suffered from "imperial overstretch."[147] Like great nations of the past (Spain and Great Britain), the United States could expect its power to erode unless its restored its productive vitality and marketplace competitiveness. Education, research and development, and bloated military spending needed attention, he said. "Are we ready to follow that historical pattern [of decline]," he asked, "or do we want to learn from history?"[148] Although most of Kennedy's critics admitted that serious problems beset the nation, they claimed that "renewal," not "decadence," was the "American truth."[149]

The *Wall Street Journal* welcomed the Gulf War because it "lets America, and above all else its elite, recover a sense of self-confidence and self-worth."[150] Bush exclaimed that henceforth "people are going to listen" to the United States because of its "reestablished credibility."[151] Armchair analysts hailed the Gulf victory as the first electronics war in which the sight of smart bombs and cruise missiles homing in on targets would deter other Saddam Husseins from challenging high-tech militaries. Yet anyone "who considered air power the linchpin of a new Pax Americana," as one writer put it, "needed only to recall Vietnam to remember the limitation of bomber fleets against a determined foe sheltered by mountains and thick foliage."[152] Debunking the "gloomsayers," as Bush called the declinists, the "revivalists" forecast a unipolar world with the United States at the top.[153] The doubters replied that U.S. officials postured just like leaders of bygone empires: claiming continued preeminence and denying trouble, and thereby ensuring that decline would persist. One senator who worried about U.S. economic competitiveness in the face of German and Japanese expansion, asked: "If we can make the best smart bomb, can't we make the best VCR?"[154] Military victory over a small Mideast nation, critics warned, could not sustain U.S. power in a world in which economic clout counted at least as much as military muscle.

The "new world order" trumpeted by Bush turned out to be an empty slogan, for the world descended into vicious local rivalries and wars that powerful nations seemed unable to stop.[155] Bush's neglect of the domestic front, moreover, cost him politically. Economic recession, huge federal deficits, stalled educational reform, retreat from environmental protection, and insensitivity to women's rights caused the president's standing in the polls to plummet. "SADDAM HUSSEIN STILL HAS HIS JOB. HOW ABOUT YOU?" ran a popular bumper sticker in 1992.[156]

To the surprise and welcome of many, the Gulf War spurred the Arab-Israeli peace process. When Bush took office in early 1989 the peace process had stalled. *Intifada* deaths continued to mount as Israelis used uncompromising military force to quell the insurrection. Israel slumped into economic recession, and debate erupted over its questionable human-rights record. Prospects for peace dimmed further in mid-1990 when the conservative Likud party took power in Israel, vowing never to give up the occupied territories. Radical Palestinian factions at the same time refused to abandon their "Holy war" *(jihad)* against the Jewish state. U.S. officials continued to meet with PLO representatives, but Israeli officials stiff-armed talks. Secretary Baker pressed both sides, but he particularly implored Israel to negotiate: "Lay aside, once and for all, the unrealistic vision of a greater Israel." He went on: "Forswear annexation. Stop settlement activity. . . . Reach out to the Palestinians as neighbors who deserve political rights."[157] Despite an Israeli rebuff to Baker's appeal, U.S. foreign aid flowed as usual to Israel: $3 billion in 1989 and $4.7 billion in 1992, for example.

The end of the Cold War, the Persian Gulf War, and growing dissatisfaction with Israel's hard-line stance among American Jews improved the diplomatic climate. The Soviet Union's collapse robbed the PLO of outside support. Yasir Arafat's ill-fated backing of Iraq during the Gulf War caused the oil-rich governments of Saudi Arabia and the Gulf states, in retaliation, to curtail their financial assistance to the PLO. Hard-line Islamic fundamentalists in the *Hamas* movement challenged Arafat's leadership within the PLO. Thus when Israel showed restraint in the face of Iraqi missile attacks and the United States promised moderate Arabs an expanded peace process after the Gulf War, Arafat decided to negotiate. Secretary Baker traveled to the Mideast eight times in 1991 to arrange for multilateral negotiations in Madrid in 1992. President Bush pressed Israel by withholding $10 billion in loan guarantees so long as the hard-line Likud government expanded Israeli settlements in the occupied territories; this pressure helped to elect a more flexible Labor government, headed by Yitzhak Rabin and Shimon Peres, in July 1992. Regarding Rabin, Arafat said: "He is not a de Gaulle. Let him at least be a de Klerk."[158]

The breakthrough came little more than a year later, after secret meetings between Israeli and PLO representatives in Norway. "Neither Israel nor the PLO could afford another year, or two, or three of conflict," a Norwegian diplomat explained.[159] In Washington on September 13, 1993, Arafat and Rabin signed a

PLO-Israeli Agreement. On September 13, 1993, President Clinton acted as stage manager on the South Lawn of the White House when Israeli prime minister Yitzhak Rabin (b. 1922), on the left, and Palestine Liberation Organization chairman Yasir Arafat, on the right, signed an historic accord for Palestinian self-rule in the Gaza Strip and Jericho—first steps, perhaps, toward a Palestinian homeland. After Rabin and Arafat affixed their signatures, Clinton shook hands with both men and then stepped back and gestured with his arms. Arafat reached his hand out, and after several long seconds, Rabin responded. (Courtesy of The White House)

declaration of principles for eventual Palestinian self-rule in the Gaza Strip and in the Jericho area of the West Bank. Prompted by President Clinton, the two leaders then shook hands. "It was a handshake with someone who just a moment ago was the devil in person," an Israeli official remarked, "and from now on is your partner in negotiation."[160] An Arab American recalled that "Jewish guys sitting on each side of me grabbed for me. From that moment on . . . there was physical embracing. We were being Semites together."[161]

Although the declaration called for self-rule by November, terrorist activities by extremists on both sides caused the Israeli government to delay its implementation. When a Brooklyn-born Israeli settler, Baruch Goldstein, killed forty Palestinians praying in a Hebron mosque in February 1994, the PLO broke off talks. After Rabin described Goldstein as a crazy person, one Palestinian remarked: "When they kill us they are crazy, and when we kill them we are terrorists."[162] Resumed talks finally produced agreement in May 1994, when Israeli forces withdrew from the Gaza Strip and Jericho and Palestinian antonomy began in those two areas. Israel and Jordan signed a peace accord in July.

SOMALIA, BOSNIA, AND THE NEW WORLD DISORDER

Peace processes also worked ever so slowly in other parts of the world. In December 1992, after he had lost the election, President Bush ordered 28,150 U.S. troops to Somalia on a humanitarian mission to feed the starving people of that civil-war-torn country of Africa (see map page 353). Ghastly television pictures of emaciated children and other skin-and-bones people starving while armed thugs stole food from their bowls had stirred Americans. The accusation from UN secretary general Boutros Boutros-Ghali that the United States showed more concern for "the rich man's war" in Bosnia than for the fate of starving Somalis, and perhaps a desire to prove that "American power was a force for good in the world and that a President should not shrink from applying it," had also contributed to Bush's decision.[163] Somalia ranked as "a tragedy of major proportions," Acting Secretary of State Eagleburger emphasized, "and, underline this, *one that we had to do something about.*"[164] The president deployed troops despite the Pentagon's reservations and a prediction from the U.S. ambassador to Kenya that "if you liked Beirut, you'll love Mogadishu."[165] Bush hoped that U.S. forces could restore order, move relief supplies to desperate Somalis, and then turn peacekeeping duties over to the United Nations by the time of Clinton's inauguration. Boutras-Ghali enthusiastically backed the plan, saying that "such a force could obtain stability very quickly. I know Somalia. I have been there many times."[166] Both men proved much too optimistic.

Somalia ranked as one of America's Cold War orphans. When the Soviet Union in 1977 began wooing the Marxist regime in Ethiopia, the Carter administration backed Somalian dictator Siad Barre, a former Soviet client, and thus gained access to the former Soviet air base at Berbera on the Gulf of Aden. Somalia became a pivotal pro-West ally in what Zbigniew Brzezinski called the "arc of crisis" stretching from the Red Sea to the Persian Gulf.[167] Over the next decade, despite human-rights violations and harsh repression of internal dissent, Siad Barre received nearly $1 billion in U.S. assistance. As the Cold War waned, Somalia's strategic importance diminished. When the Reagan and Bush administrations slashed military aid to Somalia, "we took away one of [Siad Barre's] most important tools, his repressive ability," a U.S. diplomat recalled.[168] Clan rivalries led to a ferocious civil war that destroyed half of the capital city of Mogadishu and forced Siad Barre to flee in January 1991. The United States at that point pulled out its diplomatic mission. "There are no geopolitical stakes in . . . the Horn of Africa any more," the State Department announced.[169] As a former ambassador to Somalia put it, Washington "turned out the light, closed the door and forgot about the place."[170] The civil war intensified, disrupted the economy, and produced mass starvation. In the two years following Siad Barre's ouster, some 300,000 Somalis died.

Bush's Operation Restore Hope succeeded at first. The first marines landed with more than seventy-five reporters and camera crews waiting on the beach with microphones and video cameras. U.S. officials initiated cooperative relations with

U.S. Marines in Somalia.   Armed with
M-16A2 5.56mm rifles equipped with grenade
launchers, these marines escorted relief work-
ers in December 1991 as they delivered sacks
of grain to a Somalian village during Operation
Restore Hope. (Courtesy of U.S.
Navy/Department of Defense, Still Media
Records Center)

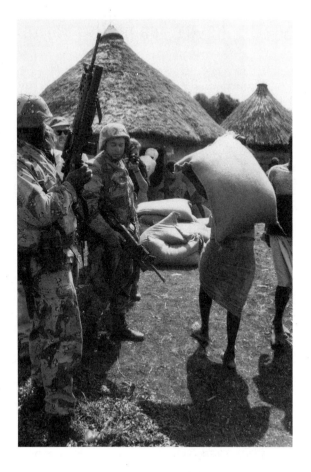

the most powerful Somali warlord, General Mohamed Farah Aidid, who controlled
the Mogadishu area. Relief operations fed the hungry, and mediation efforts progressed, with clan leaders agreeing to negotiate national reconciliation. President
Clinton began to pull U.S. forces out. "You have proved again," he told the troops,
"that our involvement in multilateral efforts need not be open-ended, that we can
go abroad and accomplish some distinct objectives and then come home again
when the mission is accomplished."[171] Not quite.

   With starvation stopped, the United Nations launched an "unprecedented enterprise aimed at nothing less than the restoration of an entire country."[172] Without
consulting Congress, the Clinton administration left 8,000 U.S. logistical troops in
Somalia, along with a 1,000-person quick-reaction force. Such attempts at nation
building, even under UN auspices, aroused nationalist resentment. In June 1993
General Aidid's forces attacked Pakistani peacekeeping troops, killing twenty-four.

The Security Council protested, and U.S. forces under UN command tried unsuccessfully to kill Aidid in a "decapitation mission" in early July.[173]

In early October, after the Clinton administration had begun to rethink its policy of pursuing Aidid, the warlord's forces killed eighteen U.S. Army Rangers in a bloody firefight. A shocked Clinton watched television pictures of dead U.S. soldiers being dragged through the streets of Mogadishu by seemingly jubilant Somalis. "It turned my stomach," he told aides.[174] "It's Vietnam all over again," charged Senator Ernest Hollings. "There's no education in a second kick of a mule."[175] Clinton quickly backtracked, claiming that "it is not our job to rebuild Somalia's society."[176] He withdrew all U.S. forces by the end of March 1994, leaving the mission to the United Nations. Having "first impersonated Mother Teresa and now John Wayne," as one journalist put it, Clinton finally sought a political solution to what had always been a political problem.[177]

More dangerous to the post–Cold War order was the crisis in the former Yugoslavia. In October 1990 the CIA predicted that, with the collapse of communism, Yugoslavia would disintegrate into bloody ethnic violence and Serbia would use force to seize as much of the country as possible. "The messenger wasn't shot, he was just ignored," an official later recalled.[178] The Bush administration essentially deferred to its European allies when they recognized the independence of Croatia and Slovenia in summer 1991 (see map, page 549). Serbia, in turn, proclaimed a new Federal Republic of Yugoslavia (including Montenegro) and incited Serbs living in the other republics—especially in Bosnia—to take up arms. Croats living in Bosnia declared an independent state. After Bosnia-Herzegovina became independent in April 1992, Serbs began to shell Sarajevo, the city where a 1914 assassination had triggered World War I and where the 1984 Winter Olympics had met. Bosnian Serbs grabbed territory and began to displace Bosnia's Muslim population through the horrors of "ethnic cleansing." One Serbian method of conquering their neighbors was mass rape in "rape camps" where Serbian fighters brutalized Muslim women.[179]

The European Community, having failed in mediation efforts, imposed trade sanctions on Serbia-Montenegro and handed the issue over to the United Nations. As UN mediators, headed by former secretary of state Cyrus Vance and former British foreign secretary David Owen, tried futilely to negotiate a peace settlement, Serbian militia seized approximately 70 percent of the Bosnian hinterland while systematically bombarding and starving the people of Sarajevo. France and Britain dispatched "Blue Helmets" (UN troops) to safeguard relief supplies in Bosnia, but recoiled from military intervention. Germany also did little, its constitution prohibiting military action beyond self-defense and alliance defense. Only in the last weeks of his administration did Bush intercede when the United States backed the Security Council's declaration of a flight ban over Bosnia. By the end of 1992 perhaps as many as 150,000 people had perished.

Clinton inherited this "problem from hell," as Secretary of State Warren Christopher once characterized the Bosnian crisis.[180] During the campaign, Clinton had criticized Bush for not saving the Muslims, saying that "there are things that can be done" in Bosnia.[181] Yet Americans, although moved by the bloodshed and suffering in Bosnia, feared getting bogged down in age-old ethnic rivalries impervious

Europe, America, and Bosnia.   The European nations tried diplomacy to settle the Bosnian crisis in the former Yugoslavia and deployed some peacekeeping troops to protect Muslim communities from attack by Bosnian Serbs. But as the crisis deepened and the Serbs perpetuated their ugly "ethnic cleansing," European leaders seemed paralyzed if not inhumane. Their hesitancy to act prompted this critical cartoon. (© 1993 Jimmy Margulies, *The Record*/New Jersey. Reprinted by permission)

to outside influence. When Clinton asked for military options, moreover, the Pentagon took note of the rugged terrain in the region and reportedly told him: "We do deserts, we don't do mountains."[182] The pressure to act mounted during spring 1993. At the dedication of the U.S. Holocaust Memorial Museum in Washington in April, Nobel Laureate Elie Wiesel pleaded with Clinton to "stop the bloodshed. . . . Something, anything, must be done" to help the Bosnian Muslims.[183] Ambassador to the United Nations Madeline Albright, prominent senators and members of Congress, and many State Department officials urged air strikes to halt Serbian aggression. Senator Hank Brown of Colorado opposed them, citing Vietnam as "a very pertinent analogy because when Americans suffer casualties in Yugoslavia, support for American involvement is going to fade."[184] A cautious Joint Chiefs of Staff chairman Colin Powell quietly admonished: "You punish from the air, you do not enforce from the air."[185] Issuing statements warning the Serbs and proclaiming America's humane concern, Clinton lacked foreign support and a domestic consensus for a major display of force. He backed away. "He doesn't want a solution that's OK for the next few weeks but then leaves you so inherently unstable that you're there a year or more from now," a top aide explained.[186] The administration appeared adrift in its foreign policy, unable to take a stand and stick to it.

The same scenario of tough talk followed by second thoughts repeated itself in August when a Serbian military push threatened to cut off Sarajevo and stop all relief supplies. When Clinton again pressed NATO for air strikes, the Serbs retreated a few miles from the mountain heights surrounding the city, thus forestalling NATO attacks. The desk officer for Bosnia thereupon resigned, protesting that the weak-kneed Department of State "will not act against genocide."[187] One journalist ridiculed "the absolutely final, ultimate, don't-mess-with-us, push-me-and-see-what-happens Clintonian deadline."[188] Clinton delivered a mixed message: "I will not let Sarajevo fall," he told a member of Congress. Then the president added, "Don't take that as an absolute. I'll do my part."[189]

Not until early February 1994 did the United States become more decisive. When a mortar shell exploded amid a Saturday crowd in Sarajevo's open market, killing at least 68 civilians and wounding 200 more, television's graphic coverage of the carnage prompted Clinton to act. The next day American C-130s and C-9 planes swept into Sarajevo to evacuate the wounded. After obtaining NATO approval, Clinton delivered an ultimatum: The Serbs must either pull back their tanks and artillery beyond the 12.4-mile exclusion zone around Sarajevo or turn them over to UN peacekeepers. If they did not, they would be attacked. Clinton appealed directly to Boris Yeltsin to press the Serbs to comply. The Serbs met the deadline, barely. On February 28, U.S. jets downed several Serbian planes that violated the "no fly" zone—the first combat action for NATO in its forty-five-year history. The diplomats continued to toil against great odds to protect Muslim enclaves and arrange cease-fires and territorial agreements that might hold.

FEUDING AND TRADING WITH CHINA, VIETNAM, AND JAPAN

Human rights and trade issues continued to dominate U.S. relations with Asia under Bush and Clinton. During the night of June 3–4, 1989, Chinese soldiers and tanks stormed into Beijing's Tiananmen Square. There they slaughtered hundreds—perhaps thousands—of unarmed students and citizens who for weeks had been holding peaceful prodemocracy rallies and appealing for talks with government leaders. The movement had attracted wide support, including the backing of some Chinese party officials. China's octogenarian rulers, however, in contrast to their counterparts in much of Eastern Europe, chose repression over constructive change—"to haul China back twenty years to terror and Orwellian groupthink."[190] The most powerful leader in the Chinese government, Deng Xiaoping, himself victimized by a popular movement two decades earlier, saw the students' call for political liberalization to match economic reforms as an attempt "to create chaos under the heavens."[191] Deng not only crushed the prodemocracy movement; he also purged the government of reformers, ordered the arrest and execution of protesters, and launched a campaign against "bourgeois liberalization." "Do not fear world opinion," he exhorted hard-line officials.[192] But world opinion became outraged, becaused "Tiananmen was a record-breaking world event on television."[193]

Although Bush officials initially expressed revulsion over the brutal events in China, their response gradually softened. Washington suspended weapons sales to China (and then soon lifted the ban) and deferred consideration of new World Bank loans to China. Yet Bush rejected stronger economic sanctions, continuing, for example, Beijing's most-favored-nation trade status. On the basis of his stint in 1974–1975 as chief of the U.S. Liaison Office in Beijing, Bush claimed to "know how the Chinese leadership thinks."[194] He calculated that China's aging leaders would once again travel the reform path; and he argued that America's global security required stable and friendly Sino-American ties. China, Bush implored, should not be isolated in the international community. In December 1989, National Security Affairs Adviser Brent Scowcroft traveled to China, where he said that "we believe it is important that we not exhaust ourselves in placing blame for the problems that exist."[195]

The Bush administration also fought a congressional move to grant extended visa status to some 40,000 fearful PRC students studying in the United States. Many of them had supported the prodemocracy campaign, and they worried that on their return to China they would face jail or worse. After offering assurances that he would honor the requests of students who wished to remain in the United States, Bush vetoed the bill. Critics charged that the United States was shortsightedly allying itself with China's elderly clique, whose rule could not last much longer, while alienating the nation's younger, progressive, future leaders. Bush cheered such leaders in Bucharest, Prague, and Warsaw but snubbed them in Beijing. The debate centered on two classic questions. First, when calls for human rights and calculations of global power politics collide, which must give way? And, second, do economic sanctions work to change the internal policies of other nations?

Prodemocracy Courage, Tiananmen Square, Beijing, China.   In early 1989 university students and sympathizers camped in Beijing's great square. They made hopeful speeches about democracy and even built a towering replica of the Statue of Liberty. Drawing inspiration from Poland's Solidarity movement, the young prodemocracy activists pleaded with their nation's aged leaders to liberalize China's politics. In June the military swept into the square. After the massacre, one person—probably a student—braved tanks in a sobering example of the classic contest between the courageous individual and the powerful state. As the historian Jonathan D. Spence has written, "The brutality of the crackdown, and the cynicism of the lies the Chinese government then told the world, could not but affect tens of thousands of China's brightest students who were currently studying abroad. These students . . . now formed a potent overseas source for disaffection." (AP/Wide World Photos)

Despite glacial progress on human rights, China's economy boomed during the early 1990s, and Americans joined the PRC's quest for riches. U.S. trade with China reached $33 billion in 1992 (with an $18.3 billion surplus in China's favor). America's two-way trade with all of East Asia soared to more than $300 billion, surpassing trade with Europe by a third, suggesting that the "Asia card" of market growth might ensure "success in the revitalization of the U.S. economy."[196] According to World Bank projections, "Greater China"—PRC, Taiwan, and Hong Kong (scheduled to return to China in 1997)—would purchase $639 billion in imports by the year 2002, in contrast with an expected $521 billion for Japan. "Greater China's" projected gross domestic product of $9.8 trillion would surpass the estimated $9.7 trillion for the United States that same year. Although Bill Clinton had criticized the Bush administration for supporting the status quo from "Beijing to the Baltics," the Clinton administration renewed China's most-favored-nation trading privileges in June 1993 after the Beijing government released several prominent dissidents.[197] Beijing's establishment of diplomatic ties with South Korea in 1992, its growing trade with Seoul, and its quiet pressure on North Korea to permit international nuclear inspection also pleased Washington.

Clinton announced, however, that China must improve its human-rights performance before another renewal of most-favored-nation status. The Chinese government responded with contempt. When Secretary Christopher visited China in March 1994, authorities arrested dissidents and then bluntly lectured that "it is futile to apply pressure against China." Chinese Premier Li Peng warned that the United States endangered "its share of the big China market."[198] Differences also continued over China's growing military strength and its sale of M-1 missile components to Pakistan and chemicals to Iraq. To Americans, China seemed "prickly, mulish and fiercely independent—France cubed," as one analyst put it.[199] Whatever its political future, China's growing economic power made it impossible, one Asian leader predicted, "to pretend that this is just another big player. This is the biggest player in the history of man."[200] In 1994, when Clinton again granted most-favored-nation status, he frankly declared that human rights and trade issues were henceforth delinked.

History-mindedness also characterized U.S. relations with Vietnam. In fall 1992, President Bush announced that "we can begin writing the last chapter of the Vietnam War."[201] Bush referred to the protracted negotiations with Hanoi to reach a full accounting for the 2,265 American military personnel still listed as missing in action (MIAs) from the Vietnam War. In February 1994, after the Clinton administration satisfied itself that Vietnamese officials had made a sincere effort to identify and return remains, Washington lifted the nineteen-year-old trade embargo with the government of Vietnam. Within hours PepsiCo erected a giant, inflated can of soda in the middle of Ho Chi Minh City (formerly Saigon) and gave away 40,000 cans of the international soft drink to presumably thirsty Vietnamese. Caterpillar, Otis, and other companies hoped to win contracts worth billions of dollars to repair Vietnam's infrastructure. Mobil expected to begin pumping oil in the South China Sea. Planned for the site of the prison that American POWs called the Hanoi Hilton was a $45 million twin-tower hotel and office complex. Despite a devastating war and two decades of isolation, many of the 71 million Vietnamese apparently retained a certain attraction to things American. "English is the language of money, the language of our future," said a Vietnamese diplomat.[202] Having opened its economy to foreign investment and trade since 1987, Hanoi undoubtedly saw a strong U.S. economic presence as a possible counter to its giant neighbor China. Full normalization of U.S.-Vietnamese diplomatic relations lay ahead.

Trade issues also dominated the Japanese-American relationship. Anti-Americanism in Japan and "Japan bashing" *("Nihon tataki")* in the United States be-deviled the world's two largest economies.[203] In 1990 the world's ten largest banks had headquarters in Japan, and several of the world's largest public companies were Japanese. Japan's biggest company, NTT, was more than twice the size of America's leading corporation, IBM. The best-selling car in America in 1989 was the Honda Accord. A former Japanese prime minister claimed that the United States was no longer number one in the world economy but rather "first among equals."[204] The best-known America-bashing book, Akio Morita's and Shintaro Ishihara's *The Japan That Can Say "No"* (1989), angered U.S. leaders. When President Bush vomited and collapsed at a state dinner in Japan in January 1992, a television camera videotaped Prime Minister Kiichi Miyazawa holding up the stricken American chief executive, heightening "the perception of a changing relationship between the two nations."[205]

The evidence mounted: The Japanese *were* more astute in marketing techno-logically advanced products; they saved more in order to invest more; they had vir-tually no illiteracy; they devoted substantial resources to education and manpower training; and they involved workers in management decisions. Not all was well in Japan, of course. The nation still depended on imports of scarce raw materials; la-borers and professional people, working twelve-hour days, seemed to produce but not to enjoy; conformity characterized their society; corruption marked the politi-cal system; and a hostility toward foreigners revealed traces of xenophobia.

"The Japanese Have Bought Pearl Harbor." Huge Japanese investments in the United States prompted the cartoonist Don C. Wright to remember December 7, 1941, when Japan attacked Pearl Harbor. By the 1980s Japan had become an economic behemoth. Americans grumbled that the Japanese were buying up the United States. But, remarked Chrysler Corporation chair Lee Iacocca, Americans had no-body but themselves to blame. "You can't get mad at them [Japanese] for saying. 'We'll take as much as you give us.'" (© 1988 Don Wright, *The Miami News*)

Many Americans especially worried that the dollar-rich Japanese were buying up too many businesses in the United States. By 1990 Japanese interests controlled 25 percent of California's banking assets and owned almost half of downtown Los Angeles. The year before, Sony bought Columbia Pictures, sounding alarms that the expansionistic Japanese were not only taking over American companies but also gaining influence over American opinion through the ownership of the nation's culture industries.

How did the Japanese get all that money? The answer emerges from fundamental economics. The huge U.S. trade deficit, built up by Americans' buying more from abroad (imports) than they sold abroad (exports), put vast sums of dollars in the hands of foreigners. The total trade deficit in 1989 reached $115 billion (about $50 billion of that figure with Japan). Japanese investors and others began to plow their accumulating dollars into the United States, buying U.S. Treasury bonds, companies, stocks, and real estate. This investment brought needed capital to America, whose citizens maintained a low savings rate, in part because they bought Japanese videocassette recorders and television sets rather than deposit their money in banks that then could have used the funds for loans to American companies that wished to expand. Japanese direct investments in the United States climbed to more than $50 billion in 1990, and Japanese portfolio investments topped $160 billion. Foreign-owned dollars also helped Washington finance the mounting federal debt. By 1989 the total U.S. foreign debt stood at $500 billion. As someone put it, the Japanese (and British, Swiss, Dutch, Canadians, and Germans) were not buying America; rather, Americans were selling it. The United States, in fact, went from being a creditor (lender) to a debtor (borrower) nation in the Reagan 1980s.

Washington applauded Japan's close military alliance with the United States (more than 50,000 American military personnel still served there) and its shouldering of more of the mutual defense costs. American officials praised Tokyo for applying Japanese funds to relieve the international debt problem and for providing economic assistance to developing nations such as the Philippines. But Washington pressed for a closing of the trade gap by opening Japanese markets more widely to American products such as grains, timber, and supercomputers. The Japanese answered that the United States' slipping competitiveness stemmed not from Japanese trade restrictions but from obsolete equipment, a deteriorating educational system, lazy workers, low savings, inadequate spending on research and development, and large payments on its foreign debt (amounting to billions of dollars a month that could more sensibly have been invested in the crumbling American infrastructure, medical research, environmental protection, and the like). "Victory for capitalism?" asked Japanologist Chalmers Johnson of the University of California. "Which capitalism? . . . Some might say the Cold War had indeed ended, and the Japanese won."[206]

Although some analysts predicted a destructive trade war in the 1990s, others noted that with the two economies so intricately linked, an economic downturn in either nation caused by economic competition would prove mutually destructive. Indeed, "a divorce is unthinkable even if the marriage remains troubled," observed a longtime Asia watcher.[207] American firms made modest headway in the large

Japanese marketplace. By 1994 McDonald's had become Japan's largest restaurant chain, and Apple Computer ranked as the second largest vendor of personal computers behind NEC, the huge Japanese company. A recession in Japan caused imports to shrink, however, and the U.S. trade deficit with Japan soared to a record $59 billion in 1993. Although observers still predicted a "Pacific Century" and a "Pax Japonica," Japan looked less imposing, with "no more of these giant sumo wrestlers and giant samurai taking over Wall Street," the historian John Dower remarked in early 1994.[208] As U.S. economic competitiveness seemed on the upswing, the Japanese themselves began to speak of the "Rising Sam."[209]

At a Group of Seven (G-7) summit in Tokyo in July 1993, President Clinton emphasized that "in hard times we shouldn't react like porcupines. We should open up like sunflowers."[210] Tokyo and Washington reached agreement on a framework for future trade pacts to create larger Japanese markets for key U.S. industries, including autos, computers, telecommunications, satellites, medical equipment, financial services, and insurance. But when Japan balked at implementation, the Clinton administration hinted that the Japanese had cheated. Washington vowed retaliation. The heated rhetoric caused one journalist to joke that Japanese and U.S. negotiators might "show up at the table in camouflage fatigues and shout: 'Ready! Aim! Sanction.'"[211]

Everything Everywhere: Global Crossroads

"Gosh, I miss the Cold War," President Clinton half-joked after American soldiers were killed in Somalia.[212] Indeed, the post–Cold War era seemed less manageable than the bipolar system that had preceded it—so full of "outlaws," so rife with religious, tribal, and ethnic tensions (especially evident in Rwanda), so overarmed, so wracked by economic catastrophes, so divided on the basis of gender, so plagued by illicit drugs, crime, and AIDS, so threatened by the proliferation of nuclear weapons and the deterioration of the natural environment, so burdened by overpopulation and famines, so disunited just when it appeared that the United Nations had emerged as a major builder of coalitions.[213]

Arms sales accelerated across the post–Cold War world. "If you have kept your eyes mainly on the U.S. and the Soviet Union," wrote *The Economist* magazine of London, "you probably think the world is becoming a safer place to live in. Well, look elsewhere."[214] Surface-to-surface missiles were showing up in the world arms market. So were U.S. Stinger missiles that the Reagan administration had given in the 1980s to radical Islamic rebels for their war against the Soviet-backed government in Afghanistan. After the Soviet withdrawal, Reagan's Afghan "freedom fighters" used the weapons against their rivals, became traffickers in heroin, and trained *jihad* terrorists and assassins. The CIA called such unintended consequences "blowbacks."[215] A multimillion-dollar covert CIA program in the early 1990s to buy back 1,000 Stingers failed. As the Afghan case demonstrated, the United States had long fed the world arms market. Experts predicted a two-thirds U.S. share of this market by the mid-1990s, as Third World nations, which might better spend their limited resources on human services, lined up to buy Patriot missiles and other expensive weapons.

Nuclear proliferation remained a threat to all nations. Although Argentina and Brazil signed a pact never to build nuclear weapons and South Africa publicly announced in 1993 that it had dismantled its nuclear weapons program, Israel, Pakistan, and India had joined the elite nuclear club—and each refused to sign the nonproliferation treaty. U.S. intelligence learned in May 1990 that Pakistan had deployed as many as ten nuclear weapons on American-made F-16 fighter planes and seemed poised to strike India. Apparently only an eleventh-hour U.S. plea defused a crisis that one CIA official called "far more frightening than the Cuban missile crisis."[216] As for the former Soviet republics, Belarus and Kazakhstan promised to relinquish nuclear arms but delayed actually doing so. Ukraine, suddenly the world's third largest nuclear power, obtained $700 million in economic aid from the United States before agreeing to dismantle its 1,600 nuclear warheads. Others worried that a deadly chemical, combined with a ballistic missile, might become the weapon of choice. To prevent such a calamity, the UN Conference on Disarmanent in Geneva reached agreement in January 1993 on a chemical-weapons treaty requiring signatories to destroy all chemical weapons by the year 2005 and to submit to rigorous inspection.

The discovery that Kim Il Sung's North Korean regime had built facilities that could produce small nuclear weapons spawned a major crisis in the early 1990s. Pyongyang refused to cooperate with the International Atomic Energy Agency, which sought to inspect suspected plants, and threatened to withdraw from the Treaty on the Non-Proliferation of Nuclear Weapons, which North Korea had signed in 1985. Why the octogenarian Kim, who had ruled his country since the 1940s, resorted to nuclear poker remained unclear. Even if the North Koreans acquired one or two nuclear weapons, their use "would mean the end of their country as they know it," as President Clinton so bluntly put it.[217] Some feared that the dictator, whose agents had blown up half the South Korean cabinet in 1983, might actually send his army of 1.2 million soldiers across the thirty-eighth parallel in one last attempt to succeed where he had failed in 1950. Others suggested that Kim intended to create a North Korean deterrent to American nuclear weapons stationed in South Korea since 1957, or to take a cost-saving step to reduce his large and expensive conventional forces. Perhaps Pyongyang played its nuclear card to gain a "Kim's ransom"—trade concessions and access to international finance to keep the isolated communist country from falling apart.[218] Whatever Kim's motives, North Korea posed a post–Cold War nightmare for Washington—a "backlash state" with nuclear weapons.[219] In spring 1994, Washington demanded that Kim disband his nuclear project. The United States also began to beef up South Korean military forces, stage military maneuvers in the region, and suggest economic sanctions against North Korea. Kim's death in mid-1994 and the ascension of his son Kim Jong Il reminded everyone that the half-century civil war on the Korean peninsula, in short, had not ended.

"Until now the cold war provided an alibi" to avoid tackling many global issues, wrote a leading analyst. "No longer."[220] The deterioration of the international

Famine in Civil War–Torn Sudan.   Since its independence in 1956, Sudan has been troubled by political disorder, including ineffective military-led regimes, a rebellion by the non-Muslim south against the Muslim north, and the Khartoum (the capital) government's effort to re-press protest by killing hundreds of thousands of southern civilians. In the 1980s and 1990s, rocked by civil strife that disrupted agricultural production, bankrupt because of a huge international debt, and staggered by drought, Sudan suffered a famine that claimed hundreds of thousands more victims. Because of the civil war, relief supplies often did not reach desperate people like this man too weak to walk. (© James Nachtwey/Magnum Photos)

environment not only endangered economic prosperity; it also threatened to undermine international stability. Any sample of data revealed problems:

- The world's population in 1994 reached 6 billion and was rising at a rate of 90 million every year.

- In Mexico City, air pollution was so bad that seven out of ten babies were born with excessive levels of lead in their blood.

- "In 1989, the world had 157 billionaires, perhaps 2 million millionaires, and 100 million homeless. Americans spend $5 billion each year on special diets to lower their calorie consumption, while 400 million people around the world are so undernourished that their bodies and minds are deteriorating."[221]

- In 1990, 40,000 children died every day from malnourishment or sickness that could have been prevented by vaccination.

- The World Food Council reported in 1991 that 45 million people faced imminent starvation.

- Americans used about one-third of all chlorofluorocarbons (CFCs) in the world—the chemical most responsible for the depletion of the ozone layer that shields the earth from the sun's deadly ultraviolet rays.

- In Sweden, at least 4,000 lakes have been so afflicted by acid rain that they are barren of fish.

- In 1991, Chinese industries emitted 11 trillion cubic meters of waste gases and 16 million metric tons of soot, largely from burning coal, thus causing acid rains that damaged forests in Korea and Siberia. Experts predict that China will become the world's biggest producer of acid rain by 2010.

- Since the late 1940s, according to the UN Environmental Program, 4.6 million square miles of land have undergone mild to extensive soil degradation—an area equivalent to China and India combined.

- As much as 75 percent of the surface water in Russia is dangerous to drink.

- Because of the diversion of water to Central Asia for agricultural irrigation, the Aral Sea, situated on the border between Kazakhstan and Uzbekistan and originally larger than Lake Huron, shrank by two-thirds.

- "Tropical forests cover only 7 percent of Earth's land surface," according to the World Resources Institute, "but they contain more than half of all living species. Yet these forests are being cut and cleared at a very rapid rate—an area of about 40 million acres (about the size of the state of Washington) every year."[222]

- The U.S. government alone annually discards more than 250,000 tons of waste paper—the equivalent of more than 4 million trees.

Whether threatened by acid rain, global warming, ozone-layer depletion, toxic wastes, water pollution, or deforestation, the world faced a host of borderless issues. The catapulting growth in population meant a greater use of scarce resources, more pollution, more disease, and more famines like those that wracked Africa in the 1980s. Overgrazing and tree-cutting in many parts of the Third World, as in Bangladesh, produced quick runoffs of rainfalls and flooding, washing away precious topsoil and killing hundreds. In turn, these ecological/economic problems generated political instability and social disintegration. Food riots and migrations of refugees challenged governments, many of which seemed immobilized. Yet the Bush administration vetoed monies for the UN Population Fund in 1989 because the agency supported birth control programs that allowed abortions. The Law of the Sea Treaty lay dormant because Washington did not want the agreement's provisions governing the marine environment to restrict private American business.

Third World nations hesitated to place restraints on their economic development even though they courted environmental crisis. And they resented lectures from industrialized nations that had practiced environmental wrongs for decades. The president of Brazil, for example, whose tropical forests (important for the absorption of carbon dioxide from the earth's air) were disappearing under slash-and-burn logging operations, snapped at North Americans: "They are the worst plunderers."[223] At the Earth Summit held in Rio de Janeiro, Brazil, in June 1992 and attended by 178 nations, Bush spoke against strong environmental protection rules, charging that they would cost jobs. He refused to sign the Biodiversity Treaty designed to slow the loss of endangered species. Clinton, however, signed the treaty in April 1993 and also agreed to reduce emissions of greenhouse gases to 1990 levels by the year 2000. The Clinton administration's increased attention to environmental issues was due in no small measure to Vice President Al Gore, who had gained a reputation as a specialist on the environment and whose book *Earth in the Balance: Healing the Global Environment* (1992) had established his credentials.

"We do not have generations," noted the Worldwatch Institute's Lester R. Brown. "We only have years in which to turn things around."[224] In the United States itself, the movement for recycling gathered momentum, and grassroots activists found receptive audiences. Pressure from environmentalists forced the U.S. tuna industry to stop using fish-netting techniques that killed 100,000 dolphins annually. Entertainers regularly supported environmental causes through such events as the 1989 "Don't Bungle the Jungle" concert staged by Madonna and the Grateful Dead. At the same time, the United States helped establish an international ban on ivory in order to save the vanishing elephant. The Clean Air Act of 1990 took steps to reduce acid rain and toxic wastes in the air. Washington also began "debt-for-nature swaps" wherein Third World nations willing to undertake major programs to protect the environment enjoyed some debt reduction.[225]

The UN Environmental Program kept "global commons" issues alive. Eighty-six nations agreed at Helsinki in mid-1989 to phase out the manufacture and use of

Deforestation of the Amazon.   The burning of tropical forests in order to open land to farming, grazing, and settlement has eliminated hundreds of plant and animal species. The clearing has also accelerated soil erosion and filled the atmosphere with carbon dioxide, one of the greenhouse gases causing global warming. In the years 1981–1990, more than 40 million acres of tropical forests were lost each year. The photograph on the left was taken by Skylab 2 in 1973 on a partly cloudy day in the Amazon basin. The photograph on the right, taken by the crew of the space shuttle *Discovery* in 1988, reveals the effects of burning as thick smoke covers the same area. (Courtesy of NASA)

ozone-destroying chemicals by the year 2000; by 1994 their efforts had reduced by half the *increase* in the concentration of CFCs in the atmosphere. Through the efforts of the World Health Organization (WHO), infectious diseases such as smallpox and malaria have nearly been eliminated. Combating the global spread of AIDS is the organization's next daunting task. Genetic-engineering programs funded by the World Bank hope to launch a "gene revolution" to improve farm productivity.[226] Finally, in 1991, twenty-six nations renewed the Antarctica Treaty of 1959—thus banning the dumping of nuclear waste on this frozen land, prohibiting oil exploration and mining, and preserving the area for scientific research, especially on global warming.

In early 1994 the State Department focused for the first time on the treatment of women in its annual human-rights report. Its grim findings included: forced sterilizations and abortions in China; coerced prostitution in Thailand and Burma; ritual genital mutilation in the Sudan and Somalia; females spending one-third as much time in school as males in Zaire; "dowry deaths" in India (husbands killing their wives because of insufficient dowries); laws making adultery illegal for women but not for men in Morocco and the Republic of the Congo. Half the world's people are women, said a State Department official, "and until you improve their situation, you're not going to improve human rights around the world."[227] The UN Children's Fund reported in 1992 that "in many countries, boys get better care than girls. As a result, an estimated 1 million girls die each year because they are born female."[228] The Worldwatch institute has estimated that medical complications relating to pregnancy kill 1 million women in Third World countries each year. Issues of equal rights for women and other gender issues necessarily climbed high on the world's agenda.

International communications issues also challenged leaders. Since the 1970s developing nations had been calling for a "New Information Order" in which the powerful developed nations would have to democratize access to information and to report news accurately and fairly. Third World critics charged that the control of information by developed nations—especially the United States—created dependency and retarded economic growth. These dissenters protested that because of its remote-sensing satellites, the United States could marshal greater information (data on weather and market conditions, mineral deposits, and agricultural output) than weaker states in negotiations on tariffs and other issues. American intelligence officers had high-tech devices, for example, that could home in on telephone conversations, telex and fax messages, and bank transfers around the world. Through the International Telecommunications Satellite Consortium (INTELSAT), founded in 1964 to coordinate the use of satellites, the United States has also preserved control of the majority of the electromagnetic spectrum for itself and its allies. Third World critics complained, too, that the mass communication system, dominated by American films, television, and syndicated news reports, preferred to report foreign events that were dramatic—often the aberrational or violent—and ignored deeply rooted traditions, long-term trends, or examples of achievement. Thus American ignorance has been perpetuated through false images of uncivilized foreigners; and cultural stereotypes have been formed that becloud reality and hence obstruct sound policymaking. One student of the Gulf War has written that "the ability of the

American-led coalition to drive its military message home and abroad by superior technology and by controlling international communications systems and news organizations had demonstrated . . . that the New World Order and the New Information Order had merged into one."[229] The questions of differential access to information and the use of outer space for telecommunications satellites crowded onto the long list of disputes discussed at international conferences.

Another aspect of communications technology revealed that powerful governments could be rendered powerless to silence critics who had easy access to inexpensive equipment for disseminating their messages. In the 1980s, videocassettes of American and Japanese newscasts of the assassination of Benigno Aquino were smuggled into the Philippines, where they were copied and distributed to home viewers. VCRs thus helped create the strong antigovernment sentiment that weakened and helped topple the dictatorship of Ferdinand Marcos, an American ally. In 1989 protesting Chinese students, cut off from most forms of communication by their government, listened to Voice of America radio broadcasts to follow events throughout China and used fax machines to communicate with the outside world. International revulsion against the Chinese crackdown was so extensive largely because the bloody events appeared on worldwide television. Communications technology, suggested some, played a central role in the revolutions of 1989 in Europe. With pocket radios, cassette players, VCRs, and portable television sets, more people had access to more information than ever before in world history. The increased flow of information seemed to possess the power to persuade governments to act. "Television images of starvation and privation will always tug at our emotions,"

American Decline, American Ignorance.
Peter C. Vey's cartoon speaks to a major point that "declinists" made to explain why U.S. power slipped: The American educational system needed reform. American students were ignorant of the wider world. A 1989 Gallup poll discovered that 14 percent of the American respondents could not pick out the United States on a world map and that 50 percent did not know that the Sandinistas and U.S.-backed *contras* were battling in Nicaragua. A 1990 Gallup survey found that one-third of the interviewees did not know whether the United States had fought on the side of the South Vietnamese or North Vietnamese in America's longest war. (P.C. Vey, reprinted from the *New York Times*)

Superpower in the New World Order. The United States' role in the post–Cold War world became unsettled, as Mike Keefe suggested in his 1992 cartoon. The United States could still wield massive military power, of course, but perhaps the USA needed other talents—especially economic competitiveness—to remain a superpower in world affairs.

(Courtesy of Mike Keefe, *The Denver Post*)

Anthony Lake admitted. But he warned that "CNN is not a compass for American interests. We cannot . . . respond to every crisis."[230] Former defense secretary James Schlesinger agreed, noting that "starvation continues in the Sudan or Mozambique, suppression in East Timor or India, ethnic war in parts of the former Soviet Union, but it is Somalia or Bosnia that draw the attention, because the cameras are there."[231]

As the 1990s began, the United States not only faced a global agenda of unusual complexity; it also had to deal with profound domestic problems. Americans ballyhooed victory in the Cold War and the triumph of capitalism. "So then why doesn't it feel better?" asked one journalist.[232] One reason was a decreasing competitive position in the world economy, and another was a federal debt that devoured revenues. The staggering trade deficit, urban decay, soaring health-care costs, stagnant productivity, and wobbly infrastructure reduced America's capacity to lead and serve as a model for the future. Georgi Arbatov, Russia's leading scholar of America, suggested that "both countries neglected their real problems, *inside* the country, and now have to pay for it. We have to pay more, you maybe less."[233] Whereas Bush had not, President Clinton acknowledged the point: "The currency of national strength in this new era will be denominated not only in ships and tanks and planes, but in diplomas and patents and paychecks."[234]

Still, even after the end of the Cold War, new arguments came from Clinton officials and others for old hegemonic policies, a major global if not interventionist role for the United States, and continued high-profile military readiness. First, it was argued, the end of the Cold War had not reduced the level of international threat. The world remained "a jungle filled with a bewildering variety of poisonous snakes," according to CIA director James Woolsey.[235] The National Security

Agency, which eavesdrops on potential enemies, laid off Russian speakers to hire specialists in Swahili and Farsi. Second, the end of Soviet-American bipolarity led to greater complexity and instability. "The real threat is the unknown," claimed Colin Powell, who urged vigilance and military preparedness.[236] Third, only the United States had the power to fashion global solutions. Fourth, the United States held a unique moral responsibility to uphold humanitarian ideals and serve human rights. Fifth, the United States could not pass up the opportunity to promote free-market capitalism in the wake of communism's demise. Sixth, because the U.S. economy intermeshed with the world economy, "we'll need to control the seas regardless of what happens in Moscow," as Secretary of Defense Richard Cheney once put it.[237]

Others made a seventh point about domestic economic imperatives. In 1992, for example, Representative Sam Gedjenson of Connecticut, one of the most liberal Democrats in Congress, fought to rescue the multibillion-dollar Seawolf submarine project after the Bush administration had cut it from the Pentagon budget. He battled to save a program that even the military wanted to eliminate. Why? Because the nuclear submarines were constructed at the Electric Boat shipyards in Groton, part of Gedjenson's home district, where cutbacks in defense spending meant high unemployment rates. As Bush had claimed: "If you throw another 50,000 kids on the street because of cutting recklessly in troop levels, you're going to put a lot more out of work."[238] Thus, despite promised reductions in military spending, the Pentagon budget was projected at $1.3 trillion for 1994–1998.

"Great tests" existed everywhere by the mid-1990s, Czech Republic president Václav Havel reminded Americans, because "everything is interrelated." Americans should know, he wrote, that "the future of the United States or the European Union is being decided in suffering Sarajevo or Mostar, in the plundered Brazilian rain forests, in the wretched poverty of Bangladesh or Somalia." When he implored Americans to exercise "global responsibility," they debated his meaning and his advice—much as they had done with other prescriptions throughout their history.[239]

FURTHER READING FOR THE PERIOD SINCE 1989

Some of the works listed in Chapter 11 also cover topics in this period.

For general assessments of George Bush, see William C. Berman, *America's Right Turn* (1994); Michael R. Beschloss and Strobe Talbott, *At the Highest Levels* (1993); Colin Campbell and Bert A. Rockman, *The Bush Presidency* (1991); Michael Duffy and Dan Goodgame, *Marching in Place* (1992); Fred Halliday, *From Kabul to Managua* (1989); and Richard A. Melanson, *Reconstructing Consensus* (1991).

For the dramatic changes in the Soviet Union and Eastern Europe, for why the Cold War ended, and for the consequences of these changes for U.S. foreign relations, see Timothy Garton Ash, *The Magic Lantern* (1990) and *The Uses of Adversity* (1989); David Armstrong and Erik Goldstein, eds., *The End of the Cold War* (1990); Anders Åslund, *Gorbachev's Struggle for Economic Reform* (1989); J. F. Brown, *Surge to Freedom* (1991); James Chace, *The Consequences of the Peace* (1992); Dusko Doder and Louise Branson, *Gorbachev* (1990); John Lewis Gaddis, *The United States and the End of the Cold War* (1992); Charles Gati, *The Bloc That Failed* (1990); Jeffrey E. Garten, *A Cold Peace* (1992); Ronald H. Hinckley, *People, Polls, and Policymakers* (1992); Michael Hogan, ed., *The End of the Cold War* (1992); Geoffrey Hosking, *The Awakening of the Soviet Union* (1990); William G. Hyland, *The Cold War Is Over* (1990); Robert Jervis and Seweryn Bialer, eds., *Soviet-American*

Relations after the Cold War (1991); Robert G. Kaiser, *Why Gorbachev Happened* (1991); William W. Kaufmann, *Glasnost, Perestroika, and U.S. Defense Spending* (1990); Charles W. Kegley, Jr., *The Long Postwar Peace* (1991); Richard Ned Lebow and Janice Gross Stein, *We All Lost the Cold War* (1993); Allen Lynch, *The Cold War Is Over—Again* (1992); Sean M. Lynn-Jones, ed., *The Cold War and After* (1991); Michael MccGwire, *Perestroika and Soviet National Security* (1991); Kenneth A. Oye et al., eds., *Eagle in a New World* (1992); Thomas G. Paterson, *On Every Front* (1992); Nicholas X. Rizopoulos, ed., *Sea-Changes* (1990); and Robert W. Tucker and David C. Henrickson, *The Imperial Temptation* (1992).

For Germany and reunification, see Timothy Garton Ash, *In Europe's Name* (1993); Michael A. Freney and Rebecca S. Hartley, *United Germany and the United States* (1991); Stephen F. Szabo, *The Diplomacy of German Unification* (1992); Gregory F. Treverton, *America, Germany, and the Future of Europe* (1992); and Peter Wyden, *Wall* (1989).

For the thesis that the United States has suffered decline, see David P. Calleo, *Beyond American Hegemony* (1987); Paul Kennedy, *The Rise and Fall of the Great Powers* (1987); Jim Hanson, *The Decline of the American Empire* (1993); Walter Russel Mead, *Mortal Splendor* (1987); Michael E. Porter, *The Competitive Advantage of Nations* (1990); and Thomas J. McCormick, *America's Half-Century* (1989). Critics of the declinist thesis are Joseph S. Nye, Jr., *Bound to Lead* (1990); Henry Nau, *The Myth of America's Decline* (1990); and Richard Rosecrance, *America's Economic Resurgence* (1990).

The United States in the international economy is treated in Richard J. Barnet and John Cavanagh, *Global Dreams: Imperial Corporations and the New World Order* (1994); Michael A. Bernstein and David E. Adler, eds., *Understanding American Economic Decline* (1994); Barry Eichengreen and Peter H. Lindert, eds., *The International Debt Crisis in Historical Perspective* (1990); Edward M. Graham and Paul Klugman, *Foreign Direct Investment in the United States* (1989); Otis L. Graham, *Losing Time: The Industrial Policy Debate* (1992); Gary G. Hufbauer and Jeffrey J. Schott, *North American Free Trade* (1992); Patrick Low, *Trading Free* (1993); and Wayne Sandholtz et al., *The Highest Stakes* (1993).

Environmental issues are explored in Richard E. Benedick, *Ozone Diplomacy* (1991); David E. Fisher, *Fire and Ice* (1990); Alexander King and Bertrand Schneider, *The First Global Revolution* (1991); Paul Klugman, *The Age of Diminished Expectations* (1990); Jim MacNeill et al., *Beyond Interdependence* (1991); Jessica T. Mathews, *Preserving the Global Environment* (1990); World Resources Institute, *Environmental Almanac* (1991); and Donald Worster, ed., *The Ends of the Earth* (1989).

Other topics on the international agenda for the United States are treated in William E. Burrows and Robert Windrem, *Critical Mass* (1994) (weapons development); Gil Loescher, *Beyond Charity* (1993) (refugees); Leonard S. Spector, *Nuclear Ambitions* (1990); Reed Ueda, *Postwar Immigrant America* (1994); and Donald Wilhelm, *Global Communications and Political Power* (1990).

For Japan, China, and Asia, see Chu-yuan Cheng, *Behind the Tiananmen Massacre* (1990); Stephen D. Cohen, *Cowboys and Samurai* (1991); Craig C. Garby and Mary Brown Bullock, eds., *Japan* (1994); John Gittings, *China Changes Face* (1990); Harry Harding, *A Fragile Relationship* (1992) (China); Sheila K. Johnson, *The Japanese Through American Eyes* (1990); Paul Klugman, ed., *Trade with Japan* (1992); Edward J. Lincoln, *Japan's Unequal Trade* (1990); Kenneth Pyle, *The Japanese Question* (1992); Jonathan Spence, *The Search for Modern China* (1990); and Lester Thurow, *Head to Head* (1992).

For Africa, see Michael Clough, *Free at Last?* (1992); Heidi Holland, *The Struggle* (1990) (ANC in South Africa); Jeffrey A. Lefebvre, *Arms for the Horn* (1991) (Ethiopia and Somalia); Fatima Meer, *Higher than Hope* (1990) (Mandela); and Peter J. Schraeder, *United States Foreign Policy Toward Africa* (1994).

The Palestinian question, Israel, and the Middle East are discussed in Deborah J. Gerner, *One Land, Two Peoples* (1990); F. Robert Hunter, *The Palestinian Uprising* (1991); Louis Kriesberg, *International Conflict Resolution* (1992); David McDowall, *Palestine and Israel* (1990); William B. Quandt, *Peace Process* (1993) and *The United States and Egypt* (1990); David Schoenbaum, *The United States and the State of Israel* (1993); and Daniel Yergin, *The Prize* (1991).

Iraqi-U.S. relations and the Persian Gulf War and its impact are the subject of Deborah Amos, *Lines in the Sand* (1992); Rick Atkinson, *Crusade* (1993); Lawrence Freedman and Efraim Karsh, *The Gulf Conflict* (1993); Stephen R. Graubard, *Mr. Bush's War* (1992); Efraim Karsh and Inari Rautsi, *Saddam Hussein* (1991);

John R. MacArthur, *Second Front* (1992) (censorship); Ken Matthews, *The Gulf Conflict and International Relations* (1993); Judith Miller and Laurie Mylroie, *Saddam Hussein* (1990); John Mueller, *Policy and Opinion in the Gulf War* (1994); Joseph S. Nye, Jr., and Roger K. Smith, eds., *After the Storm* (1992); Michael A. Palmer, *Guardians of the Gulf* (1992); Jean Edward Smith, *George Bush's War* (1992); Philip M. Taylor, *War and the Media* (1992); and Kenneth R. Timmerman, *The Death Lobby: How the West Armed Iraq* (1991).

For Canada, see Robert Bothwell, *Canada and the United States* (1992) and Seymour M. Lipset, *Continental Divide* (1990).

For U.S. relations with Latin America, see Jan S. Adams, *A Foreign Policy in Transition* (1992) (Central America); John Booth and Thomas Walker, *Understanding Latin America* (1993); Guy Gugliotta and Jeff Leen, *Kings of Cocaine* (1989); Susanne Jonas, *The Battle for Guatemala* (1991); Walter LaFeber, *Inevitable Revolutions* (1993); Abraham F. Lowenthal, *Partners in Conflict* (1990); Abraham F. Lowenthal and Katrina Burgess, eds., *The California-Mexico Connection* (1993); Donald J. Mabry, ed., *The Latin American Narcotics Trade and U.S. National Security* (1989); Christopher Mitchell, ed., *Western Hemisphere Immigration and United States Foreign Policy* (1992); Robert A. Pastor, *Integration with Mexico* (1993) and *Whirlpool* (1992); Brenda Gayle Plummer, *Haiti and the United States* (1992); Susan K. Purcell and Robert M. Immerman, ed., *Japan and Latin America in the New Global Order* (1992); W. Dirk Raat, *Mexico and the United States* (1992); Peter D. Scott and Jonathan Marshall, *Cocaine Politics: Drugs, Arms, and the CIA in Central America* (1991); Howard J. Wiarda, *American Foreign Policy toward Latin America in the 80s and 90s* (1992); and Sidney Weintraub et al., eds., *U.S.-Mexican Industrial Integration* (1991).

For Panama and the War against Noriega, consult Kevin Buckley, *Panama* (1991); John Dinges, *Our Man in Panama* (1990); Frederick Kempe, *Divorcing the Dictator* (1990); R. M. Koster and Guillermo Sanchez, *In The Time of the Tyrants* (1990); Walter LaFeber, *The Panana Canal* (1989); and Margaret E. Scranton, *The Noriega Years* (1991).

See also the General Bibliography and the following notes.

NOTES TO CHAPTER 12

1. *Newsweek, CXIV* (November 20, 1989), 28.
2. Christoph Hein, "East Berlin Diary," *New York Times Magazine,* December 17, 1989, p. 36.
3. Quoted in *Newsweek, CXIV* (November 20, 1989), 27.
4. Timothy Garton Ash, "The German Revolution," *New York Review of Books,* December 21, 1989, p. 14.
5. Quoted in *New York Times,* November 13, 1989.
6. Ash, "German Revolution," p. 14.
7. Quoted in Michael R. Beschloss and Strobe Talbott, *At the Highest Levels* (Boston: Little, Brown, 1993), p. 132.
8. Michael Meyer, "Days of the Whirlwind," *Newsweek, CXIV* (December 25, 1989), 27.
9. Quoted in *Time, CXXXIV* (November 20, 1989), 29; *Washington Post National Weekly Edition,* November 20–26, 1989.
10. *Time, CXXXIV* (November 20, 1989), 25.
11. Quoted in *Washington Post National Weekly Edition,* January 1–7, 1990.
12. Michael Howard, "The Springtime of Nations," *Foreign Affairs: America and the World, 1989/90, LXIX* (1990), 20.
13. Quoted in Richard Ned Lebow and Janice Gross Stein, "Reagan and the Russians," *The Atlantic Monthly, CCLXXIII* (February 1994), 36.
14. Quoted in Jim Hoagland, "Europe's Destiny," *Foreign Affairs: America and the World, 1989/90, LXIX* (1990), 38.
15. Quoted in Lucy Komisar, "Europe Erupts," *Bulletin of the Atomic Scientists, XLVI* (January–February 1990), 8.
16. Quoted in Amos Elon, "A Reporter at Large: Prague Autumn," *The New Yorker, LXV* (January 22, 1990), 130.
17. Quoted in Timothy Garton Ash, "The Revolution of the Magic Lantern," *New York Review of Books,* January 18, 1990, p. 42.
18. Blaine Harden and Mary Battiata, "A Revolution Built on Pride, Not Power," *Washington Post National Weekly Edition,* December 11–17, 1989.
19. Quoted in Elon, "Prague Autumn," 131.
20. Quoted in *New York Times,* February 23, 1990.
21. Quoted in *Time, CXXXV* (January 1, 1990), 53.
22. Quoted *ibid.,* p. 36.
23. Robert G. Kaiser, "The End of the Soviet Empire," *Washington Post National Weekly Edition,* January 1–7, 1990.
24. Quoted in *Time, CXXXV* (January 1, 1990), 50.
25. Quoted in Beschloss and Talbott, *Highest,* p. 134.
26. Quoted in *Newsweek, CXV* (January 8, 1990), 18.
27. Michael MccGwire, *Perestroika and Soviet National Security* (Washington, D.C.: Brookings, 1991), p. 205.
28. Quoted in *Great Decisions 1990* (New York: Foreign Policy Association, 1990), p. 5.
29. Quoted in Jane Kramer, "Letter from Europe," *The New Yorker, LXVI* (March 12, 1990), 82.

30. *Ibid.*, p. 81.
31. Quoted in Beschloss and Talbott, *Highest*, p. 296.
32. Quoted in *Hartford Courant*, December 13, 1991.
33. Quoted in Beschloss and Talbott, *Highest*, p. 466.
34. Richard J. Barnet, "Reflections: After the Cold War," *The New Yorker*, LXV (January 1, 1990), 66.
35. Quoted in Elizabeth Drew, "Letter from Washington," *ibid.*, LXV (November 22, 1989), 122.
36. Quoted in *Newsweek*, CXV (January 29, 1990), 35.
37. Quoted in *New York Times*, April 3, 1989.
38. Quoted in *Congressional Quarterly Weekly Reports*, XLVI (July 23, 1988), 2026.
39. Quoted in *Washington Post National Weekly Edition*, August 14–20, 1989.
40. Quoted in Beschloss and Talbott, *Highest*, p. 205.
41. *New York Times*, February 11, 1990.
42. Quoted in *Washington Post National Weekly Edition*, October 23–29, 1989.
43. Quoted in *Time*, CXXXII (August 1, 1988), 21.
44. Quoted in Beschloss and Talbott, *Highest*, p. 41.
45. Elizabeth Drew, "Letter from Washington," *The New Yorker*, LXVI (March 19, 1990), 104.
46. Quoted in Alan Tonelson, "Superpower Without a Sword," *Foreign Affairs*, LXXII (Summer 1993), 167.
47. Thomas L. Friedman in *New York Times*, November 28, 1993.
48. Quoted in Sidney Blumenthal, "Letter from Washington," *The New Yorker*, LXIX (January 24, 1994), 40.
49. Fred I. Greenstein, "The Presidential Leadership Style of Bill Clinton," *Political Science Quarterly*, CVIII (Winter 1993–1994), 593–594.
50. Quoted in *New York Times*, December 23, 1992.
51. Quoted in *Washington Post National Weekly Edition*, January 18–24, 1993.
52. Quoted *ibid.*, October 25–31, 1993.
53. Quoted in *Time*, CXL (November 30, 1992), 36.
54. Quoted in *Washington Post National Weekly Edition*, December 27, 1993–January 2, 1994.
55. Quoted in Richard Falk, "The Free Marketeers," *The Progressive*, LVIII (January 1994), 18.
56. Quoted in *Washington Post National Weekly Edition*, October 25–31, 1993.
57. Lee Hamilton quoted in Dick Kirschten, "How Will Bosnia Play This Fall," *National Journal*, XXVI (February 5, 1994), 336.
58. Thomas L. Friedman in *New York Times*, November 28, 1993.
59. *Ibid.*
60. Quoted in *New York Times*, September 28, 1993.
61. Arnold L. Horelick, "U.S.–Soviet Relations," *America and the World, 1989/90*, pp. 54–55.
62. Quoted in *New York Times*, April 9, 1989.
63. Quoted in Elizabeth Drew, "Letter from Washington," *The New Yorker*, LXV (January 1, 1990), 80.
64. Quoted in *New York Times*, May 14, 1989.
65. Quoted *ibid.*, May 25, 1989.
66. James A. Baker III, "Points of Mutual Advantage," speech, October 16, 1989, U.S. Department of State.
67. Quoted in *Washington Post National Weekly Edition*, December 11–17, 1989.
68. Quoted in *New York Times*, August 5, 1990.
69. Quoted in Beschloss and Talbott, *Highest*, p. 281.
70. Quoted *ibid.*, p. 318.
71. Quoted *ibid.*, p. 323.
72. Quoted *ibid.*, p. 415.
73. Quoted in William J. Crowe, Jr., *The Line of Fire* (New York: Simon and Schuster, 1993), p. 297.
74. Quoted in Beschloss and Talbott, *Highest*, p. 434.
75. Quoted in Leon Sigel, "The Last Cold War Election," *Foreign Affairs*, LXXI (Winter 1992/93), 7; *New York Times*, October 2, 1992.
76. Quoted in Alexei K. Pushkov, "Letter from Eurasia," *Foreign Policy*, No. 93 (Winter 1993–94), p. 83.
77. Quoted in Charles William Maynes, "A Workable Clinton Doctrine," *ibid.*, p. 3; Paul D. Wolfowitz, "Clinton's First Year," *Foreign Affairs*, LXXIII (January/February 1994), 41.
78. David Callahan, "The Tsar of Russia Policy," *Foreign Service Journal*, LXX (July 1993), 30.
79. Quoted in *Time*, CXLIII (January 17, 1994), 26.
80. Zbigniew Brzezinski, "The Premature Partnership," *Foreign Affairs*, LXXIII (March/April 1994), 67.
81. Philip Zelikov, "Beyond Boris Yeltsin," *ibid.*, LXXIII (January/February 1994), 48–49.
82. Stephen Sestanovich, "Russia Turns the Corner," *ibid.*, p. 11.
83. Jim Hoagland, "Europe's Destiny," *America and the World, 1989/90*, p. 41.
84. Quoted *ibid.*, 41–42.
85. Quoted in *New York Times*, February 13, 1990.
86. Richard Helms in *Hartford Courant*, March 4, 1990.
87. Quoted in *Newsweek*, CXV (February 26, 1990), 17.
88. Quoted in Elizabeth Drew, "Letter from Washington," *The New Yorker*, LXV (March 19, 1990), 104.
89. Quoted in *New York Times*, March 21, 1990.
90. Quoted in *Time*, CXXXV (June 4, 1990), 36.
91. Stanley Hoffmann, "Bush Abroad," *New York Review of Books*, November 5, 1992, p. 54.
92. Stephen R. Graubard, "A Common Discontent," *Foreign Affairs*, LXXII (Summer 1993), 5.
93. Joseph Joffe, "The New Europe," *Foreign Affairs: America and the World 1992/93*, LXXII (January 1993), 39.
94. Fritz Stern, "Freedom and Its Discontents," *Foreign Affairs*, LXXII (September/October 1993), 121.
95. Quoted in John T. Rourke, *International Politics on the World Stage* (Guilford, Conn.: Dushkin, 1993; 4th ed.), p. 170.
96. Mark Eyskens quoted in Bernard Lewis, "Rethinking the Middle East," *Foreign Affairs*, LXXI (Fall 1992), 108.

97. Rourke, *International Politics,* p. 324.
98. Quoted in *Time, CXXXV* (February 5, 1990), 31.
99. Quoted in *New York Times,* February 12, 1990.
100. Tokyo Sexwale quoted in *Washington Post National Weekly Edition,* February 26–March 6, 1994.
101. Quoted in *Time, CXXXVI* (July 2, 1990), 16.
102. Patrick Laurence, "After Victory, What?" *Africa Report* (January/February 1994), 63.
103. Brian Attwood quoted in *Boston Globe,* March 6, 1994.
104. Quoted in *Washington Post National Weekly Edition,* February 5–11, 1990.
105. Cheryl Payer quoted in *Great Decisions 1989* (New York: Foreign Policy Association, 1989), p. 30.
106. Harlan Cleveland, *Birth of a New World* (San Francisco: Jossey-Bass, 1993), p. 172.
107. Inter-American Dialogue, *Convergence and Community: The Americas in 1993* (Washington, D.C.: Aspen Institute, 1992), p. 9.
108. Quoted *ibid.,* p. 57.
109. Quoted in Morris J. Blachman and Kenneth E. Sharpe, "The War on Drugs," *World Policy Journal, VII* (Winter 1989–1990), 135.
110. Quoted in "The Talk of the Town," *The New Yorker, LXV* (January 1, 1990), 21.
111. Guy Gugliotta and Jeff Leen quoted in Michael Massing, "Desperate Over Drugs," *New York Review of Books,* March 30, 1989, p. 22.
112. Robert A. Pastor and Jorge G. Castañada, *Limits of Partnership* (New York: Alfred A. Knopf, 1988), p. 244.
113. Quoted in William O. Walker III, "Drug Control and National Security," *Diplomatic History, XII* (Spring 1988), 188.
114. Sol M. Linowitz, "Latin America," *Foreign Affairs, LXVII* (Winter 1988/89), 56.
115. Tom Miller, *On the Border* (1981), quoted in W. Dirk Raat, *Mexico and the United States* (Athens: University of Georgia Press, 1992), p. 173.
116. Norman A. Bailey quoted in *Newsweek, CXV* (January 15, 1990), 15–16.
117. Linda Robinson, "Dwindling Options in Panama," *Foreign Affairs, LXVIII* (Winter 1988/89), 191.
118. Quoted in *Washington Post National Weekly Edition,* December 25–31, 1989.
119. David S. Broder in *ibid.,* September 18–24, 1989.
120. Quoted *ibid.,* January 1–7, 1990.
121. Quoted in *Time, CXXXV* (January 1, 1990), 23.
122. Quoted in *Washington Post National Weekly Edition,* January 8–14, 1990.
123. Quoted in *Time, CXXXV* (January 1, 1990), 23.
124. George McGovern in *Washington Post,* January 16, 1990.
125. Quoted in *Time, CXXXV* (January 29, 1990), 28.
126. Quoted in *New York Times,* January 21, 1990.
127. Quoted in Deborah Amos, *Lines in the Sand* (New York: Simon and Schuster, 1992), p. 82.
128. Quoted in Thomas G. Paterson, *On Every Front* (New York: W. W. Norton, 1992; rev. ed.), p. 226.
129. Quoted in Hoffmann, "Bush Abroad," p. 56.
130. Quoted in Kenneth R. Timmerman, *The Death Lobby* (Boston: Houghton Mifflin, 1991), p. x.
131. Quoted in Lawrence Freedman and Efraim Karsh, *The Gulf Conflict, 1990–1991* (Princeton: Princeton University Press, 1993), p. 53.
132. Quoted in John T. Rourke, *Presidential Wars and American Democracy* (Washington, D.C.: Paragon, 1993), p. 14.
133. Jean Edward Smith, *George Bush's War* (New York: Holt, 1992), p. 169.
134. Quoted in Pierre Salinger and Eric Laurent, *Secret Dossier* (New York: Penguin, 1991), p. 110.
135. Quoted in Rourke, *Presidential Wars,* p. 47.
136. Rick Atkinson, *Crusade* (Boston: Houghton Mifflin, 1993), p. 55.
137. Quoted in *Hartford Courant,* January 13, 1991.
138. Quoted in Freedman and Karsh, *Gulf,* p. 293.
139. Quoted in Rourke, *Presidential Wars,* p. 59.
140. Quoted in Stephen E. Ambrose, *Rise to Globalism* (New York: Penguin, 1993; 7th rev. ed.), p. 387.
141. *Weekly Compilation of Presidential Documents, XXVII* (March 1, 1991), 233.
142. Quoted in Robert W. Tucker and David C. Hendrickson, *The Imperial Temptation* (New York: Council on Foreign Relations Press, 1992), p. 76.
143. Quoted in Atkinson, *Crusade,* p. 490.
144. Quoted *ibid.,* p. 491.
145. Freedman and Karsh, *Gulf,* p. 429.
146. Quoted in Atkinson, *Crusade,* p. 496.
147. Paul Kennedy, *The Rise and Fall of the Great Powers* (New York: Random House, 1987), p. 515.
148. Paul Kennedy in *New York Times,* April 17, 1988.
149. Samuel P. Huntington, "The U.S.—Decline or Renewal?" *Foreign Affairs, LXVII* (Winter 1988/89), 77.
150. *Wall Street Journal,* January 18, 1991.
151. Quoted in *New York Times,* March 2, 1991.
152. Atkinson, *Crusade,* p. 494.
153. Quoted in *Hartford Courant,* January 14, 1992.
154. George Mitchell quoted in *New York Times,* March 4, 1991.
155. Quoted in Tucker and Hendrickson, *Temptation,* p. 29.
156. Quoted in Atkinson, *Crusade,* p. 500.
157. James Baker, "Principles and Pragmatism," May 22, 1989, Department of State Current Policy No. 1176.
158. Quoted in Amos Elon, "A Visit with Arafat," *New York Review of Books,* August 12, 1993, p. 28.
159. Jan Egeland quoted in *Washington Post National Weekly Edition,* September 6–12, 1993.
160. Oded Ben-Ami quoted in *Time, CXLII* (September 27, 1993), 28.
161. Quoted in Sidney Blumenthal, "Letter from Washington," *The New Yorker, LXIX* (October 4, 1993), 74.
162. Quoted in *New York Times,* March 6, 1994.

163. Quoted in *Time*, CXLI (January 18, 1993), 34; Brit Hume, "The Making of a Quagmire," *National Review*, XLV (November 1, 1993), 21.

164. Quoted in *Washington Post National Weekly Edition*, December 14–20, 1992.

165. Quoted in Glenn Hastedt, ed., *American Foreign Policy 94/95* (Guilford, Conn.: Dushkin, 1994), p. 156.

166. Quoted in John R. Bolton, "Wrong Turn in Somalia," *Foreign Affairs*, LXXIII (January/February 1994), 59.

167. Quoted in *Washington Post National Weekly Edition*, October 26–November 1, 1993.

168. Quoted in Jeffrey A. Lefebvre, *Arms for the Horn* (Pittsburgh: University of Pittsburgh Press, 1991), p. 214.

169. Quoted *ibid.*, p. 272.

170. T. Frank Crigler quoted in *Washington Post National Weekly Edition*, October 26–November 1, 1993.

171. Quoted in *New York Times*, May 6, 1993.

172. Madeline Albright quoted in Bolton, "Wrong," p. 62.

173. Quoted in *Washington Post National Weekly Edition*, October 18–24, 1993.

174. Quoted in *Time*, CXLII (October 18, 1993), 38.

175. Quoted in *Hartford Courant*, October 4, 1993.

176. Quoted in *New York Times*, October 8, 1993.

177. Lance Morrow in *Time*, CXLII (October 18, 1993), 39.

178. Quoted in John Newhouse, "No Exit, No Entrance," *The New Yorker*, LXIX (June 28, 1993), 44.

179. Andrew Bell-Fialkoff, "A Brief History of Ethnic Cleansing," *Foreign Affairs*, LXXII (Summer 1993), 120.

180. Quoted in Richard J. Barnet, "Groping for a Security Blanket," *The Progressive*, LVIII (January 1994), 21.

181. Quoted in *New York Times*, October 12, 1992.

182. Quoted in Newhouse, "No Exit," 46.

183. Quoted in *Time*, CXLI (May 3, 1993), 48.

184. Quoted in *New York Times*, April 26, 1993.

185. Quoted in Newhouse, "No Exit," p. 48.

186. Quoted in *Time*, CXLI (May 10, 1993), 49.

187. Marshall Freeman Harris quoted in *U.S. News & World Report*, CXV (August 16, 1993), 40.

188. Christopher Hitchens in *Washington Post National Weekly Edition*, August 23–29, 1993.

189. Quoted in *Time*, CXLI (August 16, 1993), 31.

190. Winston Lord, "China and America," *Foreign Affairs*, LXVIII (Fall 1989), 3.

191. Quoted in Roderick MacFarquhar, "The End of the Chinese Revolution," *New York Review of Books*, July 20, 1989, p. 8.

192. Quoted in John Fincher, "Zhao's Fall, China's Loss," *Foreign Policy*, No. 76 (Fall 1989), p. 24.

193. John K. Fairbank, "Why China's Rulers Fear Democracy," *New York Review of Books*, September 28, 1989, p. 33.

194. Quoted in *Newsweek*, CXV (January 29, 1990), 35.

195. Quoted in "The Talk of the Town," *The New Yorker*, LXV (December 25, 1989), 31.

196. Yoichi Funabashi, "The Asianization of Asia," *Foreign Affairs*, LXXII (November/December 1993), 85.

197. Quoted in *New York Times*, August 14, 1992.

198. Quoted in *Hartford Courant*, March 13, 1994.

199. Nicholas D. Kristof, "The Rise of China," *Foreign Affairs*, LXXII (November/December 1993), 73.

200. Lee Kuan Yew quoted *ibid.*, p. 74.

201. Quoted in Robert B. Oxnam, "Asia/Pacific Challenges," *Foreign Affairs: America and the World 1992/93*, LXXII (January 1993), 71.

202. Quoted in *New York Times*, February 6, 1994.

203. Quoted in James Fallows, "Getting Along with Japan," *The Atlantic Monthly*, CCLXIV (December 1989), 55.

204. Noboru Takeshita quoted in *Great Decisions 1990*, p. 18.

205. Maymi Itoh, "Japanese Perceptions of the United States," *Asian Survey*, XXXIII (December 1993), 1123.

206. Quoted in *Washington Post National Weekly Edition*, February 26–March 4, 1990, March 5–11, 1990.

207. Robert A. Scalapino, "Asia and the United States," *America and the World, 1989/90*, p. 105.

208. Quoted in *New York Times*, February 6, 1994.

209. Quoted in *Washington Post National Weekly Edition*, February 28–March 6, 1994.

210. Quoted in *Time*, CXLII (July 5, 1993), 20.

211. Thomas L. Friedman quoted in *New York Times*, March 6, 1994.

212. Quoted in *Washington Post National Weekly Edition*, October 25–31, 1993.

213. Anthony Lake, "Confronting Backlash States," *Foreign Affairs*, LXXIII (March/April 1994), 55.

214. Quoted in *Great Decisions 1990*, p. 48.

215. Tim Weiner, "Blowback From the Afghan Battlefield," *New York Times Magazine*, March 13, 1994, p. 53.

216. Richard J. Kerr quoted in Seymour M. Hersh, "On the Nuclear Edge," *The New Yorker*, LXIX (March 29, 1993), 55.

217. Quoted in *Newsweek*, CXXIII (February 21, 1994), 29.

218. Michael Shapiro, "Kim's Ransom," *ibid.* (January 31, 1994), p. 32.

219. Lake, "Confronting," p. 45.

220. Strobe Talbott in *Time*, CXXXV (January 1, 1990), 72.

221. Alan B. Durning, "Ending Poverty," in Lester R. Brown, *State of the World 1990* (New York: W. W. Norton, 1990), p. 134.

222. World Resources Institute, *Environmental Almanac* (Boston: Houghton Mifflin, 1992), p. 13.

223. José Sarney quoted in *New York Times*, May 2, 1989.

224. Quoted in *Time*, CXXXIII (January 2, 1989), 30.

225. James Baker, "Diplomacy for the Environment," February 26, 1990, Department of State Current Policy No. 1254.

226. Quoted in Cleveland, *Birth*, p. 46.

227. Nancy Ely-Raphael quoted in *New York Times*, February 3, 1994.

228. Quoted in Rourke, *International Politics*, p. 561.

229. Philip M. Taylor, *War and the Media* (Manchester, Eng.: Manchester University Press, 1992), p. 266.

230. Quoted in *Washington Post National Weekly Edition*, December 27–January 2, 1994.

231. James Schlesinger, "The Quest for a Post–Cold War Foreign Policy," *Foreign Affairs: America and the World, 1992/93, LXXII* (January 1993), 18.

232. Maureen Dowd in *New York Times*, March 4, 1990.

233. Quoted in *Boston Globe*, September 20, 1992.

234. Quoted in Jonathan Clarke, "The Conceptual Poverty of U.S. Foreign Policy," *The Atlantic Monthly, CCLXXII* (September 1993), 62.

235. Quoted *ibid.*, p. 56.

236. Quoted in "Comment: The Economics of Peace," *The New Yorker, LXIX* (April 9, 1993), 4.

237. Quoted in *Hartford Courant*, April 5, 1990.

238. Quoted in Sigel, "Last," p. 12.

239. Václav Havel, "A Call for Sacrifice," *Foreign Affairs, LXIII* (March/April 1994), 7.

APPENDIX

Makers of American Foreign Relations

Presidents	Secretaries of State	Chairs of the Senate Foreign Relations Committee
George Washington (1789–1797)	Thomas Jefferson (1790–1794) Edmund Randolph (1794–1795) Timothy Pickering (1795–1800)	
John Adams (1797–1801)	Timothy Pickering (1795–1800) John Marshall (1800–1801)	
Thomas Jefferson (1801–1809)	James Madison (1801–1809)	
James Madison (1809–1817)	Robert Smith (1809–1811) James Monroe (1811–1817)	James Barbour (1816–1818)
James Monroe (1817–1825)	John Quincy Adams (1817–1825)	James Barbour (1816–1818) Nathaniel Macon (1818–1819) James Brown (1819–1820) James Barbour (1820–1821) Rufus King (1821–1822) James Barbour (1822–1825)
John Quincy Adams (1825–1829)	Henry Clay (1825–1829)	Nathaniel Macon (1825–1826) Nathan Sanford (1826–1827) Nathaniel Macon (1827–1828) Littleton W. Tazewell (1828–1832)
Andrew Jackson (1829–1837)	Martin Van Buren (1829–1831) Edward Livingston (1831–1833) Louis McLane (1833–1834) John Forsyth (1834–1841)	Littleton W. Tazewell (1828–1832) John Forsyth (1832–1833) William Wilkins (1833–1834) Henry Clay (1834–1836) James Buchanan (1836–1841)
Martin Van Buren (1837–1841)	John Forsyth (1834–1841)	James Buchanan (1836–1841)
William H. Harrison (1841)	Daniel Webster (1841–1843)	William C. Rives (1841–1842)
John Tyler (1841–1845)	Daniel Webster (1841–1843)	William C. Rives (1841–1842)

Makers of American Foreign Relations *(continued)*

Presidents	Secretaries of State	Chairs of the Senate Foreign Relations Committee
	Abel P. Upshur (1843–1844)	William S. Archer (1842–1845)
	John C. Calhoun (1844–1845)	
James K. Polk (1845–1849)	James Buchanan (1845–1849)	William Allen (1845–1846)
		Ambrose H. Sevier (1846–1848)
		Edward A. Hannegan (1848–1849)
		Thomas H. Benton (1849)
Zachary Taylor (1849–1850)	John M. Clayton (1849–1850)	William R. King (1849–1850)
Millard Fillmore (1850–1853)	Daniel Webster (1850–1852)	Henry S. Foote (1850–1851)
	Edward Everett (1852–1853)	James M. Mason (1851–1861)
Franklin Pierce (1853–1857)	William L. Marcy (1853–1857)	James M. Mason (1851–1861)
James Buchanan (1857–1861)	Lewis Cass (1857–1860)	James M. Mason (1851–1861)
	Jeremiah S. Black (1860–1861)	
Abraham Lincoln (1861–1865)	William H. Seward (1861–1869)	Charles Sumner (1861–1871)
Andrew Johnson (1865–1869)	William H. Seward (1861–1869)	Charles Sumner (1861–1871)
Ulysses S. Grant (1869–1877)	Elihu B. Washburne (1869)	Charles Sumner (1861–1871)
	Hamilton Fish (1869–1877)	Simon Cameron (1871–1877)
Rutherford B. Hayes (1877–1881)	William M. Evarts (1877–1881)	Hannibal Hamlin (1877–1879)
		William W. Eaton (1879–1881)
James A. Garfield (1881)	James G. Blaine (1881)	Ambrose E. Burnside (1881)
		George F. Edmunds (1881)
Chester A. Arthur (1881–1885)	Frederick T. Frelinghuysen (1881–1885)	William Windom (1881–1883)
		John F. Miller (1883–1887)
Grover Cleveland (1885–1889)	Thomas F. Bayard (1885–1889)	John F. Miller (1883–1887)
		John Sherman (1887–1893)
Benjamin Harrison (1889–1893)	James G. Blaine (1889–1892)	John Sherman (1887–1893)
	John W. Foster (1892–1893)	
Grover Cleveland (1893–1897)	Walter Q. Gresham (1893–1895)	John T. Morgan (1893–1895)
	Richard Olney (1895–1897)	John Sherman (1895–1897)
William McKinley (1897–1901)	John Sherman (1897–1898)	William P. Frye (1897)
	William R. Day (1898)	Cushman K. Davis (1897–1901)
	John Hay (1898–1905)	
Theodore Roosevelt (1901–1909)	John Hay (1898–1905)	William P. Frye (1901)
	Elihu Root (1905–1909)	Shelby M. Cullom (1901–1913)
	Robert Bacon (1909)	
William Howard Taft (1909–1913)	Philander C. Knox (1909–1913)	Shelby M. Cullom (1901–1913)

Makers of American Foreign Relations *(continued)*

Presidents	Secretaries of State	Chairs of the Senate Foreign Relations Committee
Woodrow Wilson (1913–1921)	William Jennings Bryan (1913–1915) Robert Lansing (1915–1920) Bainbridge Colby (1920–1921)	Augustus O. Bacon (1913–1915) William J. Stone (1915–1919) Henry Cabot Lodge (1919–1924)
Warren G. Harding (1921–1923)	Charles E. Hughes (1921–1925)	Henry Cabot Lodge (1919–1924)
Calvin Coolidge (1923–1929)	Charles E. Hughes (1921–1925) Frank. B. Kellogg (1925–1929)	Henry Cabot Lodge (1919–1924) William E. Borah (1925–1933)
Herbert C. Hoover (1929–1933)	Henry L. Stimson (1929–1933)	William E. Borah (1925–1933)
Franklin D. Roosevelt (1933–1945)	Cordell Hull (1933–1944) Edward R. Stettinius, Jr. (1944–1945)	Key Pittman (1933–1941) Walter F. George (1941) Tom Connally (1941–1947)

Presidents	Secretaries of State	Chairs of the Senate Foreign Relations Committee	Secretaries of Defense	Assistants to the President for National Security Affairs
Harry S. Truman (1945–1953)	Edward R. Stettinius, Jr. (1944–1945) James F. Byrnes (1945–1947) George C. Marshall (1947–1949) Dean G. Acheson (1949–1953)	Tom Connally (1941–1947) Arthur H. Vandenberg (1947–1949) Tom Connally (1949–1953)	James V. Forrestal (1947–1949) Louis A. Johnson (1949–1950) George C. Marshall (1950–1951) Robert A. Lovett (1951–1953)	
Dwight D. Eisenhower (1953–1961)	John F. Dulles (1953–1959) Christian A. Herter (1959–1961)	Alexander Wiley (1953–1955) Walter F. George (1955–1957) Theodore F. Green (1957–1959) J. W. Fulbright (1959–1975)	Charles E. Wilson (1953–1957) Neil H. McElroy (1957–1959) Thomas S. Gates, Jr. (1959–1961)	Robert Cutler (1953–1955; 1957–1958) Dillon Anderson (1955–1956) William H. Jackson (1956) Gordon Gray (1958–1961)
John F. Kennedy (1961–1963)	Dean Rusk (1961–1969)	J. W. Fulbright (1959–1975)	Robert S. McNamara (1961–1968)	McGeorge Bundy (1961–1966)
Lyndon B. Johnson (1963–1969)	Dean Rusk (1961–1969)	J. W. Fulbright (1959–1975)	Robert S. McNamara (1961–1968) Clark M. Clifford (1968–1969)	McGeorge Bundy (1961–1966) Walt W. Rostow (1966–1969)

Makers of American Foreign Relations *(continued)*

Presidents	Secretaries of State	Chairs of the Senate Foreign Relations Committee	Secretaries of Defense	Assistants to the President for National Security Affairs
Richard M. Nixon (1969–1974)	William P. Rogers (1969–1973) Henry A. Kissinger (1973–1977)	J. W. Fulbright (1959–1975)	Melvin R. Laird (1969–1973) Elliot L. Richardson (1973) James R. Schlesinger (1973–1976)	Henry A. Kissinger (1969–1975)
Gerald R. Ford (1974–1977)	Henry A. Kissinger (1973–1977)	J. W. Fulbright (1959–1975) John Sparkman (1975–1979)	James R. Schlesinger (1973–1976) Donald Rumsfeld (1976–1977)	Henry A. Kissinger (1969–1975) Brent Scowcroft (1975–1977)
Jimmy Carter (1977–1981)	Cyrus R. Vance (1977–1980) Edmund Muskie (1980–1981)	John Sparkman (1975–1979) Frank Church (1979–1981)	Harold Brown (1977–1981)	Zbigniew Brzezinski (1977–1981)
Ronald Reagan (1981–1989)	Alexander M. Haig, Jr. (1981–1982) George P. Shultz (1982–1989)	Charles Percy (1981–1985) Richard G. Lugar (1985–1987) Claiborne Pell (1987–)	Caspar Weinberger (1981–1987) Frank C. Carlucci (1987–1989)	Richard Allen (1981) William P. Clark, Jr. (1981–1983) Robert C. McFarlane (1983–1985) John M. Poindexter (1985–1986) Frank C. Carlucci (1986–1987) Colin L. Powell (1987–1989)
George Bush (1989–1993)	James A. Baker III (1989–1992) Lawrence Eagleburger (1992–1993)	Claiborne Pell (1987–)	Richard B. Cheney (1989–1993)	Brent Scowcroft (1989–1993)
Bill Clinton (1993–)	Warren M. Christopher (1993–)	Claiborne Pell (1987–)	Les Aspin (1993–1994) William J. Perry (1994–)	Anthony Lake (1993–)

General Bibliography

General Reference Works

See also countries, regions, and subjects in "Overviews" below and your library's computerized data bases.

Annual Surveys and Chronologies: Lester H. Brune, *Chronological History of U.S. Foreign Relations* (1985, 1991); Council on Foreign Relations, *Foreign Affairs Chronology, 1978–1989* (1990) and *The United States in World Affairs* (1932–1972); Robert H. Ferrell and John S. Bowman, eds., *The Twentieth Century* (1984); Bernard Grun, *The Timetables of History* (1991); *Keesing's Record of World Events* (1931–); London Institute of World Affairs, *The Yearbook of World Affairs* (1947–); Thomas Parker and Douglas Nelson, *Day by Day: The Sixties* (1983); Alan F. Pater and Jason R. Pater, eds., *What They Said In . . . : The Yearbook of World Opinion* (1971–); *Political Handbook of the World* (1928–); Royal Institute of International Affairs, *Survey of International Affairs, 1920–1963* (1972–1977); *The Statesmen's Year-Book World Gazetteer* (1864–); United Nations, *Demographic Yearbook* (1948–).

Atlases and Gazetteers: Ewan W. Anderson and Don Shewan, *An Atlas of World Political Flashpoints* (1993); Andrew Boyd, *An Atlas of World Affairs* (1992); Anna Bramwall, *The Atlas of Twentieth Century History* (1989); Gérard Chaliand and Jean-Pierre Rageau, *Strategic Atlas* (1990); *Hammond Atlas of the World* (1992); Robert Ferrell and Richard Natkiel, *Atlas of American History* (1987); Michael Kidron and Daniel Smith, *The New State of War and Peace* (1991); George Kurian, *Atlas of the Third World* 1983; Catherine Mattson and Mark T. Mattson, *Contemporary Atlas of the United States* (1990); David Munro, ed., *Chambers World Gazetteer* (1988); National Geographic Society, *Historical Atlas of the United States* (1988); *National Geographic Atlas of the World* (1992); Richard Natkiel et al., eds., *Atlas of the Twentieth Century* (1982); *The New York Times Atlas of the World* (1992); *Oxford Atlas of the World* (1992); Rand McNally, *Today's World* (1992); *The Times Atlas of World History* (1992); Andrew Wheatcroft, *The World Atlas of Revolutions* (1983).

Bibliographies: Samuel Flagg Bemis and Grace Gardner Griffin, *Guide to the Diplomatic History of the United States, 1775–1921* (1935); Richard Dean Burns, ed. *A Guide to American Foreign Relations Since 1700* (1982); Council on Foreign Relations, *Foreign Affairs Bibliography* (1933–1972); Byron Dexter, ed., *The Foreign Affairs 50-Year Bibliography* (1972); Wilton B. Fowler, *American Diplomatic History Since 1890* (1975); Frank Freidel, ed., *Harvard Guide to Amer-*

ican History (1974); Norman A. Graebner, ed., *American Diplomatic History Before 1900* (1978); Linda Killen and Richard L. Lael, *Versailles and After* (1983); David B. Knight and Maureen Davies, *Self-Determination* (1988); Francis P. Prucha, *Handbook for Research in American History* (1987). The journal *Diplomatic History* regularly publishes articles that review the historiography of major topics and periods and provide extensive bibliographical guidance. The *Journal of American History* regularly lists recent publications in the field.

Biographies: David Crystal, ed., *The Cambridge Biographical Encyclopedia* (1994); *Current Biography* (1940–); *Dictionary of American Biography* (1928–); John A. Garraty, ed., *Encyclopedia of American Biography* (1974); Bernard K. Johnpoll and Harvey Klehr, eds., *Biographical Dictionary of the American Left* (1986); *International Who's Who* (1935–); Warren F. Kuehl, ed., *Biographical Dictionary of Internationalists* (1983); Philip Rees, *Biographical Dictionary of the Extreme Right Since 1890* (1991); Frank W. Thackery and John E. Findling, eds., *Statesmen Who Changed the World* (1993); *Who's Who in America* (1899–); *Who's Who in the World* (1971–).

Encyclopedias: Alexander DeConde, ed., *Encyclopedia of American Foreign Policy* (1978); Margaret Denning and J. K. Sweeney, *Handboook of American Diplomacy* (1992); John Drexel, ed., *The Facts on File Encyclopedia of the 20th Century* (1991); Graham Evans and Jeffrey Newnham, eds., *The Dictionary of World Politics* (1990); John E. Findling, *Dictionary of American Diplomatic History* (1989); Stephen A. Flanders and Carl N. Flanders, *Dictionary of American Foreign Affairs* (1991); Jack P. Greene, ed., *Encyclopedia of American Political History* (1984); Joel Krieger et al., eds., *The Oxford Companion to the Politics of the World* (1993); Richard B. Morris, *Encyclopedia of American History* (1982); Jack C. Plano and Ray Olton, *The International Relations Dictionary* (1988); Jack E. Vincent, *A Handbook of International Relations* (1968).

Statistics: Erik W. Austin and Jerome C. Clubb, *Political Facts of the United States Since 1789* (1986); Ruth L. Sivard, *World Military and Social Expenditures* (1974–); Victor Showers, *World Facts and Figures* (1989); Charles L. Taylor and David A. Jodice, *World Handbook of Political and Social Indicators* (1983); U.S. Agency for International Development, *United States Overseas Loans and Grants and Assistance from International Organizations, July 1, 1945–Sept. 30, 1980* (1981); U.S. Bureau of the Census, *Historical Statistics of the United States* (1975) and *Statistical Abstract of the United States* (1879–   ); U.S. Central Intelligence Agency, *The World Factbook* (1981–   ).

Overviews of Relations with Countries and Regions, including Atlases (A), Annual Surveys (AS), Bibliographies (B), Biographical Dictionaries (BD), Chronologies (C), Encyclopedias (E), and Statistics (S)

See also U.S. Library of Congress book-length "country studies" which provide extensive historical and current information on most nations of the world.

Afghanistan: Anthony Arnold, *Afghanistan* (1985); Henry S. Bradsher, *Afghanistan and the Soviet Union* (1985); Louis Dupree, *Afghanistan* (1973); B. S. Gupta, *Afghanistan* (1986); Nancy P. Newell and Richard S. Newell, *The Struggle for Afghanistan* (1981); Stanley Wolpert, *Roots of Confrontation in South Asia: Afghanistan, Pakistan, India & the Superpowers* (1982).

Africa: Edward W. Chester, *Clash of Titans* (1974); Peter Duignan and Lewis H. Gann, *The United States and Africa* (1987); Lawrence C. Howard, *American Involvement in Africa South of the Sahara, 1800–1860* (1988); Henry F. Jackson, *From the Congo to Soweto* (1982); Colin Legum, ed., *Africa Contemporary Record* (1968–   ) (AS); Michael McCarthy, *Dark Continent* (1983); Lysle E. Meyer, *The Farther Frontier* (1992); Peter J. Schraeder, *United States Foreign Policy Toward Africa* (1994); Elliot P. Skinner, *African-Americans and U.S. Policy Toward Africa, 1850–1924* (1992). See also individual countries.

Alaska: Paul S. Holbo, *Tarnished Expansion* (1983); Ronald J. Jensen, *The Alaska Purchase* (1975); Walter A. McDougall, *Let the Sea Make a Noise* (1993). Also see Kushner in "Russia and the Soviet Union."

Algeria: See "North Africa."

Angola: Lawrence W. Henderson, *Angola* (1979); John A. Marcum, *The Angolan Revolution* (1969, 1978); Kenneth Mokoena and Nicole Gaymon, eds., *The Angola Crises* (1991). See also "Africa."

Antarctica: Peter J. Beck, *The International Politics of Antarctica* (1986); Christopher C. Joyner and Sudhir K. Chopra, eds., *The Antarctic Legal Regime* (1989); Frank G. Klotz, *America on the Ice* (1990); Jeffrey D. Myhre, *The Antarctic Treaty System* (1986).

Argentina: David Rock, *Argentina* (1985); Harold F. Peterson, *Argentina and the United States* (1964); Joseph Tulchin, *Argentina and the United States* (1990); Arthur P. Whitaker, *The United States and the Southern Cone* (1976). See also "Latin America."

Asia and the Pacific: Alexander Besher, *The Pacific Rim Almanac* (1991) (E); Jessica S. Brown et al., eds., *The United States in East Asia* (1985) (B); I. C. Campbell, *A History of the Pacific Islands* (1989); Sucheng Chan, *Asian-Americans* (1991); Warren I. Cohen, ed., *New Frontiers in American–East Asian Relations* (1983); Arthur P. Dudden, *The American Pacific* (1992); Ainslie T. Embree, *Encyclopedia of Asian History* (1988) (E); Roger W. Gale, *The Americanization of Micronesia* (1979); Selig S. Harrison, *The Widening Gulf: Asian Nationalism and American Policy* (1978); Akira Iriye, *Across the Pacific* (1967); Ernest R. May and James C. Thomson, Jr., eds., *American–East Asian Relations* (1973); Deryck Scarr, *The History of the Pacific Islands* (1990); Gerald Segal, *Rethinking the Pacific* (1990); James C. Thomson, Jr., et al., *Sentimental Imperialists* (1981). See also individual countries.

Australia: Glen St. John Barclay, *Friends in High Places* (1985); Norman Bartlett, *Australia and America Through 200 Years* (1976); Norman Harper, *A Great and Powerful Friend* (1987); Trevor R. Reese, *Australia, New Zealand, and the United States* (1969). See also "Asia and the Pacific."

Austria: Audrey K. Cronin, *Great Power Politics and the Struggle over Austria, 1945–1955* (1986); Barbara Jelavich, *Modern Austria* (1988); Karl S. Stadler, *Austria* (1971). See also "Europe."

Bangladesh: See Brown in "India."

Belgium: Frank E. Hugget, *Modern Belgium* (1969). See also "Europe."

Bolivia: Lawrence Whitehead, *The United States and Bolivia* (1969); J. W. Wilkie, *The Bolivian Revolution and U.S. Aid Since 1952* (1969). See also "Latin America" and Pike in "Peru."

Brazil: Jan Black, *United States Penetration of Brazil* (1977); Elizabeth A. Cobbs, *The Rich Neighbor Policy: Rockefeller and Kaiser in Brazil* (1992); Roger W. Fontaine, *Brazil and the United States* (1974); Stanley Hilton, *Brazil and the Great Powers* (1975); Ruth Leacock, *Requiem for Revolution* (1990); Frank McCann, *The Brazilian-American Alliance, 1937–1945* (1973); Joseph Smith, *Unequal Giants* (1991); W. Michael Weis, *Cold Warriors and Coups d'etat* (1993); Robert Wesson, *The United States & Brazil* (1981). See also "Latin America."

Burma: John F. Cady, *The United States and Burma* (1976).

Cambodia: David P. Chandler, *The Tragedy of Cambodian History* (1991); Michael Haas, *Cambodia, Pol Pot, and the United States* (1991); Prakash C. Pradhan, *Foreign Policy of Kampuchea* (1983); William Shawcross, *The Quality of Mercy* (1984). See also "Southeast Asia."

Cameroon: Julius A. Amin, *The Peace Corps in Cameroon* (1992); Mark DeLancy, *Cameroon* (1989). See also "Africa."

Canada: J. B. Brebner, *North Atlantic Triangle* (1966); Robert Bothwell, *Canada and the United States* (1992); Charles Doran, *Forgotten Partnership* (1984); Charles Doran and John H. Sigler, *Canada and the United States* (1985); William T. Fox, *A Continent Apart* (1985); Jack Granatstein and Robert Bothwell, *Pirouette* (1990); Lansing Lamont and Duncan Edmonds, eds., *Friends So Different* (1989); Seymour Martin Lipset, *Continental Divide* (1990); Lawrence Martin, *The Presidents and the Prime Ministers* (1982); J.F. Rooney, Jr., et. al., eds., *This Remarkable Continent* (1982) (A); Reginald C. Stuart, *United States Expansionism and British North America, 1775–1871* (1988).

Caribbean: David Healy, *Drive to Hegemony* (1988); Lester D. Langley, *Struggle for the American Mediterranean: United States–European Rivalry and the Caribbean, 1900–1970* (1976) and *The United States and the Caribbean in the Twentieth Century* (1989); Whitney T. Perkins, *Constraint of Empire* (1981). See also "Central America," "Latin America," and individual countries.

Central America: Thomas P. Anderson, *Politics in Central America* (1982); Morris J. Blachman et al., eds., *Confronting Revolution* (1986); John Booth and Thomas Walker, *Understanding Central America* (1993); John Coatsworth, *Central America and the United States* (1994); Kenneth M. Coleman and George C. Herring, eds., *Understanding the Central American Crisis* (1991); John E. Findling, *Close Neighbors, Distant Friends* (1987); Phil Gunson et al., eds., *The Dictionary of Contemporary Politics of Central America and the Caribbean* (1991) (E); Walter LaFeber, *Inevitable Revolutions* (1993); Thomas M. Leonard, *Central America and the United States* (1991) and *Central America and U.S. Policies, 1820s–1980s* (1985) (B); Thomas D. Schoonover, *The United States in Central America, 1860–1911* (1991); Ralph L. Woodward, *Central America* (1985). See also "Caribbean," "Latin America," and individual countries.

Chile: Michael Monteón, *Chile in the Nitrate Era* (1982); Frederick B. Pike, *Chile and the United States, 1880–1962* (1963); William F. Sater, *Chile and the United States* (1990); Paul E. Sigmund, *The United States and Democracy in Chile* (1993). See also "Latin America" and Whitaker in "Argentina."

China (and Taiwan): Gordon Chang, *Friends and Enemies* (1990); Warren I. Cohen, *America's Response to China* (1990); John K. Fairbank, *China Perceived* (1974) and *The United States and China* (1983); John Gittings, *The World and China, 1922–1972* (1974); Jonathan Goldstein et al., eds., *America Views China* (1991); Harry Harding, *A Fragile Relationship* (1992); Michael H. Hunt, *The Making of a Special Relationship* (1983); Arnold Xiangze Jiang, *The United States and China* (1988); Ernest R. May and John K. Fairbank, eds., *America's*

China Trade in Historical Perspective (1986); Stuart C. Miller, *The Unwelcome Immigrant: The American Image of the Chinese, 1785–1882* (1969); Michael Schaller, *The United States and China in the Twentieth Century* (1990); Henry Shih-Shan Tsai, *The Chinese Experience in America* (1986); Shu Guang Zhang, *Deterrence and Strategic Culture* (1992). See also "Asia and the Pacific."

Colombia: David Bushnell, *The Making of Modern Colombia* (1993); Richard L. Lael, *Arrogant Diplomacy* (1987); Stephen J. Randall, *Colombia and the United States* (1992) and *The Diplomacy of Modernization* (1977). See also "Latin America" and "Panama."

Cuba: Leslie Bethell, ed., *Cuba* (1992); Juan del Aguilar, *Cuba: Dilemmas of a Revolution* (1988); José M. Hernández, *Cuba and the United States: Intervention and Militarism, 1868–1933* (1993); Morris H. Morley, *Imperial State and Revolution* (1987); Thomas G. Paterson, *Contesting Castro* (1994); Louis A. Pérez, Jr., *Cuba* (1988), *Cuba* (1988) (B), and *Cuba and the United States* (1990); Ramón Ruíz, *Cuba* (1968). See also "Caribbean," "Latin America," and "Spanish-American-Cuban-Filipino War."

Cyprus: See Stearns in "Greece."

Czechoslovakia: Walter Ullmann, *The United States in Prague, 1945–1948* (1978); Betty Miller Unterberger, *The United States, Revolutionary Russia, and the Rise of Czechoslovakia* (1989). See also "Eastern Europe."

Dominican Republic: G. Pope Atkins and Larman C. Wilson, *The United States and the Trujillo Regime* (1972); Ian Bell, *The Dominican Republic* (1981); Bruce J. Calder, *The Impact of Intervention* (1984); Piero Gleijeses, *The Dominican Crisis* (1978); Rayford W. Logan, *Haiti and the Dominican Republic* (1968). See also "Caribbean" and "Latin America."

Eastern Europe: Robert F. Byrnes, *U.S. Policy Toward Eastern Europe and the Soviet Union* (1989); Stephen A. Garrett, *From Potsdam to Poland* (1986); Bennett Kovrig, *Of Walks and Bridges* (1991). Also see individual countries, "Russia and the Soviet Union," and "Europe."

Ecuador: See "Latin America" and Pike in "Peru."

Egypt: Geoffrey Aronson, *From Sideshow to Center Stage* (1986); William J. Burns, *Economic Aid and American Policy Toward Egypt, 1955–1981* (1985); Peter L. Hahn, *The United States, Great Britian, and Egypt, 1945–1956* (1991); Gail E. Meyer, *Egypt and the United States* (1980); Lawrence R. Murphy, *The American University in Cairo, 1919–1986* (1987); William B. Quandt, *The United States and Egypt*

(1990). See also "Israel, Palestine, and Arab-Israeli Conflict" and "Middle East."

El Salvador: America's Watch, *El Salvador's Decade of Terror* (1991); Cynthia Arnson, *El Salvador* (1982); Enrique A. Baloyra, *El Salvador in Transition* (1982); Raymond Bonner, *Weakness and Deceit* (1984); T. S. Montgomery, *Revolution in El Salvador* (1982); Alastair White, *El Salvador* (1973). See also "Central America" and "Latin America."

Ethiopia: David A. Korn, *Ethiopia, the United States, and the Soviet Union* (1986); Jeffrey S. Lefebvre, *Arms for the Horn* (1991); Harold G. Marcus, *Ethiopia, Great Britain, and the United States, 1941–1974* (1983). Also see "Africa."

Europe: Richard Barnet, *The Alliance* (1983); Peter Coffey, *The EC and the United States* (1993); *The Economist Atlas of the New Europe* (1992) (A); Nicholas V. Gianaris, *The European Community and the United States* (1991); Lawrence Kaplan, ed., *American Historians and the Atlantic Alliance* (1991); Ethan B. Kapstein, *The Insecure Alliance: Energy Crises and Western Politics Since 1914* (1990); Jacques Portes, ed., *Europe and America* (1987); Pascaline Winand, *Eisenhower, Kennedy, and the United States of Europe* (1993). See also "Eastern Europe," "NATO," individual countries, and specific wars.

Finland: Max Jacobson, *Finnish Neutality* (1969); Robert Rinehart, ed., *Finland and the United States* (1993). See also "Europe" and "Scandinavia."

France: Henry Blumenthal, *A Reappraisal of Franco-American Relations, 1830–1871* (1959), *France and the United States* (1970), and *Illusion and Reality in Franco-American Diplomacy, 1914–1945* (1986); Frank Costigliola, *The Cold Alliance* (1992); Nicholas Wahl and Robert O. Paxton, eds., *De Gaulle and the United States, 1930–1970* (1993); Irwin M. Wall, *The United States and the Making of Postwar France* (1991); Marvin Zahniser, *Uncertain Friendship* (1975). See also "Europe."

Germany: Dennis L. Bark and David R. Gross, *A History of West Germany* (1993); Hans W. Gatzke, *Germany and the United States* (1980); Wolfram F. Hanrieder, *Germany, America, Europe* (1989); Manfred Jonas, *The United States and Germany* (1984); Roger P. Morgan, *The United States and West Germany, 1945–1973* (1974); Frank Ninkovich, *Germany and the United States* (1988); Cathal J. Nolan and Carl C. Hodge, eds., *Shepherd of Democracy?* (1992); Hans-Jürgen Schröder, ed., *Confrontation and Cooperation* (1993); Thomas A. Schwartz, *America's Germany* (1991); Frank Trommler and Joseph McVeigh, eds., *America and the Germans* (1985). See also "Europe," "Holocaust," "World War I," and "World War II."

Great Britain: C. J. Bartlett, *"The Special Relationship"* (1992); Kenneth Bourne, *Britain and the Balance of Power in North America, 1815–1908* (1967); Charles S. Campbell, *From Revolution to Rapprochement* (1974); Robert M. Hathaway, *Great Britain and the United States* (1990); David A. Lincove and Gary R. Treadway, eds., *The Anglo-American Relationship* (1988) (B); Wm. Roger Louis and Hedley Bull, eds., *The Special Relationship* (1986); H. G. Nicholas, *The United States and Great Britain* (1975); D. C. Watt, *Succeeding John Bull* (1984). See also "Canada" and "War of 1812."

Greece: Louis Cassimatis, *American Influence in Greece, 1917–1929* (1988); Theodore A. Couloumbis, *The United States, Greece, and Turkey* (1983); Theodore A. Couloumbis and John O. Iatrides, eds., *Greek-American Relations* (1980); John O. Iatrides, ed., *Ambassador MacVeagh Reports: Greece, 1933–1947* (1980); Jon V. Kofas, *Intervention and Underdevelopment: Greece During the Cold War* (1989); Monteagle Stearns, *Entangled Allies* (1991); Lawrence S. Wittner, *American Intervention in Greece, 1943–1949* (1982). See also "Europe."

Grenada: Peter M. Dunn and Bruce W. Watson, eds., *American Intervention in Grenada* (1985); Gordon K. Lewis, *Grenada* (1987); Kai P. Schoenhals and Richard A. Melanson, eds., *Revolution and Intervention in Grenada* (1985). See also "Caribbean."

Guatemala: Paul J. Dosal, *Doing Business with the Dictators: A Political History of United Fruit in Guatemala, 1899–1944* (1993); Piero Glejeses, *Shattered Hope* (1991); Jim Handy, *Gift of the Devil* (1985); Richard Immerman, *The CIA in Guatemala* (1982). See also "Central America" and "Latin America."

Haiti: Rayford W. Logan, *Diplomatic Relations of the United States with Haiti, 1776–1891* (1941); David Nicholls, *From Dessalines to Duvalier* (1979); Brenda Gayle Plummer, *Haiti and the United States* (1992); Robert I. Rotberg, *Haiti* (1971). See also "Caribbean," "Latin America," and Logan in "Dominican Republic."

Hawaii: Helena G. Allen, *The Betrayal of Queen Liliuokalani* (1982); Merze Tate, *The United States and the Hawaiian Kingdom* (1965). See also "Asia and the Pacific."

Guam: Timothy P. Maga, *Defending Paradise* (1988); Earl S. Pomeroy, *Pacific Outpost* (1951). See also "Asia and the Pacific."

Honduras: Alison Acker, *Honduras* (1988). See also "Central America."

Iceland: Donald E. Neuchterlein, *Iceland* (1975).

India: William J. Barnds, *India, Pakistan, and the Great Powers* (1972); H. W. Brands, *India and the United States* (1990); W. Norman Brown,

The United States and India, Pakistan, and Bangladesh (1972); Gary R. Hess, *America Encounters India, 1941–1947* (1971); Harold R. Issacs, *Images of Asia* (1958); Robert J. McMahon, *The Cold War on the Periphery* (1994); Dennis Merrill, *Bread and the Ballot* (1990); Norman D. Palmer, *The United States and India* (1984). See also "Asia and the Pacific" and Wolpert in "Afghanistan."

Indonesia: Michael Leifer, *Indonesia's Foreign Policy* (1983); Robert J. McMahon, *Colonialism and Cold War* (1981). See also "Asia and the Pacific."

Iran: James A. Bill, *The Eagle and the Lion* (1988); Richard W. Cottam, *Iran and the United States* (1988); Alvin J. Cottrell, ed., *The Persian Gulf States* (1980); Mark J. Gasiorowski, *U.S. Foreign Policy and the Shah* (1991); James F. Goode, *The United States and Iran, 1946–51* (1989); Nikki R. Keddie, *Roots of Revolution* (1981); Mark H. Lytle, *The Origins of the Iranian-American Alliance, 1941–1953* (1987); Rouhollah K. Ramazani, *Iran's Foreign Policy, 1941–1973* (1975) and *Revolutionary Iran* (1986); Barry Rubin, *Paved with Good Intentions* (1980); Kuross A. Samii, *Involvement by Invitation* (1987). See also "Middle East" and "Persian Gulf."

Iraq: Rick Atkinson, *Crusade* (1993); Lawrence Freedman and Efraim Karsh, *The Gulf Conflict, 1990–1991* (1993); William Stivers, *Supremacy and Oil* (1982). See also "Middle East," Cottrell in "Iran," and Palmer in "Persian Gulf."

Ireland: Donald H. Akenson, *The United States and Ireland* (1973); Thomas N. Brown, *Irish-American Nationalism, 1870–1890* (1966); Francis M. Carroll, *American Opinion and the Irish Question, 1910–1923* (1978); Seán Cronin, *Washington's Irish Policy, 1916–1986* (1987); David N. Doyle and Owen D. Edwards, eds., *America and Ireland, 1776–1976* (1980); Alan J. Ward, *Ireland and Anglo-American Relations, 1899–1921* (1969). See also "Europe" and "Great Britain."

Israel, Palestine, and Arab-Israeli Conflict: George W. Ball and Douglas B. Ball, *The Passionate Attachment* (1992); Abraham Ben-Zvi, *The United States and Israel* (1994); Ian J. Bickerton and Carla L. Klausner, *A Concise History of the Arab-Israeli Conflict* (1991); Martin Gilbert, *Atlas of the Arab-Israeli Conflict* (1993) (A); Peter Grose, *Israel and the Mind of America* (1983); Wm. Roger Louis and Robert W. Stookey, eds., *The End of the Palestine Mandate* (1986); William B. Quandt, *Peace Process* (1993); John Quigley, *Palestine and Israel* (1990); Bernard Reich, *The United States and Israel* (1984); Cheryl Rubenberg, *Israel and the American National Interest* (1986); David Schoenbaum, *The United States and the State of Israel* (1993); Mohammed K. Shadid, *The United States and the Palestinians* (1981); Steven Spiegel, *The Other Arab-Israeli Conflict* (1985); Edward Tivnan, *The Lobby* (1987). See also "Middle East."

Italy: Alexander DeConde, *Half-Bitter, Half-Sweet* (1971); H. Stuart Hughes, *The United States and Italy* (1979); James E. Miller, *The United States and Italy, 1940–1950* (1986); David F. Schmitz, *The United States and Fascist Italy, 1922–1940* (1988); Leo J. Wollemborg, *Stars, Stripes, and Italian Tricolor* (1990). See also "Europe."

Japan: Roger Buckley, *US-Japan Alliance Diplomacy, 1945–1990* (1992); John K. Emmerson and Harrison M. Holland, *The Eagle and the Rising Sun* (1988); Sydney Giffard, *Japan Among the Powers, 1890–1990* (1994); Akira Iriye, *Pacific Estrangement: Japanese and American Expansion, 1897–1911* (1972); Akira Iriye and Warren I. Cohen, eds., *The United States and Japan in the Postwar World* (1989); Rita E. Neri, *U.S. and Japan Foreign Trade* (1988) (B); Charles E. Neu, *The Troubled Encounter* (1975); William L. Newman, *America Encounters Japan* (1963); Edwin E. Reischauer, *The United States and Japan* (1965); Michael Schaller, *The American Occupation of Japan* (1985). See also "Asia and the Pacific" and "World War II."

Korea: Frank Baldwin, ed., *Without Parallel* (1974); Jongsuk Chay, *Diplomacy of Asymmetry* (1990); Bruce Cumings, *The Origins of the Korean War* (1981, 1990); Yun-Bok Lee and Wayne Patterson, eds., *One Hundred Years of Cooperation* (1984); Stewart Lone and Gavan McCormack, *Korea Since 1850* (1993); Donald S. Macdonald, *U.S.-Korean Relations from Liberation to Self-Reliance* (1992); Keith McFarland, *The Korean War* (1986) (B); James I. Matray, ed., *Historical Dictionary of the Korean War* (1991) (E); Joo-Hong Nam, *America's Commitment to South Korea* (1987); Harry G. Summers, Jr., *Korean War Almanac* (1990) (C and E). See also "Asia and the Pacific."

Laos: Timothy N. Castle, *At War in the Shadow of Vietnam* (1993); Arthur J. Dommen, *Laos* (1985); Charles A. Stevenson, *The End of Nowhere* (1972). See also "Vietnam and Southeast Asia."

Latin America: Cole Blasier, *The Hovering Giant* (1976); Simon Collier et al., eds., *The Cambridge Encyclopedia of Latin America and the Caribbean* (1985) (E); Jack W. Hopkins, ed., *Latin America and Caribbean Contemporary Record* (1983–) (AS); John J. Johnson, *A Hemisphere Apart* (1990); Lester D. Langley, *America and the Americas* (1989); Abraham F. Lowenthal, ed., *Exporting Democracy* (1991); Carlos Marichal, *A Century of Debt Crises in Latin America* (1988); John D. Martz, *United States Policy in Latin America* (1988); J. Lloyd Mecham, *The United States and Inter-American Security, 1889–1960* (1961); Michael C. Meyer, ed., *Supplement to a Bibliography of United States-Latin American Relations Since 1810* (1979) (B); Harold Molineu, *U.S. Policy Toward Latin America* (1990); C. Neale Ronning and Albert P. Vanuncci, eds., *Ambassadors in Foreign Policy* (1987); David Shavit, *The United States in Latin America* (1992) (E); Joseph Smith, *Illusions of Conflict: Anglo-American Diplomacy Toward Latin America, 1865–1896* (1979); Barbara Stallings, *Banker to the Third*

World (1988); David F. Trask et al., *A Bibliography of United States–Latin American Relations Since 1810* (1979) (B). See also "Caribbean," "Central America," and individual countries.

Lebanon: Thomas L. Friedman, *From Beirut to Jerusalem* (1989); P. Edward Haley and Lewis W. Snider, eds., *Lebanon in Crisis* (1979); Dilip Hiro, *Lebanon* (1993); Itamar Rabinovich, *The War for Lebanon, 1970–1985* (1986). See also "Middle East."

Liberia: D. Elwood Dunn, *The Foreign Policy of Liberia During the Tubman Era, 1944–1971* (1979); Katherine Harris, *The United States and Liberia* (1985); Hassan B. Sisay, *Big Powers and Small Nations* (1985); Charles M. Wilson, *Liberia* (1985). See also "Africa."

Libya: Mahmoud G. ElWarfally, *Imagery and Ideology in U.S. Policy Toward Libya, 1969–1982* (1988); P. Edward Haley, *Qaddafi and the United States Since 1969* (1984). See also "Africa" and "Middle East."

Malaysia: James W. Gould, *The United States and Malaysia* (1969). See also "Asia and the Pacific."

Mexico: Leslie Bethel, ed., *Mexico Since Independence* (1991); Lester D. Langley, *Mexico and the United States* (1991); David E. Lorey, ed., *United States–Mexico Border Statistics Since 1900* (1990) (S); W. Dirk Raat, *Mexico and the United States* (1992); Karl M. Schmitt, *Mexico and the United States, 1821–1973* (1974); Norman E. Tutorow, ed., *The Mexican-American War* (1981) (B); Josefina Vázquez and Lorenzo Meyer, *The United States and Mexico* (1985); Barbara G. Valk et al., *Borderline* (1988) (B); David J. Weber, *The Mexican Frontier, 1821–1846* (1982); Sidney Weintraub, *A Marriage of Convenience* (1990). See also "Latin America."

Micronesia: See "Asia and the Pacific."

Middle East: L. Carl Brown, *International Politics and the Middle East* (1984); Thomas A. Bryson, *American Diplomatic Relations with the Middle East, 1784–1975* (1977) and *U.S.–Middle East Diplomatic Relations* (1979) (B); Uriel Dann, ed., *The Great Powers in the Middle East, 1919–1939* (1988); John A. DeNovo, *American Interests and Policies in the Middle East, 1900–1939* (1963); James A. Field, *America and the Mediterranean World, 1776–1882* (1969); T. G. Fraser, *The USA and the Middle East Since World War 2* (1989); Colin Legum et al., eds., *Middle East Contemporary Survey* (1978–) (AS); George Lenczowski, *American Presidents and the Middle East* (1989) and *The Middle East in World Affairs* (1980); William R. Polk, *The Arab World Today* (1991); David Shavit, *The United States in the Middle East* (1988) (E); Sanford R. Silverburg and Bernard Reich, *U.S. Foreign Policy and the Middle East/North Africa* (1989) (B); William Stivers, *America's Confrontation with Revolutionary Change in the Middle East, 1948–83*

(1986); Robert W. Stookey, *America and the Arab States* (1975); Alan R. Taylor, *The Superpowers and the Middle East* (1991). See also individual countries and "Persian Gulf."

Morocco: Leon B. Blair, *Western Window in the Arab World* (1970); Luella J. Hall, *The United States and Morocco, 1776–1956* (1961). See also "Africa" and "North Africa."

The Netherlands: Hans Loeber, ed., *Dutch-American Relations, 1945–1969* (1992); J. W. Schulte Nordholt and Robert P. Swierenga, eds., *A Bilateral Centennial: A History of Dutch-American Relations, 1783–1982* (1982); Cornelis van Minnen, *American Diplomats in the Netherlands, 1815–50* (1993). See also "Europe."

New Zealand: See "Australia."

Nicaragua: Karl Berman, *Under the Big Stick* (1986); Paul C. Clark, Jr., *The United States and Somoza* (1992); Peter Kornbluh, *Nicaragua* (1987); Richard Millett, *Guardians of the Dynasty* (1977); Morris H. Morley, *Washington, Somoza, and the Sandinistas* (1994); Neil Narr, *Sandinista Nicaragua* (1990) (B); Thomas W. Walker, *Nicaragua* (1991), ed., *Reagan versus the Sandinistas* (1987), and ed., *Revolution & Counterrevolution in Nicaragua* (1991). See also "Central America" and "Latin America."

Nigeria: Bassey E. Ate, *Decolonization and Dependence* (1987); Robert B. Shepard, *Nigeria, Africa, and the United States* (1991); Joseph E. Thompson, *American Policy and African Famine* (1990). See also "Africa."

North Africa: Charles F. Gallagher, *The United States and North Africa* (1963); Richard S. Parker, *North Africa* (1984). See also "Africa."

Norway: Wayne S. Cole, *Norway and the United States, 1905–1955* (1989); Ronald C. Popperwell, *Norway* (1972); Sigmund Skard, *The United States in Norwegian History* (1976); Rolf Tamnes, *The United States and the Cold War in the High North* (1991). See also "Scandinavia" and "Europe."

Pakistan: Iftikhar Malik, *U.S.–South Asian Relations, 1940–1947* (1991); Leo E. Rose and Noor A. Husain, eds., *U.S.–Pakistan Relations* (1985); Shirin Tahir-kheli, *The United States and Pakistan* (1982); M. S. Venkataramani, *The American Role in Pakistan, 1947–1958* (1982). See also Wolpert in "Afghanistan" and Barnds and McMahon in "India."

Panama (and Panama Canal): Michael L. Conniff, *Panama and the United States* (1992); David N. Farnsworth and James W. McKenney, *U.S.–Panama Relations, 1903–1978* (1983); Walter LaFeber, *The*

Panama Canal (1990); John Major, *Prize Possession* (1993); George D. Moffett III, *Limits of Victory* (1985). See also "Latin America."

Persian Gulf: Bruce R. Kuniholm, *The Persian Gulf and United States Policy* (1984) (B); Charles A. Kupchan, *The Persian Gulf and the West* (1987); Michael A. Palmer, *Guardians of the Gulf* (1992). See also "Middle East" and Cottell in "Iran."

Peru: James C. Carey, *Peru and the United States, 1900–1962* (1964); Frederick B. Pike, *The United States and the Andean Republics* (1977). See also "Latin America."

Philippines: Teodoro A. Agoncillo, *A Short History of the Philippines* (1969); David H. Bain, *Sitting in Darkness* (1984); Raymond Bonner, *Waltzing with a Dictator* (1987); H. W. Brands, *Bound to Empire* (1992); Stanley Karnow, *In Our Image* (1989); Glenn A. May, *Battle for Batangas* (1991); Peter W. Stanley, *A Nation in the Making* (1974) and ed., *Reappraising an Empire* (1984); George E. Taylor, *The Philippines and the United States* (1964). See also "Asia and the Pacific," "Spanish-American-Cuban-Filipino War," and Thomson in "Asia and the Pacific."

Poland: Piotr Wandycz, *The United States and Poland* (1980). See also "Eastern Europe" and "Europe."

Puerto Rico: Raymond Carr, *Puerto Rico* (1984); Arturo Morales Carríon, *Puerto Rico* (1984); Truman B. Clark, *Puerto Rico and the United States, 1917–1933* (1975); Ronald Fernandez, *The Disenchanted Island* (1992). See also "Caribbean."

Rumania: Joseph F. Harrington and Bruce J. Courtney, *Tweaking the Nose of the Russians* (1991). See also "Eastern Europe."

Russia and the Soviet Union: N. N. Bolkhovitinov and J. Dane Hartgrove, *Russia and the United States* (1987) (B); Philip J. Funigiello, *American-Soviet Trade in the Cold War* (1988); John Lewis Gaddis, *Russia, the Soviet Union, and the United States* (1990); Raymond L. Garthoff, *Détente and Confrontation* (1985); Howard Kushner, *Conflict on the Northwest Coast: American-Russian Rivalry in the Pacific Northwest, 1790–1867* (1975); James K. Libbey, *American-Russian Economic Relations* (1989) (B); Norman E. Saul, *The United States and Russia, 1763–1867* (1991); David Shavit, *United States Relations with Russia and the Soviet Union* (1993) (E); Nikolai Sivachev and Nikolai N. Yakovlev, *Russia and the United States* (1979). See also "Cold War," "Eastern Europe," and "Europe."

Samoa: Richard P. Gilson, *Samoa, 1830–1900* (1970); Paul Kennedy, *The Samoan Tangle* (1974). See also "Asia and the Pacific."

Saudia Arabia: Irvine H. Anderson, *Aramco, the United States, and Saudi Arabia* (1981); Lee Grayson, *Saudi-American Relations* (1982); David E. Long, *The United States and Saudi Arabia* (1985); Aaron D. Miller, *Search for Security: Saudi Arabian Oil and American Foreign Policy, 1939–1949* (1980); Nadav Safran, *Saudi Arabia* (1986). See also "Middle East."

Scandinavia: Franklin D. Scott, *Scandinavia* (1975) and *The United States and Scandinavia* (1950). See also individual countries and "Europe."

Somalia: See "Africa" and Lefebvre in "Ethiopia."

South Africa: James Barber and John Barratt, *South Africa's Foreign Policy* (1990); Thomas Borstelmann, *Apartheid's Reluctant Uncle* (1993); Christopher Coker, *The United States and South Africa, 1968–1985* (1986); Terrel D. Hale, *United States Sanctions and South Africa* (1993) (B); Richard W. Hull, *American Enterprise in South Africa* (1990); C. T. Keto, *American–South African Relations, 1784–1980* (1985) (B); William Minter, *King Soloman's Mines Revisited* (1986); Thomas J. Noer, *Briton, Boer, and Yankee* (1978) and *Cold War and Black Liberation* (1985). See also "Africa."

Spain: Raymond Carr, *Spain* (1982); James W. Cortada, *Two Nations over Time* (1978) and ed., *Spain in the Twentieth-Century World* (1980). See also "Europe" and "Spanish-American-Cuban-Filipino War."

Switzerland: Heinze K. Meier, *Friendship Under Stress: U.S.–Swiss Relations, 1900–1950* (1970) and *The United States and Switzerland in the Nineteenth Century* (1963). See also "Europe."

Syria: David W. Lesch, *Syria and the United States* (1992); Patrick Seale, *Asad* (1989) and *The Struggle for Syria* (1965). See also "Middle East."

Taiwan (Formosa): See "China (Taiwan)."

Thailand: Richard Aldrich, *The Key to the South* (1993); Robert J. Muscat, *Thailand and the United States* (1990). See also "Vietnam and Southeast Asia."

Tunisia: See "North Africa."

Turkey: David J. Alvarez, *Bureaucracy and Cold War Ideology* (1980); George S. Harris, *Troubled Alliance* (1972); Harry H. Howard, *Turkey, the Straits, and U.S. Policy* (1974). See also "Europe" and Couloumbis and Stearns in "Greece."

Uruguay: See "Latin America" and Whitaker in "Argentina."

Venezuela: Sheldon B. Liss, *Diplomacy and Independence* (1978); Stephen G. Rabe, *The Road to OPEC* (1982). See also "Latin America" and "Oil."

Vietnam and Southeast Asia: David L. Anderson, ed., *Shadow on the White House* (1993); Eric M. Bergerud, *The Dynamics of Defeat* (1991); John S. Bowman, ed., *The Vietnam War* (1986) (C); Lester H. Brune and Richard Dean Burns, eds., *America and the Indochina Wars, 1945–1990* (1991) (B); Phillip B. Davidson, *Vietnam at War* (1988); William J. Duiker, *Historical Dictionary of Vietnam* (1989) (E); Frances Fitzgerald, *Fire in the Lake* (1972); Lloyd C. Gardner, *Approaching Vietnam* (1988); Leslie Gelb and Richard Betts, *The Irony of Vietnam* (1979); George C. Herring, *America's Longest War* (1986); Gary R. Hess, *Vietnam and the United States* (1990); George McT. Kahin, *Intervention* (1986); Stanley Karnow, *Vietnam* (1991); Gabriel Kolko, *Anatomy of a War* (1985); James S. Olson, *Dictionary of the Vietnam War* (1988) (E) and *The Vietnam War* (1993) (B); Andrew J. Rotter, *The Path to Vietnam* (1987); Robert Shaplen, *Time Out of Hand* (1970); Anthony Short, *The Origins of the Vietnam War* (1989); Harry G. Summers, Jr., *Vietnam War Almanac* (1985) (C); William S. Turley, *The Second Indochina War* (1986); Marilyn Young, *The Vietnam Wars* (1991). See also "Asia and the Pacific," "Peace Movements," and "Military, U.S. Army, and Wars."

Virgin Islands and West Indies: William W. Boyer, *America's Virgin Islands* (1983); Cary Fraser, *Ambivalent Anti-Colonialism: The United States and the Genesis of West Indian Independence, 1940–1964* (1993). See also "Caribbean."

Yemen: Ahmed Nomen Al-Madhaqi, *Yemen and the USA* (1994); Fred Halliday, *Revolution and Foreign Policy: The Case of South Yemen, 1967–1987* (1989). See also "Middle East."

Yugoslavia: Phylis Auty, *Yugoslavia* (1965); John R. Lampe et al., *Yugoslav-American Relations Since World War II* (1991). See also "Eastern Europe."

Zaire (Congo): David N. Gibbs, *The Political Economy of Third World Intervention* (1991); Madeline G. Kalb, *The Congo Cables* (1982); Sean Kelly, *America's Tyrant: The CIA and Mobutu of Zaire* (1993). See also "Africa."

Overviews of Subjects, including Atlases (A), Annual Surveys (AS), Bibliographies (B), Biographical Dictionaries (BD), Chronologies (C), Encyclopedias (E), and Statistics (S)

Air Force and Air Power: Charles D. Bright, ed., *Historical Dictionary of the U.S. Air Force* (1992) (E); Alan P. Dobson, *Peaceful Air Warfare* (1991); John B. Rae, *Climb to Greatness* (1968); Michael S. Sherry, *The Rise of American Air Power* (1987); Jeffrey S. Underwood, *The Wings of Democracy* (1991); Bruce W. Watson and Susan W. Watson, *The United States Air Force* (1992) (E). See also "Military, U.S. Army, and Wars" and specific wars.

Alliance for Progress: Jerome Levinson and Juan de Onís, *The Alliance That Lost Its Way* (1970); L. Ronald Scheman, ed., *The Alliance for Progress* (1988). See also "Latin America."

American Revolution: Richard Blanco, ed., *The American Revolution* (1993) (E); Mark M. Boatner III, *Encyclopedia of the American Revolution* (1974) (E); Lester J. Cappon, ed., *Atlas of Early American History: The Revolutionary Era, 1760–1790* (1976) (A); John M. Faragher, ed., *The Encyclopedia of Colonial and Revolutionary America* (1990) (E); Jack P. Greene and J. R. Pole, eds., *The Blackwell Encyclopedia of the American Revolution* (1991) (E); John W. Raimo, ed., *Biographical Directory of American Colonial and Revolutionary Governors, 1607–1789* (1980) (BD). For histories, see Chapter 1 of Volume 1.

Anti-Americanism: "Anti-Americanism," *The Annals,* May 1988; Denis Lacorne et al., eds., *The Rise and Fall of Anti-Americanism* (1990); Alvin Z. Rubenstein and Donald E. Smith, eds., *Anti-Americanism in the Third World* (1985); David Strauss, *Menace in the West: The Rise of French Anti-Americanism in Modern Times* (1978). See also "Latin America."

Anti-Communism and McCarthyism: Jeff Broadwater, *Eisenhower and the Anti-Communist Crusades* (1992); Peter H. Buckingham, *America Sees Red* (1987) (B); Richard M. Fried, *Nightmare in Red* (1990); Robert Griffith, *The Politics of Fear* (1987); John E. Haynes, *Communism and Anti-Communism in the United States* (1987) (B); Joel Kovel, *Red Hunting in the Promised Land* (1994); Stanley I. Kutler, *The American Inquisition* (1982); Stephen J. Whitfield, *The Culture of the Cold War* (1991). See also, "Cold War."

Arms Sales: Michael T. Klare, *American Arms Supermarket* (1984); Andrew J. Pierre, ed., *Arms Transfers and American Foreign Policy* (1979). See also "Military, U.S. Army, and Wars."

Atlantic Charter: Douglas Brinkley and David Facey-Crowther, eds., *The Atlantic Charter* (1994); Theodore A. Wilson, *The First Summit* (1991). See also "World War II."

Bricker Amendment: Duane Tananbaum, *The Bricker Amendment Controversy* (1988).

Bureaucracy: Graham Allison, *Essence of Decision* (1971); I. M. Destler, *Presidents, Bureaucrats, and Foreign Policy* (1974); Louis

Galambos, ed., *The New American State* (1987); Morton H. Halperin, *Bureaucratic Politics and Foreign Policy* (1974); Irving L. Janis, *Groupthink* (1983). See also "President (General)."

Central Intelligence Agency (CIA): See "Intelligence, CIA, and Covert Action."

Chemical Weapons: G. M. Burck and Charles C. Flowerree, *International Handbook on Chemical Weapons Proliferation* (1991) (E); Anthony H. Cordesman, *Weapons of Mass Destruction in the Middle East* (1991); Victor A. Utgoff, *The Challenge of Chemical Weapons* (1991).

Cold War: Stephen Ambrose, *Rise to Globalism* (1993); Joseph L. Black, *Origins, Evolution, and Nature of the Cold War* (1986) (B); H. W. Brands, *The Devil We Knew* (1993); John Lewis Gaddis, *The Long Peace* (1987); Walter LaFeber, *America, Russia, and the Cold War* (1993); Thomas J. McCormick, *America's Half-Century* (1988); Thomas G. Paterson, *Meeting the Communist Threat* (1988) and *On Every Front* (1992). See also "Russia and the Soviet Union."

Communications: James L. Baughman, *The Republic of Mass Culture* (1992); David H. Culbert, *News for Everyman* (1976) (radio); Julian Hale, *Radio Power* (1975); Daniel R. Headrick, *The Invisible Weapon: Telecommunications and International Politics, 1851–1945* (1991); James Schwoch, *The American Radio Industry and Its Latin American Activities* (1990); Anthony Smith, *Geopolitics of Information* (1980). See also "Cultural Relations."

Congress: Congressional Quarterly, *Congress and the Nation, 1945–1984* (1965–1985) (E); Robert U. Goehlert and John R. Sayre, *The United States Congress* (1981) (B); James A. Robinson, *Congress and Foreign Policy-Making* (1967); John Rourke, *Congress and the Presidency in U.S. Foreign Policymaking* (1983); Göran Rystad, ed., *Congress and American Foreign Policy* (1982); John Spanier and Joseph Nogee, eds., *Congress, the Presidency, and Foreign Policy* (1980); U.S. Congress, *Biographical Directory of the United States Congress, 1774–1989* (1989) (BD); Gerald F. Warburg, *Conflict and Consensus* (1989). See also "President" and "War Powers."

Constitution: Henry B. Cox, *War, Foreign Affairs, and Constitutional Power, 1829–1901* (1984); Louis Fischer, *Constitutional Conflicts Between the President and Congress* (1985); Leonard W. Levy et al., eds., *Encyclopedia of the American Constitution* (1986); Louis Henken, *Foreign Affairs and the Constitution* (1972); Joan E. Smith, *The Constitution and American Foreign Policy* (1989); Abraham Sofaer, *War, Foreign Affairs, and Constitutional Power* (1976). See also "War Powers."

Containment: Terry L. Deibel and John Lewis Gaddis, eds., *Containment* (1986); Charles Gati, ed., *Caging the Bear* (1974);

Deborah Larson, *Origins of Containment* (1985); John Lewis Gaddis, *Strategies of Containment* (1982); Thomas G. Paterson, ed., *Containment and the Cold War* (1973). See also "Cold War."

Counterinsurgency: Benjamin R. Beede, *Intervention and Counterinsurgency* (1984) (B); Douglas S. Blaufarb, *The Counterinsurgency Era* (1977); Michael T. Klare and Peter Kornbluh, eds., *Low-Intensity Warfare* (1988); Michael McClintock, *Instruments of Statecraft* (1992); D. Michael Shafer, *Deadly Paradigms* (1988). See also "Intelligence, CIA, and Covert Action."

Cultural Relations: Paul Braisted, ed., *Cultural Affairs and Foreign Relations* (1968); Jongsuk Chay, ed., *Culture and International Relations* (1990); Morrell Heald and Lawrence S. Kaplan, *Culture and Diplomacy* (1977); Clayton R. Koppes and Gregory D. Black, *Hollywood Goes to War* (1987); James F. Larson, *Global Television and Foreign Policy* (1988); Frank Ninkovich, *The Diplomacy of Ideas* (1981); Emily Rosenberg, *Spreading the American Dream* (1982); Thomas J. Saunders, *Hollywood in Berlin* (1994); Anthony Smith, *The Geopolitics of Information* (1980); Kristin Thompson, *Exporting Entertainment* (1985). See also "Communications," "Philanthropy and Foundations," and "Propaganda."

Decline Thesis: David P. Calleo, *Beyond American Hegemony* (1987); Paul Kennedy, *The Rise and Fall of the Great Powers* (1987); Henry Nau, *The Myth of America's Decline* (1990); Joseph P. Nye, Jr., *Bound to Lead* (1990).

Decolonization: Franz Ansprenger, *The Dissolution of Colonial Empires* (1989); Prosser Gifford and Wm. Roger Louis, eds., *Decolonization and African Independence* (1988); D. A. Low, *Eclipse of Empire* (1991); Brian Urquhart, *Decolonization and World Peace* (1989).

Department of State, Foreign Service, and Diplomatic Practice: Robert U. Goehlert and Elizabeth Hoffmeister, *The Department of State and American Diplomacy* (1986) (B); Warren F. Ilchman, *Professional Diplomacy in the United States, 1779–1939* (1961); Charles S. Kennedy, *The American Consul* (1990); Robert H. Miller et al., *Inside an Embassy* (1992); Henry E. Mattox, *The Twilight of Amateur Diplomacy* (1989); Barry Rubin, *Secrets of State* (1985); Martin Weil, *A Pretty Good Club* (1978); Elmer Plischke, *United States Diplomats and Their Mission* (1979); Robert D. Schulzinger, *The Making of the Diplomatic Mind* (1975); Richard H. Werking, *The Master Architects* (1977). See also "President (General)."

Dependency: Fernando Henrique Cardoso and Enzo Faletto, *Dependency and Development in Latin America* (1979); André Gunder Frank, *Capitalism and Underdevelopment in Latin America* (1967); Vincent A. Mahler, *Dependency Approaches to International Political*

Economy (1980); Robert A. Packenham, *The Dependency Movement* (1992). See also "World-System Analysis."

Deterrence: Alexander L. George and Richard Smoke, *Deterrence in American Foreign Policy* (1974); Robert Jervis et al., *Psychology and Deterrence* (1985). Also see "Nuclear Arms."

Disarmament and Arms Control: Richard Dean Burns, ed., *Encyclopedia of Arms Control and Disarmament* (1993) (E); Jeffrey M. Elliot and Robert Reginald, *The Arms Control, Disarmament, and Military Security Dictionary* (1989) (E); Milton S. Katz, *Ban the Bomb* (1986); Stockholm International Peace Research Institute, *SIPRI Yearbook: International Armaments and Disarmament* (1969–) (AS and S); United Nations, *Disarmament Yearbook* (1976–) (AS); Lawrence S. Wittner, *One World or None* (1993). See also "Nuclear Arms."

Drug Trade: Donald J. Mabry, ed., *The Latin American Narcotics Trade and U.S. National Security* (1989); Arnold H. Taylor, *American Diplomacy and the Narcotics Traffic, 1900–1931* (1969); William O. Walker III, *Drug Control in the Americas* (1981) and *Opium and Foreign Policy* (1991).

Economic Relations and Business: William H. Becker and Samuel F. Wells, eds., *Economics and World Power* (1984); David P. Calleo, *The Imperious Economy* (1982); Alfred E. Eckes, *The United States and the Global Struggle for Minerals* (1979); Michael J. Freeman, *Atlas of World Economy* (1991) (A); John N. Ingham, *Biographical Dictionary of American Business Leaders* (1983) (BD); John N. Ingham and Lyness B. Feldman, *Contemporary American Business Leaders* (1990) (BD); Thelma Liesner, *One Hundred Years of Economic Statistics* (1989) (S); Wahib Nasrallah, *United States Corporation Histories* (1991) (B); Timothy O'Donnell et al., eds., *World Economic Data* (1991) (S); Richard Robinson, *United States Business History* (1990) (E); Gordon B. Smith, ed., *The Politics of East-West Trade* (1984); Joan E. Spero, *The Politics of International Economic Relations* (1981); United Nations, *International Trade Statistics Yearbook* (1985–) (AS and S), *World Economic Survey* (1955–)(AS and S), and *Yearbook of International Trade Statistics* (1950–1982) (AS and S); Herman Van Der Wee, *The Search for Prosperity: The World Economy, 1945–1977* (1977); Mira Wilkins, *The Emergence of Multinational Enterprise* (1970) and *The Maturing of Multinational Enterprise* (1975). See also "Economic Sanctions and Export Controls," "Export-Import Bank," "Tariff and Protectionism," and Funigiello in "Russia and the Soviet Union."

Economic Sanctions and Export Controls: Margaret P. Doxey, *Economic Sanctions and International Enforcement* (1980); Gary C. Hufbauer and Jeffrey J. Schott, *Economic Sanctions Reconsidered* (1990); William J. Long, *U.S. Export Control Policy* (1989); Donald Losman, *International Economic Sanctions* (1979); Homer E. Moyer, Jr., and

Linda L. Mabry, *Export Controls as Instruments of Foreign Policy* (1988); Sidney Weintrub, ed., *Economic Coercion and U.S. Foreign Policy* (1982). See also "Economic Relations and Business" and "Tariffs and Protectionism."

Environment: Robert Broadman, *International Organization and the Conservation of Nature* (1981); Lester R. Brown et al., *State of the World* (1984–) (AS); Lynton K. Caldwell, *International Environmental Policy* (1990); John McCormick, *Reclaiming Paradise: The Global Environmental Movement* (1989); Organisation for Economic Co-operation and Development, *The State of the Environment* (1991) (E and S); Kirkpatrick Sale, *The Green Revolution* (1993); World Resources Institute, *Environmental Almanac* (1992) (E); World Resources Institute (or International Institute for Environment and Development), *World Resources* (1976–) (AS). See also "Law of the Sea."

Ethics: Gerald Elfstrom, *Ethics for a Shrinking World* (1990); Ernest W. Lefever, *Ethics and United States Foreign Policy* (1957); J. E. Hare and Carey B. Joynt, *Ethics and International Affairs* (1982); Dorothy V. Jones, *Code of Peace* (1991); Kenneth W. Thompson, ed., *Ethics and International Relations* (1985) and ed., *Moral Dimensions of American Foreign Policy* (1984).

Ethnic Groups and Immigration: Mohammed E. Ahrari, ed., *Ethnic Groups and U.S. Foreign Policy* (1987); Francesco Cordasco, ed., *Dictionary of American Immigration History* (1990) (E); Alexander DeConde, *Ethnicity, Race, and American Foreign Policy* (1992); Robert A. Divine, *American Immigration Policy, 1924–1952* (1963); Louis L. Gerson, *The Hyphenate in Recent American Politics and Diplomacy* (1964); David M. Reimers, *Still the Golden Door: The Third World Comes to America* (1992); Stephen Thernstrom, ed., *Harvard Encyclopedia of American Ethnic Groups* (1980) (E) ; Robert W. Tucker et al., eds., *Immigration and U.S. Foreign Policy* (1990). See also "Refugees."

Executive Agreements: Wallace M. McClure, *International Executive Agreements* (1941); Lawrence Margolis, *Executive Agreements and Presidential Power in Foreign Policy* (1986). See also "President (General)."

Export-Import Bank: Frederick C. Adams, *Economic Diplomacy* (1976); Richard E. Feinberg, *Subsidizing Success* (1982); Rita M. Rodriquez, ed., *The Export-Import Bank at Fifty* (1987). See also "Economic Relations and Business."

Extraterritoriality: Wesley R. Fishel, *The End of Extraterritoriality* (1952).

Food Diplomacy and Relief: Nicole Ball, ed., *World Hunger* (1981) (B); Raymond F. Hopkins and Donald J. Puchala, *Global Food*

Interdependence (1980); Don Paarlberg, *Toward a Well-Fed World* (1988); Vernon W. Ruttan, ed., *Why Food Aid?* (1993); Hans W. Sinder et al., *Food Aid* (1987); Ross B. Talbott, *The Four World Food Agencies in Rome* (1990). See also "Foreign Aid."

Foreign Aid: David Baldwin, *Economic Development and American Foreign Policy, 1943–1962* (1966); Herbert Feis, *Foreign Aid and Foreign Policy* (1964); David H. Lumsdaine, *Moral Vision in International Politics: The Foreign Aid Regime, 1949–1989* (1993); Robert A. Packenham, *Liberal America and the Third World* (1973); Roger Riddell, *Foreign Aid Reconsidered* (1987). See also "Food Diplomacy and Relief."

Foreign Investment in the United States: Mira Wilkins, *The History of Foreign Investment in the United States to 1914* (1989). See also "Economic Relations and Business."

Genocide: Leo Kuper, *Genocide* (1981); Lawrence J. LeBlanc, *The United States and the Genocide Convention* (1991); Ervin Staub, *The Roots of Evil* (1989). See also "Holocaust" and "War Crimes and Trials."

Guano: Jimmy M. Skaggs, *The Great Guano Rush* (1994).

Health and Medical History of Leaders: Kenneth R. Crispell and Carlos F. Gomez, *Hidden Illness in the White House* (1988); Robert H. Ferrell, *Ill-Advised* (1992); Bert E. Park, *Ill-Fated History* (1993) and *The Impact of Illness on World Leaders* (1986). See also "President (General)" and "Presidents (By Administration)."

Holocaust: Richard Breitman and Alan M. Kraut, *American Refugee Policy and European Jewry* (1987); Leonard Dinnerstein, *America and the Survivors of the Holocaust* (1982); Israel Gutman, ed., *Encyclopedia of the Holocaust* (1990) (E); Deborah E. Lipstadt, *Beyond Belief* (1993); Michael R. Marrus, *The Holocaust in History* (1987); David Wyman, *Paper Walls* (1968) and *The Abandonment of the Jews* (1984). See also "Genocide," "Germany," "War Crimes and Trials," and "World War II."

Human Rights: America's Watch Staff (periodic reports on Latin American countries); Amnesty International, *The Amnesty International Report* (1977–) (AS); Jack Donnelly and Rhoda E. Howard, eds., *International Handbook of Human Rights* (1987) (E); Charles Humana, *World Human Rights Guide* (1992); Natalie Kaufman, *Human Rights Treaties and the Senate* (1990); Edward Lawson, *Encyclopedia of Human Rights* (1991) (E); A Glenn Mower, *Human Rights and American Foreign Policy: The Carter and Reagan Experiences* (1987) and *The United States, the United Nations, and Human Rights* (1979); Lars Schoultz, *Human Rights and United States Policy Toward Latin America* (1981); Kenneth

W. Thompson, ed., *The Moral Imperatives of Human Rights* (1980); Sandy Vogelgesang, *American Dream, American Nightmare* (1980). See also "Holocaust" and "War Crimes and Trials."

Ideology: Richard J. Barnet, *Roots of War* (1972); Edward M. Burns, *The American Idea of Mission* (1957); Arthur A. Ekirch, Jr., *Ideas, Ideals, and American Diplomacy* (1966); Michael H. Hunt, *Ideology and U.S. Foreign Policy* (1987); David M. Potter, *People of Plenty* (1954); E. L. Tuveson, *Redeemer Nation* (1968); William A. Williams, *The Tragedy of American Diplomacy* (1962). See also "Manifest Destiny" and "Race and Racism."

Immigration: See "Ethnic Groups and Immigration."

Imperialism: Michael B. Brown, *The Economics of Imperialism* (1974); Benjamin J. Cohen, *The Question of Imperialism* (1973); Philip Darby, *Three Faces of Imperialism* (1987); Michael Doyle, *Empires* (1986); Gabriel Kolko, *The Roots of American Foreign Policy* (1969); Dexter Perkins, *The American Approach to Foreign Policy* (1968); Tony Smith, *The Pattern of Imperialism* (1981); Richard W. Van Alstyne, *The Rising American Empire* (1960). See also "Dependency" and "World-System Analysis."

Indians (Native Americans): Brian W. Dippie, *The Vanishing American* (1982); Michael Green, *The Politics of Indian Removal* (1982); Barry Klein, ed., *Reference Encyclopedia of the American Indian* (1993) (E); Calvin Martin, ed., *The American Indian and the Problem of History* (1986); Francis Paul Prucha, *Atlas of American Indian Affairs* (1990) (A) and *The Indian in American Society* (1985); Michael Rogin, *Fathers and Sons* (1975); Paul Stuart, *Nation Within a Nation* (1987) (S); Carl Waldman, *Atlas of the North American Indian* (1985) (A); Philip Weeks, *Farewell My Nation* (1990).

Intelligence, CIA, and Covert Action: Stephen Ambrose, *Ike's Spies* (1981); Charles D. Ameringer, *U.S. Foreign Intelligence* (1990); Bruce D. Berkowitz and Allan E. Goodman, *Strategic Intelligence for American National Security* (1989); Paul W. Blackstock and Frank L. Schaf, eds., *Intelligence, Espionage, Counterespionage, and Covert Operations* (1978) (B); Marjorie W. Cline et al., *Scholar's Guide to Intelligence Literature* (1983) (B); George C. Constantinides, *Intelligence & Espionage* (1983) (B); Arthur B. Darling, *The Central Intelligence Agency* (1990); Rhodri Jeffreys-Jones, *The CIA and American Democracy* (1989); Rhodri Jeffrey-Jones and Andrew Lownie, eds., *North American Spies* (1991); Loch K. Johnson, *America's Secret Power* (1989); Mark Lowenthal, *U.S. Intelligence* (1992); Ernest R. May, ed., *Knowing One's Enemies* (1985); Nathan Miller, *Spying for America* (1989); Harvey Nelsen, "U.S. Intelligence," *Choice* (1992) (B); Neal H. Petersen, *American Intelligence, 1775–1990* (1992) (B); John Prados, *The Presidents' Secret Wars* (1986); John Ranelagh, *The Agency*

(1986); Harry H. Ransom. *The Intelligence Establishment* (1970); W. Michael Reisman and James E. Baker, *Regulating Covert Action* (1992); Bradley F. Smith, *The Shadow Warriors* (1983); Gregory F. Treverton, *Covert Action* (1987); Bruce W. Watson el al., eds., *United States Intelligence* (1990) (E); Robin W. Winks, *Clock & Gown* (1987).

International Law and Hague Conferences: Robert L. Bledsoe and Boleslaw A. Boczek, *The International Law Dictionary* (1987) (E); Calvin D. Davis, *The United States and the First Hague Conference* (1962) and *The United States and the Second Hague Conference* (1976); Ingrid Delupis, ed., *Bibliography of International Law* (1975) (B); Richard Falk et al., eds., *International Law* (1985); James Fox, *Dictionary of International and Comparative Law* (1991) (E); Daniel P. Moynihan, *The Law of Nations* (1990). See also "Law of the Sea."

International Monetary Fund: Mary Elizabeth Johnson, *The International Monetary Fund, 1944–1992* (1993) (B); Brian Tew, *The Evolution of the International Monetary Fund, 1945–81* (1982).

International Organizations: Sheikh Ali, *The International Organization and World Order Dictionary* (1992) (E); George W. Baer, ed., *International Organizations, 1918–1945* (1981) (B); Edward J. Osmańczyk, *The Encyclopedia of the United States and International Organizations* (1990) (E); Union of International Associations, *Yearbook of International Organizations* (1948–) (AS). See also specific international organizations.

Isolationism: Selig Adler, *The Isolationist Impulse* (1957); Wayne S. Cole, *Roosevelt and the Isolationists* (1983); Justus D. Doenecke, *Anti-Intervention* (1987) (B); Manfred Jonas, *Isolationism in America, 1935–1941* (1966).

Korean War: See "Korea."

Labor: Philip S. Foner, *U.S. Labor Movement and Latin America* (1988); Ronald Radosh, *American Labor and United States Foreign Policy* (1969); Federico Romero, *The United States and the European Trade Union Movement, 1944–1951* (1992).

Law of the Sea: Jack N. Barkenbus, *Deep Seabed Resources* (1979); Ann L. Hollick, *U.S. Foreign Policy and the Law of the Sea* (1981); D. P. O'Connell, *The International Law of the Sea* (1982); Clyde Sanger, *Ordering the Oceans* (1987); United Nations, *The Law of the Sea* (1991) (B). See also "Environment" and "International Law."

League of Nations: Denna F. Fleming, *The United States and the League of Nations* (1932); Warren F. Kuehl, *Seeking World Order* (1969); F. S. Northedge, *The League of Nations* (1985). See also "International Organization" and "United Nations."

Low Intensity Warfare: See "Counterinsurgency."

Manifest Destiny: Norman A. Graebner, ed., *Manifest Destiny* (1968); Thomas R. Hietala, *Manifest Design* (1985); Albert K. Weinberg, *Manifest Destiny* (1935). See also "Ideology" and "Racism."

Marshall Plan: Michael J. Hogan, *The Marshall Plan* (1987); Alan S. Milward, *The Reconstruction of Western Europe, 1945–51* (1984); Imanuel Wexler, *The Marshall Plan Revisited* (1983). See also "Europe" and "Foreign Aid."

Marine Corps: Allan R. Millett, *Semper Fidelis* (1980). See also "Military, U.S. Army, and Wars" and specific wars.

Military, U.S. Army, and Wars: James L. Abrahamson, *American Arms for a New Century* (1981); William M. Arkin et al., *Encyclopedia of the U.S. Military* (1990) (E); Benjamin R. Beede, *Military and Strategic Policy* (1990) (B); John W. Chambers, *To Raise an Army* (1987); Edward M. Coffman, *The Old Army* (1986); E. Ernest Dupuy and Trevor N. Dupuy, *The Harper Encyclopedia of Military History* (1993) (E); John C. Fredriksen, *Shield of the Republic/Sword of Empire* (1990) (B); Kenneth J. Hagan and William R. Roberts, eds., *Against All Enemies* (1986); Robin Higham and Donald J. Mrozek, eds., *A Guide to the Sources of United States Military History* (1975–) (B); International Institute for Strategic Studies, *The Military Balance* (1959/60–) (AS); *International Military and Defense Encyclopedia* (1993) (E); Kenneth Macksey and William Woodhouse, *The Penguin Encyclopedia of Modern Warfare* (1992) (E); Allan R. Millett and Peter Maslowski, *For the Common Defense* (1994); Herbert K. Tillema, *International Armed Conflict Since 1945* (1991) (B); Roger J. Spiller and Joseph G. Dawson III, eds., *Dictionary of American Military Biography* (1984) (BD); Peter G. Tsouras et al., *The United States Army* (1991) (E); U.S. Military Academy, *The West Point Atlas of American Wars, 1689–1953* (1959) (A); Cynthia Watson, *U.S. National Security Policy Groups* (1990) (E); Russell F. Weigley, *The American Way of War* (1973) and *History of the United States Army* (1984). See also individual services and specific wars.

Missionaries: John K. Fairbank, ed., *The Missionary Enterprise in China and America* (1974); Patricia Hill, *The World Their Household* (1985); Jane Hunter, *The Gospel of Gentility* (1984); William R. Hutchison, *Errand to the World* (1987); Paul A. Varg, *Missionaries, Chinese, and Diplomats* (1958). See also "Cultural Relations" and "Ideology."

Monroe Doctrine: Dexter Perkins, *A History of the Monroe Doctrine* (1963); Gaddis Smith, *The Last Years of the Monroe Doctrine* (1994). See also "Latin America."

Navy and Naval Issues: George W. Baer, *One Hundred Years of Sea Power* (1994); James C. Bradford, ed., *Admirals of the New Steel Navy* (1990), ed., *Captains of the Old Stream Navy* (1986), and ed., *Command Under Sail* (1985); William B. Cogar, *Dictionary of Admirals of the United States Navy* (1989) (BD); Denneth J. Hagan, ed., *In Peace and War* (1984) and *This People's Navy* (1991); Paolo E. Coletta, *A Selected and Annotated bibliography of American Naval History* (1988) (B); Paolo E. Coletta et al., eds., American Secretaries of the Naby (1980) (BD); John B. Hattendorf and Lynn C. Hattendorf, *A Bibliography of the Works of Alfred Thayer Mahan* (1986) (B); Stephen Howarth, *To Shining Sea* (1991); David F. Long, *Gold Braid and Foreign Relations* (1988); Barbara A. Lynch and John E. Vajda, *United States Naval History* (1993) (B); Nathan Miller, *U.S. Navy* (1990); Elmer B. Potter, ed., *Sea Power* (1981); Harold Sprout and Margaret Sprout, *The Rise of American Naval Power* (1966); Jack Sweetman, ed., *American Naval History* (1984) (C); Bruce W. Watson and Susan M. Watson, *The United States Navy* (1991) (E). See also "Military, U.S. Army, and Wars" and specific wars.

Neutralism and Nonalignment: H. W. Brands, *The Specter of Neutralism* (1989); K. C. Chaudhary, *Non-aligned Summitry* (1988); Steven R. David, *Choosing Sides* (1991); Richard L. Jackson, *The Non-aligned, the UN, and the Superpowers* (1983); Lawrence W. Martin, ed., *Neutralism and Nonalignment* (1962).

North Atlantic Treaty Organization (NATO): Timothy Ireland, *Creating the Entangling Alliance* (1981); Robert S. Jordan, Jr., ed., *Generals in International Politics* (1987); Lawrence S. Kaplan, ed., *American Historians and the Atlantic Alliance* (1991), *NATO and the United States* (1988), and *The United States and NATO* (1984); Augustus R. Norton et al., *NATO* (1985) (B); Joseph Smith, ed., *The Origins of NATO* (1990). See also "Cold War," "Europe," and "Nuclear Arms."

Nuclear Arms: Paul Boyer, *By the Bomb's Early Light* (1985); McGeorge Bundy, *Danger and Survival* (1990); Robert A. Divine, *The Sputnik Challenge* (1993); Lawrence Freedman, *The Evolution of Nuclear Strategy* (1989); Gregg Herken, *Counsels of War* (1985); David Holloway, *The Soviet Union and the Arms Race* (1984); Fred Kaplan, *The Wizards of Armageddon* (1983); John Newhouse, *War and Peace in the Nuclear Age* (1989); Charles R. Morris, *Iron Destinies, Lost Opportunities* (1988); Ronald E. Powaski, *March to Armageddon* (1987); Scott D. Sagan, *The Limits of Safety* (1993); Richard Smoke, *National Security and the Nuclear Dilemma* (1987); Spencer R. Weart, *Nuclear Fear* (1988); Allan M. Winkler, *Life Under a Cloud* (1993). See also "Cold War," "Scientists and Science," and "Space and Satellites."

Oil: Gerald D. Nash, *United States Oil Policy, 1890–1964* (1968); David S. Painter, *Oil and the American Century* (1986); Stephen J. Randall, *United States Foreign Oil Policy, 1919–1984* (1985); Michael B. Stoff, *Oil, War, and American Security* (1980); Daniel Yergin, *The Prize* (1991). See also "Mexico," "Middle East," "OPEC," "Venezuela," and Anderson and Miller in "Saudi Arabia."

The Olympics: Allen Guttmann, *The Games Must Go On: Avery Brundage and the Olympic Movement* (1984) and *The Olympics* (1992); Christopher R. Hill, *Olympic Politics* (1992); David Wallechinsky, *The Complete Book of the Olympics* (1992) (E).

Organization of Petroleum Exporting Countries (OPEC): M. E. Ahrari, *OPEC* (1986); Albert L. Danielson, *The Evolution of OPEC* (1982); Ian Skeet, *OPEC* (1988). See also "Oil" and Rabe in "Venezuela."

Pan-Americanism: J. Floyd Mecham, *The United States and Inter-American Security, 1889–1960* (1961); Arthur P. Whitaker, *The Western Hemisphere Idea* (1954). See also "Latin America."

Peace Movements: Harriet Hyman Alonso, *Peace As a Women's Issue* (1993); Peter Brock, *Pacifism in the United States* (1968); Charles Chatfield, *The American Peace Movement* (1992); Charles DeBenedetti, ed., *Peace Heroes in Twentieth Century America* (1986) and *The Peace Reform in American History* (1980); Charles F. Howlett, *The American Peace Movement* (1990) (B); Harold Josephson et al., eds., *Biographical Dictionary of Modern Peace Leaders* (1985) (BD); Elvin Laszlo and Jong Youl Yoo, eds., *World Encyclopedia of Peace* (1986) (E); Robert S. Meyer, *Peace Organizations Past and Present* (1988) (E); David S. Patterson, *Toward a Warless World* (1976); Nancy L. Roberts, *American Peace Writers, Editors, and Periodicals* (1991) (BD); Lawrence S. Wittner, *Rebels Against War* (1984); Valarie H. Ziegler, *The Advocates of Peace in Antebellum America* (1992). See also specific wars.

Peace Corps: T. Zane Reeves, *The Politics of the Peace Corps & Vista* (1988); Robert Ridinger, *The Peace Corps* (1989) (B); Gerald T. Rice, *Bold Experiment* (1985). See also "Cultural Relations" and Amin in "Cameroon."

Peacekeeping: Paul F. Diehl, *International Peacekeeping* (1993); William J. Durch, ed., *The Evolution of UN Peacekeeping* (1993); Alan James, *Peacekeeping in International Politics* (1990). See also "United Nations."

Pearl Harbor, 1941: Stanley L. Falk, "Pearl Harbor," *Naval History* (1988) (B); Robert W. Love, Jr., ed., *Pearl Harbor Reexamined* (1990); Martin V. Melosi, *The Shadow of Pearl Harbor* (1977); Frank P. Mintz, *Revisionism and the Origins of Pearl Harbor* (1985); Gordon W. Prange, *Pearl Harbor* (1986); Myron J. Smith, Jr., *Pearl Harbor* (1991) (B). Also see "World War II" and Chapter 6 of Volume 2 for histories.

Philanthropy and Foundations: Edward H. Berman, *The Influence of the Carnegie, Ford, and Rockefeller Foundations on American Foreign Policy* (1983); Merle Curti, *American Philanthrophy Abroad* (1963); Robert L. Daniel, *American Philanthropy in the Near East, 1820–1960* (1970). See also "Cultural Relations" and Cobbs in "Brazil."

President (General): James Barber, *The Presidential Character* (1992); E. S. Corwin, *The President* (1957); Robert A. Divine, *Foreign Policy and U.S. Presidential Elections, 1940–1960* (1974); Leonard W. and Louis Fisher, eds., *Encyclopedia of the American Presidency* (1993) (E); Robert U. Goehlert and Fenton S. Martin, *The Presidency* (1985) (B); Theodore Lowi, *The Personal President* (1985); John E. Mueller, *War, Presidents, and Public Opinion* (1973); Richard E. Neustadt, *Presidential Power and the Modern Presidents* (1990); Arthur M. Schlesinger, Jr., *The Imperial Presidency* (1973); Robert Sobel, ed., *Biographical Directory of the United States Executive Branch, 1774–1977* (1977) (BD). See also "Bureaucracy," "Congress," "Constitution," "Health and Medical History of Leaders," "Presidents (By Administration)," and "War Powers."

Presidents (By Administration): Harry Ammon, *James Monroe* (1991) (B) Peter H. Buckingham, *Woodrow Wilson* (1989) (B); Richard Dean Burns, *Harry S. Truman* (1984) (B); John Ferling, *John Adams* (1993) (B); Otis L. Graham, Jr., and Meghan R. Wander, eds., *Franklin D. Roosevelt* (1985) (E); Richard S. Kirkendall, ed., *The Harry S. Truman Encyclopedia* (1989) (E); Merrill D. Peterson, *Thomas Jefferson* (1986) (E); Robert A. Rutland, ed., *The James Madison Encyclopedia* (1992) (E). See also "Health and Medical History of Leaders" and "President (General)."

The Press and Journalism: James L. Baughman, *Henry R. Luce and the Rise of the American News Media* (1988); Bernard C. Cohen, *The Press and Foreign Policy* (1963); Joseph P. McKerns, ed., *Biographical Dictionary of American Journalism* (1989) (BD); Brigitte Lebens Nacos, *The Press, Presidents, and Crises* (1990); James Reston, *The Artillery of the Press* (1967); Ronald Steel, *Walter Lippmann and the American Century* (1980); William H. Taft, ed., *Encyclopedia of Twentieth-Century Journalists* (1986); John Tebbel and Sarah Miles Watts, *The Press and the Presidency* (1985). See also "Public Opinion."

Privateering: Carl E. Swanson, *Predators and Prizes* (1991). See also "Navy and Naval Issues."

Propaganda: Alexandre Lauien, *The Voice of America* (1988); Leo Bogart, *Premises for Propaganda* (1976) (USIA); Robert E. Elder, *The Information Machine* (1968); Sig Mickelson, *America's Other Voice* (1983); Holly C. Shulman, *The Voice of America* (1990); Thomas C. Sorensen, *The Word War* (1968); Allen M. Winkler, *The Politics of Propaganda* (1978). See also "Communications" and "Cultural Relations."

Public Opinion: Gabriel Almond, *The American People and Foreign Policy* (1950); Richard J. Barnet, *The Rockets' Red Glare* (1990); Bernard C. Cohen, *The Public's Impact on Foreign Policy* (1973); H. Schuyler Foster, *Activism Replaces Isolationism: U.S. Public Attitudes, 1940–1975* (1983); George Gallup, *The Gallup Poll: Public Opinion* (1972–) (AS and S); Ralph B. Levering, *The Public and American Foreign Policy* (1978). See also "President (General)" and "Press and Journalism."

Race and Racism: Reginald Horsman, *Race and Manifest Destiny* (1981); Paul Gordon Lauren, *Power and Prejudice* (1988); George E. Shepherd, ed., *Racial Influence on American Foreign Policy* (1971); Jay A. Sigler, ed., *International Handbook on Race and Race Relations* (1987) (E); Rubin F. Weston, *Racism in U.S. Imperialism* (1972). See also Ethnic Groups and Immigration," "Ideology," and "Manifest Destiny."

Recognition Policy: Thomas M. Franck, *The Power of Legitimacy Among Nations* (1990); L. Thomas Galloway, *Recognizing Foreign Governments* (1978).

Refugees: Anna Bramwell, ed., *Refugees in the Age of Total War* (1988); David W. Haines, *Refugees in the United States* (1985); Gil Loescher, *Beyond Charity* (1993); Gil Loescher and John A. Scalan, *Calculated Kindness* (1986); J. Bruce Nichols, *The Uneasy Alliance: Religion, Refugee Work, and U.S. Foreign Policy* (1988). See also "Ethnic Groups and Immigration."

Scientists and Science: Robert Gilpin and Christopher Wright, eds., *Scientists and National Policy-making* (1964); Greta Jones, *Science, Politics and the Cold War* (1988); Stuart W. Leslie, *The Cold War and American Science* (1993); Joseph Rotblat, ed., *Scientists, the Arms Race, and Disarmament* (1982); Alice K. Smith, *A Peril and a Hope: The Scientists' Movement in the United States, 1945–47* (1965). See also "Nuclear Arms."

The South (U.S.): Alfred Hero, *The Southerner and World Affairs* (1965); Charles O. Lerche, *The Uncertain South* (1964); Tennant S. McWilliams, *The New South Faces the World* (1988).

Space and Satellites: Walter A. McDougall, *The Heavens and the Earth* (1985); Jeffrey T. Richelson, *America's Secret Eyes in Space* (1990); Paul B. Stares, *The Militarization of Space* (1985). See also "Nuclear Arms."

Spanish-American-Cuban-Filipino War: Benjamin R. Beede, ed., *The War of 1898 and U.S. Interventions, 1899–1934* (1994) (B); James C, Bradford, ed., *Crucible of Empire* (1993); Anne C. Venzon, *The Spanish-American War* (1990) (B). Also see "Military, U.S. Army, and Wars" and Chapter 6 of Volume 1 and Chapter 1 of Volume 2 for histories.

Summit Conferences: Keith Eubank, *The Summit Conference* (1966); Elmer Plischke, *Diplomat in Chief* (1986) and *Summit Diplomacy* (1958); Robert D. Putnam and Nicholas Bayne, *Hanging Together: The Seven-Power Summits* (1984); Gordon R. Weihmiller and Dusko Doder, *U.S.–Soviet Summits* (1986). See also "Cold War."

Tariffs and Protectionism: Edward S. Kaplan and Thomas W. Ryley, *Prelude to Trade Wars: American Tariff Policy, 1890–1922* (1994); David A. Lake, *Power, Protection, and Free Trade* (1988); James M. Lutz, *Protectionism* (1988) (B); Robert A. Pastor, *Congress and the Politics of U.S. Foreign Economic Policy, 1929–1976* (1980); Sidney Ratner, *The Tariff in American History* (1972); Frank W. Taussig, *Tariff History of the United States* (1931); Tom E. Terrill, *The Tariff, Politics, and American Foreign Policy, 1874–1901* (1973); Paul Wolman, *Most Favored Nation* (1992); Thomas Zeiler, *American Trade and Power in the 1960s* (1992). See also Economic Relations and Business" and "Economic Sanctions and Export Controls."

Terrorism: Christopher Dobson and Ronald Payne, *The Never Ending War* (1987); Lawrence Freedman et al., *Terrorism and International Order* (1986); Walter Laqueur, *The Age of Terrorism* (1987); Edward F. Mickolus et al., *International Terrorism in the 1980s* (1989) (C), *Terrorism, 1988–1991* (1993) (C), and *Transnational Terrorism . . . , 1968–1979* (1980) (C); Suzanne R. Ontiveros, *Global Terrorism* (1986) (B); Barry Rubin, ed., *The Politics of Terrorism* (1990); John R. Thackrah, *Encyclopedia of Terrorism and Political Violence* (1987) (E).

Think Tanks: David M. Ricci, *The Transformation of American Politics* (1993); Robert D. Schulzinger, *The Wise Men of Foreign Affairs: The History of the Council on Foreign Relations* (1984); Bruce L. R. Smith, *The Rand Corporation* (1966); James A. Smith, *The Idea Brokers* (1991).

United Nations: Joseph P. Baratta, *Strengthening the United Nations* (1987) (B); Robert A. Divine, *Second Chance* (1967); Seymour M. Finger, *American Ambassadors at the United Nations* (1987); Thomas M. Frank, *Nation Against Nation* (1985); Max Harrelson, *Fires All Around the Horizon* (1989); Robert C. Hilderbrand, *Dumbarton Oaks* (1990); Evan Luard and Derek Herter, *The United Nations* (1993); Kumiko Matsuura et al., *Chronology and Fact Book of the United Nations, 1941–1991* (1992) (C); Edmund Jan Osmanczyk, *The Encyclopedia of the UN and International Agreements* (1985) (E); William Preston, Jr. et al., *Hope and Folly* (1989) (UNESCO); John G. Stoessinger, *The United Nations and the Superpowers* (1973). See also "International Organizations,""League of Nations," and "Peacekeeping."

Vietnam War: See "Vietnam and Southeast Asia."

War Crimes and Trials: Richard L. Lael, *The Yamashita Precedent: War Crimes and Command Responsibility* (1982); John R. Lewis, *Uncertain Judgment* (1979) (B); Philip R. Piccigallo, *The Japanese on Trial* (1979); Telford Taylor, *Nuremberg and Vietnam* (1970); Norman E. Tutorow, ed., *War Crimes, War Criminals, and War Crimes Trials* (1986) (B). See also "Holocaust" and "Human Rights."

War of 1812: John C. Fredriksen, *Free Trade and Sailors' Rights* (1985) (B); Dwight L. Smith, *The War of 1812* (1985) (B). See also "Military, U.S. Army, and Wars" and Chapter 2 of volume 1 for histories.

War Powers: Christopher N. May, *In the Name of War* (1989); W. Taylor Revely, *War Powers of the President and Congress* (1981); John H. Sullivan, *The War Powers Resolution* (1982); Francis D. Wormuth and Edwin B. Firmage, *To Chain the Dog of War* (1989). See also "Congress," "Constitution," and "President (General)."

West (U.S.) and Frontier: William A. Beck and Ynez D. Haase, *Historical Atlas of the American West* (1989) (A); J. Norman Heard, *Handbook of the American Frontier* (1987) (E); Howard R. Lamar, ed., *The Reader's Encyclopedia of the American West* (1977) (E); Dan L. Thrapp, *The Encyclopedia of Frontier Biography* (1988) (BD). See also "Indians (Native Americans)."

Women and Gender Issues: Homer L. Calkin, *Women in the Department of State* (1978); Edward P. Crapol, ed., *Women and American Foreign Policy* (1992); Rebecca Grant and Kathleen Newland, eds., *Gender and International Relations* (1991); Nancy W. McGlen and Meredith Reid Sarkes, *Women in Foreign Policy* (1993).

World Court: Michael Dunne, *The United States and the World Court, 1920–1935* (1988); D. F. Fleming, *The United States and the World Court* (1945).

World-System Analysis: Thomas J. McCormick, *America's Half-Century* (1989); Immanuel Wallerstein, *Geopolitics and Geoculture* (1991), *The Modern World-System* (1974), *Politics of the World-Economy* (1984), and *World Inequality* (1975). See also "Dependency."

World War I: Arthur Banks, *A Military History Atlas of the First World War* (1975) (A); Holger H. Herwig and Neil M. Heyman, *Biographical Dictionary of World War I* (1982) (BD). See also "Military, U.S. Army, and Wars" and Chapter 8 in Volume 1 and Chapter 3 in Volume 2 for histories.

World War II: Marcel Baudot et al., eds., *The Historical Encyclopedia of World War II* (1980) (E); David G. Chandler and James Lawton

Collins, Jr., eds., *The D-Day Encyclopedia* (1983) (E); Robert Goralski, *World War II Almanac* (1981) (C); John Keegan, ed., *The Times Atlas of the Second World War* (1989) (A); Thomas Parrish, ed., *The Simon and Schuster Encyclopedia of World War II* (1978) (E); Norman Polmar and Thomas B. Allen, *World War II* (1991) (E); John J. Sbrega, *The War Against Japan* (1989) (B); Louis L. Snyder, *Louis L. Snyder's Historical Guide to World War II* (1982) (E); Ronald Spector, "The Scholarship on World War II," *Journal of Military History* (1991) (B); U.S. Military Academy, *Campaign Atlas to the Second World War* (1980) (A); Peter Young, ed., *Atlas of the Second World War* (1973) (A). See also "Military, U.S. Army, and Wars" and Chapter 6 of Volume 2 for histories.

INDEX

Note: Page numbers in italics indicate illustrations.